CASES AND MATERIALS
ON
INTERNATIONAL TRADE LAW

AUSTRALIA
Law Book Co.
Sydney

CANADA AND USA
Carswell
Toronto

HONG KONG
Sweet & Maxwell
Asia

NEW ZEALAND
Brookers
Wellington

SINGAPORE AND MALAYSIA
Sweet & Maxwell Asia
Singapore and Kuala Lumpur

CASES AND MATERIALS
ON
INTERNATIONAL TRADE LAW

By

PAUL TODD
University of Wales

FIRST EDITION

LONDON
SWEET & MAXWELL
2003

First Edition (2002)

Published in 2002 by Sweet and Maxwell Limited
100 Avenue Road
London NW3 3PF
(http://www.sweetandmaxwell.co.uk)

Computerset by Interactive Sciences Ltd, Gloucester
Printed and bound in Great Britain by T.J. International, Ltd, Padstow, Cornwall

No natural forests were destroyed to make this product;
only farmed timber was used and re-planted.

ISBN 0421 827106

A CIP catalogue record for this book is available
from the British Library.

PREFACE

I have taught courses on the law of international trade for over 20 years, including recently at LL.M. level, but have found difficulty in finding suitable books to recommend to students. That is not to say that other books on international trade are poor, rather that international trade law courses differ, and books that are excellent for one type of course can be relatively useless for another. On the LL.M. programme to which I currently contribute, admiralty, marine insurance, carriage of goods by sea and international trade are all taught as separate modules. There are other specialist books on admiralty, marine insurance and carriage of goods by sea, to which students are referred by the teachers of those modules. International trade also deserves its own specialist book, but some international trade books also cover these other subjects. They therefore tend to offer too little detail on international trade itself, to be of use for my course. The programme on which I teach is by no means unique, so there must be other lecturers, and students, both at undergraduate and postgraduate levels, in a similar position.

My international trade course (for which this book would be suitable) is narrow but deep, concentrating on c.i.f. and f.o.b. contracts and variations thereon, and the traditional documentation including the shipped bill of lading. Some might argue that in the days of containerisation and multimodal transport this is anachronistic, but the c.i.f. contract in particular is still the mainstay of the bulk commodity trade,[1] which in terms of tonnage (if not value) still far exceeds containerised transport. C.i.f. and f.o.b. contracts also continue to account for a far greater proportion of reported cases. Moreover, if instead of grouping into one book all international sale contracts with a marine element, you decide to concentrate on contracts which raise similar legal issues, you would not place the c.i.f. contract along with, *e.g.* ex works, or delivered duty paid; they have practically nothing in common with each other. The coverage of this book may be quite narrow, but common themes run through it.

This is also a book on English law.[2] Again, in an era of harmonisation and globalisation (or so we are told), surely this cannot be justified? It is still the case, though, that English standard form contracts are used throughout the world, and the principles in this book continue to apply, to a considerable extent, throughout the common law world. Much of the content would apply with little or no modification, for example, in Australia, New Zealand, Canada, India, Malaysia, Singapore, Hong Kong, and many parts of Africa. Some of the principles would apply in the United States. Civil law systems have entirely different traditions, of

---

[1] For dry cargo at least; f.o.b. is still commonly used in bulk oil sales.
[2] By which I mean, of course, the law of England and Wales.

course, and I am frankly sceptical about the wisdom of imposing harmonisation, often based on such traditions, upon English law, at any rate in the areas discussed here. The CISG,[3] for example, would simply not work as well, in the bulk commodity trade, as the English common law, a truth well recognised by the commercial parties, whose standard forms often exclude it, just in case it ever becomes part of UK law. In any case, with the exception of the original Hague Rules, harmonisation initiatives have enjoyed relatively little success in this area, and so although they are covered, I have not devoted detailed discussion to them. (These comments apply only to this area of law; in other fields of human activity, European initiatives in particular are very much to be welcomed.)

So the book concentrates on the two main international sale contracts, the c.i.f. and f.o.b. contract (and variations thereon). There is not also detailed coverage, for example, on the law of carriage of goods by sea (which I have also taught for quite a long time, with the assistance of other excellent books on the subject). Nevertheless, the sale contracts cannot be studied entirely in a vacuum. One of the parties will be required to ensure that there is a carriage contract, and about a quarter of the book is devoted to various aspects of carriage. Ultimately, however, this is a book on international sale contracts, and the carriage elements are introduced so as properly to explain international sales. Similarly with finance; it is not possible fully to understand f.o.b. and c.i.f. contracts without dealing with bankers' documentary credits, to which three chapters are therefore devoted. But this is no more a detailed book on finance than it is on carriage. This emphasis is a deliberate choice of mine; the main reason I have found other international books unsuitable for my course is that they cover too much, and necessarily leave too little space for adequate detail on the main part of the subject.

The last two chapters consider where the law is going. There is no doubt that international trade is changing, and that the legal frameworks developed in the nineteenth century are no longer entirely suitable, in the twenty-first. This is true as much (or more) in, *e.g.* the bulk oil trade as it is in multimodal transport. These issues are discussed, as are some of the harmonisation initiatives, and the (probably inevitable) vulnerability of the system to fraud. The last chapter looks at the likely impact of computers and the Internet. This is still tentative at present; it is by no means clear that the commercial parties will actually embrace electronic documentation, for example, but if they do, they will need a legal framework within which to operate (just as the c.i.f. contract was itself unable to develop until the necessary legal framework was put in place, in the middle of the nineteenth century).

This was conceived as a book for teaching. Its aim is to provide teaching materials, and although I would hope that it could also be a useful research tool, that is not its primary purpose. It is a collection of the

---

[3] United Nations Convention on Contracts for the International Sale of Goods (Vienna Convention) 1980.

material I have found useful for teaching, structured in (what is to me at least) a logical and comprehensible fashion, with comments, links and appropriate cross-references. It is a cases and materials book, rather than a textbook, partly because there is no similar book in the marketplace, but also because, as a student, I greatly preferred cases and materials books to textbooks. Apart from the fact that they were generally more interesting, they were also more useful when I was working at home, or at weekends or in the vacation, or at any other time when the library was closed, or access to it difficult. My student days are admittedly quite a long time ago now, and in particular before widespread access to the Internet became available. Much of the material in this book could be obtained via the Internet (though not without quite a bit of searching, nor necessarily free of charge). Even so, it would take quite a time to collect and download it. In any case, I hope that my own text and commentary will add some value to the otherwise raw collection of materials.

On an issue of language convention, nearly all the actors in this book are companies. A company has legal personality, and therefore cannot be "it", but there are not two types, so "he or she" would also be entirely inappropriate. A company is therefore "he", in line with what I take to be conventional English usage. Ships and countries are female, however. Nothing should be read into these conventions, any more than into the convention in French that a cat is male and a car is female—it is just language convention.

The law is stated as at September 22, 2002.

Paul Todd

ACKNOWLEDGMENTS

Grateful acknowledgment is made to the following authors and publishers for permission to quote from their works:

ADAMS AND BROWNSWORD: *Key Issues in Contract* (1995). Reprinted by Permission of LexisNexis Butterworths Tolley.

ATIYAH: *The Sale of Goods* (P.S. Atiyah and John N. Adams, 10th ed., 2001). Reprinted by Permission of Pearson Education Limited.

BENNETT: F.O.B. Contracts: Substitution of Vessels [1990] L.M.C.L.Q. 466. Reprinted by Permission of LLP Professional Publishing, a division of Informa Group Plc.

Bolero Rulebook, 1999. © Bolero International Limited. Reprinted with the permission of Bolero International Limited.

CHRISPEELS: The Convention and the Multimodal Transport Document, UNCTAD. Reprinted by Permission of the UN.

CLARKE: *How the City of London Works* (5th ed., 1999). Reprinted by Permission of Sweet & Maxwell Ltd.

CMI: Rules on Electronic Bills of Lading. Reprinted by Permission of CMI

—: Uniform Rules for Sea Waybills. Reprinted by Permission of CMI

COLINVAUX: Revision of the Hague Rules Relating to Bills of Lading [1963] J.B.L. 341. Reprinted by Permission of Sweet & Maxwell Ltd.

CONWAY: *The Piracy Business* (1981), pp 23–25. Reprinted by Permission of The Hamlyn Trust and Sweet and Maxwell Ltd.

DEBATTISTA: *The Sale of Goods Carried by Sea* (2nd ed., 1998), Chapter 5. Reprinted by Permission of LexisNexis Butterworths Tolley.

DIAMOND: The Hague-Visby Rules [1978] L.M.C.L.Q. 225. Reprinted by Permission of LLP Professional Publishing, a division of Informa Group Plc.

Encyclopaedia Britannica CD (Primary commodity markets: Operation of the market). Reprinted by Permission of Encyclopaedia Britannica, Inc.

FELTHAM: The Appropriation to a C.I.F. Contract of Goods Lost or Damaged at Sea [1975] J.B.L. 273. Reprinted by Permission of Sweet & Maxwell Ltd.

GRUNFORS: Container Bills of Lading and Multimodal Transport Documents, UNCTAD Seminar on Ocean Transport Documentation and its Simplification, 1980. Reprinted by Permission of the UN.

GOFF: Commercial Contracts and the Commercial Court [1984] L.M.C.L.Q. 382. Reprinted by Permission of LLP Professional Publishing, a division of Informa Group Plc.

HINDELANG: No Remedy for Disappointed Trust—The Liability Regime for Certification Authorities Towards Third Parties Outwith the EC Directive in England and Germany Compared, Journal of Information, Law & Technology (JILT), 2002 (1) (http://elj.warwick. ac.uk/jilt/02-1/hindelang.html). Reprinted by Permission of JILT.

ICC: Publication No. 560, Incoterms 2000, © (1999) International Chamber of Commerce. Available from ICC Publishing S.A., 38, Cours Albert 1er, 75008 Paris.

ICC: Publication No. 500/2, Supplement to UCP 500 for electronic presentation (eUCP) Version 1.0 - © (2002) International Chamber of Commerce. Available from ICC Publishing, Inc., 156 Fifth Avenue, Suite 417, New York, NY 10010, USA.

INCE & CO.: International Trade Law Update (Tradewatch), Spring 2000 (Issue 4). Reprinted by Permission of Ince & Co.

LIGHTBURN & NIENABER: Out-turn Clauses in C.I.F. Contracts in the Oil Trade [1987] 2 L.M.C.L.Q. 177, 178–179. Reprinted by Permission of LLP Professional Publishing, a division of Informa Group Plc.

P&O CONTAINERS: Merchants Guide (International Edition, 1995), p. 43. Reprinted by Permission of P&O Nedlloyd.

REED: What is a Signature?, Journal of Information, Law & Technology (JILT), 2000 (3) (http://elj.warwick.ac.uk/jilt/00-3/reed.html). Reprinted by Permission of JILT.

REYNOLDS: Rejection of Documents [1984] L.M.C.L.Q. 191. Reprinted by Permission of LLP Professional Publishing, a division of Informa Group Plc.

SCHMITTHOFF: *Schmitthoff's Export Trade* (ed. D'Arcy L., Murray C. and Cleave B., 10th ed., 2000), p. 51. Reprinted by Permission of Sweet & Maxwell Ltd.

SELVIG: The Relationship between the Contract of Sale and Contracts relating to Transportation, Insurance and Banking Services, UNCTAD Seminar on Ocean Transport Documentation and its Simplification, 1980. Reprinted by Permission of the UN.

SASSOON: The Origin of F.O.B. and C.I.F. Terms and the Factors Influencing their Choice [1967] J.B.L. 32. Reprinted by Permission of Sweet & Maxwell Ltd.

TEIK: Transnational Fraud [1985] L.M.C.L.Q. 418. Reprinted by Permission of LLP Professional Publishing, a division of Informa Group Plc.

TODD: CEP Interagra S.A. v. Select Energy Trading G.m.b.H. (The Jambur) [1991] 5 Oil and Gas Law and Taxation Review D58. Reprinted by Permission of Sweet & Maxwell Ltd.

—: The Sormovskiy 3068 [1994] 8 Oil and Gas Law and Taxation Review D91–D92. Reprinted by Permission of Sweet & Maxwell Ltd.

—: Delivery Against Forged Bill of Lading [1999] L.M.C.L.Q. 449–456. Reprinted by Permission of LLP Professional Publishing, a division of Informa Group Plc.

—: *Bills of Lading and Bankers' Documentary Credits*: (3rd ed., 1998), Chapter 8. Reprinted by Permission of LLP Professional Publishing, a division of Informa Group Plc.

—: *Cross-Border Electronic Banking*: Dematerialisation of Shipping Documents (ed. Reed, Walden and Edgar, 2nd ed., 2000), Chapter 3. Reprinted by Permission of LLP Professional Publishing, a division of Informa Group Plc.

—: The Captain Gregos and The Captain Gregos (No. 2) [1990] 10 Journal of International Banking Law N232–N234 [1989/90] 4 Oil and Gas Law and Taxation Review D47–D50. Reprinted by Permission of Sweet & Maxwell Ltd.

—: Incorporation of Arbitration Clauses into Bills of Lading [1997] J.B.L. 331. Reprinted by Permission of Sweet & Maxwell Ltd.

—: The Heidberg [1994] 6 Oil and Gas Law and Taxation Review D67. Reprinted by Permission of Sweet & Maxwell Ltd.

—: *Documentary Credits Insight*: Rejection of Shipping Documents. Publication No. 500, ICC Uniform Customs and Practice for Documentary Credits UCP 500, © (1993), International Chamber of Commerce. Available from ICC Publishing, Inc., 156 Fifth Avenue, Suite 417, New York, NY 10010, USA.

TREITEL: Passing of Property Under C.I.F. Contracts and the Bills of Lading Act 1855 [1990] L.M.C.L.Q. 1. Reprinted by Permission of LLP Professional Publishing, a division of Informa Group Plc.

—: Time of Shipment in F.O.B. Contracts [1991] L.M.C.L.Q. 147. Reprinted by Permission of LLP Professional Publishing, a division of Informa Group Plc.

—: Rights of Rejection under C.I.F. Sales [1984] L.M.C.L.Q. 565, at p. 568. Reprinted by Permission of LLP Professional Publishing, a division of Informa Group Plc.

WINSTONE: *Financial Derivatives* (1995), p. 63, pp. 72–73, Thomson Learning. Reprinted by Permission of Thomson Publishing.

UN: United Nations Convention on Contracts for the International Sale of Goods, 1980 (CISG). Reprinted by Permission of the UN.

—: United Nations Convention on the Carriage of Goods by Sea (1978). Reprinted by Permission of the UN.

UNCTAD's Trade and Development Board Ad hoc Intergovernmental Group to Consider Means of Combating All Aspects of Maritime Fraud, including Piracy. Second session, October 1985. Chapter III. Reprinted by Permission of the UN.

While every care has been taken to establish and acknowledge copyright, and contact the copyright owners, the publishers tender their apologies for any accidental infringement. They would be pleased to come to a suitable arrangement with the rightful owners in each case.

CONTENTS

	Page
Preface	*v*
Acknowledgments	*ix*
Table of Cases (UK)	*xxii*
Table of Cases (International)	*l*
Table of National Statutes, etc	*liii*
Table of Statutory Instruments	*lxii*
Table of Treaties and Conventions	*lxiii*

PART A: INTRODUCTION

	Para.
1. OVERVIEW	1–001
(1) Historical Perspective	1–003
(a) The Early f.o.b. (and f.a.s.) Contract	1–006
(b) Development of c.i.f. from f.o.b. Contract	1–009
(c) Buyer's Desire to Move Away from Original f.o.b. and the Problems of so Doing	1–010
(d) Ensuring Performance by the Parties	1–011
(e) Development of the Bill of Lading as a Document of Title	1–012
(f) Contract of Carriage Issues and their Resolution by the Bills of Lading Act 1855	1–013
(2) Finance of International Sales	1–014
(a) Development of Bankers' Documentary Credit	1–014
(3) Modern Day Problems	1–015
(a) Development of Chains f.o.b. and c.i.f.	1–015
(b) Retreat from Traditional Documentation	1–049
(c) Summary of Advantages and Disadvantages of Traditional Bill of Lading	1–050
(d) Fraud	1–051

PART B: THE CONTRACT OF SALE

2. C.I.F. CONTRACTS AND VARIATIONS: RIGHTS AND DUTIES OF THE PARTIES	2–001
(1) General Observations on Contracts of Sale	2–001
(a) Role of the Sale Contract in International Trade	2–001

(b) Common Law Definitions—Some General Consid-
    erations   2–002
(2) C.I.F. Contracts and Variations Thereon: Basic
    Definition   2–004
(3) Limit of Seller's Duties in Relation to the Goods   2–014
    (a) c.i.f. Delivered Contracts   2–019
    (b) The c.i.f. Out-turn Contract   2–024
(4) Relationship Between Sale and Carriage Contracts   2–028
(5) Continuing Duties After Shipment   2–039

3. F.O.B. CONTRACTS AND OTHER INTERNATIONAL SALE
CONTRACTS: RIGHTS AND DUTIES OF THE PARTIES   3–001

(1) f.o.b. Contracts   3–001
    (a) Flexibility of f.o.b. Term   3–001
    (b) Issues on Range of f.o.b. Contracts   3–003
    (c) The Three Main *Pyrene v Scindia* Varieties   3–004
    (d) Nomination of Vessel   3–017
    (e) Export Licences   3–046
    (f) Delivery   3–051
    (g) Market Fluctuation Risks   3–056
(2) Other International Sale Contracts   3–058

4. RISK AND RELATED ISSUES   4–001

(1) Relevance of Passing of Risk   4–001
(2) The General Rule   4–002
    (a) Risk Passes on (or as from) Shipment   4–002
    (b) Exact Point of Transfer of Risk   4–003
(3) Application of General Rule   4–004
    (a) Divorce of Risk from Property   4–004
    (b) Role of Documentation in Evidencing a Valid
        Contract   4–007
    (c) Role of Documentation in Passing Property   4–010
(4) Genuine Expectations   4–020
    (a) Sales of Goods Act 1979, s.32(3)   4–021
    (b) Application to f.o.b. Contracts   4–022
    (c) Application to c.i.f. Contracts   4–026
(5) Other Contractual Issues Relating to Risk   4–029
    (a) Implied Condition of Merchantable Quality   4–030
    (b) Later Legislation and the durability term   4–037
    (c) Estoppel   4–040
(6) Enforceability of Contract   4–046
    (a) Repudiation   4–046A

(b)	Mistake	4–046B
(c)	Frustration	4–051

5. PROPERTY — 5–001

(1) **Consequences of Passing of Property** — 5–001
    (a) General Considerations — 5–002
    (b) Consequences of Passing of Property in International Sales — 5–005
(2) **Passing of Property: The General Scheme** — 5–006
    (a) Sale of Goods Act Provisions — 5–006
    (b) Specific and Unascertained Goods — 5–007
    (c) Unascertained Goods — 5–008
    (d) Ascertained or Specific Goods — 5–012
    (e) Equitable Property — 5–026
(3) **Property in Specific or Ascertained Goods: Evidence of Intention** — 5–030
    (a) Summary of Legal Development Since 1850 — 5–033
    (b) Early Cases and Cases Establishing General Principles — 5–040
    (c) Development of Modern Forms of Finance — 5–055
    (d) Form of Bill of Lading and Reservation to Order of Seller — 5–060
    (e) Effect of Method of Financing Transaction — 5–065
(4) **The 1995 Amendments to the Sale of Goods Act** — 5–080
(5) **The Passing of Property and the Action for the Price** — 5–081
    (a) The General Position — 5–081
    (b) Waiver of Right of Disposal — 5–085

6. THE DOCUMENTS — 6–001

(1) **Introduction** — 6–001
(2) **Role of the Documents** — 6–002
(3) **Function of Document Title** — 6–003
    (a) Right to Refuse to Deliver — 6–004
    (b) Right to Deliver Against Original Document — 6–008
    (c) Set of Three — 6–009
    (d) Delivery Without Production — 6–015
    (e) Developments Since *Sze Hai Tong* — 6–021A
    (f) The Present State of the Law — 6–025
    (g) Limits on Value of Document of Title — 6–036
    (h) When is Bill of Lading Spent? — 6–040
(4) **Which Documents can be Documents of Title?** — 6–043
    (a) Shipped Bill of Lading Document of Title Without Proof of Custom — 6-043
    (b) Which Other Documents are Documents of Title? — 6–046
    (c) Mate's Receipts as Documents of Title — 6–047

(d) Received for Shipment Bills of Lading   6–050
(e) Effect of Custom   6–052
(5) Documentation under c.i.f. and f.o.b. Contracts: Bills of Lading   6–057
(a) Requirements for Shipped Bills   6–057
(b) Clean Bill of Lading   6–066
(c) Charterparty Bills   6–071
(d) Through Bills of Lading   6–076
(e) Tender of One of a Set   6–080
(f) When Tendered?   6–084
(g) Other Requirements   6–095
(6) Other Documentation   6–096
(a) Delivery Orders   6–096
(b) Commercial Invoice   6–101
(c) Quality Certificates, etc.   6–102
(7) Insurance Requirements   6–107
(a) Requirement to Tender Insurance Policy   6–108
(b) Extent of Cover Required   6–109

7. Remedies for Breach   7–001

(1) General Principles of the Law of Contract   7–001
(a) Market Variations and Remedies   7–001
(b) Conditions, Warranties and Innominate Terms   7–006
(c) Anticipatory Breach   7–007
(d) Effect of Repudiation   7–015
(2) Terms Relating to the Goods   7–018
(a) Sale of Goods Act Implied Terms   7–018
(3) Rejection of Documents and Goods by the Buyer   7–021
(4) Loss of Right to Reject   7–032
(a) The Issues   7–032
(b) Refinements to the Reasoning in *Kwei Tek Chao*   7–039
(c) What Right to Reject has Been Lost?   7–050
(5) Carrier Indemnities   7–065

PART C: FINANCE

8. Methods Financing International Sales   8–001

(1) Bills of Exchange   8–001
(a) Definition   8–002
(b) Parties   8–003
(c) Negotiation With and Without Recourse   8–004
(d) Sight Draft/Time Draft   8–005
(2) The Documentary Bill   8–006

(3) **Documentary Credits: Fundamental Principles** 8–007
    (a) The Four Contracts in a Confirmed Irrevocable
        Credit 8–009A
    (b) Contracts Autonomous 8–010
    (c) Contracts Interconnected 8–011
    (d) Banks Deal in Documents Not Goods 8–012
(4) **Uniform Customs and Practice on Bankers' Commercial**
    Credits 8–013
    (a) The U.C.P. 8–013
    (b) Application of U.C.P. 8–014
(5) **Types of Documentary Credit** 8–016
    (a) Revocable and Irrevocable Credits 8–017
    (b) Irrevocable Credits 8–020
    (c) Methods of Payment under Irrevocable Credits 8–021
    (d) Confirmed Credits 8–022
    (e) Unconfirmed Negotiation Credits 8–026
    (f) Advantages and Disadvantages of Confirmed and
        Unconfirmed Credits 8–028
    (g) Other Types of Documentary Credit 8–029
    (h) Standby Letters of Credit 8–030
(6) **Nature of Bank's Security Under a Documentary**
    Credit 8–031
    (a) Constructive Possession 8–032
    (b) Legal Title 8–037
    (c) Equitable Title 8–041
    (d) Legal and Equitable Title Defeated by Fraud 8–043
(7) **Relationship Between Seller and Confirming Bank** 8–047
    (a) The Problem 8–047A
    (b) Possible Solutions 8–050

9. DOCUMENTARY CREDITS AND THE SALE CONTRACT 9–001

(1) **Sale Contract Requirements for Credit** 9–001
    (a) Implied Requirement for Irrevocable Credit 9–002
    (b) Terms of Credit 9–005
(2) **Credit More that Simply Means Paying the Price** 9–009
    (a) Provision of Credit Condition Precedent to Seller's
        Performance 9–010
    (b) Time of Opening of Credit 9–014
(3) **Waiver and Estoppel** 9–020
    (a) General Principles 9–020
    (b) Waiver and Periodic Actions 9–023
    (c) Only Unilateral Benefits May be Waived 9–027
(4) **Credit of Mutual Advantage of Seller and Buyer** 9–028
    (a) No Short-circuiting 9–028
    (b) Conditional Nature of Payment: Duty to Provide a
        Reliable and Solvent Paymaster 9–031

10. THE DOCUMENTS — 10–001

   (1) Documentary Requirements — 10–001
   (2) Documents Conform but Goods do Not — 10–002
   (3) The Doctrine of Strict Compliance — 10–025
      (a) Rationale of the Doctrine — 10–026
      (b) Trivial Defects — 10–030
      (c) What is an Original Document? — 10–034

PART D: CARRIAGE

11. SUBSTANCE OF CARRIAGE CONTRACTS — 11–001

   (1) General Principles of the Common Law — 11–002
      (a) From Bailment to Contract — 11–003
      (b) Other Implied Terms — 11–005
      (c) Contracting Out — 11–006
      (d) Duties of the Cargo-Owner — 11–007
      (e) The First Legislation — 11–008
   (2) Legislative Intervention and the *Hague-Visby Rules* — 11–014
      (a) Reasons for the *Hague Rules* — 11–015
      (b) General Principles and Effect — 11–021
      (c) Reason for the *Visby* Amendments — 11–031
      (d) The *Hague-Visby* Rules — 11–043
      (e) *Hague-Visby* Rules: Residual Problems — 11–061
   (3) *Hamburg Rules* — 11–081

12. THE BILL OF LADING AND THE CONTRACT OF CARRIAGE — 12–001

   (1) Relationship Between Bill of Lading and Carriage Contract — 12–001
      (a) Bill of Lading Not the Carriage Contract — 12–001
      (b) Position Where Bill of Lading Negotiated — 12–004
      (c) Consignee or Indorsee Also Charterer — 12–007
   (2) Incorporation of Charterparty Terms into Bills of Lading — 12–011
      (a) General Principles — 12–011
      (b) Ancillary Obligations — 12–012
      (c) Article III(8) — 12–013
      (d) Arbitration Clauses — 12–020
      (e) Manipulation — 12–027
      (f) From Which Charterparty? — 12–029
   (3) Identity of Carrier — 12–037
      (a) Demise Charterparty — 12–038
      (b) Time and Voyage Charters — 12–040

(c) Demise Clauses in Bills of Lading 12–044
(d) Other Factors 12–045
(e) Bailment of Terms 12–046

13. TRANSFER OF CARRIAGE CONTRACTS 13–001

(1) General Principles 13–001
  (a) Value of Bill of Lading Reduced 13–002
  (b) Common Law did not Transfer Contract with
    Bill of Lading 13–003
(2) Bill of Lading Act 1885, s.1 13–005
  (a) The 1885 Act 13–005
  (b) A Summary of the Problem 13–007
  (c) Documentation 13–008
  (d) Property Link 13–009
  (e) Rights and Liabilities Linked 13–010
  (f) Bulk Cargoes 13–011
  (g) Banks 13–012
  (h) Late Bills 13–013
  (i) Exemption Clauses 13–014
  (j) Law Commission 13–015
(3) Carriage of Goods by Sea Act 1992 13–016
  (a) The 1992 Act in General 13–016
  (b) Section 1 (Documentation) 13–017
  (c) Documentation not Covered by the Act 13–018
  (d) Specific Enumeration of Documents Covered 13–019
  (e) Section 2 (Rights Under Shipping Documents) 13–020
  (f) Residual Rights of Shipper and Intermediate
    Holders 13–021
  (g) Shipper or Intermediate Holder also Charterer 13–037
  (h) An Independent Tort or Action? 13–041
  (i) Section 3 (Liabilities Under Shipping Documents) 13–042
(4) *Brandt v Liverpool* Contracts 13–056
  (a) Application of the *Brandt v Liverpool* Doctrine to Bills
    of Lading 13–056
  (b) No Contract Implied on Facts 13–066
  (c) Conclusions on *Brandt v Liverpool* Today 13–071
(5) Tort Actions Against Carriers 13–072
(6) Other Privity Contracts 13–085

14. REPRESENTATION IN BILLS OF LADING 14–001

(1) Introduction 14–001
  (a) Importance of Representations in Bills of Lading 14–001
  (b) Initial Observations 14–002
  (c) Conflicting Viewpoints of Holder and Shipowner 14–005

(2) Who Provides the Information?		14–007
(3) Legal Effect of Representations		14–015
(a) Evidence of Truth		14–015
(b) Warranty of Truth?		14–016
(c) Estoppels		14–021
(d) Fraudulent and Negligent Misstatement		14–024
(e) Nature of Master's Obligation to State Truth		14–025
(4) Statements as to Quantity		14–033
(a) *Grant v Norway*		14–033
(b) *Grant v Norway* Not Extended		14–036
(c) Legislation		14–048
(d) Quantity Statements and Tort Actions		14–054
(e) Breach of Warranty of Authority		14–055

PART E: THE FUTURE

15. PROBLEMS AND PROPOSED SOLUTIONS		15–001
(1) Standardisation and Unification of International Sales		15–002
(a) Standard Forms and Definitions of Trade Terms		15–002
(b) Harmonisation and Globalisation		15–004
(c) Incoterms 2000		15–006
(d) Chains and Circles		15–009
(e) Negotiability of Documents		15–010
(f) Reluctance to Embrace *Hongkong Fir*		15–011
(g) U.L.I.S. and the Vienna Convention		15–014
(2) Containerisation and Multimodal Transport		15–017A
(a) Fast Ships and Use of Non-negotiable Documentation		15–018
(b) Combined Transport Operations		15–024
(3) Oil Cargoes and Standby Letters of Credit		15–032
(4) Fraud and Maritime Crime		15–037
(a) Types of Maritime Crime		15–038
(b) Prevention and Cure		15–053
16. COMPUTERISATION		16–001
(1) Contracting Over the Internet		16–001
(a) How Much Do You Need to Agree?		16–002
(b) When is a Contract Made?		16–005
(c) Writing and Signatures		16–007
(2) Facilitation of Paperless Documentation		16–015
(3) Paperless Bills of Lading in Reality		16–016
(a) Open and Closed Systems		16–017
(b) Electronic Signatures		16–019

(c) Transmission of Document   16–024
(d) Contracts Between Holder and Carrier   16–025
(e) Transfer of Property   16–026
(f) Two Models   16–027
(g) Security of Electronic Bills of Lading   16–038
(h) Conclusions   16–040

APPENDICES

APPENDIX A:
  Sale of Goods Act 1979   A–001
APPENDIX B:
  Incoterms 2000   B–001
APPENDIX C:
  Uniform Customs and Practice on Documentary Credits
  (1993 Revision) of the International Chambers of
  Commerce   C–001
APPENDIX D:
  Carriage of Goods by Sea Act 1971   D–001
APPENDIX E:
  Carriage of Goods by Sea Act 1992   E–001
APPENDIX F:
  Factors Act 1889   F–001
APPENDIX G:
  The Uniform Law on the International Sale of Goods   G–001
APPENDIX H:
  United Nations Convention on Contracts for the
  International Sale of Goods, 1980 (CISG)   H–001
APPENDIX I:
  Text and Commentary on the Hamburg Rules   I–001
APPENDIX J:
  CMI Uniform Rules for Sea Waybills   J–001
APPENDIX K:
  CMI Rules on Electronic Bills of Lading   K–001
APPENDIX L:
  Bolero Notebook   L–001
APPENDIX M:
  eUCP (Supplement to UCP 500 for Electronic
  Presentation—Version 1   M–001

TABLE OF CASES (UK)

AV Pound & Co v MW Hardy & Co Inc [1956] A.C. 588; [1956] 2 W.L.R.
683; [1956] 1 All E.R. 639; [1956] 1 Lloyd's Rep. 255; 100 S.J. 208, HL 1–005,
3–002, 3–013, 3–014, 3–047, 3–050, 3–059, 4–045, 15–003, B–002
Adams v Lindsell (1818) 1 B. Ald. 681 16–005
Adler v Dickson (No.1) [1955] 1 Q.B. 158; [1954] 3 W.L.R. 696; [1954] 3 All
E.R. 397; [1954] 2 Lloyd's Rep. 267; 98 S.J. 787, CA 11–038
Aegean Sea Traders Corp v Repsol Petroleo SA (The Aegean Sea) [1998] 2
Lloyd's Rep. 39; [1998] C.L.C. 1090, QBD (Comm Ct) 13–042, 13–053,
13–055
Afovos Shipping Co SA v R Pagnan & Fratelli (The Afovos) [1983] 1
W.L.R. 195; [1983] 1 All E.R. 449; [1983] 1 Lloyd's Rep. 335; [1983]
Com. L.R. 83; (1983) 127 S.J. 98, HL 3–042, 7–012, 7–029
Agricultores Federados Argentinos Sociedad Cooperativa v Ampro SA
Commerciale, Industrielle et Financiere [1965] 2 Lloyd's Rep. 157,
QBD 1–016, 3–040, 3–043, 3–045, 4–043, 4–045
Agrosin Pty Ltd v Highway Shipping Co Ltd (The Mata K) [1998] 2
Lloyd's Rep. 614; [1998] C.L.C. 1300, QBD (Comm Ct) 14–050, 14–051,
14–053
Aktieselskabet de Danske Sukkerfabrikker v Bajamar Compania Naviera
SA (The Torenia) [1983] 2 Lloyd's Rep. 210, QBD (Comm Ct) .. 11–024, 11–030
Al Hofuf, The. See Scandinavian Trading Co A/B v Zodiac Petroleum
SA.
Albazero, The. See Owners of Cargo Laden on Board the Albacruz v
Owners of the Albazero.
Alfred C Toepfer v Continental Grain Co [1974] 1 Lloyd's Rep. 11; (1973)
117 S.J. 649, C 6–102, 6–104A
Aliakmon, The. See Leigh & Sillivan Ltd v Aliakmon Shipping Co Ltd.
Allen v Coltart & Co (1882–83) L.R. 11 Q.B.D. 782, QBD 13–045, 13–047, 13–056
Almak, The. See Rudolph A Oetker v IFA Internationale Frachtagentur
AG.
American Accord, The. See United City Merchants (Investments) Ltd v
Royal Bank of Canada.
Andrea v British Italian Trading Co Ltd See Giacomo Costa Fu Andrea v
British Italian Trading Co Ltd.
Andreas Lemos, The. See Athens Maritime Enterprises Corp v Hellenic
Mutual War Risks Association (Bermuda).
Anglo-Russian Merchant Traders & John Batt & Co (London), Re. See
Arbitration between Anglo Russian Merchant Traders Ltd and John
Batt & Co (London) Ltd, Re.
Annefield, The. See Owners of the Annefield v Owners of Cargo Lately
Laden on Board the Annefield.
Anns v Merton LBC; sub nom. Anns v Walcroft Property Co Ltd [1978] A.C.
728; [1977] 2 W.L.R. 1024; [1977] 2 All E.R. 492; 75 L.G.R. 555; (1977)
243 E.G. 523; (1988) 4 Const. L.J. 100; [1977] J.P.L. 514; (1987) 84 L.S.G.
319; (1987) 137 N.L.J. 794; 121 S.J. 377, HL 13–076, 13–078
Anonima Petroli Italiana SpA and Neste Oy v Marlucidez Armadora SA
(The Filiatra Legacy) [1991] 2 Lloyd's Rep. 337, CA 1–049, 5–013, 5–014,
5–034, 5–060, 5–065, 5–068, 5–070, 5–072, 5–074, 5–077, 8–030, 15–032,
15–036
Antares, The. See Kenya Railways v Antares Co Pte Ltd.

Antclizo, The. *See* Food Corp of India v Antclizo Shipping Corp.
Anthony Hordern & Sons Ltd v Commonwealth and Dominion Line Ltd
  [1917] 2 K.B. 420, KBD 11–013
Aramis, The [1989] 1 Lloyd's Rep. 213; *Financial Times*, November 22,1988,
  CA 5–024, 13–009, 13–015, 13–045, 13–046, 13–055, 13–067, 13–068, 13–069,
                                                           13–070, 13–071, 16–029
Arbitration between Anglo Russian Merchant Traders Ltd and John Batt &
  Co (London) Ltd, Re [1917] 2 K.B. 679, CA 3–049
Arbitration between Weis & Co Ltd and Credit Colonial et Commercial
  (Antwerp), Re [1916] 1 K.B. 346, KBD 4–015
Arctic Trader, The. *See* Trade Star Line Corp v Mitsui & Co Ltd.
Ardennes, The. *See* Owners of Cargo Lately Laden on Board the Ardennes
  v Owners of the Ardennes.
Argonaut Navigation Co Ltd v Ministry of Food (The Argobec) [1949] 1
  K.B. 572; [1949] 1 All E.R. 160; (1948–49) 82 Ll. L. Rep. 223; 65 T.L.R.
  40; [1949] L.J.R. 353; 93 S.J. 58, CA 11–073
Armagas Ltd v Mundogas SA (The Ocean Frost) [1986] A.C. 717; [1986] 2
  W.L.R. 1063; [1986] 2 All E.R. 385; [1986] 2 Lloyd's Rep. 109; (1986) 83
  L.S.G. 2002; (1986) 130 S.J. 430, HL 14–035, 14–042, 14–043, 14–054
Arnhold Karberg & Co v Blythe Green Jourdain & Co; Theodor Schneider
  & Co v Burgett & Newsam [1916] 1 K.B. 495, CA; affirming [1915] 2
  K.B. 379, KBD 2–013, 4–008, 4–009, 4–015, 4–017, 4–050, 5–037
Associated Distributors Ltd v Hall [1938] 2 K.B. 83, CA 4–044
Associated Japanese Bank (International) Ltd v Credit du Nord SA [1989]
  1 W.L.R. 255; [1988] 3 All E.R. 902; [1989] Fin. L.R. 117; (1989) 86(8)
  L.S.G. 43; (1988) 138 N.L.J. Rep. 109; (1989) 133 S.J. 81, QBD 4–049
Astro Valiente Compania Naviera SA v Pakistan Ministry of Food and
  Agriculture (The Emmanuel Colocotronis) (No.2) [1982] 1 W.L.R.
  1096; [1982] 1 All E.R. 823; [1982] 1 Lloyd's Rep. 286, QBD (Comm
  Ct) 12–022, 12–023
Athanasia Comninos and Georges Chr Lemos, The [1990] 1 Lloyd's Rep.
  277, QBD (Comm Ct) 3–009
Athens Maritime Enterprises Corp v Hellenic Mutual War Risks Associa-
  tion (Bermuda) (The Andreas Lemos) [1983] Q.B. 647; [1983] 2 W.L.R.
  425; [1983] 1 All E.R. 590; [1982] 2 Lloyd's Rep. 483; [1982] Com. L.R.
  188; (1982) 79 L.S.G. 1257; 126 S.J. 577, QBD (Comm Ct) 10–018, 15–038
Atlas, The. *See* Noble Resources Ltd v Cavalier Shipping Corp.
Aughton Ltd (formerly Aughton Group Ltd) v MF Kent Services Ltd
  (1991) 57 B.L.R. 1; 31 Con. L.R. 60, CA 12–020

BP Exploration Co (Libya) Ltd v Hunt (No.2) [1983] 2 A.C. 352; [1982] 2
  W.L.R. 253, HL; affirming [1981] 1 W.L.R. 232; 125 S.J. 165, CA;
  affirming [1979] 1 W.L.R. 783; 123 S.J. 455, QBD 7–048
Bain v Field & Co Fruit Merchants Ltd (1920) 5 Ll. L. Rep. 16, CA;
  reversing in part (1920) 3 Ll. L. Rep. 26, KBD (Comm Ct) 1–005
Baker v Dening (1838) 8 A. & E. 94 .... 16–009, 16–010, 16–011, 16–013
Balli Trading Ltd v Afalona Shipping Ltd (The Coral) [1993] 1 Lloyd's Rep.
  1; (1992) 89(34) L.S.G. 40; (1992) 136 S.J.L.B. 259; *The Times*, August 18,
  1992, CA 11–077, 12–06, 12–017
Banco Santander SA v Bayfern Ltd; *sub nom.* Banco Santander SA v
  Banque Paribas [2000] 1 All E.R. (Comm) 776; [2000] Lloyd's Rep.
  Bank. 165; [2000] C.L.C. 906, CA 15–037
Bangladesh Chemical Industries Corp v Henry Stephens Shipping Co and
  Tex-Bilan Shipping Co (The SLS Everest) [1981] 2 Lloyd's Rep. 389;
  [1981] Com. L.R. 176, CA 5–061, 12–030, 12–031, 12–032, 12–033, 12–035
Bank Line Ltd v Arthur Capel & Co [1919] A.C. 435, HL 7–010

Bank Melli Iran v Barclays Bank (Dominion Colonial & Overseas) [1951] 2
 Lloyd's Rep. 367; [1951] 2 T.L.R. 1057, KBD 10–026
Bank of Boston Connecticut (formerly Colonial Bank) v European Grain &
 Shipping Ltd (The Dominique); *sub nom.* Colonial Bank v European
 Grain & Shipping Ltd [1989] A.C. 1056; [1989] 2 W.L.R. 440; [1989] 1
 All E.R. 545; [1989] 1 Lloyd's Rep. 431; (1989) 86(11) L.S.G. 43; (1989)
 133 S.J. 219, HL 15–039
Bank of England v Vagliano Bros; *sub nom.* Vagliano Bros v Bank of
 England [1891] A.C. 107, HL 4–022, 11–029
Bank Tejarat v Hong Kong and Shanghai Banking Corp (CI) Ltd [1995] 1
 Lloyd's Rep. 239, QBD (Comm Ct) 15–040, 15–053
Bankers Trust Co v State Bank of India [1991] 2 Lloyd's Rep. 443; *The
 Times*, June 25, 1991; *Independent*, August 14, 1991; *Financial Times*,
 June 28, 1991, CA 8–011, 10–030, 10–031, 10–032, 10–033, 16–028
Banner Ex p. *See* Tappenbeck Ex p. Banner, Re.
Banque de l'Indochine et de Suez SA v JH Rayner (Mincing Lane) Ltd
 [1983] Q.B. 711; [1983] 2 W.L.R. 841; [1983] 1 All E.R. 1137; [1983] 1
 Lloyd's Rep. 228; (1983) 127 S.J. 361, CA 10–031, 10–033
Barber v Meyerstein. *See* Meyerstein v Barber.
Barclays Bank Ltd v Customs and Excise Commissioners [1963] 1 Lloyd's
 Rep. 81, QBD (Comm Ct) ... 6–005, 6–026, 6–027, 6–029, 6–035, 6–040, 6–041,
 13–029
Barder v Taylor (1839) 9 L.J. Ex. 21 6–091
Bartletts de Reya v Byrne (1983) 133 N.L.J. 1101; (1983) 127 S.J. 69, CA ... 16–013
Baumwoll Manufactur Von Carl Scheibler v Furness; *sub nom.* Baumvoll
 Manufactur Von Scheibler v Gilchrist & Co; Baumvoll Manufactur
 Von Scheibler v Gilchrest & Co [1893] A.C. 8, HL 12–038, 12–041
Bayerische Vereinsbank AG v National Bank of Pakistan [1997] 1 Lloyd's
 Rep. 59; [1997] 6 Bank. L.R. 319; [1996] C.L.C. 1443, QBD (Comm
 Ct) 10–033
Beauvais v Green, 22 T.L.R. 816 16–013
Bekol BV v Terracina Shipping Corp, July 13, 1988, unreported, HC 11–059
Bell v Lever Bros Ltd; *sub nom.* Lever Bros Ltd v Bell [1932] A.C. 161,
 HL 4–048
Bennett v Brumfitt (1867–68) L.R. 3 C.P. 30, CCP 16–013
Bentsen v Taylor Sons & Co [1893] 2 Q.B. 283, CA 9–025
Berge Sisar, The. *See* Borealis AB (formerly Borealis Petrokemi AB and
 Statoil Petrokemi AB) v Stargas Ltd.
Berkshire, The [1974] 1 Lloyd's Rep. 185, QBD (Adm Ct) 12–044
Besseler Waechter Glover & Co v South Derwent Coal Co Ltd [1938] 1 K.B.
 408; (1937) 59 Ll. L. Rep. 104, KBD 4–044
Biddell Bros v E Clemens Horst Co; *sub nom.* E Clement Horst Co v Biddell
 Bros [1912] A.C. 18, HL; reversing [1911] 1 K.B. 934, CA; reversing
 [1911] 1 K.B. 214, KBD 2–008, 2–009, 2–010, 2–012, 4–012, 4–014, 6–061,
 6–065, 6–073, 6–095, 6–101, 6–114, 9–030
Blankenstein, The. *See* Damon Compania Naviera SA v Hapag-Lloyd
 International SA.
Blyth & Co v Richard Turpin & Co (1916) 114 L.T. 753 1–005
Bolivinter Oil SA v Chase Manhattan Bank NA [1984] 1 W.L.R. 392; [1984]
 1 Lloyd's Rep. 251; (1984) 128 S.J. 153, CA 10–015, 14–005
Borealis AB (formerly Borealis Petrokemi AB and Statoil Petrokemi AB) v
 Stargas Ltd (The Berge Sisar) [2001] UKHL 17; [2001] 2 W.L.R. 1118;
 [2001] 2 All E.R. 193; [2001] 1 All E.R. (Comm) 673; [2001] 1 Lloyd's
 Rep. 663; [2001] C.L.C. 1084; (2001) 98(20) L.S.G. 43; (2001) 145 S.J.L.B.
 93; *The Times*, March 27, 2001, HL 13–033, 13–036, 13–042, 13–043, 13–055,
 13–057

Boukadoura Maritime Corp v Marocaine de l'Industrie et du Raffinage SA
　　(The Boukadoura) [1989] 1 Lloyd's Rep. 393; *Independent*, November
　　25, 1988; *Financial Times*, November 1, 1988, QBD (Comm Ct) 14–029
Bowes v Shand; *sub nom*. Shand v Bowes (1876–77) L.R. 2 App. Cas. 455
Court: HL 3–025, 3–031, 4–015, 6–061, 6–063, 7–004, 7–018, 7–019, 7–021, 7–032,
　　　　　　　　　　　　　　　　　　　　　　　7–051, 7–052, 15–011
Braithwaite v Foreign Hardwood Co [1905] 2 K.B. 543, CA 7–025, 7–028
Brandt v Liverpool Brazil and River Plate Steam Navigation Co Ltd; *sub
　　nom*. Brandt & Co v River Plate Steam Navigation Co Ltd [1924] 1 K.B.
　　575; (1923–24) 17 Ll. L. Rep. 142, CA 5–025, 6–038, 7–068, 8–049, 11–062,
　　　　　　　12–006, 13–014, 13–017, 13–045, 13–046, 13–048, 13–055, 13–056, 13–057,
　　　　　　　　　13–058, 13–059, 13–060, 13–061, 13–062, 13–063, 13–064, 13–065,
　　　　　　　　　13–066, 13–067, 13–068, 13–069, 13–071, 13–073, 13–074, 13–076,
　　　　　　　　　　　　　　13–079, 13–082, 14–020, 14–022, 14–023, 16–029
Bremer Handelsgesellschaft GmbH v JH Rayner & Co [1979] 2 Lloyd's
　　Rep. 216, CA; reversing [1978] 2 Lloyd's Rep. 73, QBD (Comm Ct) 3–026
Bremer Vulkan Schiffbau und Maschinenfabrik v South India Shipping
　　Corp Ltd; *sub nom*. Bremer Vulkan Schiffbau und Maschinenfabrik v
　　South India Shipping Cor; Gregg v Raytheon [1981] A.C. 909; [1981]
　　2 W.L.R. 141; [1981] 2 All E.R. 289; [1981] 1 Lloyd's Rep. 253; [1981]
　　Com. L.R. 19; [1981] E.C.C. 151; 125 S.J. 114, HL 12–020
Bridge v Campbell Discount Co Ltd; *sub nom*. Campbell Discount Co Ltd
　　v Bridge [1962] A.C. 600; [1962] 2 W.L.R. 439; [1962] 1 All E.R. 385; 106
　　S.J. 94, HL 4–044
Brinkibon v Stahag Stahl und Stahlwarenhandels GmbH; *sub nom*. Brinki-
　　bon Ltd v Stahag Stahl und Stahlwarenhandelsgesellschaft mbH
　　[1983] 2 A.C. 34; [1982] 2 W.L.R. 264; [1982] 1 All E.R. 293; [1982] 1
　　Lloyd's Rep. 217; [1982] Com. L.R. 72; [1982] E.C.C. 322; 126 S.J. 116,
　　HL 16–006
Britain & Overseas Trading (Bristles) Ltd v Brooks Wharf & Bull Wharf
　　Ltd [1967] 2 Lloyd's Rep. 51, QBD 13–060
British & Beningtons Ltd v North West Cachar Tea Co Ltd; *sub nom*.
　　Baintgoorie (Dooars) Tea Co Ltd v British & Beningtons Ltd; Maz-
　　dehee Tea Co Ltd v British & Beningtons Ltd; North-Western Cachar
　　Tea Co Ltd v British & Beningtons Lt; British & Beningtons Ltd v
　　Baintgoorie (Dooars) Tea Co Ltd; British & Beningtons Ltd v Maz-
　　dahee Tea Co Ltd; North-Western Cachar Tea Co Ltd v Same [1923]
　　A.C. 48; (1922) 13 Ll. L. Rep. 67, HL 7–010, 7–026
British Estate Investment Society v Jackson (HM Inspector of Taxes), 50 R.
　　& I.T. 33; 37 T.C. 79; (1956) 35 A.T.C. 413; [1956] T.R. 397, Ch D 16–013
British Imex Industries v Midland Bank Ltd [1958] 1 Q.B. 542; [1958] 2
　　W.L.R. 103; [1958] 1 All E.R. 264; [1957] 2 Lloyd's Rep. 591; 102 S.J. 69,
　　QBD 6–069
Brogden v Directors of Metropolitan Railway Co (1876–77) L.R. 2 App.
　　Cas. 666, HL 16–005
Brown Jenkinson & Co Ltd v Percy Dalton (London) Ltd [1957] 2 Q.B. 621;
　　[1957] 3 W.L.R. 403; [1957] 2 All E.R. 844; [1957] 2 Lloyd's Rep. 1; 101
　　S.J. 610, CA 6–021, 6–029, 7–066, 15–049
Browne v Hare (1859) 4 H. & N. 822, Exchequer Chamber 4–003, 4–004, 5–033,
　　　　　　　　　　　　　　　　　　　　5–040, 5–041, 5–042, 5–049, 5–083
Browner International Ltd v Monarch Shipping Co Ltd (The European
　　Enterprise) [1989] 2 Lloyd's Rep. 185, QBD (Comm Ct) 11–077
Bryans v Nix (1839) 4 M. & W. 775; 150 E.R. 1634 13–044
Brydges v Dix (1891) 7 T.L.R. 215 .... 16–009, 16–013
Bunge & Co v Tradax England [1975] 2 Lloyd's Rep. 235, QBD (Comm
　　Ct) 3–018, 3–020, 15–011, 15–012

Bunge Corp v Tradax Export SA [1981] 1 W.L.R. 711; [1981] 2 All E.R. 540; [1981] 2 Lloyd's Rep. 1; 125 S.J. 373, HL; affirming [1981] 2 All E.R. 524; [1980] 1 Lloyd's Rep. 294, CA; reversing [1979] 2 Lloyd's Rep. 477, QBD (Comm Ct) .. 1–017, 1–048, 2–029, 3–023, 3–024, 3–029, 3–036, 3–039
Burstall v Grimsdale (1906) 11 Com. Cas. 280 6–111
Byrd, Re, 3 Curt. 117 16–010

CN Vasconzala v Churchill. *See* Compania Naviera Vasconzala v Churchill & Sim.
C Groom Ltd v Barber [1915] 1 K.B. 316, KBD 1–005, 2–018, 4–002, 4–010, 4–011, 4–013, 4–015, 4–017, 4–019, 4–027, 4–047, 5–010, 6–073, 6–111, 6–114, 7–021, 15–010, 15–016, 16–028, 16–036
Cahn v Pockett's Bristol Channel Steam Packet Co Ltd [1899] 1 Q.B. 643, CA 5–005, 6–032, 8–006
Calcutta, The. *See* Steamship Calcutta Co Ltd v Andrew Weir & Co.
Canadian Highlander, The. *See* Gosse Millard Ltd v Canadian Government Merchant Marine Ltd.
Cap Palos, The. *See* Owners of the Cap Palos v Alder.
Caparo Industries plc v Dickman [1990] 2 A.C. 605; [1990] 2 W.L.R. 358; [1990] 1 All E.R. 568; [1990] B.C.C. 164; [1990] B.C.L.C. 273; [1990] E.C.C. 313; [1955–95] P.N.L.R. 523; (1990) 87(12) L.S.G. 42; (1990) 140 N.L.J. 248; (1990) 134 S.J. 494; *The Times*, February 12, 1990; *Independent*, February 16, 1990; *Financial Times*, February 13, 1990; *Guardian*, February 15, 1990; *Daily Telegraph*, February 15, 1990, HL ... 14–024, 14–027, 14–032
Cape Asbestos Co Ltd v Lloyd's Bank Ltd (1921) W.N. 274, KBD .. 8–018, 9–026
Captain Gregos, The. *See* Cia Portorafti Commerciale SA v Ultramar Panama Inc.
Cargill UK Ltd v Continental UK Ltd [1989] 2 Lloyd's Rep. 290, CA; affirming [1989] 1 Lloyd's Rep. 193, QBD (Comm Ct) ... 3–042, 3–045, 4–042
Carlos Federspiel & Co SA v Charles Twigg & Co Ltd [1957] 1 Lloyd's Rep. 240, QBD (Comm Ct) 1–013, 3–015, 3–016, 3–057, 5–005, 5–009, 5–010, 5–011, 5–014, 5–054, 15–003
Carlsberg v Wemyss (1915) S.C. 616 6–035
Carr v London and North Western Railway Co (1874–75) L.R. 10 C.P. 307, CCP 5–083
Cartledge v E Jopling & Sons Ltd [1963] A.C. 758; [1963] 2 W.L.R. 210; [1963] 1 All E.R. 341; [1963] 1 Lloyd's Rep. 1; 107 S.J. 73, HL 13–083
Caspiana, The. *See* GH Renton & Co Ltd v Palmyra Trading Corp of Panama.
Castle v Playford (1871–72) L.R. 7 Ex. 98, Ex Chamber 2–017
Cattle v Stockton Waterworks Co (1874–75) L.R. 10 Q.B. 453; [1874–80] All E.R. Rep. 492, QBD 13–075
Cehave NV v Bremer Handels GmbH (The Hansa Nord); *sub nom.* Cehave NV v Bremer Handelsgesellschaft mbH (The Hansa Nord) [1976] Q.B. 44; [1975] 3 W.L.R. 447; [1975] 3 All E.R. 739; [1975] 2 Lloyd's Rep. 445; 119 S.J. 678, CA 3–025
Central London Property Trust v High Trees House Ltd [1947] K.B. 130; [1956] 1 All E.R. 256 (Note); 62 T.L.R. 557; [1947] L.J.R. 77; 175 L.T. 333, KBD 9–026
Central Newbury Car Auctions v Unity Finance [1957] 1 Q.B. 371; [1956] 3 W.L.R. 1068; [1956] 3 All E.R. 905; 100 S.J. 927, CA 7–041
Cerealmangimi SpA v Alfred C Toepfer (The Eurometal) [1981] 3 All E.R. 533; [1981] 1 Lloyd's Rep. 337; [1981] Com. L.R. 13, QBD (Comm Ct) 7–049

Ceval Alimentos SA v Agrimpex Trading Co Ltd (The Northern Progress) (No.2) [1996] 2 Lloyd's Rep. 319; [1996] C.L.C. 1529, QBD (Comm Ct) 2–031, 2–034

Chanda, The. *See* Wibau Maschinefabrik Hartman SA v Mackinnon Mackenzie.

Charge Card Services Ltd, Re [1989] Ch. 497; [1988] 3 W.L.R. 764; [1988] 3 All E.R. 702; (1988) 4 B.C.C. 524; [1988] B.C.L.C. 711; [1988] P.C.C. 390; [1988] Fin. L.R. 308; (1989) 8 Tr. L.R. 86; (1988) 85(42) L.S.G. 46; (1988) 138 N.L.J. Rep. 201; (1988) 132 S.J. 1458; *The Times*, July 7, 1988; *Independent*, July 6, 1988; *Financial Times*, July 8, 1988; *Guardian*, July 7, 1988; *Daily Telegraph*, July 7, 1988, CA 9–037

Chargeurs Réunis Compagnie Francaise de Navigation à Vapeur (The Ceylan) v English & American Shipping Co (The Merida) (No.2) (1921) 9 Ll. L. Rep. 464, CA 13–075

Chartered Mercantile Bank of India, London and China v Netherlands India Steam Navigation Co Ltd (1882–83) L.R. 10 Q.B.D. 521, CA 12–005

Cheetham & Co Ltd v Thornham Spinning Co Ltd [1964] 2 Lloyd's Rep. 17, QBD (Comm Ct) 5–069

Chemical Venture, The. *See* OK Petroleum AB v Vitol Energy SA.

Cia Portorafti Commerciale SA v Ultramar Panama Inc (The Captain Gregos) (No.1) [1990] 3 All E.R. 967; [1990] 1 Lloyd's Rep. 310; *Financial Times*, December 22, 1989; Lloyd's List, February 9, 1990, CA 11–003, 11–030, 11–061, 11–062, 11–063, 11–068, 11–081, 13–002, 13–007, 13–014, 13–018, 13–072

Cia Portorafti Commerciale SA v Ultramar Panama Inc (The Captain Gregos) (No.2) [1990] 2 Lloyd's Rep. 395, CA 11–030, 11–061, 11–062, 11–063, 11–068, 11–081, 13–002, 13–007, 13–014, 13–018, 13–062, 13–068, 13–069, 13–071, 16–029

Cie Commerciale Sucres et Denrees v C Czarnikow Ltd (The Naxos) [1990] 1 W.L.R. 1337; [1990] 3 All E.R. 641; [1991] 1 Lloyd's Rep. 29; (1990) 134 S.J. 1301; *Financial Times*, October 17, 1990, HL 3–016, 3–021, 3–029, 3–031, 3–032, 3–033, 3–039, 3–050, 15–002

Ciudad de Pasto, The. *See* Mitsui & Co Ltd v Flota Mercante Grancolombiana SA.

Clarke, Re, 27 L.J.P.M. & A. 18 .... 16–010, 16–011, 16–013

Cock v Taylor (1811) 13 East. 399; 104 E.R. 424 .... 13–045, 13–056

Colin & Shields v W Weddel & Co Ltd [1952] 2 All E.R. 337; [1952] 2 Lloyd's Rep. 9; [1952] 2 T.L.R. 185; [1952] W.N. 420; 96 S.J. 547, CA ; affirming [1952] 1 All E.R. 1021; [1952] 1 Lloyd's Rep. 390; [1952] 1 T.L.R. 1191, QBD 6–097, 13–060

Colley v Overseas Exporters (1919) Ltd [1921] 3 K.B. 302; (1921) 8 Ll. L. Rep. 127, KBD 3–040, 4–003, 4–045, 5–014, 5–082

Compania Naviera Vasconzada v Churchill & Sim; Compania Naviera Vasconzada v Burton & Co [1906] 1 K.B. 237, KBD .. 7–068, 13–056, 14–003, 14–017, 14–019, 14–020, 14–021, 14–022, 14–023, 14–024, 14–025, 14–027, 14–028, 14–029, 14–030, 14–033, 14–054, 14–060

Comptoir d'Achat et de Vente du Boerenbond Belge SA v Luis de Ridder Limitada (The Julia) [1949] A.C. 293; [1949] 1 All E.R. 269; (1948–49) 82 Ll. L. Rep. 270; 65 T.L.R. 126; [1949] L.J.R. 513; 93 S.J. 101, HL 1–049, 2–003, 2–015, 2–018, 2–021, 3–014, 3–060, 4–007, 4–009, 4–017, 5–017, 5–059, 6–001, 6–095, 6–096, 6–098, 6–100, 6–112, 7–021, 13–060, 15–008

Concordia Trading BV v Richco International Ltd [1991] 1 Lloyd's Rep. 475, QBD (Comm Ct) 1–001, 1–013, 1–018, 3–006, 5–010, 6–087, 6–094, 12–010, 15–009, B–015

Conoco (UK) v Limai Maritime Co (The Sirina) [1988] 2 Lloyd's Rep. 613, QBD (Comm Ct) 5–066, 13–013

Convoy Intercontinental Container Transport v Open Bulk Carriers Ltd,
   July 26, 1990 .... 11–054, 11–055
Cook, In the Estate of; *sub nom.* Murison v Cook [1960] 1 W.L.R. 353; [1960]
   1 All E.R. 689; 75 A.L.R.2d 892; 104 S.J. 311, PDAD 16–009, 16–013
Cooper (Inspector of Taxes) v Stubbs [1925] 2 K.B. 753, CA 1–039
Cooperative Centrale Raiffeisen-Boerenleenbank BA v Sumitomo Bank
   (The Royan, The Abukirk, The Bretagne, The Auvergne) [1988] 2
   Lloyd's Rep. 250; [1988] 2 F.T.L.R. 27, CA; affirming in part [1987] 1
   Lloyd's Rep. 345; [1987] 1 F.T.L.R. 233; [1987] Fin. L.R. 275, QBD
   (Comm Ct) 10–033
Coral, The. *See* Balli Trading Ltd v Afalona Shipping Ltd.
Cordova Land Co Ltd v Victor Bros Inc; Cordova Land Co v Black
   Diamond Steamship Corp [1966] 1 W.L.R. 793; 110 S.J. 290, QBD 4–035,
                                                                                   4–036
Couturier v Hastie (1856) 5 H.L. Cas. 673 ... 2–003, 3–056, 4–002, 4–046C, 4–047,
                                                          4–048, 4–049, 4–050, 15–002
Cowas-Jee v Thompson (1845) 3 Moore Ind. App. 422; 18 E.R. 560, PC 1–004,
            1–005, 1–007, 1–008, 1–011, 1–013, 5–005, 5–033, 5–035, 6–047
Cox, Patterson, & Co v Bruce & Co (1887) L.R. 18 Q.B.D. 147, CA 14–017,
                                                                             14–035, 14–040
Craven v Ryder (1816) Taunt. 433, 128 E.R. 1103 .... 1–004, 1–008, 1–011
Credit Industriel et Commercial v China Merchants Bank [2002] EWHC
   973, QBD (Comm Ct) 10–002, 10–033, 10–037
Crooks & Co v Allan; *sub nom.* Crooks v Allan (1879–80) L.R. 5 Q.B.D. 38,
   QBD 12–003
Cubazukar v Iansa. *See* Empresa Exportadora de Azucar (Cubazukar) v
   Industria Azucarera Nacional S.A. (Iansa).
Cunningham, Re, 29 L.J.P.M. & A. 71 16–011

Damon Compania Naviera SA v Hapag-Lloyd International SA (The
   Blankenstein) [1985] 1 W.L.R. 435; [1985] 1 All E.R. 475; [1985] 1
   Lloyd's Rep. 93; (1985) 82 L.S.G. 1644; (1985) 129 S.J. 218, CA 16–002
Daval Aciers D'Usinor et de Sacilor v Armare Srl (The Nerarno) [1996] 1
   Lloyd's Rep. 1, CA; affirming [1994] 2 Lloyd's Rep. 50, QBD (Adm
   Ct) 12–020, 12–028
Dawes v Peck (1799) 8 Term. Rep. 330; 101 E.R. 1417 13–045
Delfini, The. *See* Enichem Anic SpA v Ampelos Shipping Co Ltd.
Denbigh Cowan & Co v R Atcherley & Co (1921) 6 Ll. L. Rep. 383, CA 6–098
Diamond Alkali Export Corp v Bourgeois [1921] 3 K.B. 443; (1921) 8 Ll. L.
   Rep. 282, KBD 2–010, 6–050, 6–051, 6–060, 6–065, 6–111, 13–008, 15–011
Diana Prosperity, The. *See* Reardon Smith Line Ltd v Hansen-Tangen.
Discount Records Ltd v Barclays Bank Ltd [1975] 1 W.L.R. 315; [1975] 1 All
   E.R. 1071; [1975] 1 Lloyd's Rep. 444; (1974) 119 S.J. 133, Ch D 10–012,
                                          10–014, 14–002, 14–005, 15–037, 15–049, 15–053
Dobell & Co v Steamship Rossmore Co Ltd [1895] 2 Q.B. 408, CA .. 11–039, 11–040
Doe d. Phillips v Evans, Re 2 L.J. Ex. 193 16–010
Dominique, The. *See* Bank of Boston Connecticut (formerly Colonial Bank)
   v European Grain & Shipping Ltd.
Dona Mari, The. *See* Peter Cremer GmbH v General Carriers SA.
Donald H Scott & Co Ltd v Barclays Bank Ltd; *sub nom.* Donald H Scott &
   Co v Barclays Bank Ltd [1923] 2 K.B. 1; (1923) 14 Ll. L. Rep. 142, CA;
   reversing (1922) 12 Ll. L. Rep. 502, KBD 6–112
Donoghue v Stevenson; *sub nom.* McAlister v Stevenson [1932] A.C. 562;
   1932 S.C. (H.L.) 31; 1932 S.L.T. 317; [1932] W.N. 139, HL 11–038, 13–083
Doyle v Olby (Ironmongers) Ltd [1969] 2 Q.B. 158; [1969] 2 W.L.R. 673;
   [1969] 2 All E.R. 119; 113 S.J. 128, CA 7–032, 7–056, 15–049, 15–053

Dublin City Distillery Ltd v Doherty [1914] A.C. 823, HL (UK-Irl) 13–044
Dulieu v White & Sons [1901] 2 K.B. 669, KBD 6–063
Duncan v Koster; *sub nom.* Teutonia, The (1871–73) L.R. 4 P.C. 171, PC
    (UK) 11–029
Dunelmia, The. *See* President of India v Metcalfe Shipping Co Ltd.
Dunlop v Lambert (1839) 6 Cl. & F. 600; 7 E.R. 824 .... 1–010, 1–013, 2–027, 5–063,
                                                             13–038, 13–039, 13–040
Dunlop Pneumatic Tyre Co Ltd v Selfridge & Co Ltd [1915] A.C. 847,
    HL 11–0038

ED&F Man Ltd v Nigerian Sweets & Confectionery Co [1977] 2 Lloyd's
    Rep. 50, QBD (Comm Ct) 9–037
E Hardy & Co (London) Ltd v Hillerns & Fowler; *sub nom.* Hardy & Co v
    Hillerns [1923] 2 K.B. 490; (1923) 15 Ll. L. Rep. 194, CA 7–036
East West Corp v DKBS 1912. *See* Utaniko Ltd v P&O Nedlloyd BV
    (No.1).
Edgington v Fitzmaurice (1885) L.R. 29 Ch. D. 459, CA 15–049, 15–053
Edward Owen Engineering Ltd v Barclays Bank International Ltd [1978]
    Q.B. 159; [1977] 3 W.L.R. 764; [1978] 1 All E.R. 976; [1978] 1 Lloyd's
    Rep. 166; 6 B.L.R. 1; 121 S.J. 617, CA 10–002, 10–010, 10–022
Effort Shipping Co Ltd v Linden Management SA (The Giannis NK) [1998]
    A.C. 605; [1998] 2 W.L.R. 206; [1998] 1 All E.R. 495; [1998] 1 Lloyd's
    Rep. 337; [1998] C.L.C. 374; (1998) 95(7) L.S.G. 32; (1998) 148 N.L.J.
    121; (1998) 142 S.J.L.B. 54; *The Times*, January 29, 1998; *Independent*,
    January 27, 1998, HL 11–010, 13–047
El Amria, The and El Minia, The; *sub nom.* El Amria, The (No.3) [1982] 2
    Lloyd's Rep. 28; [1982] Com. L.R. 121; 126 S.J. 411, CA 1–013, 3–008, 3–009,
                                                             12–001, 12–010
Elafi, The. *See* Karlshamns Oljefabriker A/B v Eastport Navigation
    Corp.
Elder Dempster & Co v Paterson Zochonis & Co *See* Paterson Zochonis &
    Co Ltd v Elder Dempster & Co Ltd.
Elli II, The. *See* Ilyssia Compania Naviera SA v Ahmed Abdul-Qawi
    Bamaodah.
Elliott Steam Tug Co Ltd v Shipping Controller [1922] 1 K.B. 127; (1921) 8
    Ll. L. Rep. 462, CA 13–075
Emmanuel Colocotronis, The. *See* Astro Valiente Compania Naviera SA v
    Pakistan Ministry of Food and Agriculture.
Empresa Exportadora De Azucar (CUBAZUCAR) v Industria Azucarera
    Nacional SA (IANSA), February 29, 1980, QBD 2–040
Empresa Exportadora De Azucar (CUBAZUCAR) v Industria Azucarera
    Nacional SA (IANSA) (The Playa Larga and Marble Islands) [1983] 2
    Lloyd's Rep. 171; [1983] Com. L.R. 58; *The Times*, December 13, 1982,
    CA 2–040, 2–041, 2–042, 2–043, 2–045, 4–009, 15–053
Enichem Anic SpA v Ampelos Shipping Co Ltd (The Delfini) [1990] 1
    Lloyd's Rep. 252; *The Times*, August 11, 1989, CA; affirming [1988] 2
    Lloyd's Rep. 599, QBD (Comm Ct) .. 1–047, 1–049, 2–027, 5–010, 5–033, 5–060,
                        5–062, 5–065, 5–066, 5–067, 5–068, 5–069, 5–072, 5–073, 6–041, 6–042,
                        7–038, 7–030, 13–004, 13–007, 13–009, 13–013, 13–015, 13–029, 13–046,
                                                 13–055, 15–008, 15–032, 15–036
Enrico Furst & Co v WE Fischer Ltd [1960] 2 Lloyd's Rep. 340, QBD
    (Comm Ct) 8–028, 9–021
Entores Ltd v Miles Far East Corp; *sub nom.* Newcomb v De Roos [1955]
    2 Q.B. 327; [1955] 3 W.L.R. 48; [1955] 2 All E.R. 493; [1955] 1 Lloyd's
    Rep. 511; 99 S.J. 384, CA 16–005, 16–006
Epaphus, The. *See* Eurico SpA v Philipp Bros.

Equitable Trust Co of New York v Dawson Partners Ltd (1927) 27 Ll. L.
Rep. 49, HL 10–026, 10–031
Etablissement Esefka International Anstalt v Central Bank of Nigeria
[1979] 1 Lloyd's Rep. 445, CA 10–020, 14–003, 15–047, 15–048, 15–049
Etablissements Chainbaux SARL v Harbormaster Ltd [1955] 1 Lloyd's
Rep. 303, QBD 9–014
Eurico SpA v Philipp Bros (The Epaphus) [19x87] 2 Lloyd's Rep. 215;
[1987] 2 F.T.L.R. 213; *The Times*, May 18, 1987, CA; affirming [1986] 2
Lloyd's Rep. 387, QBD (Comm Ct) 2–038, 4–048, 16–028, 16–036
Eurometal, The. *See* Cerealmangimi SpA v Alfred C Toepfer.
European Asian Bank AG v Punjab & Sind Bank (No.2) [1983] 1 W.L.R.
642; [1983] 2 All E.R. 508; [1983] 1 Lloyd's Rep. 611; [1983] Com. L.R.
128; (1983) 127 S.J. 379, CA 8–035
European Enterprise, The. *See* Browner International Ltd v Monarch Ship-
ping Co Ltd.
Eurus, The. *See* Total Transport Corp v Arcadia Petroleum Ltd.
Evans v Nichol (1841) 3 M. & G. 614; 133 E.R. 1286 13–044

FE Napier v Dexters Ltd (1926) 26 Ll.L. Rep. 184, CA 5–086
F&G Sykes (Wessex) Ltd v Fine Fare Ltd [1967] 1 Lloyd's Rep. 53, CA ... 16–004
Factortame Ltd v Secretary of State for Transport. *See* R. v Secretary of
State for Transport Ex p. Factortame Ltd (No.1).
Federal Bulk Carriers v C Itoh & Co (The Federal Bulker) [1989] 1 Lloyd's
Rep. 103, CA 12–020, 12–025, 12–028
Fercometal Sarl v MSC Mediterranean Shipping Co SA (The Simona)
[1989] A.C. 788; [1988] 3 W.L.R. 200; [1988] 2 All E.R. 742; [1988] 2
Lloyd's Rep. 199; (1988) 138 N.L.J. Rep. 178; (1988) 132 S.J. 966, HL 7–017
Fetim BV v Oceanspeed Shipping Ltd (The Flecha) [1999] 1 Lloyd's Rep.
612, QBD (Adm Ct) 12–045
Field, Re, 3 Curt. 752, 16–011, 16–013
Field v Metropolitan Police Receiver [1907] 2 K.B. 853, KBD 15–039
Filiatra Legacy, The. *See* Anonima Petroli Italiana SpA and Neste Oy v
Marlucidez Armadora SA.
Filipinas I, The. *See* R Pagnan & Fratelli v NGJ Schouten NV.
Finlay v The Liverpool and Great Western Steamship Company Limited
(1870) 23 L.T. 251 .... 6–023, 13–034
Finska Cellulosaforeningen (Finnish Cellulose Union) v Westfield Paper
Co Ltd [1940] 4 All E.R. 473; (1940) 68 Ll. L. Rep. 75, KBD 6–072, 6–074
Flecha, The. *See* Fetim BV v Oceanspeed Shipping Ltd.
Foley v Classique Coaches Ltd [1934] 2 K.B. 1, CA 16–002, 16–003
Food Corp of India v Antclizo Shipping Corp (The Antclizo) [1988] 1
W.L.R. 603; [1988] 2 All E.R. 513; [1988] 2 Lloyd's Rep. 93; [1988] 2
F.T.L.R. 124; (1988) 138 N.L.J. Rep. 135; (1988) 132 S.J. 752, HL 12–033
Foreman & Ellams Ltd v Federal Steam Navigation Co Ltd [1928] 2 K.B.
424; (1928) 30 Ll. L. Rep. 52, KBD 11–029
Forestal Minosa v Oriental Credit [1986] 1 W.L.R. 631; [1986] 2 All E.R. 400;
[1986] 1 Lloyd's Rep. 329; [1986] Fin. L.R. 171; (1986) 83 L.S.G. 779;
(1986) 130 S.J. 202, CA 8–014, 8–023
Fort Shipping Co Ltd v Pederson & Co (1924) 19 Ll. L. Rep. 26, KBD 12–022
Forward v Pittard (1785) 1 T.R. 27; 99 E.R. 953 11–018
Fox v Nott (1861) 6 H. & N. 630; 158 E.R. 260 13–047
France v Dutton [1891] 2 Q.B. 208, QBD 16–009, 16–013
Fraser v Telegraph Construction & Maintenance Co (1871–72) L.R. 7 Q.B.
566, QBD 12–005

Frebold v Circle Products; *sub nom.* Frebold and Sturznickel (t/a Panda OHG) v Circle Products [1970] 1 Lloyd's Rep. 499; (1970) 114 S.J. 262, CA 2–003, 2–025, 2–026, 3–052, 3–057, 4–003

Freedom, The. *See* Owners of the Ship Freedom v Simmonds, Hunt, & Co.

Freeman & Lockyer v Buckhurst Park Properties (Mangal) Ltd [1964] 2 Q.B. 480; [1964] 2 W.L.R. 618; [1964] 1 All E.R. 630; 108 S.J. 96, CA 14–035, 14–043

Future Express, The [1993] 2 Lloyd's Rep. 542, CA; affirming [1992] 2 Lloyd's Rep. 79, QBD (Adm Ct) ... 1–051, 5–005, 6–026, 6–037, 6–039, 6–040, 6–041, 6–042, 8–029, 13–030, 13–032

Fyffes Group Ltd v Reefer Express Lines Pty Ltd [1996] 2 Lloyd's Rep. 171, QBD (Comm Ct) 11–024

GH Renton & Co Ltd v Palmyra Trading Corp of Panama (The Caspiana) [1957] A.C. 149; [1957] 2 W.L.R. 45; [1956] 3 All E.R. 957; [1956] 2 Lloyd's Rep. 379, HL 6–018, 12–013, 12–014, 12–018

Gabbiano, The [1940] P. 166, PDAD 5–014, 5–069

Galatia, The. *See* M Golodetz & Co Inc v Czarnikow-Rionda Co Inc.

Garbis Maritime Corp v Phillipine National Oil Co (The Garbis) [1982] 2 Lloyd's Rep. 283, QBD (Comm Ct) 2–033, 12–012

Garcia v Page & Co Ltd (1936) 55 Ll. L. Rep. 391, KBD 9–014

Gardano & Giampieri v Greek Petroleum George Mamidakis & Co [1962] 1 W.L.R. 40; [1961] 3 All E.R. 919; [1961] 2 Lloyd's Rep. 259; 106 S.J. 76, QBD (Comm Ct) 2–027

Garnac Grain Co Inc v HMF Faure & Fairclough Ltd; *sub nom.* Bunge Corp v HMF Faure & Fairclough Ltd [1968] A.C. 1130; [1967] 3 W.L.R. 143; [1967] 2 All E.R. 353; [1967] 1 Lloyd's Rep. 495; 111 S.J. 434, HL; affirming [1966] 1 Q.B. 650; [1965] 3 W.L.R. 934; [1965] 3 All E.R. 273; [1965] 2 Lloyd's Rep. 229; 109 S.J. 571, CA; reversing [1965] 2 W.L.R. 696; [1965] 1 All E.R. 47; [1964] 2 Lloyd's Rep. 296; 108 S.J. 693; *The Times*, August 1, 1964, QBD (Comm Ct) 1–016, 1–018, 1–021, 1–022, 1–023, 1–031, 1–046

Gatoil International Inc v Tradax Petroleum Ltd (The Rio Sun); Gatoil International Inc v Panatlantic Carriers Corp [1985] 1 Lloyd's Rep. 350, QBD (Comm Ct) 1–048, 2–044, 4–020, 4–033, 4–036, 12–010

Gebruder Metalmann GmbH & Co KG v NBR (London) [1984] 1 Lloyd's Rep. 614; (1984) 81 L.S.G. 515, CA 1–018, 1–038, 1–039, 1–043, 9–004

George Whitechurch Ltd v Cavanagh [1902] A.C. 117, HL 14–035, 14–038, 14–040, 14–041, 14–044

Giacomo Costa Fu Andrea v British Italian Trading Co Ltd; *sub nom.* Andrea v British Italian Trading Co Ltd [1963] 1 Q.B. 201; [1962] 3 W.L.R. 512; [1962] 2 All E.R. 53; [1962] 1 Lloyd's Rep. 151; (1962) 106 S.J. 219, CA 7–042

Giannis NK, The. *See* Effort Shipping Co Ltd v Linden Management SA.

Giddens v Anglo-African Produce Co Ltd (1923) 14 Ll. L. Rep. 230, KBD 9–003

Gill & Duffus SA v Berger & Co Inc; *sub nom.* Berger & Co v Gill & Duffus SA [1984] A.C. 382; [1984] 2 W.L.R. 95; [1984] 1 All E.R. 438; [1984] 1 Lloyd's Rep. 227; (1984) 81 L.S.G. 429; (1984) 128 S.J. 47, HL 1–014, 2–003, 2–021, 2–038, 4–030, 4–033, 4–036, 6–103, 7–006, 7–022, 7–026, 7–027, 7–028, 7–029, 7–031, 7–064, 10–011, 14–002, 14–005, 15–010, 15–037, 15–048

Gillett v Hill (1834) 2 Cromp. & M. 530 5–019

Ginzberg v Barrow Haematite Steel Co and McKellar [1966] 1 Lloyd's Rep. 343; 116 N.L.J. 752, QBD 5–005, 5–039, 5–054, 5–058, 5–059, 5–060, 5–064

Glencore Grain Rotterdam BV v Lebanese Organisation for International
Commerce (The Lorico) [1997] 4 All E.R. 514; [1997] 2 Lloyd's Rep.
386; [1997] C.L.C. 1274, CA; reversing [1997] 1 Lloyd's Rep. 578, QBD
(Comm Ct) 3–014, 6–002, 7–049, 9–007, 9–022
Glencore International AG v Bank of China [1996] 1 Lloyd's Rep. 135;
[1996] 5 Bank. L.R. 1; [1996] C.L.C. 111; [1998] Masons C.L.R. Rep. 78;
The Times, November 27, 1995, CA 1–016, 1–017, 10–030, 10–031, 10–032,
10–033, 10–035, 10–036, 10–037, 10–039, 10–040, 10–041, 10–042,
10–044
Glendarroch, The [1894] P. 226, CA 11–024, 11–030
Glengarnock Iron and Steel Co Ltd v Cooper & Co (1895) 22 R. 672 11–075
Glenroy, The. *See* Procurator General v MC Spencer (Controller of Mitsui
& Co Ltd).
Glyn Mills Currie & Co v East and West India Dock Co (1881–82) L.R. 7
App. Cas. 591, HL .. 6–010, 6–013, 6–014, 6–015, 6–019, 6–027, 6–031, 6–032,
6–033, 6–035, 6–040, 6–080, 6–082, 12–005, 13–044, 15–023, 15–050,
15–053, 16–029
Glynn v Margetson & Co; *sub nom.* Margetson v Glynn [1893] A.C. 351,
HL 6–018, 6–030, 6–034, 11–007, 11–027, 11–070, 12–004, 12–014
Goodman v J Eban Ltd [1954] 1 Q.B. 550; [1954] 2 W.L.R. 581; [1954] 1 All
E.R. 763; 98 S.J. 214, CA 16–010, 16–011, 16–013
Goodwin Ferreira & Co Ld v Lamport Holt Ld (1929) 141 L.T. 494 11–076
Gosse Millard Ltd v Canadian Government Merchant Marine Ltd (The
Canadian Highlander); American Can Co Ltd v Canadian Govern-
ment Merchant Marine Ltd [1929] A.C. 223; (1928) 32 Ll. L. Rep. 91,
HL 11–039
Granit SA v Benship International Inc [1994] 1 Lloyd's Rep. 526, QBD
(Comm Ct) 16–004
Grant v Norway (1851) 10 C.B. 665 .... 11–031, 14–006, 14–017, 14–023, 14–024,
14–033, 14–034, 14–035, 14–036, 14–037, 14–038, 14–040, 14–041, 14–044,
14–045, 14–046, 14–047, 14–049, 14–053, 14–054, 14–055, 14–056
Green v Sichel (1860) 7 C.B.N.S. 747 9–008
Guaranty Trust Co of New York v Hannay & Co [1915] 2 K.B. 536; 12
A.L.R. 1, CA 8–035
Gudermes, The. *See* Mitsui & Co Ltd v Novorossiysk Shipping Co.
Gundulic, The. *See* Itoh & Co Ltd v Atlantska Plovidba.

HMF Humphrey Ltd v Baxter Hoare & Co Ltd (1933) 46 Ll. L. Rep. 252;
[1933] All E.R. 457, KBD 13–060
HO Brandt & Co v HN Morris & Co; *sub nom.* HO Brandt & Co v HN
Morris & Co Ltd [1917] 2 K.B. 784, CA ... 1–006, 1–048, 3–013, 3–014, 3–046,
3–047, 3–048, 3–049, B–002
Hain SS Co Ltd v Tate & Lyle Ltd *See* Tate & Lyle Ltd v Hain Steamship
Co Ltd.
Hamilton & Co v Mackie & Sons (1889) 5 T.L.R. 677 12–026
Hamzeh Malas & Sons v British Imex Industries Ltd [1958] 2 Q.B. 127;
[1958] 2 W.L.R. 100; [1958] 1 All E.R. 262; [1957] 2 Lloyd's Rep. 549;
102 S.J. 68, CA 8–010, 8–049, 9–009, 9–019, 10–010, 10–030
Hannah Blumenthal, The. *See* Paal Wilson & Co A/S v Partenreederei
Hannah Blumenthal.
Hansa Nord, The. *See* Cehave NV v Bremer Handels GmbH.
Hansen v Harrold Bros [1894] 1 Q.B. 612, CA 12–009
Hansen-Tangens Rederi III A/S v Total Transport Corp (The Sagona)
[1984] 1 Lloyd's Rep. 194, QBD (Comm Ct) 6–007, 13–030, 15–032, 15–034,
15–035, 15–036

Hansson v Hamel & Horley Ltd [1922] 2 A.C. 36; (1922) 10 Ll. L. Rep. 507,
　　HL 6–001, 6–059, 6–077
Happy Ranger, The. *See* Parsons Corp v CV Scheepvaartonderneming
　　Happy Ranger.
Hardy & Co (London) Ltd v Hillerns & Fowler. *See* E Hardy & Co
　　(London) Ltd v Hillerns & Fowler.
Harland & Wolff v Burns and Laird Lines; *sub nom.* Harland & Wolff Ltd
　　v Burns & Laird Lines Ltd (1931) 40 Ll. L. Rep. 286; 1931 S.C. 722; 1931
　　S.L.T. 572, 1 Div 11–076
Harris v Best, Ryley & Co (1892) 68 L.T. 76 11–073
Hawk, The. *See* Oceanfocus Shipping Ltd v Hyundai Merchant Marine Co
　　Ltd.
Hayes v Brown [1920] 1 K.B. 250, KBD 16–009
Healey v Healey [1915] 1 K.B. 938, KBD 5–028
Hector, The. *See* Sunrise Maritime Inc v Uvisco Ltd.
Hedley Byrne & Co Ltd v Heller & Partners Ltd [1964] A.C. 465; [1963] 3
　　W.L.R. 101; [1963] 2 All E.R. 575; [1963] 1 Lloyd's Rep. 485; 107 S.J. 454,
　　HL 13–078, 14–002, 14–024, 14–027, 16–039
Heidberg, The. *See* Partenreederei M/S Heidberg v Grosvenor Grain &
　　Feed Co Ltd.
Heilbert Symons & Co Ltd v Harvey Christie-Miller & Co (1922) 12 Ll. L.
　　Rep. 455, KBD 6–098
Hellenic Dolphin, The [1978] 2 Lloyd's Rep. 336, QBD (Adm Ct) 11–024, 11–025
Henderson v Merrett Syndicates Ltd (No.1); *sub nom.* McLarnon Deeney v
　　Gooda Walker Ltd; Gooda Walker Ltd v Deen; Hallam-Eames v
　　Merrett Syndicates Ltd; Hughes v Merrett Syndicates Ltd; Feltrim
　　Underwriting Agencies Ltd v Arbuthnott; Deeny v Gooda Walker Ltd
　　(Duty of Care) [1995] 2 A.C. 145; [1994] 3 W.L.R. 761; [1994] 3 All E.R.
　　506; [1994] 2 Lloyd's Rep. 468; (1994) 144 N.L.J. 1204; *The Times*, July
　　26, 1994; *Independent*, August 3, 1994, HL 14–024
Henry Smith & Co v Bedouin Steam Navigation Co Ltd [1896] A.C. 70;
　　(1895) 23 R. (H.L.) 1, HL 14–015, 14–052
Hern v Nichols (1701) 1 Salk. 289 14–038
Heskell v Continental Express Ltd [1950] 1 All E.R. 1033; (1949–50) 83 Ll.
　　L. Rep. 438; [1950] W.N. 210; 94 S.J. 339, KBD 3–012, 7–064, 12–001, 14–003,
　　　　　14–007, 14–008, 14–019, 14–024, 14–029, 14–033, 14–036, 14–049, 14–050,
　　　　　　　　　　　　　　　　　　14–055, 14–058,14–059, 14–060
Heyman v Darwins Ltd [1942] A.C. 356; [1942] 1 All E.R. 337; (1942) 72 Ll.
　　L. Rep. 65, HL 7–009
Hick v Raymond & Reid; *sub nom.* Hick v Rodocanachi; Pantland Hick v
　　Raymond & Reid [1893] A.C. 22; [1891–4] All E.R. Rep. 491, HL 9–014
Hickox v Adams (1876) 34 L.T. 404 6–110
Hill v Hill [1947] Ch. 231; [1947] 1 All E.R. 54; 176 L.T. 216; 91 S.J. 55, CA 16–009,
　　　　　　　　　　　　　　　　　　　　　　16–010, 16–013
Hill v R. [1945] K.B. 329, KBD 16–009
Hindley & Co v East Indian Produce Co [1973] 2 Lloyd's Rep. 515, QBD
　　(Comm Ct) 2–012, 7–030, 7–031, 7–062, 7–064, 14–003, 14–005, 14–050,
　　　　　　　　　　　　　　　　　　　　　15–053, 15–054
Hinds, Re, 16 Jur. 1161 16–010
Hispanica de Petroles SA v Vencedora Oceanica Navegacion SA (The
　　Kapetan Markos NL) (No.2) [1987] 2 Lloyd's Rep. 321, CA 13–009
Hochster v De la Tour (1853) 2 E. & B. 678; 118 E.R. 922 7–009
Hogarth Shipping Co Ltd v Blyth Greene Jourdain & Co Ltd [1917] 2 K.B.
　　534, CA 2–033, 2–038, 12–022
Hollandia, The. *See* Owners of Cargo on Board the Morviken v Owners of
　　the Hollandia.

Homburg Houtimport BV v Agrosin Private Ltd (The Starsin); Owners of Cargo Lately Laden on Board the Starsin v Owners of the Starsin; Hunter Timber Ltd v Agrosin Private Ltd [2001] EWCA Civ 56; [2001] 1 All E.R. (Comm) 455; [2001] 1 Lloyd's Rep. 437; [2001] C.L.C. 696, CA; reversing in part [1999] 2 All E.R. (Comm) 591; [2000] 1 Lloyd's Rep. 85; [1999] C.L.C. 1769, QBD (Comm Ct) 12–045, 12–046, 13–072, 13–083, 14–001, 14–036, 14–041

Hongkong Fir Shipping Co Ltd v Kawasaki Kisen Kaisha Ltd (The Hongkong Fir) [1962] 2 Q.B. 26; [1962] 2 W.L.R. 474; [1962] 1 All E.R. 474; [1961] 2 Lloyd's Rep. 478; (1961) 106 S.J. 35, CA ... 3–025, 3–028, 7–006, 15–011, 15–015

Hordern v Commonwealth and Dominion Line. *See* Anthony Hordern & Sons Ltd v Commonwealth and Dominion Line Ltd.

Horst (E Clemens) Co v Biddell Bros. *See* Biddell Brothers v E. Clemens Horst Co.

Houda, The. *See* Kuwait Petroleum Corp v I&D Oil Carriers Ltd.

Houldsworth v Glasgow City Bank (1879–80) L.R. 5 App. Cas. 317, HL 14–040, 14–044

Household Fire and Carriage Accident Insurance Co Ltd v Grant (1879) 4 Ex. D. 216, CA 16–005

Hughes v Metropolitan Railway Co (1876–77) L.R. 2 App. Cas. 439, HL 4–044, 7–048

Huilerie L'Abeille v Societe des Huileries du Niger (The Kastellon) [1978] 2 Lloyd's Rep. 203, QBD (Comm Ct) 7–058

Huntoon Co v Kolynos (Inc) [1930] 1 Ch. 528, CA 7–026

Ian Stach Ltd v Baker Bosly Ltd; *sub nom.* Ian Stach Ltd v Baker Bosley Ltd [1958] 2 Q.B. 130; [1958] 2 W.L.R. 419; [1958] 1 All E.R. 542; [1958] 1 Lloyd's Rep. 127; 102 S.J. 177, QBD 3–014, 3–016, 3–018, 9–013, 9–016, 9–017, 15–003, 15–010

Ignazio Messina & Co v Polskie Linie Oceaniczne [1995] 2 Lloyd's Rep. 566, QBD (Comm Ct) 16–004

Ilyssia Compania Naviera SA v Ahmed Abdul-Qawi Bamaodah (The Elli 2); Kition Compania Naviera v Ahmed Abdul-Qawi Bamaodah; Lemython Compania Naviera v Ahmed Abdul-Qawi Bamaodah [1985] 1 Lloyd's Rep. 107, CA 13–061, 13–062, 13–068, 13–069

Imperial Land Co of Marseilles, Re; *sub nom.* Harris's Case (1871–72) L.R. 7 Ch. App. 587, CA in Chancery 16–005, 16–006

Indian Oil Corp Ltd v Greenstone Shipping Co SA (Panama) (The Ypatianna); Greenstone Shipping Co SA v Indian Oil Corp Ltd [1988] Q.B. 345; [1987] 3 All E.R. 893; [1987] 2 Lloyd's Rep. 286; [1987] 2 F.T.L.R. 95; (1987) 84 L.S.G. 2768; (1987) 131 S.J. 1121; *The Times*, April 23, 1987, QBD (Comm Ct) 15–052

Ines, The. *See* MB Pyramid Sound NV v Briese Schiffahrts GmbH & Co KG MS Sina.

Inglis v Stock; *sub nom.* Stock v Inglis (1884–85) L.R. 10 App. Cas. 263, HL; affirming (1883–84) L.R. 12 Q.B.D. 564, CA 2–017, 3–036, 4–003, 4–005, 4–006, 5–034, 5–040, 5–041, 5–044, 5–083

International Factors v Rodriguez [1979] Q.B. 351; [1978] 3 W.L.R. 877; [1979] 1 All E.R. 17; 122 S.J. 680, CA 13–032, 13–034

Inverkip Steamship Co Ltd v Bunge & Co [1917] 2 K.B. 193, CA 3–038

Ireland v Livingston (1871–72) L.R. 5 H.L. 395, HL 1–044, 1–005, 2–006, 2–009, 2–010, 3–006, 4–012, 4–014, 6–061, 6–065, 6–073, 6–091, 6–101, 9–030, 15–003

Ishag v Allied Bank International, Fuhs and Kotalimbora (The Lycaon) [1981] 1 Lloyd's Rep. 92, QBD (Comm Ct) 6–051

Itoh & Co Ltd v Atlantska Plovidba (The Gundulic) [1981] 2 Lloyd's Rep.
418, QBD (Comm Ct) 11–041

JH Rayner & Co Ltd v Hambros Bank Ltd [1943] K.B. 37; (1942) 74 Ll. L.
Rep. 10, CA 10–026, 10–028, 10–31
JH Tucker & Co v Board of Trade [1955] 1 W.L.R. 655; [1955] 2 All E.R. 522;
99 S.J. 385, Ch D 16–009
JI MacWilliam Co Inc v Mediterranean Shipping Co SA (The Rafaela S)
[2002] EWHC 593, QBD (Comm Ct) 11–079
J&J Cunningham Ltd v Robert A Munro & Co Ltd (1922) 13 Ll. L. Rep. 216,
KBD ... 3–017, 3–018, 3–045, 4–040, 4–043, 4–045, 5–084, 9–016, 9–017, B–017
J&J Cunningham v Guthrie (1886) 26 Sc. L.R. 208 13–060
Jackson v Rotax Motor and Cycle Co [1910] 2 K.B. 937, CA 4–015
Jambur, The. *See* CEP Interagra S.A. v Select Energy Trading GmbH.
James Finlay & Co Ltd v NV Kwik Hoo Tung Handel Maatschappij; *sub*
nom. James Finlay & Co Ltd v NV Kwik Hoo Tong Handel Maat-
schappij [1929] 1 K.B. 400; [1928] All E.R. Rep. 110; (1928) 32 Ll. L.
Rep. 245, CA; affirming [1928] 2 K.B. 604; (1928) 31 Ll. L. Rep. 220,
KBD ... 7–030, 7–032, 7–034, 7–036, 7–047, 7–052, 7–055, 7–056, 7–057, 7–058,
7–060, 7–062, 7–064
James McNaughton Paper Group Ltd v Hicks Anderson & Co [1991] 2
Q.B. 113; [1991] 2 W.L.R. 641; [1991] 1 All E.R. 134; [1990] B.C.C. 891;
[1991] B.C.L.C. 235; [1991] E.C.C. 186; [1955–95] P.N.L.R. 574; (1990)
140 N.L.J. 1311; *Independent*, September 11, 1990, CA 14–027
Jarvis v Williams [1955] 1 W.L.R. 71; [1955] 1 All E.R. 108; 99 S.J. 73, CA 13–032,
13–034
Jenkins v Gaisford & Thring, In the Goods of Jenkins (1863) 3 Sw. & Tr.
93 16–013
Johnson v Agnew [1980] A.C. 367; [1979] 2 W.L.R. 487; [1979] 1 All E.R.
883; (1979) 38 P. & C.R. 424; (1979) 251 E.G. 1167; 123 S.J. 217, HL ... 7–026
Johnson v Taylor Bros & Co Ltd [1920] A.C. 144; (1919) 1 Ll. L. Rep. 183,
HL 6–061, 6–073
Joseph Thorley Ltd v Orchis Steamship Co Ltd [1907] 1 K.B. 660, CA 11–003
Julia, The. *See* Comptoir d'Achat et de Vente du Boerenbond Belge SA v
Luis de Ridder Limitada.
Junior Books Ltd v Veitchi Co Ltd [1983] 1 A.C. 520; [1982] 3 W.L.R. 477;
[1982] 3 All E.R. 201; 1982 S.C. (H.L.) 244; 1982 S.L.T. 492; [1982] Com.
L.R. 221; 21 B.L.R. 66; (1982) 79 L.S.G. 1413; 126 S.J. 538, HL 13–076, 13–078,
13–082

KH Enterprise (cargo owners) v Pioneer Container (owners). *See* Pioneer
Container, The.
K/S A/S Seateam & Co v Iraq National Oil Co (The Sevonia Team) [1983]
2 Lloyd's Rep. 640, QBD (Comm Ct) 1–048, 3–007, 3–010, 3–011, 5–061,
12–029, 12–031, 12–032, 12–035, 13–002, 16–028
Kapetan Markos NL, The. *See* Hispanica de Petroles SA v Vencedora
Oceanica Navegacion SA.
Karaganda Ltd v Midland Bank plc; Kredietbank Antwerp v Midland
Bank plc [1999] 1 All E.R. (Comm.) 801; [1999] Lloyd's Rep. Bank. 219;
[1999] C.L.C. 1108; *The Times*, May 12, 1999; *Independent*, May 7, 1999,
CA 10–031, 10–035, 10–036, 10–039, 10–040, 10–041, 10–042, 10–044
Karlshamns Oljefabriker A/B v Eastport Navigation Corp (The Elafi)
[1982] 1 All E.R. 208; [1981] 2 Lloyd's Rep. 679; [1981] Com. L.R. 149,
QBD (Comm Ct) ... 5–013, 5–014, 5–015, 5–023, 5–025, 5–075, 5–080, 13–009,
13–067, A–022
Kastellon, The. *See* Huilerie L'Abeille v Societe des Huileries du Niger.

Kenya Railways v Antares Co Pte Ltd (The Antares) (No.1) [1987] 1 Lloyd's Rep. 424, CA 11–070

Kleinjan & Holst NV, Rotterdam v Bremer Handels GmbH, Hamburg; *sub nom.* Kleinjan Holst NV Rotterdam v Bremer Handelsgesellschaft mbH Hamburg [1972] 2 Lloyd's Rep. 11, QBD ... 7–045, 7–048, 7–057, 7–060, 7–062, 7–064

Kleinwort, Sons & Co v Associated Automatic Machine Corp (1934) 50 T.L.R. 244; (1934) 151 L.T. 1 .... 14–038, 14–044

Konstantinidis v World Tankers Corp Inc (The World Harmony) [1967] P. 341; [1965] 2 W.L.R. 1275; [1965] 2 All E.R. 139; [1965] 1 Lloyd's Rep. 244, PDAD 13–075

Kredietbank Antwerp v Midland Bank plc. *See* Karaganda Ltd v Midland Bank plc.

Kriti Rex, The. *See* Fyffes Group Ltd v Reefer Express Lines Pty Ltd.

Kronprinsessan Margareta, The [1921] 1 A.C. 486, PC (UK) 1–005, 5–013, 5–014, 5–033, 5–034, 5–038, 5–040, 5–050, 5–051, 5–054, 5–055, 5–058, 5–059

Kuwait Petroleum Corp v I&D Oil Carriers Ltd (The Houda) [1994] 2 Lloyd's Rep. 541; *Independent*, August 17, 1994, CA 6–007, 6–008, 6–019, 6–020, 6–025, 6–027, 6–029, 6–033, 15–032, 15–036

Kwei Tek Chao (t/a Zung Fu Co) v British Traders & Shippers Ltd (No.1); *sub nom.* Chao v British Traders & Shippers Ltd (No.1) [1954] 2 Q.B. 459; [1954] 2 W.L.R. 365; [1954] 1 All E.R. 779; [1954] 1 Lloyd's Rep. 16; 98 S.J. 163, QBD 1–048, 5–023, 5–068, 7–021, 7–027, 7–032, 7–033, 7–038, 7–039, 7–048, 7–049, 7–055, 7–058, 7–060, 7–062, 14–002, 14–005, 14–024, 15–051, 15–053, 16–038

L Schuler AG v Wickman Machine Tool Sales Ltd; *sub nom.* Wickman Machine Tool Sales Ltd v L Schuler AG [1974] A.C. 235; [1973] 2 W.L.R. 683; [1973] 2 All E.R. 39; [1973] 2 Lloyd's Rep. 53; 117 S.J. 340, HL 12–023

La Société Anonyme de Remorquage a Helice v Bennetts [1911] 1 K.B. 243, KBD 13–075

Lambert (Iris Frances) v Lewis (Donald Richard); *sub nom.* Lexmead (Basingstoke) Ltd v Lewis [1982] A.C. 225; [1981] 2 W.L.R. 713; [1981] 1 All E.R. 1185; [1981] 2 Lloyd's Rep. 17; [1981] R.T.R. 346; 125 S.J. 310, HL 4–036

Landauer & Co v Craven and Speeding Bros [1912] 2 K.B. 94, KBD ... 6–061, 6–078, 6–095

Laveroni v Drury (1852) 8 Ex. 166; 155 E.R. 1304 11–018

Law & Bonar Ltd v British American Tobacco Co Ltd [1916] 2 K.B. 605, KBD 2–003, 2–016, 2–018, 2–021, 2–022, 4–017, 4–026, 4–027

Lazarus Estates Ltd v Beasley [1956] 1 Q.B. 702; [1956] 2 W.L.R. 502; [1956] 1 All E.R. 341; 100 S.J. 131, CA 16–009

Le Lievre v Gould [1893] 1 Q.B. 491, CA 14–024

Leduc & Co v Ward (1888) L.R. 20 Q.B.D. 475, CA 12–004, 12–006, 12–010, 12–035, 14–020, 16–007

Leigh & Sillivan Ltd v Aliakmon Shipping Co Ltd (The Aliakmon) [1986] A.C. 785; [1986] 2 W.L.R. 902; [1986] 2 All E.R. 145; [1986] 2 Lloyd's Rep. 1; (1986) 136 N.L.J. 415; (1986) 130 S.J. 357, HL; affirming [1985] Q.B. 350; [1985] 2 All E.R. 44; [1985] 1 Lloyd's Rep. 199; (1985) 82 L.S.G. 203; (1985) 135 N.L.J. 285; (1985) 129 S.J. 69, CA 3–060, 4–001, 5–005, 5–016, 5–027, 5–028, 5–029, 11–021, 11–063, 13–002, 13–032, 13–041, 13–046, 13–059, 13–061, 13–072, 13–073, 13–083, 13–084, 14–024, 14–037

Leon Corp v Atlantic Lines and Navigation Co Inc (The Leon) [1985] 2 Lloyd's Rep. 470, QBD (Comm Ct) 15–052

Lep Air Services Ltd v Rolloswin Ltd *See* Moschi v Lep Air Services
    Ltd.
Lickbarrow v Mason (1787) 2 T.R. 63, KBD 6–044, 6–045, 6–046, 6–050, 6–062,
                                                8–039, 13–003, 13–044, 14–034
Lickbarrow v Mason (1794) 5 T.R. 683; 101 E.R. 380, KBD .. 6–044, 6–045, 6–046,
                                                6–050, 6–062, 6–065, 8–039
Liver Alkali Co v Johnson (1873–74) L.R. 9 Ex. 338, Ex Chamber 11–018
Lloyd v Grace Smith & Co [1912] A.C. 716, HL 14–006, 14–024, 14–035, 14–038,
                                                14–040, 14–044
Lloyds Bank Ltd v Bank of America National Trust and Savings Associa-
    tion [1938] 2 K.B. 147, CA 5–005, 6–032, 8–044
Lockwood v Wood (1844) 6 Q.B. 31 6–054
London & Provincial Leather Processes Ltd v Hudson [1939] 2 K.B. 724;
    (1939) 64 Ll. L. Rep. 352, KBD 15–047
London CC v Agricultural Food Products; London CC v Vitamins [1955]
    2 Q.B. 218; [1955] 2 W.L.R. 925; [1955] 2 All E.R. 229; 59 L.G.R. 350; 99
    S.J. 305, CA 16–009, 16–013
London Joint Stock Bank v British Amsterdam Maritime Agency (1910) 16
    Com. Cas. 102 13–029
Lorico, The. *See* Glencore Grain Rotterdam BV v Lebanese Organisation
    for International Commerce.
Lycaon, The. *See* Ishag v Allied Bank International, Fuhs and Kotalim-
    bora.
Lyell v Kennedy (No.3) (1884) L.R. 27 Ch. D. 1, CA 16–009

MB Pyramid Sound NV v Briese Schiffahrts GmbH & Co KG MS Sina (The
    Ines) (No.2) [1995] 2 Lloyd's Rep. 144, QBD (Comm Ct) ... 5–307, 6–030, 6–033
MCC Proceeds Inc v Lehman Brothers International (Europe) [1998] 4 All
    E.R. 675; [1998] 2 B.C.L.C. 659; (1998) 95(5) L.S.G. 28; (1998) 142
    S.J.L.B. 40; *The Times*, January 14, 1998; *Independent*, January 19, 1998
    (C.S.), CA 5–029, 13–082
M Golodetz & Co Inc v Czarnikow-Rionda Co Inc (The Galatia) [1980] 1
    W.L.R. 495; [1980] 1 All E.R. 501; [1980] 1 Lloyd's Rep. 453; 124 S.J. 201,
    CA 4–016, 6–001, 6–002, 6–067, 6–070, 10–001
McDougall v Aeromarine of Emsworth [1958] 1 W.L.R. 1126; [1958] 3 All
    E.R. 431; [1958] 2 Lloyd's Rep. 345; 102 S.J. 860, QBD (Comm Ct) 3–027
Mackay v Dick, 6 App. Cas. 251 5–084
Manbre Saccharine Co Ltd v Corn Products Co Ltd [1919] 1 K.B. 198,
    KBD 2–008, 2–010, 4–008, 4–009, 4–010, 4–014, 4–017, 4–019, 4–020, 4–046B,
                                                6–111, 7–03, 7–021, 15–053
Manchester Trust v Furness; *sub nom.* Manchester Trust Ltd v Furness
    Withy & Co Ltd [1895] 2 Q.B. 539, CA 12–037, 12–039, 12–040, 12–043,
                                                12–044, 12–045, 15–048, 15–053
Manila, The. *See* Procter & Gamble Phillipine Manufacturing Corp v Peter
    Cremer GmbH & Co.
Maran Road Saw Mill v Austin Taylor & Co Ltd *See* Ng Chee Chong, Ng
    Weng Chong, Ng Cheng and Ng Yew (A Firm t/a Maran Road Saw
    Mill) v Austin Taylor & Co.
Maredelanto Compania Naviera SA v Bergbau-Handel GmbH (The Miha-
    lis Angelos) [1971] 1 Q.B. 164; [1970] 3 W.L.R. 601; [1970] 3 All E.R.
    125; [1970] 2 Lloyd's Rep. 43; 114 S.J. 548, CA 3–027, 7–004
Margarine Union GmbH v Cambay Prince Steamship Co (The Wear
    Breeze) [1969] 1 Q.B. 219; [1967] 3 W.L.R. 1569; [1967] 3 All E.R. 775;
    [1967] 2 Lloyd's Rep. 315; 111 S.J. 943, QBD (Comm Ct) 5–017, 13–046,
                                                13–059, 13–061, 13–076, 13–081, 13–083

Mash & Murrell Ltd v Joseph I Emanuel Ltd [1962] 1 W.L.R. 16; [1962] 1
All E.R. 77 (Note); [1961] 2 Lloyd's Rep. 326; 105 S.J. 1007, CA;
reversing [1961] 1 W.L.R. 862; [1961] 1 All E.R. 485; [1961] 1 Lloyd's
Rep. 46; 105 S.J. 468, QBD (Comm Ct) 4–017, 4–018, 4–030, 4–031, 4–033,
4–035, 4–036, 4–039, A–001
Mata K, The. *See* Agrosin Pty Ltd v Highway Shipping Co Ltd.
May & Butcher Ltd v King, The [1934] 2 K.B. 17; [1929] All E.R. Rep. 679,
HL 16–003
Merak, The. *See* TB&S Batchelor & Co Ltd v Owners of the SS Merak.
Merida, The. *See* Chargeurs Réunis Compagnie Francaise de Navigation à
Vapeur (The Ceylan) v English & American Shipping Co.
Meyerstein v Barber; *sub nom.* Barber v Meyerstein (1869–70) L.R. 4 H.L.
317, HL; affirming (1866–67) L.R. 2 C.P. 661, Ex Chamber; affirming
(1866–67) L.R. 2 C.P. 38, CCP 1–051, 6–041, 6–042, 6–045, 13–029
Midland Bank Ltd v Seymour [1955] 2 Lloyd's Rep. 147, QBD 8–005, 8–027,
10–028, 15–049
Mihalis Angelos, The. *See* Maredelanto Compania Naviera SA v Bergbau-
Handel GmbH.
Mirabita v Imperial Ottoman Bank (1877–78) L.R. 3 Ex. D. 164, CA ... 4–004, 5–003,
5–014, 5–034, 5–040, 5–041, 5–042, 5–045, 5–046, 5–047, 5–049, 5–050,
5–060, 5–062
Miramar Maritime Corp v Holborn Oil Trading (The Miramar) [1984] A.C.
676; [1984] 3 W.L.R. 1; [1984] 2 All E.R. 326; [1984] 2 Lloyd's Rep. 129;
(1984) 81 L.S.G. 2000; (1984) 128 S.J. 414, HL 2–033, 5–014, 12–018, 12–027,
12–028
Missouri Steamship Co, Re (1889) L.R. 42 Ch. D. 321, CA 11–018
Mitsui & Co Ltd v Flota Mercante Grancolombiana SA; Ciudad de Pasto,
The and The Ciudad de Neiva [1988] 1 W.L.R. 1145; [1989] 1 All E.R.
951; [1988] 2 Lloyd's Rep. 208; *The Times*, April 27, 1988, CA 5–033, 5–037,
5–039, 5–042, 5–060, 5–062, 5–065, 5–072, 5–074
Mitsui & Co Ltd v Novorossiysk Shipping Co (The Gudermes) [1993] 1
Lloyd's Rep. 311, CA 13–045, 13–055, 13–068, 13–071
Mmecen SA v Inter Ro-Ro SA and Gulf Ro-Ro Services SA (The Samah
and The Lina V) [1981] 1 Lloyd's Rep. 40, QBD (Comm Ct) 16–004
Moakes v Nicholson 19 C.B. (N.S.) 290 5–052
Morris v CW Martin & Sons Ltd; *sub nom.* Morris v Martin [1966] 1 Q.B.
716; [1965] 3 W.L.R. 276; [1965] 2 All E.R. 725; [1965] 2 Lloyd's Rep. 63;
109 S.J. 451, CA 11–003, 12–049
Morton v Copeland (1855) 16 C.B. 517 .... 16–011, 16–013
Moschi v Lep Air Services Ltd; *sub nom.* Moschi v Rolloswin Investments
Ltd; Lep Air Services v Rolloswin Investments [1973] A.C. 331; [1972]
2 W.L.R. 1175; [1972] 2 All E.R. 393; 116 S.J. 372, HL 7–017
Motis Exports Ltd v Dampskibsselskabet AF 1912 A/S (No.1); *sub nom.*
Dampskibsselskabet AF 1912 A/S v Motis Exports Ltd [2000] 1 All
E.R. (Comm) 91; [2000] 1 Lloyd's Rep. 211; [2000] C.L.C. 515; (2000)
97(3) L.S.G. 37; *The Times*, January 26, 2000, CA; affirming [1999] 1 All
E.R. (Comm) 571; [1999] 1 Lloyd's Rep. 837; [1999] C.L.C. 914; *The
Times*, March 31, 1999, QBD (Comm Ct) 1–051, 6–019, 6–025, 6–026, 6–027,
6–028, 6–030, 6–031, 6–032, 6–033, 6–036, 10–035, 13–036, 14–050,
15–050, 15–053, 16–031, 16–038
Muncaster Castle, The. *See* Riverstone Meat Co Pty Ltd v Lancashire
Shipping Co Ltd.

NV Handel My J Smits Import-Export v English Exporters (London) Ltd
[1957] 1 Lloyd's Rep. 517, QBD (Comm Ct) 3–013, 3–014, 3–016, 15–003

Nai Matteini, The. *See* Navigazione Alta Italia SpA v Svenske Petroleum AB.

National Bank of South Africa v Banca Italiana di Sconto (1922) 10 Ll. L. Rep. 531, CA 3–060

National Carriers Ltd v Panalpina (Northern) Ltd [1981] A.C. 675; [1981] 2 W.L.R. 45; [1981] 1 All E.R. 161; (1982) 43 P. & C.R. 72; 125 S.J. 46; *The Times*, December 17, 1980, HL 15–039

National Petroleum Co v Owners of the Athelviscount (1934) 48 Ll. L. Rep. 164, KBD 14–028

Naviera Mogor SA v Societe Metallurgique de Normandie (The Nogar Marin) [1988] 1 Lloyd's Rep. 412; [1988] 1 F.T.L.R. 349; *The Times*, January 22, 1988; *Independent*, February 16, 1988; *Financial Times*, January 26, 1988, CA 14–009, 14–014, 14–020, 14–027, 14–030

Navigazione Alta Italia SpA v Svenske Petroleum AB (The Nai Matteini) [1988] 1 Lloyd's Rep. 452, QBD (Comm Ct) 12–027, 12–028, 12–032, 12–033, 12–035

Naxos, The. *See* Cie Commerciale Sucres et Denrees v C Czarnikow Ltd.

Nea Tyhi, The [1982] 1 Lloyd's Rep. 606; [1982] Com. L.R. 9, QBD (Adm Ct) 12–037, 13–081, 13–083, 14–019, 14–036, 14–037, 14–041, 14–044, 14–045

Nerarno, The. *See* Daval Aciers D'Usinor et de Sacilor v Armare Srl.

New Chinese Antimony Co Ltd v Ocean Steamship Co Ltd [1917] 2 K.B. 664, CA 14–052

Newborne v Sensolid (Great Britain) Ltd [1954] 1 Q.B. 45; [1953] 2 W.L.R. 596; [1953] 1 All E.R. 708; 97 S.J. 209, CA 16–009, 16–013

Newman Industries v Indo-British Industries (Govindram Bros, Third Parties) [1957] 1 Lloyd's Rep. 211, CA; reversing [1956] 2 Lloyd's Rep. 219, QBD 9–034

Ng Chee Chong, Ng Weng Chong, Ng Cheng and Ng Yew (A Firm t/a Maran Road Saw Mill) v Austin Taylor & Co [1975] 1 Lloyd's Rep. 156, QBD (Comm Ct) 8–005, 8–027, 8–028, 9–004, 9–036, 9–037, 16–031

Nichimen Corp v Gatoil Overseas Inc [1987] 2 Lloyd's Rep. 46, CA 9–022

Niru Battery Manufacturing Co v Milestone Trading Ltd [2002] EWHC 1425, QBD (Comm Ct) 15–049

Nissos Samos, The. *See* Samos Shipping Enterprises v Eckhardt and Co KG.

Njegos, The [1936] P. 90; (1935) 53 Ll. L. Rep. 286, PDAD 12–020, 12–022, 12–026

Noble Resources Ltd v Cavalier Shipping Corp (The Atlas) [1996] 1 Lloyd's Rep. 642; [1996] C.L.C. 1148, QBD (Comm Ct) 5–078, 14–052

Nogar Marin, The. *See* Naviera Mogor SA v Societe Metallurgique de Normandie.

Nordskog & Co Ltd v National Bank (1922) 10 Ll. L. Rep. 652, KBD 8–029

Norsk Bjergningskompagni A/S v Owners of the Pantanassa (The Pantanassa); *sub nom.* Norsk Bjergningskompagni A/S v Owners of the Steamship Pantanassa, her Cargo and Freight [1970] P. 187; [1970] 2 W.L.R. 981; [1970] 1 All E.R. 848; [1970] 1 Lloyd's Rep. 153; 114 S.J. 372, PDAD 2–029

North Western Bank Ltd v John Poynter Son & MacDonalds [1895] A.C. 56, HL 8–042

Northern Progress, The. *See* Ceval Alimentos SA v Agrimpex Trading Co Ltd.

Northern Shipping Co v Deutsche Seereederei GmbH (formerly Deutsche Seereederei Rostock GmbH) [2000] 2 Lloyd's Rep. 255; [2000] C.L.C. 933, CA 11–025

Northumbria, The [1906] P. 292, PDAD 12–023

Nova Petroleum International Establishment v Tricon Trading Ltd [1989] 1 Lloyd's Rep. 312 7–017

Nugent v Smith (1876) 45 L.J. (C.L.) 697 11–018

OK Petroleum AB v Vitol Energy SA (The Chemical Venture and The Jade) [1995] 2 Lloyd's Rep. 160; *The Times*, May 29, 1995, QBD (Comm Ct) 2–033, 2–035, 12–020

Obestain Inc v National Mineral Development Corp Ltd (The Sanix Ace) [1987] 1 Lloyd's Rep. 465, QBD (Comm Ct) 13–020, 13–040

Ocean Frost, The. *See* Armagas Ltd v Mundogas SA.

Oceanfocus Shipping Ltd v Hyundai Merchant Marine Co Ltd (The Hawk) [1999] 1 Lloyd's Rep. 176, QBD (Comm Ct) 14–027, 14–045

Oinoussin Pride, The. *See* Pride Shipping Corp v Chung Hwa Pulp Corp.

Okehampton, The [1913] P. 173, CA 12–043, 12–045

Olympia Oil & Cake Co & Produce Brokers' Co, Re. *See* Produce Brokers Co Ltd v Olympia Oil and Cake Co Ltd.

Orient Co v Brekke & Howlid [1913] 1 K.B. 531, KBD 6–110

Oulo Osakayetio v Arnold Laver & Co Ltd [1940] 1 K.B. 750; (1940) 66 Ll. L. Rep. 167, CA 1–005

Owners of Cargo Laden on Board the Albacruz v Owners of the Albazero; *sub nom.* Concord Petroleum Corp v Gosford Marine Panama SA [1977] A.C. 774; [1976] 3 W.L.R. 419; [1976] 3 All E.R. 129; [1976] 2 Lloyd's Rep. 467; 120 S.J. 570, HL; reversing [1975] 3 W.L.R. 491; [1975] 3 All E.R. 21; [1975] 2 Lloyd's Rep. 295; 119 S.J. 609, CA 1–048, 2–002, 2–027, 5–033, 5–039, 5–058, 5–059, 5–060, 5–062, 5–063, 5–064, 12–001, 13–020, 13–038, 13–040, 13–045, 13–080, 15–008

Owners of Cargo Lately Laden on Board the Ardennes v Owners of the Ardennes (The Ardennes); *sub nom.* Torneo v Owners of the Ardennes [1951] 1 K.B. 55; [1950] 2 All E.R. 517; (1950) 84 Ll. L. Rep. 340; (1950) 66 T.L.R. (Pt. 2) 312; 94 S.J. 458, KBD 12–002, 12–006

Owners of Cargo Lately Laden on Board the David Agmashenebeli v Owners of the David Agmashenebeli [2002] EWHC 104, QBD (Adm Ct) 14–024, 14–026

Owners of Cargo Lately Laden on Board the Rewia v Caribbean Liners (Caribtainer) Ltd (The Rewia); *sub nom.* Owners of the Cargo Lately Laden on Board the Rewia v Caribbean Liners (Caribtainer) Ltd; Rewia, The [1991] 2 Lloyd's Rep. 325; [1993] I.L.Pr. 507; *Financial Times*, July 12, 1991, CA 12–045, 12–049

Owners of Cargo Lately Laden on Board the River Gurara v Nigerian National Shipping Line Ltd (The River Gurara) [1998] Q.B. 610; [1997] 3 W.L.R. 1128; [1997] 4 All E.R. 498; [1998] 1 Lloyd's Rep. 225; [1997] C.L.C. 1322; (1997) 94(33) L.S.G. 27; (1997) 141 S.J.L.B. 175; *The Times*, July 29, 1997, CA 11–058, 11–060, 14–023, 14–029, 14–050, 14–052, 14–054

Owners of Cargo on Board the Morviken v Owners of the Hollandia (The Hollandia and The Morviken) [1983] 1 A.C. 565; [1982] 3 W.L.R. 1111; [1982] 3 All E.R. 1141; [1983] 1 Lloyd's Rep. 1; [1983] Com. L.R. 44; 126 S.J. 819, HL 11–035, 11–045, 11–047, 11–059

Owners of the Annefield v Owners of Cargo Lately Laden on Board the Annefield [1971] P. 168; [1971] 2 W.L.R. 320; [1971] 1 All E.R. 394; [1971] 1 Lloyd's Rep. 1, CA ... 12–020, 12–022, 12–023, 12–025, 12–026, 12–027, 12–028

Owners of the Cap Palos v Alder; *sub nom.* Cap Palos (The v Alder) [1921] P. 458; (1921) 8 Ll. L. Rep. 309, CA 6–018

Owners of the Ship Freedom v Simmonds, Hunt, & Co (1869–71) L.R. 3 P.C. 594, PC (UK) 13–033

Paal Wilson & Co A/S v Partenreederei Hannah Blumenthal (The Hannah Blumenthal) [1983] 1 A.C. 854; [1982] 3 W.L.R. 1149; [1983] 1 All E.R. 34; [1983] 1 Lloyd's Rep. 103; [1983] Com. L.R. 20; 126 S.J. 835, HL 4–051

Pacific Molasses Co and United Molasses Trading Co v Entre Rios Compania Naviera SA (The San Nicholas) [1976] 1 Lloyd's Rep. 8, CA 2–027, 3–011, 5–001, 5–011, 5–032, 5–033, 5–034, 5–039, 5–060, 5–061, 5–062, 5–066, 12–020, 12–029, 12–030, 12–031, 12–032, 12–033, 12–035, 12–036

Pagnan SpA v Tradax Ocean Transportation SA; *sub nom.* Tradax Ocean Transportation SA v Pagnan [1987] 3 All E.R. 565; [1987] 2 Lloyd's Rep. 342, CA 2–033

Panchauds Frères SA v Etablissements General Grain Co [1970] 1 Lloyd's Rep. 53, CA 7–040, 7–048, 7–049, 7–064

Panda OHG v Circle Products Ltd *See* Frebold v Circle Products.

Panoutsos v Raymond Hadley Corp of New York [1917] 2 K.B. 473, CA 8–022, 9–021, 9–024, 9–026, 9–027

Pantanassa, The. *See* Norsk Bjergningskompagni A/S v Owners of the Pantanassa.

Parchim, The [1918] A.C. 157, PC (UK) ... 2–003, 2–016, 3–014, 3–056, 3–057, 5–014, 5–033, 5–034, 5–036, 5–037, 5–040, 5–047, 5–048, 5–050, 5–051, 5–053, 5–054, 5–055, 5–058, 5–060

Parsons Corp v CV Scheepvaartonderneming Happy Ranger (The Happy Ranger) [2002] EWCA Civ 694; [2002] 2 All E.R. (Comm) 24, CA 11–078, 11–079, 16–017

Partenreederei M/S Heidberg v Grosvenor Grain & Feed Co Ltd (The Heidberg) (No.2) [1994] 2 Lloyd's Rep. 287, QBD (Comm Ct) 12–020, 12–033, 12–034, 12–035, 12–036, 16–007

Paterson Zochonis & Co Ltd v Elder Dempster & Co Ltd; *sub nom.* Paterson Zochnois & Co Ltd v Elder Dampster & Co Ltd; Elder Dempster & Co Ltd v Paterson Zochonis & Co Lt; Griffiths Lewis Steam Navigation Co Ltd v Paterson Zochonis & Co Ltd [1924] A.C. 522; (1924) 18 Ll. L. Rep. 319, HL; reversing [1923] 1 K.B. 420; (1922) 13 Ll. L. Rep. 513, CA 12–045, 12–047, 12–049

Patten v Thompson (1816) 5 M. & S. 350; 105 E.R. 1079 13–032

Pavia & Co SpA v Thurmann Nielsen [1952] 2 Q.B. 84; [1952] 1 All E.R. 492; [1952] 1 Lloyd's Rep. 153; [1952] 1 T.L.R. 586; 96 S.J. 193, CA 9–012, 6–014, 9–015, 9–016, 9–017, 9–018, 9–019, 9–021

Peacock v Pursell (1863) 14 C.B.N.S. 728 9–035

Pepper (Inspector of Taxes) v Hart [1993] A.C. 593; [1992] 3 W.L.R. 1032; [1993] 1 All E.R. 42; [1992] S.T.C. 898; [1993] I.C.R. 291; [1993] I.R.L.R. 33; [1993] R.V.R. 127; (1993) 143 N.L.J. 17; [1992] N.P.C. 154; *The Times*, November 30, 1992; *Independent*, November 26, 1992, HL 13–016

Peter Cremer GmbH v General Carriers SA (The Dona Mari) [1974] 1 W.L.R. 341; [1974] 1 All E.R. 1; [1973] 2 Lloyd's Rep. 366; (1973) 117 S.J. 873, QBD (Comm Ct) 6–096, 13–056, 13–058, 13–068, 14–004, 14–021, 14–022, 14–023

Peter der Grosse, The (1875–76) L.R. 1 P.D. 414, PDAD 14–028

Petroships Pte Ltd of Singapore v Petec Trading & Investment Corp of Vietnam (The Petro Ranger) [2001] 2 Lloyd's Rep. 348, QBD (Comm Ct) 15–039

Photo Production Ltd v Securicor Transport Ltd [1980] A.C. 827; [1980] 2 W.L.R. 283; [1980] 1 All E.R. 556; [1980] 1 Lloyd's Rep. 545; 124 S.J. 147, HL ... 3–025, 6–034, 7–013, 7–014, 7–015, 7–025, 11–005, 11–009, 11–070, 12–004

Pinchon's case (1612) 9 Co Rep. 866 16–012

Pioneer Container, The; *sub nom*. Owners of Cargo Lately Laden on Board
the KH Enterprise v Owners of the Pioneer Container [1994] 2 A.C.
324; [1994] 3 W.L.R. 1; [1994] 2 All E.R. 250; [1994] 1 Lloyd's Rep. 593;
(1994) 91(18) L.S.G. 37; (1994) 138 S.J.L.B. 85; *The Times*, March 29,
1994, PC (HK) 12–020, 12–049
Pirelli General Cable Works Ltd v Oscar Faber & Partners [1983] 2 A.C. 1;
[1983] 2 W.L.R. 6; [1983] 1 All E.R. 65; (1983) 265 E.G. 979; *The Times*,
December 11, 1982, HL 13–083
Playa Larga and Marble Islands, The. *See* Empresa Exportadora De Azucar
(CUBAZUCAR) v Industria Azucarera Nacional SA (IANSA).
Pordage v Cole (1669) 1 Wms. Saund. 319 7–026
Portsmouth, The. *See* TW Thomas & Co Ltd v Portsea Steamship Co
Ltd.
Power Curber International Ltd v National Bank of Kuwait SAK [1981] 1
W.L.R. 1233; [1981] 3 All E.R. 607; [1981] 2 Lloyd's Rep. 394; [1981]
Com. L.R. 224, CA 8–034
President of India v Metcalfe Shipping Co Ltd (The Dunelmia) [1970] 1
Q.B. 289; [1969] 3 W.L.R. 1120; [1969] 3 All E.R. 1549; [1969] 2 Lloyd's
Rep. 476; 113 S.J. 792, CA 3–009, 11–079, 12–007, 12–010, 12–020
Pride Shipping Corp v Chung Hwa Pulp Corp (The Oinoussin Pride)
[1991] 1 Lloyd's Rep. 126, QBD (Comm Ct) 12–028
Procter & Gamble Phillipine Manufacturing Corp v Becher [1988] 2
Lloyd's Rep. 21; [1988] F.T.L.R. 450, CA 7–027, 7–032, 7–044, 7–048, 7–050,
7–062, 7–063, 7–064, 7–064, 14–004
Procter & Gamble Phillipine Manufacturing Corp v Peter Cremer GmbH
& Co (The Manila) (No.2) [1988] 3 All E.R. 843; *Independent*, April 15,
1988 .... 7–049, 7–064
Procurator General v MC Spencer (Controller of Mitsui & Co Ltd) (The
Glenroy) [1945] A.C. 124, PC (UK) 5–039, 5–065, 5–072, 5–074
Produce Brokers Co Ltd v Olympia Oil and Cake Co Ltd; *sub nom*.
Olympia Oil and Cake Co Ltd and the Produce Brokers Co Ltd, Re
[1916] 1 A.C. 314, HL [1915] 1 K.B. 233, KBD 4–010, 4–014, 4–016, 4–017,
4–018
Pyrene Co Ltd v Scindia Steam Navigation Co Ltd [1954] 2 Q.B. 402; [1954]
2 W.L.R. 1005; [1954] 2 All E.R. 158; [1954] 1 Lloyd's Rep. 321; 98 S.J.
354, QBD 1–005, 1–008, 1–013, 3–002, 3–004, 3–005, 3–006, 3–008, 3–013,
3–014, 3–039, 3–059, 4–003, 5–011, 5–014, 9–008, 11–002, 11–042, 11–053,
11–064, 11–065, 11–067, 11–071, 11–072, 11–077, 11–079, 11–081,
12–015, 12–016, 12–018, 13–068, 13–072, 13–085, 15–002, 15–008, B–015

R Pagnan & Fratelli v NGJ Schouten NV (The Filipinas I) [1973] 1 Lloyd's
Rep. 349, QBD (Comm Ct) 1–018, 1–020, 1–021, 1–022, 1–031, 1–046, 1–048,
3–009, 15–009
R. v International Trustee for the Protection of Bondholders AG; *sub nom*.
International Trustee for the Protection of Bondholders AG v King,
The [1937] A.C. 500; (1937) 57 Ll. L. Rep. 145, HL 11–034
R. v Moore Ex p Myers (1884) 10 V.L.R. 322 16–011
R. v Secretary of State for Transport Ex p. Factortame Ltd (No.1) [1990] 2
A.C. 85; [1989] 2 W.L.R. 997; [1989] 2 All E.R. 692; [1989] 3 C.M.L.R. 1;
[1989] C.O.D. 531; (1989) 139 N.L.J. 715; *The Times*, May 19, 1989;
Independent, May 26, 1989; *Financial Times*, May 23, 1989; *Guardian*,
May 25, 1989; *Daily Telegraph*, June 5, 1989, HL 13–016
Rafaela S, The. *See* JI MacWilliam Co Inc v Mediterranean Shipping Co
SA.
Rafsanjan Pistachio Producers Cooperative v Bank Leumi (UK) Ltd [1992]
1 Lloyd's Rep. 513, QBD (Comm Ct) 10–010

Ralli v Universal Marine Insurance Co (1862) 6 L.T. 34 6–110
Raymond Burke Motors Ltd v Mersey Docks and Harbour Co [1986] 1
    Lloyd's Rep. 155, QBD (Comm Ct) 11–038
Reardon Smith Line Ltd v Hansen-Tangen (The Diana Prosperity); Han-
    sen-Tangen v Sanko Steamship Co Ltd [1976] 1 W.L.R. 989; [1976] 3
    All E.R. 570; [1976] 2 Lloyd's Rep. 621; 120 S.J. 719, HL 3–025
Redding, Re (1850) 14 Jur. 1052; 2 Rob. Ecc. 339 .... 16–009, 16–013
Rena K, The [1979] Q.B. 377; [1978] 3 W.L.R. 431; [1979] 1 All E.R. 397;
    [1978] 1 Lloyd's Rep. 545; 122 S.J. 315, QBD (Adm Ct) 12–027, 12–028
Rewia, The. *See* Owners of Cargo Lately Laden on Board the Rewia v
    Caribbean Liners (Caribtainer) Ltd.
Rex v International Trustee for, etc., Bondholders AG. *See* R. v Inter-
    national Trustee for the Protection of Bondholders AG.
Rhodes v Peterson, 1971 S.C. 56; 1972 S.L.T. 98, OH 16–013
Rio Sun, The. *See* Gatoil International Inc v Tradax Petroleum Ltd.
River Gurara, The. *See* Owners of Cargo Lately Laden on Board the River
    Gurara v Nigerian National Shipping Line Ltd.
Riverstone Meat Co Pty Ltd v Lancashire Shipping Co Ltd (The Muncaster
    Castle) [1961] A.C. 807; [1961] 2 W.L.R. 269; [1961] 1 All E.R. 495;
    [1961] 1 Lloyd's Rep. 57; 105 S.J. 148, HL 11–031, 11–039, 11–039, 11–040,
                                                                         11–041, 11–042
Robin, The. *See* Veba Oil Supply & Trading GmbH v Petrotrade Inc.
Rosa S, The [1989] Q.B. 419; [1989] 2 W.L.R. 162; [1989] 1 All E.R. 489;
    [1988] 2 Lloyd's Rep. 574, QBD (Adm Ct) ... 11–050, 11–051, 11–054, 11–056,
                                                                         11–057, 11–060
Ross T Smyth & Co Ltd v TD Bailey & Co; *sub nom.* TD Bailey Son & Co
    v Ross T Smyth & Co Ltd [1940] 3 All E.R. 60; (1940) 67 Ll.L. Rep. 147,
    HL 1–001, 1–005, 2–004, 2–011, 2–013, 3–006, 5–037, 5–039, 5–046, 5–050,
                                                          5–056, 5–058, 5–060, 8–035
Rossiter v Miller (1877–78) L.R. 3 App. Cas. 1124, HL 16–002
Royal Bank of Scotland Plc v Cassa di Risparmio delle Provincie Lom-
    barde SA; Royal Bank of Scotland Plc v Istituto Bancario San Paolo Di
    Torino, *Financial Times*, January 21, 1992, CA 8–014
Royan, The. *See* Cooperative Centrale Raiffeisen-Boerenleenbank BA v
    Sumitomo Bank.
Ruck v Hatfield (1822) 5 B. & Ald. 632, 106 E.R. 1321 ..... 1–004, 1–008, 1–011, 1–013
Rudolph A Oetker v IFA Internationale Frachtagentur AG (The Almak)
    [1985] 1 Lloyd's Rep. 557, QBD (Comm Ct) 14–004, 14–014, 14–019, 14–020

SIAT di del Ferro v Tradax Overseas SA [1980] 1 Lloyd's Rep. 53, CA;
    affirming [1978] 2 Lloyd's Rep. 470, QBD (Comm Ct) 2–029, 6–074, 6–075,
                                                                         10–026, 15–012
SLS Everest, The. *See* Bangladesh Chemical Industries Corp v Henry
    Stephens Shipping Co and Tex-Bilan Shipping Co.
Sagona, The. *See* Hansen-Tangens Rederi III A/S v Total Transport
    Corp.
Sale Continuation Ltd v Austin Taylor & Co Ltd [1968] 2 Q.B. 849; [1967]
    3 W.L.R. 1427; [1967] 2 All E.R. 1092; [1967] 2 Lloyd's Rep. 403; 111 S.J.
    472, QBD (Comm Ct) 5–037, 5–038
Salem, The. *See* Shell International Petroleum Co Ltd v Gibbs.
Samah, The. *See* Mmecen SA v Inter Ro-Ro SA and Gulf Ro-Ro Services
    SA.
Samos Shipping Enterprises v Eckhardt and Co KG (The Nissos Samos)
    [1985] 1 Lloyd's Rep. 378, QBD (Comm Ct) 16–004
San Nicholas, The. *See* Pacific Molasses Co and United Molasses Trading
    Co v Entre Rios Compania Naviera SA.

Sanders Bros v Maclean & Co (1882–83) L.R. 11 Q.B.D. 327, CA ... 1–011, 1–051, 2–045, 2–046, 6–013, 6–027, 6–045, 6–084, 6–087, 6–089, 6–090, 6–094, 10–001, 13–044, 15–037

Sanders v Vanzeller (1843) 4 Q.B. 260; 114 E.R. 897 .... 13–045, 13–056

Sanix Ace, The. *See* Obestain Inc v National Mineral Development Corp Ltd.

Sara D, The [1989] 2 Lloyd's Rep. 277; *Financial Times*, May 16, 1989, CA 12–004

Saudi Crown, The [1986] 1 Lloyd's Rep. 261, QBD (Adm Ct) 14–005, 14–024, 14–035, 14–036, 14–039, 14–041, 14–045

Saunders v Edwards [1987] 1 W.L.R. 1116; [1987] 2 All E.R. 651; (1987) 137 N.L.J. 389; (1987) 131 S.J. 1039, CA 7–032, 7–056

Scandinavian Trading Co A/B v Zodiac Petroleum SA (The Al Hofuf); *sub nom.* Scandinavian Trading Co A/B v William Hudson [1981] 1 Lloyd's Rep. 81, QBD (Comm Ct) 1–047, 3–016, 3–020, 3–028, 3–033, 3–034, 3–036, 3–037, 3–038, 3–039

Schneider v Norris, 2 M. & S. 286 16–010

Scruttons Ltd v Midland Silicones Ltd; *sub nom.* Midland Silicones Ltd v Scruttons Ltd [1962] A.C. 446; [1962] 2 W.L.R. 186; [1962] 1 All E.R. 1; [1961] 2 Lloyd's Rep. 365; 106 S.J. 34, HL 11–030, 11–031, 11–037, 11–038, 11–041, 11–043, 11–061, 11–067, 11–081, 12–049, 13–072

Seaconsar (Far East) Ltd v Bank Markazi Jomhouri Islami Iran (Service Outside Jurisdiction) [1994] 1 A.C. 438; [1993] 3 W.L.R. 756, HL; reversing [1993] 1 Lloyd's Rep. 236; *The Times*, November 25, 1992, CA 10–032

Seng Co Ltd v Glencore Grain Ltd *See* Soon Hua Seng Co Ltd v Glencore Grain Ltd.

Serraino & Sons v Campbell [1891] 1 Q.B. 283, CA 12–022

Sevonia Team, The. *See* K/S A/S Seateam & Co v Iraq National Oil Co.

Sewell v Burdick (The Zoe); *sub nom.* Sewell v Owners of the Zoe; Burdick v Sewell and Nephew; Burdick v Sewell and Nephew (1884–85) L.R. 10 App. Cas. 74, HL 5–005, 6–014, 8–038, 8–039, 12–003, 13–002, 13–012, 13–032, 13–042, 13–044, 13–046, 13–047, 13–048, 13–056, 16–029, 16–031

Sharpe v Nosawa [1917] 2 K.B. 814 .... 2–004, 6–087, 6–089, 6–090

Shell International Petroleum Co Ltd v Gibbs (The Salem) [1983] 2 A.C. 375; [1983] 2 W.L.R. 371; [1983] 1 All E.R. 745; [1983] 1 Lloyd's Rep. 342; [1983] Com. L.R. 96; (1983) 133 N.L.J. 400; (1983) 127 S.J. 154; *The Times*, February 18, 1983, HL 15–010, 15–040, 15–041, 15–044, 15–045, 15–047, 15–048, 15–051

Shepherd v Harrison (1871–72) L.R. 5 H.L. 116, HL 5–033, 5–043, 5–052, 7–023, 7–030

Silver v Ocean Steam Ship Co; *sub nom.* Silver v Ocean Steamship Co Ltd [1930] 1 K.B. 416; (1929) 35 Ll. L. Rep. 49, CA 7–068, 14–028, 14–045, 14–054

Simona, The. *See* Fercometal Sarl v MSC Mediterranean Shipping Co SA.

Simpson & Co v Thomson; Simpson & Co v Burrell (1877–78) L.R. 3 App. Cas. 279; (1877) 5 R. (H.L.) 40, HL 13–075

Sirina, The. *See* Conoco (UK) v Limai Maritime Co.

Skarp, The [1935] P. 134; [1935] All E.R. Rep. 560; (1935) 52 Ll. L. Rep. 152; 51 T.L.R. 541; 104 L.J. P. 63, PDAD 14–021, 14–023

Skips A/S Nordheim v Syrian Petroleum Co and Petrofina SA (The Varenna) [1984] Q.B. 599; [1983] 3 All E.R. 645; [1983] 2 Lloyd's Rep. 592; *The Times*, October 6, 1983, CA 12–020, 12–021, 12–025, 12–033

Smidt v Tiden (1873–74) L.R. 9 Q.B. 446, QBD 12–032

Smith Hogg & Co Ltd v Black Sea & Baltic General Insurance Co Ltd [1940] A.C. 997; (1940) 67 Ll. L. Rep. 253, HL 11–004

Smurthwaite v Wilkins (1862) 11 C.B.N.S. 842; 142 E.R. 1026 ..... 13–042, 13–047, 13–054

Smyth v Bailey. *See* Ross T Smyth & Co Ltd v TD Bailey & Co.

Société Anonyme de Remorquage à Helice v Bennetts. *See* La Société Anonyme de Remorquage a Helice v Bennetts.

Solholt, The. *See* Sotiros Shipping Inc v Shmeiet Solholt.

Soon Hua Seng Co Ltd v Glencore Grain Ltd [1996] 1 Lloyd's Rep. 398; [1996] C.L.C. 729; Lloyd's List, February 21, 1996, QBD (Comm Ct) 2–029, 10–026, 15–013

Soproma SpA v Marine & Animal By-Products Corp [1966] 1 Lloyd's Rep. 367; 116 N.L.J. 867, QBD (Comm Ct) 9–005, 9–006, 9–021, 9–022, 9–023, 9–028, 9–029, 9–031, 9–033, 9–035, 9–036, 10–027

Sormovskiy 3068, The. *See* Sucre Export SA v Northern River Shipping Ltd.

Sotiros Shipping Inc v Shmeiet Solholt (The Solholt) [1983] 1 Lloyd's Rep. 605; [1983] Com. L.R. 114; (1983) 127 S.J. 305, CA; affirming [1981] 2 Lloyd's Rep. 574; [1981] Com. L.R. 201, QBD (Comm Ct) 16–003

Soules Caf v PT Transap (Indonesia) [1999] 1 Lloyd's Rep. 917, QBD (Comm Ct) 2–029, 2–030, 2–043, 6–071, 10–026, 15–012

Spiros C, The. *See* Tradigrain SA v King Diamond Marine Ltd.

Spring v Guardian Assurance plc [1995] 2 A.C. 296; [1994] 3 W.L.R. 354; [1994] 3 All E.R. 129; [1994] I.C.R. 596; [1994] I.R.L.R. 460; (1994) 91(40) L.S.G. 36; (1994) 144 N.L.J. 971; (1994) 138 S.J.L.B. 183; *The Times*, July 8, 1994; *Independent*, July 12, 1994, HL 14–027

Stag Line Ltd v Foscolo Mango & Co Ltd; *sub nom.* Foscolo Mango & Co Ltd v Stag Line Ltd; Foscolo, Mango & Co Ltd, and HC Vivian Ltd v Stag Line Ltd; Foscolo, Mango & Co Ltd, and HC Vivian Ltd v Stag Line Ltd; Foscolo, Mango & Co Ltd, v Stag Line Ltd [1932] A.C. 328; (1931) 41 Ll. L. Rep. 165, HL 11–005, 11–027, 11–039, 11–059

Starsin, The. *See* Homburg Houtimport BV v Agrosin Private Ltd.

Steamship Calcutta Co Ltd v Andrew Weir & Co (The Calcutta) [1910] 1 K.B. 759, KBD 12–010

Sterns v Vickers; *sub nom.* Sterns Ltd v Vickers Ltd [1923] 1 K.B. 78, CA 2–017

Stettin, The (1889) L.R. 14 P.D. 142, PDAD 6–005, 6–023, 6–026, 6–035

Stindt v Roberts (1848) 17 L.J.Q.B. 166 .... 13–045, 13–056

Stumore Weston & Co v Breen (1887) L.R. 12 App. Cas. 698, HL 14–013

Sucre Export SA v Northern River Shipping Ltd (The Sormovskiy 3068) [1994] 2 Lloyd's Rep. 266; *The Times*, May 13, 1994, QBD (Adm Ct) 6–020, 6–021, 6–022, 6–026, 6–027, 6–029, 6–032

Suisse Atlantique Societe d'Armement SA v NV Rotterdamsche Kolen Centrale [1967] 1 A.C. 361; [1966] 2 W.L.R. 944; [1966] 2 All E.R. 61; [1966] 1 Lloyd's Rep. 529; 110 S.J. 367, HL; affirming [1965] 1 Lloyd's Rep. 533, CA 6–034, 11–009, 11–070

Sunrise Maritime Inc v Uvisco Ltd (The Hector) [1998] 2 Lloyd's Rep. 287; [1998] C.L.C. 902, QBD (Comm Ct) 14–044

Swallow and Pearson v Middlesex CC [1953] 1 W.L.R. 422; [1953] 1 All E.R. 580; 51 L.G.R. 253; 3 P. & C.R. 314; 97 S.J. 155, QBD 16–019

Sze Hai Tong Bank v Rambler Cycle Co [1959] A.C. 576; [1959] 3 W.L.R. 214; [1959] 3 All E.R. 182; [1959] 2 Lloyd's Rep. 114; 103 S.J. 561, PC (Sing) 6–016, 6–020, 6–021, 6–025, 6–026, 6–030, 6–034, 6–035, 6–036, 8–035, 11–070, 15–018

TB&S Batchelor & Co Ltd v Owners of the SS Merak (The Merak) [1965] P. 223; [1965] 2 W.L.R. 250; [1965] 1 All E.R. 230; [1964] 2 Lloyd's Rep. 527; 108 S.J. 1012, CA 12–020, 12–023, 12–024, 12–026, 12–028

TW Thomas & Co Ltd v Portsea Steamship Co Ltd (The Portsmouth) [1912] A.C. 1, HL 12–011, 12–012, 12–020, 12–021, 12–022, 12–023, 12–026

Tappenbeck Ex p. Banner, Re (1875–76) L.R. 2 Ch. D. 278, CA 5–052

Tarrabochia v Hickie (1856) 1 Hurl. & N. 183 3–027

Tate & Lyle Ltd v Hain Steamship Co Ltd; *sub nom.* Hain Steamship Co v Tate & Lyle Ltd [1936] 2 All E.R. 597; (1936) 55 Ll. L. Rep. 159; 52 T.L.R. 617; 41 Com. Cas. 350; [1936] W.N. 210, HL 11–003, 11–005

Taylor v Oakes Roncoroni & Co (1922) 127 L.T. 267; (1922) 18 T.L.R. 349 .... 7–026, 7–041

Taylor & Sons v Bank of Athens; Pennoid Bros v Bank of Athens (1922) 10 Ll. L. Rep. 88; (1922) 27 Com. Cas. 142, KBD 7–032, 7–046, 7–047, 7–052, 7–053, 7–055, 7–056, 7–057, 7–062, 7–063, 7–064

Teheran-Europe Co Ltd v ST Belton (Tractors) Ltd [1968] 2 Q.B. 545 4–036

Teutonia, The. *See* Duncan v Koster.

Texaco Ltd v Eurogulf Shipping Co Ltd [1987] 2 Lloyd's Rep. 541, QBD (Comm Ct) 3–040

Thompson v Dominy (1845) 14 M. & W. 403; 153 E.R. 532, Exchequer 1–013, 6–045, 13–003, 13–004, 13–006, 13–045

Toepfer v Continental Grain Co *See* Alfred C Toepfer v Continental Grain Co.

Torenia, The. *See* Aktieselskabet de Danske Sukkerfabrikker v Bajamar Compania Naviera SA.

Total Transport Corp v Arcadia Petroleum Ltd (The Eurus) [1998] 1 Lloyd's Rep. 351; [1998] C.L.C. 90; (1998) 95(1) L.S.G. 24; (1998) 142 S.J.L.B. 22; *The Times*, December 16, 1997, CA 14–004

Tradax Export SA v Italgrani di Francesco Ambrosio; Italgrani Di Francesco Ambrosio V Sosimage S.p.a.; Sosimage SpA v Italgrani di Francesco Ambrosio [1986] 1 Lloyd's Rep. 112, CA 3–020, 3–021, 3–022, 3–031

Trade Star Line Corp v Mitsui & Co Ltd (The Arctic Trader); Mitsui & Co Ltd v Jauritzen A/S [1996] 2 Lloyd's Rep. 449; [1997] C.L.C. 174, CA 12–019, 14–014, 14–020, 14–025, 14–027, 14–029, 14–030, 14–031

Tradigrain SA v King Diamond Marine Ltd (The Spiros C); *sub nom.* Tradigrain SA v King Diamond Shipping SA (The Spiros C) [2000] 2 All E.R. (Comm) 542; [2000] 2 Lloyd's Rep. 319; [2000] C.L.C. 1503; *Independent*, October 9, 2000 (C.S), CA 15–052

Trans Trust S.P.R.L. v Danubian Trading Co Ltd [1952] 2 Q.B. 297, CA 9–011, 9–013

Tregelles v Sewell (1862) 7 H. & N. 574, 158 E.R. 600 ..... 1–004, 1–005, 1–009, 1–011, 10–13, 2–005, 2–010, 4–004, 4–007, 15–002, 15–003

Trendtex Trading Corp v Central Bank of Nigeria [1977] Q.B. 529; [1977] 2 W.L.R. 356; [1977] 1 All E.R. 881; [1977] 1 Lloyd's Rep. 581; [1977] 2 C.M.L.R. 465; 121 S.J. 85, CA 10–020, 15–048

Tsakiroglou & Co Ltd v Noblee Thorl GmbH; Albert D Gaon & Co v Societe Interprofessionelle des Oleagineux Fluides Alimentaires [1962] A.C. 93; [1961] 2 W.L.R. 633; [1961] 2 All E.R. 179; [1961] 1 Lloyd's Rep. 329; 105 S.J. 346, HL 5–051, 4–052

Tweddle v Atkinson (1861) 1 B. & S. 393 11–038

Ultramares Corporation v Touche (1931) 174 N.E. 441 14–024

United Baltic Corp Ltd v Dundee Perth & London Shipping Co Ltd (1928) 32 Ll. L. Rep. 272, KBD 7–068

United City Merchants (Investments) Ltd v Royal Bank of Canada (The American Accord) [1983] 1 A.C. 168; [1982] 2 W.L.R. 1039; [1982] 2 All E.R. 720; [1982] 2 Lloyd's Rep. 1; [1982] Com. L.R. 142, HL 7–030, 7–064, 8–008, 8–009, 8–011, 8–047, 8–048, 8–049, 10–003, 10–005, 10–010, 10–011, 1–014, 10–019, 14–002, 14–005, 14–050, 15–048, 15–049

Universal Cargo Carriers Corp v Citati (No.1) [1957] 1 W.L.R. 979; [1957] 3 All E.R. 234, CA; affirming [1957] 2 Q.B. 401; [1957] 2 W.L.R. 713; [1957] 2 All E.R. 70; [1957] 1 Lloyd's Rep. 174; (1957) 101 S.J. 320, QBD 3–034, 3–038, 7–007, 7–011

Universal Petroleum Co v Handels und Transport GmbH [1987] 1 W.L.R. 1178; [1987] 2 All E.R. 737; [1987] 1 Lloyd's Rep. 517; [1987] 1 F.T.L.R. 429; (1987) 84 L.S.G. 1238, CA 15–008

Urquhart Lindsay & Co Ltd v Eastern Bank Ltd [1922] 1 K.B. 318; (1921) 9 Ll. L. Rep. 572, KBD 8–048, 9–034

Utaniko Ltd v P&O Nedlloyd BV (No.1); *sub nom.* East West Corp v Dampskibsselskabet AF 1912 A/S; East West Corp v DKBS 1912 [2002] EWHC 83; [2002] 1 All E.R. (Comm) 676, QBD (Comm Ct) ... 13–022, 13–041, 13–072, 14–047

Uxbridge Permanent Benefit Building Society v Pickard [1939] 2 K.B. 248, CA 14–038, 14–044

V/O Rasnoimport v Guthrie & Co Ltd [1966] 1 Lloyd's Rep. 1, QBD (Comm Ct) ... 14–002, 14–005, 14–019, 14–020, 14–024, 14–029, 14–036, 14–038, 14–047, 14–049, 14–054, 14–055, 14–058, 14–059, 14–060, 15–051, 15–053, 16–039

Varenna, The. *See* Skips A/S Nordheim v Syrian Petroleum Co and Petrofina SA.

Vargas Pena Apezteguia y Cia SAIC v Peter Cremer GmbH & Co [1987] 1 Lloyd's Rep. 394, QBD (Comm Ct) 7–058, 7–060

Veba Oil Supply & Trading GmbH v Petrotrade Inc (The Robin); *sub nom.* Veba Oil Supply & Trading Ltd v Petrotrade Inc (The Robin) [2001] EWCA Civ 1832; [2002] 1 All E.R. 703; [2002] 1 All E.R. (Comm) 306; [2002] 1 Lloyd's Rep. 295; [2002] C.L.C. 405; [2002] B.L.R. 54; *Independent*, January 14, 2002 (C.S), CA 7–022

Vitol SA v Esso Australia Ltd (The Wise) [1989] 2 Lloyd's Rep. 451; *Financial Times*, July 18, 1989, CA; reversing [1989] 1 Lloyd's Rep. 96; *The Times*, February 1, 1988, QBD (Comm Ct) 2–003, 2–019, 2–020, 2–023

WJ Alan & Co Ltd v El Nasr Export & Import Co [1972] 2 Q.B. 189; [1972] 2 W.L.R. 800; [1972] 2 All E.R. 127; [1972] 1 Lloyd's Rep. 313; 116 S.J. 139, CA 9–032, 9–036, 9–037

WN White & Co Ltd v Furness Withy & Co Ltd [1895] A.C. 40, HL 13–056

Wackerbarth v Masson (1812) 3 Camp. 270 1–004

Wait, Re [1927] 1 Ch. 606, CA 5–005, 5–027, 5–028, 13–046

Wait v Baker (1848) 2 Ex. 1; 154 E.R. 380 .... 5–033, 5–040, 5–041, 5–042, 5–045, 5–048, 5–049

Wait & James v Midland Bank (1926) 24 Ll. L. Rep. 313; (1926) 31 Com. Cas. 172, KBD 5–018, 5–019, 5–021, 5–022, 5–023

Waring v Cox (1808) 1 Camp. 369; 170 E.R. 989 13–032

Wear Breeze, The. *See* Margarine Union GmbH v Cambay Prince Steamship Co.

Weis & Co & Credit Colonial et Commercial (Antwerp), Re. *See* Arbitration between Weis & Co Ltd and Credit Colonial et Commercial (Antwerp), Re.

White v Jones [1995] 2 A.C. 207; [1995] 2 W.L.R. 187; [1995] 1 All E.R. 691; [1995] 3 F.C.R. 51; (1995) 145 N.L.J. 251; (1995) 139 S.J.L.B. 83; [1995] N.P.C. 31; *The Times*, February 17, 1995; *Independent*, February 17, 1995, HL 14–024

Wibau Maschinefabrik Hartman SA v Mackinnon Mackenzie (The Chanda) [1989] 2 Lloyd's Rep. 494; *Independent*, April 28, 1989; *Financial Times*, May 3, 1989, QBD (Comm Ct) 11–070

Wickman Machine Tools Sales Ltd v L Schuler AG. *See* L Schuler AG v Wickman Machine Tool Sales Ltd.

Wilson Holgate & Co Ltd v Belgian Grain and Produce Co Ltd [1920] 2 K.B. 1, KBD 6–111

Wimble v Rosenberg; *sub nom.* Wimble Sons & Co v Rosenberg & Sons [1913] 3 K.B. 743, CA .. 1–013, 1–013, 3–001, 3–002, 3–005, 3–006, 4–003, 4–022, 4–028, 5–083, B–012

Wise, The. *See* Vitol SA v Esso Australia Ltd.

World Harmony, The. *See* Konstantinidis v World Tankers Corp Inc.

Yelo v SM Machado & Co Ltd [1952] 1 Lloyd's Rep. 183, QBD 6–001, 6–058, 6–065

Young v Moeller (1855) 5 E. & B. 755; 119 E.R. 662 .... 13–045, 13–056

Ypatianna, The. *See* Indian Oil Corp Ltd v Greenstone Shipping Co SA (Panama).

Zoe, The. *See* Sewell v Burdick.

TABLE OF CASES (INTERNATIONAL)

Arbib & Houlberg v Second Russian Insurance Co, 294 F. 811 (2nd Cir. 1923) 11–028

Australasian United Steam Navigation Co Ltd v Hiskens (1914) 18 C.L.R. 646 11–018

Blue Nile Shipping Co Ltd v emery Customs Brokers (S) Pte Ltd [1990] 2 M.L.H. 385 14–054

Brown Boveri (Australia) Pty v Baltic Shipping Co (The Nadezhda Krupskaya) [1989] 1 Lloyd's Rep. 518, CA (NSW) 11–054

Bunga Seroja, The [1999] 1 Lloyd's Rep. 512, HC (Aus) 11–018, 11–024, 11–030, 15–038

CEP Interagra S.A. v Select Energy Trading GmbH (The Jambur) L.M.L.N. 289; [1991] 5 Oil and Gas Law and Taxation Review D58 .... 2–003, 2–021, 2–021, 4–048, 5–010, 5–025, 7–031, 15–010

CP Henderson & Co v Comptoir d'Escompte de Paris (1873–74) L.R. 5 P.C. 253; (1874) 2 Asp. 98; (1874) 21 W.R. 873; (1874) 42 L.J. P.C. 60; (1874) 29 L.T. 192, PC (HK) 11–080

Canadian Klockner Ltd v D/S A/S Flint (The Mica); *sub nom.* Canadian Klockner Ltd v Federal Commerce & Navigation Co Ltd (The Mica); Federal Commerce & Navigation Co Ltd v Canadian Klockner Ltd [1975] 2 Lloyd's Rep. 371, CA (Can); reversing [1973] 2 Lloyd's Rep. 478; 1974 A.M.C. 467, Fed Ct (Can) 12–044

Candlewood Navigation Corp v Mitsui Osk Lines (The Mineral Transporter and The Ibaraki Maru) [1986] A.C. 1; [1985] 3 W.L.R. 381; [1985] 2 All E.R. 935; [1985] 2 Lloyd's Rep. 303; (1985) 82 L.S.G. 2912; (1985) 135 N.L.J. 677; (1985) 129 S.J. 506, PC (Aus) 13–076, 13–078

Center Optical (Hong Kong) Ltd v Jardine Transport Services (China) Ltd [2001] 2 Lloyd's Rep. 678, HC (HK) 11–060

Compania de Navigacion la Flecha v Brauer, 168 U.S. 104 (1897) 11–018

Gian Singh & Co Ltd v Banque de L'Indochine [1974] 1 W.L.R. 1234; [1974] 2 All E.R. 754; [1974] 2 Lloyd's Rep. 1; [1974] 1 W.W.R. 1234; 118 S.J. 644; [1974] 1 Lloyd's Rep. 56, CA (Sing) 10–006

Glebe Island Terminals Pty v Continental Seagram Pty; Antwerpen, The [1994] 1 Lloyd's Rep. 213, CA (NSW) 6–025

Goldcorp Exchange Ltd (In Receivership), Re; *sub nom.* Kensington v Unrepresented Non-Allocated Claimants; Goldcorp Finance Ltd, Re [1995] 1 A.C. 74; [1994] 3 W.L.R. 199; [1994] 2 All E.R. 806; [1994] 2 B.C.L.C. 578; (1994) 13 Tr. L.R. 434; (1994) 91(24) L.S.G. 46; (1994) 144 N.L.J. 792; (1994) 138 S.J.L.B. 127; *The Times*, June 2, 1994, PC (NZ) ... 5–027, 5–029

Greenough v Munroe (1931) 53 Fed. Rep. 2d. 262, CA (USA) 9–034

Groban and Union Tractor Ltd v SS Pegu and Elder Dempster Lines Ltd (1971) 331 F.Supp. 883 14–029

Henry Dean & Sons (Sydney) Ltd v O'Day Pty Ltd (1927) 39 C.L.R. 330 .... 7–024, 7–026, 7–029, 7–064

Hindley & Co v Tothill, Watson & Co (1894) 13 N.Z.L.R. 13, CA (NZ) 9–034

Isis, The. *See* May v Hamburg-Amerikanische Packetfahrt Aktiengesellschaft.

Kum v Wah Tat Bank Ltd [1971] 1 Lloyd's Rep. 439, PC (Mal) [1967] 2 Lloyd's Rep. 437, CA (Mal) 6–053, 6–056, 13–044

Liverpool and Great Western Steam Co v Phoenix Insurance Co, 129 U.S. 397 (1889) 11–018

McGregor v Huddart Parker Ltd (1919) 26 C.L.R. 336, HC (Aus) 11–019
McRae v Commonwealth Disposals Commission (1951) 84 C.L.R. 377, HC (Aus) 4–048, 4–049, 4–050
Mahkutai, The [1996] A.C. 650; [1996] 3 W.L.R. 1; [1996] 3 All E.R. 502; [1996] 2 Lloyd's Rep. 1; [1996] C.L.C. 799; (1996) 146 N.L.J. 677; (1996) 140 S.J.L.B. 107; *The Times*, April 24, 1996, PC (HK) 12–049
Marlborough Hill, The; *sub nom.* Owners of the Marlborough Hill v Alex Cowan & Sons Ltd [1921] 1 A.C. 444; (1920) 5 Ll. L. Rep. 362, PC (Aus) 6–051, 6–063, 6–064, 6–065
Maxine Footwear Co Ltd v Canadian Government Merchant Marine Ltd [1959] A.C. 589, PC 11–025
May v Hamburg-Amerikanische Packetfahrt Aktiengesellschaft (The Isis) 290 U.S. 333 (1933) 11–019
Maynegrain Pty. Ltd v Compafina Bank [1982] 2 N.S.W.L.R. 141 13–034
Mears v London and South Western Rly Co (1862) 11 C.B.N.S. 850 13–035
Mica, The. *See* Canadian Klockner Ltd v D/S A/S Flint.

Nadezhda Krupskaya, The. *See* Brown Boveri (Australia) Pty v Baltic Shipping Co.
Nelson Pine Industries Ltd v Seatrans New Zealand Ltd (The Pembroke) [1995] 2 Lloyd's Rep. 290, HC (NZ) 11–070
New Zealand Shipping Co Ltd v AM Satterthwaite & Co Ltd (The Eurymedon); *sub nom.* AM Satterthwaite & Co Ltd v New Zealand Shipping Co Ltd [1975] A.C. 154; [1974] 2 W.L.R. 865; [1974] 1 All E.R. 1015; [1974] 1 Lloyd's Rep. 534; 118 S.J. 387, PC (NZ) 11–038, 13–068
Newis v General Accident Fire & Life Assurance Corporation (1910) 11 C.L.R. 620, HC (Aus) 16–019
Nippon Yusen Kaisha v Ramjiban Serowgee; *sub nom.* Nippon Yusen Kaisha v Ramjiban Serowjee [1938] A.C. 429; (1938) 60 Ll. L. Rep. 181; [1938] 3 W.W.R. 136, PC (Ind)x8>1–008, 6–048, 6–053

Ornstein v Hickerson (1941) 40 Fed. Supp. 305 9–033

Paterson Steamships Ltd v Canadian Cooperative Wheat Producers Ltd; *sub nom.* Canadian Cooperative Wheat Producers Ltd v Paterson Steamships Ltd [1934] A.C. 538; (1934) 49 Ll. L. Rep. 421, PC (Can) 11–004
Pembroke, The. *See* Nelson Pine Industries Ltd v Seatrans New Zealand Ltd.
Pennsylvania, Bell v Moss (1839) 5 Whart. 189 9–035
Peter Turnbull & Co Pty v Mundas Trading Co (Australasia) Pty [1954] 2 Lloyd's Rep. 198, HC (Aus) 3–026
Phoenix Insurance Co v Erie and Western Transportation Co, 117 U.S. 312 (1886) 11–018
Propeller Niagara v Cordes, 62 U.S. 7 (1859) 11–018

Railroad Co v Lockwood, 84 U.S. 357 (1873) 11–018
Rowley v Bigelow (1832) 12 Pick. 307 6–063
Russo Chinese Bank v Li Yau Sam [1910] A.C. 174, PC (HK) 14–038

SS Rosario, The, November 3, 1967, HC (Brussels) 14–029
Saffron v Societe Miniere Cafrika (1958) 100 C.L.R. 231 9–033
Stone Gemini, The [1999] 2 Lloyd's Rep. 255, Fed Ct (Aus) (Sgl judge) 6–020,
                                                          6–021, 8–033, 8–034
Stzejn v J Henry Schroder Banking Corp (1941) 31 N.Y.S. 2d. 631, CA
      (NY) 10–005, 10–010, 10–012, 10–013, 10–014

Turnbull (Peter) & Co Pty Ltd v Mundas Trading Co (Australasia) Pty Ltd
      See Peter Turnbull & Co Pty v Mundas Trading Co (Australasia)
      Pty.
Turner v Haji Goolam Mahomed Azam [1904] A.C. 826, PC (Ind) 12–009

UCM v Royal Bank of Canada 7–025
United Bank Ltd v Banque Nationale de Paris [1992] 2 S.L.R. 64, HC
      (Sing) 10–032

Vita Food Products Inc v Unus Shipping Co Ltd (In Liquidation) [1939]
      A.C. 277; (1939) 63 Ll. L. Rep. 21, PC (Can) 11–031, 11–032, 11–033, 11–035,
                                                          11–036, 11–044, 11–046, 11–047, 11–048
Vivacqua Irmaos S.A. v Hickerson (1939) 190 Southern Rep. 657 9–033
Voest-Alpine Trading USA Corps. v Bank of China,167 F. Supp. 2nd 940,
      DC (US) 10–044

William Holyman & Sons Pty Ltd v Foy & Gibson Pty Ltd (1945) 73 C.L.R.
      622 11–019

TABLE OF NATIONAL STATUTES, ETC.

*[Page references in **bold** type indicate extracts of the statute]*

UNITED KINGDOM
1677 Statute of Frauds 1677
(29 Car. 2 c. 3) 16–012
1837 Wills Act (7 Will. 4 & 1
Vict. c. 26)—
s.9 16–013
1845 Gaming Act 1845 (8 & 9
Vict. c. 109) 1–039
s.18 1–036
1855 Bills of Lading Act 1855
(18 & 19 Vict. c.
111) 1–004, 1–009, 1–012,
1–013, 1–014, 2–027, 3–009,
3–010, 3–011, 5–062, 5–063,
5–066, 6–038, 6–062, 6–063,
6–065, 8–039, 12–005,
12–006, 13–004, 13–005,
13–007, 13–009, 13–010,
13–012, 13–013,
13–015,13–033,13–039,
13–040, 13–041, 13–042,
13–044, 13–045, 13–046,
13–047, 13–048, 13–049,
13–054, 13–056, 13–057,
13–068, 13–072, 13–079,
14–018, E–006

s.1 .... 1–013, 2–027, 3–010,
3–011, 3–039, 4–010, 5–005,
5–015, 5–023, 5–024, 5–061,
5–062, 5–066, 5–067, 5–072,
5–080, 6–038, 6–039, 6–041,
6–042, 6–062, 6–079, 6–091,
8–039, 11–062, 12–006,
12–034, 12–044, 13–004,
13–005, 13–006, 13–007,
13–008, 13–012, 13–013,
13–045, 13–046, 13–047,
13–048, 13–059, 13–067,
13–069, 13–073, 13–074,
13–075, 13–076, 13–080,
14–004, 16–018

s.2 ...... 6–062, **13–006**, 13–042,
13–045

s.3 .... **6–062**, 6–065, 13–006,
13–048, 14–047, 14–048,
14–049, 14–059

1861 Admiralty Court Act
1861 (24 & 25 Vict. c.
10)—
s.6 .... 6–051, 6–063
1870 Coinage Act 1870 (33 &
34 Vict. c. 10) 11–052
1882 Bills of Exchange Act
1882 (45 & 46 Vict. c.
61) 4–022, 11–029
s.3 .... **8–002**
s.3(1) 16–007
s.23 8–002
1889 Factors Act 1889 (53 & 53
Vict. c. 45) A–068
s.1 .... **F–001**
s.2 .... 8–045, **F–002**
s.2(1) 8–006, 8–044, 8–045,
8–046
s.3 .... **F–003**
s.4 .... **F–004**
s.5 .... **F–005**
s.6 .... **F–006**
s.7 .... **F–007**
s.8 .... **F–008**
s.9 .... **F–009**
s.10 .... **F–010**
s.11 .... **F–011**
s.12 .... **F–012**
s.13 .... **F–013**
s.17 .... **F–013**
Arbitration Act 1889 (52
& 53 Vict. c. 49) 12–020
Interpretation Act 1889
(52 & 53 Vict. c.
63) 4–022
s.38(1) D–013
1890 Factors (Scotland) Act
1890 (53 & 54
Vict.) A–068
1893 Sale of Goods Act 1893
(56 & 57 Vict. c. 71) ... 4–014,
4–021, 4–032, 5–028,
5–083, 7–015, 7–016,
7–023, 7–030, 7–048,
A–001, A–004,
A–012, A–069
s.1 5–082

1893 Sale of Goods Act
        1893—*cont.*
    s.11(1)(c) 7–046
    s.11(2) 7–048
    s.13 .... 4–015, 6–104, 6–105
    s.14(1) ... 4–031, 4–032, 4–033,
                        4–035
    s.14(2) ... 4–030, 4–031, 4–032,
            4–033, 4–035, 4–036, A–001
    ss.16–19 5–028
    s.16 .... 5–017, 5–018, 5–019,
            5–020, 5–022, 5–023, 5–083
    s.17 .... 5–017, 5–037, 5–083
    s.18 .... 4–003, 5–083, 13–046
    s.18(2) 13–046
    s.19(1) 5–060
    s.19(2) ... 5–034, 5–046, 5–062,
            5–064, 8–006, 13–046
    s.19(3) 5–033, 5–043
    s.20 .... **3–054**, 5–009
    s.25(1) **8–006**
    s.25(2) 8–006
    s.28 5–082
    s.32 .... 4–022, 5–083
    s.32(1) 4–022, 4–024
    s.32(2) 4–022
    s.32(3) ... 4–022, 4–023, 4–024,
            4–025, 4–026, 4–027, 4–028,
                        4–029
    s.35 .... 7–036, 7–041
    s.35(1) 7–039
    s.49 5–082
    s.49(1) **5–082**, 5–083
    s.49(2) **5–082**, 5–083
    s.53 7–046
    s.53(2) 7–057
    s.62 6–104
1906 Marine Insurance Act
        1906 (6 Edw.7 c.
        41) 6–060, 6–111
    s.50(3) 6–110, 6–111
1918 Income Tax Act 1918
        (8 & 9 Geo.5 c. 40)—
    Sch.D 1–040
1924 Carriage of Goods by
        Sea Act 1924 (14 &
        15 Geo.5 c. 22) 11–028,
                        11–029, 11–031,
                        11–032, 11–039,
                        11–046, 11–049,
                        11–053, 11–054,
                        11–063, 11–077,
                        D–013
    s.1 11–074
    s.3 .... **11–029, 11–032**, 11–046,
                    11–071, 11–073

1924 Carriage of Goods by
        Sea Act 1924—*cont.*
    Sch. 3–004, 4–003, 5–063,
        6–038, 6–075, 11–002, 11–009,
            11–013, 11–014, 11–015,
            11–019, 11–020, 11–021,
            11–022, 11–023, 11–024,
            11–026, 11–030, 11–031,
            11–032, 11–033, 11–035,
            11–036, 11–037, 11–040,
            11–041, 11–045, 11–049,
            11–050, 11–052, 11–053,
            11–054, 11–055, 11–056,
            11–057, 11–059, 11–060,
            11–061, 11–063, 11–064,
            11–065, 11–066, 11–068,
            11–070, 11–071, 11–072,
            11–073, 11–077, 11–082,
            11–083, 12–013, 12–037,
            13–072, 13–079, 13–082,
            14–030, 14–031, 14–032,
            15–004, 15–005, 15–030
    Art.1(b) 11–073, 11–074,
                        11–076, 11–077
    Art.1(e) 11–073, 11–074,
                        11–075, 11–077
    Art.II 11–073, 11–074,
            11–075, 11–076, 11–077
    Art.III 11–021, 13–079,
                        14–029, 14–032
    Art.III(1) 11–022, 11–025,
                        11–042, 11–074
    proviso, Art.III(1) **11–041**
    Art.III(2) 11–025, 11–075,
            12–014, 12–015, 12–016,
                        15–038
    Art.III(3)–(5) 11–059
    Art.III(3) 11–076, 12–036,
            14–029, 14–030, 14–031,
                        14–032, **14–053**
    Art.III(3)(a) 14–030
    Art.III(3)(b) 14–030
    Art.III(3)(c) 14–025, 14–030
    Art.III(4) 11–031, 13–079,
            14–029, 14–030, **14–053**
    Art.III(5) 13–079, 14–029,
                        14–030
    Art.III(6) 11–068, 13–079
    Art.III(8) 11–021, 11–052,
            12–013, 12–014, 12–016,
                        12–044
    Art.IV 11–021, 11–025,
                    11–052, 13–079
    Art.IV(1) 11–019, 11–025,
                        11–039
    Art.IV(2) 11–025

1924 Carriage of Goods by
        Sea Act 1924—*cont.*
        Art.IV(2)(b) 11–025
        Art.IV(2)(c) ... 11–027, 15–038
        Art.IV(4) 11–027, 11–029,
                                    13–079
        Art.IV(5) 11–025, 11–041,
                              11–052, 11–053,
                              11–056,11–058, 11–070,
                              11–073, 13–079
        Art.IV(5)(c) 11–031
        Art.IV(6) 11–025, 13–079
        Art.V 11–021
        Art.VII 11–075
        Art.IX **11–052**, 11–053,
                              11–056, 11–073
1932 Solicitors Act 1932 (22 &
        23 Geo.5 c. 37)—
        s.65(2) **16–013**
1943 Law Reform (Frustrated
        Contracts) Act 1943
        (6 & 7 Geo.6 c. 40) ... 4–051
1950 Arbitration Act 1950 (14
        Geo.6 c. 27) 12–035
        s.32 12–020
1965 Carriage of Goods by
        Road   Act   1965
        (c. 37) 15–030
        Sch. 15–019
        Nuclear Installations Act
        1965 (c. 57)—
        s.12(4) D–013
        Hire-Purchase Act 1965
        (c. 66)—
        s.58(3) A–078
        s.58(5) A–078
        Hire-Purchase   (Scot-
        land)   Act   1965
        (c. 67)—
        s.54(3) A–078
        s.54(5) A–078
1966 Hire-Purchase   Act
        (Northern   Ireland)
        1966—
        s.65(3) A–078
        s.65(5) A–078
1967 West Indies Act 1967
        (c. 4)—
        s.1(3) D–012
        Misrepresentation   Act
        1967 (c. 7) 7–056, A–001
        s.5 .... A–004

1967 Uniform   Laws   on
        International   Sales
        Act 1967 (c. 45) 15–014,
                                    15–017
        s.1(3) **15–015**, 15–016
        s.1(4) **15–015**
        Sch.1 ... 15–015, G–001, **G–002**
        Art.1 .... **G–002**
        Art.2 .... **G–003**
        Art.3 .... **G–004**
        Art.4 .... **G–005**
        Art.5 .... **G–006**
        Art.6 .... **G–007**
        Art.7 .... **G–008**
        Art.8 .... **G–009**
        Art.9 .... **G–010**
        Art.10 .... **G–011**
        Art.11 .... **G–012**
        Art.12 .... **G–013**
        Art.13 .... **G–014**
        Art.14 .... **G–015**
        Art.15 .... **G–016**
        Art.16 .... **G–017**
        Art.17 .... **G–018**
        Art.18 .... **G–019**
        Art.19 .... **G–020**
        Art.19(2) G–073
        Art.19(3) G–101
        Arts 20–53 .... G–056
        Art.20 .... **G–021**, G–023
        Art.21 .... **G–022**, G–023
        Art.22 .... **G–023**
        Art.23 .... **G–024**
        Arts 24–32 .... G–052
        Art.24 .... **G–025**
        Arts 25–32 .... G–025
        Art.25 .... **G–026**
        Art.26 .... **G–027**
        Art.27 .... **G–028**
        Art.28 .... **G–029**
        Art.29 .... **G–030**
        Art.30 .... **G–031**, G–032
        Art.31 .... **G–032**
        Art.32 .... **G–033**
        Art.33 .... **G–034**, G–035
        Art.33(1)(d), (e), (f) G–037
        Art.34 .... **G–035**
        Art.35 .... **G–036**
        Art.36 .... **G–037**
        Art.37 .... **G–038**
        Art.38 .. **G–039**, G–040, G–041
        Art.39 .. **G–040**, G–041, G–050
        Art.40 .... **G–041**
        Arts 41–49 .... G–052
        Art.41 .... **G–042**
        Arts 42–46 .... G–042

1967 Uniform Laws on
     International Sales
     Act 1967—*cont.*
     Art.42 .... **G–043**
     Art.42(2) G–044
     Arts 43–46 .... G–043, G–049
     Art.43 .. **G–044**, G–045, G–046
     Art.44 .... **G–045**, G–046
     Art.45 .... **G–046**
     Art.46 .... **G–047**
     Art.47 .... **G–048**
     Art.48 .... **G–049**
     Art.49 .... **G–050**
     Art.50 .... **G–051**, G–052
     Art.51 .... **G–052**
     Art.52 .... **G–053**, G–054
     Art.53 .... **G–054**
     Art.54 .... **G–055**
     Art.55 .... **G–056**
     Art.56 .... **G–057**
     Art.57 .... **G–058**
     Art.58 .... **G–059**
     Art.59 .... **G–060**
     Art.60 .... **G–061**
     Art.61 .... **G–062**
     Art.62 .... **G–063**
     Art.63 .... **G–064**
     Art.64 .... **G–065**
     Art.65 .... **G–066**
     Art.66 .... **G–067**
     Art.67 .... **G–068**
     Art.68 .... **G–069**
     Art.69 .... **G–070**
     Art.70 .... **G–071**
     Art.71 .... **G–072**
     Art.72 .... G–072, **G–073**
     Art.73 .... **G–074**
     Art.74 .... **G–075**
     Art.75 .... **G–076**, G–078
     Art.76 .... **G–077**, G–078
     Art.77 .... **G–078**
     Art.78 .... **G–079**
     Art.79 .... **G–080**, G–081
     Art.80 .... **G–081**
     Art.81 .... **G–082**
     Art.82 .... G–025, G–030,
            G–033, G–042, G–048,
            G–053, G–056, G–064,
            G–069, G–071, **G–083**,
                              G–088
     Art.83 .. G–064, G–082, **G–084**
     Arts 84–87 ...... G–025, G–042,
            G–053, G–056, G–064,
            G–069, G–071, G–078
     Art.84 .... **G–085**, G–087
     Art.85 .... **G–086**, G–087

1967 Uniform Laws on
     International Sales
     Act 1967—*cont.*
     Art.86 .... **G–087**
     Art.87 .... **G–088**
     Art.88 .... **G–089**
     Art.89 .... **G–090**
     Art.90 .... **G–091**
     Art.91 .. **G–092**, G–095, G–096
     Art.92 .. **G–093**, G–095, G–096
     Art.93 .... **G–094**
     Art.94 .... **G–095**, G–097
     Art.95 .... **G–096**
     Art.96 .... **G–097**
     Art.97 .... **G–098**
     Art.98 .... **G–099**
     Art.99 .... **G–100**
     Art.100 .... **G–101**
     Art.101 .... **G–102**
     Criminal Law Act 1967
        (c. 58)—
        s.12(1) A–004
1968 Hovercraft Act 1968
        (c. 59)—
        s.1(1)(i)(ii) D–013
1971 Carriage of Goods by
        Sea Act 1971
        (c. 19) 11–027, 11–031,
                        11–043, 11–046,
                        11–053, 11–060,
                        11–063, 11–070,
                        15–021, 16–017,
                              D–001
        s.1 .... **D–002**, E–006
        s.1(2) 11–046, **11–063**,
                              11–071
        s.1(3) D–012
        s.1(4) **11–071**, 11–079
        s.1(6) **11–071**, 11–077
        s.1A **D–008**
        s.2 .... **D–009**
        s.3 .... **D–010**
        s.4 .... **D–011**
        s.5 .... **D–012**
        s.6 .... **D–013**
        Sch. 3–004, 5–063, 6–075,
               11–002, 11–009, 11–013,
               11–014, 11–015, 11–016,
               11–022, 11–024, 11–026,
               11–030, 11–031, 11–035,
               11–036, 11–038, 11–040,
               11–043, 11–044, 11–045,
               11–046, 11–048, 11–050,
               11–051, 11–057, 11–060,
               11–061, 11–062, 11–063,
               11–067, 11–068, 11–069,

1971 Carriage of Goods by
    Sea Act 1971—*cont.*
    Sch.—*cont.* 11–070, 11–077,
        11–078, 11–079, 11–080,
        11–081, 11–082, 11–083,
        12–001, 12–013, 12–016,
        12–037, 13–014, 13–018,
        13–069, 13–070, 13–072,
        13–082, 13–085, 14–026,
        14–027, 14–030, 14–030,
        14–031, 14–032, 15–005,
        15–023, 15–030, 16–017,
        D–013, E–006
    Art.I **D–013**
    Art.I(b) **11–071**, 11–079
    Art.I(c) D–004
    Art.I(e) **11–069, 11–071**
    Art.II 11–061, **11–063,**
        11–069, 11–071, **D–014**
    Art.III 14–031, 14–032,
        D–003, **D–015**
    Art.III(1) 11–042, 11–071,
        D–015
    Art.III(2) 11–069, 12–017,
        12–018, 15–038, **D–015**
    Art.III(3) 6–031, 14–027,
        14–028, 14–030, 14–031,
        14–032, 16–017, **D–015**,
        D–018
    Art.III(3)(c) 14–025
    Art.III(4) 11–043, 14–026,
        14–030, 14–049, **D–016**
    Art.III(5) 14–030, **D–016**
    Art.III(6) 11–062, 11–063,
        11–068, 11–069, **D–016**
    Art.III(6)bis 11–068, **D–018**
    Art.III(8) 11–045, 12–013,
        15–039, **D–018**
    Art.IV D–008, D–015,
        D–019
    Art.IV(2)(c) 15–038
    Art.IV(4) 11–005
    Art.IV(5) 11–065, D–003
    Art.IV(6) 11–010
    Art.IVbis 11–043, 11–061,
        11–063, D–003, D–017,
        D–021
    Art.IVbis(1) **11–063**
    Art.V 11–079, **D–022**
    Art.VI 11–063, 11–069,
        D–014, **D–023**
    Art.VII **D–024**
    Art.VIII D–013, **D–025**
    Art.IX **D–026**

1971 Carriage of Goods by
    Sea Act 1971—*cont.*
    Art.X **11–044**, 11–045,
        11–046, 11–047, 11–077,
        D–002, **D–027**
    Art.X(c) 11–071, D–003
    Arts 11–16 .... D–027
    Coinage   Act   1971
        (c. 24) 11–052
1973 Supply of Goods (Im-
    plied   Terms)   Act
    1973 (c. 13) A–001
    s.18(5) A–004
1974 Consumer Credit Act
    1974 (c. 39) ... A–031, A–077,
        F–009
    s.192(4) A–004
1977 Unfair Contract Terms
    Act 1977 (c. 50) 11–048,
        A–001, A–062
    Pt.I A–068
    s.25(1) A–068
    s.31(2) A–004
1978 Interpretation Act 1978
    (c. 30)—
    s.1 .... **16–007**
    s.17 .... A–070
1979 Arbitration   Act   1979
    (c. 42)—
    s.7(1)(e) 12–020
    Sale of Goods Act 1979
    (c. 54) 4–014, 5–083,
        7–006, 7–018, 7–023,
        8–041, 13–047,
        15–011, 15–015,
        A–001, A–003
    s.1 .... **A–004**
    s.1(2) A–004
    s.2 .... **A–005**
    s.3 .... **A–006**
    s.4 .... **A–007**
    s.5 .... **A–008**
    s.6 .... 4–049, **4–050**, A–009
    s.7 .... **A–010**
    s.8 .... **A–011**
    s.9 .... **A–012**
    s.10 .... **A–013**
    s.11 ...... A–002, **A–014**, A–073
    s.11(2) 7–006
    s.11(3) 7–006
    s.11(4) A–073
    ss.12–15 .... 7–018, 15–015,
        A–001, A–086, A–090
    ss.13–15 7–018
    s.12 .... 2–041, 2–046, 5–021,
        A–015, A–073, A–086

1979 Sale of Goods Act
    1979—*cont.*
    s.12(2) ... 2–041, 2–044, 2–045,
                      7–018
    s.12(3) 2–041
    ss.13–15 .... A–001
    s.13 ...... 4–039, **A–016**, A–019,
                  A–076, A–086
    s.13(1A) A–015
    s.13(3) A–076
    s.14 .... 2–045, 4–039, A–001,
          A–017, A–019, A–077,
          A–078, A–079, **A–080**,
                      A–086
    s.14(2) ... 2–044, **4–037**, 4–038,
                      7–018
    ss.14(2)–(2C) A–017
    s.14(2A) **4–038**
    s.14(2B) **4–038**
    s.14(2C) **4–038**
    s.14(6) A–015
    s.15 ...... 4–039, A–017, **A–018**,
            A–019, A–078, A–081,
                      A–086
    s.15(3) A–015, A–081
    s.15A ... **4–039**, 7–018, 15–011,
          A–001, A–012, **A–019**
    ss.16–19 .... 5–028, 5–071
    ss.16–20 5–006
    s.16 .... 5–008, 5–024, 5–071,
          5–080, 13–067, A–002,
                     A–020
    ss.17–20 5–030
    s.17 .... 5–012, 5–032, 5–071,
          16–026, 16–029, **A–021**
    s.17(1) **5–012**
    s.17(2) **5–012**
    s.18 .... 3–015, 5–012, 5–032,
          5–071, 5–072, 13–046, **A–022**
    s.18(2) 13–046
    s.18,r.5 .... 5–009, **5–012**,5–014,
          5–020, 5–021, 5–022, 5–023,
                  5–071, 5–080
    s.18,r.5(1) **5–012**, 5–017,
                      5–071
    s.18,r.5(2) **5–012, 5–071**
    s.18,r.5(3) A–022
    s.18,r.5(4) A–022
    s.19 .... 5–012, 5–032, 5–072,
                      A–023
    s.19(1) .. 5–027, **5–071**, 13–073,
                     13–082
    s.19(2) ... **5–012**, 5–013, 5–039,
          5–060, 5–062, 5–065, 5–067,
          5–068, 5–069, 5–070, **5–071**,

1979 Sale of Goods Act
    1979—*cont.*
    s.19(2)—*cont.* 5–073, 5–074,
          13–046, 16–026, 16–029
    s.19(3) ... 5–005, **5–071**, 6–032,
               8–006,16–031
    s.20 .... **A–024**
    s.20(1) 5–005
    s.20(2) ... 2–044, **2–045**, 2–046,
                 4–020, 4–029
    s.20A ... 5–008, A–002, **A–020**,
          A–025, A–026, A–068
    s.20B A–002, **A–026**, A–068
    s.21 .... **A–027**
    s.22 .... A–028, A–082
    s.22(1) A–082
    s.23 .... **A–029**
    s.24 .... **5–037, 8–006**, A–030,
                      A–032
    s.25 ...... **A–031**, A–032, A–083
    s.25(2) A–083
    s.26 .... **A–032**
    s.27 .... **A–033**
    s.28 .... 2–009, 7–018, **A–034**
    s.29 .... **A–035**
    s.30 .... **A–036**
    ss.30(2)–(2C) A–036
    s.31 .... **A–037**
    s.32 .... **A–038**
    s.32(1) **4–021**
    s.32(2) ... 2–035, 2–044, **2–045**,
                 4–020, 4–029
    s.32(3) ... 4–020, **4–021**, 4–029,
                      B–012
    s.33 .... **A–039**
    ss.34–35A 7–018
    s.34 .... **A–040**
    s.35 .... 7–036, 7–041, 7–049,
          A–040, **A–041**, A–084
    s.35(1) A–084
    s.35A ... A–002, A–014, **A–042**
    s.36 .... **A–043**
    s.37 .... **A–044**
    ss.38–47 5–035
    s.38 .... 5–005, **A–045**
    s.38(2) **5–037**
    s.39 .... 5–005, 5–035, **A–046**
    s.40 .... **A–047**
    s.41 .... **A–048**
    s.41(1) 5–037
    s.42 .... **A–049**
    s.43 .... **A–050**
    s.43(1)(a) 5–035
    s.43(1)(b) 5–037
    s.44 .... 5–005, **A–051**
    s.45 .... **A–052**

1979　Sale of Goods Act
　　　1979—*cont.*
　　　s.46 .... **A–053**
　　　s.47 .... **A–054**
　　　s.48 .... **A–055**
　　　s.49 .... 5–081, 5–083, **A–056**
　　　s.49(1) **5–081**
　　　s.49(2) **5–081**, 5–083
　　　s.50 .... **A–057**
　　　s.51 .... **A–058**
　　　s.52 .... **A–059**
　　　s.53 .... 7–006, 7–052, 7–054,
　　　　　　　　　　　　　　 A–060
　　　s.53(1) **7–060**
　　　s.53(2) 7–057, 7–058, **7–060**
　　　s.54 .... **A–061**
　　　s.55 .... 15–015, **A–062**, A–085,
　　　　　　 A–086, A–087, **A–088**,
　　　　　　　　　　　　　　 A–090
　　　s.56 .... 15–015, **A–063**, A–089,
　　　　　　　　　　　　　　 A–090
　　　s.57 .... **A–064**
　　　s.58 .... **A–065**
　　　s.59 .... **A–066**
　　　s.60 .... **A–067**
　　　s.61 .... 7–006, A–002, **A–068**
　　　s.61(1) A–091, A–092
　　　s.62 .... **A–069**
　　　s.63 .... **A–070**
　　　s.64 .... **A–071**
　　　Sch.1 .... A–004, **A–072**
　　　Sch.1,para.2 .... A–014
　　　Sch.1,para 3 .... A–015
　　　Sch.1,para.4 .... A–016
　　　Sch.1,para.5 .... A–017
　　　Sch.1,para.6 .... A–017
　　　Sch.1,para.7 .... A–018
　　　Sch.1,para.9 .... A–031
　　　Sch.1,para.10 .... A–041
　　　Sch.1,para.11 .... A–062
　　　Sch1,para.13 .... A–063
　　　Sch.1,para.14 .... A–068
　　　Sch.1,para.15 .... A–068
　　　Sch.2 .... A–070
　　　Sch.3 .... A–070
　　　Sch.4 .... A–070
1981　Merchant Shipping Act
　　　1981 (c. 10) 11–049
　　　s.2(1) D–002
　　　s.2(3) D–020
　　　s.2(4) D–020
　　　s.2(5) D–020
1982　Civil Jurisdiction and
　　　Judgments Act 1982
　　　(c. 27)—
　　　Sch.1, Art.5 8–14

1984　Telecommunications Act
　　　1984 (c. 12) E–006
1985　Companies Act 1985
　　　(c. 6)—
　　　s.395 5–004
1989　Law of Property (Miscel-
　　　laneous Provisions)
　　　Act 1989 (c. 34)—
　　　s.1(2) 16–011
　　　s.1(3) 16–011
　　　s.1(4) **16–011**
　　　s.2(1) 16–011
　　　s.2(3) 16–011
1990　Contracts (Applicable
　　　Law) Act 1990
　　　(c. 36) 11–048
　　　Art.3 .... **11–048**
　　　Art.3(1) **11–048**
　　　Art.3(2) **11–048**
　　　Art.3(3) **11–048**
　　　Art.3(4) **11–048**
　　　Art.7(2) **11–048**
　　　Art.8 11–048
　　　Art.9 11–048
　　　Art.11 11–048
　　　Art.21 .... **11–048**
1992　Carriage of Goods by
　　　Sea Act 1992 (c. 50) ... 1–013,
　　　　　　　 1–049, 2–027, 2–038,
　　　　　　　 3–010, 3–011, 4–010,
　　　　　　　 5–004, 5–005, 5–003,
　　　　　　　 5–023, 5–024, 5–066,
　　　　　　　 5–077, 5–080, 6–014,
　　　　　　　 6–026, 6–033, 6–036,
　　　　　　　 6–039, 6–065, 6–079,
　　　　　　　 6–091, 6–096, 6–099,
　　　　　　　　 6–100, 11–035,
　　　　　　　　 11–038, 11–061,
　　　　　　　　 11–079, 11–080,
　　　　　　　　 12–006, 12–032,
　　　　　　　　 13–004, 13–006,
　　　　　　　　 13–007, 13–014,
　　　　　　　　 13–015, 13–016,
　　　　　　　　 13–017, 13–018,
　　　　　　　　 13–026, 13–027,
　　　　　　　　 13–028, 13–029,
　　　　　　　　 13–031, 13–032,
　　　　　　　　 13–033, 13–034,
　　　　　　　　 13–035, 13–036,
　　　　　　　　 13–037, 13–040,
　　　　　　　　 13–041, 13–042,
　　　　　　　　 13–044, 13–045,
　　　　　　　　 13–048, 13–050,
　　　　　　　　 13–053, 13–054,
　　　　　　　　 13–061, 13–067,
　　　　　　　　 13–069, 13–071,

1992 Carriage of Goods by
        Sea Act 1992—*cont.*
    c. 50 .... 13–072, 14–023,
            14–050, 14–055, 14–058,
            15–023, 15–031, 15–052,
            16–017, 16–024, **E–001**
    ss.1–3 13–016
    s.1 .... 13–017, 13–019, **E–002**
    s.1(1) 13–017
    s.1(2) 14–050
    s.1(2)(a) 13–017
    s.1(2)(b) 13–017
    s.1(3) 13–017
    s.1(3)(b) E–006
    s.1(4) **6–100**, 13–017
    s.1(5) .. 6–033, 13–017, 16–024,
                                        16–029
    s.1(5)(a) 13–017
    s.1(5)(b) 13–017
    ss.2–3 5–005
    s.2 .... 13–040, 13–048, 13–050,
            13–053, 14–032, **E–003**
    s.2(1) 13–026, 13–034,
            13–048, 13–049, 13–050,
            13–053, 13–054, E–004
    s.2(1)(a) 13–020
    s.2(1)(b) 13–020
    s.2(1)(c) 13–020
    s.2(2) 13–028, 13–031,
                            13–048, E–006
    s.2(2)(a) 13–020
    s.2(2)(b) 13–020, 13–021,
                                        13–022
    s.2(3) 13–020
    s.2(4) 13–020, 13–048
    s.2(4)(b) 13–021
    s.2(5) 13–020, 13–021,
            13–022, 13–026, 13–027,
            13–034, 13–037, 13–048,
                                        13–053
    s.3 ...... 8–039, 13–042, 13–049,
            13–050, 13–053, 13–055,
                            14–004, **E–004**
    s.3(1) 13–048, 13–049,
            13–050, 13–052, 13–053,
                                        13–054
    ss.3(1)(a)–(c) **13–042**
    s.3(1)(a) 13–049, 13–050,
                                        13–051
    s.3(1)(b) 13–049, 13–050
    s.3(1)(c) 13–050, 13–051,
                                        13–052
    s.3(2) 13–042
    s.3(3) 13–042, 13–053,
                                        13–055

1992 Carriage of Goods by
        Sea Act 1992—*cont.*
    s.4 .... 13–016, 14–019, 14–036,
            14–044, 14–049, **14–050**,
            14–051, 14–054, 14–055,
            14–060, **E–005**, E–006
    s.4(a) 14–052
    s.4(b) 14–052
    s.5 .... 13–016, **E–006**
    s.5(1) 13–017, 13–021
    s.5(2) 13–031, 13–048
    s.5(2)(a) 13–026
    s.5(2)(b) 13–028
    s.5(2)(c) 13–028
1994 Sale and Supply of
        Goods Act 1994 (c.
        35) ... 4–038, 15–011, A–001,
            A–002, A–012, A–014,
                            A–015, A–017,
                            A–019, A–028,
                            A–036, A–040,
                            A–042, A–068
1995 Merchant Shipping Act
        1995 (c. 21)—
    s.186 .... D–013
    s.314(2) D–002, D–007,
                            D–013, D–020
    Sale of Goods (Amend-
        ment) Act 1995 (c.
        28) ... 13–009, A–002, A–020,
            A–022, A–026, A–068
    s.1(1) 5–008
    Civil Evidence Act 1995
        (c. 38)—
    s.13 16–009
1996 Arbitration Act 1996
        (c. 23)—
    s.5 12–020
1999 Contracts (Rights of
        Third Parties) Act
        1999 (c. 31) ... 8–050, 11–038,
                            12–037, 12–046,
                                        13–072
    s.1(1)(a) **13–085**
    s.1(1)(b) 13–085
    s.1(3) 13–085
2000 Electronic Communica-
        tions Act 2000
        (c. 7)—
    s.7 16–023

AUSTRALIA
1904 Carriage of Goods by
        Sea Act 1904 11–013,
                            11–017, 11–018,
                            11–019, 11–039

1904 Carriage of Goods by
       Sea Act 1904—*cont.*
       s.8(2) 11–018
1909 Marine Insurance Act
       1909—
       Second Sch., r.7 11–020

CANADA
1910 Water Carriage of Goods
       Act 1910 .... 11–013, 11–017,
                          11–018, 11–019
                          11–034, 11–039

NEWFOUNDLAND
1932 Carriage of Goods by
       Sea Act 1932—
       s.3 11–033

NEW ZEALAND
       Shipping and Seamen
       Act 11–018

SWEDEN
1667 Swedish Maritime Code
       1667 15–019

UNITED STATES
1893 Harter Act 1893 .. 6–064, 11–011,
                          11–013, 11–105,
                          11–017, 11–018,
                          11–019, 11–030,
                          11–034, 11–039,
                          11–040, 14–025,
                          14–029
       s.1 .... **11–012**, 11–018
       s.2 .... **11–012**, 11–018
       s.3 ..... **11–012**, 11–018, 11–039
       s.4 .... **11–012**, 14–025, 14–027,
                          14–028, 14–029
       s.5 .... **11–012**
1924 Harter Act 1924 11–018
1936 Carriage of Goods by
       Sea Act 1936 11–037,
                          11–057, L–052
       Uniform Commercial
       Code 10–008, 10–009
       Art.2 5–002
1996 Utah Digital Signature
       Act 1996 15–004

TABLE OF STATUTORY INSTRUMENTS

1998 Civil Procedure Rules
          (S.I.   1998   No.
          3132)—
          Sched. 1, RSC—
          Ord. 11, r. 1 5–061

TABLE OF TREATIES AND CONVENTIONS

*[Page references in **bold** type indicate extracts of the treaty or convention]*

1890 Convention on Rail Transport 15–019

1924 International Convention for the unification of certain rules of law relating to Bills of Lading (Hague Rules) 3–004, 4–003, 5–063, 6–038, 6–075, 11–002, 11–009, 11–013, 11–014, 11–015, 11–016, 11–017,11–018, 11–019,11–020, 11–022, 11–023, 11–024, 11–026, 11–030, 11–033, 11–036, 11–049, 11–051, 11–052, 11–053, 11–059, 11–081, 12–034, 13–072, 13–079, 15–005, 15–038, D–002, I–033, I–039, I–040, I–041, I–042, I–043, I–044, I–045, I–046, I–047, I–050, I–052, I–053, I–054, I–056, I–058, I–059

Warsaw Convention on Air Carriage 15–019

1956 Convention on Road Transport ... 15–019, 15–030

1956 Geneva Convention on Carriage of Goods by Road 15–030

1960 Paris Convention on Third Party Liability in the Field of Nuclear Energy (as amended by the Additional Protocol of January 28, 1964) I–027

1963 Vienna Convention on Civil Liability for Nuclear Damage I–027

1964 Convention relating to a Uniform Law on the International Sale of Goods (Hague Sales Convention) 15–010, 15–014, 15–016, 15–017, A–012, G–005, H–100
    Art.2 .... G–002
    Art.4 15–015
    Art.5 15–015
    Art.7 .... G–017
    Art.9 .... 15–015, 15–016
    Art.10 15–015
    Art.19.2 15–016
    Art.19.3 15–016
    Arts 52–53 15–015
    Art.97.1 15–016
    Art.99.1 15–016
    Art.99.2 15–016
    Art.100 15–016

1964 Uniform Law on the Formation of Contracts for the International Sale of Goods (Hague Formation Convention) 15–014, 15–017, H–100

1968 Brussels Protocol to amend the International Convention of certain rules relating to Bills of Lading signed at Brussels on August 25, 1924 (Visby Protocol) 5–063, 6–075, 11–002, 11–009, 11–013, 11–014, 11–015, 11–036, 11–051, 11–068, 11–081, 11–082, 11–083, 13–069, 13–070, 13–072, 15–005, D–002, I–033, I–047, I–053, I–058

1974　United Nations Conven-
　　　tion on Prescription
　　　(Limitation) in the
　　　International Sale of
　　　Goods 15–017
1978　United Nations Conven-
　　　tion of the Carriage
　　　of Goods by Sea
　　　(Hamburg Rules) ... 11–014,
　　　　　　　　11–081, 11–082,
　　　　　　　　11–083, 13–023,
　　　　　　　　15–030, **I–001**, I–038,
　　　　　　　　I–039, I–042, I–043,
　　　　　　　　I–044, I–045, I–046,
　　　　　　　　I–047, I–050, I–051,
　　　　　　　　I–052, I–053, I–054,
　　　　　　　　I–055, I–056, I–057,
　　　　　　　　I–058, I–059
　　　Art.1 .... **I–003**
　　　Art.1(6) 15–030
　　　Art.1(7) I–017
　　　Art.2 ...... 11–081, **I–004**, I–033
　　　Art.3 .... **I–005**
　　　Art.4 ...... 13–023, **I–006**, I–007
　　　Art.4(2) I–021
　　　Art.5 .... **I–007**, I–008, I–015
　　　Art.5(1) I–011
　　　Art.5(2) 11–082
　　　Art.6 .... **I–008**, I–010, I–011,
　　　　　　　　　　　　I–028, I–035
　　　Art.6(4) I–018
　　　Art.7 .... **I–009**
　　　Art.7(2) I–010, I–012
　　　Art.7(3) I–012
　　　Art.8 .... I–009, **I–010**, I–011
　　　Art.8(2) I–012
　　　Art.9 .... **I–011**
　　　Art.10 .... **I–012**
　　　Art.10(1) I–013
　　　Art.10(2) I–013
　　　Art.11 .... **I–013**
　　　Art.12 .... **I–014**
　　　Art.13 .... **I–015**
　　　Art.14 .... **I–016**
　　　Art.15 .... **I–017**
　　　Art.15(1)(k) I–018
　　　Art.16 .... **I–018**
　　　Art.17 .... **I–019**
　　　Art.18 .... 11–081, **I–020**
　　　Art.19 .... **I–021**
　　　Art.20 .... **I–022**, I–026
　　　Art.21 .... **I–023**, I–027
　　　Art.21(1) I–013
　　　Art.21(2) I–013
　　　Art.22 .... **I–024**, I–027
　　　Art.22(4) I–027

1978　United Nations Conven-
　　　tion of the Carriage
　　　of Goods by Sea
　　　(Hamburg Rules)
　　　—*cont.*
　　　Art.23 .... **I–025**
　　　Art.23(3) I–018
　　　Art.24 .... **I–026**
　　　Art.25 .... **I–027**
　　　Art.26 .... I–008, **I–028**
　　　Art.26(1) I–035
　　　Art.26(2) I–035
　　　Art.26(3) I–035
　　　Art.27 .... **I–029**
　　　Art.28 .... **I–030**
　　　Art.29 .... **I–031**
　　　Art.30 .... **I–032**
　　　Art.30(1) I–033
　　　Art.31 .... **I–033**
　　　Art.32 .... **I–034**, I–035
　　　Art.33 .... **I–035**
　　　Art.34 .... **I–036**
1979　Brussels Protocol to
　　　amend the Interna-
　　　tional Convention
　　　of certain rules re-
　　　lating to Bills of
　　　Lading signed at
　　　Brussels on August
　　　25, 1924 (1979 Addi-
　　　tional Protocol) D–002,
　　　　　　　　　　　　I–039, I–047
1980　Berne Convention Con-
　　　cerning Internation-
　　　al Carriage by
　　　Rail 15–030
1980　Protocol amending the
　　　United Nations
　　　Convention on Pre-
　　　scription (Limita-
　　　tion) in the Interna-
　　　tional Sale of
　　　Goods 15–017
1980　United Nations Conven-
　　　tion on Contracts
　　　for the International
　　　Sale of Goods (Vien-
　　　na Convention) 1–001,
　　　　　　　　　　15–005, 15–010,
　　　　　　　　　　15–014, 15–015,
　　　　　　　　　　15–016, 15–017,
　　　　　　　　　　　　　　H–001
　　　Pt.I **H–002**
　　　Art.1 .... 1–001,**H–002**
　　　Art.1(1) H–093
　　　Art.1(1)(a) H–101

1980 United Nations Convention on Contracts for the International Sale of Goods (Vienna Convention) —*cont.*

Art.1(1)(b) H–096, H–101
Art.2 .... **H–003**
Art.3 .... **H–004**
Art.4 .... **H–005**
Art.5 .... **H–006**
Art.6 .... **H–007**
Art.7 .... **H–008**
Art.8 .... **H–009**
Art.9 .... 15–015, **H–010**
Art.10 .... **H–011**
Art.11 .... **H–012**, H–013, H–097
Art.12 .... H–007, **H–013**, H–097
Art.13 .... **H–014**
Pt.II ... H–013, **H–015**, H–093, H–102
Art.14 .... **H–015**
Art.15 .... **H–016**
Art.16 .... **H–017**
Art.17 .... **H–018**
Art.18 .... **H–019**
Art.19 .... **H–020**
Art.20 .... **H–021**
Art.21 .... **H–022**
Art.22 .... **H–023**
Art.23 .... **H–024**
Art.24 .... **H–025**
Pt.III ... **H–026**, H–093, H–102
Art.25 .... 15–015, **H–026**
Art.26 .... **H–027**
Art.27 .... **H–028**
Art.28 .... **H–029**
Art.29 .... H–013, **H–030**, H–097
Art.30 .... **H–031**
Art.31 .... **H–032**
Art.32 .... **H–033**
Art.33 .... **H–034**
Art.34 .... **H–035**
Art.35 .... **H–036**
Art.36 .... **H–037**
Art.37 .... **H–038**, H–051
Art.38 .... **H–039**, H–041, H–083
Art.39 .... **H–040**, H–041, H–047
Art.39(1) H–045
Art.40 .... **H–041**
Art.41 .... **H–042**, H–044

1980 United Nations Convention on Contracts for the International Sale of Goods (Vienna Convention) —*cont.*

Art.42 .... 15–015, H–042, **H–043**, H–044
Art.43 .... **H–044**
Art.43(1) H–045
Art.44 .... **H–045**
Art.45 .... **H–046**
Arts 46–50 .... H–052
Arts 46–52 .... H–046
Art.46 .... **H–047**
Art.47 .... **H–048**
Art.47(1) H–050
Art.48 .... **H–049**, H–051
Art.48(2) H–050
Art.49 .... H–049, **H–050**
Art.50 .... H–045, **H–051**
Art.51 .... **H–052**
Art.52 .... **H–053**, H–100
Art.53 .... **H–054**
Art.54 .... **H–055**
Art.55 .... **H–056**
Art.56 .... **H–057**
Art.57 .... **H–058**
Art.58 .... **H–059**
Art.59 .... **H–060**
Art.60 .... **H–061**
Art.61 .... **H–062**
Arts 62–65 .... H–062
Art.62 .... **H–063**
Art.63 .... **H–064**
Art.63(1) H–065
Art.64 .... **H–065**
Art.65 .... **H–066**
Art.66 .... **H–067**
Art.67 .... **H–068**, H–070, H–071
Art.67(2) 15–016
Art.68 .... **H–069**, H–070, H–071
Art.69 .... **H–070**, H–071
Art.70 .... **H–071**
Art.71 .... **H–072**
Art.72 .... **H–073**
Art.73 .... **H–074**
Arts 74–77 .... H–046, H–062
Art.74 .... **H–075**, H–076, H–077, H–079
Art.75 .... **H–076**, H–077
Art.76 .... **H–077**
Art.77 .... **H–078**
Art.78 .... **H–079**

1980   United Nations Conven-
          tion on Contracts
          for the International
          Sale of Goods (Vien-
          na   Convention)
          —*cont.*

Art.79 .... **H–080**
Art.80 .... **H–081**
Art.81 .... **H–082**
Art.82 .... **H–083**, H–084
Art.83 .... **H–084**
Art.84 .... **H–085**
Art.85 .... **H–086**, H–089
Art.86 .... **H–087**, H–089
Art.87 .... **H–088**
Art.88 .... **H–089**
Pt.IV **H–090**
Art.89 .... **H–090**
Art.90 .... **H–091**
Art.91 .... **H–092**
Art.92 .... **H–093**, H–100
Art.93 .... **H–094**

1980   United Nations Conven-
          tion on Contracts
          for the International
          Sale of Goods (Vien-
          na   Convention)
          —*cont.*

Art.94 .... **H–095**, H–098
Art.95 .... **H–096**
Art.96 .... **H–097**
Art.97 .... **H–098**
Art.98 .... **H–099**
Art.99 .... **H–100**
Art.100 .... **H–101**
Art.101 .... **H–102**
Art.96 .... H–013

1980   United Nations Conven-
          tion on Internation-
          al   Multimodal
          Transport   of
          Goods 15–029

PART A

INTRODUCTION

Chapter 1

OVERVIEW

THIS is a book on international sales of goods, their finance and carriage. Article **1–001**
1 of the Vienna Convention[1] effectively defines international sales as contracts of
sale of goods between parties whose places of business are in different states.
While this definition will be adopted for the purposes of this book, the main
concentration will be on a much narrower range of contracts, namely the "c.i.f."
(cost insurance freight) and "f.o.b." (free on board), and variations thereon.

One reason for concentrating on these particular contracts is that some of the
international sales contracts within the Vienna Convention definition raise no
international issues. They are, in effect, domestic sale contracts, albeit that the
parties may be from different states. For this reason Michael Bridge, for example,
excludes ex-works contracts from his book,[2] limiting coverage to those contracts
"where the seller assumes responsibility for at least some of the export
arrangements."[3]

C.i.f. and f.o.b. contracts share important features lacking from other varieties
of international sale contract. Under these contracts, the seller's duties regarding
the goods themselves generally end on loading.[4] In all c.i.f., and arguably in many
f.o.b. contracts,[5] possession is transferred constructively, by means of the shipping
documents, which represent the goods. Further, the documents can then be used
to resell or pledge the goods while they are still at sea, and the buyer, or if there
is a series of chain sales the eventual buyer, presents the documents to obtain the
goods from the carrier at their destination. In these contracts, the documents take
on a much greater importance than in other types of contract.[6]

With this type of transaction the seller loads the goods at the port of loading,
and obtains shipping documents which the buyer uses to discharge the goods at
the port of destination. There is no need for the parties ever to meet in order to
perform the transaction. Dealings can be wholly documentary in form, and
neither buyer nor seller need leave his country of business.

In *Ross T. Smyth & Co Ltd v T.D. Bailey, Son & Co* Lord Wright said of the c.i.f.
contract[7]:

> "It is a type of contract which is more widely and more frequently in use than
> any other contract used for purposes of sea-borne commerce. An enormous

---

[1] "United Nations Convention On Contracts For The International Sale Of Goods" (1980)
("CISG"). See further para. 15—014 and App. H, below.
[2] M. Bridge, *The International Sale of Goods, Law and Practice* (Oxford University Press,
1999).
[3] See his explanation, *ibid.*, at para. 1.06.
[4] Risk of loss or damage thereafter passes to the buyer, subject to the exceptions described
in Ch. 4, below. See also the extensive discussion in Ch. 2 (c.i.f.), below.
[5] See, *e.g. Concordia Trading BV v Richco International Ltd* [1991] 1 Lloyd's Rep. 475, in Ch. 6,
below, where the documents in a classic f.o.b. contract appear to be performing the same
function as they would c.i.f.
[6] The bill of lading plays the role described in Chap. 6, below.
[7] [1940] 3 All E.R. 60 at 67; (1940) 67 LL.L.R. 147 at 156. This case is considered more fully
at para. 5—056, below.

number of transactions, in value amounting to untold sums, are carried out every year under c.i.f. contracts."

1–002   Times have moved on since 1940, however; the traditional c.i.f. and f.o.b. contracts are undoubtedly less well-suited to modern trading conditions than to those of 60 years ago, and there are even those who regard them as obsolete. Indeed, a view was taken when Incoterms was last revised, in 2000, that the traditional maritime terms be abolished as anachronistic.[8] Undoubtedly, they are poorly-suited to containerisation and multi-modal transport, probably the most important development in the liner trade in the last half century.[9] Martin Stopford talks of two recent revolutions in shipping technology, containerisation and bulk transport, the latter revolution being characterised by use of much larger vessels, and improved cargo-handling. Of the latter, he says[10]:

> "The bulk shipping revolution was no less wide-ranging [than containerisation] in its effects. Bulk transport of raw materials by sea was, for the first time, viewed as part of an integrated materials handling operation in which investment could improve productivity. By employing economies of scale, investing in high speed cargo handling systems and integrating the whole transport systems, bulk transport costs were reduced to such an extent that it is often cheaper to import raw materials by sea from suppliers thousands of miles away than by land from suppliers only a few hundred miles away . . . Bigger ships played a central part in this process. Over a period of 50 years from 1945 to 1995 oil tankers became twenty times bigger and dry bulk vessels ten to fifteen times bigger. Improved cargo handling in ports and bigger integration with land transport completed the transformation."

C.i.f. and f.o.b. contracts remain the mainstay of the bulk transport trade. Stopford continues (at p. 15):

> "There is a long history of carrying cargo in shiploads—Roman grain ships, tea clippers, bulk timber and the fleets of colliers in the nineteenth century are examples—but bulk shipping did not develop as the major sector of the shipping industry [until][11] the decades following the Second World War. A fleet of specialist crude oil tankers was built to service the rapidly expanding economies of Western Europe and Japan, with smaller vessels for the carriage of products and liquid chemicals. In the dry bulk trades, several important industries, notably steel, aluminium and fertilizer manufacture, turned to foreign suppliers for their raw materials and a fleet of large bulk carriers was built to service the trade. As a result, bulk shipping became a rapidly-expanding sector of the shipping industry and bulk tonnage now accounts for about three-quarters of the world merchant fleet."

On page 18, he produces a table, based on Fernley's Annual Review 1995, Table 1, and World Bulk Trades (1985 and 1995), Table 1, which shows that of 4,506 million tons of cargo shipped in 1994, 3,040 million (or about two thirds) was bulk cargo, compared with just 336 million containerised (estimated). In tonnage terms at any rate, therefore, the traditional contracts retain their dominant position. In value terms, the position is admittedly different, since containerised goods tend to have a much higher value, per ton, than bulk cargoes.

---

[8] See further para. 15—007, below.
[9] See further the discussion in Ch. 15, below.
[10] M. Stopford, *Maritime Economics* (2nd ed., Routledge, 1997), p. 4.
[11] The original text has "in", which must surely be a misprint?

It is probably true to say that f.o.b. and c.i.f. contracts, and variations thereon, continue to dominate the bulk shipping trade, but are less relevant in liner shipping, which is generally responsible for containerised cargo. Stopford observes (at p. 15) that "Bulk and liner shipping are as different in their character as it is possible for two industries to be", and this is also true of the nature of legal disputes to which each gives rise. Moreover, a perusal of the law reports suggests that bulk shipping continues to generate the majority of legal disputes.

Nevertheless, the c.i.f. contract was an invention of the late nineteenth century, the f.o.b. contract probably earlier, although modern varieties evolved along with c.i.f. Trading practices have changed significantly since then, and even in bulk shipping, neither the contracts nor the documentation they call for remains entirely appropriate. Unfortunately, the solutions that work in the liner trade have no application to bulk transport.

(1) Historical Perspective

The historical development of f.o.b. and c.i.f. contracts to a large extent explains their present logical basis.   **1–003**

SASSOON, THE ORIGIN OF F.O.B. AND C.I.F. TERMS AND THE FACTORS INFLUENCING THEIR CHOICE

[1967] J.B.L. 32

[Footnotes are as in the original, but renumbered for inclusion in this book.]

F.O.B. Contracts

The first of the terms to make its appearance was the f.o.b. term.   **1–004** Though the earliest reported decisions date back to the turn of the [nineteenth] century[12] the contract for the sale of goods "free on board" had probably been current in the trade for some time prior thereto.

That the f.o.b. term precedes the c.i.f. term is not in the least surprising. The reason for this becomes apparent once the conditions of the international seaborne trade of the late eighteenth and early nineteenth centuries are recalled. Prior to the establishment of regular shipping lines, when documents as symbols of goods afloat were only beginning to gain recognition and before modern telegraph, radio and postal services were inaugurated, the mechanics and methods of the overseas trade were very different from those prevailing today. The merchant of that epoch would normally have to charter a vessel to call at different foreign ports to purchase whatever goods were available there. He, or his agent, would normally have to personally undertake the adventure—for it was indeed an adventure—by accompanying the ship and by being present on it throughout the entire voyage. If suitable merchandise were found, he

---

[12] The first reported cases are *Wackerbarth v Masson* (1812) 3 Camp. 270; *Craven v Ryder* (1816) Taunt. 433 (f.o.b.); and *Tregelles v Sewell* (1862) 7 H. & N. 574; *Ireland v Livingston* (1872) L.R. 5 H.L. 395 (c.i.f.).

would order them to be delivered to "his" vessel where he would presumably finally inspect them, and for which he would, if they conformed
to any sample he had previously seen, then and there tender the price or
other consideration. It was probably to circumstances such as these that
the f.o.b. term owes its inception. And it is probably for this reason that
originally the f.o.b. buyer was considered to be the shipper of the goods
to whom the bill of lading would normally be furnished.[13] With technological progress the conditions of international trade also rapidly
changed. Regular shipping lines were established. Information was more
readily available. Foreign contacts could be maintained on a permanent
basis. Documents could be posted. The Bills of Lading Act 1855 was
enacted conferring upon the indorsee the right to sue on the contract of
affreightment where no such right for enforcement in his own name
previously existed. Means of finance were devised and banks began
participating in transactions as "buyers of exchange." The net result was
that foreign trade soon grew in volume while business adapted itself to
these changing conditions by the application of new methods and means
more suited to those concerned. In short, the currently familiar pattern of
international trade began to emerge.

C.I.F. Contracts

1–005   The c.i.f. term evolved with the expansion of commerce, though as may
be seen from the first reported cases decided in 1862 and 1871,[14] respectively, the initials were originally spelled out in a different order, *viz.*
"c. f. & i."[15] Where the buyer or his agent was not physically present at
the point of delivery as he no longer had to be, and payment, as a result,
was deferred to a subsequent date, the c.i.f. term better served the interests of the seller. He was the shipper and the person to whom the bill of
lading was issued. Thus no question could arise as to his right to his
possession.[16] Moreover, he was certain that insurance had been procured
and was therefore less concerned than an f.o.b. seller would be about the
prospects of recovering the value of the goods in the event of loss or
damage before payment. Finance and banking credit facilities, therefore,
were also much easier to arrange. The c.i.f. term, however, had certain

---

[13] As stated by Lord Brougham in *Cowas-Jee v Thompson* (1845) 3 Moore Ind. App. 422, 429:
"It is proved beyond all doubt, indeed it is not denied, that when goods are sold in London,
'free on board,' the cost of shipping then falls on the seller, but the buyer is considered as
shipper." It is of interest to note that the recurrent theme of the first fifty years of f.o.b.
litigation is the claim against a carrier by an unpaid seller to whom a mate's receipt has been
issued for having delivered the bill of lading to the f.o.b. buyer: see, *e.g. Craven v Ryder* (1816)
Taunt. 433; *Ruck v Hatfield* (1822) 5 B. & Ald. 632 and the *Cowas-Jee* case.

[14] *Tregelles v Sewell; Ireland v Livingston;* see n. 12, above.

[15] The term c.i.f. is sometimes supplemented by one of more initials, *e.g.* "c.i.f. & e.", "c.i.f.
& c.", "c.i.f.c. & i". As to the meaning of the foregoing terms, see Schmitthoff, *The Export
Trade* (4th ed.), p. 34 [this book is now in its 10th ed.: Leo D'Arcy, Carole Murray and Barbara
Cleave, *Schmitthoff's Export Trade, The Law and Practice of International Trade* (10th ed., Sweet
& Maxwell, 2000)].

[16] [Note 15 is repeated here].

clear advantages for the buyer also. He was, for instance, relieved of the responsibility for securing the necessary shipping space and for arranging the insurance of the goods. And he, too, benefited from the easier finance and credit facilities. Because of reasons such as these, the c.i.f. contract soon began gaining ground and gradually replaced the f.o.b. term as the most widely used term of delivery in the overseas trade. By the beginning of the present century the volume of business transacted on c.i.f. terms far exceeded that transacted on any other basis.[17] This era, which lasted until the advent of the First World War, can probably be described as the "golden age" of the c.i.f. contract. This is not to say that the f.o.b. term was entirely abandoned. It still performed a useful function, for example, in situations where, because of the size or nature of the cargo purchased or for any other reason, the buyer had chartered a vessel under hire. But where this was not the reason for the choice of the f.o.b. term, and often it was not, the term frequently acquired some of the attributes of the c.i.f. contract. In particular, the seller often undertook to secure the shipping space for the buyer and he would also normally procure the bill of lading and assume the status of shipper.[18] So, the f.o.b. term survived and was still in frequent use.[19] With the scarcity of shipping space caused by the First World War the volume of trade transacted

---

[17] See Lord Wright's speech in *Ross T. Smyth & Co Ltd v T.D. Bailey Son & Co* [1940] 3 All E.R. 60 at 68 where he described the c.i.f. contract as one " . . . which is more widely and frequently in use than any other contract used for purposes of seaborne commerce. An enormous number of transactions, in value amounting to untold sums, are carried out every year under c.i.f. contracts."

[18] As Devlin J. stated in *Pyrene Co Ltd v Scindia Navigation Co Ltd* [1954] 2 Q.B. 402, 424: "The f.o.b. contract has become a flexible instrument. In what counsel called the classic type . . . the buyer's duty is to nominate the ship, and the seller's to put the goods on board for account of the buyer and procure a bill of lading . . . Sometimes the seller is asked to make the necessary arrangements; and the contract may then provide for his taking the bill of lading in his own name and obtaining payment against the transfer, as in a c.i.f. contract." Because of this latter practice Bailhache J., in *Bain v Field & Co Fruit Merchants* (1920) 3 LL.L.R. 26, 29, even challenged the rule that under an f.o.b. contract the buyer invariably assumes the onus of securing the tonnage. He drew significant distinctions between the sale of cargoes (where the vessel would presumably be under charter to the buyer and the choice of f.o.b. term would therefore be clearly apparent) and the purchase of smaller items where no such apparent reason existed, as well as between domestic (see [next note]) and other f.o.b. transactions. He said as follows: "As a matter of fact . . . in f.o.b. contracts for the sale of comparatively small parcels, as distinguished from cargoes, it is the universal practice now for sellers at the port of shipment, when that port is abroad, to busy themselves in securing the shipping space, and I am inclined to think that the court, in holding the view that the duty is still on the buyer and that the seller is merely acting in a friendly way or as an agent for the buyer, is deciding in a manner not in accordance with the commercial practice or the views of commercial men."

[19] Mention should also be made of the fact that, throughout this and later periods, a substantial volume of domestic business was transacted on f.o.b. terms. This was due to orders placed by exporters with domestic suppliers. Although the exporter might be sending goods to his clients abroad on similar (f.o.b.) or other (c.i.f. or ex ship) terms, the domestic supplier would normally be requested to deliver the goods f.o.b. a vessel nominated by the exporters. This form of business could not be conducted on c.i.f. terms for in such a case there would normally be no need for an intermediary between the seller and the overseas buyer. It should be noted, however, that the division of responsibilities between seller and buyer under a domestic f.o.b. contract may be different from those governing an export transaction: see: *e.g.* observations in *AV Pound & Co Ltd v MW Hardy & Co Inc.* [1956] A.C. 588.

on c.i.f. terms soon began to contract. As sellers were reluctant to undertake the onus of securing tonnage with the uncertainty of rapid fluctuations in the price and in the availability of freight[20] a corresponding increase in trade handled upon f.o.b. terms soon began to manifest itself. The situation lasted until the re-establishment of normal shipping conditions in the late twenties, whereupon the c.i.f. contract regained the position of prominence it had previously enjoyed, a revival that lasted until the advent of the Second World War. By the time this was was over and concluded, and sufficient tonnage was once again available, a new factor influencing the preference for transacting business on f.o.b. terms had arisen. This was the development and establishment of many new national shipping and insurance industries and the general scarcity of foreign exchange. In order to preserve foreign currency or support domestic industries, governments have often restricted the allocation of foreign currency to the f.o.b. value of the goods at the foreign port of embarkation, compelling the importer to procure carriage and insurance in the local market in domestic currency. In the absence of import regulations, or other measures having a similar effect, pressure was nonetheless exerted to restrict imports to f.o.b. terms in order to support and promote national shipping an insurance industries.

Note

Many of the authorities cited here are covered in this book: *Cowas-Jee v Thompson* in this chapter; *Tregelles v Sewell* and *Ireland v Livingston* in chapter 2, below; *Pyrene Co Ltd v Scindia Navigation Co Ltd* and *A.V. Pound & Co Ltd v M.W. Hardy & Co Inc.* in chapter 3, below; *C. Groom Ltd v Barber* in chapter 4, below; *The Kronprinsessan Margareta* in chapter 5, below; and *Ross T. Smyth & Co Ltd v T.D. Bailey Son & Co* in this chapter and in chapter 5, below.

(a) The Early f.o.b. (and f.a.s.) Contract

1–006   From the above passage it can be seen that the f.o.b. contract pre-dated modern forms of communication, yet survives to this day, in part because of exchange controls, freight being payable in advance, etc., but also because it can be used for domestic supply to the loading port, even where the international sale contract is c.i.f.[21]

Until around the end of the 18th century it was not possible to carry on export trade in its modern day form. This was before regular shipping lines were established, before the inauguration of modern telegraph, radio and postal services, and before the establishment of modern finance and insurance facilities.

International trade would often have been carried out by the buyer chartering a vessel and calling personally at foreign ports of call. Sellers would have brought

---

[20] The situation is well described in *Blyth & Co v Richard Turpin & Co* (1916) 114 L.T. 753. During the period of hostilities a similar situation prevailed with respect to insurance premiums, in particular the cost of covering war risks: see observations in *The Kronprincessan Margareta and Other Ships* [1921] 1 A.C. 486. It should, however, be noted that in the absence of an express stipulation to the contrary the c.i.f. seller is not normally required to procure war risk insurance. See, *e.g. C. Groom Ltd v Barber* [1915] 1 K.B. 316, 321. Where the insurance is to include war risk it is often provided that any increase in the premium prevailing on the contract date shall be for the account of the buyer. See, *e.g. Oulu Osakeytio v Laver* [1940] 1 K.B. 750.

[21] As in *Brandt v Morris*, discussed in para. 3—046, below.

their goods alongside or on board the buyer's ship and trading would have thereupon been concluded, with the buyer paying the price. It is probable that free alongside ship (f.a.s.) and free on board (f.o.b.) contracts would have had their origin in this way, at around the end of the 18th century (the first reported cases using the term, cited by Sassoon, above, are early 19th century cases).

At this stage the buyer would have been entirely responsible for carriage of the goods (either on board his own ship, or a vessel chartered by him) and the bill of lading (receipt of the carrier) would have been issued to him, not to the seller.

COWAS-JEE V THOMPSON

Privy Council. (1845) 3 Moore Ind. App. 422; 18 E.R. 560

Facts:
The sellers contracted to sell goods (pigs of lead) f.o.b., paid for by six-   **1–007**
month time bills. (Note that the election to accept bills was at the sellers' option; they could have elected instead to take cash at 2.5 per cent discount.) The sellers delivered the goods on board the ship, and took mate's receipts for them,[22] which they retained. The purchasers accepted the bills drawn by the sellers, and bills of lading were issued to them. Before the bills matured, the purchasers became insolvent.

Held:
The Judicial Committee held that the sellers were not entitled to stop the goods, for once delivered to the ship they were no longer *in transitu*,[23] and that the retention of mate's receipts by the sellers was immaterial (indeed, they had no right to retain them, and the mate's receipts should have been given up).

LORD BROUGHAM: It is proved beyond all doubt, indeed it is not denied, that when goods are sold in London, "free on board," the cost of shipping then falls on the seller, but the buyer is considered as shipper . . .

We are clearly of the opinion, that the non-delivery of the receipt can operate nothing whatever, and on this plain ground, that [the sellers] ought to have delivered it up; it was their clear and bounden duty to do so; and it would be preposterous that they should avail themselves of their own wrong against the other party, whom they had injured. What possible right, could they have to retain the receipt, which belonged to [the purchasers], as much as any chattel in their possession? . . .

. . .

The question in all the cases between buyer and seller, which is the case here, is, whether, or not, anything remained to be done as between these two parties . . . In the present case, it is quite clear, that nothing whatever remained to be done, between the buyer and the seller, unless it be that

---

[22] Mate's receipts are preliminary documents, issued before loading, acting primarily as receipts by the carrier. They are discussed in detail in paras 6—046 and 14—007, below.
[23] This is also relevant to the discussion of liens in 5—035, below; the unpaid seller here, having no property, also had no other protection against the buyers' insolvency.

the former ought most certainly to have delivered up the mate's receipt, which he wrongfully, or by oversight, kept possession of, without the shadow of a right to it; and whether it be wrong or error, he is not the party to take advantage of this . . .

Notes

1–008   This was an early f.o.b. contract, where delivery was to the ship, treated in cases such as *Ruck v Hatfield*,[24] and *Craven v Ryder*,[25] as the buyer's warehouse.[26] The buyer was also regarded as shipper (note also that the vessel was chosen by the purchasers). Not only was delivery to the ship, but risk and property would typically pass on shipment in f.o.b. contracts at that time.

It must have been assumed that property had passed in *Cowas-Jee* itself, since otherwise no right of stoppage would have arisen. However, the goods were no longer *in transitu*, having been delivered to the ship. Effectively, therefore, delivery is regarded as complete at the buyer's warehouse, and the only way in which this differs from an ordinary domestic sale of goods is that the warehouse floats.

The result in *Cowas-Jee* was that the f.o.b. sellers were unprotected against the buyer's bankruptcy after shipment, but before the maturity of six-month bills. They had attempted to protect themselves by having mate's receipts issued to them, in the hope that bills of lading would not be issued to the buyers except on delivery up of the mate's receipts, but the bills of lading were issued without delivery up of mate's receipts, and the sellers were unprotected.[27]

Some facets of this early transaction remain in the modern f.o.b. contract (*e.g.*, the third type described in *Pyrene v Scindia* below, where the buyer is shipper; this is probably in fact the commonest variety today, and also FOB Incoterms in Appendix B): for types of f.o.b. contract, see *Pyrene Co Ltd v Scindia Navigation Co Ltd*[28] For Incoterms, see chapter 15 and Appendix B, below.

(b) DEVELOPMENT OF C.I.F. FROM F.O.B. CONTRACT

1–009   It is clear from the extract from Sassoon that though f.o.b. and f.a.s. contracts were well-suited to trading before the technological and legal advances of the nineteenth century, the form of trading common then was very inconvenient, particularly for buyers, and the c.i.f. contract developed as soon as the necessary technological and legal structures were in place. (Note that it required both; the technology for c.i.f. contracts predated the development of the necessary legal structures, but only after both were in place could the c.i.f. contract develop.)

Two features of the early f.o.b. contract are worth noting. First, delivery was to the vessel, and property and risk would have passed from seller to buyer at that time. As will become apparent in chapters 3 and 5, below, delivery remains to the vessel today, and risk continues to pass then, although property today can pass later. Secondly, all shipping arrangements, including if necessary the conclusion of a carriage contract, were made by the buyer. Today, although the f.o.b. contract

---

[24] (1822) 5 B. & Ald. 632, 106 E.R. 1321.
[25] (1816) Taunt. 433, 128 E.R. 1103.
[26] All these cases are also cited by Sassoon in the extract at para. 1—004, above.
[27] It is now clear from cases such as *Nippon Yusen Kaisha v Ramjiban Serowgee* [1938] A.C. 429, PC, discussed in para. 6—048, below, that the shipowner is not obliged, where the buyer is shipper, to demand delivery up of mate's receipts. See also generally in paras 6—046 *et seq.* and 14—007, below, discussion on the role of the mate's receipt.
[28] [1954] 2 Q.B. 402, discussed fully in 3—004, below.

can still retain those features, it need not do so, and once more effective communications had become available, it was often more convenient to place a greater degree of responsibility on the sellers.

The logical development of this process, of shifting responsibility for making shipping arrangements on to the sellers, was the c.i.f. contract, where the seller is the shipper, and also insures. Another feature of the c.i.f. contract is the quotation of an inclusive price, including freight and insurance (probably the single feature distinguishing the c.i.f. contract from modern variants of f.o.b.). This development towards the c.i.f. contract required not only a technological infrastructure that was lacking until the nineteenth century, in particular good communication and postal services, but also modern forms of marine insurance, and the recognition of the role of the bill of lading as a document of title. It also depended on a legal infrastructure that was lacking prior to the enactment of the Bills of Lading Act 1855, and it is noteworthy that there are no reported c.i.f. cases prior to that legislation.[29]

The place of physical delivery, however, of the goods to the ship, remains c.i.f. as with the f.o.b. contract, from which it developed. In this respect the c.i.f. contrasts sharply with the apparently similar ex-ship contract, where delivery is to the port of discharge. For this reason the c.i.f. contract is better suited to the documentary sale than ex-ship, and presumably this accounts for its significantly greater popularity.[30]

(c) Buyer's Desire to Move Away from Original f.o.b. and the Problems of so Doing

Buyers were concerned, as early as they could, to place a greater responsibility   **1–010**
for arranging shipment on the sellers (who were generally better placed to make the arrangements). This became theoretically possible early in the nineteenth century, with the establishment of regular shipping lines, and the setting up of efficient postal and telegraph services. Ideally, the buyer could now arrange the transaction at a distance, no longer needing to travel personally. We can see some development in this direction even quite early in the nineteenth century,[31] but neither its logical conclusion, the c.i.f. contract, where the seller takes on all the responsibilities of shipment, nor the modern f.o.b. varieties, could develop until after 1855. This was because there were other difficulties, some of a legal nature, which needed to be resolved before the modern form of international sales contract could develop.

(d) Ensuring Performance by the Parties

Compared with most domestic sales of goods, the parties to an international   **1–011**
sale are unlikely to deal often with one another, or to know much about each other. A look at nineteenth-century case law suggests that this was even more likely to be the case then than it is now, most of the parties being small traders dealing in relatively trivial commodities (*e.g.*, old iron rails, etc.).[32]

This may not matter very much where the seller delivers the goods, and is paid, at the buyer's vessel (or "floating warehouse"), but it is another matter altogether when the transaction takes place at a distance. Even with the original form of

---

[29] Sassoon notes that the first reported c.i.f. case (or c.f. & i.) is *Tregelles v Sewell* (1862) 7 H. & N. 574; despite its many advantages over the earlier f.o.b. and f.a.s. contracts, the c.i.f. contract could not develop until after the enactment of the Bills of Lading Act 1855.

[30] See also the discussion of chain sales below.

[31] See the discussion of *Dunlop v Lambert*, in para. 13—040, below.

[32] The cargoes in *Sanders v Maclean* (see para. 6—080, below) and *Tregelles v Sewell*.

transaction, it appears that sellers attempted to protect themselves against buyers sailing away without paying.[33] With a transaction at a distance the position is worse, for the seller possibly knows nothing of the financial standing of the buyer or buyers, faces the possibility (in the event of default by the buyer) of having to sue overseas, and is taking a great risk is consigning goods unless he can be reasonably certain of being paid for them. Once the goods have gone, the seller has lost control over them, and cannot get them back, or use them as security against non-payment.

On the other hand, the buyer cannot inspect the goods until he receives them at the port of discharge, nor can he trust the seller to ship goods or cargo of the promised quantity and description, any more than the seller can trust him. Thus, the ideal solution for the seller, that of demanding payment in advance, has no appeal to buyers. There is therefore a fundamental conflict between the interests of the parties—the seller wants payment before consigning goods, but the buyer does not want to pay until he is sure of the seller's trustworthiness.

(e) Development of the Bill of Lading as a Document of Title

1–012   The solution to the conflict of interests outlined above was to use the bill of lading as security.[34] The role played by the bill of lading as a document of title is considered in detail in chapter 6, but in principle, it performs the following functions:

(a) It is a receipt for the goods, usually issued by the master on the shipowner's behalf. As such, it typically contains statements describing the quantity and apparent quality of the goods,[35] the fact and date of shipment and name of the ship.[36] The master is a disinterested party, so the statements ought to be reliable, and ideally the shipowner ought to be liable to anybody who relies on them, if they are false; however, as will become apparent in chapter 14, this ideal situation is not always achieved.

(b) During the eighteenth and nineteenth centuries the bill of lading developed into a document of title; transferring the document could also transfer the property in the goods, and the right to possess them when the vessel arrived at her destination. The legal support to this last right, of constructive possession, is considered in detail in chapter 6, below.

The bill of lading can be mailed ahead of the goods to the purchaser, and the purchaser needs to obtain it in order to claim the goods themselves when they arrive. If it can be arranged for the seller only to release the bill against payment,[37] if the buyer does not pay or goes bankrupt, the seller can still use the bill of lading to deal with the goods, even though at sea. Thus, the danger of consigning goods to a faraway destination to an unknown buyer is to some extent mitigated. Moreover, the purchaser, by inspecting the bills, obtains an assurance that they

---

[33] In *Cowas-Jee v Thompson*, above, mate's receipts were issued to, and retained by the sellers, and in *Ruck v Hatfield* (1822) 5 B. & Ald. 632, 106 E.R. 1321 and *Craven v Ryder* (1816) Taunt. 433, 128 E.R. 1103, transferred to the buyers against payment, the idea being that the buyers could only obtain bills of lading by exchanging the mate's receipts for them. *Cowas-Jee* showed that the device did not generally work, since the shipowner was normally entitled, and indeed obliged, to issue bills of lading to the buyer as shipper, to whom property had passed on shipment.

[34] For a history of the early development of the bill of lading, see Bools, *The Bill of Lading: A Document of Title to Goods*, (LLP, 1997), Ch. 1, and pp. 149–58.

[35] Note apparent, since the master may be unaware of the actual quality.

[36] Assuming a shipped bill—other documents are considered in paras 6—043, *et seq.*, below.

[37] Mechanisms for ensuring this are covered in Ch. 8, below.

have been loaded, and some evidence that, on loading, they complied with the terms of the sale contract. Therefore, the buyer may be content to pay against production of the bill of lading, before he is able actually to inspect the goods themselves.

To the development of modern f.o.b. and c.i.f. contracts, the development of the bill of lading as a document of title was a necessary precondition, but not sufficient. The seller's protection was still less than ideal, until enhanced by the later development of the documentary credit, as described in Part II of the book. Also, the bill of lading could state only the situation on shipment, and since carriage by sea is hazardous, may not represent the current state of the goods. Modern sales contracts therefore also need to stipulate who is to insure the goods, and for the use of assignable marine insurance policies. Moreover, the carrier must be liable should the goods be lost or damaged at sea through his fault.

It was this last requirement that delayed development of the c.i.f. contract until after 1855. In a c.i.f. contract the seller makes all the arrangements for carriage,[38] including contracting with the carrier. If the buyer is to be required to pay against the bill of lading, the seller's entitlement to payment must necessarily depend only on the condition of the goods on shipment. Therefore, it is only the buyer who is interested in suing the carrier for loss or damage that occurs post-shipment. If the buyer has no contractual relationship with the carrier, that creates problems which were initially addressed by the Bills of Lading Act 1855.

(f) Contract of Carriage Issues, and their Resolution by the Bills of Lading Act 1855

The development of the bill of lading allowed sellers to ship goods to distant   **1–013**
buyers, with some security to all parties, and f.o.b. contracts developed into more varied forms. As communications developed, buyers attempted to get sellers, who were better placed in the exporting country, to perform a greater variety of functions, so that a division of responsibilities (f.o.b.), where the buyer nominated the vessel but the seller made the arrangements for shipment became common. However, it was usually desirable for the buyer to contract with the carrier, so that in making the shipping arrangements, the seller was usually regarded as acting only as agent for the buyer. If the seller obtained a bill of lading it would normally be in the buyer's name, and would not be used as security for payment as it is today.[39] This form of f.o.b. contract also continues to this day.

However, neither the c.i.f. contract, nor the first two varieties of f.o.b. contract described in *Pyrene v Scindia*, in chapter 3, could develop until 1855.[40] For even if the seller were prepared to undertake aspects of arranging carriage, there were two reasons why it was better for him to do so as buyer's agent, rather than contracting with the carrier as principal. First, since property and risk passed to the buyer on shipment,[41] it was arguable that only he would be able to sue the carrier for substantial damages if they were lost or damaged at sea, and that if the

---

[38] He can alternatively purchase goods which have already been shipped, but this was a later development (see further the discussion in para. 2—004, below).

[39] Under the c.i.f., but also modern forms of f.o.b. contract, as can be seen clearly from *Concordia Trading BV v Richco International Ltd* [1991] 1 Lloyd's Rep. 475, in para. 6—087, below.

[40] The first reported c.i.f. case is *Tregelles v Sewell* (1862) 7 H. & N. 574—the leading classic f.o.b. authority does not seem to be until *Wimble, Sons v Rosenberg & Sons* [1913] 3 K.B. 743, and even that case is by no means clear cut. See further the discussion of *Pyrene v Scindia* in para. 3—004, below, and *Wimble v Rosenberg* in para. 4—022, below.

[41] A necessary conclusion from the floating warehouse arguments, such as in *Cowas-Jee* above, which regards the sale as complete on shipment. Comments in *Ruck v Hatfield* (1822) 5 B. & Ald. 632, 106 E.R. 1321 also suggest that in f.o.b. sales the ship was considered to be the warehouse of the buyer, the contract providing for delivery thereto.

contract was made by the seller, he would be able to recover only nominal damages. This problem was thought to have been resolved by the House of Lords decision in *Dunlop v Lambert*,[42] but even if the decision there was that a seller as shipper had a useful action against the carrier, it would usually be the buyer who had an interest in suing, and a much more important (and inconvenient) decision was that of *Thompson v Dominy*: the transfer of a bill of lading does not enable the transferee to bring an action in his own name on the carriage contract.[43] *Thompson v Dominy* was the second, and more substantial reason, delaying the development of modern contractual forms. It was only after *Thompson v Dominy* had been overturned by the Bills of Lading Act 1855, s.1, that contracts could develop with the seller as principal party to the carriage contract. This provision (in summary at least) transferred contractual rights against the carrier with the bill of lading.[44]

Thus, the 1855 Act facilitated the development of the c.i.f. contract. It also allowed for the development of varieties of f.o.b. contract where the seller contracted as principal, rather than merely as buyer's agent, *e.g.* (possibly) *Wimble, Sons v Rosenburg & Sons* [1913] 3 K.B. 743; *The El Amria and El Minia* [1982] 2 Lloyd's Rep. 28 (where the buyer cannot have contracted as principal), and *Carlos Federspiel & Co, S.A. v Charles Twigg & Co Ltd* [1957] 1 Lloyd's Rep. 240 (where the seller undertook to contract as principal). Varieties of f.o.b. contract are discussed in chapter 2, below.

(2) FINANCE OF INTERNATIONAL SALES

(a) DEVELOPMENT OF BANKERS' DOCUMENTARY CREDIT

1–014 Though the use of the bill of lading made it safer for sellers to ship goods for which they had not yet been paid, and for buyers to pay for goods that they had not yet had the opportunity to inspect, and the Bills of Lading Act 1855 made possible the development of the c.i.f., and more modern forms of f.o.b. contract, the situation as described above is still far from ideal. From the viewpoint of the seller, the following problems remained:

(a) The seller still necessarily lost control of the documents, when he forwarded them to the buyer. How, then, was he to enforce his security in fact, should the buyer default? A partial solution to this problem developed, and is described at the start of chapter 8, but it was not ideal.

(b) If the buyer defaulted after the goods had been shipped, the seller has incurred significant costs by then. Assuming he can retain the bill of lading, he can resell the goods, or collect them at their destination, but the latter alternative, necessitating collection of the goods from a foreign country, is unlikely to be attractive.

(c) If, on the other hand, the seller chooses to resell the goods, some goods may simply be unsaleable to anybody else, apart from the original buyer. An obvious example would be a component manufactured specifically for plant or machinery owned by the buyer.

---

[42] (1839) 6 Cl. & Fin. 600, (1839) 7 E.R. 824. What this case actually decided is far from clear; it is discussed fully in para. 13—040, below.
[43] (1845) 14 M. & W. 403; 153 E.R. 532, also covered in para. 13—003, below.
[44] The Act was unsatisfactory in a number of respects, and has since been replaced by the Carriage of Goods by Sea Act 1992: see Ch. 13, below.

(d) Probably of greater practical importance is that the seller cannot protect himself against market falls, should his original buyer default, since he will be forced to make a new contract of sale, at the new current market price, which on a falling market, will be lower than the contract price.[45]

From the viewpoint of the buyer, he has to pay against documents, whose time of tender he cannot accurately predict. He needs the documents to resell the goods, so he needs liquid capital. Far better would be to use the proceeds of the resale to pay the seller, since then (unless he has sold at a loss) no liquidity is required.

Fortunately, the bill of lading can be used more than once, to transfer property and constructive possession in the goods. This allows one or more banks to step in as intermediaries, to guarantee payment to the seller, and to finance the sale for the buyer. Moreover, giving the banks possession of the shipping documents provides them with security, should the buyer default.

The bankers' commercial credit, especially where irrevocable and confirmed, performs the following functions.

(a) The seller no longer takes the risk of the buyer's solvency—he need do nothing until the credit is received.

(b) If the credit is confirmed, he never needs to sue outside his own jurisdiction.

(c) He may use the security of the credit to raise money from his own bank, in order to finance the transaction from his end.

(d) The buyer also benefits, because the bank provides liquidity for the transaction, and he need not repay the bank until he can re-sell the goods.

In its most basic form, the workings of an irrevocable credit are as follows:

(a) There is a term in the sale contract that payment is to be by irrevocable documentary credit.

(b) The buyer instructs the nominated bank, or first class banker, to open a credit in the seller's favour, payment to be against delivery of shipping documents.

(c) The bank then notifies the seller that this has been done. By so doing the bank is in effect guaranteeing the creditworthiness of the buyer. The bank represents to the seller that if he ships the goods and tenders the documents, it will pay the price come what may. It is then up to the bank to recover the money eventually from the buyer. Note that the shipping documents are tendered to the bank, so they have a security against the goods should the buyer not pay.

(d) Only at this stage, once the seller has received this guarantee, is he required to make arrangements to ship the goods, and procure the necessary bills of lading.

(e) The seller ships the goods and thereby obtains the shipping documents. He forwards these to the banker, who will either pay in cash or provide a bill of exchange for the price to be drawn on the bank.

Documentary credits are described in full detail in chapters 8 to 10, below. It is worth observing that they provide advantages to both sellers and buyers. The

---

[45] Sellers are therefore naturally anxious to keep contracts alive on falling markets; it was probably for this reason that the sellers in *Gill & Duffus v Berger* (in para. 7—002, below) were so reluctant initially to repudiate.

buyer can benefit, because once the bank has received the bills of lading it can advance to the buyer credit for their value until he is able to resell them (see the description of the trust receipt in chapter 8, below). The buyer no longer needs liquidity, still less to have cash available at the indeterminate time at which the documents are presented.

A confirmed credit works similarly, but with the addition of a confirming bank in the seller's country of business. The confirming bank adds a second independent undertaking, protecting seller against the need to sue abroad. Pretty well all credits issues in the U.K. are irrevocable, but not all are confirmed; the seller may not need the additional security they provide, justifying the payment of two commissions.

(3) Modern Day Problems

(a) Development of Chains f.o.b. and c.i.f.

1–015 The early cases considered in this chapter, and at the start of chapter 2, below, were single sales between relatively small trading parties. Once the idea of constructive delivery through tender of documents became established in the c.i.f. contract, however, it was appreciated that the same documents could be used to pledge the goods, as with the documentary credit described above.

Alternatively, the buyer could re-sell the goods, on c.i.f. terms. Nor was it necessary for a c.i.f. seller actually to ship the goods himself; he could obtain documents relating to goods already afloat.

It has been observed that the c.i.f. contract remains widely used in the bulk commodity trade. This was not its original use, but it (and to a lesser extent the f.o.b. contract) were adopted because of their ideal suitability for such trade, which differs in important respects from trade in manufactured goods, for which the traditional contracts are less well suited. Most of the cases concern either grains and other foodstuffs, or bulk oil; these are not the only bulk commodities shipped, however, and the markets differ from each other in various respects.

(i) *Trade in Grains and Other Foodstuffs*

Intermediaries and chains

1–016 If we consider the trade in grain and other foodstuffs, some striking features stand out.[46]

First, many of the traders, especially at the importing end, are relatively small concerns, unable to take large tonnages. Many international sales are therefore of quite small amounts, for example for 2,000 tons of Plate maize in *Ampro*,[47] in Ch. 3, below. However, economies of scale, and particularly cargo-handling considerations, make it much cheaper to ship the cargo in much larger quantities.[48] It is, therefore, almost inevitable that much of the trade is performed by intermediaries. These intermediaries might, for example, purchase amounts large enough to be economical to ship from a number of sellers, selling them on in smaller amounts to end users. In *Garnac Grain*, below, for example, it was the practice of the ill-fated Allied physically to collect the commodity (in that case lard) into large storage depots, from which it could be conveniently exported.

---

[46] For a general description of dry bulk commodity sales, see, *e.g.* M. Stopford, *Maritime Economics*, (2nd ed., Routledge, 1997), pp. 314–331.
[47] [1965] 2 Lloyd's Rep. 157 (an f.o.b. contract).
[48] M. Stopford, *op. cit.*, nn. 10, 11 and 46.

Commodity brokers might purchase sufficient cargo to fill an entire vessel, but often with a view to splitting the cargo for delivery to a number of sub-purchasers, at the port of discharge.

It follows that a bulk commodity cargo is likely to be resold at least once; chain sales are therefore virtually inevitable. A contract which can be performed by transfer of documents is ideal for purchase and sale by intermediaries, who may have no desire (or indeed capability) to take physical possession of the cargo itself. It also follows that it would be common for a single cargo, often stored as an undivided bulk on board the vessel, to be split between a number of eventual purchasers, none of whom would wish to take the entire tonnage.[49]

For this type of contract to work, it is desirable for each sale and resale to be on identical terms, apart from quantity and price. Standard forms are therefore essential, and ideally the same documents should be used for each contract.[50] Moreover, an event which terminates one contract, for example by frustration or breach, should terminate them all.[51]

C.i.f. and f.o.b. contracts are well suited to this role. The products are relatively standardised, wheat (for example) of a particular grade being commercially identical, whoever the supplier. Contracts of this type can therefore often be generic, with no need to stipulate the identity of the supplier, name of ship or even (necessarily) country of origin. Apart from the price, and a generic specification, only the port of loading (f.o.b.) or discharge (c.i.f.) might be determined. In c.i.f. sales in particular, the seller can often satisfy the contract with any goods of the contract description, shipped from anywhere, as long as they are shipped within the contract period, aboard a vessel destined for the discharge port.[52]

Market fluctuations

1–017

A second feature of trade in grains and other foodstuffs is that traders like to contract for supplies well ahead. For example, in *Bunge v Tradax*,[53] in chapter 3, below, the contract, concluded in January 1974, was for 5,000 tons of soya bean meal to be shipped in each of the months May, June, and July 1975, well over a year ahead. End users obviously like to secure future supplies, but intermediaries too will therefore need to enter into similar contracts, for sale and purchase of cargoes to be delivered well into the future.

Another consequence of trading so far ahead is that market prices can fluctuate significantly between contract and delivery. The wheat trade is used by Lipsey & Crystal, in their classic economics textbook,[54] as a paradigmatic example of a classical free market, in the sense that no individual trader, or group of traders, controls prices. Certainly, individual buyers of wheat have insufficient market strength to be anything other than price-takers. Moreover, there can be significant spot market price fluctuations, due, for example, to changes in agricultural conditions, and political events. David Winstone notes that[55]:

"Buyers of commodities are concerned that prices might rise in the future. Sellers have the opposite concern, that prices might fall. One way of ensuring certain prices in the future is to enter into an agreement, a forward delivery

---

[49] For the particular problems posed by this additional complication, see further the discussion of delivery orders in paras 6—096, *et seq.*, below.

[50] Except where delivery orders are used for the sub-sale, but they too should ideally match the bill of lading originally issued.

[51] Otherwise a trader might be left with documents which cannot be used for the sub-sale, and be forced to enter new sales, inevitably at a market disadvantage.

[52] *e.g.*, the contract in *Glencore v Bank of China* [1996] 1 Lloyd's Rep. 135, discussed in paras 10—030, *et seq.*, below.

[53] [1981] 1 W.L.R. 711, [1981] 2 All E.R. 513, [1981] 2 Lloyd's Rep. 1.

[54] Lipsey & Chrystal, *Positive Economics* (8th ed., Oxford University Press, 1995).

[55] Winstone, *Financial Derivatives*, at p. 63: see para. 1—033.

contract,[56] to sell/buy at an agreed price in the future. Regardless of what happens to the spot market price between the date the agreement is made and the date of exchange, the parties to the agreement, buyer and seller, have removed price risk from their transaction."

Where there is a well-developed futures market,[57] as there is in grain and food trades, the futures market is better suited for both hedging against or speculating on long-term price fluctuations, but especially in rapidly fluctuating markets there might also be a temptation to speculate on c.i.f. and f.o.b. contracts, which (unlike fully-fledged futures markets) normally envisage eventual delivery of cargo. Futures markets, with delivery dates usually fixed at three month intervals,[58] are not well-suited to dealing with short-term fluctuations.

This can manifest itself in two main ways. First, a c.i.f. or f.o.b. buyer will try to find any reason to get out of the sale contract on a falling market, since equivalent goods can now be bought elsewhere, more cheaply.[59] Conversely, the seller will attempt to repudiate on a rising market, re-selling the goods at a higher price. This assumes, of course, the existence of a ready market in equivalent goods, which in turn demands a degree of standardisation of goods, but the bulk commodity market in grain and foodstuffs provides this. Secondly, it is inevitable that the intermediaries, who will normally be commodity brokers, will have many sale and purchase contracts. Ideally, of course, sale and purchase commitments will match, but a trader who expects a market fall would be tempted to re-sell goods purchased under existing contracts. His sale commitments would now exceed his purchases (in market terminology, he would go short), but he could meet his sale commitments by buying back equivalent goods later, at a lower price if his market predictions had been correct. Similarly, a trader who was already short would be tempted to remain short, hoping to take advantage of the expected market fall. The converse would of course be true where the market was expected to rise; traders would be tempted to go long, entering into further purchase commitments now, hoping to sell off excess goods (at a higher price) later. This is all possible only if the c.i.f. or f.o.b. contracts are not for the sale of specific goods, so that the seller can satisfy his commitments to his purchaser by supplying any goods matching the contractual description.

There is, in any case, a relationship between futures and physical markets, as described below.

Circles

1–018　　Even in the absence of market fluctuation, a trader who has matched his purchase and sale commitments can find himself short if a purchase falls through, for any reason, long if a sale. The *Gebruder* case, below, is an example of the latter, where a trader was left long by the breach of contract of his sub-buyer. In that case he remedied the situation by selling the excess on the futures market. In *The Filipinas I*, below, Pagnan purchased from Tradax 21,000 tons of maize, f.o.b., which they re-sold to Schouten. Later, they re-purchased the same cargo from Schouten.[60] The report does not make clear why they did this. Perhaps they had

[56] *i.e.* a contract envisaging delivery of cargo in the future. With a small number of exceptions, discussed below, c.i.f. and f.o.b. contracts envisage the eventual delivery of cargo, whereas contracts on the future exchange markets do not. (Footnote author's own.)

[57] See further below.

[58] Usually theoretical, in that in the overwhelming majority of cases, there will be no eventual delivery.

[59] See, *e.g. Glencore v Bank of China*, [1996] 1 Lloyd's Rep. 135 discussed in 10—030, *et seq.*, below.

[60] Technically, the cargo sold to Schouten was not necessarily the same cargo as that purchased from Tradax. Any 21,000 tons would do, but in reality, the expectation was clearly that the same cargo would be used.

always intended to make the re-purchase, since the market appeared to be falling, but if so they gambled incorrectly, since the market rose between the sale and re-sale. Alternatively, they may have been left short, perhaps with the failure of another purchase, and needed to buy cargo to fulfil sale commitments elsewhere. Whatever the correct explanation, Pagnan as sellers had ended up as purchasers later in the chain, thereby creating a circle (albeit a simple one, of only two parties).

Circles are usually created accidentally (unlike in futures markets proper, where "closing out" is the norm). As long as all the parties in a circle remain solvent, there is little point in requiring the transfer of documents or goods around the parties, and many standard form commodity contracts contain a circle clause, the effect of which is instead to allow simply for settlement of price differences (see the GAFTA 100 circle clause, set out below). The effect of this, if the original seller creates the circle by purchasing later in the chain, is to negate any requirement to ship any goods at all.[61] It would therefore be theoretically possible to use circles, deliberately created, for pure speculation, but in reality, this level of speculation is confined to fully-fledged futures markets.

In *The Filipinas I*, Pagnan, under their original contract as f.o.b. purchasers from Tradax, were obliged to nominate the vessel. When it became clear that the vessel nominated by them (and indeed, effectively taken over from Schouten) would not arrive in time, they re-sold the cargo back to Tradax,[62] this time deliberately to create another circle, and agreeing to close out the original purchase, with a price adjustment.

We see another example of a circle, unusually brought about deliberately, in *Garnac Grain*, below, and again (though accidentally this time) in *Concordia v Richco*, in chapter 6, below. In both of these cases there was a circle clause in each of the contracts, but one of the parties had become insolvent, rendering the clause inapplicable.

GATFA 100 CIRCLE CLAUSE (29)

[Footnotes are author's own.]

Where Sellers re-purchase from their Buyers or from any subsequent **1–019**
buyer the same goods or part thereof, a circle shall be considered to exist as regards the particular goods so repurchased, and the provisions of the Default Clause shall not apply.[63] (For the purpose of this clause the same goods shall mean goods of the same description, from the same country of origin, of the same quality, and, where applicable, of the same analysis warranty, for shipment to the same port(s) of destination during the same period of shipment).[64] Different currencies shall not invalidate the circle. Subject to the terms of the Prohibition Clause in the contract,[65] if goods are not appropriated, or, having been appropriated documents are not presented, invoices based on the mean contract quantity shall be settled

---

[61] Indeed, this was part of Schouten's successful argument in the case; see further below.

[62] Or again, to be more accurate, sold 21,000 tons of cargo of the same description.

[63] Clause 28. It is necessary to exclude this provision where a circle arises, since it would otherwise be triggered by non-shipment of goods, or non-tender of documents.

[64] Bulk commodity contracts will normally be for the sale of generic goods, where the seller can satisfy the contract with any goods matching the contract description. It would not normally be the case, therefore, for the seller in a circle to re-purchase exactly the same goods as sold.

[65] Clause 21, which cancels obligations affected by prohibition of export, blockade or hostilities.

by all buyers and their sellers in the circle by payment by all Buyers to their Sellers of the excess of the Sellers' invoice amount over the lowest invoice amount in the circle. Payment shall be due not later than 15 consecutive days after the last day for appropriation, or, should the circle not be ascertained before the expiry of this time, then payment shall be due not later than 15 consecutive days after the circle is ascertained. Where the circle includes contract(s) expressed in different currencies the lowest invoice amount shall be replaced by the market price on the first day for contractual shipment and invoices shall be settled between each Buyer and his Seller in the circle by the payment of the differences between the market price and the relative contract price in currency of the contract.

All sellers and buyers shall give every assistance to ascertain the circle and when a circle shall have been ascertained in accordance with this clause same shall be binding on all parties to the circle.

As between Buyers and Sellers in the circle, the non-presentation of documents by Sellers to their Buyers shall not be considered a breach of contract.

Should any party in the circle prior to the due date of payment commit any act comprehended in the Insolvency Clause of his contract,[66] settlement by all parties shall be calculated at the closing out price as provided for in the Insolvency Clause, which shall be taken as a basis for settlement, instead of the lowest invoice amount in the circle. In this event respective Buyers shall make payment to their Sellers or respective Sellers shall make payment to their Buyers of the difference between the closing out price and the contract price.

R. PAGNAN & FRATELLI v N.G.J. SCHOURLEN N.V., THE FILIPINAS I

Queen's Bench Division (Commercial Court). [1973] 1 Lloyd's Rep. 349

Facts:

1–020   Tradax Ltd sold 21,000 tons of maize, f.o.b., to Pagnan; the buyers were to nominate the vessel, and nomination once made was to be irrevocable. Pagnan sold the same quantity of maize to Schouten, on identical terms but at a slightly lower price ($47.90 per ton, compared with $49.25); although this was a contract for the sale of unascertained goods, Pagnan clearly intended to use the same cargo. Schouten chartered *The Filipinas I* to carry the maize, and nominated *The Filipinas I* under their contract with Pagnan.

---

[66] Clause 30. The effect of this clause, in the event of the insolvency of either party to a sale contract, is to close out the contract at the market price. Thus a seller to a buyer who becomes insolvent re-purchases from him, and the sub-buyer from the insolvent party re-sells to him, at the market price. This would enable documents to move from seller to sub-buyer, by-passing the insolvent party.

Schouten later resold to the same quantity of maize to Pagnan at a higher price ($51.50), and "transferred" the charterparty to Pagnan (by creating a sub-charter on the same terms as the head charterparty). Again, though the contract could theoretically have been satisfied using any cargo, this was in reality a resale of the same cargo back to Pagnan, and indeed, the sale was tied to the sub-charter of *The Filipinas I*. Moreover, the parties cancelled the earlier contract and agreed a price difference adjustment; as a result of market fluctuations, Schouten had profited from the two transactions, at Pagnan's expense.

Pagnan then nominated *The Filipinas I* under their original contract with Tradax (of which the evidence suggested that Schouten were unaware). Then they discovered that *The Filipinas I* would be late in arriving at the loading port. In fact, *The Filipinas I* was not ready to load by the cancelling date, and Pagnan cancelled their sub-charter with Schouten. On the same day, they resold the maize to Tradax at a higher price still ($54.50, again cancelling their original contract with Tradax and taking a price adjustment). On this transaction Pagnan profited, on a continuing rising market, at Tradax's expense.

Schouten claimed their price adjustment from Pagnan, but Pagnan now wanted to get out of this disadvantageous deal. They argued that they were entitled to repudiate the sub-charterparty for breach by Schouten of the expected readiness to load clause, that the price adjustment agreement and sub-charter were part of one transaction, which stood or fell as one, and that they were therefore entitled to repudiate the entire transaction. They also claimed that there had been a total failure of consideration under the resale contract, because no goods were ever shipped nor documents tendered.

Held:

(a) There was no total failure of consideration since the "sale" contract from Schouten to Pagnan clearly did not envisage shipment of any goods, and was merely a price adjustment mechanism. Kerr J. noted that the price could not have been intended to be paid against shipping documents, because it was payable before the vessel was likely to arrive. Also the charter of only one vessel made it impossible to envisage two cargoes being shipped under the earlier and later contracts. In any case, under Pagnan's argumemt, they would have remained obliged, under their earlier contract with Schouten, to sell them 21,000 tons of cargo.

(b) The charterparty and sale contract were separate contracts, their commercial purpose being entirely different, so that even if Pagnan were correct in their contention that Schouten were in breach of the expected readiness clause, that did not entitle them to repudiate the price adjustment contract. (The question whether there had been a breach of charter was remitted to arbitration.)

1–021   KERR J.: *(on the total failure of consideration argument)* [This submission rests] on a foundation that the contract of May 13/14 [second sale contract between Schouten and Pagnan] is to be regarded as a real contract, in the sense that the parties intended goods to be shipped and documents to be presented in pursuance of it. In my view, this is not only fallacious, but would produce a situation of commercial impracticability which, with due respect to Mr Davenport's ingenious argument [for Pagnan], can on analysis be seen to be little short of absurd. What the parties in my view clearly intended to achieve by the contract of May 13/14, was—as expressly stated in the document of May 13—the cancellation of the converse contract of Jan. 26 ([the earlier sale contract] under which Pagnan had been the sellers and Schouten the buyers) in consideration of a payment by Pagnan to Schouten of a price difference of $3.60 per ton which had arisen from the intervening rise in the market price of Brazilian maize,[67] and which they agreed should be payable on 21,000 tons as the notional mean quantity, since the contract provided for options of 5 per cent more or less. This price difference was not to be payable immediately but on or before June 15, no doubt because this was approximately the date by which both parties would have had to perform obligations under the contract of Jan. 26 if it had not been agreed that it should be cancelled. By that date Schouten would have been obliged to nominate a vessel and thereafter to provide it for loading by Pagnan. Pagnan would have been obliged to have goods ready for shipment and thereafter to deliver them on board. Schouten had indeed chartered *The Filipinas I* for this very purpose, but when the contract of Jan. 26 was cancelled by the contract of May 13/14, Schouten also required Pagnan to take the vessel off their hands. In this way the transaction makes perfect sense commercially. It could not have been intended that the sum of $54,000 payable on or before June 15, was only to be payable against shipping documents, since it can be seen from the dates that it was on any view highly unlikely that shipping documents would have been available—let alone in Holland or Italy—by that date.

I asked Mr Davenport for his analysis of the position. He said that the terms of the contract of May 13/14, in particular the inclusion of a new price as opposed to a mere reference to the settlement of a price difference, showed that it was intended to be what the parties expressed it to be, *viz.* a true contract of "resale". This expression is in itself a misnomer. Since one is not dealing with specific or ascertained goods one is not dealing with sales and resales but agreements to sell and resell. But even using the words sale and resale in their colloquial sense, I asked Mr Davenport what, on his analysis, had happened to the contract of sale of Jan. 26. I think that his ultimate answer was that it subsisted and that one must disregard the express reference in the document of May 13, which shows that it was intended to be cancelled by the later contract of "resale". I agree that for the purposes of his contentions Mr Davenport

---

[67] $51.50 as against $47.90.

logically constrained to argue that the contract of Jan. 26 remained in force. For if the contract of May 13/14 is to be regarded as a true "resale", *i.e.* as an agreement by Schouten to resell to Pagnan the goods or documents which under the January contract Pagnan were obliged to sell to Schouten, then it must necessarily follow that the January contract also remained in force. But if one then asks oneself—as I asked Mr Davenport —how the matter would on this basis have worked out in practice if both contracts had been performed, one gets to a situation which could only be analysed in terms of Alice in Wonderland. Was each party to provide and ship 21,000 tons of maize from these two ports, obtain the appropriate shipping documents, and were they then solemnly, in effect, to exchange them on payment of the two respective prices so that apart from the price difference they would then both be in precisely the same position as in the beginning? Was each party to nominate a ship to the other for this purpose? Which of them, on this basis, would be entitled to nominate *The Filipinas I* of which both were sub-charterers at different levels, since she could only carry one full and complete cargo of about 21,000 tons? It is obvious to me, as it clearly was to the umpire and Court of Appeal at G.A.F.T.A., that the parties never intended anything of the kind. They only contemplated one quantity of 21,000 tons and one carrying vessel, *The Filipinas I.* They did not intend that the contract of Jan. 26 should remain in force but that it should be cancelled. They therefore did not intend that the contract of May 13/14 should be a contract of "resale" which was to be performed as such, but they merely concluded it as a means of wiping out the contract of Jan. 26 and leaving the payment of the difference in price as the only obligation which they in fact intended to be performed under it.

As was pointed out by Mr Hallgarten on behalf of Schouten, there is nothing at all unusual in commodity dealers using contracts of sale or resale as a means of arriving at a position in which the true nature of the transaction is the settlement of a price difference. As he put it, and as one often hears it put in the context of commodity, share or currency dealings for future performance, traders like to have contracts on their books. For reasons which appear sensible to them as a matter of business, or because of the law relating to gaming transactions, they do not make bare contracts for the settlement of price differences but clothe these in contracts of sale or re-sale or both. An extreme illustration of this can be found in *Garnac Grain Co v Faure & Fairclough Ltd*, in particular in the report of the full judgment of Mr Justice Megaw (as he then was) in [1964] 2 Lloyd's Rep. 296, at 309. If they use this means in order to gamble on future price differences and for no other purpose, it being in effect agreed between them that neither party should be entitled to call for performance, then the contract will be unenforceable as being a gaming transaction . . . But no objection can be raised to the contract of May 13/14, on any such ground. If the true intention of the parties was, as to which I have no doubt, that it was merely a convenient means whereby Schouten agreed to the cancellation of the contract of Jan. 26 in consideration of the payment by Pagnan of the price difference between the two contracts, then the Court should give effect to their intention.

I therefore hold that upon the conclusion of the contract of May 13/14, and the charter-party of the latter date the contract of Jan. 26 was cancelled and the only remaining obligation, under the contract of May 13/14, was the obligation of Pagnan to pay to Schouten on or before June 15, a price difference which had by that date been agreed in the sum of $54,000. On this basis Mr Davenport's primary argument fails.

Notes

1–022   What Kerr J. effectively decided was that, although Pagnan and Schouten had purported to enter into an f.o.b. contract which envisaged the shipment of cargo, the real intention was simply to close out the earlier transaction made between them. Had *The Filipinas I* arrived in time, Pagnan could have used her to perform the original contract with Tradax, but when that contract was also closed out, there was no longer any need to ship goods at all.

Separate issues would have arisen over *The Filipinas I*, which had been chartered to carry the (now non-existent) cargo of maize, initially by Schouten who then sub-chartered to Pagnan, but whether either or both of these charterparties could be repudiated was not decided by Kerr J. (the sub-charter issue being sent back to the arbitrators).

Garnac Grain Co v Faure & Fairclough Ltd referred to in the above judgment, eventually went to the House of Lords ([1968] A.C. 1130). The case is unusual in that a circle was deliberately created by the initial seller, who did not intend to ship goods. The dispute was between other parties in the circle, however, neither of whom (it was decided) were party to the seller's plans. As far as these two parties were concerned, the contract (in this case c.i.f.) was (unlike that in *The Filipinas I*) exactly what it purported to be, a contract which envisaged the shipment of goods and tender of documents. Courts are, of course, concerned only to interpret the contract before them, the only relevant intentions being those of the parties to that contract. In *The Filipinas I*, by contrast, the parties were the only people forming the circle, and it could reasonably be inferred that their intention was not to ship goods and tender documents.

GARNAC GRAIN CO v FAURE & FAIRCLOUGH LTD

House of Lords. [1968] A.C. 1130, on appeal from [1966] 1 Q.B. 650

Facts and issues:

1–023   Allied had succeeded in securing more or less a monopoly in regard to the export of fats and vegetable oils on the Atlantic seaboard of the United States. They purchased these foodstuffs from various merchants, and collected it into large storage facilities. Generally they would arrange to export it to Unilever in the U.K., but instead of doing so directly, they sold via a number of intermediaries, with each intermediary purchasing from the last in the chain, for $2 a ton less than the sale price to the next party in the chain, prices being calculated back from the eventual sale price to Unilever. Hence, each intermediary was guaranteed a profit. Allied, however, required the intermediaries to advance funds to finance the transaction, on the security of warehouse receipts.

In the particular case, Allied sold 15,000 tons of lard, c.i.f., to Gersony for $191 per ton, who then re-sold on identical terms to Garnac, for $193 a ton. Garnac re-sold for $195 to Faure, the normal expectation being that Faure would re-sell for $197 to Unilever. However, Unilever were unable to proceed with the transaction, and so Allied themselves re-purchased the goods from Faure, thereby deliberately creating a circle. Allied had, of course, received the usual advances of funds from the intermediaries, each of which stood to make a profit of $30,000 on its c.i.f. purchase and re-sale, in addition to interest on the advances.

Unfortunately for all parties concerned, Allied went into liquidation, there being insufficient goods to satisfy the security of the warehouse receipts. Of course, no goods had been shipped, and assignees of Faure's contract (Bunge) sued Garnac for non-delivery. Gersony were of course in no position to deliver goods or documents to Garnac, nor to pay damages to them.

Garnac unsuccessfully sought a declaration that they had lawfully rescinded the c.i.f. contract between themselves and Faure. They unsuccessfully claimed that the c.i.f. contract was a sham, not being in reality what it purported to be, a contract which envisaged the shipment of goods. They also claimed (also unsuccessfully) that Allied were guilty of fraudulent misrepresentation, and that Faure were party to the fraud.

Held:
The c.i.f. contract was not a sham, since both Garnac and Faure had envisaged that lard would eventually be shipped, and delivered eventually to Unilever. Allied, who were aware of the truth, were guilty of fraudulent misrepresentation, but Faure were not party to the fraud. Nor were Faure acting as Allied's agents, but entered into the contract in their own right, as principals. Garnac were therefore liable for damages for non-delivery.[68]

SELLERS L.J.: Allied Crude Vegetable Oil Refining Corporation (referred **1–024** to as "Allied") until it went into liquidation on November 18, 1963, had been carrying on in the United States of America a very extensive exporting trade in vegetable oils and its crash brought very heavy and widespread losses. That event brought about the present litigation.

On Monday July 15, 1963, four contracts, one of which has been the subject of this action, were entered into. They in fact established a circle of contracts which was brought about by the activities of Allied. The reason for this and the effect of what was done form the basis of this controversy. I refer to them as contracts, as ostensibly they are, but it is in issue whether the last is an effective contract binding in its terms.

At the outset of that day the plaintiffs, Garnac Grain Company Incorporated (referred to as "Garnac") agreed to buy from Allied 15,000 tons of

---

[68] The damages were considerable, since Allied's collapse had resulted in a world shortage of lard, and hence a substantial rise in market price.

United States lard for December/January shipment c.i.f. Bromborough / Purfleet on the usual Unilever terms at a price of $193 per ton.

It was later arranged, at the instigation of Allied, that Garnac, instead of buying this consignment from Allied, should buy it from an American company, Gersony Strauss Incorporated (referred to as "Gersony"), who would be interposed. There is a written contract of July 15, 1963, whereby Allied sold to Gersony 15,000 tons of prime steam lard Unilever specifications at $191 per ton c.i.f. Bromborough/Purfleet December 1963/January 1964 at buyer's call (Contract "A").

This purchase by Gersony was passed to Garnac at $193 (Contract "B"). Garnac sold to the first defendants H.M. Faure & Fairclough Ltd, in London (referred to as "Faure") the same quantity to the specification North American prime steam lard December 1963/January 1964 shipment at $195 (Contract "C"), and the series of contracts closed on the same day by Allied buying back from Faure at a price of $197 the consignment which they had sold a few hours earlier at $191 for purported shipment in December/January (Contract "D"). These were all contracts for unascertained goods and there were slight variations in description or specification but these do not affect this appeal.

In order that these transactions of one day should be seen in their setting a number of other transactions prior and subsequent thereto were investigated at the trial and the evidence both oral and of documents became extensive and complicated.

In many trades it may be that in the ordinary working of the market where goods are sold along a line or string, goods after changing hands will be bought back by the original seller and so a circle may be created. That is not this case. Here this circle was not fortuitous but was designed by Allied when it made the first sale and the reason was to raise finance.

1–025   Allied's method of trading was summarised in the judgment of Megaw J. as follows:

> "Allied, whose business dealings have led to these, and I understand other, great financial losses, were a corporation carrying on business at Bayonne, New Jersey, as suppliers in a very large way of vegetable oils and animal fats. It would appear that they had built up a very large business, amounting in some of the commodities at least to almost a monopoly in the eastern seaboard of the United States, of buying oils and fats, often in comparatively small quantities, from the producers in the interior of the United States, accumulating these stocks in store in tanks owned by two warehousing companies in Bayonne, and then selling these accumulated stocks in large consignments, primarily at least for export. The export sales might be either to commercial users, such as Unilever in the United Kingdom, or to governmental organisations in what are called 'developing countries' under the provisions of certain United States legislation known as Public Law No. 480. The

provisions of that law are not in evidence and are not material for this case. Suffice it to say that Allied, somehow or other, apparently had access to advance information as to the probability of such sales. They used advance knowledge as a means of interesting merchants dealing in vegetable oils and fats; for Allied did not, apparently, normally themselves sell direct for export. They sold to merchants who in turn re-sold, or hoped to re-sell, on the export market."

The volume and extent of Allied's business attracted merchants eager to trade and willing to do so very much as Allied directed. Indeed this appears to have been necessary as Allied would not normally trade with those who would not finance them. One method of finance was to lend Allied money on the security of warehouse warrants or receipts. An advance would be 80 per cent. of the market price at the date of the loan, so that there was some margin for a fall in value. Garnac had advanced very large sums in this way and established a position which led and would be expected to lead to business coming to them when sales arose. When the crash came the goods were not in the warehouse to meet the warrants but for the purposes of this case nothing turns on loans secured by warrant except the inducement of trade.

The ultimate finance came from the consumers of the goods, and Unilevers were very large and regular buyers. When they were bidding, Allied would be informed of the market price and would generally sell through Faure, whom they had appointed as general agents to transact this business. The goods would be sold to Faure at a price of $2 less than Faure's selling price to Unilever and if Allied so wished, as they generally did for financial purposes, they would put Garnac alone or one or two others behind them each with a $2 margin. I have described the sales the reverse way because I understand the price would depend on what the consumer contracted to pay. Garnac would advance on such a sale and would have the security of their sale to Faure and would have the benefit of the $2 uplift on price, or commission as it was sometimes called, and a good interest on the money lent. As the quantities were large this was substantial business. The 15,000 tons under the present contract would give a total payment to Garnac of nearly $3,000,000.

It was not suggested that the string contracts, so contrived by Allied where there was the final sale to Unilever or a similar buyer, were not binding contracts enforceable according to their tenor. They would involve shipment by Allied of the goods specified on the relevant date, followed by payment by Unilever and the adjustment of the price down the string.

The plaintiffs' complaint is with regard to the transactions of July 15, 1963. By contract "C" Garnac were required to ship or to have arranged for the shipment of the goods specified by the end of January, 1964, at the latest. By reason of their collapse in November, 1963, Allied were unable to fulfil their contract "A" with Gersony, who in turn have been unable to fulfil contract "B" with Garnac and are not in a financial position to pay damages.[69] Garnac were therefore confronted with their liability to Faure. Faure have in fact assigned the benefit of this contract to the second defendants (referred to as "Bunge") but it has been conceded that Bunge are in no better position than Faure in their legal rights and further consideration of the assignment does not arise.

By this action Garnac claim that they are not liable to Faure and Megaw J. has upheld their claim. Garnac, through their solicitors, purported to rescind contract "C" on January 17, 1964, and they claim that they were entitled to rescind and have rescinded. The other relief asked depends on the success of this contention.

The statement of claim alleged fraudulent misrepresentation inducing Garnac to enter into contract "C" by both Faure and Allied. The misrepresentation alleged was that both the defendants dishonestly led Garnac to believe that Faure had resold or were to resell to Unilever and it was alleged that Garnac were induced to enter into the bargain in the belief that it was an ordinary commercial transaction and that they were not informed that Unilever had postponed a purchase for the time being, as both defendants knew when the four contracts of July 15, 1963, were entered into. Garnac had no knowledge that Allied were to buy back from Faure and so create a circle. The plaintiffs made an alternative claim, in the event of the claim in fraud against Faure failing (as it did), that, on the transactions and circumstances viewed as a whole, Faure, in entering into contract "C" with Garnac, were acting as agents for Allied as undisclosed principals and if so, the contract could be rescinded because it had been brought about by the fraud of Allied, the undisclosed principals.
[Sellers L.J. refused to interfere with the finding at first instance that Faure were not party to the fraud, and continued . . .]

1–026   As Faure were not fraudulent it is said for the defence that contract "C" was an ordinary commercial contract for the sale of goods where in the ordinary way delivery would not be expected because of the nature of the transaction but where there was always the legal obligation to perform according to its tenor if things went wrong. It was not, it was argued, a sham contract. It was in every way a complete contract for the sale of goods and there was no other independent contract which it purported to conceal.

Similarly, with contract "D" between Faure and Allied.

The main questions in this appeal, so far, depend on whether the judge was right in treating contract "D" as not a binding contract and, if it was not, whether, as Garnac allege, it makes Allied the undisclosed principals of Faure when they entered into contract "C" with Garnac and, if so, what is the effect of that.

I have been inclined, in agreement with Megaw J., to view this particular circle transaction with suspicion. I doubt if any aid is to be found from the other transactions to which detailed reference was made, to throw any real light on these transactions. A circle may arise fortuitously

---

[69] It appears that they had themselves gone into liquidation.

but it must be unusual to have it designed with the original supplier deciding who shall constitute the members of the circle and in what order and specifying for each a standard "uplift" of price. Such a circle does not look like a sale of goods, for the supplier by his ultimate purchase relieves himself of the obligation to ship any goods and in the meantime has acquired finance to 80 per cent of the market value of the goods (plus probably advances on goods represented by warehouse warrants) at a cost of $2 a ton multiplied by the number of transactions in the circle and the interest on the money advanced.

Then too there was no guarantee that, if and when a consumer was available, the same parties as constituted the circle would be allowed to enter the line which led to the ultimate sale to the consumer, although such, no doubt, was the hope and the understanding of each of the parties. Allied were, as far as I understand it, free to ignore or by-pass any such party although their financial requirements might restrain them from regarding it as good business so to do. They were not beyond ignoring Faure in making a sale to Unilever after they had agreed with Faure to act as their agents for that business.

On the other hand each transaction had its formal documents which in every way indicated a genuine transaction. It was pointed out forcibly that Garnac had protected themselves, or hedged, against the large loan to Allied by contracting forthwith with Faure, who were first-class traders in this business with the highest reputation and who would be expected to honour their contract if for some reason Faure's purchasers were to fail.

The judgment does not condemn the circle of July 15, 1963, as a whole as consisting of sham documents not revealing the true deals between the parties. It finds that Garnac—and presumably Gersony—were ignorant of the circle and believed that the line of sales would end with Unilever. It is the transaction "D" between Faure and Allied which the judgment finds to be a sham or "fictitious," as one witness described it, perhaps viewing it from his own approach. Obviously Faure and Allied knew that there was to be no immediate sale to Unilever and that the circle from Allied back to Allied was complete.

It was strongly urged for the defendants Faure, which Bunge sup-   **1–027** ported, that there was no underlying or alternative bargain proved differing from that to be read on the face of the written contract. If there were a different contract which was the agreement of the parties it can only be derived by inference. Faure would know that they would not have to deliver to Allied 15,000 tons December/January shipment, for the effect of the transactions was that Allied had, so to speak, bought back their obligation to ship. But is that enough?

In the course of exonerating Faure from the allegation of fraud the judge considered the reasons given by Eric Faure for what the judge described as "the curious use of re-sale contracts to Allied as a frequent feature of their financing operation." He deals not with the transaction of

July 15, where Faure did not make an advance, but with other transactions where any dishonest intention in respect of the resale was disproved.

The judge accepted Faure's evidence that it had a business purpose. The buying and reselling tied the transaction to business, to the eventual export business which he hoped was going to come. "Whenever we lent money we were always given a programme by Allied of the exports which we envisaged."

The judge said:

> "I am confirmed by other evidence in my belief that a reasonable business man could have thought that transactions such as this served a sensible business purpose, even though their legal effect might appear to be nil."

The other evidence was that of the vice-president of Bunge, Fornari, "a most impressive witness," who had said that such a transaction—that is, a purchase from Allied and an immediate resale to them—was the sort of transaction in which Bunge used to participate.

I do not find this in all the circumstances very satisfactory, but if Faure so regarded such transactions I find it difficult to denounce their apparent transaction, contract "D," with Allied as a sham so as to open up consideration of what function they did play in the completion of the circle involving as it does their purchase from Garnac, contract "C."

If fraud had been found against Faure then Garnac's position would have been clear and their rescission or right of rescission established. But as an alternative to that case which has failed, I do not find the evidence sufficient to establish some other agreement between Faure and Allied than that which the documents record.

[Sellers L.J. then rejected the claim that Faure were acting as agents for Allied.]

Note

The decision of the Court of Appeal was upheld in the House of Lords, where only the agency point was at issue.

1–028   LORD PEARSON: My Lords, there are only two questions to be dealt with, one relating to an alleged agency of a contracting party for an undisclosed principal, and the other relating to the assessment of damages for breach of the contract. In view of the length and complexity of the case counsel were requested to confine their arguments in the first instance to these two questions, postponing any argument on other questions raised in the appeal. A similar course had been taken in the Court of Appeal. In consequence of your Lordships' conclusions on the agency question, the other questions became immaterial and were not argued or considered, and they will be referred to only so far as may be necessary for the purpose of explaining the course of the proceedings.

The appellants are an American corporation named Garnac Grain Company Incorporated, who will be referred to as "Garnac." The respondents are an English company named H.M.F. Faure & Fairclough Ltd, who will be referred to as "Faure," and an American corporation named Bunge Incorporated, who will be referred to as "Bunge." Two other American corporations come into the story, one being Allied Crude Vegetable Oil Refining Corporation, who will be referred to as "Allied," and the other (playing only a minor part) being Gersony Strauss Company Incorporated, who will be referred to as "Gersony."

The litigation arose from the financial collapse of Allied, which occurred on November 18, 1963, and caused very heavy losses to the merchants (including Garnac, Faure and Bunge) who had been dealing with and making loans to Allied.

Allied had carried on business at Bayonne, New Jersey, as suppliers in a very large way of vegetable oils and animal fats. They would buy oils and fats, often in comparatively small quantities, from the producers in the interior of the United States; they would accumulate stocks of these commodities in tanks owned by two warehousing companies in Bayonne; and they would sell the stocks in large consignments to merchants, primarily for export to consumers overseas. The consumers included Unilever (Raw Materials) Ltd, belonging to the Unilever group of companies and having depots or wharves at Bromborough (on the Mersey) and Purfleet (on the Thames) and making large purchases of the commodities from time to time. Other consumers were governmental agencies in developing countries in Asia and Africa. The business was attractive to the merchants, and they were willing to fall in with suggestions from Allied as to the transactions to be undertaken and the modes of carrying them out. In particular Allied, who needed finance for buying and collecting the stocks, were able to insist that the merchants, if they were to have the business, must make loans to Allied. The merchants made their loans normally on the security of "revolving" warehouse receipts for specified quantities of the commodities, and in anticipation of participating in impending or projected transactions in the commodities. The transactions were so large that the merchants would not wish to be "long" of the commodities, and so a sale by Allied to the merchants and a resale by the merchants to the consumers would be negotiated concurrently, and a "string" of purchases and sales would be arranged. In the simplest form a string would contain only three parties—Allied as first sellers, the merchants as buyers and resellers, and the consumers as last buyers. But Allied operated in complicated and devious ways and might arrange to have more than three parties in a string.

A difficult situation would arise if the hoped-for transaction fell **1–029** through, the negotiations with the consumers being unsuccessful. In such a situation Faure, if they were the merchants concerned, would expect to participate in a later transaction and might enter into a strange pair of contracts with Allied of a circular or "back-to-back" character. Allied would agree to sell a quantity of the commodity to Faure at a stated price, and Faure would agree to sell a like quantity of the same commodity to Allied (or sometimes nominally to a subsidiary company of Allied) at a higher price, which was usually $2 per ton higher. This circular or back-to-back transaction would give to Faure a remuneration for making their loan, in addition to the interest charged for it, and was considered by Faure to have further advantages as a step on the way to participation in a later transaction of a normal commercial kind, and as tying the loans to trading. Faure were used to entering into pairs of contracts of this character with Allied, but Garnac had no experience or knowledge of them. There was evidence that Bunge also entered into such pairs of contracts with Allied, but apparently not in connection with loans of money to Allied.

The merchants dealing with Allied were making good profits and were not incurring any serious risks so long as Allied remained solvent and able to fulfil their contracts. Even if Allied became insolvent, the merchants would still be protected (except against falls in the market price) by their warehouse receipts so long as these were covered by actual stocks of the commodities in the warehouses.

The contract sued on was one of four contracts made on July 15, 1963, which will be referred to as contracts A, B, C and D. The parties were Allied, Gersony, Garnac and Faure. Each contract was for the sale of 15,000 long tons of prime steam lard complying with Unilever specifications for shipment in December, 1963, or January, 1964, at a price c.i.f. Bromborough / Purfleet and on the conditions of contract form 34 of the London Oil and Tallow Trades-Association. Contract A was for sale by Allied to Gersony at a price of $191 per ton. Contract B was for sale by Gersony to Garnac at a price of $193 per ton. Contract C was for sale by Garnac to Faure at $195 per ton, and this was the contract sued on. Contract D was for sale by Faure to Allied at $197 per ton. Thus Allied were both first sellers and last buyers in this string of contracts, and the four contracts would have formed a "circle" under clause 14 of contract form 34 but for the fact that in these contracts (at any rate in contract C) clause 14 was struck out. If clause 14 had been retained as a clause of the contract, only price differences would have been payable and as between buyers and sellers in the circle the non-delivery of documents by each seller to his buyer would not have been considered a breach of contract. That is subject to the question, which has not been discussed and on which I express no opinion, whether the insolvency of Allied would have affected the operation of clause 14. Without clause 14, there would still be an expectation that the parties would be content with payment of differences, but, subject to the questions raised in the action, either party to any of these four contracts would be entitled to require literal performance of the contract by delivery of documents and payment of the price.

In the event things went wrong and the parties' expectations were disappointed. Allied had their financial collapse on November 18, 1963, before the time for shipment (December/January) under the four contracts of July 15, 1963. Allied were insolvent and unable to perform their contracts: they could not deliver documents in respect of lard under contract A and they could not take up and pay for documents in respect of lard under contract D. The merchants who had been lending money to Allied suffered heavy losses. They had believed themselves to be secured, but in fact they had no security because the stocks which ought to have been in the warehouses covering the revolving warehouse receipts were not there. Faure were in grave difficulties and came under the control of their creditor banks. Gersony went into liquidation. Garnac and Bunge were affected to some extent but less severely. There remained outstanding, subject to the questions raised in the action, the rights and obligations under contract C. Faure were entitled to have the documents delivered to them by Garnac under contract C, and in default of such delivery to claim damages for non-delivery. Owing to the insolvency of Allied and Gersony, Garnac could not obtain shipping documents from Gersony and so were unable to effect delivery to Faure. The market price at all material times was above the contract price, because the withdrawal of Allied as a large collector and supplier of lard caused a scarcity and a consequent rise in the price.

There is therefore a claim by Faure as the buyers under contract C, or by Bunge, who are assignees of Faure, against Garnac for a very large sum of damages for non-delivery of the shipping documents under contract C. Prima facie the claim is well founded because the contract was not fulfilled.

This claim was made by way of counterclaim in the action, which had **1–030** been commenced by Garnac. Garnac's defence to it was that contract C was unenforceable against them and had been or should be rescinded on either or both of two grounds:

(a) The first ground was that Garnac were induced to enter into the contract by fraudulent misrepresentations made by Allied and by Faure, to the effect that the transaction, of July 15, 1963, was a normal commercial transaction, and that Faure were reselling to Unilever and were not reselling to Allied.

(b) The second ground was that Faure in making the contract acted as agents for Allied as undisclosed principals, that Garnac were induced to enter into the contract by fraudulent misrepresentations made by Allied, and that the fraud of the undisclosed principals rendered the contract unenforceable by the agents.

It was conceded at the hearing in the Court of Appeal that Bunge as assignees of Faure could not be in any better position than Faure.

At the trial before Megaw J. Garnac failed on the first ground because the judge held that Faure had not made any fraudulent misrepresentation, but Garnac succeeded on the second ground. The judge decided that Faure in making contract C acted as agents for Allied as undisclosed principals, that Garnac was induced to enter into the contract by fraudulent misrepresentations made by Allied, and that the fraud of the undisclosed principals rendered the contract unenforceable by the agents. Accordingly, he gave judgment in favour of Garnac on this issue.

Faure and Bunge appealed to the Court of Appeal. Garnac did not challenge the judge's finding that Faure did not make any fraudulent misrepresentation, and Garnac relied solely on the second ground. The Court of Appeal concentrated on the issue of agency, because if it were decided that there was no agency, Faure and Bunge would succeed with their counterclaim and would not need to establish their other contentions. Their principal other contentions were that Allied had not made fraudulent misrepresentations or had not thereby induced Garnac to enter into the contract, and that Garnac had affirmed the contract. The Court of Appeal decided that there was no agency and gave judgment accordingly in favour of Faure and Bunge on their counterclaim for damages for breach of contract C.

Were the Court of Appeal right in deciding that there was no agency?

[LORD PEARSON concluded that they were.]

Note

1–031   Even leaving aside the circle, and assuming that the normal sale to Unilever had gone ahead, these c.i.f. contracts have some notable features. The intermediaries' sole purpose appears to have been to finance the transaction by providing Allied with an advance.

It is clear that these sales are quite unlike domestic sales of goods. The intermediaries have no tangible interest in the underlying product. In *Garnac Grain* they were essentially engaged in lending money for a substantial return. In *The Filipinas I*, Pagnan may have sold to Schouten and re-purchased, simply speculating on the market continuing to fall. Even where there is no speculative element (and there might not have been in *The Filipinas I*), most of the sellers and buyers will be in the middle of a chain, with neither the intention nor capability of physically dealing in the goods themselves. Indeed, in *The Filipinas I*, it was really immaterial in the end that no goods were ever shipped, and in practical terms this will usually be true where there is a circle of contracts.

(ii) *Commodity futures markets*

1–032   Because c.i.f. and f.o.b. contracts normally envisage the eventual delivery of goods, even if postponed into the future, David Winstone would categorise them as forward delivery contracts "to arrive". They can to some extent be used to hedge against price fluctuations, in that the seller is protected against a fall in the market prior to delivery, the buyer against a market rise.[70] There are, however, other problems using this type of contract for hedging (or indeed speculation).

---

[70] It is in the nature of a hedge, however, that the parties cannot take advantage of movements the other way—that would be speculating.

WINSTONE, FINANCIAL DERIVATIVES

(Thomson Learning, 1995), p. 63

Whilst [the parties] have removed risk as to price, they have not removed **1–033** all risk. Their agreement is not free of default risk. If the spot market price were to rise above the agreed price between the date of the agreement and the agreed date of the sale, there would be a temptation for the seller to ignore the agreement and sell at the higher, prevailing spot price. Equally, there would be a temptation for the buyer to renege upon the agreement were the price to fall. There is also the problem that one of the parties will not be able, even if willing, to meet their obligations.

There are also other problems in using this type of forward agreement as a matter of routine in hedging price risk. Seller and buyer have to locate each other, therefore search costs arise. There is also the problem of negotiating not only the price, but the quantity of the commodity, its quality and where it should be delivered, as well as compliance with these terms.

Default risk, search costs and non-standardisation are therefore draw-backs to this type of forward delivery contract, often described as a **to arrive** contract because it is fully intended that the commodity will be delivered and taken up at the agreed future date.

[Emphasis as in original text.]

Comments

As we shall see in chapters 8–10, below, a documentary credit can protect **1–034** sellers, at least to a limited extent, from default risk, whereas a performance bond can protect buyers.

There is, however, no need for the parties to put up with the problems of the physical market where the product is capable of being sufficiently standardised for a futures market to develop; a futures market is much better, both for hedging and speculation, than a physical market, and it was natural for the parties to develop such markets in times of uncertainty.[71] Much of the speculation in bulk commodities takes place in the futures markets,[72] where it is expected neither for the sellers ever to deliver, nor the buyers ever to receive the goods. Indeed, bulk commodity futures markets are similar in many respects to money markets.

WILLIAM CLARKE, HOW THE CITY OF LONDON WORKS

(5th ed., Sweet & Maxwell, 1999), p. 101

Forward Markets . . . The essential characteristics of a forward contract **1–035** are: (i) it is undertaken for any required volume, (ii) the commodity . . . is

---

[71] David Winstone notes that the modern futures market in grain developed in Chicago (Chicago Board of Trade) in the mid-nineteenth century, fuelled by price uncertainty, especially during the American Civil War—Winstone, *Financial Derivatives*, (Thomson Learning, 1995), p. 61.

[72] Futures in wheat, for example, have been traded since 1870. For a description of the commodity futures markets in London today, see Clarke, *How the City of London Works*, (5th ed., Sweet & Maxwell 1999), Ch. 12.

expected to be delivered, (iii) the contract cannot be transferred or sold to second or third parties (*i.e.* it cannot be "traded"), (iv) the contract need not be published.

Futures Markets Like forward markets, they offer a place where contracts are arranged between traders, promising to deliver an agreed amount of a commodity... on an agreed date, at a price. They offer the same protection as a forward contract.

The essential characteristics of a futures market, in contrast to a forward market are: (i) the contracts are standardised, (ii) the business is open and prices published, (iii) the contracts can thus be traded (*i.e.* the obligations can be subsequently bought and sold), (iv) dealings are usually organised by a clearing house, providing protection to the participants.

Comments

1–036   Clarke describes the delivery contract to arrive (into which category c.i.f. and f.o.b. contracts fall) as a forward contract, contrasting them with futures markets.

Futures markets trade in the contracts themselves, so that someone who has, *e.g.* contracted to take delivery of 10,000 bushels of wheat in March can sell that contract in the market. The market in such contracts varies in a manner that it closely related to the market in the physical commodity itself.[73]

Trade in such contracts is only possible if there is standardisation, not only as to the type of commodity, but also as to quantity, and time and place of delivery. The only variable factor should be price. Delivery dates are usually standardised to every three months, and there will be a number of possible delivery points.

Trading takes place in commodity exchanges, which can be used to bring together traders who are both numerous and disparate. This avoids the search costs referred to by Winstone, in the above passage. Dealings are essentially public, enabling a market price to be determined. There is also a clearing house, which acts as counterparty, taking the opposite side in all transactions after clearing, and thereby removing any default risk.[74] It also enables all parties to close out their contracts later, with the counterparty again taking the opposite side, there being no need (as in the physical market) to find the other original parties to establish a circle.

In reality, although actual delivery is a theoretical possibility,[75] deals are usually closed out, with sellers of futures later repurchasing, or vice-versa, with a price adjustment but no actual movement of goods. The hedger can thus use the futures, rather than the physical market, to guard against market fluctuations, but without any of the other risks associated with the physical market. Thus, someone with a stock of wheat, *i.e.* long in wheat, fearful of a market fall, can sell on the futures market, buying back an equivalent quantity when the wheat is sold. Because movements of the physical and futures markets are closely related to each other, any loss made from the long position on a falling physical market will be compensated (approximately) by the short position taken on the futures market. Similarly, someone wishing to purchase wheat (*i.e.* short in wheat) in the future would take a long position in the futures market, re-selling in the futures

---

[73] See Winstone, *op. cit.* at pp. 65 *et seq.*
[74] See Winstone, *op. cit.* at pp. 70 *et seq.*
[75] This always enabled such transactions to avoid problems caused by s.18 of the Gaming Act 1845, even before recent relaxations to that legislation. It also helps to ensure that futures prices remain related to those of the physical commodity.

market at the same time as purchasing in the physical market. If the market were to rise, any losses consequent on being short in the physical market would be compensated by the long position taken in the futures market.[76] The hedge depends on the possibility of closing out the position taken in the futures market, at a later date; closing out is essential to the operation of the hedge.

WINSTONE, FINANCIAL DERIVATIVES

(Thomson Learning, 1998), pp. 72–73

Should a trader with a short position [in the futures market] actually want to make delivery at the expiry of the futures contract, they will tell the clearing house and the trader with the oldest long position will be informed by the clearing house that delivery is to take place. For every holder of a short futures position there will be a holder of a long futures position . . . Because the clearing house is counterparty to both positions settlement is guaranteed.

1–037

Comments

A trader with a short position in the futures market, wishing to make delivery, will logically have a long position in the physical market, since this is effectively selling physical goods on the futures market, as in *Gebruder*, below. It may well be that it is this relationship, between physical and futures markets, which keeps the prices approximately in line.[77]

This should be regarded as unusual, however. The overwhelming majority of futures contracts are closed out, and physical delivery is rarely made.

1–038

COOPER v STUBBS

Court of Appeal. [1925] 2 K.B. 753

Issues:

The issue was whether Stubbs, who was a member of a firm of cotton brokers and cotton merchants, but who also engaged in private speculations in the futures markets, in which his firm had no interest, was liable to pay tax on his profits. Holding that he was, the court rejected Stubbs' argument that because he had no intention of taking actual delivery of the cotton, these were simply gambling transactions.

1–039

Atkin L.J.:

---

[76] In both cases, the opposite position would obtain were the market to go the other way.
[77] See, however, Chaikin & Moher, below, at p. 398, and references therein. Clearly it is possible to have a futures market where no physical delivery occurs, as with BIFFEX, the Baltic International Freight Futures Market, which opened in 1985, and is traded on the London Commodity Exchange. See, *e.g.* William Clarke, *How the City of London Works*, (5th ed., Sweet & Maxwell, 1999), p. 112. With BIFFEX there is no physical commodity to deliver, but prices are calculated mathematically, on the basis of the Baltic Freight Index (BFI). Even though a market of this type is theoretically possible, however, there are advantages in the interrelationship between physical and futures markets, as shown by *Gebruder*, below.

. . . All the contracts that were entered into by the appellant, whether they were entered into by him through his firm or through other brokers, were in fact real transactions. They gave rise to real contractual rights: they were contracts either for the purchase or for the sale of cotton in the future which could be enforced, and so far as the other party to the contract, who might be a dealer in this country, or a dealer in America, was concerned, he would not know whether the contract into which he had entered would be eventually closed by a contra contract or whether it would not. For these reasons it seems to me to be plain law that transactions such as the appellant entered into were real transactions and were not mere bets.

It seems that because futures contracts envisaged the theoretical delivery of goods, they avoided any difficulties with the Gaming Act 1845, even before it was relaxed for financial securities.[78] However, the main interest of the case, for present purposes, lies in the findings of the Special Commissioners, describing how the market operated.

Findings of fact made by Special Commissioners [Footnotes are author's own]

1–040   1. At a meeting of the Special Commissioners held on January 18, 1924, for the purpose of hearing appeals the appellant, Henry Stubbs, appealed against assessments to income tax . . . for the years ended April 5, 1921, April 5, 1922, and April 5, 1923, respectively, made upon him by the Additional Commissioners for the Division of Liverpool under the provisions of the Income Tax Acts.

2. The assessments under appeal were made upon the appellant under Sch. D of the Income Tax Act, 1918, in respect of profits from private transactions in cotton futures entered into by him in the circumstances hereinafter set out.

3. The appellant was a partner in the firm of Richard Stubbs & Co, which carried on the business of cotton brokers (*i.e.,* selling on commission to spinners and merchants and buying and selling for clients on future delivery contracts) and cotton importers (*i.e.,* acting as merchants on their own account). In all material years up till the death of Richard Stubbs, Senior, in 1919, the partners in the firm were Richard Stubbs, Senior, the appellant and Richard Stubbs, Junior. After the death of Richard Stubbs, Senior, the partners were the appellant and Richard Stubbs Junior. On the death of Richard Stubbs, Junior, on October 2, 1922, the business ceased, and the appellant retired temporarily from business. He resumed business after an interval of about six months.

4. The course of business of cotton merchants in general and of the appellant's firm was as follows:

---

[78] See the discussion in Chaikin & Moher, "Commodity Futures Contracts and the Gaming Act" [1986] L.M.C.L.Q. 390.

(a) Owing to the uncertainty of the quantity and quality of the cotton crop the price of cotton was subject to violent and rapid fluctuations. In order to protect himself against such fluctuations between the time of buying and selling or vice versa, a merchant usually effected a cover or hedge each time he made a purchase or sale of actual cotton.

(b) On a purchase by a merchant of actual cotton, for which he had not yet found a purchaser,[79] the merchant effected a hedge by making a contract for the sale of the same quantity of cotton for delivery in some month in the future.[80] Conversely on a sale of actual cotton not yet purchased the merchant effected a hedge by making a contract for the purchase of the same quantity of cotton for delivery in some month in the future.

These hedging contracts were known as future delivery contracts.[81] The future delivery contract, though differing in some important respects from the contract for the purchase or sale of actual cotton, provided for the delivery of actual cotton, but it was only exceptionally that a future delivery contract was entered into with the intention of taking up actual cotton, and it was almost invariably closed out, as explained in para. (d) below, by entering into another future delivery contract to cancel out with the one originally entered into.

(c) By means of these hedges at any given time the total amount of cotton bought or contracted to be bought by the merchant (whether as actual cotton or under a future delivery contract) balanced his total commitments for sale of cotton (either as actual cotton or under future delivery contracts), and thus the risk of any rise or fall in the general price of cotton between the time of purchase and sale of actual cotton was eliminated. On the subsequent sale or purchase of the actual cotton the relative hedging contract was nearly always closed out by the merchant.

(d) Future delivery contracts were dealt in on the Liverpool, New York and New Orleans cotton markets. Under the rules of the Liverpool Cotton Association, of which the appellant was a member, there was a provision that where purchases and sales were made between the same members of the Association for the same quantity of cotton for delivery in the same month, the contracts were closed out, and the transaction was concluded by the receipt or

---

[79] *i.e.* being long in cotton.
[80] *i.e.* taking a short position in the futures market.
[81] It is obvious that the terminology here differs from that used earlier. These are the contracts in the futures market.

payment of differences. The vast majority of future delivery contracts were closed in this way, both in Liverpool, New York and New Orleans.

(e) Besides the ordinary future delivery contracts, the appellant's firm from time to time entered into the operation known as a straddle, which consisted of entering into a future delivery purchase contract in Liverpool and a future delivery sale contract for the same amount of cotton in New York or New Orleans, or vice versa. When actual cotton was bought or sold one side of the straddle would be closed, leaving the firm with the other side of the straddle as a hedge against the actual cotton. Straddles were entered into in anticipation of subsequent transactions in actual cotton, and in some cases these straddles would be closed without any actual cotton being bought. While a complete hedge against fluctuations in the price could be effected by the ordinary future delivery contract, the straddle was useful in the import business as a protection against fluctuations in the rate of exchange and in the cost of shipping actual cotton.

(f) The firm varied their hedges frequently in consequence of fluctuations in the market: for instance, they altered a future delivery contract for one month into a future delivery contract for another month, or they sold future delivery contracts in Liverpool and bought corresponding future delivery contracts in New York or New Orleans, if they thought that the course of business would make the alteration advantageous.

(g) In accordance with a common custom among cotton merchants, the firm employed an arrivals salesman to transact on the Exchange the future delivery contract business of the firm. In addition to the future delivery contracts necessary to the firm or their clients for hedging, which were bought or sold on the instructions of the firm, the arrivals salesman was allowed to deal on his own initiative in future delivery contracts not required for hedging. This dealing was entered into not so much with the object of profit as with the object of enabling the arrivals salesman to keep in touch with the futures market. All these deals were closed at the end of the day, so that no great risk of loss was involved. It was the common practice of cotton merchants to authorize their arrivals salesman to enter into such deals. The arrivals salesman received 30 per cent. of the profits on these deals, the balance going to the firm, who bore any losses. The average number of these transactions was between 1000 and 1100 a year. The firm's profits or losses on these transactions were included in the accounts of their business.

5. The Commissioners stated that they were satisfied that the appellant's firm entered into future contracts, including the straddles, as a protection or hedge against their transactions in actual cotton, that the

contracts formed a legitimate and in fact an essential part of their business of cotton merchants, and that the speculative deals entered into by the arrivals salesmen were ancillary to this business.

6. Future delivery contracts were also entered into by members of the Liverpool Cotton Association and others, not as hedges to transactions in actual cotton, but purely as speculative transactions, with a view to making a profit on the rise or fall, as the case might be, in the market price of the contracts. Future delivery contracts entered into with this object were always closed out by entering into a similar contra contract, as described in para. 4 (d), differences being received or paid. The profit or loss on the transaction was then ascertained. This form of transaction constituted in the opinion of the Commissioners nothing more nor less than gambling in differences.

7. During the material years the appellant entered into speculative transactions on his own behalf in future delivery contracts without any intention of taking up actual cotton, or of using the contracts as hedges for actual cotton transactions. His partners had knowledge of, but no interest in, these transactions. Nearly all the transactions were done through the appellant's own firm, which, except in the last year, charged him brokerage on buying or selling the contracts. These transactions differed from the speculative transactions entered into by the arrivals salesman of the firm, as the appellant's transactions were generally open for more or less lengthy periods, while the firm's speculative transactions were invariably closed on the same day.

Comments

Not all commodities are suitable for trade on futures markets.

ENCYCLOPAEDIA BRITANNICA CD (PRIMARY COMMODITY MARKETS: OPERATION OF THE MARKET)

The great bulk of commodity trading is in contracts for future delivery. **1–041** The purpose of trading in futures is either to insure against the risk of price changes (hedging) or to make a profit by speculating on the price trend. If a speculator believes that prices will rise, he buys a futures contract and sells it when he wishes (*e.g.*, at a more distant delivery date). The speculator either gains (if prices have risen) or loses (if they have fallen), the difference being due to the change in price.

"Hedging" means the offsetting of commitments in the market in actuals by futures contracts. A producer who buys a commodity at spot (current) prices but does not normally resell until three months later can insure himself against a decline in prices by selling futures: if prices fall he loses on his inventories but can purchase at a lower price; if prices rise he gains on his inventories but loses on his futures sales. Since price movements in the actuals market and the futures market are closely related, the loss (or gain) in actual transactions will normally be offset by a comparable gain (or loss) in the futures market.

The operation of futures markets requires commodities of uniform quality grades in order that transactions may take place without the buyer having to inspect the commodities themselves. This explains why there is no futures market, for example, in tobacco, which varies too much in quality. A steady, unfluctuating supply also is needed; this is referred to technically as "low elasticity of supply," meaning that the amount of a commodity that producers supply to the market is not much affected by the price at which they are able to sell the commodity. If supply could be adjusted relatively quickly to changes in demand, speculation would become too difficult and risky because exceptionally high or low prices, from which speculators are able to profit, are eliminated as soon as supply is adjusted. Monopolistic control of demand and supply is also unfavourable to the operation of a futures market because price is subject to a large extent to the control of the monopolist and is thus unlikely to fluctuate sufficiently to provide the speculator with an opportunity for making profits. There is, for example, no market in diamonds, because there is only one marketing cooperative. In 1966 the London market in shellac ceased to function after the Indian government applied control of exporters' prices at the source.

Before World War II London was the centre of international trade in primary goods, but New York City has become at least as important. It is in these two cities that the international prices of many primary products are determined. Although New York often has the bigger market, many producers prefer the London market because of the large fluctuations in local demand in the United States that influence New York market prices. In some cases international commodity agreements have reduced the significance of certain commodity markets.

There are markets in both New York and London for numerous primary goods, including cotton, copper, cocoa, sugar, rubber, coffee, wool and wooltops, tin, silver, and wheat. Tea, wool, and furs are auctioned in London, but in the case of many other commodities, auctions have been superseded by private sales. In London the metal market is much more a "spot" or delivery market than other futures markets. Many countries have their own markets: Australia for wool, Sri Lanka and India for tea, and Malaysia for rubber and tin.[81a]

(iii) *Relationship Between Physical and Futures Markets*

1–042   C.i.f. and f.o.b. contracts for bulk commodities, then, are delivery contracts "to arrive", and not true futures contacts. There is, however, a relationship between physical and futures markets. In particular, a trader who is left long in the physical market can sell into the futures market, as occurred in the following case.

[81a] Copyright 1994–1998 Encyclopaedia Britannica.

GEBRUDER METELMANN GMBH & CO KG v NBR (LONDON) LTD

Court of Appeal. [1984] 1 Lloyd's Rep. 614

Facts and issues:

The case arose from the breach, on a falling market, of an f.o.b. contract   **1–043**
for 2,000 tons of sugar, by N.B.R. (the buyers). At first instance N.B.R.
denied the existence of the contract, but Mustill J. found against them,
and there was no appeal on that issue. The issue in the Court of Appeal
was whether it was reasonable for Metalmann, as innocent sellers, to
mitigate their loss by selling on the sugar futures (or "terminal" market),
rather than the physical market for sugar. The Court of Appeal held that
it was.

MUSTILL J.: *(at first instance)* [MUSTILL J. having found the defendant   **1–044**
buyers liable for breach of contract, continued on the quantum (footnotes
are added):] By way of introduction, it is convenient to say something
about the world market in sugar: There are two relevant markets in which
transactions are effected for the sale and purchase of sugar. First, there is
the "physicals" market. This is not a market in the sense of being a place
where bargains are made, but is a general description of transactions
which are being made all the time for sales of sugar by sellers, to
identified buyers, the parties intending that the contracts shall be performed by physical delivery of the sugar, and payment of the price.
Second, there is the "terminal" market. Here there are market organizations, through which transactions are made—such as the Paris and London exchanges. Here A. does not sell to B., intending that when the due
date arrives he will deliver sugar to B. Instead, A. makes a contract with
a broker for the sale of a stipulated quantity, ostensibly calling for delivery on a future date. In reality, it is not contemplated that A. will make
delivery to anyone—either the broker or a buyer. Instead, all concerned in
the transaction know that before the due date A. will close out his "short"
position by making a purchase of an equal quantity for the same delivery
date. Conversely, a person B. on the opposite side of the market who has
purchased a quantity for delivery at a future date will close his "long"
position, by making an equivalent sale.[82] On the face of the contract, and
perhaps in law—it does not matter for present purposes—the parties can
insist on actual performance. But in reality this does not happen. Buyers
and sellers are not matched: the traders are dealing with the market, not
with other traders; the sugar and the price do not change hands; and the
profit is made, not by purchase and onward sale (as in the physicals
market) but by sale and repurchase. Essentially, the traders are dealing in
differences.

[82] Sellers sell short and buyers buy long. A party with purchases exceeding sales is therefore
left long, which was Metalmann's position after the failure of the disputes f.o.b. sale
contract.

Since the physicals and terminal markets are concerned with sales of the same commodity, the prices ruling in the two markets on any particular date, in respect of contracts for delivery at a given future date, will follow the same general trend. But they will not necessarily be identical. Moreover, it is to some extent misleading to speak of "prices ruling". Although the London and Paris markets do publish "daily prices" these are fixed by the authorities quite early in the day by reference to recent transactions. The sugar futures market is extremely volatile, and may change by tens of dollars within a single day, so that the quoted price may bear only a distant relation to the price at which bargains are being struck even in the same market, later in the same day. Still less will they be closely connected with the price at which a transaction in physical sugar is effected at some time on the day in question. Comparisons between prices are also made more difficult by the fact that if the prices are reduced to (say) a common U.S. dollar basis, they will be affected by changes in the parities of the U.S. dollar, the pound sterling and the French franc.

One further comment should be made. Some confusion arose during the trial from the use of the words "spot" or "prompt" to describe the prices fixed by the authorities in the London and Paris markets. These are not prices for immediate delivery, but for delivery (as I understood the evidence) at any time up to the end of the following month. To avoid misunderstanding I will call the price fixed by the authorities as "daily price".

Against this background I turn to the present dispute. The problem arises from the fact that the contract sued upon, and the contract effected in mitigation, were made in different markets.

The contract sued upon, which I have held was made on Dec. 1, 1980, was a "physicals" contract.[83] It was made between an identified buyer and an identified seller. The intention was that Metelmann would procure sugar, transport it to the port of shipment, cause it to be shipped within the shipment period, transfer the shipping documents to N.B.R., and obtain payment of the price.

The contract made in mitigation was of a different character. As I have said, on Jan. 21, 1981, Metelmann by telex accepted N.B.R.'s conduct as a wrongful repudiation of the contract. At or about the time when they sent this telex—the precise moment can no longer be ascertained—they effected a sale on the Paris terminals market for the May, 1981, position. When making this contract, it was not contemplated by Metelmann that it would ever be consummated by physical delivery. Essentially, it was intended as a device to freeze the loss on what was believed to be a falling market.

The reason why a forward sale will, in many circumstances, act as a stop-loss transaction where a physical sale has gone awry may be illustrated by the following example. Imagine that a seller has made a forward

[83] For shipment in January 1981.

sale of 200 tons of a commodity for June delivery, at a price of $100 per ton. Imagine also that the sale goes wrong, and that the seller has to retain the goods until he disposes of them in (say) March, at the then current market price of $80 per ton, thus making a loss of $4000. Assume now that at the moment when the original sale goes off the seller makes another sale in the futures market for March delivery at $95 per ton. When March arrives, he can buy back his futures contract at the ruling market price of $80 per ton, making a profit of $15 per ton, or $3000, which does to diminish his loss in respect of the goods themselves. By making his futures sale, he has held his loss at $5 per ton, and the loss will remain the same, no matter whether the market falls to $80 per ton, or $60 or any other figure.

This is of course a great oversimplification. The practice is much more complicated than the theory. Nevertheless, in principle a short sale will act as a hedge against a fall in the market, to protect a long physical position; and it was to hold the loss at the market price as it stood on the date of repudiation that Mr Robertson sold against N.B.R. on the Paris terminal market

. . .

Certain facts can be stated with reasonable confidence. In order not to   **1–045** prolong still further an already lengthy judgment, I will simply state the following findings without analysing the evidence on which they are based:

(1) The sugar market had been in the course of a rapid decline for several weeks at the time when N.B.R. repudiated the contract. It had reached a high point of about U.S. $1000 during the previous November, but had then turned downhill. From time to time there were brief recoveries, but the overall trend was consistently downwards.

(2) A reasonable person in the position of Mr Robertson [of Metelmann] would have concluded that the adverse trend would continue, although such a person could also anticipate that there might be occasional brief rallies.

(3) There was in fact a brief rally just after Jan. 21. This may be illustrated by taking the dollar equivalent of the French daily prices for the trading days beginning Jan. 21 and ending Jan. 30—635.15; 682.45; 694.30; 723.99; 736.04; 700.10; 695.89; 668.04.

(4) Although it could be foreseen that a brief rally might occur, there was no way in which Mr Robertson could have predicted that one would actually occur during the few days following Jan. 21.

(5) Mr Robertson never gave more than momentary consideration (if that) to the possibility of finding a buyer who needed 2000 tonnes of sugar for physical delivery f.o.b. Hamburg or Antwerp during

the remaining 10 days of January, 1981. His reflex action as a trader was to make a stop-loss sale in the terminal market. Whether a buyer for immediate delivery of physical sugar could have been found cannot be precisely ascertained on the evidence, but I think it legitimate to infer that such a sale was an unlikely prospect, and that if Metelmann had been lucky enough to find a buyer, the fact that the sale was obviously being made on a distress basis would have pushed the price to a discount of perhaps $20 per tonne by comparison with the daily price.

(6) Metelmann could probably "within a week" have found a buyer for 2000 tonnes of sugar for delivery at some more distant date: say February or the first half of March, 1981. Towards the end of the trial doubts were expressed as to what Mr Robertson meant when he used the expression "within a week". In my judgment, he intended to convey that a sale of physical sugar might have taken a week, or it might have taken less.

(7) At the material time, sales of physical sugar were being effected for forward positions at prices which were generally (though apparently not always) at a premium by comparison with the prices obtainable for the same contract position in the Paris terminal market.

(8) At the material time, the prices obtainable on the Paris terminal market in respect of sales for the March position stood at a premium by comparison with sales for the May position.

(9) Notwithstanding that a sale for March offered a better price than a sale for May, Mr Robertson chose to effect his stop-loss sale for May rather than March. It is sufficient to say, without going into detail, that he did so because there was less risk, in relation to a sale for the May position, that Metelmann would find themselves squeezed into paying a high price for the repurchase which would in due course close out their short sale.

I now turn to the . . . intended source and the ultimate fate of the goods which had been sold to N.B.R. When the trial began, the plaintiffs were asserting that the intended source was a contract dated Dec. 4, 1980, whereby they had bought from Nordeutschezuker G.m.b.H. & Co ("Nordzuker") a quantity of 12,000 tonnes for delivery between January and June, 1981. If this had indeed been the intended source, it should have been possible to discover whether, for example, the goods intended for delivery to N.B.R. were already in the port of shipment on Jan. 21, and were subsequently utilized to fulfil a contract with some other buyer when the sale with N.B.R. fell through; or whether the goods remained at Nordzuker's factory until they were brought down to the port and delivered to another of Metelmann's buyers; or whether the contract with Nordzuker simply remained unfufilled as regards 2000 tonnes. It soon became clear, however, that no such investigation could be based on the evidence available at the trial. The contract of Dec. 4 was only one of dozens made with Nordzuker during 1981, and Metelmann also bought large quantities from other sellers, so that no supplier and no contract could be identified as the origin of the goods to be delivered. By the same token, no goods were ever earmarked as those to be delivered to N.B.R., so that it is impossible to investigate when, where, to whom and at what price "the contract goods" were ultimately delivered. In my judgment, the only legitimate assumption upon which to approach the computation of damages—and this was an assumption with which Mr Robertson ultimately agreed—is that because of N.B.R.'s default the total quantity of sugar received by Metelmann from its suppliers, and the total quantity delivered to its buyers, were each reduced by 2000 tonnes.

Comments

1. The Court of Appeal disagreed with Mustill J.'s view that Metelmann's **1–046** decision to sell on the "terminal" market, for a (theoretical) May delivery was unreasonable mitigation. In the view of the Court of Appeal, this was a perfectly reasonable method of protecting against an expected market fall. In fact, a sale on the physical market would have obtained a better price, but only because of a temporary and unforseeable market rise, at the end of January.

2. The "terminal" market was being used by Metelmann not for speculation, but to hedge against the expected market fall. The price obtained on the January sale, though for a May delivery, would have been related to the January physical price. Usually, a trader using the "terminal" market to hedge by selling in January would close out by purchasing the equivalent quantity in May. If the market had fallen, the May price ought to be lower than the January, giving a profit on the "terminal" market, approximately offsetting any loss caused by the falling price on the physical market. In the particular case, there would be no later repurchase, since the breach by N.B.R. had left Metelmann long, *i.e.* with more sugar than required to fulfil its other sale contracts.

3. The f.o.b. contract was on the physical, not the "terminal" market. The contract presupposed an actual delivery, and would not normally be closed out. It seems to have been suggested that it would be satisfied out of a larger cargo (12,000 tons) of sugar purchased previously. In that event there would have been at least one resale, and the larger shipment would have been split, presumably between several buyers. It is common with contracts of this type for there to be at least one resale, for large cargoes to be split up, and for the particular cargo not to have been identified at the time the resale contract is made.

4. Though it is not normally intended for contracts on the physical market to be closed out, it can happen, as in *The Filipinas I* and *Garnac Grain*, above, in neither of which were any goods actually shipped.

(iv) *Bulk Oil*

Oil shares some, but not all, the features of trade in foodstuffs. The bulk oil **1–047** trade is not a free market,[84] but although OPEC sellers (producers) operate a cartel, they do not have a monopoly; moreover, the purchasers (refiners) are not altogether without power, and prices fluctuate quite rapidly. Unlike grain and foodstuffs, both importers and exporters will usually be able to deal with entire

[84] Lipsey & Crystal instance OPEC as a classic example of a cartel see n. 54, above.

tanker loads of cargo, so the problem of splitting cargoes does not arise. However, many contracts are for the sale of more than one shipment, so some organisation of cargoes is required.[85] There are also usually margins as to quantities supplied, to enable flexibility in shipping arrangements.[86]

Until about 30 years ago the major oil companies ("majors"), as purchasers, were able fairly successfully to secure supplies with long-term contracts, and presumably because, in a time of surplus supplies,[87] buyers were able to determine prices, there was no futures market, nor any great degree of speculation. This era ended with the Yom Kippur war and OPEC crisis of 1973.[88] Since then, and more particularly since the Gulf war beginning in 1979 (Iran against Iraq), power shifted to the producers. They refused to contract on a long-term basis, and the spot market, which has been very unstable at times, came to predominate. For a time, at least, oil prices rose very rapidly. This, and the general disorganisation of the market since 1973, attracted independent oil companies as intermediaries. To a large extent these seem to have become necessary for the operation of a disorganised market, but no doubt there have also been speculative opportunities. Stopford observes (at p. 309) that:

> "as the oil market has become more volatile the prominence of oil traders, who act as intermediary between the producer and the refinery, has become more prominent. They now often own the oil during shipment and because their interests are very different from those of the traditional oil majors, this has altered the supply side of the business."

As with bulk dry cargo trades, most of the intermediaries have no oil storage facilities. Moreover, the need to use the physical market for hedging and speculation was exacerbated by the late development of a fully-fledged futures market in bulk oil,[89] and continues where price fluctuations are particularly rapid.

There is a description in *The Al Hofuf*, in chapter 3, below, where a circle of f.o.b. oil sales developed.

(v) *Some Conclusions on Commodity Contracts*

1–048   It is clear, then, that bulk commodity contracts differ in important respects from many other sale contracts. Although, unlike with a fully-fledged futures market, it is usually envisaged that goods will be shipped from a port of loading to port of discharge,[90] they may be bought and re-sold by many intermediaries, none of whom have the intention, or indeed the capability, of taking the goods themselves. For bulk dry cargo, the intermediaries are necessary for the collection and distribution of the cargo, and intermediaries have also become essential to the operation of the oil market. On volatile markets, the intermediaries may also engage in speculation, although fully-fledged futures markets are generally better suited for this function.

---

[85] *e.g. The Delfini* [1990] 1 Lloyds Rep. 252 (see para. 5—066, below).
[86] In *The Al Hofuf* [1981] 1 Lloyd's Rep. 81, discussed further in Ch. 3, below, the total quantity was 40,000 tonnes of gas oil plus or minus 10 per cent in buyers' option, giving considerable flexibility to the buyers.
[87] The USA maintained its own emergency reserves.
[88] At any rate crisis from a Western viewpoint; presumably producers saw it differently.
[89] The International Petroleum Exchange was incorporated only in 1980, and oil is now the most heavily traded cash commodity in the world: see Clarke, *op. cit.*, at pp. 95 and 97. See in general on these developments Daniel Yergin, *The Prize*, (Touchstone, 1991), especially Pt V.
[90] Since even with circles, it is unusual for them to be formed deliberately.

Commodity sales therefore commonly involve long chains of re-sales, some-times as many as 50 or even 100 in the case of bulk oil.[91] This is only possible because physical delivery is to the ship, not to the port of discharge; this is why the c.i.f. contract, rather than the ex-ship, finds favour where multiple re-sales are envisaged. Once the cargo has been loaded and the shipping documents obtained, all further transactions can be performed by transfer of documents alone, there being no further need to investigate the goods. Bulk commodity shipments still account for nearly three-quarters of the total world tonnage, so it is not surprising that whereas a very large proportion of the world's shipping tonnage is carried c.i.f., relatively small proportions are carried ex-ship.

As has been seen, f.o.b. contracts, as well as c.i.f., may be used in chains and circles. Where the f.o.b. contract is being used for domestic supply,[92] as in *Brandt v Morris*, in chapter 3, below, there will inevitably be at least one further sale, for the export of the goods (another example is the *Kwei Tek Chao* case in chapter 7, below, where the c.i.f. sale in the case was preceded by an f.o.b. supply contract). Alternatively, a buyer under a true f.o.b. export sale may sell on, on c.i.f. terms (*e.g. The Rio Sun*, in chapter 2, below; *The Albazero*, in chapters 5 and 13, below). But f.o.b. contracts themselves can be used back to back in re-sales (*e.g. The Sevonia Team*, in chapter 3, below; *The Filipinas I* [1973] 1 Lloyd's Rep. 349, above); this is especially appropriate where it is intended that the ultimate receiver pay the freight (the eventual result in *The Sevonia Team*). In *The Filipinas I*, the buyer in each case was responsible for securing tonnage, and this was effected for the successive re-sales by sub-chartering the same vessel.

So by contrast with the early cases, most modern decisions on c.i.f. and f.o.b. contracts involve chain sales, or even circles. The development of the law, the contractual aspects of which are said to give effect to the intentions of the parties, has been affected by the existence of these chains and circles. Other developments might be desirable, and the parties themselves need to be mindful of this commer-cial reality. These issues are all examined in chapter 15. Long chains also exacer-bate the problem in the next section.

(b) Retreat from Traditional Documentation

It is clear from the discussion at the start of this chapter that the development **1–049** of the c.i.f. contract, and also modern varieties of f.o.b., depended upon con-structive delivery being made by transfer of documents. This presupposes that the documents arrive before the goods. Today, however, this can no longer always be assumed.

Containerised and manufactured goods are not normally resold on the voyage, but the increased speed of modern vessels can again cause problems, given that there has been no commensurate increase in the speed of airmail. The goods may

---

[91] In a paper given to a conference organised by Legal Studies and Services Ltd, "Bills of Lading: Changes to the English Law and the Commercial Implications", April 2 and 3, 1990, Brian Davenport Q.C. noted of oil cargoes: "The chains may be long. A banker once told me that he had seen a chain of 104 buyers." In a later paper given to a conference organised by the same group, "Carriage of Goods by Sea Act 1992: The Practical and Legal Implications", February 11, 1993, he notes that this is also a relatively recent phenomenon. Comparing the present day to 1960, he observes that: " . . . the mineral oil trade . . . was carried out very differently from today. The world's oil industry was dominated by the seven largest oil companies. There was no oil trading as we all know it today: if there were sales outside the group at all, they were only from one major to another."
A similar pattern can be seen in bulk commodity sales. In *Scandinavian Trading Co A/B v Zodiac Petroleum SA and William Hudson Ltd (The Al Hofuf)* [1981] 1 Lloyd's Rep. 81, Mocatta J. observed that strings are especially common in sales of soya beans (the cargo in *Bunge v Tradax*).
[92] See also nn. 19 and 21, above.

still arrive before the documents, but at any rate if finance by documentary credit is not required, there is no need for negotiable documentation to be used in this type of trade. The problems here are relatively easily solved, by using waybills and other documentation discussed in chapters 6 and 15, below. However, the traditional c.i.f. and f.o.b. contracts are no longer really suitable for this type of trade. Some alternatives are examined in chapter 15, below.

Even with bulk commodities, the traditional documentation is no longer ideal. Part of the problem is caused by the long chains, particularly where voyages are relatively short, and each transaction is financed by a documentary credit, necessitating checking of the documents by each of the banks involved. In *The Delfini*, a case involving the carriage of oil considered further in chapter 5, below, Purchas L.J. observed that:

> " . . . in the modern conditions prevailing in the shipment not only of oil cargoes but perhaps also other bulk cargoes, and where there is a string of sellers and buyers and a short journey between loading and delivery it is frequently the case that the ship arrives at the port of discharge before any of the shipping documents, including the original bills of lading, find their way down the chain into the hands of the ultimate purchaser to whom the delivery of the cargo is to be made. Thus it is that the procedure of issuing letters of indemnity of the kind issued in this case has grown up so as to enable the discharge of the cargo to take place with expedition and to avoid delaying the ship until the arrival of the formal documents."

The consequences of the carrier delivering without production of an original bill of lading, which are considered in chapter 6, below, can be serious, and to date no very satisfactory solution to this problem has been implemented.[93] Electronic documentation, considered in chapter 16, below, may be the answer.

Another problem in the dry cargo bulk trade, especially in foodstuffs, is that (as described above) the cargo frequently needs to be split between a number of buyers. Bills of lading are not always suitable for this, and delivery orders do not always provide the parties with adequate security. See further *The Julia*, described in chapter 2, below, and also the discussion in chapter 4, below.

Sometimes it is argued that the law should be changed to accommodate the parties' trading practices. This was done with the enactment of the Carriage of Goods by Sea Act 1992, considered in chapter 13, below. Legislation might also be desirable to facilitate the operation of electronic bills of lading, considered in chapter 16, below. However, where a group of traders asks effectively for the law to accord them special treatment, it is legitimate to ask whether they could resolve any problems by altering their trading practices, or if not, whether their trading practices are so beneficial to society as to require the special protection of the law. Many may question, for example, whether the law should be changed to encourage speculation in bulk commodity markets, especially where a fully-developed futures market exists, alongside the physical market. On the other hand, intermediaries, especially for dry cargo, are necessary for the physical trade to run efficiently at all, and there are some commodities (*e.g.* tobacco) for which a futures

---

[93] In *The Delfini* the cargo was delivered against a letter of indemnity. Payment was by standby letter credit, which did not require the bill of lading to be tendered. It is difficult to see that the bill of lading can be performing any of the functions described above in *The Delfini*, or in cases such as *The Filiatra Legacy*, for example, both analysed further in paras 5—066, et seq., below.

market would be impracticable. There might therefore be a case, even for legislation to protect trade in the physical bulk commodity trade.

(c) SUMMARY OF ADVANTAGES AND DISADVANTAGES OF TRADITIONAL BILL OF LADING

Central to the story of international trade law, over the last thirty years or so, **1–050**
has been the actual or proposed replacement of the traditional shipped bill of
lading with alternative documentation. Much of that story, which is ongoing, is
covered in this book, and in particular in chapter 15, below. In summary, however,
the bill of lading is useful:

(a) Where a number of re-sales are contemplated. For the most part this affects
only bulk oil and dry-cargo commodity sales (which however continue to
account for nearly three quarters of the world's tonnage).

(b) In any other case where the seller needs the security of a document of
title.

(c) Where payment is by documentary credit.

The bill of lading is not so useful where:

(a) The goods not re-sold during transit (especially container shipments). If
there is also no problem about payment, for example in the case of sales to
another branch of a multi-national company, or an associated company,
then a bill of lading is not needed, and indeed is often not used.

(b) The bill of lading will not reach the consignee before the goods arrive at
their destination. Particular problems include:

(i) Fast ships on short (*e.g.* North Atlantic container) voyages. Non-negotiable waybills are usually used instead.
(ii) Oil cargoes and bulk dry cargo commodities (because of the number of
re-sales). No satisfactory solution has yet appeared, but the developments described in chapter 16 could bear fruit eventually, should the
trading parties so choose.

(c) The bill of lading is also a port-to-port document, and is not well-suited to
modern multimodal forms of transport.

(d) FRAUD

Fraud is not a modern problem as such, but it is a fairly major modern industry. **1–051**
It will become apparent at various places in the book that the law and practice of
international trade has developed to protect traders against the consequences of
the bankruptcy, but not the fraud of the other parties with whom they deal. As
Bowen L.J. observed in *Sanders v Maclean* (on the issue of original bills of lading
in triplicate)[94]:

"The object of mercantile usages is to prevent the risk of insolvency, not of
fraud; and anyone who attempts to follow and understand the law merchant
will soon find himself lost if he begins by assuming that merchants conduct
their business on the basis of attempting to insure themselves against fraudulent dealing. The contrary is the case. Credit, not distrust, is the basis of

---

[94] (1883) 11 Q.B.D. 327 at 343.

commercial dealings; mercantile genius consists principally in knowing whom to trust and with whom to deal, and commercial intercourse and communication is no more based on the supposition of fraud than it is on the supposition of forgery".

Similar sentiments can be found in *The Future Express*, and in Willes J.'s judgment in *Barber v Meyerstein*[95]:

"all arguments founded upon the notion that the Court is to pronounce a judgment in this case which will protect those who deal with fraudulent people, are altogether beside the facts of this case, and foreign from transactions of this nature."

Generally then, international law and trading practices protect the parties against the insolvency, but not the fraud, of other trading parties. An unusual exception is *Motis Exports*, discussed in chapter 6, below.

---

[95] (1870) L.R. 4 H.L. 317.

PART B

THE CONTRACT OF SALE

C.I.F. CONTRACTS AND VARIATIONS: RIGHTS AND DUTIES OF THE PARTIES

(1) GENERAL OBSERVATIONS ON CONTRACTS OF SALE

(a) ROLE OF THE SALE CONTRACT IN INTERNATIONAL TRADE

THE sale contract is central to international trade transactions, because it allocates **2–001** the responsibility for entering into carriage and insurance contracts, and determines the terms upon which those contracts, and any contract with a financing bank, are to be entered. Though the sale contract cannot directly affect the terms of any other contract made (or vice versa), it stipulates the terms on which third party contracts are to be entered, so that the sale contract may be broken if contracts with third parties are entered into on different terms. Thus, where payment is by documentary credit,[1] the sale contract determines the type and terms of the credit which must be provided.

In this chapter and chapter 3, below the rights and obligations of seller and buyer, under the main international sale contracts, are covered in general terms. Property and risk (and related issues) are covered in the following two chapters (4 and 5). The parties also have obligations in respect of the shipping documents, and there is a correlation between these duties and duties by and towards banks where payment is by commercial credit. Issues arising from shipping documents can be quite complex, and the subject deserves a chapter of its own.[2]

(b) COMMON LAW DEFINITIONS—SOME GENERAL CONSIDERATIONS

The common law definitions of trade terms, such as c.i.f., or f.o.b., may be **2–002** regarded as convenient shorthand, from which various consequences follow; indeed, in the extreme case, as long as the goods are identified, a sale contract "f.o.b. London" (where London is the port of loading) or "c.i.f. London" (where London is the port of discharge), ought in principle to be enforceable. If the parties have not filled out more precisely their contractual rights and liabilities, the courts can do it for them, on the basis of presumptions.[3]

For the reasons considered in chapter 15, however, international sales are rarely made simply on f.o.b. or c.i.f. terms, but typically make detailed provision for the responsibilities of the parties. There is a variety of standard forms in use, or the parties may adopt trade terms, such as Incoterms 2000. The standard common law c.i.f. or f.o.b. contract may therefore be comparatively rare. As Roskill L.J. observed in *The Albazero*[4]:

---

[1] See further Chs 8 and 9, below.
[2] See Ch. 6, below (and see also Ch. 7, below for the remedies).
[3] There is fairly full discussion at least of the f.o.b. presumptions, below. For c.i.f., see also Ch. 6 (on documents), below.
[4] [1975] 3 W.L.R. 491, 523. See also paras 5—063 and 13—038, below for full coverage of this case.

"It is a trite observation that what is sometimes called a true f.o.b. or a true c.i.f. contract is a comparative commercial rarity. Contracts vary infinitely according to the wishes of the parties to them. Though a contract may include the letters f.o.b. or c.i.f. amongst its terms, it may well be that other terms of the contract clearly show that the use of those letters is intended to do no more than show where the incidence of liability for freight or insurance will lie as between buyer and seller but is not to denote the mode of performance of the sellers' obligations to the buyer or of the buyer's obligations to the seller."

He continued, specifically on property issues, which are considered in detail in chapter 5, below.[5]

2–003   In spite of Roskill L.J.'s observations, the common law definitions still have a role to play, both as shorthand, and to fill out the terms which are not covered by the detailed agreement, since it is very unlikely that the detailed agreement will cover everything. Incoterms 2000, for example, sets out the duties of seller and buyer in considerable detail, but none of its terms would resolve the problems over property considered in chapter 5, nor indeed, the questions over rejection of documentation considered in Chapter 7.[6] Even the more detailed standard forms, such as G.A.F.T.A. 100,[7] do not deal with the timing of the passing of property.

Thus, however detailed the terms of the contract, it is assumed that certain consequences are intended to follow from the designation of a contract as, *e.g.* c.i.f., or f.o.b., and the courts give effect to the intention of the parties as far as they can. Difficulties can obviously arise where there is a conflict between the designation, *e.g.* c.i.f., and the remainder of the terms, in which case the courts have to interpret the contract as best they can. Sometimes, terms which are inconsistent with the designation are struck out,[8] but it may be possible to interpret them so as to be consistent with the designation.[9] No doubt, the second approach is more likely to accord with the intentions of the parties than the first, but if the parties have expressed inconsistent intentions within the same document, it is obviously more difficult to give effect to (or indeed to determine) their wishes. Where neither of these is possible, the designation itself may have to give. Thus, even if a contract is expressed on its face to be, *e.g.* c.i.f., that is not necessarily conclusive. In *The Julia*,[10] the House of Lords held that a contract which purported to be c.i.f. was in fact an ex-ship contract. The outcome of the case depended on this, since the rules as to risk which apply to c.i.f. contracts (on which, see further chapter 4,

---

[5] The case was reversed on other grounds [1977] A.C. 774; see para. 13—038, below.

[6] It may also be worth observing that the trade terms in Incoterms were themselves based on the common law definitions, since the purpose of the I.C.C. was to standardise and codify, rather than change the law. Incoterms, and other attempts at standardisation and unification, are discussed in Ch. 15, below.

[7] The Grain and Feed Trade Association standard form c.i.f. contract for feedingstuffs in bulk.

[8] In *Gill & Duffus SA v Berger & Co Inc.* [1984] A.C. 382, [1984] 2 W.L.R. 95, [1984] 1 Lloyd's Rep. 227, under a contract described as c.i.f., one of the shipping documents required was a quality certificate on discharge. The first tender included no such document, but the buyers were held not to be entitled to reject the tender, the implication being that a c.i.f. contract could not stipulate the tender of such a document; see further paras 6—102 *et seq.*, below. See also *Law and Bonar Ltd v British American Tobacco Ltd* [1916] 2 K.B. 605, covered in para. 4—027, below. For f.o.b., the delivery term in *Frebold and Sturznickel (Trading as Panda OHG) v Circle Products Ltd* [1970] 1 Lloyd's Rep. 499 (in para. 3—052 below) was interpreted so as to be consistent with the f.o.b. designation.

[9] *Vitol SA v Esso Australia Ltd (The Wise)* [1989] 1 Lloyd's Rep. 96, reversed on other grounds [1989] 2 Lloyd's Rep. 451, CA.

[10] *Comptoir d'Achat et de Vente du Boerenbond Belge SA v Luis de Ridder Limitada (The Julia)* [1949] A.C. 293 (see further below). See also *C.E.P. Interagra SA v Select Energy Trading GmbH (The Jambur)* L.M.L.N. 289 (also below), where insufficient weight was (arguably) placed by the court on the c.i.f. designation.

below) were held inapplicable. The result arguably fails to accord proper weight to the parties' designation of the contract as c.i.f., but only because there are inconsistent terms elsewhere in the contract, making it difficult to ascertain their overall intention.[11]

(2) c.i.f. Contracts and Variations Thereon: Basic Definition

The c.i.f. contract represents the logical conclusion of the developments con-   **2–004**
sidered in chapter 1, above. Under a c.i.f. contract, the seller always undertakes to secure shipping space, make all the shipping arrangements, ship the goods and make the carriage contract as principal (or purchase goods which have already been shipped), and secure insurance. Freight and insurance are included in the price; it follows that fluctuations in rates fall upon the seller, not the buyer. In all these respects, the c.i.f. contract differs from the original f.o.b. contract, as described by Sassoon in the article at the start of the chapter.

Nonetheless, the c.i.f. contract developed from the f.o.b., and retains some of its features. As with the f.o.b. contract, delivery of the goods themselves is to the vessel, and risk transfers from the seller to the buyer at that point. It follows that, as with the f.o.b. contract, the seller is obliged to ship goods which accord with the contractual description, and bear all the costs up to that point.

There are, however, two stages to delivery in a c.i.f. contract. It is completed by transfer of documents, which transfer to the buyer, while the goods are at sea, constructive possession, or the right to take them from the vessel on arrival. In *Sharpe v Nosawa* [1917] 2 K.B. 814, Atkin J. (at 818) termed this "constructive delivery." Physical delivery is not postponed until the goods arrive, unlike an ex-ship contract, and the c.i.f. seller does not undertake to ensure that the goods arrive at their eventual destination.

It is also possible to purchase and sell goods which are already afloat, on c.i.f. terms (see the extract from *Ross T. Smyth v Bailey*, below). In that case the seller need not ship the goods himself, but can tender documents representing goods already shipped, of the contract description.

The common law definition of the term had become established by early in the twentieth century, the following being among the authorities.

TREGELLES v SEWELL

Court of Exchequer. (1862) 7 H. & N. 574; 158 E.R. 600

Decision:

The contract was for 300 tons of rails, delivered at Harburgh, c.f. & i., and   **2–005**
the court held that the seller did not undertake to deliver the rails at Harburgh, but to put in on board a ship bound for Harburgh and hand to the buyer a policy of insurance and other documents, after which his liability ceased and the goods were at the risk of the purchaser.

[11] In *The Parchim* [1918] A.C. 157, the contract between the German and the Dutch company was described as c.i.f., but Lord Parker of Waddington, having concluded that neither freight nor insurance were included in the price, said (at 164): "the price is really for cost only, and the contract has far more of the characteristics of a contract f.o.b. Taltal than it has of a contract c.i.f. European port." It is not clear whether anything turned on this, but property was certainly held to pass earlier than would be usual under a c.i.f. contract, and no effect was given to the description of the contract as c.i.f. See further para. 5—048, below. See also the discussion of *Couturier v Hastie* (1856) 5 H.L.C. 673, in para. 4—046, below.

Note

Pollock C.B. (at 602 of the E.R.) decided the case on the basis that in "the absence of any evidence of what the parties meant, the general principle must prevail, *viz.* that where money is paid under a contract it cannot be recovered back unless it is clear that such was the intention of the parties. Wilde B. also emphasised that payment had been on delivery to the ship. But Martin B. construed the document according to the known practice of merchants, and effectively therefore defines the term "c.f. & i."

Even so, the court is concerned primarily to determine what these particular merchants meant. The common law is not generally well-suited to standardising definitions. This is an issue further addressed in chapter 15, below.

This was the first reported c.i.f. (or c.f. & i.) contract case. It is clear, then, that from the outset it was accepted that delivery was to the vessel, not to the destination port, and that risk passed on shipment. Refinements of this general (and fundamental) position are discussed in chapter 3, below.

IRELAND v LIVINGSTON

House of Lords. (1872) L.R. 5 H.L. 395

2–006   The case concerned the interpretation by an agent of equivocal instructions by the principal, to procure goods on c.i.f. terms, but the main importance of the case lies in the following passage taken from the following observations of Blackburn J. in advising the House of Lords, at 406, 407:

2–007   BLACKBURN J.: The terms at a price, "to cover cost, freight, and insurance, payment by acceptance on receiving shipping documents," are very usual, and are perfectly well understood in practice. The invoice is made out debiting the consignee with the agreed price (or the actual cost and commission, with the premiums of insurance, and the freight, as the case may be), and giving him credit for the amount of the freight which he will have to pay to the shipowner on actual delivery, and for the balance a draft is drawn on the consignee which he is bound to accept (if the shipment be in conformity with his contract) on having handed to him the charterparty, bill of lading, and policy of insurance. Should the ship arrive with the goods on board he will have to pay the freight, which will make up the amount he has engaged to pay. Should the goods not be delivered in consequence of a peril of the sea, he is not called on to pay the freight, and he will recover the amount of his interest in the goods under the policy. If the non-delivery is in consequence of some misconduct on the part of the master or mariners, not covered by the policy, he will recover it from the shipowner. In substance, therefore the consignee pays, though in a different manner, the same price as if the goods had been bought and shipped to him in the ordinary way.

If the consignor is a person who has contracted to supply the goods at an agreed price, to cover cost, freight and insurance, the amount inserted in the invoice is the agreed price, and no commission is charged. In such a case it is obvious that if freight is high, the consignor gets the less for the goods he supplies, if freight is low he gets the more. But inasmuch as he has contracted to supply the goods at this price he is bound to do so, though, owing to the rise in prices at the port of shipment making him pay more for the goods, or of freight causing him to receive less himself, because the shipowner receives more, his bargain may turn out a bad one. On the other hand, if owing to the fall in prices in the port of shipment, or of freight, the bargain is a good one, the consignee still must pay the full agreed price. This results from the contract being one by which the one party binds himself absolutely to supply the goods in a vessel such as is stipulated for, at a fixed price, to be paid for in the customary manner, that is, part by acceptance on receipt of the customary documents, and part by paying the freight on delivery, and the other party binds himself to pay that fixed price. Each party there takes upon himself the risk of the rise or fall in price, and there is no contract of agency or trust between them, and therefore no commission is charged.

Note

The importance of this passage is that it shows how freight and insurance is **2–008** included in the c.i.f. price. More commonly in the nineteenth century than today, freight under the carriage contract was payable on delivery of the goods from the vessel, at the destination port, and consequently would normally be paid, if the goods arrived, by the buyer. The commercial invoice therefore credits the buyer with the freight he will be obliged to pay.

Today, freight is more commonly payable in advance, especially under dry-cargo carriage contracts, and therefore this problem does not arise. In such cases, the seller will obtain the freight, and obtain freight prepaid bills of lading.

Freight is still commonly paid on delivery in the bulk oil trade, however.

The standard definition of the c.i.f. contract is often taken to be that in *Biddell Bros. v E. Clemens Horst Co* (but discussion can also be found in *Manbre Saccharine Co Ltd v Corn Products Co Ltd*, in para. 4—014, below).

BIDDELL BROTHERS v E. CLEMENS HORST CO

[1912] A.C. 18, HL, affirming [1911] 1 K.B. 214 (Hamilton J.) and reversing [1911] 1 K.B. 934, CA

Facts and issues:

A c.i.f. contract also provided for "Terms net cash." The sellers success- **2–009** fully argued that this meant net cash against documents. The buyer unsuccessfully argued that he was not obliged to pay until the goods had arrived at their destination, and a reasonable opportunity had been allowed to him for examination to see if they were in conformity with the contract. The buyer's argument, that the "expression c.i.f. standing alone is merely a means of calculating the price to be paid for the goods by adding together the various items of which the price is composed" and that the "letters c.i.f. have nothing to say to delivery" was rejected.

Hamilton J.'s judgment, which was approved in the House of Lords., contains what may be regarded as the standard definition of the c.i.f. contract:

HAMILTON J.: *(at first instance, reversed in the Court of Appeal but whose decision was reinstated in the House of Lords)* The meaning of a contract of sale upon cost, freight, and insurance terms is so well settled that it is unnecessary to refer to authorities upon the subject. A seller under a contract of sale containing such terms has firstly to ship at the port of shipment goods of the description contained in the contract; secondly to procure a contract of affreightment, under which the goods will be delivered at the destination contemplated by the contract; thirdly to arrange for an insurance upon the terms current in the trade which will be available for the benefit of the buyer; fourthly to make out an invoice as described by Blackburn J. in *Ireland v Livingston* (1872) L.R. 5 H.L. at 406 or in some similar form; and finally to tender these documents to the buyer so that he may know what freight he has to pay and obtain delivery of the goods, if they arrive, or recover for their loss if they are lost on the voyage. Such terms constitute an agreement that the delivery of the goods, provided they are in conformity with the contract, shall be delivery on board ship at the port of shipment. It follows that against tender of these documents, the bill of lading, invoice, and policy of insurance, which completes delivery in accordance with that agreement, the buyer must be ready and willing to pay the price.

KENNEDY L.J.: *(dissenting in the Court of Appeal, but whose views were upheld in the House of Lords)* How is such a tender to be made of goods afloat under a c.i.f. contract? By tender of the bill of lading, accompanied in case the goods have been lost in transit by the policy of insurance. The bill of lading in law and fact represents the goods.

EARL LOREBURN L.C.: *(in the House of Lords)* This is a contract usually called a c.i.f. contract, under which the seller is to ship a cargo of hops and is to contract for freight and to effect insurance; and he is to receive 90s. per 112 lbs. of hops. The buyer is to pay cash. But when is he to pay cash? The contract does not say. The buyer says that he is to pay cash against physical delivery and acceptance of the goods when they have come to England.

Now s.28 of the Sale of Goods Act says in effect that payment is to be against delivery. Accordingly we have supplied by the general law an answer to the question when this cash is to be paid. But when is there a delivery of goods which are on board ship? That may be quite a different thing from delivery of goods on shore. The answer is that delivery of the bill of lading when the goods are at sea can be treated as delivery of the goods themselves, this law being so old that I think it is quite unnecessary to refer to authority for it.

Now in this contract there is no time fixed at which the seller is entitled to tender the bill of lading. He therefore may do so at any reasonable time; and it is wrong to say that he must defer the tender of the bill of lading until the ship has arrived, and it is still more wrong to say that he must defer the tender of the bill of lading until after the goods have been landed, inspected, and accepted.

Notes

There was further elaboration of the c.i.f. seller's duty in Kennedy L.J.'s judg-   **2–010**
ment in the Court of Appeal, in a passage considered in *Manbre Saccharine Co Ltd
v Corn Products Co Ltd* [1919] 1 K.B. 198, in para. 4—014, below.

Hamilton J.'s judgment makes clear that while delivery of the goods is on board
the vessel, the process of delivery is completed by transfer of documents. This
second stage in the delivery process transfers the right to take delivery from the
vessel, or the right to take possession, or constructive possession.

It is, therefore, necessary for the documents to be able to transfer constructive
possession. One of the reasons for the rejection by McCardie J. in *Diamond Alkali
Export Corp. v Fl Bourgeois* [1921] 3 K.B. 443 of the received for shipment bill of
lading as good tender c.i.f. was because the tender of documents is the method by
which the goods are delivered. *Ireland v Livingston* and Hamilton J.'s judgment in
Biddell Bros. v E Clemens Horst Co were among the authorities cited for this
proposition. See further chapter 6, below.

CONCLUSION FROM THE ABOVE CASES

From the above we can see that the c.i.f. term, like the f.o.b. from which it evolved,
implies physical delivery of the goods to the ship, not to the port of discharge,
even where (as in *Tregelles*) the port of discharge is stated in the contract. It is also
clear from the *Ireland v Livingston* that the c.i.f. price covers cost, freight and
insurance, and the seller not the buyer therefore bears the risk of freight and
insurance fluctuations. This is probably the main difference between the c.i.f.
contract and the f.o.b. with additional duties, where freight and insurance, even
if paid by the seller, are for buyer's account.

In summary, then, by saying that in a normal c.i.f. sale, the responsibilities of
the seller are to ship goods which accord with the contract description, to enter
into a contract of carriage, to insure the goods during carriage on terms usual in
the trade, and to tender the shipping documents to the buyer. The shipping
documents must be capable of completing the delivery process, and are described
in detail in chapter 6, below.

ROSS T SMYTH & CO LTD v TD BAILEY SON & CO

House of Lords. [1940] 3 All E.R. 60

The importance of the case, for present purposes, lies in the description of the c.i.f.   **2–011**
contract in Lord Wright's speech.

LORD WRIGHT: The contract in question here is of a type familiar in
commerce, and is described as a c.i.f. contract. The initials indicate that
the price is to include cost, insurance and freight. It is a type of contract
which is more widely and more frequently in use than any other contract
used for purposes of sea-borne commerce. An enormous number of
transactions, in value amounting to untold sums, are carried out every
year under c.i.f. contracts. The essential characteristics of this contract
have often been described. The seller has to ship or acquire after that
shipment the contract goods, as to which, if unascertained, he is generally
required to give a notice of appropriation. On or after shipment, he has to
obtain proper bills of lading and proper policies of insurance. He fulfils
his contract by transferring the bills of lading and the policies to the

buyer. As a general rule, he does so only against payment of the price, less the freight, which the buyer has to pay. In the invoice which accompanies the tender of the documents on the "prompt"—that is, the date fixed for payment—the freight is deducted for this reason.

Notes

1. From this it can again be deduced that:

  (i) freight and insurance are included in the c.i.f. price;

  (ii) where is it envisaged that, under the carriage contract, the buyer will be required to pay the freight, as for example where it is payable on delivery, the freight is deducted from the price in the invoice;

  (iii) delivery is effected by transfer of documents;

  (iv) the seller is entitled to purchase goods already afloat; he is not required to obtain and ship them himself.[12]

2. This case is also of importance for the passing of property, and is considered in more detail in para. 5—056.

Goods must be shipped

HINDLEY & CO LTD v EAST INDIAN PRODUCE CO LTD

Queen's Bench Division (Commercial Court). [1973] 2 Lloyd's Rep. 515

2–012   C. & f. sellers, of 50 tons of Siamese jute, were themselves parties in a string of contracts, and obtained a bill of lading which appeared in all respects proper on its face. They tendered this to the buyers against payment, but it later transpired that no goods had been loaded on board the vessel. The buyers successfully claimed return of the price paid, and damages for breach of contract. The sellers' argument, that the contract was one for the sale of documents or one to be performed by the delivery of documents, was rejected, even though the sellers were not themselves the shippers of the goods.

KERR J.: The sellers' submission can be summarized as follows: They submit that there is no liability because contracts of sale on c.i.f. or c. & f. terms are contracts for the sale of documents or to be performed by the delivery of documents. They point out that the bill of lading was in all respects proper on its face, that they themselves relied on the truth of its contents, and that they had no reasonable or any means of checking the accuracy of its contents.

They also point out—and in my view this must be a crucial limb of their argument—that they were not the shippers of these goods, but merely parties in a string who were on any view unconnected with whatever may have been the circumstances which gave rise to the issue of this bill of lading without any goods having been shipped.

---

[12] This is also arguably a difference between the f.o.b. and c.i.f. contract, but if the varieties of f.o.b. have extended as far as is suggested in s.3.1.3, and the shipping documents can take on the same security function, it is difficult to see why this should not be possible f.o.b. also.

Finally they contend that in the circumstances the buyers have a remedy against the carriers and submit that the buyers should be confined to that remedy and should have no remedy against the sellers, who were on any view innocent of what may have happened.

In my judgment none of these considerations can avail the sellers, and the award in favour of the buyers is correct. The reported cases and textbooks contain many authoritative statements defining or describing the obligations of sellers under c.i.f. or c. & f. contracts. I do not propose to add to these save in so far as is necessary for present purposes. It is sufficient to say that a seller under such contracts has what can broadly be described as a duality of obligations relating respectively to the goods which are the subject-matter of the contract and the documents covering the goods which have to be tendered to the buyer. On the facts of the present case I consider that the sellers are in breach of both these aspects of their obligation.

I will deal first with the aspect relating primarily to the goods. The obligation of the seller under this type of contract is either to ship or to procure the shipment of goods of the contract description under a proper contract of affreightment, and to do so in accordance with any terms of the contract relating to their shipment as regards, for instance, time and place of shipment. Alternatively, the seller's obligation, if he does not himself ship or procure the shipment, is to procure documents—and in this connection one is referring to a bill of lading or a number of bills of lading—which cover such goods so shipped. In either event the obligation of the seller is thereafter to deliver such documents to the buyer.

I need only refer to a few passages which deal with the seller's obligations relating to the goods, but most of these appear to have had in mind the position of sellers who are also the shippers. There is for instance the classic passage in the judgment of Mr. Justice Hamilton (as he then was) in *Biddell Brothers v E Clemens Horst Co* [1911] 1 K.B. 214, at p. 220, where he said:

" . . . A seller under a contract of sale containing such terms [—and he was dealing with a c.i.f. contract—] has firstly to ship at the port of shipment goods of the description contained in the contract; secondly to procure a contract of affreightment, under which the goods will be delivered at the destination contemplated by the contract; thirdly to arrange for an insurance under the terms current in the trade which will be available for the benefit of the buyer; fourthly to make out an invoice . . . and finally to tender these documents to the buyer" [—I am not quoting the passage in full because the further details do not matter—]

That well-known passage was cited with approval by Lord Justice Warrington in *Arnhold Karberg & Co v Blythe, Green, Jourdain & Co* in the Court of Appeal, [1916] 1 K.B. 495, at p. 513. That case and other cases also show that it is an over-simplification to say that a c.i.f. contract is merely a **2–013** contract for the sale of documents. It is, as Lord Justice Bankes put it in that case (at p. 510, with whom Lord Justice Warrington agreed at p. 514) a contract for the sale of goods to be performed by the delivery of documents.

Another passage in which that part of the seller's obligation which relates to the shipment of the goods is stressed is to be found in the speech of Lord Wright in *Ross T Smyth & Co Ltd v TD Bailey, Son & Co* [1940] 3 All E.R. 60, at p. 67; (1940) 67 Ll.L. Rep. 147, at 156. He there said:

[Kerr J. quoted the passage from the case set out above and continued:]

Turning to the text-books, there are only two to which I propose to refer. In what is now vol. 5 of *British Shipping Laws*, dealing with c.i.f. and f.o.b. contracts, one has in the first part an up-dated version of the well-known work of Mr. Justice Kennedy (as he then was), on c.i.f. contracts. In par. 1 on p. 3 of that work one finds the following description of the seller's obligations.

"Under this form of contract the seller performs his obligations by shipping, at the time specified in the contract or, in default of express provision in the contract, within a reasonable time, goods of the contractual description in a ship bound for the destination named in the contract, or by purchasing documents in respect of such goods already afloat, and by tendering to the buyer, as soon as possible after the goods have been destined to him, the shipping documents."

Similarly, in the 17th edition of Scrutton on *Charter-Parties and Bills of Lading*, at p. 173 there is the following note on c.i.f. contracts:

"In a contract for the sale of goods upon 'c.i.f.' terms, the contract, unless otherwise expressed, is for the sale of goods to be carried by sea, and the seller performs his part by shipping goods of the contractual description on board a ship bound to the contractual destination, or purchasing afloat goods so shipped, and tendering, within a reasonable time after shipment, the shipping documents, to the purchaser [—then there should be a comma—] the goods during the voyage being at the risk of the purchaser. . . . "

It follows from all these passages—and is indeed a matter of elementary law—that a c. & f. or c.i.f. contract is to be performed by the tender of documents covering goods which have been shipped either by the seller or by someone else in accordance with the terms of the contract. If no goods have in fact been shipped the sellers have not performed their obligation. I cannot see any basis for the distinction which the sellers here seek to draw between a seller who is also the shipper and a seller who is not the shipper. At the date of the contract it may well be unknown which means of performance the particular seller will employ, and in an ordinary c.i.f. or c. & f. contract, as in the present case, there will be nothing in the contract which restricts his choice between the two alternative methods of performance.

Since there was no shipment of any goods in the present case, either by these sellers or by anyone else, this is in my judgment sufficient to enable the buyers to succeed in recovering damages for breach of that part of the sellers' obligations.

Notes

1. The argument that a c.i.f. contract is a sale of documents alone is considered further in chapter 4, below.

2. Kerr J. held that the sellers were also in breach of their obligation to tender accurate documents. This aspect of the case is considered further in chapter 6, below.

Variations on c.i.f.

Variations on c.i.f. contracts are possible, which still retain the main features of the transaction. A common one is the c. & f. contract, which places the obligation to insure on the buyer. It is a positive obligation, and not merely a release of the seller's obligation to insure. This is because the seller may also have an interest in insurance, for example if the buyer does not pay or goes bankrupt, and the seller is left to reclaim the goods.

(3) Limit of Seller's Duties in Relation to the Goods

The seller's duties regarding the goods generally finish when they are loaded **2–014** on board, and he is under no obligation to deliver them to the intended port of destination. As long as the goods are loaded according to contract, the seller will not generally be liable if they are later lost or damaged on the voyage; the goods are at the buyer's risk after shipment (see chapter 4, below). A contract requiring him actually to deliver the goods to their destination is not a c.i.f. contract.

Note that in the following case the contract was described as c.i.f., but the documentary requirements were inconsistent with that designation. The designation and the documentary requirements could not both therefore stand. It was not possible to alter the documentary requirements (since these were all the seller had agreed to). Logically, therefore, the only other possibility was to strike down the c.i.f. designation.

COMPTOIR D'ACHAT ET DE VENTE DU BOERENBOND BELGE SA v LUIS DE RIDDER LIMITADA (THE JULIA)

House of Lords. [1949] A.C. 293

The action concerned a contract for the sale of part of a bulk parcel of rye (500 tons **2–015** out of just over 1,000), which was expressed to be "c.i.f. Antwerp". After the ship had sailed and the buyer had paid for the goods, against presentation of the shipping documents on 30 April 1940, Antwerp was occupied by the Germans (around 10 May 1940), so it was impossible to deliver the rye to the intended destination. For various reasons (including that it was part of an undivided bulk parcel) the property in the goods had not at that stage passed to the buyer, who claimed repayment of the money he had paid, on the grounds that there had been a total failure of consideration (*i.e.* total non-performance) on the part of the seller.

Held

The contract was not what it purported to be, and was in fact a contract for the delivery of the goods to Antwerp. An important factor in the reasoning was that the contract called for a delivery order which was neither issued by the carrier (or his agent), nor attorned to by him. It was not therefore a c.i.f. contract at all, but an ex-ship contract. That being so, there was no part performance by the seller. There was a total failure of consideration, and the buyer could recover.

2–016   LORD PORTER: My Lords, the obligations imposed upon a seller under a c.i.f. contract are well known, and in the ordinary case include the tender of a bill of lading covering the goods contracted to be sold and no others, coupled with an insurance policy in the normal form and accompanied by an invoice which shows the price and, as in this case, usually contains a deduction of the freight which the buyer pays before delivery at the port of discharge. Against tender of these documents the purchaser must pay the price. In such a case the property may pass either on shipment or on tender, the risk generally passes on shipment or as from shipment, but possession does not pass until the documents which represent the goods are handed over in exchange for the price. In the result the buyer after receipt of the documents can claim against the ship for breach of the contract of carriage and against the underwriter for any loss covered by the policy. The strict form of c.i.f. contract may, however, be modified: a provision that a delivery order may be substituted for a bill of lading or a certificate of insurance for a policy would not, I think, make the contract concluded upon something other than c.i.f. terms, but in deciding whether it comes within that category or not all the permutations and combinations of provision and circumstance must be taken into consideration. Not every contract which is expressed to be a c.i.f. contract is such. Sometimes, as in *The Parchim* [in chapters 3 and 5], terms are introduced into contracts so described which conflict with c.i.f. provisions. In the present case therefore it is not as if a usual form of delivery order had been given and accepted or an insurance certificate covering the parcel was in the hands of Van Bree as agents for the buyers, nor can a solution be found in the mere designation of the contract as c.i.f. This is not a case in which the overriding provision is the term c.i.f. under which antagonistic terms can be neglected on the ground that they are repugnant to the transaction, as was done by Rowlatt J. in *Law & Bonar Ld v British American Tobacco Co Ld* [1916] 2 K.B. 605 [see chapter 3]. The true effect of all its terms must be taken into account, though, of course, the description c.i.f. must not be neglected. It is true, no doubt, to say that some steps had been taken towards the performance of this contract, *e.g.* the goods had been shipped, an invoice sent, the customary so-called delivery order had been transmitted and that delivery order amongst its provisions contained a declaration by the sellers' agents, Belgian Grain and Produce Co Ld that they gave a share of the present delivery order of $4,973 in a certificate of insurance. But the taking of steps towards performance is not necessarily a part performance of a contract. The question is whether the purchaser has got what he is entitled to in return for the price. Of course, if the buyers paid the sum claimed in order to obtain the delivery order and the share purported to be given by it in the certificate of insurance, the contract would have been performed in part at least, but I do not so construe the contract, even when illuminated by the practice adopted by the parties. That practice seems to me rather to show that the payment was not made for the documents but as an advance payment for a contract afterwards to be performed. With all due respect to the learned judge and the Master of the Rolls, I can see no sufficient reason for supposing either that the delivery order had some commercial value or that Van Bree undertook a personal liability by their indorsement of the document. There was no evidence of commercial value and the document itself was merely an instruction by one agent of the sellers to another. In my view, if the Belgian Grain and Produce Co Ld were sued upon the document they would rightly reply that they were acting only as agents and Van Bree could make the same defence. The document appears to me to be no more than an indication that a promise already made by the sellers would be carried out in due course, but in no way increases their obligations or adds to the security of the buyers.

In my opinion, the method by which the contract was customarily **2–017** carried out supports this view. No doubt the contract could have been so performed as to make it subject to the ordinary principles which apply to a c.i.f. contract. The tender of a bill of lading or even of a delivery order upon the ship, at any rate if attorned to by the master, and a policy or a certificate of insurance delivered to or even held for them might well put it in that category. But the type of delivery order tendered in the present case was a preliminary step only. A complicated procedure had to be followed before the goods would be released. The buyers had to hand the sum due for freight to their agents; those agents would then pay the freight and present the delivery order to the Belgian Grain and Produce Co Ld, who would sign a note on it acknowledging receipt of the freight: the agents thereupon would hand the delivery order to Van Bree who would retain it and issue a "laissez suivre" or release to themselves authorizing delivery to the agents. But before physical delivery of the goods could take place Van Bree must have received a "Captain's laissez suivre" authorising delivery to them. "It was thus," as the umpire says, "the effective document upon which Van Bree obtained physical possession of the goods; it was issued to Van Bree and was never physically in the buyers' hands." Similarly, "the insurance certificates," as the umpire also finds, "were received by Van Bree from the Belgian Grain and Produce Co Ld and would not have passed through the hands of, or even have been seen by, the buyers." He further finds that Van Bree "were at no time and in no respect agents of the buyers and that the sellers did not, by delivering the certificates to Van Bree, constructively deliver them to the buyers nor did Van Bree at any time hold the certificates (whether countersigned by the Belgian Grain and Produce Co Ld or not) at the disposal of the buyers." In these circumstances the fact that the sellers twice collected the insurance money for a total loss and handed it to the buyers does not lead very far. It was a convenient method of settling accounts between the parties and, despite the extra two percent, is in substance no more than a repayment of the money given for the goods.

My Lords, the object and the result of a c.i.f. contract is to enable sellers and buyers to deal with cargoes or parcels afloat and to transfer them freely from hand to hand by giving constructive possession of the goods which are being dealt with. Undoubtedly the practice of shipping and insuring produce in bulk is to make the process more difficult, but a ship's delivery order and a certificate of insurance transferred to or held for a buyer still leaves it possible for some, though less satisfactory, dealing with the goods whilst at sea to take place. The practice adopted between buyers and sellers in the present case renders such dealing well nigh impossible. The buyer gets neither property nor possession until the goods are delivered to him at Antwerp, and the certificate of insurance, if it enures to his benefit at all, except on the journey from ship to warehouse, has never been held for or delivered to him. Indeed, it is difficult to see how a parcel is at the buyers' risk when he has neither property nor possession except in such cases as *Inglis v Stock* [see para. 4—005, below] and *Sterns Ld v Vickers Ld* [1923] 1 K.B. 78, where the purchaser had an interest in an undivided part of a bulk parcel on board a ship, or elsewhere, obtained by attornment of the bailee to him.

The vital question in the present case, as I see it, is whether the buyers paid for the documents as representing the goods or for the delivery of the goods themselves. The time and place of payment are elements to be considered but by no means conclusive of the question: such considerations may, on the one hand, indicate a payment in advance or, on the other, they may show a payment postponed until the arrival of the ship, though the property in the goods or the risk have passed to the buyer whilst the goods are still at sea, as in *Castle v Playford* (1872) L.R. 7 Ex. 98.[13] But the whole circumstances have to be looked at and where, as, in my opinion, is the case here, no further security beyond that contained in the original contract passed to the buyers as a result of payment, where the property and possession both remained in the sellers until delivery in Antwerp, where the sellers were to pay for deficiency in bill of lading weight, guaranteed condition on arrival and made themselves responsible for all averages, the true view, I think, is that it is not a c.i.f. contract even in a modified form but a contract to deliver at Antwerp. Nor do I think it matters that payment is said to be not only on presentation but "in exchange for" documents. There are many ways of carrying out the contract to which that expression would apply, but in truth whether the payment is described as made on presentation of or in exchange for a document, the document was not a fulfilment or even a partial fulfilment

---

[13] There were express provisions as to the passing of property and risk on tender of bills of lading in that case, though cash was to be paid on arrival at the discharge port *[author's footnote]*.

of the contract: it was but a step on the way. What the buyers wanted was delivery of the goods in Antwerp. What the sellers wanted was payment of the price before that date, and the delivery of the documents furnished the date for payment, but had no effect on the property or possession of the goods or the buyers' rights against the sellers. If this be the true view there was plainly a frustration of the adventure—indeed the sellers admit so much in their pleadings—and no part performance and the consideration had wholly failed. The buyers are accordingly entitled to recover the money which they have paid. I would allow the appeal and pronounce for the alternative award with costs in your Lordships' House and in the courts below.

Notes

1. Had this contract been as designated, a c.i.f. contract, the buyer would have **2–018** failed. In relation to the goods the seller had performed all the duties appropriate to a c.i.f. contract, and if documentation appropriate to a c.i.f. contract had also been tendered, the buyer have had no claim at all merely because the goods could not actually be discharged at Antwerp.

2. The case is authority (*obiter*) that ship's delivery orders can be tendered instead of bills of lading in a bulk sale c.i.f., as long as the contract so provides. See further paras 6—096, *et seq.*, below.

3. The problem with the documents tendered here was that they gave (nor indeed could give) the purchaser no rights directly against the shipowner. Therefore they could not transfer constructive possession, so that there could be no constructive delivery of the goods. Effectively, therefore, the goods could not be delivered until they arrived.

4. The documentary requirement was therefore repugnant to the c.i.f. One of the terms had therefore to be struck out. In *Law and Bonar Ltd v British American Tobacco Ltd*,[14] which was approved by the House of Lords in *The Julia*, Rowlatt J. held that a printed clause stating that the goods were at the seller's risk until actual delivery had no application to a c.i.f. contract, being repugnant to it. His judgment begins:

> "Some points in this case, I think, are quite clear. In the first place, the tender of documents representing goods duly shipped in accordance with the contract and insured against marine risks as required by the contract was not vitiated by the fact that the goods had actually been lost. That is plain.[15] Secondly, the printed clause at the end of the form used in this case stating that the goods are at seller's risk till actual delivery has no application to the present contract. The buyers paying c.i.f. terms were actually paying for the insurance against all contemplated risks from the moment of shipment. It seems to me that a term that, for a period after shipment, the goods were to be at the risk of the seller is repugnant to that, and the clause to that effect printed on the form used in this case is inapplicable to the transaction that actually was entered into."

In other words, the c.i.f. term prevailed. In *The Julia*, however, it was not possible to alter the documentary requirement, which in any case accorded with the intentions of the parties; therefore the c.i.f. term had to be struck out.

5. Another possibility is to interpret a term which is capable of bearing more than one interpretation, so as to be consistent with the c.i.f. designation.

---

[14] [1916] 2 K.B. 605.
[15] See further the discussion of *C. Groom Ltd v Barber* in para. 4—011, below.

(a) c.i.f. Delivered Contracts

2–019   The two cases in this section concern c.i.f. delivered contracts, which are commonly used in the bulk oil trade. Delivery at the discharge port is constrained either to be at latest by a certain date, or between two dates. The problem is that if the goods are lost, the delivery condition will certainly not be met; thus, to interpret the delivery clause literally would be to shift the risk of loss during the voyage back on to the seller, which would seem to be repugnant to the c.i.f. designation. In *The Wise*, it was possible to interpret the delivery clause consistently with the designation, but *The Jambur* is a more problematic case.

VITOL SA v ESSO AUSTRALIA LTD (THE WISE)

Queen's Bench Division (Commercial Court). [1989] 1 Lloyd's Rep. 96

(reversed on other grounds Court of Appeal, [1989] 2 Lloyd's Rep. 451)[16]

2–020   The contract (for the sale of a cargo of oil) was expressed to be c. & f., title and risk to pass at the vessel's manifold flange at loadport. The vessel was not specified. The buyers were however entitled to reject the cargo unless it was delivered between two dates, supposedly (according to Leggatt J.) because of the importance of dates of delivery at the discharge port. So this was a "c. & f. delivered" contract.

     LEGGATT J.: *(interpreting the clause as imposing a requirement)* (at 101, col. 1) It seems to me that since the parties have chosen to designate the contract as a c. & f. contract, I should approach the construction of it in the expectation that that is what it is. When I look at the delivery clause, I find that it is to be performed by a vessel to be nominated followed by the words "*Arrival*: March 15–30 1986". It seems to me that the natural construction of the clause is that the nominated vessel shall be such as is expected to arrive within the period mentioned. It does not wear the air of a contract to procure the guarantee of delivery within the period stipulated, especially since to do so would be inconsistent with a c.i.f. contract in classic form.

Note
     Leggatt J.'s interpretation of the clause is possible only where the sellers have a choice of vessel; the interpretation was not possible in the following case.

CASENOTE BY THE AUTHOR ON CEP INTERAGRA SA v SELECT ENERGY TRADING GMBH (THE JAMBUR) L.M.L.N. 289

[1991] 5 Oil and Gas Law and Taxation Review D58

[Footnotes are the author's own—there are none in the original.]
C.i.f. contract—effect of delivery clause

---

[16] The appeal was on the interpretation of a "without prejudice" agreement, which is irrelevant to the present discussion.

Facts:

C.i.f. buyers of a cargo of gasoil purported to treat the contract as at an **2–021** end when some 2,500 tons of the cargo was lost as a result of a collision with another vessel. They claimed that by virtue of a delivery clause in the sale contract,[17] the sellers were obliged actually to deliver the full cargo to the port of discharge. Since the sellers were unable to do so, they were in anticipatory breach of contract.[18]

Held:

The buyers were entitled to repudiate the contract.

Comment

If this case is correct, it has extremely far-reaching consequences, since it has long been thought that a c.i.f. seller does not have to effect physical delivery of the cargo, and that a clause in the contract requiring him to do so is repugnant to the transaction. In *Law and Bonar Ltd v British American Tobacco Ltd* [1916] 2 K.B. 293 (approved by the House of Lords in *The Julia* [1949] A.C. 293), for example, Rowlatt J. held that a printed clause stating that the goods were at the seller's risk until actual delivery had no application to a c.i.f. contract, being repugnant to it. In *Gill & Duffus SA v Berger & Co Inc.* [1984] 1 A.C. 382, 389, Lord Diplock took the view that a certificate of quality on discharge could not be included among shipping documents required to be tendered under a normal c.i.f. contract, since it could not be obtained until physical discharge had occurred.[19]

The sellers in *The Jambur* argued that the only effect that could be given to a delivery clause was negative, to make it clear that the sellers would be in breach if they did anything actually to prevent delivery. Phillips J. rejected the argument on the grounds that the wording of the clause was clear and emphatic, that it imposed upon the sellers an obligation physically to deliver the cargo to the port of discharge by a certain date, and that this obligation was a condition of the contract. There was no reason not to give this clause, which unlike the printed form in *Law and Bonar* had been expressly considered by the parties, its stated effect. The c.i.f. and other established types of contract were the servants of those who used them, and there could therefore be variations from the classic forms. It may be difficult to fit the requirements of certain trades within the classic c.i.f. and f.o.b. frameworks, the oil trade being a case in point, where the cargo commonly arrives before the seller can tender the bill of lading.

Whether so liberal an interpretation, in particular to the c.i.f. contract, can be justified in the light of earlier authorities, is perhaps open to doubt, but if it can, then clearly there can also be no objection to the c.i.f. out-turn contract,[20] where the price payable depends on the actual quantity delivered. On the basis of previous authorities, the effect of such a clause was far from clear.

PHILLIPS J.: Mr. Simon [for the sellers] is . . . correct to submit that the **2–022** starting point when considering the Delivery Clause is that it falls to be construed in the context of a CIF contract. It is natural to seek a construction which is not antagonistic to such a contract. Such an approach does not, in my judgment, justify construing the Delivery Clause as the negative covenant suggested by Mr Simon in his alternative submission. The

---

[17] Which required delivery of the cargo "Latest by 30th April 1990".
[18] This contention is not unproblematic: see further Ch. 7, below.
[19] See further para. 6—102.
[20] Discussed in the following section.

emphatic wording of the clause is not consistent with such a limited effect.

Mr Simon's primary submission that the clause should be disregarded as inconsistent with a CIF contract implicitly acknowledged that the natural meaning of the clause is that contended for by the Buyers. In my judgment the clear meaning of the Delivery Clause is that the Sellers have to procure physical delivery of the cargo by the 30th April.

I turn then to consider the submission that the designation of the contract as CIF should override the Delivery Clause as being antagonistic. In *Law and Bonar Ltd v British American Tobacco Co Ltd* Rowlatt J. adopted such an approach where the antagonistic clause was part of a printed form to which the parties had added the conflicting provisions of a CIF contract. Here the Delivery Clause is a term expressly agreed and incorporated into the contract by the parties. It can only be legitimate to disregard such a clause if it is impossible to give sensible effect to it having regard to conflicting provisions in the remainder of the contract. In the present case I find no such conflict.

It is important to bear in mind that established types of contract for the sale of goods are the servants of those who use them, not *vice versa*. New trades have grown up and old trades have altered with the result that the contractual requirements of buyers and sellers of goods cannot always be accommodated within the framework of the classic CIF or FOB contract. The oil trade is a case in point.

It is not uncommon for oil cargoes sold on CIF terms to reach their destination before the seller can tender the bill of lading.[21] The ship may then give delivery to the buyer in exchange for an indemnity and the buyer may pay the seller against a letter of indemnity. Payment may precede delivery or *vice versa*. The contract in the present case permits of such variations to the classic CIF transaction.

I can see no reason why the Delivery Clause should not be permitted to take effect according to its natural meaning as a further variation to the classic CIF contract. It is not hard to imagine commercial justification for such a clause. It may well be that the Buyers wanted the cargo to arrive by 30th April to meet a specific delivery obligation under a delivered contract. Both Buyers and Sellers were traders. I can see no reason in principle why they should not have agreed that the risk of an untoward delay in the voyage should be born by the Sellers rather than by the Buyers.

Accordingly I hold that the Delivery Clause bears the meaning contended for by the Buyers and that due effect falls to be given to the clause in accordance with that meaning.

This conclusion raises the question of whether the obligation imposed by the Delivery Clause was a condition, an innominate term or a warranty. Mr. Eder [for the buyers] came armed with formidable authority to support the proposition that the term was a condition. In the event, while

---

[21] See further the discussion in para. 15—032 *et seq.*, below.

not conceding this, Mr. Simon raised no positive challenge to that construction. In that he showed his customary sensible discretion. I rule that the obligation imposed on the Sellers by the Delivery Clause was a condition of the contract.

Notes

1. Unlike *The Wise*, the vessel was named, so Leggatt J.'s interpretation was impossible. **2–023**

2. Here, it seems that the risk of *marine* loss remained with the seller, so that the distinctions drawn in the following section could not be made.

3. The parties could have contracted ex-ship, but chose instead to contract c.i.f. Arguably little weight is being given to the c.i.f. designation. A possible explanation is that the delivered clause appeared to have been carefully considered by the parties.

4. Another explanation is also possible, however. Not only had some of the cargo been forever lost, but because of the damage to the vessel, even if no goods had been lost, the vessel would still not have arrived on time. A possible interpretation, therefore, is that only the risk of delay, rather than loss of the cargo as such, remained on the seller.

(b) The c.i.f. Out-turn Contract

Under this variant, used primarily in the bulk oil trade, price is payable on delivered quantity. Arguably, therefore, risk remains on the seller during the voyage, since he will not be paid for whatever is lost. The point of these clauses, however, was to protect buyers from the consequences of inevitable losses, such as evaporation, sedimentation, and clingage to tanks, rather than the consequences of accident. These clauses only appeared after the price increases consequent on OPEC production restrictions in the 1970s, after which buyers became reluctant to pay for losses that (at that time) could easily exceed 0.5 per cent of the cargo carried. **2–024**

LIGHTBURN & NIENABER: "OUT-TURN CLAUSES IN C.I.F. CONTRACTS IN THE OIL TRADE"

[1987] 2 L.M.C.L.Q. 177, 178–179

[Footnotes are as in the original, but renumbered for inclusion in this book.]
Prompted by sky-rocketing prices following the Arab-Israeli war in 1973 and the overthrow of the Shah of Iran in 1979, the c.i.f. out-turn contract gained increased currency in the international oil industry. Its popularity among buyers results from the fact that the out-turn clause relieves them from having to pay on the basis of the quantities shown on the bill of lading as is normally the case under a standard c.i.f. contract. Thus delivery shortfalls, which became increasingly costly to buyers as the price of oil climbed, were shifted to the sellers. **2–025**

Although the insertion of an out-turn clause in an otherwise c.i.f. contract will cause unavoidable loss to be for the account of the seller, its use gives conflicting views regarding the apportionment of other risks. According to one view, the appropriate moment for the passing of risk under a c.i.f. out-turn contract remains in accordance with the essential c.i.f. concept, *i.e.* the risk passes from the seller to the buyer on shipment. This approach treats the out-turn clause basically as a price adjustment mechanism with regard to unavoidable transit losses while the risk of marine loss remains on the buyer. The second and more far-reaching interpretation is that an out-turn loss clause essentially changes the time at which the risk of loss, whether marine or transportation, passes from the seller to the buyer from the point of shipment to the port of destination.[22] Such an approach would not take into account the distinctions between "unavoidable" and "extraordinary" loss or, in the parlance of the oil trade, between transportation and marine loss. According to that view, this is the straightforward and ordinary meaning of an out-turn clause—since the clause states that the buyer need only pay for the actual quantity that is to be received, there can be no liability if nothing arrives due to marine risk . . . [They discuss the practical difficulties involved in distinguishing between the different types of risk] . . . Would it not be simpler, it may be asked, simply to place the risk of loss on the seller until delivery?

The answer to this last question, it is suggested, is no. To the extent parties to a contract use a recognised trade term, *prima facie* effect should be given to that term . . . If the parties did not intend to contract on a c.i.f. basis, then they would not have specified "c.i.f." in the contract.[23]

The reasons for admitting an exception to normal c.i.f. rules are not compelling in this case. Out-turn terms have traditionally been a shorthand way of dealing with transportation losses as opposed to marine losses. These concepts are clearly recognised in the oil trade and the risks have been extensively analysed by industry specialists. A party seeking to overcome the accepted meaning of a particular term should have the burden of showing that the parties intended to disregard the legal consequences that would normally flow from its use. The expression "out-turn" addresses itself to a specific and well-defined problem, namely, unavoidable transit losses. To broaden the scope to include marine losses would be an unjustified incursion into the normal c.i.f. rules.

---

[22] Note what is meant when it is said that the risk of loss is shifted. This discussion assumes that even if the risk of marine loss were shifted from the buyer to the seller under an out-turn clause, the contract would remain subject to general c.i.f. principles. Thus, if a casualty did occur the seller could still perform by presenting normal c.i.f. shipping documents and the buyer in such a case would not have a claim for damages, but, rather, the right to withhold payment. The issue addressed goes further; this comment questions the assumption that the c.i.f consequences are avoided by the out-turn clause so that the buyer is no longer obliged to pay for the shortfall due to marine loss.
[23] In *Panda OHG v Circle Products Ltd* [1970] Lloyd's Rep. 499, 504, CA, it is stated with regard to the f.o.b. standard term that, "*prima facie*, when two commercial men use a well-known phrase of that kind, they must be presumed to give it its established meaning".

[They go on to suggest that buyers who want to shift the risk on to the sellers can easily insist on an ex-ship contract, based on out-turn quantity.]

Notes

1. *Panda OHG v Circle Products Ltd* [1970] Lloyd's Rep. 499, 504 is set out in para. 3—052, below.

2. This is an attempt to interpret the out-turn clause so as to be consistent with c.i.f. notions of passing of risk. There may be difficulties operating such an interpretation in practice. For example, if the entire ship and cargo are lost due to accident, how much does the buyer pay? Classifying the losses might also be difficult, for example if one of the ship's pumps is accidentally damaged, causing more of the cargo to be unpumpable on arrival, and hence not discharged from the ship.

3. In principle, however, these clauses may give rise to problems no more difficult than other types of clause making provision for a price adjustment. For example, suppose the contract allows a choice of discharge ports at different prices (perhaps to reflect differences in freight rates). Surely, such a contract could be encompassed within the c.i.f. term, but suppose the ship sinks before the discharge port is nominated? There is no real difference between this example and the out-turn loss clause.

4. Where there is an out-turn loss the carrier might be liable for breach of carriage contract. Alternatively and additionally, or if there is an out-turn loss clause or cargo-retention clause in the carriage contract, the cargo owner might be able to deduct the value of the shortfall from freight. In a c.i.f. out-turn contract where seller is charterer, and there is an out-turn loss clause in the charterparty, the seller's deduction from freight under the charterparty could, in principle, compensate him for the price reduction under the sale contract. If the buyer also attempts to sue the shipowner on the bill of lading contract, he will presumably be met with the defence that he has suffered no loss, having had the benefit of the price reduction. If, on the other hand, there were no out-turn clause in the sale contract, the shipowner could find himself facing both a freight deduction from the seller/charterer, and a damages action from the buyer. For this reason, the cargo retention clause in the BPVOY4 tanker voyage charterparty contains the following provision:

"33.4 Charterers hereby agree to indemnify Owners against any liability to a Bill of Lading holder resulting from non-delivery of any such cargo in respect of which a deduction from freight is made under this Clause 33 provided always that Charterers shall under no circumstances be liable to indemnify Owners in an amount greater than the amount of freight so deducted."

See further the discussion in Yates, *Contracts for the Carriage of Goods by Land, Sea and Air*, (LLP, 1993), para. 1.1.6.2.15.

GARDANO & GIAMPERI v GREEK PETROLEUM GEORGE MAMIDAKIS & CO

Queen's Bench Division. [1962] 1 W.L.R. 40, [1961] 2 Lloyd's Rep. 259

Issues:

Charterers as c. & f. sellers claimed against the shipowners in respect of a shortfall of a cargo of kerosene. The shipowners claimed that they had

2—026

2—027

no right to sue, the only right to sue having passed to the c. & f. buyers (the Greek government) under the Bills of Lading Act 1855, s.1.

Note that the entire cargo of kerosene was sold, and the bill of lading named the buyers as consignee. The shipowners claimed that the 1855 Act was triggered because property passed on consignment.

Held:

McNair J. held that the charterers had a right to sue, either because the Bills of Lading Act 1855, s.1 did not operate because (contrary to the shipowners' assertions) property had not passed, or alternatively (*i.e.* even if the buyer had an action based on s.1) on *Dunlop v Lambert* principles.

Notes

1. The latter part of the case was overruled in *The Albazero* [1977] A.C. 774. The narrow views expressed on the 1855 Act were approved in *The Delfini* [1990] 1 Lloyd's Rep. 252, but that Act has now been replaced by the Carriage of Goods by Sea Act 1992. See further chapter 13 on these aspects of the case.

2. However, the case may still be regarded as an authority on the passing of property. This was an unusual contract, where the risk provisions bore some similarities to a c. & f. out-turn contract (but were perhaps closer still to an ex-ship or delivered contract, as Mustill L.J. later pointed out in *The Delfini*, because the entire risk of loss of cargo during the voyage (marine and transportation), apart from the first 0.5 per cent, was placed on the charterer/sellers), and McNair J. held that the normal c. & f. incidents did not apply. Property was held not to have passed in *Gardano*, although it would have passed had this been an ordinary c. & f. contract.

3. The case was distinguished on this point by Lord Denning M.R. in *The San Nicholas* [1976] 1 Lloyd's Rep. 8 (see further para. 5—061, below), where an order bill of lading was used, and property was held (at any rate by Lord Denning M.R.) to have passed on indorsement.

4. The relevance of the case for present purposes is that the out-turn provision affected (and hence to some extent prevailed against) the c. & f. designation.

(4) Relationship Between Sale and Carriage Contracts

2–028   Additionally to shipping the goods according to the contract description, the seller is required to enter into an appropriate carriage contract. If the bill of lading tendered discloses a carriage contract which is inconsistent with the contract of sale, the buyer is entitled to reject it.

SOULES v CAF V PT TRANSAP OF INDONESIA

Commercial Court. [1999] 1 Lloyd's Rep. 917

Issues and decision

2–029   The contract concerned the sale of Java tapioca chips, c.i.f. "one port out of Lorient/Brest/Montoir/La Pallice". Bills of lading were tendered which provided for "freight payable as *per* charterparty" (although in fact freight had been prepaid), and gave a significantly wider range of discharge ports than the four specified in the contracts. It was held that the buyers were entitled to reject them.

TIMOTHY WALKER J.: ... I will summarize the relevant principles of law as to which there can be no dispute, borrowing copiously, without direct attribution, from the judgments of Megaw L.J. in *SIAT di dal Ferro v Tradax Overseas SA* [1980] 1 Lloyd's Rep. 53, and Mance J. in *Seng Co Ltd v Glencore Grain Ltd* [1996] 1 Lloyd's Rep. 398:

   (i) A c.i.f. contract is an essentially documentary transaction under which the buyers part with their money in return for continuous documentary protection against the carrier,

  (ii) The documentary requirements of the contract must be strictly complied with, and the buyer is not obliged to evaluate how significant any documentary discrepancy may prove to be; he is entitled to know where he stands. In this context he is not obliged to accept assurances outside the bills of lading.

 (iii) It is the bill of lading to which the buyers are entitled to look as being definitive of the contract of carriage binding upon the shipper,

 (iv) The bill of lading must provide for the carriage of the goods to the agreed destination.

Thus in summary it is fundamental to the whole transaction that the buyers can look to the carrier for a remedy under documents which accurately reflect the terms of the contract of sale.

   ... However, if the documents do not conform, the buyers, as a matter of law, are entitled to reject them. ...

As to the port of discharge point, it is clear from the findings of fact that the bills of lading as issued gave a significantly wider range of discharge ports than the four specified in the contract, the four French ports for which the French buyers based in Boulogne had contracted. On the face of the bills the goods could in theory have ended up in England or Spain. Mr. Merriman's submission [for the sellers] that a bill of lading which provides for carriage to a range wider than the contractual range cannot be defective, is in any event expressly gainsaid by the holding of Megaw L.J. in *Tradax* (*op. cit.*) that in the case of a contract of sale c.i.f. Venice, tender of a bill of lading which, by reference to the charter-party, provided for discharge at Venice or Ravenna, would be a bad tender (see [1980] 1 Lloyd's Rep. 53 at p. 60, col. 1 centre, read with p. 63, col. 2 last paragraph, and p. 64, col. 1 first paragraph).

As to the payment of freight point (which was of course an entirely separate discrepancy) Mr. Merriman submitted that there is no general rule that a c.i.f. contract requires a freight paid bill of lading. That may be so, but this contract did. The contract price was "US $ 168.50 per metric tonne c.i.f. free out". Mr. Merriman accepted that the buyers must have been invoiced for the full c.i.f. price. The full c.i.f. price included freight. Thus the clear statement of the law by Brandon J. (as he then was) in *The Pantanassa* [1970] 1 Lloyd's Rep. 153 at p 163, col 1, directly covers the point. He said:

> "In the case of c.i.f. contracts, payment of the freight element in the price may be effected in one of two ways. The first way is for the seller to prepay the freight and invoice the buyer for the full c.i.f. price, which is payable by the buyer against the shipping documents.
> . . . When the first method is used, the seller provides freight prepaid bills of lading."

Turning back to the facts of the present case, a bill of lading stating "freight payable as per charter-party" leaves wide open the possibility that the shipowners would demand freight at the discharge port. Thus the Board were obviously right in regarding the bills of lading as discrepant in the two specified respects.

Comments

2–030   One of the problems in *Soules* was that the carriage contract gave the seller a greater range of discharge ports than the sale contract. The problem in the next case is the opposite; at a time of regional conflict, the shipowner insisted on incorporating into the carriage contract a greater degree of freedom regarding discharge ports than the buyers had agreed to under the sale contract, and the shipowner refused to discharge at the buyers' preferred port.

One way of dealing with the problem is for the sale contract to incorporate carriage contract terms, but the carriage contract will usually not be entered into until later. The courts take the view that it is legitimate to incorporate into a contract terms of a contract not yet in existence, but a cautious view is taken, partly because the carriage contract is not open for the buyers' inspection.

CEVAL ALIMENTOS SA v AGRIMPEX TRADING CO LTD (THE NORTHERN PROGRESS) (NO. 2)

Queen's Bench Division (Commercial Court). [1996] 2 Lloyd's Rep. 319

Facts:

2–031   Under the c. & f. sale contract, delivery was to be one safe port out of Rijeka/Koper at buyers' option to be declared when vessel passing Gibraltar. The sale contract further provided: "All other terms conditions and exceptions as per Charterparty". The charterparty later entered into contained a special diversion clause (55) which provided that:

> "In the event that Yugoslavian ports are closed to merchant shipping or the area is subject to an insurance premium due to war-like conditions then Owners to declare this to Charterers and Charterers to nominate alternative port within Italian Adriatic. Extra insurance premium for

this to be for Charterers' account. Any deviation incurred to be compensated to the Owners by the Charterers at cost duly substantiated."

This allowed the shipowners a wider deviation right than the sale contract, since Rijeka and Koper could still be regarded as safe, even if the insurance premium had been increased to trigger cl. 55. An amendment was later agreed to allow Hamburg as an alternative discharge port, and the sale contract was also amended to allow Hamburg as a discharge port. However, the buyers were unaware of the existence of cl. 55, which was not a term that was usual or reasonable in the trade, and unless cl. 55 were incorporated into the sale contract, the position remained that the buyers were entitled to nominate Rijeka or Koper, as long as they remained safe.

The London insurance market gave notice that Yugoslavia was to be added to the war risk additional premiums areas, but Koper at any rate remained safe and undisturbed, at all material times. The buyers insisted on Rijeka as discharge port, with Koper as an alternative, whereas the sellers insisted on discharging at Hamburg, the shipowner having refused to proceed to Yugoslavia.

Eventually the buyers accepted Hamburg (which involved them in significant additional overland transport costs) under protest, and sued for breach of the sale contract. At the ensuing arbitration proceedings, the case proceeded on the assumption that the bill of lading tendered incorporated cl. 55. On appeal from arbitration, the sellers claimed to change their grounds of appeal to argue the contrary.[24]

Decision:

1. The sale contract did not incorporate cl. 55. Consequently the   **2–032**
   buyers were entitled to treat the bills of lading tendered as non-contractual.

2. The sellers were not allowed, at the appeal stage from arbitration proceedings, to argue for the first time that cl. 55 was not incorporated into the bill of lading, so that the bill of lading would have conformed to the sale contract. Even if they had been allowed to amend their grounds of appeal, they would still have been in breach of the sale contract, in ordering discharge at Hamburg.

The issues on appeal:

RIX J.: The three questions of law for which leave to appeal was granted are as follows:

---

[24] The terms of the bill of lading do not appear in the report, but the description in Rix J.'s judgment of the arbitration proceedings suggest that the incorporation clause was similar to that of the sale contract. It appears, however, that different considerations apply to bills of lading incorporating the terms of an existing charterparty than to sale contracts incorporating terms of a charterparty yet to be agreed.

(a) Whether or not, on the facts found, sellers were in breach of any of their obligations under the contract of sale (as amended)?

(b) Whether or not, on the facts found, buyers waived any rights to treat the bills of lading as non-contractual or are estopped from so contending?

(c) Whether or not the words: "All other terms, conditions and exceptions" in the contract of sale were effective to incorporate the terms of the charter-party, including cl. 55, into the contract of sale?

Before me, the primary issue debated has been whether cl. 55 was incorporated into the sale contract (part of question (c)). The issue of waiver (question (b)) has been pursued, but in very much a secondary role. Question (a) was intended to raise the issue of what breach of contract remained in the light of the sellers' submission that the award found that cl. 55 was not incorporated into the bill of lading. I made it clear already at the hearing that I did not read the award as so deciding.

In the circumstances two subsidiary or alternative submissions were advanced before me, one by the sellers, and the other, if needed, by the buyers. The sellers' alternative submission was that, if I were to uphold the award in concluding that cl. 55 was not incorporated into the sale contract, then I should go on to hold that cl. 55 was not incorporated into the bill of lading either. On that basis, I should hold overall that there was no breach of the sale contract to found the buyers' claim for damages and the appeal should succeed. The buyers' riposte was in the first place that I should not permit the sellers now for the first time on appeal to raise a new question of law to the effect that cl. 55 was never incorporated into the bill of lading; and secondly that in such a case there was in any event a breach of the sale contract in that the diversion to Hamburg was ordered not by the buyers, whose option under the amended contract it was, but by the sellers against the wishes and despite the protests of the buyers. Both these alternative submissions were subject to the argument that they had not been raised before the board of appeal and/or had not been made the specific subject matter of an application for leave to appeal. I shall therefore deal with them only after I have considered the issues plainly before me.

Is cl. 55 incorporated in to the sale contract?

2–033   On behalf of the sellers Mr. Eder submitted that it was. The incorporation clause was broad, and being express permitted limitation only on the ground of a term being insensible or inconsistent when read together with the parent contract, but not on the ground of a term being unreasonable or abnormal in the trade. *Prima facie* therefore cl. 55 was incorporated. Moreover, it was neither insensible nor inconsistent. It was sensible, because it was germane to and indeed part of the essential subject matter of shipment, carriage and delivery. It was consistent, because although it qualified or modified the contractual arrangements for delivery in Yugoslavia, it did so only in a way which was analogous to other terms of this or any other sale contract, such as the safe port warranty, or the war risk clause. Qualification was not the same as inconsistency: only a term which was repugnant could amount to inconsistency. The clause required a degree of manipulation when read within the context of the sale contract because of being written in terms of owners and charterers: but that was easily solved by substituting "sellers" for "owners" and "buyers" for "charterers". Such a degree of manipulation was readily permitted. As for the incorporation of terms in a charter-party not yet entered into nor nominated to the buyers, that was contemplated by the sale contract itself which referred to the sellers cabling buyers with the vessel's name and port of loading either five days prior to the expected time of loading or "upon chartering" whichever earlier.

In the context of these submissions Mr. Eder referred me to authorities on the closely analogous question of the incorporation of charter-party terms into bills of lading, such as Scrutton on *Charterparties* at pp. 63–65, *The Garbis* [1982] 2 Lloyd's Rep. 282, and *Miramar Maritime Corporation v Holborn Oil Trading Ltd* [1984] 2 Lloyd's Rep. 129; [1984] 1 A.C. 676. On the distinction between incorporated terms which merely qualify the parent contract and terms which cannot be incorporated because of inconsistency amounting to repugnancy, he referred me to *Pagnan SpA v Tradax Ocean Transportation SA* [1987] 2 Lloyd's Rep. 342 and *Hogarth Shipping Co Ltd v Blyth, Greene, Jourdain & Co Ltd* [1917] 2 K.B. 534. On the question of the incorporation of terms from a future contract, he referred me to *OK Petroleum AB v Vitol Energy Ltd* [1995] 2 Lloyd's Rep. 160.

On behalf of the buyers, on the other hand, Mr. Cordara, Q.C. sub- **2–034** mitted that cl. 55 was not incorporated into the sale contract. Logically his first point was that there could not in any event be any incorporation of a charter-party which at the time of the sale contract had not even come into existence. Secondly, reasonableness in matters of construction was an essential test, and there was nothing reasonable about incorporating a term, found by the Board of Appeal to be itself unreasonable and unusual in the trade, into a c & f sale contract which required the sellers to procure a contract of carriage which was reasonable and usual. As for the requirement of consistency, cl. 55 failed that test: not only did it provide for a different destination from that which would otherwise be the contractual one, but it did so in terms different from those otherwise specifically incorporated to deal with the problem of war, such as the US War Risk clauses and the Sept 17 amendment. In this context, moreover, it did not even fall within the express scope of the incorporation clause because it was not within the expression "All *other* terms . . . " (*emphasis added*). Furthermore, even though the manipulation required to make sense of the clause within the sale contract might be small, the Courts would not be prepared to manipulate a clause to make sense of an incorporation which would have an unreasonable effect. For the purposes of these submissions Mr. Cordara was prepared to rely on much the same authorities as those cited by Mr. Eder.

I will deal first of all with Mr. Cordara's submission that the sale contract's incorporation clause was ineffective because the charter-party was not yet in existence and the clause therefore had nothing to bite on. It was submitted that words of incorporation generally relate to pre-existing contractual arrangements which, for brevity's sake, parties are content to adopt as the measure of their own mutual obligations: the standard example is the incorporation of the terms of an existing charter-party into a bill of lading. Such words are not easily to be read as relating to some future transaction between one only of the contracting parties and some third party over which the other contracting party will have no control. If, however, the words of incorporation were to be confined to an existing charter-party, then the buyers could at least in theory have called for and reviewed it at the time of contracting.

The initial question raised by this submission is whether it was indeed the case that the sale contract predated the charter-party. The award merely finds that those two contracts were both made on the same day, Sept 13, 1991. However, Mr. Cordara submits that there was no relevant charter-party until *Northern Progress* was nominated to the buyers, which was only on Sept 18. Mr. Eder did not, I think, take issue with that approach, and I am prepared to accept it as correct.

I have some sympathy with Mr. Cordara's submission, but in my judgment it goes too far. The very fact just considered, that a charter-party, even if already in existence as a matter of fact, only becomes relevant to the sale contract when a vessel is nominated to the buyers, demonstrates that any charter-party, whether already made or not, is for these purposes to come into existence only in the future. Moreover, Mr. Eder is in my judgment correct to point out that the sale contract itself contemplates that a charter-party may be fixed only after the sale contract has been made (see the provision for nomination of the vessel "upon chartering"). The incorporation clause therefore contemplates a future contract. Indeed, that is typical of c.i.f. contracts, under which a seller is obliged to procure a contract of carriage for the sale: such carriage contracts must regularly be entered into only after the sale contract in question. Not only is there quite frequently reference in the sale contract to the (at that time unknown) terms of a future carriage contract, *e.g.* to its demurrage provisions, but through the bill of lading the buyer is going in his turn to become party to all the terms of the contract of carriage arranged between seller and shipowner. There is nothing unheard of, therefore, in such an arrangement. And to broaden the argument still further, it is frequently the case that parties enter into contracts which incorporate terms which, although already in existence, are at the relevant time unknown to one contracting party and perhaps extremely difficult for him to consult. In practice, therefore, even if not in theory, the vice of the incorporation complained of in this case is commonly found, but the incorporation is not on that ground ineffective.

It could also be said that the danger adverted to, that one party will contract in terms over which the other party will have no control, will be in any event limited by well-known doctrines such as the requirement that any term to be incorporated must be capable of being read sensibly and consistently in the context of the parent contract.

There is, so far as the researches of Counsel have taken them, only one **2–035** case in which the problem of the incorporation of a future contract has been specifically considered and that is *OK Petroleum AB v Vitol Energy Ltd* [1995] 2 Lloyd's Rep. 160. That too was a case concerned with a c.i.f. contract which incorporated charter-party conditions at any rate so far as demurrage was concerned. The particular issue there was whether the charter-party demurrage time bar provision was also incorporated. That issue was decided in favour of the plaintiff seller on the basis that the time bar provision was merely ancillary and therefore was not incorporated. At p. 168 Colman J. said this:

"In my judgment the correct analysis of the authorities is that in a case, such as the present, where the incorporated contract does not exist when the incorporating contract is entered into and cannot be presumed by the parties to the latter to contain any specific wording or terms, the established approach to construction is that general words of incorporation will not normally be construed as wide enough to incorporate any provision from the other contract unless that provision is part of the subject-matter of that contract and not merely ancillary to it, such, for example, as an arbitration clause or a jurisdiction clause. Such ancillary provisions will not normally be treated as relevant or germane to the rights and obligations of the parties under the incorporating contract."

Colman J. did not, therefore, decide the point on the broad basis of Mr. Cordara's current submission, although he had the nature of the problem of the incorporation of a contract not yet in existence well in mind, as is clear from the following passage of his judgment where he is contrasting the differences raised by the incorporation of charter-party terms into bills of lading as distinct from the incorporation of charter-party terms into sale contracts (at p. 163):

"By contrast, in the case of these sale contracts, as would normally be the case with such contracts, the charter-parties whose terms as to demurrage are said to have been incorporated had not been brought into existence at the time when the sale contracts were entered into. Nothing in the terms of the sale contracts specified the precise terms of the charter-party which the seller might enter into. He had complete freedom to contract on any terms provided that he procured delivery of the goods in accordance with the terms of the sale contract and tendered a bill of lading consonant with his obligations as a c.i.f. seller."

If, however, Colman J. had regarded the sale contract demurrage provision as providing for an indemnity against the seller's liability to the shipowner in demurrage, then—

> " . . . there would be much to be said for the argument that the time bar could not have been intended to operate for the benefit of the buyer since the seller might only receive notification of a claim for demurrage which was so late within the 90 days that he was unable to preserve his right of indemnity by giving notice to the buyer within the 90 day period . . . (at p. 164)."

. . . it is of course a well known rule of c.i.f. contracts that the c.i.f. seller is under a duty to make or procure a proper contract of affreightment and procure a proper bill of lading: see, for instance, Benjamin's *Sale of Goods*, 4th ed., 1992, at par. 19–023. A proper contract of affreightment or bill of lading is one which will *inter alia* provide for the carriage of the goods to the contractual destination, contain no deviation clauses other than those which are usual and customary, and generally be in a form which is "reasonable and acceptable in the trade" or "usual and customary" (*ibid.* at par. 19–022, 19–029–19–032, Halsbury's *Laws of England*, 4th ed. 1983, vol. 41, at par. 917). These duties are reflected in s.32(2) of the Sale of Goods Act, 1979, *viz*:

> "Unless otherwise authorised by the buyer, the seller must make such contract with the carrier on behalf of the buyer as may be reasonable having regard to the nature of the goods and the other circumstances of the case . . . "

. . . in the context of the c.i.f. sale it seems to me to be well established that the seller is bound not to impose upon his buyer a contract of carriage which contains unreasonable or unusual terms.

2–036   To revert to Mr. Cordara's first submission, that an incorporation clause is ineffective to incorporate any terms of a contract not yet in existence, the authorities that I have considered above confirm my judgment that that submission goes too wide and is mistaken. It may be, but it will always depend on the circumstances, that an incorporation clause will not readily be understood as referring to future as distinct from existing contracts. But in the present case of a c & f sale, the sale contract will naturally look forward to a future charter-party, and the wording of this particular contract ("upon chartering") merely goes to underline that inherent assumption. The incorporation of cl. 55 cannot, therefore, fail on that broad ground. Nevertheless, the duty is to procure a reasonable and usual contract of carriage, and in the light of Mr. Eder's acceptance that he is bound by the award's finding that cl. 55 is not a term that is reasonable or usual in the trade, there is obvious strength in the submission that the incorporation clause in this case does not incorporate a clause that would otherwise render the sellers in breach of their basic duties.

Mr. Eder nevertheless submits that an express incorporation clause of sufficient width overrides such considerations. Here the clause is "All other terms, conditions and exceptions as per Charter Party". "All", he submits, means all, and there is therefore *prima facie* incorporation subject to cl. 55 being sensible in its new context (the sale contract) and not inconsistent with it. Clause 55 does make sense, with a small and necessary degree of manipulation; and it merely qualifies the sale contract without being inconsistent. Express incorporation overrides implied duties or the role of any further requirement of reasonableness.

In my judgment, however, the most fundamental rule of construction is to seek to ascertain, by objective means, the true intention of the parties. Principles of construction are developed in certain contexts, among them the problem of incorporation clauses, to assist in this process; but such principles, like all maxims of construction, cannot be allowed to take on a life of their own divorced from the ultimate goal of seeking to ascertain the parties' true intent. That goal may require an ultimate judgment to be developed which seeks a compromise of even conflicting principles, or principles which push in different directions. . . .

In my judgment the question of construction in this case has to take account of the following factors:

(1) The incorporation clause is not a particularly emphatic one. "All" is immediately qualified by "other" in circumstances where the sale contract had already immediately before provided for the deemed incorporation (in the charter-party) of specific clauses designed to deal with the problem of war, . . .

(2) Even without the qualification introduced by the word "other", it is common ground that the word "All" does not mean quite what it seems to say, as so often happens. Thus charter-party terms which do not deal with the shipment, carriage or delivery of the goods would not be incorporated. Terms which cannot be manipulated to make sense in the context of the sale contract are not incorporated. Inconsistent terms are not incorporated. Ancillary terms are not incorporated. . . .

(4) Clause 55 was an unreasonable and unusual term in the trade. It may be that this factor by itself would be enough to exclude its incorporation. After all, the parties can hardly have contemplated that the sellers would procure a contract of affreightment which, because it was not in a form reasonable and customary in the trade, rendered the sellers in breach of their duty as c. & f. sellers. But even if that factor does not entirely by itself go to override or exclude what might otherwise be a *prima facie* incorporation, it is highly relevant in the overall consideration of what the parties must be regarded as intending by their incorporation clause.

(5) There is then the element of rationality or commercial common-sense. I do not agree with Mr. Eder that it plays no part in the process of construction in this context. . . . Indeed, it seems to me that the doctrine of the exclusion of terms which do not make sense . . . as well as the doctrine of inconsistency are but aspects of the overall process of arriving at the true intention of the parties in which the concept of rationality and commercial commonsense must play their appropriate and fundamental roles. Parties may of course agree to unreasonable terms or terms which fly in the face of commercial reality (and all the more readily of course where the commercial difficulty is not manifest): if however a Court is to conclude that, by means of something as imprecise as an incorporation clause, the parties have intended to agree what is manifestly unreasonable, then the parties must make that intention clear. As Scrutton states, at p. 64:

"Where the intention is doubtful, the court will not hold that the term is incorporated."

. . .

In my judgment the incorporation of cl. 55 into the sale contract, and *a fortiori* the sale contract as amended, in the absence of specific negotiation between the parties, lacks rationality and flies in the face of commercial commonsense.

. . .

For these reasons I am quite satisfied that the award's holding that cl. 55 was not incorporated into the sale contract should be upheld. I am confirmed in my views by the Board of Appeal's findings, already set out above, that the inclusion of such a clause, which allowed owners to sail elsewhere than to the contractual destination because an additional insurance premium had been announced, cannot be viewed as reasonable; also that the clause was different in kind and in conflict with specific contract clauses concerning renomination of the discharge port.

. . .

Incorporation of cl. 55 into the bill of lading

. . .

2–037   In my judgment Mr. Cordara is right in his submission that it is now too late for the sellers to seek to obtain leave to appeal on the ground that cl. 55 was never incorporated into the bill of lading. . . . Moreover, even if I were to have given leave to the sellers to argue before me that cl. 55 was not incorporated into the bill of lading, I would not in any event have considered it just to do so without also permitting the buyers, if they indeed needed my leave in this respect, to argue that even if the clause was not so incorporated, there was a breach by the sellers in ordering the vessel to discharge at Hamburg. As it is, I do not see what possible defence the sellers have to such an alternative argument, and none was suggested to me by Mr. Eder.

Comments

Whether the seller enters into a bill of lading contract or a voyage charterparty, the carriage contract will fix a freight payment for the voyage, which will be independent of the time the voyage takes. Since cargo-owners can influence loading and discharge times, shipowners protect themselves by requiring cargo-handling operations to be completed within the laytime determined in the contract. If the laytime is exceeded, the carriage contract invariably makes provision for the cargo-owner to pay demurrage, which is liquidated damages for detention. This has the effect of shifting some or all of the risk of delay from shipowner to cargo-owner during the loading and discharge process.   **2–038**

If the seller is shipper then he can become liable to pay make demurrage, and this liability is not divested on transfer of the shipping documents, by the Carriage of Goods by Sea Act 1992.[25] Yet the buyer can influence cargo-handling times, especially on discharge, and also where the buyer has a choice of discharge ports. Sellers may wish to protect themselves, therefore, against incurring demurrage payments, through the fault of the buyers.

One way to do this, if the seller is charterer, is to procure the incorporation of a cesser clause into the charterparty, which requires the shipowner to proceed against the receiver, rather than the shipper/charterer, for demurrage incurred at discharge. The other way is to provide in the sale contract, for buyers to pay demurrage to them. One way of doing this is to provide for demurrage to be payable as per charterparty.[26]

Where the seller is time charterer, no demurrage will be payable under the carriage contract, but the seller will have to pay hire for the period of any delay. In such circumstances, if the seller wishes the buyer to compensate for such hire payments, he will have to make appropriate provision in the sale contract.

(5) Continuing Duties After Shipment

Though physical delivery takes place on shipment, the seller may be in a position to interfere with the goods subsequently, and prevent them from arriving at their destination. For example, if he is charterer of the vessel, the charterparty may give him a choice of discharge ports. Suppose, after shipping the goods, he diverts the vessel to a port other than that named as the discharge port in the c.i.f. contract. We have already seen that he would be in breach of his obligation to enter into a reasonable carriage contract.   **2–039**

There may be other possibilities for interference, as in the following two cases. In both these cases, the carrier may have obeyed non-contractual instructions given by the seller, in which case he might himself have been in breach of the carriage contract, but in the present context, we are concerned primarily with the seller's liability on the contract of sale.

---

[25] See further Ch. 13, below.

[26] See, *e.g. Eurico SpA v Philipp Brothers (The Epaphus)* [1987] 2 Lloyd's Rep. 215; *Gill & Duffus SA v Rionda Futures Ltd* [1994] 2 Lloyd's Rep. 67; *OK Petroleum AB v Vitol Energy SA* [1995] 2 Lloyd's Rep. 160. Note however that once incorporated the clause is interpreted in its own right within the sale contract, and is not regarded as simply an indemnity for demurrage actually paid under the charterparty.

EMPRESA EXPORTADORA DE AZUCAR v INDUSTRIA AZUCARERA NACIONAL SA (THE PLAYA LARGA AND MARBLE ISLANDS)

Court of Appeal. [1983] 2 Lloyd's Rep. 171

On appeal from (and upholding) Cubazukar v Iansa Queen's Bench Division (Commercial Court), SJ/160/78, February 29, 1980

Facts:

2–040   Under a contract made in February 1973, Iansa purchased from Cubazukar a quantity of sugar c. & f., to a Chilean port, shipments to be effected between January and October, 1973. Because of an uprising in Chile, and the replacement of a regime friendly to Cuba with one less so, the performance of the contracts was affected by decisions made at high level in the Cuban government. Later, performance of the contracts became illegal under Cuban law.

  As a consequence of the government action (and instructions by Cubazukar), *The Playa Larga*, which was in the process of delivering cargo (which had already been paid for) in Chile left port, before completion of the delivery; *The Marble Island*, which was *en route* for Chile, was diverted elsewhere (although documents were tendered under the documentary credit, against which the price was paid). The charterparty for *The Aegis Fame*, which was about to load, was cancelled. Thus, some sugar never reached Iansa although they had paid for it, and although (in the case of *The Playa Larga* and *The Marble Island*) the cargo had been loaded by Cubazukar. The sellers had thus arguably performed their duties c.i.f., by loading the cargo aboard the vessels, and argued that they were not responsible for its delivery to the buyers.

  After the coup, there was no further performance of the contract by either party. The market had steadily risen since the contract had been made, and continued to rise after the coup, and Iansa sued Cubazukar.

Held:

Playa Larga

2–041   In respect of *The Playa Larga* cargo, IANSA could succeed on the basis of the Sale of Goods Act 1979, s.12, and in the tort of conversion (the Court of Appeal upholding Mustill J. on this point); it was accepted, however, that s.12(2) could not be applied without limitation, and that the seller could not be responsible where the buyer's possession was disturbed by the wrongful act of a third party totally unconnected with the seller. That was not the situation in the case, however. Mustill J. did not see that any term could have been implied apart from s.12(2), but the Court of Appeal would have been prepared to imply a term at common law also, had s.12(2) not been enacted:

"In a contract of sale, other than one to which subsection (3) below applies, there is also an implied term that—

. . .

(b) the buyer will enjoy quiet possession of the goods except so far as it may be disturbed by the owner or other person entitled to the benefit of any charge or encumbrance so disclosed or known."

The conversion claim depended on the buyer having sufficient immediate right to possession to found the claim. Since property had passed to him, this was not a problem here.

Marble Island

In respect of *The Marble Island*, the contract was frustrated prior to any **2–042** breach by Cubazukar, nor did IANSA ever obtain sufficient title to sue in conversion, and IANSA was unable to recover damages (but it could reject the documents, which were discrepant, and recover the price already paid); again, the Court of Appeal upheld Mustill J.

Aegis Fame

In respect of the unshipped balance, the contract was frustrated and Cubazukar was therefore not in breach.

Comments

The main importance of the case is in establishing the nature of the liability of **2–043** c.i.f. sellers who, having loaded the goods in accordance with the contract, later act in such a manner as to prevent them from reaching the buyer.

In the Court of Appeal, the rejection in respect of *The Marble Island* cargo was justified on the grounds that the documents were discrepant, but Mustill J. also considered the validity of tender of documents representing carriage contracts that were no longer being, or could not be carried out. This aspect of the case is considered further in chapter 4, below.

Note also *Soules CAF v PT Transap of Indonesia* [1999] 1 Lloyd's Rep. 917, where bills of lading giving the seller (as shipper) a range of discharge ports, other than destinations specified in the contracts, were held discrepant.

GATOIL INTERNATIONAL INC. v TRADAX PETROLEUM LTD (THE RIO SUN)

Queen's Bench Division (Commercial Court). [1985] 1 Lloyd's Rep. 350

Issues:

The case main importance of this case is in the application of ss.12(2), **2–044** 14(2), 20(2) and 32(2) of the Sale of Goods Act 1979 to c.i.f. contracts.

Facts:

Panatlantic (shipowners) time chartered the vessel to Ocean Tanker (OTC), who sub-chartered to Ocean Energy (OER) and thence (for a voyage) to Tradax. Only the head charterparty made any provision for the cargo (of oil) to be heated.

IEOC (an affiliate of Agip) sold a cargo of oil to Tradax f.o.b., and Tradax nominated the *Rio Sun*; Tradax re-sold the cargo c.i.f. to Gatoil. (The parties to the action were Gatoil, Panatlantic and Tradax.)

Gatoil were late in nominating a discharge port, and the vessel was held for a considerable time at Augusta. Tradax claimed entitlement to compensation (having incurred a demurrage liability over this period), and a lien against the cargo. Later (and consequently), they delayed the eventual discharge of the cargo (ordering the master not to enter the discharge port). An injunction having been obtained against them, Tradax eventually withdrew the instruction.

Tradax also tendered an "L.O.I." (letter of indemnity—as they were entitled to under the letter of credit), rather than the original bills of lading which were in their possession.[27] Even after Tradax had withdrawn their instructions not to discharge, the master refused to do so except against production of all the original bills, and on the express instructions of Panatlantic (who asserted a lien on sub-freights). (Gatoil had apparently obtained original bills by this time.)

Because of solidification of the cargo there was further delay at discharge, and short delivery (around 3.68 per cent R.O.B.[28]—a very high percentage—the norm would be around 0.25–0.5 per cent).

Gatoil claimed against Tradax in respect of both shortfall and delay, and Panatlantic for the delay, the latter because they had insisted on delivering only against original bills. Tradax counterclaimed in respect of the delay, and in respect of demurrage at discharge.

---

[27] See Ch. 6, below for a discussion of the legal consequences, in general terms, of delivery without production of an original bill.
[28] Remaining on board.

Contractual Relationships in The Rio Sun

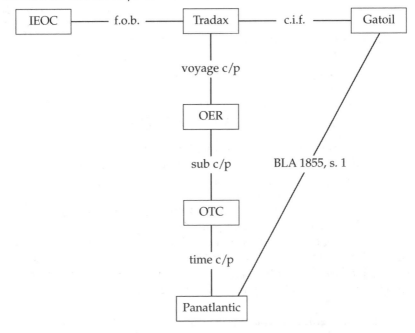

Held by Bingham J. (in respect of the c.i.f. contract):

(Only the claims by Gatoil (c.i.f. buyers) against Tradax (c.i.f. sellers) are **2–045** relevant to the discussion in this chapter):

1. The cargo was neither unmerchantable nor unfit for the purpose of being carried to a destination within the range agreed. There was therefore no breach of s.14 of the Sale of Goods Act 1979. Section 14 is further considered in chapter 4, below.

2. Tradax were not in breach of contract in failing to stipulate (in the carriage contract) for the heating of the cargo. Gatoil's claim was based on the Sale of Goods Act 1979, s.32(2), which requires the seller to make a reasonable carriage contract, but it was held that Tradax were entitled to assume that the cargo would survive the voyage contemplated without deterioration even if unheated. The section is as follows:

> "Unless otherwise authorised by the buyer, the seller must make such contract with the carrier on behalf of the buyer as may be reasonable having regard to the nature of the goods and the other circumstances of the case; and if the seller omits to do so, and the goods are lost or damaged in course of transit, the buyer may decline to treat the delivery to the carrier as a delivery to himself or may hold the seller responsible in damages."

3. Tradax were however liable for the delay, in purporting to exercise an unjustified lien over the cargo, refusing to allow the vessel to proceed to the discharge port. The claim was based on the Sale of Goods Act 1979,

s.12(2), set out above, which requires the goods to be transferred free from encumbrance, and that the buyer be entitled to enjoy quiet possession of them, but would succeed anyway at common law on the basis of *The Playa Larga and Marble Islands* [1983] 2 Lloyd's Rep. 171 (see above).

4. Bingham J. also thought that in principle, Tradax would have been liable under s.20(2) of the Sale of Goods Act 1979, but did not need to decide this point. In principle, Bingham J.'s view (set out below) is not easy to reconcile with delivery c.i.f. being to the ship, rather than at the port of discharge. Section 20(2) is in the following terms:

> "But where delivery has been delayed through the fault of either buyer or seller the goods are at the risk of the party at fault as regards any loss which might not have occurred but for such fault."

5. Tradax were also liable for failing promptly to forward bills of lading to Gatoil. The basis of this claim was the Court of Appeal decision of *Sanders v Maclean* (see further para. 6—084, below). Although Tradax claimed that Gatoil could have obtained the cargo using the L.O.I., Bingham J. observed that the vessel would have been under no obligation to discharge the cargo to anyone not holding the bills of lading.[29]

BINGHAM J.: *(on the s.20(2) point)* [The seller's] argument is that s.20(2) is not directly applicable to c.i.f. contracts because the "delivery" referred to is delivery of the goods and the c.i.f. seller is not under any obligation to deliver the goods at the agreed destination. Were the point crucial to the outcome of this case it would be necessary to consider it in some detail. It is not. I shall, therefore, confine myself to a tentative expression of opinion. Despite the peculiar features of a c.i.f. contract, what the buyer wants at the end of the day is actual delivery of the goods, and he wants them in good condition. The seller need do nothing after tendering the shipping documents against payment. But if the seller does wrongfully delay actual delivery of the goods, whatever other breach of contract may be involved, I see no reason why the sub-section should not have the effect of putting upon him the risk of any loss which might not have occurred but for the delay which he caused.

Comments

2–046   Here, delivery to the ship was not delayed, but discharge was. Bingham J. thought that the sellers were in breach of s.20(2), but even if this is correct, since in any circumstance where s.20(2) is breached, s.12 will almost certainly also be breached, it may be that this controversy has no practical application.

Another possibility is that s.20(2) is triggered by a delay in constructive delivery, *i.e.* tendering documents, but since liability would arise (as in the case itself) under *Sanders v Maclean*, it is difficult to see that s.20(2) would add anything in that situation either.

---

[29] See further generally, Ch. 6, below.

CHAPTER 3

F.O.B. AND OTHER INTERNATIONAL SALE
CONTRACTS: RIGHTS AND DUTIES OF THE PARTIES

(1) F.O.B. CONTRACTS

(a) FLEXIBILITY OF F.O.B. TERM

WHILE the c.i.f. contract described in the previous section developed from the   3–001
f.o.b., it differs from the original f.o.b. contract in many fundamental respects; the
seller always undertakes to secure shipping space, ship the goods, and to make
the carriage contract as principal (or purchase goods which have already been
shipped). Freight and insurance are included in the price; it follows that fluctuations in rates fall upon the seller, not the buyer.

This is a far cry from the original f.o.b. contract, where the buyer was always
considered shipper. There was no need for this situation to continue after 1855,
however, and the parties were free to develop contracts which shared some, but
not all the features of c.i.f. For example, it might be sensible, even where the buyer
wishes to nominate the vessel, for the seller to make the shipping arrangements;
he will often be best placed to do so, at the loading port.

The courts were initially slow to catch on to the development of the f.o.b.
contract. In *Wimble, Sons & Co v Rosenberg & Sons* [1913] 3 K.B. 743 (set out later
in para. 4—022), the f.o.b. sellers nominated the vessel, made the shipping
arrangements and paid the freight (for buyers' account), but it is not clear that
they were regarded as contracting with the carrier as principal. Nor were they
contractually obliged to take on these duties, which in Buckley L.J.'s words were
"in the nature of a request to the sellers with which they were not bound to, but
as matter of courtesy in business no doubt would, comply." The view still seems
to have been taken at this stage that fundamentally under an f.o.b. contract, the
ship was provided by the buyers, and that if the sellers were involved in the
shipping arrangements, it was as agent for the buyers, or merely by way of
request, rather than as a contractual undertaking.

As the twentieth century progressed, however, contracts where the sellers made   3–002
the carriage contract, or even nominated the vessel, came to be regarded as
varieties of f.o.b. contract, and in *Pyrene v Scindia Navigation* [1954] 2 Q.B. 402,
Devlin J. observed (in a rather unsatisfactory passage set out below) that the
"f.o.b. contract has become a flexible instrument".

Because a range of contracts can be described as f.o.b., it is sensible for the
parties to spell out the detailed terms (see further para. 15—002, *et seq.*, below),
although the courts operate presumptions, in the absence of contrary evidence.
Even where the parties spell out the detailed terms, the courts must give some
weight to the description of the contract as f.o.b. Other terms that are ambiguous
can then be interpreted so as to be consistent with the f.o.b. designation, or if they
are clearly repugnant to the essence of the f.o.b. contract, the courts must decide
which of two inconsistent terms should prevail.

Even accepting the flexibility of the term, it is necessary, therefore, to determine
the limits of the f.o.b. concept (especially bearing in mind that the parties have not

chosen the c.i.f. designation). The term certainly determines place of delivery and (in general) allocation of costs[1]; the seller undertakes to place the goods on board the ship, and to bear all costs up to that time. The buyer bears all costs thereafter. The basic obligation is stated by Buckley L.J. in *Wimble Sons v Rosenburg & Sons* [1913] 3 K.B. 743, 752:

> "An f.o.b. contract is one under which the seller is to put the goods on board at his own expense on account of the buyer, . . . "

Sassoon (at para. 438) provides a fuller version of this definition, and describes as the essence of the f.o.b. contract that:

> "(i) the seller must pay the cost and bear the responsibility of putting goods 'free on board,' in other words, bear full responsibility for the cost and safety of the goods until the point of their passing the ship's rail, and (ii) that upon this being accomplished delivery is complete and the risk of loss in the goods is there and then transferred to the buyer."

Apart from that, the f.o.b. contract was described in *Pyrene v Scindia* as a flexible instrument, and little else is determined by the term (except freight and insurance market risks—see further below).

It is not even necessary for an f.o.b. contract to be an international sale, in the sense in which that term is used in this book. For example, a c.i.f. or f.o.b. exporter may wish to enter a contract for supply of the goods to be delivered to his ship. This will be a wholly domestic contract, whose performance is entirely completed within the exporting country, although it envisages a subsequent export sale. The domestic supply variety of f.o.b. contract is conceptually very similar to the original type of f.o.b. contract, described in chapter 1, above.

Given the wide variety of f.o.b. contracts, it is perhaps not surprising that it is difficult to lay down general principles as to the rights and duties of the parties: see further para. 3—046, below.

(b) Issues on Range of f.o.b. Contracts

3–003   In considering the meaning of the f.o.b. term, regard should be had to the following:

(a) What the parties contracted to do may differ from what they actually did (although, of course, the latter can be used as evidence for the former). Thus, for example, the mere fact that an f.o.b. seller enters a carriage contract as principal does not necessarily imply that he contracted to do so.

(b) However flexible the f.o.b. term, there are limits to the flexibility. It is reasonable to suppose that if the parties have contracted f.o.b., the courts will need very strong evidence that they have agreed to an arrangement outside the limits of the f.o.b. concept. If there is an express term, they will have to decide to which of two inconsistent terms they will give effect.

(c) The use of term f.o.b. can create presumptions as to what the parties agreed, in the absence of other evidence. It is necessary to distinguish, therefore, between what can be encompassed within the f.o.b. concept, and what the term means when there is no other evidence as to what the parties agreed.

---

[1] But see, *e.g. A.V. Pound & Co Ltd v M.W. Hardy & Co Inc.* [1956] A.C. 588, in para. 3—047, below.

In the latter context, f.o.b. may admit far less flexibility than in the former.

(c) The Three Main Pyrene v Scindia Varieties

The differences between the main vareties of f.o.b. contract revolve around who 3–004 nominates the vessel, and who is responsible for making the contract of carriage. The variations were described by Devlin J. in *Pyrene Co Ltd v Scindia Navigation Co Ltd*.

PYRENE CO LTD v SCINDIA NAVIGATION CO LTD

Queen's Bench Division. [1954] 2 Q.B. 402; [1954] 1 Lloyd's Rep. 321

Facts and issues:
Note that the facts are more fully stated at the start of the passage set out from Devlin J.'s judgment in para. 11—072, below.

The cargo (a fire tender) was dropped and damaged by the negligence of the shipowner during loading. At this stage, before the goods had passed the ship's rail, they were still the property of the seller.[2] The seller sued the carrier, for the full value of the damage (£966), in tort for negligence. The issue was whether the shipowner could claim the benefit of a clause written into the contract of carriage by virtue of the Hague Rules, the effect of which (at that time) was to limit his liability to £200.[3] It was essentially a question of privity of contract, in effect whether the seller was party to the contract of carriage. The seller claimed that he was not, and that therefore he was not bound by the clause. On of the issues, therefore, was whether the seller could be regarded as the shipper under an f.o.b. contract.

Held:

1. The shipowner was entitled to the benefit of the clause limiting liability to £200.

2. After discussion of the varieties of f.o.b. contract, that the buyer was shipper.[4]

3. The Hague Rules, incorporating the clause, applied to the loading process. See further on this issue para. 11—072, below.

4. Although the buyer was shipper, the seller was party to an implied contract with the carrier, even though he did not expressly make the contract of carriage. See further paras 11—064 *et seq.*, and 13—085 below, on this aspect of the case.

---

[2] The sale contract expressly provided for property not to pass till delivery over the ship's rail: see at 413, 424.

[3] The £200 limit was derived from the British Maritime Law Association's Agreement of August 1, 1950, which is no longer in force, the limit under the Hague-Visby Rules being generally higher. See further paras 11—049, *et seq.*, and 11—064, *et seq.*, below.

[4] The sale contract expressly provided that freight was to be engaged by the buyer (see at 423), and the actual process of making the carriage contract is described at 424.

Diagrammatic Representation of Express Contractual Relationships: Pyrene v Scindia Navigation Ltd

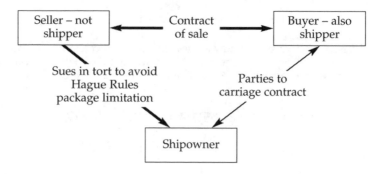

Devlin J.: *(on the varieties of f.o.b. contract)*

3–005   The f.o.b. contract has become a flexible instrument. In what counsel called the classic type as described, for example, in *Wimble, Sons & Co Ltd v Rosenberg & Sons* [1913] 3 K.B. 743, the buyer's duty is to nominate the ship, and the seller's to put the goods on board for account of the buyer and procure a bill of lading in terms usual in the trade. In such a case the seller is directly a party to the contract of carriage at least until he takes out the bill of lading in the buyer's name. Probably the classic type is based on the assumption that the ship nominated will be willing to load any goods brought down to the berth or at least those of which she is notified. Under present conditions, when space often has to be booked well in advance, the contract of carriage comes into existence at an earlier point of time. Sometimes the seller is asked to make the necessary arrangements; and the contract may then provide for his taking the bill of lading in his own name and obtaining payment against the transfer, as in a c.i.f. contract. Sometimes the buyer engages his own forwarding agent at the port of loading to book space and to procure the bill of lading; if freight has to be paid in advance this method may be most convenient. In such a case the seller discharges his duty by putting the goods on board, getting the mate's receipt and handing it to the forwarding agent to enable him to obtain the bill of lading.[5] The present case belongs to this third type[6]; and it is only in this type, I think, that any doubt can arise about the buyer being a party to the contract.

---

[5] In this case the bill of lading is therefore issued to an agent of the buyer, and will be in the name of the buyer.

[6] The type of contract where the buyer is shipper is described by Sassoon as "strict" f.o.b., "because it entails the performance of a lesser number of responsibilities on behalf of the seller than under any other interpretation or usage": Sassoon, *C.i.f. and f.o.b. Contracts* (4th ed., Sweet & Maxwell, 1995), para. 443. Schmitthoff however describes the classic type as "strict", preferring "f.o.b. contract (buyer contracting with carrier)" for the third type: Leo D'Arcy, Carole Murray and Barbara Cleave, *Schmitthoff's Export Trade, The Law and Practise of International Trade* (10th ed., Sweet & Maxwell, 2000), p. 20. Clearly, no standard usage should be assumed, except for "classic f.o.b." itself, which since *Pyrene v Scindia* has been taken as meaning that the seller ships the goods on a vessel nominated by the buyer.

[DEVLIN J. then describes the process by which the buyers made the contract of carriage.]

Notes

1. The most important aspect of this case, for present purposes, is Devlin J.'s view that f.o.b. is a flexible term, from which it follows that the parties themselves should ideally spell out the detailed terms—see further chapter 15, below. In *Pyrene* itself, the buyer's undertaking to ship was clear from the terms of the sale contract, and the facts also clearly pointed to the buyers having made the carriage contract. The decision does not make clear what the obligations of the parties would be in the absence of a clear term. To some extent this problem has been filled out by later cases (see further below).

3–006

2. This passage, though oft-quoted, is unsatisfactory in some respects, and in particular as to its description of the classic type. In the first place, the contract in *Wimble, Sons & Co Ltd v Rosenberg & Sons* is probably not correctly classified as classic f.o.b., the first type of contract described here. If one considers what the seller actually did in *Wimble v Rosenberg* (the facts of which are set out in detail in chapter 4, below), he may well have made the carriage contract as principal, but he also made pretty well all the shipping arrangements, paid the freight and chose the vessel, so on this basis it looks most like the second type of contract described here.[7] However, the seller appears not to have been under any contractual obligation to do any of these things, Buckley L.J. commenting, for example, (at 753) that:

"The further request that the seller should pay the freight formed no part of the contract and was a matter with which the seller was not bound to comply."

Nor is it even clear that the seller in *Wimble* even undertook to be shipper, and therefore on the basis of contractual undertakings, *Wimble* should probably be analysed as a variety of the third type.

3. The sentence about the bill of lading is also very puzzling. If the seller is acting as buyer's agent, then he will not directly be party to the carriage contract at all. If he contracts as principal, then he should be able to take the bill of lading in his own name. Morevoer, in that case the contract can only be transferred to the buyer on the principles discussed in chapter 13, below.

4. Perhaps the problem facing Devlin J. was that, at the time *Pyrene v Scindia* was decided, *Wimble v Rosenberg* was the best example he could find. It is clear from subsequent authorities that encompassed within the f.o.b. term is the seller contracting as principal (see below). Moreover, in *Concordia Trading BV v Richco International Ltd*,[8] Evans J., describing the classic f.o.b. contract, said:

"In the normal case, although the goods have been shipped on a vessel nominated by the buyer, the seller for his own protection will have reserved the right of disposing of the goods, as unpaid seller, and the bill of lading will require delivery to him or to his order."

The case, which is set out in chapter 6, below, turned on the documents performing the same function as in a c.i.f. sale. It therefore seems safe to conclude that it is acceptable, in a classic f.o.b. contract, for the seller to take out a bill of lading in his own name.

5. Three main varieties of f.o.b. contract were identified:

---

[7] Far from nominating the vessel, the buyer did not even know her name—that was how the issue in the case arose.

[8] [1991] 1 Lloyd's Rep. 475. See also para. 6—087, below.

Types x 3 (handwritten marginalia)

(a) Seller makes the contract of carriage, but buyer nominates the vessel ("classic" f.o.b.).

(b) Seller nominates the vessel, and also makes the contact of carriage. This is probably the rarest variety, and the type that most closely resembles a c.i.f. contract. Schmitthoff describes the f.o.b. contract with additional duties, which is of this type, where the seller also pays the freight and insurance.[9] Unlike the true c.i.f. contract, freight and insurance are for buyer's account, rather than being included in the cost. The freight and insurance rate fluctuation risks are thus borne by the buyer, not the seller.

(c) Buyer nominates the vessel, and makes the contract of carriage (as in Incoterms 2000 and *Pyrene* itself).[10] This is probably the most common variety today.

6. Devlin J. held that the contract in *Pyrene* was of the third type, with buyer as shipper.

7. The "classic" variety of f.o.b. contract is still probably the most common, and is the basis of the definition adopted by the Institute of Export, where the parties choose their standard terms. The buyer nominates the ship (his duty is to nominate an effective ship), but the seller is required to load the goods on board and pay all costs incurred up to that point. The seller also makes the contract of carriage, though the cost of so doing will be charged to the buyer's account. The seller having loaded the goods will obtain bills of lading which will be forwarded to the buyer, and against which normally the buyer will pay the price. It is more appropriate than the third type where the seller is better placed actually to make the arrangements for carriage, and the contract of carriage. Abundant shipping space is assumed, in other words that any ship nominated by the buyer will in fact be able to take the goods.

8. If shipping space is short, and the buyer does not require a special variety or nationality of ship (usually where the items shipped are small), the seller may nominate the ship as well. This is the second type described in *Pyrene*.

9. There are a number of reasons why the parties might choose to contract f.o.b., rather than c.i.f.:

(a) Under the carriage contract, freight does not become payable until on or even after delivery. It may be preferable in that case for the purchaser, not the seller, to take on the responsibility for paying freight. While it is clear from *Ireland v Livingston* and *Ross T. Smyth* (above) that this can be accommodated within the c.i.f. contract, it can still be more convenient to use the f.o.b. form. Bulk oil sale contracts are commonly f.o.b., probably for this reason.

(b) Either the buyer's goods are of such a nature that a particular type of vessel is required (*e.g.* refrigerated cargo), or there are, *e.g.* foreign currency restrictions which encourage the buyer to use ships of his own national shipping line. In such cases the buyer would wish to nominate the ship.

(c) The buyer is charterer of the vessel. This would argue for a contract of the third type described in *Pyrene* (note however that the buyer had not chartered the vessel in *Pyrene v Scindia* itself).

10. Where the seller is shipper, the buyer may demand tender of a shipped bill of lading as evidence that the seller has performed his obligations, and loaded the goods. This bill of lading can be used as security by the seller as in c.i.f. sales, if

---

[9] Schmitthoff, *op. cit.*, p. 18.
[10] The full text of Incoterms is set out in App. B, below.

taken to seller's order,[11] and sales can be financed by banks on documentary credits. The buyer can use also use the shipped bill as a document of title, for pledge or resale. So whereas not all f.o.b. contracts make use of the bill of lading as a document of title, the documents can nevertheless perform the same function as in c.i.f. sales.

(i) *Seller contracting as principal*

Devlin J. envisages that in contracts of type 1 and 2, the seller can contract as   **3–007** principal, and not merely as agent for the buyer. This is now clearly encompassed within the f.o.b. term.

There are, however, a number of separate issues:

(a) Merely because a seller in fact contracts with the carrier as principal does not imply that, under the sale contract, he was obliged to do so.

(b) It follows that, merely because cases can be found where the seller ships as principal, that does not prove that the f.o.b. term is also capable of encompassing situations where he is contractually obliged to do so.

(c) Even if the f.o.b. contract is capable of encompassing this situation (for example, where there is an express term to that effect), there may still be a strong presumption, in the absence of evidence to the contrary, that an f.o.b. buyer undertakes to ship the goods. In many cases, the courts have to construe the contractual obligations from relatively little evidence, for example letters and telephone conversations rather than detailed standard forms. In such cases, presumptions can take on an enhanced importance.

(d) It is not uncommon for both the f.o.b. seller and buyer to enter into carriage contracts, with different carriers (see *The Sevonia Team*, below).

THE EL AMRIA AND THE EL MINIA

Court of Appeal. [1982] 2 Lloyd's Rep. 28

Facts and decision:

F.o.b. sellers (of Egyptian onions bound for European ports) were parties   **3–008** to what was probably a contract of affreightment, through co-ordination of Supreme Onion Shipping Committee (the "SOSC"). They also took order bills of lading—the contract of affreightment contained no exclusive jurisdiction clause but the bill of lading did (in favour of the Egyptian courts).

The cargo having arrived damaged, the cargo-owners (f.o.b. buyers) sued the shipowners in England and the Court of Appeal held that they were barred by the jurisdiction clause, because their only contract was on bill of lading terms.

It is, therefore, part of the ratio that it is not a *Pyrene* category 3 case, and that the sellers were not acting as agents for the buyers in entering the carriage contract, since otherwise the buyers' relationship with the carrier would have been governed by the contract of affreightment (see further below). In fact, this was an f.o.b. contract with additional duties.

---

[11] As in *Concordia v Richco*, see above.

Donaldson L.J.: We do not regard the fact that there is no charter-party to which the cargo-owners are a party as necessarily fatal to their contention that the terms of the contract of carriage are other than as stated in the bill of lading and that the bill of lading in their hands was merely a receipt. But we do consider that it would require extremely clear and cogent evidence to establish so unusual an arrangement. In *Pyrene & Co v Scindia Navigation Co* [1954] 1 Lloyd's Rep. 321; [1954] 2 Q.B. 402, at 332 and 424 Devlin J. instanced three types of f.o.b. contract.

In the first, or classic type, the buyer nominates the ship and the seller puts the goods on board for account of the buyer, procuring a bill of lading. The seller is then a party to the contract of carriage and if he has taken the bill of lading to his order, the only contract of carriage to which the buyer can become a party is that contained in or evidenced by the bill of lading which is endorsed to him by the seller. The second is a variant of the first, in that the seller arranges for the ship to come on the berth, but the legal incidents are the same. The third is where the seller puts the goods on board, takes a mate's receipt and gives this to the buyer or his agent who then takes a bill of lading. In this latter type the buyer is a party to the contract of carriage *ab initio*.

It would avail the receivers nothing that the sellers in shipping the goods should have made separate contracts of carriage for each parcel on the terms of the Continent contract, unless they did so as agents for the buyers. In any other case, the buyers only became parties to any contract of carriage and able to sue on it when the bills of lading were endorsed to them and the only contract of which they could avail themselves is that contained in or evidenced by the bill of lading. No doubt some documentary or other evidence exists of the arrangements made between the buyers and the sellers as to the shipment of the goods and the making of the contract of carriage, but none has been drawn to our attention.

Accordingly, all we know is that the sellers arranged for the ship to become available, that the sellers shipped the onions, that the sellers took an order bill of lading and that the sellers endorsed that bill of lading in favour of the receivers and delivered it to the receivers on payment of the price. Using Mr Justice Devlin's classification, this is a type 2 f.o.b. contract, and the buyer's only rights are under the bill of lading.

Note

3–009   It was accepted that if the receivers had been party to the contract of affreightment, then that and not the bill of lading would have governed their relationship:

> "Accordingly, the position is that if the receivers were the charterers of the vessel on the terms of the Continent contract, the bills of lading would be bare receipts and not contracts of carriage in their hands (see *President of India v Metcalfe Shipping Co* [1970] 1 Q.B. 289).[12] It is true that in that case the charterparty required the master to sign bills of lading "without prejudice to this charterparty" and there is no equivalent clause in the Continent contract, but

[12] See further para. 12—008, below.

part of the ratio of the decision was that a master normally has no authority to vary the terms of a charter-party and that to issue a contractual bill of lading to a charterer would have this effect."

But the receivers were held not to be party to that contract (*i.e.* the contract of affreightment), only the sellers being party as principals.

Diagrammatic Representation of Contractual Relationships: The El Amria Case—Relationships Created

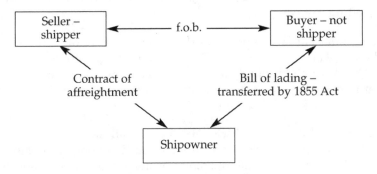

Other cases

From *The El Amria and The El Minia*, it is clear that f.o.b. sellers can contract with the carrier as principal, and not merely as buyers' agents. Another case where the seller clearly contracted as principal is *The Athanasia Comninos* [1990] 1 Lloyd's Rep. 277, where the f.o.b. seller, as shipper, was held directly liable to the carrier for shipping dangerous cargo. Mustill J. observed that:

"Under many forms of f.o.b. contract it can be inferred that the property of the goods passes on shipment, that the entire carriage is performed on behalf of the buyer as owner of the goods, and that the seller participates in the contract primarily (if not exclusively) as agent for the buyer. In my view, this is not the position here."

In reality, it may be too simplistic to think of one or other party entering into a carriage contract. Even where the buyer undertakes to provide tonnage, he may do so by chartering a vessel, and successive sales, on similar terms, can be effected by each sub-buyer taking an assignment of the charterparty, or a sub-charter, as in *The Filipinas I* in chapter 1, above. The buyer will certainly have made a contract of carriage, but only with the disponent owner under his immediate charterparty (in *The Filipinas I* the buyer had in fact chartered the vessel from his immediate seller). The question can then arise as to the relationship, if any, between the parties to the contract of sale, and the shipowner.

K/S A/S SEATEAM & CO v IRAQ NATIONAL OIL CO (THE SEVONIA TEAM)

Commercial Court. [1983] 2 Lloyd's Rep. 640

The plaintiffs (Seateam) were owners of the vessel *Sevonia Team*, which **3–010** was on charter to Colocotronis S.A. A cargo of nearly 90,000 tons of crude oil was shipped f.o.b. by INOC (shippers) at Khor-al-Amaya for delivery at Portland, Maine. There were a number of re-sales, and the eventual owners were the defendants Petrofina Canada. Petrofina Canada also took a sub-charterparty of the vessel.

Property in the oil passed (instantaneously through the intermediate buyers) to Petrofina Canada on shipment, when the oil passed through the vessel's permanent hose connection. Freight was payable at destination.

The bill of lading, signed by the master on behalf of the owners, provided for delivery:

> "unto order Portland Pipeline Corporation for Order of Petrofina Canada on behalf of Pannac Limited or to their assigns upon payment of freight as per charter party all conditions and exceptions of which the charter party including the negligence clauses, are deemed to be incorporated in this Bill of Lading."

The oil was delivered and discharged, but not all the freight due under the charter was paid. The owners originally sued not only the defendants but also the shippers and intermediate consignees, but these claims were settled or withdrawn. "Thus the claim against the third defendants, Petrofina Canada, is the only live issue before the court". The shipowners had to argue that the bill of lading contract was enforceable against Petrofina Canada.

The shipowners had to argue first that liability to pay freight was imposed upon the eventual consignees by virtue of the Bills of Lading Act 1855, s.1, and secondly, that the bill of lading incorporated the head charter, to which they were party, rather than a sub-charter to which Petrofina, but not the owners were party.

Held (for the shipowners):

1. The head charter was incorporated by the bill of lading. See further on this issue para. 12—031, below.

2. Petrofina were consignees, and property passed to them "upon consignment", so they could be sued under the 1855 Act. This aspect of the decision has been overtaken by the replacement of the 1855 Act by the Carriage of Goods by Sea Act 1992.

Notes

3–011   1. The main issue in *The Sevonia Team*, as to the interpretation of the Bills of Lading Act 1855, s.1, is no longer relevant in the light of its replacement by the Carriage of Goods by Sea Act 1992.

2. One of the arguments, however, was whether there could be a consignment by the shipper, required to trigger the 1855 Act, where the buyer had nominated the vessel:

> "Mr. Gilman [for Petrofina Canada] argued that there never was any consignment in the present case, since the vessel was nominated by the buyers. But in my view that argument was hopeless."

3. It must be part of the *ratio* of the case, however, that the contract with the shipowner in *The Sevonia Team* was made by the original sellers as principals, liabilities under which were imposed on the successive f.o.b. buyers by the 1855 Act. Had the successive sellers contracted with the shipowner as buyer's agents, there would have been no need to argue the Bills of Lading Act points at all, since Petrofina Canada would have been directly party to the bill of lading contract. (Note that the Bills of Lading Act points are no longer of importance, given its replacement by the Carriage of Goods by Sea Act 1992.)

4. The contract in *The Sevonia Team* seems, therefore, to have been classic f.o.b., with seller contracting with the shipowner as principal.

5. The case is noted by the author in "Contracts with Consignees and Indorsees" [1984] L.M.C.L.Q. 476–487.

6. The facts are similar to those in The San Nicholas, in para. 5—061, below, which again concerned an f.o.b. contract where the buyers were sub-charterers, where their only relationship with the shipowner was the contract of carriage made by the sellers as principals, rights under which were transferred to them the Bills of Lading Act 1855, s.1.

Diagrammatic Representation of Contractual Relationships: The Sevonia Team

Contractual relationships in *The Sevonia Team*

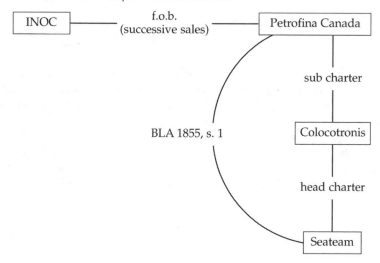

Further issues:

There are, however, two separate issues, first, whether an f.o.b. seller can contract **3–012** with the carrier as principal, and secondly, whether he can be obliged to do so by the contract. It seems reasonably clear from the above authorities that the answer to the first question is "yes", but the second is less clear-cut. However, Devlin J. himself appears to have countenanced this possibility in *Heskell v Continental Express* [1950] 1 All E.R. 1033, in chapter 14. Of a contract that could probably not be categorised as c.i.f. he observed:

"I shall now set out the particular facts of this case . . . It was arranged that, in accordance with the usual course of business, the plaintiff should see to the packing and shipment of the goods . . . , make the necessary disbursements, insure the goods . . . , and charge for the whole on the invoice. He was then to receive payment against documents. The plaintiff says that this was a c.i.f. contract . . . It is true that the price agreed on was not inclusive of insurance and freight, and that the total amount . . . on the invoice that was ultimately rendered by the plaintiff sets out the cost of packing, insurance and freight separately. But I do not think that the transaction can fairly be split up into separate parts. The plaintiff received no separate remuneration as agent or otherwise for arranging the shipment . . . The fact that payment was made against documents, and not earlier or otherwise, is, in my judgment, an important factor. It is worth noting that the plaintiff took out the bill of lading in his own name . . . Whether it can properly be labelled c.i.f. or not, I am satisfied that it was an essential term of this contract that the plaintiff should procure the shipment of the goods."

The conclusion, therefore, is that the plaintiff (seller) was obliged to procure shipment. Yet this does not seem to have been a c.i.f. contract. Insurance and freight were for buyer's account, and it is probably an f.o.b. contract with additional duties.

N.V. HANDEL MY. J. SMITS IMPORT-EXPORT v ENGLISH EXPORTERS (LONDON), LTD

Commercial Court. [1957] 1 Lloyd's Rep. 517

Facts:

3–013 The case concerned a contract for the sale of glacial acetic acid, f.o.b. Rotterdam, under which it had been agreed that the sellers would do their best to secure shipping space. In the event, no ship was nominated, and the issue was who was at fault.

The sellers argued that as a "fundamental proposition, where, in a written contract, you find the words or symbol 'f.o.b.', that necessarily imports, or imports unless excluded by very clear language, that there shall rest upon the buyers the obligation to nominate a ship."

Held:

The f.o.b. contract, which fell to be interpreted, was formed from two letters and an order form.

McNair J. found that there was no obligation upon the buyers to find a vessel, since in the first letter the sellers had said that:

"We are now arranging shipment for Hong Kong as early as possible in June and as soon as we are in the position to give you the name of the steamer we shall not fail to do so immediately."

In the second letter the buyers wrote:

"It has been agreed that you [—that is, the sellers—] will do your best to obtain shipping space as soon as possible. We hope you will succeed in getting the consignment shipped in May."

McNair J. therefore held that the sellers had merely undertaken to "do their best" to obtain shipping space. Since they had done so, it followed that neither party was liable to the other for the failure to nominate.

MᴄNᴀɪʀ J.: *(on the argument of the sellers)* It is quite true, and I accept without qualification, that in what has been called the "classic form" of f.o.b. contract the obligation does, if nothing else is said, rest upon the buyers to nominate a ship. That has been well-established for many years, and a statement to that effect can be found, in particular, in the case of *H.O. Brandt & Co v H.N. Morris & Co Ltd* [1917] 2 K.B. 784, in the speeches of Viscount Reading, C.J., and Lord Justice Scrutton. But, as has been observed in a number of cases, these expressions "f.o.b." and "c.i.f.", as applied to sale contracts, do not of themselves standardize the legal indicents falling upon one party or the other.

By way of illustration, I have been referred to the judgment of Delvin J. in *Pyrene Company, Ltd v Scindia Navigation Company, Ltd* [1954] 2 Q.B. 402; [1954] 1 Lloyd's Rep. 321 ... *[McNair J. set out the passage set out above]* ...

Similarly, in a more recent case in the House of Lords of *A.V. Pound & Co Ltd v M.W. Hardy & Co Inc.* [1956] A.C. 588; [1956] 1 Lloyd's Rep. 255; it was again emphasized that in construing the obligations arising under a f.o.b. contract, and, in particular, the question upon whom rested the duty of obtaining an export licence, it was not sufficient merely to reach the conclusion that the contract was f.o.b. but you must look at all the surrounding circumstances. Of the case of *H.O. Brandt & Co v H.N. Morris & Co Ltd sup.* (to which I have already made reference in another connection), it was said by Viscount Kilmuir, L.C., (at pp. 603 and 264 of the respective reports) that that case laid down no general rule that on every f.o.b. or f.a.s. contract the buyer must supply a ship into which, or alongside which, the goods can legally be placed where there exists a prohibition on export except with a licence.

[Mᴄɴᴀɪʀ J. *reviewed the facts, and in particular the contents of the two letters, and continued:*]

... [The sellers'] obligation [to secure shipping space] seems to me, again, to co-exist quite consistently with the contract being otherwise upon f.o.b. terms; the f.o.b. terms still remain effective and important for two purposes at least, namely, to specify the exact price and what is included in the price, namely, all charges up until free on board, and, secondly, those words are apt for determining the place and moment at which the property and risk passes; and there is nothing inconsistent in those provisions with the obligation to find shipping space which I have endeavoured to state.

Notes

McNair J. emphasised that both f.o.b. and c.i.f. contracts could vary con- **3–014** siderably. He cited as f.o.b. authorities *Pyrene Company Ltd v Scindia Navigation*

Company Ltd, above, and *A.V. Pound & Co Ltd v M.W. Hardy & Co Inc.* [1956] A.C. 588, distinguishing *H.O. Brandt & Co v H.N. Morris & Co Ltd* [1917] 2 K.B. 784, both of which are discussed below. *Brandt v Morris* (a classic f.o.b. contract) was relied on strongly by the seller.

For the c.i.f. proposition, McNair J. cited *Comptoir d'Achat et de Vente du Boerenbond Belge, SA v Luis de Ridder, Limitada (The Julia)* [1949] A.C. 293, and *The Parchim* [1918] A.C. 157 (which was described as, but was probably not in reality a c.i.f. contract, since freight and insurance were for buyer's account). Both these cases have already been considered.

Here, the sellers were held to have undertaken to provide shipping space, and not merely to act out of friendship to the buyers. It is clearly part of the *ratio* of the case that the buyers were under no obligation to provide it. However, the sellers' obligation was not absolute, and this led Sassoon to observe at para. 521 (commenting on *Handel* but citing no other authority) that:

> " . . . unless an express agreement to the contrary can be shown to exist, the seller would, in the case of f.o.b. shipment to destination contracts, always undertake merely a conditional obligation to do his best to secure the ship."

Since, however, the limited undertaking was inferred from the express terms of the second letter, and was therefore dependant on the particular facts found, it is surely inappropriate to draw general conclusions from it, as Sassoon does here.

What is clear, however, is that McNair J. thought that in the absence of contrary evidence, the f.o.b. term implied that the duty to secure shipping space would be on the buyers.[13] The normal position could be displaced by contrary evidence, as in the case before him.

See also *Glencore Grain Rotterdam BV v Lebanese Organisation for International Commerce (LORICO)* [1997] 2 Lloyd's Rep. 386 (upholding Longmore J. on this issue, [1997] 1 Lloyd's Rep. 578), where the Court of Appeal refused to imply into a letter of credit (there being no express term) an entitlement for buyers that payment under the letter of credit need only be made if the bills of lading are marked "freight pre-paid", on the grounds that such a term is inconsistent with the operation of an f.o.b. contract, in the absence of express provision to the contrary in the sale contract. Even if an f.o.b. seller can undertake to pay the freight for buyer's account, such an undertaking will not be inferred in the absence of an express term.

CARLOS FEDERSPIEL & CO SA v CHARLES TWIGG & CO LTD

Queen's Bench Division (Commercial Court). [1957] 1 Lloyd's Rep. 240

Facts:

3–015   The case involved a contract for the sale of bicycles, expressed to be f.o.b. British port, insurance and freight to be charged as extras. The price had been paid by the buyers, and preparations for shipment made by the sellers, but the sellers were wound up before the goods were shipped. The buyers claimed that property had already passed to them.

Held:

Property would not pass until the goods were appropriated under s.18, Rule 5 of the Sale of Goods Act 1979, which would not occur until

---

[13] See also the *Ian Stach* case, below.

shipment. This aspect of the decision is considered further in chapter 5, below.

The importance of the case for present purposes is that the contract was regarded as f.o.b., although the seller was under a contractual obligation to make the carriage contract. The delivery was to be f.o.b., with freight and insurance as extras.

PEARSON J.: I agree . . . that fundamentally [this] is to be regarded as an f.o.b. contract, but one has to add that it has some c.i.f. features attached to it. The delivery expressly is to be f.o.b., but freight and insurance are to be extras, . . . It would seem that the intention is that the sellers are, in the first instance, to arrange the insurance and the contract of affreightment, and they are to pay the freight and insurance and charge them as extras to the buyers; and the intention seems to be that they should charge the cost price to the buyers, so that any rise or fall in rates of freight or insurance would be for the account of the buyers and of no interest to the sellers. That seems to be the nature of the contract.

It is, in my view, an f.o.b. contract, but one can also consider what the position would be if that is a wrong view and if it is in truth to be regarded as predominantly a c.i.f. contract.

Notes

The classification of the contract as f.o.b. is certainly not part of the *ratio* of the   **3–016**
case, since appropriation would not have been earlier, had the contract been c.i.f. Indeed, Pearson J. went on to consider the position, were the contract in reality c.i.f., and concluded that it would make no difference:

"It . . . therefore, that if and so far as this contract was in its true nature an f.o.b. contract, the natural time at which the property would pass would be on shipment. Undoubtedly this contract also contained some c.i.f. features, and there is an express reference to what is called "approximate c.i.f. charges" in the *pro forma* invoice. If and in so far as it was a c.i.f. contract, the effect of the authorities is that the property would pass not earlier than shipment, perhaps later than shipment. But for the purpose of the present case there is no need to consider whether it would be on shipment or at some later time."

(On property issues generally, see chapter 5, below).

(ii) *Conclusion on Carriage Contract*

The authorities would seem to support the conclusion that the f.o.b. term is   **3–016A**
sufficiently flexible to encompass first, either party making the carriage contract as principal, and secondly, either party undertaking to make the carriage contract. The second statement cannot be made quite as categorically, given that the views expressed in *Federspiel v Twigg* were clearly *obiter*.

Given the development of the f.o.b. term, however, it would be expected that in the absence of contrary evidence, duties regarding shipment are *prima facie* on the buyer. Thus, Diplock J. observed in *Ian Stach Ltd v Baker Bosley Ltd* [1958] 2 Q.B. 130, 138 that:

"On the face of the written contract . . . , it may be a matter of doubt as to whose was to be the responsibility for finding shipping space and for determining shipping port and shipping date. *Prima facie*, under an f.o.b. contract that is the duty and responsibility of the buyer; but there are probably as many exceptions to the rule as there are examples of it."[14]

The duty may be shifted by express terms or strong evidence. In *N.V. Handel My. J. Smits Import-Export v English Exporters (London) Ltd*, above, McNair J. thought that an obligation to ship could be placed on the seller, while still giving meaning to the f.o.b. term. There, the obligation was not absolute, but it does not appear to have been qualified in *Federspiel v Twigg*.

It may perhaps be concluded that fairly strong evidence is needed to justify a conclusion, in any given case, that the seller has undertaken to make the carriage contract. Even where he has, there may be a presumption that the undertaking is qualified, although the latter conclusion is not clearly justified on the basis of the authorities.

Where the buyer is shipper, he will, in principle, be liable for demurrage, should delay be incurred at loading and discharge, unless he is a time charterer, in which case he will incur hire for the period of the delay. Yet whether there is delay at the loading port might well be entirely within the control of the seller. The specification of a period for loading gives the buyer only limited protection against the consequences of seller's delay in loading, unless there is a provision such as that in *The Naxos*, below. Another possibility is to require the seller to pay any demurrage that becomes due, or otherwise to compensate a buyer who is time charterer. The voyage charter laytime and demurrage provisions were therefore incorporated into the sale contract in the *Al Hofuf*, below, and interpreted as they would have been in a carriage contract.

(d) NOMINATION OF VESSEL

3–017   It is clear from the above discussion that the obligation to nominate the vessel can be placed on either party, but that in the absence of any evidence of contrary intention, the obligation is on the buyer. The obligation is to nominate an effective ship, defined in *J. & J. Cunningham v Munro* (1922) 13 Lloyd's Rep. 62 and 216, at 216 (col. 2). There is a fuller extract in chapter 4, below, but the relevant paragraph is:

> "The contract under consideration was for 200 tons of Dutch bran for shipment during October, 1920, price £13 per ton f.o.b. Rotterdam, buyers finding freight room. Under such an arrangement it was the duty of the purchasers to provide a vessel at the appointed place, Rotterdam, at such a time as would enable the vendors to bring the goods alongside the ship and put them over the ship's rail, so as to enable the purchasers to receive them within the appointed time—in this case October. It would not, for example, be sufficient for the vendors to bring them to a warehouse at five minutes before midnight on Oct 31. The usual practice under such a contract is for the buyer to nominate the vessel and to send notice of her arrival to the vendor in order that the vendor may be in a position to fulfil his part of the contract. When the vendors tender the goods in question to the purchasers theoretically by placing them on the ship's rail, it is open to the purchasers to reject if the goods are not in accordance with the contract."

---

[14] He concluded that the evidence, in the form of various letters, pointed to the contract being classic f.o.b.

(i) *Shipment Period*

It is also clear from *J. & J. Cunningham v Munro* that where a period for shipment   **3–018**
is agreed, and at any rate where the obligation is on the buyers to nominate the
vessel, they have the freedom to choose the time within the shipment period
(subject to the estoppel arguments advanced, unsuccessfully, in *J. & J. Cunningham*
itself).[15] In that case, the shipment period was October, and the buyers were held
entitled to take the cargo of bran at any time during that month. They were
required to ensure that the vessel arrived in Rotterdam in time for the sellers to
load the cargo by the end of October, but they were under no obligation to ensure
an earlier arrival.

BUNGE & CO LTD v TRADAX ENGLAND LTD

Queen's Bench Division (Commercial Court) [1975] 2 Lloyd's Rep. 235

Facts:
In a "buyers' call" contract, the vessel arrived too late for the sellers to be
able to load within the shipment period. The sellers commenced loading,
but were unable to complete it before the shipment period expired. The
sellers offered to continue loading the next day but the weather was
unsuitable, and thereafter the sellers demanded the market rate for further cargo loaded, which the buyers refused to pay. The balance of the
cargo was never loaded.

Held:
The buyers had broken a condition of the contract by failing to nominate
an effective vessel, capable of loading the cargo within the period. The
sellers had elected to keep the contract alive, but their obligation to load
did not extend beyond the shipment period.

DONALDSON J.: The sellers protested that if the vessel arrived on Friday,   **3–019**
Jan. 19, there would be insufficient time to load the cargo within the
shipment period, which expired at midnight on Saturday, Jan. 20. The
normal working hours of the port ended for the week at 17:00 hours on
the Friday, but the sellers offered to load on the Saturday, subject to the
buyers meeting the cost of overtime. The sellers also offered to complete
loading after Jan. 20, provided that the buyers paid the market rate for
this part of the cargo. The buyers ultimately agreed to pay overtime for
Saturday working, but it rained and in the event nothing could be loaded
that day. They did not agree to pay for any of the cargo at market rates.
Only 110 tons was or could be loaded on the Friday and the balance of the
contract quantity was never shipped.

The award states two questions for the opinion of the Court, but only
one is now relevant. This is whether upon the true construction of the
contract and upon the facts found, the sellers were in breach of contract

[15] (1922) 13 L.L.L.R. Also Diplock J.'s assumption in *Ian Stach Ltd v Baker Bosley Ltd* [1958] 2
Q.B. 130, 139 and 142. This case considered further in para. 9—017, below.

by not causing the full contract quantity of barley to be shipped on the vessel.

The vessel was not ready to load before 15:00 hours on Friday, Jan. 19, and it is now common ground that this late arrival constituted a breach of contract upon the part of the buyers. As a result, the sellers could, if they had wished, have rejected the vessel and treated the contract as repudiated. But they did not do so and it is upon this fact that Mr Eckersley, for the buyers, founds his argument. In his submission, the sellers, by starting to ship the barley, waived their right to rely upon the late arrival of the vessel as discharging them from their obligation under the contract. That obligation was, he says, to ship the cargo in accordance with the custom of the port, that is to say, in the case of Berwick, within a reasonable time. Thence-forward their only remedy was to claim damages for any loss or expense which they incurred as a result of the late arrival of the vessel. Mr Hallgarten, who has appeared for the sellers, submits that a partial loading of the vessel under a very clearly defined protest does not amount to a waiver of the sellers' rights. Even if this is wrong, the sellers' obligation to ship does not continue after the expiry of the agreed shipment period at midnight on Saturday, Jan. 20, 1973.

In my judgment the sellers succeed. The buyers have the right to nominate the vessel which is to carry the cargo. They also have the right to send her to the port of loading at a time of their choice. But both these rights are subject to two qualifications. First, that the vessel shall be suitable for the cargo and for the port. Second, that the time when she is tendered shall be within the shipment period and such that the cargo can thereafter be shipped in accordance with the custom of the port and shipment completed at or before the expiry of that period. The sellers for their part have an obligation to start shipping as soon as the vessel is tendered and to continue to do so in accordance with the custom of the port. This obligation continues irrespective of whether this leads to the completion of shipment at or before the end of the shipment period. But this obligation to ship ceases at the end of the shipment period. The contract itself says "Delivery . . . between 1st and 20th January, 1973, (both dates inclusive)". Under no circumstances are they under any obligation to continue to ship after that period has expired.

Notes

3–020   In *Bunge,* the sellers had the cargo ready when the ship arrived, and loaded it as quickly as they could. If the vessel arrives in good time within the shipment period, the question of the sellers' obligation to load was considered in *Tradax Export SA v Italgrani di Francesco Ambrosio* [1986] 1 Lloyd's Rep. 112, where Kerr L.J. rejected the following finding of the arbitrators:

> "It is the duty of an F.O.B. Seller to have the contractual goods ready for delivery to the Buyer's Vessel on call within the contractual period of delivery. Therefore, an F.O.B. Seller is in default of his obligation under the Contract if, on receiving a notice of readiness from a buyer's vessel, he does not, at that moment in time, have the goods ready for delivery."

He went on to make the following observations, at p. 117:

"If [the *Bunge* conditions] on the side of the buyers are complied with, then the seller is obliged, also as a condition of the contract, to load the goods before the end of the shipment period (or any extension of it). All these matters were common ground between the parties . . .

The question which is not covered by any authority is whether—assuming that the buyers have complied with the conditions on their side mentioned above—the sellers can be in breach of condition before the expiry of the shipment period if they in fact load the contractual goods by this date, or are ready, able and willing to do so when the buyers nevertheless purport to declare them to be in default—*i.e.*, in breach of condition—before this date. I have never previously heard of any such contention . . .

Similarly, there is nothing in the passages which I have quoted from Benjamin on *Sale* to suggest that, by failing to complete the loading within a reasonable time, or within the time prescribed by the loading rate (if any) laid down in the contract, the sellers can be held to be in breach of condition even if the loading is completed before the expiry of the shipment period. *Prima facie* the sellers would be liable in damages in the first case and for demurrage in the second. Thus, if a contract calls for shipment in, say, March, with payment against documents, and the sellers tender properly dated March bills of lading, I have never heard it suggested that the buyers are nevertheless entitled to reject the tender and treat the sellers as being in default, on the ground that the loading should have been completed more quickly or that the bills of lading should have borne some earlier date in March."

From this it appears that:

1. The sellers do not need to have a cargo ready for loading when the ship arrives;

2. The sellers however have an obligation to load within a reasonable time of the arrival of the vessel, and "within the time prescribed by the loading rate (if any) laid down in the contract";

3. The obligations in 2. are not conditions: see further *The Al Hofuf*, below (where however the contract of sale incorporated laytime and demurrage provisions from the carriage contract).

(ii) *Additional Contractual Terms*

As with many other aspects of f.o.b. contracts, the parties may add terms to clarify or vary the common law position. A "buyer's call" contract, for example, clarifies the common law position, that the buyers have the right to determine the shipment date, within the period. The words "buyer's call" probably do little more than that. Kerr L.J. continued in *Italgrani*, at 118: **3–021**

"A requirement that the goods should previously have been available and ready for loading would, in my view, introduce a novel obligation into f.o.b. contracts. No such obligation, let alone in the nature of a condition, can, in my view, be extracted from the words "at buyers' call". Their purpose and effect are merely that the buyers have the option of calling for the goods to be loaded at any time during the shipment period when the vessel provided by them is ready to do so."

This seems merely to restate the common law requirement. In *Compagnie Commerciale Sucres et Denrees v Czarnikow Ltd (The Naxos)*,[16] on the other hand (below), the House of Lords held rule 14(1) to be a condition of the contract:

" . . . the seller shall have the sugar ready to be delivered to the buyer at any time during the contract period."

One of the arguments advanced by the sellers was that rule 14(1) added nothing (let alone an obligation that could be construed as a condition) to the common law position where a shipment period is agreed and the buyer undertakes nomination of the vessel. Indeed, Gatehouse J. had taken the view at first instance that:

"I do not think that the first paragraph [of r. 14] imposes a separate and further duty upon the seller in addition to his duty under the classic f.o.b. contract."

In the Court of Appeal [1989] 2 Lloyd's Rep. 462 and House of Lords, it was felt necessary to construe rule 14 as a whole:

"[1] In cases of f.a.s., f.o.b., and free stowed in hold (f.o.b. stowed) contracts the Seller shall have the sugar ready to be delivered to the Buyer at any time within the contract period.
[2] The Buyer, having given reasonable notice, shall be entitled to call for delivery of the sugar between the first and last working day inclusive of the period of delivery.
[3] If the vessel (or vessels) has presented herself in readiness to load within the contract period but has failed to be presented within 5 calendar days of the date contained in the notice above calling for delivery of the sugar the Buyer shall be responsible for any costs incurred by the Seller by reason of such delay exceeding the 5 calendar days.
[4] If the vessel (or vessels) has presented herself in readiness to load within the contract period, but loading has not been completed by the last working day of the period, the Seller shall be bound to deliver and the Buyer bound to accept delivery of the balance of the cargo or parcel up to the contract quantity."

3–022 In the Court of Appeal Sir Michael Kerr, dissenting in the Court of Appeal, but whose judgment was upheld by a majority in the House of Lords, said:

"In *Italgrani* the arbitrators concluded that in f.o.b. contracts generally, or on the true construction of the words "buyer's call" alone, the legal position is as follows:

'It is the duty of an FOB Seller to have the contractual goods ready for delivery to the Buyer's Vessel on call within the contractual period of delivery.'

That was rejected by this Court. In the present case, on the other hand, r. 14(1) provides expressly as follows:

' . . . the Seller shall have the sugar ready to be delivered to the Buyer at any time within the contract period.'

I agree with Mr Johnson [for the buyers] that in substance this is identical with the implied obligation which the arbitrators upheld in *Italgrani*, but which this Court rejected in the absence of some express term to that effect. In the present case, on the other hand, we have the express term which was absent in *Italgrani*.

---

[16] [1990] 1 W.L.R. 1337.

Against this background I then return to the two issues which I stated earlier after setting out the relevant parts of the award.

The first is whether r.14(1) is no more than a general statement of the sellers' position at common law or whether it casts some additional express obligation on the sellers. Mr Moore-Bick [for the sellers] contended for the former. He submitted that r.14(2) was no more than a general statement of the rights at common law of buyers under this form of contract, and that r.14(1) should therefore be regarded as no more than a statement of the converse from the point of view of the sellers. However, I cannot agree. The decision in *Italgrani*, which approved the analysis of the obligations of parties to "classic" f.o.b. contracts at common law as set out in Benjamin on *Sale*, clearly shows that r.14(1) imposes on the sellers a succinct additional express obligation which would not otherwise exist. Moreover, when read together, as they should be, it is clear that pars (1) to (4) of r.14 provide a special code of rights and obligations concerning delivery which differs substantially from what would be the position at common law in the absence of these provisions, save possibly of par. (2) if this had stood alone . . . "

In the House of Lords, Lord Ackner said: **3—023**

"It is clear from the award that the arbitrators were satisfied that r.14(1) imposed an additional contractual obligation on the sellers. The arbitrators did not accept the sellers' submission that r.14(1) added nothing to the buyers' obligations to be found in the contract, and was therefore merely a restatement in general terms of their obligations.

The construction of r.14(1)

It is common ground that r.14(1) falls to be construed against the background of the general law relating to f.o.b. contracts and in the context of the rules. It is quite clear that r.14 taken as a whole cannot be said to contain mere statements of general principle, adding nothing to the contractual obligations to be found in the form contract used by the parties . . . True enough, if r.14(2) had stood alone it could be said that it would have added nothing to the contract . . . However, r.14(2) does not stand alone and indeed is not in itself a separate rule but part of r.14, to which the numbering has been added merely as a matter of convenience."

It is fairly clear from this that while rule 14(2) (had it stood alone) probably states the common law position, rule 14(1) does not, but imposes an additional obligation on the seller, which was held to be a condition (see further paras 7—006, *et seq.*, below).

The parties can, if they wish, modify the common law position significantly. Incoterms 2000, for example, allows the seller the choice of shipment date, the delivery clauses A4 and B4 providing respectively:

"The seller must deliver the goods on the date or within the agreed period at the named port of shipment and in the manner customary at the port on board the vessel nominated by the buyer."

"The buyer must take delivery of the goods when they have been delivered in accordance with A4."

Notice stipulations are also often agreed by parties. In *Bunge Corporation., New York v Tradax Export SA, Panama* [1981] 1 W.L.R. 711, in a buyer's call contract, the following clause appeared:

"Period of delivery—during [May 1975] at buyers' call. Buyers shall give at least [15] days' notice of probable readiness of (vessels) . . . "

This clause imposed on the buyer an obligation, which was held to be a condition, an effect of which was significantly to reduce his normal option to call for the goods at any time, under a buyer's call contract.

BUNGE CORPORATION, NEW YORK v TRADAX EXPORT SA, PANAMA

House of Lords. [1981] 1 W.L.R. 711, [1981] 2 Lloyd's Rep. 1

Facts:

3–024 The case concerned an f.o.b. contract (on the GAFTA 119 standard form) for the sale of soya bean meal, under which (as amended) the sellers' last day for shipment was June 30, 1975. The buyers were required (under clause 7) to give 15 days' notice of probable readiness of the vessels, but in the event did not do so until June 17. This was too late to allow the sellers to perform the contract within the shipment period, and on a falling market the sellers claimed repudiation of the contract, on the grounds that the buyers had broken a condition.

Held:

The sellers were entitled to damages for wrongful repudiation by the buyers.

3–025   LORD WILBERFORCE: The appeal depends upon the construction to be placed upon clause 7 of GAFTA form 119 as completed by the special contract. It is not expressed as a "condition" and the question is whether, in its context and in the circumstances it should be read as such.

Apart from arguments on construction . . . , the main contention of Mr Buckley for the appellant [buyers] was based on the decision of the Court of Appeal in *Hongkong Fir Shipping Co Ltd v Kawasaki Kisen Kaisha Ltd* [1962] 2 Q.B. 26, as it might be applied to clause 7. Diplock L.J. in his seminal judgment illuminated the existence in contracts of terms which were neither, necessarily, conditions nor warranties, but, in terminology which has since been applied to them, intermediate or innominate terms capable of operating, according to the gravity of the breach, as either conditions or warranties. Relying on this, Mr Buckley's submission was that the buyer's obligation under the clause, to "give at least [15] consecutive days' notice of probable readiness of (vessels) and of the approximate quantity required to be loaded," is of this character. A breach of it, both generally and in relation to this particular case, might be, to use Mr Buckley's expression, "inconsequential," *i.e.*, not such as to make performance of the seller's obligation impossible. If this were so it would be wrong to treat it a breach of condition: *Hongkong Fir* would require it to be treated as a warranty.

This argument, in my opinion, is based upon a dangerous misunderstanding, or misapplication, of what was decided and said in *Hongkong Fir*. That case was concerned with an obligation of seaworthiness, breaches of which had occurred during the course of the voyage. The decision of the Court of Appeal was that this obligation was not a condition, a breach of which entitled the charterer to repudiate. It was pointed out that, as could be seen in advance the breaches, which might occur of it, were various. They might be extremely trivial, the omission of a nail; they might be extremely grave, a serious defect in the hull or in the machinery; they might be of serious but not fatal gravity, incompetence or incapacity of the crew. The decision, and the judgments of the Court of Appeal, drew from these facts the inescapable conclusion that it was impossible to ascribe to the obligation, in advance, the character of a condition.

Diplock L.J. then generalised this particular consequence into the analysis which has since become classical. The fundamental fallacy of the appellants' argument lies in attempting to apply this analysis to a time clause such as the present in a mercantile contract, which is totally different in character. As to such a clause there is only one kind of breach possible, namely, to be late, and the questions which have to be asked are, first, what importance have the parties expressly ascribed to this consequence, and secondly, in the absence of expressed agreement, what consequence ought to be attached to it having regard to the contract as a whole.

The test suggested by the appellants was a different one. One must consider, they said, the breach actually committed and then decide whether that default would deprive the party not in default of substantially the whole benefit of the contract. They invoked even certain passages in the judgment of Diplock L.J. in the *Hongkong Fir* case [1962] 2 Q.B. 26 to support it. One may observe in the first place that the introduction of a test of this kind would be commercially most undesirable. It would expose the parties, after a breach of one, two, three, seven and other numbers of days to an argument whether this delay would have left time for the seller to provide the goods. It would make it, at the time, at least difficult, and sometimes impossible, for the supplier to know whether he could do so. It would fatally remove from a vital provision in the contract that certainty which is the most indispensable quality of mercantile contracts, and lead to a large increase in arbitrations. It would confine the seller—perhaps after arbitration and reference through the courts—to a remedy in damages which might be extremely difficult to quantify. These are all serious objections in practice. But I am clear that the submission is unacceptable in law. The judgment of Diplock L.J. does not give any support and ought not to give any encouragement to any such proposition; for beyond doubt it recognises that it is open to the parties to agree that, as regards a particular obligation, any breach shall entitle the party not in default to treat the contract as repudiated. Indeed, if he were not doing so he would, in a passage which does not profess to be more than clarificatory, be discrediting a long and uniform series of cases—at least from *Bowes v Shand* (1877) 2 App. Cas. 455 onwards which have been referred to by my noble and learned friend, Lord Roskill. It remains true, as Lord Roskill has pointed out in *Cehave NV v Bremer Handelsgesellschaft mbH (The Hansa Nord)* [1976] Q.B. 44, that the courts should not be too ready to interpret contractual clauses as conditions. And I have myself commended, and continue to commend, the greater flexibility in the law of contracts to which *Hongkong Fir* points the way (*Reardon Smith Line Ltd v Yngvar Hansen-Tangen (trading as H. E. Hansen-Tangen)*) [1976] 1 W.L.R. 989, 998). But I do not doubt that, in suitable cases, the courts should not be reluctant, if the intentions of the parties as shown by the contract so indicate, to hold that an obligation has the force of a condition, and that indeed they should usually do so in the case of time clauses in mercantile contracts. To such cases the "gravity of the breach" approach of the *Hongkong Fir* case [1962] 2 Q.B. 26 would be unsuitable. I need only add on this point that the word "expressly" used by Diplock L.J. at p. 70 of his judgment in *Hongkong Fir* should not be read as requiring the actual use of the word "condition": any term or terms of the contract, which, fairly read, have the effect indicated, are sufficient. Lord Diplock himself has given recognition to this in this House: *Photo Production Ltd v Securicor Transport Ltd* [1980] A.C. 827, 849. I therefore reject that part of the appellants' argument which was based upon it, . . .

3–026   In conclusion, the statement of the law in Halsbury's *Laws of England*, 4th ed., vol. 9 (1974), paras. 481–482, including the footnotes to paragraph 482 . . . appears to me to be correct, in particular in asserting (1) that the court will require precise compliance with stipulations as to time wherever the circumstances of the case indicate that this would fulfil the intention of the parties, and (2) that broadly speaking time will be considered of the essence in "mercantile" contracts—with footnote reference to authorities which I have mentioned.

The relevant clause falls squarely within these principles, and such authority as there is supports its status as a condition: see *Bremer Handelsgesellschaft mbH v J.H. Rayner & Co Ltd* [1978] 2 Lloyd's Rep. 73 and see *Turnbull (Peter) & Co Pty Ltd v Mundas Trading Co (Australasia) Pty Ltd* [1954] 2 Lloyd's Rep. 198. In this present context it is clearly essential that both buyer and seller (who may change roles in the next series of contracts, or even in the same chain of contracts) should know precisely what their obligations are, most especially because the ability of the seller to fulfil his obligation may well be totally dependent on punctual performance by the buyer.

3–027   LORD LOWRY: . . . The law having been established, why should we regard the term here in question as a condition? I start by expressing my full agreement with the reasons given in your Lordships' speeches. Among the points which have weighed with me are the following:

(1) There are enormous practical advantages in certainty, not least in regard to string contracts where today's buyer may be tomorrow's seller.

(2) Most members of the string will have many ongoing contracts simultaneously and they must be able to do business with confidence in the legal results of their actions.

(3) Decisions would be too difficult if the term were innominate, litigation would be rife and years might elapse before the results were known.

(4) The difficulty of assessing damages is an indication in favour of condition: *McDougall v Aeromarine of Emsworth Ltd* [1958] 1 W.L.R. 1126, 1133.

(5) One can at least say that recent litigation has provided indications that the term is a condition. Parties to similar contracts should (failing a strong contra indication) be able to rely on this: *The Mihalis Angelos* [1971] 1 Q.B. 164, 199F *per* Edmund-Davies L.J.

(6) To make "total loss" the only test of a condition is contrary to authority and experience, when one recalls that terms as to the date of sailing, deviation from a voyage and the date of delivery are regarded as conditions, but that failure to comply with them does not always have serious consequences.

(7) Nor need an implied condition pass the total loss test: see (6) above.

(8) If the consequences of breach of condition turn out to be slight, the innocent party may treat the condition as an innominate term or a warranty.

(9) While the sellers could have made time of the essence, if it were not so already, this would require reasonable notice, which might well not be practical either in a string contract or at all.

(10) In *Tarrabochia v Hickie* (1856) 1 H. & N. 183, 188 upon which the appellants strongly relied, Bramwell B. said:

> "No doubt it is competent for the parties, if they think fit, to declare in express terms that any matter shall be a condition precedent, but when they have not so expressed themselves, it is necessary for those who construe the instrument to see whether they intend to do it. Since, however, they could have done it, those who construe the instrument should be chary in doing for them that which they might, but have not done for themselves."

But in that very case both Pollock C.B. and Bramwell B., without the benefit of any express term, said that, where the agreement was that a ship should sail on a particular day, that was a condition precedent.

(11) To accept the argument that conditions ought not to be implied "because the parties themselves know how to describe a term" would logically condemn the entire doctrine of implied terms.

(12) Arbitrators and courts might if the term were innominate, give different answers concerning the effect of a breach in very similar transactions, and parties could never learn by experience what was likely to happen in a given situation. So-called string contracts are not made, or adjudicated on, in strings.

The only arguments against treating the term as a condition appear to me to be based on generalities, whereas the considerations which are peculiar to this contract and similar contracts tell in favour of its being a condition. For these reasons, and for the reasons given by my noble and learned friends, I would concur in dismissing both the appeal and the cross-appeal.

3–028   LORD ROSKILL: To my mind the most important single factor in favour of Mr Staughton's submission [for the sellers] is that until the requirement of the 15-day consecutive notice was fulfilled, the respondents could not nominate the "one Gulf port" as the loading port, which under the instant contract it was their sole right to do. I agree with Mr Staughton that in a mercantile contract when a term has to be performed by one party as a condition precedent to the ability of the other party to perform another term, especially an essential term such as the nomination of a single loading port, the term as to time for the performance of the former obligation will in general fall to be treated as a condition. Until the 15 consecutive days' notice had been given, the respondents could not know for certain which loading port they should nominate so as to ensure that the contract goods would be available for loading on the ship's arrival at that port before the end of the shipment period.

Notes

1. The passage from Lord Wilberforce's speech is chosen to show that some terms are still characterised as conditions, in spite of *Hongkong Fir*. That case might apply to a term which can be broken in a wide variety of ways, from the very trivial to the catastrophic, but there is only one way to break a time term. Lord Lowry gives commercial, and Lord Roskill legal, reasons why this particular term should be regarded as a condition. The arguments for preferring conditions to innominate terms are examined again in paras 15—011, *et seq.*, below.

2. It is unusual for sellers to repudiate on a falling market, but they would have been buyers one stage earlier in the chain, and their suppliers might similarly have repudiated.

3. The House of Lords upheld the decision of the Court of Appeal, [1980] 1 Lloyd's Rep. 294, which was applied in *The Al Hofuf*, below (at least to the buyers' obligations).

COMPAGNIE COMMERCIALE SUCRES ET DENREES v CZARNIKOW LTD (THE NAXOS)

House of Lords. [1990] 1 W.L.R. 1337, [1991] 1 Lloyd's Rep. 29

The case concerned an f.o.b. contract (under which the buyer was respon-   **3–029**
sible for nominating the vessel, or vessels) for the sale of a quantity of
sugar, with a shipment period covering May and June 1986. The contract
incorporated the rules of the Refined Sugar Association, rule 11 of which
provided that the buyer had the option of taking delivery in one or more
lots during the contract period, and rule 14(1) provided that:

" . . . the seller shall have the sugar ready to be delivered to the buyer
at any time during the contract period."

The sellers did not have cargo ready for the vessel nominated by the
buyers, which was ready to load on May 29, and the buyers claimed that
this entitled them to treat the contract as terminated.

Held:

1. The sellers had broken the contract by not having the cargo ready
   for loading. Although rule 14(1) did not require them to have cargo
   ready at all times during the contract period, it did require them to
   have sugar available for loading without delay or interruption as
   soon as the vessel nominated by the buyers presented herself ready
   to load.

2. The obligation imposed on the sellers by rule 14(1) was a condition,
   and therefore the buyers were entitled to treat the contract as
   terminated. It was effectively a time clause, especially when construed along with cl.7: "Buyer to give Seller not less than 14 days'
   notice of vessel(s) expected readiness to load", and following *Bunge
   v Tradax Exports* [1981] 1 W.L.R. 711, time clauses in mercantile
   contracts should usually be held to be conditions. Additionally, in
   this case the arbitrators had found that rule 14(1) was of the utmost
   importance, as the buyers required prompt delivery in order to
   fulfil onward commitments.

Lord Brandon dissented on the second issue only. In his view, the contract
treated other obligations, breaches of which would cause delay, as
breaches of warranty, and logically all similar obligations should be
classified in the same way, *i.e.* as warranties.

Notes:

Among the arguments that were used by the sellers against rule 14(1) being   **3–030**
construed as a condition, were that it added nothing to the normal duties of an
f.o.b. buyer, and that it was insufficiently precise to be construed as a condition.

The refutation of the former argument was considered above. The latter argument is essentially that, if a term is such that any breach, however, slight, allows the other party to repudiate, that term needs to be defined with precision.

TREITEL, "TIME OF SHIPMENT IN F.O.B. CONTRACTS"

[1991] L.M.C.L.Q. 147

[Footnotes are as in the original, but renumbered for inclusion in this book.]

3–031   ... Under the general law, a mere failure by an f.o.b. seller to ship goods within a reasonable time of receipt would not of itself amount to a breach of condition, so as to give the buyer the right to rescind; that right would only arise if the seller had failed to load by the end of the shipment period.[17] At the other extreme, it has been suggested that, if the contract stipulated for shipment within a specified number of days after receipt of shipping instructions, that stipulation probably would be classified as a condition[18]; it would lay down a precise time-table and would thus fall within the general rule that time clauses which lay down specific dates for the performance are normally to be classified in this way. The crucial provision in *The Naxos* fell somewhere between these two extremes. While [r. 14] did not, of itself, lay down a precise time-table, it did (in conjunction with cl. 7) enable the parties, in the light of events subsequent to the contract, to determine exactly when the goods had to be available for loading: namely, "at the expiration of the notice given under clause 7 and as soon as the vessel presents herself ready to load within the contract period".[19] Had r. 14 stood alone, the requirement of "reasonable notice" in its para. (2) would have involved "questions of degree"[20] ... The main purpose of classifying time clauses as conditions is to promote certainty by enabling the injured party to tell exactly when he can rescind; that purpose cannot be achieved when the time stipulation is itself vague. Had r. 14 not been supplemented by cl. 7, it would have fallen into this category since the requirement of "reasonable notice" in para. (2) would have failed to specify how much notice had to be given.

The classification of a time clause as a condition most clearly promotes certainty where the clause is one which fixes a date for performance, so that it is possible to tell, without doubt, from the time of contracting exactly when performance is to become due. The stock example of this type of provision is one specifying a shipment period, which (in the absence of a contrary indication) is a condition.[21] But the same classification has also been adopted where the contract specified, not a date, but an event on (or within a stated interval from) which performance was to become due ... [In] *The Naxos* ... the specified event (the arrival of the ship) did not precede, but followed, the specified interval of time ... -

[17] *Tradax Export SA v Italgrani di Francesco Ambrosio* [1986] 1 Lloyd's Rep. 112, 117.
[18] Benjamin's *Sale of Goods* (3rd. ed.), §1830 [now 5th ed., paras. 20–028 ff.]
[19] [1990] 1 W.L.R. 1337, 1347.
[20] *ibid.*
[21] *Bowes v Shand* (1877) 2 App. Cas. 455, see para. 7—019, below.

[but] ... once the 14 days' notice had been given and the ship had arrived, there could be no doubt that the sellers' failure to have the cargo ready was a breach. It is when a time clause is one which indicates clearly on what day the stipulated act is to be done (so that its breach can be clearly and easily established) that certainty is most obviously promoted by classifying the term as a condition. As a practical matter, the *fact* of breach cannot be disputed where performance has not been rendered at the end of the stipulated time, or on the occurrence of the stipulated event. And if the term is classified as a condition the injured party is not concerned with any question as to the *effect* of the breach: he can safely rescind and enter into a substitute transaction. This, indeed, was exactly the course of action followed by the buyers in *The Naxos*.

Notes:

The argument examined here is that the time clause in *The Naxos* was precise,   3–032
but Treitel then examines another argument that appears to have appealed to Lord Ackner, that even an imprecise time clause can be a condition when there is a finding of fact that its performance is regarded as commercially vital—note the reliance on the finding of the arbitrators in held (2) above.

Treitel then examines the dissenting approach of Lord Brandon, and a test where the intention of the parties is collected from the terms of the agreement itself. Lord Brandon's view is, in effect, that since other time terms within the same contract are clearly not conditions, it is "illogical" to hold r.14(2) to be a condition. Treitel concludes on this issue as follows:

"The arguments of the majority and of Lord Brandon seem largely to pass each other by. On the other hand, Lord Brandon is surely right to resist the argument that a time clause should be classified as a condition *merely* because it is a time clause and specifies a definite time of performance ... It is submitted that the classification of the disputed term in *The Naxos* as a condition is most readily justified by reference to the combination of the two factors already mentioned: the ease of establishing the breach and the importance to the buyer of strict performance of that term."

Implicit in this discussion is the high desirability of the promotion of certainty in this type of transaction, and the willingness of the courts to construe terms as conditions, in pursuit of this objective.

(ii) *Incorporation of Carriage Terms into f.o.b. Sale Contracts*

The common law position might not adequately protect a buyer who is also   3–033
shipper. The problem is really the reverse of that for c.i.f. contracts described in the previous chapter, in that the buyer might become liable for demurrage payments under the carriage contract if cargo-handling is delayed, but at loading cargo-handling is to a large extent within the seller's control, especially as the common law does not require him to have a cargo ready when the vessel arrives. One way of protecting the buyer is to enter into a contract such as that in *The Naxos* (although this would not cover delays in the loading process). Another is to incorporate the carriage contract laytime and demurrage provisions into the sale contract, as in *The Al Hofuf*.

Note that more of the judgment is set out than is strictly necessary for this particular discussion, the case also being of interest in other respects.

SCANDINAVIAN TRADING CO A/B v ZODIAC PETROLEUM SA (THE AL HOFUF)

Queen's Bench Division (Commercial Court). [1981] 1 Lloyd's Rep. 81

Facts:

3–034   The case concerned a classic f.o.b. contract for 40,000 tonnes of gas oil, plus or minus 10 per cent. in buyers' option. The contract further provided, against the word "laytime", "36 hours SHINC" (Sundays and Holidays included) "plus 6 NOR" (6 hours notice of readiness) (*i.e.* 42 hours' in total from notice of readiness being given), and against the word "Demurrage" "charter-party rate of vessel to apply"; the effect of this incorporation was to impose on the sellers liability to pay demurrage, at the charterparty rate, if loading was not completed within the laytime.[22]

There were in fact two shipments, and in respect of 19,800 tons a circle developed. The issue arose over the balance of about 23,000 tonnes under the sale contract.

There was a custom in the oil trade that an f.o.b. buyer had to give in succession notices of expected time of arrival of the vessel at the refinery or the lifting port, 72, 48 and 24 hours in advance of the anticipated date of arrival.

No such notice was given by the buyer, and the vessel nominated (*Al Hofuf*) could not arrive in time to load all the cargo by the end of the shipment period (28 Feb 1977). The market was steadily falling, however, and in particular for the winter oil which was the subject matter of the contract, so the sellers accepted the nomination but subject to extending loading until 2nd March (but accepting demurrage liability). The vessel gave no notice of readiness, and sailed away without loading, the buyers claiming that the sellers were in repudiatory breach of contract.

Held:

1. The buyers' failure to nominate a vessel that could load the cargo within the shipment period constituted a breach of condition by them, but the sellers had elected to keep the contract alive.

2. Applying the same principles as apply to laytime and demurrage in carriage contracts, the sellers would only be in repudiatory breach themselves if they failed (or refused) to load within a frustrating time, and the facts did not support that contention (Devlin J.'s principles from *Universal Cargo Carriers Corporation v Citati*

---

[22] Note that only the demurrage rate, and not the laytime provision, are incorporated from the charterparty. Many tanker voyage charterparties at this time would have provided for 72 hours' total laytime for loading and discharge, and there would be no logic in making the sellers responsible for demurrage at discharge. 36 hours (plus NOR) for loading therefore seems a reasonable allocation.

[1957] 2 Q.B. 401, [1957] 1 Lloyd's Rep. 174 were applied). The buyers were not therefore justified in sailing the vessel away.

MOCATTA J.: In the pleadings in this action the plaintiffs [sellers], the   3–035
Scandinavian Trading Co. A.B., claimed . . . a declaration that the first defendants [buyers] repudiated and/or broke the contract of sale between the parties which was for 40,000 tonnes of gas oil, plus or minus 10 per cent at the buyers' option, and that the first and second defendants, and each of them, were liable to indemnify the plaintiffs in respect of their resulting loss. The second defendants guaranteed the performance by the first defendants of the contract of sale entered into between the first defendants and the plaintiffs. The points of claim further claimed U.S. $169,625 or their equivalent, as damages and, finally, they claimed interest.

There was a counterclaim by the defendants for the non-shipment by the plaintiffs of 23,000 tonnes of gas oil. The consequence of that non-shipment, according to the counterclaim, was that the defendants were unable to make the profit they would have made on a sub-contract, which would have produced, after allowing for the price the defendants would have had to pay the plaintiffs, a profit of U.S. $ 40,250 . . .

The facts of this case I have found of considerable interest. Indeed, from the three excellent witnesses who gave evidence I learnt a great deal which was novel to me in relation to the oil trade. In speaking of the oil trade I am speaking of something which appears to have come into existence as a trade of some size relatively recently and for the major part since the traumatic events both in Israel and throughout the world in relation to the Yom Kippur war and its consequences and the very rapid rise in the price of crude oil ever since.

Although the Court is dealing with a claim for damages of breach of contract of sale, the sale being f.o.b. at a refinery in Cagliari, at a place called Sarroch, the name of the refinery itself being Saras, the contract naturally contains a number of provisions in relation to laytime, demurrage and other measures with which one is more familiar in their setting in a charter-party. Indeed, the use of terms more frequently used in charter-parties than in contracts of sale has made it, perhaps, more difficult than it would otherwise be to keep one's mind clear one some of the points that have arisen in considering the fairly substantial body of telex communications which have been put before the Court. Furthermore, the language used in some of those telexes has been, I think, somewhat confusingly used by their authors.

The plaintiffs are basically an oil trading company with their head office in Stockholm and a substantial London office—which is looked after by the vice-president of the plaintiffs, a Mr Rapp. He describes himself, apart from being vice-president of the mother company in Stockholm, as general manager of the subsidiary company in London. He was a wholly admirable witness and spoke almost impeccable English. The plaintiffs, as I understood Mr Rapp's evidence, are really a substantially larger company than the other oil traders about whom I heard evidence. The plaintiffs, as a matter of history, started their career, as I understood Mr Rapp, by importing Russian oil into Sweden. They now, apparently, own some 35 per cent. of the outlets for petroleum products in Sweden; they also export oil to other countries, including the United States of America, and, I think, do a certain amount of chartering of ships with which to carry the oil they sell.

The first defendants, Zodiac Petroleum S.A., is a Swiss company whose head office is in Geneva. This is an oil trading company. It buys and sells quantities of different petroleum products, in liquid form. There are, I believe, a number of other sister companies whose names all incorporate the word Zodiac. Certainly there is in London, or there was at the material time, a London company, an English company, called Zodiac Petroleum Ltd who acted as agents for the first defendants in some of the communications that passed between the first defendants and either the plaintiffs or the brokers, who are a concern called Petroder. It would seem that Petroder, who certainly carry on business in London and no doubt elsewhere, may be a subsidiary of a Bahamian company in whose name the word Bassett is included. Certainly the commissions earned by Petroder were paid to the Bassett company.

One of the remarkable things about this trade in oil between these relatively small companies (I say relatively small because when one thinks of oil companies one naturally, as a layman, thinks of mammoth companies like Exxon, Esso, Shell, British Petroleum, Petrofina, and so forth) is that they do deals with each other through a single broker who acts both for the sellers and for the buyers and receives a commission of 2 1/2 per cent from the sellers. This system, which is wholly at odds with the general approach of English law to the position of agents, apparently works to the complete satisfaction of both sellers and buyers although, naturally enough, a seller wants to get as much as he can for his oil and the buyer wants to pay as little as he can for his.

The second defendants, Williams Hudson Ltd, guaranteed the performance by the first defendants, who, I think, are their wholly owned subsidiary, of their purchase contract with the plaintiffs. I was told by Miss French, who at the time worked for the first defendants, that there is a whole building in Maltravers Street occupied both by the second defendants themselves and by units of their subsidiary and related companies . . .

[Mocatta J. *described communications between the parties and continued:*]

3–036   It follows from what I have said, I think, and anyhow it is common ground, that this was the classic type of f.o.b. contract in that the provision of the ship was the duty of the buyer. Quite frequently, particularly I think in post-war years, the duty of providing the ship as well as the goods has fallen upon the seller; but not so in this case. This follows the

19th century practice which is well demonstrated in the well known case of *Inglis v Stock* (1885) 10 App. Cas. 263 ...

It is common ground that in this interesting and relatively new trade it is the custom that the buyer who buys f.o.b. must give, in succession, notices of expected time of arrival of the vessel at the refinery or lifting port in question, 72, 48 and 24 hours in advance of the anticipated date of arrival.

On Feb. 14 the first defendants sold on what they had agreed to purchase from the plaintiffs to a buyer whose name was to be nominated, as I understand it, by a concern called Motoroil Hellas. The name subsequently nominated was the A. and G. Oil and Shipping Co., Ltd, briefly referred to in a number of documents as "Argoil". That company is one of the companies in the very large and well known Green group of companies headed by either an individual or a company, or both, under the name of "Vardinoyannis". That group of companies deals in oil and owns and charters ships. It may be, I do not know, that the shipping interest is its main interest. The sale on was of the same quantity, with the same option as to variation of quantity, at a modest profit because the price was U.S. $ 123.50 f.o.b. Cagliari; it had exactly the same provisions as regards laytime and demurrage and also the same provisions as regards the payment of commission to Bassett Investments.

Argoil undoubtedly sold on to sub-purchasers. But their name does not emerge from the documents before me. It may be, though I am quite uncertain about this, that they were another company in the Vardinoyannis empire. However, it does appear from the evidence, though one cannot be quite certain of this, that the sale between Argoil and their purchasers (whom I shall call "company X") were probably made, as regards price, on a moveable basis associated with the prices published in Platt's Oil Price List, from day to day. It also appears as if company X chartered a Saudi Arabian tanker, called *Al Hofuf*, on an Exxonvoy charter form to pick up the gas oil which that company had purchased from Argoil, Argoil had purchased from Zodiac and Zodiac had purchased from the plaintiffs.

It appears that shortly after the main contract was made the market prices of petroleum and its various products went into decline. The fall was not catastrophic but it seems to have been fairly steady. It obviously had not begun by Feb. 14 but the high seems to have been reached for gas oil about Feb. 9 and for kerosene about Feb. 14. To show the fall that subsequently ensued I merely quote prices taken from Platt's Oil Price List on Mar. 7, with regard to gas oil, ranging between U.S. $ 114 and U.S. $ 117. It is thought that the first figure was for f.o.b. sales and the second for c.i.f. sales.

It was admitted between Counsel that the provision in the head contract for delivery between Feb. 20 and 28 was a condition of the contract and of its essence and it was further admitted that timely notices of expected time of arrival of the vessel in accordance with the custom already mentioned was also a condition and of the essence of the contract.

It was natural that Counsel should have agreed on those points, both because, if I may say so with respect, the decision is fairly obvious and, what is more important, had been laid down fairly recently in an extremely interesting and important judgment of the Court of Appeal is *Bunge Corporation v Tradax Export SA* [1980] 1 Lloyd's Rep. 294. One is very tempted, so interesting is the judgment, to quote extensively from it, but that would be clearly an unnecessary expenditure of time in view of the agreement between Counsel . . .

. . . The other deals that took place before the events in this action, had the effect that (just as so often happens with other products, and in particular with soya beans, with which we are all so very familiar these days) a circle developed and, whereas the plaintiffs themselves sold to the defendants, the defendants sold on, I think to a German concern called Mabanaft, that concern sold back to the plaintiffs. The amount in question was 19,800 tonnes and the four parties concerned settled this by paying the differences. In fact, I think that the plaintiffs did quite well out of it, but that is wholly immaterial. That left a balance under this contract which has turned out to be about 23,000 tonnes.

[MOCATTA J. *described various communications between the parties, regarding the late nomination of the vessel, and continued:*]

3–037   . . . It is right that I should say that although this nomination by the first defendants was clearly late and in breach of contract, because plainly it was impossible to load 23,000 tonnes between 18:00 hours on Monday Feb. 28 and midnight. The average rate of loading being something like 800 to 1000 tonnes per hour, the plaintiffs were quite happy, if they could arrange things, to accept this departure from, and variation of, the charter because the price was a good one. The market had slightly fallen, though only slightly by Feb. 25, but nevertheless the plaintiffs took the view that it was on a downward trend.

In relation to that, I should add that in the Mediterranean basin the boundary between winter and summer comes round about Mar. 1 or very soon thereafter. In the winter there is a demand for gas oil with a pourability (if I may use such a word) down to −15 deg. C., but with the oncoming of the summer there is no demand for such a resistance to cold weather because such cold weather is not expected, and the demand changes to gas oil of a pourability of −12 deg. C. Apart from that the demand for gas oil generally tends to fall because one of the purposes to which it is put is for central heating. I add that the resistance to low temperature, so as to produce a gas oil which remains pourable down to a temperature of −15 deg. C., is achieved by adding kerosene to the gas oil—I think in a percentage of 15 per cent, kerosene to 85 per cent. gas oil—and kerosene is a more expensive refined product of petroleum than is gas oil. Accordingly, not unnaturally, the plaintiffs were happy if they could retain the price agreed on Jan. 31 although it was on Feb. 25 and they were very near the formal end of the winter. Then they would enter a period when nobody would be interested in buying gas oil which remained pourable even though the temperature was as low as −15 deg. C.

The plaintiffs were prepared to accept liability for demurrage; it will be remembered that the contract provided "charter party rate of the vessel to apply". We have no evidence what the charter-party rate of demurrage was in this case. However we do have a scintilla of evidence to which I have already referred, namely, that the vessel was chartered on the Exxon voyage form, that is to say it was a voyage charter and not a time charter, and therefore in all probability did provide for a rate of demurrage. It sometimes happens that there is no such provision, particularly in a time charter, and a seller who has delayed the loading of the ship provided by the f.o.b. buyer cannot be brought to book for holding the vessel up and causing the buyer to pay hire for the time lost. In this case the plaintiffs did not hesitate to offer to pay any demurrage that there might be because they had been sufficiently far-sighted, in the process of the agreement which they had made with the client in Sardinia, as to laytime, namely 36 hours, and notice of readiness and for demurrage to provide—"all time spent in excess of the laytime allowed which was to be paid by your hirer calculated as *per* charter party except for vessels on time-charter", when the London Tanker Broker Monthly Average Freight Rate assessment was to be applied . . .

In fact *Al Hofuf* arrived in Sarroch Roads on Sunday Feb. 27, at 19_00 hours, and sailed on Monday Feb. 28 at 22:00 hours. It appears that she gave no notice of readiness to anybody. The evidence available to the Court does not indicate where she went or whether it was Argoil or company X that ordered her to leave or what it was that she was engaged in doing; presumably picking up some other cargo at some other port.

. . . the defendants tried to justify their position of sailing their vessel away, at 22:00 hours on Monday, without any cargo, on the basis that the sellers had loaded none and it was uncertain when they were going to load it. They took the view that the sellers had repudiated their obligations under the agreement which had been made and accordingly the buyers, or the sub-buyers, were justified in sailing *Al Hofuf* away from Cagliari.

[MOCATTA J. *reviewed the quality of the evidence and continued:*]

It is well established in charter-party law that the time for the provision **3–038** of cargo to load as well as the time taken in loading it are neither conditions which are of the essence of the contract. You may break the contract and be liable in damages for not providing the cargo when you should have or for taking a very long time to load the ship. But unless you take so long a time that you reach what the Courts call "a frustrating time" the ship is not entitled to say that such conduct is a repudiation and to sail away, but has to be content with the demurrage which it can earn, when there is provisions for damage, or damages for detention if there is no specific provision for demurrage. This was established in the well known decision of Devlin J. (as he then was) in the famous case of *Universal Cargo Carriers Corporation v Citati* [1957] 1 Lloyd's Rep. 174; [1957] 2 Q.B. 401, which is a bible for decisions on a number of points in this particular field, and which followed the very well known case of *Inverkip Steamship Co Ltd v Bunge & Co* [1917] 2 K.B. 193, where Lord Justice Scrutton said the same thing about delay in loading a ship and that it was not enough that the charterer was taking an unreasonable time in loading the ship to entitle it to more than demurrage unless the time was what is called "frustrating". Admittedly it is somewhat difficult to define what is and what is not a frustrating time but that is the law —beyond peradventure.

Accordingly, I do not think that, in the present case, even if I had not accepted Mrs. Riben's evidence, that the buyers could in any way justify the sailing away of *Al Hofuf* when she did sail . . .

I therefore consider that the counterclaim fails and will be dismissed and there must be judgment for the amount claimed.

Notes

3–039   1. Mocatta J. mentioned two breaches of condition by the buyers, the first of which would apply to any f.o.b. contract where the buyer was responsible for nominating the vessel, and the second of which applied in particular to the customs within the oil trade (the successive notices). To treat these obligations as conditions seems consistent with the law as it later developed in the House of Lords in *Bunge v Tradax* and *The Naxos*, above.

2. Mocatta J. did not think, however, that the obligation of the sellers to load within the laytime was a condition. His reasoning was that it was well-established from charterparty cases that it was an innominate term, and clearly he saw no reason to apply different reasoning in a sale contract context.[23]

3. Though the contract is described as classic f.o.b., the laytime and demurrage provisions only make sense if the buyer is shipper, or at any rate liable to pay demurrage incurred at loading (since otherwise why require the sellers to pay demurrage to the buyers?).[24] This was most probably a *Pyrene* type 3 contract.[25]

Further observations

The passages taken from this judgment are more extensive than strictly necessary to support the above observations, in the notes. *The Al Hofuf* is also of interest for its description of the oil trade at that time (the contract was made in January 1977, for shipment in February, only a few years after the breakdown in orderly oil trading, following the Yom Kippur war). Apart from the incorporation of demurrage provisions into the sale contract, and the notice provisions that were a custom of the trade, we see a long chain of relatively small traders, some of whom

---

[23] It might be questioned whether the wholesale importation of charterparty law into the sale contract is appropriate, given that the chain sale considerations do not arise in charterparties. On the other hand, the provision for demurrage as liquidated damages probably argues against the seller's obligation being classified as a condition.

[24] It is possible, but surely unlikely, that the seller was shipper and the buyers' liability was under the Bills of Lading Act 1855, s.1.

[25] The authors of Schmitthoff's *Export Trade*, (10th ed.), agree (at p. 18, n. 41) that *The Al Hofuf* was not classic f.o.b., but f.o.b. (buyer contracting with carrier)—*i.e. Pyrene* type 3.

appear to be tanker owners, others of whom clearly have no oil storage facilities, and can therefore only be acting as middlemen. We even see a circle developing, with price adjustments, regarding the part of the cargo that was not at issue in the case. See further on oil markets in para. 1—047, above.

(iv) *Substitution*

If the originally-nominated ship fails to arrive, or is ineffective for any other   **3–040**
reason, the buyer can substitute a fresh nomination. In *Colley v Overseas Exporters Ltd*, in chapter 5, below, no fewer than five nominations were made, none of which (due to a series of misfortunes) was effective. It was never suggested that the buyer was not entitled to substitute, after the failure of the first nomination.

AGRICULTORES FEDERADOS ARGENTINOS SOCIEDAD COOPERATIVA LIMITADA v AMPRO SA COMMERCIALE

Queen's Bench Division. [1965] 2 Lloyd's Rep. 157

Facts:
The contract was for the sale, f.o.b. Rosario, of 2000 metric tons of Plate maize, f.o.b. Rosario, shipment from Sept. 20 to Sept. 29, 1960. The vessel nominated by the buyers was delayed, and the sellers purported to repudiate the contract (on a rising market) on the ground of her inability to load in time. The buyers had been able to nominate an alternative vessel, which would have been able to load after working hours, during overtime on 29th, but were unable to secure any co-operation from the sellers.

Held:
The sellers' purported cancellation of the contract was wrongful. The buyers were entitled to substitute, the original nomination having been delayed.

WIDGERY J.: There is nothing expressly in this contract to provide the circumstances in which a particular vessel shall be nominated, and the rights of the parties are to be regulated by the general law as it applies to an f.o.b. contract. As I understand it, the general law applying in [an f.o.b.] contract merely is that the buyers shall provide a vessel which is capable of loading within the stipulated time, and if, as a matter of courtesy or convenience, the buyers inform the sellers that they propose to provide vessel A, I can see no reason in principle why they should not change their minds and provide vessel B at a later stage, always assuming that vessel B is provided within such a time as to make it possible for her to fulfil the buyers' obligations under the contract.

Notes
The general rule is subject to normal contractual principles. For example, if the nominated vessel could not possibly have arrived in time, and there was no

possibility of a substitute, the buyer would be in anticipatory breach (*e.g. Texaco v Eurogulf* [1987] 2 Lloyd's Rep. 541).

TEXACO LTD v EUROGULF SHIPPING CO LTD

Queen's Bench Division (Commercial Court). [1987] 2 Lloyd's Rep. 541

Facts:

3–041   The final date for loading was 13 Feb 86, in Milford Haven, but the vessel nominated by the buyers (*Giray*) on 5 Feb was trading in the Eastern Mediterranean. On 10 Feb, the plaintiff sellers discovered that *Giray* was at Istanbul, and communicated their concerns to the buyers. The next day the defendant buyers communicated their inability to perform the contract, claiming to be the victims of a fraudulent misrepresentation by their sub-buyers, and the sellers repudiated. The sellers claimed damages, and the buyers claimed that they had wrongfully repudiated on 10th.

Held:

The sellers had not repudiated the contract on 10th, but even if they had, they were entitled to do so; nomination of *Giray* was manifestly false in the sense that it could never possibly be fulfilled and the notion of a substitute nomination was wholly artificial and fanciful and without any conceivable practical reality. The plaintiffs were entitled to damages.

3–042   HIRST J.: Firstly, I consider that the nomination was manifestly false, though, of course, through no fault of the defendants. Mr Gaisman [for the buyers] accepts that, to use his words, a "Mickey Mouse" nomination would amount to a repudiation; whether or not this particular nomination merits the Walt Disney epithet I need not decide, but I am quite satisfied that it was false in the sense that it could never possibly be fulfilled, and the fact that the parties only discovered this subsequently to the actual making of the nomination I consider to be neither here nor there. Secondly, the notion of a substitute nomination by Mr Robinson is on the facts of this case wholly artificial and fanciful, and without any conceivable practical reality, as the telex of Feb 11 plainly demonstrates.

Notes

1. It is not entirely clear what the basis of this decision is. When no vessel arrived to take the oil by 13th, the buyers would clearly have broken their obligation to nominate an effective vessel, and it is clear from authorities discussed above that that is a breach of condition. However, there is authority that the doctrine of anticipatory breach does not apply to breaches of conditions (see further *The Afovos* in para. 7—012, below), and there is nothing in the case to suggest that an effective nomination could not have been made within a frustrating time. If the case is correct, therefore, for the buyers to make a "Mickey Mouse" nomination must itself be a breach of condition, entitling the sellers to repudiate. That is clear from the following extract:

"Firstly, I consider that the nomination was manifestly false, though, of course, through no fault of the defendants. [Counsel for the buyers] accepts that, to use his words, a 'Mickey Mouse' nomination would amount to a repudiation; whether or not this particular nomination merits the Walt Disney epithet I need not decide, but I am quite satisfied that it was false in the sense that it could never possibly be fulfilled, and the fact that the parties only discovered this subsequently to the actual making of the nomination I consider to be neither here nor there . . . "

The conclusion might be justified conceptually, if the Mickey Mouse nomination is regarded as a refusal by the buyers to perform the contract.

2. In *Ampro*, the contract had no notice provisions, or other restrictions on nomination. *Ampro* was distinguished in *Cargill UK Ltd v Continental UK Ltd*. [1989] 1 Lloyd's Rep. 193, where it would have been impossible, within the provisions of the contract, to make a substitute nomination.

CARGILL UK LTD v CONTINENTAL UK LTD

Court of Appeal. [1989] 1 Lloyd's Rep. 193

Facts:
The contract provided for a provisional notice of nomination (containing   **3–043** vessel's name and itinerary) followed by a definite final notice. This procedure was followed, but later the buyers attempted to make a substitute nomination (the original vessel could not arrive in time), by giving a second final notice. This was rejected by the sellers, who refused to load cargo on board the substituted vessel.

Decision:
The buyers were held not to be entitled to make a substitution after the final notice; the notice that they gave in respect of the substitute was too late to be good as either a provisional or a final notice in respect of that vessel. Therefore the notice terms in the contract precluded them from making the substitute nomination.

PARKER L.J.: I find little assistance from the later authorities. So far as authority is concerned the matter in my view depends upon the decision in the *Ampro*. So far as that case is concerned much reliance is placed on Widgery J.'s reference to substitution but in my judgment such reliance was misplaced. The problem in that case was whether the nomination of vessel A prohibited the later nomination of vessel B, even if:

(a) the nomination of vessel B was a good nomination in itself and

(b) there was nothing in the contract to provide the circumstances in which a particular vessel should be nominated.

In my judgment the decision does not establish or purport to establish any general rule of law.

In the present case the contract expressly provided for a series of notices. It also provided specific details as to the suitability of the vessel to be provided by buyers. On the facts, the provisions of the nomination clause were complied with in respect of *Cobetas* but by the time the first notice in respect of *Finnbeaver* was given it was too late to be good as either a provisional or a final notice in respect of that vessel. The notice of readiness was timeous in respect of it but the notice of readiness clause requires that the vessel is to present notice of readiness—

" . . . having complied with all the requirements of the Nomination Clause above."

Buyers' argument involves reading this clause as if it read "having complied with all the requirements of the nomination clause above in respect of some vessel" whereas Mr Johnson [for the sellers] contends that it should be read as "having complied with all the requirements of the nomination clause above in respect of herself" or "in respect of that vessel". He accepts that, had buyers, having given a provisional notice in respect of *Cobetas*, desired to nominate or substitute another vessel they would have been entitled to do so provided that there was time to comply with the notice provisions in respect of that vessel, but in the present case there was not. There was not even time to give a valid definite notice.

3–044   I have no hesitation in preferring sellers' construction to that of buyers'. If parties specifically stipulate for the vessel's name and itinerary to be given eight clear days before ETA and nine running days before expiry of the shipping period, to be followed by a definite notice six running days before such expiry, and finally a notice of readiness to be given by the vessel having complied with such requirements, I find it impossible to attribute to the parties the mutual intention that buyers could nominate another vessel with a different itinerary, notwithstanding that it was too late to give either a provisional or final notice in respect of her. Buyers' argument must in my view involve, if right, the further consequence that having given provisional and definite notice under the nomination clause and a valid notice of readiness in respect of vessel A they could have actually tendered for loading another vessel. This in my judgment is unacceptable.

It appears to me impossible also to import an implied term in favour of buyers. If buyers are right as to construction no implied term is needed. If however sellers are right on construction the implied term contended for would be inconsistent with the express term.

Mr Rokison [for the buyers] contended with great force that the fundamental obligation of the buyers was to provide a suitable vessel within the delivery period, that in tendering *Finnbeaver* they were merely seeking to comply with that obligation when they could no longer do so with *Cobetas* and that they would have so complied but for sellers' refusal to accept her. The Court should uphold contracts where possible and not enable the sellers to escape when they had clearly demonstrated by their own action that the vessel was suitable, that they could have loaded and that their only reason for refusing to do so was to take advantage of a market change. While I appreciate the force of these arguments I am unable to accept that they can prevail over what in my judgment is the plain meaning of the contract. It is common place for parties, if they can, to cancel contracts in order to take advantage of changes in the market when, but for the change, they would have been content to refrain from cancellation; but if the right to cancel is there they are entitled to exercise it notwithstanding that the sole reason for doing so is some commercial advantage.

Note

1. There was absolutely nothing wrong with the substituted vessel, nor was **3–045** there any obvious commercial reason for the provisional notice to require the vessel's name. The only reason for rejection (by the sellers) was that the market was rising; indeed, the sellers offered to load the substitute at a new price.

2. The *Ampro* position is, in the light of this decision, subject to any express terms of the contract to the contrary. In the view of Parker L.J., *Ampro*:

"established no more than that the nomination of vessel B is not barred by the previous nomination of vessel A provided that the nomination of vessel B is itself a good contractual nomination. Here it was not."

3. *Cargill* is noted by Howard Bennett, [1990] L.M.C.L.Q. 466. Among the issues he discusses are the consequences of a substitution that causes loss to the sellers. This is bound up with the discussion of *J. & J. Cunningham v Munro*, in paras 4—040, *et seq.*, below.

(e) Export Licences

In *H.O. Brandt & Co v H.N. Morris & Co Ltd* [1917] 2 K.B. 784, the Court of **3–046** Appeal held that the obligation to provide an export licence fell on the buyers, Scrutton L.J. expressing the view that the obligation to provide an effective ship meant to provide a ship which can legally carry the goods. If this were the correct view, then the obligation to provide the export licence would fall on whichever party had agreed to nominate the vessel.

As with other aspects of f.o.b. contracts, however, the courts are concerned to find the intention of the parties, and no invariable rules can therefore be laid down. *Brandt* was an unusual case where the f.o.b. purchasers had themselves sold the goods on to American buyers (in other words, the f.o.b. buyers were the exporters, the f.o.b. contract concerned being merely one of domestic supply to the vessel). Moreover, only the buyers had the information necessary to apply for the licence.

A.V. POUND & CO LTD v M.W. HARDY & CO INC.

House of Lords. [1956] A.C. 588, [1956] 1 Lloyd's Rep. 255

Facts:

The case concerned an f.a.s. sale, which was silent as to the provision of **3–047** an export licence.[26] No licence could be obtained, and the ship nominated

---

[26] Note that no distinction was drawn, for the purposes of the case, between f.o.b. and f.a.s. contracts.

by the buyers was therefore unable to load the cargo. The sellers claimed damages.

The sellers were aware of the eventual destination of the goods (required for this cargo, which was to be shipped from Portugal to East Germany), and only they knew the name of their suppliers, who alone could apply for the licence.

Held:

The sellers were not entitled to damages, because no obligation in this case fell upon the buyers to provide the licence (indeed, a qualified obligation fell upon the sellers). *Brandt* did not establish any general rule for f.o.b. or f.a.s. contracts, where the buyer had contracted to nominate the vessel, that an obligation on the buyers would be implied, to obtain an export licence for the goods (where necessary), or to supply a ship into or alongside which the goods can lawfully be placed, in default of express stipulation between the parties; each case depends on the contract and surrounding circumstances in that case.

3–048   Viscount Kilmuir L.C.: The first broad issue between the parties is whether it was the duty of the buyers to provide a vessel alongside which the sellers could lawfully place the turpentine, or whether, on the licence for the destination desired by the buyers being refused, the buyers were excused from the performance of the contract. It was common ground before this House, and it had been so accepted by McNair J., and the Court of Appeal, that the proper law of the contract was English. Counsel for the sellers submitted that the proper law of the contract was English. Counsel for the sellers submitted that the impact of Portuguese law was restricted to modes of performance, in accordance with the limitations which well-known decisions on that subject have indicated.

The sellers' main contention, in accordance with the judgment of McNair J., on which they relied, was that the principles applicable were those laid down by the Court of Appeal in *H.O. Brandt & Co v H.N. Morris & Co Ltd* [1917] 2 K.B. 784. In that case, the goods had been sold f.o.b. Manchester by English merchants to English merchants seeking to export from England. Subsequent to the contract, an order rendering a licence necessary was made in the United Kingdom under United Kingdom statutory powers. In these circumstances, the court held that it was for the buyers to supply any necessary licence which is required to enable the goods to be placed on the ship. In my opinion, it is necessary to remember, in comparing *Brandt v Morris* with any other case in this field, (i) that the parties had not contracted with reference to an existing licensing system; (ii) that a United Kindgom licensing system overtook their contract; (iii) that either party could have applied to the British authorities; (iv) that the buyers alone knew the facts which it was necessary to state when a licence was applied for. The sellers, however, argued that the effect of this decision, and especially of the judgment of Scrutton L.J., was that, in the case of any f.o.b. contract it was the duty of the buyers to provide a ship alongside which the goods could legally be place~, therefore, their duty to procure any licence required.

In my opinion, the decision in *Brandt v Morris* is authority only for the **3–04**> proposition that, where a British buyer has bought goods for export from Britain, and a British prohibition on export except with a licence supervenes, then there is a duty on such a buyer to apply for a licence, because not only is he entitled to apply to the relevant British authority but he alone knows the full facts regarding the destination of the goods. It is not without importance to note that Scrutton L.J., introduces the part of his judgment which deals with this point by saying ([1917] 2 K.B. at p. 798):

> "This is a contract to sell sixty tons of aniline oil f.o.b. Manchester. At the date of the contract there was no prohibition against the export of aniline oil. In *Re Anglo-Russian Merchant Traders & John Batt & Co (London)* [1917] 2 K.B. 679, the contract was a c. and f. contract, and at the date thereof there was an existing prohibition against export except under a licence. A question arose as to whose duty it was to obtain a licence. Bailhache J., held that the person who had contracted to sell undertook to obtain the licence or to pay damages. This court held that, as there was a finding of fact that the seller had done all in his power to get a licence, at any rate his obligation was not higher than that, and that therefore he was not liable. In this case it becomes necessary to go further and to decide whether in this f.o.b. contract the obligation to obtain a licence, in case there should after the making of the contract be a prohibition against export, lies upon the sellers or the buyers. In my opinion it lies upon the buyers."

In my view, significance must be attached to the words "in this f.o.b. contract". Further, it must be observed that the Lord Justice draws attention not only to the fact that one was a c. and f. contract while the other was f.o.b., but also to the fact that in one case the prohibition was existing and that in the other it supervened. It is in the second case that the words following become applicable, namely:

> "The buyers must provide an effective ship, that is to say, a ship which can legally carry the goods."

Also, in the case of a supervenient prohibition, once it has become the duty of the buyers to obtain the licence and so legalise the ship, it is immaterial that there is a duty on the sellers to perform the act subsidiary to export, namely, to bring the goods through customs on to the quay. Moreover, it is, in my view, essential for us, thirty-nine years later, to read that judgment as Scrutton L.J., was delivering it, in contradistinction to his decision in *Re Anglo-Russian Merchant Traders & John Batt & Co (London)*. I draw attention to the words in which the Lord Justice there posed the problem ([1917] 2 K.B. at p. 688):

"The sellers could only export aluminium under a licence. They contracted to export it. There are two alternatives suggested. Have they
contracted to get a licence or pay damages though it may be illegal to
export? Or have they contracted to use reasonable diligence to get a
licence, and, having been unable to obtain one, are they relieved from
any liability because a contract which is illegal cannot be enforced?"

Scrutton L.J., reaches the conclusion that the second of these alternatives
is the term that must be implied in the contract.

Against that background, I cannot extract from *Brandt v Morris* a
general rule that, on every f.o.b. or f.a.s. contract, the buyer must supply
a ship into which, or alongside which, the goods can legally be placed
where there exists a prohibition on export except with a licence . . .

The sellers can only succeed in this action if they can establish that
there was a breach of contract by the buyers. In my opinion, they have
failed to do so. The essential facts seem to me to be (i) that the sellers
knew that the buyers wished to export to Eastern Germany, and (ii) that
only the suppliers (whose identity the sellers deliberately withheld from
the buyers) could apply for the necessary licence. In these circumstances,
it was for the sellers to do their best to obtain a licence for Eastern
Germany through the suppliers and, if they found that they could not,
further performance of the contract was excused . . .

Notes

3–050   It is, therefore, not possible to lay down any general rules for the provision of
export licences in f.o.b. contracts. The editors of Schmitthoff distinguish between
export contracts (duty on sellers) and supply contracts (duty on buyers),[27] but
though this distinction is clearly an important factor, *Pound v Hardy* cautions
against any general rule.

(f) DELIVERY

3–051   All of the terms discussed so far as flexible, in that within the f.o.b. designation,
it is open for the parties to vary the allocation of duties between the parties. There
are nonetheless limits to the flexibility of the f.o.b. term. Delivery is to the ship,
and for a contract to provide for delivery at any other time would be inconsistent
with the designation f.o.b.[28]

If a contract contains two clearly inconsistent terms, the court has to decide how
much weight to attach to each. In a contract that is stated to be f.o.b., however, a
term that is capable of more than one interpretation will probably be interpreted
in a way that is inconsistent with the designation.

---

[27] Schmitthoff's *Export Trade* (10th ed.), p. 28.
[28] Even this allows of variation, however, as in the f.o.b. stowed contract in *The Naxos* (see
para. 3—029, above).

FREBOLD AND STURZNICKEL (TRADING AS PANDA OHG) v CIRCLE PRODUCTS LTD

Court of Appeal. [1970] 1 Lloyd's Rep. 499

Facts:

The case concerned a contract for the sale of children's toys, which was **3–052** expressed to be f.o.b. Rotterdam, it was a condition of the contract that delivery would be effected in good time for the buyers (in London) to catch the Christmas trade. Delivery to the vessel was made in good time, but delay occurred subsequently, after the arrival of the goods in the U.K., so that the toys did not reach the buyers in time for Christmas. The purchasers purported to repudiate the contract, and were sued by the sellers for wrongful repudiation; the purchasers counter-claimed for non-delivery.

Held:

The contract was held, on its facts, to be on f.o.b. terms, in spite of the sellers' instruction to their shipping agents only to deliver the goods against payment. The sellers were held not to be in breach of contract, since in an f.o.b. contract, delivery is to the vessel.

WIDGERY L.J.: There was no formal or written agreement, and the terms **3–053** of the contract must be discovered in the correspondence passing between the parties, supplemented by the oral evidence. The first point to notice is that both parties contemplated that the transaction should be "on f.o.b. terms", and the substance of the plaintiffs' case in this Court is that these terms restricted the plaintiffs' obligation to delivery of the goods over the ship's rail at Rotterdam, an operation which was certainly concluded within the time contemplated in the contract. If this is correct, it would follow that the property and risk in the goods passed to the buyers at that moment, and the buyers cannot hold the sellers responsible for the muddle or worse which occurred between British Rail and Schenkers when the goods arrived in London.

The buyers' case is that this was not a normal f.o.b. contract and that the reference to f.o.b. terms did no more than provide that the buyers should be responsible for the freight payable from the point of shipment onwards. It remained the obligation of the sellers (so it is said) to secure the delivery of the goods to Schenkers in London, and if such delivery was not effected the sellers were in breach . . .

The issue is now reduced to a very narrow one: "Was the sellers' obligation in regard to delivery discharged when the goods were put on board the ship in Rotterdam, or did the sellers remain responsible for seeing that the goods were duly delivered to Schenkers in London?" I have not found this an easy question, but in the end I am persuaded that the Judge gave insufficient weight to the fact that this was a contract on f.o.b. terms. *Prima facie*, when two commercial men use a well-known phrase of this kind they must be presumed to give it its established meaning. I do not think that this presumption is rebutted by the fact that the sellers instructed Schenkers not to hand over the goods until payment had been secured, and I think that the fact that Schenkers were to act as the buyers' agents to receive the goods in London sufficiently explains the references to "delivery to Schenkers" upon which so much reliance is placed in the buyers' argument.

3–054   SIR FREDERICK SELLERS: The essence of an f.o.b. contract is that the goods are to be shipped free on board a ship (*i.e.*, at the seller's expense) and consigned to the buyer or his agent. On shipment the goods are appropriated to the contract and the seller cannot thereafter rightfully withdraw or otherwise dispose of the goods. The property in them passes to the buyer, who is responsible for the freight and the goods are at the buyer's risk. I might refer to s.20 of the Sale of Goods Act, 1893:

> "Unless otherwise agreed, the goods remain at the seller's risk until the property therein is transferred to the buyer, but when the property therein is transferred to the buyer, the goods are at the buyer's risk whether delivery has been made or not."

A term which required delivery in London would be totally inconsistent with an f.o.b. contract, and in my view there was no evidence which supported an overthrow of the agreed f.o.b. terms.

It was also contended that the provision which the parties agreed that the goods should not be handed over by Schenkers to the buyers until the freight was paid altered the essential terms of the contract. This provision is quite a customary one under an f.o.b. contract. If, as here, the arrangement is merely to secure the contract price by requiring cash before the goods are handed over, and is not made with the intention of withdrawing the goods from the contract, it shows, and it does, nothing inconsistent with the intention to pass the property on shipment.

Notes

3–055   Two observations can perhaps be made here. First, the term f.o.b. clearly implies delivery to the vessel. Secondly, the court attached considerable weight to the f.o.b. designation, to the extent of interpreting the arguably inconsistent delivery term to be consistent with that designation. Sir Frederick Sellers' interpretation is set out in the above passage. In Edmund Davies L.J.'s view, the instruction to the shipping agents should be interpreted as reserving only a right of disposal until payment, and hence postponing the transfer of property, but not possession, which passed to the buyers on delivery (to the vessel).

There is a difference between these views, but only as to the timing of the passing of property, not as to the interpretation of the f.o.b. term. See further chapter 5, below, on the passing of property.

(g) MARKET FLUCTUATION RISKS

3–056   As we have seen, sometimes f.o.b. contracts include additional duties for the seller, *e.g.* provision of carriage and insurance. The difference between an f.o.b.

contract with additional duties and a c.i.f. contract becomes clear if insurance and freight rates fluctuate. In the former case, the actual cost of insurance and freight is added to the price, to the buyer's account, so that if (say) the rates increase the buyer pays the extra. In a c.i.f. contract, the price of the entire package is fixed in advance, so the risk of insurance or freight rates increasing falls on the seller, not the buyer. Conversely, it is the seller who benefits if rates fall, unlike the position with the f.o.b. contract with additional duties.[29]

THE PARCHIM

Privy Council. [1918] A.C. 157

The facts are set out at para. 5—048. The main issue was when property passed, but the correct classification of the contract was also considered. Though it was expressed to be c.i.f., Lord Parker of Waddington thought that it had more of the characteristics of an f.o.b. contract.

LORD PARKER OF WADDINGTON: This . . . is not an ordinary c.i.f. contract. The insurance is separately provided for and the premium is not included in the price, and, although the price includes freight, it is only the freight under the charterparty which the buyer is to take over. If the right to cancel that charterparty arises and the option to do so is exercised, the buyer has the responsibility of finding another ship to take the intended cargo. He has to pay any excess of freight over the chartered freight; also he has to pay the storage for the nitrate until loaded on another vessel. As the sum included for freight in the price is a mere matter of calculation and would be payable separately by the buyer and deducted from the price, the price is really for cost only, and the contract has far more of the characteristics of a contract f.o.b. Taltal than it has of a contract c.i.f. European port.

Notes

In this case the insurance was not included in the cost, and though freight was included, it was tied into a particular charterparty; if the charterparty was cancelled, risk of fluctuation in freight rate would fall on the buyers, not the sellers. This is consistent with freight and insurance market fluctuation risks being on the sellers c.i.f., but the buyers f.o.b., and this is probably the fundamental difference between the two types of contract.

3—057

Conclusions

The flexibility of the f.o.b. term implies that the parties have considerable flexibility over the allocation of duties between themselves, within that designation. There are however fairly strong presumptions, however, which allow the courts to give meaning to the term, in the absence of evidence to the contrary.

There are nonetheless terms which are clearly repugnant to the f.o.b. contract, for example the delivery term argued by the buyers in *Frebold*, and terms which include freight and insurance within the cost. *Frebold* suggests that where the

[29] Probably, therefore, the contract in *Couturier v Hastie* (1856) 5 H.L. Cas. 673, discussed in paras 4—046 *et seq.*, below, was in reality a c.i.f. contract, although the term had not been coined by then: freight and insurance were included in the price (note also that the goods had already been shipped).

parties express the contract as f.o.b., the courts are reluctant to give effect to terms which are repugnant to that designation, and will interpret ambiguous terms so as to be consistent with it.

In both *The Parchim* and *Federspiel v Twigg*, the question was whether the contract was correctly classified as f.o.b. or c.i.f. It is probable that in neither case did anything turn on that distinction; though the presumptions as to when property passes may differ as between the two types, other factors are so much more important in the passing of property that it is doubtful whether the classification will ever be conclusive. See further para. 5—048.

If, on the other hand, the courts had given effect to the postponed delivery term, argued by the buyers in *Frebold*, this would have been significant, since it would have prevented risk passing until delivery.

(2) OTHER INTERNATIONAL SALE CONTRACTS

3–058   The other varieties of sale contract used in international trade are defined by the time at which delivery takes place. They are relatively rare compared to f.o.b. and c.i.f. contracts and variations thereon, and the bill of lading does not take on the same role as a document of title. They are included here primarily for completeness, because they have little in common with the f.o.b. and c.i.f. contracts discussed elsewhere in the book. There is further discussion of alternative varieties of contract in chapter 15, below, however, in the context of present problems with the traditional contracts, and proposals for reform.

EXTRACT FROM A PAPER ENTITLED "THE RELATIONSHIP BETWEEN THE CONTRACT OF SALE AND CONTRACTS RELATING TO TRANSPORTATION, INSURANCE AND BANKING SERVICES", BY ERLING SELVIG, PROFESSOR OF LAW AT THE UNIVERSITY OF OSLO, TO THE UNCTAD SEMINAR ON OCEAN TRANSPORT DOCUMENTATION AND ITS SIMPLIFICATION, 1980

3–059   Delivery is the decisive point in the performance of the contract by the seller. In international sales involving carriage of goods the delivery and the carriage are closely interrelated. Generally speaking, three alternative solutions have to be taken into account: delivery may be effected (1) at the beginning of the carriage, (2) when the goods are received by a carrier having undertaken the carriage of the goods to their destination, and (3) at the termination of the carriage. Which of the three applies in a particular case depends on the delivery term incorporated by the parties in the contract.

By delivery terms we usually refer to a set of standard clauses expressed by way of some abbreviation, the legal meaning of which has been defined by national laws as well as the customs of the trade. The International Chamber of Commerce has elaborated a set of rules for a number of the important delivery terms, defining in considerable detail the meaning of each term. These standard definitions are called Inco-terms, and such a definition is intended to be applied by express reference in the sales contract.

The delivery terms having the greatest practical importance as regards sales involving carriage by sea are:

"Ex Works/Warehouse"

The seller must then deliver the goods by placing them at the buyer's disposal at his factory or warehouse and it is for the buyer to arrange that the goods are received and then carried to their destination. [Footnote: Frequently, in particular when the goods are to be shipped by liner service, the seller undertakes to arrange on behalf of the buyer the carriage of the goods to their destination.] Thus, the clause belongs in group (1) above.

"FAS" or "FOB" a named port of loading

the seller must then deliver the goods alongside (FAS) or on board (FOB) a ship named by the buyer, who has, therefore, to charter or otherwise reserve the necessary shipping space in the designated vessel. *[Footnote above repeated.]* Thus, these clause belong in group (2) above.[30]

"CIF" or "CF" [more usually c. & f.]

a named destination: the seller must then deliver the goods by shipping them to their destination, viz. procure an appropriate contract of carriage to that end, pay the freight and other costs charged by the carrier and —under CIF, but not CF—arrange and pay for customary insurance of the goods in transit. Even under such clauses, however, delivery takes place, generally speaking, when the goods are taken in charge by the carrier or loaded on board the ship, and also these clauses belong in group (2) above.

"Ex Ship", "Ex Quay" or "Delivered" a named destination—

the seller must then arrange that the goods be carried to the destination and there placed at the disposal of the buyer, from the ship (Ex Ship), from the pier after landing (Ex Quay), or from the carrier's warehouse (Delivered). Thus, these clauses belong in group (3) above. It should be noted that clauses like FOB, free on truck, rail, etc. are also used in relation to a named destination.

Delivery is a key concept in sales law

The time of delivery shows whether the seller has complied with the stipulations in the contract as to when he is to perform or whether he is in breach by delay. In sales involving carriage, the time for delivery is

---

[30] The f.a.s. contract is treated as essentially similar to the third type of f.o.b. contract in *Pyrene v Scindia*; the contract in *A.V. Pound & Co Ltd v M.W. Hardy & Co Inc.* [1956] A.C. 588 was f.a.s., but the House of Lords treated the case as being subject to the same rules as apply to an f.o.b. contract.

regularly fixed in relation to shipment of the goods by the seller, *e.g.* shipment within a period or fixed time limit, shipment by a certain liner to leave at a certain time, etc.

Whether the seller has delivered goods in conformity with the contract is also determined at the time of delivery. On delivery the risk of loss [see following Chapter], damage or delay relating to the goods normally passes from the seller to the buyer. In sales based on FAS, FOB, CIF or CF this is the time when the goods are taken in charge by the carrier or loaded in the ship.

Finally, delivery is very often decisive for the distribution of costs, the seller paying all costs incurred up to the time of delivery and the buyer those incurred thereafter. However, as we have seen, for instance in CIF/CF sales the seller pays certain cost incurred after delivery.

Notes

3–060   1. The f.a.s. (free alongside ship) contract is in some respects similar to the f.o.b. contract, and developed from the same historical process, but the seller will usually obtain a mate's receipt or received for shipment bill of lading, rather than a shipped bill of lading. It is unlikely that a seller f.a.s. would be able to tender a received for shipment bill to a bank on a documentary credit (see chapter 8, below), and the received for shipment bill does not usually perform all the functions of a document of title (see further chapter 6, below).

2. The other varieties of contract described are not truly international in character at all, but in reality varieties of domestic sales. Even though the two parties may happen to be from different countries, and carriage of the goods may involve a sea element, this is irrelevant to the rights and duties of the parties. In ex-ship and ex-quay contracts the buyer may receive a delivery order, but neither that nor the bill of lading can be said truly to represent the goods, both property and risk remaining in the seller until at least the end of the voyage, whatever documentary transactions are effected. An ex-warehouse contract might also require tender of a delivery order rather than a bill of lading: see, *e.g. National Bank of South Afrcia v Banca Italiana* (1922) LL.L.R. 531.

3. *The Julia*, paras 2—015 *et seq.*, above, is an example of an ex-ship contract. In *The Aliakmon*, in paras 13—073, *et seq.*, below, a c. & f. contract was varied to become an ex-warehouse contract, though with the unusual feature that risk remained with the buyer as from shipment.

4. In addition to the above contracts, use is beginning to develop of special contracts for combined transport and container operations. These are covered further in paras 15—017, *et seq.*, below.

CHAPTER 4

RISK, AND RELATED ISSUES

(1) Relevance of Passing of Risk

THE seller is not generally responsible for loss of or damage to the goods after risk **4–001** passes. If they are so lost or damaged he can nevertheless claim payment from the buyer. In *Leigh & Sillivan Ltd v Aliakmon Shipping Co Ltd (The Aliakmon)* in the Court of Appeal [1985] Q.B. 350 (affd. on other grounds [1986] A.C. 785), Sir John Donaldson M.R. thought that:

"the true analysis [of the goods being at the buyer's risk] is that he has contracted to buy and pay for the goods in whatever state they may be when the voyage ends."

If the goods are lost or damaged after risk has passed, the buyer should look to the carrier or the insurance policy, and not to the seller, for compensation. If neither the insurance policy covers the loss (as in many of the cases discussed below, though rare in practice), nor is the carrier liable, the buyer must bear the loss himself.

(2) The General Rule

(a) Risk Passes On (or as from) Shipment

The general principle is easy both to state and to justify. Delivery f.o.b. is to the **4–002** ship, and it is therefore appropriate for risk to pass then. Though the c.i.f. contract differs in many respects from f.o.b., it shares the same delivery point, and it is therefore appropriate for risk to pass at the same time.

The general rule is, therefore, that for both f.o.b. and c.i.f. contracts, risk passes to the buyer on shipment. Where goods are purchased afloat, as in many c.i.f. sales, risk passes retrospectively as from shipment. In other words, risk is deemed to have passed from a time before the contract was concluded.

Though the rule's original justification must surely have been that shipment is the time at which delivery of the goods is regarded as taking place, it also turns out to be very convenient. As J.D. Feltham noted in [1975] J.B.L. 273[1]:

"The passage of risk on or as from shipment is convenient in eliminating difficult questions of proof of the time goods were lost or damaged while at sea."

We saw in chapter 1, above that the c.i.f. contract, and to a lesser extent the f.o.b., came to dominate bulk commodity carriage. The main reason is probably that

---

[1] See below for further extracts from this article.

these are documentary sales, and certainly the conventional rule as to risk is essential if the documents are to be freely transferable. If risk passed later than shipment, reselling the goods while they are at sea could be difficult. The first buyer in a chain may have innocently taken up documents for goods which (unbeknown to him) have been lost, and find himself unable to make the resale. If that were the general rule, the first (or any subsequent) buyer in a chain would be unwise to accept documents without also inspecting the present condition of the goods. Since the goods are at sea this would be difficult to say the least, and the effect would be that sales and purchases of goods afloat could not safely be made.

It may be argued that inspection of the goods at sea is no longer a problem with modern communications technology, such as INMARSAT. Whatever the state of communications technology, however, it is still desirable for there to be a clear delivery point, and for that delivery point to be the same for all the contracts in the chain, so that the same documents can be used for each sub-sale. Realistically, the only possible delivery points are at loading and at discharge, and the advantage of loading is that it enables the documents to be negotiated earlier.

Though the goods are therefore at the buyer's risk during the sea carriage, he can usually protect himself against the consequences of this. He can tell from the documents that the goods were loaded apparently in good condition,[2] and if they have subsequently deteriorated either he will know that the seller has insured them, or he can take out insurance himself.[3] Ideally, he ought also to be able to resell them on similar terms, but the doctrine of common mistake, considered below, places limits on this, at any rate where the contract is for the sale of specific goods which perish before the resale contract is made (see further below).

At any rate, there seems little doubt that the main reason why most of the world's tonnage is carried on c.i.f. terms, rather than ex-ship, is because delivery is to the ship, and risk passes on, or as from shipment.

(b) Exact Point of Transfer of Risk

4–003   There are no c.i.f. authorities as to *exactly* when the risk passes, and the f.o.b. cases are equivocal. In *Frebold and Sturznickel (Trading as Panda OHG) v Circle Products Ltd* [1970] 1 Lloyd's Rep. 499,[4] Widgery L.J. talks of delivery being at the ship's rail, but in a different context Devlin J. was unimpressed by arguments that the ship's rail should a point at which responsibilities are defined in *Pyrene Co Ltd v Scindia Navigation Co Ltd* [1954] 2 Q.B. 198 (and see further chapter 11, below):

> " . . . the division of loading into two parts is suited to more antiquated methods of loading than are now generally adopted and the ship's rail has lost much of its nineteenth-century significance. Only the most enthusiastic lawyer could watch with satisfaction the spectacle of liabilities shifting uneasily as the cargo sways at the end of a derrick across a notional perpendicular projecting from the ship's rail."

In *Colley v Overseas Exporters* [1921] 3 K.B. 302, 307,[5] the view appears to be taken that neither property nor risk normally pass until loading is complete:

---

[2] Subject to the problems discussed in Ch. 14, below.
[3] In many of the cases below, such as *Groom v Barber*; *Manbre Saccharine*; *Law & Bonar*; and *Couturier v Hastie*, the goods were in fact uninsured against the consequences which befell them, so that the party at risk really did bear the loss. No wonder they were worth litigating, then, but such cases appear to be very rare; indeed, the first three arose from the sudden and unexpected outbreak of a world war.
[4] See para. 3—052, above.
[5] See further para. 3—004, above.

"I need only deal with f.o.b. contracts. The presumed intention (see s. 18 of the Act) of the parties has been settled. It seems clear that in the absence of special agreement the property and risk in goods does not in the case of an f.o.b. contract pass from the seller to the buyer till the goods are actually put on board: see *Browne v Hare* (1859) 4 H. & N. 822; *Inglis v Stock* (1885) 10 App. Cas. 263; *Wimble v Rosenberg* [1913] 3 K.B. 743, 747; *Benjamin on Sale* (6th ed.), p. 785, where several useful cases are collected."

This passage is equivocal, however, since it depends on an interpretation of "actually put on board". Moreover, the issue in *Pyrene* was as to the scope of application of the Hague Rules, and Devlin J.'s remarks were not addressed directly to the passing of risk. Earlier in his judgment, he seems to accept that delivery f.o.b. is to the ship's rail, which would therefore be the appropriate place for risk to pass.

(3) APPLICATION OF GENERAL RULE

(a) DIVORCE OF RISK FROM PROPERTY

Historically, f.o.b. transactions were complete at the ship's rail, and as early as **4–004** *Tregelles v Sewell* (1862) 7 H. & N. 574, 158 E.R. 600,[6] it was established that risk c.i.f. passed, as for f.o.b., on shipment. The buyer could therefore be required to pay as long only as the goods were shipped; there was no additional requirement that they should arrive at their destination. For reasons already rehearsed, there seems little doubt that this is why the c.i.f. contract is now so widely used, compared to the ex-ship, where risk passes at the port of discharge, especially where reselling the goods is envisaged, while they are at sea.

It is also probably true, though, that at the time of *Tregelles v Sewell*, it was thought that property also generally passed on shipment f.o.b. (see *e.g. Browne v Hare* (1858) 3 H. & N. 484, 4 H. & N. 822; 157 E.R. 1067),[7] and hence by implication also c.i.f. Risk and property generally pass together in contracts for the sale of goods. It only became clear later that property might pass later than shipment, either:

1. because the seller took the bill of lading to his own order and hence reserved a right of disposal (as in *Mirabita v Imperial Ottoman Bank* (1878) 3 Ex. D. 164 (CA)), or

2. because it came to be recognised, in the c.i.f. contract, that delivery was a two-stage process, involving physical delivery to the vessel, followed by constructive delivery on transfer of documents, and therefore that property need not pass until the second stage, or

3. because the goods were part of an undivided bulk, as in *Inglis v Stock*.

Inglis v Stock determined that risk f.o.b. nonetheless passed on shipment, even where the passing of property were postponed.

---

[6] See para. 2—005, above.
[7] See further para. 5—041, below.

INGLIS v STOCK

Court of Appeal. 12 Q.B.D. 564 (Affirmed House of Lords. (1885) 10 App. Cas. 263)

Facts and issues:

4–005 The case involved a bulk consignment of sugar shipped f.o.b. Hamburg, on board the City of Dublin, for Bristol. The ship and entire consignment were lost after shipment, after which the seller appropriated to the respondent buyer's contract the 200 tons due under that contract, and the remaining 190 tons on board the same vessel to another contract (under which—unbeknown to both the seller and the respondent—the respondent was also the ultimate purchaser). The goods were then paid for by the buyer (the price being variable depending on saccharine content).

The action was not between buyer and seller, but related to the buyer's insurance policy. He was insured in floating policies upon "any kind of goods and merchandises" between Hamburg and Bristol, and the issue was whether he had an insurable interest in the goods.

Held:

The buyer had an insurable interest in the goods because they were at his risk from shipment under an f.o.b. contract. Because the goods were at the buyer's risk from shipment, he could claim on the policy, since in the event of the non-arrival of the goods, the buyer would suffer a financial loss.

BRETT M.R.: Now if the goods dealt with by the contract were specific goods, it is not denied but that the words "free on board," according to the general understanding of merchants, would mean more than merely that the shipper was to put them on board at his expense; they would mean that he was to put them on board at his expense on account of the person for whom they were shipped; and in that case the goods so put on board under such a contract would be at the risk of the buyer whether they were lost or not on the voyage.

Now that is the meaning of those words "free on board" in a contract with regard to specific goods, and in that case the goods are at the purchaser's risk, even though the payment is not to be made on the delivery of the goods on board, but at some other time, and although the bill of lading is sent forward by the seller with documents attached in order that the goods shall not be finally delivered to the purchaser until he has either accepted bills or paid cash.

Then the question arises, can there be a contract with the terms "free on board" which can be fulfilled without the delivery of specific goods at the time of shipment? Is there any mercantile or legal reason why a person should not agree to sell so much out of a bulk cargo on board or *ex* such a ship upon the terms that if the cargo be lost the loss shall fall upon the purchaser, and not upon the seller? I can see no reason why he should not; and if such a contract can be made, and in a contract to buy and sell a certain quantity *ex* ship or *ex* bulk there is put in the terms "free on board," one must, with regard to that contract, give some meaning to those words "free on board." What meaning can be given to them with regard to the unseparated part of the goods which is the subject-matter of the contract, but the same meaning as is given to those words with regard to goods attributed to the contract? What is there unreasonable or contrary to business or law in those words "free on board," meaning in such a contract "I sell you twenty tons out of fifty upon the terms that you shall pay such a price for those twenty, I paying the costs of the shipment, that is, 'free on board,' and you bearing the risk of whether they are lost or not?" It does not seem to me that there is anything more inconsistent with business or law that parties should make such a contract with regard to a portion of a cargo than that they should make it with regard to a whole cargo or with regard to a specific part of a cargo, . . .

BAGALLAY L.J.: It has not been denied that, where the contract deals with specified goods, the introduction of the provision that they are to be "free on board" places the goods at the risk of the buyer. But it has been suggested that such is not the case when the goods are not specific, but are, as they were in the present case, a certain proportion of goods to be delivered out of a larger quantity. . . . What authority is there for a suggested difference between the case of specific goods, and goods of the class which I have just now mentioned? Why should there be any difference between the two? No authority has been cited to shew that there is a difference. . . .

LINDLEY L.J.: It is said, however, that you cannot have a contract by which the goods are to be at the risk of the buyer, that is, that the buyer is to pay for the goods shipped, lost or not lost, unless those goods were appropriated to him when they were shipped. That seems to me too wide a proposition. I see no reason why a person should not agree to buy and pay for a portion of a cargo, say of sugar in bags or of corn in bulk, although the actual sugar or corn to be delivered may not be ascertained before the ship is unloaded. . . .

Note

That in an f.o.b. sale risk passes on shipment had been known for some time **4–006** prior to the case, because delivery f.o.b. is to the ship, and had the contract been for specific goods no issue would have arisen, but the goods here were unascertained, and therefore property could not have passed by the time the damage occurred (see further chapter 5, below, on passing of property). Prior to *Inglis v Stock*, it had probably been assumed that risk passed along with property,[8] but in *Inglis* risk passed although property could not.

Though the seller's obligations under the sale contract were not directly at issue, there are also *dicta* in Lord Blackburn's speech in the House of Lords, that he was entitled to appropriate to the buyer's contract goods which he knew to be

---

[8] From which it must necessarily have been assumed that an f.o.b. contract could not be made for goods which remained unascertained at the time of shipment.

lost. (Note that the seller had in fact appropriated 200 tons of sugar which had been destroyed, to perform his contract with the buyer.)

An argument was rejected that the seller was in breach of contract by allowing the cargoes to become mixed, and that therefore he (rather than the buyer) should bear the risk of loss on the voyage.

(b) ROLE OF DOCUMENTATION IN EVIDENCING VALID CONTRACT

4–007   *Tregelles v Sewell* established that risk (c.i.f.) passed, as for f.o.b., on shipment, and that the buyer could therefore be required to pay so long only as the goods were shipped. Emphasis then moved to the documentation. The importance of documentation giving rights against the carrier is clear from *The Julia,*[9] and given that risk passes on shipment, if loss or damage occurs subsequently the buyer's rights against the carrier and insurance company are obviously paramount.

ARNHOLD KARBERG & CO v BLYTHE, GREEN, JORDAIN & CO

Court of Appeal. [1916] 1 K.B. 495

Facts:

4–008   Under two c.i.f. contracts made in peacetime, the goods were shipped on two German vessels, and in one case, under a German policy of insurance. At the outbreak of the First World War on August 14, 1914, both vessels entered ports of refuge, where they remained. The issue was whether the tender of shipping documents was valid.

Decision:

A bill of lading is good tender c.i.f. only if it evidences a "subsisting" contract of carriage. There the further performance of the contract had become illegal as a result of the war, and the bill of lading was held not to be good tender.

Note that the bills of lading had both been issued in peacetime, being dated July 6 and 11, 1914, and therefore at the time of issue would have evidenced valid contracts of carriage. The ships went into refuge on the first day of the war. War risk insurance had been taken out by the buyers, on July 29, on part of cargo only (they could not get insurance for whole cargo, and to that extent, therefore, had to bear the loss themselves).

Note

At first instance [1915] 2 K.B. 379, Scrutton J. observed that:

"I am strongly of opinion that the key to many of the difficulties arising in c.i.f. contracts is to keep firmly in mind the cardinal distinction that a c.i.f. sale is not a sale of goods, but a sale of documents relating to goods."

However, although his decision was affirmed in the Court of Appeal, doubt was cast upon this observation, Bankes and Warrington L.JJ. indicating their view that a c.i.f. contract is a contract for the sale of goods to be performed by the delivery

---

[9] See paras 2—015, *et seq.*, above.

of documents. In *Manbre Saccharine* (below), however, McCardie J. thought that "the difference is one of phrase only."

Further commentary

The question is how far *Arnhold Karberg* extends. The contracts there were ren-   **4–009**
dered illegal under English law. It is clear, however, from the cases discussed below, that a bill of lading can be tendered even after the destruction of the goods and the vessel, which might arguably at least frustrate the carriage contract, rendering it void.

In *Empresa Exportadora de Azucar (Cubazukar) v Industria Azucarera Nacional SA (Iansa)*, Queen's Bench Division (Commercial Court), SJ/160/78, February 29, 1980, upheld by the Court of Appeal in *The Playa Larga* (in respect of a c. & f. contract),[10] sugar was shipped aboard a Cuban vessel destined for buyers in Chile. After the *coup d'etat* in Chile in 1973, further performance of the carriage contract relating to *The Marble Island* cargo became illegal under the law of Cuba, but not under UK law. The vessel was diverted away from the Chilean buyers, and one of the issues was whether tender of a bill of lading in respect of that cargo could be valid. Mustill J. concluded (in the light of cases such as *Arnhold Karberg & Co v Blythe, Green, Jourdain & Co* [1915] 2 K.B. 379, [1916] 1 K.B. 495 and *Manbre Saccharine Company Limited v Corn Products Co Ltd* [1919] 1 K.B. 198, below) that:

"(1) The seller is obliged to tender documents representing contracts which are valid and effective at the time of tender.

(2) This requirement does not however entail that the contracts must necessarily give the buyer enforceable rights against the carrier in relation to the future performance of the contract. Thus, the tender of a bill of lading representing a contract which has already been frustrated can, in appropriate circumstances, be a proper compliance with the contract of sale.

(3) Where the bill of lading contract has already ceased to confer enforceable rights as to future performance at the moment of tender, it is not clear on the cases how the line is to be drawn between those documents which are and those which are not a valid tender. There are three possible views as to the type of document which can properly be rejected: (a) Those relating to contracts of carriage which have become illegal under English law (as the lex fori); (b) Those relating to contracts whose performance has become illegal either by the lex fori or by the proper law of the contract; (c) Those relating to contracts which have been discharged by frustration on any ground, except the destruction of the goods themselves.

In my opinion, the authorities are best reconciled by holding that documents in category (b) are open to rejection."

In that case the contract of carriage had been frustrated by Cuban but not UK law, and Mustill J. thought that tender of the bill of lading bad. The point did not need to be decided, however, because the documents were in any case discrepant.

The documents in *Arnhold Karberg* differed from those in *The Julia* (chapter 2, above) in that they were capable, at the time of issue, of giving the holder valuable rights against the carrier, whereas those in *The Julia* were not. The cases in the following section suggest that it is not generally necessary for the documents still to have any value at the time of transfer. In that case, *Arnhold Karberg* represents an exception to the normal position. This exception is clearly justified by public

---

[10] See para 2—040, above.

policy, but there is a case for limiting it, I would suggest, to cases where the UK itself is at war.

In the Court of Appeal, there was no discussion of this precise issue, but Ackner L.J. said:

"We also agree with the learned Judge that the circumstances in which the change of destination was made resulted in the documents being defective at the moment of tender. They related to a contract of carriage to a destination which was not the one named in the contract of sale, and they were false in that they purported to represent a contract which had in fact been privately varied."

This was a different issue, whether the seller could tender documents relating to a carriage contract under which he had the power to divert the vessel to a different destination, and had in fact done so.

The actual decision in each case, however, was that the documents were otherwise discrepant and had been validly rejected on those grounds.

(c) ROLE OF DOCUMENTATION IN PASSING PROPERTY

4–010   The next issue was whether it should be necessary that the documents could pass property. Note that under the general law of sale of unascertained goods the seller can only appropriate goods which are in existence at the time of appropriation. Also, given the emphasis on giving the buyer enforceable rights against the carrier, it is perhaps noteworthy that the Bills of Lading Act 1855, s.1, was not triggered unless property passed to the buyer (this is no longer the case under the 1992 Act: see further chapter 13, below).

The normal sale of goods position does not apply to a c.i.f. contract, according to Atkin J. in *C. Groom Ltd v Barber*, although "[the] seller must be in a position to pass the property in the goods by the bill of lading if the goods are in existence", but in the case itself the goods had been lost (uninsured)[11] prior to the tender of the bill of lading. The seller was held entitled to tender the bill.

It was not clear in *Groom* whether the seller knew of the loss at the time of tender, and there was authority (in *Re Olympia Oil & Cake Co and Produce Brokers' Co* [1915] 1 K.B. 233) that a seller cannot appropriate to a contract goods which he knows at time of appropriation to be lost, but this was not a c.i.f. contract proper (probably ex-ship), was decided on the construction of the particular contract, and was in any case later doubted [1917] 1 K.B. 320. *Dicta* in *Manbre Saccharine*, below, suggest that the seller can so appropriate, and *The Galatia*, also below, is consistent with this proposition.

C. GROOM LTD v BARBER

King's Bench Division. [1915] 1 K.B. 316

Briefly:

4–011   Risk passes on shipment under a c.i.f. contract. Atkin J. held that a seller may validly and effectively tender documents relating to goods lost at sea at the time of the tender.

---

[11] See further para. 6—114, below, on the insurance issue.

Facts and issues:

100 bales of Hessian cloth were shipped c.i.f., "War risk for buyer's account", on board the *City of Winchester* on July 15, 1914. The ship was captured, and subsequently sunk by a German cruiser on August 6, before (or so Atkin J. assumed) the goods were appropriated to the buyer's contract. The seller tendered a bill of lading and an f.c. and s. policy of insurance. The buyers refused to pay the price. The case arose on an appeal from arbitration.

Held:

1. The buyer was not entitled to reject the documents tendered. On the issue of risk, a c.i.f. seller may validly and effectively tender documents relating to goods lost at sea at the time of the tender.

2. On the issue as to whether the seller had to procure insurance against war risk, he was entitled to tender an f.c. and s. policy (see further para. 6—114). "War risk for buyer's account" did not mean that the seller was to effect war risk at buyer's expense, but that war risk was the concern of the buyer alone. It should also be noted that the contract of sale had been made in peacetime (July 8), and the loss occurred right at the beginning of the war.

ATKIN J.: (*on the issue of loss of the vessel*) The next point raises a question **4–012** of general interest in reference to contracts of sale on c.i.f. terms. It is said that the seller cannot tender documents representing goods which were lost at the time of tender because at the time of the loss no goods had been appropriated to the contract so as to pass the property to the buyer. It is said, therefore, that the goods tendered were non-existent and consequently that the documents were not in order. The appeal committee deal, or appear to deal, with the point by saying "As regards the second contention the committee were of the opinion that the seller fulfilled his obligation under the contract by intimating to the buyers that he was in a position to deliver the documents deliverable under the contract and that it was the buyer's obligation to take up such documents, and that the fact that the goods had been lost by a war peril and were in consequence not in a deliverable state was not a sufficient ground to relieve the buyers from their obligation under the contract"; but I am not sure that that fully deals with the question of the property not being in the buyers at the time of the loss. It was contended by the buyers that in a c.i.f. contract the seller's duty was so to act as to pass the property to the buyer, either on shipment or at any rate in case of loss at some time before the loss, and that if this were not done the seller could not make a valid delivery under the contract inasmuch as there were no goods in existence that could be said to be the buyer's goods or would be so appropriated as to become his goods.

The committee have not dealt with the question of fact as to whether there had been any appropriation of goods to this contract by or on behalf of the seller. In the view that I hold the question is immaterial, but if it becomes material I think I should, in the absence of any admission, have to refer the case back to the committee for a finding. Upon the evidence as disclosed in the case there does not appear to have been any appropriation, and I shall assume there was none. What is the meaning of a contract on c.i.f. terms? I think the answer has been given authoritatively in the judgment of Hamilton J. in *Biddell Brothers v E. Clemens Horst Co* [1911] 1 K.B. 214, at p. 220 where he said this: "The meaning of a contract of sale upon cost, freight, and insurance terms is so well settled that it is unnecessary to refer to authorities upon the subject. A seller under a contract of sale containing such terms has firstly to ship at the port of shipment goods of the description contained in the contract; secondly to procure a contract of affreightment, under which the goods will be delivered at the destination contemplated by the contract; thirdly to arrange for an insurance upon the terms current in the trade which will be available for the benefit of the buyer; fourthly to make out an invoice as described by Blackburn J. in *Ireland v Livingston* (1872) L.R. 5 H.L. at p. 406 or in some similar form; and finally to tender these documents to the buyer so that he may know what freight he has to pay and obtain delivery of the goods, if they arrive, or recover for their loss if they are lost on the voyage.

In my opinion the result is that the contract of the seller is performed by delivering to the buyer within a reasonable time from the agreed date of shipment the documents, ordinarily the bill of lading, the invoice, and the policy of insurance, which will entitle the buyer to obtain on arrival of the ship delivery of goods shipped in accordance with the contract, or in case of loss will entitle him to recover on the policy the value of the goods if lost by a peril agreed in the contract to be covered, and in any case will give him any rightful claim against the ship in respect of any misdelivery or wrongful treatment of the goods. It therefore becomes immaterial whether before the date of the tender of the documents the property in the goods was the seller's or buyer's or some third person's. The seller must be in a position to pass the property in the goods by the bill of lading if the goods are in existence, but he need not have appropriated the particular goods in the particular bill of lading to the particular buyer until the moment of tender, nor need he have obtained any right to deal with the bill of lading until the moment of tender. If it were otherwise the shipper of goods in bulk, or of goods intended for several contracts, or the intermediate seller who may be the last of a chain of purchasers from an original shipper, might find it impossible to enforce a contract on c.i.f. terms. The seller's obligation cannot depend upon whether the goods are lost or not, and if when there is no loss the property has to pass to the buyer before delivery of the documents, at what stage of the transaction must it pass? Unless it be at the time of shipment I can see no reason for fixing upon any other time than on delivery of the documents, and if it be the law that a tender of documents is ineffectual unless in fact at the moment of shipment the property actually passed to the ultimate buyer, it appears to me that business operations would be very seriously embarrassed.

I do not think that the above is inconsistent with the judgment of Kennedy L.J. in *Biddell Brothers v E. Clemens Horst Co* [1911] 1 K.B. at p. 956 in the Court of Appeal. Difficult questions arise as to the time when in performance of a contract on c.i.f. terms the property passes to the buyer. But the question when in fact the property passes is distinct from the question whether the seller undertakes as a term of the contract that the property shall pass at a given time, and the Lord Justice in the passage cited, in my view, is only dealing with the former question. After the decision of the House of Lords in the same case[12] I do not think it is necessary to consider former cases. The object of the Courts in construing commercial contracts is to try to give effect to the intention of both the contracting parties and not to impose upon business men terms which they never contemplated. If old forms are now used to express different meanings from those read into them in earlier days the Courts should be prompt to recognise the altered use if they are satisfied that there is in fact a change. I do not say that a contract on c.i.f. terms means to-day anything different to what it ever meant, but if the Courts at other times have rightly imputed to the contract a different meaning to what has been suggested, in my judgment the true meaning of the words is now altered.

Notes

1. A major part of the *rationale* for this decision was a recognition of the use of **4–013** the c.i.f. contracts in chain sales: "If it were otherwise the shipper of goods in bulk, or of goods intended for several contracts, or the intermediate seller who may be the last of a chain of purchasers from an original shipper, might find it impossible to enforce a contract on c.i.f. terms."

2. There was a chain in *Groom v Barber* itself; the seller had himself purchased on identical terms, apart from the price. It seems that he too was unaware of the name of the vessel until the documents were tendered to him by his seller, about an hour before he tendered them to the buyer in the case.[13]

3. It was not clear whether or not the seller knew of the loss at the time of tender of documents (indeed, his position in the chain suggests that he possibly did not), but probably this would make no difference, as is shown by the following case.

MANBRE SACCHARINE CO LTD v CORN PRODUCTS CO LTD

King's Bench Division. [1919] 1 K.B. 198

Facts:

The sale contract (c.i.f.) was for (among other items) a number of 280 lb. **4–014** bags of starch. Bags of 140 lb. and 220 lb. were actually shipped aboard the *Algonquin*, which was later sunk by a German submarine, with the loss of all the goods aboard. The defendant sellers, knowing of this, two

[12] See 2—009, above.
[13] In fact only an invoice was ever actually tendered, but it was assumed that the seller was in a position to deliver the other documents required under the contract.

days later tendered documents including a letter which declared that the goods were insured, but no policy of insurance.

The buyers refused to accept the documents and sued the sellers for damages for breach of the sale contract (the market value of equivalent goods having risen considerably above the original price).

Held:

1. A c.i.f. seller is generally able to tender bills of lading for goods, even though he knew that the goods had been lost at sea.

2. But in the particular case the buyer was able validly to reject them and sue for damages, because there was no policy of insurance tendered, and because the goods were of the wrong size.

McCARDIE J.: (*on the bill of lading issue*) The first question arising can be briefly stated as follows: Can a vendor under an ordinary c.i.f. contract effectively tender appropriate documents to the buyer in respect of goods shipped on a vessel which at the time of tender the vendor knows to have been totally lost? In opening the case for the plaintiffs [buyers] Mr. Hogg K.C. submitted that the answer to this question was "No," and he relied upon *In Re Olympia Oil & Cake Co and Produce Brokers' Co* [1915] 1 K.B. 233. If that case so decides, and if it be still an authority, I should feel bound to follow it, inasmuch as the judgments were given by three learned judges sitting as a Divisional Court after full argument and consideration. It has undoubtedly been the view of many lawyers and of many commercial men that the *Olympia Case* [1915] 1 K.B. 233 was a decision to the effect submitted by Mr. Hogg. It has been assumed that the contract there in question was in fact a c.i.f. contract and some colour is perhaps given to the assumption by the words of one of the members of the Court (*ibid.,* 237). But in the course of his argument before me Mr. MacKinnon K.C. [for the sellers] has produced a print of the actual contract discussed before the Divisional Court in the *Olympia Case* [1915] 1 K.B. 233, and it is now clear beyond doubt that the bargain there in question was not a c.i.f. contract at all. On the contrary, it was possessed of certain characteristics inconsistent with and opposite to a c.i.f. bargain. The terms of the agreement were of a special nature. At the close of the case before me Mr. Hogg expressly and frankly conceded that the document in the *Olympia Case* [1915] 1 K.B. 233 was not a c.i.f. contract, and he stated that he would not further rely on that decision as possessing any relevance to the point now before me. . . .

The nature of a c.i.f. contract has been described by Blackburn J. in *Ireland v Livingston* (1872) L.R. 5 H.L. 395, by Lord Sumner, then Hamilton J., in *Biddell Brothers v E. Clemens Horst Co* [1911] 1 K.B. 214, 220, and by Kennedy L.J. in his dissenting judgment in the Court of Appeal in the same case [1911] 1 K.B. 934, 955. The judgment of Kennedy L.J. was approved by the House of Lords: [*see chapter 3, above*].

I conceive that the essential feature of an ordinary c.i.f. contract as compared with an ordinary contract for the sale of goods rests in the fact that performance of the bargain is to be fulfilled by delivery of documents and not by the actual physical delivery of goods by the vendor. All that the buyer can call for is delivery of the customary documents. This represents the measure of the buyer's right and the extent of the vendor's duty. The buyer cannot refuse the documents and ask for the actual goods, nor can the vendor withhold the documents and tender the goods they represent. The position is stated with weight and clearness in the treatise on charterparties by Scrutton L.J., 8th ed., p. 167 [now Scrutton on *Charterparties*, 20th ed., 1998], in the notes to article 59 as follows: "The best way of approaching the consideration of all questions on c.i.f. sales is to realise that this form of the sale of goods is one to be performed by the delivery of documents representing the goods—*i.e.* of documents giving the right to have the goods delivered or the possible right, if they are lost or damaged, of recovering their value from the shipowner or from underwriters. It results from this that various rules in the Sale of Goods Act, 1893 [re-enacted in 1979], which is primarily drafted in relation to the sale and delivery of goods on land, can only be applied to c.i.f. sales *mutatis mutandis*. And there may be cases in which the buyer must pay the full price for delivery of the documents, though he can get nothing out of them, and though in any intelligible sense no property in the goods can ever pass to him—*i.e.* if the goods have been lost by a peril excepted by the bill of lading, and by a peril not insured by the policy, the bill of lading and the policy yet being in the proper commercial form called for by the contract.

In *Arnhold Karberg & Co v Blythe, Green, Jourdain & Co* [1915] 2 K.B. 379, **4–015** 388, Scrutton L.J., when a judge of first instance, described a c.i.f. contract as being a sale of documents relating to goods and not a sale of goods. But when the Court of Appeal considered that case [1916] 1 K.B. 495, 510, 514 Bankes L.J. and Warrington L.J. commented on the language of Scrutton J. and indicated their view that a c.i.f. contract is a contract for the sale of goods to be performed by the delivery of documents. But I respectfully venture to think that the difference is one of phrase only. For in reality, as I have said, the obligation of the vendor is to deliver documents rather than goods—to transfer symbols rather than the physical property represented thereby. If the vendor fulfils his contract by shipping the appropriate goods in the appropriate manner under a proper contract of carriage, and if he also obtains the proper documents for tender to the purchaser, I am unable to see how the rights or duties of either party are affected by the loss of ship or goods, or by knowledge of such loss by the vendor, prior to actual tender of the documents. If the ship be lost prior to tender but without the knowledge of the seller it was, I assume, always clear that he could make an effective proffer of the documents to the buyer. In my opinion, it is also clear that he can make an effective tender even though he possess at the time of tender actual knowledge of the loss of the ship or goods. For the purchaser in case of loss will get the documents he bargained for; and if the policy be that required by the contract, and if the loss be covered thereby, he will secure the insurance moneys. The contingency of loss is within and not outside the contemplation of the parties to a c.i.f. contract. The views I have expressed are, I feel, in full accord with the observations of Atkin J. in *C. Groom, Ltd v Barber* [above] as to the requirements of a c.i.f. contract, and with the judgment of Bailhache J. in *Re Weis & Co and Credit Colonial et Commercial (Antwerp)* [1916] 1 K.B. 346. I therefore hold that the plaintiffs were not entitled to reject the tender of documents in the present case upon the ground that the *Algonquin* had, to the knowledge of the defendants, sunk prior to the tender of documents. This view will simplify the performance of c.i.f. contracts and prevent delay either through doubts as to the loss of ship or goods or through difficult questions with regard to the knowledge or suspicion of a vendor as to the actual occurrence of a loss . . .

The above observations suffice to dispose of the case, but two other points were argued before me. Mr Hogg submitted that the tender in respect of the starch was in any event bad, inasmuch as the contract was for the sale of starch in 280 lb. bags, whereas the starch shipped by the defendants was, as appears from the invoice, partly in 220 lb. bags and partly in 140 lb. bags. Mr MacKinnon K.C. [for the defendants] argued that the words "280 lb. bags" were not a material part of the bargain. But, in my opinion, it is clear that such words were an essential part of the contract requirements. They constitute a portion of the description of the goods. The size of the bags may be important to a purchaser in view of sub contracts or otherwise. A man may prefer to receive starch either in small or large or medium bags. If the size of the bags was immaterial I fail to see why it should have been so clearly specified in the contract. A vendor must supply goods in accordance with the contract description, and he is not entitled to say that another description of goods will suffice for the purposes of the purchaser: see s.13 of the Sale of Goods Act, 1893; *Bowes v Shand* (1877) 2 App. Cas. 455, 480–1 per Lord Blackburn; *Jackson v Rotax Motor and Cycle Co* [1910] 2 K.B. 937. The tender by the defendants of starch in bags other than 280 lb. bags was a failure to comply with their contract.

Notes

4–016　　1. Because of the eventual decision, paragraph 2 of the decision (above) is *dicta* only.

2. McCardie J. regarded the *Olympia Oil and Cake Co* case [1915] 1 K.B. 233 as not laying down any general principle for c.i.f. contracts; he did not think the contract there was c.i.f. at all, and indeed, it looks more like an ex-ship contract.

3. In *The Galatia* [1980] 1 W.L.R. 495, the cargo (sugar) was damaged by fire just after loading, and discharged. This was before the bill of lading was even issued, and indeed the bill of lading was claused to show the damage to the goods:

> "Cargo covered by this Bill of Lading has been discharged Kandla view damaged by fire and/or water used to extinguish fire for which general average declared."

Yet the Court of Appeal held that the c. & f. buyer must accept the documents tendered. This is consistent with the general principle that the goods are at the buyer's risk once loading is complete. Note also that because of the clausing, the seller must have known of the condition of the goods at the time the bill of lading was tendered.[14]

EXTRACT FROM J.D. FELTHAM, "THE APPROPRIATION TO A C.I.F. CONTRACT OF GOODS LOST OR DAMAGED AT SEA"

[1975] J.B.L. 273

[*Footnotes are as in the original, but renumbered for inclusion in this book.*]

4–017

It is well known that a contract for the sale of goods c.i.f. is a contract for the sale of goods to be performed by delivery of documents,[15] normally an invoice, a bill of lading and a policy of insurance. The risk of loss or damage to the goods (so far as it is not covered by the contractual obligations of the parties)[16] passes from the seller to the buyer on or as from shipment. The passage of risk on or as from shipment is convenient in eliminating difficult questions of proof of the time goods were lost or damaged while at sea. The reference to the passage of risk retrospectively as from shipment is necessary to cover the option of a seller c.i.f. of performing his contract by the appropriation thereto of documents relating to goods previously shipped by himself or a third party and to cover the case of the sale of goods afloat.[17] In the event of loss or damage at sea there may well be a claim under the policy of insurance or against the shipowner under the contract of affreightment evidenced by the bill of lading. But *pace* Lord Normand[18] the fact that a particular form of loss or damage at sea is not covered by the policy of insurance does not prevent the risk from passing to the buyer.[19]

[*Feltham describes the facts of* Groom v Barber *and continues:*]

. . . On a case stated by the arbitrators Atkin J. held that a seller c.i.f. may validly and effectively tender documents relating to good lost at sea at the time of tender and [the buyer] was held to be bound to pay. In *Manbre Saccharine Company Limited v Corn Products Co Ltd*[20] there is a statement by McCardie J. that a seller c.i.f. can validly tender documents in respect of goods shipped on a vessel which at the time of tender the

---

[14] This case is discussed in greater detail in para. 6—067, below.

[15] *Arnhold Karberg & Co v Blythe, Green, Jordain & Co* [1916] 1 K.B. 495, 510, 514.

[16] In a contract of sale c.i.f. the seller's promises, express and implied, as to the quality and condition of the goods will normally be construed as promises as to the state of the goods at the time when risk passes, *i.e.* shipment: *Mash & Murrell Ltd v Joseph I Emmanuel Ltd* [1961] 2 Lloyd's Rep. 326. See *Benjamin's Sale of Goods*, paras. 829, 1442.

[17] *Mash & Murrell Ltd v Joseph I Emmanuel Ltd* (*supra*).

[18] *Comptoir d'Achat et de Vente du Boerenbond Belge SA v Luis de Ridder Limitada (The Julia)* [1949] A.C. 293, 319.

[19] *Groom v Barber* [1915] 1 K.B. 316; *Law & Bonar Ltd v British American Tobacco Ltd* [1916] 2 K.B. 605 [para. 4—027, below].

[20] [1919] 1 K.B. 198. See also *Law & Bonar Ltd v British American Tobacco Ltd*, *supra*.

seller knows to have been totally lost. The question arises whether these statements are correct in a case where the seller has not, prior to the time of the loss, appropriated the goods in question to the c.i.f. contract in question so as to make those goods the goods he is obliged to deliver under the contract.

[*Feltham describes the* Olympia Cake *case, and continues:*]

. . . In the new *Benjamin's Sale of Goods*,[21] Mr G.H. Treitel expresses the view that a c.i.f seller may validly tender documents relating to goods lost at sea prior to the time of tender only if he has appropriated the goods in question before the time of the loss. He points to the general principle of the law of sale that a seller of generic goods by description is not relieved because the particular goods which he intended to appropriate but has not yet appropriated are destroyed. As against this it may be argued that the c.i.f. contract is a special case because the seller performs by delivery of documents and the consideration obtained by the buyer is not simply the goods but the goods and/or rights under the contracts of insurance and affreightment. Whether the goods are lost or not, the buyer gets rights under the ancillary contracts which may or may not cover the loss in question.[22]

Mr Treitel shows that the statement of Atkin J. in *Groom v Barber*[23] that "[t]he seller must be in a position to pass the property in the goods by the bill of lading if the goods are in existence, but he need not have appropriated the particular goods in the particular bill of lading to the particular buyer until the moment of tender, nor need he have obtained any right to deal with the bill of lading until the moment of tender" was made in reply to an argument that at the time of loss the goods must have been appropriated to the contract so as to pass the property to the buyer. The passage may not use "appropriation" in the sense of merely attaching the contract to the particular goods. But on the facts given on the reports of *Groom v Barber* and the *Manbre Saccharine Co* case,[24] there is room for argument whether there had been appropriation in the sense that the seller had bound himself to deliver the particular goods in question and it does not appear that in either case the court gave attention to the question. In *Groom v Barber* there can hardly have been any more than an appropriation of whatever goods might be appropriated to the seller by the Calcutta merchant from whom he was buying. In the *Manbre Saccharine Co* case, the contracts were for the sale c.i.f. of unascertained goods by

---

[21] Paras. 1549–1550. [See now Benjamin's *Sale of Goods*, 5th ed., 1997, para. 19–094.] Contrast Schmitthoff, *The Export Trade*, 6th ed., pp. 33–34. [*See now, 10th ed., 2000.*]

[22] *Cf.* Scrutton J. in *Arnhold Karberg & Co v Blythe, Green, Jordain & Co* [1915] 2 K.B. 379, 388. But this is the passage in which Scrutton J. described a c.i.f. contract as a sale of documents relating to goods, with which Bankes and Warrington L.JJ. in the Court of Appeal disagreed, stating that a c.i.f. contract was a contract for the sale of goods to be performed by the delivery of documents. See note [12], *supra*.

[23] Note [16], *supra*, at p. 324.

[24] *Supra*, note [17].

description and so far as communications between the seller and buyer are concerned the first mention by the seller of a shipment on the *Algonquin*, the ship in fact lost, was a letter of March 14 (two days after the ship was sunk) enclosing bills of lading for goods shipped on the *Algonquin* and invoices. Any appropriation must then have been one involving no communication with the buyer.[25] In *Groom v Barber*, Atkin J. appears to speak of appropriation in a general sense, *e.g.* in stating:

"The committee have not dealt with the question of fact as to whether there had been any appropriation of goods to this contract by or on behalf of the seller. . . . Upon the evidence as disclosed in the case there does not appear to have been any appropriation, and I shall assume there was none."

He justifies his decision in the case by the argument that otherwise the shipper of goods in bulk or of goods intended for several contracts or the intermediate seller who may be the last in a chain of purchasers from an original shipper, might find it impossible to enforce a contract on c.i.f. terms. It seems probable that a seller in the middle of a chain will be unable to appropriate particular goods to his contract until he receives an appropriation from the seller to him. The most he may be able to do is to appropriate to the contract whatever goods may be appropriated to him by his predecessor in the chain and it is doubtful whether such an appropriation is crucial for the present purpose.

In the *Olympia Oil & Cake Co* case,[26] Rowlatt J. in the Divisional Court, **4–018** in an argument against the right to appropriate a lost cargo to the contract, put the case of a person in whose hands the cargo was lost. He pointed out that, if he could validly appropriate to a contract of sale a shipment known to be lost, then he could afterwards enter a contract to sell a cargo, and, if the price fell, buy a cargo afloat, tender it and pocket the difference, and, if the price rose, tender the lost ship and escape from the speculation without loss. But the first branch of this principle merely illustrates what any seller may do on a falling market and the seller remains saddled with the loss of the original cargo so far as this is not covered by insurance; the second branch depends on the question under discussion but involves the additional variation that the goods have been lost prior to the making of the contract under which they are tendered. This variation will be discussed below.

If one considers the question of damage to the goods rather than the loss thereof, it is suggested that a seller c.i.f. may validly appropriate to his contract goods which have been damaged at sea prior to the time of appropriation. In *Mash & Murrell Ltd v Joseph I. Emmanuel Ltd*,[27] a case on a contract of sale c. & f. on July 8 of goods afloat, the Court of Appeal assumed that the risk of over-heating in the hold at Famagusta prior to

---

[25] See *Benjamin's Sale of Goods*, para. 1503. [*See now 5th ed., 1997.*]
[26] [[1915] 1 K.B. 233.]
[27] Note [13], *supra.*

July 4 was on the buyer. But it is not suggested that the seller knew of the damage before the arrival of the ship at Liverpool on July 18. ... It is suggested that the law is the same even if the seller knows of the damage at the time he appropriates the goods to the contract; the seller's knowledge does not appear to make a material difference. If a seller c.i.f. may validly appropriate to a contract goods known to have been damaged at sea prior to the time of appropriation (and can pass the risk of such damage to the buyer as from shipment), it is hard to see why the rule should not be the same if the goods are lost prior to the time of appropriation. There does not appear to be a good reason for a difference in principle between a case of serious damage and a case of loss.

[*Feltham then goes on to consider the situation where the goods are lost before the contract is made; see further below on this issue.*]

Notes

4–019   The issue is really how far *Manbre Saccharine* extends, assuming that it determines the proposition that a c.i.f. seller can appropriate, for the purposes of passing property, goods which he knows, at the time of such appropriation, to have been lost. From the discussion later in the chapter, it appears that a seller cannot, knowing goods to have been lost at sea, later enter into a c.i.f. contract, passing the risk of such loss retrospectively to the new buyer, as from shipment. It follows from this that if in a chain sale, one of the c.i.f. buyers goes into liquidation after the goods have been lost at sea, his immediate seller, who has had to take up and pay for the documents, cannot protect his position by entering into a new sale contract, and tendering the same documents. Were the principles of the documentary transaction to be taken to their logical conclusion, this would be possible, and it is arguably regrettable that it is not.

There are however two meanings of appropriation. (On the different meanings of appropriation, see further chapter 5, below) The appropriation under discussion in *Groom* and *Manbre*, it is argued, is the unconditional appropriation needed to pass the property. It does not follow, Treitel is said to argue, that the seller can appropriate to the contract goods which he knows to be lost, in the other sense of the meaning of appropriation, that of deciding that those goods are going to be used for that contract. Against this, Feltham argues that there had not been an appropriation in either sense in *Groom* or *Manbre*, and in *Groom v Barber* at any rate, where the seller himself was unaware of the identity of the vessel until an hour before tender of documents to the buyer, this would seem to be quite a strong argument. Feltham argues against the distinction drawn by Treitel, and also argues that the same position should apply to damage or deterioration to the goods; *Mash & Murrell*, cited in the last paragraph set out above, is considered further below.

As for the Rowlatt J. example, in the first branch the lost cargo is really irrelevant; on a falling market one would expect the contract price to be higher than the current value of the cargo, and if the seller buys a cargo at current price and sells it at contract price he will of course make a profit. He can always do that, whether or not there is another lost cargo in existence. In any case, he presumably purchased the lost cargo at a higher price and has made a loss on that transaction. In the second branch the market is rising, so he pays the current high rate for the cargo afloat; if (as is likely on a rising market) he paid less for the lost cargo, by tendering it he will make a profit, but he will make nothing on the other cargo, and he would have made the same profit had the cargo not been lost. It is difficult to see why these consequences are assumed to be undesirable.

(4) Genuine Exceptions

The transfer of risk under the contract depends on the contract remaining **4–020** enforceable at the seller's suit, which will not be the case if the buyer validly rejects the documents (as in *Manbre Saccharine*) or the goods, thereby re-vesting risk in the seller. There are also problems if the contract is void for mistake, or frustrated. Though in practice these affect the transfer of risk, they are not genuine exceptions to the rules, and are dealt with later in this chapter.

There are also genuine exceptions to the rules on risk, considered here.

We have already come across (in *The Rio Sun*, in para. 2—044, above) the Sale of Goods Act 1979, s.20(2) (delay in delivery), which if applicable expressly alters the risk position, and s.32(2) (reasonable carriage contract), which by delaying delivery in practice alters risk. Neither was dealt with in any sense conclusively in *The Rio Sun*, s.32(2) because the carriage contract was reasonable, and s.20(2) because it was unnecessary to do so. If delivery is construed as being to the vessel, as would be natural in an f.o.b. or c.i.f. contract, s.20(2) will have no application to any delays occurring after shipment. If on the other hand, delivery is construed as including constructive delivery under a c.i.f. contract, any delay up to the time of tender is covered.

Another genuine exception to the normal rules on risk is s.32(3).

(a) Sale of Goods Act 1979, s.32(3)

This section re-enacts an identical section from the 1893 Act). **4–021**

Sale of Goods Act 1979, s.32(3)

Unless otherwise agreed, where goods are sent by the seller to the buyer by a route involving sea transit, under circumstances in which it is usual to insure, the seller must give such notice to the buyer as may enable him to insure them during their sea transit, and if the seller fails to do so, the goods are at his risk during such sea transit.

Notes

1. Since the section is a re-enactment of an earlier identical section (in the Sale of Goods Act 1893), it follows that any case since 1893 is authoritative. Moreover, the 1893 Act was itself a codification of the common law (a point which Vaughan Williams L.J. regarded as relevant to its construction, in the following case).

2. Where the section applies, the goods may remain at the seller's risk even after shipment, if he does not give the buyer sufficient information to enable him to insure.

3. The section needs to be read along with s.32(1):

"Where, in pursuance of a contract of sale, the seller is authorised or required to send the goods to the buyer, delivery of the goods to a carrier (whether named by the buyer or not) for the purpose of transmission to the buyer is *prima facie* deemed to be a delivery of the goods to the buyer."

(b) Application to f.o.b. Contracts

WIMBLE SONS & CO LTD v ROSENBERG & SONS

Court of Appeal. [1913] 3 K.B. 743

Facts:

4–022   The case involved the shipment of 200 bags of rice f.o.b. Antwerp. The sellers had not told the buyers the name of the ship (which was selected by them). The reason was probably to do with postal delays, because the ship sailed on a Sunday. Shortly after shipment the ship was stranded, and the cargo became a total loss. The buyers did not have an open cover, but their practice was to take out insurance only after being notified of the name of the ship. Thus they were uninsured, and refused to pay the price. The sellers sued for the price.

Held (Vaughan Williams L.J. dissenting):
The sellers were entitled to the price.

Vaughan Williams L.J.: . . . The case in substance turns on the construction of s. 32 of the Sale of Goods Act, 1893, and in particular of sub-s. 3 of that section. It is to be remembered, I think, throughout the interpretation of this Act that it is a codifying Act and subject, therefore, to the provisions of the Interpretation Act, 1889, and subject also to the canon of construction when dealing with a codifying Act laid down by Lord Herschell, in the House of Lords, in *Bank of England v Vagliano* [1891] A.C. 107, 144, a case on the Bills of Exchange Act, 1882, which was also a codifying Act: "The proper course is in the first instance to examine the language of the statute and to ask what is its natural meaning, uninfluenced by any considerations derived from the previous state of the law, and not to start with inquiring how the law previously stood, and then, assuming that it was probably intended to leave it unaltered, to see if the words of the enactment will bear an interpretation in conformity with this view." . . .

An argument before us was on the basis that sub-s. 3 of s. 32 had and could have no application to a contract of sale f.o.b. It was argued also that the buyers did not require a notice, because they might have insured these goods by "a general cover contract" or by a "ship or ships" contract . . . At the conclusion of Mr. Leck's argument on behalf of the plaintiffs [sellers], . . . his junior put forward a new point, that notice already had been given, enabling the buyers to insure, for that the contract of purchase itself was notice. . . .

This case turns to my mind on construction. No facts are in dispute. I am of opinion that sub-s. 3 of s. 32 of the Sale of Goods Act covers an f.o.b. contract. To say generally that sub-s. 3 does not cover an f.o.b. contract seems to me to be a conspicuous illustration of departure from Lord Herschell's canon of construction which I have already quoted. The natural meaning of the words of sub-s. 3 does not exclude an f.o.b. contract. The real ground for the suggested exclusion is that the sub-section, construed according to its natural meaning, is hard to reconcile with some of the previous law laid down in the cases relating to the carriage of goods under an f.o.b. contract, and that it is highly improbable that the Legislature intended to alter or modify law which is the result of a series of decisions laid down by great commercial lawyers.

Mr Leck, in his excellent argument on behalf of the plaintiffs, to my mind was evidently pressed by a strong desire to avoid a breach of Lord Herschell's canon of construction of codifying statutes and argued that sub-s. 3, read in the light of sub-s. 1, has no application to a case where, in pursuance of a contract of sale, the seller is "authorized or required" to send goods to the buyer, and says that under an f.o.b. contract the seller is never authorized nor required to send the goods to the buyer, but completely performs his duty when he puts the goods on board the steamer. Bailhache J. based his judgment on this contention of Mr. Leck and, as I understand his judgment, in effect held that an f.o.b. contract is excluded unless it includes some words whereby the vendor undertook to send the goods by some ship selected by himself, and that in this case the shipping instructions ought not to be regarded as part of the contract, in which case Bailhache J. thought sub-s. 3 would have applied.

I construe the word "send," . . . in sub-s. 3 in the sense of "forward" or "despatch," and in my opinion the word "send" covers every obligation of the seller in reference to effecting or securing the arrival of the goods the subject of sale at the destination intended. It is not true in fact to say that the purchased goods are being sent to the ship on which they are placed for the purpose of delivery at the port of destination. The purchased goods are not the less being sent to the buyer at the port of destination because delivery f.o.b. is *prima facie* delivery to the buyer, or because the property has passed to the buyer. Sub-s. 3, in my opinion, casts a duty on the seller forwarding the goods to the buyer by a route involving sea transit, under circumstances in which it is usual to insure, to give such notice as may enable the buyer (to whom be it observed the property in the purchased goods has passed), to insure them during their sea transit. The penalty for not performing this duty is that goods, though the goods of the buyer, shall be at the risk of the seller during such sea transit. Moreover the same result is arrived at if the words "where goods are sent by the seller to the buyer," at the beginning of sub-s. 3, are construed as describing the whole transaction.

I have already said that I cannot agree with the argument of [the sellers] that the contract of sale itself was notice within the meaning of sub-s. 3, and I have arrived at this conclusion not only on the ground that the contract did not afford sufficient information to enable the buyer to insure the purchased goods during their sea transit, but also on the ground that knowledge of the buyer, actual, inferred, or assumed, which would enable the buyer to insure, does not dispense with the statutory obligation of the seller, where the route involves sea transit under circumstances in which it is usual to insure, to give such notice to the buyer as may enable him to insure the goods during their sea transit. The obligation . . . on the seller is to give such notice, with such details, to the buyer as may be necessary to effect insurance of the goods during sea transit. It is to my mind impossible to construe the words as meaning that the obligation to insure does not arise in case the buyer happens to have sufficient information from some other source than the statutory notice to enable him to insure the goods.

I have only to add that, whichever of the suggested constructions relieving the seller from obligation to give the statutory notice in the case of an f.o.b. contract is adopted, the practical utility and application of sub-s. 3 of s. 32 are reduced to nil.

4–023   BUCKLEY L.J.: Before Bailhache J. counsel for the seller contended that under an f.o.b. contract the seller is never "authorized or required to send the goods to the buyer," a contention which the learned judge seems to have adopted, adding "more particularly as I cannot bring myself to believe that sub-s. 3 applies to an ordinary f.o.b. contract of sale." This contention has been repeated before us. I propose in the first instance to consider it.

The contention is that sub-s. 3 is a qualification of sub-s. 1 and may be read as if it were prefaced by the words "provided always that." To this I agree. Then it is said sub-s. 1 applies only where the seller is authorized or required to send the goods to the buyer, and that is not the case where the contract of sale is f.o.b., inasmuch as the delivery is complete so soon as the goods are handed over the ship's rail: that the sending by the seller to the buyer is then complete. In my opinion this is erroneous. The sending of the goods is not, within the language of the section, equivalent to the delivery of the goods to the buyer. The first sub-section uses the word "send" and the word "transmission" and the word "delivery." The word "send" is so used as to bear the same meaning as that for which the word "transmission" is next employed, and both the one and the other are contrasted with "delivery," the word last used. In sub-s. 1 the word "send" means, I think, "despatch" or "transmit," in a physical sense, and not "deliver" so as to pass the property at law. The same meaning is, I think, to be attributed to the word "sent" in sub-s. 3. After the property has passed by placing the goods on shipboard under an f.o.b. contract, the goods may, I think, within the meaning of sub-s. 3, be "sent," that is to say, transmitted or despatched by the seller to the buyer. Goods are capable of being sent by the vendor, in whom the property is not, to the buyer, in whom it is. . . .

The effect of the section seems to me to be as follows: Where in pursuance of a contract of sale goods are to be sent, it shall be an incident of every contract, as it already is of an f.o.b. contract, that delivery to a carrier is delivery to the buyer, with the result that the goods at sea will be at the risk of the buyer. But nevertheless (unless otherwise agreed), if the seller fails to comply with sub-s. 3, the risk shall be that not of the buyer but of the seller. From these provisions I can find no exception of an f.o.b. contract, but on the contrary I find a reduction of every contract for this purpose to the position of an f.o.b. contract.

So far, therefore, it seems to me that the appellants are right and that it is necessary to see whether in the present case sub-s. 3 has been complied with.

Sub-s. 3 requires the seller to give such notice to the buyer as will enable the latter to insure. These words will be satisfied if either (a) the buyer is already in possession of knowledge of all the facts which it is necessary to know in order that he may insure the goods, in which case nothing is wanting to enable him to insure them, or (b) if such notice (if any) as has been given him completes his knowledge of the facts so as to enable him to insure. . . .

. . . But . . . it seems to me that no notice to "enable" the buyer was wanted, for he already had ability: he had all materials necessary to enable him to insure. Those words of the section, therefore, which require the seller to give notice do not apply, for no notice was wanted to enable the buyer to insure. But if this is not so and the seller was under an obligation to give him such notice, &c., then I think he had done so. The contract itself of June 27, 1912, was a sufficient notice. It gave the buyer knowledge of all the necessary particulars other than knowledge which rested with himself, or was determinate by himself, namely, first, the port of discharge, and, secondly, the name of the ship. The former lay within his own knowledge and was supplied by him in August. The latter was not necessary to enable him to insure, and in fact he waived knowledge of it by leaving it to the seller to select the ship. For these reasons I am of opinion that, although sub-s. 3 is applicable to this case notwithstanding that the contract was an f.o.b. contract, yet the seller has not failed to do anything which by sub-s. 3 he was bound to do.

HAMILTON L.J.: Bailhache J. decided that s. 32, sub-s. 3, of the Sale of **4–024** Goods Act did not apply to this case. This is the subject of the appeal. The question is whether he was right. I think he was.

The "sending" of the goods in sub-ss. 1 and 3 of s. 32 is the same thing in each case, an actual forwarding or transmission. The use of the same word "send" in s. 29 shews this. But in sub-s. 1 the case is, "where the seller is authorised or required to send the goods" and that too "in pursuance of a contract of sale"; in sub-s. 3 the case is, "where the goods are sent by the seller to the buyer" simply. In the former, which is a provision in favour of the seller limiting his responsibility, the questions are, Was he authorized or required to send the goods, that is, to transmit or forward them, to start them on their journey? Has he done so? When and where does his responsibility cease? A further question was raised, which we need not decide, namely, does "in pursuance of a contract of sale" mean "in performance of" or "as required under the terms of'? On the other hand the latter sub-s. 3 is one in favour of the buyer and makes his responsibility in certain circumstances conditional on the seller's giving a certain notice. Here the question is not merely have the goods been "sent" in the above sense, but have they been so sent by the seller to the buyer, that is, by the sender as seller to the receiver as buyer, or, in the language of sub-s. 1, sent "in pursuance of a contract of sale." Hence, in spite of the use of the same verb "to send," it does not necessarily follow that a contract involving sending, if within sub-s. 1, must therefore also be within sub-s. 3. It is well settled that, on an ordinary f.o.b. contract, when "free on board" does not merely condition the constituent elements in the price but expresses the seller's obligations additional to the bare bargain of purchase and sale, the seller does not "in pursuance of the contract of sale" or as seller send forward or start the goods to the buyer at all except in the sense that he puts the goods safely on board, pays the charge of doing so, and, for the buyer's protection but not under a mandate to send, gives up possession of them to the ship only upon the terms of a reasonable and ordinary bill of lading or other contract of carriage. There his contractual liability as seller ceases, and delivery to the buyer is complete as far as he is concerned. In such a case the goods are not "sent by the seller to the buyer," though they then begin a journey which will end in the buyer's hands. In law, as between buyer and seller, they are then and there delivered by the seller to the buyer, and thereafter it is by the buyer and his agent, the carrier, and not by the seller, that the goods are "sent" to their destination. It is in this sense that I understand the words of Bailhache J., "what one generally understands by an f.o.b. contract is that the goods are not sent by sea by the vendor but are delivered by him at the rail of the ship and are then taken over by the shipowner nominated by the buyer and conveyed by him across the sea." So understood, I agree with them. . . .

It has been argued that, in signing and sending to the buyer the contract note itself, the seller, to the benefit of whose acts the plaintiffs succeed, did give to the buyer such notice as might enable him to insure the goods. Literally this is undeniably true. The appellants say that this is a paradox, which would make every f.o.b. contract its own enabling notice and so, also, so far nullify the sub-section. I think this is true too, but my conclusion is that the paradox helps to shew that f.o.b. contracts are not within the sub-section. It is a *reductio ad absurdum*.

Notes

4–025   1. Although two members of the Court of Appeal thought that the section applied, in principle, to f.o.b. contracts (Vaughan Williams and Buckley L.JJ.), the majority view (Buckley and Hamilton L.JJ.) was that, at any rate, the section did not apply to this particular contract. The majority view can probably be extended to any f.o.b. contract, but not necessarily to a c. & f. contract (see further below).

2. Hamilton L.J. thought the section did not apply in principle to this f.o.b. contract, because the seller does not send the goods to the buyer by a route involving sea transit, but merely puts them on board a ship for dispatch to the buyer. This reasoning would not necessarily apply to an f.o.b. contract where the

seller is under an obligation to ship the goods, nor would it necessarily apply to a c. & f. contract.

3. Vaughan Williams and Buckley L.JJ. both disagreed with Hamilton L.J.'s view, adopting a wider definition of "send", and holding that the section applied in principle to f.o.b. contracts; they disagreed with each other as to the manner of its application.

4. Vaughan Williams L.J. thought that the seller should have provided more information, and that the risk remained with him because of his failure to do so, but his was the dissenting judgment.

5. Buckley L.J. thought that the seller had given sufficient information to comply with the terms of the section, and indeed the buyer can always take out a general policy of insurance, without needing to know the name of the ship. But as Hamilton L.J. pointed out, if this view is correct the section imposes no obligations on an f.o.b. seller, because the buyer always already knows sufficient information to take out a general insurance policy anyway.

6. It would seem, then, that whether or not s. 32(3) applies in principle to f.o.b. contracts, it is unlikely ever to apply in practice.

7. Note that the buyers knew the description of the goods (from the contract), the port of discharge (because it was selected by them) and the port of loading (from the contract). This is sufficient information to insure the goods, and one would expect an f.o.b. buyer always to have this information.

(c) Application to c.i.f. Contracts

Obviously, s.32(3) will not usually apply to c.i.f. contracts (though it might to c. & f.), because the duty to insure is on the seller. However, the seller is not necessarily obliged to provide full insurance cover, in which case there may still be room for its application, where the buyer would wish to take out additional insurance. An argument to this effect failed (c.i.f.) in *Law & Bonar*, but the case is inconclusive on the case where war risk insurance is usual, and provided by the buyer.   **4–026**

LAW & BONAR LTD v BRITISH AMERICAN TOBACCO LTD

King's Bench Division. [1916] 2 K.B. 605

Facts:

The facts were similar to those in *C. Groom v Barber*, set out earlier in this chapter, and indeed the action arose out of the sinking of the same vessel, *City of Winchester* by a German cruiser in August 1914.   **4–027**

In *Law & Bonar*, the sale contract was made in May 1914. The bill of lading was dated July 20th. War did not break out until August 4th. Therefore, both the conclusion of the sale contract, and shipment, occurred in peacetime. The vessel was captured and eventually sunk by a German cruiser on or about August 13th (or possibly earlier). The goods (Calcutta Hessian, like those in *Groom v Barber*) were likewise uninsured against war risks, but in this case the buyers claimed that since they had not been informed of the name of the vessel, or the fact that she had been sunk, until after the goods were lost, they had been given insufficient information to enable them to take out war risks insurance on their own account. Therefore risk remained with the sellers on the basis of section 32(3).

Note that it was assumed that it would be for the buyers to take out war risk (evidence showed that war risk insurance was available from August 4th onwards).

Decision:

The 32(3) argument was rejected on the grounds that section 32(3) does not apply at any rate to a c.i.f. contract which was made in peacetime.

Rowlatt J. left open the possibility that it may apply to a contract made at a time when insurance against war risk was usual (but arguably in that case the seller would be under an obligation to provide war risk cover anyway: see further the discussion in chapter 6, below).

ROWLATT J.: The next question is whether s.32(3) of the Sale of Goods Act, 1893, applies to this case. It clearly does not apply to a c.i.f. contract in times when no one contemplates war, and when, therefore, war is not usually insured against. It does not apply because the contract c.i.f. provides for all the insurance that is contemplated or usual and the seller is to effect it. That was the nature of the contract when made. It dealt exclusively and expressly with all the insurance that was in view. But now it is said that, on war becoming imminent, another form of insurance emerged and the contract ceased to be one which dealt exhaustively with the question of insurance and a new obligation arose for the seller. I cannot agree. This sub-section annexes a term to the contract, and the question whether it is applicable or not falls to be decided at the time when the contract is made. I say nothing as to whether the sub-section could apply to a contract c.i.f. made at a time when insurances other than those to be provided by the seller—*e.g.*, against war risks—are usual. That point does not arise. In this case I do not think that there is any real evidence that it was usual to insure against war risks at any material time . . . I am not at all certain whether [the buyers] themselves had made up their minds whether they would insure against war risks or not . . .

Comments

4–028   1. This passage leaves open the possibility that s.32(3) may apply, in very limited circumstances, to a c.i.f. contract, and it would be easier to argue that it might apply to c. & f. However, Rowlatt J. does not advance this question far, so we still need to consider arguments based on *Wimble v Rosenberg*. On that basis, in principle:

(a) If it is accepted that delivery is to the vessel, and that consequently the goods are not sent to the buyer by a route involving sea transit, then there is no basis for the application of 32(3) to any f.o.b. or c.i.f. contract, but even Hamilton L.J. did not construe "send" this narrowly in *Wimble*.

(b) To deliver is not necessarily to send. Thus, Hamilton L.J.'s interpretation ought not generally to apply c.i.f., since on no basis can the seller be regarded as undertaking the shipment as the buyer's agent.

(c) Buckley L.J. (the other majority view in *Wimble*) would have applied the section in principle, but held that the buyer already had sufficient information. However, in *Wimble* the buyer was aware of the port of loading, and could therefore obtain a floating policy of insurance, whereas this would not necessarily be the case c.i.f. / c. & f., since the seller may have a choice of loading ports (especially with a c.i.f. or c. & f. sale afloat).

2. If war risk is usual, arguably a c.i.f. seller is required to provide it, in which case again, the section would have no application. The c.i.f. seller must provide such insurance as is customary in the trade; surely this would include such insurance as is usual. See further chapter 6, below.

(5) Other Contractual Issues Relating to Risk

Section 32(3), if it applies, genuinely postpones the transfer of risk, as does **4–029** s.20(2), considered in chapter 2, above (at least where the delay contributes to the loss or damage complained of) and, in effect, s.32(2). This section is concerned with contractual terms or doctrines which have a similar effect to altering the timing of the transfer of risk, where the party who has to make good the loss is not the party at risk.

(a) Implied Condition of Merchantable Quality Sale of Goods Act 1893, s.14(2)

Where goods are bought by description from a seller who deals in **4–030** goods of that description (whether he is the manufacturer or not), there is an implied condition that the goods will be of merchantable quality; but if the buyer has examined the goods, there is no implied condition as regards defects which such examination ought to have revealed.

Notes

The cases set out here were decided under this provision. It was altered, but not materially, in 1979, and again in 1994. The 1994 changes may affect the discussion, and are considered further below.

The principle in *Mash & Murrell*, below, is "that merchantability in the case of goods sold c.i.f. or c. & f. means that the goods must remain merchantable for a reasonable time, and that in the case of such contracts a reasonable time means time for arrival and disposal on arrival."[28] This implies that they should be capable of withstanding a normal sea voyage. The case has been heavily criticised, but if the principle is correct, then s.14(2) may, in limited situations, have the effect of partially re-vesting risk in the seller, even after shipment. For example, suppose the goods deteriorate after shipment. Although the buyer remains technically at risk, he may nevertheless have recourse against the seller where, though the goods were of the contract description and quality when loaded, they were not capable of enduring a normal voyage, and hence, on the *Mash & Murrell* principle, not of merchantable quality.

Arguably, any adjustment to the normal principles on risk is unfortunate, especially in a chain sale. Unlike the normal situation where damage occurs after shipment, however, the buyer's only recourse is against the seller. The risk will not be covered by marine insurance, and since the cause of loss is inherent vice, there will be no action against the carrier. Moreover, although breach of s.14(2) is

---

[28] Elsewhere, Diplock J. applies the same reasoning to f.o.b. contracts, on the grounds that they too envisage sea transit.

a breach of *condition*,[29] entitling the buyer to reject, the right is probably limited to rejection of goods on their arrival, and does not extend to rejection of the shipping documents, which will typically conform on their face: see further *Gill & Duffus SA v Berger & Co Inc* [1984] A.C. 382 (see further paras 7—021, *et seq.*, below).

MASH & MURRELL LTD v JOSEPH I EMMANUEL LTD

Queen's Bench Division. [1961] 1 Lloyd's Rep. 46, [1961] 1 W.L.R. 862

Facts:

4–031   The buyers dealt in potatoes for human consumption. They entered into a contract with the sellers for the sale of potatoes (afloat), which had been shipped from Cyprus c. & f. Liverpool. The sellers knew that the purchasers dealt in fruit and vegetables for human consumption. Though the goods were properly stowed, on arrival at Liverpool they were found to be affected by soft-rot and unfit for human consumption (they were sold as pig-food at £3 per ton, whereas had they arrived in sound condition they would have been worth 32s per cwt., or £32 per ton). In an action for damages by the buyers:

Held (by Diplock J.):
The sellers were in breach of s.14(2) (of the 1893 Act). To be of merchantable quality, goods loaded under a c.i.f. or f.o.b. contract must be capable of withstanding a normal sea-voyage.

Note
The sellers were also held to be in breach of s. 14(1) (requiring that the goods be fit for their purpose).

4–032   DIPLOCK J.: I am satisfied that when the potatoes, the subject-matter of this action, were loaded at Limassol they were "not fit to travel" to Liverpool on the *Ionian* on the voyage which she was taking, which I have held was a normal voyage, in the sense that they were in such a condition that in the ordinary course of events they would, on arrival at Liverpool, be unfit for human consumption, which is the purpose for which Cyprus spring crop potatoes in bags are normally used.

On those findings of fact a question of law, which has been hotly debated, arises. I have so far travelled through my legal life under the impression, shared by a number of other judges who have sat in this court, that when goods are sold under a contract such as c.i.f. contract, or f.o.b. contract, which involves transit before use, there is an implied warranty not merely that they shall be merchantable at the time they are put on the vessel, but that they shall be in such a state that they can endure the normal journey and be in a merchantable condition on arrival. It has been strenuously argued by counsel for the defendants in this case

---

[29] Subject to the 1994 amendments, considered in para. 4—039, below.

that that impression under which I have been for so long is quite erroneous ... It is, therefore, necessary to analyse the way in which the plaintiffs put their case.

The plaintiffs have put their case in three different ways. First, founding themselves on s.14(1) of the Sale of Goods Act, 1893, they say that here was a case where the buyer by implication made known to the seller the particular purpose for which the goods were required so as to show that they relied on his skill and judgment, and that accordingly they rely on the implied condition that the goods were fit for that purpose, namely, the purpose of being carried by the *Ionian* on her voyage to Liverpool and for the purpose of being carried to Liverpool for sale for use after arrival for human consumption. Alternatively, they rely on s.14(2), namely, on an implied condition as to merchantable quality, and they say that the merchantable quality as regards these potatoes is that at the time of shipment they should be merchantable as potatoes sold for carrying and delivery to Liverpool by the *Ionian*. The third way in which the plaintiffs put their case is that there is an implied warranty in a c.i.f. or c.& f. contract, as this was, that the goods should be fit to stand the voyage from Cyprus to Liverpool on which the *Ionian* was about to embark, a normal voyage from Cyprus to Liverpool, and should arrive sound and fit for sale for human consumption after arrival. ...

It does not seem to me that there is really any very great distinction between the three alternative ways in which the plaintiffs put their case. Had the case been tried before the Sale of Goods Act, 1893, was passed, it would have been unnecessary to put it in the first two ways, and it seems to me, in a case of this kind, that sub-s. (1) and sub-s. (2) of s.14 of the Sale of Goods Act, 1893, are really two sides of the same coin. If a buyer makes known a particular purpose—those, of course, are the words of sub-s. (1)—to the seller so as to show that he relies on the seller's skill and judgment, then the suitability for that particular purpose is a warranty and implied condition of the contract. If he does not make known any particular purpose, then, the assumption being that he requires them for the ordinary purposes for which such goods are intended to be used, the implied condition is one that they are fit for those ordinary purposes, that is to say, that they are merchantable, and I venture to think that there is no other distinction between sub-s. (1) and sub-s. (2).

If it were possible for the coin to have three sides, I should have said that the implied term on which counsel for the plaintiffs relies as a third ground, applicable to c.i.f., and f.o.b. contracts, was a third side of the same coin. I think it really comes to no more than this, that merchantability in the case of goods sold c.i.f. or c. & f. means that the goods must remain merchantable for a reasonable time, and that in the case of such contracts a reasonable time means time for arrival and disposal on arrival.

[DIPLOCK *J. reviewed the authorities and concluded*:]

I accordingly hold that the defendants were in breach of an implied condition to ship goods in such a condition as to be capable of standing a normal voyage to Liverpool and to be of merchantable quality at the time of arrival.

Notes

4–033   The case went to the Court of Appeal, [1961] 2 Lloyd's Rep. 326, [1962] 1 W.L.R. 16, where Diplock J. was reversed on the facts, because it was held that this was not a normal sea-voyage: the potatoes had remained unventilated for 5 days continuously in hot summer weather. Diplock J.'s views on the extent of the warranty implied by s. 14(2) were assumed to be correct.

The principle was also assumed (but not decided) to be correct in *The Rio Sun* [1985] 1 Lloyd's Rep. 350, in chapter 2, where Bingham J. said:

> "In *Mash & Murrell Ltd v Joseph I. Emanuel Ltd* [1961] 1 Lloyd's Rep. 46; [1961] 1 W.L.R. 862, Diplock J. (as he then was) regarded it as axiomatic that when goods were sold under a c.i.f. contract which involved transit before use there was an implied warranty not merely that they should be merchantable at the time they were put on the vessel but that they should be in such a state that they could endure the normal journey and be in a merchantable condition upon arrival. Mr. Rokison, Q.C., for Gatoil [the c.i.f. buyers] relied on this principle. The principle itself has been the subject of some criticism (see Sassoon *C.I.F. and F.O.B. Contracts*, 2nd ed., at pp. 214–219 [note that this book is now in its 4th ed.—see paras. 319ff]) but Mr. Merriman for Tradax [the c.i.f. sellers] did not challenge its correctness or its applicability in this case. Instead, he laid stress on the reference to a normal journey, his contention, of course, being that this was not a normal journey because of the vessel's long wait at Augusta."

Bingham J. appears to have accepted that the particular voyage was not normal, because of a long delay before discharge (the problem concerned the partial solidification of an oil cargo—see further chapter 2, above).

Criticisms of the Mash & Murrell principle:

1. Though the action was for damages, the term in s. 14(2) is a condition, and would have allowed the buyers to reject the goods (but probably not the documents—see further chapter 6, below, and in particular *Gill & Duffus v Berger*).
2. There was an alternative reason for the decision, based on s.14(1), that the goods were not fit for the purpose required (that purpose being known to the defendants). This would have been sufficient to decide the case.
3. This was not a typical c. & f. contract, in that the goods were intended to be used by the purchaser, rather than re-sold.
4. The case is criticised by Sassoon, who also cites counter-authorities: see paras. 319, *et. seq.*

The following case limited the application of Diplock J.'s views.

CORDOVA LAND CO LTD v VICTOR BROS INC

Queen's Bench Division. [1966] 1 W.L.R. 793

Facts:

4–034   The sellers, who were an American company with no assets in the United Kingdom, agreed to sell a quantity of skins c.i.f. Hull. The skins were shipped in Boston, and clean bills of lading were issued, but were badly damaged upon arrival in Hull. The buyers applied for leave to serve writs in America, and in order to do so had (under R.S.C., Ord. 11, r.1 (g)) to show a breach of contract within the jurisdiction.

Held:

There was no implied warranty that the skins would be of contract description on arrival at Hull, and therefore no breach of contract within the jurisdiction.

There was a second action against the shipowners for fraudulent misrepresentation in issuing clean bills of lading, which is irrelevant for present purposes. (The action failed because if there had been a fraudulent misrepresentation, it had been committed outside the jurisdiction.)

WINN J.: It is said, belatedly, as Mr. Mustill, on behalf of the plaintiffs **4–035** [buyers], frankly admitted, because it was not said in the first place when leave was sought, that there is an arguable case that a breach of one or both of these contracts was committed within the jurisdiction. That is a very interesting matter, but, as he frankly admits, he has no authority for maintaining that a contract to ship goods c.i.f. to Hull comprises a warranty that the goods will on discharge in Hull be of the contract description and contract quality other than one passage in a judgment of Diplock J. in *Mash & Murrell Ltd v Joseph I. Emmanuel Ltd*. It would be otiose to refer to this case at any length. After Diplock J. had considered the case made under s.14(1) and the case made under s.14(2) of the Sale of Goods Act 1893, by buyers of potatoes which had been shipped from Cyprus to purchasers who to the knowledge of the sellers dealt in such fruit and vegetables for human consumption, he went on to say:

"If it were possible for the coin to have three sides, I should have said the implied term on which Mr. Roche [for the buyers] relies as a third ground, applicable to c.i.f., c. & f. and f.o.b. contracts, was a third side of the same coin. I think it really comes to no more than this, that merchantability in the case of goods sold c.i.f. or c. & f. means that the goods must remain merchantable for a reasonable time, and that, in the case of such contracts, a reasonable time means time for arrival and disposal upon arrival."

I would understand those words to mean that the vendor undertook that the goods which he sold and shipped would be merchantable not only at the time of shipment or at the time of the contract or throughout the voyage, but also for such a time after arrival as would reasonably be required for the disposal of the goods for the purpose of the buyer. I think that understanding is shown to be right by the paragraph in which the judge said:

"I accordingly hold that the defendants were in breach of their warranty to ship goods in such a condition as to be capable of standing a normal voyage to Liverpool and to be of merchantable quality at the time of arrival."

In fact that case went to the Court of Appeal but there the decision of the court was upon factual grounds; this matter of law was not decided by the court. All that was said about it was in the passage in the judgment of Harman L.J., when he said [1961] 2 Lloyd's Rep. 326, 328:

> "I shall assume, for the present purpose, that, under the contract in question, there was implied this warranty, namely, that the potatoes, when put on board, were in such a state that, assuming a normal voyage, they would on arrival be in such a condition as to be suitable for the purpose for which the plaintiffs required them, namely, sale to retailers for human consumption."

That may be a narrower statement of the warranty. Be that as it may, the "Third side of the coin" was not an essential ground for the judgment of Diplock J. Furthermore it was not essential for him to draw such a distinction between breach in Liverpool and breach in Limassol, Cyprus, in that case as is of vital importance in the present case. I do not think that passage in the judgment of Diplock J. founds "a good arguable case" that the vendors in the present matter, the present transactions, entered into a warranty to be performed in Hull that the goods on arrival there would there and then be of the contract description and quality. It seems to me, whilst obviously this topic will call for some further consideration in some future case, that there is a real distinction between the obligations undertaken by a vendor who ships perishable goods and those undertaken by a vendor who ships goods such as skins, which though plainly vulnerable to some extent to deterioration in transit are not nearly so vulnerable as potatoes; the latter may, *inter alia*, mature and ferment. I cannot accept the submission that there is here any good arguable case of breach of contract within the jurisdiction . . .

Notes

4–036

1. Even if the Diplock view had been applied in *Cordova*, it would have been difficult to show that the breach had occurred in the UK.

2. It is arguable that any obligation on the seller relating to the condition of the goods after shipment will reduce the negotiability of bills of lading, and *Mash & Murrell* was criticised by Diplock L.J. himself (as he had by then become) in *Teheran-Europe Co Ltd v ST Belton (Tractors) Ltd* [1968] 2 Q.B. 545, admittedly in a wholly different type of case:

> "The plaintiffs, I am sorry to say, also relied on some observations of my own in the case of *Mash & Murrell, Ltd v Joseph I. Emmanuel Ltd* [1961] 1 All E.R. 485 at p. 489, which, though I think that they were correct in the context of that case, where the description of the goods was generic, were expressed with incautious wideness."

There was, of course, no resale in *Mash*, and the case is more like a domestic sale of goods than most international sales.

3. There are also good arguments for limiting *Mash* to perishable goods, because it is difficult to see why non-perishable goods should deteriorate without the carrier's fault, or a marine peril covered by the marine insurance policy. In *Cordova*, the suggestion was made that the goods had been in poor condition when loaded, the bill of lading (fraudulently) not stating their true condition (of course, if this was true, then the sellers were in breach anyway, but not necessarily on *Mash* principles).

4. Nevertheless Lord Diplock, as he later became, supported his earlier view by remarks in *Lambert v Lewis* [1982] A.C. 225. The Law Commission has also taken the view that there should be an implied term of durability written into the Sale of Goods Act (Working Paper No. 85 (1983), pp. 19–20). These remarks apply primarily to domestic sales, however, where considerations of negotiability do not apply. However, there is now an implied durability term, which applies in principle to all sales of goods (see further below).

5. An unsuccessful s.14(2) argument, based on *Mash & Murrell*, was also advanced by Gatoil against Tradax in *The Rio Sun* (in chapter 2), but was rejected because the voyage was not normal, and had the vessel sailed straight to any port within the agreed range and discharged within a reasonable time, no unusual ROB would have formed. The cargo was entirely fit to withstand a voyage of the kind and length contemplated by the contract.

Arguments in favour of the durability term:

1. There was no question of re-sale in *Mash*, and the sellers knew that the potatoes were intended for human consumption, after completion of a sea voyage.

2. Although s.14(2) creates a condition, the documents will usually be in order, so the buyer will be unable to reject them, on the basis of *Gill and Duffus v Berger*, however narrowly that later case is interpreted (see further paras 7—021, *et seq.*, below); note that there was no question of rejection in *Mash & Murrell* itself.

3. Unlike the usual situations, where the loss is occasioned by a marine risk, the buyers will not be covered on the insurance policy, nor will they be able to claim against the carrier.

(b) LATER LEGISLATION AND THE DURABILITY TERM

All the cases are in the previous section were decided on the basis of the original 1893 section, but it was altered in the 1979 Act to the following: **4–037**

SALE OF GOODS ACT 1979, s.14(2)

Where the seller sells goods in the course of a business, there is an implied condition that the goods supplied under the contract are of merchantable quality, except that there is no such condition—

(a) as regards defects specifically drawn to the buyer's attention before the contract is made; or

(b) if the buyer examines the goods before the contract is made, as regards defects which that examination ought to reveal.

Note

It seems unlikely that the 1979 changes affect the discussion, but the section was further amended in 1994, as follows:

SALE OF GOODS ACT 1979, s.14(2), AS AMENDED BY THE SALE AND SUPPLY OF GOODS ACT 1994

4–038 Where the seller sells goods in the course of a business, there is an implied term that the goods supplied under the contract are of satisfactory quality.

(2A) For the purposes of this Act, goods are of satisfactory quality if they meet the standard that a reasonable person would regard as satisfactory, taking account of any description of the goods, the price (if relevant) and all the other relevant circumstances.

(2B) For the purposes of this Act, the quality of goods includes their state and condition and the following (among others) are in appropriate cases aspects of the quality of goods—

(a) fitness for all the purposes for which goods of the kind in question are commonly supplied,

(b) appearance and finish,

(c) freedom from minor defects,

(d) safety, and

(e) durability.

(2C) The term implied by subsection (2) above does not extend to any matter making the quality of goods unsatisfactory—

(a) which is specifically drawn to the buyer's attention before the contract is made,

(b) where the buyer examines the goods before the contract is made, which that examination ought to reveal, or

(c) in the case of a contract for sale by sample, which would have been apparent on a reasonable examination of the sample.

Notes

1. The 1994 Act came into force on January 3, 1995, and which carried into effect the recommendations of the Law Commission (Law Com. No. 160 (Scot. Law. Com. No. 104) (1987), *Sale and Supply of Goods*).

2. The Act also added the new section, s.15A:

SALE OF GOODS ACT 1979, s.15A

(1) Where in the case of a contract of sale—   4–039

(a) the buyer would, apart from this subsection, have the right to reject goods by reason of a breach on the part of the seller of a term implied by section 13, 14 or 15 above, but

(b) the breach is so slight that it would be unreasonable for him to reject them, then, if the buyer does not deal as consumer, the breach is not to be treated as a breach of condition but may be treated as a breach of warranty.

(2) This section applies unless a contrary intention appears in, or is to be implied from, the contract.

(3) It is for the seller to show that a breach fell within subsection (1)(b) above.

(4) This section does not apply to Scotland.

Notes

The effect of the 1994 changes is to:

1. Make clear that durability is included within the concept of merchantable quality; durability is now expressly brought within s.14, and this will tend to strengthen arguments for the *Mash & Murrell* term.

2. Alter the effect of minor breaches (s.15A), by making them breaches of warranty only. This will prevent the buyer rejecting the goods for breaches of the term whose effect is slight.

(c) Estoppel

The next case countenances the reverse situation, where the buyer may be   4–040
responsible for loss of or damage to goods even before shipment.

J & J CUNNINGHAM LTD v ROBERT A MUNRO & CO LTD

King's Bench Division. (1922) 13 Lloyd's Rep. 62, 216

Facts:

The contract of sale was for 200 tons of Dutch bran for shipment during October 1920, f.o.b. Rotterdam. The sellers were in a hurry to remove the bran from their own factory, and took the goods down to the dock on board a lighter on October 14th. They duly informed the buyer of this, but the buyers protested that:

"This is an October shipment; we have got all October in which to take shipment from you. You have no right to force this bran upon us and we are not ready to take it, but we will do our best as we are reselling it."

In the event the ship nominated by the buyer did not begin loading until October 28th. During loading some of the bran was discovered to be bad (it had overheated). The buyers rejected it and the matter went to arbitration, who found that the risk of heating was on the buyers, and that the buyers were liable for the expenses in connection with the goods after their arrival at Rotterdam on 14th. A special case was stated for the court.

Held:

The buyers were entitled to reject the bran, it being at sellers' risk until shipment.

4–041   AVORY L.C.J.: Before giving our opinion in this case it will be advisable to state the principles of law appertaining to an f.o.b. contract so far as they are applicable to the circumstances.

The contract under consideration was for 200 tons of Dutch bran for shipment during October 1920, price £13 per ton f.o.b. Rotterdam, buyers finding freight room. Under such an arrangement it was the duty of the purchasers to provide a vessel at the appointed place, Rotterdam, at such a time as would enable the vendors to bring the goods alongside the ship and put them over the ship's rail, so as to enable the purchasers to receive them within the appointed time—in this case October. It would not, for example, be sufficient for the vendors to bring them to a warehouse at five minutes before midnight on Oct. 31. The usual practice under such a contract is for the buyer to nominate the vessel and to send notice of her arrival to the vendor in order that the vendor may be in a position to fulfil his part of the contract. When the vendors tender the goods in question to the purchasers theoretically by placing them on the ship's rail, it is open to the purchasers to reject if the goods are not in accordance with the contract.

That being the relationship between the parties the liability on either side may be varied (1) by express contract altering the place or date of loading (2) by the conduct of the parties. For example, there may be circumstances which disentitle the purchaser to reject the goods when they are placed on the ship's rail, as for instance when he has by his conduct already accepted them before their arrival there; there may also be circumstances where, although the purchaser may be entitled to reject the goods when the goods are being placed over the ship's rail, yet the vendor may be entitled to recover damages in respect of the deterioration of the goods. Assuming the sale of a perishable cargo, say of fresh vegetables for October shipment, suppose the purchasers nominate their vessel and write to the vendors saying "she will be at the quayside in three days time." The vendors gather their vegetables and send them to the quayside; but the nominated ship does not arrive for a fortnight, during which time the vegetables go bad. It may be that the purchasers are entitled to reject the vegetables which have so deteriorated, but the vendors are then entitled to rely upon and bring into play another legal principle. It is not exactly an estoppel which prevents the purchasers from rejecting, but it is the doctrine that where one person makes a statement to another meaning that statement to be relied upon and acted upon by that other, if the other suffers damage by so relying and acting upon it he is entitled to recover such damage from the person making the statement. In the case put forward the damage would be the loss of the price which the vendors would otherwise have obtained from the purchasers. This legal doctrine might be put in ordinary language as it is put in the case stated by the arbitrator, *viz.*, that under such circumstances after the vendor has brought the goods to the quay at the invitation of the purchaser the goods remained at the purchaser's risk.

We now turn to the facts of this case. The contract was a contract for the sale of bran as above stated. It appears that the vendors, although they had sold for October delivery, were obliged to take the goods from their own vendors early in October; and the lighter with the bran on board arrived at Rotterdam about the 14th of the month. Correspondence then took place between the vendors and the purchasers sending the ship forward. The ship, in fact, arrived on Oct. 24, loading began on the 28th; and after 15 tons had been loaded, the bran underneath was discovered to be bad, when the buyers claimed to reject and refused the remainder. The arbitrators have found that the bran went bad between the 14th and the 28th, while it was in the lighter; and the vendors contend that the purchasers were not entitled to reject, having regard to the circumstances. They say in effect that owing to the correspondence between the parties, either there was an agreement by the purchasers to take delivery on the 14th or that after the 14th the bran remained at the risk of the purchasers. The purchasers contend that there was no evidence upon which the arbitrators could uphold the contention of the vendors. It should be stated that no witness was called and the whole of the facts depend upon the correspondence.

Applying the law, as above stated, to the facts, we are of the opinion (1) That there is no evidence on which the arbitrators could find that the contract between the parties was either expressly or impliedly varied. (2) It therefore remains to be considered whether by their conduct the purchasers had so acted that the vendors can say "You induced us to send the bran to Rotterdam much earlier than we would otherwise have done, with the consequences that it has gone bad while waiting the arrival of your ship, and the risk of deterioration falls upon you." As above stated, the vendors had to take the bran from their sellers early in October and were therefore naturally anxious to get their purchasers to take it as soon as possible after its arrival from the mills. What is the proper inference to be drawn from the letters—is it that the purchasers were doing their best to help the vendors out of a difficulty by getting the ship as soon as possible to Rotterdam without making any definite promise or is it, having regard to the fact that by Oct. 14 the bran had already been selected and put upon board the lighter, that the purchasers must be taken to have accepted it on or about that date? We do not think that the mere fact of nominating the vessel can be construed as an acceptance of the goods, even though they had already been placed on the lighter to be sent forward; nor do we think the mere fact of a sub-sale by the purchasers is evidence of acceptance by them of the goods. An inference cannot be drawn that by either of such usual acts they disentitle themselves to exercise their right of rejection when the goods are tendered at the ship's rail.

It is clear that on Oct. 14 the purchasers were not expecting the bran to reach Rotterdam for another week and they were only thinking of giving shipping instructions in the course of a day or two. Down to that date there appears to have been nothing done which could be construed either as an acceptance of the goods or as any invitation to send them forward.

With regard to the rest of the correspondence we cannot say that it discloses any evidence of conduct misleading the vendors and inducing them to send the goods forward at an earlier date. It appears to us that it was the vendors who were in a difficulty and that the purchasers were doing their best to help them by trying to get the vessel to Rotterdam as soon as possible, but that the purchasers did not make any such representation as would entitle the vendors to say they acted upon it to their damage.

We accordingly answer the questions addressed to us as follows:

Were Robt. A. Munro & Co Ltd. entitled to reject the goods tendered to them under the contract?—Yes.

Were they bound in law to take delivery of the goods before Oct. 28, 1920, the day on which they were ready to take them?—No.

On whom was the risk after the arrival of the goods in Rotterdam and before the loading on the ship commenced?—On the vendors . . .

Note

4–042 On the facts as found by Avory L.C.J., risk remained in the sellers until the goods were actually shipped, and the buyers were not obliged to take early delivery of the goods. This was an f.o.b. contract for an October shipment where, because the buyers nominated the vessel, they were entitled to take the goods at any time within the shipment period.[30]

Avory L.C.J. also envisaged (in the above passage) that the result would have been different had the buyers' conduct led either to the conclusion that the original contract had been varied, or to an estoppel. An estoppel could have operated had the buyers by their conduct induced the sellers to send the goods down to the dock early, with the sellers acting in reliance to that inducement. No such inducement had been shown to occur in the case, but if it had done Avory L.C.J. thought that risk would shifted to the buyer even before shipment.

Suppose, for example, a classic f.o.b. contract provides for October shipment. The buyer is thus entitled (as in the case itself) to nominate any ship which is able to load the goods at any time in October. He tells the seller that the ship he has nominated will arrive and be ready to load on 1st October. Relying upon this information the seller sends the goods down to the dock for loading on 1st. The ship is not in fact ready to load until 28th October, and in the meantime the goods

---

[30] See further Ch. 3, above.

have deteriorated on the dock. An estoppel would operate in such circumstances.

A related issue was considered by Howard Bennett, in a casenote on *Cargill UK Ltd v Continental UK Ltd*, a substitution case discussed in para. 3—043, above.

HOWARD BENNETT, "F.O.B. CONTRACTS: SUBSTITUTION OF VESSELS"

[1990] LMCLQ 466

[*Footnotes are as in the original, but renumbered for inclusion in this book.*]

Arguably the most vexed question surrounding nomination of vessels **4–043** under f.o.b. contracts is whether the sellers can recoup from the buyers any additional expenditure or loss incurred as a result of a substitution. No problem arises if the substitution constitutes a breach of contract, the only pertinent questions which arise relating to availability of remedies and assessment of loss, referred to above.

However, suppose the buyers nominate vessel A to arrive at a specified date. In reliance thereon, the sellers transport the goods to the port of loading. The buyers then substitute vessel B, which will not arrive for a further two weeks. The sellers in consequence incur additional storage costs. On the assumptions that the buyers are not in breach of their basic nomination obligation[31] and that the substitution is *prima facie* valid, in the sense that the contract does not prohibit it absolutely nor have any relevant contractual time limits expired, can the sellers claim against the buyers for the additional costs of storage? Although *Cargill* does not contribute to this particular point, it is so closely connected to the other aspects of substitution that a brief comment is apposite.

To the extent that f.o.b. buyers may, within the terms of any individual contract, be said to have a right of substitution, it is difficult to see how the exercise thereof may give the sellers a ground of recovery. Insofar as the *Ampro* case supports such a right, it is regarded as authority against any such recovery. This view is, furthermore, supported by a powerful argument to the effect that the situation involves a paradigm arm's length commercial contract. The sellers could have protected themselves by prohibiting any substitution or rendering the exercise of any substitution rights expressly subject to reimbursement of any loss or additional expenditure thereby caused. They have only themselves to blame if they failed to do so. On the other hand, it is argued that,if the sellers' loss is directly attributable to their reasonable and foreseeable reliance on the buyers' nomination, they ought to be able to recover.

---

[31] [The footnote refers back to the following text: "The buyers' basic obligation is merely to inform the sellers of the name of the vessel in time for the sellers to be able to load within the contractual shipment period; there is no legal obligation to communicate a nomination prior thereto."]

In *Cunningham v Munro*,[32] Lord Hewart C.J., postulated the sale of a perishable cargo of vegetables which is sent to the port of loading in response to and in reliance upon a nomination by the buyers. The nominated vessel is late (or is substituted in favour of a vessel arriving later) by which time the cargo has become unmerchantable. What is the legal position?

> It may be that the purchasers are entitled to reject the vegetables which have so deteriorated, but the vendors are then entitled to rely upon and bring into play another legal principle. It is not exactly an estoppel which prevents the purchasers from rejecting, but it is the doctrine that where one person makes a statement to another meaning that statement to be relied upon and acted upon by that other, if the other suffers damage by so relying and acting upon it he is entitled to recover such damage from the person making the statement. In the case put forward the damage would be the loss of the price which the vendors would otherwise have obtained from the purchasers.[33]

4–044   It is difficult to know how to interpret this *dictum*. On the one hand, it appears that Lord Hewart C.J., is invoking the rule in *Hughes v Metropolitan Railway*,[34] which is supposed, however, to be prayed in aid as a shield rather than wielded as a sword.[35] However, it may be that, by nominating a vessel before they have to, in circumstances where reliance by the sellers is foreseeable and such reliance ensues, the buyers waive their rights to substitute so that the date of arrival of the vessel is definitively fixed, permitting the sellers to sue for breach, recovering any additional wasted expenditure as special damages.[36] It is, nevertheless, highly unlikely that performance of a contractual obligation within the agreed terms can constitute an unequivocal representation not to do something *prima facie* permitted by the contract.

An alternative approach would be to construe the buyers' right to substitute as subject—in the absence of any relevant express terms—to an implied restriction. The nature of such a restriction is, however, not immediately apparent, even assuming that any implication could be sustained could be sustained on the ground of business efficacy. An implied reimbursement obligation would transform a right of substitution into an option to be purchased, the price determined by reference to the sellers' reasonable responses to the original nomination. However, while the concept of the exercise of a contractual right carrying an express

---

[32] [(1922) 28 *Com. Cas.* 42.]
[33] *ibid.*, 46.
[34] (1877) 2 App. Cas. 439.
[35] Benjamin's *Sale of Goods* (3rd edn. 1987), para. 1846, n. 72. [See now 5th ed., 1997.]
[36] By analogy with waiver of delivery times generally: *Bessler Waechter Glover & Co v South Derwent Coal Co* [1938] 1 K.B. 408.

price is well established,[37] whether the implication of such a price is consistent with arm's length bargaining must be doubtful. Alternatively, the implied restriction could take the form of limiting any exercise of any substitution rights to a reasonable time after the original nomination. The reasonable time would expire either once the sellers had acted in reliance upon the nomination to the knowledge of the buyers, or once the sellers might reasonably be supposed to have so reacted and have indeed done so, whichever was the earlier. This might, of course, prejudice a seller actuated not just by the buyers' nomination but also by other commercially reasonable motives of which the buyers could not reasonably be expected to be aware.

One is perhaps driven, albeit not too reluctantly, to the conclusion that, if the sellers wish to be protected financially against the consequences of substitution, they ought to insert appropriate terms into the contract. If they fail so to do, it is inappropriate for the courts to intervene to smooth the rough edges of a commercial bargain by essentially artificial devices.

Comments

It cannot surely be the case, in the perishable goods example from *Cunningham* **4–045** *v Munro*, adopted in a slightly different context by Bennett, that as Avory L.C.J. says:

"under such circumstances after the vendor has brought the goods to the quay at the invitation of the purchaser the goods remained at the purchaser's risk."

How the *J. & J. Cunningham* estoppel might work can be seen by analogy with the property estoppel unsuccessfully argued in *Colley v Overseas Exporters* in para. 5—084, below; if the purchasers make a representation that the vessel will arrive early in the month, which is relied upon by the sellers, the buyers could be estopped from claiming that the goods remained at the sellers' risk from the time they were sent down to the dock until shipment. Thus, although the goods are still technically at the seller's risk, the buyer may have no recourse against him for their deterioration, and must accept and pay for them.

Howard Bennett observes that an estoppel of this type cannot be used as a shield, only as a sword, but that is not a problem where the goods deteriorate. The estoppel would prevent the buyers from claiming damages in respect of the deterioration. If the buyers rejected the goods and were sued by the sellers, they would not be able to use the deterioration as the basis of a defence. There would be no need, in either case, to use the estoppel as a sword.

The storage cost example used by Bennett is different, however, because the sellers would have to use the estoppel as a sword in order to claim damages. On the analysis adopted here, the action would fail.

Both examples work in exactly the same way where the buyer substitutes a late nomination for an earlier one, if the earlier nomination constitutes a representation that a vessel will pick up the cargo at an early date in the shipment period, whereas in fact, the substituted vessel arrives later. The fact that there are two different vessels involved surely cannot affect the *Cunningham* analysis, nor I

---

[37] *Associated Distributors v Hall* [1938] 2 K.B. 83; *Bridge v Campbell Discount* [1962] A.C. 600.

would suggest does it make any difference whether the substitution is allowed on *Ampro* principles (see para. 3—040). Howard Bennett would probably disagree:

"It is, nevertheless, highly unlikely that performance of a contractual obligation within the agreed terms can constitute an unequivocal representation not to do something *prima facie* permitted by the contract."

But that would also be true of the example used in *Cunningham* itself, where the early nomination, which is within the contractual terms, constitutes the representation by the buyers.

Bennett concludes with a view that the courts should not intervene to protect the sellers in an "arm's length commercial contract", where terms have not been expressly agreed. In the absence of express terms, however, the courts have no option but to fill in the contract. Sometimes they do this by presumption, as with the flexible f.o.b. terms considered in chapter 3, above. Sometimes they refuse (at any rate explicitly) to operate presumptions, taking the view that "each case depends on the contract and surrounding circumstances", as in *Pound* v *Hardy* in chapter 3, above. Whichever approach is adopted will inevitably benefit one of the parties. The argument that the courts should not intervene to protect the sellers loses much of its force, given that they have already intervened to protect the buyers in *Ampro*, even where the contract contains no express substitution right.

Pound v Hardy approach will tend to lead to a lottery, but if the parties have not agreed, and there is no trade custom, it is difficult to see how a lottery can be avoided. If there is a trade custom or usage, a presumption based on that usage seems sensible to apply. That may well be how the presumptions for interpreting f.o.b. contracts in chapter 3 were arrived at, including probably the position in *Ampro*. There are also the well-known business efficacy and officious bystander tests for implying additional terms, and of course, the working of the estoppel doctrine is also well-known. If they do not apply then it is difficult to see why the courts should intervene; in his substitution example, estoppel probably protects the seller against the consequences of deterioration of the goods, but not against increased storage costs. In the last case, it is indeed difficult to see why the courts should intervene to protect the seller.

(6) Enforceability of Contract

4–046   It is clearly essential if the shipping documents are to be freely transferable that the risk is in the buyer after shipment, and as seen above this is indeed the general position.

(a) Repudiation

4–046A   The transfer of risk depends on the contract continuing to be enforceable by the seller. It will not be if the seller commits a repudiatory breach of contract, allowing the buyer to reject either documents or goods. If the seller is in repudiatory breach of contract, for example by not loading goods of the contract description, or shipping the wrong quantity, or shipping late, the buyer has the option of rejecting the goods. If the seller tenders the wrong documents, the buyer can reject those. A valid rejection of documents or goods by the buyer effectively re-vests the risk in the seller as from shipment. See, *e.g. Manbre Saccharine Co v Corn Products Co*, above.

(b) Mistake

Further, if the contractual doctrines of mistake or frustration apply, the agreement will be rendered unenforceable by either party, and the risk will lie where it falls.

4–046B

It is unlikely that frustration has any significant application in this area of law, but common mistake may have at least a limited role to play.

COUTURIER v HASTIE

House of Lords. (1855) 5 H.L.C. 673, 10 E.R. 1065

Facts and decision:

A contract was made for the sale of an identified cargo of Salonika Indian corn. The contract was expressed to be f.o.b., but since freight and insurance were included in the price, and the goods had already been shipped, it had the characteristics of what later came to be called a c.i.f. contract.[38] Unknown to either seller or buyer the goods had perished at sea before the contract was made, but after shipment (they had become overheated and been lawfully sold by the ship's master at Tunis to prevent further deterioration).

4–046C

The seller unsuccessfully sued for the price, the buyer being held not liable.

Lord Cranworth L.C.: . . . I may state shortly that the whole question turns upon the construction of the contract which was entered into between the parties . . . If this had depended not merely upon the construction of the contract but upon evidence . . . of what mercantile usage had been, I should not have been prepared to say that a long-continued mercantile usage interpreting such contracts might not have been sufficient to warrant, or even compel your Lordships to adopt a different construction. But in the absence of any such evidence, looking the contract itself alone, it appears to me clearly that what the parties contemplated, those who bought and those who sold, was that there was an existing something to be sold and bought, and if sold and bought, then the benefit of insurance should go with it. . . . The contract plainly imports that there was something which was to be sold at the time of the contract, and something to be purchased. No such thing existing, . . . there must be judgment . . . for the Defendants . . .

What did the case decide?

If *Couturier v Hastie* were of general application it would be very undesirable, since the risk of loss was effectively borne by the seller. We have already seen the undesirability of this, after shipment in a c.i.f. contract (which this probably was).

4–047

If the case is of general application, then it also introduces distinctions which are difficult to justify. Suppose, for example in *Groom v Barber*, the sale contract

[38] See Ch. 2, above.

had been made after the loss of the goods. In principle, the buyer obtains exactly the same rights on transfer to him of the documents, and surely it should make no difference whether the loss precedes the contract. But a wide reading of *Couturier v Hastie* might suggest otherwise.

In the case the buyers were held not liable for the price. The case does not decide whether the sellers would also have been liable for non-delivery. However, the passage above suggests that the existence of the goods at the time of contracting was fundamental to the contract, from which it might be inferred that the contract was void:

> "It was for many years thought that the case was decided in this way on the ground that the contract was void for mistake."[39]

This view is no longer widely accepted, however, and indeed, there is no mention of the concept of mistake in the case itself. See, *e.g.*, the extensive discussion in Treitel, *The Law of Contract* (10th ed., 1999), pp. 270–273.

If on the other hand, the case decides only that a seller who cannot deliver the goods to the buyer is not normally entitled to the price, it may be rationalised as a case where the seller warranted the existence of the goods, or even more narrowly, that the requirements for payment of the price (on which see further chapter 5) were not met. Whatever the true explanation, however, it is clear from the above passage that it is wrong to generalise from the decision, which depended on the construction of the particular contract.

Common mistake and modern international sales contracts

4–048/9   Though *Couturier v Hastie* itself was limited to the particular contract, if the common mistake doctrine applies generally to international sales contracts, the effect will be for risk to lie where it falls, since if the contract is void neither party can sue the other.

It is likely to be a problem only for c.i.f. (or c. & f.) sales of cargo that is already afloat, which is not in existence when the contract is made. The problem also arises where the seller is suing, since denial of an action for damages or the price might put the risk of loss on to him. Even for chain sales, all contracts are usually made before the goods are shipped, and a sale of goods afloat is likely to be pretty well limited to the rare situation in *The Epaphus*,[40] where the original sale contract had fallen through:

> "In consequence, there came into existence something which is in my experience, and in the experience of Counsel, a rare phenomemon: the sale of a cargo afloat by a named vessel."[41]

Had the cargo on board *The Epaphus* perished by the time of this second contract, the case would have been similar to *Couturier v Hastie*, at least insofar that the cargo had perished by the time the contract was made.

The test for common mistake propounded by Lord Atkin in *Bell v Lever Brothers Ltd* [1932] A.C. 161 (at 218) was that:

> "a mistake will not affect assent unless it is the mistake of both parties, and is as to the existence of some quality which makes the thing without the quality essentially different from the thing as it was believed to be."

[39] Atiyah, Adams and MacQueen, *The Sale of Goods* (10th ed., Longman, 2002) at p. 93. (The authors do not share this view.)
[40] *Eurico SpA v Philipp Brothers, The Epaphus* [1987] 2 Lloyd's Rep. 215. *The Jambur* in para. 2—021, above, is another example of the sale of a cargo already afloat.
[41] From Staughton J.'s judgment at first instance [1986] 2 Lloyd's Rep. 387.

Lord Thankerton's test (at 235) was similar, that common mistake:

"can only properly relate to something which both must necessarily have accepted in their minds as an essential and integral element of the subject matter."

Non-existence of the goods would seem, at first sight, to satisfy this test, but it was held not to do so in the High Court of Australia in *McRae v Commonwealth Disposals Commission* (1951) 84 C.L.R. 377; there, the seller was taken to have warranted the existence of the goods, and a similar explanation was adopted of *Couturier v Hastie* itself (see paras. 11–19 of the judgments of Dixon and Fullagar JJ.). *Couturier v Hastie* was also regarded as turning on construction of the particular contract, and therefore not of general application.

In *Associated Japanese Bank (International) Ltd v Credit du Nord SA* ([1989] 1 W.L.R. 255, 268), Steyn J. said:

"Logically, before one can turn to the rules as to mistake, whether at common law or in equity, one must first determine whether the contract itself, by express or implied condition precedent or otherwise, provides who bears the risk of the relevant mistake. It is at this hurdle that many pleas of mistake will either fail or prove to have been unnecessary. Only if the contract is silent on the point, is there scope for invoking mistake."

If one takes the view that the international sales contracts considered in this chapter place the risk of non-existence of the goods after shipment on the buyer, then clearly there is no room for the application of the doctrine of mistake. Even if the *McRae* interpretation is adopted of *Couturier v Hastie*, which puts the risk of non-existence on the seller, it was an interpretation of the particular contract, where the parties contemplated that there was an existing something to be sold bought. Surely it is true only, in the case of a c.i.f. (or c. & f.) contract for goods already afloat, that the parties contemplated only that goods existed when they were shipped. If so, the case has no application to modern international sales contracts.[42]

I would suggest, therefore, that *Couturier v Hastie* does not affect the risk principles discussed in this chapter. Unfortunately, however, the mistake doctrine as enacted in s.6 of the Sale of Goods Act 1979 will affect the transfer of risk under c.i.f. contracts, at any rate for specific goods.

SALE OF GOODS ACT 1979, s.6

Where there is a contract for the sale of specific goods, and the goods **4–050** without the knowledge of the seller have perished at the time when the contract is made, the contract is void.

Notes

This section (re-enacting an identical provision from the 1893 Act) appears to be a statutory entrenchment of the view that the contract in *Couturier v Hastie* was void for mistake. As was observed in *McRae* (at para. 20): "This has been generally supposed to represent the legislature's view of the effect of *Couturier v Hastie*". The section (or the equivalent provision in the law of Victoria) did not apply in

---

[42] Although the contract in *Couturier v Hastie* has similarities with a c.i.f. contract, the c.i.f. term was not used at that time, so the parties could not be taken to have appreciated its full implications.

McRae itself, where "the goods never existed, and the seller ought to have known that they did not exist." Thus they had not perished, without the seller's knowledge.

The section applies only to contracts for the sale of specific goods, and only where they once existed, and have now perished. Effectively, this limits its operation to either manufactured goods, or entire cargoes on board a bulk vessel. The effect of s.6 is that, because neither party can bring an action on a void contract, in effect the risk is always on the plaintiff, whichever party he may be.

It is difficult to see any coherent policy behind this position, and the effect of this section, which appears to have been based on a misreading of *Couturier v Hastie*, is unfortunate. It has been argued that the section may only give rise to a presumption: for further discussion see, in general on this issue, Atiyah, *The Sale of Goods* (10th ed., 2000), pp. 93–98, and especially p. 97, but this flies in the face of its wording, especially when compared to other sections, which expressly create only presumptions. In this respect, it is perhaps a pity that Scrutton J.'s view that a c.i.f. sale is not a sale of goods, but a sale of documents relating to goods, has not been accepted (see the discussion of *Arnhold Karberg & Co v Blythe, Green, Jourdain & Co*, above). Had it been, the Sale of Goods Act would not have applied at all.

(c) Frustration

4–051   The courts appear to be unwilling to apply the frustration doctrine to sales of goods, at any rate merely because the goods have been lost or damaged.

If a contract is frustrated, both parties are discharged from any further obligations under it, whether performance of duties or payment of money. Thus, for example, if the contract were frustrated before the price had been paid, the buyer would be relieved of the obligation to pay the price. At common law, payments that had already been made could not generally be recovered back, and payments that had became due before the frustrating event generally remained due, even if they had not yet been paid. Under the Law Reform (Frustrated Contracts) Act 1943, however, which applies to sale contracts (although not to carriage contracts on bill of lading terms), sums which had already become payable at the time of frustration cannot be claimed by the other party, and any sums actually paid are recoverable. Thus, if the contract is frustrated after the price has been paid, the buyer can recover it back, and if the price has become due but not yet been paid, the seller cannot claim it.

In *Paal Wilson and Co v Partenreederei Hannah Blumenthal (The Hannah Blumenthal)* [1983] 1 A.C. 854, Lord Brandon said, summarising earlier authorities:

"... there are two essential factors which must be present in order to frustrate a contract. The first essential factor is that there must be some outside event or extraneous change of situation, not foreseen or provided for by the parties at the time of contracting, which either makes it impossible for the contract to be performed at all, or at least renders its performance something radically different from what the parties contemplated when they entered into it. The second essential factor is that the outside event or extraneous change of situation concerned, and the consequences of either in relation to the performance of the contract, must have occurred without the fault or the default of either party to the contract."

Although Lord Brandon talks in terms of two essential factors, there are in reality three requirements which can be discerned from this passage. First, the outside event must not have been foreseen or provided for by the parties at the time of contracting. Secondly, it must be sufficiently serious to undermine the whole basis upon which the contract was to be performed (the event must "go to the root of the contract"). Thirdly, it must have occurred without the fault of either party to the contract.

Because the event must not have been contemplated by the parties when the contract was made, it follows that nothing which is provided for in the contract can frustrate it. Clearly, the destruction of the goods may "go to the root of the contract", but since the risk of loss or damage has clearly been placed on one or other party under an f.o.b. or c.i.f. contract, it cannot be said to be an unforeseen event.

Since it is also necessary that the consequences flowing from a frustrating event to be sufficiently serious to undermine the very basis upon which it has been made, it might be thought that nothing less than total loss of the goods could frustrate the contract. In a c.i.f. contract, however, the seller is under an obligation to pay the freight, and this could well increase significantly if, for example, the Suez Canal were closed after the contract had been made. In fact, Suez cases have nearly all concerned carriage contracts, from which it can be inferred that it is very unlikely that increase in the length of a voyage will ever be considered sufficiently serious to frustrate a contract. In the one Suez case concerning a c.i.f. contract, the same result was reached as in the carriage cases. In *Tsiroglou & Co Ltd v Noblee Thorl GmbH* [1962] A.C. 93, the effect of the closure of the canal in 1956 was approximately to double the length of the voyage, and also its freight cost to the shippers, but the House of Lords refused to hold the c.i.f. contract frustrated. As with the other Suez cases, the voyage via the Cape was not fundamentally different from a voyage via Suez, although it was, of course, considerably more expensive. Extra expense is not, however, sufficient reason to frustrate a contract.[43]

TSAKIROGLOU & CO LTD v NOBLEE THORL GmbH

House of Lords. [1962] A.C. 93

The case concerned a sale of groundnuts, c.i.f., from Port Sudan to Hamburg. The parties envisaged shipping through the Suez Canal, but the canal was closed after the contract was concluded.   **4–052**

Held:
The contract was not frustrated as the ship could go round via the Cape of Good Hope (there being no implied term that carriage was to be via Suez). The greater cost of the freight, borne by the c.i.f. seller, was not so great as to render this a fundamentally different adventure.

VISCOUNT SIMONDS: it hardly needs reasserting that an increase of expense is not a ground of frustration . . . It is a question of law whether a contract has been frustrated, and it is commonly said that frustration occurs when conditions arise which are fundamentally different from those contemplated by the parties.

---

[43] Freight rates rose from £7 10s per ton to £15, *i.e.* doubled, but the increase was quite a small fraction of the c.i.f. cost of £68 15s. Of course, with a c.i.f. contract, it is the seller who bears the risk of fluctuations in the freight rate.

Comment

Frustration of a c.i.f. contract will be very rare, and clearly the parties have made provision for the loss of the goods. Possible frustrating events might include the destruction of the ship, where the contract provides for shipment on board a particular ship (or where only one vessel is capable of carrying the goods), and illegality of performance (*e.g.* declaration of war). The contract could also presumably be frustrated if performance became impossible, for example where the only available route was blocked.

Frustration is also possible under s.7 of the Sale of Goods Act 1979, but this will rarely apply to a c.i.f. or f.o.b. contract.

SALE OF GOODS ACT 1979, s.7

4–053   Where there is an agreement to sell specific goods, and subsequently the goods, without any fault on the part of seller or buyer, perish before the risk passes to the buyer, the agreement is hereby avoided.

Note

This is a form of statutory frustration of the sale contract, though the courts have shown themselves unwilling to apply the frustration doctrine to sales of goods. Like s.6, the section was a codification of what was supposed to be the case law at the time. It is unlikely to be of major consequence in international sales. Because it only operates where risk has not passed, it can only apply to a contract for specific goods which perish *before shipment*, where usually the risk would fall upon the seller. It might be thought that it could apply after shipment where ss.20(2), 32(2) or 32(3) apply, since these sections postpone the passing of risk, but in each case there would be a breach of contract by the seller, and thus frustration would be excluded.

If the agreement is avoided, however, the buyer cannot sue for non-delivery in these circumstances.

CHAPTER 5

PROPERTY

(1) CONSEQUENCES OF PASSING OF PROPERTY

EVEN the most detailed standard form sale contracts rarely deal with the passing **5–001** of property. There is no mention of it in the GAFTA contracts, nor in INCO-TERMS. Sometimes the contract states expressly when property should pass, as in, *e.g. The San Nicholas* [1976] 1 Lloyd's Rep. 8, below, but even there the agreement did not (at least in Lord Denning's view) determine when it actually passed. This is usually determined by common law rules, and presumptions which are said ultimately to be about what the parties to the sale contract intended. One consequence of this is that it can be difficult to determine, in advance of litigation, precisely when property passes. Fortunately, the question has recently become far less important than once it was.

(a) GENERAL CONSIDERATIONS

At the start of chapter 18 of "The Sale of Goods" by Atiyah (10th ed., 2001), **5–002** edited by John Adams and Hector MacQueen, the consequences of the passing of property in sales of goods are discussed. Not only are the consequences disparate, but they are also subject to numerous exceptions, leading to doubts about whether they should be determined by a single concept of property at all. Arguably, it would be better if the courts determined each of the consequences separately, leaving the property concept simply to resolve priorities, when one of the parties is insolvent. However, the discussion in Atiyah ends as follows (on p. 314):

" . . . Questions will still arise (for instance) as to who is the proper plaintiff to sue a third person when goods are damaged en route; questions will still arise about risk, and the right to sue for the price. Above all, questions will still arise about the claims of a buyer against an insolvent seller (and those claiming through him) as well as about the claims of a seller against an insolvent buyer (and likewise those claiming through him). These claims must be disposed of by the law somehow. One way of doing it is the traditional common law way of trying to use a concept like 'property' to decide most of the problems, while recognizing that many exceptions must be made. This has the disadvantage . . . that the exceptions sometimes seem to eat up the rule.

Alternatively, the law might have abandoned the 'conceptual' approach altogether and adopted the 'specific issue' approach, that is, have dealt with each specific question, such as the buyer's ability to pass title to a third party, the passing of risk, liability for the price, etc., without reference to the passing of property. This is the approach of Article 2 of the Uniform Commercial Code which is now in force throughout nearly all of the United States.[1] But the

---

[1] The footnote here states: "It is enacted in all states except Louisiana, which adopted the Code Napoleon in the early nineteenth century."

alternative approach, while it has many attractions, fails to provide answers to new problems unforeseen by the law, or indeed to problems newly created by subsequent laws. For the 'specific issue' approach avoids general solutions by use of general organizing concepts like property, and may therefore offer no solution at all (except perhaps by way of arguments by analogy) to new problems. The traditional common law approach has at least the virtue that in principle there is always a way of meeting new problems, namely by looking to see who has the property in the goods at the relevant moment, and treating that person as owner, with consequences which are assumed to meet the new problems. . . . "

5–003   This is no doubt sensible enough where the new issues are similar to those which are clearly central to the property concept, *e.g.* competing claims against a bankrupt, but there is surely no obvious logic in using a concept which has developed to deal with a particular type of problem, to determine an entirely different type of problem.

In a simple domestic sale of goods, say of an item of furniture, the transfer of the property completes the transaction, logically entitling the seller to claim the price. There is a logic in transferring the risk at the same time, and with the property go privileges. If, after the transfer of property, the seller goes bankrupt the goods can no longer be claimed by his trustee in bankruptcy, or liquidator, and if the goods are negligently damaged or converted, the buyer is the obvious plaintiff. These are all incidents of the property concept in an ordinary domestic sale. Also, once the property has passed, the goods are necessarily appropriated to the contract, in the sense that the seller cannot unilaterally take them back and substitute others, even if those others match the contract description.

These attributes of property really have little in common, however, although this is masked by there being only one delivery point in a simple domestic sale, where it is convenient that all these attributes pass. The international sales considered in this book differ in that there are, certainly for c.i.f. and often for f.o.b. contracts, not one delivery point but two, physical and constructive delivery. It is less obvious now that all the incidents of property should pass at the same time. As we saw in chapters 2–4, it is convenient for risk to pass with physical delivery, but the seller may wish to retain the security of property until constructive delivery has taken place. Actions against third parties, whether in contract or tort, might more logically depend on the passage of risk, rather than property.[2] Yet if physical delivery has occurred, and the seller is prepared to make constructive delivery, it is not easy to justify denying him the right to the price, just because property has not yet passed.

In fact, from as early as *Mirabita v Imperial Ottoman Bank* (1878) 3 Ex.D. 164, below, the courts have accepted that different attributes of property might pass at different times. There it was recognised that while the seller might retain property as security against payment, other incidents often associated with property, such as the right to prevent the seller from selling the goods elsewhere, might nonetheless have passed to the buyer.[3] There is no necessity for the same concept to perform two inherently disparate tasks (only the first of which affects third parties), and the law has been improved by recognising this.

5–004   In international trade, then, the trend has been away from allowing too much to depend on the property concept, so as to allow different incidents of property to be in seller and buyer simultaneously. In this chapter we can see how property and risk have become unlinked, certainly in the c.i.f., and largely also in the f.o.b. contract; there is simply no reason why the one concept should be tied in with the

---

[2] The Carriage of Goods by Sea Act partly implements this principle for contract, but not for tort actions: see further para. 13—072, below.

[3] Effectively, this is the origin of the two meanings of appropriation, discussed below.

other.[4] Rights of suit against third parties, on the other hand, are probably (in general) better tied in with passage of risk rather than property, but until 1992 were in fact almost dependent on property. Most people seem to agree that the law was immeasurably improved in 1992 by the divorce of rights of suit from the whereabouts of property. Moreover, many of the problems of the 1992 Act are caused by the residual relevance of property, for example in tort actions: see further chapter 15, below.

Obviously, the "specific issue" approach is better where the issues are sufficiently disparate that they bear little relation to the original concept. In international sales, this approach seems to be gaining ground over the "conceptual" approach. Consistently with this, especially since the enactment of the Carriage of Goods by Sea Act 1992, on which see further chapter 13, the importance of property has been significantly reduced in international sales, and is probably less important than in domestic sales of goods.

Nonetheless, there is still a single time at which property passes, and on which some consequences, not necessarily closely related, depend. On the previous page in Atiyah (p. 313), the main consequences flowing from the passing of property are identified as follows (emphasis in original text):

> "1. If the property in the goods has passed to the buyer he will generally have a good title to them if the seller becomes insolvent while the goods remain in the seller's possession.
>
> 2. If the goods are delivered subject to a reservation of title (or property) by the seller, the seller *may* have a good title to the goods should the buyer become insolvent.[5]
>
> 3. The right to sue a third party for damage to, or loss of, the goods, may depend on who has property.
>
> 4. The risk passes prima facie when the property passes.
>
> 5. Generally speaking, the seller can only sue for the price if the property has passed."

The editors of Atiyah also note that the first three in the list can affect parties other than the seller and buyer, and observes that:

> "it is a serious question whether contracting parties should be permitted to adjust the passing (or non-passing) of the property in a contract of sale to protect themselves against the risk of the other party's insolvency, without any regard to the interests of third party creditors."

He observes that the interests of third parties, in respect of the first two, are often in fact protected by the Companies Act 1995, s.395, but this provision generally has no application to c.i.f. and f.o.b. contracts.

As far as international sales are concerned, consequences 1 and 2 apply. Moreover, any bank financing the sale by documentary credit can be affected by the timing of the passing of property, so it is perhaps strange that it is ultimately determined only by the intentions of the parties to the sale contract.

Arguably, the property concept is central only to consequences 1 and 2, and should not be used to determine consequences 3 to 5. For international sales, consequence 3 has been largely (but not entirely) unlinked from property by the Carriage of Goods by Sea Act 1992. Consequence 4 is no more than a *prima facie*

---

[4] Fundamentally, property rights affect third parties, whereas risk is irrelevant except to the parties to the transaction.
[5] Emphasis in original, and there is a cross-reference elsewhere in Atiyah.

presumption, which is probably sensible enough where the parties have made no provision for risk. Risk does not affect third parties, however, and there is no reason therefore why the parties to the sale contract cannot vary it; in fact they do in c.i.f. and f.o.b. contracts, making separate provision for risk as we have seen in chapter 2. Consequence 5 applies to c.i.f. and f.o.b. contracts, although there is no obvious link between the concepts; a possible justification is that the transfer of property completes the transaction and therefore entitles the seller to the agreed price.

(b) Consequences of Passing of Property in International Sales

5–005   In international sales, the passing of property is less important than it was prior to the Carriage of Goods by Sea Act 1992, but it still has the following consequences:

1. The most important consequence of property is that it can protect against the bankruptcy of the other party, since if one of the parties goes bankrupt, in general the trustee in bankruptcy only has any claim on the property of the bankrupt. In a sale context see, *e.g. Carlos Federspiel & Co, SA v Charles Twigg & Co Ltd* [1957] 1 Lloyd's Rep. 240, below and also in chapter 3, above, where the buyers had paid for goods but had not obtained property at the time of the seller's bankruptcy, and *Ginzberg v Barrow Haemetite Steel Co* [1966] 1 Lloyd's Rep. 343, below, where c.i.f. sellers were protected against receivership of the buyers because property had not passed to them. This was undoubtedly one of the original motivations for sellers retaining bills of lading against payment, or taking bills of lading to their own order. An early case, where the sellers failed to retain property, is *Cowas-Jee v Thompson* (1845) 3 Moore Ind. App. 422, 430; 18 E.R. 560, 563, PC, in chapter 1, above. See also the discussion of the Sale of Goods Act 1979, s.19(3), described in chapter 8, below.

2. The importance is not limited to the sale contract, since where payment is by banker's commercial credit, transfer of the documents of title to it can transfer the special legal title of a pledgee (described by Lord Selborne in *Sewell v Burdick* (1884) 10 App. Cas. 74 as a pledge accompanied by a power to obtain delivery of the goods when they arrive, and (if necessary) to realise them for the purpose of the security), which protects the bank against its customer's bankruptcy before it is reimbursed. Since it is the seller who creates the pledge, it is generally assumed to be desirable that the seller retains title until tender of the documents to the confirming or correspondent bank. If property has already passed to the buyer, the tender of documents by the seller cannot give the bank any security (this was one of the problems in *The Future Express* [1993] 2 Lloyd's Rep. 542, in chapter 6).

3. However, there are limitations on the efficacy of retention of property. If the bankrupt (whether seller or buyer) has resold the goods to a third party, the property of the other party may not avail him, because there are a number of circumstances where good title can be passed to a third party even by someone who has no title himself (see, *e.g.* Atiyah, *The Sale of Goods* (10th ed., 2001), Ch. 19). In a sale context, see *Cahn v Pockett's* [1899] 1 Q.B. 643, and in a bankers' commercial credit context, see *Lloyds Bank v Bank of America National Trust and Savings Association* [1938] 2 K.B. 147. Both these cases are in chapter 8, below. Both were fraud cases, and in general, retention of property gives no protection against the fraud of the other party.

4. Further, in the event of the buyer becoming bankrupt while the goods are still at sea, the seller who has not been paid the price is protected by a lien (if he retains possession) or a right of stoppage in transit (if he has parted with possession) even if the property in the goods has already passed (note that stoppage in transit protects only against bankruptcy, not other forms of non-payment—Sale of Goods Act, s.44). See generally, *e.g.* Sale of Goods Act, s.39, the unpaid seller being defined in s.38. The efficacy of the lien is considered further below.

5. In principle, equitable title can also confer protection against bankruptcy (as where a trust receipt, described in chapter 8, below, is used under a documentary credit). However, apart from that situation, where there is an express declaration of trusteeship, the courts have taken the view that the Sale of Goods Act provisions for passing of legal title form a complete code—see, *e.g.* Atkin L.J.'s views in *Re Wait* [1927] 1 Ch. 606, expressly upheld by the House of Lords in *The Aliakmon* [1986] A.C. 785.

6. The holder of legal (but not the holder of merely an equitable) title can bring tort actions against the carrier, in negligence and conversion. This is of lesser importance given the greater likelihood of a contract action following the Carriage of Goods by Sea Act 1992, but may be relevant to double liability issues (see para. 13—040, below). An immediate right to possession will also suffice for a conversion action, however (*e.g.* in the event of misdelivery by the carrier)—it is not necessary also for property to have passed.

7. Many of the cases in this chapter are on the application of the Bills of Lading Act 1855, s.1, but see now Carriage of Goods by Sea Act 1992, ss.2–3 (in chapter 13, below), which removes property considerations from the transfer of rights and obligations under the carriage contract. Property may still be relevant, however, in some circumstances; for example, there could be a double liability problem where property passes late, since both seller and buyer may be able to sue for substantial damages—this point will be further considered in chapter 13, below.

8. Determination of risk—s.20(1) of the Sale of Goods Act 1979 provides that unless otherwise agreed risk follows property. Probably this was the original reason why risk was held to pass on shipment in f.o.b., and later c.i.f. contracts. Today, however, while this *prima facie* presumption, that risk and property pass together, may often hold in domestic sales of goods, it rarely does in international sales, where property often passes later than risk.

9. The seller's action for the price usually depends on property having passed to the buyer. See further below.

10. Property can have relevance in Prize cases arising from seizures of vessels and cargoes in wartime. Details of Prize law are beyond the scope of this book.

(2) Passing of Property: The General Scheme

(a) Sale of Goods Act Provisions

The relevant provisions of the Sale of Goods Act 1979, on passing of property, **5–006** are ss.16–20 ("Transfer of property as between seller and buyer"). They are set out in full in Appendix A, below.

(b) Specific and Unascertained Goods

5–007   Whereas in a contract for the sale of specific goods, the goods can be identified
from the time of contract as being destined for the buyer and him alone, where the
goods are unascertained the buyer cannot point to the particular goods which are
destined for him. A common example of the sale of specific goods might be the
sale of a particular manufactured item. Unascertained goods can be either purely
generic or part of an undivided but specific bulk. An example of the former might
be a contract for 150 tons of copra, c.i.f. London, October shipment. The seller can
supply goods satisfying the contract description from anywhere in the world. An
example of the latter might be 200 tons of copra from a specified ship. The buyer
cannot say which 200 tons are his until the bulk is divided.

The processes by which unascertained goods can become ascertained are
described below.

(c) Unascertained Goods

Notes

5–008   1. Prior to the addition, by the Sale of Goods (Amendment) Act 1995, s.1(1), of
s.20A of the Sale of Goods Act (which is considered below) s.16 operated as an
absolute bar on the passing of property in unascertained goods. It still does,
except in the limited situations where s.20A applies.

2. Goods that are part of an undivided bulk cannot be ascertained, and the
effect of s.16 used to be that property in them could not therefore pass until they
were discharged from the vessel, and hence became ascertained. This conclusion
is now subject to s.20A, considered below.

3. Where the sale can be satisfied by one or more of a number of identical goods,
they will be ascertained when the seller appropriates them to the contract. Such
appropriation is irrevocable; the seller is committing himself to using those goods,
and none other, to perform the sale contract, and will be in breach of contract if
he later substitutes other goods. It is unlikely that such commitment will be
inferred before shipment.

CARLOS FEDERSPIEL & CO, SA v CHARLES TWIGG & CO, LTD

Queen's Bench Division (Commercial Court). [1957] 1 Lloyd's Rep. 240

Decision:

5–009   Property in a consignment of bicycles sold f.o.b. did not pass until
shipment. The buyer had already paid, but was held not to have obtained
any property in them, the seller having been wound up before the goods
had been shipped. The seller had not finally appropriated the goods to
the contract, within rule 5 of Sale of Goods Act 1979, s.18, prior to their
shipment.

Pearson J.: *(after categorising the contract as f.o.b.—see chapter 3, below
—and reviewing authorities on appropriation)* On those authorities, what are
the principles emerging? I think one can distinguish these principles.
First, Rule 5 of Sect. 18 of the Act is one of the Rules for ascertaining the
intention of the parties as to the time at which the property in the goods
is to pass to the buyer unless a different intention appears. Therefore the

element of common intention has always to be borne in mind. A mere setting apart or selection of the seller of the goods which he expects to use in performance of the contract is not enough. If that is all, he can change his mind and use those goods in performance of some other contract and use some other goods in performance of this contract. To constitute an appropriation of the goods to the contract, the parties must have had, or be reasonably supposed to have had, an intention to attach the contract irrevocably to those goods, so that those goods and no others are the subject of the sale and become the property of the buyer.

Secondly, it is by agreement of the parties that the appropriation, involving a change of ownership, is made, although in some cases the buyer's assent to an appropriation by the seller is conferred in advance by the contract itself or otherwise.

Thirdly, an appropriation by the seller, with the assent of the buyer, may be said always to involve an actual or constructive delivery. If the seller retains possession, he does so as bailee for the buyer. There is a passage in Chalmers' *Sale of Goods Act*, 12th ed., at p. 75, where it is said:

> "In the second place, if the decisions be carefully examined, it will be found that in every case where the property has been held to pass, there has been an actual or constructive delivery of the goods to the buyer."

I think that is right . . .

Fourthly, one has to remember Sect. 20 of the Sale of Goods Act, whereby the ownership and the risk are normally associated. Therefore as it appears that there is reason for thinking, on the construction of the relevant documents, that the goods were, at all material times, still at the seller's risk, that is *prima facie* an indication that the property had not passed to the buyer.

Fifthly, usually but not necessarily, the appropriating act is the last act to be performed by the seller. For instance, if delivery is to be taken by the buyer at the seller's premises and the seller has completed his part of the contract and has appropriated the goods when he has made the goods ready and has identified them and placed them in position to be taken by the buyer and has so informed the buyer, and if the buyer agrees to come and take them, that is the assent to the appropriation. But if there is a further act, an important and decisive act to be done by the seller, then there is *prima facie* evidence that probably the property does not pass until the final act is done.

Applying those principles to the present case I would say this. Firstly, the intention was that the ownership should pass on shipment (or possibly at some later date) because the emphasis is throughout on shipment as the decisive act to be done by the seller in performance of the contract. Secondly, it is impossible to find in this correspondence an agreement to a change of ownership before the time of shipment. The letters . . . do not contain any provision or implication of any earlier change of ownership. Thirdly, there is no actual or constructive delivery; no suggestion of the seller becoming a bailee for the buyer. Fourthly, there is no suggestion of the goods being at the buyer's risk at any time before shipment; no suggestion that the buyer should insist on the seller arranging insurance for them. Fifthly, the last two acts to be performed by the seller, namely, sending the goods to Liverpool and having the goods shipped on board, were not performed.

Therefore, my decision that the *prima facie* inference which one would have drawn from the contract is that the property was not to pass at any time before shipment, is in my view not displaced by the subsequent correspondence between the parties. It follows, therefore, that there was no appropriation of these goods and therefore the action fails.

Notes

5–010   Taking the five principles in turn:

1. There must be shown "an intention to attach the contract irrevocably to those goods, so that those goods and no others are the subject of the sale and become the property of the buyer." Prior to shipment, unless the precise goods are identified in the sale contract, it is usually reasonable to accord to the seller the right to substitute other conforming goods. Since very few f.o.b. or c.i.f. contracts identify the precise goods to be sold,[6] it would be very rare for property to pass before shipment in either of these types.

2. The need for both parties to agree to an appropriation is discussed further below. It is sometimes possible to infer the assent of one or both parties.

3. Here, appropriation is tied in with actual or constructive delivery. In the context of an f.o.b. contract, or at least the early type of f.o.b. contract described at the beginning of chapter 1, delivery is to the vessel, and the presumption would be that property would also pass then. With a c.i.f. contract, constructive delivery is later, on transfer of documents, and the presumption seems to be that property passes c.i.f., on tender of documents against payment of the price.

It is also often said that the presumption with an f.o.b. contract is that property passes on shipment. With more modern forms of f.o.b. contract, however, where the documents are used in a manner similar to c.i.f.,[7] there is a lot to be said for the view that, as with a c.i.f. contract, passing of property is postponed until tender of documents. In *Federspiel v Twigg* itself, of course, where payment had already been made, there would have been no need for the seller to retain any right of disposal, and property would probably have passed on shipment.

These are in any case only presumptions; in *The Ciudad de Pasto* (in this chapter), property under an f.o.b. contract did not pass before tender of documents, whereas in *The Delfini* (also in this chapter), property under a c.i.f. contract passed earlier. Factors apart from the classification of the contract are more likely to determine the issue. From *Federspiel v Twigg*, however, we can say at least that property is unlikely to pass before shipment, whether the contract is f.o.b. or c.i.f.

---

[6] An exception might be a contract for all the cargo on board a particular ship, as in *The Jambur* in para. 2—020, above. This was a contract for the sale of specific goods, but they were already afloat when the contract was made, so clearly, property could not have passed prior to shipment. (Note that contracts for the sale of cargo that is already afloat are quite rare.)

[7] See, *e.g. Concordia v Richco*, in para. 6—086, below.

4. The presumption that property and risk pass at the same time is often rebutted in an international sale, where risk passes before property. Here, however, the argument is that property at any rate does not pass before risk, and that is generally true in international sales.

5. Appropriation will usually be the seller's last act. Until then the seller will not be taken irrevocably to have committed himself, as required by the first principle. Appropriation is therefore unlikely to be before shipment, but could be later. Suppose, for example, a number of identical goods are shipped for more than one buyer; appropriation could be delayed until those due to each buyer are identified by transfer of bills of lading. In a case like *C. Groom v Barber* in chapter 4, the seller was himself unaware of the identity of the contract goods until about an hour before tender of documents, so could hardly have appropriated them before then.

Comment

The requirement in *Federspiel v Twigg* is effectively for irrevocable commitment **5–011** on the part of the seller; the seller can withdraw the goods up until shipment, so that will usually be the earliest time when ascertainment can occur. There seems also to be a strong presumption that property will not in any case pass earlier than shipment, *even* where the seller appears to be irrevocably committed before then. In *Pyrene Co Ltd v Scindia Navigation Co Ltd* [1954] 2 Q.B. 402,[8] the seller had surely relinquished control over the goods as soon as they had been picked up by the stevedores' crane, but the inference must surely be drawn from the case that the property in them nevertheless did not pass until they had crossed the ship's rail.[9] The contract was f.o.b., but the principles of s.16 clearly apply similarly to c.i.f. contracts.

On the other hand, in *The San Nicholas* [1976] 1 Lloyd's Rep. 8, Roskill L.J. speculated that property might have passed before consignment. But this was no more than speculation; neither Roskill L.J. nor Lord Denning M.R. were prepared to decide the issue finally on an interlocutory appeal, and in any case, Lord Denning M.R. thought that property passed on tender of documents (see further below).

(d) Ascertained or Specific Goods

Once the goods have been appropriated, and hence become ascertained, the **5–012** general principle is stated in s.17:

> "(1) Where there is a contract for the sale of specific or ascertained goods the property in them is transferred to the buyer at such time as the parties to the contract intend it to be transferred.
>
> (2) For the purpose of ascertaining the intention of the parties regard shall be had to the terms of the contract, the conduct of the parties and the circumstances of the case."

Since it may be difficult to discern intention, presumptions are created in ss.18 and 19, the most important of which are:

---

[8] Described in detail in Ch. 3, above, and Chs. 11 and 13, below.
[9] The seller's action in tort depended on this, as did Devlin J.'s reasoning on the conversion action, were the seller not to be party to some kind of contract with the carrier. On the latter, see further Ch. 15, below.

18. Unless a different intention appears, the following are rules for ascertaining the intention of the parties as to the time at which the property in the goods is to pass to the buyer. . . .

Rule 5

(1) Where there is a contract for the sale of unascertained or future goods by description, and goods of that description and in a deliverable state are unconditionally appropriated to the contract, either by the seller with the assent of the buyer or by the buyer with the assent of the seller, the property in the goods then passes to the buyer; and the assent may be express or implied, and may be given either before or after the appropriation is made.

(2) Where, in pursuance of the contract, the seller delivers the goods to the buyer or to a carrier or other bailee or custodier (whether named by the buyer or not) for the purpose of transmission to the buyer, and does not reserve the right of disposal, he is to be taken to have unconditionally appropriated the goods to the contract. . . .

19. (2) Where goods are shipped, and by the bill of lading the goods are deliverable to the order of the seller or his agent, the seller is *prima facie* to be taken to reserve the right of disposal."

Section 19(2), which will often apply to c.i.f. contracts, and by no means rarely to f.o.b., is considered further below—the presumption there created is strong but not conclusive.

Only rule 5 of s.18 appears to have any relevance to f.o.b. and c.i.f. contracts. Note that s.17 looks to the intention of both parties, and that the appropriation under rule 5(1) requires the assent of both parties. By contrast, rule 5(2) and s.19(2) look only at the position of the seller.

5–013   The unconditional appropriation in Rule 5 is referred to in Benjamin's *Sale of Goods*[10] as "proprietary" appropriation, and is necessary to pass property. This is contrasted with "contractual" appropriation, which ascertains the goods (see above). It seems that, unless the ascertainment of the goods is by means of an unconditional appropriation within this section, for example if the seller reserves a right of disposal, a later unconditional appropriation must occur to transfer property. There is often in other words a contractual appropriation, which ascertains the goods (see above), and a later proprietary appropriation. This is really saying no more than that property cannot pass until the goods are ascertained, but does not necessarily pass then; often it passes later.

The editors of Benjamin take the view that appropriation in the contractual sense "depends primarily on the intention of the seller." Bools advances a "control rationale" for the passing of property (based in part upon *The Kronprinsessan Margareta*, below, and in part on s.19(2)), which emphasises the intention of the seller, and enables him to control whether property passes.[11] The seller's control is emphasised even for the proprietary appropriation. He says that:

"the requirement of an unconditional proprietary appropriation in rule 5 is nothing more than evidence of the seller's intention to pass the property as required by s.17."[12]

---

[10] (5th ed., 1997), para. 18–157.
[11] Bools, *The Bill of Lading: A Document of Title to Goods*, (Lloyd's of London Press, 1997), esp. pp. 22–24.
[12] At p. 24. His footnote argues that: " . . . the argument in *Karlshamns Oljefabriker v Eastport Navigation Corp (The Elafi)* [1981] 2 Lloyd's Rep. 679, 685 and *Anonima Petroli Italiana SpA and Neste Oy v Marlucidez Armadora SA, (The Filiatra Legacy)* [1991] 2 Lloyd's Rep. 337, 342 that property can pass without an unconditional appropriation is unsustainable."

There seems little doubt that the seller can, should he so wish, control property and prevent it from passing. Bools goes on to observe that because proprietary appropriation "is dependent upon the seller's presumed intention, a reservation, even in breach of the sale contract, will be effective."[13] Physical retention of the bill of lading, as in *The Kronprinsessan Margareta*, below, might also allow the seller unilaterally to prevent property from passing. But to assert that it is always for the seller unconditionally to appropriate, and that property cannot pass without the necessary unconditional appropriation, is to fly in the face of the authorities. Such an assertion is certainly inconsistent with *The Elafi* and (perhaps) *The Filiatra Legacy* (both cases dealt with in detail below). Moreover, the emphasis on physical control in *The Kronprinsessan Margareta* has not been repeated in more recent cases.

Undoubtedly, property cannot pass before the goods are ascertained. Unless the   **5–014** contract is for the sale of specific or ascertained goods, this will require a contractual appropriation, which the seller can prevent from occurring.[14] Sometimes the buyer can also prevent it from occurring, as in *Colley v Overseas Exporters*, below. Once the goods have been ascertained, however, I would suggest that any of the following may occur:

(a) The contractual appropriation, necessary to ascertain the goods may be intended to be unconditional, in which case it also takes effect as a proprietary appropriation, and property passes immediately, by virtue of s. 18 rule 5; the seller may have no reason to retain title, the most obvious situation being where he has already been paid: in both *Federspiel v Twigg*, above, and *Pyrene Co Ltd v Scindia Navigation Co Ltd*,[15] if the goods had been ascertained, it is reasonable to suppose that property would have passed immediately.

(b) The seller may have intended to retain the property subject to a condition, usually payment of the price,[16] in which case if the condition is satisfied property passes without need for further action on his part—see, *e.g. Mirabita v Ottoman Bank* below, and if property passed after shipment, *The Filiatra Legacy*, also below.[17] Both these cases are inconsistent with Bools' view, above.[18]

(c) Alternatively, any conditions might already have occurred, prior to ascertainment—as in *The Elafi*, below, another case which is inconsistent with Bools' view,[19] in which case property can pass automatically without the

---

[13] If this is correct, and the authorities suggest that it is, Debattista's conclusion on intention, below, is wrong.

[14] In *The Elafi*, below, the goods apparently became ascertained without any intervention from the seller, but the seller could have prevented ascertainment from occurring by not shipping the goods and tendering the documents. The seller had in fact done all he could to ascertain the goods, but was prevented from so doing only by operation of law.

[15] See Ch. 3, above.

[16] Exceptionally, the seller may be interested in retaining property even after payment of the price, as in *The Gabbiano* [1940] P. 166, where the price was payable on out-turned quantity, so that if the price was paid before discharge, some or all of the price might need to be repaid—in the case itself, the goods were seized as Prize after payment of the price had been paid, and the sellers successfully claimed that they had retained the property.

[17] In *Mirabita*, tender of the price was sufficient to trigger the passing of property; it was not necessary for the seller to accept it. It is not clear whether property passed on or after shipment in *The Filiatra Legacy*. If the former, then this is simply a case of unconditional appropriation by the seller on shipment; if the latter, then the passing of property was triggered by an event which was completely outside the seller's control—see further below.

[18] As he admits regarding the latter; he contends that it is wrong.

[19] The other case that he contends is wrong, for this reason.

need for further action by the seller. In *The Elafi*, though, the seller had already done everything he could unconditionally to appropriate the goods to the contract, and it was not through his omission that property was still unable to pass; passing of property was effectively deferred, by operation of law, until ascertainment. It is inconceivable to suppose that once ascertainment had occurred in *The Elafi*, either that the seller retained any control over the goods (after all, he had already been paid, against tender of documents), or that anything else remained to be done by the buyer. To require some further act by the seller to pass property in these circumstances, as Bools seems to, is surely absurd.

(d) Alternatively, the seller may *physically* retain control, as in *The Kronprinsessan Margareta*. There, from the physical retention was inferred unilateral retention of property also by the seller. In many cases, the seller will physically retain the documents, but the emphasis on physical control in *The Kronprinsessan Margareta* seems not to be as prevalent in more recent cases; it does not seem to be the decisive factor. The Privy Council was concerned to distinguish *The Parchim* (an inconvenient decision, also considered below), and the physical retention of the bill of lading was a device to do this. Now that *The Parchim* is no longer regarded as a strong authority, the courts seem to place less emphasis on physical control.

KARLSHAMNS OLJEFABRIKER v EASTPORT NAVIGATION CORP (THE ELAFI)

Queen's Bench Division (Commercial Court). [1981] 2 Lloyd's Rep. 679

Facts:

5–015 The claimant buyers had purchased 6,000 tonnes of copra c.i.f. from East Asiatic, under four identical contracts. The sellers used 12 bills of lading, each for 500 tons of cargo aboard *The Elafi*, to satisfy this contract. Total bill of lading quantities for cargo aboard *The Elafi* were for 22,000 tons, but in fact slightly more had been loaded. All the cargo had been originally shipped by the International Copra Export Corporation (ICEC), who had negotiated the bills of lading in favour of East Asiatic. The bills of lading were further negotiated in favour of the claimant receivers, who paid against them.

The receivers also purchased 500 tons, from the same consignment on board *The Elafi*, from Frank Fehr. This cargo, which had itself been purchased by Frank Fehr, also from the shippers (ICEC), was not covered by a bill of lading.

The goods were being shipped from the Philippines to Sweden, and at intermediate ports of call during the voyage (Hamburg and Rotterdam) some of the cargo was discharged to other buyers, after which all that remained on the ship was destined for the claimant buyers, albeit under a number of different contracts, involving two different sellers. This occurred some time after the bills of lading had been indorsed in favour of the claimants.

At some time later than this some of the cargo was damaged by water entering a hold as the result of the shipowners' negligence and breach of contract. On an appeal from arbitration, the question arose whether the buyers could sue the respondent shipowners in contract and tort. The shipowners' defence to the tort action was that property had not passed to the receivers by the time the damage had occurred, and their defence to the contract action was that property had not passed upon or by reason of indorsement (as required by the Bills of Lading Act 1855, s.1, which was in force at the time).

Held:

1. In order to be able to sue in tort the buyers had to show that they **5–016** were owners of the goods at the time the damage occurred. The case on this point has been subsequently approved by the House of Lords in *The Aliakmon* [*see para. 13—072, below*].

2. Property had passed before the damage occurred, appropriation occurring by process of exhaustion, without the need of any further act by the seller. There was no additional need for the goods to be appropriated to each of the separate contracts under which the buyers purchased the goods for the property to pass.

MUSTILL J.: The validity of the claimants' first way of putting their **5–017** claim, namely that they were entitled to sue in negligence as owners of the goods, depends upon whether (as they contend) the property passed to them at the moment when, upon completion of discharge at Hamburg, it could be said for certain that all the cargo on board was destined for them, or whether (as the respondents maintain) the property did not pass until the goods were discharged at Karlshamn, by which time the damage had already occurred.

There is no doubt as to the general principles to be applied when deciding an issue of this nature. Whatever the intentions of the parties, where the contract is for the sale of unascertained goods no property can pass until the goods are ascertained: s.16 of the Sale of Goods Act, 1893. Once ascertainment has taken place, the passing of the property depends on the intention of the parties, which is to be collected from the terms of the contract, the conduct of the parties, and the circumstances of the case: s.17. As part, but only part, of the process of drawing the necessary inference, the Court must have regard to the *prima facie* presumption, created by s.18, r.5(1) that the parties intended the property in unascertained goods to pass when goods of the contract description in a deliverable state were unconditionally appropriated to the contract, either by the seller with the assent of the buyer, or by the buyer with the assent of the seller.

It is convenient to approach the present case in stages, in the light of these general principles. First, what would have been the position if the entire cargo had been sold to the claimants under a single contract? Here, since the contract was on c.i.f. terms, it is very probable that the property would have passed to the claimants when the shipping documents were negotiated, for the cargo was ascertained and appropriated from the outset, and the general rule is that under a c.i.f. contract the property passes with the documents. The only cause for uncertainty is the fact that the claimants had a right to reject goods in excess of the stipulated quantity, so that it would not be possible to know during the voyage whether any individual portion of cargo might not ultimately revert to the vendors. I believe, however, that in such a situation the property in the entire cargo would pass conditionally to the claimants, subject to a retransfer of any excess if the claimants so elected, and that this would be sufficient to found a claim in tort in respect of all such cargo as the claimants chose to accept.

Next, there is the situation which would exist if (say) half of the cargo was sold to each of two buyers. Here, it would be clear that no property would pass until the goods had been discharged, and a physical separation effected between the goods delivered under each contract; notwithstanding that the contract was on c.i.f. terms: see, for example, *The Julia* [1949] A.C. 293 [*in chapter 2, above*]. The absence of any ascertainment during the voyage would mean that s.16 prevented the property from passing, whatever the parties may have intended; hence there could be no claim in tort: *Margarine Union GmbH v Cambay Prince Steamship Co Ltd* . . .[20]

5–018   The next step is to see what the position would have been if the whole of the cargo had been sold to the claimants, under four rather than one contract of sale. There was no physical separation of the goods in the holds of the vessel, as between the various contracts. Did this prevent the property from passing before delivery? Here, there is an authority very close to the point, in the shape of *Wait and James v Midland Bank Ltd* (1926) 24 Ll.L. Rep. 313; (1926) 31 Com. Cas. 172. The dispute was between the claimants, who were unpaid vendors of grain to Redlers & Co and a bank, to whom part of the grain was pledged as security for an overdraft. The question was whether in the circumstances the property had passed to Redlers, so that they could confer a proprietary interest on the bank. What happened was as follows. The claimants were owners of an entire shipload of wheat, which was delivered into a warehouse. By the three contracts in question, the plaintiffs sold part of the shipload to Redlers, giving them delivery orders, against which Redlers took delivery of part, and left the remainder in the warehouse. As time went by, the claimants made sales of the cargo to other purchasers, until at last there were no goods in the warehouse except those which had been left behind by Redlers. The latter then pledged the goods to the bank. On the application of the warehouse, the rights of the claimants and the bank were decided by interpleader proceedings. At the trial, the claimants argued that under s.16 the property in the goods sold from bulk did not pass until the goods had been separated from the bulk and ascertained; and since the goods had never been appropriated as between the three contracts, the property could not pass, even though the bank was pledgee of the entire quantity remaining. All that Redlers could transfer to the bank was the right to get

---

[20] [1969] 1 Q.B. 219.

the cargo weighed out of the warehouse, a right which was never exercised. On the other side, the bank argued that as soon as all the goods
which the claimants had in the warehouse had been disposed of, and the
amount sold to Redlers was all that was left, that amount became ascertained by the process of exhaustion, and the property passed to Redlers,
who were in a position to pass it on to the bank.

The judgment of Roche J. in favour of the bank proceeded by two
stages. First, the learned judge held that although weighing *ex warehouse*
was the usual method of ascertainment for the purpose of s.16, it was not
the only effective method. Here the matter had been dealt with "automatically by the facts", in the sense that the goods had become ascertained by
a process of exhaustion.

Second, while it was true that there had been no differentiation of the
goods between the different contracts, this did not mean that there had
been no sufficient ascertainment, for the purpose of s.16. As the learned
Judge held:

> "These contracts were always in one hand . . . In my judgment it is
> sufficient if, where there are contracts for the sale of unascertained
> goods to one buyer, it is ascertained what the goods are which are
> covered by those contracts; and I hold that that is the permissible and
> proper construction of section 16."

In the present case, Mr. Eder for the respondents [shipowners] did not
question that there might be ascertainment of goods by exhaustion, rather
than by an explicit separation of each consignment from the bulk; and I
am sure that he was right to make this concession. He does, however,
make two criticisms of the judgment of Roche J.

First, Mr. Eder contends that Roche J. was mistaken in giving a broad   **5–019**
interpretation to s.16. If the section is looked at in isolation, there is force
in this argument. The section refers to "a contract for the sale of unascertained goods", and says that the property shall not pass "unless and until
the goods are ascertained". In their most natural sense the words "the
goods" would be read as referring to the goods which are the subject of
the contract in question, so that one can say of them that "these are the
goods which refer to that contract". But when one comes to deal with an
unusual situation, such as exists here, it is in my view legitimate to look
at the reasoning which underlies the legislation. This is quite plain. The
passing of property is concerned with the creation of rights *in rem*, which
the purchaser can assert, not only against the vendor, but against the
world at large, and which he can alienate in such a way as to create
similar rights in a transferee. Where there are multiple contracts of sale in
the hands of different buyers, in relation to an undivided bulk, there are
only two possible solutions. First, to hold that the buyers take as joint
owners in undivided shares. English law has rejected this solution. The
only alternative is to hold that the property does not pass until the goods
are not only physically separated, but separated in a way which enables

an individual buyer to say that a particular portion has become his property under his contract of sale: for until then, to adopt the words of Bayley B. in *Gillett v Hill* (1834) 2 Cromp. & M. 530 at p. 535, no one can say which part of the whole quantity the seller has agreed to deliver. There is, however, no need to impose this solution on a case where there are parallel contracts between the parties, together comprising the whole of the bulk. Here, it is known which part of the whole the seller has agreed to deliver, namely, all of the parts. I am unable to envisage a situation in which it would make the least practical difference whether or not the purchaser of an entire cargo from the same seller under a series of contracts for homogeneous goods is able to identify which ton or bag of the whole relates to which contract. So far as the creation of rights *in rem* are concerned it does not matter; nor does it for the purposes of a claim arising from non-delivery or short delivery. If the seller delivers nothing at all, the buyer sues in respect of the whole quantity. If he delivers only part, then he can appropriate the delivery to whichever of the contracts he prefers, paying the price fixed by that contract, and claiming damages in accordance with the prices under the other contracts.

In the present case, there is nothing in the award to suggest that the contracts differed even as regards price. This being so, it seems to me quite unnecessary to read s.16 so as to produce a different result in the case of four contracts comprising the entire bulk from the one which would have been reached if there had been a single contract for the whole.

There is, moreover, a serious practical objection to the defendants' argument. Their analysis stops short at the moment of discharge. But if it is valid, it must apply, not only while the goods were in the hold, but also after discharge. The property therefore would not pass until such time, at Karlshamn or somewhere else, as the goods were physically allocated between the various contracts. No doubt the bulk was ultimately sub-divided in some way, but there is no reason to suppose, and nothing in the award to suggest, that the division bore any relation to the four contracts. Logically, therefore, it must follow that the property never passed at all, whatever the intention of the parties may have been. Even if it were possible to imply a term passing the property when the goods were taken into the possession of the claimants—and I can see no very convincing grounds for this—it could not stand with s.16, the provisions of which are paramount. Mr. Eder was unable to suggest any escape from this absurd result, consistent with the defendants' argument. In my judgment, the only acceptable course is to adopt the same common sense approach to ascertainment as was applied in *Wait and James v Midland Bank Ltd, sup,* the reasoning in which I therefore adopt as follows.

5–020   There is, however, another criticism which Mr. Eder directs at the judgment of Roche J., namely, that it omits any mention of s.18(5). Whatever may be the position, he says, as regards ascertainment, there was here no appropriation of the goods to the individual contracts before the moment of loss.

In my judgment, this objection adds nothing to the argument in relation to ascertainment. If is true that in some cases the ascertainment of goods may not be the same as the unconditional appropriation of them, although the distinction will usually be difficult if not impossible to draw. But here I cannot see any difference. On the hypothesis that all the goods were the subject of parallel contracts between the same parties, the facts which constituted the ascertainment of the goods so as to release the inhibition created by s.16 on the passing of the property must have seen the same as those which constituted appropriation for the purpose of ascertaining the parties' intention as to the passing of the property for the purposes of s.18, r.5. Mr. Eder did not suggest how, in a case like this, it would be possible to have ascertainment without appropriation, or *vice versa*. This being so, it appears legitimate to place appropriation on the same broad basis as ascertainment, and hold that it is sufficient if the whole of the bulk can be identified with the contracts taken as a group.

Before leaving the question of appropriation, I should draw attention to one other factor, namely, that the want of an unconditional appropriation is not an absolute bar to the passing of property, but merely one of the factors to be taken into account when ascertaining the presumed intentions of the parties. Whatever the provisions of r.5, I can see no reason why the parties should be presumed to have intended that the passing of the property should be held up beyond the time when all the bills of lading had been negotiated and the price paid as to 95 per cent; and when it was known that all the cargo remaining on board was destined for the plaintiffs. I am reinforced in this view by the findings of the arbitrators, to which I have already referred.

For these reasons, I conclude that if all the Karlshamn cargo had been sold directly by International Copra to the claimants, the property would have passed when the goods became ascertained, as soon as discharge had finished at Hamburg. In fact, however, part of the cargo devolved along a different chain of title, *via* Frank Fehr. Does this make any difference?

The first ground upon which Mr. Eder contended that the interposition of Frank Fehr makes all the difference is as follows. Imagine that Frank Fehr had not resold that amount of the Karlshamn cargo remaining after the deduction of 6000 tonnes. The cargo would then have consisted, after delivery of the Rotterdam and Hamburg portions, of two consignments: one sold to the claimants, and one to Frank Fehr. Quite clearly neither the claimants nor Frank Fehr would have had title before discharge at Karlshamn, for it was only then that the goods would have been ascertained. Since neither had title, neither could confer it, on the principle *nemo dat quod non habet*.

In my judgment this argument is unsound. The maxim *nemo dat* is a **5–021** useful summary of the law applicable to a case where the vendor of specific goods for immediate delivery purports to make title by virtue of a title which he himself claims to possess. But it is not the law that the seller of unascertained goods warrants that he himself will be the owner at the time when the property is to pass. Section 12 creates an implied condition that the seller "will have a right to sell the goods". This involves no promise about the seller's own proprietary rights; only that he will be able to create the appropriate rights in the buyer. A contract of sale can perfectly well be performed by a seller who never has title at any time, by causing a third party to transfer it directly to the buyer. So there is nothing anomalous in holding that Frank Fehr could, by reselling to the claimants, immediately create in them a right of property which would not have accrued to Frank Fehr themselves until a later occasion, if the goods had not been resold.

So the question comes to this, whether the reasoning of *Wait and James v Midland Bank Ltd* can be taken one stage further, so as to hold that the uniting of all purchase contracts in the hands of a single buyer is capable of passing the property in the bulk, even though the purchases are made from different sellers. (For the moment I am speaking only of ascertainment; the question of intent must be considered later.)

For my part, I can see no reason why the principle should not be the same. What is needed for ascertainment is that the buyer should be able to say, "Those are my goods". This requirement is satisfied if he can say, "All those are my goods". There is no need to be able to say that any particular goods came from any particular source.

The question of appropriation is less straight-forward, and here I think there may be a difference from the simpler case, where all the contracts are made with the same seller, since the attribution of the cargo to individual contracts may have a real practical significance. For example, if it had unexpectedly been found, when the time came for discharge that there was a shortage rather than a surplus, the question would have arisen whether the claimants should sue Frank Fehr for non-delivery, or the carriers under the bill of lading. The only way to deal with this question would be to look for some event happening at or after the moment of discharge which could be treated as an appropriation by the sellers, the carrier or the claimants. The same analysis must, I believe, apply if there is over–, not under-delivery: so that if r.5 were to make an appropriation a precondition of the transfer of property, the claimants would not acquire title until the completion of discharge.

5–022   Rule 5 does not, however, have this effect. It merely creates a rebuttable presumption that an appropriation is necessary for the transfer of title. Ultimately, the question is one of intent. It is true that the property in an undivided bulk will not normally pass before appropriation. But this is because in most cases the act of ascertainment is simultaneous with the act of appropriation, and without ascertainment there can be no transfer of title. The present case is, however, an exception: for if the reasoning of *Wait and James v Midland Bank Ltd* is applicable here, there was an ascertainment during the voyage. This released the inhibition on the passing of property, and all that remains to be considered is the intention of the parties. Did they intend that the transfer of title should be held up until the completion of discharge, or did they intend that the claimants should be able to say of the cargo "That is all ours", from the moment at Hamburg when the interests of all the other buyers had been satisfied.

The answer to this question may be reached by two stages. First, as regards the goods purchased direct from International Copra. These were the subject of a c.i.f. sale. I can see nothing to displace the ordinary presumption that property under such a sale is intended to pass upon the negotiation of the documents. This happened during the ocean voyage. It is true that the intention of the parties could not immediately be fulfilled, since the goods were not yet ascertained. As soon as this happened, however, upon the completion of discharge at Hamburg, there was no longer anything to prevent the presumed intention from taking effect. Second, as regards the Frank Fehr portion, the award supplies the answer to the question; for the arbitrators have found that, as between the respective parties to the purchase from International Copra and the resale to the claimants, the intention was that upon completion of the discharge of the cargo destined for Hamburg there should pass to the buyers the property in whatever surplus goods then remained on board the vessel. There is nothing surprising in such a finding, or any ground for believing that the arbitrators may have misdirected themselves by (for example) giving insufficient weight to r.5. On the contrary, they have stated in their reasons that:

> "We do not think it artificial to conclude that the goods became ascertained within the meaning of section 16 of the Sale of Goods Act, albeit that the goods may not have been appropriated to any of the contracts for the purposes of section 18(5) of the Act."

This shows that the arbitrators were well aware of r.5; and I agree with the view of the law which they express. Their finding on intention is one of fact, which the Court could not disturb even if it suspected that it might be wrong; which I do not.

In the result, therefore, I agree with the conclusion of the arbitrators that the claimants became owners of the goods upon the completion of discharge of the Hamburg consignment, and that they accordingly had title to sue in tort, in respect of the damage caused during discharge at Karlshamn.

Notes

1. Mustill J. also commented on an alternative claim in contract based on the **5–023** Bills of Lading Act 1855, s.1, which failed, because it could not be shown that the damaged goods were covered by the bills of lading (theoretically, all the damaged goods could have come from the Frank Fehr consignment). This aspect of the case has probably not been altered by the Carriage of Goods by Sea Act 1992 (see further chapter 13, below), since exactly the same reasoning could be applied.

2. The case is by no means typical, and (at least subject to the 1995 amendments) it is the exception for property in an undivided bulk to pass during the voyage. No aspect of this case would be affected by the 1995 amendments, which are discussed below.

3. Bools' problem with this case is that although ascertainment might occur through exhaustion (Mustill J. following *Wait and James v Midland Bank Ltd* (1926) 24 Ll.L. Rep. 313; (1926) 31 Com. Cas. 172), the seller did nothing amounting to an unconditional appropriation to pass the property. Mustill J. appears to have assumed that appropriation could also occur automatically, or alternatively that appropriation is not a condition precedent for the passing of property. He observes that r.18(5) creates only a presumption, not a rule of law.

4. The correct analysis is surely this. Property cannot pass prior to ascertainment, and after ascertainment it passes when the parties intend it to pass. By the time ascertainment had occurred, through the process of exhaustion, there is no doubt that the goods were irrevocably committed to the four sale contracts, since the bills of lading had been negotiated; payment had been made, so there was no need for the sellers to retain a right of disposal. All that prevented property from passing was s.16, which ceased to have any effect once ascertainment had occurred. There was also nothing to prevent property passing of the Frank Fehr consignment. The only real problem was that the sellers did not do anything positive unconditionally to appropriate the goods to pass property, but Mustill J. did not think they needed to.

5. Suppose there was a reason (apart from the ascertainment problem) why property could not pass under the Frank Fehr contract, for example because the plaintiffs had not yet paid for that part of the cargo. In that case, property could not pass in any of the cargo. Presumably property in the entire cargo would remain with the original shippers (International Copra Export Corporation), although, if Frank Fehr and East Asiatic had both paid for their shares, under the 1995 amendments (considered below) they would have property in the entire cargo as tenants in common. That would also presumably be the case if Frank Fehr had originally shipped their own part of the cargo, thereby mixing it with cargo of East Asiatic, rather than purchasing it from ICEC. Whichever of these situations obtained, property in the entire cargo would pass to the plaintiffs on payment to Frank Fehr.

6. On the conditional transfer of property, see further the discussion of the *Kwei Tek Chao* case in chapter 7, below.

7. The next case is included here, really only for comparison (the main point of the case being left until chapter 13). It is similar to *The Elafi*, except that there were two buyers, and *The Elafi* reasoning could therefore not apply.

THE ARAMIS

Court of Appeal. [1989] 1 Lloyd's Rep. 213

Facts:

5–024   The two plaintiffs, Unigrain and Van der Valk, had each purchased consignments of a little over 200 tonnes of Argentine linseed expellers, and were holders of bills of lading in respect of these consignments. Their cargo was part of an undivided bulk, being mixed also with other consignments of Argentine linseed expellers, destined for other receivers.

The trial was conducted without oral evidence or full discovery, so that the facts found were rather sparse, but it seems that the vessel called at various ports *en route*, where some of the bulk was discharged in favour of other buyers. It seems that there was over-discharge, because when the vessel arrived (at Rotterdam) there was insufficient cargo left aboard to satisfy the plaintiffs' bills of lading. Only 11,550 kilos was discharged in favour of Van der Valk, and none at all in favour of Unigrain.

Decision and comment:

Both plaintiffs sued the carrier, and lost. Various grounds were advanced, Van der Valk bringing a claim based on s.1 of the 1855 Act. Their problem was that property in their part of the undivided bulk cargo could not pass to them until division of the bulk at discharge (this is no longer a problem in the light of the Carriage of Goods by Sea Act 1992). Until then it was not ascertained, and property could not therefore pass by virtue of the Sale of Goods Act 1979, s.16. Van der Valk therefore failed (because the passing of property was insufficiently closely connected with the transfer of the bill of lading).

Unigrain did not even attempt to advance an argument based on s.1 in *The Aramis*, facing as they did the additional difficulty that none of their cargo at all was discharged. Hence, they never obtained any property in any of the cargo.

Notes

1. This case differs from *The Elafi*, where all the cargo that remained aboard was   5–025
destined for the *same* buyer, so that it could be said to have been ascertained by process of exhaustion. Here, even after the over-discharge had occurred *en route*, there were two rival claims, and the remaining cargo could not be said to belong to Van der Valk, rather than Unigrain, until discharge had taken place at Rotterdam. It is essentially like *The Elafi* would have been in the example used by Mustill J., had Frank Fehr not resold their part of the cargo to the claimants; clearly then no property could have passed.

2. The above discussion applies only to **undivided** bulks. If an entire bulk cargo is sold to a single buyer (as often happens with oil cargoes—*e.g. The Jambur* in para. 2—020, above), the cargo is ascertained and the principles discussed below, on ascertaining the parties' intention, apply. Similarly if the cargo is divided, for example by being carried in a number of holds, if the whole of the cargo in the same hold is destined for the same buyer, the cargo is ascertained.

3. The main importance of this case concerns *Brandt v Liverpool* contracts, and it is considered in detail in para. 13—056, below.

(e) EQUITABLE PROPERTY

The Sale of Goods Act provisions described above determine when property   5–026
passes at common law. They do not expressly determine whether property in part of an undivided bulk might pass in equity. It might be supposed, then, that a buyer can argue that he is owner in equity, whatever the common law position, as determined by the Sale of Goods Act.

RE WAIT

Court of Appeal. [1927] 1 Ch. 606

After the buyer had paid for part of a bulk cargo of wheat, purchased   5–027
c.i.f., the seller went bankrupt. In order not to lose both money and goods

to the seller's trustee in bankruptcy, he tried to claim equitable property in the goods.

Held:
The buyer failed because he had no property in the goods.

Notes
   1. The case was approved by the House of Lords in *Leigh & Sillavan Ltd v Aliakman Shipping Co Ltd (The Aliakmon)*—see para. 13—072, below. In the later case Lord Brandon thought it extremely doubtful that the concept of equitable ownership has any application to an ordinary contract of sale. The later case is of more general application than *Re Wait*, because it did not involve a bulk cargo. *Re Wait* was also approved by the Privy Council in *Re Goldcorp Exchange* [1995] 1 A.C. 74.
   2. *The Aliakmon* involved an attempt by a c. & f. buyer to sue a shipowner in tort. Property had not passed to the buyer, because of an express reservation of title clause under s.19(1) of the Sale of Goods Act, but the buyer argued that he had equitable title, and that that was sufficient to provide a cause of action. Lord Brandon disagreed on both issues.

LORD BRANDON'S SPEECH IN THE ALIAKMON

[1986] A.C. 785

5–028   My Lords, . . . counsel for the buyers put forward two propositions of law. The first proposition was that a person who has the equitable ownership of goods is entitled to sue in tort for negligence anyone who by want of care causes them to be lost or damaged without joining the legal owner as a party to the action. The second proposition was that a buyer who agrees to buy goods in circumstances where, although ascertained goods have been appropriated to the contract, their legal ownership remains in the seller acquires on such appropriation the equitable ownership of the goods. Applying those two propositions to the facts of the present case, counsel for the buyers submitted that the goods the subject matter of the c & f contract had been appropriated to the contract on or before shipment at Inchon, and that from then on, while the legal ownership of the goods remained in the sellers, the buyers became the equitable owners of them, and could therefore sue the shipowners in tort for negligence for the damage done to them without joining the sellers.
   In my view, the first proposition cannot be supported. There may be cases where a person who is the equitable owner of certain goods has also a possessory title to them. In such a case he is entitled, by virtue of his possessory title rather than his equitable ownership, to sue in tort for negligence anyone whose want of care has caused loss of or damage to the goods without joining the legal owner as a party to the action: see, for instance, *Healey v Healey* [1915] 1 K.B. 938. If, however, the person is the equitable owner of the goods and no more, then he must join the legal owner as a party to the action, either as co-plaintiff if he is willing or as co-defendant if he is not. This has always been the law in the field of

equitable ownership of land and I see no reason why it should not also be so in the field of equitable ownership of goods.

With regard to the second proposition, I do not doubt that it is possible, in accordance with established equitable principles, for equitable interests in goods to be created and to exist. It seems to me, however, extremely doubtful whether equitable interests in goods can be created or exist within the confines of an ordinary contract of sale. The Sale of Goods Act 1893, which must be taken to apply to the c & f contract of sale in the present case, is a complete code of law in respect of contracts for the sale of goods. The passing of the property in goods the subject matter of such a contract is fully dealt with in ss.16 to 19 of the Act (now ss.16 to 19 of the Sale of Goods Act 1979). Those sections draw no distinction between the legal and the equitable property in goods, but appear to have been framed on the basis that the expression "property", as used in them, is intended to comprise both the legal and the equitable title. In this connection I consider that there is much force in the observations of Atkin L.J. in *Re Wait* [1927] 1 Ch. 606 at 635–636, from which I quote only this short passage:

> "It would have been futile in a code intended for commercial men to have created an elaborate structure of rules dealing with rights at law, if at the same time it was intended to leave, subsisting with the legal rights, equitable rights inconsistent with, more extensive, and coming into existence earlier than the rights so carefully set out in the various sections of the Code."

These observations of Atkin L.J. were not necessary to the decision of the case before him and represented a minority view not shared by the other two members of the Court of Appeal. Moreover, Atkin L.J. expressly stated that he was not deciding the point. If my view on the first proposition of law is correct, it is again unnecessary to decide the point in this appeal. I shall, therefore, say no more than that my provisional view accords with that expressed by Atkin L.J. in *Re Wait*.

Notes

1. Since this case, the conclusion on the first proposition has been supported by the Court of Appeal in *MCC Proceeds Inc v Lehman Brothers International (Europe)* [1998] 4 All E.R. 675; [1998] 2 B.C.L.C. 659, and that on the second proposition by the Privy Council in *Re Goldcorp Exchange* [1995] 1 A.C. 74.   **5–029**

2. The first proposition is considered further in chapter 13, below. As for the second, clearly it would be inappropriate, in a case like *The Aliakmon*, where the seller had expressly reserved a right of disposal against payment, for equitable property effectively to defeat that. It is by no means as clear that it should not have a role in resolving bulk undivided cargo problems.

3. It may, however, be assumed that equitable ownership has in fact no significant application in this area of law, and that it is impossible to avoid by this means the common law position described above.

(3) PROPERTY IN SPECIFIC OR ASCERTAINED GOODS: EVIDENCE OF INTENTION

5–030   Where the sale is of specific goods, or once goods are ascertained, the general principle is that property in the goods passes when the parties intend it to pass, guidelines being provided by sections 17–20 of the Sale of Goods Act 1979. The intention of the parties can be difficult to determine, and can vary considerably between different transactions.

DEBATTISTA, CONTRACTS FOR THE SALE OF GOODS CARRIED BY SEA—"THE TRANSFER OF PROPERTY IN THE INTERNATIONAL SALE OF GOODS CARRIED BY SEA"

(2nd ed., Butterworths, 1998), Ch. 5

5–031   It is difficult to over-emphasise the significance of express clauses in the contract of sale determining when ownership is to pass. If the parties have made clear in their contract where they intend property to be transferred, the presumptions set out in the Act for the discernment of their intention become irrelevant. For the present, though, we shall assume that the parties have failed to make their intention clear and that the courts are therefore thrown upon the five presumptions set out in the Act.

Notes

5–032   1. The presumptions mentioned here are the rules in s.18.

2. Obviously, since property depends upon intention, an express clause will carry considerable weight, and will often be conclusive. The assertions in the above passage, however, need to be qualified:

(a) It seems to be fairly rare for sale contracts expressly to state when property is to pass.

(b) There are cases where the courts have held that the seller can unilaterally control the passing of property, it must follow that he can delay its passing, even if it is in breach of the express terms of the sale contract. It has also been held that for the seller to retain a right of disposal, for security purposes only, does not entail a breach of the sale contract, even where under the sale contract property should have already passed. To this extent, therefore, even express terms of the sale contract will certainly not be decisive. It is difficult to square Debattista's remarks with *The San Nicholas*, for example (below).

3. Though s.17 in the terms of the intention of both parties, the rules in s.18 and (more particularly) the presumptions in s.19 depend primarily on the seller's intention alone.

(a) SUMMARY OF LEGAL DEVELOPMENT SINCE 1850

5–033   It is clear from the cases that the passing of property depends on a number of factors, and that bold general statements should be treated with caution.

For example, from the authorities below might be inferred as a starting point, that property f.o.b. passes on actual delivery,[21] to the vessel, whereas property c.i.f. passes on constructive delivery, on tender of documents. Even if this is a justifiable inference, however, it is only a starting point. Where in an f.o.b. contract the documents perform a role similar to that in a c.i.f., property will pass later, as in *The San Nicholas* [1976] 1 Lloyd's Rep. 8 and *The Ciudad de Pasto* [1988] 1 W.L.R. 1145; [1988] 2 Lloyd's Rep. 208 (see below). Conversely, in both *The Albazero* [1977] A.C. 774, [1975] 3 W.L.R. 491 and *The Delfini* [1990] 1 Lloyd's Rep. 252, (see below) property passed before tender of documents in a c.i.f. contract, where the documents were not being used for their traditional security function. It is necessary to look at all the relevant facts, and beware of broad generalisations.

There follows a framework, a personal view of mine of course, intended to place the cases in some kind of context.

Early Cases

The delivery point for the early f.o.b. contract, described at the start of chapter 1, above, was shipment, to the buyer's floating warehouse, and there was a very strong presumption that both risk and property passed then (see, for example, *Cowas-Jee v Thompson* (1845) 3 Moore Ind. App. 422; 18 E.R. 560, in para. 1—007, above).

On the assumption that the seller was contractually obliged to transfer property on shipment, the courts were initially reluctant to infer an intention to transfer later (see *Browne v Hare* (1858) 3 H. & N. 484; 4 H. & N. 822; 157 E.R. 1067, and perhaps also *The Parchim* [1918] A.C. 157, below).[22] However, acts by the seller which were clearly inconsistent with an intention to pass property were effective to retain it, of to transfer it to a third party, as in *Wait v Baker* (1848) 2 Ex. 1, set out more fully below. In reaching this conclusion, however, a great deal of emphasis seems to have been placed on the physical control of the bill of lading (*Shepherd v Harrison* (1871) L.R. 5 H.L. 116, which was codified as s.19(3) of the Sale of Goods Act (see chapter 8, below); *The Parchim*; *The Kronprinsessan Margareta* [1921] 1 A.C. 486). Except in *The Parchim*, no distinction has been drawn in these cases between f.o.b. and c.i.f. contracts, and of course the physical delivery point is no different. In none of the cases (except possibly *The Kronprinsessan Margareta*) were modern methods of international finance adopted, and there is no reason to suppose that, in the unlikely event that similar facts occurred today, each would be decided any differently today.

The reasoning in *Mirabita v Imperial Ottoman Bank* (1878) 3 Ex. D. 164, by **5—034** contrast, depends (at least at face value) on the form of the bill of lading, rather than its physical retention. It is also assumed by the Court of Appeal that merely to retain security against payment is not a breach of contract by the seller, even if the contract provides for property to pass on shipment. Therefore, there is less need for any reluctance to hold that property passes after shipment.[23] The inference was drawn (later to be codified as s.19(2) of the Sale of Goods Act) that from reserving the bill of lading to his order could be inferred an intention to retain title against payment, a conditional appropriation, in other words. Once the condition had occurred (in this case, tender of the price by the buyer) property passed, without the need for further intervention on the part of the seller. *Mirabita* was applied in *The San Nicholas*, and the reasoning in *The Filiatra Legacy* [1991] 2 Lloyd's Rep. 337 has obvious similarities. *Mirabita* was effectively the origin of the

---

[21] With the original f.o.b. contract, considered in Ch. 3, above, the bill of lading would have been issued to the buyer, and there would have been no constructive delivery.

[22] Note that similar reasoning need not apply c.i.f., since although the physical delivery point is the same, constructive delivery is postponed until tender of documents.

[23] It also became clear in *Inglis v Stock*, considered in para. 4—005, above, that an f.o.b. seller was not necessarily in breach merely because property did not pass on shipment.

two meanings of appropriation; whereas contractual appropriation, preventing the seller from selling the goods elsewhere, might take place on physical delivery, the seller could retain property as security against payment until a later time, such as transfer of documents, or tender of payment.

The courts did not initially fully embrace *Mirabita*, which was distinguished in *The Parchim*, primarily on the grounds that in *The Parchim*, the seller did not retain physical control over the bill of lading. The Parchim was in turn distinguished, on essentially the same grounds, in *The Kronprinsessan Margareta* a few years later, and has since come to be regarded as an exceptional case, not of general application. The reasoning in *The Parchim*, at least in general terms, was that since risk in what was regarded as an f.o.b. contract passed on shipment, it would take fairly strong evidence to infer an intention to pass property later. Retention of title after shipment, simply to secure the price should not be lightly inferred, since the seller is adequately protected by the unpaid seller's lien.

The Lien Argument

5–035 The unpaid seller's lien is regulated by the Sale of Goods Act 1979, ss.38–47, which are set out in Appendix A. It can be seen from s.39 that it gives a right of withholding delivery, even though property has passed to the buyer, and a right of re-sale. However, under s.43(1)(a), the lien terminates when the seller "delivers the goods to a carrier . . . for the purpose of transmission to the buyer without reserving the right of disposal of the goods." Thereafter the seller has only the right of stoppage in transit, which continues to protect him against an insolvent buyer. However, it protects only against the buyer's insolvency, and of course lasts only during transit. If transit continues until discharge, since the buyer should only be able to obtain the bill of lading against payment, there is a case for taking the view that the lien and right of stoppage provide the seller with adequate security. However, *Cowas-Jee v Thompson* (in chapter 1) suggests that this may not always be the case. There the Privy Council held that after delivery to the f.o.b. buyer's floating warehouse the goods were no longer in transit; for this variety of f.o.b. contract, therefore, neither lien or stoppage in transit will protect an unpaid seller after shipment.

Development of Modern International Finance

5–036 During the 1920s and 1930s, it became more common to finance international sales by documentary credit (see chapter 7, below). This affected the property debate in two ways, which pulled against each other (and both strands of reasoning remain extant today). First, it is argued that the bank needs to obtain from the seller a special property in the goods as pledgee. This will happen only if the seller has not before tender to the bank passed all property to the buyer. This argues against property passing on shipment, and against the reasoning in *The Parchim*. The argument has gained widespread acceptance.

The second line of reasoning is that only the intentions of seller and buyer are taken into account in the Sale of Goods Act, not that of the bank. From the viewpoint of the seller, he can look to payment from a first class bank, and therefore does not need to retain title against payment. There is therefore no reason why property should pass after shipment. This second argument, which is directly contrary to the first, did not find favour at all until recently, but has gained currency in a narrow class of case. It will be considered below.

Effect of Documentary Credit on Passing of Property

5–037 Where payment is by documentary credit, the bank is best protected if property passes on tender of the shipping documents, against which the seller will be paid.

In *Ross T Smyth & Co Ltd v TD Bailey Son & Co* [1940] 3 All E.R. 60, below, Lord Wright observed that:

"In general . . . , the importance of the retention of the property is not only to secure payment from the buyer but for purposes of finance. The general course of international commerce involves the practice of raising money on the documents so as to bridge the period between shipment and the time of obtaining payment against documents. . . . The general property in the goods must be in the seller if he is to be able to pledge them. The whole system of commercial credits depends on the seller's ability to give a charge on the goods and the policies of insurance. A mere unpaid seller's lien would, for obvious reasons, be inadequate and unsatisfactory."

In his view, for a c.i.f. sale at least, final appropriation (to pass property) does not generally take place until indorsement. He admits that there might be exceptional cases, such as *The Parchim*, but these are not of general application. Gone is the reluctance to infer retention of property after shipment, not because of the needs of the seller, but because of those of international finance.

He does not explain why the lien would be inadequate and unsatisfactory for reasons which are "obvious", but a similar view is taken by the editors of Benjamin's *Sale of Goods* (5th ed.), page 1133, para. 18–156[24]:

"The suggestion[25] that such a seller has adequate security for the payment of the price by reason of his rights of lien or stoppage in transit has not been accepted by the courts; and their refusal to accept it is based on a realistic appreciation of modern methods of financing overseas sales. A bank willing to advance money on the security of property in goods would be much less ready to accept the somewhat perilous security of the rights of lien or stoppage.[26] These rights may be useful, in the last resort, when other methods of securing payment have failed; but it is unlikely that a bank (or consequently a seller wanting to raise money on the security of shipping documents) would intend to rely solely on them. In overseas sales, there is, therefore, a fairly strong presumption that the seller does not intend to part with property until he has either been paid or been given an adequate assurance of payment."[27]

Again, the obvious weaknesses of the lien and right of stoppage are not explained. Perhaps those identified above are sufficient. More probably, the bank will not normally be able to use the lien, not being a seller. Thus, s.38(2) provides:

"In this Part of this Act 'seller' includes any person who is in the position of a seller, as, for instance, an agent of the seller to whom the bill of lading has been indorsed, or a consignor or agent who has himself paid (or is directly responsible for) the price."

This would not normally include a bank under a documentary credit, who will ultimately be the agent of the buyer not the seller (so that the lien will terminate

[24] This passage is unchanged since at least as far back as the 3rd edition.
[25] The note in the original refers to *The Parchim*.
[26] The authors cite, among other authorities, *Arnhold Karberg*, and *Smyth v Bailey*, but contrast *Sale Continuation Ltd v Austin Taylor & Co* [1968] 2 Q.B. 849, where property had passed earlier—the bank went into liquidation, and the authors cryptically note (in one of the few jokes in Benjamin): "Perhaps the fate of the bank suggests that this was not good business practice."
[27] The authors cite, among other authorities, *The Ciudad de Pasto* [1988] 1 W.L.R. 1145, 1153 (and see below) and *The Ines* [1995] 2 Lloyd's Rep. 144, 156.

under s.43(1)(b)). Even if the bank were (unusually) agent for the seller, the lien does not apply to credit sales by virtue of s.41(1), unless the buyer becomes insolvent; this will not necessarily adequately protect the bank.

Sassoon argues (paras. 571ff) that the unpaid seller's lien is sufficient even where payment is by documentary credit, because the seller can pass a title to the bank, even if he has parted with property, by virtue of s.24 of the Sale of Goods Act 1979:

> "Where a person having sold goods continues or is in possession of the goods, or of the documents of title to the goods, the delivery or transfer by that person, or by a mercantile agent acting for him, of the goods or documents of title under any sale, pledge, or other disposition thereof, to any person receiving the same in good faith and without notice of the previous sale, has the same effect as if the person making the delivery or transfer were expressly authorised by the owner of the goods to make the same."

However, surely the bank would normally know of the previous sale (it is, after all, the sale that they are financing), thereby rendering the section inapplicable.

It seems, therefore, that Lord Wright was correct in *Smyth v Bailey* to reject the view that the lien provides adequate protection. Certainly his approach seems to be the one usually adopted, however, at any rate for c.i.f. contracts.

Contrary arguments:

5–038

1. Banks do not always demand security of property. One reason for this is that even if the bank does not obtain legal title on tender of documents, it will usually only release the documents on the terms that the buyer constitutes himself trustee of the goods for the bank. Thereafter, at least, the bank will be adequately protected by its equitable property as beneficiary under the trust. In *Sale Continuation Ltd v Austin Taylor & Co Ltd* [1968] 2 Q.B. 849, for example, property passed from seller to buyer before the documents were pledged, so that the bank could not have obtained a possessory title as pledgee (property passed on shipment by express clause in the sale contract).[28] However, the documents were later released to an agent of the seller against a trust receipt the effect of which was expressly to constitute the agent trustee of the goods for the bank. The second transaction, creating a trust of property that had already passed, was not in any way dependent on the original pledge, so the bank could obtain equitable title under the trust even though it had obtained no legal title under the pledge. Consequently, the bank's possessory title will often only be of importance for a relatively short time (*i.e.* between tender of documents and the time that they are released to the buyer). See further chapter 7, below.

2. The position of the bank is ignored under the Sale of Goods Act provisions, and if the seller knows that he is to be paid, it is arguable that he should not need to reserve property. In other words, you could argue that payment by documentary credit is a good ground for holding that property passes on shipment. An early expression of such a view can be found in *The Kronprinsessan Margareta* (below). Lord Sumner observed:

---

[28] Property passed on shipment by virtue of an express clause in the sale contract: [1968] 2 Q.B. 849, 855E; [1967] 2 Lloyd's Rep. 403, 406 (col. 2). The bank went into liquidation, and the editors of Benjamin's *Sale of Goods* observe (presumably tongue in cheek): " . . . the bank appears to have accepted pledge of documents from the seller after the property had passed to the buyer. Perhaps the fate of the bank suggests that this was not good business practice": Benjamin, *Sale of Goods* (5th ed.), para. 18–156, n. 96.

"It is said that, as a matter of business, the confirmed credit relieved the consignors of all further concern in the goods, for they could have no doubt that they would be paid by the bank in any event and that the failure to insure is proof positive of this."

In the event, however, property passed on indorsement, Lord Sumner taking the view that the bank had not in fact given the benefit of any enforceable undertaking to the consignor, so that in other words there was no irrevocable or confirmed credit in existence. In any case, he said, payment by documentary credit is no more than indirect evidence of the intention of the parties under s.17:

"The special circumstance of the existence of a confirmed banker's credit . . . is only indirectly relevant. It no doubt enhances the likelihood that the bills of lading will eventually be taken up and the goods be paid for, and so diminishes the importance to the seller of being still able to say that the goods are his, but it is not direct evidence of intention; it is only a reason why a particular intention is more likely to have been formed in such a case than in others. The intention has still to be inferred . . . "

On the other hand, given that the only relevant intention is that of the parties under the sale contract, there is a certain logic in the view that if the seller knows that he is going to be paid by a reputable bank, there is less need for him to reserve a right of disposal. If property passes before tender of documents that may well prejudice the security of the bank, but that is arguably not the concern of the parties to the sale contract. (This argument is dealt with further below.)

3. It is a feature of property that it affects third parties, here the bank. There is a good argument that the timing of its passing should not depend (as in fact it does) entirely on the intentions of the parties to the sale contract.

A summary of the law today

As will be seen in *Ginzberg*, and *The Albazero*, Lord Wright's view in *Smyth v Bailey* that property c.i.f. generally passes on indorsement has gained wide acceptance. Moreover, *Ginzberg* in no way depends on control being retained by the seller, since he did not have the bill of lading, and positively facilitated delivery of the goods to the buyer. **5–039**

Nor does any distinction appear generally to be drawn between f.o.b. and c.i.f. contracts; where the documents are used to perform the same function, passing of property is delayed until indorsement and payment, just as with c.i.f. (see *The San Nicholas* and *The Ciudad de Pasto*, both of which concerned f.o.b. contracts).

However, s.19(2) creates only a presumption, even where bills of lading are taken to seller's order. The evidence may suggest that they are retained for a reason other than to secure payment, as in *The Albazero*. There, they were retained to allow flexibility of distribution within a group of companies; once they were posted, they were no longer capable of fulfilling this role, and therefore property was not retained beyond that time.

Recent cases also see the resurgence of the argument that if the seller is guaranteed payment by a first class banker, he need not retain title, so that the presumption in s.19(2) is rebutted. This argument has generally been rejected in documentary credit cases (see *The Glenroy* [1945] A.C. 124 and *The Ciudad de Pasto*), but has found favour with standby letters of credit, where the bank has in any case relinquished any property security in the goods, and the bill of lading is not required to trigger the payment mechanism.

(b) Early Cases and Cases Establishing General Principles

5–040 Because in the early cases it was assumed that an f.o.b. seller would be in breach of contract in retaining property after shipment, this inference was not lightly drawn. However, the Court of Appeal took the view in *Mirabita v Imperial Ottoman Bank* that it was not a breach of contract merely to retain property against payment. It also became clear in *Inglis v Stock*, considered in chapter 3, above, that an f.o.b. seller was not necessarily in breach merely because property did not pass on shipment. Nonetheless, the reluctance to postpone passing of property, especially for f.o.b. contracts, continued to be shown in *The Parchim*, contrasting with a more modern view, a few years later, in *The Kronprinsessan Margareta*.

Browne v Hare demonstrates the reluctance of the courts to infer an intention to pass property after shipment, on the grounds that this would be a breach of contract by the seller. *Wait v Baker* shows that the inference can be drawn, however, if the bill of lading is dealt with in a manner which is clearly inconsistent with an intention to pass property. It may be that the correct analysis of *Wait v Baker*, though, is that the sellers never appropriated the property to the contract.

BROWNE v HARE

Exchequer Chamber. (1858) 3 H. & N. 484, 4 H. & N. 822; 157 E.R. 1067

Decision:

5–041 Property (and hence risk, which was the real issue in the case) was held to pass on shipment f.o.b., although the bill of lading was made deliverable "unto shipper's order." *Wait v Baker* (1848) 2 Exch. 1 was distinguished.

Note

There seems to have been an assumption that property and risk would pass at the same time, and indeed, that if the seller had reserved title after shipment that would have constituted a breach of contract (*e.g.* the following statement, at p. 498):

> "If, at the time the oil was shipped at Rotterdam, the plaintiffs had intended to continue their ownership, and had taken the bill of lading in the terms in which it was made for the purpose of continuing the ownership and exercising dominion over the oil, they would in our opinion have broken their contract to ship the oil 'free on board,' and the property would not have passed to the defendants; but if when they shipped the oil they intended to perform their contract and deliver it 'free on board' for the defendants, we think they did perform it, and the property in the oil passed from them to the defendants."

Obviously, strong evidence would be required to infer an intention on the seller to break the sale contract, but this view about the passing of property (that an f.o.b. seller is necessarily in breach if he reserves title after shipment) must be revised in the light of later cases, and in particular *Mirabita v Ottoman Bank*, which suggests the possibility of conditional appropriation. It is also clear that in appropriate circumstances, the necessary intention will be inferred.

The risk aspects of *Browne v Hare* are not open to objection, however, and were applied in *Inglis v Stock*, (see chapter 4, above) where property could not have passed by the time the goods were lost, because the goods were part of an unascertained bulk.

WAIT v BAKER

Exchequer (Parke B.). (1848) 2 Ex. 1; 154 E.R. 380

Facts and issues:

An f.o.b. seller of barley (who also appears to have shipped the goods, **5–042** although possibly as agent for the defendant buyer) took bills of lading to his own order, and after a dispute with the defendant over the quality of the barley, indorsed the bills to the plaintiffs, having refused the defendant's tender of money. The market had risen considerably.

When the vessel arrived, the defendant (without production of the bills) obtained some of the cargo, and the plaintiffs successfully sued in trover; property had never passed to the defendant.

Notes:

1. Here, then, the seller unilaterally prevented property passing to the purchaser.

2. This was not a contract for specific goods, but could be satisfied by the delivery of any cargo satisfying the contractual description, and the seller, not having indorsed the bill of lading in his favour, had not appropriated the goods to the contract in order to pass property to the defendant.

3. The seller was not party to the action, and it was not clear whether the seller had broken the f.o.b. contract of sale, although presumably he had, delivery having been made to a third party. In *Browne v Hare* (above) it was clearly assumed not only that the seller in *Wait v Baker* was in breach of contract, but also that it would generally be a breach of an f.o.b. contract for the seller to reserve title after delivery to the ship. This view is now difficult to support: see especially Staughton L.J.'s remarks in *The Ciudad de Pasto*, below.

4. *Wait v Baker* was distinguished in *Mirabita v Ottoman Bank*, where property was held to have passed on the tender of the price by the buyers—the distinction appears to have been that there the seller reserved title merely to secure the price, whereas here there was never any appropriation of any goods at all to the f.o.b. contract.

SHEPHERD v HARRISON

House of Lords. (1871) L.R. 5 H.L. 116

Bills of lading for a consignment of cotton were retained by agents of the **5–043** sellers, and one of the bills of lading, together with a bill of exchange for the price of the cotton, was sent to the purchasers, Shepherd, upon whom the bill of exchange was drawn. Shepherd, disputing the quality of the cotton, refused to accept the draft. It was held that property had not passed to him, and that the carriers should not deliver the cotton to him (the sellers having interposed prior to delivery). The sellers had retained property by retaining control of the bill of lading, although risk was said to have passed to Shepherd on shipment. Property would only pass to Shepherd conditionally upon his acceptance of the draft.

The decision was codified in s.19(3) of the Sale of Goods Act (on which see further chapter 8, below). For present purposes, the importance of the case lies in the seller's ability to control the passing of property by the physical retention of the bill.

5–044   LORD WESTBURY: ... [The sellers] shipped the cotton on board the Olinda—I am speaking of the 200 bales—and when they delivered the cotton to the captain of the Olinda, they took from him the ordinary bill of lading to their own order.

Now, what was the effect of that transaction in law and according to mercantile usage? The effect was this—that they controlled the possession of the captain, and made the captain accountable to deliver the cotton to the holder of the bill of lading. The bill of lading was the symbol of property, and by taking the bill of lading they kept to themselves the right of dealing with the property shipped on board the vessel. They also kept to themselves the right of demanding possession from the captain. They had, therefore, all the incidents of property vested in themselves. Now, that was by no means inconsistent with the special terms of the shipment, namely, that the cotton was shipped on account of and at the risk of the buyers. That is perfectly consistent with the property, as evidenced by the bill of lading, remaining in the possession of the vendors of the cotton in question.

Then, if that be so, it is incumbent on the buyer to adduce circumstances to control the legal effect of that transaction, and to shew that the evidence of ownership and of the right to deal with the property consequent on the authority of the bill of lading, are controlled by other facts, and that it was not intended to retain the right of possession, and the interest in the property shipped, and the right of disposing of it, in the holder of the bill of lading. Undoubtedly the obligation to shew this lies upon the individual who contradicts what would otherwise be the ordinary legal conclusion from that transaction.

[*Lord Westbury reviewed the facts and concluded that Shepherd never obtained property in the cotton.*]

Note
The House clearly recognised the possibility that property and risk might pass at different times. See further also *Inglis v Stock* in para. 4—005, above.

MIRABITA v IMPERIAL OTTOMAN BANK

Court of Appeal. (1878) 3 Ex. D. 164

Facts:
5–045   Phatsea & Pappa (P & P) sold goods to the plaintiff (Mirabita), taking a bill of lading to their own order. A bill of exchange was presented to the plaintiff, who declined to accept it except only against the bill of lading, which was not tendered to him. P & P then drew a second bill of exchange, and tendered it with the bill of lading to the defendant, who discounted the bill of exchange. Eventually both bill of lading and bill of

exchange were tendered to Mirabita, who were prepared to pay the bill on maturity,[29] but not to accept the bill. Later Mirabita tendered full payment. The defendants refused to give up the bill of lading to enable the plaintiff to claim the goods from the warehouse into which they had been put (in the defendant's name). The plaintiff successfully sued for conversion. The sole issue was whether the property in the goods had passed to the plaintiff.

Held:

The Court of Appeal held that property had passed to the plaintiff in spite of the bill of lading being taken to the order of the sellers. The intention was to pass the property (with the risk) on shipment, subject only to the condition that the plaintiff paid the price. The plaintiff, by tendering the price, had satisfied the condition, and therefore the property had passed. *Wait v Baker* was distinguished on the grounds that there:

> "the vendor originally took the bill of lading to order, and kept it in his possession, to deal with as he thought fit, and never intended that the property should pass until he handed the bill of lading to the vendee on such terms as he choose to exact."

If in *Mirabita* the sellers had resold the cargo to a third party before the plaintiff had tendered the price, it seems to have been accepted that property would have passed to the third party, although this would have been a breach by the sellers of the sale contract. This was not the situation in the case itself, and indeed the sellers were not in breach of contract in *Mirabita*.

Notes

The following passage in Cotton L.J.'s judgment was cited in *Smyth & Co v* **5–046**
Bailey & Co as the foundation for s.19(2) of the Sale of Goods Act (see further below):

> "If, however, the vendor, when shipping the articles which he intends to deliver under the contract, takes the bill of lading to his own order, and does so not as agent or on behalf of the purchaser, but on his own behalf, it is held that he thereby reserves to himself a power of disposing of the property, and that consequently there is no final appropriation, and the property does not on shipment pass to the purchasers."

The emphasis in *Mirabita* is on the form of the bill of lading, rather than the physical control (since, after all, the bill of lading was not, in the end, handed to the plaintiff). It is important for the view that for a seller merely to retain property against payment is not a breach of contract, even where delivery is on shipment. It surely follows from this that presumptions against property being retained ought to be weaker. It also introduces the notion of conditional appropriation, which can pass property once the condition is triggered, without the need for any further intervention on the part of the seller. To this extent the case appears to be

---

[29] It was a 60-day time draft.

inconsistent with the view expressed by Bools, that property cannot pass without an unconditional appropriation—here the only appropriation was conditional, but property passed when the condition was satisfied, without further intervention on the seller's behalf.

Mirabita led to the enactment of s.19(2) (on which see further below) and the presumption that the seller intended to retain property where the bill of lading was taken to his own order.

Conclusions so far:

5–047
1. There is a presumption with an f.o.b. contract that property and risk pass on delivery, on shipment.

2. However, even where a contract envisages that property will pass on shipment, the seller will not necessarily be in breach if he retains title after shipment, as long as it is only as security. It would however be a breach for the seller to deliver the goods, which have on shipment been contractually/conditionally appropriated to the contract, to a third party.

3. Where the bill of lading is taken to the order of the seller, there is a presumption that he retains a right of disposal. This presumption has now been given a statutory basis, and would appear to apply equally to an f.o.b. as to a c.i.f contract.

4. There might also be cases where the seller retains property through retention of physical control of the bill of lading.

Further developments:

Nonetheless, the courts continued, at any rate for a time, to apply a strong presumption that for f.o.b. contracts, at any rate, property passed on shipment, the seller being adequately protected thereafter by his lien. The notion that the seller might deprive himself of the possibility of dealing with the goods contrary to his contract with the buyer (*i.e.* have appropriated the goods contractually), while nevertheless retaining property as security, did not immediately find favour. In *Mirabita*, and in other cases where property had been retained after shipment, the seller had arguably retained control of the bill of lading, so as to enable him to transfer the property to a third party, should he so wish. In *The Parchim* he did not. In the following two cases, the physical dealings with the bill were of paramount importance in the passing of property. *The Parchim* is the last case, however, where the courts display a clear reluctance to pass property after shipment, whether the contract be truly classified as f.o.b. or c.i.f.

THE PARCHIM

Privy Council. [1918] A.C. 157

Facts and issues:

5–048
The case concerned a shipment from a German to a Dutch company during the First World War. The cargo was seized by the British Government as Prize. If the goods had still been German owned the seizure would have been lawful, and Prize law prevents property passing from enemy to neutral at sea. The Dutch company had paid for the goods, and therefore had to show that property had passed on shipment.

The issue was when property passed under a contract which though described as c.i.f., had more of the characteristics of an f.o.b. contract (only cost and charterparty freight—not insurance—being included in the price). As Lord Parker observed at pp. 163–164:

"This . . . is not an ordinary c.i.f. contract. The insurance is separately provided for and the premium is not included in the price, and, although the price includes freight, it is only the freight under the charterparty which the buyer is to take over. If the right to cancel that charterparty arises and the option to do so is exercised, the buyer has the responsibility of finding another ship to take the intended cargo. He has to pay any excess of freight over the chartered freight; also he has to pay the storage for the nitrate until loaded on another vessel. As the sum included for freight in the price is a mere matter of calculation and would be payable separately by the buyer and deducted from the price, the price is really for cost only, and the contract has far more of the characteristics of a contract f.o.b. Taltal than it has of a contract c.i.f. European port."

[See further chapter 3, above, on the distinguishing features of these types of contract.]

Bills of lading were taken to sellers' order, and payment was not due until 90 days after sight; the sellers' bank held on to them until payment.

Held:

In these circumstances Lord Parker of Waddington held that property in the goods had passed with risk on shipment, so the seizure was unlawful. He said (at 171) that where:

"the seller deals with the bill of lading only to secure the contract price, and not with the intention of withdrawing the goods from the contract [as in *Wait v Baker*], he does nothing inconsistent with an intention to pass the property, and therefore the property may pass either forthwith subject to the seller's lien or conditionally on performance by the buyer of his part of the contract".

He also said that where the seller was sufficiently protected by the lien the inference that property would pass only conditionally upon payment by the buyer was necessarily weak, and easily rebutted. [*Lien arguments are discussed above.*]

LORD PARKER OF WADDINGTON (at 170 *et. seq.*): The English cases, how-   **5–049**
ever, on which the Sale of Goods Act was founded seem to show that the appropriation would not be such as to pass the property if it appears or can be inferred that there was no actual intention to pass it. If the seller takes the bill of lading to his own order and parts with it to a third person, not the buyer, and that third person, by possession of the bill of lading, gets the goods, the buyer is held not to have the property so as to enable him to recover from the third party, notwithstanding that the act of the seller was a clear breach of the contract: *Wait v Baker* . . . This seems to be because the seller's conduct is inconsistent with any intention to pass the

property to the buyer by means of the contract followed by the appropriation. On the other hand, if the seller deals with the bill of lading only to secure the contract price, and not with the intention of withdrawing the goods from the contract, he does nothing inconsistent with an intention to pass the property, and therefore the property may pass either forthwith subject to the seller's lien or conditionally on performance by the buyer of his part of the contract: *Mirabita v Imperial Ottoman Bank* . . . *Browne v Hare* . . . The *prima facie* presumption in such a case appears to be that the property is to pass only on the performance by the buyer of his part of the contract and not forthwith subject to the seller's lien. Inasmuch, however, as the object to be attained, namely, securing the contract price, may be attained by the seller merely reserving a lien, the inference that the property is to pass on the performance of a condition only is necessarily somewhat weak, and may be rebutted by the other circumstances of the case.

Having regard to the doctrine that the master of a ship who gives to the shipper of goods a bill of lading becomes bailee of the goods to the person indicated by the bill of lading, a seller holding a bill of lading to his order would have a sufficient possession of the goods to maintain his lien, even if he had on shipment parted with the property. The seller in such a case makes the ship (even if it belongs to the buyer or is chartered by him) his warehouse so far as these goods are concerned, and the case, as pointed out by Pollock C.B. in *Browne v Hare*, is to be governed by the same rules as that of a person contracting to buy goods in a warehouse of the seller where they are to remain until paid for, so that the seller retains a lien. They may or may not become the buyer's property before he pays for them, according to the terms of the contract. . . .

Their Lordships have come to the conclusion, after carefully considering all the facts, that it was the intention of the parties to the contract that the property in the cargo should pass to the buyer upon shipment, but that the buyer was not intended to have possession of the cargo, or of the bills of lading which represented the cargo, until actual payment at due date of the purchase price. With the exception of the form of the bills of lading, everything points to this conclusion. The contract is for the sale of the whole cargo of a named ship. On shipment, or at any rate on notification of shipment, the cargo is at the risk of the buyer, who has to pay for it whether it arrives or not. The cargo is to be insured for buyer's account and benefit and insured at its arrived value, including profit, which the buyer alone could make. The buyer takes over the charterparty and names the port of discharge. The only matter which seems to point to an intention not to pass the property on shipment is the form in which the bills of lading were taken. But this form was determined by the seller's agent without knowledge of the contract, and though it may have been determined on general instructions from his principal, without particular instructions given in view of the particular contract. The way in which the seller subsequently deals with the bills of lading points rather to a desire to support his lien than to a desire to retain the property or any *jus disponendi* incident to the property. As soon as the bills of lading arrive in Europe he places them at the buyer's disposal, subject only to payment of the purchase price at due date. As soon as this is done he loses the possibility of withdrawing them from the contract, even if otherwise he could have done so. Under these circumstances the form of the bills of lading is, in their Lordships' opinion, quite insufficient to displace the strong inference of an intention to pass the property on shipment arising from the terms of the contract and the other facts.

Notes

1. The basic presumption here is that property passes with risk, on shipment, **5–050** and that the seller's security is not to reserve property but possession. The basis for distinguishing *The Mirabita* appears to have been that the bank in *The Parchim* held the bills of lading "as it were, *in medio*", whereas the bank in *Mirabita* was acting clearly for the sellers. There was also no realistic possibility of substituting other goods (or buyers) in *The Parchim*.

2. For c.i.f. contracts at any rate, the notion that the seller is adequately protected by the lien has not generally found favour, as this is thought not to accord banks adequate protection under a documentary credit—see further *Ross T Smyth v Bailey*, and the discussion below. The contract in *The Parchim* was clearly treated as being f.o.b., however. Perhaps the presumptions operate differently as between f.o.b. and c.i.f. sales. Yet though the shipping documents can be less important f.o.b., in many cases they perform exactly the same function as in c.i.f. sales. In principle, in such cases, the two types should arguably be treated similarly.

3. It should probably not be assumed that *The Parchim* is of general application. In *The Kronprinsessan Margareta*, *The Parchim* was regarded as turning on its own facts—in that case the bill of lading was reserved to the buyer's order, but possession and control over it were retained by the seller. In *The Parchim* it was taken to seller's order, but there was no presumption of retention of title. These two cases place greater emphasis on physical control, than the form of the bill of lading.

THE KRONPRINSESSAN MARGARETA, THE PARANA, AND OTHER SHIPS

Privy Council. [1921] 1 A.C. 486

Facts and issues:
Like *The Parchim*, this was a First World War Prize case, but the contract **5–051** this time was c. & f. This time, to avoid seizure of the goods, the cargo-owners had to argue that property had passed before shipment. This was because of the twin application of the doctrine of infection, a Prize rule which condemns goods owned by the same owner as other goods on board the same vessel which are liable to condemnation, and the doctrine that property in goods cannot move from enemy to neutral while the goods are at sea. Only by showing that property had passed to them prior to shipment, therefore, could they avoid the application of the doctrine of infection.

Held:

The seizure of the goods was lawful. Property had passed after shipment. Even though the bill of lading made the goods deliverable to the order of the purchaser, no intention was thereby shown to pass property before payment. Lord Sumner also regarded *The Parchim* as an exceptional case, and thought it should be virtually limited to its own facts.

5–052   Lord Sumner (at 514 *et seq.*): Now two things are quite plain. The consignors did not propose at any time to rely for payment on the mere personal credit of the consignees, and they carefully kept the bills of lading in their own agents' hands until the draft was met: see *Moakes v Nicholson* 19 C.B. (N.S.) 290. But for the absence of a policy of insurance they strictly pursued the same course of dealing with the documents, as if there had been a c.f. and i. sale.

In these circumstances what can be inferred as to the passing of the general property? What is there to show an intention to pass that property for anything less than payment, and what motive is there for such an intention? The appellants, Messrs. Lundgren & Rollven, have to show that it passed to them and passed, too, before the beginning of the voyage. It if did, then the consignors no longer owned the goods and had nothing to show against them except a draft of their own, which could not be enforced, and a bill of lading, which would not entitle them to delivery of the goods, though its retention might seriously inconvenience the new owners, the consignees. Rights to stop *in transitu* or to exercise an unpaid vendors' lien need hardly be discussed, for, on a question of intention in fact as to which there is a good deal of evidence, it would be artificial to assume that the consignors' minds were actually determined to the contrary by consideration of legal remedies, of which it is not shown that they had any knowledge, let the legal presumption be what it will. It is said that, as a matter of business, the confirmed credit relieved the consignors of all further concern in the goods, for they could have no doubt that they would be paid by the bank in any event and that the failure to insure is proof positive of this. It may be so, though their Lordships do not desire to express any opinion as to the rights of the parties if the coffee were known to be already lost at the time of the presentation of the draft, but it seems clear that the consignors desired to retain an interest in the goods, otherwise why should they retain the bill of lading in their agents' hands? It is said that this only points to an intention to reserve a special property as security, but the omission to insure would be equally significant in this case, and there is no reason why, as a matter of actual intent, a special and not the general property should have been reserved. The case might be very different if the bills of lading had been forwarded to Lundgren & Rollven direct: *Ex parte Banner* (1876) 2 Ch.D. 278. As it is, *Shepherd v Harrison* (1871) L.R. 5 H.L. 116 would surely apply, if on presentation of the bills of lading with the draft there had been a retention of the first without payment of the second. There may be explanations of the shipper's election to be his own insurer of the coffee till the sight draft should be met, but, however this may be, there is nothing to outweigh the significance of a dealing with the documents so nearly identical with that in an ordinary transaction c.f. and i.

No authority was forthcoming which proved to be completely in point.   **5–053** Cases, in which it has been held that taking the bill of lading in the shipper's own name negatives any unconditional appropriation to the buyer by the delivery of the goods on shipboard and indicates one conditional on the documents being taken up, can throw only an indirect light on the question here involved. Certainly no case was found, in which it was held that taking the bill of lading in the buyer's name, while withholding delivery of it until presentation and taking up of the documents, would not be, as an appropriation, equally conditional. Much reliance was placed on *The Parchim* [see above], a case not only decided on very special facts, but on facts so different from those arising in the present appeal as not in any way to rule it. That case did not in any degree substitute the incidence of the risk for the passing of the general property as the test to be applied. There the sellers of the entire cargo of a named ship took the bills of lading to their own order, but it was held that the presumption of an intention to retain the property till something was done by the buyer after shipment was rebutted by the special circumstances of the case. The contract was unusual. It was on cost and freight terms, but was by no means similar to that now under discussion. With the exception of the form of the bills of lading, which itself was determined by the sellers' agent without either particular instructions or actual knowledge of the terms of the contract, everything pointed to the intention that the property should pass to the buyer on shipment, though he was only to have possession of the cargo and of the bills of lading representing it on subsequently paying the price. Special significance was attached to the fact that, on shipment or at least on notification of it, the cargo was to be at the buyer's risk and he had to pay, lost or not lost. Meantime the documents were held by a bank *in medio*, neither to be transferred to the buyers without payment, nor to be placed at the sellers' disposal, unless and until the buyers failed to take them up. Incidentally it may be observed that, although the loading was only completed after the outbreak of war, the interval was short, the shipment was made in pursuance of a contract entered into before the war, and no point was taken on behalf of the captors, even if any arose, as to the passing of property afloat during war from an enemy seller to a neutral buyer by delivery of documents. The case does not purport to lay down any general rule, that a particular mode of dealing with a bill of lading must, whenever it occurs and in whatever circumstances, always prove a particular intention. It is not an authority for the contention, that, if the bill of lading is taken in the buyer's name this necessarily proves that the goods shipped are appropriated to the contract, and delivered to the captain as the buyer's bailee, with a consequent inference of the passing of the property to the buyer on shipment.

In the present case it appears to their Lordships that the retention by the seller of the bill of lading was inconsistent with an intention to pass the property. They think that it was "clearly intended by the consignor to preserve his title to the goods until he did a further act by transferring the bill of lading." The special circumstances of the existence of a confirmed banker's credit in this case is only indirectly relevant. It no doubt enhances the likelihood that the bills of lading will eventually be taken up and the goods be paid for, and so diminishes the importance to the seller of being still able to say that the goods are his, but it is not direct evidence of intention; it is only a reason why a particular intention is more likely to have been formed in such a case than in others. The intention has still to be inferred, principally from what was done and from the communications made with reference to it, and these point to an intention not to pass the property till the drafts were paid, and it is really rather a reason for intending to get the documents presented and taken up as soon as possible, than for an intention not to retain the ownership even until that could be effected. If the seller was paid or was holder of an enforceable contract from a bank for payment, the sooner he passed the property the better, for he was uninsured, but if he was neither he gained nothing by passing the property away. It was not onerous property.

Notes

5–054   1. The argument that property passed prior to shipment was thought only to be possible at all because the bills were not taken to the sellers' order, but to the order of the consignees. Lord Sumner observed that:

> "If the shippers had insured the goods and had attached the policy to the draft, and if they had taken the bills of lading to their own order, no question could have arisen."

But the bills were taken to the buyers' order and retained by the sellers.

2. Unlike *The Parchim* there was a bankers' credit opened in The *Kronprinsessan Margareta*, but the bank had not apparently accepted any irrevocable commitment to pay the consignors (see at 513). This was probably therefore a revocable letter of credit, which was not used as security for payment (it was opened partly as protection against exchange rate fluctuations).

3. Lord Sumner also assumed, and thought it relevant that the insurance (effected in Europe by the consignees) was for the consignees' benefit only (the reason appears to have been difficulty in obtaining war risk insurance in the US). This assumption (which obviously would not apply to c.i.f. contracts) clearly strengthened the argument that the consignors had abandoned their interest in the goods from before shipment. However, Lord Sumner noted that the consignors had retained the bills of lading, and that the only possible reason for doing so would be to retain title until payment. If the bills had been forwarded to the consignees, then (in his view) different considerations might apply.

4. *The Parchim* was effectively limited to its facts.

5. Bools argues that this is very much a control theory case; the sellers retained title not because the carriers remained their agents (as would have been the case had the bills of lading been retained to their own order), but because they retained control over them. While this is no doubt true, it surely does not follow that control is the governing consideration in all cases. Certainly, however, physical control of the bill of lading was regarded as of great significance in this case, and

in *The Parchim*. Here, the sellers retained control of the bills; in *The Parchim* they did not. However, it is rarely emphasised in more modern cases: *cf. Ginzberg*, below.

6. Even if Lord Sumner in *The Kronprinsessan Margareta* had had greater regard to the form of the bill of lading it is unlikely that the cargo-owners would have succeeded, because where the presumptions in s. 19 do not apply, there seems to be a very strong presumption that property will not pass earlier than shipment, as the cargo-owners needed to argue, even if the goods are appropriated before then. See further the discussion of *Federspiel v Twigg*, above.

(c) Development of Modern Forms of Finance

In none of the cases in the last section, except perhaps *The Kronprinsessan* **5–055** *Margareta*, were the transactions financed by documentary credit. Modern international finance was an important development between the First and Second World wars. It clearly influenced the following case, where the House of Lords decisively rejected *The Parchim* as being of general application. Gone is the reluctance to postpone passing of property after physical delivery (shipment), and the emphasis on the unpaid seller's lien. The case clearly entrenches the distinction between contractual and proprietary appropriation, and establishes that for c.i.f. contracts at any rate, where constructive delivery is by tender of documents, property generally passes on tender of documents. One of the justifications is the practice of finance by documentary credit, and the consequential inadequacy of the unpaid seller's lien.

ROSS T SMYTH & CO LTD v TD BAILEY SON & CO

House of Lords. [1940] 3 All E.R. 60

Facts and issues:
The sellers gave notice of appropriation of about 15,444 quarters of corn, **5–056** as they were entitled to do under the sale contract, and sent a provisional invoice. The buyers wrongly rejected the provisional invoice as not being in accordance with the contract, and the sellers made a second appropriation, of 15,000 quarters. The House of Lords held that the sellers did not thereby waive the buyers' breach. The buyers also argued that the second appropriation was a repudiatory breach of contract, on the grounds that the sellers had already passed property in a larger quantity of corn, by virtue of the earlier appropriation. The House of Lords disagreed; the appropriation had been conditional, and did not pass property.

Importance of case:
The importance of the case, for present purposes, lies in the views taken, in Lord Wright's speech, on the passing of property under a c.i.f. contract. *[This extract follows immediately from the extract in para. 2—011, above].*

Lord Wright: *(after describing the c.i.f. contract—see chapter 2, above)* In **5–057** this course of business, the general property in the goods remains in the seller until he transfers the bills of lading. These rules, which are simple enough to state in general terms, are of the utmost importance in commercial transactions. I have dwelt upon them perhaps unnecessarily, because the judgment of the Court of Appeal might seem to throw doubt on one of their most essential aspects. The property which the seller retains while he or his agent, or the banker to whom he has pledged the documents, retains the bills of lading is the general property, and not a special property by way of security. In general however, the importance of the retention of the property is not only to secure payment from the buyer but for purposes of finance. The general course of international commerce involves the practice of raising money on the documents so as to bridge the period between shipment and the time of obtaining payment against documents. These credit facilities, which are of the first importance, would be completely unsettled if the incidence of the property were made a matter of doubt. By mercantile law, the bills of lading are the symbols of the goods. The general property in the goods must be in the seller if he is to be able to pledge them. The whole system of commercial credits depends on the seller's ability to give a charge on the goods and the policies of insurance. A mere unpaid seller's lien would, for obvious reasons, be inadequate and unsatisfactory. I need not observe that particular contracts may contain special terms, or otherwise indicate a special intention, taking the contract outside these rules.

Notes

5–058   One of the main issues in this case, which arose on detailed points of construction of a c.i.f. contract, was whether the seller had finally appropriated goods to the contract. Lord Wright made clear that appropriation identified the goods, and tied them irrevocably into the particular contract, but did not necessarily pass property. Indeed, the normal inference in c.i.f. contracts, especially where the bill of lading was made out to seller's order, was that property passed on tender of documents—the finance of international sales could hardly be carried on on any other basis, since the seller had to retain property to create the pledge on a documentary credit. The distinction adopted here is the same as that between contractual and proprietary appropriation, discussed earlier.

The Parchim is regarded as exceptional, as it was in *The Kronprinsessan Margareta*. Though in *Smyth v Bailey* the sellers physically retained the bills, this was in no sense the basis of the decision.

There is now authority that as a general proposition property passes on indorsement, at least for c.i.f. contracts. See, *e.g.* the statements of Roskill L.J. in *The Albazero* [1977] A.C. 774 (considered in detail in paras 5—063 and 13—038, below), and of McNair J. in *Ginzberg v Barrow Haemetite Steel Co* [1966] 1 Lloyd's Rep. 343.

GINZBERG v BARROW HAEMETITE STEEL CO

Commercial Court. [1966] 1 Lloyd's Rep. 343

Main issues:

5–059   This was a c.i.f. contract where, because the bills of lading had not arrived before the vessel herself arrived, the sellers gave the buyers delivery orders to enable them to take delivery. The buyers went into receivership (and subsequent liquidation), after taking delivery, but before paying for the goods. McNair J. held that property remained with the sellers, who were able to assert their legal title.

McNair J. accepted that it was common for the parties to a c.i.f. contract to intend that property in the goods should pass only when payment is made. In *Ginzberg* itself, the usual presumption was not rebutted by delivery having already been made to the buyers under delivery orders, bills of lading not having become available by the time the goods arrived at the port of discharge. An argument, based on *The Julia* (see chapter 2, above), that by substituting this method of delivery, the parties had varied the contract from c.i.f. to ex-ship, was rejected. All that had happened was that the sellers had agreed to provide a mechanism to expedite delivery, the ship having arrived before the bills of lading. No fundamental variation to the contract had been agreed. It remained a c.i.f. contract.

It is surely difficult to regard this as a case where the sellers controlled the passing of property, as they had in *The Kronprinsessan Margareta*, for example. They did not have the bills of lading themselves prior to discharge of the cargo, and did everything they could to facilitate its delivery.

McNair J.'s general proposition on the passing of property c.i.f. was referred to with approval by Roskill L.J. in *The Albazero* (see below).

(d) FORM OF BILL OF LADING AND RESERVATION TO ORDER OF SELLER

Smyth v Bailey and *Ginzberg* both concerned c.i.f. contracts. In *The Parchim*, the   **5–060** contract was said to have more of the characteristics of an f.o.b. contract. From this it might be assumed that the form of the contract is crucial. I would suggest that this is a mistaken assumption; of far greater importance is the form of the bill of lading, and the seller's dealings with it.

Whether f.o.b. or c.i.f., property passes later than shipment if the seller reserves a right of disposal in the goods (typically reservation of property against payment). Such reservations are effective by virtue of s.19(1) of the Sale of Goods Act, above. The operation of this section was the reason that property did not pass in *The Aliakmon* (see para. 13—072, below, for detailed coverage). Express reservations of this type are rare in international sales, however.

A seller is *prima facie* deemed to reserve a right of disposal where the bill of lading is reserved to his order, by virtue of Sale of Goods Act 1979, s.19(2), a codification of Cotton L.J.'s views in *Mirabita v Imperial Ottoman Bank*. The effect of this presumption is that property passes on indorsement of the bill of lading. This will usually occur only against payment of the price, either directly from the buyer, or on a commercial credit from a bank.

The presumption is rebuttable. *The San Nicholas* and *The Ciudad de Pasto* suggest a fairly strong presumption, but the presumption was rebutted in the Court of Appeal in *The Albazero* (which *on this issue* was upheld by the House of Lords), and in both *The Delfini* and *The Filiatra Legacy*, paras 5—066 and 5—070.

PACIFIC MOLASSES CO AND UNITED MOLASSES TRADING CO LTD V ENTRE RIOS COMPANIA NAVIERA (S.A.) (THE SAN NICHOLAS)

Court of Appeal. [1976] 1 Lloyd's Rep. 8

Facts and issues:

5–061 The defendant shipowners let *The San Nicholas* under a voyage charter-party from Brazil to the United States Gulf. This charterparty was expressly governed by the law of England. The vessel was sub-chartered to the plaintiffs. The sub-charter was expressed to be governed by the law of the Flag of the vessel.

The plaintiffs, the United Molasses Trading Co Ltd, agreed to buy a quantity of molasses which were shipped aboard the vessel, and thus also became indorsees of a bill of lading issued by the defendant shipowners. The contract for the sale of the molasses contained a clause that property and risk in the goods were to pass to the buyers at the permanent hose connection of the vessel at the loading port. The bill of lading contained a clause incorporating "the Charter", but because blank spaces in the document were not filled in, it was not clear from the document which charter was incorporated. The plaintiffs received the documents and paid 95% of the cost by letter of credit against them. The ship and cargo later sank. In seeking leave to serve a writ on the defendant shipowners out of the jurisdiction, the plaintiffs needed to show (by virtue of RSC, O. 11, r. 1 (f) (iii)) a good *prima facie* case:

1. That the head charter (and not the sub-charter) was incorporated (because that charter specified English law as the proper law), and

2. That they were entitled to sue by virtue of the Bills of Lading Act 1855, s.1, although they were not party to the original contract of carriage.

Held:

There was a good arguable *prima facie* case that the plaintiffs could sue on a statutorily implied contract, expressly or impliedly governed by English law, and leave to serve the writ out of the jurisdiction would therefore be given.

The relevant passages on the incorporation issue were further considered in *The S.L.S. Everest* and *The Sevonia Team [see paras 12—030 and 12—032, below]*.

5–062 LORD DENNING M.R.: *(On the Bills of Lading Act)* Who were the parties to the contract? Who can sue? Mr. Gilman for the shipowners said that the United Molasses Co were not entitled to sue as parties to the contract because they did not fall within the Bills of Lading Act 1855. He submitted the property passed to United Molasses (under the f.o.b. contract of July, 1971) when the molasses passed through the permanent hose to the ship at Recife. It did not pass to them "upon or by reason of the consignment or endorsement" of the bill of lading. ... By reserving it "to order", the shipper reserved to himself power of disposing of the property and the property did not pass to the purchaser on shipment, see *Mirabita v Ottoman Bank* (1878) 3 Ex. D. 173. In order to obtain delivery, the bill of lading would have to be indorsed specially or in blank. When produced by United Molasses, it would be evidence that they had taken it by indorsement and were entitled to the goods by reason of it. I think that there is at least a *prima facie* case that the property did pass to them by indorsement so as to entitle them to sue under the Bills of Lading Act, 1855.

Notes

Lord Denning M.R. thought that property passed on indorsement in spite of the clause in the contract of sale, because the bill of lading was reserved to the order of the shippers. His view was based on the Sale of Goods Act 1893 (now 1979), s.19(2). But this section creates only a rebuttable presumption of reservation of property where the bill of lading is reserved to the order of the shippers. The presumption was rebutted, *e.g.* in *The Albazero*, and it might be argued that an express stipulation in the contract of sale is evidence of sufficient weight to rebut the presumption. Certainly this is the logic of the passage from Debattista's textbook, set out earlier in the chapter. On the other hand, it may be that merely to reserve a right of disposal against payment of the price would not entail a breach of contract, for the same reason that there was no breach in *Mirabita* itself.

In the event, the court did not need to make a final decision on when property passed, and Roskill L.J. did not adopt Lord Denning M.R.'s view. However, Roskill L.J.'s view, that the precise timing of passing of property was unimportant for the purposes of s.1 of the 1855 Act, cannot be correct in the light of *The Delfini*, discussed on this issue in chapter 13, below. If *The San Nicholas* is correct, therefore, it must be on the basis of Lord Denning M.R.'s reasoning, that property passed on indorsement.

In *Mitsui & Co Ltd v Flota Mercante Grancolumbiana SA (The Ciudad de Pasto)* [1989] 1 All E.R. 951, the bill of lading made the goods deliverable to the order of the seller. 80 per cent of the price had been paid before shipment, but the Court of Appeal applied the s.19(2) presumption, and inferred that the seller retained the bill as security against payment of the remaining 20 per cent. Since there was no evidence that the balance of the purchase price was ever paid, it was impossible to infer that property ever passed to the buyer.

Note that both of these cases concern f.o.b. contracts, and in neither was property held to pass on shipment.

The presumption is rebuttable, however.

(ALBACRUZ (CARGO OWNERS) v ALBAZERO (OWNERS) (THE ALBAZERO)

House of Lords. [1977] A.C. 774

Facts:

C.i.f. sellers (from f.o.b. buyers) of goods were also time charterers of a   **5–063** vessel called *The Albacruz*, sister ship to *The Albazero*. A bill of lading was issued to them as shippers pursuant to the charterparty. During the voyage *The Albacruz* and her goods sank and were totally lost, due to a breach of the charterparty, and also of the bill of lading contract, by the shipowners.

At the time of the loss the bill of lading had been posted to the c.i.f. buyers but had not been received by them. The Court of Appeal held that property had passed to the buyers on posting of the bill, and this view was upheld in the House of Lords (though the actual decision of the Court of Appeal was reversed). See further on this point the notes, below.

If the Court of Appeal were correct in holding that property had passed, the buyers as indorsees could, in principle, have sued on the bill of lading (relying on the 1855 Act). They could not do so in reality, however, because they were time-barred by the Hague Rules.

However, the shippers were a company in the same group as the indorsees, and they therefore decided to sue, in their own right but on behalf of the buyers, on the charterparty. The Hague Rules did not apply to charterparties (nor do the amended Hague-Visby Rules today—see further chapter 11, below), so effectively this was an action to avoid the time bar.

The Albazero, belonging as it did to the same owners as *The Albacruz*, was arrested for the action. The shippers claimed (on the basis of *Dunlop v Lambert* (1839) 6 Cl. & F. 600, in para. 13—040, below) substantial damages to be held in trust for the indorsee. The shipowners argued that property in the goods having passed to the indorsees by the time of their loss, the shippers were entitled to nominal damages only. This argument was based on the general contractual principle that damages are compensatory only, and that the shippers had suffered no loss.

Diagrammatic representation (action brought by B) of the Contracts in the Albazero

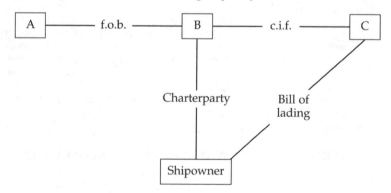

Held in the House of Lords:

1. Upholding on this point the decision of the Court of Appeal, and necessarily to reach the decision in the House of Lords, the property in the goods had passed to the plaintiffs.

2. Reversing on this point the decision of the Court of Appeal, property in the goods having passed to the indorsees, the shippers could recover only nominal damages on the charterparty. We return to this issue in chapter 13, below.

Note

The property issue was dealt with in the Court of Appeal (also reported in **5–064** [1977] A.C. 774), and Lord Diplock was content to agree with Roskill L.J. Roskill L.J. began by stating the usual position that property in c.i.f. contacts passes on tender of documents and payment against them:

> "I unreservedly accept that, in the absence of any contrary intentions appearing from the contract, the conduct of the parties and the circumstances of the case, where goods are sold on c.i.f. terms the property will not pass from the seller to the buyer except against tender of documents by the seller to the buyer and payment by the buyer to the seller against these documents."

Thus Roskill L.J. accepted as a general principle that at least in c.i.f. sales, property should be presumed to pass on tender of documents. This is also in line with *Ginzberg v Barrow Haemetite Steel Co* [1966] 1 Lloyd's Rep. 343 (see para. 5—059, above). Though this is an important statement of general application, *The Albazero* actually represents an exception to the usual position because a contrary intention *could* be found, even though the bill of lading was reserved to seller's order.

Payment was not due until 180 days after sight (*i.e.* the seller was extending credit), and a common reason for rebuttal of the s.19(2) presumption is where the seller extends credit to the buyer. There is of course no need to reserve property against payment in this situation. This of itself was not thought to be conclusive, but it was also found that the only reason for the bill of lading being reserved to seller's order was that the group's business arrangements required flexibility of distribution, which in turn required the sellers to hold the bill of lading initially. They could, for example, use the bill to transfer the goods to a different buyer within the group, should that have been regarded as desirable. This flexibility was lost once they no longer had possession of the bill, *i.e.*, once it had been posted.

It was, therefore, held that property passed on posting of the bill of lading to the purchasers. There was no need to infer an intention on the part of the sellers to retain property until indorsement. This aspect of the case is unlikely to be of general application, except to show that the normal presumption stated by Roskill L.J. can be displaced.

(e) Effect of Method of Financing Transaction

In general, the courts have been reluctant to infer that the existence of a **5–065** documentary credit is a reason for passing property on shipment. In *The Glenroy* [1945] A.C. 124, a cargo shipped from Japan to Germany was seized as enemy property in October 1939 (which was, of course, before Japan entered the war), and in order to justify the seizure the British Crown had to argue that property had already passed to the German buyers at the time of the seizure. One of their arguments was that because the sellers had obtained an undertaking from a bank under a letter of credit, they were no longer interested in the goods, because they had been assured of payment in full. Lord Porter, rejecting this argument, observed that "the bank might fail" (at 135).

In *The Ciudad de Pasto* [1989] 1 All E.R. 951, 957j, sellers agreed to sell a quantity of prawns f.o.b. 80 per cent of the price had been paid before shipment, the balance to be paid (or so the Court of Appeal assumed) by letter of credit. The bill of lading made the goods deliverable to the order of the seller, but the Court of Appeal applied the section 19(2) presumption, and inferred that the seller retained the bill as security against payment of the remaining 20 per cent. There was no evidence either as to when or if the remaining 20% was paid, or that the bill of lading was indorsed in favour of the purchasers, although the cargo was eventually discharged (in a damaged condition) to them. The evidence was indeed described as "woefully inadequate" (at 953c), but on the limited facts available the Court of Appeal refused to infer that property had ever passed to the f.o.b. purchaser.

On the effect on passing of property of the letter of credit, Staughton L.J. said ([1989] 1 All E.R. 951, 957j):

"Nor can I attach much weight to the fact that the balance of the price was (as I assume) payable by letter of credit. Even the most copper-bottomed letter of credit sometimes fails to produce payment for one reason or another; and the seller who has a letter of credit for 100 per cent of the price will nevertheless often retain the property in his goods until he has presented the documents and obtained payment."

On the other hand, the existence of a stand-by letter of credit guaranteeing payment was treated as a reason for holding that property in an oil cargo had passed before indorsement, although the bill of lading was to sellers' order, in both *The Delfini* and *The Filiatra Legacy*. In such cases, the bill of lading is not even required to trigger payment. In *The Filiatra Legacy*, there was no question of the seller using the bill of lading to control property. The bill of lading did not come into the seller's possession until long after discharge, by which time any property would almost certainly have been consumed or destroyed.

ENICHEM ANIC SpA v AMPELOS SHIPPING CO LTD (THE DELFINI)

Court of Appeal. [1990] 1 Lloyds Rep 252

5–066   In an alleged short-delivery claim, the main importance of this case lay in its narrow interpretation given to section 1 of the Bills of Lading Act 1855 (disapproving contrary statements by Roskill L.J., *obiter* in *The San Nicholas* [1976] 1 Lloyd's Rep. 8, and Lloyd J. in *The Sevonia Team* [1983] 2 Lloyd's Rep. 640). This aspect of the case is no longer directly relevant in the light of the replacement of that Act by the Carriage of Goods by Sea Act 1992. Nevertheless, the case is still of importance on the property issue. The reasoning on the 1855 Act is also important to the extent that it makes Roskill L.J.'s reasoning in *The San Nicholas*, above, unsustainable.

Facts:

The plaintiffs, Enichem, were c.i.f. purchasers of a cargo of bulk oil from Vanol, who had themselves purchased a larger quantity of oil from Sonatrach. Under the contract between Vanol and Enichem, payment was to be made four days after discharge, against documents or seller's letter of indemnity in respect of missing documents. Vanol was also required to open a bank guarantee, which was in fact given before shipment. Under the contract between Sonatrach and Vanol, property passed on shipment.

Bills of lading were issued to Sonatrach, who indorsed them to Vanol in blank, so that in Vanol's hands they were bearer documents. Delivery of the cargo was effected against charterers' (Vanol's) letter of indemnity. Payment was made four days later, and the bills of lading reached Enichem about a week after that.

There was a short delivery, and Enichem sued the shipowners in contract. Under the Bills of Lading Act 1855, s.1, which was then in force, they had to show that property had passed to them upon or by reason of indorsement (see further chapter 15, below).

Held at first instance:
At first instance Phillips J. held that the bills of lading had ceased to be effective as transferable documents of title when the cargo was discharged (even though it had not been discharged against those documents, and the cargo in respect of which the claim was made had not been discharged at all). Hence the ultimate receivers (who claimed short delivery) could not rely on s.1.[30] Phillips J. reiterated these views in *The Sirina*,[31] a case heard on the same day as *The Delfini* and essentially similar to it. See further chapter 4, above and chapter 15, below, on this aspect of the case.

Held in the Court of Appeal:
Phillips J.'s decision in *The Delfini* was affirmed by the Court of Appeal, **5–067** but on the narrower grounds that there was no causal relationship between indorsement and the passing of property. The Court of Appeal took the view that property passed on discharge: since this occurred before indorsement it could not be said that indorsement played an essential causal part in the passing of property. The plaintiffs had argued that the effect of s.19(2) was that property passed on indorsement of the bills of lading, and that even though this had occurred after discharge, this was sufficient to trigger s.1.[32]

Passing of property:
The bill of lading was not indorsed in the plaintiff's favour until some time after discharge, and as it was made out to seller's order, it was argued that the sellers had retained a right of disposal, and that property did not therefore pass until indorsement.

The Court of Appeal rejected this contention, holding that property passed (at latest) on discharge, under the provisions of the sale contract. Purchas L.J.'s view was that[33]:

---

[30] *Enichem Anic SpA v Ampelos Shipping Co Ltd (The Delfini)* [1988] 2 Lloyd's Rep. 599, 607 (col. 2).

[31] *Conoco UK Ltd v Limni Maritime Co Ltd (The Sirina)* [1988] 2 Lloyd's Rep. 613. It is clear from 616 (col. 1), that he is directly adopting his own remarks from *The Delfini*.

[32] Note that *Delfini*–type situations still raise issues under the new law, but these issues are quite different from those under s.1.

[33] [1990] 1 Lloyd's Rep. 252, 266 (col. 2).

"I have no doubt that the consensual intention of the parties was that upon delivery of the cargo in accordance with the shippers' request the property in the cargo passed to Enichem Anic . . . "

It followed that the statutory presumption contained in s.19(2) was rebutted.[34] The reason was that the bills of lading could not in any meaningful sense be used as security. It had always been envisaged that the cargo may be delivered without production of a bill of lading. Furthermore, payment was assured by stand-by letter of credit, so that there was no reason to reserve a right of disposal. Mustill L.J. concluded[35]:

" . . . it is sufficient to remind oneself that the inference to be drawn from the taking of an order bill is rebuttable. I think it clear that the shipowners have rebutted it here."

Mustill L.J. clearly thought the seller's argument that passing of property be postponed until indorsement absurd, given that this could be months after discharge, and indeed even after cargo had become admixed with other cargo belonging to the receivers.

Thus, s.19(2) of the Sale of Goods Act 1979 was rebutted, in spite of the sale contract being on c.i.f. terms, where payment was by standby letter of credit which guaranteed payment to the seller, and which could operate entirely independently of the bill of lading. Property therefore passed at latest on discharge (when the cargo was delivered under the contract of sale), and arguably earlier, when the buyers were invoiced for payment, and independently of the later indorsement.

Notes

5–068   1. In *The Delfini*, the Court of Appeal neither adopted nor disapproved the view of Phillips J. at first instance that the bill of lading was incapable of passing property after the discharge of the cargo because it had become exhausted (even though, because of the short delivery not all the property had been discharged). This issue remains undecided, and is considered further in chapter 6, below.

2. *The Filiatra Legacy* (see below) raised similar issues—there property was held to pass earlier still, perhaps as early as shipment, but certainly before discharge, s.19(2) again being rebutted, for similar reasons. The material factor appears to have been that the bill of lading played no part at all in the mechanism for payment, so that there was no possible reason for the sellers to reserve title.

3. In *Kwei Tek Chao v British Traders and Shippers Ltd* [1954] 2 Q.B. 459, in chapter 7, below, it was postulated that if a buyer accepted the documents and later validly rejected the goods, he might obtain a conditional property on tender of documents, which later re-vested in the seller. In *The Delfini*, the cargo-owners attempted unsuccessfully to argue this reasoning in reverse, "that the acceptance of the goods on delivery was conditional on the bills of lading proving to be in

---

[34] Even if this was wrong, the right of disposal would be reserved only against payment, and this too occurred before indorsement: [1990] 1 Lloyd's Rep. 252, *per* Mustill L.J. at 272 (col. 1).

[35] [1990] 1 Lloyd's Rep. 252, 271 (col. 2).

accordance with the contract: so that the property did not finally come to rest in Enichem until the bills of lading were available for inspection." This is a quote from Mustill L.J.'s judgment, who did not think the *Kwei Tek* reasoning could be adapted in this way.

TREITEL, "PASSING OF PROPERTY UNDER C.I.F. CONTRACTS AND THE BILLS OF LADING ACT 1855"

[1990] L.M.C.L.Q. 1

[Footnotes are as in the original, but renumbered for inclusion in this book.]

Passing of property under c.i.f. contracts commonly occurs on transfer **5–069** of shipping documents, including a bill of lading, against payment of the price. Property passes at this point, not because there is any rule of law to this effect, but because of an inference as to the intention of the parties, and in particular the intention of the seller: it is assumed that he would intend to retain property, until payment, by way of security for that payment.[36] Where he holds a bill of lading to his own order, this inference is raised to the level of a statutory presumption by s.19(2) of the Sale of Goods Act 1979. In *The Delfini* the statutory presumption did not apply, since the bill of lading was not to the order of Vanol (and was at all material times in their hands a bearer document). And the inference which might normally be drawn from retention by a seller of the bill of lading was displaced by many circumstances. In the first place, the sellers did not retain the bill of lading to secure the price: the reason for their delay in forwarding it to the buyer was simply that it had not come into their hands. Secondly, the sellers did not need the bill of lading as security for the price: they had the security of a bank guarantee even before shipment and had been paid in full shortly after discharge of the goods. It is not impossible for a seller to intend to retain property after he has been paid in full, but the inference that he intended to do so will only be drawn in exceptional circumstances,[37] none of which existed in *The Delfini*. . . . [Such an] intention would have to be clearly proved and would not be inferred from a setting in which the seller had no commercial reason for deferring the passing of property in this way. The retention of a "spent" bill of lading might support an inference of intention to retain property in goods after delivery where the seller had *not* been paid,[38] but it is highly unlikely to have this effect after payment in full.

---

[36] Benjamin's *Sale of Goods* (3rd ed., 1987), para. 1690 *[now 5th ed.]*.
[37] *e.g.* in *The Gabbiano* [1940] P. 166, where the outbreak of war and consequent operation of Prize rules can be said to have influenced the intention of the seller.
[38] *e.g. Cheetham & Co Ltd v Thornham Spinning Co Ltd* [1964] 2 Lloyd's Rep. 17.

ANONIMA PETROLI ITALIANA SpA AND NESTE OY v MARLUCIDEZ ARMADORA SA (THE FILIATRA LEGACY)

Court of Appeal. [1991] 2 Lloyd's Rep. 337

5–070 This was a case of an alleged theft by shipowners of part (4,502 Mt.) of an oil cargo. The cargo-owners successfully established that they had title to sue, but failed on the substantive claim (on the evidence).

Title to sue:
The sellers had purchased f.o.b. and resold c.i.f. They had a bill of lading but were also charterers, and the charterparty had an arbitration clause. Hence they had no claim on the bill of lading, and any claim on the charterparty had to go to arbitration (and was possibly time-barred).

The buyers had no claim on the bill of lading, since it came into their possession some time after discharge. They could only succeed in tort, and needed to show that property had passed to them in respect of the cargo alleged to have been converted.

The shipowner argued that property passed (at the earliest) on discharge, and hence never passed in respect of any oil remaining on board (r.o.b.), because it had never been discharged. The bill of lading was taken out to the sellers' order, as required by the (standby) letter of credit.

Held on passing of property:
The Court of Appeal held (rebutting the presumption in s. 19(2) of the Sale of Goods Act 1979) that property had passed to the buyers on shipment, or at latest when discharge commenced, so that they had title to sue in respect of the r.o.b., but in the event the plaintiffs' claim was rejected on the substantive issues (see below).

MUSTILL L.J.: *(on title to sue)*

Title to Sue—The Law

5–071 This is to be found in sections 16 to 19 of the Sale of Goods Act 1979. In the case of a contract for the sale of unascertained goods, as here, no property in the goods is transferred to the buyer unless and until they are ascertained (section 16). Where there is a contract for specific or ascertained goods, the property is transferred when the parties intend it to be transferred, having regard to the terms of the contract, the conduct of the parties and the circumstances of the case (section 17). Section 18 sets out rules for ascertaining the intention of the parties "unless a different intention appears", including rule 5:

> "(1) Where there is a contract for the sale of unascertained or future goods by description, and goods of that description and in a deliverable state are unconditionally appropriated to the contract, either by the seller with the assent of the buyer or by the buyer with the assent of the seller, the property in the goods then passes to the buyer; and the assent may be express or implied, and may be given either before or after the appropriation is made.

(2) Where, in pursuance of the contract, the seller delivers the goods to the buyer or to a carrier or other bailee for custodier (whether named by the buyer or not) for the purpose of transmission to the buyer, and does not reserve the right of disposal, he is to be taken to have unconditionally appropriated the goods to the contract."

Also important is section 19:

"(1) Where there is a contract for the sale of specific goods or where goods are subsequently appropriated to the contract, the seller may, by the terms of the contract or appropriation, reserve the right of disposal of the goods until certain conditions are fulfilled; and in such a case, notwithstanding the delivery of the goods to the buyer, or to a carrier or other bailee or custodier for the purpose of transmission to the buyer, the property in the goods does not pass to the buyer until the conditions imposed by the seller are fulfilled.
(2) Where goods are shipped, and by the bill of lading the goods are deliverable to the order of the seller or his agent, the seller is prima facie to be taken to reserve the right of disposal.
(3) Where the seller of goods draws on the buyer for the price, and transmits the bill of exchange and bill of lading to the buyer together to secure acceptance or payment of the bill of exchange, the buyer is bound to return the bill of lading if he does not honour the bill of exchange, and if he wrongfully retains the bill of lading the property in the goods does not pass to him."

As is plain from sections 18 and 19, the inference that a seller is   5–072
reserving the right of disposal, if he obtains a bill of lading which makes the goods deliverable to his own order, can be rebutted by the circumstances of a particular case. It has twice been decided that a requirement in the sale contract for a letter of credit to secure payment of the price does not necessarily rebut that inference. Lord Porter so held in *Part Cargo ex Glenroy* [1945] A.C. 124, 135 ("the bank might fail"); and this court reached the same conclusion in *Mitsui & Co Ltd v Flota Mercante Grancolombiana SA* [1988] 2 Lloyd's Rep. 208, 214 ("even the most copper-bottomed letter of credit sometimes fails to produce payment for one reason or another"). Neither of these cases was concerned with a short voyage, when it was possible (and indeed contemplated) that the goods might arrive before the bill of lading.

In *Enichem Anic SpA v Ampelos Shipping Co Ltd (The Delfini)* [1990] 1 Lloyd's Rep. 252 the issue was whether the buyer had a cause of action in contract against the shipowner, for the purposes of R.S.C. Order 11. That in turn depended on whether a right to sue on the bill of lading had been vested in the buyer under section 1 of the Bills of Lading Act 1855. It was a case of a short voyage, where the sale contract itself contemplated that the goods might be discharged before tender of the bill of lading, and required the buyer to provide a bank guarantee. In the event both tender of the bill of lading and payment of the price occurred after completion of discharge—as in the present case. The Court of Appeal rejected an argument that the property did not pass until the bill of lading was tendered or the price paid. There are some passages in the judgments which support the view that it passed on discharge of the goods; but there was no need in that case to consider whether it might have passed at some earlier time.

The shipowners in the present case argue that the property did not pass until discharge of the oil, and then only in such of the oil as was discharged, not any which (as the buyers say) remained on board the *Filiatra Legacy*. The bill of lading was made out to the order of the sellers—indeed the contract required that it should be, since that was the term of the letter of credit referred to in the sale contract. Therefore, it is said, the sellers reserved the right of disposal, and there was no unconditional appropriation of the oil to the contract except in that part of it which was discharged. The shipowners' argument would have the property to pass on payment of the price by the buyers, if that had occurred before discharge; but it did not. The argument for the buyers and sellers was that, as Leggatt J. held, the property passed when payment of the price was secured; this in effect occurred when the oil was shipped, since the letter of credit had already been opened and the only document required from the buyers for its operation had already been supplied. Alternatively it was said in the written outline argument, and the judge would have held, that the property passed when the sellers provided a letter of indemnity. This argument may involve some confusion between the letter of indemnity provided by the sellers to the shipowners, on 28th and 29th November 1983, and the letter of indemnity addressed to the buyers, which was executed on 13th December 1983. The point was not pursued in oral argument. The third argument, which would also have been accepted by the judge, was that the property in all the oil passed when any part of it was delivered.

Title to Sue: Conclusion

5–073   It is common ground that the buyers must show that the whole cargo became their property no later than 19th December 1983, when discharge at Falconara came to an end and any substantial quantity of oil remaining on board was wrongfully converted by the shipowners.

In our judgment the whole of the oil had by then become the property of the buyers. The voyage foreseen by the contract was a short one. It was plainly contemplated that the oil might be delivered at Falconara, mixed with other oil, and even refined and distributed, before payment of the price became due. The contract nevertheless provided for a thirty-day period of credit. It also contemplated that the bill of lading might not reach the buyers before discharge of the cargo. In those circumstances the parties can scarcely have intended that passing of the property should depend either on payment of the price or on transfer of the bill of lading, at all events unless they expressly said so.

But Mr. Rokison, for the shipowners, observes that the sellers still took a bill of lading to their own order. We suspect that this was done as a matter of routine. No doubt it gives rise to the presumption in section 19(2), that they were reserving the right of disposal. But, as Mustill L.J. asked in the *Delfini* [1990] 1 Lloyd's Rep 252 (at page 271), subject to what condition was it reserved? Plainly not a condition which would be fulfilled by payment of the price, or tender of the bill of lading to the buyers. It may well be that some unconditional act of appropriation was still necessary before the property passed. If so, there was an appropriation either when the sellers sent their invoice to the buyers, or when they ordered the shipowners to proceed to Falconara and deliver the cargo to the buyers, or when the master on their instructions tendered notice of readiness and started to discharge the cargo.

We need not decide between those possible conclusions. The property in all the oil passed to the buyers when discharge commenced, if not before. Mr Rokison's final argument was that, in their letter of indemnity executed on 13th December 1983, the sellers wrote:

"We expressly warrant title to and have the full right and authority to transfer such title and to effect delivery of the crude oil . . . "

By that date the vessel had already discharged for five hours, on 30th November. We decline absolutely to read the letter of indemnity as a statement only of present title on 13th December. In our judgment what the letter meant was that the sellers warranted their title as at the time when they purported to pass property to the buyers, whenever that might be.

In agreement with Leggatt J., we hold that the buyers have title to sue in these proceedings.

Notes

It was necessary to distinguish two cases where the s.19(2) presumption was **5–074** not rebutted merely because sale was by documentary credit, the argument being that the seller did not need to retain property: *The Glenroy* [1945] A.C. 124 135 ("the bank might fail"); and *Mitsui & Co Ltd v Flota Mercante Grancolombiana SA* [1988] 2 Lloyd's Rep. 208, 214, CA ("even the most copper-bottomed letter of credit sometimes fails to produce payment for one reason or another"). Important factors in the reasoning in *The Filiatra Legacy* was that the voyage was short, and that it was always contemplated that the bill of lading may not arrive in time. In any case the price was secured by the standby letter of credit, so there was no need for the sellers to reserve title (but this does not appear to have been expressly part of the reasoning).

The Court of Appeal therefore held (upholding Leggatt J.) that the buyers had title to sue. The property in all the oil passed to the buyers when discharge commenced, if not before. The court did not decide when it passed.

Note on apparent lack of unconditional appropriation:
If property passed after shipment, there does not appear to have been any **5–075** positive act by the seller, unconditionally appropriating the goods to pass property. See Bools' criticism of *The Elafi*, which also applies to this case (but only if

Bools is right). Note that if property passed on shipment, Bools' criticism is not apposite anyway, but the Court of Appeal did not decide exactly when it passed, only that it was sometime before final discharge.

Shortfall:

5–076 There was an apparent shortage on figures from one of the two shore tanks of 4,502 tonnes. The buyers alleged that this quantity must have been deliberately retained on board the ship, and thus was stolen and converted by the shipowners or their employees (for use as bunker fuel). They claimed agreed damages of $946,230. Leggatt J found in their favour, finding that the missing oil had been intentionally admixed with ballast water in the cargo tanks, and perhaps later disposed of or used as fuel.

The shipowners maintained that all the cargo on board was discharged with the exception of a small quantity amounting to 30 tonnes, which was unpumpable. If this were correct, it would follow that the buyers' records of the quantity discharged were inaccurate or incomplete.

The owners claimed that the cargo had been lost in the refinery, either by having been deliberately but negligently misrouted before it reached tanks 55 and 61, or after it reached those tanks but before they were measured on 13th and 19th December respectively, or had leaked from one or both of those tanks into other parts of the refinery system. They claimed that this could easily go undetected.

Note that there was no allegation that cargo was lost on the voyage, or in the sea-line at discharge. There was simultaneous ballasting with discharge of 3 cargo holds (which had been crude oil washed), not just double-bottom and wing tanks. The owners claimed this was to speed turnaround, or perhaps because of failure of ballast-pumps.

The Court of Appeal held in the owners' favour on the shortfall issue—this was essentially a question of assessment of the evidence, the plaintiffs having failed to prove, in the manner appropriate to a case which involved the assertion of a serious crime, that their version of events was correct.

Further observations:

5–077 1. In *The Filiatra Legacy*, the bank had no interest in when property passed, since unlike a bank under a conventional documentary credit, it obtained no security under the stand-by letter of credit whatever happened. Property was held to have passed on shipment.

2. From the seller's point of view the position ought to be the same where he accepts a time draft under a documentary credit, since there too he is content with the personal promise of the bank, but the bank in those circumstances might want property, and the position would probably be different.

3. In cases such as these, the seller does not need to produce a bill of lading to procure payment, nor is it envisaged that the bank will necessarily obtain a document of title as security. Even if it did, it is envisaged that delivery will be made without production of an original bill. The buyer and the bank are being asked to take the seller on trust regarding payment. In such cases, which are quite common, it is difficult to see how the bill of lading is providing any security to anyone.

4. As long as the buyers eventually obtained the bill of lading, were the facts to arise today, there would be a contractual action, under the Carriage of Goods by Sea Act 1992.

NOBLE RESOURCES LTD v CAVALIER SHIPPING CORP. (THE ATLAS)

Queen's Bench Division (Commercial Court). [1996] 1 Lloyd's Rep. 642

Issues:

The plaintiffs were f.o.b. purchasers from Russian exporters of a cargo of steel   **5–078**
billets which were alleged to have been short-delivered. The contract was a barter
contract, which contemplated that the steel would be exchanged for metallurgical
equipment of equivalent value, but also that the plaintiffs, Noble Resources,
would, within 10 days of signing the contract, provide an irrevocable bank
guarantee for payment of the full value of the steel products.

In an action against the shipowner for short delivery, the main issue was
whether the bills of lading stated a quantity of goods loaded; this aspect is
discussed in chapter 16, below. A subsidiary issue was whether the plaintiffs had
title to sue.

Held:

Property had passed on shipment, and the f.o.b. buyers therefore had title to sue
in negligence. Since the contract was on f.o.b. terms, consisted of a barter arrangement and provided for the fall back of a guarantee, property in goods shipped
must have been intended to pass on appropriation, *i.e.* on shipment.

Longmore J.: Noble Resources Ltd acquired the steel billets from the   **5–079**
Russian exporters pursuant to an f.o.b. contract of barter dated Nov. 30,
1990; the contract contemplated that the steel would be exchanged for
metallurgical equipment of equivalent value but that Noble Resources
Ltd would, within 10 days of signing the contract, provide an irrevocable
bank guarantee for payment of the full value of steel products. There was
no provision for payment against documents although there was a provision for the Russian exporters to nominate an account number and a bank
where money was to be remitted if the steel was supplied before Noble
Resources Ltd fulfilled its obligations for "counter supply". Invoices
together with original bills of lading, mate's receipts and other documents were to be given to Noble Resources Ltd's Moscow representative
within seven days of vessel's departure. Since the contract was on f.o.b.
terms, consisted of a barter arrangement and provided for the fall back of
a guarantee, property in goods shipped must, in my view have been
intended to pass on appropriation (*viz.* on shipment) rather than on
performance of any subsequent condition such as payment, see Benjamin,
Sale, par 18–073. No guarantee was, in fact, provided but that fact did not
alter the intention of the parties as to the passing of property and I shall
refer to Noble Resources Ltd hereafter as the "cargo-owners". . . .

Notes

Longmore J. referred to the then current edition of Benjamin's *Sale of Goods*; see
now 5th ed., Sweet & Maxwell, 1997, para. 18–164.

This is another case where the existence of a guarantee negatived any presumption that might otherwise have arisen that the sellers retained a right of disposal
in the property.

(4) The 1995 Amendments to the Sale of Goods Act

5–080   Before 1995, sales of undivided bulk cargo, whether in liquid or dry cargo form, were sales of unascertained goods if parts of the bulk were sold to a number of different buyers: no individual buyer could state which part of the bulk will be his until it is appropriated to him (by being divided out). This would usually occur on the splitting of the bulk on discharge, and only then did the cargo become ascertained. Because of the absolute rule stated in s.16, therefore, property in part of an undivided bulk cargo could not usually pass until delivery, and clearly whether or not payment is by irrevocable documentary credit could have no effect on this. It also followed that where an undivided bulk cargo was sold to a number of different buyers, the original seller had property to pledge to the bank on tender of documents, but if one of the buyers re-sold, he had no property to pledge to any bank financing the sub-sale.

Before 1992, this also had major implications for buyers of undivided bulk cargoes under the regime of the 1855 Act, since s.1 could never apply in their favour, and therefore they could not sue the carrier in contract if the goods were lost or damaged on the voyage. The Law Commission, in its Working Paper No. 112 (*Rights to Goods in Bulk*), 1989, considered amending both s.1 and s.16, in order to deal with this problem. It appeared however that the main problem was with s.1, which was eventually replaced by the Carriage of Goods by Sea Act 1992. This resolved all the problems discussed in chapter 13, below, on bulk cargoes. In 1995, however, the Sale of Goods Act was amended, in accordance with the Law Commission proposals, to allow property in undivided bulks to pass to all the buyers as tenants in common, once the cargo had been paid for. This is subject to the definition of a bulk; the 1995 amendments would not work, for example, where cargo from two or more sellers was loaded on board, and mixed in undivided holds.[39]

If an entire bulk cargo is sold to a single buyer (as often happens with oil cargoes), the cargo is ascertained and the principles discussed in the previous sections apply. Similarly if the cargo is divided, for example by being carried in a number of holds, if the whole of the cargo in the same hold is destined for the same buyer, the cargo is ascertained.

(5) The Passing of Property and the Action for the Price

(a) The general position

SALE OF GOODS ACT 1979, s.49

5–081   (1) Where, under a contract of sale, the property in the goods has passed to the buyer, and the buyer wrongfully neglects or refuses to pay for the goods according to the terms of the contract, the seller may maintain an action against him for the price of the goods.

(2) Where, under a contract of sale, the price is payable on a day certain irrespective of delivery, and the buyer wrongfully neglects or refuses to

---

[39] This would not be a problem on the facts of *The Elafi* in para. 5—015 above, whose result was enacted in the amendment to s.18, r.5, since all the cargo was originally shipped by one person, who sold to both the plaintiffs and Frank Fehr, Frank Fehr then selling on to the plaintiffs. Prior to ascertainment by exhaustion, if the 1995 amendments had applied, Frank Fehr and the plaintiffs would have shared the entire cargo as tenants in common.

pay such price, the seller may maintain an action for the price, although the property in the goods has not passed, and the goods have not been appropriated to the contract.

Notes

1. It would be uncommon to make the price payable on a certain date to allow the seller to take advantage of s.49(2). The buyer does not normally wish to pay before tender of documents, while the seller wishes to retain the documents as security against payment. Thus the price will often be made payable against tender of documents.

2. Only if the seller extends credit to the buyer is it likely that the price will be payable on a certain date, and even then it is more common to grant a fixed duration of credit, *e.g.* payment 180 days after sight of documents.

3. Thus, the passing of property is usually critical in actions for the price. If the buyer refuses to take delivery, or refuses to pay before property has passed, the seller can sue for damages for breach of contract, but not for the price.

4. The advantages of the action for the price are that it is not necessary for the seller to go through the expense and hazard of proving loss—he can claim the fixed sum representing the price whatever happens. Further, his remedy is not subject to the contractual doctrines of mitigation and remoteness of damage.

5. Where the seller sues for the price to and it is necessary for him to rely on s.49(1) (*i.e.* to show that property in the goods has passed), it is irrelevant that it has not done so because of the fault of the buyer.

COLLEY v OVERSEAS EXPORTERS

King's Bench. [1921] 2 K.B. 302

F.o.b. buyers failed (after no fewer than five attempts) to nominate an effective ship, and the goods (which were unascertained) were therefore left stranded on the dock. The sellers had done everything they could to perform the contract, and sued for the price.

5–082

Held:
They were unable to maintain an action the price, because property f.o.b. does not pass until shipment, and that had not occurred. It was immaterial that it was through the buyers' breach of contract that shipment had not occurred.

MᶜCᴀʀᴅɪᴇ J.: ... Such are the facts. The defendants committed no deliberate breach of contract; they suffered a series of misfortunes. They failed however to name an effective ship. The plaintiff on his part did all he could to carry out his obligations. Under these circumstances the plaintiff seeks to recover the price of the goods in question. ...

... The contention of Mr. Willes [for the plaintiff sellers] before me was that inasmuch as the defendants' own fault had here prevented the goods from being put on board they were disabled from saying that the price, which would have been payable if and when the goods had actually been put on board, was not now due to the plaintiff. This is a novel and interesting submission. An action for the price of goods is, of course, essentially an action for a liquidated sum. It involves special and techni-cal elements. By special bargain the price of goods may be payable before delivery or before the property has passed from vendor to buyer: see . . . s.49 of the Sale of Goods Act, 1893. In ordinary cases and unless otherwise agreed delivery of the goods and payment of the price are concurrent conditions: see s.28 of the Sale of Goods Act, 1893. Now the full meaning of the word "price" is not actually defined by the Sale of Goods Act, except perhaps in s.1, which says:

> "A contract of sale of goods is a contract whereby the seller transfers or agrees to transfer the property in goods to the buyer for a money consideration, called the price."

The circumstances however under which a claim to the price may be made (as distinguished from a claim of damages for breach of contract) are indicated in s.49 of that Act. Sect. 49 provides, sub-s.1:

> "Where, under a contract of sale, the property in the goods has passed to the buyer, and the buyer wrongfully neglects or refuses to pay for the goods according to the terms of the contract, the seller may maintain an action against him for the price of the goods."

Sub-s.2:

> "Where, under a contract of sale, the price is payable on a day certain irrespective of delivery, and the buyer wrongfully neglects or refuses to pay such price, the seller may maintain an action for the price, although the property in the goods has not passed, and the goods have not been appropriated to the contract."

5–083 Here sub-s.2 of s.49 does not apply . . . The parties before me here made no special agreement as to the payment of the price. Nor can it be said that sub-s.1 of s.49 applies here, for the property in the goods has not in fact and law passed to the buyer. Several rules for the passing of property in sale of goods contracts are indicated in ss.16, 17, 18, and also in s.32. The Act does not deal specifically with f.o.b. or c.i.f. contracts. Judicially settled rules exist however with respect to them. I need only deal with f.o.b. contracts. The presumed intention (see s.18 of the Act) of the parties has been settled. It seems clear that in the absence of special agreement the property and risk in goods does not in the case of an f.o.b. contract pass from the seller to the buyer till the goods are actually put on board: see *Browne v Hare* (1859) 4 H. & N. 822; *Inglis v Stock* (1885) 10 App. Cas. 263; *Wimble v Rosenberg* [1913] 3 K.B. 743, 747 . . .

. . . In my view the law as to the circumstances under which an action will lie for the price of goods has not been changed by the Sale of Goods Act 1893 [now 1979, referred to in this passage as "the code"]. The enactment seems to crystallise and confirm the old law . . . The existing condition of the law is put in Benjamin on *Sale*, 6th ed., p. 946, where it is rightly stated that the old principles "are by implication preserved by s.49 of the code." And the learned editor adds:

> "Where the property has not passed, the seller's claim must, as a general rule, be special for damages for non-acceptance."

An exception to the general rule is to be found is the cases provided for by s.49(2) of the code. In my opinion . . . no action will lie for the price of the goods until property has passed, save only in the special cases provided for by s.49(2). This seems plain both on the code and on common law principle. I have searched in vain for authority to the contrary. . . .

. . . Towards the close of his argument Mr. Willes submitted a further point—namely, that the defendants were estopped from denying that the property had passed to them. Estoppel is a vague word. It is often used to support a submission not capable of precise juristic formulation. The only estoppel which can be suggested is estoppel by conduct. . . . The main rule was clearly put in *Carr v London and North Western Ry Co* (1875) L.R. 10 C.P. 307, 317 as follows:

> "If a man, whatever his real meaning may be, so conducts himself that a reasonable man would take his conduct to mean a certain representation of facts, and that it was a true representation, and that the latter was intended to act upon it in a particular way, and he with such belief does act in that way to his damage, the first is estopped from denying that the facts were as represented."

This is a useful rule. It is quite distinct from what is called "waiver" . . . If therefore the defendants in this case represented to the plaintiffs facts showing that the property in the goods had passed to them, and if also the plaintiff had believed that representation and had acted upon it to his damage, then the defendants would, I conceive, be estopped from denying that the property had passed to them and that the price was therefore payable to the plaintiff: . . . I am satisfied that there is no estoppel on the facts and documents here before me. The defendants made no misrepresentation of fact. The plaintiff has not acted on any statement or relied on any misleading conduct of the defendants. He knew the circumstances as fully as the defendants knew them. None of the elements of estoppel are here present. It follows therefore for the reasons given that the plaintiff is not entitled to recover the price of the goods in question. If he desires to claim damages he must amend his writ. On the record at present before me he cannot ask for judgment.

Notes

1. Where property **has** passed, but payment of the price is made subject to a condition subsequent, the buyer cannot prevent the price becoming payable by   **5–084**

preventing the condition from occurring: *Mackay v Dick* 6 App. Cas. 251 (which was distinguished in *Colley*).

2. The observations on the unsuccessful estoppel argument are set out here because, with risk substituted for property, they may help to explain the estoppel suggested in *J & J Cunningham v Munro* in para. 4—040, above; if the estoppel had worked in that case, the buyers would have been estopped from denying that risk had passed to them. The two examples are not on all fours, however, because McCardie J., is talking about representations of fact, whereas the representations in Avory L.C.J.'s example were as to intention. Later developments in promissory estoppel could retrospectively explain Avory L.C.J.'s judgment, however.

(b) Waiver of Right of Disposal

5–085   If property has not passed only because of a right of disposal reserved by the seller, there is (not particularly strong) authority that the seller can waive that right in order to pass the property. So, for example, if the seller has reserved a right of disposal against payment (and thereby prevented property from passing), and the buyer has not paid, the seller can waive the right of disposal and sue the buyer for the price.

F.E. NAPIER v DEXTERS LTD

Court of Appeal. (1926) 26 Ll.L. Rep. 184

5–086   In an action for the price it was held that property had passed, and that the seller had not retained a right of disposal (or *jus disponendi*) by the use of a clause in the sale contract: "Cash against mate's receipt." Alternatively, he could waive his right of disposal to pass the property.

BANKES L.J.: *(after holding that the seller had not retained a right of disposal)* There is a further point that Roche J took. He apparently took the view that it may be that the buyers' contention is right, and that the seller reserved the *jus disponendi* by virtue of his contract, and this document. But assuming that to be so, in my opinion (he says) it was competent for the seller in the circumstances to waive the condition precedent in his favour; and waiving that condition precedent in his favour the acceptance of the goods was sufficient to justify the claim for the price at the contract rate.

I can see no fault in law in that view of the learned Judge . . .

Note

The issue did not arise directly, since the CA held that the seller had not retained a right of disposal.

CHAPTER 6

THE DOCUMENTS

(1) Introduction

It is obvious that the shipping documents have an essential role to play in a c.i.f.   **6–001**
contract, and that their role in an f.o.b. contract can depend on the type of f.o.b.
contract with which we are concerned.

The c.i.f contract was based around the traditional shipped bill of lading, policy
of marine insurance and invoice, and in the absence of evidence to the contrary,
those will be the documentary requirements under a c.i.f. contract. However, the
traditional documentation may be inconvenient for a number of reasons (see
further chapter 15, below), so the parties have some freedom to depart from them.
Moreover, the terms of the trade may affect the documentary requirements.

Nevertheless there are limits to the degree of variation allowed by the courts,
both c.i.f. and (where applicable) f.o.b. To stipulate too great a variation may
prevent a sale contract being regarded as, *e.g.* c.i.f. at all, as in *The Julia* (see para.
2–015), set out in chapter 2, above. Alternatively, very strong evidence, for example of an agreement or a trade custom, might be required to displace the normal
documentary requirements. Of course, the shipping documents will often have to
be handled not only by the immediate purchasers, but also by sub-purchasers in
chain sales and, where payment is to be by commercial credit, banks. The courts
are keen to promote negotiability of documents, but the pursuit of negotiability
demands a high degree of standardisation within a given trade, both of the
contractual terms and of the required documents. It is very difficult to operate
chain sales if widely different documents are required at each stage. Thus for
example, Lord Sumner in *Hansson v Hamel and Horley Ltd* thought that[1]:

> "It is essential that they should so conform to the accustomed shipping docu-
> ments as to be reasonably and readily fit to pass current in commerce."

It is worth observing the reference to accustomed shipping documents. Ultimately, the courts are concerned to interpret the intentions of the parties, but in
the absence of intention being expressed, what is usual in the particular trade may
be the best evidence. However, this passage from Lord Sumner's speech was used
in *The Galatia*, below, to justify a refusal to allow trade practices to determine what
the law should be. Trade practices may be evidence of intention, but they should
not be allowed to dictate development of the law.[2]

Given that the c.i.f. documentary requirements, in the absence of evidence to
the contrary, are known, one question to be addressed in this chapter is the extent
to which f.o.b. requirements differ. Other questions are the strength of evidence
needed to vary the normal requirements, and the absolute limits placed by the
courts on variation, where as in *The Julia*, the courts consider the documentary
requirements repugnant to the very nature of the transaction.

---

[1] [1922] 2 A.C. 36, at 46. See further below, on the discussion of clean bills of lading, and
through bills of lading.
[2] See also Sellers J.'s views of trade practices in *Yelo v S.M. Machado*, below.

(2) Role of the Documents

6–002   In a c.i.f. contract, the documents, in principle, can perform the following functions:

(a) Provide evidence that the seller has shipped goods of the contractual description, within the contractual shipment period;

(b) Transfer constructive possession to the goods, and perhaps also property;

(c) Transfer rights and liabilities under the carriage contract (see chapter 13, below);

(d) Provide evidence that the goods are insured, and transfer the benefit of any insurance policy to the purchaser.

A shipped bill of lading and assignable policy of marine insurance can perform all of these functions, and the issues are therefore the extent to which other documents can also fulfil the role, and the extent to which these other documents are acceptable tender c.i.f.

In an f.o.b. contract the documents need not perform any function at all, but can perform any or all of them; the different types of f.o.b. contract may impose no obligation on the seller, or require him to obtain a bill of lading in the name of the buyer, or allow him to take a bill of lading to his own order. In an f.o.b. contract with additional duties there is no reason why the shipping documents should not perform exactly the same role as with c.i.f. Also, whether a freight prepaid or freight collect bill is required will depend on the duties undertaken by the seller. In the absence of evidence of contrary intention, however, the courts assume that an f.o.b. buyer is responsible for freight (see the discussion of *Glencore Grain Rotterdam BV v Lorico* at para. 2–006 and para. 3–014, above). Conversely, a freight prepaid bill is normally required in a c.i.f. contract, unless the buyer is credited with the amount of the freight: see the discussion in *Ireland v Livingston* in chapter 2, above.[3]

(3) Function of Documents of Title

6–003   It has already been explained in Chapter 1 how the bill of lading, as a document of title, can represent the goods, and how the transfer of the bill of lading transfers constructive possession of the goods. A document of title transfers constructive possession of the goods. The shipped bill of lading is recognised, by custom of merchants, as a document of title at common law (the extent to which other documents can also be documents of title is considered later in this chapter). Only the holder of a document of title can demand the goods from the ship at destination (see para. 1–012, above).

The bill of lading can therefore be negotiated, to enable the holder either to re-sell the goods (especially in the case of bulk commodity sales), or pledge them with a bank to raise money on their security (see further chapters 8–10, below). Thus, in a contract where the seller is shipper, and obtains the bill of lading, after shipment the shipper sends the shipping documents to the purchaser, indorsed if it is made out to his order, or if payment is to made by banker's commercial credit, to a bank for payment. The holder of the bill for the time being, by transferring it again, can transfer constructive possession of the goods themselves, and the right to demand delivery of the goods from the carrier at their

---

[3] Note that the bill of lading did not evidence freight having been paid in *The Galatia*, at para. 6–067, below, but was held to be good tender c. & f.

destination. Thus, dealings in the goods themselves can be effected by transfer of the documents.

For a document of title to work, the following requirements need to be met:

(a) The carrier should not be required to deliver except against production of a document of title. He should, however, be under an obligation to deliver to the holder.

(b) The carrier who delivers against a document of title should incur no liability towards anybody else. He must be protected from suit, even if the person to whom he delivers (against presentation of an original document) does not have title to the goods.

(c) The carrier who delivers without production of a document of title should be liable to the person entitled to the goods.

(a) Right to Refuse to Deliver

The carrier should not be entitled to refuse to deliver against production of an original document of title. If the transfer of the document of title transfers property in the goods, even if only the special property of a pledgee (see para. 5–036, above), the carrier who refuses to deliver, or who delivers to someone who is not entitled to delivery, will be liable in conversion. If the property is not transferred, then the holder will usually have to fall back on a contract action, which until 1992 was fraught with difficulty (but no longer—see further chapter 13, below). The carrier may also be liable in bailment, but unless he attorns, only to the original bailor, who will usually be the shipper. In general, therefore, for the first condition to obtain, it is necessary for the document of title to transfer either property or a cause of action in contract, or both, but since 1992, the contract action has generally been unproblematic. **6–004**

The carrier should, however, be entitled to refuse to deliver, except against production of an original bill of lading (or other document of title).

BARCLAYS BANK LTD v COMMISSIONERS OF CUSTOMS & EXCISE

Queen's Bench Division (Commercial Court). [1963] 1 Lloyd's Rep. 81

Issues:

A bill of lading was pledged to the plaintiff bank after the shipowner had discharged the goods into the custody of a warehouse at the port of discharge. The Commissioners of Customs & Excise claimed possession of the goods as judgment creditors, on the grounds that purchase tax was due on them from the pledgors. The bank claimed that it had title to the goods. **6–005**

Held:

Diplock L.J. held that the document remained a document of title until the goods had been surrendered to the person entitled to them, and that until that time:

"the shipowner is not bound to surrender possession of the goods to any person whether named as consignee or not, except on production of the bill of lading". Consequently, the bank was lawful holder of the bill, and the Commissioners were not entitled to possession of the goods.

DIPLOCK L.J.: *(sitting at first instance at 88)* The contract for the carriage of goods by sea, which is evidenced by a bill of lading, is a combined contract of bailment and transportation under which the shipowner undertakes to accept possession of the goods from the shipper, to carry them to their contractual destination and there to surrender possession of them to the person who, under the terms of the contract, is entitled to obtain possession of them from the shipowners. Such a contract is not discharged by performance until the shipowner has actually surrendered possession (that is, has divested himself of all powers to control any physical dealing in the goods) to the person entitled under the terms of the contract to obtain possession of them.

So long as the contract is not discharged, the bill of lading, in my view, remains a document of title by indorsement and delivery of which the rights of property in the goods can be transferred. It is clear law that where a bill of lading or order is issued in respect of the contract of carriage by sea, the shipowner is not bound to surrender possession of the goods to any person whether named as consignee or not, except on production of the bill of lading (see *The Stettin* (1889) 14 P.D. 142). Until the bill of lading is produced to him, unless at any rate, its absence has been satisfactorily accounted for, he is entitled to retain possession of the goods and if he does part with possession he does so at his own risk if the person to whom he surrenders possession is not in fact entitled to the goods.

Note

6–006   Note especially the following from the above extract:

"Such a contract is not discharged by performance until the shipowner has actually surrendered possession (that is, has divested himself of all powers to control any physical dealing in the goods) to the person entitled under the terms of the contract to obtain possession of them."

The precise grounds for discharge of the contract are considered further below.

KUWAIT PETROLEUM CORP. v I. & D. OIL CARRIERS LTD (THE HOUDA)

Court of Appeal. [1994] 2 Lloyd's Rep. 541

6–007   There were two main issues in this case. First, did the master have the right to delay performance of a time charterer's order as to employment to check that it was genuine, and secondly, did the charterers have the right to order the master to deliver without production of a bill of lading, given the existence of an express indemnity in the charterparty.

Only the second issue is relevant here. *The Houda* is authority for the proposition that time charterers have no general right to order owners to deliver cargo otherwise than to the holders of a bill of lading. The charterparty contained the following clause:

"Charterers hereby indemnify owners against all consequences or liabilities that may arise from the master, charterers or their agents signing bills of lading or other documents or from the master otherwise complying with charterers' or their agent's orders, (including delivery of cargo without presentation of bills of lading, or at port(s) different from the port(s) shown on the bills of lading) as well as from any irregularities in papers supplied by charterers or their agents. Letter of indemnity to owners' P. & I. club wording to be incorporated in this charterparty."

However, it conferred on the charterers no express right to demand delivery without production, and the Court of Appeal refused to imply one.

Though the case involves the interpretation of a time charterparty, it is implicit in the issue of a bill of lading to order that under the bill of lading contract, the shipowner will deliver only to a lawful holder of the bill[4]:

"Under a bill of lading contract a shipowner is obliged to deliver goods upon production of the original bill of lading. Delivery without production of the bill of lading constitutes a breach of contract even when made to the person entitled to possession. . . .

It is an incident of the bill of lading contract that delivery is to be effected only against the bill of lading." (Leggatt L.J. in *The Houda*.)

When charterers direct the shipowner to issue an order bill of lading, that implies (*per* Millett L.J.):

"an instruction, not merely to sign bills of lading, but to deliver the cargo to the persons who provided evidence of their entitlement thereto by producing the bills of lading."

NEILL L.J.: It is by no means uncommon in the oil cargo trade for the cargo to be discharged before the bill of lading is received. This practice was noticed by Staughton J. in *The Sagona* [1984] 1 Lloyd's Rep. 194 at 201. As Staughton J. explained, there may be a number of reasons for this practice, but it does not seem to me that the existence of the practice or the right to a letter of indemnity can impose on the owners a contractual obligation which does not otherwise exist. [*The charterparty clauses*] do not in my view impose any express obligation on the charterers to discharge a cargo in the absence of the bill of lading. They merely provide for a letter of indemnity if such discharge takes place. But I do not construe the clauses as imposing a contractual duty on the owners.

(b) RIGHT TO DELIVER AGAINST ORIGINAL DOCUMENT

The converse of the right of the shipowner to refuse to deliver except against production of an original bill is that he should be required to deliver when one is tendered, and should also be protected against a claim from anybody else. His

6–008

---

[4] Note the breach of contract action. The contract is of course originally made with the shipper, but transferred to the lawful holder on the principles discussed in chapter 13, below.

concern is that the person who has property, or an immediate right of possession, is not the same as the person holding the document of title, and that he may therefore be liable in conversion if either he refuses to deliver to the person with the immediate right to possession, or if he delivers to anybody else. Of course this should not happen, but bills of lading issued in sets of three originals can be separately negotiated (see further below). Another possibility, which seems to be less common, is for the goods to have been stolen prior to shipment.

In *The Houda*, Millett L.J. made the following observations about the contractual obligation of a shipowner who issues an order bill:

> "Once the master has signed a bill of lading and parted with it, he has subjected the shipowners to a contractual obligation, enforceable at the suit of any person to whom the bill of lading has been negotiated, to deliver the cargo to that person. Their right to deliver the cargo to the first person who claims it and produces an endorsed bill of lading, provided that they have no notice of any better title, is well established, even though the person presenting the bill of lading has in fact no title to the goods."

Leggatt L.J. said that "It is an incident of the bill of lading contract that delivery is to be effected only against the bill of lading", but also observed that "Under a bill of lading contract a shipowner is obliged to deliver goods upon production of the original bill of lading. Delivery without production of the bill of lading constitutes a breach of contract even when made to the person entitled to possession. But the shipowner is not discharged by delivery to the holder if he has notice or knowledge of any defect of title."

These observations concentrate on the shipowner's obligations (and right to deliver) under the carriage contract, and provide him with a contractual defence where the person entitled is party to a carriage contract. If he holds a bill of lading he normally will be (see chapter 13, below), but the shipowner will not be able to rely on a contractual defence if the cargo was stolen prior to shipment, and the person entitled (the victim of the theft) has no connection with the shipment. Another possible defence is considered in the next section.

(c) Sets of Three

6–009   The requirement to deliver against production of an original bill, and the protection afforded to the carrier who does so, would not be a problem were only one original bill of lading issued. In fact, bills of lading are usually issued in sets of three originals, "one of which being accomplished, the others stand void." The reason for this originated in early days of international trade, when there was a significant risk of a document being lost; if three were issued and sent separately, there was a good chance that at least one bill of lading would reach the consignee. The practice causes no difficulties when all the parties are acting in good faith, but it is obviously a possible source of fraud, for example if two or more of the originals are separately negotiated.

GLYN MILLS CURRIE & CO v EAST AND WEST INDIA DOCK CO

House of Lords. (1882) 7 App. Cas. 591

6–010   Goods were shipped, and three original bills of lading were issued, under which the cargo was deliverable to "Cottam & Co or their assigns". The bills were marked "First", "Second" and "Third". Each bill also contained the clause,

"In witness whereof the master or purser of the said ship hath affirmed to three bills of lading, all of this tenor and date, the one of which bills being accomplished, the others to stand void."

During the voyage Cottam & Co., who were in possession of all three bills, indorsed the bill of lading marked "First" to a bank to raise money by way of loan. Upon arrival, the goods were unloaded into the custody of a dock company. Cottam & Co. produced the bill of lading marked "Second", unindorsed, and the dock company (in good faith and without any knowledge of the pledge to the bank) delivered the goods to third parties upon delivery orders issued by Cottam & Co. The bank sued the dock company for conversion.

Held:

The dock company was not guilty of conversion. Its duties (and *a fortiori* those of a shipowner) extended no further than to deliver the goods to the first person to present a bill of lading, as long as it had no notice of any competing claims. It was under no obligation to require all three, nor to take further steps to ensure that the presenter of the document was in fact the consignee.

EARL CAIRNS: Now if there were only one part of the bill of lading the 6–011 process, as it appears to me, would be an extremely simple one. The bill of lading would be the title deed, and whoever came to the shipowner or to the master of the ship and demanded delivery of the goods, in whatever right he claimed—whether as the original consignee or as a person coming by order of the consignee, or as the assign of the contract or of the property—in any of those cases all that the master of the ship (who is not a lawyer and has not, perhaps, a lawyer at his side) would have to say is, "Where is your title deed? Produce it." If he had not a title deed the master would be entitled to say "I will not deliver these goods to you." If, on the other hand, he had the bill of lading, and if there was no fraud and no notice of any different title brought home to the master, all that the master would have to do would be to deliver to the person having that title deed, and then the master would be free from any responsibility.

But the confusion, the difficulty, and embarrassment have arisen from there not being what I have supposed, one title deed, but there being more than one, in this case three parts of the title deed, that it to say of the bill of lading. I asked the question, For whose benefit is it that there are those three parts? Certainly not for the benefit of the shipowner, or for the benefit of the master. To them the presence of three parts of the bill of lading is simply an embarrassment. It is for the benefit of the shipper or of the consignee. I do not stop to inquire whether to them it is really a benefit or whether at this time of day (many if not all of the reasons for having bills of lading in parts being very much modified) it would not be better for every one that there should be only one part; that is a question for the mercantile world to consider. It is quite sufficient for me to say that it is certainly not for the benefit or for the convenience of the shipowner or of the master that there are three parts of the bill of lading.

Then what has the shipowner to do? The shipowner has to protect himself from that which is liable to cause difficulty or embarrassment to him, and the way in which it appears to me he does protect himself is by stating that although "the master or purser hath affirmed to three bills of lading"—that is to say has signed three bills of lading "all of the same tenor and date"—yet notwithstanding that fact "one of these bills of lading being accomplished the others shall stand void", which I understand to mean that if upon one of them the shipowner acts in good faith he will have "accomplished" his contract, will have fulfilled it, and will not be liable or answerable upon any of the others. If one is produced to him in good faith he is to act upon that and not to embarrass himself by considering what has become of the other bills of lading. That appears to me to be the plain and natural interpretation of these words, having regard to the purpose for which they are introduced. I put it to the learned counsel who argued the case whether he could suggest any other explanation of these words which would give them a rational meaning, but I could not learn from the bar that there was any other explanation that could be suggested.

6–012   That being the case, there has occurred exactly one of those instances in which the shipowner requires protection. I use the term "shipowner" because for this purpose I assume that the dock company is in the position of the shipowner. He has had, in good faith, one of the parts of the bill of lading presented to him—he has had no notice of any title at variance with that—he has acted upon the bill of lading so produced, and it appears to me that if he or those who stand in his place, are not to be protected, the final clause might as well be struck out of the bill of lading.

It is said that this will cause inconvenience to those who advance money upon bills of lading. I do not think that it need do so in the least. There are, at all events, three courses open to them, either of which they may take. The mercantile world may, if they think right, alter the practice of giving bills of lading in more parts than one. That would be one course which might be taken. But even supposing that the bill of lading is in more parts than one all that any person who advances money upon a bill of lading will have to do, if he sees, as he will see, on the face of the bill of lading, that it has been signed in more parts than one, will be to require that all the parts are brought in, that is to say, that all the title deeds are brought in. I know that this is the practice with regard to other title deeds, and it strikes me with some surprise that anyone would advance money upon a bill of lading without taking that course of requiring the delivery up of all the parts. If the person advancing the money does not choose to do that, another course which he may take is, to be vigilant and on the alert and to take care that he is on the spot at the first arrival of the ship in the dock. If those who advance money on bills of lading do not adopt one or other of these courses, it appears to me that if they suffer, they suffer in consequence of their own act.

Whether that be so or not, it seems to me that the dock company, standing in the position of the shipowner, require to be protected—that they have done that which it was their positive duty to do, and that the judgment of the Court below ought to be affirmed.

Notes

1. The effect of this decision is to protect the shipowner. Where bills of lading **6–013** are issued in sets of three originals, the shipowner is protected as long as he delivers against production of any original; he need not require tender of all three, nor need he take steps to enquire whether the holder of the original presented is in fact entitled to take delivery of the cargo.[5] Earl Cairns noted that the practice of issuing bills in sets of three was for the benefit of either the shipper or consignee, if indeed it was a benefit at all, and was certainly not for the benefit of the shipowner.

2. The practice has continued to the present day, long after the need for it has disappeared, and obviously risks of fraud can occur as a result of it (*e.g.* a consignee having received all three sets fraudulently enters into three separate sub-sales of the same goods).

3. Buyers and banks can protect themselves by paying only against all three originals. Where payment is by bankers' documentary credit (see chapters 8–10, below), banks usually demand all three sets as security for their advance.[6] In an ordinary sale contract, however, the buyer must pay against one: see *Sanders v Maclean*, later in this chapter.

4. *Glyn Mills* is also consistent with a principle that it is for merchants, rather than carriers, to take the risk of the fraud of other merchants. In general, this seems an eminently reasonable principle, but as we will see below, it is not uniformly adopted.

Juristic basis of the decision:

The juristic basis of *Glyn Mills* is not entirely clear, but it would make a difference, **6–014** were the facts to be altered slightly.

In *Glyn Mills*, the plaintiff (who failed in a conversion action) was a bank with whom a bill of lading had been deposited as pledgee, the defendant having delivered the goods to the holder of another original bill. In most cases today, the holder would be party to a contract with the shipowner, on the basis of the Carriage of Goods by Sea Act 1992 (on which see further chapter 13), in which case the shipowner would have a contractual defence; the document made clear on its face that there were three bills, "one of which bills being accomplished, the others to stand void", from which it could be inferred that the shipowner was entitled to deliver against the first bill presented.

After the decision two years later in *Sewell v Burdick*,[7] it became clear that the plaintiff in *Glyn Mills* was not in privity of contract with the defendant, so a contractual defence would not have been possible, but Lord Blackburn observed that the plaintiffs must have been aware that there was more than one bill, since their bill was marked "first" and also bore the words: " . . . one of which bills being accomplished, the others shall stand void." Lord Watson's view also seems to depend on the plaintiff's notice, and the form of the bill of lading.[8] This would be consistent with a *volenti* defence, but if that is the basis of the decision, it would not apply if the plaintiff was unaware that there was more than one original in circulation, nor if the plaintiff had no bill of lading at all. The view of Lord Selborne L.C.,[9] depending on mercantile usage, does not appear to be so limited, and another possible explanation of the case is that conversion requires a wrongful act by the carrier, whereas to deliver against production of an original bill,

---

[5] Although Lord Blackburn took the view, at 613, that the shipowner should interplead if he had notice that the parts had been separately negotiated.
[6] *e.g.* U.C.P. 500, art. 23(a)(iv), set out in App. C, below.
[7] (1884) 10 App. Cas. 74.
[8] See at 606 and 614.
[9] At 596.

without notice of competing claims, is not wrongful.[10] If this is the correct explanation of the case, it provides the carrier with a general protection, but the explanation applies only to documents of title recognised as such, because of mercantile usage, by the common law.[11]

(d) DELIVERY WITHOUT PRODUCTION

6–015   The *Glyn Mills* decision only protects a shipowner who delivers against production of an original bill of lading, albeit that he is not required to deliver only against production of the full set. The logic of using a document of title to transfer constructive possession implies, however, that the shipowner who delivers without production of a bill of lading should not be protected, and indeed should be liable should he deliver to the wrong person.

SZE HAI TONG BANK LTD v RAMBLER CYCLE CO LTD

Privy Council. [1959] A.C. 576

Facts:

6–016   The carrier (through his authorised agent), delivered goods without production of a bill of lading, against an indemnity in his favour, from the consignee's bank. This was a common practice at the port of Singapore. The consignee did not pay the seller for the goods, and the seller/consignor sued the carrier. The appellant bank was involved in the action because it admitted liability to indemnify the carrier were the carrier liable.

Held:
The carrier was liable to the seller for both breach of contract, and conversion. Further, an exemption clause in the carriage contract would not lightly be construed so as to protect the carrier against this breach of contract.

6–017   LORD DENNING: *(footnotes to official reports taken from judgment)* It is perfectly clear law that a shipowner who delivers without production of the bill of lading does so at his peril. The contract is to deliver, on production of the bill of lading, to the person entitled under the bill of lading. In this case it was "unto order "or his or their assigns," that is to say, to the order of the Rambler Cycle Company, if they had not assigned the bill of lading, or to their assigns, if they had. The shipping company did not deliver the goods to any such person. They are therefore liable for breach of contract unless there is some term in the bill of lading protecting them. And they delivered the goods, without production of the bill of

[10] Bools, *The Bill of Lading: A Document of Title to Goods*, (L.L.P., 1997), at p. 166. For a general definition of conversion, see, *e.g.* Rogers, *Winfield & Jolowicz on Tort*, (15th ed., Sweet & Maxwell, 1998), Ch. 17.
[11] See further Chs 15 and 16, below, on the difficulties of extending *Glyn Mills* protection to other types of documentation.

lading, to a person who was not entitled to receive them. They are therefore liable in conversion unless likewise so protected.

In order to escape the consequences of the misdelivery, the appellants say that the shipping company is protected by clause 2 of the bill of lading, which says that:

"During the period before the goods are loaded on or after they are discharged from the ship on which they are carried by sea, the following terms and conditions shall apply to the exclusion of any other provisions in this bill of lading that may be inconsistent therewith, *viz.,*

- (a) so long as the goods remain in the actual custody of the carrier or his servants" (here follows a specified exception);
- "(b) whilst the goods are being transported to or from the ship" (here follows another specified exemption);
- "(c) in all other cases the responsibility of the carrier, whether as carrier or as custodian or bailee of the goods, shall be deemed to commence only when the goods are loaded on the ship and to cease absolutely after they are discharged therefrom."

The exemption, on the face of it, could hardly be more comprehensive, **6–018** and it is contended that it is wide enough to absolve the shipping company from responsibility for the act of which the Rambler Cycle Company complains, that is to say, the delivery of the goods to a person who, to their knowledge, was not entitled to receive them. If the exemption clause upon its true construction absolved the shipping company from an act such as that, it seems that by parity of reasoning they would have been absolved if they had given the goods away to some passer-by or had burnt them or thrown them into the sea. If it had been suggested to the parties that the condition exempted the shipping company in such a case, they would both have said: "Of course not." There is, therefore, an implied limitation on the clause, which cuts down the extreme width of it: and, as a matter of construction, their Lordships decline to attribute to it the unreasonable effect contended for.

But their Lordships go further. If such an extreme width were given to the exemption clause, it would run counter to the main object and intent of the contract. For the contract, as it seems to their Lordships, has, as one of its main objects, the proper delivery of the goods by the shipping company, "unto order or his or their assigns," against production of the bill of lading. It would defeat this object entirely if the shipping company was at liberty, at its own will and pleasure, to deliver the goods to somebody else, to someone not entitled at all, without being liable for the consequences. The clause must therefore be limited and modified to the extent necessary to enable effect to be given to the main object and intent of the contract: see *Glynn v Margetson & Co*[12]; *GH Renton & Co Ltd v Palmyra Trading Corporation of Panama*.[13]

To what extent is it necessary to limit or modify the clause? It must at least be modified so as not to permit the shipping company deliberately to disregard its obligations as to delivery. For that is what has happened here. The shipping company's agents in Singapore acknowledged: "We are doing something we know we should not do." Yet they did it. And they did it as agents in such circumstances that their acts were the acts of the shipping company itself. They were so placed that their state of mind can properly be regarded as the state of mind of the shipping company itself. And they deliberately disregarded one of the prime obligations of the contract. No court can allow so fundamental a breach to pass unnoticed under the cloak of a general exemption clause: see *The Cap Palos*.[14]

Comments (on the liability issue)

6–019   1. The requirement that delivery be made only against production of a bill of lading is not a problem as long as the consignee receives it before the goods arrive, but it can cause severe problems for shipowners on, *e.g.* North Atlantic container routes where the ship often arrives before the documents. It can also be a problem where a negotiable bill is issued, and there are multiple re-sales on a relatively short voyage. This can happen with any bulk commodity, but the greatest problems seem to have arisen with oil cargoes.

2. These problems are considered further in paras 15–018 *et seq.*, below. Many shipowners would prefer to see the replacement of bills of lading with non-negotiable waybills, precisely because of these liability problems. Sometimes one of the three original bills of lading is carried on board the ship in an envelope, and given to a named person (the consignee), who presents it back to the ship to obtain delivery. It is by no means clear that shipowners are protected by this practice,[15] given the obvious likelihood that the consignor will negotiate the other two originals (and why retain them otherwise?). Shipowners who engage in this practice usually require an indemnity similar to that in the above case.

3. The shipping company's representative said in evidence:

"It is an accepted fact that, in absence of bills of lading, goods are released on an indemnity. I agree we are supposed to deliver on the bill of lading being produced to us. I agree that, when we do not have the bill of lading produced, we cover ourselves by getting an indemnity. When it is suggested to me that we get these indemnities because we know we are doing what we should not do, I say that if no risk, we would not need indemnity. I agree we get indemnity because we are doing something we know we should not do, but it is common practice. It is an everyday occurrence. We rely on the bank's guarantee."

The case concerned, then, delivery to someone not entitled, where the carrier was aware that he was doing something wrong. It is now apparent that neither of

---

[12] [1893] A.C. 351.

[13] [1957] A.C. 149, 164.

[14] [1921] P. 458, 471.

[15] It differs from *Glyn Mills* in two respects. First, it can no longer be said that the practice is not for the benefit of the shipowner. Secondly, the shipowner is put on notice of possible competing claims. As to whether the indemnity would be effective protection, see further para. 6–021, below.

these are prerequisites. In *The Houda* (see above), the shipowner was held entitled to refuse (and therefore should have refused?) to deliver to someone who was entitled, but had no bill of lading. In *Motis Exports* (see below), the shipowner was held liable, although he believed (wrongly) that he was delivering against an original bill.

Comments (on exemption clauses protecting a misdelivering carrier)

In *The Houda*, there was no express contractual provision entitling the charterers **6–020** to demand delivery without production of the bills of lading, and one would not be implied from the existence of an indemnity, but Millett L.J. suggested that the position would have been different if there were an express contractual term:

> "In the absence of express contractual provision entitling them to do so, it was in my judgment thereafter no longer open to the Charterers to countermand or vary their instructions by directing the Owners to deliver the cargo otherwise than against presentation of the bills of lading, thereby depriving the Owners of the protection to which their original instructions had entitled them."

This is also consistent with *Sze Hai Tong Ltd v Rambler Cycle Co*, above, where Lord Denning observed of shipowners who had delivered without production of a bill of lading that:

> "They are, therefore, liable for breach of contract unless there is some term in the bill of lading protecting them."

Presumably, this implies that they could have been protected by an express contractual provision (although that case also makes clear that very clear words would be required). See further below.

In the Australian case *The Stone Gemini*,[16] there was a clause in the charterparty allowing delivery without production, against an indemnity, and the bill of lading incorporated all terms and conditions of the charterparty (on which see further chapter 12, below). Tamberlin J., following *The Sormovskiy 3068* (where there had been a similar clause), observed that making provision for a letter of indemnity amounted to an admission that the shipowners would become liable to the lawful holder for wrongful delivery, and the clause could not therefore be used as a defence to a conversion action.

Comments (on the indemnity)

The indemnity was assumed to be enforceable in *Sze Hai Tong*, no argument **6–021** being addressed to the court on this issue, as the bank admitted liability on the indemnity. If, however the shipowner knew that he was delivering to someone not entitled, an indemnity against what would in effect be theft should be unenforceable as an illegal contract, on the basis of *Brown Jenkinson v Percy Dalton*—see chapter 7, below. The carriers in *Sze Hai Tong* knew that what they were doing was wrong, but did not know, or presumably even suspect, that they were delivering to someone who was not entitled. Probably that would not attract the *Brown Jenkinson* principle. In *The Stone Gemini*,[17] the Australia Federal Court, New South Wales District Registry in Admiralty held an indemnity enforceable on similar facts.

---

[16] [1999] 2 Lloyd's Rep. 255, paras 49 *et seq.*
[17] Above, paras 67 *et seq.* The possibility was there discussed of waiver operating against the holder of a bill of lading, who had consented to the goods being delivered without production, against a letter of indemnity, but the evidence did not support waiver: para. 48.

It might be different had an original bill been carried on the ship, since there would be little point in doing that unless the other originals were to be negotiated, and there would be a real risk that the person taking delivery might not be entitled. If delivery were construed as a fraud on the holder of the other two originals, that would attract the *Brown Jenkinson* principle. *Brown Jenkinson* also demonstrates that merely because a fraudulent practice is common does not lead the courts to looking on it any more kindly.

(e) Developments Since *Sze Hai Tong*

There were a number of cases since *Sze Hai Tong* which suggested there might be exceptions, for example where a bill of lading were lost, and an explanation for its absence provided.

CASENOTE BY THE AUTHOR ON *THE SORMOVSKIY 3068*

The Times, 13 May 1994. Later reported at [1994] 2 Lloyd's Rep. 266; published in [1994] 8 "Oil and Gas Law and Taxation Review" D91–D92

Bill of lading

6–022 Delivery without production of bill of lading—whether delivery made to persons entitled to possession of the cargo—whether shipowner entitled to deliver to such persons without demanding production of original bill of lading

Sucre Export SA v Northern River Shipping Ltd (The "Sormovskiy 3068"). Queen's Bench Division, 25 April 1994. Clarke J.

Facts:

The plaintiffs were sub-charterers of the vessel, "Sormovskiy 3068", of which the defendants were owners. The plaintiffs were also f.o.b. purchasers of 3,000 tonnes (60,000 bags) of sugar. Three original bills of lading had been issued evidencing the shipment, and indorsed in blank in favour of the plaintiffs, who thereupon became owners of the cargo.

The plaintiffs re-sold the sugar c.i.f. to Forfar, the sale eventually being agreed as cash against documents, and Forfar re-sold to BMH. BMH paid Forfar for the sugar, but Forfar did not pay the plaintiffs, at any rate the full amount for the cargo. Because of a reservation of title clause in the contract between the plaintiffs and Forfar, title did not pass to Forfar. When the vessel arrived at the Commercial Sea Port (CSP) at Vyborg (near St. Petersburg), discharge began without the knowledge or consent of the plaintiffs, and without production of an original bill of lading, and over 2,000 tonnes had been discharged before the plaintiffs discovered the situation.

The main issue in the case involved the claim by the plaintiffs that the defendant shipowners were liable in contract and conversion, on the grounds that they had delivered without requiring production of an original bill of lading.

The defendants claimed that they were entitled to deliver the cargo to the persons entitled to it, even in the absence of an original bill of lading, and that they had indeed delivered to the parties entitled to possession since they (CSP) were the agents of the plaintiffs. They claimed that there is no authority for a term being implied into the carriage contract prohibiting the shipowner from delivering to the persons entitled to the cargo, in the absence of an original bill of lading.

In the alternative, the defendants claimed that they delivered in accordance with the practice, custom and local law of the port.

Other relevant facts are that the bill of lading was consigned to order, and that the address of BMH was given as the notify address.

Held:

1. The defendants were liable for delivering without production of an original bill of lading.

2. In any event, the defendants did not deliver to a person entitled to possession as an agent of the plaintiffs.

3. The defendants did not deliver in accordance with the practice, custom and local law of the port.

Comment

The most significant aspect of the case relates to delivery without production of **6–023** an original bill of lading.

The conventional view was probably that the defendants' case was almost unarguable, but surprisingly, there was little previous authority on the requirement for tender of an original bill of lading prior to delivery to a person entitled to possession of the cargo, such authority as was cited mostly concerning delivery to someone not entitled to possession of the cargo. The defendants also made the point that there must be some circumstances where the shipowner was entitled (and indeed obliged) to deliver without production, since an original bill of lading would not always be available, for example where it had been lost or stolen. They also cited *Finlay v The Liverpool and Great Western Steamship Company Ltd* (1870) 23 L.T. 251, where Martin B. held that the shipowners were not entitled to deliver, even against an original bill of lading, where it was known by the time of delivery that the bill of lading had been obtained fraudulently. The only authority cited which was clearly contrary to the defendants' case was *The Stettin* (1889) 14 P.D. 142, but the remarks made in that case were *dicta*, since the actual decision there was based on German rather than English law.

Nevertheless, Clarke J. was not convinced by the defendants' argument, summarising his conclusion as follows:

"It makes commercial sense to have a simple rule that in the absence of an express term of the contract the master must only deliver the cargo to the holder of the bill of lading who presents it to him. In that way both the shipowners and the persons in truth entitled to possession of the cargo are protected by the terms of the contract. Where the master or shipowner delivers the cargo in breach of contract otherwise than in return for an original bill of lading the person entitled to possession will of course only be entitled to recover substantial damages if he proves that he has suffered loss and damage as a result. So for example if the cargo is delivered to the person entitled to possession he will not ordinarily be able to show that he has suffered a loss."

He was prepared to accept that there may be exceptions to the general rule, for example, where there is an express contractual term requiring the master to deliver the cargo against a letter of indemnity or bank guarantee. Indeed, such a clause was here incorporated from the charterparty (but the owners did not comply with it as they did not take a letter of indemnity or a bank guarantee). He would also have been prepared, had the issue arisen, to imply terms to cater for the loss or theft of the original bills, and for the situation where it was proved to the master's reasonable satisfaction that the person seeking delivery of the goods was entitled to possession, and an explanation was given as to the absence of the bills of lading. But Clarke J. was not prepared to accept the general proposition advanced by the defendants.

6–024   Even if he had been prepared to accept that argument, he did not accept that the shipowners had delivered to the persons entitled to possession of the sugar. The defendants argued that the plaintiffs constituted BMH (and hence CSP as agent of BMH) as their agents by selling the cargo to sub-buyers who in turn re-sold it to BMH, or alternatively by representing in the bill of lading and the charterparty that they would nominate agents, by stating in the bill of lading that BMH was the notify party and by sending a copy of the bill of lading, and the invoice between Forfar and BMH (stating that BMH were the buyers of the sugar) with the vessel. Clarke J. refused to hold that these facts led to the agency conclusion contended by the defendants.

The defendants' argument that they delivered in accordance with the practice, custom and local law of the port was also rejected. This was essentially an issue of fact, where there was a conflict of evidence between two experts on Russian law. Again, part of the argument was that CSP were agents of the plaintiffs, but this time it was conceded that Russian rather than English law should determine the matter. This aspect of the case raises no issues of general principle for English law.

The defendants also argued that they were protected by the following clause in the bill of lading:

" . . . The Carrier shall in no case be responsible for loss of or damage to cargo arisen prior to loading or after discharging."

The argument was rejected on the grounds that the breach by the shipowners was permitting discharge without requiring production of an original bill of lading, and that but for the breach discharge would not have begun. Hence, it could not be said that the plaintiffs' loss had arisen only after discharging.

(f) THE PRESENT STATE OF THE LAW

6–025   The exceptions to the general rule, for example to cater for the loss or theft of the original bills, were doubted in *The Houda*, and can now be said almost certainly to be incorrect. The authorities were reviewed by Professor Wilson in "The Presentation Rule Revisited" [1995] L.M.C.L.Q. 289. A clause exempting the carrier from liability might in principle work, but it would need very explicit drafting, and none of the clauses considered since *Sze Hai Tong* has been successful. Professor Wilson observes, at pp. 297–298, that:

"Perhaps the neatest solution to the problem was provided by the draftsman of the bill of lading in the Australian case of *The Antwerpen*.[18] The New South Wales Court of Appeal initially held that, on its true construction, a standard exemption clause . . . did not absolve the carrier from liability for delivery of

---

[18] [1994] 1 Lloyd's Rep. 213.

goods without production of the relevant bill. Nevertheless a majority of the court was of the view that he was afforded complete protection by the addition of a further clause to the effect that:

'The exemptions limitations terms and conditions in this bill of lading shall apply whether or not loss or damage is caused by . . . actions constituting fundamental breach of contract.' "

It is now also clear that it is not a defence for the carrier to be unaware that he is not delivering against an original bill of lading.

CASENOTE BY THE AUTHOR ON RIX J.'S DECISION IN *MOTIS EXPORTS LTD v DAMPSKIBSSELSKABET AF 1912 (AKTIESELSKAB)* ENTITLED "DELIVERY AGAINST FORGED BILL OF LADING"

[1999] L.M.C.L.Q. 449–456

[Footnotes as in the original, but renumbered for present purposes.]

    Motis Exports Ltd v Dampskibsselskabet AF 1912 (Aktieselskab)[19] is the **6–026** latest of a line of cases, extending the liability of a shipowner for delivering without production of an original bill of lading; the shipowner believed the bill of lading tendered to be an original, but it was in fact a forgery. The issue was the liability of the shipowner to the holder of an original bill.

Some Background

    Much of the value of a document of title to merchants and their bankers lies in its ability to transfer the right to possession of the goods while the goods are at sea; only the holder of an original document is entitled to take delivery of the goods at the port of discharge. Without this feature, much of the security given by such a document to an unpaid seller, or bank under a documentary credit, would be lost. If the bill of lading is retained, but the shipowner delivers to a buyer who has not paid for the goods, the holder will of course have an action against the buyer, but this is of no value if the buyer is insolvent; the security of the document lies in the liability of the shipowner for misdelivery in such cases. The law and practice of international trade was developed to protect the parties against the insolvency of others.

    The use of a document of title can also protect the shipowner, however, since it identifies the only person to whom he is both entitled and obliged to deliver. It is therefore necessary that[20]:

---

[19] [1999] 1 Lloyd's Rep. 837; [1999] 1 All E.R. (Comm.) 571.
[20] (a) and (b) were examined by Wilson, "The Presentation Rule revisited" [1995] L.M.C.L.Q. 289. For completeness, it is also necessary for the holder of an original document to be able to require the shipowner to deliver to him; that requirement is not relevant to this note.

(a) if the shipowner delivers other than against production of an original document, he should be liable to the holder of the original document;

(b) the shipowner should be entitled to refuse to deliver except against production of an original document[21];

(c) the shipowner should be protected if he delivers against production of an original document.

In recent years the courts have asserted these principles rigorously, at least for the shipped bill of lading, admitting few exceptions. Proposition (a) was established at least as long ago as 1889 in *The Stettin*,[22] and reasserted in *Barclays Bank Ltd v Commissioners of Customs and Excise*,[23] but probably the best-known authority is *Sze Hai Tong Ltd v Rambler Cycle Co*,[24] where a shipping company was held liable to the shipper for delivering, against an indemnity but without production of an original bill of lading, to a consignee who had not paid for the goods. In *Sze Hai Tong*, the shipping company knew that it was acting wrongly in delivering without production, but the principle was extended in *The Sormovskiy 3068*,[25] where the shipowners believed that they were delivering to the person entitled to take delivery. Both Diplock J. in *Barclays Bank Ltd v Commissioners of Customs and Excise* and Clarke J. in *The Sormovskiy 3068* suggested that there might be limited exceptions to the shipowner's liability, however (see further below).[26]

6–027   For proposition (b), *Barclays Bank Ltd v Commissioners of Customs and Excise* is also an authority,[27] but the best authority is *The Houda*,[28] where the shipowners were held by the Court of Appeal justified in refusing to deliver without production of bills of lading on the instructions of their time charterers. In contrast to the *Barclays* and *Sormovskiy* decisions,

---

[21] In *Motis Exports*, Rix J. considered (but rejected) the argument that though the shipowners might be entitled to refuse to deliver against a forged bill, whether or not they knew of the forgery, they might nonetheless be entitled to deliver in the absence of such knowledge. See further [nn. 21, 45] and text thereto.

[22] (1889) 14 P.D. 142, where the bill of lading was made out in favour of a named consignee or his assigns.

[23] [1963] 1 Lloyd's Rep. 81; the statements of Diplock J. are *dicta*, the issue in the case being when the bill of lading ceased to be a document of title.

[24] [1959] A.C. 576. The main issue was whether the shipping company could rely on a contractual exemption clause—see further [nn. 35 and 39] and text thereto.

[25] *Sucre Export SA v Northern River Shipping Ltd (The Sormovskiy 3068)* [1994] 2 Lloyd's Rep. 266. On the facts, the shipowners were held to have delivered to someone not entitled to take delivery, but the decision would have been the same even if the shipowners' beliefs had been true.

[26] [n. 32] and text thereto. There are also unusual cases, such as *The Future Express* [1993] 2 Lloyd's Rep. 542, noted [1994] L.M.C.L.Q. 350, where the holder of the original bill has no cause of action; were the facts to arise today, however, he would have a contractual action under the Carriage of Goods by Sea Act 1992.

[27] Again *dicta*, the issue being as described [n. 23].

[28] *Kuwait Petroleum Corporation v I. & D. Oil Carriers Ltd (The Houda)* [1994] 2 Lloyd's Rep. 541. This case and *The Sormovskiy 3068* form the backbone of the discussion in Wilson [1995] L.M.C.L.Q. 289.

however, no support can be found in *The Houda* for the existence of any exceptions, save express provision in the carriage contract.

For proposition (c), the best authority is probably *Glyn Mills Currie & Co v East and West India Dock Co*,[29] where the House of Lords held that a shipowner who delivered against the first original bill tendered of a set of three, would be protected against the claim of the true owner (of whose title the shipowner had no notice). In *Glyn Mills* itself, a pledgee pledged only one bill of a set of three, retaining one of the others, which he used to collect the goods, without first having repaid the loan.

Analytically, *Motis Exports* is an extension of the category (a) authorities, Rix J. taking the view (contrary to *Barclays* and *Sormovskiy*) that the only exception is where there is an express clause protecting the shipowner in the carriage contract. The shipowner was held liable to the lawful holder of an order bill for delivering against production of a forged bill. A second issue was the interpretation of a clause purporting to protect the carrier against the consequences of misdelivery; here the case does little more than apply well-established principles.

Though *Motis Exports* is no doubt properly classified in category (a), factually it is very different from the other cases in that category; more than one document purporting to be an original bill of lading was in existence, and the shipowners delivered against what they believed to be a valid original bill. It is difficult to see how this situation can arise in the absence of fraud. In this respect, the case with the greatest similarity to *Motis Exports* is *Glyn Mills*, the difference being that in *Glyn Mills* delivery was made against presentation of a real original, rather than a forgery. In *Glyn Mills* too there was a fraud (by the pledgor), and in both cases the shipowners both intended to and believed that they were acting properly. In *Glyn Mills*, however, the shipowners were protected, whereas in *Motis Exports* they were not.

It is not particularly difficult to justify giving the holder of a bill of lading an action against a shipowner who has chosen to deliver without production, in order to protect the holder against the bankruptcy of a third party. Justifying an action against an innocent shipowner, to protect the holder against the fraud of another party, is more difficult. "The object of mercantile usages is to prevent the risk of insolvency, not of fraud".[30] The mercantile usages were developed for the benefit of merchants, not shipowners, and arguably they, rather than the shipowners, should bear the risk of fraud. The result in *Glyn Mills* accords with this principle; that in *Motis Exports* does not.

Motis Exports: facts and main issues:
Motis Exports was a trial of preliminary issues on assumed facts which, **6–028** simply stated, were these. The plaintiffs shipped various consignments

---

[29] (1882) 7 App. Cas. 591. The action was against a dock company, but the principles are equally applicable to shipowners.
[30] *Sanders v Maclean* (1883) 11 Q.B.D. 327, 343, *per* Bowen L.J.

aboard the defendants' ships, taking order (Maersk Line) bills of lading, containing the following clause (cl. 5.3.b):

> Where the carriage called for commences at the port of loading and/ or finishes at the port of discharge, the Carrier shall have no liability whatsoever for any loss or damage to the goods while in its actual or constructive possession before loading or after discharge over ships rail, or if applicable, on the ships ramp, however caused.

Forged bills of lading were used to obtain delivery orders in respect of the goods, the fraudsters using these delivery orders to obtain delivery of the goods themselves at the discharge ports.

The plaintiffs sued the defendant shipowners for breach of the bill of lading contracts, and for conversion, in misdelivering the goods to persons not entitled to them. The defendants claimed that they were entitled to deliver against the forged bills, assuming that the forgery was neither known nor reasonably apparent, or alternatively that they were protected from liability by cl. 5.3.b.

Rix J. held that the plaintiffs were entitled to succeed.

Delivery against forged bills of lading:

6–029 It had never been previously decided whether a shipowner is protected if he delivers against bills of lading which purport to be original, but which are in fact forged. The defendants argued that there were exceptions to the "simple rule that in the absence of an express term of the contract the master must only deliver the cargo to the holder of the bill of lading who presents it to him".[31] They relied primarily on *dicta* in *Barclays Bank Ltd v Commissioners of Customs and Excise* and *The Sormovskiy 3068*,[32] where respectively Diplock and Clarke JJ. envisaged an exception where the bill of lading had been lost, and its absence satisfactorily accounted for. The defendants' purpose in arguing the existence of this exception appears to have been simply to argue that the rule was not absolute. Once any exception is admitted, the list of exceptions can be extended, for example to cover a shipowner who is deceived by a forged bill of lading, since far from intending to deny the bill of lading holder's right, he is attempting as best he can to acknowledge it. Moreover, the shipowner has acted entirely without fault.

Rix J.'s view, however, based primarily on views expressed by all three judges in the Court of Appeal in *The Houda*,[33] was that there were no exceptions to the general rule against delivery without production, even where the bill of lading was missing, unless there was a contractual term protecting the carrier. Rix J. therefore disapproved Clarke J.'s *dicta* in *The Sormovskiy 3068*. To the problem of the lost bill of lading, either the owner who was unable to produce the bill should persuade the shipowner to

---

[31] [1994] 2 Lloyd's Rep. 266, 274, *per* Clarke J.
[32] [nn. 23 and 25] at pp. 89 and 272, respectively.
[33] [n. 28].

deliver against an indemnity,[34] or the directions of the court should be sought, in the exercise of its equitable jurisdiction to grant relief in the case of lost bills.

Since Rix J. was prepared to admit (in the absence of an express contractual term) of no exceptions to the "simple working rule", it was necessary to interpret it, to consider whether a forged bill of lading is as good as a genuine bill of lading for the purposes of the rule. In holding that it was not, Rix J. did not think that a shipowner could be obliged to deliver against a forged bill, whether he was or was not aware of the forgery. Nor would he be entitled to deliver if he was aware of the forgery. Rix J. was reluctant to imply a term entitling him to do so, in ignorance of the forgery, primarily because (in his view) it would subvert the bill of lading's role as the key to the warehouse.

The shipowners had also argued that that the contractual position should be analogous to that in conversion, and that "it is only where a bailee intends to deny the owner's right or to assert a right inconsistent with the owner's right that he is liable in conversion: therefore, a shipowner deceived by a forged bill of lading does not intend to deny the bill of lading holder's right, but to acknowledge it, and cannot be liable in conversion." After fully reviewing the authorities, Rix J. analysed the situation differently, however: the shipowners had committed "an intentional act inconsistent with the true owner's rights, albeit done in ignorance of them and without intending to challenge them; and is a conversion."

The exemption clause issue:

The loss to the cargo occurred after discharge, and the shipowners argued   **6–030** that they were in any event protected by cl. 5.3.b. The clause does not, however, expressly mention misdelivery, and could be construed as covering only accidental losses, and possibly theft. Rix J. was prepared so to interpret it, restrictively, relying on cases such as *Sze Hai Tong Bank Ltd v Rambler Cycle Co Ltd*,[35] and *The Ines*.[36] Moreover, even if the clause could be construed so as to cover theft, there was a difference between physical theft and obtaining by deception, as had occurred here; even if the former was covered by the clause, the latter was not.

Motis Exports adds little here to existing jurisprudence. Such clauses are interpreted *contra preferentem*, much as was the deviation clause in *Glynn v Margetson & Co*,[37] and limited and modified to the extent necessary to enable effect to be given to the main object and intent of the contract. As to what this is, one "of the key provisions of the bill of lading, so far as the shipper is concerned, is the promise not to deliver the cargo other

[34] There is a clear assumption that such indemnities are enforceable, although this has never been directly tested. If, however, the shipowner knew that he was delivering to someone other than the true owner, the indemnity would be unenforceable on the principles stated in *Brown Jenkinson & Co Ltd v Percy Dalton (London) Ltd* [1957] 2 Q.B. 621.
[35] [1959] A.C. 576.
[36] [1995] 2 Lloyd's Rep. 144.
[37] [1893] A.C. 351.

than in return for an original bill of lading",[38] and clear words would be needed to contract out of this.

Earlier in the judgment, however, Rix J. had emphasised that the one exception to the "simple working rule" was a contractual term protecting the carrier. He must therefore have envisaged the possibility that such a term could exist, and indeed, that must be the case, since the rule is one of construction.[39] The type of clause that might suffice was fully discussed by Wilson a few years ago in this Quarterly.[40]

Comment:

(i) Who should bear the risk of fraud?

6–031   It is arguable that the result in *Motis Exports* is just. Rix J. observed that "as between shipowner and true goods owner, it is the shipowner who controls the form, signature and issue of his bills . . . If one of two innocent people must suffer for the fraud of a third, it is better that the loss falls on the shipowner, whose responsibility it is both to look to the integrity of his bills and to care for the cargo in his possession and to deliver it aright, rather than on the true goods owner, who holds a valid bill and expects to receive his goods in return for it." Arguably it should indeed be the shipowner who should suffer from the fraud of the third party. He could, after all, produce bills which are more difficult to forge, or where forgeries are easier to detect.

By contrast, in *Glyn Mills* it was the true owner, rather than the shipowner, who suffered from the fraud, but there Earl Cairns asked[41]: "For whose benefit is it that there are those three parts? Certainly not for the benefit of the shipowner, or for the benefit of the master. To them the presence of three parts of the bill of lading is simply an embarrassment. It is for the benefit of the shipper or of the consignee." Justice in that case therefore dictated that the loss should fall on the cargo-owner, not the shipowner.

Superficially attractive though they may be, however, these arguments do not justify the decision in *Motis Exports*. Just as in *Glyn Mills*, it is not in the shipowners' interests to issue bills in sets of three, many shipowners, especially on container routes, would probably prefer not to have to issue bills of lading at all.[42] It is the merchants, not the shipowners, who require negotiable documentation. Shipowners are obliged by the

---

[38] *Per* Clarke J. in *The Ines*, [n. 36] at p. 152, a passage quoted by Rix J. in *Motis Exports* at p. 846. See also [n. 50], where a similar view is quoted.

[39] Although parts of Lord Denning's speech in *Sze Hai Tong* almost take the now-discredited fundamental breach as a rule of law approach, even that decision was in fact based on the construction of the clause.

[40] [1995] L.M.C.L.Q. 289, at 296–298.

[41] (1882) 7 App. Cas. 591, 599.

[42] See, *e.g.* Sir Anthony Lloyd, "The bill of lading: do we really need it?" [1989] L.M.C.L.Q. 47.

Hague-Visby Rules to issue bills of lading,[43] but it can be argued that the attendant risks should be borne by the merchants, and not by the ship-owners.

For there to be no action at all against the shipowner for misdelivery **6–032** would be entirely to negate the value of the bill of lading as "the key to the warehouse", however, and a better argument might be to allow shipowners, in some circumstances, to refuse to issue bills of lading, for example where a waybill, or electronic document, might be more appro-priate. Such an argument is beyond the scope of this note. Where an order bill *is* issued, it is clear that it might be negotiated, and it is therefore necessary for there to be rules about delivery. The "simple rule" pro-pounded in *The Sormovskiy 3068* and *Motis Exports* gives the merchants the security of a document of title, in protecting them against delivery of their goods to someone who is not entitled to them, and who may be insolvent. The "simple rule" also protects shipowners, since they know to whom delivery is to be made; this also justifies the refusal to make an exception where the bill of lading is lost.

It does not follow, merely because that exception is not justified, that no exception is justified, and I have already suggested that a distinction can be drawn between protecting merchants against insolvency and fraud. The use of documents of title to represent goods is inevitably fraud-prone, and since the benefit is entirely for the merchants, so arguably should be the risk. Moreover, merchants normally bear the risk of fraud.[44] In *Glyn Mills* the merchant was unable to pass the risk on to the ship-owner; nor should he have been able to do so in *Motis Exports*.

In *Glyn Mills* the shipowner was entitled to deliver against the first original bill presented, not having notice of the true owner's claim. If he had had notice, he would not have been so entitled. In the case of a forged bill, clearly the shipowner should neither be obliged, or entitled, to deliver against a bill which he knows to be forged, but it is difficult to see why he should not be accorded the same protection as in *Glyn Mills*, in the absence of such knowledge.[45] Rix J.'s view, that this would undermine "the integrity of the bill as the key to a floating warehouse" is unconvinc-ing, since the key concept was developed to protect merchants against insolvency, not fraud. Little more convincing is the argument that the shipowner controls the form of the bill, since even the most sophisticated

---

[43] Article III(3).

[44] *e.g.* the property provisions in s.19(3) of the Sale of Goods Act 1979 protect the seller who uses a documentary bill against the buyer's bankruptcy but not his fraud: *Cahn v Pockett's Bristol Channel Steam Packet Co Ltd* [1899] 1 Q.B. 643; a trust receipt protects a bank against a bankrupt but not a fraudulent customer: *Lloyd's Bank v Bank of America National Trust and Savings Association* [1938] 2 K.B. 147. Mercantile usages generally protect against bankruptcy not fraud.

[45] Rix J. thought that he should be entitled to refuse to deliver, even if he were in ignorance of the forgery. Clearly if the fraudsters themselves sued the shipowner for such refusal they would be met with an *ex turpi causa* defence. The position would be more difficult were the forged bill subsequently negotiated, but it is difficult as a matter of logic to see why the ignorant shipowner should not be entitled to refuse, but also to be protected if he does deliver.

bill is unlikely to be proof against forgery by a sufficiently determined fraudster.

It is suggested, therefore, that the decision in *Motis Exports* is undesirable. Since, moreover, it was based on Rix J.'s interpretation of the carriage contract, and in particular on taking a particularly strong view of its main object, to deliver only on presentation of an original bill of lading,[46] there would be no conceptual difficulty in reaching a different result, on a different interpretation of the contract.

(ii) Extensions of Motis Exports reasoning

6–033 Professor Wilson queries "whether it is advisable or expedient at the present day to rely to so great an extent on a procedure for releasing goods which is dependent on the production of a unique piece of paper", and observes that the "time may have come to make greater use of the waybill and the various electronic data information services which are available."[47] There seems also to have been a move away from the traditional shipped bill of lading in recent years, towards non-negotiable documentation such as the waybill, and documentation which can be issued earlier, such as the mate's receipt or the received for shipment bill. No doubt the future will bring increased use of electronic documentation.[48] It is at least arguable, however, that the common law recognises only the shipped bill of lading as a document of title without proof of custom.[49] To what extent, then, can the reasoning protecting merchants in cases such as *Motis Exports*, be extended to other forms of documentation?

Motis Exports depends on the interpretation of the bill of lading contract, and the implication that it "is an incident of the bill of lading contract that delivery is to be effected only against the bill of lading."[50] It therefore follows that the same reasoning can apply to any document to which a similar implication is applicable, as long as, if the action is not brought by the original shipper, the Carriage of Goods by Sea Act 1992 applies. It probably applies to a received for shipment bill, therefore,[51] and to a ship's delivery order. The implication would be inappropriate for a waybill, although they come within the 1992 Act, but the parties could presumably make, *e.g.*, NODISP provision by an express contractual term. The *Motis Exports* implication would probably be inappropriate to a mate's receipt and to a merchant's delivery order, and in any case neither document comes within the 1992 Act.

---

[46] [n. 38 and n. 50].

[47] [1995] L.M.C.L.Q. 289, 298.

[48] See, *e.g.* Diana Faber, "Electronic Bills of Lading" [1996] 2 L.M.C.L.Q. 323.

[49] This is beyond the scope of this note, but see, *e.g.*, Benjamin, *Sale of Goods* (5th ed., Sweet & Maxwell, 1997), para. 18–045.

[50] *per* Leggatt L.J. in *The Houda* [n. 28] at 553, a passage quoted by Rix J. A similar passage is quoted, [n. 38].

[51] Indeed, the bill of lading in *The Ines* was received for shipment: [n. 36].

As for electronic documentation, a similar implication ought to apply to an electronic bill of lading as to a paper bill, or at any rate that delivery will be made only to the lawful holder (if that is the appropriate term), but the parties would probably be wiser to incorporate an express term to that effect. It is by no means certain that an electronic document would be brought within the 1992 Act,[52] but schemes such as that envisaged by C.M.I.[53] involve the carrier at each transfer, so that it would be possible for each merchant to contract with the carrier directly.

There are two further observations to make on electronic bills of lading. First, since the parties would almost certainly make express provision as to delivery, they could decide whether the risk of fraud should be borne by the carrier or by the merchants.[54] I have suggested that a case can be made for the risk being borne by the merchants. Secondly, there would be a problem with the present law if the goods were stolen before shipment, since there would be no privity of contract between the true owner and the carrier, and hence no possibility of the carrier raising a contractual defence (to a conversion action). If conventional bills of lading are issued, and the carrier delivers against production of an original, he is protected by *Glyn Mills*. It seems unlikely, however, that *Glyn Mills* applies to electronic documentation, or indeed to any document apart from the bill of lading.

Developments since the publication of the casenote

Rix J.'s decision was upheld in the Court of Appeal ([2000] 1 Lloyd's Rep. 211). On the issue of the exemption clause Stuart Smith L.J. made the following observations, after setting out the passages from *Sze Hai Tong*, above: **6–034**

"Mr. Dunning [for the shipowners] points out that in that case the agents knew that they were effecting delivery to someone who was not entitled to them, whereas in the present case the defendants did not know that. But as I have pointed out, if Mr. Dunning is right, the clause would appear to be wide enough to exempt liability whether or not the defendant knew this, or where negligent. Mr. Dunning also submits that Lord Denning's reference to fundamental breach cannot now stand in the light of the authorities of *Suisse Atlantique Societe v NV Rotterdamsche Kolern Centrale* [1967] 1 A.C. 361, and *Photo Productions Ltd v Securicor Transport Ltd* [1980] A.C. 827. But these decisions do not affect the reasoning based on *Glyn v Margetson and Co* [1893] A.C. 357. In that case the bill of lading under which oranges were shipped from Malaga to Liverpool had a wide deviation clause; the ship diverted very substantially from the direct route to Liverpool with the result that the oranges had been damaged by the delay. Lord Herschell L.C. at 355 said:

'My Lords, the main object and intent, as I have said, of this charterparty is the carriage of oranges from Malaga to Liverpool. That is the matter with which the shipper is concerned; and it seems to me that it would be to defeat what is the manifest object and intention of such a contract to hold that it was entered into with a power to the shipowner to proceed anywhere that he

---

[52] It would depend on the Secretary of State making provision within s.1(5).
[53] "Rules for Electronic Bills of Lading" (1990).
[54] Frauds could be perpetrated, for example, by the interception of keys by outsiders (who could therefore take control of the electronic bill), or by unauthorised transfers made by employees of the company.

pleased, to trade in any manner that he pleased, and to arrive at the port at which the oranges were to be delivered when he pleased.

Then is there any rule of law which compels the construction contended for? I think there is not. Where general words are used in a printed form which are obviously intended to apply, so far as they are applicable, to the circumstances of a particular contract, which particular contract is to be embodied in or introduced into that printed form, I think you are justified in looking at the main object and intent of the contract and in limiting the general words used, having in view that object and intent. Therefore, it seems to me that the construction contended for would be an unreasonable one, and there is no difficulty in construing this clause to apply to a liberty in the performance of the stipulated voyage to call at a particular port or ports in the course of the voyage.'

6–035   In his reply Mr. Dunning submitted that the object of the contract was the carriage of goods by sea from the Far East to West African ports and not the delivery of goods against production of the original bill of lading. The express language of the bill of lading does not in terms make delivery conditional on production of the original bill of lading. The relevant wording appears to be:

'... for delivery unto Consignee mentioned herein or to his or their assigns where the Carriers responsibilities shall in all cases and in all circumstances whatsoever finally cease ... IN WITNESS whereof the number of original Bills of Lading stated on this side have been signed, one of which being accomplished the other(s) to be void.'

But it has been established for well over a century that under a bill of lading contract a shipowner is both entitled and bound to deliver the goods against production of an original bill of lading, provided he has no notice of any other claim or better title to the goods (see *Glyn Mills Currie & Co v East and West India Dock Co* (1882) 7 App. Cas. 591, *The Stettin* (1889) 14 P.D. 142, *Carlsberg v Wemyss* (1915) S.C. 616 at 624, *Sze Hai Tong Bank Ltd v Rambler Cycle Co Ltd* [1959] A.C. 576, and particularly the passage I have cited at p. 586, *Barclays Bank Ltd v Commissioners of Customs and Excise* [1994] 2 Lloyd's Rep. 81, and *The Houda* [1994] 2 Lloyd's Rep. 541, particularly at 550, 552–3 and 556). It seems probable that the importance of this obligation stems from the negotiable nature of the bill of lading.

In my judgment Rix J. was correct to characterise what occurred as mis-delivery. A forged bill of lading is in the eyes of the law a nullity; it is simply a piece of paper with writing on it, which has no effect whatever. That being so delivery of the goods, or in this case the delivery order which was tantamount to the delivery of the goods, was not in exchange for the original bill of lading but for a worthless piece of paper. No doubt so far as the owner of the goods is concerned there is little difference between theft of the goods by taking them without consent of the bailee and delivery with his consent where the consent is obtained by fraud. Mr. Dunning, adopting the colourful phrase sometimes used of a bill of lading, that it is the key to the floating warehouse, or in this case the container yard, said that it made no difference whether the thief used a duplicate key to break in and steal or a forged metaphorical key. But one cannot take the metaphor too far. In my judgment clause 5.3(b) is not apt on its natural meaning to cover delivery by the carrier or his agent, albeit the delivery was obtained by fraud. I also agree with the judge that even if the language was apt to cover such a case, it is not a construction which should be adopted, involving as it does excuse from performing an obligation of such fundamental importance. As a matter of construction the courts lean against such a result if adequate content can be given to the clause. In my view it can, as I have indicated in para. 13; it is wide enough also to cover loss caused by negligence, provided the loss is of the appropriate kind."

(g) Limits on Value of Document of Title

The rights accorded to the holder in cases such as *Sze Hai Tong* and *Motis* **6–036**
Exports depend upon a cause of action against the carrier. Usually, the holder will
have a contract action, under the Carriage of Goods by Sea Act 1992 (on which see
further chapter 13, below). Where the bill of lading confers an immediate right to
possession, the holder can also sue in conversion. In the absence of a cause of
action, however, even a shipped bill of lading is useless as security.

THE FUTURE EXPRESS

Court of Appeal, [1993] 2 Lloyd's Rep. 542, upholding Diamond J.
[1992] 2 Lloyd's Rep. 79

Summary:
The importance of this case is that even where a document which is **6–037**
capable of being a document of title to goods, such as a shipped bill of
lading, is transferred, it gives no security unless the transferee has a cause
of action against the carrier.

Facts:
Bills of lading, naming the bank as consignee, were presented under a
documentary credit about a year after the goods (a cargo of wheat) had
been discharged to the purchaser, a fraudster who made off with the
cargo and failed to reimburse the bank. By the time the bills of lading
reached the bank, not only had the cargo long been discharged, but it no
longer existed.

The bank had acquiesced in the sense that it had allowed the credit to
be extended, on the buyer's instructions, and certainly by the final extension, the bank knew that the goods had by then been delivered. The
reason for the bank agreeing to the extensions was apparently that they
were short of foreign currency. The credit also provided that stale documents were acceptable, but this was merely to get around UCP (1983
revision), Art. 47 (set out in Appendix C).

Delivery was against a letter of indemnity provided by the seller (who
was also charterer of the vessel, and himself f.o.b. purchaser, to whom
property in the cargo passed on shipment).

Held at first instance:
Even where a carrier had delivered without production of an original bill **6–038**
of lading, in order for a consignee named in a bill of lading to sue, he had
to show either that he was party to a contract with the carrier, or that
the carrier had attorned (so as to create a bailment), or (in order for the
consignee to sue in tort) that he had property in, or a right to possess the
goods.

The bank had conceded that it had no action in contract; it was not an
original contracting party, and the 1855 Act did not apply in its favour.
Nor would it have had any chance of success in a *Brandt v Liverpool* action

[see chapter 13, below], neither having taken delivery of the cargo, nor having paid freight or any other charges.

The bank had no action in tort:

The bank never obtained property in the goods, since property had passed to the purchaser before the bills of lading were tendered. In Diamond J.'s view, property passed to the buyer on discharge. The intention had been to constitute the bank pledgee, with special property, but only once the bills of lading were tendered, and by the time this happened, the sellers had no property to pledge. Possession also passed to the buyer before constructive possession could pass to the bank. Therefore, the bank never obtained either property or possession, necessary to sue in tort.

The carrier had not attorned. The attornment in advance theory, which would allow any consignee or indorsee to sue in bailment, would have negated the need for the Bills of Lading Act 1855, s.1.

The bill of lading was not however stale—it would only be stale once delivery had been made to someone entitled to delivery, otherwise even a purchaser who obtained all the original bills of lading in a set would not necessarily thereby obtain a security (see further below). Indeed, but for the problems over the cause of action, the shipowners had certainly committed a tort by misdelivering the goods.

Diamond J. left open the question whether the shipowners were protected by the one-year time-bar in the *Hague Rules*.

Held in the Court of Appeal:

Diamond J.'s view was upheld on the grounds that property had passed to the buyer before the bank obtained the bills of lading, and that therefore the seller was not in a position to pledge the goods, and that the carrier had not attorned. The Court of Appeal dealt only with the cause of action issues, but appeared to differ from Diamond J. on the issue whether the bill of lading was a stale document at the time it was tendered.

Attornment was defined in the Court of Appeal as follows:

"There is an attornment when, in simple terms, a bailee of goods acknowledges that he holds the goods on behalf of a person other than the original bailor. The relationship of bailment then springs up between the bailee and that other person, enabling him to sue in conversion for non-delivery."

The argument was rejected that

"the defendants 'attorned' by issuing bills of lading in which the plaintiffs were named as consignees, and that the attornment was "perfected" when the bills of lading reached the plaintiffs over a year later."

Notes

The observation was made in the Court of Appeal that the law protects against   **6–039**
bankruptcy not fraud, and that if "the documents had come forward in the usual
way, and Dalali [purchaser] had been insolvent, instead of fraudulent, the plaintiffs would have been fully secured."

The bank also sued the sellers in Geneva, but the outcome was not known by
the time of the case against the carrier.

This was actually the third consignment under a revolving letter of credit—nothing in the case turns on this, but revolving letters of credit are relatively
rare (see further para. 8–029, below).

Relevance of the case today

This was one of the last cases that arose under the regime of the Bills of Lading
Act 1855, s.1 (see further chapter 13, below). Under the Carriage of Goods by Sea
Act 1992 the position would be different, because the bank would have an action
in contract. This will usually give a contract action to the holder of a bill of lading,
but the 1992 Act does not apply to all documents. Mate's receipts are not covered
by the Act, but they can be documents of title on proof of custom (see below).
Alter the facts of *The Future Express* by substituting such a document for a bill of
lading, and the result would be the same today.

(h) WHEN IS BILL OF LADING SPENT?

It follows from *Barclays Bank Ltd v Commissioners of Customs & Excise*, above,   **6–040**
that the bill of lading remains a document of title, even when the goods have been
discharged, until they are discharged to the lawful owner. Were it otherwise the
carrier would be able to use his own wrongful act to evade liability. It has not been
decided whether the bill can remain a document of title where although delivery
has been made to the true owner, the bill has not been produced (for example,
where delivery is made against an indemnity). In *The Future Express*, Diamond J.
reviewed the inconclusive authorities, and concluded[55]:

> "I regard it as a difficult question whether the mere delivery of goods against
> an indemnity to a person who was rightfully entitled to them had he surren-
> dered the bill of lading exhausts that bill as a document of title. I would,
> however be reluctant to hold that a bill of lading becomes exhausted as a
> document of title once the carrier has delivered the goods against an indemnity
> to a person authorised to receive delivery. In such a situation the bill of lading
> has not been surrendered and can be passed to third parties who may take it for
> valuable consideration without notice that the goods have meanwhile been
> discharged. This would mean that, even if the purchaser took the precaution of
> ensuring that all parts of the bill were delivered to him (see the precautionary
> measure recommended by Earl Cairns in *Glyn Mills v East and West India Dock
> Co* (1882) 7 App. Cas. 591 at p. 600) still he could not be sure that he had
> acquired a good possessory title to the goods. To hold that a bill of lading
> becomes spent when goods are delivered against an indemnity would greatly
> detract from the value of bills of lading as documents of title to goods, would
> diminish their value to bankers and other persons who have to rely on them for
> security and would facilitate fraud. . . . It is not, however, necessary in the
> present case to express any concluded view on the question I have just dis-
> cussed since it is clear in any event that delivery of the goods was not made to
> some person having a right to claim them under the bills of lading . . . "

The bill of lading made the goods deliverable only to the bank.

[55] At 99–100.

6–041	The opposite view has been expressed, however, and the position not conclusively determined. The Court of Appeal in *The Future Express* made no comment on Diamond J.'s views, above. *The Delfini* has already been discussed in para. 5–066. In that case, a cargo of oil (with the exception of the 275 tons to which the short delivery claim related) was delivered to the plaintiffs, who did not obtain the bills of lading until several days after discharge. The plaintiffs (who were the persons lawfully entitled to the cargo) sued the shipowners in contract, under s.1 of the Bills of Lading Act 1855, but failed at first instance on the grounds that the bills of lading were stale by the time they reached the plaintiffs. The case is not a particularly useful authority, because both parties accepted that the bills would have been stale had all the cargo been delivered (a view that is, of course, contrary to that taken by Diamond J., above), but that it had not, and the cargo-owners argued that, at least in respect of the 275 tons that had not been delivered, the bills of lading remained effective documents of title. The following is an extract from Phillips J.'s judgment:

> "Mr. Hirst [for the plaintiffs, submitted that] . . . on the facts of the present case the bill of lading remained a document of title at the time that it was delivered to the second plaintiffs. He submitted that, applying the words of Willes J. in *Meyerstein v Barber* [(1866) L.R. 2 C.P. 38; (1870) L.R. 4 H.L. 317] there had not been complete discharge because 275 tonnes of cargo had been short-landed. Applying the words of Diplock J. [*in Barclays Bank Ltd v Customs and Excise, above*] the contract of carriage had not been discharged, because the cargo had not been completely delivered to the person entitled to it. It followed that the bill of lading remained a valid transferable document of title. Mr. Hirst elaborated this proposition by submitting that the bill of lading remained a document of title not in respect of all the cargo covered by it, but solely in respect of the portion of 275 tonnes not delivered.
>
> "The concept of a bill of lading remaining an effective document of title for an undelivered part of a single bulk cargo covered by the bill is a novel one. Whether or not there are circumstances in which a bill of lading can so operate, I am satisfied that it did not do so on the facts of this case.
>
> "In *Meyerstein v Barber* the issue was whether discharge to a sufferance wharf subject to the shipowners' lien for freight robbed the bill of lading of further efficacy. Willes J. ruled that it did not because there had not been 'complete delivery of possession' to the person entitled to the cargo. In speaking of complete delivery of possession he had in mind the quality of the delivery of possession—not the question of whether 100 per cent of the quantity loaded had been delivered.
>
> "I agree with Mr. Hirst that the test to be applied is that of Diplock J. in *Barclays Bank Ltd v Customs and Excise*. Where I differ from Mr. Hirst is in respect of his contention that the contract of carriage is not discharged unless the vessel delivers 100 per cent of the goods loaded. The discharge of the contract referred to by Diplock J. occurs, in my view, when the primary obligations of the contract of carriage come to an end, notwithstanding that the carrier may have incurred secondary obligations as a consequence of breach of those primary obligations. In this case once *Delfini* had arrived at Gela, discharged the vast majority of the cargo loaded (if one postulates short landing of 275 tonnes) and sailed away the contract of carriage was discharged by performance. Thereafter any remedy against the defendants lay in a claim for damages for breach."

6–042	This is necessarily inconsistent with Diamond J.'s view, who would have held the bills of lading to be valid documents of title, even had the entire cargo been discharged, including the disputed 275 tons.

The Delfini was upheld in the Court of Appeal, but on the different ground that property did not pass upon or by reason of indorsement, as required by s.1 of the 1855 Act (see further chapter 5, above and chapter 13, below). It was not therefore necessary to consider whether the bills of lading remained valid as documents of title. Nevertheless, Mustill L.J. said: [1990] 1 Lloyd's Rep. 252 , at p. 269 (col. 2).

> "Finally, I should mention the continued status of the bill of lading after the goods have arrived at destination, and have been discharged from the ship. It is, I think, quite clear from *Meyerstein v Barber*.[56] that when the goods have been actually delivered at destination to the person entitled to them, or placed in a position where the person is entitled to immediate possession, the bill of lading is exhausted 'and will not operate at all to transfer the goods to any person who has either advanced money or has purchased the bill of lading'. It is equally clear that until the buyer has actually received delivery, the fact that the goods have been discharged at destination subject (say) to a lien for freight, does not entail that the bill is exhausted."

This suggests that the test is whether delivery has been made to the person entitled, whether or not he has been required to produce the bill of lading. The point remains open, however, since neither *The Delfini* nor *The Future Express* turned on it in the end. I would suggest, however, that Diamond J.'s argument seems forceful.

(4) Which Documents can be Documents of Title?

(a) Shipped Bill of Lading Document of Title Without Proof of Custom

Early in the development of international trade it was accepted that transfer of   **6–043**
the bill of lading could at any rate also transfer the property in the goods.

LICKBARROW v MASON

King's Bench. (1787) 2 Term Rep. 63 (original decision). (1794) 5 Term Rep. 683; 101 E.R. 380 (new trial on point of pleading)

Bills of lading were indorsed in favour of the plaintiffs against payment to an   **6–044**
agent of the seller. The agent went bankrupt before the seller was paid. The sellers attempted to stop the goods *in transitu*.

Held:
Though the consignor may stop the goods *in transitu* before the bill of lading is indorsed, property passes to the consignee on indorsement, whether the indorsement be to a named person or in blank.

Buller J.: *(original trial)* According to a note of *Wright and Campbell*, which I took in Court, Lord Mansfield said, that since the case in Lord Raymond, it had always been held that the delivery of a bill of lading transferred the property at law.

---

[56] (1870) L.R. 4 H.L. 317, especially at 330 and 335.

Notes

6–045   1. The special verdict of the jury in the second trial was that:

> "by the custom of merchants, bills of lading, expressing goods or merchandizes to have been shipped by any person or persons to be delivered to order or assigns, have been, and are, at any time after such goods have been shipped, and before the voyage performed, for which they have been shipped, negotiable and transferable by the shipper or shippers of such goods to any other person or persons, by such shipper or shippers indorsing such bills of lading with his, her or their name or names, and delivering or transmitting the same so indorsed, or causing the same to be so delivered or transmitted to any such other person or persons; and that by such indorsement and delivery, or transmission, the property in such goods hath been, and is transferred and passed to such other person or persons . . . "

2. Note that the principle applies only to the shipped bill of lading, but it is based on the custom of merchants, so that if the custom of merchants altered, similar conclusions may also be drawn of other documents.

3. *Lickbarrow v Mason* refers only to the transfer of property, not to constructive possession. Of course, property usually carries with it a right of possession, but during the nineteenth century, the courts developed the modern notion that the bill of lading could transfer constructive possession, independently of any question about property. In *Barber v Meyerstein* (1866) L.R. 2 C.P. 38, affirmed (1870) L.R. 4 H.L. 317, the bill of lading was seen as the symbol of the goods, and its transfer conferred on the holder the key to the warehouse.[57] But the transferee was a pledgee, and Willes J. thought that property only passed to a pledgee on delivery of the goods (which could be actual or constructive delivery). The transfer of the bill of lading operated as a constructive delivery. Hence, property passed because constructive possession had passed, not the other way around. Passing of property is not a prerequisite. Certainly, it is now clear that it is constructive possession which the bill of lading transfers, whether or not it also transfers property.

4. *Lickbarrow v Mason* is described in detail in Bools, *The Bill of Lading: A Document of Title to Goods* (L.L.P., 1997), Ch. 1.

Comments (on passing of property):

1. The case does not decide that the bill of lading always transfers the property, and it later became clear that though it is quite common for property in the goods to pass on indorsement of the bill of lading, it does not always do so. See further chapter 5, above.

2. Nor does the decision make the bill of lading a negotiable instrument. It cannot transfer to the indorsee a better title than that of the transferor (unlike, *e.g.* a banknote).

3. Though the transfer of a bill of lading can at common law pass the property in the goods, it does not automatically pass to the consignee the rights and liabilities under the contract of carriage. See further chapter 13, below, and in particular *Thompson v Dominy*, which represents the common law position.

(b) Which Other Documents are Documents of Title?

6–046   It is clear from *Lickbarrow v Mason*, therefore, that for over 200 years, the courts have recognised that shipped bills of lading are always, by custom of merchants,

---

[57] As it was in *Sanders Brothers v Maclean & Co* (1883) 11 Q.B.D. 327 (considered further at paras 6–081, *et seq.*, below), where however, property had also passed.

documents of title, and there is no need to prove a local (or more widespread) custom. Other documents can become documents of title by custom. However, it is part of the essence of a document of title that it can be negotiated, so a non-negotiable document can never be a document of title.

It is not clear, however, whether any other document, apart from the shipped bill of lading, is always treated as a document of title, even without proof of custom. A mate's receipt is not, and this is perhaps not surprising, given that it is usually intended to be merely a preliminary document, to be given up in exchange for a document which might be a document of title. (However, if there is a local custom that the mate's receipt is not given up, but itself negotiated, then it might locally be regarded as a document of title.)

(c) MATE'S RECEIPTS AS DOCUMENTS OF TITLE

We have come across mate's receipts in the discussion of *Cowas-Jee v Thompson* **6–047** in chapter 1, above, and their role is described more fully at the start of chapter 14, below. In chapter 14, below, the important point is made that the statements in them, which are transferred on to the bill of lading, are made by the shipper, not the carrier. We also saw in *Cowas-Jee v Thompson* that they are preliminary documents, which should be given up, in return for the bill of lading, although the shipowner is entitled to issue the bill of lading to the shipper, whether the mate's receipts are given up or not (see further below).

For present purposes, two points should be made. First, the mate's receipt is a preliminary document, issued earlier than the bill of lading. If speed is important, therefore, one can see why there are temptations to negotiate it, rather than the bill of lading. Secondly, however, it is not intended to be the final document issued; it is intended to be given up, in exchange for the bill of lading. It would surely be inappropriate for any document which is intended to be preliminary only to be regarded as a document of title.

NIPPON YUSEN KAISHA v RAMJIBAN SEROWGEE

Privy Council. [1938] A.C. 429

Summary:
The case demonstrates the importance of a document of title—here **6–048** Ramjiban Serowgee had no document of title, and had no claim against the carrier when he delivered the cargo to the holder of a shipped bill of lading, bills of lading having been issued without the mate's receipts being given up.

Facts:
Serowgee were (intermediate) sellers f.a.s. to International Export Company, Ltd (Export). The sale was expressed to be cash against mate's receipts, and the shipowners had issued mate's receipts to Ramjiban Serowgee when the goods were received alongside ship. However, the shipowners later issued shipped bills of lading, against a letter of indemnity, to the buyers (International Export Co. Ltd), without the mate's receipts being given up in exchange.

Export did not pay Serowgee, but negotiated bills of lading to Japanese purchasers, to whom Nippon Yusen delivered, against production of the bills. Serowgee (who were still in possession of the mate's receipts) sued the shipowners.

Held:

Property had passed to Export when the goods were delivered alongside the vessel; from that time Ramjiban Serowgee, as holder of the mate's receipt, had neither the property in nor possession of the goods. They were thereafter left only with an equitable lien, enforceable against Export.[58] The mate's receipt was not a document of title, and the carrier was not put on notice not to issue bills of lading to the person (Export) who had booked the freight space with the carrier (the carrier had no notice of equitable lien prior to issuing bills). Thus the carrier had committed no wrong enforceable at the suit of Serowgee.

There was no general principle that the mate's receipt had to be given up before the bill of lading could be issued—the carrier was indeed bound to issue the bill of lading to the shipper who had contracted for the freight.

There was no conversion by the carrier since property had passed alongside ship.

6–049   LORD WRIGHT: (at 445) The mate's receipt is not a document of title to the goods shipped. Its transfer does not transfer property in the goods, nor is its possession equivalent to possession of the goods. It is not conclusive, and its statements do not bind the shipowner as do the statements in a bill of lading signed with the master's authority. It is, however, *prima facie* evidence of the quantity and condition of the goods received, and *prima facie* it is the recipient or possessor who is entitled to have the bill of lading issued to him. But if the mate's receipt acknowledges receipt from a shipper other than the person who actually receives the mate's receipt, and, in particular, if the property is in that shipper, and the shipper has contracted for the freight, the shipowner will *prima facie* be entitled, and indeed bound, to deliver the bill of lading to that person. . . .

Note

Serowgee's problem was that they had no cause of action, because they had neither property nor, in the absence of a document of title, right to possession. Property had passed to Export on delivery alongside the vessel. Moreover, since the Privy Council held that the mate's receipts were not documents of title, it followed that Ramjiban Serowgee did not retain possession of the goods either. As f.a.s. sellers, they had no contract with the ship, Export being the shippers. Lord Wright observes that the situation would have been very different if the sellers had delivered the goods to the ship in their own name as shippers, because then they would have been entitled to call for the bills of lading. They would (as

---

[58] The lien was provided under the terms of sale contract, which provided for payment against mate's receipts, but retention of the lien suggested property had passed as soon as the goods had been appropriated, and that there was no reservation of right of disposal. See further para. 5–035, above, on the relationship between property and liens.

shippers) have had a contractual cause of action against the shipowners, whether or not they also had a document of title.

(d) RECEIVED FOR SHIPMENT BILLS OF LADING

Where there is no proof of custom, *Diamond Alkali Export Corporation v Fl* **6–050** *Bourgeois* (dealt with more fully below) suggests that the shipped bill of lading may continue to be the only document recognised as a document of title at common law. The editors of Benjamin's *Sale of Goods* also take the view that the reasoning in *Lickbarrow v Mason* should not extend beyond shipped bills, so that even a received for shipment bill of lading should not be accepted as a document of title without proof of custom. The following justification for distinguishing between shipped and received for shipment bills is made[59]:

"There is . . . a practical reason for distinguishing, for this purpose, between shipped and received bills. Once goods have been shipped, it is impossible or extremely difficult for the shipper or consignee to deal with them physically and it is that impossibility or extreme difficulty which led to the recognition of shipped bills of lading as documents of title. There is no such impossibility or extreme difficulty in dealing with goods before they have been shipped, and correspondingly less need to regard documents relating to them as documents of title. On the other hand, refusal to recognise received bills as documents of title need not hamper dealings in such goods once they have been shipped, for it is then a simple matter to turn the received into a shipped bill by a notation recording the fact of shipment."

The argument effectively is that there is no need for a document of title to pass constructive possession unless it is impossible, or extremely difficult, to transfer physical possession, and that will only be true once the goods have been shipped.

Another argument against recognising the received for shipment bill as a document of title is that there is no clear notion of what a received for shipment bill is. It may clearly state that the goods have been received for shipment aboard a particular vessel, or it may leave the carrier with a discretion as to the identity of the vessel. It may state that the carrier has received the goods personally, or it may merely state receipt by an agent. It must be more difficult to establish a custom where the document itself can admit of so wide a variation.

Ultimately, however, *Diamond Alkali* decides not that a received for shipment **6–051** bill cannot be a document of title without proof of custom, but that it is not good tender under a c.i.f. contract. Observations about its status as a document of title are *dicta*. In *The Marlborough Hill*,[60] the Privy Council held that a received for shipment bill was a bill of lading for the purposes of the Admiralty Court Act 1861, section 6. Though it was not part of the *ratio*, Lord Phillimore was not disposed to distinguish in any regard between shipped and received for shipment bills of lading, and it might therefore be inferred that received for shipment bills were now to be regarded as documents of title[61]:

"It is a matter of commercial notoriety, and their Lordships have been furnished with several instances of it, that shipping instruments which are called bills of lading, and known in the commercial world as such, are sometimes framed in the alternative form 'received for shipment' instead of 'shipped on board,' and

---

[59] Benjamin, *Sale of Goods* (5th ed., Sweet & Maxwell, 1997), at para. 18–045.
[60] [1921] 1 A.C. 444.
[61] At 451.

further with the alternative contract to carry or procure some other vessel . . . to carry, instead of the original ship.

"There can be no difference in principle between the owner, master or agent acknowledging that he has received the goods on his wharf, or allotted portion or quay, or his storehouse awaiting shipment, and his acknowledging that the goods have actually been put over the ship's rail. The two forms of bill of lading may well stand, as their Lordships understand that they stand, together. The older is still in the more appropriate language for whole cargoes delivered and taken on board in bulk; whereas 'received for shipment' is the proper phrase for the practical business-like way of treating parcels of cargo to be placed on a general ship which will be lying alongside the wharf taking in cargo for several days, and whose proper stowage will require that certain bulkier or heavier parcels shall be placed on board first, while others, though they have arrived earlier, wait for the convenient place and time of stowage."

In *Ishag v Allied Bank International (The Lycaon)*,[62] Lloyd J. held that a received for shipment bill, naming the particular ship on which the goods were to be carried, should be regarded as a document of title, in the light of *The Marlborough Hill*. Again, however, it was not part of the *ratio*. The issue remains open.

(e) Effect of Custom

6–052   A document can become a document of title on proof of custom, which may be a local custom. The document must be capable, in principle, of being a document of title, however; it must, for example, be a negotiable document.

KUM v WAH TAT BANK LTD

Privy Council. [1971] 1 Lloyd's Rep. 439, on appeal from the Malaysian Court of Appeal ([1967] 2 Lloyd's Rep. 437)

Facts:

6–053   Wah Tat Bank had taken mate's receipts (naming the bank as consignee) as security, where they advanced credit to the shipper of a cargo. It was envisaged that when the bank was reimbursed, the bank would hand back the mate's receipts endorsed to the shippers so that they could obtain delivery of the goods. It was therefore contemplated that the mate's receipts would in fact operate as documents of title, in the sense that delivery would not take place except against their production, and that no other document of title would be issued for the cargo.

The charterers, on the instructions of the shippers, released the goods back to the shipper (against an indemnity) without production the mate's receipts (no bills of lading having been issued).

The action by the bank:

The bank sued the charterers in conversion and what was then (before the statutory changes made in 1977) trover, but failed to establish that as holder of the mate's receipt, it had (constructive) possession of the goods. The bank could not be a common law pledgee without delivery.[63] So their action depended on

---

[62] [1981] 1 Lloyd's Rep. 92.
[63] There was no doubt that the bank was an equitable pledgee, giving it an interest which would have been enforceable against the shipper, but the bank had not given notice to the ship, which was therefore not bound by the equitable pledge.

whether there was symbolic delivery, and that depended on whether the mate's receipts constituted documents of title.

The bank claimed that by custom of trade between Sarawak and Singapore (but not necessarily the other way), mate's receipts were treated as documents of title.[64] Note that the custom was that a bill of lading was not issued, so that the only document which would be transferred was the mate's receipt, an understandable practice on the relatively short route involved. This differed from *Nippon Yusen Kaisha v Ramjiban Serowgee*, where the mate's receipts were envisaged as preliminary documents only, which would normally later be given up. Indeed, had it been usual for the mate's receipt to be given up for a bill of lading, it is difficult to see how any local custom that they were used as documents of title could be established. There was also evidence that even where a bill of lading was issued, it was never issued without the mate's receipt being given up.

View taken on mate's receipt:
A The court would have been prepared to regard it as such in the particular case were it not for the fact that it was expressly marked "not negotiable".

LORD DEVLIN: *(starting at 443)* Their Lordships can see no reason in 6–054 principle why a document of title should not be created by local custom. As the Chief Justice pointed out in the Federal Court, a custom is unlikely to be "applicable all over the world" until it has first been applied in various localities. The test imposed by the trial Judge, their Lordships consider with respect, shows a misunderstanding of the nature and effect of a mercantile custom. On the other side a somewhat similar misunderstanding is shown in the respondents' notice of appeal to the Federal Court in which the custom or practice contended for is described as one

"whereby merchants, bankers and carriers by sea acknowledged and accepted that mate's receipts were documents of title".

Their Lordships will consider these two matters together.

In speaking of a custom of merchants the law has not in mind merchants in the narrow sense of buyers and sellers of goods. A mercantile custom affects transactions either in a particular trade or in a particular place, such as a market or a port, and binds all those who participate in such transactions, whatever the nature of their callings. It is true that a document relating to goods carried by sea and said to be negotiated through banks could hardly be recognised as a document of title if the evidence did not show it to be treated as such by shipowners, shippers and bankers. But the limits of the custom, if it be established, are not to be defined by reference to categories of traders or professional men; if established, it binds everyone who does business in whatever capacity. To describe a custom as belonging to particular callings diverts attention from its true character which consists in its attachment to a trade or place.

[64] The evidence showed that from Sarawak to Singapore between 90 per cent. and 95 per cent. of the traffic was being carried on mate's receipts, without a bill of lading whereas, in the opposite direction the percentage was between 75 per cent. and 80 per cent.

Universality, as a requirement of custom, raises not a question of law but a question of fact. There must be proof in the first place that the custom is generally accepted by those who habitually do business in the trade or market concerned. Moreover, the custom must be so generally known that an outsider who makes reasonable enquiries could not fail to be made aware of it. The size of the market or the extent of the trade affected is neither here nor there. It does not matter that the custom alleged in this case applies only to part of the shipping trade within the State of Singapore, so long as the part can be ascertained with certainty, as it can here, as the carriage of goods by sea between Sarawak and Singapore. A good and established custom

" ... obtains the force of a law, and is, in effect, the common law within that place to which it extends. [*Lockwood v Wood* (1844) 6 Q.B. 31, per Tindal, C.J., at 64.]"

Thus the custom in this case, if proved, takes effect as part of the common law of Singapore. As such it will be applied by any Court dealing with any matter which that Court treats as governed by the law of Singapore. In this sense it is binding not only in Singapore but on anyone anywhere in the world.

6–055   The common law of Singapore is in mercantile matters the same as the common law of England ... Accordingly, the question whether the alleged custom, if proved in fact as their Lordships hold that it is, is good in law must be determined in accordance with the requirements of the English common law. These are that the custom should be certain, reasonable and not repugnant. It would be repugnant if it were inconsistent with any express term in any document it affects, whether that document be regarded as a contract or as a document of title.

In their Lordships' opinion the custom alleged is neither uncertain nor unreasonable. The form of mate's receipt used is similar to a bill of lading and there is no difficulty about treating it as an equivalent. ... Their Lordships can see nothing unreasonable in using the mate's receipt in this case as a document of title. The law knows that to require the physical delivery of goods whenever they change hands in trade would be unreasonable and recognises the need of merchants for a document that will represent the goods. It was by the custom of merchants that the bill of lading became such a document. But no documentary form is immutable. It is quite a natural development, first for the mate's receipt to become more elaborate and then for merchants to feel that in certain cases the bill of lading can be dispensed with. The function of the commercial law is to allow, so far as it can, commercial men to do business in the way in which they want to do it and not to require them to stick to forms that they may think to be outmoded. The common law is not bureaucratic.

There would be uncertainty or unreasonableness if in relation to the same consignment a bill of lading and a mate's receipt, both documents of title, could be in circulation at the same time. The evidence was however unanimous that the bill of lading, when it was issued in this trade, was issued only in exchange for the appropriate mate's receipt. This is indeed the normal practice throughout the world, but, so long as possession of the mate's receipt is only evidence of title (the mate's receipt not being a document of title), the master must be at liberty at his peril to issue the bill of lading on such other evidence as he chooses to accept. The establishment of the mate's receipt as a document of title would necessarily deprive the master of this degree of liberty, for he would then be as much at fault in issuing a bill of lading without the delivery up of the mate's receipt as he would be if he issued a second set of bills of lading without delivery up of the first. It has not however been argued—rightly so, their Lordships think—that in this respect the treatment of the mate's receipt as a document of title would be repugnant to any principle of law.

Up to this stage their Lordships find themselves in agreement with the judgment of the Chief Justice [Wee Chong Jin CJ]. The factor that in the end compels them to differ from his conclusion is the presence on the mate's receipt of the words "NOT NEGOTIABLE".

These words are part of the printed form. Their presence on a mate's receipt which is to be used simply as such may be superfluous, but it is not incongruous. The only meaning, whether it be a popular or a legal meaning, that can be given to this marking is that the document is not to pass title by endorsement and delivery. Unfortunately businessmen frequently do not trouble themselves about such points. These documents were from the beginning of the practice, which goes back at least 40 years, handled just as if they were negotiable and transferable by endorsement. ...

... The Chief Justice found "that everybody connected with this trade has ignored these printed words".

The question is whether a Court of law can also ignore them. The **6–056** Courts are well aware of the tendency of businessmen to retain in the documents they use inapplicable or outmoded expressions; and they endeavour, albeit with reluctance since the retention is inevitably a source of confusion—to give effect to what they take to be the true nature of the document. There are well established rules of construction which permit the Court to disregard printed words when they are inconsistent with written words or with the paramount object which the document appears from its language to be designed to achieve. But these rules can be used only when there is a conflict between one part of the document and another or between the effect of a part and the effect of the whole. They are rules for reconciling different expressions in or of the document itself. They cannot be used to introduce into the document, either by implication or by force of custom, what is outside it. The rule is plain and clear that inconsistency with the document defeats the custom. If this document had "Negotiable" printed in the right hand corner and "Not negotiable" in the left, the argument could begin. But if the right-hand corner is blank, custom cannot be used to fill it. Whichever way the argument for the respondents is put, it amounts in the end to a submission that the force of custom should expel from the document words that are on it: this is not permissible by law.

The decision (on appeal from the Malaysia Court of Appeal)

The bank nevertheless succeeded (in conversion) on the grounds that "the shipment of the goods was a delivery to the ship as bailee for the bank so that thereby the pledge was completed and the bank given the possessory title on which it relies." Since the bank was named as consignee, and had advanced the full amount of the money, shipment constituted delivery to the bank, and passed special property to the bank as pledgee. If the bank had instead been a buyer under a contract of sale, shipment in similar circumstances would likewise have transferred property to it.

The situation in *Kum v Wah Tat Bank* was however rather unusual; the bank succeeded only because shipment of the goods could be regarded as delivery to the bank—in a normal documentary credit, the pledge is not created until tender of documents after shipment, and property does not pass until then. *Kum v Wah Tat Bank* is not therefore of general application, and gives no general protection to banks which advance money on the security of a document which is not a document of title.

(5) Documentation under c.i.f. and f.o.b. Contracts: Bills of Lading

(a) Requirement for Shipped Bill

6–057   For an f.o.b. contract, the justification for requiring a shipped bill may be no more than to provide evidence that the seller has loaded conforming goods. There is a case, then, for relaxing the requirement should the parties agree, or should there be strong evidence of a trade custom to the contrary.

For a c.i.f. contract, the bill of lading must also be a document of title, and be capable of transferring the carriage contract. If only a shipped bill of lading can perform those functions, then there is a case for a rigid requirement for a shipped bill under a c.i.f. contract. Since 1992 the carriage contract has been capable of being transferred by a received for shipment bill (see para. 13–017). Other documents can be documents of title, with proof of custom (and perhaps otherwise). In that case, there is no justification for adopting different requirements for c.i.f. than for f.o.b. contracts.

YELO v S.M. MACHADO & CO LTD

Queen's Bench Division. [1952] 1 Lloyd's Rep. 181

Facts:

6–058 F.o.b. sellers of mandarin oranges from a Spanish port claimed that they were entitled to tender received for shipment bills, by virtue of a trade custom in the Spanish ports concerned.

Held:

They were not. An f.o.b. seller would need very strong evidence of a trade custom in order successfully to argue the contrary.

This was technically *obiter dicta*, because the buyers had an alternative defence based on non-compliance with the documentary credit requirements (the effect of which was that the credit had expired).

SELLERS J.: (at 192) The plaintiff adduced evidence that "Received for shipment" bills of lading were frequently used by shipowners whose vessels were chartered to carry fruit from the Spanish ports concerned, but the shipments went to Scandanavia, Holland, Denmark and various United Kingdom ports. Many of the shipments may have been consignments for sale on arrival. I do not regard this evidence as establishing, even if in the circumstances the custom of the trade could be implied into the contract at all, that for an f.o.b. shipment a "Received for shipment" bill of lading was customarily accepted in the trade between the ports involved. It would, in my opinion, require strong evidence of an agreement, express or implied, to supplant the requirement of a "Shipped" bill of lading in an f.o.b. contract where the seller undertook to find the ship. The date of shipment in this contract was vital, as it would normally be in an f.o.b. contract, and a "Received for shipment" bill of lading, unless specially indorsed with the date of shipment, is of itself no evidence of the date when the goods were put on board and acknowledged to be so by the shipowner.

Note

The justification for the requirement is essentially evidential, but it is not entirely inflexible, since it can be supplanted by sufficiently strong evidence to the contrary.

6–059

General observations

Sellers J. was reluctant to imply into an f.o.b. contract, where the seller was required to find the ship, a term allowing them to tender a received for shipment bill of lading, because evidence of shipment was required, and also because the date of shipment was important (shipment date was in December specifically for the Christmas trade). Evidence of a trade custom was relied upon by the sellers, but Sellers J. thought that strong evidence of an agreement, express or to be implied, would be needed to rebut the requirement of a shipped bill. Such evidence was lacking here because many of the contracts in the trade in question (fruit from Spanish ports) were ex-ship. In any case, as Sellers J. observed:

"The parties were not, in my opinion, contracting on the basis of the custom or practice of the port or trade. It was their first contract together and neither was familiar with the then circumstances of the trade or, as I find, placing any reliance upon it."

We may presume that an express term would however have sufficed, and would not have been repugnant to an f.o.b. contract. Sellers J. also thought that a received for shipment bill, specially indorsed with the date of shipment, might have sufficed—presumably this would have been the equivalent of a shipped bill.

Another of Sellers J.'s grounds was the well-known passage from Lord Sumner's speech in *Hansson v Hamel & Horley, Ltd* [1922] 2 A.C. 36, at 46 (also quoted above):

"These documents have to be handled by banks, they have to be taken up or rejected promptly and without any opportunity for prolonged inquiry, they have to be such as can be re-tendered to sub-purchasers, and it is essential that they should so conform to the accustomed shipping documents as to be reasonably and readily fit to pass current in commerce."

The sellers also failed on another ground, relating to the documentary credit. This is of no particular general importance, except that Sellers J. observed that his views on the received for shipment bills were not necessary for the decision.

DIAMOND ALKALI EXPORT CORP v FL BOURGEOIS

King's Bench Division. [1921] 3 K.B. 443

6–060 The question at issue was whether a c.i.f. seller could tender received for shipment bill of lading and a certificate of insurance.

Held:
The buyers were entitled to reject the documents.

1. A received for shipment bill of lading is not good tender c.i.f. because it does not acknowledge shipment.

2. For valid tender c.i.f. an insurance *policy* must be tendered falling within the provisions of the Marine Insurance Act 1906 (see further below).

6–061 McCardie J.: *(on the bill of lading)* What then are a seller's duties and buyer's rights under a c.i.f. contract? They were stated by Lord Blackburn in *Ireland v Livingston* (1872) L.R. 5 H.L. 395, 406, where he refers to a "bill of lading." So, too, the well-known judgment of Hamilton J. in *Biddell Brothers v E. Clemens Horst Co* [1911] 1 K.B. 214, 221, where he says:

"It follows that against tender of these documents, the bill of lading, invoice, and policy of insurance, which completes delivery in accordance with that agreement, the buyer must be ready and willing to pay the price."

So Kennedy L.J. says in his judgment in the same case in the Court of Appeal [1911] 1 K.B. 934, 956:

"How is such a tender to be made of goods afloat under a c.i.f. contract? By tender of the bill of lading, accompanied in case the goods have been lost in transit by the policy of insurance. The bill of lading in law and fact represents the goods":

see too the judgment of Scrutton J. in *Landauer & Co v Craven* [1912] 2 K.B. 94, 107. The latest statement is the opinion of Lord Birkenhead in *Johnson v Taylor Bros & Co* [1920] A.C. 144, 149, where he says in speaking of the duties of a vendor under a c.i.f. contract:

"He is bound in the second place to tender to the purchaser within a reasonable time after shipment the shipping documents, for example, the bill or bills of lading and a policy of insurance reasonably covering the value of the goods."

I should mention also the notes to Scrutton on *Charterparties*, 10th ed., Art. 59. If then a vendor under an ordinary c.i.f. contract is bound to tender a bill of lading, the question next arising is: What is meant by a bill of lading within such a contract?

The contract decides the rights of the buyer. The question is not as to the meaning of the phrase in a particular Act of Parliament or as to the possible meaning under other forms of contract. Nor is it material that a buyer objects to the document for ulterior motives: see, for example, Lord Cairns' judgment in *Bowes v Shand* (1877) 2 App. Cas. 455, 465, 476 and Lord Hatherley's judgment in the same case. A buyer, as these noble Lords pointed out, is entitled to insist on the letter of his rights. As Lord Hatherley said: "If you seek to fasten upon him the engagement, you must first bring him"—the buyer—"within the four corners of the contract." A buyer, moreover, may have obvious business reasons for so insisting, as he may have to implement his own bargain with rigorous sub-vendees. Now I consider that the phrase "bill of lading" as used with respect to a c.i.f. contract means a bill of lading in the sense established by a long line of legal decisions. Unless this meaning be given the matter is thrown into confusion.

In Art. 3 of Scrutton on *Charterparties*, 10th ed., is a definition which says: "A bill of lading is a receipt for goods shipped on board a ship signed by the person who contracts to carry them or his agent and stating the terms on which the goods were delivered to and received by the ship." This statement suggests at once an obvious and serious distinction between a receipt for goods actually shipped on board a particular ship and a receipt for goods which are at some future time to be shipped on board either a particular ship or an unnamed ship to follow her. The business distinction and varying results of the two seem to me to be plain. The legal distinction seems to me to be equally plain.

From the earliest times a bill of lading was a document which acknow- **6–062** ledged actual shipment on board a particular ship. In Bennett's *History of the Bill of Lading* (Cambridge Press, 1914), at p. 8, is this passage: "Desjardins says that towards the close of the 16th century the use of the Bill of Lading was widespread—he quotes a definition from Le Guidon de la mer, a document of that epoch, which defines the Bill of Lading as 'the acknowledgment which the master of the ship makes of the number and quality of the goods loaded on board'": see Desjardin's *Traité de Droit Commercial Maritime*, Tome 4, Art. 904 (Paris, 1885). It is clear, I may add, that the bill of lading sprang from the ship's book of lading, which was a document of recognized importance showing the goods actually put on board.

The famous case of *Lickbarrow v Mason* (1794) 5 T.R. 685 was decided in 1794. It decided that bills of lading were transferable by the custom of merchants. The finding of the jury as to the custom is set out as follows: It begins:

"By the custom of merchants, bills of lading, expressing goods or merchandises to have been shipped by any person or persons to be delivered to order or assigns, have been, and are, at any time after such goods have been shipped, and before the voyage performed, for which they have been or are shipped, negotiable and transferable by the shipper or shippers of such goods."

The word "negotiable" in that special verdict really means no more than the word "transferable" or "assignable": see Scrutton on *Charterparties*, Art. 56 (note).

I am not aware of any decision which has modified the finding of the jury in *Lickbarrow v Mason* (1794) 5 T.R. 683, 685 as to the subject-matter to which alone the custom of transferability applied. Apparently that custom, and that custom only, was operative when the Bills of Lading Act, 1855 (18 & 19 Vict. c. 111), was passed. Now that Act expressly recites the custom found in *Lickbarrow v Mason* (1794) 5 T.R. 683, 685, and then proceeds: "And whereas it frequently happens that the goods in respect of which bills of lading purport to be signed have not been laden on board." It thus seems plain that the Act was referring to documents acknowledging an actual shipment on board a specified ship. I need not refer to ss. 1 and 2 of the Act. But s.3 says: "Every bill of lading in the hands of a consignee or endorsee for valuable consideration representing goods to have been shipped on board a vessel shall be conclusive evidence of such shipment as against the master or other persons signing the same." It seems clear that no assignee can invoke the benefits, for example, of s.3 of the Act, unless the document actually asserts the goods to have been shipped on board.

6–063   The whole point of the section seems to go if the document does not contain such an assertion. I will refer to this Act later.

Now in Blackburn on *Sale*, 3rd ed. (1910), p. 421, is this statement.

"A bill of lading is a writing signed on behalf of the owner of the ship in which goods are embarked, acknowledging the receipt of the goods, and undertaking to deliver them at the end of the voyage (subject to such conditions as may be mentioned in the bill of lading)."

The common form of a bill of lading is given in Carver on *Carriage by Sea*, 6th ed., Sect. 54. It is worthy of observation that in an American case, *Rowley v Bigelow* (1832) 12 Pick. 307 (Mass.), Shaw C.J. said: "The bill of lading acknowledges the goods to be on board and regularly the goods ought to be on board before the bill of lading is signed": see note (3.) in Parsons on *Shipping* (Boston), vol. i., p. 187, where the learned author somewhat pointedly says: "It is a fraud on the part of the Master to sign the bills before the goods are on board." In Benjamin on *Sale*, 6th ed., p. 846, is this passage, giving the result of the cases: "When delivery is to be made by a bill of lading the rule is that the seller makes a good delivery if he forward to the buyer, as soon as he reasonably can after the shipment, a bill of lading, whereunder the buyer can obtain delivery, duly indorsed and effectual to pass the property in the goods, made out in terms consistent with the contract of sale, and purporting to represent goods in accordance with the contract, and which are in fact in accordance therewith." Apart from any authority to the contrary it seems to me that I must hold that the document here is not a bill of lading within the c.i.f. contract before me. It does not acknowledge the goods to be on board a specific ship, nor does it acknowledge a shipment on board at all. It leaves it uncertain as to whether the goods will come by the *Anglia* or some following ship. The word "following" is loose and ambiguous in itself. The document does not even say "immediately following," nor does it indicate that the "following ship" will belong to or be under the control of the person who issues the bill of lading. The document seems to me to be (in substance) a mere receipt for goods which at some future time and by some uncertain vessel are to be shipped. It is not even in the form of the New York Produce Exchange bill of lading set out in Carver, 6th ed., Appendix A, p. 971. The buyer is left in doubt as to actual shipment and actual ship.

The sellers, however, submit that I am bound by the opinion of the Privy Council in *Marlborough Hill (Ship) v Cowan & Sons* [1921] 1 A.C. 444. The buyers, on the other hand, contend that that opinion is erroneous and that I ought not to follow it. I need scarcely state the deep diffidence and embarrassment which I feel in discussing that weighty opinion. As Lord Phillimore himself, however, pointed out in *Dulieu v White & Sons* [1901] 2 K.B. 669, 683, a Privy Council advice is not binding on the King's Bench Division even as to the *res decisa*. I wish to point out first that the actual decision in the *Marlborough Hill* Case was merely that the bill of lading there in question (which closely resembles the one now before me) fell within s.6 of the Admiralty Court Act, 1861. It may be that the phrase "bill of lading" in that section permits of a broad interpretation. I point out next that there is no express statement in the *Marlborough Hill* Case that the document there in question actually fell within the Bills of Lading Act, 1855. In the third place it seems to me to be clear that the Board did not consider the nature and effect of an ordinary c.i.f. contract or the decisions thereon in relation to the question before them. The case of *Bowes v Shand* (1877) 2 App. Cas. 455 moreover was not even cited to the Board. Lord Phillimore, in reading the advice of the Privy Council, said [1921] 1 A.C. 451:

"There can be no difference in principle between the owner, master, or agent acknowledging that he has received the goods on his wharf, or allotted portion of quay, or his storehouse awaiting shipment, and his acknowledging that the goods have been actually put over the ship's rail."

6–064 With the deepest respect I venture to think that there is a profound difference between the two, both from a legal and business point of view. Those differences seem to me clear. I need not state them. If the view of the Privy Council is carried to its logical conclusion, a mere receipt for goods at a dock warehouse for future shipment might well be called a bill of lading. Again the Board say [1921] 1 A.C. 444, 452:

> "Then as regards the obligation to carry either by the named ship or by some other vessel; it is a contract which both parties may well find it convenient to enter into and accept. {453} The liberty to tranship is ancient and well established, and does not derogate from the nature of a bill of lading, and if the contract begin when the goods are received on the wharf, substitution does not differ in principle from tranship-ment."

I do not pause to analyse these words. I only say that in my own humble view substitution and the right of transhipment are distinct things, and rest on different principles. The passage last cited can, I think, have no application at all to a c.i.f. contract, which provides for a specific date of shipment. It will suffice if I say two things. First, that in my view the *Marlborough Hill* Case does not apply to a c.i.f. contract such as that now before me. Secondly, that grounds for challenging the *dicta* of the Privy Council will be found in Art. 22, and the notes and cases there cited, in Scrutton on *Charterparties*, 10th ed., as to what are called "through bills of lading," in the lucid article in the Law Quarterly Review of October, 1889, vol. v., p. 424, by Mr Harold D. Bateson; and of July, 1890, vol. vi., p. 289, by the late Mr Carver, and in Carver on *Carriage*, 6th ed., notes to Sect. 107. I do not doubt that the document before me is a "shipping docu-ment" within the U.S.A. Harter Act, 1893. I feel bound to hold, however, that it is not a bill of lading within the c.i.f. contract of sale made between the present parties.

Notes

6–065 The bill of lading stated only that the goods were

> "Received in apparent good order and condition from D.A. Horan to be transported by the S.S. Anglia now lying in the Port of Philadelphia . . . or failing shipment by said steamer in and upon a following steamer, . . . "

Thus the bill of lading did not even unequivocally identify the ship upon which the goods were to be shipped (although the *Anglia* was named, shipment could be on board a subsequent steamer). McCardie J. observed (at 451) that: "The docu-ment seems to me to be (in substance) a mere receipt for goods which at some future time and by some uncertain vessel are to be shipped." Nonetheless, although he emphasised the lack of specificity in this bill of lading, his remarks apply to all received for shipment bills. The distinction he adopts is "between a receipt for goods actually shipped on board a particular ship and a receipt for goods which are at some future time to be shipped on board either a particular ship or an unnamed ship to follow her". Thus, he takes the same view of all received for shipment bills. Moreover, in spite of the last sentence from the above passage, which on its face applies only to the contract before him, his views would appear to apply to any c.i.f. contract. The reasoning can therefore be stated generally: received for shipment bills are not good tender under a c.i.f. contract. Moreover, by contrast with *Yelo v Machado*, there is no suggestion that trade practices can alter the position at all.

The main reasoning was that:

1. The tender of documents is the method by which the goods are delivered.[65]

2. The received for shipment bill of lading is not a document of title at common law.[66]

3. The received for shipment bill of lading is not a bill of lading within the 1855 Act.[67] (The 1855 Act, and its successor, the Carriage of Goods by Sea Act 1992, are discussed in chapter 13, below.)

McCardie J. reached his decision in spite of strong evidence of a trade custom, "inasmuch as the form of the document before me is of frequent use at American ports",[68] but it does not necessarily follow that a term expressly providing for tender of a received for shipment bill would be repugnant to a c.i.f. contract.

Times have changed since this decision, however. From the authorities considered earlier, it is arguable that the received for shipment bill is now recognised as a document of title, and the 1855 Act has been replaced by the Carriage of Goods by Sea Act 1992, which applies equally to the received for shipment as to the shipped bill of lading. Arguably, therefore, much of the basis for *Diamond Alkali* has been weakened.

It remains the case, however, that a c.i.f. seller is required to ship the goods, and that only a shipped bill of lading can provide evidence that he has done so. That is also true f.o.b., and it may therefore be that the c.i.f. position is similar to f.o.b. *Yelo v Machado* suggests that for f.o.b. contracts, where the seller is required to tender a bill of lading, normally a shipped bill is required, but that the normal presumption can be rebutted by very strong evidence to the contrary.

Note also that in *Diamond Alkali*, the buyers were also entitled to reject because a certificate of insurance was tendered, not an assignable policy. This aspect of the case is considered further below.

(b) Clean Bill of Lading

There is also a requirement for a clean bill in a c.i.f. or f.o.b. contract, which **6–066** means that the carrier must state in the bill that the goods were loaded on board in apparent good order and condition. The bill may not be claused (*i.e.* there must

---

[65] At 448 (and see the above passage); McCardie J. cited *Ireland v Livingston* (1872) L.R. 5 H.L. 395, 406, and the judgments of Hamilton J. and Kennedy L.J. (dissenting) in *Biddell Bros v E. Clemens Horst Co* [1911] 1 K.B. 214, 221 and [1911] 1 K.B. 934, 956. Kennedy L.J. observed that "the bill of lading in law and fact represents the goods", and his judgment was later upheld in the House of Lords [1912] A.C. 18.

[66] At p. 450 (and see the above passage); *Lickbarrow v Mason* (1794) T.R. 685 and the Preamble and s.3 of the Bills of Lading Act 1855 were relied on in support of this view.

[67] At 452–453 (and see the above passage); *The Marlborough Hill* [1921] 1 A.C. 444 (P.C.) was criticised and not followed.

[68] At 447 (and see the above passage).

be no qualifications in the margin as to the condition of the goods on loading). A bill of lading will still be clean, however, if it is claused by notations indicating that the goods have deteriorated, or been been damaged or destroyed *after* shipment.

M. GOLODETZ & CO v CZARNIKOW-RIONDA CO INC (THE GALATIA)

Court of Appeal. [1980] 1 W.L.R. 495

6–067 The case concerned a contract for shipment of a quantity of about 13,000 tons of sugar c. & f. Bandarshapur, Iran, incorporating the rules of the Refined Sugar Association. Payment was to be made cash, ship lost or not lost, against clean "On Board" bills of lading evidencing freight having been paid. The R.S.A. rules expressly required the buyer to insure the cargo.

The sellers shipped the goods according to contract, but after loading some 200 tons were destroyed by fire and discharged. The separate bill of lading issued in relation to these discharged goods acknowledged that they had been shipped in apparent good order and condition, but bore a typewritten notation:

> "Cargo covered by this Bill of Lading has been discharged Kandla view damaged by fire and/or water used to extinguish fire for which general average declared."

The sellers claimed entitlement to the price, and on an appeal from arbitration, the question therefore arose whether the buyers were entitled to reject the bill of lading for the 200 tons discharged.

In fact, the buyers had accepted the documents, without prejudice, to see if they would be accepted by their sub-buyers. However, when the buyers tendered the documents to the confirming bank under the sub-sale, they were rejected on the grounds that they bore a superimposed clause or notation. They had also previously been rejected, by the seller's own bank, when the bill of lading was tendered by the original shippers under the f.o.b. supply contract. The buyers argued that the bill of lading was unacceptable in the trade and hence unmerchantable, having been rejected by two banks. Whether the banks were correct to reject the bill of lading is considered further in chapter 10, below.

Held:
That the bill of lading was clean, and that the buyers must therefore accept it—the clausing did not invalidate it, relating as it did to damage after shipment.

DONALDSON J. at first instance: *(also reported at [1980] 1 W.L.R. 495, whose decision the Court of Appeal upheld), on the bill of lading issue)*

6–068   (i) *The practical test.* Mr Johnson *[for the buyers]* submits that there are two possible tests to be applied, the practical and the legal. The practical test is whether a bill of lading in this form is acceptable to banks generally as being a "clean" bill of lading. Since 1962, virtually all banks have accepted the international rules set out in a document issued by the International Chamber of Commerce entitled "Uniform Customs and Practice for Documentary Credits." Rule 16 provides[69]:

---

[69] The modern provision is art. 32 of UCP 500—see App. C.

"A clean shipping document is one which bears no superimposed clause or notation which expressly declares a defective condition of the goods and/or the packaging. Banks will refuse shipping documents bearing such clauses or notations unless the credit expressly states clauses or notation which may be accepted."

This definition fails to specify the time with respect to which the notation speaks. The bill of lading and any notations speak *at* the date of issue, but they may speak about a state of affairs which then exists or about an earlier state of affairs or both. If the rule refers to notations about the state of affairs at the time of the issue of the bill of lading or, indeed, at any time after shipment of the 200 tons was completed, the bill of lading is not "clean" within the meaning of that word in the rule for the notation clearly draws attention to the cargo being damaged. If, however, it refers to notations about the state of affairs upon completion of shipment, the bill of lading is equally clearly clean for it shows that the goods were in apparent good order and condition on shipment and suggests only that they were damaged after shipment.

Mr Johnson draws attention to the fact that this bill of lading was rejected by two different banks. The first rejection was by the sellers' own bank when the bill of lading was tendered by the shippers under the f.o.b. supply contract. The second rejection was by the buyers' sub-purchasers when it was tendered to them by the buyers without prejudice to the rights of the parties as between sellers and buyers. On these facts, Mr Johnson invites me to hold that this bill of lading is not a "clean" bill in commercial or practical terms. . . .

There is, I think, more than one answer to this "practical test" objection. First, the contract called for cash against documents, which no doubt assumes a documentary credit. But the board has not found that it was a custom of the trade, and the contract does not provide, that the documents shall be such as to satisfy the U.C.P. rules as to "clean" bills of lading, which rules do not have the force of law. Furthermore, if there is ambiguity as to the meaning of those rules, that ambiguity should if possible be resolved in a way which will result in the rules reflecting the position under general maritime and commercial law. So construed they add nothing to the legal test which I consider hereafter.

Second, the evidence does not disclose that banks generally would reject such a bill of lading as that relating to the 200 tons as not being a "clean" bill of lading or that, if they would do so, it would be for any better reason than that they were applying what they thought the U.C.P. rules required.

Third, I am not satisfied that it is right to apply a practical test, other than in the context of the merchantability of the documents to which I will return hereafter. What is really being said here is that the very fact that the buyers and two banks rejected these documents proves that they are not "clean." This is a proposition which I decline to accept.

6–069   (ii) *The legal test.* I, therefore, proceed to apply the legal test. As Salmon J. remarked in *British Imex Industries Ltd v Midland Bank Ltd* [1958] 1 Q.B. 542, 551, a "clean bill of lading" has never been exhaustively defined. I have been referred to a number of textbooks and authorities which support the proposition that a "clean" bill of lading is one in which there is nothing to qualify the admission that the goods were in apparent good order and condition and that the seller has no claim against the goods except in relation to freight. Some clearly regard the relevant time as being that of shipment. Some are silent as to what is the relevant time. None refers expressly to any time subsequent to shipment.

As between the shipowner and the shipper (including those claiming through the shipper as holders of the bill of lading) the crucial time is shipment. The shipowner's prime obligation is to deliver the goods at the contractual destination in the like good order and condition as when shipped. The cleanliness of the bill of lading may give rise to an estoppel and the terms of the bill of lading contract may exempt the shipowner from a breach of this obligation, but everything stems from the state of the goods as shipped. As between seller and c.i.f. or c. & f. buyer, the property and risk normally pass upon the negotiation of the bill of lading, but do so as from shipment. Thus, the fact that the ship and goods have been lost after shipment or that a liability to contribute in general average or salvage has arisen is no reason for refusing to take up and pay for the documents.

In these circumstances, it is not surprising that there appears to be no case in which the courts or the textbook writers have had to consider a bill of lading which records the fate of the goods subsequent to shipment and, indeed, I have never seen or heard of a bill of lading like that in the present case. Nor is it surprising that some of the judgments and textbooks do not in terms say that when reference is made to the condition of the goods what is meant is their condition on shipment.

However, I have no doubt that this is the position. The bill of lading with which I am concerned casts no doubt whatsoever on the condition of the goods at that time and does not assert that at that time the shipowner had any claim whatsoever against the goods. It follows that in my judgment this bill of lading, unusual though it is, passes the legal test of cleanliness.

Notes

6–070   Donaldson J. went on to say that he accepted unreservedly the observation already quoted, that:

> "These documents have to be handled by banks, they have to be taken up or rejected promptly and without any opportunity for prolonged inquiry, they have to be such as can be re-tendered to sub-purchasers, and it is essential that they should so conform to the accustomed shipping documents as to be reasonably and readily fit to pass current in commerce."

He continued, however:

"A tender of documents which, properly read and understood, call for further inquiry or are such as to invite litigation is clearly a bad tender. But the operative words are 'properly read and understood.' I fully accept that the clause on this bill of lading makes it unusual, but properly read and understood it calls for no inquiry and it casts no doubt at all upon the fact that the goods were shipped in apparent good order and condition or upon the protection which anyone is entitled to expect when taking up such a document whether as a purchaser or as a lender on the security of the bill."

The decision clearly limits (and surely correctly) the extent to which trade practices can determine the law. The mere fact that the bill of lading had twice been rejected by a bank did not render it unclean. On whether the banks were correct to reject the bill, see further chapter 10. Donaldson J. thought the banks' position wrong, but in any case irrelevant in an interpretation of the sale contract.

The decision in *The Galatia* is consistent with the general rules as to risk (see chapter 4, above). The sellers had fully performed all their obligations regarding the goods, and risk in them passed to the buyer on shipment. However, while Donaldson J. thought that the buyers might be liable for damages simply on the basis of risk, the entitlement to the price arose only on and against the tender of contractual documents. Thus, the case depended on the bill of lading being clean; it could not be decided on the basis of risk alone.

The judgment of Megaw L.J. (the only substantive judgment in the Court of Appeal) does little more than uphold Donaldson J.'s views.

(c) Charterparty Bills

The obligation on a c.i.f. seller is enter into a contract of carriage which is **6–071** reasonable, and not otherwise in conflict with the sale contract.[70] The bill of lading may itself set out the terms of the carriage contract,[71] but bills of lading are often almost silent on their face, incorporating terms from a charterparty.[72] There is an obvious logic to this; if for example, it is intended for the receiver to pay demurrage incurred at discharge, it is sensible for the laytime and demurrage provisions from the charterparty to be incorporated. There is however the obvious difficulty that the indorsee may be unaware of the charterparty terms, especially if a charterparty bill can be good tender whether or not the charterparty itself is also tendered.

FINSKA CELLULOSAFORENINGEN v WESTFIELD PAPER CO LTD

King's Bench Division. [1940] 4 All E.R. 473

The question at issue was whether a seller of woodpulp c.i.f. could **6–072** validly tender a bill of lading containing the clause "All conditions and exceptions as per charterparty dated (blank)" when no charterparty was produced, and a further clause ("F.A.A. Current War Risk Clause") which gave the master a discretion, in the case of war or hostilities rendering the prosecution of the voyage unsafe, to land the goods at any port he may

---

[70] On the latter point, see *Soules CAF v PT Transap of Indonesia*, at para 2–029, above.
[71] See paras 12–001, *et seq.* for the relationship between the bill of lading and the carriage contract.
[72] See paras 12–001, *et seq.* for a discussion of precisely which terms are incorporated.

consider safe, where for all purposes the voyage should be considered terminated.

On a voyage to Leith (Scotland) beginning in February 1940, the goods (aboard a Finnish ship) were discharged at Kotka in Finland. The sellers tendered the documents and sued for the price.

Held:
The sellers were entitled to the price.

6–073   VISCOUNT CALDECOTE, L.C.J.: If the proper shipping documents were tendered by the plaintiffs to the buyers or their agents, the plaintiffs are entitled to recover these amounts. By their points of defence, the defendants say that they were entitled to reject the tendered documents, and they specify two grounds on which the documents were defective. Their first ground is that no charterparty has been produced or identified or tendered to the defendants. The bill of lading contained a clause as follows:

"All conditions and exceptions as per charterparty dated (blank)."

. . . I think that the defendants and their agents well understood what was intended by the clause, and were aware that shipments would take place, as in the past, in vessels chartered on the terms of the Baltpulp charter. The fact that no objection was raised on the score of this clause until after the action was commenced goes some way to confirm me in this opinion. Counsel for the defendants put his case as high as to say that, in all cases of c.i.f. contracts, the charterparty must be tendered where it is a relevant document. As authority for that proposition, he referred to a passage from the judgment of Blackburn J. in *Ireland v Livingston* (1872) L.R. 5 H.L. 395, 406:

"... for the balance a draft is drawn on the consignee which he is bound to accept (if the shipment be in conformity with his contract) on having handed to him the charterparty, bill of lading and policy of insurance."

It is to be observed that neither in the judgment of Hamilton J. in *Horst (E. Clemens) Co v Biddell Brothers* nor in the judgment of Kennedy L.J. in that case in the Court of Appeal is there any mention of the charterparty as one of the necessary documents to complete delivery in accordance with the agreement. Nor, again, in *Johnson v Taylor Brothers & Co Ltd* [1920] A.C. 144, 155, 156, where Lord Atkinson once more stated the sellers' duties under a c.i.f. contract, was there any mention of the charterparty as a necessary document to be produced by the seller, together with the invoices, bill of lading and policy of insurance, in order to entitle him to receive payment.

In the circumstances of this case, at any rate, the tender of the bill of lading duly indorsed was, in my opinion, a sufficient compliance with the contract of sale to entitle the sellers to payment of the price of the goods, subject, however, to the second ground on which the defendants allege that the bill of lading was defective. . . . [The second ground concerned the insurance provision made; see further the discussion of C. *Groom v Barber*, below (on this issue).]

Notes (on acceptability of charterparty bill)

The view expressed in this passage depends on the circumstances of the **6–074** particular case. Here the charterparty concerned was on the Baltpulp form, as both parties knew from previous dealings, and which was also the standard form used for the particular trade. Nor does it appear to have been amended since the previous dealings. Possibly the case depended upon this. In *SIAT Di Del Ferro v Tradax Overseas SA*, Donaldson J. observed[73]:

"The mere fact that a bill of lading refers to a charterparty does not require the production of that charter, if its terms are not incorporated into the bill of lading contract or do not affect the buyers' rights. . . . Nor need the charter-party be produced if the bill of lading refers to a known standard form and it is only the printed clauses of that form which are relevant, *e.g.* "Centrocon Arbitration clause". If the decision in *Finska Cellulosaforeningen v Westfield Paper Company Ltd* is correct, it is justified upon this ground."

This places quite serious limits on *Finska*; if the charterparty is not on a known **6–075** standard form, or (more likely) has been heavily amended, or differs from that used in past dealings between the parties, the seller is probably under an obligation to tender it in addition to the bill of lading. There is an obvious circularity problem, though: how is the buyer to know that, if the charterparty is not tendered?

In *SIAT* itself, the bills of lading did not state the destination (and the charterparty destination differed from the contractual destination). Donaldson J. continued:

"They were also defective in that, in the absence of an accompanying copy of the charterparty, they did not show whether the other terms of the contract of carriage were consistent with the sale contract. Had the charterparty been produced, both the buyers and the banks could have discovered that the provisions as to discharging laytime were in fact inconsistent with the sale contract."

The buyers were therefore entitled to reject the bills, a conclusion affirmed by the Court of Appeal.[74]

Up to and including the 1983 revision, the U.C.P. (which normally applies to documentary credits) stated that, unless otherwise stipulated in the credit, banks would reject a charterparty bill, no doubt because of the fear that they might be bound by terms of which they have no knowledge. However this prompted Ventris to comment[75]:

---

[73] [1978] 2 Lloyd's Rep. 470, 492 (col.2).
[74] [1980] 1 Lloyd's Rep. 53.
[75] F.M. Ventris, *Bankers' Documentary Credits*, (3rd ed., Lloyd's of London Press Ltd, 1990), p. 30. See also *UCP 500 & 400 Compared*, (I.C.C. Publication No. 511, 1993), at p. 74, where it is pointed out that the applicant and beneficiary will be aware of the terms of the carriage contract. However, they will not necessarily be aware of the terms of the carriage contract if there is a long chain, and banks themselves may be interested in the terms of the carriage contract.

"In view of other startling innovations made in the 1983 Revision it is disappointing to find that the rules still make the acceptance of a charter-party bill of lading subject to the credit including its specific acceptance. Today, more and more products are shipped in bulk which means that, unless the cargo is carried in the owner's own vessel, it is carried in a chartered vessel. Having regard to the modifications made in order to accommodate container traffic[76] there seems no valid reason to continue this ban on charter-party bills of lading . . . "

However, Article 25 of UCP 500 (see Appendix C below) now makes express provision for them.

Notes (on substance of carriage contract)

There may be more than one charterparty, and in any case, not all charterparty terms are appropriate for incorporation into a bill of lading contract. There is a fuller discussion of this at paras 12–037, *et seq.*

Though the *Hague* and *Hague-Visby Rules* (which generally protect cargo-owners) do not apply to charterparties,[77] the indorsee of a charterparty bill of lading is protected by them (unless he is also charterer) by virtue of holding a bill of lading, assuming the bill of lading is governed by the *Hague* or *Hague-Visby Rules*.

(d) Through Bills of Lading

6–076   The bill of lading must cover the goods for the entire voyage, from shipment to port of destination. If the goods are to be transhipped during the voyage, for example where a large bulk cargo is shipped from outside Europe to a European port, and then placed aboard smaller vessels for distribution throughout Europe, then a through bill of lading is required.

The essence of the through bill of lading is that one carrier (probably the ocean carrier in the above example) takes on obligations for the whole voyage, but with a liberty to sub-contract on-carriage from the port of transhipment. (Conceptually, it is similar to the combined transport document described at paras 15–024, *et seq.*, below, except that it covers port-to-port shipment by more than one carrier, whereas a combined transport document covers mixed land and sea carriage.) There must also be an express liberty to tranship in the carriage contract, for in the absence of an express stipulation transhipment will put the carrier in breach.

Whether a through bill of lading constitutes a valid tender probably depends on what is usual and customary in the particular trade, but in any event it must provide coverage for the cargo for the entire voyage.

HANSSON v HAMEL & HORLEY LTD

House of Lords. [1922] 2 A.C. 36

Facts:

6–077   Cod guano was to be shipped c.i.f. from Braatvag, Norway to Yokohama, Japan. It was put on to a small local vessel first, for transhipment at Hamburg on to a large Japanese steamer, bound for Japan along with

---

[76] He is referring here to art. 25 of the 1983 revision, which has been split up into arts 24 and 26 of the present revision, both of which have relevance for container traffic.
[77] See Ch. 11, below.

other cargoes from elsewhere. A document called a through bill of lading was issued, but only at Hamburg by the second carrier.

Held:

In principle, a through bill of lading can be acceptable tender c.i.f. This was a bad tender, however, because it was not a through bill of lading at all. Not being issued until Hamburg, it did not cover the first (local) voyage. Had the goods been damaged at the local stage, the consignee would have had no action against the first carrier.

LORD SUMNER: These documents have to be handled by banks, they have to be taken up or rejected promptly and without any opportunity for prolonged enquiry, they have to be such as can be re-tendered to sub-purchasers, and it is essential that they should so conform to the accustomed shipping documents as to be reasonably and readily fit to pass current in commerce. I am quite sure that, under the circumstances of this case, this ocean bill of lading does not satisfy these conditions. It bears notice of its insufficiency and ambiguity on its face; for, although called a through bill of lading, it is not really so. It is the contract of the subsequent carrier only, without any complementary promises to bind the prior carriers in the through transit . . . the buyer was plainly left with a considerable *lacuna* in the documentary cover to which the contract entitled him.   **6–078**

The point is also put in a slightly different way, which equally relates especially to bills of lading. Scrutton J. points out in *Landauer & Co v Craven & Speeding Bros.* [1912] 2 K.B. 94, that in a sale of goods c.f. and i., the contract of affreightment must be procured "on shipment". Of course this is practicable and common even when a through bill of lading is necessary, containing provision for transhipment at an intermediate port from a local to an ocean steamer not in the same ownership. I do not understand this proposition as meaning that the bill of lading would be bad, unless it was signed contemporaneously with the actual placing of the goods on board.

"On shipment" is an expression of some latitude. Bills of lading are constantly signed after the loading is complete, and, in some cases, after the ship has sailed. I do not think that they thereby necessarily cease to be procured "on shipment", nor do I suppose that the learned judge so intended his words. It may also be that the expression would be satisfied, even though some local carriage on inland waters, or by canal, or in an estuary by barge or otherwise, preceded the shipment on the ocean steamer provided that the steamer's bill of lading covered that prior carriage by effectual words of contract. "On shipment" is referable both to time and place. In principle, however, and subject to what I have said, I accept this opinion of so great an authority, and I am quite sure that a bill of lading only issued thirteen days after the original shipment, at another port in another country many hundreds of miles away, is not duly procured "on shipment".

Indeed the ocean bill of lading was not procured as part of this c.f. and i. shipment at all, and "on shipment" does not at any rate mean on re-shipment or on transhipment.

Notes

6–079   The tenor of the judgment is that if this had been a genuine through bill it could in principle have constituted a good tender c.i.f. Lord Sumner continued (at p. 48):

"Accordingly, I express no opinion adverse to the sufficiency of through bills of lading, properly so-called, as a tender under a contract like this. I would add that the evidence given to prove a course of business between the contracting parties or a custom of merchants generally affecting the normal requirements of a c.f. and i. contract failed to establish any distinction in this case, and I have no observation to make on the effect of such evidence had it been sufficient."

There were some doubts whether through bills of lading triggered s.1 of the Bills of Lading Act 1855 applies to them (see chapter 13, below). However, there are no similar doubts now that that section has been replaced by the Carriage of Goods by Sea Act 1992.

(e) Tender of One of a Set

6–080   *Glyn Mills*, above, makes it expedient for a c.i.f. purchaser to obtain all the original bills in a set (the set usually being of three). It is, of course, possible for the contract expressly to require tender of all the originals, but in the absence of such an express stipulation, the Court of Appeal held, only a year after *Glyn Mills* was decided, that a c.i.f. buyer could require tender of only one original.

SANDERS BROTHERS v MACLEAN & CO

Court of Appeal. (1883) 11 Q.B.D. 327

Facts:

6–081   In a contract for the sale of a quantity of old railway iron two tenders of documents were made. The buyers refused the first tender on the ground that only two of the three bills were tendered, and the second on the ground that the bills of lading could not have been forwarded in time to arrive before the goods. The sellers sued for breach of contract.

Held:

The sellers were entitled to damages for non-acceptance. In an ordinary sale contract where payment is to be made against bills of lading, the buyer must accept and pay on one bill and cannot demand all three originals. Nor will a term be implied that the documents must be tendered in time to arrive before the goods themselves.

[*Arguments on the timing of the second tender are considered further below.*]

6–082   Brett M.R.: *(on the first tender)* . . . [The first] question is whether, by the terms of an ordinary contract of sale relating to goods shipped payment is to be made against bills of lading, is it a part of the contract that all existing copies of the bill must be offered in order to entitle the sender of the goods to payment? If only one copy of the bill of lading has been indorsed, it is plain and known law that the delivery of that copy so indorsed, with an intention to pass property in the goods, passes the property, and will entitle the person to whom it is delivered to demand possession of the goods on their arrival; and it is also known law that if it be so indorsed the person to whom it is delivered can, by indorsement for value, pass the property to someone else, and, if that one copy of the bill of lading is the first which is indorsed, it passes the property so that no subsequent indorsement of any other of the copies will have any effect upon the property in the goods. It was, however, urged before Pollock B, not that that view of the law had been altered, but that a difficulty had arisen in the mercantile world which made it unsafe for a vendee, under these circumstances, to accept the first indorsed copy of the bill of lading, because, if the original shipper remained in possession of any other copy of the bill of lading he might fraudulently indorse it, and present that subsequently indorsed copy of the bill of lading to the captain of the ship before any of the other copies had been presented to him, and then the shipowner would be absolved, as against the real owner of the goods, for having delivered the goods under such bill of lading, although such indorsement was fraudulent. That was so decided by the House of Lords in the case of *Glyn Mills & Co v East and West India Dock Co* [*above*]. I make no observation upon that decision, except that it is to be loyally followed. It was inevitable, to my mind, upon that decision by the House of Lords, that somebody who wanted to reject a cargo would avail himself of it as a ground for his doing so. That has now happened, and the question is whether there is anything in that decision which alters the old law.

Now the House of Lords, as I understand that case . . . distinctly stated that the old law with regard to the passing of property by bills of lading was not altered, and that the first copy of the bill of lading, properly indorsed for value, with an intent to pass the property, passed the property, and that no other copy of the bill of lading subsequently indorsed would have any effect in passing the property at all. They held only that although the true owner of the goods could sue the person into whose possession the goods had gone, because the goods were his, yet that he could not sue the captain or shipowner; because when he took the property in the goods by virtue of the indorsement of the first copy of the bill of lading, he took it subject to a contingency, that if the goods were delivered by the captain to any body else upon a subsequent copy of the bill of lading fraudulently indorsed by the consignor, he could not sue the shipowner, but he could sue anybody else who dealt with the goods which were his property. If that be true, could it be the meaning of this contract, which states in terms that payment is to be made against bills of lading (and which here is the same as if it had been payable on presentation of bill of lading, because bills of lading here apply to shipments in different months), that although the bill of lading offered would pass the property and give the right to possession, yet nevertheless the vendee had a right to reject the cargo, because all the three copies or parts of the bills of lading were not delivered to him? In my opinion that is not the result of the case of *Glyn Mills & Co v East and West India Dock Co*, and it would be contrary to the practice and to the known principles of mercantile law with regard to bills of lading. Therefore I cannot agree with the learned judge, Pollock B, in the decision he came to. That of itself would be sufficient to decide this case. But considering that the other point was argued, and that it is a matter of mercantile law which, in my opinion, ought not to be left in any doubt, I desire to say for myself that I think the second tender... was a good tender, even assuming that the first was bad.

Note

6–083   On the issue of the first tender, of one only of the set of three bills of lading, the commercial practices around which the law of international trade is based were developed to protect against the bankruptcy of the other party, not his fraud. They assume that all parties act in good faith, and this assumption has been necessary to allow complex documentary transactions to grow up. Fraud today is a significant problem (see paras 15–037, *et seq.*), but to alter commercial practice in an attempt to eliminate fraud may negate much of the usefulness of the present day transactions.

(f) When Tendered?

SANDERS BROTHERS v MACLEAN & CO

Court of Appeal. (1883) 11 Q.B.D. 327

6–084   The facts of this case have already been stated. The second tender was rejected on the ground that the bills of lading could not have been forwarded in time to arrive before the goods, and the Court of Appeal held this to be a bad reason for rejection.

Brett M.R.: *(on the second tender)* The objection taken to this last tender was this. It was said that it was made at such a time that the bills of lading could not have been forwarded to Philadelphia in time to be there on the ship's arrival, and that it was an implied condition in the contract of sale of the goods that the bills of lading should be delivered to the consignee or vendee in time for him to send them forward, so that they should be at the port of delivery when the ship arrived, and that if that condition was not fulfilled the consignee or vendee had a right to reject the goods. It was stated further, that if we should not go to that length at least we must hold there is implied this, that the bills of lading be delivered to the consignee in such a time as that he could forward them to the port of delivery before charges are incurred, and that that also is not merely an implied stipulation but is an implied condition in the contract, and if not fulfilled the consignee has a right to reject the cargo. The first objection to that contention seems to me to be that the Court has no right to import anything into a contract which it would not be clear to every reasonable man must have been present to the minds of both contracting parties, and agreed to by both. Take the first of these cases. The bill of lading, it is said, must be delivered in time to arrive at the place of destination at or before the ship arrives. A cargo is worth £20,000: if the bill of lading could only arrive the day after the ship it would be monstrous to say that the vendee should have a right to reject the whole cargo although no damage had been done to anybody. So, if the bill of lading is to be delivered so that it may arrive in ordinary course before charges are incurred, a cargo worth £20,000 may be shipped to a place where it would be for the benefit of the vendee that it should be, but where it would be ruin to the vendor to have it if he was obliged to sell it there again, and yet because charges of £10 may have been incurred can it be said that the vendee has a right to reject the cargo? Again, supposing even that there had been an express stipulation in the contract that the bill of lading should be delivered at such a time as that it might arrive at the port of delivery before charges were incurred, or at the time the ship arrived, yet as the rule is not to construe a stipulation in the contract to be a condition unless it is expressly stated that it is a condition, or unless the breach of it goes to the whole value of the contract, such a stipulation could never have been a condition, because obviously a breach of it would not go to the whole value of the contract. As, therefore, if it were an express stipulation, it would not amount to a condition, obviously no such condition can be implied. It is equally impossible, to my mind, to say that even a stipulation ought to be implied in the contract that the bill of lading should be delivered so that it may arrive before or at the time of the arrival of the ship or before charges are incurred.

But, on the other hand, merchants never could have contemplated that **6–085** after a cargo had been destined to a purchaser or consignee the shipper should keep the bill of lading as long as he pleased. Therefore some stipulation with regard to this must be implied. The stipulations which are inferred in mercantile contracts are always that the party will do what is mercantilely reasonable. What, then, is the contract duty which is to be imposed by implication on the seller of goods at sea with regard to the bill of lading? I quite agree that he has no right to keep the bill of lading in his pocket, and when it is said that he should do what is reasonable it is obvious the reasonable thing is that he should make every reasonable exertion to send forward the bill of lading as soon as possible after he has destined the cargo to the particular vendee or consignee. If that be so, the question of whether he has used such reasonable exertion will depend upon the particular circumstances of each case. If there is a perishable cargo or one upon which heavy charges must surely be incurred, the reasonable thing for him to do is to make even a greater exertion than he would in the case of another cargo. That is one of the circumstances which has to be considered. Another circumstance would be from whence is the shipment? How near is the consignor to the ship so as to enable him to get possession of the bill of lading? If in the present case the bill of lading had been in London I should have thought that the consignors would be bound to deliver it much sooner than where as here they had to get it from St. Petersburgh. They were bound to use all reasonable exertion to get the bill of lading from St. Petersburgh and to offer it in London as soon as under the circumstances it was reasonable for them to do so. Whether they did use such reasonable exertion, and whether what they did was under the circumstances done within a reasonable time, was a question for the jury, and in this case it seems to me that substantially the jury found that they had done all that was reasonable, and therefore even if the first tender had been bad I should have thought that the second tender was good. . . .

Notes

6–086   1. On the second tender Brett M.R. refused to imply a condition of the sale contract that the documents would arrive before the ship. This problem has become more topical recently (see paras 15–018, *et seq.*, below).

2. The term implied by Brett M.R. was that the seller must make every reasonable exertion to send it forward as soon as possible. What constitutes reasonable exertion will depend on all the circumstances, but there is no rigid rule that the documents must arrive before the ship.

3. Where an f.o.b. seller is obliged to forward shipping documents, the timing obligation is the same as for c.i.f.

CONCORDIA TRADING BV v RICHCO INTERNATIONAL LTD

Queen's Bench Division (Commercial Court). [1991] 1 Lloyd's Rep. 475

Facts:

6–087   Richco had contracted to sell, on classic f.o.b. terms, 26,250 tonnes of Argentine soya beans. This was the beginning of a chain, in which Concordia were the third buyer, and they contracted to sell the same cargo, on the same terms, to Richco. Thus, a circle of contracts had now formed. Richco never sent the documents to the first buyer, but instead retained them.

Richco then contracted to sell the beans to Panchaud, and again a chain was set up, the last two parties of which were Cargill and Exportchleb, the last of whom were the final receivers and the charterers of the vessel. The entire series of contracts thus formed a circle, in which Richco were at the beginning and the end, followed by a chain, in which Richco were at the beginning and Exportchleb at the end.

Panchaud committed an act of insolvency, so that Richco were stuck with the documents, and now no valid sale contract. In the end they were able to sell down the chain to Cargill, but presumably at a substantial loss. The documents eventually arrived with Exportchleb two months after shipment (one day before discharge).

Presumably in an attempt to recover their loss, Richco sued their own sellers in the circle, Concordia, claiming that Concordia had broken their obligation to forward the documents to Richco. There was no doubt that Concordia were in breach of this obligation, since Richco had retained the documents throughout (arguably a somewhat unmeritorious position for Richco to adopt). The only issue was the date of the breach. The buyers claimed that it was not broken until the time for discharge arose. The sellers claimed that the date of their breach was much earlier, when the market price of soya beans was below the contract price, so as to claim that the buyers were entitled only to nominal damages. By the time the goods arrived the market had risen again, and the buyers claimed substantial damages.

Held:

Evans J. held that where a (classic) f.o.b. seller was obliged to tender shipping documents (here "Bill of Lading shall be considered proof of delivery in the absence of delivery to the contrary"), he had a duty to perform the obligation forthwith, *i.e.* with all reasonable despatch, subject to their being no express provision or time limit to the contrary in the contract (there was not in the case). He equated f.o.b. duties with c.i.f., applying *Sanders v Maclean* and *Sharpe v Nosawa* [1917] 2 K.B. 814.

The case was sent back to G.A.F.T.A. Board of Appeal, who had originally found in favour of the buyers.

EVANS J.: *(after setting out the relevant terms of the GAFTA 64 contract)* So, **6–088** the sellers' obligation was the basic one under an f.o.b. contract of sale, that is, to load contractual goods on board the vessel nominated by the buyers. The bill of lading in the normal course of events would be issued to the sellers. They would present it and other documents to the buyers, requiring payment against documents. There is nothing expressed in the contract regarding the time when the obligations, to present the documents and to pay against documents, should be performed.

This has become the sole issue of law raised by the present appeal. The sellers failed to present documents, in circumstances which will appear, but they contend that the date of their default was not Sept. 29 [date of discharge] but a much earlier date in the first part of August, when the market price of the goods, or of documents representing them, was substantially lower than the contract price. Hence, the buyers' claim for damages should be nominal only.

The sellers contend that the duty of a c.i.f. seller is well established in law. It is, put briefly, to send forward the shipping documents promptly after the goods are shipped. The same duty, they say, rests upon f.o.b. sellers. Shipment took place on July 25/29 at San Nicolas and bills of lading were issued bearing those dates. These would normally become available in London by Aug. 5, so the sellers say that their default, which is not disputed, in failing to tender documents to the buyers took place on or shortly after that date.

The Board of Appeal accepted the buyers' contention that the sellers' default took place much later, on Sept 29. By that date, the vessel had carried the contract goods, and others, to the port of Odessa, and was about to commence discharging the contract goods there. Until then, the sellers could have bought the shipping documents in the market and tender them to the buyers, Richco, in time for them to be presented to the ship for discharge to take place. The board's conclusion is in par. 4:6 of the award:

> With regard to the date of default; Sellers were not in default until the day it was no longer possible for them to purchase the documents for the goods in order to fulfil the Contract, which was 28th September 1987. WE THEREFORE FIND THAT the date of default is 29th September 1987 and we are supported in this by the fact that negotiations to purchase the documents were taking place up to 28th September.

The basis for this award is that, as the contract was silent as to the time for performance of the sellers' obligation to tender the documents to the buyer, this was by legal implication a reasonable time, and such a time continued until it became impossible for the sellers to obtain the documents, if they did not already hold them, so as to enable the buyers to present them to the ship. Only then, the buyers submit, did the sellers fail to perform their obligation so as to become in default. They could, of course, have performed the contract at any earlier date, once the documents were available to them, and if they had tendered the documents at some earlier date, then the buyers would have been obliged to pay.

The c.i.f. rule

6–089   This is well established. In the words of Benjamin on *Sale* (3rd ed) par. 1663 at p. 1061:

> *"Documents to be tendered promptly.*
>   Where the contract contains no express provisions as to the time of tender, the seller must take steps to tender the documents as soon as possible after the goods have been shipped or (in the case of goods sold afloat) after the seller has 'destined the cargo to the particular vendee or consignee'. Although the contrary has been suggested a c.i.f. seller appears, according to the older authorities, to be under no absolute obligation to tender the documents before the arrival of the ship . . ."

Benjamin continues by referring to the application of this rule when the documents are passed down a "string" of buyers and sellers, but points out that cases of this kind will generally be goverened by express provisions as to the time of tender in the contracts.

The leading authorities for the general rule are *Sanders v Maclean* (1883) 11 Q.B.D. 327 *per* Sir Baliol Brett M.R. and *Sharpe v Nosawa* [1917] 2 K.B. 814 *per* Atkin J.

There is no doubt in my mind that the c.i.f. seller is obliged to send forward the documents with all reasonable despatch, or "forthwith" if a single word is preferred, and that performance of this duty is unrelated to the arrival of the ship. The formulation relied upon by the plaintiffs in the present case is "to take all reasonable steps to forward [the documents] without delay" and it is suggested, I think, that this is subtly different in its effect from an obligation to send them "forthwith". I confess that I am unable to appreciate the suggested distinction, because in both cases the time for performance is limited by reference to what the seller can reasonably do. If there is a valid difference, then as stated above I prefer the words first used.

F.O.B. sales

The first question raised by this appeal is whether the same duty rests   **6–090**
upon an f.o.b. seller, which the plaintiffs were. Benjamin (par. 1819 at p. 1172) answers this question in their favour:–

> An f.o.b. seller who undertakes to tender a bill of lading is not (any more than a c.i.f. seller) under any absolute obligation to make the tender before the arrival of the goods at their intended destination; though (like a c.i.f. seller) he is no doubt under a duty to tender the documents promptly, or within such time as may be specified by the contract.

The defendants (buyers), however, dispute this. They say that there was no breach of contract, alternatively no default for the purposes of this contract, until such time as the documents ceased to be marketable, that is, able to be bought and sold in the market; until the time, that is, when the receiver needs the documents to obtain delivery of the goods from the ship at the port of destination, allowing a reasonable time, where necessary, for the documents to be transferred through a string to the ultimate buyer or his agent at that port.

In support of this definition of the seller's duty, the defendants refer to the facts of the present case. These demonstrate how the parties conducted themselves in a real-life situation, though produced by an unusual event, namely, the failure of one of the parties involved in the string. They point to the basic difference between the transfer of documents under a c.i.f. contract, which amounts to constructive delivery of the goods, and the lesser importance of the transfer of documents under an f.o.b. contract, where the goods were delivered to the buyer by being placed on board a vessel nominated by the buyer (cl. 7 of GAFTA 64). They submit, alternatively, that the seller's duty should be modified, if not for all f.o.b.

sales, then at least for f.o.b. sales which form part of a string or for such sales when insolvency supervenes and the string, or circle, is broken.

The latter submissions will require reference to the circumstances of the present case, but before doing so I will consider the more general contentions involving all fob sales.

There is some force in Mr Young's submission [for the buyers, Richco] that *Sharpe v Nosawa* was a case of non-shipment, where Atkin J. had to decide whether the sellers were liable in damages for non-delivery of documents or for non-delivery of goods. He held at p. 818:–

> The answer depends upon the true meaning of a c.i.f. contract of this kind. It is reasonably plain that such a contract is performed by the vendor taking reasonable steps to deliver as soon as possible after shipment the shipping documents ... The delivery intended by the contract is a constructive delivery.

He also quoted, with approval, the *dictum* of Sir Baliol Brett M.R. in *Sanders v Maclean* (1883) 11 Q.B.D. 327 at p. 337:

> The stipulations which are inferred in mercantile contracts are always that the party will do what is mercantilely reasonable ...

There is good reason, in my view, why the correct inference in the case of f.o.b. contracts should be derived from what is "mercantilely reasonable" in those contracts rather than from a direct application of the c.i.f. rule. The contracts are of different kinds, and the analogy is not so close that a straight transfer should be made.

6–091   Nevertheless, there are compelling reasons why, in my judgment, the duty imposed on the f.o.b. seller should be to the same effect as has been established in the case of c.i.f. sales. The f.o.b. seller is required to obtain shipping documents and to tender them to the buyer, and the buyer is obliged to make payment against documents, as is implicit in the present contract (cl. 11; the contrary was not argued before me): see Benjamin on *Sale* par. 1818. In the normal case, although the goods have been shipped on a vessel nominated by the buyer, the seller for his own protection will have reserved the right of disposing of the goods, as unpaid seller, and the bill of lading will require delivery to him or to his order.

The delivery of documents then has the effect of transferring the property in the goods to the buyer, and of bringing about a statutory assignment of contractual rights against the shipowner under s.1 of the Bills of Lading Act, 1855.[78] It remains, therefore, a major event in the relationship between seller and buyer brought about by the f.o.b. contract

---

[78] Now Carriage of Goods by Sea Act 1992—see Ch. 15, below.

of sale. It is certainly more than a merely mechanical process of transferring the bill of lading to the buyer for his convenience some time before he has to present the bill of lading at the destination port.

So far as "mercantile reasonableness" is concerned, I cannot see any reason why the f.o.b. seller should not be required to tender the documents forthwith. Neither party suggests that there is no duty, or that the seller can retain the documents indefinitely. The only reason for holding onto them is that he might have some intention of controlling the date of default, in the event of non-payment, in a way which appears advantageous to him. There is, on the other hand, an overwhelming weight of reasons, practical as well as ones of legal principle, why he should perform rather than delay performance of the contract. Not least, the buyer may want the documents promptly, rather than having to wait until the vessel discharges or is about to discharge the goods. Moreover, the more emphasis that is placed on the fact that the buyer has nominated and is in control of the ship, the more it seems to me that the seller has placed the goods on board that ship in a capacity which is analogous to that of agent for the buyer (though acting, of course, as a principal: compare *Barder v Taylor* (1839) 9 L.J. Ex. 21, and see *Ireland v Livingston* (1872) L.R. 5 H.L. 395). As such, he may be under a duty, analogous to that of an agent, of acting promptly and with reasonable regard to the buyer's interests.

Mr Young's further submission in support of the buyers' contention is that, as the facts of the present case demonstrate, there may continue to be dealings with the documents until such time as the vessel is ready to discharge the goods. Therefore, he says, the documents continue to be capable of lawful tender until that time. This realises a question of principle, which I think can be expressed thus. If the seller is obliged to tender the documents promptly, and if his failure to do so constitutes a default, does this make any subsequent tender non-contractual and the documents worthless, so far as any f.o.b. contract relating to the goods in question is concerned? This assumes that the failure to tender the documents in time is a breach of condition, or at least amounts to a default under the contract. I will make that assumption for present purposes. Although logically any subsequent tender of the documents may be non-contractual, it does not follow that no such tender can be made, or that it cannot be accepted by the buyers. The contract may be kept open, for any number of reasons. A second reason for rejecting this submission is that the documents do not become valueless, or non-marketable, even if they cannot any longer be tendered by the sellers under a particular contract of sale. The bill of lading, in particular, remains "the key to the warehouse", whether floating or ashore, and by custom of merchants it represents the goods whilst they are in the possession or custody of the shipowner or his agents.

For these reasons, I hold that there does rest upon the f.o.b. seller, who is obliged by his contract to obtain and tender the shipping documents, a

6–092

duty to perform that obligation forthwith, that is to say, with all reasonable despatch, subject of course to any express provision or time-limit which the contract may contain. This duty, at least for all practical purposes, is commensurate with that which rests upon the c.i.f. seller in accordance with the authorities referred to above.

Criteria

6–093   In the absence of express provision, the time for performance of the obligation depends upon all the circumstances of the case. What steps it is reasonable for the sellers to take, and what is the reasonable time within which they can be taken, are questions of fact, and these in the present case are for the arbitrators, namely, the Board of Appeal, to decide. The test is likely to be most difficult to apply when there is not a single "classic" f.o.b. contract of sale, but a series of contracts forming a string, maybe with one or more circles forming part of the string, and particularly when insolvency supervenes, as it did here.

I come next, therefore, to the buyers' alternative submissions, namely, that the duty of sending forward the documents "forthwith" does not apply in circumstances such as these.

Mr Young submits that here at least the duty is to tender the documents within such time as the receiver, or ultimate buyer, needs them for the purposes of obtaining delivery from ship. The receiver may be someone other than his direct buyer, and so it would follow that some additional time would reasonably be required for onward transmission of the documents by him to the ultimate buyer. But at least, he submits, the buyer would have some direct knowledge of these factors, unlike the case where a reasonable time depends upon factors affecting the seller, which may not be known to the buyer.

In my judgment, however, the sellers' duty remains the same as in the general case, even though a string, circle or insolvency is involved. Its application in these circumstances must take account of the need for the documents to pass through several hands and of all factors which are relevant to the question whether the process has been completed with reasonable despatch. I emphasise, adopting Mr Salter's submission, that a reasonable time for performance of the individual seller's duty includes whatever allowances are reasonably necessary for performance of the corresponding duty by previous sellers before him, though he cannot claim allowances for any previous breach. So the duty is more stringent in practice than that of merely passing on the documents as soon as they are received by him. The same practical difficulties arise with regard to c.i.f. contracts, and I am not aware that any insuperable problem has arisen there.

Notes

6–094   1. In *Sanders v Maclean*, Brett M.R. apparently assumed the term was a condition, in which case any breach gives the innocent party the option of repudiating the contract, and treating it as at an end. In the context of the case, had Brett M.R. implied the condition contended for, the buyer could have rejected the documents and refused to pay the price. Breaches of terms other than conditions usually (but not always today) give rise only to a remedy in damages. Brett M.R. says that a condition is a term breach of which goes to the whole value of the contract.

2. As we saw in chapter 3, above, there are problems treating terms as vague as this as conditions, and Evans J. was less sure in *Concordia*.

3. Questions involving repudiation are further considered in chapter 7, below, but in general it can be said that buyers will pick on any breach as an excuse to reject on a falling market, and sellers will do so on a rising market.

(g) OTHER REQUIREMENTS

In addition to the above requirements, to be valid for c.i.f. tender a bill of lading **6–095** must be procured on shipment or not long afterwards,[79] must cover the contract goods and none other,[80] and must show that shipment has occurred within the time stipulated in the sale contract.[81]

(6) OTHER DOCUMENTATION

(a) DELIVERY ORDERS

We have already come across delivery orders in the discussion of *The Julia* at **6–096** para. 2–015, above. They are used for sales of parts of undivided bulk cargoes. If the seller (for example) only has a bill of lading for the entire cargo, then obviously he cannot use that for the sale. He can, however, issue an order to the carrier to deliver the requisite quantity of quantity to the purchaser.

The problem with the delivery order in *The Julia* was that it was simply an order given by the seller, to their own agents (Van Bree) in Antwerp. This document gave the purchasers no rights of any kind against the carrier, and was therefore held not to be acceptable tender under a c.i.f. contract.

By contrast, ship's delivery orders can provide rights against the carrier (see *The Dona Mari* at para. 13–058),[82] and they can be acceptable tender under a c.i.f. contract, if the contract expressly so stipulates. A ship's delivery order is either issued by the carrier, or attorned to by him (in which case he is accepting liability as bailee). It should be distinguished from the merchant's delivery order, which was held not acceptable in *The Julia* at para. 2–015, above.

COLIN & SHIELDS v W. WEDDEL & CO LTD

Court of Appeal. [1952] 2 All E.R. 337

Under a contract for the sale of goods and their shipment to Liverpool the **6–097** buyers were to make payment against a ship's delivery order. The goods

---

[79] See, *e.g.* Kennedy L.J. in *Biddell Bros v Horst Co* [1911] 1 K.B. 934, 958; *Landauer & Co v Craven & Speeding Bros.* [1912] 2 K.B. 94.
[80] *The Julia* [1949] A.C. 293, *per* Lord Porter at 309.
[81] See Ch. 7, below.
[82] Whatever difficulties might once have existed about the nature of these rights, the holder of a ship's delivery order has contractual rights against the carrier, by virtue of the Carriage of Goods by Sea Act 1992.

were shipped to Manchester and then put on to a dumb barge to carry them to Liverpool, where they were discharged. The sellers tendered a document signed by the shipowners directing the master of the hide berth in Liverpool to deliver to the buyers the goods. The buyers rejected this document or to make payment.

Held:

This was not a ship's delivery order. A ship's delivery order must be addressed to the ship and must request the ship to deliver the goods to the buyers, and it must be given and presented while the goods are in the ship's possession. This delivery order was issued by someone who was no longer in physical possession of the goods. Sellers J. ([1952] 1 All E.R. 1021) stressed that had the goods been lost after their transfer at Manchester to the dumb barge the delivery order tendered would have conferred no rights on the buyers. His view was affirmed in the Court of Appeal.

6–098   DENNING L.J.: The contract of sale was a c.i.f. contract—modified, no doubt, in some respects, but, nevertheless, a c.i.f. contract which carried with it an obligation on the sellers to provide a proper contract of affreightment in the form of a bill of lading which could be transferred to or held on trust for the buyers. The most important modification is contained in condition 3 of the official contract form of the Hide and Skin Sellers' Associations. It enables the sellers to supply a ship's delivery order instead of a bill of lading. This modification is made so as to enable a seller to split up a bulk consignment into smaller parcels and to sell them to different buyers while the goods are still at sea. A seller often only has one bill of lading for the whole consignment, and he cannot deliver that one bill of lading to each of the buyers because it contains more goods than the particular contract of sale, so in each of his contracts of sale the seller stipulates for the right to give a ship's delivery order. The bulk consignment can then be split up into small parcels each covered by a ship's delivery order instead of a bill of lading. Such being the commercial object of this clause, I agree with my Lord as to the meaning of "ship's delivery order" in this contract. It means, I think, an order given by the seller directed to the ship, whereby the seller orders the ship to deliver the contract goods to the buyer or his order. The ship's delivery order is not as good a protection for the buyer as a separate bill of lading would be, because it gives no cause of action against the ship unless the master attorns to the buyer, and then it gives a different cause of action which may not be as favourable as a bill of lading. To overcome these drawbacks so far as possible, the contract provides for the ship's delivery order "to be countersigned by a banker, shipbroker, captain, or mate, if so required". It also provides that the buyers are to be "put in the same position as they would have been if they had been in possession of a bill of lading". This can, I think, only be done by the sellers becoming themselves trustees for the buyers of the rights contained in the bill of lading so far as the contract goods are concerned. The contract, in effect, constitutes them trustees, and it requires as its basis the existence of the appropriate bill of lading. In support of what I have said I would only refer, in addition to *The Julia*, to *Re Denbigh Cowan & Co & R. Atcherley & Co*,[83] and to *Heilbut, Symons & Co, Ltd v Harvey, Christie Miller & Co*[84] Once the contract is understood in the way I have stated, this case must be decided in favour of the buyers for two reasons:

(i) the sellers did not provide a proper contract of affreightment, for the bill of lading did not provide for carriage to Liverpool, but only to Manchester, and the belated clause "in transit to Liverpool" did not remedy the position, because it did not extend the contract of carriage to Liverpool;

(ii) the sellers did not provide a proper ship's delivery order. The document which they presented was not an order on the ship, but an order to a porter at the docks at Liverpool who had nothing to do with the ship. I am inclined to think also the documents were not in law tendered in time, but I need not elaborate my reasons for so thinking. I entirely agree with the judgment which my Lord has delivered, and I agree that the appeal should be dismissed.

Notes

The Law Commission recommended inclusion of ship's delivery orders within **6–099** the Carriage of Goods by Sea Act 1992, and indeed its recommendations were carried out (see further chapter 13, below). It was concerned that the definition under the 1992 Act should conform with the common law definition, which determines c.i.f. sale contract requirements. They defined the ship's delivery order as follows[85]:

"Ship's delivery orders are either (a) documents issued by or on behalf of shipowners while the goods are in their possession or under their control and which contain some form of undertaking that they will be delivered to the holder or to the order of a named person; or (b) documents addressed to a shipowner requiring him to deliver to the order of a named person, the shipowner subsequently attorning to that person. Where the order is issued to the ship and authorises, directs or orders the carrier to deliver to a certain person, it confers no rights against the carrier until the carrier attorns to the person to whom delivery is due. Similarly, where such a delivery order is transferred, there would have to be a fresh attornment to the transferee before he acquired a right of possession against the carrier."

The definition in the 1992 Act was intended to be a codification of the common law definition.

---

[83] (1921) 90 L.J.K.B. 836.
[84] (1922) 12 Ll.L. Rep. 455.
[85] Law Com. No. 196: "Rights of Suit in Respect of Carriage of Goods by Sea" (1991), para. 5.26.

CARRIAGE OF GOODS BY SEA ACT 1992, S.1(4)

6–100 References in this Act to a ship's delivery order are references to any document which is neither a bill of lading nor a sea waybill but contains an undertaking which—

(a) is given under or for the purposes of a contract for the carriage of goods to which the document relates, or to goods which include those goods; and

(b) is an undertaking by the carrier to a person identified in the document to deliver the goods to which the document relates to that person.

Note

It is probable that *Julia*-type delivery orders are much more common than ship's delivery orders, because of the difficulty, in practice, of obtaining the latter. *Julia*-type delivery orders do not come within the 1992 Act, nor are they acceptable tender c.i.f.

(b) COMMERCIAL INVOICE

6–101 A c.i.f. seller must also tender an invoice. The form of the invoice, which is not defined in detail in the authorities on c.i.f. contracts, was originally set out by Blackburn J. in *Ireland v Livingston*[86]:

> "The invoice is made out debiting the consignee with the agreed price (or the actual cost and commission, with the premiums of insurance, and the freight, as the case may be), and giving him credit for the amount of freight which he will have to pay the shipowner on actual delivery."

In *Biddell Brothers v E. Clemens Horst Co*, Hamilton J. said that the invoice must be made out "as described by Blackburn J. in *Ireland v Livingston* or in some similar form".[87] This is not a very onerous requirement, although stricter provision is often expressly made, especially in documentary credits.

In a c.i.f. contract, the invoice would usually debit the buyer with the agreed price, and credit him with any freight or other charges he may have to pay the carrier at discharge (for example, if freight has not been paid in advance and a freight collect bill of lading is used).

(c) QUALITY CERTIFICATES, ETC.

6–102 It is open for the parties to stipulate additional shipping documents, and a common requirement is for a quality certificate. It may also be stipulated that the quality certificate is conclusive evidence of some of the facts stated within it. In *Toepfer v Continental Grain Co*,[88] the Court of Appeal held that where the sale contract provides that a certificate is to be conclusive as to the quality of goods, the buyer will be precluded from suing the seller even if, contrary to the statement contained in the certificate, they are not of the contract quality. The certificate had

---

[86] (1872) L.R. 5 H.L. 395, 406–407.
[87] [1911] 1 K.B. 214.
[88] [1974] 1 Lloyd's Rep. 11.

been issued negligently, and in arbitration proceedings the Board of Appeal said that it was:

"commercially harsh that a buyer should be left without remedy as the result of a negligent certificate."

Lord Denning M.R. thought that the buyer may have an action against the issuer of the certificate, even if not against the seller.

For a c.i.f. or f.o.b. contract, however, the seller's obligations regarding the goods generally end on shipment; they are at the buyer's risk thereafter, and any requirement for a quality certificate to be issued later (*e.g.* on discharge) will be repugnant, and will be struck out.

GILL & DUFFUS S.A. v BERGER & CO INC

House of Lords. [1984] A.C. 382

This case is considered in detail at para. 7–022, below. One of the stipulated shipping documents under a c.i.f contract was a quality certificate obtained at the port of discharge. The sellers' first tender was rejected by the buyers on the grounds that no quality certificate was tendered, and this was held to be a wrongful rejection on the ground that a quality certificate obtained at the port of discharge could not be a valid shipping document c.i.f. A second tender was however made, including a quality certificate obtained on discharge, and this was also rejected by the buyers. One of the issues was whether the buyers could assert that the goods did not conform to the contractual description, or whether the quality certificate was conclusive evidence against them.

6–103

LORD DIPLOCK: The buyers . . . rejected the documents and refused to pay against presentation on the ground that they did not include

6–104

"certificate of quality on discharge made out on behalf of all parties by GSC certifying that the goods are of the same quality as the sample sealed by GSC Paris when the business was concluded."

My Lords, a certificate by GSC as to the quality of the goods at port of discharge under the certification clause in the contract is not, and is indeed incapable of being, included among shipping documents which a seller is required to tender to his buyer in return for payment of the price under a contract of sale in ordinary c.i.f. terms. Although an argument to the contrary was apparently persisted in by the buyers up to the Court of Appeal, its hopelessness has now been recognised and it has not been advanced in the argument for the buyers in your Lordships' House.

[Lord Diplock then turned his attention to the second tender, which the buyer claimed to be entitled to reject on the grounds that the goods did not match the contractual description, and continued:]

My Lords, before turning to the fate of the instant case in the Court of Appeal, it is convenient to deal with the conclusiveness of the GSC certificate of quality. *Toepfer v Continental Grain Co* was a case of a c.i.f. sale of wheat by description alone, *viz.* "No. 3 hard amber durum wheat of U.S. origin." The contract contained no provision for a sample, but it incorporated a term: "Official certificates of inspection to be final as to quality."

The words used in a contract of sale that refer to the goods agreed to be sold (not being "specific goods" as defined in s.62 of the Sale of Goods Act 1893) often include words that describe a characteristic as to quality or condition that they possess which distinguishes them from other goods of the same general kind. What *Toepfer v Continental Grain Co* decided was that where the description of the goods agreed to be sold included a statement as to their quality and provided that a certificate as to quality was to be final, the certificate was final as to the correspondence of the goods with that part of the description of them in the contract that referred to their quality (in casu "No. 3 hard amber") notwithstanding that the certificate was proved to have been inaccurate. The conclusion reached by the Court of Appeal in *Toepfer v Continental Grain Co* is, in my opinion, plainly right. My own preferred analysis of the reason why it is consistent with s.13 of the Sale of Goods Act 1893 is that while "description" itself is an ordinary English word, the Act contains no definition of what it means when it speaks in that section of a contract for the sale of goods being a sale "*by* description." One must look to the contract as a whole to identify the kind of goods that the seller was agreeing to sell and the buyer to buy. In *Toepfer's* case, it was not "No. 3 hard amber durum wheat" simpliciter but durum wheat of U.S. origin for which a certificate had been issued by a U.S. Government official stating that its quality was that which is described in the trade as "No. 3 hard amber."

6–105   Similarly, where, as in the instant case, the sale (to use the words of section 13) is "*by* sample as well as *by* description," characteristics of the goods which would be apparent on reasonable examination of the sample are unlikely to have been intended by the parties to form part of the "description" *by* which the goods were sold, even though such characteristics are mentioned in references in the contract to the goods that are its subject matter.

My Lords, the c.i.f. contract in the instant case contains provisions opposite the rubrics "quality" and "special conditions & remarks" respectively, which make the certificate of GSC conclusive as to the conformity of the bulk shipment at port of discharge with the sample that had been submitted to the buyers while the contract was in course of negotiation and had been sealed by GSC. It must have been the intention of the parties that the conclusiveness of the certificate would be limited to those characteristics of the contract goods that would be apparent on reasonable examination of the sample; but there is no suggestion in the instant case of any disconformity between the goods as delivered at Le Havre and the sealed sample, in respect of any characteristic which reasonable examination of the sample would not have revealed. Since Lloyd J., and all three members of the Court of Appeal, accepted that such was in law the effect of these provisions of the c.i.f. contract, I need say no more about them except to express my respectful concurrence.

Note

The case could have been decided on the basis of the quality certificate being **6–106** conclusive evidence, but the House preferred to base its decision on the wider basis considered in the next chapter.

Note the observation that the requirement for a quality certificate to be issued can become part of the description of the goods.

(7) INSURANCE REQUIREMENTS

In c.i.f. contracts (see chapter 2, above) the seller has to provide a valid marine **6–107** insurance policy with reputable insurers, covering the value of the goods for the voyage.

(a) REQUIREMENT TO TENDER INSURANCE POLICY

Arguably the buyer needs an assignable policy of insurance, and needs to be **6–108** able to inspect its terms. That argues that the policy should be tendered.

MANBRE SACCHARINE CO LTD v CORN PRODUCTS CO LTD

King's Bench Division. [1919] 1 K.B. 198

The facts and issues were set out at para. 4–014, above. The buyers were held **6–109** entitled to reject (among other reasons) because the only insurance document tendered by the sellers was a letter which declared that the goods were insured.

McCARDIE J.: *(on the insurance issue)* . . . Under an ordinary c.i.f. con- **6–110** tract the vendor is obviously bound to tender a proper policy of insurance together with the other documents required. This obligation is clearly indicated by the various judgments I have already referred to when dealing with the nature of a c.i.f. contract [*see the extract in chapter 4, above*]. The policy must be tendered even if the goods have safely arrived at the time of tender—see *Orient Co v Brekke & Howlid* [1913] 1 K.B. 531 *per* Lush and Rowlatt JJ. In the present case the defendants tendered no policy of insurance at all. They merely made the following statement in their letter of March 14, 1917: "We hereby hold you covered by insurance for the amount of £4,322 in accordance with the terms of a policy of insurance in our possession re shipment ex s.s. *Algonquin*." This, as Mr Hogg K.C. [for the plaintiffs] tersely said, was the mere assurance that a policy had been issued, and not the policy of insurance itself. It was suggested on behalf of the plaintiffs that the letter amounted either to an equitable assignment of the insurance moneys to the extent of £4,322 or to a declaration of trust to such amount in respect of these moneys. Even if this suggestion be well founded yet there is a wide difference between an actual policy of insurance transferable to the defendants as contemplated by s.50(3) of the Marine Insurance Act, 1906, and such a letter as that of the defendants here. The plaintiffs, I hold, were clearly entitled to a policy and not to a mere assertion by the defendants that a policy existed and that the defendants would hold the plaintiffs covered.

Even if the defendants had tendered the policies actually held by them I should still have held the tender bad, for they were policies which covered a quantity of goods outside those mentioned in the bills of lading and invoices sent to the plaintiffs. In my opinion a purchaser under a c.i.f. contract is entitled to demand, as a matter of law, a policy of insurance which covers and covers only the goods mentioned in the bills of lading and invoices. This, I think, was settled by the decision of the Court of Appeal, consisting of Lord Cairns, Lord Coleridge C.J., and Mellish L.J., in the case of *Hickox v Adams* (1876) 34 L.T. 404. Unless the purchaser gets a policy limited to his own interests he would become one only of those who are interested in the insurance; and he is entitled, in my view, to refuse to occupy a position which may give rise to obvious complications—see per Turner L.J. in *Ralli v Universal Marine Insurance Co* (1862) 6 L.T. 34, 37 . . .

DIAMOND ALKALI EXPORT CORP v FL BOURGEOIS

King's Bench Division. [1921] 3 K.B. 443

6–111   The question at issue was whether a c.i.f. seller could tender received for shipment bill of lading and a certificate of insurance.

Held:
The buyers were entitled to reject the documents.

1. A received for shipment bill of lading is not good tender c.i.f. because it does not acknowledge shipment (see above).

2. For valid tender c.i.f. an insurance *policy* must be tendered falling within the provisions of the Marine Insurance Act 1906.

McCardie J.: *(on the insurance issue)* Is this certificate a proper policy of insurance within the c.i.f. contract here made? I have read, I believe, all the cases on the rights and obligations of buyer and seller under c.i.f. contracts . . . In all the cases a "policy of insurance" is mentioned as an essential document. The law is settled and established. I may point out that in *Burstall v Grimsdale* (1906) 11 Com. Cas. 280 it was expressly provided by the contract that a certificate of insurance might be an alternative for an actual policy. I ventured in *Manbre Saccharine Co v Corn Products Co* [see para. 4–014, above] to discuss the relevant authorities, including the lucid judgment of Atkin J. in *C Groom Ltd v Barber* [see para. 4–011, above]—a judgment which I have again most carefully read. It seems plain that a mere written statement by the sellers that they hold the buyers covered by insurance in respect of a specified policy of insurance is not of itself a policy of insurance within a c.i.f. contract: see the *Manbre Saccharine* case. It seems plain also that a broker's cover note or an ordinary certificate of insurance are not adequate agreements within such a contract: see Bailhache J. in *Wilson, Holgate & Co v Belgian Grain & Produce Co.*

Does the present document fulfil the seller's contractual duty? . . . Now the certificate is not a policy. It does not purport to be a policy. This is conceded by Mr Hastings in his able argument for the sellers. It is a certificate that a policy was issued to D.A. Horan, and it incorporates the terms of that policy. Those terms I do not know, nor is there anything before me to indicate that the buyers knew them. The certificate does not show whether the policy was in a recognized or usual form or not. The certificate does not therefore contain all the terms of the insurance. The terms have to be sought for in two documents—namely, the original policy and the certificate. But even if this document is not a policy yet the sellers say it is "equivalent to a policy" . . . This leads me to ask whether the document before me differs in any material respect from a policy of insurance. To begin with, I do not see how the buyer here could know whether the document he got was of a proper character (one he was bound to accept) unless he saw the original policy,and examined its conditions, whether usual or otherwise. In the next place I feel that the certificate of insurance falls within a legal classification, if any, different to that of a policy of insurance. The latter is a well-known document with clearly defined features. It comes within definite, established and statutory legal rights. A certificate, however, is an ambiguous thing; it is unclassified and undefined by law; it is not even mentioned in Arnould on Marine Insurance. No rules have been laid down upon it. Would the buyer sue upon the certificate or upon the original policy of insurance? If he sued simply on the certificate he could put in a part only of the contract, for the other terms of the contract—namely, the conditions of the actual policy—would be contained in a document not in his control and to the possession of which he is not entitled. Thirdly, I point out that before the buyer could sue at all he would have to show that he was the assignee of the certificate: see Arnould, 9th ed, ss. 175–177. In what way can he become the assignee? It is vital to remember the provisions of the Marine Insurance Act 1906. Now the relevant statutory provision is s.50(3) which says: "A marine policy may be assigned by endorsement thereon or in other customary manner." This sub-section, however, only applies, so far as I can see, to that which is an actual marine policy. . . I must therefore hold that the buyers were entitled to reject the documents upon the ground that no proper bill of lading and no proper policy of insurance were tendered by the sellers in conformity with the c.i.f. contract.

Note

In *Donald H. Scott & Co Ltd v Barclays Bank Ltd*, although Bankes L.J. agreed with **6–112**
McCardie J.'s view that the document tendered must show all the terms of

the policy, he was unprepared to go as far as McCardie J. in requiring the policy to comply "with the English law relating to policies of marine insurance."[89]

In this respect, the c.i.f. contract may allow for some flexibility. In *The Julia*, Lord Porter thought that a term which expressly allowed substitution of a certificate of insurance for a policy would not be repugnant to a c.i.f. contract. It may also be that some American certificates of insurance are regarded as equivalent to policies, at any rate if they contain all the terms necessary to constitute a valid policy of insurance according to English law.[90]

(b) EXTENT OF COVER REQUIRED

6–113　　In the absence of contrary stipulation, a c.i.f. seller is obliged to provide only the minimum cover current in the trade, and if the buyer requires more comprehensive cover he should so stipulate in the sale contract, or alternatively contract on terms whereby he takes on the insurance obligation himself (*e.g.* c. & f.). The terms current in a particular trade can vary between trades and routes, and over time.

A common cause of litigation occurs on the outbreak of hostilities, where ships are sunk and it is discovered that the cargo is not insured against war risk. Once hostilities have been under way for a time, it is likely that the sale contract will address the matter of war risk directly.

In general, war risk must be stipulated expressly in the sale contract, and if it is not the seller is at liberty to insure "free of capture and seizure" (f.c. and s.). The rationale is that any other conclusion could lead to very expensive rates even in peacetime.

C. GROOM LTD v BARBER

King's Bench Division. [1915] 1 K.B. 316

6–114　The issues in this case were set out at para. 4–011, above. Atkin J. held that a c.i.f. seller could tender an f.c. and s. policy of insurance, and that "War risk for buyer's account" did not mean that the seller was to effect war risk at buyer's expense, but that war risk was the concern of the buyer alone. The sale contract had been made in peacetime, ship and cargo being lost (and uninsured) in the very early days of the first world war.

ATKIN J.: *(on the insurance point)* In a contract on c.i.f. terms the seller has, as stated by Hamilton J. in *Biddell Brothers v E. Clemens Horst Co* [1911] 1 K.B. 214, to arrange for an insurance on the terms current in the trade which would be available for the buyer. I am satisfied that at the time this contract was made the terms current in the trade were terms which excluded war risk; in other words that the policy would contain the f. c. and s. clause, and therefore, apart from the special terms of this contract, a policy in such terms would be in order. The finding of the appeal committee in that respect makes the matter quite certain. But in this contract there are the words "war risk for buyer's account." It was said that this meant that the seller was bound to take out a policy covering war risk but was entitled to charge the buyer with the expense of it. That

[89] [1923] 2 K.B. 1, 13.
[90] [1923] 2 K.B. 1, 11.

would mean that at all times, even in times of peace, a war risk policy must be taken out at the expense of the buyer. I am satisfied that no seller or buyer contemplated such a thing, and if the buyer were charged with the expense of such a policy he would, in ordinary times of peace, by the very first person to object. To my mind these words mean that war risk is the buyer's concern, and if he wants to cover war risk he must get it done. It might be contended that the condition meant that the proper course of business was that the buyer was entitled to ask the seller, when he was taking out the usual policy, to take out one also covering war risk at the buyer's expense. If it could mean that, I am satisfied in this case that the buyer never requested the seller to take out a war risk policy on those terms. When he made his request the buyer never intended to pay the cost, and his intention was that the seller was bound to take out the policy at his (the seller's) expense. In those circumstances I am satisfied that the buyer's contention on this point fails and that the award that the policy was in order is right.

Note
The decision leaves open the possibility that, if hostilities on particular routes last long enough, the customary insurance practices may alter so as to place an obligation to take out war risk on the seller.

CHAPTER 7

REMEDIES FOR BREACH

(1) GENERAL PRINCIPLES OF THE LAW OF CONTRACT

(a) MARKET VARIATIONS AND REMEDIES

7–001 As already explained in chapter 1, above, a c.i.f. seller has contractual duties to ship conforming goods, and tender conforming documents relating to those goods. If the seller breaches any term of the contract, relating either to the goods or the documents, the buyer has a right to damages for breach. The right to claim damages is automatic, assuming any damage has been suffered, and is independent of any other remedy considered in this section. Contractual damages are intended to compensate the injured party for the breach, to put him as far as possible into the position he would have been in had the contract been properly performed.

It follows from this basis of calculation, that if the contract had been a good bargain for the injured party, his damages will allow him to keep the benefit of that bargain. Conversely, if the contract had turned out to be a bad bargain, the damages put him into the position he would have been in had the *bad* bargain been properly performed. In other words, he cannot get out of his bad bargain by suing for damages. Put another way, contractual damages do not normally compensate for losses caused by general market fluctuations.

Examples of damages in fluctuating markets

7–002 Suppose, for example, the goods as stipulated by the contract (for example January grain) would have been worth £4,000. In other words, it would cost £4,000 to purchase identical grain today on the open market. Inferior grain is actually shipped, in breach of contract, which is worth £2,500. In accordance with contractual principles, the damages remedy puts the buyer into the position he would have been in had the contract been properly performed. In principle, the buyer should receive a maximum of £1,500 in contract damages.

Suppose, however, that the sale contract was made some months ago, for *futures* in January grain, when grain prices were expected to be higher. The agreed price was therefore £8,000, representing the market price of January grain at the time. Since the contract was made grain prices have fallen. The buyer has made a bad bargain, because the general market price has dropped.

Contract damages do not compensate for bad bargains. the buyer's damages are still £1,500, for exactly the same reasons as before. Had the contract been properly performed the grain would have been worth £4,000. Because of its inferior quality, it is worth £2,500. However, if the buyer sues for £1,500 contractual damages, and sells the inferior grain he has received for the £2,500 it is worth, he obtains £4,000 total. Since he has paid £8,000 as the price, he is still £4,000 out of pocket. His position would have been exactly the same, of course, if the contract had been properly performed: he would still obtain only £4,000 on resale of the grain, and would still lose £4,000 as a result of his bad bargain.

Market reasons for repudiation

On the other hand, if the buyer can repudiate the contract, and reject either the **7–003** grain itself, as not being of contract description, or the documents representing the grain, and either refuse to pay the price or claim its return, he can to shift the market drop back on to the seller. The buyer can now go into the market and buy identical grain at the new price (£4,000), thereby avoiding altogether paying the £8,000 original price. Hence, on a falling market, buyers will generally wish to reject documents or goods.

Sometimes the buyer's main, or even only loss results from the market drop. Suppose, for example, the grain was shipped (in breach of contract) not in January but on 1st February. In other respects, however, it is of the contract description. It is probably worth the same as it would have been had it been shipped on 31st January, so that the buyer has lost nothing as a result of the seller's breach. The grain is worth £4,000 on whichever of the two days it was shipped. If the contract price was £8,000, however, the buyer should obviously reject the documents if he can, and buy equivalent grain at elsewhere at the current market price of £4,000, rather than pay the contract price of £8,000 for grain which is now worth only £4,000.

Sellers, on the other hand, on a falling market will generally prefer to keep the contract alive and claim the contract price. Conversely, on a rising market, the sellers will generally repudiate if they can, whereas buyers will generally prefer to keep the contract alive.

Most of the cases in this chapter concern market fluctuations of this type, but there can be other reasons for a party wishing to treat the contract as repudiated. For example, the buyers were able to reject documents on a rising market in *Manbre Saccharine v Corn Products*, considered at para. 4–014, above; the documents were worthless, however, representing goods which had been sunk by a risk which was uninsured against. Sellers might also repudiate on a falling market, and sell elsewhere if it looks as though, for example, protracted litigation will be required to obtain the contract price from the buyers.

Such cases appear to be rare, however, and market fluctuations seem to be the main reason for repudiation. Of course, the reason actually given is the breach by the other party. There is a hint of artificiality, therefore, in much of the reasoning discussed in this chapter.

ADAMS AND BROWNSWORD, KEY ISSUES IN CONTRACT

(Butterworths, 1995), pp. 164–166

[*Footnotes are as in the original, but renumbered and restyled for inclusion in this book. Emphasis is as in the original.*]

. . . the fact of the matter is that the existing law fails to take into account, **7–004** in an explicit and coherent way, the reasons underlying the innocent party's claimed right to withdraw. What this signifies is not merely that the law is indifferent to the existence of good reasons for withdrawal, but also that it has no serious concern with bad reasons for withdrawal.

Such indifference to bad reasons has implications at two levels. First, it yields the settled principle that, *if the innocent party has the right to withdraw for breach*, then it is immaterial that (in the absence of estoppel or the like) that bad reasons have been cited at the time of withdrawal.[1] Thus, in *The Mihalis Angelos*,[2] for example, the innocent charterers were rescued from having wrongly relied on force majeure as a ground for withdrawal by the Court of Appeal holding that there was actually a breach of condition by the owners of the vessel. Secondly, and more importantly, it entails that a breach may be cited as the legal ground for withdrawal when the innocent party's reasons for seeking withdrawal are wholly unrelated to the breach. In other words, as Mellish L.J. once put it, there is no requirement that the "real reason"[3] for seeking release from a contract should coincide with the cited legal reason for withdrawal. Accordingly, an innocent party may be permitted to cite a breach as the legal reason for withdrawal when the real explanation lies in some collateral economic reason—for example, when a supplier wishes to withdraw on a rising market, or a buyer wishes to withdraw on a falling market. . . .

. . . As has been intimated, where an innocent party seeks to withdraw for collateral economic reasons, the attraction of withdrawal is that it releases the party from the prices obtaining under the contract into a market with more favourable prices. Often, the price differential (between the contract and the market) will be very substantial so that large gains are to be made only if the innocent party can escape from the contract. By contrast, if the innocent party is restricted to a remedy in damages for the losses directly occasioned by the breach, no more than quite trivial sums may be recoverable. In many cases, therefore, the position is that the innocent party is not the least bit interested in recovering damages for the breach but sees great advantage in securing withdrawal. . . .

Notes

7–005   Adams and Brownsword go on to argue strongly against the present regime, preferring what they describe as a reason-centred regime, where in order to withdraw "the innocent party must have good reasons for saying that *the breach* is such that damages simply would not be adequate relief." The courts have shown themselves reluctant to go down that route, at any rate in commercial contracts of the type considered in this book. Part of that reluctance is premised on the reasoning at the start of chapter 15, which I would suggest is fairly convincing, again given the nature of the particular transactions. There are additionally arguments based on certainty; there is also a feeling that commercial parties are capable of looking after themselves, and that if the law is certain they

---

[1] See K.E. Lindgren, J.W. Carter, and D.J. Harland, *Contract Law in Australia* (Sydney, Butterworths, 1986) para. 1969.
[2] *Mardelanto Cia Naviera SA v Bergbau-Handel GmbH: The Mihalis Angelos* [1971] 1 Q.B. 164.
[3] In *Shand v Bowes* (1876–7) 2 Q.B.D. 112, 115, Mellish L.J. observed that, if the defendant buyers' contention was accepted, then the consequence would be 'that purchasers would, without any real reason, frequently obtain an excuse for rejecting contracts when prices had dropped'. On appeal, however, the House was not impressed by this consideration, see *Bowes v Shand* (1877) 2 App. Cas. 455, 465–466 (Lord Cairns L.C.), and 476 (Lord Hatherley) [*also below*].

can draft their own contracts to give whatever protection they need; they do not need the courts to do that job for them.[4]

(b) Conditions, Warranties and Innominate Terms

Not all breaches of contract entitle the innocent party to repudiate, and if one party repudiates when he is not entitled to do so, the other party (even though in breach of contract) may himself sue for wrongful repudiation. The Sale of Goods Act 1979 (set out in full in Appendix A, below) divides contractual terms into two main types, conditions and warranties. The legislation recognises two types of term. The condition is a term "the breach of which may give rise to a right to treat the contract as repudiated": Sale of Goods Act, s.11(3). It does not matter how slight is the breach, nor how little damage is occasioned by it to the injured party. The warranty is a term "the breach of which gives rise to a claim for damages but not to a right to reject the goods and treat the contract as repudiated": Sale of Goods Act, s.61. Damages are calculated by reference to s.53. Section 11(2) allows the buyer to opt to keep the contract alive, even where the seller has broken a condition of the contract, without jeopardising a damages action. **7–006**

Where the injured party elects to repudiate, he may additionally claim damages. The consequences of repudiation are considered further below.

In *Hong Kong Fir Shipping Co Ltd v Kawasaki Kisen Kaisha Ltd* [1962] 2 Q.B. 26, the Court of Appeal was prepared to countenance a third type of term, the "innominate" or intermediate term. Breach of an innominate term can give a right to repudiate, but does not do so automatically. Only if the breach is sufficiently serious that it "goes to the root of" the contract can the innocent party repudiate, otherwise he is limited to a claim for damages alone. The test is alternatively stated as whether the breach is sufficiently serious that it frustrates the adventure, and this is also the modern meaning of the term "fundamental breach" of contract.

Whereas with a breach of condition the consequences of the breach are irrelevant to the right of the injured party to repudiate, in innominate term cases they are of paramount importance. It might be said that *Hong Kong Fir* substituted for the classification of the term the "gravity of the breach" approach to the question whether repudiation was justified. In *Hong Kong Fir* itself, the shipowners were in breach of their obligation, to time charterers, to provide a seaworthy vessel, the consequences of which could vary from the very trivial to the catastrophic. The charterers were unable to show that the consequences of the breach were sufficiently serious to allow them to repudiate the charterparty.

Assuming that a breach has occurred which allows the injured party to repudiate, he can elect whether to do so, or instead to keep the contract alive (or in other words affirm the contract). If he has made a bad bargain he will usually wish to repudiate, but probably not otherwise. He must make the election quickly, and affirmation may be inferred from his conduct.

Repudiation by the innocent party can be risky, because if it turns out that he was not entitled to do so, he may be sued for wrongful repudiation by the other

---

[4] See, *e.g.* the sentiments expressed by Goff, "Commercial contracts and the Commercial Court" [1984] L.M.C.L.Q. 382, 392; referring to time charterparty withdrawal clauses, where shipowners use the slightest lateness in payment of hire to justify withdrawing the vessel, for purely economic reasons on a rising market, he observes that "Equitable relief [against such withdrawals] is really inconsistent with the principle that in commercial transactions parties must, so far as possible, be able to know where they stand, or at least to obtain helpful advice from their lawyers on the basis of which they can act with a reasonable degree of confidence. People who charter ships are not children in arms. If they are inexperienced, they can get the advice of brokers . . . " Clearly these sentiments, if correct, are equally apposite in the context of the present discussion.

party. This is effectively what happened in *Gill & Duffus v Berger & Co Inc*—see below.

(c) ANTICIPATORY BREACH

7–007   It is not necessary for the injured party actually to wait before repudiating, until a breach of an innominate term has become so serious as to frustrate the adventure. The contractual doctrine of anticipatory breach may allow him to repudiate earlier. The criteria were stated by Devlin J. in *Universal Cargo Carriers Corporation v Citati*.[5]

UNIVERSAL CARGO CARRIERS CORPORATION v CITATI

Queen's Bench Division. [1957] 2 Q.B. 401

Issues
7–008   The only importance of this case, for present purposes, is in Devlin J.'s discussion of anticipatory breach of contract.
A voyage charterer who fails to load cargo within the laytime allowed under the charterparty commits a breach of contract.[6] This is not a breach of condition, but on the principles discussed above, if he exceeds the laytime by so long that the delay frustrates the adventure, the shipowner can repudiate the charterparty. In *Citati* the shipowner withdrew and rechartered the vessel, believing that the charterer would substantially exceed the laytime allowed, although the withdrawal occurred even before the laytime had expired. The charterer was not in breach of contract, therefore, at least in this respect, and the shipowner could justify his action only on the basis of anticipatory breach.

Held:
The case arose on an appeal from arbitration, and the court determined only what tests were to be applied. The question whether the shipowner was in fact entitled to repudiate was referred back to the arbitrator.

7–009   DEVLIN J.: (at 436) . . . in the arbitration the main argument was on anticipatory breach, and the emphasis on one mode of it, namely, renunciation. The chief findings of the arbitrator relate entirely to renunciation. I must therefore consider the nature of anticipatory breach and the findings thereon which the arbitrator has made.
The law on the right to rescind is succinctly stated by Lord Porter in *Heyman v Darwins Ltd* ([1942] A.C. 356, 397), as follows:

"The three sets of circumstances giving rise to a discharge of contract are tabulated by Anson[7] as: (i) renunciation by a party of his liabilities under it; (ii) impossibility created by his own act; and (iii) total or

---

[5] [1957] 2 Q.B. 401.
[6] For laytime and demurrage, see the commentary at para. 2–038, above. The problem in a case such as *Citati* is that demurrage does not always fully compensate a shipowner, who therefore, when the delay in loading is likely to be very long, prefers to terminate the charterparty and obtain an alternative fixture elsewhere.
[7] See Anson's *Law of Contract* (20th ed.), p. 319. [See now Beatson, *Anson's Law of Contract* (28th ed.), Oxford University Press (2002)].

partial failure of performance. In the case of the first two the renunciation may occur or impossibility be created either before or at the time for performance. In the case of the third it can occur only at the time or during the course of performance."

The third of these is the ordinary case of actual breach and the first two state the two modes of anticipatory breach. In order that the arguments which I have heard from either side can be rightly considered, it is necessary that I should develop rather more fully what is meant by each of these two modes.

A renunciation can be made either by words or by conduct, provided it is clearly made. It is often put that the party renunciating must "evince an intention" not to go on with the contract. The intention can be evinced either by words or by conduct. The test of whether an intention is sufficiently evinced by conduct is whether the party renunciating has acted in such a way as to lead a reasonable person to the conclusion that he does not intend to fulfil his part of the contract. . . .

. . . *Hochster v De la Tour* (1853) 2 E. & B. 678, 118 E.R. 922 established that a renunciation, when acted on, became final. Thus if a man proclaimed by words or conduct an inability to perform, the other party could safely act on it without having to prove that when the time for performance came the inability was still effective.

Since a man must be both ready and willing to perform, a profession by words or conduct of inability is by itself enough to constitute renunciation. But unwillingness and inability are often difficult to disentangle, and it is rarely necessary to make the attempt. Inability often lies at the root of unwillingness to perform. Willingness in this context does not mean cheerfulness; it means simply an intent to perform. To say "I would like to but I cannot" negatives intent just as much as "I will not". In the earlier part of his argument counsel for the charterer contended that a statement of inability without unwillingness did not amount to a renunciation, but in the end he abandoned the point. He concedes that the arbitrator's conclusion that the charterer evinced an intention not to perform is sufficiently supported by the finding that his attitude was that he was willing to perform if he could, but that he could not. In the other form of anticipatory breach, counsel for the charterer, as will be seen, contends that the disablement must be deliberate and not negligent or accidental. But to the extent that inability enters into renunciation, counsel for the charterer is not concerned with the character of the inability. If a man says "I cannot perform", he renounces his contract by that statement, and the cause of the inability is immaterial.

The two forms of anticipatory breach have a common characteristic that is essential to the concept, namely, that the injured party is allowed to anticipate an inevitable breach. If a man renounces his right to perform and is held to his renunciation, the breach will be legally inevitable; if a man puts it out of his power to perform, the breach will be inevitable in

7–010

fact—or practically inevitable, for the law never requires absolute certainty and does not take account of bare possibilities. So anticipatory breach means simply that a party is in breach from the moment that his actual breach becomes inevitable. Since the reason for the rule is that a party is allowed to anticipate an inevitable event and is not obliged to wait till it happens, it must follow that the breach which he anticipates is of just the same character as the breach which would actually have occurred if he had waited. . . . If this is right, it seems to me to dispose in principle of counsel for the charterer's submission that the disablement must be deliberate. If when the day comes for performance a party cannot perform, he is in breach, quite irrespective of how he became disabled. The inability which justifies the assumption of an anticipatory breach cannot be of any different character. Anticipatory breach was not devised as a whip to be used for the chastisement of deliberate contract-breakers, but from which the shiftless, the dilatory, or the unfortunate are to be spared. It is not confined to any particular class of breach, deliberate or blameworthy or otherwise; it covers all breaches that are bound to happen.

[*On the issue of whether the shipowners were entitled to rely on later evidence to ascertain the charterers' intention, Devlin J. cited Lord Sumner in* Bank Line, Ltd v Arthur Capel & Co *[1919] A.C. 435, at 454, and continued:*]

Even if Lord Sumner's principle applied, counsel for the owners rests too much on the words "what happens afterwards may assist". This does not, in my judgment, mean that a forecast, which appeared to be the most reasonable one at the time, may be revised in the light of after events and the revised version prevail. It means simply that if there is a question as to which of two forecasts seemed at the time to be the better one, the knowledge of what happened afterwards may assist the judge in making his choice between them.

[*Devlin J. then went on to consider impossibility, citing in particular Lord Sumner in* British & Beningtons v North Western Cachar Tea Co *[1923] A.C. 48, at 70, and continued:*]

In my judgment, . . . if the owners can establish that in the words of Lord Sumner the charterer had on July 18[8] "become wholly and finally disabled" from finding a cargo and loading it before delay frustrated the venture, they are entitled to succeed. Lord Sumner's words expressly refer to the time of breach as the date at which the inability must exist. But that does not mean in my opinion that the facts to be looked at in determining inability are only those which existed on July 18; the determination is to be made in the light of all the events, whether occurring before or after the critical date, put in evidence at the trial.

---

[8] The date at which the shipowners withdrew from the charter.

Notes

In general, therefore, a party commits an anticipatory breach, allowing other party to repudiate, if either he renounces his liabilities, or it has become impossible to perform them. Renunciation may be inferred not only from express words, but also from conduct, as interpreted at the time of the repudiation (see the penultimate paragraph quoted above). In *Citati* itself, the owners' claim on renunciation failed.   **7–011**

The innocent party may also repudiate if the guilty party cannot perform the contract, or it is inevitable that his performance will involve a so serious as to frustrate the adventure. This is a wholly objective test, and does not depend at all on what the innocent party thought. The innocent party can rely on the guilty party's inability to perform even if he (the innocent party) was not aware of it, or did not even suspect it, at the time of repudiation (see the last paragraph quoted above).

So for example in *Citati*, the owners' withdrawal would have been justified, in the opinion of Devlin J., even though it took place even while laytime was still running, if at the time of the withdrawal the charterers had become wholly and finally disabled from finding and loading a cargo before the delay frustrated the adventure. They would then have succeeded on the grounds of impossibility of performance, although they had failed on renunciation. Conversely, if the charterers could have loaded before the delay had become such as to frustrate the adventure, the withdrawal by the shipowners would have been wrongful, even if the owners were certain of the charterers' inability to do so when they withdrew the vessel. The court was unable to decide this question on the facts as found by the arbitrator, so it had to be referred back to him.

As to whether anticipatory breach also applies to a breach of condition, Lord Diplock made a number of observations in *The Afovos*.[9]

AFOVOS SHIPPING CO SA v PAGNAN (THE AFOVOS)

House of Lords. [1983] 1 Lloyd's Rep. 335

Importance of case:
The importance of this case, for the purposes of the present discussion, lies in Lord Diplock's remarks on anticipatory breach of contract.   **7–012**

Facts and issues:
It was accepted that a time charterer was required punctually to pay hire, by clause 5 of the charterparty,[10] and that failure to do so would amount to a breach of condition. An argument advanced by the shipowners was that they were therefore entitled to withdraw the vessel from the charter as soon as it became impossible for the charterers to pay punctually, even though the time for payment had not yet occurred. It seems to have been assumed that failure to make punctual payment constituted a breach of condition by the charterers, but not a breach that would have gone to the root of the contract.

---

[9] *Afovos Shipping Co SA v Pagnan (The Afovos)* [1983] 1 Lloyd's Rep. 335.
[10] On a New York Produce Exchange form (a commonly used standard form dry-cargo time charterparty).

Held
The shipowners' argument would be rejected; they were not entitled to with-draw the vessel, prior to punctual payment not being made.

7–013   LORD DIPLOCK: The clause of the charterparty of which it was submitted that the charterers were in breach by anticipation as early as 1640 hrs. on Thursday, 14 June 1979 was cl. 5; and the event relied on as constituting an anticipatory breach of that clause was that by that time, as a result of the failure by the charterers' agents, their bankers Credito Italiano in Padua, to send a timeous telex correctly addressed to First National Bank of Chicago in London, the charterers had disabled themselves from making payment on 14 June 1979, in the manner specified in that clause, of the instalment of hire due on that date.

Although the findings of fact by Lloyd J. do not go quite as far as this, I will assume in the owners' favour that it would have been impossible to transfer money which would be credited on 14 June 1979 to the account specified in cl. 5, after 1640 hrs. on that date; so that, as respects the semi-monthly instalment of hire due on 14 June, breach by the charterers of cl. 5 was inevitable by the time the shipowners' telex of the 14 June 1979 was sent. Nevertheless the doctrine of anticipatory breach by conduct which disables a party to a contract from performing one of his primary obliga-tions under the contract has in my view no application to a breach of such a clause.

The relevant portions of cl. 5 have been set out by Lord Hailsham L.C. The first part of the clause imposes on the respondents as charterers a primary obligation to pay the "said hire" (which by cl. 4 had been fixed at a monthly rate and *pro rata* for any part of a month) punctually and regularly in advance by semi-monthly instalments in the manner speci-fied, which would involve the payment of a minimum of 42 and a maximum of 54 instalments, during the period of the charter. Failure to comply with this primary obligation by delay in payment of one instal-ment is incapable in law of amounting to a "fundamental breach" of contract by the charters in the sense to which suggested in *Photo Produc-tion Ltd v Securicor Transport Ltd* [1980] A.C. 827 at 849 this expression, if used as a term of legal art, ought to be confined [see below]. The reason is that such delay in payment of one half-monthly instalment would not have the effect of depriving the owners of substantially the whole benefit which it was the intention of the parties that the owners should obtain from the unexpired of the time charter extending over a period of between 21 and 27 months.

The second part of cl. 5, however, starting with the word "otherwise" goes on to provide expressly what the rights of the owners are to be in the event of any such breach by the charterers of their primary obligation to make punctual payment of an instalment. The owners are to be at liberty to withdraw the vessel from the service of the charterers; in other words they are entitled to treat the breach when it occurs as a breach of condi-tion and so giving them the right to elect to treat it as putting an end to all their own primary obligations under the charterparty then remaining unperformed. But although failure by the charters in punctual payment of any instalment, however brief the delay involved may be, is made a breach of condition it is not also thereby converted into a fundamental breach; and it is to fundamental breaches alone that the doctrine of anticipatory breach is applicable.

The general rule is that a primary obligation is converted into a secondary obligation (whether a "general secondary obligation" or an "anticipatory secondary obligation" in the nomenclature of the analysis used in my speech in *Photo Production Ltd v Securicor Transport Ltd*) when and only when the breach of the primary obligation actually occurs. Up until then the primary obligations of both parties which have not yet been performed remain intact. The exception is where one party has manifested to the other party his intention no longer to perform the contract and the result of the non-performance would be to deprive the other party of substantially the whole benefit which it was the intention of the parties that that other party should obtain from the primary obligations of both parties remaining to be performed. In such a case, to which the term "repudiation" is applicable, the party not in default need not wait until the actual breach: he may elect to treat the secondary obligations of the other party as arising forthwith.

The doctrine of anticipatory breach is but a species of the *genus repudiation* and applies only to fundamental breach. If one party to a contract states expressly or by implication to the other party in advance that he will not be able to perform a particular primary obligation on his part under the contract when the time for performance arrives, the question whether the other party may elect to treat the statement as a repudiation depends on whether the threatened non-performance would have the effect of depriving that other party of substantially the whole benefit which it was the intention of the parties that he should obtain from the primary obligations of the parties under the contract then remaining unperformed. If it would not have that effect there is no repudiation, and the other party cannot elect to put an end to such primary obligations remaining to be performed. The non-performance threatened must itself satisfy the criteria of a fundamental breach.

Similarly, where a party to a contract, whether by failure to take timeous action or by any other default, has put it out of his power to perform a particular primary obligation, the right of the other party to elect to treat this as a repudiation of the contract by conduct depends on whether the resulting non-performance would amount to a fundamental breach. Clearly, in the instant case delay in payment of one semi-monthly instalment of hire would not.

Notes

1. These remarks of Lord Diplock are technically *obiter dicta*, since the ship- **7–014** owners did not repudiate the charterparty, but instead purported to invoke the anti-technicality provisions prior to withdrawal. The *ratio* of the case is simply

that the anti-technicality provisions could not be invoked until the time for punctual payment had actually passed, and punctual payment not been made.

2. Nothing in the above passage suggests that anticipatory breach cannot apply to breaches of condition, where the effect of the breach of condition is sufficiently serious that it also amounts to a fundamental breach.

3. In *Photo Production*, below, Lord Diplock also allows that deviations might be a special case, to which the doctrine applies.

(d) Effect of Repudiation

PHOTO PRODUCTION LTD v SECURICOR TRANSPORT LTD

House of Lords. [1980] A.C. 827

Relevance of case:

7–015 This is not an international trade case, and its only relevance, for present purposes, is in Lord Diplock's analysis of the effect of repudiation on the parties' contractual obligations.

Lord Diplock: My Lords, it is characteristic of commercial contracts, nearly all of which today are entered into not by natural legal persons, but by fictitious ones, *i.e.*, companies, that the parties promise to one another that something will be done, for instance, that property and possession of goods will be transferred, that goods will be carried by ship from one port to another, that a building will be constructed in accordance with agreed plans, that services of a particular kind will be provided. Such a contract is the source of primary legal obligations on each party to it to procure that whatever he has promised will be done is done. (I leave aside arbitration clauses which do not come into operation until a party to the contract claims that a primary obligation has not been observed.)

Where what is promised will be done involves the doing of a physical act, performance of the promise necessitates procuring a natural person to do it; but the legal relationship between the promisor and the natural person by whom the act is done, whether it is that of master and servant, or principal and agent, or of parties to an independent subcontract, is generally irrelevant. If that person fails to do it in the manner in which the promisor has promised to procure it to be done, as, for instance, with reasonable skill and care, the promisor has failed to fulfil his own primary obligation. This is to be distinguished from "vicarious liability", a legal concept which does depend on the existence of a particular legal relationship between the natural person by whom a tortious act was done and the person sought to be made vicariously liable for it. In the interests of clarity the expression should, in my view, be confined to liability for tort.

A basic principle of the common law of contract, to which there are no exceptions that are relevant in the instant case, is that parties to a contract are free to determine for themselves what primary obligations they will accept. They may state these in express words in the contract itself and, where they do, the statement is determinative; but in practice a commercial contract never states all the primary obligations of the parties in full; many are left to be incorporated by implication of law from the legal nature of the contract into which the parties are entering. But if the parties wish to reject or modify primary obligations which would otherwise be so incorporated, they are fully at liberty to do so by express words.

Leaving aside those comparatively rare cases in which the court is able to enforce a primary obligation by decreeing specific performance of it, breaches of primary obligations give rise to substituted secondary obligations on the part of the party in default, and, in some cases, may entitle the other party to be relieved from further performance of his own primary obligations. These secondary obligations of the contract breaker and any concomitant relief of the other party from his own primary obligations also arise by implication of law, generally common law, but sometimes statute, as in the case of codifying statutes passed at the turn of the century, notably the Sale of Goods Act 1893. The contract, however, is just as much the source of secondary obligations as it is of primary obligations; and like primary obligations that are implied by law secondary obligations too can be modified by agreement between the parties, although, for reasons to be mentioned later, they cannot, in my view, be totally excluded. In the instant case, the only secondary obligations and concomitant reliefs that are applicable arise by implication of the common law as modified by the express words of the contract.

Every failure to perform a primary obligation is a breach of contract. **7–016** The secondary obligation on the part of the contract breaker to which it gives rise by implication of the common law is to pay monetary compensation to the other party for the loss sustained by him in consequence of the breach; but, with two exceptions, the primary obligations of both parties so far as they have not yet been fully performed remain unchanged. This secondary obligation to pay compensation (damages) for non-performance of primary obligations I will call the "general secondary obligation". It applies in the cases of the two exceptions as well.

The exceptions are: (1) where the event resulting from the failure by one party to perform a primary obligation has the effect of depriving the other party of substantially the whole benefit which it was the intention of the parties that he should obtain from the contract, the party not in default may elect to put an end to all primary obligations of both parties remaining unperformed (if the expression "fundamental breach" is to be retained, it should, in the interests of clarity, be confined to this exception); (2) where the contracting parties have agreed, whether by express words or by implication of law, that any failure by one party to perform a particular primary obligation ("condition" in the nomenclature of the Sale of Goods Act 1893), irrespective of the gravity of the event that has in fact resulted from the breach, shall entitle the other party to elect to put an end to all primary obligation of both parties remaining unperformed (in the interests of clarity, the nomenclature of the sale of Goods Act 1893, "breach of condition", should be reserved for this exception).

Where such an election is made (a) there is substituted by implication of law for the primary obligations of the party in default which remain unperformed a secondary obligation to pay monetary compensation to the other party for the loss sustained by him in consequence of their non-performance in the future and (b) the unperformed primary obligations of that other party are discharged. This secondary obligation is additional to the general secondary obligation; I will call it "the anticipatory secondary obligation".

In cases falling within the first exception, fundamental breach, the anticipatory secondary obligation arises under contracts of all kinds by implication of the common law, except to the extent that it is excluded or modified by the express words of the contract. In cases falling within the second exception, breach of condition, the anticipatory secondary obligation generally arises under particular kinds of contracts by implication of statute law; though in the case of "deviation" from the contract voyage under a contract of carriage of goods by sea it arises by implication of the common law. The anticipatory secondary obligation in these cases too can be excluded or modified by express words.

When there has been a fundamental breach or breach of condition, the coming to an end of the primary obligations of both parties to the contract at the election of the party not in default is often referred to as the "determination" or "rescission" of the contract or, as in the Sale of Goods Act 1893, "treating the contract as repudiated". The first two of these expressions, however, are misleading unless it is borne in mind that for the unperformed primary obligations of the party in default there are substituted by operation of law what I have called the secondary obligations.

Notes

7–017   1. This passage distinguishes between primary obligations, which are the actual contractual undertakings to perform, and secondary obligations, which are the obligations, *e.g.* to pay damages for failure to perform a primary obligation.

2. If the innocent party is entitled, and elects to repudiate, from that moment both parties are relieved from any further requirement to perform the primary obligations under the contract (that is to say, the primary obligations that remain unperformed). This is the effect of the two paragraphs beginning "The exceptions are: . . . ". It is also clear, however, that the secondary obligations survive repudiation.[11]

3. If the innocent party affirms the contract, the primary obligations remain in force, and if he elects to repudiate, they remain in force until such time as

---

[11] *e.g.* in *Nova Petroleum International Establishment v. Tricon Trading Ltd* [1989] 1 Lloyd's Rep. 312, c.i.f. sellers nominated a vessel that could not arrive within the contract period. The buyers thereupon repudiated, but Evans J. (citing *Lep Air Services Ltd v. Rolloswin Ltd* [1973] A.C. 331) held the sellers liable to pay damages for non-performance of delivery obligation, which was not of course due until after the repudiation. The contract appears to have been a variation on c.i.f. delivered (see paras 2–019 *et seq.*, above).

repudiation actually occurs.[12] In either case, the secondary obligation, *e.g.* to pay damages, arises in respect of primary obligations already broken.

4. Anticipatory breach is dealt with in the last two paragraphs, which suggest that while the doctrine applies generally to anticipated fundamental breaches, it applies only exceptionally to breaches of conditions.

(2) Terms Relating to the Goods

(a) Sale of Goods Act Implied Terms

International sale contracts are subject to the terms of the Sale of Goods Act 1979, set out in Appendix A. Note that in sections 12 to 15 are implied conditions as to the goods, but that there is a modification in section 15A, preventing the buyer from rejecting for very slight breaches. Sections 12(2), 14(2) and 15A have already been discussed, in chapter 4, above.   **7–018**

Section 28 makes payment and delivery concurrent conditions, and sections 34–35A deal with the buyer's right to accept or reject non-conforming goods.

In c.i.f. and f.o.b. contracts the seller is obliged to ship conforming goods, or in the case of a c.i.f. contract, purchasing goods which, when shipped, conformed to the contractual description. Shipping non-conforming goods will often amount to a breach of one of the conditions implied by ss.13–15 of the Sale of Goods Act 1979. Moreover, in *Bowes v Shand*,[13] the House of Lords held that the shipment date was part of the description of the goods; therefore, shipping outside the contract period can also amount to a breach of condition.

BOWES v SHAND

House of Lords. (1877) 2 App. Cas. 455

Facts
The case concerned two identical contracts for the sale of 300 tons "of Madras rice, to be shipped at Madras, or coast, for this port, during the months of March and/or April, 1874, per Rajah of Cochin." Nearly all the rice was shipped in February, as the bills of lading clearly showed.   **7–019**

Held
The buyers were entitled to reject the rice.

Lord Blackburn: (at 480–481) It was argued, or tried to be argued, on one point, that it was enough that it was rice, and that it was immaterial when it was shipped. As far as the subject-matter of the contract went, its being shipped at another and a different time being (it was said) only a breach of a stipulation which could be compensated for in damages. But I think that that is quite untenable. I think, to adopt an illustration which was used a long time ago by Lord Abinger, and which always struck me as being a right one, that it is an utter fallacy, when an article is described,   **7–020**

[12] *e.g. The Simona* [1989] 1 A.C. 788.
[13] (1877) 2 App. Cas. 455.

to say that it is anything but a warranty or a condition precedent that it should be an article of that kind, and that another article might be substituted for it. As he said, if you contract to sell peas, you cannot oblige a party to take beans. If the description of the article tendered is different in any respect it is not the article bargained for, and the other party is not bound to take it. I think in this case what the parties bargained for was rice, shipped at Madras or the coast of Madras. Equally good rice might have been shipped a little to the north or a little to the south of the coast of Madras. I do not quite know what the boundary is, and probably equally good rice might have been shipped in February as was shipped in March, or equally good rice might have been shipped in May as was shipped in April, and I dare say equally good rice might have been put on board another ship as that which was put on board the Rajah of Cochin. But the parties have chosen, for reasons best known to themselves, to say: We bargain to take rice, shipped in this particular region, at that particular time, on board that particular ship, and before the Defendants can be compelled to take anything in fulfilment of that contract it must be shewn not merely that it is equally good, but that it is the same article as they have bargained for—otherwise they are not bound to take it.

(3) REJECTION OF DOCUMENTS AND GOODS BY THE BUYER

7–021   In *Kwei Tek Chao v British Traders and Shippers Ltd*, considered in detail below, Devlin J. suggested that the buyer would have to right to reject non-conforming goods after inspection on their arrival. It is also clear that where the wrong documents are tendered, the buyer may reject them, and the same is true where the documents do not conform on their face, because then they show that non-conforming goods have been shipped.[14] In *Manbre Saccharine v Corn Products*, considered at para. 4–014, above, the buyer was able to reject on both of these grounds.[15] In *Kwei Tek Chao*, Devlin J. also took the view that there were two separate rights to reject, one relating to the documents and the other to the goods, arising at different times, in a c.i.f. contract.

On the principles already discussed in this chapter, however, it might also be thought that if, before the documents are tendered, the buyer discovers that the seller has shipped non-conforming goods, he should be able to treat the contract as repudiated, and therefore reject the documents, even if the documents themselves are in conformity with the contract. Of course, even if he accepts the documents and pays the price, he will later have the chance to reject the goods and claim back the price paid and damages for breach of contract, but it is far preferable to reject the documents and refuse to pay the price. The former course of action is not very satisfactory in international sales, where the seller trades in a foreign country and where his solvency may be in doubt: the use of bills of lading is intended in part precisely to protect buyers against paying the price and

---

[14] Where the goods have been lost, as in *The Julia; C. Groom v Barber* or *Manbre Saccharine*, the rights contained in, or evidenced by the documents are the totality of the value that the buyer obtains.

[15] The bill of lading also showed that the goods were non-conforming in *Bowes v Shand*.

being left with only contractual remedies, where the goods are not shipped according to contract.

Even if the buyer only suspects that non-conforming goods have been shipped, he should be able to rely upon knowledge that subsequently comes to light to justify his rejection of the documents, whether or not the documents themselves conform. It appears, however, that this may not be the law, at least as far as c.i.f. contracts are concerned.

GILL & DUFFUS SA v BERGER & CO INC

House of Lords. [1984] A.C. 382

Facts and issues:
The contract for sale was for 500 tonnes of Argentine Bolita beans c.i.f. Le Havre.   **7–022**
Payment was to be cash against documents, and there was to be a quality certificate issued at port of discharge.

The correct quantity was shipped within the shipment period, but only 445 tonnes was delivered at Le Havre, the other 55 tonnes being carried on to Rotterdam and then transhipped. On the principles discussed in chapter 2, above, the seller was not responsible for this deviation after shipment.

However, the sellers could not obtain the quality certificate for 500 tonnes after discharge, and the buyers refused to pay against the bill of lading and insurance documents alone. This was a wrongful rejection, because a quality certificate issued after discharge could not be a shipping document (see chapter 6, above). The sellers could at that stage have elected to treat the buyers' wrongful rejection as repudiating the contract, and sued for damages. They did not do so, presumably because the market price of Bolita beans had fallen, and they wanted to keep the contract alive (so as to claim the original contract price).

The sellers therefore obtained a certificate for the 445 tonnes discharged, and attempted a second tender. Again the buyers rejected (presumably because the market price had fallen). The documents were of course again in order, but the buyers contended that when the goods arrived, they did not conform to the contractual description (because they included a number of coloured beans, whereas Argentine Bolita beans are supposed to be white). This time the sellers elected to treat the buyers' rejection as repudiating the contract.

The issue, on an appeal from arbitration, was whether the buyers were entitled to reject the documents.

Held
The buyers were not entitled to reject. Since they were held to be bound by the quality certificate, they should have been unable to argue that the goods were not of the contractual description.[16] However, Lord Diplock thought that, in principle, a c.i.f. buyer was bound to accept the documents, even where the seller shipped goods which were defective, but presented documents for them which conformed on their face to the contractual requirements.

LORD DIPLOCK: That being so it is, in my view, a legal characteristic of   **7–023** a c.i.f. contract so well established in English law as to be beyond the

---

[16] See further the discussion of quality certificates at para. 6–102 *et seq.*, above. A quality certificate can be made conclusive evidence of the statements therein, even if negligently made. It may, however, be invalid if there is a departure from the instructions, where for example the wrong sampling method is used, since the test method is part of the specification: *Veba Oil Supply & Trading GmbH v Petrotrade Inc* [2002] All E.R. 703. There was no evidence of any irregularities in *Gill & Duffus*.

realm of controversy that the refusal by the buyer under such a contract to pay to the seller, or to a banker nominated in the contract if the contract so provides, the purchase price upon presentation at the place stipulated in the contract, of shipping documents which on their face conform to those called for by the contract, constitutes a fundamental breach of contract, which the seller is entitled to elect to treat as rescinding the contract and relieving him of any obligation to continue to perform any of his own primary obligations under it; or, to use the terminology of the Sale of Goods Act 1893 [now replaced by the 1979 Act], "to treat the contract as repudiated." So far as concerns the instant case the relevant primary obligation of the sellers of which they were relieved, was any further obligation to deliver to the buyers any of the goods that were the subject matter of the contract.

That a refusal of the buyer to accept the tender of shipping documents which on the face of them conform to the requirements of a c.i.f. contract and upon such acceptance to pay the contract price amounts to a breach of condition (in the meaning given to that expression in the Sale of Goods Act 1893) has been taken for granted so universally by English courts as not to have attracted any subsequent positive exposition worthy of citation, ever since Lord Cairns put it thus in *Shepherd v Harrison* (1871) L.R. 5 H.L. 116, 132, a case where payment was to be by acceptance of a documentary bill of exchange:

> "I hold it to be perfectly clear that when a cargo comes in this way, protected by a bill of lading and a bill of exchange, it is the duty of those to whom the bill of lading and the bill of exchange are transmitted in a letter, either 'to approbate or to reprobate' entirely and completely, then and there."

Recognition of the principle so stated (to which I have myself supplied the emphasis) is implicit in all judgments dealing with bankers' confirmed credits as a mode of payment including the most recent judgments of this House.

7–024   I have not overlooked a case decided in the High Court of Australia, *Henry Dean & Sons (Sydney) Ltd v O'Day Pty Ltd* (1927) 39 C.L.R. 330, to which deprecative reference is made in Benjamin's *Sale of Goods*, 2nd ed. (1981), para. 1717.[17] The case turned largely on a question of pleading which in New South Wales in 1927 followed the system that applied in England before the Judicature Act. By a majority of three to two (Knox C.J., Higgins and Starke JJ., Isaacs and Powers JJ. dissenting), it was held that when a buyer under a c.i.f. contract who was suing the seller for damages for non-delivery of goods which corresponded to the contract description, was met by a plea by the seller that by reason of the buyer's previous non-acceptance of a documentary bill of exchange accompanied by conforming documents, the buyer had failed to prove the essential

---

[17] Now Benjamin, *Sale of Goods* (5th ed., 1997), paras. 19–142 *et seq.*

allegation in his pleading that he was ready and willing to perform the contract at the time when tender of the actual goods that had been shipped under the bill of lading had been made. The two judges in the High Court who formed the minority took the orthodox view that the buyer's refusal to accept the documentary bill on presentation made him unable to establish his readiness and willingness to perform the contract. Of the majority, Knox C.J. and Higgins J. appear to have held that a c.i.f. buyer is entitled to reject conforming shipping documents, if it should subsequently turn out that the actual goods shipped under the conforming documents did not in fact conform to the contract; a view which, if correct, would destroy the very roots of the system by which international trade, particularly in commodities, is enabled to be financed. Starke J., although he concurred with Knox C.J. and Higgins J. in the outcome of the action, did not adopt this *ratio decidendi*. He regarded the case as a special one turning upon its particular facts; and I must confess that I have been unable to discover in his judgment any clear statement of some legal principle that he was treating as applicable to those facts.

There was thus no *ratio decidendi* that commanded the support of a majority of the High Court of Australia. Maybe for this reason, so far as I have been able to ascertain, *Henry Dean & Sons (Sydney) Ltd v O'Day Pty Ltd* has never been regarded as meriting citation in any later case. It has for more than half a century justifiably remained one of those submerged cases which lawyers in general have tacitly accepted as being a total loss, until it was dredged up in the course of the hearing of the instant case in your Lordships' House to provide, in the judgments of Knox C.J. and Higgins J., a *tabula in naufragio* for the buyers. In my opinion what was expressed to be the *ratio decidendi* of those judgments is not the law of England.

Notes

1. At its narrowest, the case decided only that the buyer was unable to reject **7–025** conforming documents, being precluded by the quality certificate from raising any issue on the quality or description of the goods.[18] Lord Diplock's view on liability did not depend on the quality certificate, however, which implies that he would have taken the same view even in the absence of any certificate. On its widest interpretation, his view (with which all the other members of the House agreed) was that a c.i.f. buyer is not entitled reject documents which conform on their face to the contractual requirements, whether or not conforming goods have been shipped. This position seems at first sight unfair on buyers, but a justification it is that if the bill of lading is truly to be a negotiable document, the law must cater for chain sales, as well as the simple position between single buyer and single seller. Had the opposite view been taken an intermediate buyer, who had innocently taken up the documents without knowing the condition of the goods on shipment, could find himself unable to use those documents to effect a re-sale.

2. Lord Diplock also said that "nothing that I say is intended to cover cases of fraud"; where fraud on the part of the seller is proven, the *ex turpi causa* doctrine will be invoked against him, and no liability will attach to the buyer. This

---

[18] See further paras 6–012 *et seq.*, above, on this issue.

therefore constitutes an exception, but probably not a very wide one. No doubt, it will often be difficult for the seller to procure proper shipping documents for defective goods without fraud on somebody's part, but it must be the fraud of the seller, and it must be proven.

3. The previous year the House of Lords had had to decide essentially the same issue as between seller and bank (where payment is by documentary credit) in *UCM v Royal Bank of Canada* (see chapter 10, below). *Gill & Duffus* brought the position as between seller and buyer into line with that as between seller and bank, though the policy reasons are different: a justification in the *UCM* case is that banks deal only with documents, and have no expertise in goods, whereas obviously buyers may be expected to be interested in the quality of the goods themselves.

4. The contract considered in *UCM* is probably unilateral (see the discussion at the end of chapter 8, below), in which case it is not meaningful to talk of the seller being in breach. The c.i.f. contract in *Gill & Duffus* is an ordinary bilateral contract, however; one might have thought that if the seller had shipped defective goods, the buyer should be able to reject on ordinary contractual principles, treating the contract as discharged because of the seller's prior repudiatory breach. Lord Diplock's reasoning is apparently inconsistent with the general contractual position. One way around this would be to treat the seller's obligation to ship conforming goods and the buyer's to accept and pay against documents as independent covenants, in which case a breach by the seller has no effect on the buyer's independent obligation.

5. Later in his speech, Lord Diplock suggests that, in principle, where in a case such as this a seller sues for wrongful repudiation, his damages might:

> "fall to be reduced by any sum which the buyers could establish they would have been entitled to set up in diminution of the contract price by reason of a breach of warranty as to description or quality of the goods represented by the shipping documents that had been actually shipped by the sellers if those goods had in fact been delivered to them."

This is in line with *Photo Production*, since the sellers' breaches would have occurred before their (valid) repudiation of the contract, but creates some difficulty with the old case of *Braithwaite v Foreign Hardwood Co* [1905] 2 K.B. 543. Discussion of this issue is beyond the scope of this book, but see, *e.g.* Carter (1985) L.Q.R. 167, 170 and also Benjamin's *Sale of Goods* (5th ed., 1997), chapter 9.

TREITEL, "RIGHTS OF REJECTION UNDER C.I.F. SALES"

[1984] L.M.C.L.Q. 565, at p. 568

[Footnotes are as in the original article, but renumbered for inclusion in this book.]

7–026   [The] remedies of the buyer against the seller are based on the assumption that the buyer is not himself in repudiatory breach of his obligations under the contract of sale. *Prima facie*, the buyer's failure or refusal to pay against conforming documents is such a breach and therefore gives the seller the right to rescind the contract. This, however, is subject to the important qualification that the buyer's refusal to pay against conforming documents would not be wrongful if before such refusal the seller had himself committed such a repudiatory breach. In that case, the buyer would himself be entitled to rescind the contract on account of the seller's breach; and his refusal to pay against documents could be regarded as an exercise of that right to rescind, even though at the time of refusal he gave a different ground for it, or no ground at all.[19] Nor would a claim for damages by the buyer be inconsistent with the view that he had rescinded; for it is now well settled that the victim of a repudiatory breach can both rescind and claim damages.[20] These general rules relating to the effect of repudiatory breaches are, however, subject to an exception where the obligations of the contracting parties were (to use somewhat old-fashioned terminology) "independent covenants".[21] In such a case, breach by one party did not give the other a right to rescind, but only one to claim damages.

[*Professor Treitel goes on to discuss* Henry Dean & Sons (Sydney) Ltd v O'Day Pty Ltd,[22] *continuing on p. 570:*]

In that case, too, c.i.f. buyers had refused to pay against conforming documents and it later turned out that the goods shipped by the sellers had not been of the contract description. The case differed from *Gill & Duffus SA v Berger and Co Inc* in two ways: (1) it was *the buyers* who claimed damages; and (2) it does not seem that any attempt was made by either party to rescind the contract. The buyers' claim succeeded, Knox, C.J., and Higgins, J., taking the view that the buyers' refusal to pay was "justified by the result",[23] *i.e.* by the discovery that the goods were not of the contract description. Lord Diplock has now declared that this view "is not the law of England."[24] Hence, even if the first breach was committed by the sellers, that breach did not justify the buyers' repudiation of the contract. In a c.i.f. contract, the buyer's duty to pay against documents is an independent covenant which must be performed even though the seller has failed to perform his duty to ship conforming goods (or to buy such goods afloat and appropriate them to the contract). This view follows from the commercial risks taken by the parties to such a contract. The buyer's duty to pay without examining the goods necessarily means that he is to part with the money before he has any assurance about the quality of the goods. The risk that the goods might not be of the right quality is one that the buyer takes, to the extent of being bound to assert remedies in respect of defects by action, rather than the quicker (and perhaps more efficacious) method of withholding the price. The c.i.f. buyer must thus, as a general rule,[25] pay against documents even though

---

[19] On the principles stated in cases such as *Taylor v Oakes Roncoroni & Co* (1922) 127 L.T. 267 and *British & Beningtons v North Western Cachar Tea Co Ltd* [1923] A.C. 48.
[20] *Johnson v Agnew* [1980] A.C. 637.
[21] See, *e.g. Pordage v Cole* (1669) 1 Wms. Saund. 319; *Huntoon Co v Kolynos (Inc)* [1930] 1 Ch. 528.
[22] (1927) 39 C.L.R. 330.
[23] *Ibid.*, p. 338; cf. pp. 350–351.
[24] [1984] A.C. 382, 391.
[25] Possible exceptions are considered *infra*, . . .

the goods are not in conformity with the contract; and he must do so even though he is entitled later to reject these goods.

Notes

7–027   1. Professor Treitel's conclusion is based upon his own logical assessment of the position, rather than on what Lord Diplock expressly stated. Independent covenants appear to be rare, and the conclusion is effectively that special rules apply to c.i.f. contracts because of the risks assumed by the buyer. While this is no doubt a possible argument, it does not seem to me necessarily to follow that because a buyer normally has to accept the documents in the absence of any knowledge of the quality of the goods, he should also be required to accept them when he in fact knows the goods to be defective.

2. In cases such as *Kwei Tek Chao*, considered later in this chapter, and certainly in *Procter & Gamble v Becher*, it seems to have been assumed that a c.i.f. buyer was entitled to reject a backdated bill of lading, although the bill of lading would have conformed on its face with the contractual description. This requires Treitel to distinguish the *Kwei Tek Chao* line of cases. The distinctions are considered later in the chapter, but they are arguably unconvincing. He suggests that a backdated bill of lading is not covered by *Gill & Duffus*, because it is not genuine.

3. Professor Treitel is really taking a very wide interpretation of Lord Diplock's view. Perhaps the case stands for a narrower proposition, easier to reconcile with the general law of contract.

FRANCIS REYNOLDS, "REJECTION OF DOCUMENTS"

[1984] L.M.C.L.Q. 191

[*Footnotes are as in the original article, apart from n. 27, but renumbered for inclusion in this book.*]

7–028   The decision of the House of Lords in *Gill & Duffus SA v Berger and Co Inc*[26] considers some fundamental problems relating to rejection of documents in documentary sales. The case involved a c.i.f. sale of Argentine Bolita Beans to be accompanied by a certificate of quality indicating conformity on discharge with samples taken earlier. The goods arrived at Le Havre, the port of discharge, before the documents were tendered, but not all were discharged; a small portion was carried to Rotterdam and brought back a few days later. The sellers tendered documents, which were rejected because they did not include the certificate of quality. This was of itself without more a repudiatory breach, as the certificate did not relate to quality on shipment and therefore could not be a shipping document under such a contract. The [sellers],[27] however, did not treat the contract as discharged, but set about obtaining such a certificate. Subsequently they tendered the documents again, accompanied this time by a certificate. This could not relate to all the goods, since not all had at

---

[26] [1984] 2 W.L.R. 95. The case has many similarities with the notorious *Braithwaite v Foreign Hardwood Co Ltd* [1905] 2 K.B. 343; see *Benjamin's Sale of Goods*, 2nd ed., paras. 1728–1731.
[27] The word "buyers" in the original must be a typing error.

the time of its issue arrived, and therefore covered only the first and larger portion discharged.

The buyers, who presumably believed that the goods did not conform to sample whatever the certificate said, again rejected the documents. This was of itself a further repudiatory breach, which the sellers this time accepted. They sued the buyers, who in the House of Lords were held liable for wrongful repudiation by rejecting the second presentation of documents.

The case was decided in three different ways at first instance,[28] in the Court of Appeal[29] and in the House of Lords, and a proper analysis of the many points raised would require a full article or more. It is the purpose of this note only to direct attention to certain points of general principle arising out of the case.

First, the documents were correct on their face and no indication is given that they were false in any material particular; thus the buyers' claim was in the end treated as one to reject documents because the contract goods were defective. Put in one way such a claim is clearly inadmissible. The notion that a buyer is entitled to reject conforming documents if it should *subsequently turn out*[30] that the actual goods shipped under them did not in fact conform to the contract is inconsistent with the presuppositions behind a c.i.f. contract—though it may of course go to damages if the buyer is sued.

On the other hand, if the buyer can establish that the seller *had already* **7–029** committed a breach of contract and was at the time of tender of documents wholly and finally disabled from performing the contract, for example because the contract concerns specific goods which were when shipped not in conformity with sample, or because the seller has made an irrevocable contractual appropriation of such non-conforming goods, there is more to be said for rejection of documents being justified. In such a case it can be argued that there is *already* a breach, and no principle requires the innocent party to wait until a particular stage (parting with his money) before treating the contract as discharged. The position is similar to that discussed in the previous note [*on* The Afovos], save that there is an actual, not merely an anticipatory breach. Only a special rule relating to documentary sales and presumably based on the importance of quick handling of documents would displace this conclusion. A decision of the High Court of Australia, *Henry Dean & Sons (Sydney) Ltd v O'Day Pty Ltd*,[31] provides some support for allowing rejection in such a case, though it is not clear whether the two judges whose decision prevailed in that case based themselves on the fact that a breach *already* had been committed or not.

In the *Gill & Duffus* case the buyers were presumably unable to prove such a pre-existing breach, for they were bound by the certificate of

---

[28] [1982] 1 Lloyd's Rep. 101.
[29] [1983] 1 Lloyd's Rep. 622.
[30] See the speech of Lord Diplock at p. 101.
[31] (1927) 39 C.L.R. 330.

quality on discharge, and it would be fanciful to seek to prove that the goods had been nonconforming when loaded when they must be assumed to have been conforming on arrival. True, there was no certificate relating to the small portion overcarried, but only proof that such a certificate could not have been obtained would permit the conclusion that some of the goods did not conform (which would have been enough to constitute a breach). The judgment of Robert Goff, L.J., in the Court of Appeal suggests that in such a case the buyers might have been *entitled* to reject the documents, but the point is not, with respect, made entirely clear and in any case the buyers lacked the necessary finding of fact. The judgment of Lord Diplock in the House of Lords is, however, perfectly clear. What was expressed to be the *ratio decidendi* of the prevailing judges in *Henry Dean & Sons (Sydney) Ltd v O'Day Pty Ltd*[32] is said not to be the law of England; and the possibility of proving that the further certificate would not have been issued went to damages only.

7–030   It may still be possible to argue that the decision does not prevent a contrary result where it can be proved that the goods were not in conformity with the contract on shipment and that there was no possibility of further appropriation or substituted tender; but the tenor of Lord Diplock's speech is against it. The principal explanation of his view seems to lie in these words[33]:

> "Under the original c.i.f. contract a right of the buyer at his election to reject shipping documents and a right at his election to reject the goods themselves upon delivery are separate and successive rights. The latter does not become exercisable until the seller has unconditionally appropriated the goods to the contract. Under a c.i.f. contract this does not happen until his reservation of the right of disposal of the goods by his withholding from the buyer the shipping documents which represent them is terminated by his transferring the shipping documents to the buyers."

The words "unconditional appropriation" usually refer to the passing of property and require the goods to become ascertained by the appropriation. They should exclude therefore cases where the bill of lading tendered relates to part of a larger cargo, the whole of which is non-conforming, in respect of which unconditional appropriation does not occur until discharge and allocation to the contract.

    The duty of a c.i.f. buyer to pay against documents is expressed in very wide form in an earlier passage[34]:

> "That a refusal of the buyer to accept the tender of shipping documents which on the face of them conform to the requirements of a c.i.f. contract and upon such acceptance to pay the contract price amounts to

---

[32] *Supra.*
[33] At p. 104.
[34] At p. 100.

a breach of condition (in the meaning given to that expression in the Sale of Goods Act 1893) has been taken for granted so universally by English courts as not to have attracted any subsequent positive exposition worthy of citation, ever since Lord Cairns put it thus in *Shepherd v Harrison* (1871) . . . Recognition of the principle so stated (to which I have myself supplied the emphasis) is implicit in all judgments dealing with bankers' confirmed credits as a mode of payment including the most recent judgments of this House."[35]

It is perhaps permissible to assume that this passage is not intended to deny, nevertheless, that the buyer can refuse to pay against documents which are actually false. Falsity, whether or not the result of fraud, has usually been assumed to be a valid ground for rejecting.[36] But the assimilation of the buyer's duty to that of the bank is certainly a parallel carrying implications. For whereas the banker deals in documents alone, the buyer participates in a sale of goods to be performed by the transfer of documents; hence there has hitherto been at least a case for treating the buyer differently.

Notes

1. Two possible limitations are at least alluded to here. First, if, unlike *Gill & Duffus* (because of the quality certificate) the buyers can establish a pre-existing breach by the sellers, they should be able to repudiate then and there, on ordinary contractual principles. Secondly, in the last paragraph Professor Reynolds suggests that the buyer might be able to refuse to pay against documents which are actually false, which presumably means documents that do not accurately describe the goods. This would cover the backdated bills of lading considered later in the chapter, but might also cover a clean bill of lading issued for goods which clearly do not conform (not the situation in *Gill & Duffus*, where the alleged defects would probably not have been apparent to the master).   **7–031**

2. The limitations alluded to allow the decision to conform to the normal law of contract, but they might also be thought to place significant limits on the decision, which surely cannot have been contemplated by Lord Diplock.

3. However, suppose it is accepted that if the buyer can establish a pre-existing breach of condition by the seller, he can repudiate the contract then and there. To establish such a breach might not be all that easy. For a c.i.f. contract, the seller can use any conforming goods, so that (as Reynolds observes) even if the buyer clearly establishes that non-conforming goods have been shipped, the seller will only be breach if the contract is for those specific goods, or those goods have been unconditionally appropriated to the buyer's contract. Often (and certainly in the bulk commodity market with which Lord Diplock's remarks are mainly concerned) the appropriation will occur only on the actual tender of documents, in which case the buyer will never be able to establish a pre-existing breach; moreover, as soon as the documents are tendered the price becomes payable, so it is then too late for the buyer to repudiate. This explanation is consistent with general

---

[35] A leading example is *United City Merchants Ltd v Royal Bank of Canada* [1983] A.C. 168. [Single quotation marks within the original quote have been omitted here, since they appear to be a typing error.]

[36] See, *e.g. James Finlay & Co Ltd v N.V. Kwik Hoo Tong Handel Maatschappij* [1928] 2 K.B. 604, 613 (affirmed [1929] 1 K.B. 400); *Hindley & Co v East Indian Produce Ltd* [1973] 2 Lloyd's Rep. 515.

principles of the law of contract, but implies that *Gill & Duffus* would not apply in a case like *The Jambur*, for example, considered at para. 2–021, above, where the contract was for the sale of specific goods. Interestingly, however, the buyer was allowed to reject conforming documents in that case.

4. Professor Reynolds also suggests that a buyer ought to be able to reject a false bill of lading—this would presumably (in his view) include a backdated bill, as considered in the cases at the end of this chapter, but also perhaps a bill of lading that did not represent the goods, by being issued clean for clearly defective goods.[37] The logic of Lord Diplock's remarks are against this, however, and perhaps we should try and find another explanation for the cases considered later in this chapter.

5. Though the case concerns c.i.f. contracts, if the principle upon which it is decided is as outlined in n. 3 above, it should apply also to f.o.b. sales, where there are separate obligations on the seller both to ship goods and to tender valid documents. If Professor Treitel's independent covenant explanation is correct, however, then its logic may be limited to the c.i.f. contract.

(4) Loss of Right to Reject

(a) The Issues

7–032   Typically, the cases concern c.i.f. sales of commodity futures, where (for example) January shipment is required. Shipment is actually made in early February, but the bill of lading is backdated to show January shipment. The market is falling, so that the buyers have made what has turned out to be a bad bargain. If the true shipment date had been stated on the bill of lading, they would have rejected it on grounds of late shipment (see *Bowes v Shand* (1877) App. Cas. 455, above, where the House of Lords stated that the shipment period stipulated in a c.i.f. contract forms part of the description of the goods). In that event, instead of paying the contract price, the buyers would have gone back into the market to purchase equivalent goods at the current (*i.e.* lower) market price. Thus, by rejecting the documents, they would been able to shift the market loss back on to the sellers.

Because the bill of lading has been backdated, however, the buyers are unaware of the true shipment date, and so accept the documents, and pay the high contract price against them. If they sue for late shipment, the sellers will counter that damages should be nominal, or very small, arguing that the basis of their assessment is the difference in market value between goods shipped in late January and the same goods shipped in February, usually an insignificant sum. This was the view taken by McCardie J. in *Taylor & Sons, Ltd v Bank of Athens* (1922) 27 Com. Cas. 142. Clearly, therefore the buyers bear the market loss, whereas had they rejected the documents the sellers would have borne it.

Taylor & Sons, Ltd v Bank of Athens was distinguished by the Court of Appeal in *James Finlay & Co v M.V. Kwik Hoo Tong HM* [1929] 1 K.B. 400, where the buyers instead claimed that the sellers had broken a separate condition, by issuing a bill of lading containing a false statement. Of course, had this condition not been broken, the shipment date would have been correctly stated, and the buyers would have rejected on the basis of *Bowes v Shand*. They would therefore have been able to shift the market loss back to the sellers, and the loss flowing from this breach of condition is therefore the entire market loss. This is, in effect, a claim for damages for loss of the right to reject the documents.

---

[37] There is no doubt, at any rate, that buyers can reject a bill of lading, even though conforming on its face, which is a nullity because no goods have been shipped: *Hindley & Co v East Indian Produce Ltd*, at para. 2–012, above.

In *James Finlay*, the buyers, having been induced to accept the falsely-dated documents, used them for a sub-sale, and therefore never took delivery of, or got a chance to inspect the goods. However, in cases where there is no sub-sale, the buyers still have a separate right to reject the goods themselves, when they arrive, and claim the price back from the sellers. They have a second chance, therefore, to shift the market loss back. They are more likely to resell them, however, albeit at a substantial loss because of the falling market: it is usually more attractive to resell immediately to defray expenses, rather than attempt to reclaim the price back from sellers who will typically be situated abroad, and whose solvency may be in doubt, and the importance to *Kwei Tek Chao* below, is that it extends the damages for loss of the right to reject reasoning in *James Finlay* to this situation also.

The cases up to *Procter & Gamble* (see below) establish that where c.i.f. buyers accept a misdated bill of lading in ignorance of the true shipment date, at any rate where the goods were actually shipped outside the contractual period, they can sue for damages for loss of the right to reject the bill, thereby shifting the market loss back on to the sellers. They do not lose this right merely because, from commercial necessity, they accept the goods when they arrive, and resell them having discovered the true shipment date. The buyers may lose the right to reject on grounds of late shipment, however, if they conduct themselves in such a way that they are estopped from asserting it, for example by taking up the documents in full knowledge of the true shipment date. If they are estopped from rejecting on grounds of late shipment, they also lose the right to claim damages for loss of the right to reject, and thus cannot shift the market loss back on to the sellers.

The assumption is made throughout that no fraud on the part of the sellers can be proved. In *Procter & Gamble*, Kerr L.J. pointed out that in cases where the sellers can be shown to have acted fraudulently, the measure of damages for fraudulent misrepresentation is such as to put the buyers into the same position as if the misrepresentation had not been made, in other words as if the bill of lading had never been tendered: *Doyle v Olby (Ironmongers) Ltd* [1969] 2 Q.B. 158; *Saunders v Edwards* [1987] 1 W.L.R. 1116. Since the buyers would not have paid the contract price had the bill of lading not been tendered, clearly this measure of damages shifts the market loss back on to the sellers.

The buyer's remedies where he is induced to accept documents and goods by alteration of the documents so that they appear to conform to contractual requirements, or where documents are wrongfully issued by the carrier so that they appear to conform, are discussed in the next case.

KWEI TEK CHAO v BRITISH TRADERS & SHIPPERS

Queen's Bench Division. [1954] 2 Q.B. 459; [1954] 1 Lloyd's Rep. 16

Facts:

London exporters agreed to sell Rongalite C (a chemical) to merchants c.i.f. Hong Kong, to be shipped on or before 31st October 1951. The goods were shipped a few days later, but the bill of lading was fraudulently altered (though not by the sellers themselves)[38] to show October shipment. Meanwhile, the general market price of Rongalite C had dropped, so as it transpired the Hong Kong merchants had made a bad bargain.

7–033

---

[38] Indeed, the sellers (British Traders) had themselves purchased the goods on a domestic supply contract that was at first on f.o.b. terms, but later altered to "c.i.f." to allow for payment by documentary credit against shipping documents (albeit that the bill of lading was in British Traders' name). The bills of lading had been altered by these suppliers, in order to obtain payment under the credit.

The buyers could find nothing wrong with the documents, which indeed conformed on their face, falsely stating as they did that the goods had been shipped within the stipulated time for shipment. They had discovered the truth by the time the goods arrived, and indeed because of the late shipment they lost their resale contract. Undoubtedly they could, at that stage, have rejected the goods, in which case they would probably have incurred storage charges, and hope eventually to reclaim the price paid, and other losses, from a seller on the other side of the world. This option seemed unattractive commercially, so they decided to use the documents to resell the goods, and at least recoup some of their loss immediately. Because of the market drop they inevitably suffered a loss, which but they sought to recover from the defendant sellers.

The sellers argued that they were limited to ordinary contractual damages (*i.e.* excluding the general market drop) because they had accepted the documents (because they could find nothing wrong with them), and also the goods (for commercial reasons). They had also transferred the documents to a third party, in order to resell the goods.

Held:
The buyers could recover all their loss, including the general market drop.

7–034   DEVLIN J: There is not, in my judgment, one right to reject; there are two rights to reject. A right to reject is, after all, only a particular form of a right to rescind the contract. Wherever there is a breach of condition there is a right to rescind the contract, and if there are successive breaches of different conditions committed one after the other, each time there is a breach there is a right to rescind in respect of that breach. A right to reject is merely a particular form of the right to rescind, which involves the rejection of a tender of goods or of documents; and a rightful rejection of either is a rescission which brings the contract to an end.

Here, therefore, there is a right to reject documents, and a right to reject goods, and the two things are quite distinct. A c.i.f. contract puts a number of obligations upon the seller, some of which are in relation to the goods and some of which are in relation to the documents. So far as the goods are concerned, he must put on board at the port of shipment goods in conformity with the contract description, but he must also send forward documents, and those documents must comply with the contract. If he commits a breach the breaches may in one sense overlap, in that they flow from the same act. If there is a late shipment, as there was in this case, the date of the shipment being part of the description of the goods, the seller has not put on board goods which conform to the contract description, and therefore he has broken that obligation. He has also made it impossible to send forward a bill of lading which at once conforms with the contract and states accurately the date of shipment. Thus the same act can cause two breaches of two independent obligations.

However that may be, they are distinct obligations, and the right to reject the documents arises when the documents are tendered, and the right to reject the goods arises when they are landed and when after examination they are found not to be in conformity with the contract. There are many cases, of course, where the documents are accepted but the goods are subsequently rejected. It may be that if the actual date of shipment is not in conformity with the contract, and the error appears from the documents, the buyer, by accepting the documents, not only loses his right to reject the documents, but also his right to reject the goods, but that would be because he had waived in advance reliance on the date of shipment.

That they are distinct obligations, and that that is the root of the reasoning in *James Finlay & Co Ltd v NV Kwik Hoo Tong* [1929] 1 K.B. 400, is to my mind apparent from the way in which the case is put in the judgment of Greer L.J., who said (at p. 413):

"The respondents say that the appellants not merely promised to ship the sugar in September but by a distinct and separate promise under-took to hand a bill of lading which would truly state that the sugar was shipped in September; so their claim is not merely for damages for breach of contract to deliver the sugar to the ship in September but for damages for breach of the undertaking to give a true bill of lading. It seems to me that that is the answer to [the] vigorous argument that the two things to be compared are the position the respondents would be in, so far as money is concerned, if the whole agreement had been performed on the one hand, and the position they would be in if the whole agreement was not performed. What has to be considered is the plaintiff's position as regards money if the particular term of the agreement had been performed, and they are to be put, so far as money is concerned, in that same position by damages for breach of that term of the contract. The judge has taken the view that the shippers prom-ised to state truly in the bill of lading the date of shipment, and the respondents say that if that had been done they would have been entitled to reject the goods. By the breach of contract in sending for-ward a bill of lading containing a false statement, the plaintiffs say they have been deprived of that right. I suggested to the appellants that if their promise to tender a correctly dated bill of lading had been in a separate contract their contention would have been unarguable. It seems to me to make no difference that the term is in the same contract which contains the obligations to ship the sugar in September."

He continued in a further passage, at p. 414:   **7–035**

"I agree . . . that the result of that is to give the plaintiffs in this case exactly the same damages as they would have received if they had successfully brought an action for fraudulent misrepresentation, but there may well be terms in a contract which, if broken, put the party complaining of the breach in the same position as if he claimed damages for false misrepresentation. That is the view that commends itself to my mind . . . "

There being, therefore, two separate and distinct obligations, there is a right to rescind arising on the breach of any one of them, and the matter has to be looked at in the way that Greer L.J. suggested, as if the two obligations were contained in two separate contracts.

It follows, therefore, as a matter of principle, that the action of the plaintiff on the second breach cannot affect his right to damages on the first breach. They are distinct not merely in law, but also as a matter of business. Having a right to reject the documents separately from a right to reject the goods, it is obvious that as a matter of business very different considerations will govern the buyer's mind as he applies himself to one or other of those questions. When he has to make up his mind whether he accepts the documents, he has not parted with any money. If he parts with his money and then has to consider whether to reject the goods, wholly different considerations would operate. In the interval he may have had dealings with the goods; he may have pledged them to his bank, he may have agreed to resell the specific goods, and the position may have been entirely altered.

Let me leave aside the position of a bank and take the simple case of a buyer who has not dealt with the property in any way, but has accepted the documents believing them to be accurate; and suppose that when the goods arrive the market has fallen by, say, five per cent. The buyer is faced with the choice, if he rejects the goods and wants to put himself back into the same position, of having to go out into the market and buy a new lot of goods at 95 per cent of the purchase price. He might well feel, if the seller to him was somebody about whom he knew little, that he was not going to part with the goods by rejecting them and pay out another 95 per cent of the price (which he might pay to the seller himself if the seller was selling the goods in the market, the property having returned to him) and be faced merely with an unsecured claim for the recovery back from the seller of the price which he originally paid. Very different considerations would naturally govern his mind at that stage, when he was considering whether to reject the goods or not, from those which would govern his mind when he was considering whether to reject the documents.

If I might call the breach of the term to deliver correct documents breach A, and the failure to ship goods on the contract date as breach B, it seems to me that the right to damages for breach A vests when the breach is committed, that the measure is then determined as being the proper measure required to put the buyer in as good a position as he would have been in if the breach had not been committed; and that when a separate breach, breach B, is committed the buyer has a separate and independent right to elect upon that breach as to the way in which he is going to deal with it, whether he treats it as a condition or as a warranty, and that he cannot be fettered in the exercise of that right as he would be if by his election he altered the measure of damage for breach A. That measure of damage must remain the same however the buyer elects to deal with breach B . . .

There is one other matter on this aspect of the case with which I should **7–036** also deal, although it arises only indirectly. In view of the conclusion at which I have arrived that I am dealing with two separate breaches, each with their separate remedies, it is not relevant to consider whether the buyers lost their right to reject the goods. In my view they lost their right to reject the documents, and their right to reject the goods was something different which they could exercise one way or the other whichever way they chose. If there had been only one right to reject it would have been material to ascertain whether the buyers had in any event lost their right to reject by any action taken by them in relation to the documents. Had they handled the documents in such a way as to amount to an acceptance under s.35 of the Sale of Goods Act 1893 [now re-enacted in 1979, see above], and if they had committed that act before they had knowledge of the true position, then Mr Roskill [for the sellers] would have been faced with the argument that when the goods were landed the buyers were in any event obliged to accept them, having already lost their right to reject them, so that no distinction could properly be drawn between that and the *Kwik Hoo Tong* case . . .

Atkin L.J., in the course of his judgment in *Hardy & Co (London) Ltd v Hillerns and Fowler* [1923] 2 K.B. 400, dealt with the situation which is always a little puzzling under the c.i.f. contract: if the property passes when the documents are handed over, by what legal machinery does the buyer retain a right, as he undoubtedly does, to examine the goods when they arrive, and to reject them if they are not in conformity with the contract? Atkin L.J. put forward two views for consideration. One was that the property in the goods, notwithstanding the tendering of the documents, did not pass until the goods had been examined or until an opportunity for examination had been given. The other was that it passed at the time of the tendering of the documents, but only conditionally and could be revested if the buyer properly rejected the goods. Mr Roskill argues [for the defendant sellers] (and I think rightly) that for the first possible view indicated by Atkin L.J. no other authority can be found, and it would clearly create considerable complications. If there is no property in the goods, how can the buyer pledge them? It would provide a simple answer to the point had it arisen in this case, since there could not be a pledge. I think that the true view is that what the buyer obtains, when the title under the documents is given to him, is the property in the goods, subject to the condition that they revest if upon examination he finds them to be not in accordance with the contract. That means that he gets only conditional property in the goods, the condition being a condition subsequent. All his dealings with the documents are dealings only with that conditional property in the goods. It follows, therefore, that there can be no dealing which is inconsistent with the seller's ownership unless he deals with something more than the conditional property. If the property

passes altogether, not being subject to any condition, there is no ownership left in the seller with which any inconsistent act under section 35
could be committed. If the property passes conditionally the only ownership left in the seller is the reversionary interest in the property in the
event of the condition subsequent operating to restore it to him. It is that
reversionary interest with which the buyer must not, save with the
penalty of accepting the goods, commit an inconsistent act. So long as he
is merely dealing with the documents he is not purporting to do anything
more than pledge the conditional property which he has. Similarly, if he
sells the documents of title he sells the conditional property. But if, as was
done in *Hardy & Co (London) Ltd v Hillerns and Fowler* [1923] 2 K.B. 400,
when the goods have been landed, he physically deals with the goods
and delivers them to his sub-buyer, he is doing an act which is inconsistent with the seller's reversionary interest. The seller's reversionary
interest entitles him, immediately upon the operation of the condition
subsequent, that is, as soon as opportunity for examination has been
given, to have the goods physically returned to him in the place where
the examination has taken place without their being dispatched to third
parties. The dispatch to a third party is an act, therefore, which interferes
with the reversionary interest. A pledge or a transfer of documents such
as that which takes place on the ordinary string contract does not.

7–037   I observe that the view expressed in Halsbury's *Laws of England*, Hailsham, ed., vol. 29, p. 224, para. 297, seems to be that the transfer of the bill
of lading to a third party would be inconsistent with section 35. I myself
should prefer to take the view that neither of them is inconsistent for the
reasons I have given; they stand on the same level and they are both
dealing merely with conditional property. It would in my view be unsatisfactory if a court had to decide every time where there was a string of
contracts that as soon as the documents had been passed to the first in the
string with the intention to pass title in the property the right to reject was
thereby lost.

It might further be suggested that in any event, in the circumstances of
this case, the buyer having pledged the goods to a banker was not in a
position to reject, because it was his banker who exercised dominion over
them by reason of the pledge. That, again, raises a question of some
theoretical difficulty: can a buyer in effect defeat a pledge by exercising
his right of rejection? One view might be that although the property is
conditional property which is subject to a condition subsequent, he cannot by his own voluntary act in putting the condition subsequent into
operation defeat the pledge. The other view would be that it cannot have
been contemplated as between banker and seller that when the buyer
pledged the documents he was intending to abandon or impair his right
of rejection. It would certainly be very far from the circumstances of the
present case in the course the argument has taken that I should express
any view on that. It is merely a matter to which attention might be paid
by those who are concerned with it. Obviously, the banker, in dealing
with his letter of credit or his instructions, can impose what conditions he

likes, and it may be that in those matters prevention is better than cure, at any rate, if the cure involves litigation.

Notes

1. Though the buyers had undeniably accepted the goods, it could not be **7–038** inferred from that alone that they had accepted the documents as well. The two rights to reject were completely separate.

2. The reason that they had accepted the documents also was because the fault was hidden from them. Therefore, because of the seller's breach in presenting a backdated bill of lading, they had been deprived of their right to reject the documents. The basis of that right is discussed below.

3. They were able to recover, therefore, all the loss they suffered by not rejecting, and of course this included the market fall.

4. The last extract from the judgment, above, shows that where the buyer accepts the documents, and pays against them, and later rejects the goods on arrival, property in the goods will pass to him, and then back again to the seller. During this period the buyer has conditional property. In *The Delfini* in chapter 5,[39] the cargo-owners attempted to argue that property had passed only conditionally, acceptance of the goods on delivery being conditional upon conforming bills of lading being tendered. This would have involved a reversal of the normal situation, in that conditional property would have passed on acceptance of the goods, the documents arriving only later. The Court of Appeal in *The Delfini* was unprepared to extend Devlin J.'s reasoning in *Kwei Tek* to this converse situation. Purchas L.J., taking a point raised by counsel, also observed that "as a commercial possibility it would be difficult to contemplate contracting parties providing for a right to reject the cargo at some point which might be as much as 12 months later after the oil had been delivered into the receiver's tanks and most probably mixed with other oil if not actually processed in some way or another." Mustill L.J. observed that "since a bill of lading (either original or copy) was by the contract required to accompany the ship, along with the certificate of origin and other documents, plainly so that import formalities could be complied with, it must have been contemplated that the buyers or their representatives would inspect them immediately on arrival: and it seems unlikely that if they were not then rejected, the Court would entertain rejection when the full set of documents was presented nearly two weeks later." The purport of both these observations is that the second right, to reject the documents, was not a realistic possibility in *The Delfini*. Even had this not been the case, Mustill L.J. further observed that the conditional property in *Kwei Tek* supposes that the whole property passes, subject to a condition subsequent, not that the passing of property is postponed until the subsequent condition arises (otherwise property in a c.i.f. contract would not pass until the arrival of the goods).[40]

(b) Refinements to the Reasoning in *Kwei Tek Chao*

It is clear from the above discussion that the rights to reject documents and **7–039** goods are separate rights, and *Kwei Tek* tells us that it cannot be inferred merely from acceptance of the documents that the buyer also accepts the goods,[41] or *vice-versa*. However, the buyer's conduct in relation to the documents *may* lead to the inference that he also accepts the goods, or at least cannot reject them for defects which became apparent from the documents. In *Kwei Tek Chao* itself, Devlin J.

---

[39] See para. 5–066, above.
[40] Woolf L.J. in *The Delfini* agreed with this observation, and also with the view that the *Kwei Tek* reasoning could not be applied in reverse.
[41] By virtue of the Sale of Goods Act, s.35(1).

(after making the point that the two rights to reject were separate) observed that:

> "It may be that, if the actual date of shipment is not in conformity with the contract, the buyer, by accepting the documents, loses not only his right to reject the documents but also his right to reject the goods, but that would be because he had waived in advance the date of shipment."

PANCHAUDS FRÈRES SA v ETABLISSEMENTS GENERAL GRAIN CO

Court of Appeal. [1970] 1 Lloyd's Rep. 53

Facts:

7–040 The sale contract was for 5500 tonnes of Brazilian yellow maize c.i.f. Antwerp. Shipment was to take place during June/July 1965. Shipment actually took place during August, but the bill of lading was dated 31st July 1965. However, although the bill of lading was falsely dated, the true shipment date could have been ascertained from an examination of the certificate of quality. This stated: "loaded on August 10th to 12th 1965", which would obviously have told the buyers that the bill of lading was wrongly dated.

The buyers paid against the shipping documents but refused to accept the goods when they arrived at Antwerp, originally on the grounds that the number of bags did not correspond with the number stated in the bill of lading. Arbitration proceedings were commenced, the sellers claiming the purchase price, and the arbitrators upheld the buyers' claim. The sellers appealed to the Committee of Appeal of the London Corn Trade Association Ltd. At this stage the buyers altered their grounds for rejection, to contend instead that they were entitled to reject because of the false date on the bill of lading.

Held:

By taking up the documents and paying for them, the buyers were precluded from later complaining of late shipment.

7–041 LORD DENNING M.R.: It is well settled that if a buyer rejects and gives one ground for it, he is not confined to that ground. If he afterwards finds out another ground on which he was entitled to reject, then in the ordinary way he can rely on that ground also. That is clear from *Taylor v Oakes, Roncoroni & Co* (1922) 18 T.L.R. 349. It is similar to the rule that if a man dismisses a servant on one ground, he is not confined to that ground. If he afterwards finds another ground justifying his dismissal, he can rely on that too. But this rule is subject to the qualification that a man may by his conduct preclude himself from setting up the later ground. We had, a little while ago, a case where a man was dismissed for one particular piece of dishonesty. At the trial the employer realised that he would not succeed in proving that particular dishonesty. So, during an adjournment, he got evidence of another piece of dishonesty and tried to raise it. But we did not allow it. He had fought the case on the earlier ground, and it would not be fair to allow him to rake up another ground at that stage. It is not, strictly speaking, a case of waiver but of estoppel by conduct . . .

The present case is not a case of "waiver" strictly so called. It is a case of estoppel by conduct. The basis of it is that a man has so conducted himself that it would be unfair or unjust to allow him to depart from a particular state of affairs which another has taken to be settled or correct, see the cases I referred to in *Central Newbury Car Auctions Ltd v Unity Finance Ltd* [1957] 1 Q.B. 371, at 380. Applied to the rejection of goods, the principle may be stated thus: If a man, who is entitled to reject goods on a certain ground, so conducts himself as to lead the other to believe that he is not relying on that ground, then he cannot afterwards set it up as a ground of rejection, when it would be unfair or unjust to allow him to do so. Mr. Lloyd [for the sellers] gave a good illustration. Suppose, he said, in this case the bill of lading had contained the true date of shipment —Aug. 12—(whereas the last date under the contract was July 31): so that, when the buyer took up the documents, he could have seen, if he had read it, that the date of shipment was Aug. 12. If he did not trouble to read it, but instead took up the documents and paid for them, he could not afterwards reject the goods on the ground of late shipment. Even though he had not read the bill of lading—and so was ignorant of the late shipment—he could not afterwards reject the goods on that ground: for the simple reason that he had the full opportunity of finding out from the contract documents what the real date of shipment was: and yet he did not trouble to do so. It would not be fair or just to allow him afterwards to reject the goods. Mr. Evans was inclined to accept this illustration as correct. Another instance can be given from the ordinary sale of goods. If a buyer does not choose to examine the goods when they arrive, and puts it off beyond a reasonable time, he loses his right to reject: see s.35 of the Sale of Goods Act, 1893 [now 1979, see above]. Although he did not know they were not in conformity with the contract, nevertheless, by letting a reasonable time go by, he loses his right to reject.

It seems to me that this case falls within that principle. If the buyers had read the shipping documents when they took them up and paid for them—as they could and should have done—they would have read this certificate of quality and seen that the date of shipment was really Aug. 12: and that someone had put July 31 on to the bill of lading so as to make it appear that the goods had been shipped in accordance with the contract, whereas, in fact they had not. If the buyers choose not to read the documents, they must put up with the consequences. They must be treated as if they had read them. This was clearly the view of the Committee of Appeal of the London Corn Trade Association Ltd.: and, in a commercial matter like this, I like to hear the views of commercial men, just as Lord Mansfield did with his special jurymen. The Committee of Appeal held that the buyers "cannot be deemed to have been unaware" that the maize was loaded between Aug. 10 and 12, 1965. By taking up the documents and paying for them, they are precluded afterwards from complaining of the late shipment or of the defect in the bill of lading. That seems to me to be the finding of the Committee of Appeal, and I see no error of law in it. They used the word "waiver" but that does not matter. They buyers are precluded, by their conduct, from relying on the late shipment as a ground for rejecting the goods.

7–042   WINN L.J.: In approaching the discussion of "waiver" in the judgment of the learned Judge, I was affected with a subconscious recollection of the principle to which my Lord has expressly referred, which found expression in the words of Diplock L.J. in *Andrea v British Italian Trading Company Ltd* [1962] 1 Lloyd's Rep. 151. I too would deprecate any excessively scholastic approach to problems such as were presented to the commercial men in this Appeal Committee. I do not think they did use the word "waive" correctly, if the correctness of their use of it is to be judged by criteria which are familiar to and adopted by lawyers. But I do not attach any importance to this fact albeit I agree with the learned Judge's view or it. Their use of the word was not technically precisely correct, but their meaning seems to be reasonably clear.

There is a very good discussion of waiver in Chitty on *Contracts*, 23rd ed., *General Principles* volume, at para. 1241 and the following paragraphs. I do not take time to quote from those paragraphs; it is quite clear on referring to them that rightly treat, "waiver" as derived either from agreement or from a quasi estoppel. In my own judgment it does not seem possible in this case to say affirmatively that there was here either a fresh agreement, to rescind or vary the original contract, or anything which, within the scope of the doctrine as hitherto enunciated, could be described as an estoppel or a quasi estoppel. I respectfully agree with my Lord that what one has here is something perhaps in our law not yet wholly developed as a separate doctrine—which is more in the nature of a requirement of fair conduct—a criterion of what is fair conduct between the parties. There may be an inchoate doctrine stemming from the manifest convenience of consistency in pragmatic affairs, negativing any liberty to blow hot and cold in commercial conduct.

7–043   CROSS L.J.: . . . Mr. Evans [for the buyers] admitted that if the bill of lading itself had borne a date in the middle of August, then, even though these buyers had not read the bill, or if they read it, had not noticed the date, they could not have been heard to complain that the goods were not shipped within the contract period. But he invited us to draw a line between matters which had to be included in the contractual documents if they were to play their proper part in the contractual scheme and matters such as the date of loading in the certificate of inspection, which did not have to be there, but just happened to be there. I think that it would be wrong to draw such a distinction, as a matter of law. . . .

Notes

Here the buyers' conduct led to the conclusion that they had accepted the   7–044
documents, knowing the true shipment date. They were held not to be entitled to
reject the goods either, on grounds of late shipment. It must normally follow that
they would also lose the right to claim damages for loss of the right to reject on
those grounds; if they are assumed voluntarily to have accepted the documents,
in full knowledge of the truth, they cannot logically claim that they lost the right
to reject because the truth was hidden from them. That this is the general position
is also clear from *Procter & Gamble v Becher*, below.

However, even where the buyer accepts the documents in full knowledge of the
truth, he may still be entitled to *Kwei Tek* damages if he accepts them without
prejudice.

KLEINJAN & HOLST NV ROTTERDAM v BREMER HANDELGESELLSCHAFT mbH HAMBURG

Queen's Bench Division. [1972] 2 Lloyd's Rep. 11

Facts:
The sellers telexed a notice of appropriation which mistakenly misstated the name   7–045
of the vessel upon which the goods had been loaded as *The Mahout*, whereas they
had actually been loaded on board *The Mahsud*. Later, the sellers telexed the
correction, but the buyers refused to accept the correction as a fresh notice of
appropriation or as an amendment to the original message, and insisted that
shipping documents were tendered conforming with the original notice. Eventually however, they agreed to accept a bill of lading evidencing shipment on
board *Mahsud*, but adding: "we shall pay the documents as per contract reserving
our rights . . . ". The position was, therefore, that they had accepted documents
which they claimed to be faulty, in full knowledge of the truth.

The sellers claimed that they were in any case entitled to make a fresh notice of
appropriation, and that they were therefore entitled to tender the *Mahsud* bill of
lading, but that even if this was incorrect, so that they were in breach of contract,
damages were limited to the difference in value between cargoes loaded on board
the two vessels. Since this would be nothing, damages should be nominal.

Held:
Cooke J. first held that the sellers were not entitled to make a fresh notice of
appropriation. This was simply a matter of construction of the particular c.i.f.
contract, and is of no relevance to the present discussion.

He further held that the buyers could claim as damages for the breach the
difference between the contract price and the market price.

Cooke J.: *(having decided the sellers were not entitled to make a fresh notice*   7–046
of appropriation) I now come to the question of damages. The argument of
the sellers, as I understand it, is this. The buyers in this case have accepted
the documents and have accepted the goods. Therefore, by virtue of
s.11(1)(c) of the Sale of Goods Act, 1893, the breach of any condition to be
fulfilled by the sellers can only be treated as a breach of warranty. The
only breach of warranty on which it is now open to the buyers to rely is
a warranty that the goods would be shipped on the *Mahout*. Applying the
principles of s.53 of the Sale of Goods Act, the measure of damages for
such a breach is the difference in value between goods shipped on the
Mahout and goods shipped on the *Mahsud*, and since there is no such

difference in value or, at any rate, none to recover nominal damages only. That, as I understand it, is the gist of Mr. Boyd's argument [for the sellers] on this part of the case and in support of it he relies on the decision of McCardie J. in *Taylor and Sons Ltd v Bank of Athens* (1922) 27 Com. Cas. 142.

I think it is convenient to begin from what I hope are generally accepted principles. Where the sellers are in breach of a term of the contract which in Sale of Goods Act terminology is a condition, the buyers may, if they act at the right time, rescind the contract. If for any reason the buyers are unable to act at the right time or if they elect not to rescind, then the right of rescission is lost, but since the fact remains that the sellers are in breach of the term in question the buyers are entitled to recover damages for that particular breach in accordance with whatever measure is appropriate to it. No doubt in the case where the buyers elect not to rescind they may, at the same or some other time, waive also their right to recover damages for the particular breach in question. Such a waiver is perhaps in normal circumstances unlikely. In any event, an election not to rescind for the breach does not of itself import a waiver of the right to recover damages for it. One turns then to consider what happened in this case. The findings in . . . the special case appear to me to show that . . . the buyers were minded to reject the documents tendered. That is to say, the buyers were minded to rescind the contract on the ground of the sellers' breach of condition in failing to tender documents complying with the [*original*] notice of appropriation . . . [*Later*] the buyers accepted the documents and paid the contract price. They did so pursuant to he agreement contained in the exchange of telex messages on the date. By that agreement the rights of the buyers are reserved. Where a person's rights are reserved then *prima facie* it is all of his rights which are reserved and not merely some of them. I think that all of the buyers' rights were reserved in this case including their right to recover damages for the sellers' breach of contract in failing to tender shipping documents in accordance with the [*original*] notice . . .

7–047   What then is the measure of damages appropriate to that breach? In my view, it is the difference between the contract price of the goods and their market price at the date of the breach. In *James Finlay & Co Ltd v NV Kwik Hoo Tong Handel Maatschappij* [1929] 1 K.B. 400, the sellers under a c.i.f. contract tendered to the buyers a bill of lading which stated, not fraudulently but contrary to the fact, that shipment had taken place in the contract month. In the belief that the bill of lading was correctly dated, he buyers paid the contract price. Subsequently the buyers learned that the goods had not been shipped during the contract month. It was held by the Court of Appeal, affirming the judgment of Wright J. ([1928] 2 K.B. 604), that the buyers were entitled to recover damages for the breach by the sellers of their obligation to deliver a bill of lading correctly stating the date of shipment and that the measure of such damages was the difference between the market price and the contract price of the goods. Now it is true that in *Finlay's* case the buyers were misled by a wrongly-dated bill of lading and accepted the shipment on the basis that the bill of lading was correctly dated. In the present case it cannot be said that the buyers were misled into believing that the documents tendered were in accordance with the contract, for indeed at the very time when the documents were tendered the buyers were maintaining that they were not in accordance with the contract. But by accepting the documents while reserving their rights they buyers must be taken to have reserved their right to take the point that the documents were not in accordance with the contract and to recover damages on that basis. In my view, the decision in *Finlay's* case lays down a general rule as to the measure of damages in cases there the sellers have broken a condition of the contract by failing to tender proper documents and the buyers, not having rescinded, are entitled to recover damages for the breach. The reasons why the buyers have not rescinded are immaterial. Whether they have been misled or have elected not to rescind with full knowledge of the facts the position is the same, namely, that if they had rescinded, they would not have had to pay a price (*viz.* the contract price) in excess of the market price of the goods at the time of the breach.

It remains to consider the case of *Taylor and Sons Ltd v Bank of Athens*, *sup.* In that case Taylor's bought from the bank locust beans under a contract which provided that the beans should be shipped and the bills of lading dated in July and/or August, 1919. Relying on an assertion of the sellers that the bills of lading were dated Aug. 31, 1919, the buyers accepted the documents tendered, paid the price and received the goods. Subsequently the buyers discovered they had been signed in September, and that shipment had not taken place during the contract months. The buyers went to arbitration but, perhaps unfortunately, their claim for damages as formulated in the arbitration was not based on a breach of contract in tendering a bill of lading bearing the wrong date. The breach of contract complained of was a failure to ship the goods within the proper period. For that breach of contract the measure of damages was held by McCardie J. to be the difference at he material time between the market price of beans shipped in August and the market price of beans shipped in September. That was a nominal sum only. I think it is fair to say that the decision in *Taylor's* case has been generally accepted as correctly stating the measure of damages for the particular breach complained of in that case. It is clear, however, from the decisions of Wright J. and of the Court of Appeal in the *James Finlay* case that *Taylor's* case is not to be taken as laying down the measure of damages where the breach complained of is a failure to tender correct shipping documents. That is the breach complained of in this case and, in my view, the measure of damages in this case is that which I have stated. . . .

For these reasons, I am of the opinion that the measure of damages in this case is the difference between the contract price of the goods and the market price of similar goods at the time when the documents were tendered. . . .

Notes

7–048   It is now clear from *Procter & Gamble v Becher*, below, that this reasoning applies
only where the acceptance is similarly qualified.

The passage above suggests that the principles in *Panchaud* probably only
prevent the buyer from rejecting the goods, or claiming *Kwei Tek* damages. Even
where a buyer has accepted the documents, he is still in principle entitled to
pursue his remedy for ordinary contractual damages: Sale of Goods Act, s.11(2),
i.e. he can still treat the breach as a breach of warranty).[42] This assumes, however,
that the inference from the conduct in *Panchaud* is that the buyers must be taken
to have accepted the documents knowing of the late shipment. If *Panchaud* is
instead based upon some wider principle of equity, it may operate to prevent the
buyers claiming even ordinary contractual damages, if his conduct rendered it
inequitable for him to do so.

From the three very different judgments in *Panchaud* it is not obvious what the
basis of the decision is. Lord Denning M.R.'s estoppel reasoning looks unsound
since the sellers do not appear to have relied in any way on the buyers' conduct
in taking up the documents. It may be, then, that a better analysis is simply that
the conduct of the buyers led to the implication that they had accepted the
documents and the goods. Cross L.J.'s view at least is consistent with this
interpretation, and see further Benjamin, *Sale of Goods* (5th ed., 1997), para. 19–139.
In *B.P. Exploration Co (Libya) Ltd v Hunt (No. 2)* [1979] 1 W.L.R. 783 at 810–811,
Robert Goff J. took the view that *Panchaud* had nothing to do with estoppel:

> "The [estoppel] principle, therefore, presupposes three things: (1) a legal rela-
> tionship between the parties (2) a representation, express or implied, by one
> party that he will not enforce his strict rights against the other and (3) reliance
> by the representee (whether by action or by omission to act) on the representa-
> tion, which renders it inequitable, in all the circumstances, for the representor
> to enforce his strict rights, or at least to do so until the representee is restored
> to his former position. Now I do not understand the *Panchaud* case to fall within
> that principle. The case was concerned with a c.i.f. contract of sale of goods and
> the question which arose for decision was whether the buyer, who had received
> a tender of documents including a bill of lading which inaccurately stated the
> goods to have been shipped within the contract period, and a certificate of
> quality which accurately stated that they had been shipped late, and who
> (having failed to observe the late date in the certificate of quality) took up the
> documents without question, could thereafter reject the goods on the ground
> that they were shipped late. The Court of Appeal, reversing Roskill J., held that
> the buyer could not do so. Now it is well established in contracts for the sale of
> goods that, if a buyer accepts the goods (within the meaning of that expression
> as used in the Sale of Goods Act 1893), he cannot thereafter reject them he has
> a choice, and if he chooses to accept the goods his decision is final. In a c.i.f.
> contract of sale, he has two opportunities of rejection: a right to reject the
> documents, and a right to reject the goods, if they are not in accordance with
> the contract. All that the *Panchaud* case decided was that if, in a c.i.f. contract,
> the documents show that the goods were shipped late, and the buyer never-
> theless accepts the documents, then, even if he has failed to notice the late
> shipment date when he took up the documents, he will be precluded from
> thereafter rejecting the goods for that reason. The decision stems from the need
> for finality in commercial transactions, as does the doctrine of acceptance in

---

[42] A damages claim was not at issue in *Panchaud Frères* itself; the issue was whether the
buyers could justify their rejection of the goods. In *Kwei Tek* ordinary contractual damages
would have been small, and in *Kleinjan* nominal, but this need not always be the case; for
example, if the goods have to arrive in time to take advantage of a volatile market, such as
the Christmas trade, late shipment of itself may cause substantial loss.

contracts for the sale of goods, an analogy relied on by Lord Denning M.R. in his judgment in the *Panchaud* case [1970] 1 Lloyd's Rep. 53 at 57. I do not read the *Panchaud* case as arising from the principle in *Hughes v Metropolitan Rly Co* because the *Panchaud* case does not depend in any way on the representee having relied on any representation by the buyer; indeed, on the facts of the *Panchaud* case itself, the goods were (as is usually the case) on the high seas at the time when the documents were taken up by the buyer."

However, in *Procter & Gamble Philippine Manufacturing Corporation v Peter Cre-* **7–049** *mer GmbH & Co (The Manila)* [1988] 3 All E.R. 843,[43] Hirst J. preferred an estoppel explanation, on the grounds that it was supported by authority, and distinguished *Panchaud* on the grounds that in the case before him the survey report, tendered along with the shipping documents, were equivocal as to when shipment actually occurred, and that the facts stated in it were not therefore sufficient to cast doubt on the bill of lading date.

Clearly, whatever the basis of *Panchaud*, there is no reason to apply it unless the statements in the other documents clearly cast doubt on the accuracy of the bill of lading statements, since only then can the buyer be taken to have made an unequivocal representation by taking up the documents.[44]

In *Panchaud*, dealings with the documents restricted the grounds upon which the buyers could later reject the goods. In *Kwei Tek*, dealings with the goods, with full knowledge of the late shipment, did not prevent the buyers later raising the issue of the shipment date on the documents. However, subsequent dealings involving the goods can lead to inferences about the documents. In *Cerealmangimi SpA v Alfred C Toepfer (The Eurometal)* [1981] 3 All E.R. 533 the documents were tendered late, and the buyer was clearly entitled to reject them on these grounds. The goods themselves were also clearly defective, but the buyer asked for the goods to be fumigated, and from this conduct, relating to the goods, could be inferred an acceptance of both documents and goods. *Kwei Tek Chao* was distinguished.

(c) What Right to Reject has Been Lost?

PROCTER & GAMBLE PHILIPPINE MANUFACTURING CORPORATION v BECHER GmbH

Court of Appeal. [1988] 2 Lloyd's Rep. 21

Facts:

There were two contracts, numbered 83/701 and 83/703 for the sale c.i.f. **7–050** of a quantity of Philippine copra expellers, the contract incorporating the G.A.F.T.A. Form 100, clause 6 of which is headed "Period of shipment", and states:

---

[43] Noted by Cooper, [1989] L.M.C.L.Q. 397.

[44] The necessity for an unequivocal representation was also emphasised by the Court of Appeal in *Glencore Grain Rotterdam BV v Lebanese Organisation for International Commerce (LORICO)* [1997] 2 Lloyd's Rep. 386, where *Panchaud* was explained as an "application of the common law rule of acceptance, now established in s.35 of the Sale of Goods Act, in the comparatively limited circumstances of a case where a c.i.f. buyer accepts documents but rejects or purports to reject the goods." The existence of doctrines of waiver and estoppel by conduct were also recognised, but the Court of Appeal did not regard *Panchaud* as establishing any new doctrine. For either waiver or estoppel to operate, "the facts must justify a finding that there was an unequivocal representation made by one party, by conduct or otherwise, which was acted upon by the other."

"As per bill(s) of lading dated or to be dated . . . the bill(s) of lading to be dated when the goods are actually on board. Date of the bill(s) of lading shall be accepted as proof of date of shipment in the absence of evidence to the contrary . . . "

The original shipment period was extended for both contracts to include January 1984, but in the case of the contract considered in the appeal (83/703), later varied to allow the sellers the option of February shipment subject to a 3.5% price allowance.

The bills of lading were dated 31st January 1984, although loading was not completed until 10th February. The buyers accepted and paid against the documents, and later resold the goods without prejudice "in order to avoid further costs and expenses". Because the market had fallen, however, they obtained only 57% of the contract price. They claimed as damages from the sellers the difference between the contract price and the price obtained on the resale, although it was accepted that there was no great difference in the value of January and February goods. In effect, the buyers were attempting to shift the market fall back on to the sellers.

[*Note that this case arose out of the same shipment on the* Manila, *but between different parties and turning on a different set of facts, as* Procter & Gamble Philippine Manufacturing Corp v Peter Cremer GmbH & Co (The Manila) [1988] 3 All E.R. 843, above.]

Held:
The Court of Appeal unanimously held that the buyers were not entitled to damages on the basis claimed, and could not thereby shift the market loss back on to the sellers. The sellers admitted liability to a 3.5% price reduction in any event, on the basis of the express terms of the contract, as varied.

Under contract No. 83/701 (which had not been similarly varied to allow February shipment) shipment (during February) *was* made outside the contract period. This was not subject to the appeal, since it fell within already established principles.

7–051   KERR L.J.: Many commercial cases turn on the dates of bills of lading. Normally they have three common features. The date shown is the last day of a calendar month. This is also the last day of the contractual shipment period. But the cargo was in fact only loaded a few days later, during the following month. Presumably some cargoes are really loaded in full on the last day of a month and covered by a correctly dated bill of lading. But one never hears of such cases in the Courts. When we see a bill of lading dated on the last day of a month we know that it was ante-dated to serve a clear-cut, though dishonest, commercial purpose: the pretence that the goods were in fact put on board before the expiry of the contractual shipment period. The reason lies in the decision of the House of Lords in *Bowes v Shand* (1877) App. Cas. 455 (at pp. 468, 475 and 480) that the shipment period stipulated in a c.i.f. contract forms part of the description of the goods. It follows that late shipment involves a breach of condition which gives rise to a right of rejection.

In times of falling prices this rule, and its attempted avoidance by the presentation of misdated bills of lading, have given rise to innumerable disputes against the background of commodity dealings in "futures". There is usually no difference whatever between goods loaded at the end of January instead of the beginning of February. The goods are the same. But this is not a trade in goods but in contracts for the shipment of goods. A January contract may be far more valuable than one for shipment in February. More important, on a plunging market the inability to present a bill of lading evidencing shipment within the contract period can have very serious financial consequences: the difference between the right to demand payment of the contract price on the one hand, and having to deal with "spot" goods of far lesser value, possibly involving considerable expenses in their disposal, on the other hand.

The misdated bill of lading in the present case probably had its origin in commercial considerations of this nature. It would be unrealistic to attribute a misdated bill of lading at the end of a calendar month to a purely clerical error. But there is nothing to show that in this case the plaintiff sellers had any part in the misdating, or even knowledge of it. The originators may have been anywhere up a string of contracts before this bill of lading reached these sellers. This is not unusual, since proof of complicity on the part of the sellers under the contract in question is not an essential ingredient of the buyers' rights. The cases show that if the bill of lading against which payment is made had been wrongly dated within the contract period, for whatever reason, when the goods which it purported to cover had in fact only been shipped after its expiry, then the buyers' right of rejection based on *Bowes v Shand* remains *prima facie* unaffected. The unprecedented feature of the present case, however, is that although the bill of lading was falsely ante-dated, the shipment of the goods, albeit in the early part of the following month, still took place within the contract period agreed between these particular sellers and buyers. This raises a novel problem . . . Given the fact that the buyers paid the contract price against presentation of a bill of lading which had been falsely dated, as they would not have done if they had known this fact, what is the measure of damages to which they are entitled when the goods purportedly covered by this bill of lading were only shipped later, but still within the contract period?

[Kerr L.J. *stated the facts, set out clause 6 of GAFTA 100, and continued:*]

I have already mentioned that in *Bowes v Shand* (*sup*) the House of **7–052** Lords held that a stipulation in a c.i.f. contract that the goods be shipped during a particular period forms part of the description of the goods and is accordingly in the nature of a condition. In the present context there then followed a line of three important cases in which the measure of damages for breach of this condition was considered against the background of bills of lading which had been wrongly ante-dated within the contract period. In *Taylor & Sons Ltd v Bank of Athens* (1922) 10 Ll. L. Rep. 88; (1922) 27 Com. Cas. 142 the buyers did not rely on the misdating of the bill of lading as in itself constituting a breach. Having paid against documents—including a wrongly ante-dated bill of lading—without being aware of any breach, the buyers only claimed damages for late shipment when they subsequently discovered that the goods had been shipped about six days out of time, during the following month. The arbitrators held that the buyers were only entitled to nominal damages, since the late shipment made no difference to the value of the goods. This was upheld by McCardie J. on the ground that, having accepted the documents and the goods, the buyers were no longer entitled to treat the breach as a breach of condition, but only as a breach of warranty. The Judge applied the provisions which are now to be found in s.53 of the Sale of Goods Act 1979:

[KERR L.J. *set out the section—see Appendix A, and para. 7–060, below, and continued:*]

In the subsequent cases, however, the buyers relied upon the presentation of a misdated bill of lading as a breach which was separate from, and additional to, the breach of shipping the goods out of time. In that situation, it was held in *James Finlay & Co Ltd v MV Kwik Hoo Tong Handel, Maatschappij* (1928) 31 Ll. L. Rep. 220; [1928] 2 K.B. 604 by Wright J. and affirmed by Scrutton, Greer and Sankey L.JJ. in this Court in (1928) 32 Ll. L. Rep. 245: [1929] 1 K.B. 400 that the buyers were entitled to substantial damages based—broadly speaking—on the difference between the contract price and the market price of the goods realised after their arrival. Since *James Finlay* is the leading and unchallenged case in this field, and since the issue is whether or not its reasoning applies equally in the present case, it is necessary to cite some of the important passages from the judgments.

7–053   Wright J. distinguished *Taylor v Bank of Athens* (*sup*) on the ground that the point concerning the misdated bill of lading had not been taken and said at pp. 225 *et seq.* and 611 *et seq.*:

"... In any case the buyer is, I think, entitled to rely on the accuracy of the bill of lading date, and to regard the seller as impliedly guaranteeing its accuracy, unless there are express terms of the contract to the contrary... The buyer under such a contract as those in question has the right to reject the tender of documents and refuse to pay the cash or accept the draft, if the shipment is not made in the contract month. The effect of misdating the bill of lading is to deprive them of that right by rendering its exercise impossible, if he relies, as in practice he generally must rely, and in law is entitled to rely, on the accuracy of the bill of lading date. He takes delivery of the goods and pays for them, because on the face of the bill of lading he is bound to do so under the contract, whereas if the bill of lading showed because it was a true document that the sellers could not enforce the contract, because the shipment was out of date, the buyer could and would refuse the tender and could obtain the same goods at their market price, which I assume to be lower than the contract price, that is, at a great saving to himself . . . In such a case the difference between the market price and the contract price, the latter being higher than the former, represents, in my judgment, the measure of damages in favour of the buyer for breach by the seller of his obligation to deliver a correct bill of lading. The obligation is in its nature, I think, a condition, and if the breach were known in time the buyer could reject the documents; but from its very nature the breach is often only ascertainable when it is too late to reject the documents or treat the contract as repudiated, and no remedy is possible to the buyer except a claim for damages, as on the footing of a breach of warranty . . . "

He then referred to s.53 of the Sale of Goods Act and went on: **7–054**

"In the present case it seems to me clear that the parties must have contemplated that the buyers would, by taking up the documents and accepting the goods on the faith that they were bound to do so, pay the higher contract price instead of the lower market price, and lose their right to reject and suffer damage accordingly."

That decision and reasoning were unanimously affirmed on appeal to this Court. Referring to the judgment of Wright J., Scrutton L.J. said at pp. 249 and 409:

" . . . As he said, if the bill of lading had shown that the shipment was in October, the tender would have been rejected by Finlay & Co, who would have kept in their pocket the price they paid under the contract, and the loss by the fall in the market would properly have fallen on the Dutch firm, because of their breach of contract in presenting an incorrect bill of lading. I agree with that view."

Greer L.J. agreed, and said at pp. 252 and 412:

" . . . I am not at present prepared to say what I would hold if the question were whether a buyer is entitled to reject a cargo of goods where the bill of lading mentioned, say, the 5th of the month whereas in fact the goods were loaded on the 6th; but I am clearly of opinion that a buyer would be entitled to reject the documents under a contract of this kind which called for September goods and the bill of lading stated, contrary to the fact, that the goods were shipped in September. That is as far as it is necessary to go in this case . . .

"What has to be considered is the plaintiffs' position as regards money if the particular term of the agreement had been performed, and they are to be put, so far as money is concerned, in that same position by damages for breach of that term of the contract. The Judge has taken the view that the shippers promised to state truly in the bill of lading the date of shipment, and the respondents say that if that had been done they would have been entitled to reject the goods. By the breach of contract in sending forward a bill of lading containing a false statement, the plaintiffs say they have been deprived of that right. I suggested to the appellants that if their promise to tender a correctly dated bill of lading had been in a separate contract their contention would have been unarguable. It seems to me to make no difference that the term is in the same contract which contains the obligation to ship the sugar in September. I agree . . . that the result of that is to give the plaintiffs in this case exactly the same damages as they would have received if they had successfully brought an action for fraudulent misrepresentation, but there may well be terms in a contract which, if broken, put the party complaining of the breach in the same position as if he claimed damages for false representation . . . "

7–055   He then distinguished *Taylor v Bank of Athens* in the same way as Wright J. had done on the ground that no separate breach in relation to the bill of lading date had been raised. Sankey L.J. also agreed and said at pp. 254 and 416:

" . . . A c.i.f. contract is a contract for the sale of goods, but, as everyone knows, there are certain specific documents which are part of that contract, one of them being a bill of lading, as to which there is an implied obligation that it shall be dated accurately.
   " . . . No fraud is imputed to the appellants, and I assume that they are blameless in the matter; but it is admitted that they broke one of the fundamental conditions of the contract—namely, the condition or obligation to give an accurately dated bill of lading. As a result the respondents took the sugar, but they did not get what the defendants had contracted to give them. They got something different—namely, an October instead of a September shipment . . . I think the measure of damages in a case like this is the difference between what the buyers have in fact paid to the sellers and the market price of the goods. This is not in conflict with any of the earlier cases. In *Taylor v Bank of Athens* the cause of action was entirely different from that in the present case. Here the cause of action is for not having given what the contract gave a right to—namely, an accurately dated bill of lading . . . "

The decision in *James Finlay* was followed and applied by Devlin J. (as he then was) in *Kwei Tek Chao v British Traders and Shippers Ltd* [1954] 1 Lloyd's Rep. 16; [1954] 2 Q.B. 459. He analysed the position by explaining (at pp. 48 and 480) that there were two rights to reject:

"a right to reject documents, and a right to reject goods, and the two things are quite distinct."

He took the decision in *James Finlay* a stage further by holding that the buyers' entitlement to substantial damages remained intact even though they had discovered the true facts—the misdating of the bill of lading and the late shipment—before the goods had arrived, because, having paid the price, they had no viable alternative but to deal with the goods in the best way possible in the circumstances. The buyers in the present case strongly relied on this aspect in support of their submissions. . . .

. . . The essence of Mr. Russell's argument in favour of the buyers was deceptively simple . . . His submissions were designed to demonstrate the importance of correctly dated bills of lading in the context of various aspects of c.i.f. contracts and contracts for the carriage of goods by sea. No one doubts these matters for one moment. The whole basis of the decision in *James Finlay* was that one of the sellers' obligations under a c.i.f. contract is to present a correctly dated bill of lading. This obligation has the character of a condition, in the sense that the buyer is entitled to reject a tender of documents which include an incorrectly dated bill of lading, and thus entitled to refuse to pay for the goods. On a falling market it is self-evident that buyers would have availed themselves of this right if they had known that the tendered bill of lading was misdated. As Scrutton L.J. said in *James Finlay* at pp. 249 and 409, the buyers would in that event have kept the price in their pocket. And in *James Finlay* and *Kwei Tek Chao* the buyers accordingly recovered full damages on this basis. No more need be said by way of introduction.

One then comes to the buyers' seductive submission on these lines. Mr Russell said that it followed that if the buyers had known in this case that the bill of lading had been misdated they would have rejected the documents, refused to pay the price and left the sellers to face the loss resulting from the fall in the market. As a statement of what would have happened if the buyers had known the true facts this is obviously true. But it does not provide the correct test in law. The issue is not what the buyers would have done if they had known the true facts. The first question is: what would have been the buyers' rights if the sellers had not committed the breach on which the buyers rely?

7–056

That this is the correct analysis of the issue is not only apparent from the passages cited from the judgments in *James Finlay*, but also as a matter of general principle. The object of an award of damages for breach of contract is to put the innocent party in the same position so far as money can do it as if the contract had not been broken. So put, the answer to the present problem becomes obvious. If there had been no breach, then the bill of lading under contract 83/703 would have been dated Feb. 6 or 10 instead of Jan. 31. In that event the buyers would have had no right to reject it or to refuse to pay for the goods. They would only have been entitled to the contractual allowance for shipment in February. In relation to contract 83/701 the position would have been different. A correctly dated bill of lading would have revealed the sellers' breach of condition in relation to the date of shipment, whereas an incorrect date concealed this breach. On that basis, following _James Finlay_, the buyers were rightly awarded full damages under contract 83/701. But the Board of Appeal was wrong in drawing no distinction in relation to contract 83/703 and awarding full damages in both cases. The incorrectly dated bill of lading tendered under the latter contract concealed no similar breach.

The correctness of this analysis is supported by two other general considerations.

First, as was pointed out by McCardie J. in _Taylor v Bank of Athens_, the position would of course be entirely different if the sellers had themselves been involved in the false dating of the bill of lading and could therefore have been sued in fraud. In that event the buyers would have recovered full damages because the measure of damages in claims for fraud is different. In cases of fraudulent misrepresentation the innocent party is entitled to be put in the same position as if the representation had not been made, not as if it had been true; see _Doyle v Olby (Ironmongers) Ltd_ [1969] 2 Q.B. 158 and _Saunders v Edwards_ [1987] 1 W.L.R. 1116 at p. 1121. In that event, therefore, the measure of damages would have assumed that no bill of lading had been presented at all and placed the buyers in the same position as if they had kept the price of the goods in their pocket. But there was no basis for any such claim in the present case, and we also heard no argument about the possible relevance of the Misrepresentation Act 1967. I therefore say no more about this.

7–057   The second aspect which one must bear in mind is that the buyers' apparent misfortune is no different in principle from other situations where an "innocent" party may be unaware in time that the other party has committed a breach of condition. When he subsequently discovers this he may be compelled to treat it as no more than a breach of warranty. The damages recoverable for a breach of warranty may well turn out to be greatly different from what would have been the "innocent" party's position if he had known of the breach of condition in time to be able to rescind the contract. In financial terms the difference is between compensation for a breach of contract and putting the innocent party in the same position as if he had never entered into the contract at all. _Taylor v Bank of Athens_ provides a good illustration in a similar context. Unfortunately for the buyers, no reliance was placed on the breach involved in the tender of a wrongly dated bill of lading, as subsequently in _James Finlay_. The shipment had been made out of time on a falling market, and if the buyers had been aware of this they would, of course, have refused to pay against the documents. But the sellers were equally innocent, and by the time the truth came out the buyers were left only with the measure of damages under s.53(2). But no loss connected with the fall in the market flowed from the fact that the shipment was a few days late; nor any other loss. So the buyers were left with nominal damages only.

Strictly, as both Counsel agreed, if Leggatt J. had not ordered the repayment of 3 1/2 per cent of the price as damages, his order should have included an award of nominal damages. . . .

. . . In *Kleinjan & Holst NV Rotterdam v Bremer Handelsgesellschaft mbH Hamburg* [1972] 2 Lloyd's Rep. 11 the buyers objected to a notice of appropriation which named a ship different from the one on which the goods had in fact been loaded. They paid against presentation of documents, but only under a reserve of their rights. So they were only entitled to damages for breach of warranty under s.53(2). On the special facts of the case these were assessed by Cooke J. as:

" . . . the difference between the contract price of the goods and the market price of similar goods at the time when the documents were tendered . . . "

and on its facts the outcome of the case is not open to challenge. But he also said the following in general terms at p. 22:

"In my view, the decision *Finlay's* case lays down a general rule as to the measure of damages in cases where the sellers have broken a condition of the contract by failing to tender proper documents and the buyers, not having rescinded, are entitled to recover damages for the breach. The reasons why the buyers have not rescinded are immaterial. Whether they have been misled or have elected not to rescind with full knowledge of the facts the position is the same, namely, that if they had rescinded, they would not have had to pay a price (*viz.* the contract price) in excess of the market price of the goods at the time of the breach."

As was pointed out by Saville J. in *Vargas Pena Apezteguia Y Cia SAIC v Peter Cremer GmbH* [1987] 1 Lloyd's Rep. 394, that statement is too wide. The decision in *James Finlay* is not to be treated as laying down any general rule that a breach in relation to the documents presented under a c.i.f. contract automatically gives rise to damages based on the difference between contract and market prices. The true position can, in my view, be summarised as follows, apart from actions based on misrepresentation: **7–058**

1. The presentation of the documents by sellers under a c.i.f. contract implies a guarantee or warranty—or whatever term one chooses to use—in the nature of a condition that the contents of the documents are true in all material respects. In relation to the dates of bills of lading this is an express obligation under clause 6 of GAFTA 100. But the judgments in *James Finlay* show that the same result follows by implication from the mere act of tendering the documents under the contract.

2. If the contents of the documents are untrue in any material respect, then the buyers can reject them and refuse to pay the price. No

doubt, as the Judge in the present case mentioned in passing, although the point had not been argued, it may then be open to the sellers to make a second correct tender if they can. But in practice this will not often by possible.

3. Ignoring all questions of waiver, which must depend upon the circumstances, if the buyers pay against documents which are untrue in any material respect, then the next question is whether they would have been entitled to reject the documents if their contents had been correct. If they could have done so, because there would then still have been some other material breach of condition of the contract, as in *James Finlay*; *Kwei Tek Chao* and *The Kastellon* [1978] 2 Lloyd's Rep. 203; [1979] 1 K.B. 400 in relation to the date of shipment, then—but only then—will the buyers be entitled to the full measure of damages, *i.e.*, generally the difference between the contract and market prices. The reason is that in that event this would be:

> " . . . the estimated loss directly and naturally resulting, in the ordinary course of events . . . "

from the sellers' breach in presenting documents which contained untrue material statements. On that basis s.53(2) of the Sale of Goods Act would lead to this result. But not if the incorrect document did not conceal any breach on the part of the sellers.

However, there remains one additional aspect. The only discussion of these problems of which counsel were aware is to be found in paras. 1763 to 1771 of Benjamin's *Sale of Goods*, 3rd ed. (1987),[45] which I found of great assistance. The instant situation is considered in para. 1770 under the heading "Defects in the documents alone". This discusses situations:

> " . . . where the goods were in all respects in accordance with the contract but the seller tendered, for example, a certificate of insurance when he should have tendered a policy, or where the goods were in fact shipped within the shipment period but the bill of lading was not 'genuine', e.g., because it bore a false date of shipment."

The text proceeds, in line with the views expressed above:

> "If the buyer accepts documents in such a case (even in ignorance of his right to reject them) he should have no right to substantial damages; such damages cannot be awarded . . . to compensate the buyer for loss of his right to reject the goods, for in the situation now under discussion he never had any such right . . . "

---

[45] Now Benjamin, *Sale of Goods* (5th ed., 1997), para. 19–176.

I agree. However, it does not necessarily follow that in such a situation the buyers will never be able to recover substantial damages for the sellers' breach in presenting documents whose contents were incorrect in some material respect. For instance, a falsely dated bill of lading becomes effectively unmerchantable, in the sense of being non-negotiable (or, more accurately, non-transferable) once its true date is known. Its presentation by the sellers was a breach of contract even if the goods were in fact shipped during the contractual shipment period, as in the present case. In such circumstances it may well be possible for the buyers to show that they suffered loss as the result of this breach. Thus, they may have found themselves "locked in" on a falling market by holding a non-transferable bill of lading, when they might otherwise have been able to sell the goods afloat, albeit already at substantially less than their original contract price. Alternatively, they might be able to show that if the bill of lading had been correctly dated they could have used it to fulfil a previously concluded sub-sale covered by a notice of appropriation with which they were now unable to comply.

NICHOLLS L.J.: The sole question raised by this appeal concerns the measure of damages payable by the sellers in respect of their admitted breach of contract. In breach of cl. 6 of the GAFTA 100 form of contract, which was the form used by the parties, the bill of lading tendered to the buyers and accepted by them did not state correctly the date when the goods were actually on board. The bill of lading stated the date of shipment in the Philippines as Jan. 31, 1984. In fact the goods were not shipped until either Feb. 6 or 10, 1984. Shipment on those dates, and this is the feature of crucial importance in this case, was within the extended shipment period, expiring on Feb. 29, 1984, which had been agreed between the parties (subject to certain allowances). Other salient facts include the following. The relevant contract, dated Oct. 7, 1983 and numbered 83/703, was for the sale of 500 tonnes of Philippine copra expeller cake at the price of US $199.50 per tonne. Payment of 98 per cent of the full price was made by the buyers in April, 1984, on presentation of the bill of lading and other shipping documents. The m.v. *Manila* arrived in Rotterdam on July 8, 1984, and the goods were sold by the buyers one week later, at the greatly reduced price of US $ 113 per tonne.

7–059

Although the sole question on this appeal concerns damages, it is necessary to note at once, because this is at the heart of the arguments advanced on behalf of the buyers, that a right to damages is not the only remedy which a buyer has in respect of a misdated bill of lading. Before us it was common ground that the buyers in the present case were entitled to reject the bill of lading when it was tendered. They were entitled to reject the bill of lading because it misstated the date of shipment. They were entitled to reject the bill for this reason, even though the goods had been shipped within the shipment period. If the buyers had exercised that right then, unless the sellers had been able to re-tender another, correct bill of lading, that would have been the end of the matter:

the buyers would have kept the price, and they would not have suffered the loss they did by reason of the fall in the market.

That remedy, of rejection of the shipping documents when tendered, was one of the remedies available in respect of the sellers' breach of cl. 6. In the event the buyers were unable to have recourse to that remedy, because they did not know of the inaccuracy in the bill of lading when it was tendered. So, perforce, the buyers' remedy in respect of the sellers' breach of cl. 6 was confined to a right to recover damages.

7–060　　It is at this point, as it seems to me, that some confusion has crept into the buyers' case. It is trite law that the basic, general principle applicable in awarding damages for breach of contract is that the innocent party is to be placed, so far as money can do this, in the same position as he would have been in if the contract had been performed. If in the circumstances the breach caused no financial loss, only nominal damages are recoverable by the innocent party. This, on principle, will be so even if the breach in respect of which damages are being claimed is a breach of a condition which would have enabled the innocent party to reject the documents or goods altogether, had he known of the existence of the breach before, by accepting the documents or goods, it became too late for him to exercise the remedy of rejection. In such a case the remedy of rejection may afford an innocent party a much more valuable form of relief. But when that remedy ceases to be available, and the innocent party is confined to his remedy in damages, he is not entitled to assess his damages by reference to what his financial position would have been if the primary remedy of rejection had been exercised by him. For better or worse, his claim, as a claim for damages, is then confined to making good the loss sustained by him by reason of the breach of the contract. Quantifying that loss requires, in general, a comparison to be made between the innocent party's actual financial position and what his financial position would have been had the contract been duly performed.

This accords with the approach adopted in s.53(1) and (2) of the Sale of Goods Act, 1979:

> "(1) Where there is a breach of warranty by the seller, or where the buyer elects (or is compelled) to treat any breach of a condition on the part of the seller as a breach of warranty, the buyer is not by reason only of such breach of warranty entitled to reject the goods; but he may—
>
> (a) set up against the seller the breach of warranty in diminution or extinction of the price, or
> (b) maintain an action against the seller for damages for the breach of warranty.
>
> (2) The measure of damages for breach of warranty is the estimated loss directly and naturally resulting, in the ordinary course of events, from the breach of warranty."

There is no suggestion in that section that the measure of the damages recoverable for breach of warranty in a case where there has been a breach of condition which the buyer has been compelled to treat as a warranty is any different from the measure of the damages recoverable in any other case of breach of warranty.

I do not think that the existence of the disparity in the efficacy of the two remedies, rejection and damages, in a case where the breach causes little or no financial loss to a buyer, casts doubt on the correctness of this analysis of the measure of the damages recoverable for such a breach. The disparity arises from the availability of the right of rejection in such a case, namely, even where the breach of condition has caused little or no financial damage to the innocent party. If there is an anomaly here, it lies in the availability of the remedy of rejection in such a case, not in the measure of damages applicable in such a case.

With those principles regarding damages in mind, it is to be observed that, in the present case, if cl. 6 had been duly performed by the sellers, the buyers would have had no right to reject the shipping documents when tendered. This is in marked contrast with the position in *James Finlay & Co Ltd v MV Kwik Hoo Tong Handel Maatschappij* (1928) 31 Ll.L. Rep. 220; [1928] 2 K.B. 604; (1928) 32 Ll.L. Rep. 245; [1929] 1 K.B. 400, where if the bill of lading had stated the date of shipment correctly, the buyers would have been entitled to refuse to accept the shipping documents. Likewise in *Kwei Tek Chao v British Traders and Shippers Ltd* [1954] 1 Lloyd's Rep. 16; [1954] 2 Q.B. 459. To the extent that the general rule enunciated in *Kleinjan & Holst NV Rotterdam v Bremer Handelsgesellschaft GmbH Hamburg* [1972] 2 Lloyd's Rep. 11 at p. 22 is inconsistent with this approach, I agree with the observations made on that case by Mr Justice Saville in *Vargas Pena Apezteguia Y Cia SAIC v Peter Cremer GmbH* [1987] 1 Lloyd's Rep. 394 at p. 399.

As I see it, this is the short and complete answer to the buyers' **7–061** contention that damages in respect of the tender of the misdated bill of lading are to be assessed on the footing that the buyers were thereby wrongfully deprived of a right to reject the documents and the goods. They did not lose that right by reason of the breach. Had there been no breach of cl. 6 the buyers would have had no right to reject the bill of lading or the goods. What the buyers lost, in the event, was the opportunity to exercise one of the remedies (rejection) afforded by the law in respect of the breach. They lost the opportunity to exercise that remedy, not because of the breach of cl. 6, but because they did not know of the existence of the breach at the time. But, as I have sought to indicate, having lost the opportunity to exercise the remedy of rejection in respect of the breach, thenceforth the buyers' remedy in respect of the breach was confined to recovering the actual financial loss, if any, suffered by them by reason of the breach.

Mr Russell presented the buyers' case in several further ways which were superficially different but essentially the same. They all founder on the same point. In particular, it was submitted, first, that since the tender of the bill of lading was a bad tender, the comparison to be made is between the financial position of the buyers (a) having accepted the bad tender and (b) having rejected the bad tender. I cannot accept this formulation. The comparison is between the financial position of the buyers in the events which happened (*viz.* having accepted the bad tender) and what their financial position would have been if the bill of lading had stated accurately the date of shipment (*viz.* having accepted a good tender).

If that comparison is made, the extent of the loss of the buyers was that, unknown to themselves, they had been given an unmerchantable bill of lading. As to that, I do not doubt that there may be cases where a buyer suffers loss by payment of the price against a bill of lading which was unmerchantable because it misstated the date of shipment even though the actual date of shipment was within the contract period. Such a buyer might, by reason of the unmerchantability of the bill, be unable to sell the goods, or complete a prior sale of the goods, whilst the goods were still afloat. In such a case the buyers' *prima facie* measure of damages would be the difference between the market value of the goods when he ought to have been able to deal with them (*viz.* when the bill of lading was tendered and accepted) and the market value of the goods when he became able to deal with them (*viz.* when the goods were delivered). In the present case the impact of cl. 27 would also have to be considered with regard to any claim for loss of profit on sub-sales. I do not pursue these points, however, because no claim under any of these heads was advanced in this case before such a claim emerged, as an alternative claim, in the course of the argument of this appeal. Neither before the arbitrators nor before the judge did the buyers claim that pending the arrival of the cargo in Rotterdam and its delivery to the buyers they had suffered loss by reason only of the bill of lading being unmerchantable because of the inaccuracy in it. What was claimed was the difference between the price paid by the buyers on tender of shipping documents in April (plus additional shipping costs also paid by the buyers) less the proceeds of sale of the goods when sold by the buyers shortly after delivery in July. . . .

Putting aside, therefore, any claim for damages based solely on the unmerchantability of the bill, if the proper comparison is made, between the buyers' financial position in the events which happened and what their financial position would have been if the bill of lading had stated the actual date of shipment, the answer is plain: the buyers suffered no financial loss. They paid the contract price and they received goods which conformed to the contract in all respects, including as to date of shipment. Hence they are entitled to no damages (save only that, having paid 98 per cent of the price, with no deduction of the agreed allowances for a shipment made in February, the buyers are entitled to damages to the extent of the over-payment). . . .

CROOM-JOHNSON L.J.: I have read in draft both the judgments of Kerr   **7–062**
L.J. and Nicholls L.J. and I agree with them.

Note
Note that *Kleinjan* (above) is expressly limited to the situation where the buyers,
knowing the truth, accept the documents reserving their rights. In the absence of
such a reservation, *Kwei Tek* damages would not be available.

Have the buyers lost a right to reject?
It is clear from the passages cited from *James Finlay*, both in *Procter & Gamble* and
in *Kwei Tek*, that the damages in that case were for the seller's breach in tendering
a misdated bill of lading.[46] For example, Sankey L.J. said:

" . . . No fraud is imputed to the appellants, and I assume that they are
blameless in the matter; but it is admitted that they broke one of the fundamental conditions of the contract—namely, the condition or obligation to give
an accurately dated bill of lading. . . . "

Similarly from the judgment in *Hindley & Co v East Indian Produce Ltd* (discussed
at para. 2–012, above):

" . . . The leading case on this topic is *James Finlay & Co v NV Kwik Hoo Tong
Handel Maatschappij*, in 1928 reported at first instance in (1928) 31 Ll.L. Rep. 220,
and in the Court of Appeal in (1928) 32 Ll.L. Rep. 245. At first instance Wright
J. put this matter as follows at p. 225:

'A c.i.f. contract, such as those in question, is a contract for the sale and
delivery of goods which must be shipped as called for by the contract
description, but it is also a sale of documented goods. The c.i.f. seller is bound
to procure and tender to the buyer shipping documents, that is, in particular,
a bill of lading, which will, among other things, show the date of shipment,
that being a condition of the contract. In my judgment it is an implied
condition of the contract that the bill of lading so to be tendered shall be a
true and accurate document and correctly state the date of shipment. Such a
condition seems to me to be absolutely necessary to give to the transaction
such business efficacy as the parties must have intended . . . '

'In the Court of Appeal the decision of Wright J. was affirmed that the buyers
were entitled to damages from the sellers on the ground that the bill of lading,
which appeared to be perfectly proper on its face, in fact misstated the date of
shipment. Scrutton L.J. said at p. 248, that it was at any rate

' . . . an essential part of the contract that genuine documents relating to
goods complying with the contract should be furnished to the buyer'."

Had that breach not been committed, and the correct shipment date appeared on
the face of the bill, the bill would not have conformed on its face, and would have
been rejected. The price would not have been paid, and the market loss never
suffered. Damages for that breach should therefore put the buyers into the same
position, and hence to be based on the difference between the price paid and the
current market price. This basis of calculation shifts the market fall back on to the
seller.

In *Procter & Gamble* there was a crucial departure from cases such as *James
Finlay*, or *Kwei Tek*. In both those cases, shipment had been made outside the

---

[46] *Taylor v Bank of Athens* was distinguished because there, damages were not claimed for
that particular breach.

contract period, but the date in the bill of lading had been backdated within the contract period. In *Procter & Gamble*, however, even if the bill of lading had been correctly dated the buyers could not have rejected it, because shipment was actually made during the contract period. *Procter & Gamble* could therefore have been decided simply on the basis that the buyers had lost no right to reject because of the backdating of the bill. Indeed, this appears to be one basis for the decision.

Even the points made in both the main judgments about the theoretical possibility of damages for rendering the bill of lading unmerchantable do not require that the buyer ever had the right to reject it, had he known the truth. The unmerchantability has been caused directly by the seller's breach in backdating the bill, not from the buyer's loss of any right to reject it.

7–063   However, the reasoning was made more complicated by the assumption in *Procter & Gamble* that the buyers could have rejected the bill of lading that was actually tendered, had they known the true shipment date at the time of the tender, on the grounds that the shipment date stated on the bill was not correct. It was on this basis that the buyers advanced their argument for damages for loss of the right to reject. Thus, for example, Kerr L.J. said:

> "The cases show that if the bill of lading against which payment is made had been wrongly dated within the contract period, for whatever reason, when the goods which it purported to cover had in fact only been shipped after its expiry, then the buyers' right of rejection ... remains *prima facie* unaffected."

Later on in his judgment he continued:

> "Mr Russell [for the buyers] said that ... if the buyers had known in this case that the bill of lading had been misdated they would have rejected the documents, refused to pay the price and left the sellers to face the loss resulting from the fall in the market. As a statement of what would have happened if the buyers had known the true facts this is obviously true."

In *Procter*, the buyers argued that the false dating was itself a breach of condition, and that had they known the true facts when the bill of lading was tendered they would have rejected it (because it was falsely dated). Kerr L.J. held that this was not the correct test, but that the real issue was: "what would have been the buyers' rights if the sellers had not committed the breach on which the buyers rely?" Of course, they would have had to accept the documents and the goods, because no breach of any kind would have been committed.

Kerr L.J. took the view that his test followed from *Taylor v Bank of Athens* itself, since had the buyers been aware of the sellers' breach of condition at the time of tender (late shipment) they would have rejected, but they were held entitled only to ordinary damages for breach of warranty.

Problems with this approach

7–064   There is a clear assumption in *Procter*, then, that a backdated bill can be rejected, even if shipment is actually made during the contract period. This proposition is not, however, supported by any authority.

No fraud has been established in any of these cases, and in *Procter* the backdated bills conformed on their face. In the light of *Gill & Duffus SA v Berger & Co Inc.* [1984] A.C. 382, above, it is at least arguable, therefore, that no right to reject had been lost by the buyers, since they would have been unable to reject the documents, even if they had known the truth. This depends on the precise *ratio* of *Gill & Duffus*, considered earlier in this chapter. On a wide interpretation of the case, however, there are problems reconciling *Gill & Duffus* with the reasoning of Kerr L.J. in *Procter & Gamble*.

It may be that *James Finlay* does indeed stand for the proposition that presenting a falsely-dated bill is, without more, a breach of condition, and that in *Taylor* the buyers could have rejected if they had known the true facts in time. If so, then it is necessary to reconcile that position with *Gill & Duffus*. One possibility is one of the narrow rationes for *Gill & Duffus* suggested above, but for the purposes of the present discussion we will assume that the House of Lords there held that a c.i.f. buyer cannot reject a bill of lading which conforms on its face to the contractual requirements, even if the seller has shipped goods which do not so conform, unless fraud on the part of the seller can be proved.

It is true that the misrepresentation in *Gill & Duffus* was as to the quality and description of the goods, and not their shipment date. Treitel (see above at para. 7–027) suggests that a backdated bill is not a genuine bill of lading,[47] but it is difficult to see why a backdated bill should be treated differently from one which is incorrect in any other material particular. No doubt, if no goods are shipped at all, as in *Heskell v Continental Express*, discussed at para. 10–003, below or *Hindley & Co v East Indian Produce Ltd*, see above, there is a case for regarding the document tendered as non-genuine, although it looks like a bill of lading, but it is surely less convincing similarly to distinguish between a clean bill of lading issued for non-conforming goods, which appears to be covered by *Gill & Duffus*, and a backdated bill. Commenting on another case,[48] Lord Diplock said of the view "that a c.i.f. buyer is entitled to reject conforming shipping documents, if it should . . . turn out that the actual goods shipped under the conforming documents did not in fact conform to the contract", that if correct, it "would destroy the very roots of the system by which international trade, particularly in commodities, is enabled to be financed". It is difficult to see why this reasoning does not apply equally to backdated bills, which conform on their face.

Further, where payment is by confirmed irrevocable bankers' documentary credit, the House of Lords held, as part of the *ratio*, in *United City Merchants (Investments) Ltd v Royal Bank of Canada* [1983] A.C. 168 (see further chapter 10, below), that the confirming bank cannot reject a bill of lading merely because it is backdated. No doubt, the four contracts in a confirmed irrevocable credit are autonomous, and in principle the documentary requirements under the contract between seller and confirming bank can differ from those as between seller and buyer.[49] It may also be possible to justify a difference of requirements on the grounds that whereas banks deal only with documents, and are not expected to have any expertise relating to goods, buyers are clearly interested in the goods themselves.[50] Nevertheless, it is clearly inconvenient if the requirements as between seller and c.i.f. buyer differ from those as between seller and confirming bank.

Perhaps it should not be to readily assumed, then, that a c.i.f. buyer can reject an apparently conforming bill of lading merely because it is backdated.

An objection might be raised that whatever the true basis of *Panchaud Frères*, it must have depended on the buyers having the right to reject the documents tendered,[51] since otherwise nothing could have been inferred from their acceptance. The bill of lading conformed on its face in *Panchaud*, but the quality certificate did not, so the case can be explained as one where the documents did not, as a whole, conform on their face, and where the documents were inconsistent. If that is the correct explanation, however, it depends on the quality

---

[47] A distinction drawn again in "Damages for breach of a c.i.f. contract" [1988] L.M.C.L.Q. 457, essentially an extended note on *Procter & Gamble*, where the author cites *Re General Trading Co Ltd* (1911) 16 Com. Cas. 95.

[48] *Dean (Henry) & Sons (Sydney) Ltd v O'Day Pty Ltd* (1927) 39 C.L.R. 330.

[49] Indeed, the contract considered in *UCM* was probably unilateral; see the discussion at paras 8–047 *et seq.*, below.

[50] See the discussion at para. 10–002, below.

[51] Similarly in *Kleinjan*, but there the documents did not conform on their face.

certificate being a contractual document. The survey certificate in *Procter &
Gamble Philippine Manufacturing Corp v Peter Cremer GmbH & Co (The Manila)*
[1988] 3 All E.R. 843, above, by contrast, was not, but Hirst J. seemed to think that
Panchaud reasoning could apply, at least in principle (albeit that it did not apply
in fact—see further the discussion of the case above). If the argument advanced
here is correct, then the assumption that *Panchaud* could apply in a case such as
The Manila is not.

(5) CARRIER INDEMNITIES

7–065　　　Given the importance of sellers' tendering conforming documents, it should
come as no surprise that shippers sometimes persuade carriers to issue clean bills
of lading even where the goods are clearly defective, or there is some doubt about
whether they conform to contractual requirements or not.

It is generally unwise for carriers to issue clean bills for defective goods,
because they lay themselves open to actions by consignees and indorsees when
the goods are delivered (the basis of which are discussed in chapter 14, below).
On the other hand, if the goods are in apparent good order and condition, the
shipper is entitled to a clean bill of lading. If therefore there is doubt, it can most
safely be resolved by the issue of a clean bill of lading, subject to an indemnity
from the shipper should the receiver sue.

The problem in the following case is that there was no doubt; the goods were
clearly defective, and a clean bill of lading should not have been issued for
them.

BROWN JENKINSON & CO LTD v PERCY DALTON (LONDON) LTD

Court of Appeal. [1957] 2 Q.B. 621

7–066　　　The master (for the shipowners) was induced by the shippers, on the
promise that the shippers would indemnify the shipowners, to sign clean
bills of lading for a cargo of barrels of orange juice which were clearly
leaking. They were sued by the consignee, and claimed from the shipper
on the indemnity. The shipper, wholly unmeritoriously, resisted the claim
on the grounds that the indemnity was unenforceable as an illegal contract.

Held: (Lord Evershed M.R. dissenting)
The indemnity was unenforceable as an illegal contract, because it was a
fraud on the buyer.

7–067　　　MORRIS L.J.: On the facts as found, and indeed on the facts which are
not in dispute, the position was therefore that, at the request of the
defendants, the plaintiffs made a representation which they knew to be
false and which they intended should be relied upon by persons who
received the bill of lading, including any banker who might be concerned.
In these circumstances, all the elements of the tort of deceit were present.

Someone who could prove that he suffered damage by relying on the representation could sue for damages. I feel impelled to the conclusion that a promise to indemnify the plaintiffs against any loss resulting to them from making the representation is unenforceable. The claim cannot be put forward without basing it upon an unlawful transaction. The promise upon which the plaintiffs rely is in effect this: if you will make a false representation, which will deceive indorsees or bankers, we will indemnify you against any loss that may result to you. I cannot think that a court should lend its aid to enforce such a bargain.

The conclusion thus reached is one that may seem unfortunate for the plaintiffs, for I gain the impression that they did not pause to realize the significance and the implications of what they were asked to do. There was evidence that the practice of giving indemnities upon the issuing of clean bills of lading is not uncommon. That cannot in any way alter the analysis of the present transaction, but it may help to explain how the plaintiffs came to accede to the defendants' request. There may perhaps be some circumstances in which indemnities can properly be given. Thus if a shipowner thinks he has detected some faulty condition in regard to goods to be taken on board, he may be assured by the shipper that he is entirely mistaken: if he is so persuaded by the shipper, it may be that he could honestly issue a clean bill of lading, while taking an indemnity in case it was later shown that there had in fact been some faulty condition. Each case must depend upon its circumstances. But even if it could be shown that there existed to any extent a practice of knowingly issuing clean bills when claused bills should have been issued, no validating effect for any particular transaction could in consequence result.

It can further be said that in this case the issuing of a clean bill of lading did not mean that there was non-disclosure as to some defect in the quality of the orange juice itself but only of the barrels that contained it. This, however, cannot affect the analysis of the transaction. Nor can it be doubted that it would be of great consequence for a banker, who was advancing money, to know whether it was likely that the orange juice was really in the barrels or whether it was likely that some of it would have leaked away and become irretrievably lost. Such knowledge would also obviously be of great importance to a purchaser or receiver of the goods.

It is said that a result of issuing a clean bill of lading is that a shipowner **7–068** deprives himself of certain defences to claims that may be made against him. In this way advantage in one sense results for indorsees of the bill of lading and disadvantages for the shipowner. The shipowner deprives himself of the possibility of setting up certain defences, if he is sued. He cannot assert that the goods, which he has carried, were in defective condition when he received them on his ship., if he has stated on the bill of lading that they were in good condition. In *United Baltic Corporation Ltd v Dundee, Perth and London Shipping Co Ltd* (1928) 32 Ll.L. Rep. 272, 275 Wright J. expressed himself thus:

"The shipowner delivers the goods at the port of destination and the goods-owner points out to him that they are damaged. Then the ship-owner replies that he is only liable to pay for such damage as occurred during the voyage and that he had delivered the goods in the same condition as that in which he received them. The goods-owner replies: 'That may be so in fact, but you are estopped because you have stated on the bill of lading on the faith of which I take up the goods and pay for them—I have acted to my prejudice on this bill of lading—you have stated on that very authoritative document that you received them in apparent good order and condition and you cannot now be heard to say the contrary: therefore you are by this estoppel, by this fiction or convention, liable for the difference between their sound value and the actual damaged value which they show."

See also *Compania Naviera Vasconzala v Churchill & Sim* [1906] 1 K.B. 237 [at para. 14–017, below]; *Brandt v Liverpool, Brazil and River Plate Steam Navigation Co Ltd* [at para. 13–057, below] and *Silver v Ocean Steamship Co Ltd* [1930] 1 K.B. 416 to which I have already referred.

It was pointed out . . . that though there may be an estoppel against the shipowner, the holder of a clean bill of lading may still be in great difficulties if defective goods are shipped. He may have resold the goods and he may find that his purchaser will not accept, and he may some-times experience great practical difficulties in suing the shipowner if, for example, the shipowner is a foreign shipowner. If he sues the shipowner, the latter may be entitled to rely on some clause in the bill of lading which protects him; furthermore, some time limit may prove fatal to a claim. But in any event buyers and bankers who act on the faith of clean bills of lading are not seeking law suits.

Some of the considerations to which I have referred may denote that in this particular case the plaintiffs, not being actuated by bad intentions, did not realize the viciousness of the transaction . . .

But whatever features there are in this case which possibly enable one to approach it with a measure of sympathetic understanding as to how the plaintiffs came to act as they did, the undisputed facts show that a short point is involved. It may be stated thus. Can A, who does what B asks him to do, enforce against B a promise made in the following terms: 'If you will at my request make a statement which you know to be false and which you know will be relied upon by others and which may cause them loss, then, if they hold you liable, I will indemnify you'? In my judgment, the assistance of the courts should not be given to such a purpose.

7–069   PEARCE L.J.: The real difficulty that arises in the case is due to the fact that the plaintiffs, whatever may have been the defendants' intentions, appear from the evidence not to have contemplated that anybody would ultimately be defrauded. Theirs was a slipshod and unthinking extension of a known commercial practice to a point where it constituted fraud in law. In the last 20 years it has become customary, in the short-sea trade in particular, for shipowners to give a clean bill of lading against an indemnity from the shippers in certain cases where there is a *bona fide* dispute as to the condition or packing of the goods. This avoids the necessity of rearranging any letter of credit, a matter which can create difficulty when time is short. If the goods turn out to be faulty, the purchaser will have his recourse against the shipping owner, who will in turn recover under his indemnity from the shippers. Thus no one will ultimately be wronged.

This practice is convenient where it is used with conscience and circumspection, but it has perils if it is used with laxity and recklessness. It is not enough that the banks or the purchasers who have been misled by clean bills of lading may have recourse at law against the shipping owner. They are intending to buy goods, not law suits. Moreover, instances have been given in argument where their legal rights may be defeated or may not recoup their loss. Trust is the foundation of trade; and bills of lading are important documents. If purchasers and banks felt that they could no longer trust bills of lading, the disadvantage to the commercial community would far outweigh any conveniences provided by the giving of clean bills of lading against indemnities.

The evidence seemed to show that, in general, the practice is kept within reasonable limits. In trivial matters and cases of bona fide dispute, where the difficulty of ascertaining the correct state of affairs is out of proportion to its importance, no doubt the practice is useful. But here the plaintiffs went outside those reasonable limits. They did so at the defendants' request without, as it seems to me, properly considering the implications of what they were doing. They thought that they could trust the defendants' agreement to indemnify them. In that they were in error.

Notes

1. The shipowners thought that they were merely following common business **7–070** practice, and were probably surprised to be branded as fraudulent. The shippers' position, on the other hand, was wholly unmeritorious. As Morris L.J. observed (at 629), it was they who had requested the procedure, and that "they are prepared to condemn their own conduct in order to save their own pocket."

2. Nonetheless, by issuing a clean bill of lading for goods which were clearly defective, the shipowners made statements which they knew to be false, knowing also that those statements would be relied upon by subsequent purchasers. They therefore committed the tort of deceit, and (by the *ex turpi causa* doctrine) were precluded from enforcing a contract of indemnity against the shippers, being unable to claim without relying on the illegality.

3. As Morris L.J. observed, this would not necessarily prejudice the holder of such a bill, because of the principles discussed in chapter 14, below, and indeed in the case, nobody appears to have been prejudiced in fact. However, as Morris L.J. also observed, a holder could certainly be prejudiced if the shipowners were foreign, and may encounter difficulties on a re-sale, if the sub-buyer rejected the goods. The whole purpose of the indemnity was therefore to protect the shipowners from the consequences of their own fraudulent misrepresentation, and was therefore unenforceable as an illegal contract.

4. It is also clear from the above passages that by contrast, an indemnity is enforceable if the carrier has a genuine doubt about whether the goods are in apparent good order and condition, and because of the doubt is prepared to issue a clean bill only on the promise of an indemnity. No element of fraud is present in such a case.

5. It is unclear how far, if at all, the principles in this case can be extended to cover other situations, *e.g.* indemnities taken by shipowners delivering goods other than against a bill of lading. It is clear, however, that merely because a practice is common, it does not follow that the courts will necessarily look kindly upon it.

Part C

FINANCE

CHAPTER 8

METHODS OF FINANCING INTERNATIONAL SALES

(1) BILLS OF EXCHANGE

BILLS of exchange are central to the operation of the documentary bill, and **8–001** although they are not necessary to the operation of documentary credits, they are in reality almost universally used. The following (outline) features need to be understood.

(a) DEFINITION

The bill of exchange (or draft) is defined in the Bills of Exchange Act 1882, s.3 **8–002** as:

> "an unconditional order in writing, addressed by one person to another, signed by the person giving it, requiring the person to whom it is addressed to pay on demand or at a fixed or determinable future time a sum certain in money to or to the order of a specified person, or bearer."

Note that the order must be unconditional, and also that by virtue of s.23, every obligation arising under the bill must be expressed in writing and signed by the party liable.

(b) PARTIES

The original parties are the drawer, drawee and payee, but either drawer or **8–003** drawee may also be payee. The payee is the "beneficiary". The drawer issues the order in writing, requiring the drawee to pay. Primary liability to pay the bill rests with the drawee (but only if he accepts liability—clearly liability cannot be unilaterally imposed on him by the drawer).

A bill of exchange is a negotiable instrument. Bearer bills can be negotiated by delivery. Order bills are negotiated by delivery and indorsement. Performance of the obligations in the bill can be claimed by the payee, or if the bill has been negotiated, by the subsequent holder or the bill. A "holder in due course", who takes a bill which is complete and regular on its face, in good faith and for value, and without notice either of any defect in the title of the person negotiating it to him, or that the bill has been dishonoured, avoids the *nemo dat* principle, as does any subsequent holder claiming through him. That is the difference between a negotiable instrument (bill of exchange) and document of title (bill of lading).

(c) NEGOTIATION WITH AND WITHOUT RECOURSE

Where the bill of exchange is negotiated with recourse, the indorser may be **8–004** liable to the subsequent holder if the bill is dishonoured by the drawee, upon notice of such dishonour by the subsequent holder. Where the bill of exchange is negotiated without recourse, the indorser negatives this liability (*i.e.* the subsequent holder bears the loss). This is an important distinction in the operation of documentary credits (see below at para. 8–007).

(d) Sight Draft / Time Draft

8–005   A bill of exchange might be a sight bill or a time bill. A sight bill must be paid on presentation. A time bill must be paid upon presentment for acceptance, when the bill matures a fixed time (*e.g.* 90 days) after sight. Time bills can be sold for cash, but of course their value (sight rate) will be less than the face value of the bill (because of the interest element).

Both time bills and sight bills are commonly used in documentary credits (on which see below at para. 8–007). If the credit provides for cash payment or sight draft, the bank will usually provide the buyer with an advance for it against the security of the goods, but the buyer will be liable for interest until the goods are sold and he is able to make reimbursement. Conversely, a seller who obtains a time draft under a credit can usually sell it to his own bank for immediate cash, but the bank will then deduct interest until maturity (and presumably a commission).[1] Arguably, therefore, the difference between cash payment or sight draft on the one hand, and time draft on the other, comes down to a question of interest. As Devlin J. observed in *Midland Bank Ltd v Seymour*[2]:

> "Well, of course, basically the confirmed credit is designed to give the seller the security he wants before he ships the goods. He can arrange to ship the goods in the confident knowledge that as soon as he tenders documents that are in order he is bound to be paid. If the letter of credit provides for a cash payment, or a sight bill, he will get paid at once. That will mean, of course, that the buyer, unless he sells the documents for cash, will be out of his money during the period of the voyage and until he disposes of the goods on arrival. But the buyer, of course, may not like that, and then the letter of credit he furnishes will not provide for a cash payment, but, as in this case, for a bill after sight—a 90 days' bill. Then the seller, unless he sells the bill for cash, will be out of his money for 90 days. If the buyer does pay cash, he will probably do so by advance from his bank on the security of the goods. If the seller sells the bill to his bank it is only another way of getting an advance on the security of the bill. The only point of difference is, which of the two, buyer or seller, has to pay in the form of interest or discount for financing the goods during what one might call the barren period of transportation or delivery?"

This is not in fact a complete picture, in that the holder of a time draft takes the risk of the drawee's bankruptcy prior to maturity. Whether a bank that has purchased such a bill can reclaim from the seller depends on whether the bill is negotiated with or without recourse.

(2) The Documentary Bill

8–006   The documentary bill solves the practical problem how the seller releases the bill of lading only against payment, given that he must post the bill of lading to the buyer, who will usually be overseas. It would be difficult, therefore, for the

---

[1] See, *e.g. Maran Road v Austin Taylor*, below.
[2] [1955] 2 Lloyd's Rep. 147, at 165.

seller to supervise the transfer, unless he has an agent in the importing country.

In the absence of an agent, the documentary bill provides the seller with limited protection. It is a bill of exchange to which a bill of lading (drawn on the buyer) is attached. The idea is to ensure that the buyer does not receive the bill of lading until he has accepted the bill of exchange. Sale of Goods Act, s.19(3) provides:

> "Where the seller of goods draws on the buyer for the price, and transmits the bill of exchange and bill of lading to the buyer together to secure acceptance or payment of the bill of exchange, the buyer is bound to return the bill of lading if he does not honour the bill of exchange, and if he wrongfully retains the bill of lading the property in the goods does not pass to him."

The retention of property protects the seller against the bankruptcy of the buyer, but note that in spite of s.19(3), the buyer has obtained with the consent of the seller possession of the documents of title to the goods, and in *Cahn v Pockett's Bristol Channel Steam Packet Co Ltd*, the Court of Appeal held that he could pass good title under s.25(1)[3]:

> "Where a person having bought or agreed to buy goods obtains, with the consent of the seller, possession of the goods or the documents of title to the goods, the delivery or transfer by that person, or by a mercantile agent acting for him, of the goods or documents of title, under any sale, pledge, or other disposition thereof, to any person receiving the same in good faith and without notice of any lien or other right of the original seller in respect of the goods, has the same effect as if the person making the delivery or transfer were a mercantile agent in possession of the goods or documents of title with the consent of the owner."

The bill of lading is clearly a document of title, and the buyer is within the definition of a mercantile agent, for these purposes. The Court of Appeal also held that the seller's right to stoppage *in transitu* was precluded by what is now s.24[4]:

> "Where a person having sold goods continues or is in possession of the goods, or of the documents of title to the goods, the delivery or transfer by that person, or by a mercantile agent acting for him, of the goods or documents of title under any sale, pledge, or other disposition thereof, to any person receiving the same in good faith and without notice of the previous sale, has the same effect as if the person making the delivery or transfer were expressly authorised by the owner of the goods to make the same."

It is not clear whether the buyer in *Cahn v Pockett's* was fraudulent, although he negotiated the bill of lading, to obtain proceeds from a sub-sale, without accepting the draft. The limited protection provided by the documentary bill is demonstrated by the result, where the seller was left without remedy against the sub-buyer, to whom title had passed. It certainly follows from the case that there is no protection against a fraudulent buyer, who sells on the goods without paying—the seller is left with no property to assert against the sub-buyer, and the buyer himself is unlikely to be worth suing.[5] In fact, the documentary bill gives

---

[3] [1899] 1 Q.B. 643, the functionally-identical section at that time being s.25(2)).
[4] Then s.2(1) of the Factors Act 1889.
[5] In *Cahn* he was in any case insolvent, but in general there is little profit in suing fraudsters.

the seller no better (nor worse) protection than retention of title under s.19(2) (on which see chapter 5, above).

The seller is better protected by the bankers' commercial credit, where the risk of fraud is taken by the issuing bank (see further below). As with other aspects of this area of law, the parties are better protected against the bankruptcy than the fraud of the other traders with whom they deal.

(3) DOCUMENTARY CREDITS: FUNDAMENTAL PRINCIPLES

8–007　　The general workings of documentary credits, and the protection given to the parties, were described at para. 1–014, above. In its most developed form, the confirmed irrevocable credit, it provides the following main features:

1. The seller tenders documents, not to the buyer against payment, but to a confirming bank, usually in his own country of business. Instead of looking for payment to an overseas buyer whose solvency may be in doubt, he can look instead to a reliable and solvent paymaster, situated in his own country, so that he will not need to sue abroad, in the event of a dispute.

2. The buyer is relieved of liquidity difficulties, and both seller and buyer can use the credit to finance the transaction.

3. The banks obtain the security of the shipping documents, in the event of default by the buyer.

For the seller to be protected, he must be able to rely on payment by the bank as long as conforming documents are tendered, irrespective of any claims by the buyer that he in breach of the sale contract; his payment must not depend on the buyer's concurrence. Conversely, the bank needs to be able to determine whether to pay, solely on the basis of the documents tendered; it has, in any case, no other means of determining whether the seller has performed his obligations under the sale contract.

From this follows that contract 4 must not depend on contract 1; each contract is to be interpreted autonomously, and indeed the autonomy principle extends to each of the four contracts forming the confirmed irrevocable credit.

(a) THE FOUR CONTRACTS IN A CONFIRMED IRREVOCABLE CREDIT

UNITED CITY MERCHANTS (INVESTMENTS) LTD v ROYAL BANK OF CANADA, THE AMERICAN ACCORD

House of Lords. [1983] A.C. 168

8–008　This case is examined in greater detail at para. 10–003, below. Of importance for the present is Lord Diplock's analysis of the contractual relationships involved, in an irrevocable confirmed credit.

LORD DIPLOCK: *(at 182H—183C)* It is trite law that there are four autonomous though interconnected contractual relationships involved: (1) the underlying contract for the sale of goods, to which the only parties are the buyer and the seller; (2) the contract between the buyer and the issuing bank under which the latter agrees to issue the credit and either itself or through a confirming bank to notify the credit to the seller and to make payments to or to the order of the seller (or to pay, accept or negotiate bills of exchange drawn by the seller) against presentation of stipulated documents; and the buyer agrees to reimburse the issuing bank for payments made under the credit. For such reimbursement the stipulated documents, if they include a document of title such as a bill of lading, constitute a security available to the issuing bank; (3) if payment is to be made through a confirming bank, the contract between the issuing bank and the confirming bank authorising and requiring the latter to make such payments and to remit the stipulated documents to the issuing bank when they are received, the issuing bank in turn agreeing to reimburse the confirming bank for payments made under the credit; (4) the contract between the confirming bank and the seller under which the confirming bank undertakes to pay to the seller (or to accept or negotiate without recourse to drawer bills of exchange drawn by him) up to the amount of the credit against presentation of the stipulated documents.

Again, it is trite law that in contract (4), with which alone the instant appeal is directly concerned, the parties to it, the seller and the confirming bank, "deal in documents and not in goods," as article 8 of the Uniform Customs puts it.[6] If, on their face, the documents presented to the confirming bank by the seller conform with the requirements of the credit as notified to him by the confirming bank, that bank is under a contractual obligation to the seller to honour the credit, notwithstanding that the bank has knowledge that the seller at the time of presentation of the conforming documents is alleged by the buyer to have, and in fact has already, committed a breach of his contract with the buyer for the sale of the goods to which the documents appear on their face to relate, that would have entitled the buyer to treat the contract of sale as rescinded and to reject the goods and refuse to pay the seller the purchase price. The whole commercial purpose for which the system of confirmed irrevocable documentary credits has been developed in international trade is to give to the seller an assured right to be paid before he parts with control of the goods that does not permit of any dispute with the buyer as to the performance of the contract of sale being used as a ground for non-payment or reduction or deferment of payment.

Notes

The first paragraph set out here describes the four contracts which form the basis of a confirmed irrevocable credit: **8–009**

1. The contract of sale between buyer and seller;

2. The contract between buyer and issuing bank;

3. The contract between issuing and correspondent (or confirming) bank; and

4. The contract between correspondent bank and seller.

[6] This was the 1974 revision. The present provision is Article 4 (see App. C, below).

The Four Autonomous Contracts (Confirmed Irrevocable Credit)

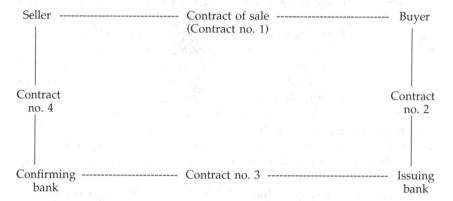

United City Merchants concerned a confirmed irrevocable credit, and Lord Diplock clearly states that the third contract only arises where the credit is confirmed: an irrevocable credit, where there is no confirming bank, consists simply of three autonomous though interconnected contractual relationships:

1. The contract of sale;

2. The contract between buyer and issuing bank; and

3. The contract between issuing bank and beneficiary.

The first three contracts are ordinary bilateral contracts between the parties. The fourth is more problematic, because neither bank is agent of the seller. No solution that is wholly satisfactory has yet been found to the relationship between seller and confirming bank: see further below.

The second of the two paragraphs above makes two fundamental (and related) points about documentary credits, that banks deal in documents rather than goods, and that the whole purpose of an irrevocable credit "is to give to the seller an assured right to be paid before he parts with control of the goods that does not permit of any dispute with the buyer as to the performance of the contract of sale being used as a ground for non-payment or reduction or deferment of payment." These points are elaborated on in chapter 10, below.

(b) Contracts Autonomous

8–010   The four contracts are autonomous in that their terms are independent of each other. So, for example, nothing in the sale contract (contract 1) can affect the terms of the credit. This is in part merely an application of the privity of contract doctrine, but were it otherwise the banks could be put into a difficult position, not necessarily being aware of the terms of the sale contract. Nor is the bank affected by subsequent variations to the sale contract, or even perhaps its subsequent repudiation by the parties to it. The bank may be entirely unaware of any such variation or repudiation, and in principle its position should not be affected by it.

It also follows that the obligation of the confirming bank to pay the beneficiary on tender of documents (contract 4), the obligation of the issuing bank to reimburse it (contract 3) and the obligation of the customer to reimburse the issuing bank (contract 2) are all independent of disputes between the parties to the sale contract (contract 1).

The autonomy of each of the four contracts is fundamental to the operation of documentary credits, and in particular to two other principles, which are vital to their operation. In *Hamzeh Malas & Sons v British Imex Industries Ltd*,[7] Jenkins L.J. observed that[8]:

"it seems to me to be plain enough that the opening of a confirmed letter of credit constitutes a bargain between the banker and the vendor of goods, which imposes upon the banker an absolute obligation to pay, irrespective of any dispute there may be between the parties as to whether the goods are up to contract or not."

This assurance of payment can be used by the seller to raise finance for the transaction, to cover the costs of shipping, obtaining, or even manufacturing the goods. The ability it gives to both seller and buyer to raise finance makes the commercial credit much more than merely a means of paying the price. The necessary security can only be given to the seller if his right to payment (under contract 4) is independent of any dispute there may be under contract 1 (sale contract). The buyer must not be allowed to prevent payment, if the seller tenders the documents required by the terms of the credit.[9]

This principle of autonomy is preserved by the *Uniform Customs and Practice for Documentary Commercial Credits*, which applies to the overwhelming majority of credits issued throughout the world.[10] Article 3(a) provides that:

"Credits, by their nature, are separate transactions from the sales or other contract(s) on which they may be based and banks are in no way concerned with or bound by such contract(s), even if any reference whatsoever to such contract(s) is included in the credit. Consequently, the undertaking of a bank to pay, accept and pay Draft(s) or negotiate and/or to fulfil any other obligation under the Credit is not subject to claims or defences by the Applicant resulting from his relationships with the Issuing Bank or the Beneficiary."[11]

It also follows that each of the credit contracts is independent of the others, and of the sale contract (the "underlying transaction"). Thus in principle (however undesirable in reality), the obligations of the confirming bank towards the beneficiary (contract 4) may differ from those owed to it by the issuing bank (contract 3), and those between the issuing bank and its customer (contract 2). If, for example, the terms of the credit differed from the customer's instructions, the confirming bank's relations with the beneficiary would be governed by the terms of the credit, whereas the relationship between issuing bank and customer would be governed by the customer's instructions.[12]

Each contract can even be governed by the law of a different jurisdiction: certainly the courts have taken the view that the state whose law governs the

---

[7] [1958] 2 Q.B. 127.

[8] [1958] 2 Q.B. 127, 129.

[9] See further paras 8–013 *et seq*, below.

[10] See further below; the full text is set out in App. C, below.

[11] The last sentence was added in 1993, primarily to deter applicants for credits from claiming that payment should be stopped because of the beneficiary's breach of his contractual obligations to the applicant: *UCP 500 & 400 Compared* (I.C.C. Publication No. 511, 1993), pp. 7–8. Only banks and not applicants were mentioned in earlier versions of the U.C.P.

[12] Article 3(b) of the U.C.P. provides: "A Beneficiary can in no case avail himself of the contractual relationships existing between the banks or between the Applicant and the Issuing Bank." This is identical to Art. 6 of the 1983 Revision.

credit (contract 4) is independent of the law governing the underlying transaction (contract 1, the contract of sale).[13]

(c) Contracts Interconnected

8–011   The situation described in the last but one paragraph, though in principle possible, is extremely undesirable in practice. It is much better for the requirements under each of the contracts to be the same. Theoretical possibility and desirable practice therefore diverge. In *The American Accord*, Lord Diplock continued later in his speech:

> "It would be strange from a commercial point of view, although not theoretically impossible in law, if the contractual duty owed by confirming and issuing banks to the buyer to honour the credit on presentation of apparently conforming documents despite the fact that they contain inaccuracies or even are forged were not matched by a corresponding contractual liability of the confirming bank to the seller/beneficiary (in the absence, of course, of any fraud on his part) to pay the sum stipulated in the credit on presentation of apparently conforming documents."

Ordinarily, of course, and ideally, the terms of the credit (contract 4), and the agreement between the banks (contact 3), will conform precisely with each other, and with the customer's instructions (contract 2). Interconnection implies that in that case, the same law will apply to each contract. Sir John Megaw elaborated on this in *Bankers Trust Co v State Bank of India* as follows[14]:

> "The metaphor 'autonomous' means only that one does not read into any one of the four contracts the terms of any of the other three contracts. But the 'genesis and the aim of the transaction' ... are not to be ignored where they may be relevant to assist in the interpretation of the terms of the contract."

In reality, therefore, the obligations of the bank towards the beneficiary should tie in with the obligations of the customer towards the bank (unless the bank exceeds its instructions in the issue of the credit). Hence contracts 2, 3 and 4, although autonomous, are interconnected. This interconnection is examined further in chapter 10, below, where it will be seen that part of the rationale for the decision in *The American Accord* was to ensure that the law on contract 4 matched that on contract 3.

(d) Banks Deal in Documents Not Goods

8–012   Article 4 of the U.C.P. provides that "In credit operations all parties concerned deal with documents, and not with goods, services and/or other performances to which the documents may relate." This reiterates a principle of the common law.

Banks do not hold themselves out as having any expertise in goods; this is one of the justifications for the principles described in chapter 10, below.

---

[13] For the purposes of this book, however, it is assumed that all contracts are governed by the domestic laws of the U.K.
[14] [1991] 2 Lloyd's Rep. 443.

(4) Uniform Customs and Practice on Bankers' Commercial Credits

(a) The U.C.P.

Attempts at unification and harmonisation of the law rarely meet with success,[15] but documentary credits are an exception. Nearly all are on the terms of the *Uniform Customs and Practice for Documentary Credits* ("U.C.P."), last revised in 1993.[16]   **8–013**

The U.C.P. was originally published by the International Chamber of Commerce (I.C.C.) in 1933, and was revised in 1951, 1962, 1974, 1983 and most recently in 1993, as a result of the deliberations of the I.C.C. Banking Commission. Revisions have therefore averaged about once a decade, and have usually been in response to changing trade and banking practices. For example, the 1983 revisions responded to new forms of documentation, particularly for combined transport operations, and this process was taken further in the 1993 revisions. Some of the ramifications of changes in commercial practised are elaborated on further in chapter 15, below.

The U.C.P. has been adopted in 146 countries, and as has already been observed, nearly all credits issued today, except in China and Rumania, are on the terms of the Uniform Customs and Practice. However, this has not always been the case. Only since the 1962 revisions have banks in the United Kingdom adopted the U.C.P., for example, since before then the U.C.P. differed in a number of fundamental ways from "London Practice".

The 1993 revision will be referred to extensively in this book, and is fully set out in Appendix C.

(b) Application of U.C.P.

Although the U.C.P. is of almost universal application, it does not have the force of law in the United Kingdom, and has to be incorporated into the contracts which form the basis of the credit (*i.e.* contracts 2, 3 and 4, above). Article 1 of the U.C.P. provides: **8–014**

"The Uniform Customs and Practice for Documentary Credits, 1994 Revision, Publication No. 500, shall apply to all documentary credits (including to the extent to which they may be applicable standby letters of credit),[17] where they are incorporated into the text of the credit. They are binding on all parties thereto unless otherwise expressly stipulated in the credit."

In the United Kingdom the U.C.P. has not been given the force of law, and English law does not recognise a principle whereby terms are compulsorily incorporated into a contract in the absence of provision to the contrary. Therefore, the last sentence of Article 1, providing that the Articles are binding on all parties thereto unless otherwise agreed, has no effect in the absence of express words of incorporation. As to what is required for incorporation, see *Forestal Mimosa Ltd v*

---

[15] See, *e.g.* the discussion of Incoterms at 15–004 *et seq.*, below.

[16] The contrast with the far less successful Incoterms is striking; perhaps it has come about because banks are able, in effect, to dictate the terms on which they will do business, and hence to impose upon the industry a code which suits them. Harmonisation seems rarely to occur without pressure.

[17] On which see further below. These were brought within the U.C.P. for the first time in 1983. As Art. 1 implies, however, not all provisions of the U.C.P. are capable of applying to the standby letter of credit.

Oriental Credit Ltd,[18] where an insertion in the left-hand margin of the document was held by the Court of Appeal to be sufficient to incorporate the provisions of the U.C.P.

U.C.P. terms will also be overridden by any terms expressly agreed between the parties. In *Royal Bank of Scotland plc v Cassa di Risparmio delle Provincie Lombard*,[19] a contract between two banks into which the 1993 revision of the U.C.P. was incorporated expressly provided for payment in New York. An argument that this should be read subject to the U.C.P., which it was said required payment to be made in London, was rejected by the Court of Appeal, Mustill L.J. observing[20]:

> "As I see it, this case is founded on the proposition that the contractual relationship is dominated by U.C.P., that the obligation of the issuing bank to reimburse [the plaintiffs] derived solely from Articles 10 and 16,[21] and that accordingly one should look there and no further to find the undertaking by the issuing bank to reimburse the accepting bank. I cannot agree. Undeniably the Uniform Customs and Practices have an important role in the conduct of international trade. They expound technical terms; they promote consistency; and they enable the parties to express their intentions briefly, without the need to negotiate and set out all the terms of the relationship at length. Nevertheless, whilst not belittling the utility of the U.C.P., it must be recognised that their terms do not constitute a statutory code. As their title makes clear they contain a formulation of customs and practices, which the parties to a letter of credit transaction can incorporate into their contracts by reference. This being so, it seems to me that the obvious place to start, when searching for a contractual term material to a particular obligation is the express agreement between the parties. If it is found that the parties have explicitly agreed such a term, then the search need go no further, since any contrary provision in U.C.P. must yield to the parties' expressed intention. If on the other hand the agreement is silent in the material respect, then recourse must be had to U.C.P., and if a relevant term is found there, that term will govern the case."

8–015   Another consequence of the fact that the U.C.P. is only given force in the UK by incorporation into the contracts which form the basis of the credit, is that its provisions cannot be used to determine whether those contracts have been made in the first place. Some of the consequences of this conclusion are elaborated upon below.

In fact, English banks have adopted the U.C.P. since the 1962 revisions, so that their standard forms will invariably incorporate the U.C.P. provisions, but that does not affect the sale contract, which will be governed by the common law unless it expressly stipulates that any credit opened under it is governed by the U.C.P.[22] In most situations this will not matter, since the provisions of the U.C.P. do not in general operate in opposition to the common law, but rather elaborate

---

[18] [1986] 1 W.L.R. 631. See below.

[19] *Financial Times*, January 21, 1992, otherwise unreported. The issue was whether the defendants could be sued in the United Kingdom under Art. 5 of Sched. 1 of the Civil Jurisdiction and Judgments Act 1982, which depended on whether the place of performance was the UK. It was held that the place of performance was New York, by virtue of express stipulation in the contract.

[20] The argument was that the U.C.P. provisions on reimbursement were silent as to where the obligation was to be performed, but that the general principle should be applied that the debtor should seek out his creditor (in which case reimbursement should be in London). Because the Court held that the place or performance was stipulated expressly, it did not need to consider whether the general principle was applicable in the context of international banking transactions.

[21] The equivalent Arts of the 1993 Revision are 9 and 14.

[22] Presumably the U.C.P. would also apply if the sale contract required the credit to be opened by a particular bank, which itself had adopted the U.C.P.

upon it. Their purpose for the most part is to clarify, rather than alter the law. There are some differences, however, between common law and U.C.P. provisions, for example regarding the requirements for the commercial invoice,[23] in which case the provisions of the sale contract may conflict with those of the other contracts underlying the credit.

Inter-bank electronic messages sent by S.W.I.F.T. (the Society for Worldwide Interbank Financial Telecommunications), do not expressly state when the credit is subject to the U.C.P., but the phrase: "unless specifically stated, the Documentary Credit is issued subject to Uniform Customs and Practice for Documentary Credits, International Chamber of Commerce, Paris, France, which are in effect on the date of issue" is incorporated into the user handbook.

Banks are also required to notify the I.C.C. of their adherence to the U.C.P.

(5) Types of Documentary Credit

The distinctions between revocable and irrevocable, and confirmed and uncon- **8–016** firmed credits, are sometimes confused. The first relates to the obligations of the issuing bank, the second to those of the correspondent bank.

(a) Revocable and Irrevocable Credits

A revocable credit is useless from the seller's point of view (though the buyer **8–017** can gain from it). Its only attraction for sellers can be its relative cheapness, where the trustworthiness of the buyer is not in doubt, because it offers no security at all. Not only can the issuing bank (on the instructions of the buyer) revoke at any time, but it need not even inform the seller that it has done so.

CAPE ASBESTOS CO LTD v LLOYD'S BANK LTD

King's Bench. (1921) W.N. 274

The correspondent bank advised the sellers that it had opened a credit in **8–018** its favour, but added: "This is merely an advice of the opening of the above-mentioned credit and is not a confirmation of the same". It was advised by the issuing bank that the credit was cancelled but did not inform the sellers of this. About 7 weeks later the sellers tendered the shipping documents for payment. The bank did not pay and the sellers sued the bank, claiming that the bank was under a duty to give them reasonable notice of the cancellation of the credit.

Held
The bank may cancel a revocable credit at any time, and is under no duty to inform the seller that a revocable credit has been cancelled.

BAILHACHE J.: It was to be observed that the letter of June 14, 1920, from the defendants to the plaintiffs announced the opening of a revocable and not of a confirmed credit. A letter in that form intimated to the person in

---

[23] See para. 6–101, above.

whose favour the credit was opened that he might find that the credit was revoked at any time. That being the representation by the defendants to the plaintiffs, were the defendants under any legal duty to give notice to the plaintiffs when the credit was revoked. On consideration his Lordship had come to the conclusion that there was no legal obligation on the defendants to give notice in the circumstances. In a case of this kind the wise course for the seller to take before making a shipment of the goods would certainly be to inquire of the bank whether or not the credit had been withdrawn. The practice of the defendants to give notice in such cases was a most prudent, reasonable and business-like practice, and his Lordship hoped that nothing that he said in this case would lead banks to alter that practice, but at the same time it did not seem to be based upon any legal obligation or duty. it had been said that the defendants regarded the giving of notice as an act of courtesy which they always performed except when, as in this case, it was unfortunately forgotten. That was the true view of the proceeding. It was an act of courtesy which it was very desirable should be performed, but it was not founded upon any legal obligation. If that conclusion was right it disposed of the case.

Notes

8–019   1. The above passage, taken from Weekly Notes, is a commentary on, rather than an exact quote from the judgment of Bailhache J.

2. The court seems to have confused the terms "revocable" and "unconfirmed". The correspondent bank made it clear that it was not confirming the credit, but did not make clear that it was also irrevocable. Nevertheless, Bailhache J. proceeded on the assumption that the credit was irrevocable, and the case is therefore authority that an irrevocable credit can be revoked without notice.

3. Revocable credits are rare in the UK.

4. Article 8(a) of the U.C.P. (in Appendix C, below) defines the revocable credit similarly to the common law, but Article 8(b) provides protection for any other bank which has already accepted and paid against documents, for example where the other bank has agreed to negotiate the documents on behalf of the seller.

(b) Irrevocable Credits

8–020   The essential workings of an irrevocable credit were described in chapter 1, above. An irrevocable credit cannot be revoked once issued (subject to the conceptual difficulties discussed at the end of this chapter). This is also provided by Article 9(d)(i) of the U.C.P.

(c) Methods of Payment Under Irrevocable Credits

8–021   Because under an irrevocable credit the seller knows that he will eventually be paid by a reliable and solvent paymaster, the seller does not usually insist upon payment of cash against documents. Credits sometimes provide for deferred cash payment. Alternatively (and more commonly), an acceptance credit may be used, in which case the bank undertakes to accept bills of exchange drawn on it by the beneficiary. Such bills can be in the form of sight drafts, but time drafts (maturing a fixed time, often 90 days, after sight) are more commonly used, and this provides an alternative method of deferring payment. Another (rare) possibility is the negotiation credit, where the issuing bank undertakes to negotiate (*i.e.* purchase) bills of exchange drawn by the beneficiary on a third party. The issuing bank can then itself, of course, present those bills to the third party (probably another bank). All these methods of payment are provided for under Article 9(a) of the U.C.P.

For an irrevocable negotiation credit it is important that the issuing bank negotiates without recourse against the drawer (*i.e.* beneficiary under the credit), so that it is the issuing bank and not the drawer who takes the risk of default by the third party when the bills of exchange are presented. See U.C.P., Article 9(a)(iv).

(d) CONFIRMED CREDITS

If a correspondent bank confirms the credit, it adds its own undertaking to that **8–022** of the issuing bank, effectively taking on towards the seller all the obligations taken on by the issuing bank, where the credit is unconfirmed. In other words, the seller need only deal with the confirming bank, and its undertakings may be regarded as irrevocable.

The confirming bank must add its own definite and irrevocable undertaking to pay to that of the issuing bank, and if for any reason it is not reimbursed by the issuing bank (for example, where the issuing bank has gone into liquidation), it must have no recourse against the beneficiary. In *Panoustos v Raymond Hadley Corporation of New York* [1917] 2 K.B. 473, it was admitted by all parties that a credit was not confirmed where the "confirming" bank stated:

"In advising you that this credit has been opened we are acting merely as agents for our foreign correspondents and cannot assume any responsibility for its continuance."

This was not confirmed because no irrevocable undertaking was entered into by the "confirming" bank.

Correspondent banks will not normally confirm revocable credits, because of the considerable risks they would incur by so doing. The workings have been described in chapter 1, above, and the nature of the undertaking is described in Article 9(b) of the U.C.P.

Again, there are various methods of payment, also provided for by the U.C.P. Under a negotiation credit, the confirming bank must negotiate without recourse to drawer, since it, rather than the beneficiary, takes the risk of non-payment by the issuing bank. Under an acceptance credit, the confirming bank undertakes to accept drafts on maturity (see Article 9(b)(iii)).

FORESTAL MIMOSA LTD v ORIENTAL CREDIT LTD

Court of Appeal. [1986] 1 W.L.R. 631

The case concerned a confirmed irrevocable acceptance credit in which **8–023** there was a marginal insertion which read: "Except so far as otherwise expressly stated this documentary credit is subject to Uniform Customs and Practice for Documentary Credits." The goods having been shipped and documents tendered, the defendants (confirming bank) alleged that there were discrepancies in the documents, and refused to acknowledge liability for acceptance and payment of the drafts under the letters of credit.

Held:
The alleged discrepancies were unarguable, and once it was accepted that the UCP applied, the defendants were required to accept and pay against the drafts.

8–024   Sir John Megaw: The defendants' contention . . . is that, when one looks at the letter of credit of the [issuing] Bank in the first instance, without referring to the Uniform Customs terms, it is clear that that credit was, by agreement between the parties, on the words that they used, only to become operative in the event that the buyers under a particular credit did in fact accept the sellers' draft when the sellers' draft, together with the other documents, was presented to them; and that, if the buyers declined to accept that draft, while the buyers might be liable under legal obligations to the sellers by virtue of the contract of sale, the sellers would obtain no help, assistance or legal right of any sort by virtue of the confirmed credit. That would be so because the confirmed credit would not have come into operation as a contract between the plaintiffs and the defendants. [The defendants] submitted, quite rightly, that that did not mean that the credit, if that was its effect, was of no benefit whatever to the sellers. It could, in certain circumstances, be of benefit to them: it would be of benefit to them if the buyers under the credit did indeed accept the draft, because then the effect of the confirmed credit would be that the bank would come under an obligation to the sellers. If the buyers thereafter failed in their obligation to pay the draft at maturity, the bank would have to pay the sellers the amount of the accepted draft. But, on [the defendants'] submission . . . , it would be a credit (if it can be so described) under which it was open to the buyers of their own volition to make the bankers' credit wholly ineffective for any purpose simply by saying, "We refuse to accept the draft." That is a contract which the parties can make if they wish. But, to my mind, it would not be regarded within the commercial community as being properly described as a confirmed irrevocable documentary credit. The purpose—or, at any rate, one of the important purposes—of such a credit, as it is understood in international finance, is that it shall not be open to the buyer by his own choice, with, it may be, no kind of legal justification whatever, when proper documents are tendered, to render the bank's obligation to the seller under the credit a wholly useless obligation and one that has no legal effect.

If it were not for the incorporation into this contract of the Uniform Customs, there would be, at any rate, a fair argument for [the defendants'] submission, and for the judge's view. In his opinion the Uniform Customs could not be treated, as he put it, as overriding the other terms of the document. . . .

To my mind, it is wrong to approach this question of construction by looking at the document first without reference to the Uniform Customs. The marginal note which I have cited provides unambiguously that, except insofar as otherwise expressly stated, this documentary credit is subject to the Uniform Customs. Unless, therefore, there is some express provision which excludes the Uniform Customs terms, they have got to be brought in. There is no such express provision excluding any relevant part of the Uniform Customs. It might be that, if it could be shown that there was some irreconcilable inconsistency between the Uniform Customs terms and the other terms of the document, the Uniform Customs terms would have to be ignored. In my judgment, there is no justification for reading into the contract any implied exclusion; and—I think this is probably part of the same proposition—there is no inconsistency between the terms which the Uniform Customs would incorporate and the terms which appear on the face of the document itself. On the contrary, those terms have been included by reference to the Uniform Customs terms, and are to be interpreted by reference to the relevant parts of the Uniform Customs terms.

Note

On the principle of autonomy discussed above, payment under a confirmed   8–025
irrevocable credit should not depend on the decision of the buyers, and the U.C.P. applies this principle to an acceptance credit. It would have been possible, were the U.C.P. not incorporated, to interpret this credit as one under which acceptance was not required unless the buyers consented, but once the U.C.P. was held incorporated, this interpretation became untenable.

(e) Unconfirmed Negotiation Credits

It is not unusual for credits to be irrevocable but unconfirmed. In this case the   8–026
correspondent bank simply negotiates the documents on behalf of the issuing bank's behalf, but does not undertake payment on its own behalf. It leaves the seller open, therefore, to the possibility of having to litigate against the issuing bank, and such litigation may take place abroad. On the other hand, so long as the issuing bank is reputable, and therefore unlikely to default, sellers may not consider worthwhile the extra commission payable for confirmation.

MARAN ROAD SAW MILL v AUSTIN TAYLOR & CO LTD

Queen's Bench Division. [1975] 1 Lloyd's Rep. 156

The plaintiffs were Malaysian sellers of timber, and the defendants acted   8–027
as their selling agents. In reality, under the agency agreement with the plaintiffs the defendants were purchasers of the timber. The defendants then arranged a sub-sale of the timber to sub-buyers, who paid cash against documents to the defendants. The transaction can be analysed, then, as Maran Road as sellers and Austin Taylor as buyers.

Payment was to be by irrevocable letter of credit, which was opened in the plaintiffs' favour by Sale Continuation Ltd, trading as Sale & Co Payment was to be made 90 days after sight, but the credits also provided that drafts were negotiable by the Bangkok Bank in Kuala Lumpur at sight rate. In other words, the plaintiffs were assured of payment on sight by the Bangkok Bank, and there was a provision for interest to be claimed by the Bangkok Bank from Sale & Co when they presented the documents for acceptance. The arrangement is described by Ackner J. as follows:

" . . . when shipment time came under the contract for the sale of the timber, the plaintiffs drew bills of exchange on Sale & Co made out to the order of the Bangkok Bank Ltd for payment 90 days after sight. The sum involved would be the price of the goods less the defendants' commission *[which in the case was 4% of the f.o.b. value]*. The plaintiffs took the bills and shipping documents to the Bangkok Bank, [and] negotiated these bills with the bank at sight rate. The Bangkok Bank then took the shipping documents and the bills and obtained Sale & Co's acceptance in exchange for the shipping documents. The shipping documents would then be handed over to the defendants by Sale & Co against payment or the provision of a trust letter."

This is similar to the purchase of time drafts described in *Midland Bank v Seymour*, above. Bangkok Bank did not confirm the credit, however.

In accordance with the arrangement the plaintiffs shipped the timber, and obtained payment at sight rate from Bangkok Bank. Bangkok Bank tendered the shipping documents to Sale & Co, who released them to the defendants.[24]

Before the bills of exchange, providing for payment 90 days after sight, had matured, Sale & Co went into liquidation, adnd the bills of exchange were dishonoured. Bangkok Bank accordingly called upon the plaintiffs to reimburse them, and the plaintiffs did so. The plaintiffs sued the defendants for recovery of the sum paid by them to the Bangkok Bank. Their claim in effect was that they had not received the purchase price for the goods, the credit having failed.

Held

The plaintiffs were entitled to succeed, the defendants having broken the sale contract, by failing to provide a reliable and solvent paymaster [see further para. 9–036, below].

One of the arguments advanced by the defendants was that the plaintiffs should not have reimbursed the Bangkok Bank, in other words that the credit had not failed and the plaintiffs had occasioned their own loss. Ackner J., in rejecting this contention, noted that a confirming bank would have had no right of recourse against the drawer, and that the beneficiary would have been under no obligation to reimburse it. He then referred to Article 3 of the U.C.P. (1962 Revision), which is substantively similar to Article 9(b) of the 1993 Revision, and continued (at 161 col. 1):

---

[24] This would be a similar arrangement to the trust receipt, described below.

"This Article makes it clear that a confirming bank may not have recourse. It is otherwise in the case of a non-confirming bank. The reason is that whereas the latter is the agent of the issuing bank for the purpose of advising the credit, it acts as principal vis-à-vis the beneficiary. He [negotiating bank] is under no duty to negotiate and if it does so, it may make whatever conditions it likes as to a pre-requisite to doing so. It follows that if the credit is available by 'time' draft, the negotiating bank may have recourse on the draft if this is ultimately unpaid."

Ackner J. also rejected a contention of the defendants that the Bangkok Bank could be taken to have confirmed the credit because they had negotiated time drafts at sight rate. He saw no reason for any such implication.

Negotiation credits are described in the U.C.P., Article 10.

(f) Advantages and Disadvantages of Confirmed and Unconfirmed Credits

Unlike the confirmed credit, therefore, the unconfirmed negotiation credit gives the beneficiary no protection against failure or refusal to pay by the issuing bank. It leaves the seller open to the possibility of having to litigate against the issuing bank, if for example the issuing bank rejects the documents, which litigation may of course take place abroad.   **8–028**

On the other hand, as long as the issuing bank is reputable, sellers may not consider worthwhile the extra commission payable for confirmation. Indeed, confirmation may in practice add very little when the issuing bank is reputable. In *Enrico Furst & Co v W.E. Fischer Ltd* [1960] 2 Lloyd's Rep. 340, a credit which was issued by a reputable bank in Italy should have been confirmed by a London bank, but the Westminster Bank in London was instructed (at 344):

"Please advise the beneficiaries of the opening of this letter of credit, without adding your confirmation."

Hence the credit was not confirmed by a London bank, but the English sellers raised no objection to the lack of confirmation, and indeed were later held to have waived their right to rely on non-confirmation of the credit when an action was brought against them by the buyers for non-delivery of the goods. It did not surprise Diplock J. that they had not taken this point (at 348):

"I have no doubt that the defendants [sellers], when they received the letter of credit, took no point on its not being 'an irrevocable credit opened in London'.[25] They took plenty of points, but they did not take that one. They treated it as valid in its nature and requested the plaintiffs [buyers] to extend it, which they did. No doubt the reason that they did not take any point about it is that, with a reputable [issuing] bank like Swiss-Israel Trade Bank, it made no real commercial difference whether the Westminster Bank, Ltd, added their own confirmation or not."

---

[25] This terminology is a little confusing. This statement appears to mean "confirmed in London", since an irrevocable credit had in fact been opened, and a London bank had advised but not confirmed the credit.

Clearly it is by no means necessary for sellers always to demand confirmation of credits, then. An unconfirmed irrevocable credit will frequently offer all the security that is required.

An irrevocable credit can, in any case, give the parties advantages apart from simply finance. In *Maran Road*, it was not the normal practice of the defendants to agree to pay shippers in Malaysia by letters of credit, because of the extra expense involved, but the plaintiffs insisted on payment under an irrevocable commercial credit, because according to Ackner J. (at 157, col. 2):

" . . . letters of credit were of advantage since *inter alia* these enabled them to borrow money from their banks against such documents. In fact, this was the very reason given by the plaintiffs to the defendants for insisting on the establishment of letters of credit in their favour. They relied upon overdrafts from their bankers and letters of credit were 'instrumental to our obtaining advances necessary for speeding up our production and shipments.' "

These advantages could be obtained without the need for confirmation.

(g) Other Types of Documentary Credit

8–029   There are a number of other types of credit, including in particular the transferable credit defined in Article 48 of the U.C.P. This is used by a seller who is selling goods which are supplied by a number of different suppliers. It can be split up, so that the benefit of the original credit can be divided to pay the various suppliers.

Irrevocable and confirmed credits are clearly defined, both at common law and under the U.C.P., as are standby credits considered below. Transferable credits are defined under the U.C.P. The remaining credits considered here have not been formally defined, so these are commercial, rather than legal definitions (although obviously, a court would define them were it necessary to do so).

In chain sales a bank may, on the security of the credit opened in the seller's favour, open a similar credit for his supplier (for a smaller sum). This is a back-to-back credit. The credits in favour of seller and his supplier will be in identical terms apart from the price.

A revolving credit allows the seller guaranteed payment for a number of shipments up to a fixed maximum sum. It is not then necessary, say in the case of a regular supply, or a number of shipments, to set up fresh credits for each shipment. On the other hand, the maximum liability of the bank is limited to the fixed sum, which will typically be less than the price for all the shipments. As the bank is reimbursed by the buyer, the credit is again extended (automatically) to the agreed sum.

In *Nordskog & Co v National Bank* (1922) 10 Lloyd's Rep. 652, Bailhache J. appeared to accept the following expert witness testimony, as to the definition of a revolving credit:

"It is a little difficult to define, but a revolving credit technically means a credit for a certain sum at any one time outstanding, which is automatically renewed by putting on at the bottom what has been taken off at the top. If you have a revolving credit for £50,000 open for three months, to be operated on by drafts at 30 days' sight as drafts are drawn, they temporarily reduce the amount of the credit below £50,000. As these drafts run off and are presented and paid they are added again to the top of the credit, and restore it again to £50,000. That is what is known technically as a revolving credit, and it is automatic in its operation and does not need any renewal."

Revolving credits seem to be rare, but the credit in *The Future Express* (see para. 6–037, above) was of this type.

(h) STANDBY LETTERS OF CREDIT

Standby credits are not true documentary credits at all, but are essentially a **8–030** form of bank guarantee. Sometimes they are used to guarantee payment where a true documentary credit cannot be used, and sometimes they are used, by way of performance bond, to guarantee performance by a seller or contractor. Nevertheless, much of the law relating to documentary credits also applies to guarantees and performance bonds, and indeed since 1983, so have the provisions of the U.C.P., so far as they can be made applicable. Both forms of stand-by credit are commonly used in international sales of goods and services.

A standby letter of credit allows for payment other than against the usual shipping documents, and they are used in situations where the seller might not reasonably be expected to have shipping documents to tender (for example in *The Delfini* and *The Filiatra Legacy*—see paras 5–066, *et seq*.). Because a document of title is not tendered, the bank obtains none of the security described in the following section, and is left with only a personal claim against the applicant. This may not matter unduly if the applicant is reputable (*e.g.* a major oil company), and unlikely to go bankrupt.

(6) NATURE OF BANK'S SECURITY UNDER A DOCUMENTARY CREDIT

Unlike a standby letter of credit, a bank under a documentary credit has **8–031** shipping documents as security, which protect it against the bankruptcy or non-payment by the buyer. It is not limited to a personal claim. It has constructive possession of the goods, and often either legal or equitable title also.

(a) CONSTRUCTIVE POSSESSION

The transfer of the bill of lading to the bank transfers constructive possession, **8–032** and as long as the bank retains it, will have an action against the shipowner who delivers the goods to anyone else, for example a purchaser who has not paid, without production of a bill of lading (see *Sze Hai Tong* at para. 6–016, above).

THE STONE GEMINI

Australia Federal Court, New South Wales District Registry in Admiralty.
[1999] 2 Lloyd's Rep. 255

Facts:

The plaintiffs (Westpac) were a negotiating bank, which had paid the **8–033** beneficiary against tender of documents, which the issuing bank (BOC) had later refused to accept. The shipowner (Navalgalaxy) delivered the goods to the purchaser (Jindalee), without production of an original bill but against a letter of indemnity, and the plaintiffs sued in conversion.

The shipowners denied the plaintiffs' title to sue, and claimed that the bank had notice that delivery was to be against a letter of indemnity, and had therefore waived, or was estopped from asserting, its rights.

Held:

The plaintiffs were entitled to succeed. The waiver and estoppel points failed on the facts.

8–034   TAMBERLIN J.: 1. In the principal action the plaintiff Westpac banking Corporation ("Westpac") by amended writ dated July 5, 1996, applied to arrest *Stone Gemini* ("the vessel") on the ground that Westpac had a claim against the owners of the vessel arising from wrongful discharge of cargo. The vessel was arrested and an application was made for release. Security was provided and the vessel was released from arrest on Oct 18, 1996.

2. Shortly summarized, the claim of Westpac is that at the time of discharge it had a special property in the nature of rights in respect of the cargo as either a pledgee, equitable mortgagee, or bearer of bills of lading issued in respect of the cargo whereby it was entitled to delivery of the cargo. Westpac contends that the cargo was wrongfully delivered without the production of the bills of lading. Westpac's case is that the cargo was released against letters of indemnity provided by other parties and that it was unaware of the existence of these indemnities until after discharge had been effected. It further says that it would not have consented to discharge of the cargo against the letters of indemnity if it had been aware of them. Accordingly, it claims damages in conversion against the vessel. . . .

Claim in conversion

27. Conversion has been described as an intentional exercise of control over goods which so seriously interferes with the right of another to control those goods that the person so acting may be required to pay its full value: see Fleming, *The Law of Torts*, 9th ed, 1998, at pp. 60 ff. The test requires an intention to deal with the goods and to exercise dominion over them on behalf of someone other than the owner. It is not necessary that the person who converts the goods should be aware that there is interference with the rights of another. The emphasis is rather on an intentional act which has the effect of interfering with the rights of others. In order to succeed in conversion the plaintiff must be able to show an entitlement to possession or delivery of the goods as at the time of conversion.

Right to delivery

28. The first matter for consideration in the present circumstances is the nature and extent of Westpac's right to require delivery of the cargo to it when it was unloaded in the period between July 11 and 14, 1995.

29. Westpac submits that, as the negotiating bank, it was the pledgee or equitable mortgagee of the cargo because it was the bearer of the bills of lading which had been delivered to it and endorsed in blank at the time when the discharge took place. It is well settled law that endorsement in

blank of a negotiable bill of lading causes it to operate as a bearer bill. Westpac says that at the time of discharge in July, the bills of lading entitled it to call for delivery of the cargo and that this entitlement was wrongfully extinguished because the cargo was discharged by the master without authority on the basis that letters of indemnity, of which it was unaware, had been provided by . . . Jindalee.

30. Westpac says that as a consequence of being furnished with the shipping documents upon negotiating the letter of credit and making payment on the drafts, it acquired a "special property" as pledgee in the cargo sufficient to entitle it to sue in conversion.

31. In response, the defendants submit that Westpac never acquired any right with respect to the goods. It was not a pledgee of the bills because there was no specific undertaking by anyone that the goods were to be pledged. The submission is that the relevant "contract" is the transfer of the letter of credit issued by BOC which calls for delivery of the bills of lading to BOC and not to Westpac. Further, so it is submitted, Westpac was not a confirming bank which undertook to become directly liable for the payment. The true position is said to be that Westpac is the bank which negotiated the letter of credit and that such negotiation did not give rise to any implied pledge over the goods represented by the bills of lading. Its right to recover was said to be against BOC provided it presented documents as required by the BOC letter of credit . . .

32. Letters of credit, which are provided for in relation to contracts for the sale of goods in international trade, are autonomous agreements in the sense that they are distinct from the contractual rights conferred by the underlying agreement for sale of the goods in question. Generally speaking the letter of credit must be honoured regardless of the rights which exist *inter se* between buyer and seller in relation to the cargo itself: see *Power Curber International Ltd v National Bank of Kuwait* [1981] 1 W.L.R. 1233 at p. 1241. Letter of credit transactions are primarily concerned with payment against documents and not with the quality or contractual terms which govern the quality or supply of the goods in question.

33. It is well settled law that a bearer bill of lading entitles the holder to call for possession of the goods. Where goods are delivered to a person other than the holder of the bill of lading then the person or corporation so delivering is exposed to risk of liability to the holder: see *Sze Hai Tong Bank Ltd v Rambler Cycle Co Ltd* [1959] A.C. 576 at 586 where Lord Denning said:

[TAMBERLIN J. referred to the paragraph set out in chapter 6, beginning: "It is perfectly clear law that a shipowner who delivers without production of the bills of lading does so at his peril", and continued:]

34. Navalgalaxy submits that it is only the issuing bank under a letter   **8–035**
of credit which is entitled to security by way of pledge of a bill of lading. This is said to be because it is the issuing bank and as such is exposed to the risk of making payment in respect of the goods delivered to its

customers. This is, so it is said, because if the goods are released without presentation of the bills of lading the customer may dispose of them and may not reimburse the issuing bank, thus exposing the issuing bank to liability. Accordingly, the security provided by the right to call for delivery is required. Westpac's response is that the negotiation and payment by it in good faith, in honouring the bank drafts, had the effect of conferring on it a right to possession of the cargo by way of security and that this right was lost as a consequence of delivery against the letters of indemnity. The delivery of the documents to Westpac was not solely to enable it to collect from BOC, but entitled it to have the goods delivered to it if its debt was not satisfied. In other words it was not merely acting as an agent for collection which held the documents only for the purpose of collection of the debt from BOC.

35. In my view, Westpac was the negotiating bank, in the present circumstances and as such it acquired rights to claim against BOC: *European Asia Bank AG v Punjab & Sind Bank (No. 2)* [1983] 1 W.L.R. 642 at pp. 657–660.

36. The bills of lading which were delivered to Westpac in early July, served several purposes. First, it was necessary to present the bills of lading to BOC in order to obtain payment by that bank, as issuing bank, in respect to the letter of credit. Second, the bills also served as security in respect of the cargo which was the subject of the bills of lading in the event that payment was not made by BOC. When Westpac received the bills and made payment for the cargo and freight, it acquired special property as the entity to delivery of the cargo. The provision of the bills to Westpac as pre-condition of the negotiation and payment of the amounts due gave rise to an implied pledge of title in the goods represented by the bills. The rationale for implication of the pledge is that the furnishing of the bills of lading to Westpac as security was a condition on which payment of the purchase price and freight was made by Westpac. The entitlement to delivery conferred by the possession of the bills of lading operated to secure Westpac against the contingency that BOC or its customers might not pay. The position is usefully summarized in *The Law of Bankers' Commercial Credits*, Gutteridge & Megrah, 1984 at p. 210 where the authors say[26]:

> "As regards the issuing bank such right [of resort to the documents of title for reimbursement of sums of moneys paid against them] is usually given by the agreement between it and its customer identified in the application for the credit. The intermediary bank has an implied pledge when it pays or negotiates documents tendered to it by the seller."

37. Further authority in support of this proposition can be found in *Guaranty Trust Co of New York v Hannay & Co* [1915] K.B. 536; *Ross T.*

---

[26] After a gap of 17 years, there is now a 2001 edition of this book, by Richard King; see further below.

Smyth & Co Ltd v TD Bailey Son & Co [1940] 3 All E.R. 60 at p. 68, and Pagets *Law of Banking*, 11th ed., 1996, at p. 694. Having regard to these authorities, in my view, at all material times during the discharge of the cargo between July 10 through July 14, 1995 Westpac, as the entity to call for delivery of the cargo, had a sufficient right to the cargo to make it a pledgee and to support its claim in conversion against the vessel for wrongful delivery.

38. Several further submissions require consideration in relation to the claim in conversion.

Possession of bills of lading

39. First it is submitted for Jindalee and the vessel that as at the time of unloading, Westpac had lost any right or interest under bills of lading, which it might have otherwise acquired, when it forwarded the bills of lading on July 6, 1995 to BOC for acceptance. It is submitted that Westpac thereby surrendered possession of the title documents and that at the time cargo was discharged from the vessel Westpac was not a bearer or holder of the bills of lading. As at July 11 when unloading began it is said that the bills of lading were either in the course of delivery to BOC or were in the physical possession of BOC for acceptance. The documents appear to have been received by BOC on July 11, 1995. In relation to this question, it is important to note that both the advice documents sent on July 6, with which the bills were enclosed for acceptance, together with the BOC letter of credit itself, incorporate the 1993 edition of the Uniform Customs and Practice for Documentary Credits (U.C.P. 500) ("the U.C.P."). The relevant U.C.P. provisions are as follows:

[TAMBERLIN *J. set out Articles 13 and 14 (see Appendix C, below), and continued:*]

40. The provisions of the U.C.P. recognize that until the documents are **8–036** accepted and taken up by the issuing bank the bills of lading are to be held for return to the presenter. This position accords with the commercial reality of the present situation where the bills were to provide security to Westpac as negotiating bank until the documents specified in the letter of credit were accepted by BOC. The documents, in my view, were despatched on the basis that until acceptance they were to retain their character as security for the moneys paid out by Westpac. The possession of the bills did not move into a legal hiatus when they were despatched on July 6. They did not pass into the "possession" of BOC. As it turned out the documents required by the letter of credit were never accepted. In my view, they therefore never left the legal possession of Westpac, notwithstanding that they were not physically in the hands of Westpac at the time when the discharge of cargo was carried out. It could not, in my view, be suggested that Westpac ever had any intention, imputed or otherwise, to surrender its security or possessory rights under the bills

before acceptance by BOC. Until the documents were accepted by BOC Westpac remained at risk in relation to the moneys which it had paid as negotiating bank.

41. A second issue, which raises a question of fact, is whether Westpac was notified on or before mid-July, 1995 of any proposal to discharge the cargo against a letter or letters of indemnity without production of bills of lading. If the answer to this question is in the affirmative, then consequential questions arise as to whether Westpac impliedly agreed or consented to this course. If it did, so the argument runs, it could not maintain its claim in conversion.

[TAMBERLIN J. *continued to examine the evidence, concluding that there was no consent.*]

Note

8–037   A bank as holder of the bill of lading can also take delivery itself, of course, and exercise any of the other rights of the holder of a document of title, discussed in chapter 6, above.

(b) LEGAL TITLE

8–038   Constructive possession protects against non-payment by the buyer, but not his bankruptcy, since there is no point taking delivery of a bankrupt's goods. Protection against bankruptcy requires property.

The House of Lords held in *Sewell v Burdick* that a bank under a documentary credit does not obtain the general property, but only the special legal title of a pledgee. It obtains no property at all, however, if the seller has, by the time of tender of documents, already passed the entire property to the buyer (see further the discussion at para. 5–036, above).

SEWELL v BURDICK

House of Lords. (1884) 10 App. Cas. 74

Facts:

8–039   Machinery shipped aboard the respondent's vessel was landed at a Black Sea port, and warehoused in a Russian custom-house. The shipper disappeared, and accordingly under Russian law, the cargo was sold to pay custom-house duty and charges. The sale realised no more than was sufficient for that purpose.

The appellants, who were bankers in Manchester, had taken bills of lading for the machinery, as security for a £300 advance to the shipper. They did not claim delivery of the cargo (which had in any case been lawfully sold), but the respondents claimed freight from the appellants, on the basis that as holders of bills of lading they became liable under the Bills of Lading Act 1855.[27]

---

[27] Section 1 depended on property in the goods passing "upon or by reason of . . . consignment or indorsement." The respondents claimed that by virtue of the decision in *Lickbarrow v Mason*, discussed in para. 6–043, above, the transfer of the bills of lading to the bank had also transferred the entire legal property in the goods to them, as required by the section.

Held:

The House held that they were unable to do so. The reasoning of Lords Blackburn, Bramwell and FitzGerald was essentially that it did not follow from the *Lickbarrow v Mason* that a bank as pledgee obtained the entire legal property in the goods in order to trigger s.1. As pledgee a bank obtains only a special property in the goods, and not the general property so that generally s.1 was inapplicable.[28]

The case remains important only for its discussion of special property. The liability of a bank today would be determined by s.3 of the Carriage of Goods by Sea Act 1992 (see chapter 13, below).

LORD FITZGERALD: My Lords, Field J. in the Court below came to the conclusion that the transaction under investigation was intended by the parties to operate as a pledge only. There can be no doubt that the inference thus drawn by the learned judge was correct in fact. It seems to follow that the pledgees acquired a special property in the goods with a right to take actual possession, should it be necessary to do so for their protection or for the realisation of their security. They acquired no more, and subject thereto the general property remained in the pledgor.

I am of opinion that the delivery of the indorsed bill of lading to the defendants as a security for their advance did not by necessary implication transfer the property in the goods to the defendants. They were not therefore "indorsees of a bill of lading to whom the property in the goods passed by reason of the indorsement," so as to make them without more "subject to the same liabilities in respect of such goods as if the contract contained in the bill of lading had been made with them."

8–040

(c) EQUITABLE TITLE

As long as the bank retains the bill of lading, then, it retains constructive possession and (often) legal title to the goods. Suppose the buyer needs to re-sell the goods in order to pay the issuing bank. He cannot re-sell the goods without obtaining the bill of lading. If the bank releases the bill of lading to him it loses its security in the goods.

8–041

The solution is for the bank to release the bill of lading to the buyer only in exchange for a trust receipt, under which the buyer declares himself trustee of the goods for the bank. Usually the buyer is also authorised to sell the goods, as agent or trustee for the bank, in which case he becomes trustee, for the bank, of the proceeds of sale.

Under this arrangement the bank becomes equitable owner of the goods until sold. This equitable property is independent of any legal title the bank has to the goods; however, legal title must have passed to the buyer, in order for him to declare himself trustee. Before the 1995 amendments to the Sale of Goods Act (see chapter 5, above), neither bank nor buyer would have had legal title to part of an undivided bulk cargo, but this will not normally now be the case. If the buyer goes bankrupt before the goods are sold, the bank can assert his equitable title against the buyer's liquidator, or trustee in bankruptcy.

If the buyer sells the goods as agent or trustee of the bank, then the bank loses any equitable title it had to the goods, but gains equitable title to the proceeds of

---

[28] *e.g.* Lord Blackburn (1884) 10 App. Cas. 74, at 95 and 102–103; Lord Bramwell at 104, and Lord Fitzgerald at 106.

sale. In the event of the buyer's non-payment, this equitable title can be asserted as long as the proceeds remain traceable in equity.

NORTH WESTERN BANK LTD v JOHN POYNTER & SON

House of Lords. [1895] A.C. 56

8–042   The pledgors of a bill of lading (Page & Co) were under a contract to sell goods represented by the bill of lading (phosphate rock) to third parties (Cross & Co). The pledgees (the appellant bank) returned the bill of lading to the pledgors to enable them to effect their sale, on the following terms:

> "It is distinctly agreed that we [the bank] are to have immediate and absolute power of sale, and that under that power we authorise and empower you [the pledgors] to enter into contracts of sale of the merchandise on our behalf in the ordinary course of business, and we expressly direct you to pay to us from time to time the proceeds of all such sales immediately and specifically as received by you to be applied towards payment of the said advance, interest, commission, and all charges.
>
> "You are at any time at our request to give us full authority to receive all sums due or to become due from any person or persons in respect of any sales of the merchandise so made by you on our behalf."

The pledgors sold the cargo to Cross & Co, and went bankrupt before reimbursing the bank. The purchase money was identifiable, and was in fact still being held by Cross & Co, not having yet been paid over to Page & Co In Scottish arrestment proceedings, the issue was whether the bank had title to the debt against Cross & Co (Poynter, another creditor of Page & Co, took arrestment proceedings against the fund, but the arrest would be invalid if the bank had title.)

Held:
Because Page & Co were merely acting as agents for the bank in selling its goods on its behalf, the debt was owed to the bank. Thus, the bank's security was unaffected by the release of documents to Page & Co, and the subsequent sale.

Notes
1. There was an additional conflict of laws point, because though both parties were domiciled in England the money was in Scotland. It was held that English law applied. The point has no general relevance to the subject matter of this chapter.
2. Though this was not an advance on a commercial credit, the result would have been unchanged had it been.

(d) Legal and Equitable Title Defeated by Fraud

The trust receipt is fine, as long as the proceeds of sale remain traceable in equity. In common with many other devices in export trade, however, it gives poor protection against the buyer's fraud, for example if the buyer resells the goods and dishonestly misappropriates the proceeds. Then the proceeds may no longer be traceable, but the bank will also have lost any title it had to the goods.   **8–043**

LLOYDS BANK LTD v BANK OF AMERICA

Court of Appeal. [1938] 2 K.B. 147

Lloyds Bank had advanced money on the security of shipping documents, which it released to the pledgor, Strauss & Co, "in order to enable the [pledgor] to sell the merchandise as trustees for the plaintiffs . . . " The pledgor signed a trust receipt, undertaking "that the proceeds of the sale of the said merchandise or any portion thereof will be received by us as your trustees and kept separate from other monies and will be remitted to you as and when received by us."   **8–044**

The pledgor did not in fact do re-sell the goods in order to reimburse the bank, but fraudulently transferred the bills of lading to the Bank of America, thereby raising further money on the goods. The pledgor then went into liquidation, without reimbursing Lloyds Bank. Presumably no proceeds were traceable, since Lloyds Bank attempted to claim the documents back from the Bank of America, or damages for their conversion. In effect, therefore, they claimed title to the goods themselves.

Held:
The pledgor was able to pass good title to the second bank, despite the property reserved by the first bank by means of the trust receipt, because of the application of the Factors Act 1889, s.2(1). This provision (set out in Appendix F) allows mercantile agents in possession of goods (or documents representing the goods) with the consent of the owner, to pass good title to a third party. Lloyds Bank was regarded as owner for these purposes, and the pledgor was held to be a mercantile agent within the meaning of the section (even though he also had the general property in the goods).

SIR WILFRED GREENE M.R.: *(at 161)* On that state of facts the first question which arises is, quite shortly, this: Were Strauss & Co, Ltd., mercantile agents in possession of those shipping documents with the consent of the owner? I will put on one side for the moment the question whether they were mercantile agents, because that is a question which is one on which we have not heard a very great deal of argument. I will proceed at once to the question on which the greater part of the argument has turned.   **8–045**

It is said: When you look at the relevant date, which is the date when Strauss & Co, Ltd., came, into possession of those documents, is it true to say that they were in possession of those documents with the consent of the owner? The argument, if I understood it correctly, was of this nature, that, where goods have been pledged, the only person whom you can with correct use of language describe as the owner is the pledgor. As justification for that it is said that the pledgor is the person who has the general property in the goods and the interest of the pledgee is merely a limited and particular interest. As an abstract proposition that, no doubt, is, in substance, correct. But the question in this case is: Who is the owner for the purpose of this section? I myself find it only confusing to go into abstract questions of what the word "owner" may mean in other contexts and for other purposes. The object of the section and the history of the legislation is too familiar to require statement. When I look at the language of s.2 of the Factors Act, 1889, itself I find in it what appears to me to be a very clear clue to the meaning of the word "owner." Sect. 2, sub-s.1, states *[His Lordship read the sub-section—see Appendix F, below].* The section, therefore, on its face is contemplating that the person it describes as the "owner" will be the person who would be in a position to give express authority with regard to the dealing in question. It seems to me that a person who would not be in a position to give that express authority cannot by himself constitute what is described as the owner. It may, of course, very well be, and it happens very frequently, that the incidents and rights of ownership are divided among two or more hands. One person may have the right to possession, which is one of the rights incident to ownership, and another person may have all the other rights incident to ownership. Nevertheless it is only the two of them who can confer on a third party the ownership of the property in question. It is only by their combining in an assignment that they can confer a good title. I am quite unable to read the word "owner" in this section as excluding such a case. It seems to me that, where the right of ownership has become divided among two or more persons in such a way that the acts which the section is contemplating could never be authorized save by both or all of them, these persons together constitute the owner. If it is with the consent of those persons that the mercantile agent is in possession of the documents, then he is in possession of them with the consent of the owner within the meaning of the section.

. . . In the present case, according to a practice which is as familiar as any mercantile practice can be, the person entrusted with the sale was not a third party at all, but the actual merchant himself. Does that make any difference from the point of view of the construction of the section? In my opinion it does not. It is perfectly true (and here for a moment I am disregarding the special language of the covering documents in this case, to which I shall return later) that the pledgor obtained possession of the documents in contemplation of a sale which was to some extent in his own interest and which would affect his own title as pledgor, and to that extent may be regarded as intending to act as a principal in the transaction. But I find nothing in the section which excludes from the case contemplated the case where the mercantile agent himself has got some interest in the property with which he is dealing. It seems to me that one may have a case, and for all I know it may be a common case, where a person who is himself a mercantile agent has in combination with somebody else the ownership of goods. A mercantile agent may have some interest in goods the remaining interest in which is vested in somebody else. It seems to me quite impossible to say that, when such a mercantile agent is allowed to have possession of the goods with the consent of the other person interested, for the purpose of selling, the section does not apply, because the mercantile agent himself has also got some interest which must be brought in in order to give a purchaser a complete title. It appears to me that that would be putting too narrow a meaning on the section. In such a case the possession would be referable in part to the mercantile agent's own interest and in part to the consent of the person having the residuary interest, who in combination with the agent would be the owner for the purposes of the section.

[He went on to conclude that Strauss & Co were mercantile agents.]

Notes

1. The Bank of America could not claim property merely by virtue of its possession of the bill of lading, because the pledgor's title was defective. If bills of lading were negotiable instruments, as opposed to being merely documents of title, the Bank of America would have been able to succeed even without invoking the Factors Act provision.   **8–046**

2. The same principles as in the case apply if under a documentary credit the buyer resells the goods and fraudulently dissipates the proceeds. Title in the goods passes to the sub-buyer under the Factors Act provision, and (if dissipated) the proceeds of sale no longer exist. So there is nothing left in which the bank can claim any property.

3. The only protection against this type of fraud is for the issuing bank to make certain of the honesty of the buyer before agreeing to open the credit. Banks should therefore take the necessary precautions before agreeing to act.

(7) Relationship Between Seller and Confirming Bank

Article 9(a) of the U.C.P. provides: **8–047**

"An irrevocable Credit constitutes a definite undertaking of the Issuing Bank [*to pay*], provided that the stipulated documents are presented to the Nominated Bank or to the Issuing Bank and that the terms and conditions of the credit are complied with . . . "

The various forms of payment are then set out, as discussed above. We will see in the next chapter that receipt of the notification of an irrevocable credit normally has immediate consequences for the seller, his liability to perform under the sale contract being contingent on that receipt. Also, after that time he is usually obliged to seek payment in the first instance from the confirming bank, and cannot sue the buyer directly (see the discussion of short-circuiting in the next chapter). Ideally, the bank should be unable to revoke from that time onwards. This position obtains in the United States.

In *United City Merchants v Royal Bank of Canada, The American Accord*, discussed in detail in chapter 10, below, Lord Diplock thought it "trite law" that the relationship between confirming bank and seller is contractual, and that the contract was autonomous (*i.e.* independent of contracts 1 and 2). If this is correct, it renders obsolete old theories as to the nature of the relationship, such as are now consigned to Appendix 5 of Gutteridge and Megrah's *Law of Bankers' Commercial Credits* (8th ed., Europa, 2001), by Richard King.

The American Accord involved a confirmed irrevocable credit, but exactly the same problems apply in an unconfirmed credit, as to the nature of the relationship between issuing bank and beneficiary.

(a) THE PROBLEM

The seller does not normally make any promise to the bank that it will perform. Usually the seller is merely notified of the opening of the credit, and need not communicate with the bank at all, prior to tender of the shipping documents. On a contractual analysis, the opening of the credit must constitute an offer by the confirming bank. Since the seller makes no promise to do anything at this stage it must be a unilateral offer (*i.e.* binding only one party, the bank). By tendering the documents the seller clearly accepts the unilateral offer, and provides considering (the requested performance), and so there are no problems in cases such as *The American Accord* itself, where the seller who had tendered documents successfully sued the confirming bank. The problem arises if the bank revokes its offer at an earlier stage, *i.e.* if it purports to revoke an irrevocable credit. The problem is merely a specific example of the more general problem, well-known to first year students of the law of contract, when does a unilateral offer become irrevocable. Whatever view you take of the general problem, the answer might be starting to perform, or maybe completion of performance, but it will not be simple receipt of the offer.

ATIYAH, *THE SALE OF GOODS*

10th ed., p. 439

[Footnotes are as in the original, but have been renumbered for inclusion in this chapter.]

8–048   In the past, doubts have even existed as to whether the seller could sue the bank if it refused to honour a confirmed credit, anyhow prior to shipment, on the ground that there is no contract between seller and bank, owing to the absence of any consideration supplied by the seller. There is no difficulty when the goods have once been shipped, because this is action by the seller in reliance on the bank's undertaking, and that should suffice as a valid consideration by any modern test. In practice, banks never take this technical point and judicial pronouncements now seem to put their liability beyond doubt.[29]

---

[29] See especially *Hamzeh Malas & Sons v British Imex Industries Ltd* [1958] 2 Q.B. 127, 129, *per* Jenkins L.J.; *Urquhart Lindsay & Co v Eastern Bank Ltd* [1922] 1 K.B. 318; *United City Merchants (Investments) Ltd v Royal Bank of Canada* [1983] 1 A.C. 168, 183, *per* Lord Diplock.

Notes

Richard King, in the new edition of Gutteridge and Megrah, also concludes (at   **8–049**
p. 77) that it is "clear that the beneficiary has contractual rights", but the cases
cited in Atiyah are not particularly convincing. In *U.C.M.* there was obviously a
contract, because the documents had been tendered by the seller, and in both the
other cases there had been a tender, which had been accepted by the bank, albeit
that the sales were by instalments, the issue arising on later instalments. *Hamzeh
Malas* in any case concerned contract 1, not contract 4.

Treitel is more doubtful, and sees that acceptance, as well as consideration, can
be problematic.[30] Of the consideration problem he concludes[31]:

> "The widely held commercial view is that the bank is bound as soon as the
> seller is notified of the credit. If (as seems probable) this view also represents
> the law, it is best regarded as an exception to the doctrine of consideration."

But in view of the retrenchment in the *Brandt v Liverpool* cases in chapter 13—see
below, where the courts have been very reluctant to extend conventional views of
offer, acceptance and consideration, it is difficult to see why they should make an
exception here. I would argue that the conclusion to the Atiyah passage above is
simply wrong.

There is also the observation that in "practice, banks never take this technical
point", and writers in the past have suggested that a reputable bank would never
revoke, and that the problem is therefore academic (the implication also being
that academic points are not worth discussing). Yet Lord Diplock observed in *The
American Accord* (see chapter 10) that:

> "I must confess that the argument that a seller should be content to rely on the
> exercise by banks of business expediency, unbacked by any legal liability, to
> ensure prompt payment by a foreign buyer does not impress me . . . "

I would argue that the following two views are not only untenable, but bordering
on outrageous:

1. That a group of businessmen is so reputable that it should be regarded as
   being above the law;

2. That special legal principles should apply to just one area of business
   activity.

(b) Possible Solutions

Elsewhere I have suggested that a bank, by revoking an irrevocable credit,   **8–050**
could put the buyer in breach of his contractual obligation to provide a "reliable
and solvent paymaster" (on which see chapter 9, below), and hence that the bank
could itself incur liability for interference with contract.[32] The difficulty with this
solution is that the liability of the banker depends on the terms of the contract of
sale, which does not accord with the principle of the autonomy of the credit.

Richard King (at p. 78) observes that the problem may have been solved by the
Contracts (Rights of Third Parties) Act 1999, since it would allow the seller to
enforce a term of contract 2, conferring a benefit on him. No doubt this is in
principle correct, but it means that the seller is enforcing contract 2, not contract
4. Neither solution, therefore, sits happily with the autonomy of the credit.

[30] Treitel, *Law of Contract* (10th ed., 1999), p. 38.
[31] At p. 140.
[32] P. N. Todd, *Sellers and Documentary Credits* [1983] J.B.L. 468.

CHAPTER 9

DOCUMENTARY CREDITS AND THE SALE CONTRACT

(1) SALE CONTRACT REQUIREMENTS FOR CREDIT

9–001   CREDIT requirements will ultimately be determined by the sale contract, which is therefore sometimes referred to as the underlying transaction.

Because the contract of sale is autonomous, it has no direct effect on the obligations of the banks under the credit. The contracts constituting the credit (contracts 2, 3 and 4) are independent of the underlying transaction (contract 1). If the required form of credit is not provided by the buyer the seller may thereby have an action against the buyer under the sale contract (contract 1), but his relationship with issuing or confirming bank will be determined by the terms of the credit actually provided (contract 4). Therefore, if the credit does not conform to the sale contract requirements the seller may sue the buyer on the contract of sale, or (as in the following case) use the buyer's non-performance as a defence to an action on the sale contract by the buyer, but can take no steps to remedy the situation against either bank directly.

(a) IMPLIED REQUIREMENT FOR IRREVOCABLE CREDIT

9–002   Where the sale contract provides for sale by documentary credit, the courts presume a requirement for an irrevocable credit unless the contrary is expressly stated.[1]

GIDDENS v ANGLO-AFRICAN PRODUCE LTD

King's Bench Division. (1923) 14 Ll.L. Rep. 230

Decision:

9–003   Giddens, c.i.f. purchasers (under two contracts) of South African yellow maize sued the sellers (Anglo-African Produce) for damages for non-fulfilment of the contracts. Bailhache J. accepted the defendant sellers' contention that the credit required by the sale contract had not been opened, so that the condition precedent for their performance had not arisen. The sellers were therefore not in breach.

BAILHACHE J.: (at 230 (col. 2)) I think this case is quite hopeless. Here is a contract which calls for an established credit and in purported satisfaction of what this contract calls for what they get is this: "Negotiations of

[1] With the 1993 revisions, the U.C.P. position has been brought into line with that of the common law: see art. 6, set out in App. C, below.

drafts under these credits are subject to the bank's convenience. All drafts hereunder are negotiated with recourse against yourselves." How that can be called an established credit in any sense of the word absolutely passes my comprehension.

Notes

1. This was not an irrevocable credit because under an irrevocable negotiation credit the drafts must be negotiated without recourse against the drawer.[2] It appears from the (very short and not very clear) report of the case that the sale contract did not call expressly for an irrevocable credit, but it is usually assumed that a requirement for an irrevocable credit was implied.

    9–004

2. There is no presumption, by contrast, that a credit is required to be confirmed, unless the sale contract expressly so states.[3]

3. The contracts provided that, in the event of default by the sellers (which the buyers unsuccessfully alleged), the contract should be closed out at a price determined by the London Corn Trade Association. The price had risen from the contract price of around 31s. per 480 lb., to over 37s., and the buyers claimed the difference as damages. If the buyers were bulk commodity traders, a possible effect of non-performance by the sellers would be to leave them short on maize. They would remedy this by purchasing on the futures market, and (had they been able to establish a breach by the sellers) their loss would be the difference between the contract price and the price determined by the futures market. Had they already been long, the effect of the alleged sellers' breach would have been to leave them less long, with less to sell on the futures market. Their loss would have been the same in that case.

4. It is interesting, anyway, that the sale contract assumed that the buyers would remedy a seller's breach by closing out, rather than buying equivalent maize on the physical market. On the relationship between physical and futures markets in general, see chapter 1, above. This is a converse situation (in fact) to *Gebruder Metelmann GmbH & Co K.G. v N.B.R. (London) Ltd* [1984] 1 Lloyd's Rep. 614 (see para. 1–043), where a seller mitigated his loss, on a buyer's breach, by selling on a futures market.

(b) TERMS OF CREDIT

The contract of sale, and the contracts making up the credit, are autonomous, so that the obligation of, *e.g.* the confirming bank to accept the documents tendered is determined by the contracts making up the credit, not the sale contract. This relationship is considered further in chapter 10, below.

    9–005

In principle, of course, the sale contract can determine the terms of the credit, in the sense that, if the terms are too onerous, the buyer will be put in breach of the sale contract. Obviously, the sale contract may make express provision, but where it does not, the courts appear reluctant to imply stipulations, so that the buyer has considerable freedom over the terms of the credit, in the absence of express stipulation to the contrary.

---

[2] See Ch. 8 on methods of payment. Although the report is rather inadequate, this appears to be a negotiation credit, where drafts are drawn on the buyer (applicant), the issuing bank undertaking merely to negotiate the drafts. This form of credit is rare, and indeed, the U.C.P. provides that "A Credit should not be issued available by Draft(s) on the Applicant" (*e.g.* arts 9(a)(iv); 9(b)(iv)).

[3] There was no implication, for example, in *Maran Road v Austin Taylor*, in para. 8–027 and also below, that the credit should have been confirmed by Bangkok Bank.

SOPROMA SPA v MARINE & ANIMAL BY-PRODUCTS CORPORATION

Commercial Court. [1966] 1 Lloyd's Rep. 367

Facts:

The buyer agreed to buy 1,000 tons of Chilean fish fullmeal from the seller c. & f., the sale contract also requiring a 70 per cent. protein content. Under the sale contract, payment was to be by irrevocable documentary credit, but apart from stipulating the identity of the advising bank (Marine and Midland Trust Co, New York), the sale contract was otherwise silent as to the details of the credit. It was unclear whether the credit was also required to be confirmed by Marine and Midland Trust Co.

The credit that was eventually opened (there were a number of variations agreed to the original sale contract, as described further below) stipulated that the shipping documents must include (among others) a certificate of analysis stating that it had a minimum protein content of 70 per cent., and full set of on board ocean bills of lading, issued to order and blank indorsed, and marked "freight prepaid".

The sellers tendered a bill of lading marked "freight collect", and naming the confirming bank as consignee, but not issued to order. A quality certificate was also tendered certifying a minimum protein content of only 67 per cent. The bank rejected the documents,[4] and the sellers attempted to make a second tender, directly to the buyers. This was also rejected.[5] The sellers went to arbitration, claiming that the buyers were in breach of the contract of sale, and the Umpire found in their favour. The buyers appealed to the Board of Appeal of the London Cattle Food Trade Association (L.C.F.T.A.), which stated a special case for decision by the High Court. One of the issues was whether the buyers, by procuring credits which stipulated additional documents to those required by the sale contract itself, were thereby acting in breach of the contract of sale.

Held:

McNair J. held that the buyers were not in breach.

9–006 McNair J.: *(on the credit requirements, at 386 (col. 1))* It may be that [*the credits opened by the buyers*] were ... defective in that they called for documents in addition to those specified in the contract itself. This was the view expressed by the Board of Appeal in par. 39 (c) of their findings of fact set out above. But as at present advised, I should not feel disposed to accept this conclusion. It seems to me to be a necessary implication from the use of the words "payment against letters of credit" that the credit itself should set out in detail the specific conditions under which it can be operated including the period of its availability and that so long as

---

[4] See further at para. 10–027, below.
[5] See further below at para. 9–029.

these conditions are fair and reasonable and not inconsistent with the terms of the contract itself no objection can be taken to them by the sellers. It is to be observed that the Board of Appeal though advancing in par. 39 (c) the view stated above, themselves, after stating in Par. 40 (1) that:

" . . . it is therefore unnecessary for the purposes of this Award to find whether the letters of credit opened by the Buyers failed to conform with the terms of the contract . . . "

found that the letters of credit were not inconsistent with the terms of the contract.

Observations
McNair J.'s view, in essence, was that the terms of the credit are contained in the credit itself, and cannot generally be implied from the sale contract, subject only to the implied requirement that the credit terms must be fair and reasonable, and must not conflict with the express terms of the sale contract. This view, which accords the buyers a discretion, is *obiter*, since the seller was in any case estopped from relying on any inconsistencies in the credit (see below). It is however consistent with a general reluctance to imply terms into commercial contracts, subject to the normal officious bystander and business efficacy tests.

The documents required in *Soproma* were consistent with the sale contract, in that the 70 per cent. protein requirement was the same, and freight prepaid bills would be usual under c. & f. contracts (although buyers will not necessarily object to freight collect bills, as long as freight is deducted from the invoice price, or a freight receipt tendered by the sellers.)[6]

Conversely, a requirement for a certificate of analysis showing 80 per cent. protein would clearly be inconsistent with the sale contract. Some documents would in any case be inconsistent with any c.i.f. (or c. & f.) contract, and could not be stipulated. We saw in para. 6–102, for example, that a requirement for a quality certificate issued on discharge, or indeed at any other time after shipment, could not be stipulated under a c.i.f. contract. Therefore, if such a document were stipulated in the credit, the terms of the credit would necessarily be inconsistent with a c.i.f. sale contract, and the buyer would be in breach.

The following case considers a similar inconsistency, but for an f.o.b. contract.

GLENCORE GRAIN ROTTERDAM BV v LORICO

Court of Appeal. [1997] 2 Lloyd's Rep. 386, noted [1997] I.T.L.Q. 46

The importance of the case is that the Court of Appeal held that f.o.b. sellers were entitled to refuse to load the cargo (of wheat), where the credit required freight prepaid bills of lading.   **9–007**

There was also an issue as to whether the sellers had waived their right to rely on the buyers' failure to open a contractual letter of credit. See below (para. 9–022).

EVANS L.J.: The first issue, therefore, is whether the buyers under a sale contract on what are described as normal f.o.b. terms are entitled to open

---

[6] McNair J., at 387 (col. 1).

a letter of credit which requires the sellers to present "freight pre-paid" bills of lading if they are to receive payment from the buyers' bank. Absent any special agreement, the sellers are entitled to see a conforming letter of credit in place before they begin shipment of the goods, and then their obligation is to ship the contract goods on board the vessel provided by the buyers, for carriage on whatever terms as to freight and otherwise the buyers have agreed with the shipowner. The sellers are expressly free of any obligation to pay freight (special terms apart, f.o.b. is the antithesis of c. & f.—cost and freight) and in the normal course they cannot be sure before shipment that the shipowner will issue freight pre-paid bills of lading, unless they are prepared if necessary to pay the amount of freight themselves, or unless some other guaranteed payment mechanism is already in place. I would put the matter broadly in that way, because it may be that an undertaking from the shipowner himself, or a third party guarantee of the payment of freight following due shipment of the goods, would suffice . . . It is abundantly clear, in my judgment, that the buyers' own assurance cannot be enough to serve as a guarantee to the sellers that "freight pre-paid" bills of lading will be issued when shipment is complete. That would mean, as the Judge pointed out, that the security of a bank guarantee for the payment of the price, which is what the letter of credit mechanism provides, would be destroyed. I therefore agree with the Judge's observations that the buyers' contention, that the letter of credit terms were in conformity with the contract, is contrary both to the underlying concept of the f.o.b. contract (subject always to what special terms may be agreed in a particular case) and to the essential commercial purpose of the letter of credit machinery.

9–008   LONGMORE J.: *(at first instance,[7] whose view was upheld in the Court of Appeal)*

. . . I fear I cannot agree with the Board of Appeal that in the circumstances it is right to imply an entitlement on the part of the buyers that payment under the letter of credit need only be made if the bills of lading are marked "freight pre-paid".

I say that for two reasons. The first reason is that such a term is inconsistent with the operation of an f.o.b. contract. It is no doubt right to say that a seller or shipper under an f.o.b. contract must normally procure and present a bill of lading. But that bill of lading will not usually be a freight pre-paid bill of lading for the simple reason that as between seller and buyer the seller has not agreed to pay the costs of carriage. It is for the buyer to make and pay for such carriage arrangements as are made. Freight may in fact be paid before bills of lading are issued but that is not within the control of the seller. A requirement that he present freight pre-paid bills of lading in order to operate a letter of credit presupposes that he can obtain such bills of lading. He cannot in fact be sure to obtain such

---

[7] [1997] 1 Lloyd's Rep. 578.

bills of lading since payment of freight is entirely within the control of the buyer.

If authority be needed for this comparatively elementary proposition, it can be found in the case of *Green v Sichel* (1860) 7 C.B.N.S. 747, in which the requirement that the f.o.b. seller produce to the buyer a bill of lading was regarded as a custom of the trade rather than, as now, a duty imposed on the seller by implication in the usual form of f.o.b. contract; see *Pyrene Co Ltd v Scindia Navigation Co Ltd* [1954] 2 Q.B. 402 at p. 424 *per* Mr Justice Devlin.

Nevertheless the facts of the older case are relevant because the ship-owner would not release the bill of lading for the goods unless a much higher rate of freight was paid than had previously and normally been charged. The jury found (1) that the price of the goods did not by custom of the trade become payable until there had been produced to the buyer a bill of lading or other document evidencing shipment and, (2), that the seller had not undertaken to pay the freight or obtain a bill of lading. The Court of Common Pleas on the further findings of the jury said that the seller had placed the goods on board the vessel with the intention of parting with control over them by way of delivering them to the buyers. The buyers could not therefore rely on the custom of the trade, that a bill of lading be produced, when they, who had the obligation to pay the freight, were preventing the bill of lading from being procured. This case is, in my view, authority for the proposition that the buyer under a normal f.o.b. contract is not entitled to insist that the seller must procure a bill of lading, if it is necessary to pay freight, in order to get the bill of lading. It is so treated in Benjamin *Sale of Goods*, 4th ed., par. 20–020,[8] and it must follow that one cannot imply into this contract of sale an entitlement on the part of the buyers to insist that a letter of credit only be operated on production of freight pre-paid bills of lading.

Notes

1. Longmore J.'s reasoning is different from that in the Court of Appeal, in that he emphasises that the buyer can actually prevent the bill of lading, in the required form, from being issued at all.

2. We saw in chapter 3, above, that some f.o.b. contracts place on sellers the obligation to pay freight, to buyers' account. In that case, a freight pre-paid bill would also be appropriate.[9] The comments above are limited to a "normal" f.o.b. contract.

(2) CREDIT MORE THAN SIMPLY MEANS OF PAYING THE PRICE

In a well-known passage in *Hamzeh Malas & Sons v British Imex Industries Ltd*, **9–009** Jenkins L.J. said[10]:

---

[8] Now Benjamin, *Sale of Goods* (5th ed., 1997), para. 20–020.
[9] See paras 3–005 and 3–014, above.
[10] [1958] 2 Q.B. 127, 129.

"it seems to me to be plain enough that the opening of a confirmed letter of credit constitutes a bargain between the banker and the vendor of goods, which imposes upon the banker an absolute obligation to pay, irrespective of any dispute there may be between the parties as to whether the goods are up to contract or not."

The sellers, relying on this absolute obligation, may incur expense and risk in manufacturing or purchasing and shipping the goods. They may themselves use the security of the credit to set up a back-to-back credit (see para. 8–029, above), as buyers. Accordingly, the courts recognise that the credit is more than simply a means of paying the price, since the seller may be relying on it to finance the transaction.

(a) Provision of Credit Condition Precedent to Seller's Performance

9–010   The importance of the following case is that (generally) the opening of the credit was a condition precedent of seller's performance under sale contract, so that the seller is under no obligation to perform at all until the credit is opened. Also, since the seller may be relying on the credit to finance the transaction, damages caused by his impecuniosity are not necessarily too remote.

TRANS TRUST SPRL v DANUBIAN TRADING CO LTD

Court of Appeal. [1952] 2 Q.B. 297

Facts and decision:

9–011   The plaintiffs agreed to sell to the defendants 1,000 tons of steel, it being agreed that the sale should be by irrevocable credit,[11] which the plaintiffs needed in order to finance the transaction. The defendant buyers failed to procure the opening of a credit in accordance with the requirements of sale contract, and Denning L.J. (as he then was) took the view that, at least in this particular case, the sellers were under no obligation to perform at all in the absence of a credit.

The sellers were also able to claim damages for loss of profit on the transaction, although the market price of the steel had risen above the contract price, so that ordinarily they would have suffered no loss. The failure to provide the sale contract made them too impecunious to purchase the steel at all, though, and therefore could be said to have led foreseeably to their loss.

9–012   Denning L.J.: *(at 304–305)* This is another case concerned with the modern practice whereby a buyer agrees to provide a banker's confirmed credit in favour of the seller. This credit is an irrevocable promise by a banker to pay money to the seller in return for the shipping documents. One reason for this practice is because the seller wishes to be assured in advance not only that the buyer is in earnest but also that he, the seller, will in fact obtain his money when he delivers the goods. Another reason is because the seller often has expenses to pay in connexion with the goods and he wishes to use the credit so as to pay those expenses. He may, for instance, be himself a merchant, who is buying the goods from the growers or the manufacturers, and has to pay for them before he can

---

[11] The credit is described as "confirmed" in the report, but it would be "irrevocable" in modern terminology.

obtain delivery, and his own bank will only grant him facilities for the purpose if he has the backing of a letter of credit. The ability of the seller to carry out the transaction is, therefore, dependent on the buyer providing the letter of credit, and for this reason the seller stipulates that the credit should be provided at a specified time well in advance of the time for delivery of the goods.

What is the legal position of such a stipulation? Sometimes it is a condition precedent to the formation of a contract, that is, it is a condition which must be fulfilled before any contract is concluded at all. In those cases the stipulation "subject to the opening of a credit" is rather like a stipulation "subject to contract". If no credit is provided, there is no contract between the parties. In other cases a contract is concluded and the stipulation for a credit is a condition which is an essential term of the contract. In these cases the provision of the credit is a condition precedent, not to the formation of the contract, but to the obligation of the seller to deliver the goods. If the buyer fails to provide the credit, the seller can treat himself as discharged from any further performance of the contract and can sue the buyer for damages for not providing the credit.

The first question is: what was the nature of the stipulation in this case? When the buyers sent their order, they stated in writing . . . that "a credit will be opened forthwith." . . . The statement was a firm promise by the buyers by which they gave their personal assurance that a credit would be opened forthwith . . . [There] was then . . . a concluded contract by the sellers to sell, and the buyers to buy, the steel for December-January delivery, and it was a part of that contract that the buyers would be personally responsible for seeing that a credit should be opened forthwith. On those findings it is clear that the stipulation for a credit was not a condition precedent to the formation of any contract at all. It was a condition which was an essential term of a contract actually made.

That condition was not fulfilled. The sellers extended the time for the credit but it never came, not even after reasonable notice. The sellers were, therefore, discharged from any further performance on their side, and are entitled to claim damages. But what is the measure of damages? That is the important question in the case. The price of the goods had steadily risen from the date of the contract onwards, and the buyers say that the sellers could at any time have resold the goods for more than the contract price, and are, therefore, only entitled to nominal damages. If the claim of the sellers had been for damages for non-acceptance of goods, or for repudiation of the obligation to take delivery, then the damages would, no doubt, be nominal. But it is none of those things. It is a claim for damages for not providing a letter of credit. The buyers say that, even so, the credit is only a way of paying the price, and that the damages recoverable on that score are only nominal, because the seller could resell the goods at a profit.

This argument reminds me of the argument we heard in *Pavia & Co v Thurmann-Nielsen* [below]. It treats the obligation to provide a credit as the same thing as the obligation to pay the price. That is, I think, a mistake. A banker's confirmed credit is a different thing from payment. It is an assurance in advance that the seller will be paid. It is even more than that. It is a chose in action which is of immediate benefit to the seller. It is irrevocable by the banker, and it is often expressly made transferable by the seller. The seller may be relying on it to obtain the goods himself. If it is not provided, the seller may be prevented from obtaining the goods at all. The damages he will then suffer will not in fact be nominal. Even if the market price of the goods has risen, he will not be able to take advantage of the rise because he will not have any goods to resell. His loss will be the profit which he would have made if the credit had been provided. Is he entitled to recover that loss? I think he is [subject to the normal rules of remoteness of damage in contract] . . .

Notes

9–013   1. It was necessary to the decision to hold that the buyers were in breach of contract, in failing to provide the credit. Had the provision of the credit been a condition precedent, both sellers and buyers would have been relieved of any obligation to perform in the absence of a credit being provided. In *Trans Trust*, only the sellers were relieved of this obligation to perform, the buyers remaining liable in damages for breach of contract. This must be the normal position, since the buyers will normally undertake to provide the credit.

2. It was not strictly necessary, however, to hold the provision of the credit to be a condition precedent to performance, since had it been a warranty only, the decision would have been the same.

3. Damages for the breach were governed by the ordinary principles applicable to remoteness of damage in contract. Here, sellers claimed as damages the loss of profit which they would have made on the sale. The buyers claimed that the credit was no more than a way of paying the price, and that since the steel market was rising, the sellers should have resold at a profit. Therefore they had suffered no loss, so the damages ought to be nominal only.

In fact, the sellers had not resold the steel at a profit, because in the absence of a credit they were unable to purchase it from the manufacturers in the first place (since they were relying on the provision of the credit to finance the transaction). This is, of course, quite normal, and Denning L.J. thought that it was wrong to treat the provision of the credit as simply an alternative way of paying the price.

This reasoning can of course equally apply on a falling market. Diplock J. applied *Trans Trust SPRL v Danubian Trading Co Ltd*, on a falling market, in *Ian Stach Ltd v Baker Bosley Ltd*.[12] The sellers were held entitled validly to repudiate the sale contract because the credit had not been opened in time. Diplock J. had held that the measure of damages was the difference between the contract price and market price at the time of repudiation. The market price having fallen between the time of entering the contract and the time of its repudiation, the damages included compensation for the market loss suffered by the sellers through having to sell on a falling market.[13] Had the buyers properly performed by opening the credit in time, they would have obtained the contract price under the credit and would not have suffered any market loss.

---

[12] [1958] 2 Q.B. 130; see further para. 9–017, below.
[13] At 145. The contract price was $205 per tonne, and the market price was found to be $194 at the time of repudiation. It will not always be easy in practice to ascertain market price, but here evidence was accepted that a Swiss company was prepared to pay $194 for the goods on the relevant date.

4. Both sellers and buyers in *Trans Trust* were in a chain, and the sellers were put in breach of their own supply contract.[14] They failed to obtain damages for this, as too remote, because the buyers were unaware that the suppliers were themselves relying on the provision of the documentary credit, to obtain the goods. Had this also been within the contemplation of the parties, then presumably it too would have been recoverable.

(b) Time of Opening of Credit

The principle that the credit is more than simply a means of paying the price **9–014** also affects the time within which it must be opened, assuming this is not stipulated in the sale contract. The usual contractual position applies, that in the absence of express provision the courts imply a reasonable time.[15] What is a reasonable time will depend on the circumstances, but buyers should not assume that they can wait until the delivery period, which may be many months ahead in bulk commodity sales (*e.g.* the cases discussed at the end of chapter 7, above). In *Etablissements Chainbaux SARL v Harbormaster Ltd*, a reasonable time of not more than a month was implied, where delivery was not to take place for eight months. In Devlin J.'s view[16]:

"It is to be observed that the provision as to the letter of credit is to be contrasted with the provision as to delivery. Delivery is not to start until the lapse of eight months . . . It is plain, therefore, that although the letter of credit is to provide for payment against shipping documents, and therefore payment could not in any event be due until some eight months, when deliveries started, the buyers offered to establish the letter of credit before that. One can well understand the business reason for that. Sometimes a letter of credit is wanted merely because the seller is unwilling to make arrangements for shipment, which may involve him in expense, unless he knows he is going to be paid. That might be the normal case where the seller has got the goods and the only expense he has to incur in relation to them is to put them on board ship or otherwise arrange for their transport, but in this case it plainly is not so: the seller had to manufacture the goods [marine engines], and what he desires is to have the letter of credit for it is plainly so that he will have the assurance, within a few weeks and before he begins manufacture, that he is certain to be paid and that the labour of manufacture will not therefore be done in vain."

There, the sellers were held justified in repudiating the contract when the buyers clearly could not have complied with their obligation to provide a letter of credit within a reasonable time.[17]

In any contract for future delivery, the seller needs to be protected against market falls between the contract and delivery dates. This is another justification for refusing to allow the buyer to delay opening the credit until the date for delivery is imminent. In the event of the buyer's bankruptcy in the meantime, the seller would be unprotected against the market fall.

In addition to the reasonable time requirement, however, the courts have consistently held that if the contract provides for shipment by the seller at any time over a stated period, then in the absence of an express stipulation, the buyer

---

[14] The suppliers were also dependent on the credit in order to obtain the goods themselves, and were therefore also able to claim damages, on a rising market.

[15] This was established as a general contractual principle in *Hick v Raymond & Reid* [1893] A.C. 22 at 32–33, *per* Lord Watson, and applied in a documentary credit context by Porter J. in *Garcia v Page & Co Ltd* (1936) 55 Ll.L. Rep. 391, at 392 (col. 1).

[16] [1955] 1 Lloyd's Rep. 303, at 305 (col. 2).

[17] As extended by the conduct of the sellers.

must open the credit and make it available by the beginning of the shipment period. The authority for a c.i.f. contract is the Court of Appeal decision in *Pavia & Co SpA v Thurmann-Nielsen*.[18]

PAVIA & CO SPA v THURMANN-NIELSEN

Court of Appeal. [1952] 2 Q.B. 84

Facts:

9–015   A c.i.f. contract for the sale of 3,000 tons of shelled Brazilian groundnuts provided for shipment of the first 1,500 tons at any time between February 1 and April 30, 1949, and as to the second 1,500 tons at any time between March 1 and May 31 (at sellers' option), payment by confirmed, irrevocable letter of credit. The sellers having obtained the export licence on February 9, pressed the buyers to open the credit, but the buyers did not do so until April 22nd. The sellers refused to ship, and claimed damages from the buyers for breach of contract in failing to open the credit.

Held:

The sellers were entitled to succeed. The headnote states:

> "In a contract for the sale of goods c.i.f., shipment at the option of the seller over a prolonged period, which provides for payment by confirmed credit, the buyer, in the absence of express stipulation, must open the credit and make it available to the seller at the beginning of the shipment period. The seller is entitled, before shipment, to be assured that he will on shipment be paid. If the buyer is anxious not to have to put the credit machinery in motion until shortly before the seller is ready to ship, a provision for that purpose must be inserted in the contract."

DENNING L.J.: *(at 88)* The question in this case is this: In a contract which provides for payment by confirmed credit, when must the buyer open the credit? In the absence of an express stipulation, I think the credit must be made available to the seller at the beginning of the shipment period. The reason is because the seller is entitled, before he ships the goods, to be assured that, on shipment, he will get paid. The seller is not bound to tell the buyer the precise date when he is going to ship; and whenever he does ship the goods, he must be able to draw on the credit. He may ship on the very first day of the shipment period. If, therefore, the buyer is to fulfil his obligations he must make the credit available at the very first date when the goods may be lawfully shipped in compliance with the contract.

---

[18] [1952] 2 Q.B. 84.

Comment

The buyers claimed that since the credit was simply a means of paying   **9–016**
the price, there was no reason why the credit should be provided before
the price became payable (*i.e.* in a c.i.f. sale, on tender of shipping
documents). The Court of Appeal took the view that this was the wrong
approach. The credit was not simply a means of paying the price, but was
also intended to provide the seller with security.

Similar reasoning was applied to an f.o.b. contract by Diplock J. in *Ian
Stach Ltd v Baker Bosley Ltd*,[19] where the contract was f.o.b., rather than
c.i.f. The contract was described as "classic" f.o.b., where the ship is
nominated by the buyer, who is entitled to call for shipment at any time
within the stipulated shipment period.[20]

IAN STACH LTD v BAKER BOSLEY LTD

Queen's Bench Division. [1958] 2 Q.B. 130

Held:
In an f.o.b. contract providing for shipment date "August-September,   **9–017**
1956", and payment by confirmed, irrevocable credit, the buyers were
required to establish the credit by August 1, 1956, at the latest. The sellers
were justified in repudiating the contract when no credit had been
opened by August 14, and were also entitled to damages.

DIPLOCK J.: [*citing the c.i.f. authorities, then continuing (at 142)* The distinction between those cases and the present case is that this is a classic f.o.b.
contract in that the buyer is entitled to call for shipment at any time
within the shipping period and up to the end of the shipping period. The
authority for that (if any be wanted) is to be found in *J. & J. Cunningham
Ltd v Robert A. Munro & Co Ltd* (1922) 28 Com. Cas. 42 [see chapter 3,
above]. So it is said that there is a distinction to be drawn between a c.i.f.
contract and a classic f.o.b. contract, and a distinction to be drawn
between a classic f.o.b. contract and those f.o.b. contracts which were the
subjects of the cases to which Mr Kerr [for the sellers] referred [where the
seller had the duty and responsibility of fixing the shipping], namely, that
in the classic f.o.b. contract, where the buyer can dictate the date of
shipment, the seller is not obliged to commence any of the operations
directed to performing his obligations under the contract until he has had
shipping instructions or calling forward instructions from the buyer. It is
urged by Mr Lawson [for the buyers] that, applying the *ratio decidendi* in
the c.i.f. contract cases the *Pavia* [above] line of cases the time at which the

---

[19] [1958] 2 Q.B. 130.
[20] *J. & J. Cunningham Ltd v Robert A. Munro & Co Ltd* (1922) 28 Com. Cas. 42 (see Ch. 3,
above). The buyers argued unsuccessfully that this was a ground for distinguishing *Pavia*,
where the sale contract was on c.i.f. terms (and the time of shipment was at sellers' call):
[1958] 2 Q.B. 130, 142.

confirmed credit must be opened is a reasonable time before the shipping instructions take effect. The rival contention by Mr Kerr is that the credit must be opened a reasonable time (as he put it) before the earliest shipping date; but in his reply he was prepared to put it as at latest by the earliest shipping date. Mr Lawson, on the other hand, says that it must be a reasonable time before the actual shipping date.

There is no authority which guides me in this matter. It seems to me, however, that the contention for which Mr Kerr argues is the sensible one, and, since it is the sensible one, and since there is no authority to the contrary, the one which I am inclined to hold, and do hold, is good law.

I am fortified in this view by the fact that it is quite apparent from the correspondence and from the conduct of the parties in this case (and, so far as one can see, from that of the parties to the other contracts) that it is their view that that was the requirement of the contract. It seems to me that, particularly in a trade of this kind, where, as is known to all parties participating, there may well be a string of contracts all of which are financed by, and can only be financed by, the credit opened by the ultimate user which goes down the string getting less and less until it comes to the ultimate supplier, the business sense of the arrangement requires that by the time the shipping period starts each of the sellers should receive the assurance from the banker that if he performs his part of the contract he will receive payment. That seems to me at least to have the advantage of providing a definite date by which the parties know they have to fulfil the obligation of opening a credit.

9–018   The alternative view put forward by Mr Lawson, namely, that the credit has to be opened a reasonable time before the actual shipping date, seems to me to lead to an uncertainty on the part of buyer and seller which I should be reluctant to import into any commercial contract. I asked Mr Lawson, when the court came to consider what was a reasonable time, which must depend upon the circumstances, whether it depended upon the circumstances known to the parties at the time of the contract, or the circumstances as ascertained later before the shipping instructions were given—or, as a third alternative, the circumstances as they actually were, whether known to the parties or not. It seems to me that that sort of uncertainty is open to the same criticism which Somervell L.J. directed to the argument put forward to him in *Pavia & Co SpA v Thurmann-Nielsen* [above]. What was argued in that case was that the buyer need not open the credit until the seller was ready to deliver and had got bills of lading; and Somervell L.J. said then [at 88]:

"My view is that the contract would be unworkable if . . . the buyer under it was under no obligation until a date, which he could not possibly know, and which there is no machinery for his finding out, namely, when the seller actually has the goods down at the port ready to be put onto the ship."

It seems to me that on Mr Lawson's argument the obligation that arises on the buyer does not arise until a date which he could not possibly know, because it is a date which must depend on circumstances which would not normally be known to him: he does not know, and would not normally know, how long a chain there was between him and the actual manufacturer or stockist to whom the credit or some subsequent back-to-back credit founded upon it has to be transferred: he would not know how long it would take to bring the goods from the place where they were and transport them to the port: he would not know in a case of this kind, and did not know, whether or not the goods had to be rolled to order or whether they were in stock or whether they were partly rolled. It seems to me that in a case of this kind, and in the case of an ordinary f.o.b. contract financed by a confirmed banker's credit, the prima facie rule is that the credit must be opened at latest (and that is as far as I need go for the purposes of this case) by the earliest shipping date. In that way one gets certainty into what is a very common commercial contract. In any other way one can, I think, only get a position in which neither buyer nor seller knows what his rights are until all the facts have been ascertained, and one, and possibly two or three, courts have directed their minds to the question whether in all the circumstances that was a reasonable time for the credit to be opened.

I therefore hold that it was the duty of the defendants under this contract to open their letter of credit or to get a banker's pre-advice of it by August 1, 1956, at the latest . . .

Comment

The buyers argued that unlike *Pavia*, it was they rather than the sellers who   **9–019**
were entitled to choose the time of shipment, within the stipulated period. Diplock J.'s view was that this made no difference to the principle in *Pavia*. He cited the remarks of Jenkins L.J. in *Hamzeh Malas & Sons v British Imex Industries Ltd.*, set out above, from which can be inferred that a commercial credit is more than simply a means of paying the price.[21]

Note also the certainty reasoning in the above passage, of particular importance where the contracts are likely to be part of a string. This point is further elaborated in chapter 15, paras 15–009 *et seq.*, below.

(3) Waiver and Estoppel

(a) General Principles

Normal principles of waiver and estoppel apply to sale contracts,[22] and we   **9–020**
have seen an application of this in para. 7–048, above. In the present context, where a sale contract calls for a particular type of credit, it is open to the seller to accept a different type, providing him with less security. Any party to a contract

---

[21] [1958] 2 Q.B. 130, 139.
[22] This is beyond the scope of this book, but see, *e.g.* Treitel, *The Law of Contract* (10th ed., Sweet & Maxwell, 1999), pp. 97 *et seq.*

can waive a benefit that is wholly for himself. It is a factual question whether he has accepted the inferior security.

SOPROMA SPA v MARINE & ANIMAL BY-PRODUCTS CORPORATION

Commercial Court. [1966] 1 Lloyd's Rep. 367

Issues:

9–021   The facts and decision, relating to the first tender, were set out above. The sellers claimed that by procuring credits which stipulated additional documents to those required by the sale contract itself, the buyers were in breach of the sale contract. McNair J. held that they were not, but even if they had been, the sellers had waived the breach, or were estopped from relying on it: after the credit had been opened, the sellers requested a variation of the sale contract, to allow them to ship in two instalments, of different tonnages to those previously agreed.[23]

McNair J.: *(on the estoppel or waiver issue)* The next question [after the issue of the second tender, which is considered below] which arises is as to the effect of the sellers' acceptance of the terms of the letter of credit. On the facts in the present case the letters of credit were admittedly defective in at least two respects, (i) they were not confirmed and (ii) they were not opened in time to cover the whole shipment period. See on the latter point *Pavia & Co, SpA v Thurmann-Nielsen* [1952] 2 Q.B. 84 [above]. It may be that they were also defective in that they called for documents in addition to those specified in the contract itself . . . [This aspect of the decision has already been considered, above.] . . . But, assuming for the purposes of the point at present being considered that the letters of credit were defective both in respect of the matters mentioned above, namely, not being confirmed and not covering the whole shipment period, and also in respect of the additional requirements, the material question is as to the effect of the sellers' acceptance of the letters of credit. On the assumption stated, the sellers could, I think, plainly have treated the buyers' failure to open proper letters of credit as a breach of condition entitling them to rescind and claim damages. In fact (i) the sellers applied for the two letters of credit to be varied by the authorization of the tender of one consolidated set of documents under the two letters of credit and (ii) in fact after this authorization had been given they operated the letters of credit by the tender of a consolidated set of documents. In my judgment, by so acting, the sellers must be taken to have accepted the position that their letters of credit were in order and, not having at any time given notice to the buyers that they required letters of credit in strict conformity with the contract, they are precluded (whether the matter is put as waiver, variation or estoppel) from now saying that the letters of credit

---

[23] The original agreement had been for a single shipment of 1,000 tons, later varied to two shipments, each of 500 tons. The contract was later varied again, after the credit had been opened, to provide for shipments of 600 and 400 tons.

were not in order and did not accurately define the contractual mode of obtaining payment including the period of availability. See *Panoutsos v Raymond Hadley Corporation of New York* [1917] 2 K.B. 473, and *Enrico Furst & Co v W.E. Fischer, Ltd* [1960] 2 Lloyd's Rep. 340.

The request by the sellers in [*Enrico*] for an extension of the defective letters of credit is indistinguishable in principle from the request in the present case for a variation of the two letters of credit by the authorisation of presentation of a single consolidated set of shipping documents. This result, as it seems to me, both accords with well-settled principles of law and is also consistent with good business sense. Unless the concession asked for by the sellers had been granted, the sellers would have been in plain default since by shipping the whole 600 tons under one bill of lading they had put it out of their power to tender two bills of lading, namely, a separate bill of lading under each letter of credit. Accordingly, they can only succeed in the present case if they can establish that in law they made a valid tender of documents under the letters of credit as so modified and within the period of availability of these letters ...

Notes

McNair J. appears to regards it as a matter of indifference whether the matter is put as waiver, variation or estoppel,[24] and all were present in *Soproma*. The sale contract had been varied, the consideration moving from the buyer being acceptance of the different instalment sizes. This also amounted to a detriment, which would have given rise to an estoppel. Waiver is perhaps best described as the exercise of a choice; the sellers could have acted in one way, treating the buyer's breach (in providing non-contractual letters of credit, had such a breach been established) as a ground for repudiating the contract. Instead they requested a variation, without objecting to the letters of credit. This reasonably communicated to the buyers that the sellers were content to accept the letters of credit provided. **9–022**

By contrast, in *Glencore Grain Rotterdam BV v LORICO* (see para. 9–007, above, and see also chapter 3, para. 3–014 above),[25] the buyers provided a non-contractual credit which required f.o.b. sellers to tender freight prepaid bills of lading. The sellers objected, but later demanded a price increase, without making further reference to the credit. The price increase demanded by the sellers was wholly unjustified, and was held to amount to a refusal by them to perform the contract. However, it was not agreed, and the sellers eventually refused to load. The issue was whether they were justified in so doing.

The Court of Appeal held that the sellers were entitled to repudiate the sale contract, on the grounds of the buyers' failure to open a contractual letter of credit. They were held not to have waived their right to rely on this breach. Ultimately, whether there had been a waiver turned on factual inferences, as to the substance of the sellers' representation. In *LORICO*, there was no unequivocal representation by the sellers that they had relinquished their rights arising out of the buyers' failure to open a letter of credit in the form required by the sale contract. Merely from the fact that the sellers made no further reference to the letter of credit, when demanding the price increase, could not be inferred that they had misled the buyers into believing that the "freight pre-paid" requirement was no longer important.

---

[24] See at 368 (col. 2).
[25] [1997] 2 Lloyd's Rep. 386.

See also *Nichimen Corp v Gatoil Overseas Inc*,[26] where merely by granting a number of fixed extensions of time to the buyer, the sellers were held not to have waived their right to continue to treat the time for opening of the letter of credit as of the essence. Nor did they impliedly agree or represent that the buyers' time for opening the letter of credit had become at large. They were held justified in repudiating the sale contract, when the final extension had expired, no credit having been opened.[27]

(b) Waiver and Periodic Actions

9–023   In *Soproma*, the waiver was a one-off choice, whereby the sellers accepted the credit provided for that particular sale contract. Where there are a number of shipments, or even a number of contracts, the seller may be taken to have waived his rights regarding future, as well as present shipments and/or contracts.

PANOUSTOS v RAYMOND HADLEY CORPORATION

Court of Appeal. [1917] 2 K.B. 473

9–024   The sale contract (for a number of shipments of flour, each shipment being deemed a separate contract) provided that payment should be by confirmed bankers' credit. The seller accepted payments for a number of shipments by means of a credit which was not confirmed.

Held:

The Court of Appeal held that he was unable to repudiate the contract when the buyer provided an unconfirmed credit for a later shipment. Because the seller had waived for a time the buyer's breach of condition in failing to provide a confirmed credit, he was held unable to repudiate the contract on that ground without giving reasonable notice.

9–025   Viscount Reading C.J.: (at 477–479) . . . It is open to a party to a contract to waive a condition which is inserted for his benefit. If the sellers chose to ship without the safeguard of a confirmed bankers' credit, they were entitled to do so, and the buyer performed his part of the contract by paying for the goods shipped, though there was no confirmed bankers' credit, inasmuch as that condition had been waived. If at a later stage the sellers wished to avail themselves of the condition precedent, in my opinion there was nothing in the facts to prevent them from demanding the performance of the condition if they had given reasonable notice to the buyer that they would not ship unless there was a confirmed bankers'

---

[26] [1987] 2 Lloyd's Rep. 46.

[27] The Court of Appeal held that the sellers were entitled to summary judgment, the buyers having no arguable defence. The case involved a bulk oil contract (Brent crude), where the price had approximately halved in the four months between contract and performance. The clear inference is that the buyers wanted to get out of the contract, but the sellers were held entitled to nearly US$6 million in damages, the difference between contract and current market prices.

Note however that the sellers would have had to bear the market fall, had the buyers gone into liquidation.

credit. If they had done that and the buyer had failed to comply with the condition, the buyer would have been in default, and the sellers would have been entitled to cancel the contract without being subject to any claim by the buyer for damages.

In *Bentsen v Taylor, Sons & Co* [1893] 2 Q.B. 283 Bowen L.J. stated the law as to waiver thus: "Did the defendants by their acts or conduct lead the plaintiff reasonably to suppose that they did not intend to treat the contract for the future as at an end, on account of the failure to perform the condition precedent?" Reading sellers for defendants and buyer for plaintiff in that passage, it applies exactly to the present case. The sellers did lead the buyer to think so, and when they intended to change that position it was incumbent on them to give reasonable notice of that intention to the buyer so as to enable him to comply with the condition which up to that time had been waived ...

... It seems to me to follow from the observations of Bowen L.J. in *Bentsen v Taylor, Sons & Co* that there must be reasonable notice given to the buyer before the sellers can take advantage of the failure to provide a confirmed bankers' credit.

[Viscount Reading agreed with Bailhache J., at first instance ([1917] 1 K.B. 767) that reasonable notice had not been given.]

Notes

The inference from the sellers' choosing to behave in one way, rather than another, is clear from this judgment. The sellers could have insisted on a contractual credit, but "chose to ship without the safeguard of a confirmed bankers' credit". From this choice was inferred the representation giving rise to the waiver.

In *Cape Asbestos Co Ltd v Lloyds Bank Ltd* (see chapter 8, para. 8–018 above) the issuing bank was held entitled to revoke, without notice, a revocable credit. The bank raised a further defence that the bill of lading tendered did not conform to the terms of the credit, since instead of being to the order of the defendant bank, it was made out to the order of the buyers. The sellers claimed, relying on *Panoustos*, that the bank having accepted a bill of lading in similar terms on a previous shipment had waived its right to reject on those grounds for the subsequent shipment. In the event the point did not arise for decision since the credit had been validly revoked, but Bailhache J. said that in any event *Panoustos* was not authority for the proposition claimed[28]:

9–026

"That case [*Panoustos*] was an authority for the proposition that where an act had to be done by the buyer of goods, such, for instance, as the opening of a confirmed banker's credit, and he did not perform that act, and the seller nevertheless went on delivering the goods with knowledge that the act had not been performed, the seller could not suddenly cancel the contract and refuse to make further deliveries without giving the buyer reasonable notice of his intention so as to give the buyer an opportunity of putting himself right. That case was no authority for the proposition, that where an act had to be done periodically, as, for instance, the delivery of a bill of lading in such a case as the present, the fact that it had been done irregularly in the past justified the

---

[28] [1921] W.N. 274 at 275 (col. 2).

assumption that the irregularity would be waived in the future. The *Panoustos* case had only reference to an act which had to be done once and for all, and not to an act which had to be done periodically."

The distinction, then, is between an act which has to be done once and for all, as in the confirmation of the credit in *Panoustos*,[29] and one which has to be done periodically, as in tendering bills of lading for each shipment in *Cape Asbestos*.

This distinction, stated as a matter of law, seems unconvincing, if it is accepted that the substance of the representation is ultimately an issue of fact. Nonetheless, looked at purely as a matter of fact, the inference to be drawn from acceptance of a one-off act would usually be of greater significance than that to be drawn from acceptance merely of one of series of periodic acts.

The waiver doctrine in *Panoustos* has obvious factual similarities with the doctrine of promissory estoppel developed later, in the well-known case of *Central London Property Trust Ltd v High Trees House Ltd*.[30] There, the landlords were precluded (except on reasonable notice) from claiming the full rent, having accepted periodic payments at a reduced rent. They had, however, initially agreed in writing to the reduced rent, so it is not clear that any inferences could be drawn from the acceptances, periodically, of the lower payments.

(c) Only Unilateral Benefits May be Waived

9–027   It is also clear from the start of the above passage in *Panoustos* that waiver is limited to "which is inserted for [the seller's] benefit". Indeed, neither waiver nor estoppel operate unless the stipulation is inserted only for the benefit of the party waiving the right, or being estopped from relying on it. By contrast, the stipulation that payment is to be made by commercial credit benefits both seller and buyer, and it is not generally open to the seller unilaterally to waive it by insisting on making payment directly to the buyer.

(4) Credit of Mutual Advantage of Seller and Buyer

(a) No Short-circuiting

9–028   In *Soproma*, above, it was stressed that payment by bankers commercial credit is to the mutual advantage of both seller and buyer, and that in general therefore sellers cannot short-circuit the credit by tendering documents directly to the buyer and demanding payment directly from him. It is only possible to waive rights which benefit only the party so waiving.

SOPROMA SPA v MARINE & ANIMAL BY-PRODUCTS CORPORATION

Commercial Court. [1966] 1 Lloyd's Rep. 367

9–029   The facts, and decision on the first tender, have already been set out. The sellers attempted a second tender, but McNair J. held that they were not entitled to do so.

---

[29] Although there were several separate shipments in *Panoustos*, confirmation of the credit should have occurred when the credit was opened. The credit opened in the seller's favour covered all the separate shipments, so that the act of confirmation was a once and for all act.

[30] [1947] K.B. 130. In both cases a party was precluded from asserting his strict legal rights, without giving reasonable notice. *Panoustos* does not appear to depend on detrimental reliance, however.

One reason was simply that the second tender was out of time, but additionally, the sellers were not entitled to short-circuit the credit by claiming payment from the buyer directly.

McNair J.: *(on the second tender)* The first fundamental point which **9–030** arises on the facts as stated is as to the effect in such a contract as this (i) of the opening of a letter of credit and (ii) of the acceptance of the terms of the letter of credit by the sellers. On behalf of the buyers it was submitted that the express term in the contract

"PAYMENT: Against Letter of Credit confirmed irrevocable with the Marine Midland Trust Co of New York . . . "

defines the contractual method of payment by buyers and the contractual method of performance by the sellers by which initially payment is to be obtained subject, of course, to the buyers' right to reject the goods themselves if not in conformity with the contract and that, whereas in a normal c.i.f. or c. & f. contract providing for payment cash against documents, the shipping documents must be tendered to the buyers, under this form of contract the tender of documents has to be made to the bank by whom the credit has been opened or, in the case of a confirmed credit, to the bank by whom the credit has been confirmed, and that such tender of documents is the only manner in which the sellers can obtain payment. Such a conclusion, as it seems to me, is of mutual advantage to both parties—of advantage to the seller in that by the terms of the contract he is given what has been called in the authorities a "reliable paymaster" generally in his own country whom he can sue, and of advantage to the buyer in that he can make arrangements with his bankers for the provision of the necessary funds, his banker retaining the drafts and the documents as his security for making payment to the seller and the buyer being freed from the necessity of having to keep funds available to make payment against presentation of documents to him at an uncertain time which is no further defined in the authorities than being at a reasonable time after shipment by the seller of documents covering goods which he has shipped or which are already afloat. Although in the classic statements as to the duties of the respective parties such as is to be found in *Ireland v Livingstone* (1872) L.R. 5 H.L. 395, and *Biddell v E. Clemens Horst Company* [1911] 1 K.B. 214, reference is made to the duty of the sellers to tender to the buyers the shipping documents in exchange for payment by the buyers, in a case like the present, in which by the express terms of the contract payment is to be made against letters of credit, as it seems to me the general principle stated in those cases must be controlled by the express words of the contract. Under this form of contract, as it seems to me, the buyer performs his obligation as to payment if he provides for the sellers a reliable and solvent paymaster from whom he can obtain payment—if necessary by suit—although it may well be that if the banker fails to pay by reason of his insolvency the buyer would be liable; but in such a case, as at present advised, I think that the basis of the liability must in principle be his failure to provide a proper letter of credit which involves (*inter alia*) that the obligee under the letter of credit is financially solvent. (This point as to the buyers' liability for the insolvency of the bank was not fully argued before me and I prefer to express no concluded opinion upon it as I understand that it may arise for decision in other cases pending in this Court.) It seems to me to be quite inconsistent with the express terms of a contract such as this to hold that the sellers have an alternative right to obtain payment from the buyers by presenting the documents direct to the buyers. Assuming that a letter of credit has been opened by the buyers for the opening of which the buyer would normally be required to provide the bank either with cash or some form of authority, could the seller at his option disregard the contractual letter of credit and present the documents direct to the buyer? As it seems to me, the answer must plainly be in the negative.

Notes

1. McNair J. emphasises that the buyer, as well as the seller, benefits from the credit, primarily in liquidity terms.

2. McNair J. seemed prepared to envisage an exception to the principle, that the seller cannot short-circuit the credit, where the bank becomes insolvent.

(b) Conditional Nature of Payment: Duty to Provide a Reliable and Solvent Paymaster

9–031   The position is different if the bank goes bankrupt and cannot pay, because the seller then loses his advantages under the credit, and the buyer has not provided a "reliable and solvent paymaster". In that event the seller can claim payment directly from the buyer, unless express provision to the contrary is made in the contract of sale.

In *Soproma*, McNair J. perhaps took the view that the only exception was insolvency of the bank,[31] but it might go further than that, to embrace any failure of the bank properly to pay.

ALAN (W.J.) & CO LTD v EL NASR EXPORT AND IMPORT CO

Court of Appeal. [1972] 2 Q.B. 189

9–032   Under the contracts of sale payment was to be by irrevocable letter of credit in Kenyan currency. The letters of credit actually opened did not conform in a number of respects with the buyer's obligations under the sale contract, but in particular were for payment in UK sterling.

Before payment was made sterling was devalued to 85.7% of its original value, but the Kenyan currency was not. The sellers claimed payment under the letters of credit and then claimed directly from the buyers an additional amount representing the difference in value between the two currencies.

Held:

Although the credits did not conform in a number of respects, and although under the sale contract payment was to be in Kenyan currency, because the sellers

[31] It is difficult to be sure, since he did not express a concluded view.

had accepted payment under the sterling letters of credit, they had waived their right to be paid in Kenyan currency. Once the price had been paid under the credits, the buyers had discharged their whole contractual obligation and could not be required to pay more.

The main importance of the case, for present purposes, lies in the statements contained in the following passage.

LORD DENNING M.R.:

The Effect of a Letter of Credit

When an irrevocable letter of credit is issued by one bank and con- **9–033** firmed by another, it may be a "conforming" credit; that is, one which conforms exactly to the contract of sale: or it may be a "non-conforming" credit; that is, one which does not conform exactly to the contract of sale, but is afterwards modified or accepted as being satisfactory to all concerned. It then becomes equivalent to a "conforming credit". In any such case the question arises whether the credit is to be regarded as absolute payment of the price, or as conditional payment of it, or as no payment at all but only a means by which payment may be obtained; that is, as collateral security.

This must be a matter of the true construction of the contract: but, in order to construe it, it is important to bear in mind what the consequences are in each case.

Absolute Payment

If the letter of credit is an absolute payment of the price, the consequences are these: the seller can only look to the banker for payment. He can in no circumstances look to the buyer. The seller must present the documents to the banker and get payment from him in cash or get him to accept sight or time drafts. If the banker does not take up the documents, the seller will retain them, resell and sue the banker for damages. If the banker takes up the documents in exchange for time drafts, and the banker afterwards becomes insolvent, the seller must prove in the liquidation. He cannot sue the buyer.

There is an observation in the High Court of Australia which suggests that a confirmed irrevocable letter of credit may amount to absolute payment. In *Saffron v Societe Miniere Cafrika* (1958) 100 C.L.R. 231, at 243–244, the High Court said:

> "a provision for payment by irrevocable and confirmed letter of credit . . . might perhaps not unreasonably be regarded as a stipulation for the liability of the confirming bank in place of that of the buyer."

And in *Soproma SpA v Marine & Animal By-Products Corporation* [above] McNair J said:

"Under this form of contract, as it seems to me, the buyer performs his obligations as to payment if he provides for the sellers a reliable and solvent paymaster . . . "

McNair J. did not, however, have all the arguments before him.

In my opinion a letter of credit is not to be regarded as absolute payment, unless the seller stipulates, expressly or impliedly, that it should be so. He may do it impliedly if he stipulates for the credit to be issued by a particular bank in such circumstances that it is to be inferred that the seller looks to that particular banker to the exclusion of the buyer. There are some cases in the United States which are to be explained in this way, such as *Vivacqua Irmaos SA v Hickerson* (1939) 190 Southern Rep. 657 and *Ornstein v Hickerson* (1941) 40 Fed. Supp. 305. And in the *Soproma* case there was a stipulation for a particular banker, which may account for McNair J.'s observation.

Conditional payment

9–034   If the letter of credit is conditional payment of the price, the consequences are these: the seller looks in the first instance to the banker for payment: but if the banker does not meet his obligations when the time comes for him to do so, the seller can have recourse to the buyer. The seller must present the documents to the banker. One of two things may then happen: (1) the banker may fail or refuse to pay or accept drafts in exchange for the documents. The seller then, of course, does not hand over the documents. He retains dominion over the goods. He can resell them and claim damages from the buyer. He can also sue the banker for not honouring the credit: see *Urquhart Lindsay & Co Ltd v Eastern Bank Ltd* [1922] 1 K.B. 318. But he cannot, of course, get damages twice over. (2) The bank may accept time drafts in exchange for the documents, but may fail to honour the drafts when the time comes. In that case the banker will have the documents and will usually have passed them on to the buyer, who will have paid the bank for them. The seller can then sue the buyer on the drafts: or if the banker fails or is insolvent, the seller can sue the buyer. The banker's drafts are like any ordinary payment for goods by a bill of exchange. They are conditional payment, but not absolute payment. It may mean that they buyer (if he has already paid the bank) will have to pay twice over. So be it. He ought to have made sure that he employed a "reliable and solvent paymaster."

There are several cases which show that in the ordinary way a letter of credit is conditional and not absolute payment . . . Thus in New Zealand in *Hindley & Co v Tothill, Watson & Co* (1894) 13 N.Z.L.R. 13, 23, the Court of Appeal said that the seller had the liability "of the bank in the first instance and on the bank's default that of the defendants (the buyers)." In the United States in *Greenough v Munroe* (1931) 53 Fed. Rep. 2d. 262, 365, the United States Court of Appeals for the second circuit (New York) said:

"the authorities favour the view that there is no presumption that the seller takes a draft drawn under a letter of credit in absolute payment of the buyer's obligation to pay for the merchandise; hence upon default by the bank upon its draft the seller may look to the buyer."

Finally in England in *Newman Industries Ltd v Indo-British Industries* [1956] 2 Lloyd's Rep. 219, at 236, Sellers J. said in regard to a time draft:

"I do not think there is any evidence to establish, or any inference to be drawn, that the draft under the letter of credit was to be taken in absolute payment. I see no reason why the plaintiffs . . . should not look to the defendants, as buyers, for payment."

Many of the textbooks treat a letter of credit as conditional payment. Thus Professor Davis in 1954 said:

"such authority as there is tends to support the view that the letter of credit constitutes conditional, and not absolute, payment. Therefore, should the issuing banker fail to honour the seller's drafts, drawn in conformity with the terms of the credit, the rights of the seller against the buyer will revive."

see *The Law Relating to Commercial Letters of Credit*, 2nd ed. (1954), p. 46; 3rd ed. (1963), p. 49, Megrah in H.C. Gutteridge's *Law of Bankers' Commercial Credits*, 4th ed. (1968), pp. 29–33 and Paget on *The Laws of Banking*, 7th ed. (1966), pp. 620–622 is to the same effect.

No Payment at All
If the letter of credit is no payment at all, but only a means by which **9–035** payment may be obtained, *i.e.*, if it is only collateral security, the consequences are these: the seller ought to present the documents to the banker. If the seller does not do so, he will be guilty of laches in enforcing his security and the buyer will be discharged: see *Peacock v Pursell* (1863) 14 C.B.N.S. 728. But if on presentation the banker fails or refuses to take up the documents, then (if the letter of credit is only collateral security) the seller will be entitled to take the documents round to the buyer (or send them to him) and demand that he takes them up and pay the price. This situation finds no place in any of the authorities. There is a statement in an old case in *Pennsylvania, Bell v Moss* (1839) 5 Whart. 189, 203, when it was said:

"A credit with a banker is not payment, but a means of payment, more or less secure according to the solidity of the depository; and the greater or less certainty of the security cannot affect the question of its character: it is but a security still."

That statement was quoted with approval by Finkelstein in 1930, in *Commercial Letters of Credit*, p. 156, who says that the seller "desires additional security without the surrender of any rights that he may have against the buyer." But the complete answer was given by McNair J. in *Soproma SpA v Marine & Animal By-Products Corporation* [above]:

> "It seems to me to be quite inconsistent with the express terms of a contract such as this to hold that the sellers have an alternative right to obtain payment from the buyers by presenting the documents direct to the buyers. Assuming that a letter of credit has been opened by the buyer for the opening of which the buyer would normally be required to provide the bank either with cash or some form of authority, could the seller at his option disregard the contractual letter of credit and present the documents direct to the buyer? As it seems to me, the answer be plainly in the negative."

Conclusion as to Payment

As a result of this analysis, I am of the opinion that in the ordinary way, when the contract of sale stipulates for payment to be made by confirmed irrevocable letter of credit, then, when the letter of credit is issued and accepted by the seller, it operates as conditional payment of the price. It does not operate as absolute payment.

It is analogous to the case where, under a contract of sale, the buyer gives a bill of exchange or a cheque for the price. It is presumed to be given, not as absolute payment, nor as collateral security, but as conditional payment. If the letter of credit is honoured by the bank when the documents are presented to it, the debt is discharged. If it is not honoured, the debt is not discharged: and the seller has a remedy in damages against both banker and buyer.

Notes

9–036   1. The *dicta* from *W.J. Alan & Co Ltd v El Nasr Export and Import Co* were applied by Ackner J., as part of the *ratio*, in *Maran Road Saw Mill v Austin Taylor Ltd.*[32] The facts of this case were set out in chapter 8, para. 8–027, above. It will be remembered that the issuing bank failed, and that the seller repaid the purchase money to the Bangkok Bank, which had purchased time drafts drawn on the issuing bank but had not confirmed the credit. The seller then brought an action against its agent, who was in the position of buyer under the commercial credit, and succeeded. The case was a direct application of the principles of *W.J. Alan & Co Ltd v El Nasr Export and Import Co*, Ackner J. taking the view that they were equally applicable to an agency agreement as to an ordinary sale by way of commercial credit. He said[33]:

> "Can it then be said that [the defendants] have discharged their contractual obligation, when, although they have established a letter of credit, payment has not been made under it? To my mind, the answer is a simple one and is in the

[32] [1975] 1 Lloyd's Rep. 156.
[33] [1975] 1 Lloyd's Rep. 156, 159 (col. 1).

negative. I respectfully adopt and slightly adapt the language used by Stephenson L.J. in *W.J. Alan & Co Ltd v El Nasr Export and Import Co*. The agents promised to pay by letter of credit not to provide by a letter of credit a source of payment which did not pay."

2. The principles of *W.J. Alan & Co Ltd v El Nasr Export and Import Co* create only a presumption, which is (in principle at any rate) rebuttable, so it is open for the courts in appropriate circumstances to treat payment under a credit as absolute rather than conditional payment. One possibility, mentioned in the case itself, is where the seller "stipulates for the credit to be issued by a particular bank in such circumstances that it is to be inferred that the seller looks to that particular banker to the exclusion of the buyer".[34] Normally, of course, the choice of issuing bank is left to the buyer, and therefore the seller should not be required to take the consequences of its failure. In *Soproma*, by contrast, the banker (the Marine and Midland Trust Co of New York) was selected by the seller, which may account for McNair J.'s limited view that only in the event of its insolvency might the seller be able to tender documents to the buyer directly.

The bank was not selected by the plaintiff sellers in *Maran Road Saw Mill v Austin Taylor Ltd*, where the presumption in *W.J. Alan & Co Ltd v El Nasr Export and Import Co* was not rebutted. Ackner J. observed[35]:

"The principal has not, for example, stipulated for the credit to be issued by a particular banker, in such circumstances that it is to be inferred that he is looking to that particular banker to the exclusion of the agent . . .

The plaintiffs did not expressly or impliedly agree that the liability of the issuing bank should be accepted by them in place of that of the defendants. Thus, the defendants were obliged to employ a reliable and solvent paymaster and if they failed to do so, despite having put him in funds, they like the buyer in the case of the contract for the sale of goods, have to pay twice over."

3. Nor is it enough to rebut the *Alan v El Nasr* presumption for the identity of **9–037** the bank to be merely agreed between the parties. In *E.D. & F. Man Ltd v Nigerian Sweets & Confectionery Co Ltd*,[36] the respondent buyers (under three contracts for the sale of white crystal sugar) argued that the opening of the credit should be treated as absolute payment because the sellers had agreed on the identity of the issuing bank. The facts were similar to those in the *Maran Road* case: the issuing bank, Merchant Swiss Ltd, was wound up after the buyers had reimbursed it, but before payment had been made to the sellers under 90 day drafts drawn on it. The sellers sued the buyers directly.

In an appeal from arbitrators on a point of law, Ackner J. held that, on the facts found, the buyers were liable. Applying *Alan v El Nasr* directly, he thought that the seller's agreement as to choice of bank was merely one factor, and not in any way conclusive[37]:

"Mr. Evans [for the buyers] sought to submit as a proposition of law, that where the identity of the bank is agreed between the parties, and not left to the choice of the buyers, it must follow that the sellers impliedly agree that the liability of the issuing bank has been accepted by them in place of that of the buyers. I do not think that this is correct. The fact that the sellers have agreed on the identity of the issuing bank is but one of the factors to be taken into account when considering whether there are circumstances from which it can be properly

---

[34] [1972] 2 Q.B. 189, at 210, *per* Lord Denning M.R.
[35] [1975] 1 Lloyd's Rep. 156 at 159 (col. 2)—160 (col. 1).
[36] [1977] 2 Lloyd's Rep. 50.
[37] [1977] 2 Lloyd's Rep. 50 at 56.

inferred that the sellers look to that particular bank to the exclusion of the buyer. It is in no way conclusive. In this case . . . , there were other circumstances which clearly supported the presumption that the letters of credit were not given as absolute payment but as conditional payment . . .

The sellers' remedy in such circumstances is to claim from the buyers either the price agreed in the contract of sale or damages for breach of their contractual promise to pay by letter of credit."

In fact the case was not particularly strong, because principal shareholders of the respondent buyers were also principal shareholders of Merchant Swiss Ltd. It seems likely, then, that the buyers chose the identity of the issuing bank and the sellers merely acquiesced. Would the position be different if the sellers had insisted on the identity of the issuing bank? No doubt the presumption of absolute payment would then be stronger, but it would still presumably not be conclusive. There appears to be a strong presumption in favour of construing letters of credit as conditional payment only, in the absence of an express stipulation to the contrary.

4. Not only does the buyer remain liable for the price, but may also be liable in damages for failure to provide a reliable and solvent paymaster: the failure to pay by the bank puts the buyer in breach of the sale contract: see *Alan v El Nasr* itself, especially *per* Stephenson L.J., and also *per* Ackner J. in *Maran Road Saw Mill v Austin Taylor & Co Ltd* [1975] 1 Lloyd's Rep. 156. Though it will normally be better for the seller to sue for the price, if provision of a reliable and solvent paymaster is a condition (not an unreasonable inference from the cases at paras 9–031 *et seq.*, above), a seller on a rising market could use the breach to repudiate and sell elsewhere. Moreover, the tort action discussed at the end of chapter 8, above depends on the bank's failure to pay putting the buyer in breach of contract.

5. These cases were distinguished by the Court of Appeal, in a different context, in *Re Charge Card Services Ltd*.[38] Payment for consumer goods under a charge card was held to be absolute payment where the charge card company went into liquidation. The principle from the documentary credit cases was held inapplicable, but no doubt was cast on their correctness; it was simply that the situation was very different. Not only was it the seller who chose to do business with the charge card company, but the majority of transactions (which were small over-the-counter sales) left the seller with no record of the buyer's address.[39] It was, therefore, reasonable to infer that he did not expect to look to the buyer for the price. These factors do not apply to documentary credit payments, which will normally be conditional.

---

[38] [1989] Ch. 497.
[39] See also Atiyah, *The Sale of Goods* (10th ed., Pitman, 2001), pp. 301–302.

CHAPTER 10

THE DOCUMENTS

(1) DOCUMENTARY REQUIREMENTS

WHERE it applies, the documentary requirements are contained in Part D of the **10–001** U.C.P., which is set out in full in Appendix C, below. A detailed discussion of these provisions is left to specialist books on documentary credits.[1]

Where a traditional bill of lading is required, the requirements are set out in Article 23, unless the credit calls for a charterparty bill of lading, in which case reference needs to be made to Article 25 (the earlier 1983 revision provided that bills of lading which were issued under and are subject to the conditions of a charterparty would be rejected unless expressly authorised, but provision has been made for charterparty bills since 1993). In most respects, these requirements mirror those for a clean shipped bill of lading under f.o.b. and c.i.f. sale contracts; thus, usually there will be no material discrepancies between contracts 1 and 4 where under a c.i.f. or f.o.b. contract, payment is by confirmed irrevocable credit to which the U.C.P. applies. In particular, Article 23(a)(ii) reflects c.i.f. and f.o.b. practice by requiring the bill of lading to indicate that the goods have been loaded on board or shipped on a named vessel. Thus a received for shipment bill will not suffice. The U.C.P. also provides, subject to the express terms of the credit, for tender of through bills of lading, as long as the entire voyage is covered by one bill of lading, in Article 23(b)–(d).

Article 23(a)(iv) is more stringent than the common law sale contract requirements, requiring tender of the full set, if issued in a set of more than one original. By contrast, under a c.i.f. sale contract, tender of one original of the set is sufficient unless the contract expressly stipulates otherwise.[2] It has long been customary for banks to demand the entire set, as a precaution against fraud, but equivalent provision should also be made in the sale contract, or buyers risk being in breach if the bank rejects tender of less than the full set.

Since 1983, the U.C.P. has also made provision for alternative documentation, and this trend continues with the 1993 revision. Non-negotiable sea waybills are covered by Article 24, multimodal transport documents by Article 26, air transport documents by Article 27, road, rail or inland waterway transport documents by Article 28, and courier and post receipts by Article 29. Alternative documentation is discussed more fully in chapter 15, below.

In *The Galatia*, in chapter 6, (see para. 6–067 above) the bill of lading, claused because of damage which had occurred after shipment, had already been rejected by two banks before it was tendered to the buyer. One of the arguments put for the buyer was that what is now Article 32(a) of the U.C.P. required their rejection. Donaldson J. doubted this interpretation of the Article, because the clause did not indicate defects at the time of shipment.

---

[1] I have myself dealt with the subject matter of this chapter in greater detail in Todd, *Bills of Lading and Bankers' Documentary Credits* (3rd ed., LLP, 1998), Ch. 6. There is also a new edition of Gutteridge & Megrah, which has been referred to in Chs 8 and 9, above.

[2] See *Sanders v Maclean* in Ch. 6, para. 6–081 above.

If this interpretation is correct, U.C.P. terms coincide with the requirements under an ordinary sale contract. In the event, Donaldson J. did not need to decide the interpretation issue, because he also thought that even if it did require rejection of the bill of lading by the banks, the contract of sale made no mention of the U.C.P. Since the U.C.P. does not have the force of law, if commercial practice conflicted with the U.C.P. rules, then on an interpretation of the sale contract commercial practice, rather than the U.C.P., should prevail.

This reasoning follows from the autonomy of the four contracts constituting the credit. In an action by seller against buyer, only the terms of the sale contract are relevant. The fact that the credit is issued on U.C.P. terms should not affect interpretation of the sale contract. It would be different, of course, had the action been against one of the banks. If the credit is to be on U.C.P. terms, therefore, an appropriate clause should ideally be incorporated into the contract of sale, to ensure that sale and credit requirements are brought into line.

It is surprising and unfortunate that the difficulty in *The Galatia* has not been resolved by revisions to the U.C.P. subsequent to the case (which was based on the 1962 revision). As Donaldson J. observed in *The Galatia*, the definition of a clean shipping document fails to specify the time with respect to which the notation speaks. It should not be too difficult to resolve this; in the case of a shipped bill of lading at least, loading is the appropriate time.

In 2002, the I.C.C. published the eUCP, which is intended to supplement the U.C.P. where electronic documents are stipulated. It is set out in full in Appendix M, below, and discussed in chapter 16, para. 16–015, below.

(2) Documents Conform but Goods do Not

10–002 This section, and the next, examine a bank's right to reject the documents tendered. Since this is not a specialist book on documentary credits, we will not examine the bank's role in tedious detail. There are, however, some preliminary observations that need to be made:

1. Banks hold themselves out as being capable of telling whether documents tendered conform to the requirements of the credit. They do not hold themselves out as having any expertise in the goods, the subject matter of the sale contract. The bank needs therefore to make a judgment on the basis of the documents alone, and must also make it quickly.[3]

2. The autonomy of the contracts constituting the credit implies that a bank, in deciding whether to accept the documents, tendered, has no interest in the consequences (if any) of its decision on the sale contract, nor should its decision be affected by disputes under the sale contract.

3. The seller is shipping goods under an assurance that he will be paid by a reliable and solvent paymaster. This implies, in particular, that the decision whether payment is made should not be at the discretion of the buyer.

4. The transaction might be part of a chain, and so the same arguments for certainty that are rehearsed in para. 15–010 apply here.

---

[3] It is also essentially a passive inspection; banks are under no obligation, for example, to perform a mathematical calculation, to check conformity between documents: *Credit Industriel et Commercial v China Merchants Bank* [2002] EWHC 973 (Comm.) (and see below at para. 10–037), at para. 25.

The leading case is entirely in conformity with these principles, but a side effect
of the decision is its failure to discourage fraud (see further chapter 15, below, on
the problems of maritime crime).

UNITED CITY MERCHANTS (INVESTMENTS) LTD v ROYAL BANK OF CANADA, (THE AMERICAN ACCORD)

House of Lords. [1983] A.C. 168

Machinery had been shipped aboard the American Accord after the contract date,   **10–003**
but the date on the bill of lading was falsified to make it appear that they were
shipped according to contract: though there may have been fraud, it was not
shown that the seller was fraudulent.

There were two main issues, one of which related to illegality involving foreign
currency controls. That issue is not relevant to commercial credits. The other issue
was whether a bank was entitled to refuse payment under a confirmed irrevocable documentary credit, in an action by the seller against the bank, where
although the documents appeared to be in order on their face, the goods were not
in fact shipped according to contract.

Held:
The bank was bound to pay unless fraud on the part of the seller was proved (it
had not been in the case).

LORD DIPLOCK: (*on the documentary credit point*) My Lords, for the propo-   **10–004**
sition on the documentary credit point, both in the broad form for which
counsel for the confirming bank have strenuously argued at all stages of
this appeal and in the narrower form or "halfway house" that commended itself to the Court of Appeal [explained below], there is no direct
authority to be found either in English or Privy Council cases or among
the numerous decisions of courts in the United States of America to which
reference was made in the judgments of the Court of Appeal in the instant
case. So the point falls to be decided by reference to first principles as to
the legal nature of the contractual obligations assumed by the various
parties to a transaction consisting of an international sale of goods to be
financed by means of a confirmed irrevocable documentary credit. It is
trite law that there are four autonomous though interconnected contractual relationships involved: (1) the underlying contract for the sale of
goods, to which the only parties are the buyer and the seller; (2) the
contract between the buyer and the issuing bank under which the latter
agrees to issue the credit and either itself or through a confirming bank to
notify the credit to the seller and to make payments to or to the order of
the seller (or to pay, accept or negotiate bills of exchange drawn by the
seller) against presentation of stipulated documents; and the buyer agrees
to reimburse the issuing bank for payments made under the credit. For
such reimbursement the stipulated documents, if they include a document of title such as a bill of lading, constitute a security available to the
issuing bank; (3) if payment is to be made through a confirming bank, the
contract between the issuing bank and the confirming bank authorising

and requiring the latter to make such payments and to remit the stipulated documents to the issuing bank when they are received, the issuing
bank in turn agreeing to reimburse the confirming bank for payments
made under the credit; (4) the contract between the confirming bank and
the seller under which the confirming bank undertakes to pay to the seller
(or to accept or negotiate without recourse to drawer bills of exchange
drawn by him) up to the amount of the credit against presentation of the
stipulated documents.

Again, it is trite law that in contract (4), with which alone the instant
appeal is directly concerned, the parties to it, the seller and the confirming
bank, "deal in documents and not in goods", as Art. 8 of the Uniform
Customs puts it.[4] If, on their face, the documents presented to the confirming bank by the seller conform with the requirements of the credit as
notified to him by the confirming bank, that bank is under a contractual
obligation to the seller to honour the credit, notwithstanding that the
bank has knowledge that the seller at the time of presentation of the
conforming documents is alleged by the buyer to have, and in fact has
already, committed a breach of his contract with the buyer for the sale of
the goods to which the documents appear on their face to relate that
would have entitled the buyer to treat the contract of sale as rescinded
and to reject the goods and refuse to pay the seller the purchase price. The
whole commercial purpose for which the system of confirmed irrevocable
documentary credits has been developed in international trade is to give
to the seller an assured right to be paid before he parts with control of the
goods and that does not permit of any dispute with the buyer as to the
performance of the contract of sale being used as a ground for non-
payment or reduction or deferment of payment.

10–005   To this general statement of principle as to the contractual obligations
of the confirming bank to the seller, there is one established exception:
that is, where the seller, for the purpose of drawing on the credit, fraudulently presents to the confirming bank documents that contain, expressly
or by implication, material representations of fact that to his knowledge
are untrue. Although there does not appear among the English authorities any case in which this exception has been applied, it is well established in the American cases, of which the leading or "landmark" case is
Sztejn v J. Henry Schroder Banking Corp (1941) 31 N.Y.S. 2d. 631. This
judgment of the New York Court of Appeals was referred to with
approval by the English Court of Appeal in *Edward Owen Engineering Ltd
v Barclays Bank International Ltd* [1978] Q.B. 159, though this was actually
a case about a performance bond under which a bank assumes obligations to a buyer analogous to those assumed by the confirming bank to
the seller under a documentary credit. The exception for fraud on the part
of the beneficiary seeking to avail himself of the credit is a clear application of the maxim *ex turpi causa non oritur actio* or, if plain English is to be

---

[4] See para. 8–012, above. The present provision is U.C.P. 500, Art. 4.

preferred, "fraud unravels all." The courts will not allow their process to be used by a dishonest person to carry out a fraud.

The instant case, however, does not fall within the fraud exception. Mocatta J. found the seller to have been unaware of the inaccuracy of Mr. Baker's notation of the date as which the goods were actually on board the *American Accord*. [Mr. Baker was the employee of the loading brokers to the carriers who was in charge of the transaction on their behalf. He had acted fraudulently in issuing the bills of lading bearing what was to his knowledge a false statement as to the date on which the plant was actually on board *American Accord*.] It believed that it was true and that the goods had actually been loaded on or before 15 December 1976, as required by the documentary credit.

Faced by this finding, the argument for the confirming bank before Mocatta J. was directed to supporting the broad proposition that a confirming bank is not under any obligation, legally enforceable against it by the seller/beneficiary of a documentary credit, to pay to him the sum stipulated in the credit against presentation of documents, if the documents presented, although conforming on their face with the terms of the credit, nevertheless contain some statement of material fact that is not accurate. This proposition which does not call for knowledge on the part of the seller / beneficiary of the existence of any inaccuracy would embrace the fraud exception and render it superfluous.

My Lords, the more closely this bold proposition is subjected to legal analysis, the more implausible it becomes; to assent to it would, in my view, undermine the whole system of financing international trade by means of documentary credits.

It has, so far as I know, never been disputed that as between confirming **10–006** bank and issuing bank and as between issuing bank and the buyer the contractual duty of each bank under a confirmed irrevocable credit is to examine with reasonable care all documents presented in order to ascertain that they appear on their face to be in accordance with the terms and conditions of the credit, and, if they do so appear, to pay to the seller/ beneficiary by whom the documents have been presented the sum stipulated by the credit, or to accept or negotiate without recourse to drawer drafts drawn by the seller/beneficiary if the credit so provides. It is so stated in the latest edition of the Uniform Customs. It is equally clear law, and is so provided by Art. 9 of the Uniform Customs,[5] that confirming banks and issuing banks assume no liability or responsibility to one another or to the buyer "for the form, sufficiency, accuracy, genuineness, falsification or legal effect of any documents." This is well illustrated by the Privy Council case of *Gian Singh & Co Ltd v Banque de l'Indochine* [1974] 1 W.L.R. 1234, where the customer was held liable to reimburse the issuing bank for honouring a documentary credit on presentation of an apparently conforming document which was an ingenious forgery, a fact

---

[5] Article 15 of the 1993 revision.

that the bank had not been negligent in failing to detect on examination of the document.

It would be strange from a commercial point of view, although not theoretically impossible in law, if the contractual duty owed by confirming and issuing banks to the buyer to honour the credit on presentation of apparently conforming documents despite the fact that they contain inaccuracies or even are forged were not matched by a corresponding contractual liability of the confirming bank to the seller/beneficiary (in the absence, of course, of any fraud on his part) to pay the sum stipulated in the credit on presentation of apparently conforming documents. Yet, as is conceded by counsel for the confirming bank in the instant case, if the broad proposition for which he argues is correct, the contractual duties do not match. As respects the conforming bank's contractual duty to the seller to honour the credit, the bank, it is submitted, is only bound to pay on presentation of documents which not only appear on their face to be in accordance with the terms and conditions of the credit but also do not in fact contain any material statement that is inaccurate. If this submission be correct, the bank's contractual right to refuse to honour the documentary credit cannot, as a matter of legal analysis, depend on whether at the time of the refusal the bank was virtually certain from information obtained by means other than reasonably careful examination of the documents themselves that they contained some material statement that was inaccurate or whether the bank merely suspected this or even had no suspicion that apparently conforming documents contained any inaccuracies at all. If there be any such right of refusal it must depend on whether the bank, when sued by the seller/beneficiary for breach of its contract to honour the credit, is able to prove that one of the documents did in fact contain what was a material misstatement.

It is conceded that to justify refusal the misstatement must be "material" but this invites the query: material to what? The suggested answer to this query was: a misstatement of fact which if the true fact had been disclosed would have entitled the buyer to reject the goods; date of shipment (as in the instant case) or misdescription of the goods are examples. But this is to destroy the autonomy of the documentary credit which is its *raison d'etre*; it is to make the seller's right to payment by the confirming bank dependant on the buyer's rights against the seller under the terms of the contract for the sale of goods, of which the confirming bank will have no knowledge.

10–007   Counsel sought to evade the difficulties disclosed by an analysis of the legal consequences of his broad proposition by praying in aid the practical consideration that a bank, desirous as it would be of protecting its reputation in the competitive business of providing documentary credits, would never exercise its right against a seller/beneficiary to refuse to honour the credit except in cases where at the time of the refusal it already was in possession of irrefutable evidence of the inaccuracy in the documents presented. I must confess that the argument that a seller should be content to rely on the exercise by banks of business expediency, unbacked by any legal liability, to ensure prompt payment by a foreign buyer does not impress me; but the assumption that underlies reliance on expediency does not, in my view, itself stand up to legal analysis. Business expediency would not induce the bank to pay the seller/beneficiary against presentation of documents which it was not legally liable to accept as complying with the documentary credit unless, in doing so, it acquired a right legally enforceable against the buyer to require him to take up the documents himself and reimburse the bank for the amount paid. So any reliance on business expediency to make the system work if the broad proposition contended for by counsel is correct must involve that, as against the buyer, the bank, when presented with apparently conforming documents by the seller, is legally entitled to the option, exercisable at its own discretion and regardless of any instructions to the contrary from the buyer, either (1) to take up the documents and pay the credit and claim reimbursement from the buyer, notwithstanding that the bank has been provided with information that makes it virtually certain that the existence of such inaccuracies can be proved, or (2) to reject the documents and refuse to pay the credit.

The legal justification for the existence of such an independently exercisable option, it is suggested, lies in the bank's own interest in the goods to which the documents relate, as security for the advance made by the bank to the buyer, when it pays the seller under the documentary credit. But, if this were so, the answer to the question, "To what must the misstatement in the documents be material?" should be, "Material to the price which the goods to which the documents relate would fetch on sale if, failing reimbursement by the buyer, the bank should be driven to realise its security." But this would not justify the confirming bank's refusal to honour the credit in the instant case; the realisable value on arrival at Callao of a glass fibre manufacturing plant made to the specification of the buyers could not be in any way affected by its having been loaded on board a ship at Felixstowe on 16 December instead of 15 December 1976.

My Lords, in rejecting this broad proposition I have dealt with it at **10–008** greater length than otherwise I would have done, because it formed the main plank of the confirming bank's argument on the documentary credit point before Mocatta J., who, however, had no hesitation in rejecting it, but found for the confirming bank on the Bretton Woods [illegality] point. It formed the main ground also in the confirming bank's notice of cross-appeal to the Court of Appeal on which the confirming bank would seek to uphold the judgment in its favour if the seller's appeal should succeed on the Bretton Woods point. It was not until halfway through the actual hearing in the Court of Appeal that the notice of cross-appeal was amended to include a narrower proposition referred to as a "halfway house" which the Court of Appeal accepted as being decisive in the confirming bank's favour. This rendered it unnecessary for that court to rule on the broad proposition that I have so far been discussing, although Stephenson L.J. indicated obiter that for this part he would have rejected it. In the confirming bank's argument before this House a marked lack of enthusiasm has been shown for reliance on the "halfway house" and the broad proposition has again formed the main ground on which the confirming bank has sought to uphold the actual decision of the Court of Appeal in its favour on the documentary credit point.

The proposition accepted by the Court of Appeal as constituting a complete defence available to the confirming bank on the documentary credit point has been referred to as a "halfway house" because it lies not only halfway between the unqualified liability of the confirming bank to honour a documentary credit on presentation of documents which on reasonably careful examination appear to conform to the terms and conditions of the credit and what I have referred to as the fraud exception to this unqualified liability which is available to the confirming bank where the seller/beneficiary presents to the confirming bank documents that contain, expressly or by implication, material representations of fact that to his own knowledge are untrue; but it also lies halfway between the fraud exception and the broad proposition favoured by the confirming bank with which I have hitherto been dealing. The halfway house is erected on the narrower proposition that, if any of the documents presented under the credit by the seller/beneficiary contain a material misrepresentation of fact that was false to the knowledge of the person who issued the document, and intended by him to deceive persons into whose hands the document might come, the confirming bank is under no liability to honour the credit, even though, as in the instant case, the persons whom the issuer of the document intended to, and did, deceive included the seller/beneficiary himself.

My Lords, if the broad proposition for which the confirming bank has argued is unacceptable for the reasons that I have already discussed, what rational ground can there be for drawing any distinction between apparently conforming documents that, unknown to the seller, in fact contain a statement of fact that is inaccurate where the inaccuracy was due to inadvertence by the maker of the document, and the like documents where the same inaccuracy had been inserted by the maker of the document with intent to deceive, among others, the seller/beneficiary himself? *Ex hypothesi* we are dealing only with a case in which the seller/beneficiary claiming under the credit has been deceived, for, if he presented documents to the confirming bank with knowledge that this apparent conformity with the terms and conditions of the credit was due to the fact that the documents told a lie, the seller/beneficiary would himself be a party to the misrepresentation made to the confirming bank by the lie in the documents and the case would come within the fraud exception, as did all the American cases referred to as persuasive authority in the judgments of the Court of Appeal in the instant case.

10–009   The American cases refer indifferently to documents that are "forged or fraudulent", as does the Uniform Commercial Code that has been adopted in nearly all states of the United States of America. The Court of Appeal reached their halfway house in the instant case by starting from the premise that a confirming bank could refuse to pay against a document that it knew to be forged, even though the seller/beneficiary had no knowledge of that fact. From this premise they reasoned that, if forgery by a third party relieves the confirming bank of liability to pay the seller/beneficiary, fraud by a third party ought to have the same consequence.

I would not wish to be taken as accepting that the premise as to forged documents is correct, even where the fact that the document is forged deprives it of all legal effect and makes it a nullity, and so worthless to the confirming bank as security for its advances to the buyer. This is certainly not so under the Uniform Commercial Code as against a person who has taken a draft drawn under the credit in circumstances that would make him a holder in due course, and I see no reason why, and there is nothing in the Uniform Commercial Code to suggest that, a seller/beneficiary who is ignorant of the forgery should be in any worse position because he has not negotiated the draft before presentation. I would prefer to leave open the question of the rights of an innocent seller/beneficiary against the confirming bank when a document presented by him is a nullity because unknown to him it was forged by some third party, for that question does not arise in the instant case. The bill of lading with a wrong date of loading placed on it by the carrier's agents was far from being a nullity. It was a valid transferable receipt for the goods giving the holder a right to claim them at their destination, Callao, and was evidence of the terms of the contract under which they were being carried.

But, even assuming the correctness of the Court of Appeal's premise as respects forgery by a third party of a kind that makes a document a nullity for which at least a rational case can be made out, to say that this leads to the conclusion that fraud by a third party which does not render the document a nullity has the same consequence appears to me, with respect, to be a non sequitur, and I am not persuaded by the reasoning in any of the judgments of the Court of Appeal that it is not.

On the documentary credit point I think that Mocatta J. was right in deciding it in favour of the sellers and that the Court of Appeal was wrong in reversing him on this point.

Notes

This case was a reaffirmation, and extension, of previous authorities. The Court **10–010** of Appeal decision of *Hamzeh Malas & Sons v British Imex Industries Ltd* established that the bank must pay on the credit if the correct documents are tendered, irrespective of any dispute under the sale contract.[6] There was no question of fraud in that case, and the buyer failed to obtain an injunction, restraining the bank from paying (an action therefore on contract 2).[7] The fraud exception was established by the decision of the New York Supreme Court in *Stzejn v J. Henry*

---

[6] [1958] 2 Q.B. 127.
[7] See also on contract 2 *Discount Records v Barclays Bank*, para. 10–012, below.

Schroeder Banking Corporation.[8] The Court of Appeal in *Edward Owen Engineering Ltd v Barclays Bank International Ltd* limited *Stzejn*, Lord Denning M.R. observing that "The only exception is when there is a clear fraud of which the bank has notice."[9] *Edward Owen* was a performance bond case, under which it was assumed that the bank's obligations to the buyer were analogous to those assumed by the confirming bank to the seller under a documentary credit. *The American Accord* applied the reasoning in these three cases to a documentary credit, where the action was brought by the beneficiary against the confirming bank (*i.e.* contract 4).

As in *Edward Owen*, the fraud exception is narrow, applying (in the documentary credit case) only where the seller can be shown himself to have been fraudulent. The exception was said by Lord Diplock to be:

"a clear application of the maxim *ex turpi causa non oritur actio* or, if plain English is to be preferred, 'fraud unravels all.' The courts will not allow their process to be used by a dishonest person to carry out a fraud."

This is however the full extent of the fraud exception. It must be fraud on the part of the seller, and it must be proved.[10] Banks must honour a credit even if they suspect fraud, if they cannot prove it (it can be difficult to prove fraud in the time available—see further below, and also chapter 15, below). They must also pay even if they know that the documents tendered are fraudulent, unless they can prove that the seller was aware of the fraud.[11] Schmitthoff commented that[12]:

"[b]anks will not like the idea that they have to honour a credit although they know that the documents tendered are fraudulent, only because it cannot be proved, before the credit is honoured, that the seller is aware of the fraud."

The justification for the fraud exception, then, is public policy. The refusal in *The American Accord* to extend it renders the system very fraud-prone (see below and paras 15–037 *et seq.*, below). One justification for this refusal is that an elaborate commercial system has been built up, on the basis that a vendor of goods, selling against a confirmed letter of credit, is selling under the assurance that nothing will prevent him from receiving the price.[13] Another is that banks are experts at dealing with documents, not goods (see further the comments at the beginning of this section). Were *U.C.M.* to have gone the other way, they would have been expected to determine whether the goods, as well as the documents, in fact conformed to the contract description.

Further observations

10–011
    1. The action in *The American Accord* was on contract 4, the juristic nature of which creates difficulties (see the discussion at the end of chapter 8, above). Here, however, the documents had been tendered, and the beneficiary had

---

[8] (1941) 31 N.Y.S. 2d. 631. It was alleged that the seller had shipped rubbish, and Megarry J. observed in *Discount Records*, below, that "the proceedings consisted of a motion to dismiss the formal complaint on the ground that it disclosed no cause of action. That being so, the court had to assume that the facts stated in the complaint were true. The complaint alleged fraud, and so the court was dealing with a case of established fraud."

[9] [1978] Q.B. 159, at 171.

[10] A rare example is *Rafsanjan Pistachio Producers Co-Operative v Bank Leumi (UK) plc* [1992] 1 Lloyd's Rep. 513, where the requisite fraud was proved.

[11] Subject perhaps to the exception that forged documents are nullities (for example where there is no ship, or the ship exists but no cargo is shipped), and therefore do not count as documents at all, for *American Accord* purposes.

[12] [1982] J.B.L. 319, at 322.

[13] Essentially the view taken from *Hamzeh Malas*, and discussed in para. 9–009, above.

done everything the bank required of him. There are therefore none of the difficulties in finding a contractual cause of action as were discussed in paras 8–047 *et seq.*, above.

2. The documentary position has now been held to be similar where apparently conforming documents are tendered to a buyer directly (*i.e.* where no bank is involved): see *Gill and Duffus v Berger* (in para. 7–022, above). Different justifications have to be found where no bank is involved, however.

3. The fraud potential is apparent in the following case.

DISCOUNT RECORDS LTD v BARCLAYS BANK LTD

Chancery Division. [1975] 1 W.L.R. 315

The plaintiffs were purchasers of a consignment of records and cassettes **10–012** from a French company (Promodisc), payment to be by confirmed irrevocable credit. Documents were tendered which conformed on their face,[14] but by then it had become clear that the cartons shipped contained largely rubbish. The purchasers had ordered 8,625 records and 825 cassettes. The cargo was packed in 94 cartons, but of these two were found to be empty, five were filled with rubbish or packing, and 28 were only partly filled. 275 records and 518 cassettes were actually delivered, but of the 518 cassettes only 25 per cent. were delivered to order.

The plaintiffs nevertheless failed to restrain the confirming bank from paying under the credit, Megarry J. distinguishing *Sztejn* on the grounds that no fraud on the part of the sellers was proven, merely alleged.

Megarry J.: During the argument on this point before me, the familiar **10–013** English phrase "Fraud unravels all" was also discussed. However, it is important to notice that in the *Sztejn* case the proceedings consisted of a motion to dismiss the formal complaint on the ground that it disclosed no cause of action. That being so, the court had to assume that the facts stated in the complaint were true. The complaint alleged fraud, and so the court was dealing with a case of established fraud. In the present case there is, of course, no established fraud, but merely an allegation of fraud. The defendants, who were not concerned with that matter, have understandably adduced no evidence on the issue of fraud. Indeed, it seems unlikely that any action to which Promodisc was not a party would contain the evidence required to resolve this issue. Accordingly, the matter has to be dealt with on the footing that this is a case in which fraud is alleged but has not been established. . . .

. . . I would be slow to interfere with bankers' irrevocable credits, and not least in the sphere of international banking, unless a sufficiently grave cause is shown; for interventions by the court that are too ready or too frequent might gravely impair the reliance which, quite properly, is

---

[14] Or at any rate, documents which were eventually accepted as conforming by an official of the plaintiffs: see at 317.

placed on such credits. The *Sztejn* case, 31 N.Y.S. 2d 631, is plainly distinguishable in relation . . . to established fraud . . . I do not say that the doctrine of that case is wrong or that it is incapable of extension to cases in which fraud is alleged but has not been established, provided a sufficient case is made out. That may or may not be the case. What I do say is that the present case falls far short of establishing any ground upon which it would be right for the court to intervene by granting the interlocutory injunction claimed . . . The motion accordingly fails and will be dismissed.

Notes

10–014   The case pre-dated *The American Accord*, which even more clearly limits *Sztejn* to established fraud. If Promodisc had been fraudulent, then this decision would have assisted them in their purpose.

In *Discount Records* itself, the report suggests that the victims (buyers) might (possibly) have had a contractual action against the issuing bank, arising from an independent breach. If so, they might therefore have been adequately protected, being able to shift the loss on to the bank. If not, position would have been very weak. They would have been left to pursue Promodisc themselves, for breach of contract and (possibly) deceit.

The American Accord was a case on contract 4, *Discount Records* on contract 2. Clearly, however, it would be intolerable if a bank were required to accept documents under contract 4 which it could not then pass (eventually) to the buyer for payment. Each contract must be treated alike by the law; they might be autonomous, but they are also interconnected. Indeed, Lord Diplock observed in *The American Accord* that:

> "It would be strange from a commercial point of view, although not theoretically impossible in law, if the contractual duty owed by confirming and issuing banks to the buyer to honour the credit on presentation of apparently conforming documents despite the fact that they contain inaccuracies or even are forged were not matched by a corresponding contractual liability of the confirming bank to the seller/beneficiary (in the absence, of course, of any fraud on his part) to pay the sum stipulated in the credit on presentation of apparently conforming documents."

He concluded, of course, that it was so matched.

The injunction (now called a freezing order in the UK, but not elsewhere in the common law world) is in any case a discretionary remedy. The principles upon which it is to be granted were stated by the Court of Appeal in the following case.

BOLIVINTER OIL SA v CHASE MANHATTAN BANK

Court of Appeal. [1984] 1 Lloyd's Rep. 251

10–015   The only importance of this case lies in the following remarks, on the limited circumstances where a buyer can restrain a bank, by injunction, from paying the beneficiary under a credit.

Sir John Donaldson M.R.: Before leaving this appeal, we should like to **10–016** add a word about the circumstances in which an *ex parte* injunction should be issued which prohibits a bank from paying under an irrevocable letter of credit or a performance bond or guarantee. The unique value of such a letter, bond or guarantee is that the beneficiary can be completely satisfied that, whatever disputes may thereafter arise between him and the bank's customer in relation to the performance or indeed existence of the underlying contract, the bank is personally undertaking to pay him provided that the specified conditions are met . . . If, save in the most exceptional cases, he is to be allowed to derogate from the bank's personal and irrevocable undertaking, given be it again noted at his request, by obtaining an injunction restraining the bank from honouring that undertaking, he will undermine what is the bank's greatest asset, however large and rich it may be, namely its reputation for financial and contractual probity. Furthermore, if this happens at all frequently, the value of all irrevocable letters and performance bonds and guarantees will be undermined.

Judges who are asked, often at short notice and *ex parte*, to issue an injunction restraining payment by a bank under an irrevocable letter of credit or performance bond or guarantee should ask whether there is any challenge to the validity of the letter, bond or guarantee itself. If there is not or if the challenge is not substantial, *prima facie* no injunction should be granted and the bank should be left free to honour its contractual obligation, although restrictions may well be imposed on the freedom of the beneficiary to deal with the money after he has received it. The wholly exceptional case where an injunction may be granted is where it is proved that the bank knows that any demand for payment already made or which may thereafter be made will clearly be fraudulent. But the evidence must be clear, both of the fact of fraud and as to the bank's knowledge. It would certainly not normally be sufficient that this rests on the uncorroborated statement of the customer, for irreparable damage can be done to a bank's credit in the relatively brief time which must elapse between the granting of such an injunction and an application by the bank to have it discharged.

BARBARA CONWAY, *THE PIRACY BUSINESS*

(Hamlyn, 1981) at pp. 23–25

The [next] type of marine fraud, the documentary fraud, is, from the **10–017** point of view of the fraudsters, both the least dramatic and the most profitable of any. . . . But from the criminal point of view, the beauty of the documentary fraud is that there is no need to have the correct amount or type of cargo on board the ship before presenting the "proof" of loading which will enable them to claim payment. In fact, it is not even necessary to have a ship.

The operation of the documentary fraud depends wholly on the "letter of credit" system . . . To understand how it can be abused, you first have to know your way around the system.

The first and crucial point to understand about the system is that it operates to a stunning degree on trust. There are any number of checkpoints on the documents concerned, but they are more to ensure that the paperwork has been prepared correctly than that its content is truthful. It is, in short, an open invitation to roguery. And the invitation has been gratefully accepted to the increasing detriment of al except the rogues. . . .

As mentioned above, the bill of lading, and its accompanying papers, "theoretically" provides the proof needed that the specified goods are indeed on board the vessel. But of course, it only does that if the bill itself is truthful and accurate. And all these documents are only of value if they happen to be genuine.

But they may not be. Forgery is a very sophisticated art (or craft) now, and none of these documents is particularly difficult to fabricate. Indeed, the forgeries do not even need to be particularly good. . . .

So how can it be possible for a bank (and virtually all the major international banking groups have been caught out at some time by forged documents presented to back up a documentary credit) to pay out large sums of money, sometimes amounting to millions, on such slender evidence? Indeed, how can it come about that letters of credit have been duly paid out even though the ship specified was nowhere near the loading port at the time it was supposed to have been receiving the goods, or may not even have existed? . . .

The banks themselves leap into the breach to defend themselves against any charge of negligence. After all, they point out, a major commercial branch will handle large numbers of such routine transactions as letters of credit every day. There are certain basic checks which are carried out, although these tend to concentrate more on whether the documents have been made out correctly than whether they are genuine. Some fraudulent efforts are indeed weeded out in this process, but not enough.

The other point made by the banks is that they are employed not as detectives, but as payment agents. If the shipper is dealing with a crooked shipowner or ship's master, then presumably the shipper's own checking system has gone badly awry. There is some validity in this view, although it cannot absolve the banks of all moral responsibility, even if they have clearly established that they are free of legal onus in the matter.

Observation

10–018 The late Barbara Conway is undoubtedly correct to observe that the documentary credit system is fraud-prone. Given the state of the law, however, that is not the fault of the banks. Given also the speed with which they have to make decisions, it seems unlikely that they could often obtain the requisite proof of fraud (by the immediate seller, remember, not, as would be far more likely, by the shipper, or an earlier seller in the chain) successfully to resist an action, whatever enquiries they made.

Barbara Conway makes similar comments in her later (updated and somewhat expanded) work, *Maritime Fraud*, (L.L.P., 1990) at pp. 8–9.[15] Both these books make a depressing read, delving the depths of human greed, but both were written before the re-emergence (in the nineties) of professional (and very violent) pirates. On the problems of maritime crime generally, see further paras 15–037 *et seq.*, below.

Limits to The American Accord?

The following case may illustrate the limits of *The American Accord*. The issuing   **10–019** bank successfully defended proceedings by the beneficiary for a *Mareva* injunction (now called a freezing order in the UK, but not elsewhere in the common law world). Brandon L.J. decided the case simply on the basis that a *Mareva* injunction was inappropriate, since there was no doubt that the defendant bank would meet its obligations if judgment was given against it, but Lord Denning M.R. also thought relevant his doubts about the claim (though fraud was not proven). Lawton L.J. was equivocal as to the relevance of suspicions of fraud by the plaintiffs.

This was not, of course, the final trial, and any equitable remedy is discretionary. Another point is that if these documents really were forged, they were not genuine documents at all, to which *The American Accord* (which was not decided until a few years later) would apply.

ETABLISSEMENT ESEFKA INTERNATIONAL ANSTALT v CENTRAL BANK OF NIGERIA

Court of Appeal. [1979] 1 Lloyd's Rep. 445

Apparently conforming documents were tendered in respect of 94,000   **10–020** tonnes of cement said to be aboard eight vessels, although there was considerable doubt whether the vessels or cargo ever existed at all. The bank successfully defended a claim for a *Mareva* injunction brought by the applicants for the credit.

LORD DENNING M.R.: This is another case involving what has been called in the papers "the cement scandal" in regard to Nigeria. It so happened a few years ago that the Ministry of Defence in Nigeria ordered vast quantities of cement from all over the world. The Central Bank of Nigeria issued letters of credit to pay for all the cement which was coming in, and a good deal of it was payable through London banks.

Great quantities of cement were shipped to Lagos: and at one time there were 300 or 400 ships waiting outside the port of Lagos to discharge the cement. There were not enough wharves or quays to take it there, let alone all the other goods coming into Nigeria. So immense demurrage

---

[15] Arguably neither of these books is appropriately titled. Most of the cases in *The Piracy Business* (unlike darker and more recent developments in, *e.g.* the South China Sea—see further chapter 15, below) do not involve piracy, part of the essence of which is violence: *Athens Maritime v Hellenic Mutual War Risks (The Andreas Lemos)* [1983] Q.B. 647. The insurance cases in *Maritime Fraud* are genuine frauds, but most of the cargo cases (including the ghost ships, and *The Salem*) are thefts rather than frauds. There might be a deception, but it is not the operative cause of the loss.

was built up on the ships which were lying outside the port of Lagos for months and months. The story of what happened will be found in the case of *Trendtex Trading Corporation v Central Bank of Nigeria* [1978] 1 Lloyd's Rep. 581, in which that bank claimed sovereign immunity and said they could not be sued. It was held in this Court that they could be sued in the ordinary Courts. That was the position in law. This is a further aspect of that "cement scandal".

In this case the Ministry of Defence ordered 240,000 tonnes of cement in December, 1974, at a price of US $ 59.90 per tonne c.i.f. Lagos. The total purchase price was US $ 14,376,000. That was ordered and agreed to be paid for by the Ministry of Defence in Lagos from a company (I will call it such) called Etablissement Esefka International Anstalt of Liechtenstein, but operating apparently from an address in the Strand, London. The Nigerian Ministry of Defence said that letters of credit would be opened accordingly—transferable, divisible letters of credit. The letters of credit were issued on Mar. 18, 1975. The advice was given by the Midland Bank here on the account of the Central Bank of Nigeria for these moneys to be paid for the goods against documents. The documents included commercial invoices (four copies), a full set of four bills of lading, an insurance policy and the like. The ordinary set of shipping documents was to come forward. The credit was irrevocable, transferable and divisible: and, furthermore, there was a special provision by annexure for demurrage to be payable in the total sum of US $ 4100 a day. That demurrage also came under the letters of credit which were issued by the Central Bank of Nigeria through the London correspondents, the Midland Bank, in favour of the Liechtenstein company, Esefka International.

10–021   I do not suppose that Esefka International had any cement at all themselves. They had to buy it; and apparently successfully in several cases. A good deal of the cement was shipped, a good many of the ships were held up, and a good deal of demurrage was payable. As to a great number of them, no question arises. But a question does arise in regard to eight vessels which were supposed to have shipped about 94,000 tonnes of this cement. With regard to those eight vessels, the shipping documents, the bills of lading, certificates and the like were presented to the Midland Bank as though everything was in good order. On being presented with those documents, the Midland Bank in London paid out huge sums in respect of these goods. Nearly $ 6,000,000 were paid out in respect of these ships.

Lo and behold. I will come almost to the end of the story in a moment. Solicitors from London have been out to Lagos on behalf of the Central Bank of Nigeria. They have been to Greece, and they have obtained very strong evidence that there were no genuine documents at all—that these bills of lading were not genuine, but were forged. There is great doubt whether these eight vessels ever existed at all. . . . In practically every one of these eight ships the bills of lading appeared as if there had been a ship which had changed its name. Nearly all the bills of lading were made out on that basis, and signed by the master, that they were shipped at a port in Greece called Volos.

When the solicitor from London went out to Greece he found that it was all "moonshine" in effect. They had never had any of these ships in Volos at all. And Volos had not got the quantity of cement or anything like it to fulfil these supposed bills of lading. What is more, the harbourmaster did not know of any being put on board or sent forward, and so forth. So a very strong case was made out that these bills of lading were not genuine at all. They were forged in respect of goods which had never existed.

. . . At all events, there it was. Esefka, the Liechtenstein company, got money on three vessels. There is a question of whether those vessels ever existed. Klemo got money on five other vessels, and the same question mark arises about those. And the long and the short of it is that on these supposedly genuine documents Mr. Klemo and the other people got US $ 6,000,000.

When the solicitor from London found this out, he advised the Central Bank of Nigeria and the Midland Bank in London that they were not to pay any more money. They were certainly not to pay any demurrage with regard to this claim under these letters of credit when this kind of fraud, as he said it was, had been perpetrated.

Was there such a fraud or not? Of course it is a debatable question. We have not got anywhere near the trial itself. But for myself, in view of the strength of the evidence which has been collected by the London solicitor in Lagos and in Greece, it seems to be elementary that, if it was a genuine transaction, Mr. Paul Harris (who was obviously the genius behind it) and Mr. Klemo (who was the person who was supposed to have supplied the goods) would have made affidavits or come forward to show that these were genuine goods and these were genuine shipments. But there are no such affidavits. . . . [There] is not a word of evidence to show that there were genuine transactions. Indeed, Mr. Paul Harris in an affidavit admits that there is an arguable case for saying that they were not genuine.

When the Central Bank of Nigeria were so advised, they said: **10–022**

"We are not going to pay any demurrage outstanding on these letters of credit on these other shipments. We say that a fraud has been going on . . . "

Now certain points of law emerge on that matter. First of all, it seems to have been one transaction. The whole letter of credit covered all the 240,000 tonnes. The documents ought to be correct and valid in respect of each parcel. If that condition is broken by forged or fraudulent documents being presented—in respect of any one parcel—the defendants have a defence in point of law against being liable in respect of that parcel. And they have a claim, not only as to any outstanding claim but also they have a counterclaim for the money which they have overpaid and which they paid on false documents. We said as much in *Edward Owen Engineering Ltd v Barclays Bank International Ltd* [1978] 1 Q.B. 159 at 169 to 170, in which I quoted what Browne L.J. said:

" . . . In my judgment, if the documents are presented by the beneficiary himself, and are forged or fraudulent, the bank is entitled to refuse payment if it finds out before payment, and is entitled to recover the money as paid under a mistake of fact if it finds out after payment . . . "

I should have thought that that was the good sense of the matter. That is so far as the actual payment and recovery are concerned. . . .

I think I have said enough about the case to show that in regard to the claim there is a good arguable defence on account of the forged or fraudulent bills of lading to show that the claim is not well-founded. . . .

That being the state of affairs, the practical question at the moment is whether or not there should be a *Mareva* injunction granted so as to prevent the Central Bank of Nigeria from removing out of the jurisdiction of England a very substantial sum of money to meet the plaintiffs' claim. I would not like to throw any doubt whatsoever upon the validity of the *Mareva* injunctions which have been granted since they were started year by year in the Commercial Court and have proved to be of the greatest value, but in order that they should operate there should at least be a good arguable case for the plaintiffs that the money is going to become due to them. On the material before us, it seems to me that there are many doubts in the plaintiffs' claim and there is so much defence to be raised against it that it would not be a case where the plaintiffs have a really good arguable case to succeed. That is one ground on which it would not be right to grant a *Mareva* injunction.

But there is another ground too. The *Mareva* injunction is only to be granted where there is danger of the money being taken out of the jurisdiction so that if the plaintiffs succeed they are not likely to get their money. That has happened, I believe, in all the cases we have had hitherto, such as one-ship companies which are going to disappear with the money and no one can get it unless a *Mareva* injunction is granted. The situation is very different indeed with the Central Bank of Nigeria. There are affidavits showing the immense funds which are available to the Central Bank of Nigeria in commercial countries all over the world including this country. It seems to me that it would not be right to say that the government of Nigeria would not honour its obligations or that there is any risk of its dishonouring its obligations if it is found to be liable by this Court.

So on these grounds, first, it seems to me that there is not a good arguable case which a *Mareva* injunction requires. Secondly, there is no danger of the assets going outside the jurisdiction. . . . Therefore, it seems to me that it would not be right to grant a *Mareva* injunction. . . .

LAWTON L.J.: I agree with the judgment delivered by Lord Denning   **10–023**
M.R. . . .

So far as the *Mareva* injunction is concerned, it seems to me that a novel point of law does arise in regard to the effect of the fraudulent conduct of the beneficiary under a letter of credit upon the continued existence of the letter of credit. There is no English authority dealing with the matter and only one American authority. In those circumstances, I myself would not be prepared to say what the chances of success are for the plaintiffs. But what I am sure about is this, that there is no evidence whatsoever in my judgment that the defendant bank will not meet its obligations if judgment is given against it. It is unrealistic to say that there is any danger of their doing so. Nigeria is a very large and one of the most prosperous of the African countries with a substantial export trade, and enjoying, so one of the affidavits says, the benefit of support from the International Monetary Fund; and, as my Lord has pointed out, it has assets all over the word, no doubt for the purpose of supporting its international trade. In those circumstances it is inconceivable that they would default from a judgment of this Court, albeit that it would be, if the plaintiffs were successful, for a sum of just over US $ 2,000,000. . . .

BRANDON L.J.: I agree that the appeal should be allowed. So far as the   **10–024**
Mareva injunction is concerned, I would base my judgment only upon the second ground mentioned by my Lord, Lawton L.J., that is to say, on the ground that there is no material from which the Court could conclude that the assets of the defendants are likely to be removed from the jurisdiction so as to avoid payment of any judgment which the plaintiffs might obtain. . . .

Note

The Nigerian cement scandal is also described by Barbara Conway in *The Piracy Business* (Hamlyn, 1981) at p. 49.

The case is unusual in that the c.i.f. buyers (the Nigerian government) agreed to pay demurrage; presumably they were forced into this position by the congestion that they had themselves created. Another (unrelated) problem was that there was no satisfactory control over the demurrage claims, which provided another fruitful opportunity for fraud.

(3) THE DOCTRINE OF STRICT COMPLIANCE

This section is, in a sense, the converse of the last. There, the documents   **10–025**
appeared to be in order, but there were doubts about the goods. Here, no doubt is cast upon the conformity of the goods, but the documents do not conform exactly to the credit requirements.

(a) RATIONALE OF THE DOCTRINE

10–026   There is a tension at work in the doctrine of strict compliance. Suppose there is a trivial defect in the documentation, but the documents are in fact just as good as those stipulated. It might be thought very unfair for the bank to be allowed to reject, especially if, for example, it is doing so on the instructions of the buyer, whose sole concern is to get out of a falling market. However, the principles from the start of the previous section all point to the documents being required to conform strictly, and banks being required to reject for even the most trivial defect. For the most part, the common law has favoured the second of these approaches.

Since neither bank is agent expressly for the seller, the mandate for each bank derives from the instructions of the buyer. At common law, the banks' mandate is to accept only the exact documents stipulated in the credit. This is the doctrine of strict compliance. If the seller deviates at all from tendering the required documents, the bank is under no obligation to pay. Indeed, unless the buyer expressly permits payment, the bank is under a positive obligation not to pay.

It is immaterial that the goods conform to the contract description. Where the U.C.P. applies, (*i.e.* in some 95% of credits), the principle is relaxed a little, by virtue of Article 37 (set out in Appendix C, below).

As in the previous section, it appears that the courts treat similarly contracts 2, 3 and 4; this is clearly desirable if banks are required to accept documents for which they cannot claim reimbursement. Many of the cases, including the following, concern contract 4,[16] but *Bank Melli Iran v Barclays Bank D.C.O.* applies the same principles to contract 3,[17] and *Equitable Trust Company of New York v Dawson Partners Ltd* to contract 2.[18] Earlier cases established the rigid common law rule.[19] The following case also considers the effect of the U.C.P., which relaxes it slightly.

SOPROMA SPA v MARINE & ANIMAL BY-PRODUCTS CORPORATION

Commercial Court. [1966] 1 Lloyd's Rep. 367

10–027   The facts have already been set out (see para. 9–005, above). Discrepant documents were tendered, which the bank rejected. It has already been observed that the buyers were not in breach of the sale contract in obtaining a credit on the terms which they did. The sellers then made a second tender, but directly to the buyers. This second tender was also rejected by the buyers. The sellers sold

---

[16] See also *J.H. Rayner & Co Ltd v Hambros Bank Ltd* [1943] 1 K.B. 37, where MacKinnon L.J. also took the view that the position between bank and beneficiary ought in principle to be the same as that between bank and customer.

[17] [1951] 2 Lloyd's Rep. 367.

[18] (1926) 27 Ll.L. Rep. 49.

[19] In *Seng Co Ltd v Glencore Grain Ltd* [1996] 1 Lloyd's Rep. 398, Mance J. adopted a test similar to common law strict compliance for documentation under a c. & f. sale contract, and in refusing leave to appeal (unreported, C.A., 4 July 1996), Hobhouse L.J. was clearly unimpressed by the seller's contention that "there is a distinction to be drawn between a case which requires documents to be tendered to the Buyer, and where they are to be tendered to a bank under a letter of credit." Mance J.' view was applied in *Soules CAF v PT Transap of Indonesia* [1999] 1 Lloyd's Rep. 917. See also *SIAT di dal Ferro v Tradax Overseas SA* [1980] 1 Lloyd's Rep. 53, where Megaw L.J. also adopted a strict test as to documentation, subject only to a *de minimis* exception.

the goods at a loss, and (unsuccessfully) sued the buyers for non-acceptance. These aspects of the case have already been considered in chapter 9, above.

McNair J. also took the view that the bank was entitled to reject the first tender, because the documents did not conform. This is an application of the doctrine of strict compliance, and is the reason for including the case here also.

McNAIR J.: (*on the strict compliance issue*) [On the first tender] I now turn **10–028** to a number of . . . points taken as to the sufficiency of the credit. First, it was said there was an inconsistency between the description of the goods in the invoice, namely, "Chilean Fish Full Meal", and the description of the goods in the bill of lading, namely "Chilean Fishmeal", and reliance was placed upon (1) *Midland Bank Ltd v Seymour* [1955] 2 Lloyd's Rep. 147, at p. 153, for the statement that the documents must be mutually consistent, and (2) upon *J.H. Rayner & Co Ltd v Hambro's Bank Ltd* [1943] 1 K.B. 37, for the proposition that the description of the goods in the shipping documents—in that case the bills of lading—must conform with the description of the goods in the letter of credit. In the present case the letters of credit as stated above incorporated the "UNIFORM CUSTOMS AND PRACTICE FOR COMMERCIAL DOCUMENTARY CREDITS" which by Art. 33 [see now Art. 37 of the 1993 revision, in Appendix C, below] provide as follows:

"The description of the goods in the Commercial Invoice must correspond with the description in the credit. Wherever the goods are described in the remaining documents, description in general terms will be acceptable."

I have already set out earlier in this judgment the findings of the Board of Appeal . . . as to the meaning and effect of the terms "Fish Full Meal" and "Fish Meal" and their conclusion that the invoice specifically states "Fish Full Meal", and anyone in the trade seeing a bill of lading would not expect to see a more specific description than "fishmeal" and could not reasonably object to such a description. In my judgment, so far as concerns the [first] tender under the letters of credit, the bill of lading contained a sufficient general description to comply with Art. 33, the invoice having described the goods in accordance with the letters of credit. There was no clause corresponding with Art. 33 in *Rayner's case, sup.*, . . .

The next point to be taken was as to the inconsistent statements as to the protein content . . . [McNair J stated the relevant facts] . . . Quite apart from the shippers' invoice, which probably in law is irrelevant, though it may well have afforded the buyers with a well-justified reason for doubting the true protein content of the goods shipped, it is in my judgment plain that the two documents relied upon by the buyers in their rejection, namely, the shippers' certificate of quality and the certificate of analysis, did not constitute valid shipping documents under the letter of credit as was in fact acknowledged by the sellers when, on making their second tender direct to the buyers, they instructed the Italian bank to withdraw these documents and to substitute in their place and analysis certificate signed by themselves dated Oct. 16 and a quality certificate also so signed and dated without any certificate as to protein content. In my judgment, the documents so tendered were not a good tender against the letter of credit.

Note

10–029   On the first tender the decision is an application of the doctrine of strict compliance. The U.C.P. relaxed the inflexible common law position: Article 37 of the present revision allows for a description in general terms, apart from in the invoice. Thus, if the only fault had been the description in the bill of lading as "Fishmeal", the tender would have been valid. Even then, it would not have been valid at common law. As it was, the U.C.P. Article did not cure the other faults.

The last revision of the U.C.P. provides, in Article 13(a), that "Compliance of the stipulated documents on their face with the terms and conditions of the Credit shall be determined by international standard banking practice as reflected in these Articles." Arguably, this allows for more flexibility to be introduced into the doctrine of strict compliance. The courts in the United States appear to apply a rule "to the effect that banks should be charged with knowledge of banking practices but are relieved from any charge to know commercial practices, *i.e.* the industry practices of the commercial parties to the underlying transaction."[20] This bears some similarities with the principle that banks do not deal in goods, but can only be workable if there are clearly defined banking practices, which are the same throughout the world (for otherwise how would you work a chain sale with banks in different countries?). Flexibility might tend to promote justice at the expense of certainty. On the importance of certainty, see further the discussion in paras 15–009 *et seq.*, below.

(b) Trivial Defects

PAUL TODD, "DISCREPANCIES BETWEEN BILLS OF LADING AND LETTERS OF CREDIT"

Letter of Credit Update (Government Information Services, USA) (1999), pp. 14–19

[Footnotes are added.]

10–030   In *Bankers Trust Co v State Bank of India* [1991] 2 Lloyd's Rep. 443, Lloyd L.J. accepted evidence "that discrepancies are found in nearly half of all credits". It may well be true that, as Sir Thomas Bingham M.R. observed in *Glencore International AG v Bank of China* [1996] 1 Lloyd's Rep. 135, the discrepancies are rarely litigated, matters usually being settled well before that stage:

---

[20] The quote is from a commentary by John F. Dolan, 8 B.F.L.R. 53, at p. 58, where American practices are described in detail. See also Dolan, "Letters of Credit: A Comparison of the U.C.P. 500 and the new U.S. Article 5" [1999] J.B.L. 521, especially at pp. 523–524.

"There are a number of reasons for this. The parties to these transactions (buyers, sellers, issuing and advising banks) are seasoned professionals, not inexperienced consumers. . . . Banks, rightly jealous of their reputation in the international market-place, are generally careful not to refuse payment on grounds of non-conformity unless the non-conformity is clear."

Nevertheless, the high rate of discrepancies, or alleged discrepancies, is disturbing, because it weakens the security of the seller. One of the main advantages to a seller of an irrevocable documentary credit is said to be that the "vendor of goods selling against a confirmed letter of credit is selling under the assurance that nothing will prevent him from receiving the price" (*per* Jenkins L.J. in *Hamzeh Malas & Sons v British Imex Industries Ltd* [1958] 2 Q.B. 127 at 129). If potential problems, and hence the potential for non-payment, exist in half of all credits, the value of such assurance is surely severely compromised.[21]

There are, I would suggest, only two possible reasons for the degree to which discrepancies, or alleged discrepancies, arise under letters of credit. One is that the credit requirements are insufficiently precise, rendering it unclear whether a credit has been complied with or not. In *Bankers Trust Co v State Bank of India* itself, for example, 967 pages of free text had to be checked. In *Glencore International AG v Bank of China*, the credit (for a sale of aluminium ingots) required "Origin: Any Western Brand", the issue being whether this covered goods which were shipped from Indonesia (see further below). Probably a degree of vagueness is inevitable in commerce, especially where a variety of goods will satisfy the buyer's requirements, but it is certain to increase the potential for disputes about discrepancies.

The only other possible reason (that I can think of) is that the credit requirements are too onerous, given that the beneficiary might have little control over the precise form of the shipping documents, and that minor technical mistakes can often creep into any document. . . .

Bank's Duties where Discrepancies Found or Suspected

. . .

This article is concerned with discrepancies, and therefore with the **10–031** doctrine of strict compliance, which is worth examining in more detail. . . . [A] bank is neither obliged nor entitled to accept non-conforming documents. To take the simplest case, of an issuing bank under an unconfirmed credit, the bank will not be obliged to accept under its contract with the beneficiary, and will not be entitled to accept under its contract with the applicant. But the non-compliance may be extremely trivial, consisting for example of obvious typing errors, where a refusal by

---

[21] There is another reason for concern. If discrepancies are rarely litigated, this implies either that the banks are deciding whether discrepancies are material or not, or that they are consulting with the applicant, neither of which states of affairs is desirable.

the buyer to accept could hardly be justified, but may be used as a device to get out of a bad bargain on a falling market (the reason, incidentally, for the rejection in *Glencore International AG v Bank of China*). Alternatively (*e.g.* on a rising market) the buyer may be only too happy to accept the documents. Two issues therefore arise. First, does the strict compliance doctrine allow of any exception where the non-compliance is really trivial; secondly, to what extent is it permissible for the bank to leave the decision whether of not to accept to the buyer, or applicant for the credit?

Very Trivial Defects

The original common law position was that the triviality of a defect was irrelevant; a bank could not be expected to know whether a defect was trivial, and therefore the documents had to comply strictly with the terms of the credit. It was no answer that the document presented was just as good. There are many authorities. In *Equitable Trust Co of New York v Dawson & Partners* (1926) 27 Ll.L. Rep. 49), Lord Sumner observed that there "is no room for documents which are almost the same or which will do just as well". In *J.H. Rayner & Co Ltd v Hambros Bank Ltd* [1943] 1 K.B. 37, an irrevocable credit required sight drafts to be accompanied by bills of lading for "Coromandel groundnuts". The sellers tendered bills of lading for "machine-shelled groundnut kernels", which were universally understood in the trade to be identical to "Coromandel groundnuts". The bank refused payment; the seller sued and failed, MacKinnon L.J. observing that it was no good that the words in the bill of lading were "almost the same, or they will do just as well". They were not the same, and as against the seller the bank was entitled to refuse payment.

As explained above, the position was relaxed by the U.C.P., except for the commercial invoice, where the full rigour of the common law continues to apply. While its rationale has obvious benefits for the banks, who need do no more than examine the documents themselves, in a complex credit a very strict position can allow buyers easily to escape a bad bargain, for example on a falling market. Moreover, there are some errors which must obviously be trivial, even on examination of the documents alone, and there is a good argument for relaxing the position, at any rate for such defects.

In *Banque de l'Indochine et de Suez SA v J.H. Rayner (Mincing Lane) Ltd* [1983] Q.B. 711, Parker J. thought "that Lord Sumner's statement cannot be taken as requiring rigid meticulous fulfilment of precise wording in all cases. Some margin must and can be allowed, but it is slight, and banks will be at risk in most cases where there is less than strict compliance." In that case the tender was held in fact to be bad, both by Parker J. and later by the Court of Appeal, but at least the possibility was alluded to that some defects are so trivial as to not to entitle a bank to reject. In *Bankers Trust Co v State Bank of India*, Lloyd L.J. described as trivial that "the telex number of the buyers' . . . office was given as 931310 instead of 981310."

As with the earlier case, nothing actually turned on the triviality of this defect, but the view earlier tentatively advanced by Parker J. was to some extent entrenched by this judgment. (A further example of a trivial defect was given in *Kredietbank Antwerp v Midland Bank plc*, Court of Appeal, 28 April 1999,[22] where Evans L.J. gave as an example an obvious typographical error, such as the possible misspelling of "Smith", as "Smithh".)

The courts have since *Bankers Trust* been reluctant to extend this category of defect, and indeed it would surely be undesirable if it applied other than to the sort of defect which is obviously trivial, on examination of the documents alone. In *Seaconsar Far East Ltd v Bank Markazi Jomhuori Islami Iran* [1993] 1 Lloyd's Rep. 236, the credit required each of the documents presented to contain the letter of credit number and the name of the buyer. The Court of Appeal refused to enquire as to the reason for this requirement and held that the bank could not ignore it. However trivial an omission, the absence of the letter of credit number and the name of the buyer from the *procès verbal* called for some explanation, and the bank were entitled to reject the documents. Lloyd L.J. observed that:

10–032

"I cannot regard as trivial something which, whatever may be the reason, the credit specifically requires. It would not, I think, help to attempt to define the sort of discrepancy which can properly be regarded as trivial. But one might take, by way of example, *Bankers Trust Co v State Bank of India* where one of the documents gave the buyer's telex number as 931310 instead of 981310. The discrepancy in the present case is not of that order."

So far then, the recognition of a special category of trivial defects, if accepted into the law at all, was restricted to a very narrow scope (see also, e.g., the decision of the High Court of Singapore in *United Bank Ltd v Banque Nationale de Paris* [1992] 2 S.L.R. 64). In particular, any defect which puts the bank on enquiry is not trivial for these purposes. In *Glencore International AG v Bank of China*, however, the letter of credit (relating to a sale of aluminium ingots) stated "Origin: Any Western Brand". The commercial invoices described the goods as "Any Western Brand—Indonesia (Inalum Brand)". The certificate of origin also certified that the material "is of Indonesian origin (Inalum brand)". Both differed, in other words, from the credit requirements. The Court of Appeal (reversing Rix J. on this point) took the view that had these been the only defects, the tender would have been good. On the commercial invoice, to which alone, of course, the common law doctrine of strict compliance still applied, Sir Thomas Bingham M.R. observed that:

"It is, we think, plain that the original specified in the credit ('Any Western brand') is expressed in very broad generic way. A banker

---

[22] Now reported in [1999] 1 Lloyd's Rep. Bank. 219.

would require no knowledge of the aluminium trade to appreciate that there could be more than one brand falling within the genus. . . . We cannot for our part accept that the additional words 'Indonesia (Inalum brand)' were such as . . . to . . . call for further inquiry or are such as to invite litigation. It seems to us quite plain on the face of the document that the additional words were to indicate the precise brand of the goods, it being implicit that that brand fell within the broad generic description which was all that was required. The additional words could not, on any possible reading of the documents, have been intended to indicate that the goods did not or might not fall within the description 'Any Western brand'."

This aspect of the decision is to be welcomed to the extent that the real reason for rejection in that case was that the market was falling, and it would be regrettable if any defect, however trivial, could allow a buyer to escape a bargain that had turned bad for that reason. The defect is clearly very different from that instanced by Lloyd L.J. in *Bankers Trust Co v State Bank of India*, and the case establishes a significant exception to the doctrine of strict compliance. However, it is clear from the above passage that Sir Thomas Bingham M.R. regards the meaning as clear from the face of the document, so that if this is true, the principle is not infringed upon that the bank should be able to determine from the documents alone whether or not to accept them.

Consultation with Applicant[23]

10–033   The observation at the start of the article was that, in spite of the number of discrepancies in documentary credits, few get to the litigation stage; one reason may be that the parties negotiate, and particularly that applicants for credits are prepared to accept documents that, strictly speaking, they would be entitled to reject. The doctrine of strict compliance, even as applied in *Glencore*, coupled with the increasing complexity of modern credits, surely makes it likely that rejection on technical grounds will be possible in a high proportion of credits.

We also observed earlier that any bank has to look to at least two contracts to determine where its duties lie. To take the simplest case, of an unconfirmed irrevocable credit, if the documents tendered do not conform the issuing bank is entitled, as against the beneficiary, to reject them. The bank can also be required to reject them by the applicant, but if the non-conformity is of no consequence the applicant may not wish to reject them. One possibility is for the bank to accept under reserve, as occurred in the *Banque de l'Indochine* case, but that is not entirely desirable because it delays the time until which the applicant can be certain of final payment. It is arguably sensible, therefore, to allow a bank, before finally

---

[23] There is further discussion of this issue in *Credit Industriel et Commercial v China Merchants Bank* [2002] EWHC 973 (Comm.).

deciding to reject, to consult with the applicant. On the other hand, it would be undesirable by so doing to prolong the decision-making process too much; moreover, the seller's security would be significantly weakened if too much control over the decision-making process were left with the buyer. The courts appear to have reached a position which while allowing banks to consult, compromises unduly neither speed nor the security of the seller.

Gatehouse J. first suggested in *The Royan* [1987] 1 Lloyd's Rep. 345 that the bank should be allowed time to consult with the applicant before deciding whether or not to accept or reject the documents. In *Bankers Trust Co v State Bank of India*, however, the unanimous view of the Court of Appeal was that on no view should a bank be allowed time to enable the buyers to examine the documents for the purpose of discovering further discrepancies. The majority view, however, with Lloyd L.J. dissenting on this point, was that a bank which had decided to reject the documents was allowed time to send them to the buyers to enable them to decide whether or not to waive the discrepancies. Both of these cases were decided under Article 16(c) of the 1983 revision of the U.C.P., which allowed banks a "reasonable time" to determine whether to accept or reject. The majority view in *Bankers' Trust* was effectively codified in Article 14(c) of U.C.P. 500:

> "If the Issuing Bank determines that the documents appear on their face not to be in compliance with the terms and conditions of the Credit, it may in its sole judgment approach the Applicant for a waiver of the discrepancy(ies). This does not, however, extend the period mentioned in Article 13(b) [time for examining documents]."

(Although it may appear on first sight that this codifies the minority position in *Bankers Trust*, by not extending the period in Article 13(b), 13(b) itself allows the reasonable time which was defined by the majority in *Bankers Trust* as including the time required to approach the applicant for a waiver.)

In *Bayerische Vereinsbank v Bank of Pakistan* [1997] 1 Lloyd's Rep. 59, Mance J. took the view that a bank which handed over to its customer the responsibility for determining whether the documents were discrepant, and then simply adopted and communicated whatever decision the customer reached was almost certain to be in breach of Article 13(b). This is also in line with the *Bankers' Trust* position, and indeed the law appears to have arrived at a good compromise position. Banks are entitled to consult with the applicant, and are allowed time to do so, but only where they have found discrepancies entitling them to reject, and their purpose is to see if the applicants are prepared to waive the discrepancies. Thus, the decision whether to reject is initially made by the bank, not the applicant, and the seller's security is not thereby compromised. It also seems unlikely that the *Bankers Trust* solution, as now codified in the U.C.P., will significantly prolong the decision-making process.

(c) What is an Original Document?

10–034   Article 23(iv) of the U.C.P. requires tender of "a sole original bill of lading or, if issued in more than one original, the full set as so issued", and there is an equivalent provision in Article 25(vi) for charterparty bills. There are also references elsewhere to "original" documents. Until about ten years ago, it was relatively easy to distinguish between an original document and a copy, but with the advent of colour scanners, high quality colour laser printers and photocopiers, etc., that is no longer the case. Ideally, however, it must also be clear to a bank what must be accepted and what rejected.

PAUL TODD, "DISCREPANCIES BETWEEN BILLS OF LADING AND LETTERS OF CREDIT" (CONTINUED)

Letter of Credit Update (Government Information Services, USA) (1999), pp. 14–19

[Footnotes are added.]

Requirement for Original Document

10–035   For obvious reasons, credits often call for original documents, and sometimes the full set of originals. With today's high quality laser printers and photocopiers, however, it is not always easy to determine what is an original document. Neither the U.C.P. nor the courts have dealt with this problem satisfactorily, and clearly a radical rethink is required.

The relevant provision of U.C.P. 500 is Article 20(b), which begins:

"Unless otherwise stipulated in the Credit, banks will also accept as originals document(s) produced or appearing to have been produced:

  i. by reprographic, automated or computerized systems;
  ii. as carbon copies;

provided that it is marked as original and, where necessary, appears to be signed."

As the Court of Appeal observed in *Kredietbank Antwerp v Midland Bank plc* (on which see further below), the use of the word "also" suggests that this Article was intended to be permissive, rather than restrictive, but in *Glencore International AG v Bank of China*, the Court of Appeal adopted a very literal, and restrictive interpretation of it. The beneficiary's certificates certifying, as required by the terms of the credit, that one full set of non-negotiable documents had been sent to the buyer, were either word-processed and laser-printed, or (more likely) photocopies of such documents; the evidence was that the photocopies were indistinguishable from those produced on the laser printer. The certificates were signed, but were not marked as original. The Court of Appeal took the view that even though they appeared to be originals, they were in fact authenticated copies, rather than original documents. The requirements of Article 20 were triggered, because the certificates (whether laser-printed or photo-copied) had been produced by reprographic, automated or computerized means. They were therefore discrepant, even though they had been signed, because they were not marked as original. If the certificates had been hand-written or typed, the provision would not have been trig-gered,[24] and there would have been no need to mark them as original, but a signature on a copy makes it an authenticated copy, not an original.

The decision in *Glencore* is not easy to justify, especially as a bank will have no ready means of distinguishing between typed, word-processed or photocopied documents, and the Court of Appeal to some extent resiled from its previous view in *Kredietbank Antwerp v Midland Bank plc*, taking the view that the Article 20(b) requirements apply only to copies, and not for example, to an original document produced by a laser printer. The reasoning in *Glencore* was thus limited to the photocopy which it was accepted had most likely been tendered in that case. Had one of the laser-printed documents been tendered, the decision in *Glencore* would there-fore (we now know) have been different.[25] Since it was accepted in *Glencore* that the photocopy was indistinguishable from the laser-printed original, the *Kredietbank Antwerp* solution is hardly any more satisfactory from the bank's viewpoint.

The law appears, then, to have got itself into a mess, but it is difficult to see what solution is possible as long as original documents are demanded, and modern reproduction methods make it impossible to distinguish copies from originals. Clearly there is a need to find some method of making originals more easily recognisable; the problem is not legal but practical. Nor is it confined to bankers' documentary credits, as the recent decision in *Motis Exports Ltd v Dampskibsselskabet AF 1912, Aktieselskab* [1999] 1 Lloyd's Rep. 837 shows; a shipowner who had delivered against a forged document of title, believing it to be an original document, was held liable to the holder of the original. Perhaps a con-sequence of the decision in *Motis Exports* will be to encourage carriers to make original shipping documents more clearly recognisable, and diffi-cult to forge, but that will not affect other documents, such as the insur-ance policy that was at issue in *Kredietbank Antwerp*. This is a matter which clearly needs urgently to be addressed by the trading parties, and the I.C.C.

Issues

Glencore looks towards certainty, requiring rejection of anything that is, or appears   **10–036** to be, produced by a printer or photocopier, unless satisfying the proviso to Article 20(b). It is a restrictive interpretation of a provision that was probably intended to be permissive, and requires rejection of almost any document that is

---

[24] They would neither have been, nor appear to have been, produced by reprographic, automated or computerized systems. The laser-printed documents and photocopies were, although they did not appear to be.
[25] This is contrary to the actual reasoning in *Glencore*, however.

not marked as original and signed. *Kredietbank* introduces flexibility, but at the expense of certainty.

Neither *Glencore* nor *Kredietbank* provides a workable solution, unless it is obvious which is the original, and which the copy. *Glencore* requires a typed original (should any such documents still exist) to be accepted, but a laser-printed document to be rejected, even though it looks original, and is therefore indistinguishable from the typed document. *Kredietbank* requires a laser-printed original to be accepted, but a photocopy to be rejected, even though they look identical.

In July 1999, the Commission on Banking Technique and Practice of the I.C.C. itself provided guidance on what should be regarded as original and what should not. It has already been observed that Article 13(a) provides that "Compliance of the stipulated documents on their face with the terms and conditions of the Credit shall be determined by international standard banking practice as reflected in these Articles." The I.C.C. could be taken to be effectively clarifying banking practice.[26] In any event, their advice was accepted as a correct interpretation by Steel J., in his attempt to reconcile the two divergent approaches of the Court of Appeal, in the following case.

CREDIT INDUSTRIEL ET COMMERCIAL v CHINA MERCHANTS BANK

Queen's Bench Division (Commercial Court). [2002] EWHC 973 (Comm.)

10–037   The issue for present purposes involved documents that had been stamped and signed in ink, and would have been accepted as original prior to U.C.P. 500. There was no evidence as to how the documents had actually been produced, so they may have been produced by computerised or automated means. Steel J. took the view that *Glencore* did not apply to documents that would have been regarded as original prior to 1993 (laser-printed documents not having been considered prior to the 1993 revision).

Credit Industriel et Commercial (CIC), a French bank, successfully claimed payment under an irrevocable documentary letter of credit issued by China Merchants Bank (CMB), a Chinese bank. CIC appear to have negotiated, but not confirmed, the credit.

10–038   STEEL J.: [39] I turn now to the principal field of battle between the parties as regards discrepancy, namely the alleged failure to tender an original of the packing list, certificate of quantity and certificate of quality.

[40] The basic rule is that at least one original is required. So far as UCP 500 is concerned, the only relevant article is Art. 20(b):

[Steel J. set out the Article, and an example of the format of the packing list, and continued:]

[42] . . . There was no evidence as to the manner in which the documents had in fact been prepared prior to stamping and signature. As regards appearances:

---

[26] See also Dolan [1999] J.B.L. 521 at p. 525.

a) The documents did not appear to have been produced on a conventional type writer,

b) The documents may have been photocopied or may have been produced by a computer controlled printer.

c) The documents may not have been wholly produced at one time: the body of the document may have been inserted on a document already containing the details of name, address and so on beneath the pecked line.

[43] In short, the documents demonstrate all the difficulties of grappling with the definition and identification of original, as opposed to copy, documents in the modern era with its word processors, laser printers, colour printers, scanner and so on. So ubiquitous has this machinery become that it must be rare indeed that any document is produced by some process other than a form of "reprographic, automated or computerised" system.

[44] It may well be uncontroversial to state that the governing law of the L/C is French law. However, not only is there no evidence of any difference between French Law and English Law, it also hardly needs saying that this field affords a paradigm example of the need for avoidance of any difference in approach to UCP 500 as between different jurisdictions. Accordingly it is immediately necessary to revisit the recent decisions of the Court of Appeal which have grappled with the issue of originality and the requirements of Art. 20.

[45] In *Glencore v Bank of China* [1996] 1 Lloyd's Rep. 135, the relevant letter of credit required the presentation of a "beneficiary's certificate . . . certifying that one full set of non-negotiable documents have been sent to the buyer". The documents were rejected *inter alia* on the ground that the beneficiary's certificates "were neither original documents nor marked as original." Strikingly, there was before the Court detailed evidence from the Claimant as to how the documents were in fact produced. A word processor would produce "the original" version which would then be photocopied many times. The eye could not distinguish between the original printed version and the photocopies. The document presented was probably a signed photocopy.

[46] Sir Thomas Bingham, giving judgment to the Court, expressed his conclusion as follows:

"Art. 20(b) is, as it seems to us, designed to circumvent this argument by providing a clear rule to apply in the case of documents produced by reprographic, automated or computerised systems. The sub-article requires documents produced in a certain way (whether 'original' or not) to be treated in a certain way. It is understandable that those framing these rules should have wished to relieve issuing bankers of the need to make difficult and fallible judgments on the technical means by which documents were produced. The beneficiary's certificates in this case may, in one sense, have been originals; but it is plain on the evidence that they were produced by one or the other of the listed means and so were subject to the rule.

Even if it is true that the certificates did not appear to have been produced by one or other of these means (which must, we think, be very doubtful) that makes no difference if in fact they were: the sub-article is clear in its reference to 'documents(s) produced or appearing to have been produced . . . '

The original signature was of course a means of authenticating the certificates, and they were not required to be signed. But a signature on a copy does not make an original, it makes an authenticated copy; and Art. 20(b) does not treat a signature as a substitute for a marking as 'original', merely as an additional requirement in some cases."

10–039 [47] Some three and a half years later, the issue of originality re-surfaced in the Court of Appeal in *Kredietbank Antwerp v Midland Bank Plc* [1999] 1 Lloyd's Rep. Bank. 219. Here the document concerned was an insurance policy. Once again, there was direct evidence as to how the relevant document had been produced, namely by feeding headed notepaper into a laser printer, the document thereafter being signed. The Defendant submitted that Art. 20(b) as interpreted in *Glencore* required the document to be marked as original in order to conform. Evans L.J. concluded:

"38. In my view, the purpose of the rule introduced as Art. 22(c) in 1984 and amplified in 1993 is clear. Previously, banks were entitled to reject documents which were not originals. The practice was established and it is recognised inferentially by the UCP. Henceforth they would accept certain documents which would previously have been rejected as non-originals, provided that specified safeguards were observed. This applied expressly to photocopies ('reprographic systems') and to carbon copies. These two are by their nature copies of some other document which is their original, although this does not prevent them from being the original contract or document required by the credit, for the reasons suggested above.

39. The question is whether the accompanying reference to documents produced 'by (in UCP 400 'by, or as the result of',) automated or computerised systems' applies to all documents of that kind, even when they are not copies of any other documents and they could not have been rejected as non-original under the existing rules. If that is the effect of these words in Art. 20(b)(i), then the rule permits the bank to refuse original documents which otherwise they are bound to accept; a strange and paradoxical result of the object was to widen the category of documents which could be tendered. If on the other hand 'produced by automated or computerised systems' refers only to documents produced by such means which are copies of other documents that can be

regarded as their originals, then this reference is consistent with 'reprographic systems' and carbon copies and with the objects of the rule.

40. It is consistent also with the introduction of the word 'also' in 1993; 'banks will also accept'. This shows that the intention was to widen the category of acceptable documents, by including some non-original (copy) documents, and there is no qualification, certainly no express qualification, of the existing duty to accept documents which clearly are the originals required by the credit.

41. In my judgment, as a matter of construction, there is nothing in Art. 20(b) which entitles the bank to reject an original document which previously was a valid tender under the credit. A document which clearly is the original, in the sense that it contains the relevant contract, and which is not itself a copy of some other document, is certainly an original for the purposes of the underlying rule."

[48] So far as to the implications of *Glencore* were concerned, Evans L.J. **10–040** continued:

"51. If, contrary to my understanding of the court's judgment in *Glencore*, the passage quoted above does not mean or imply that a document produced by word-processor and laser printer, and which is clearly the original document required by the credit, may be rejected unless 'marked as original' and where necessary signed, then it was *obiter* because in *Glencore* the document itself was a photocopy, and therefore a copy of some other document, and in my respectful view, Art. 20(b) does not entitle the bank to reject an original document (not being itself a copy document) which otherwise it is bound to accept."

[49] There is no dispute that these two decisions, both of which are binding on me sent sequential ripples of unease through the banking community. Views were divided between those concerned that *Glencore*, in the interests of certainty, required an unduly inflexible routine against the background of modern printing techniques and those concerned that *Kredietbank*, in the interests of flexibility, established an unworkable distinction between documents produced by electronic means which were obviously original and those which were not.

[50] Before turning to the reactions of the I.C.C., it is desirable to seek to apply the principles to be derived from these two cases to the present case. Notably, as already observed, there was evidence before the court in both those cases as to how the relevant documents had been produced. In the present case, there is no such evidence. Indeed it might be arguable that such evidence is inadmissible since the standards of care imposed on the bank is to exercise reasonable care to ascertain compliance "on the face" of the document. It would be a rare case where a checker will have knowledge as to how a document was prepared or any source for extracting information in that regard. Somewhat surprisingly, the relevance of

evidence as to how the document was in fact created was not an issue in either decision.

[51] The explanation may well be that Art. 20(b) refers to documents "produced or appearing to have been produced". This appears to be a genuine alternative. Thus, as appears in the decision in *Glencore*, even if it reasonably appeared to a bank that a document had not been produced by a computerised system, this would make no difference if in fact it had been. However, in the present case, it is only appearances that are material. It was Mr. Liu's evidence that the documents were rejected because they were or appeared to be "copies of the originals" but not carrying the word "original". Quite what he meant by the words "copies" in the context of this case was not investigated.

[52] The fact remains that the decision in *Glencore* is rendered the more complicated by the fact that the document involved was found in fact to have been a photocopy. The photocopy was "indistinguishable from the originals" which was produced by a laser printer. Does it follow that the decision would have been the same if it had been "an original" that had been countersigned? There is one indication that it would not necessarily have given rise to the same end result (cf. "but a signature on a copy does not make an original; it makes an authenticated copy"). However this was all in the context of a finding that "the sub-article requires documents produced in a certain way (whether original or not) to be treated in the same way". Yet it was this passage which, if taken literally, was regarded as *obiter* in *Kredietbank*.

10–041   [53] The uncomfortable but logical conclusion was that the effect of *Glencore* was that a document which appears to have been or was in fact produced by a typewriter but not stamped "original" must be accepted but such a document which appears to have been or was in fact produced by a computer must be rejected. The implications are all the greater given the almost total demise of the typewriter and the use of computers for all forms of printing. (As for carbon paper, this may possibly only now be found in a museum.)

[54] It was these concerns, or some of them, which informed the decision in *Kredietbank* to the effect that a document, despite being produced in one of the specified modes and not being stamped as an original, would nonetheless be acceptable as an original if it clearly was an original and/or would have been accepted as such prior to U.C.P. 500. (In fact Art. 20(b) of U.C.P. 400 was in material respects the same, save that the word "also" was omitted.) This was on the basis that the only commercially sensible construction of the Article is that the reference to "automatic or computerised systems" encompasses only those documents produced by such means which are in turn apparently (or in fact) copies of other documents which can be regarded as their originals.

[55] CMB [issuing bank] submitted that there was no distinction between the documents in the present case and the beneficiary's certificate held to be discrepant in *Glencore*. They appeared to be produced by automated or computerised systems (albeit it was not said that they

appeared to be produced reprographically). Despite being original in one sense, they nonetheless needed to be marked as such (albeit that, ironically, CMB did not reject the most closely analogous document to that considered in *Glencore* namely the "shipper's certificate").

[56] CIC contended, as an alternative to their primary case on the I.C.C.'s 1999 policy statement (for which see below), that the matter was determinable in their favour by virtue of *Kredietbank* in that the document were not produced by a reprographic system nor were they in any other sense a copy. The originals, as thus defined, had been authenticated as such by stamp and signature so that they would have been accepted as original before U.C.P. 500.

[57] The position is scarcely clear cut. But it seems to me that, loyally trying to follow both these decisions, I am driven to the conclusion that the ratio in *Glencore* was directed to the treatment of documents appearing or known to be copies or, in some analogous respect, of a class not prior thereto treated as originals. It was common ground between the experts that the certificates in the present case would have been accepted as originals prior to the introduction of U.C.P. 400/500. It follows that I accept the submission of CIC that the certificates were not discrepant in the light of the two decisions.

[58] I now turn to the steps taken by the I.C.C. in the wake of *Glencore* **10–042** to embark on a world-wide consultation process on the issue of the original documents. The initiating document to this consultation was paper prepared in October 1998 for distribution to all 160 national committees:

"Original documents—
What are they?
What is meant by 'Reprographic' documents?
Since the judgment in the Glencore/Bayerische Vereinsbank versus Bank of China court case, the issue of which is an original document; when does a document need to be marked as 'original' and what form of document represents a 'reprographic' document (in the context of UCP 500) have been uppermost in the thoughts of documentary credit specialists world-wide.

Whilst ICC have tried to respond to the issues when raised, we have also received a number of queries from various parts of the world which have been asked to refrain from offering an official opinion on, due to pending litigation in other court cases. The number of questions in relation to this 'original' issue are not diminishing and the Officers of the Banking Commission believe that this is an important topic which requires discussion and the development of a consensus. The outcome will, hopefully, provide a clear position of ICC. Such a viewpoint will be based on future transactions and will not necessarily be capable of being used retrospectively.

To compile a question and provide a suggested response (opinion) would not necessarily achieve the result that we wish. The Officers request that attendees at the October Banking Commission meeting consider the following issues and be prepared to voice their views and/or opinions in an open forum—following which an opinion will be produced which will represent the views of the meeting. In the discussion that will ensue, it must be remembered that we are unable to amend UCP 500—therefore the wording in sub-art. 20(b) must remain as it is but we can provide an opinion that would reflect 'international standard banking practice' in its interpretation."

[59] This paper was discussed at a meeting of the ICC Commission on Banking Technique & Practice in Florida that same month. (Notably amongst the delegates was Mr Jungzhi Shi, the Assistant president of the International Department of CMB.) Further discussion took place in a meeting at the ICC's Department of Policy and Business Practice in Paris in April 1999, during the course of which the *Kredietbank* decision was handed down. The paper under discussion included the following passage:

"ORIGINAL DOCUMENTS—THE WAY FORWARD
Following the *Glencore* decision, some banks in a few locations may have changed their practices from those that were administered previously. Other banks have ignored *Glencore* as incorrect in its interpretation of the UCP or inapplicable in their countries. Many have worried that they may be caught in the middle of a dispute over the scope and meaning of sub-art. 20(b). At the Banking Commission meeting held in Florida during October 1998 it was decided that a draft paper would be submitted for discussion at the 28–29 April 1999 meeting.

In order that the full effect may be given to the final decision of the Banking Commission, it is proposed that the published document be issued as a "Decision of the Banking Commission, that reflects the international standard banking practice as intended by the drafters of ICP 500."

10–043 [60] The final outcome was the policy statement or decision issued on 12 July 1999:

"This Decision emphasises the need to correctly interpret and apply sub-art. 20(b) of UCP 500. Consequently, ICC national committees and associated organisations are strongly urged to distribute this decision as widely as possible to help ensure the correct interpretation in the evaluation of documents issued under letters of credit. This decision does not amend sub-art. 20(b) of UCP 500 in any way, but merely indicates the correct interpretation thereof which has been adopted unanimously by the ICC Commission on Banking Technique and Practice on 12 July 1999.

Correct interpretation of sub-art. 20(b) . . .

General approach

Banks examine documents presented under a letter of credit to determine, among other things, whether on their face they appear to be original. Banks treat as original any document bearing an apparently original signature, mark, stamp, or label of the issuer of the document, unless the document itself indicates that it is not original. Accordingly, unless a document indicates otherwise, it is treated as original if it:

1. appears to be written, typed, perforated, or stamped by the document issuer's hand; or
2. appears to be on the document issuer's original stationery; or
3. states that it is original, unless the statement appears not to apply to the document presented (e.g. because it appears to be a photocopy of another document and the statement of originality appears to apply to that other document)

Hand signed documents

Consistent with sub-paragraph (A) above, banks treat as original any document that appears to be hand signed by the issuer of the document. For example, a hand signed draft or commercial invoice is treated as an original document, whether or not some or all other constituents of the document are preprinted, carbon copied or produced by reprographic, automated or computerised systems . . .

4. What is not an 'Original'?

A document indicates that it is not an original if it:

1. appears to be produced on a telefax machine:
2. appears to be a photocopy of another document which has not otherwise been completed by hand marking the photocopy or by photocopying it on what appears to be original stationery; or
3. states in the document that it is a true copy of another document or that another document is the sole original.
5. Conclusion

Based upon the comments received from ICC national committees, members of the ICC Banking Commission and other interested parties, the statements in cls. 3 and 4 above reflect international standard banking practice in the correct interpretation of UCP 500 sub-art. 20(b)."

[61] It is of course common ground that, if it is appropriate to apply this decision to the documents that are at issue in the present case, they were

not discrepant on the ground of lack of originality. But it was the Defendant's submission that, despite the express recognition of the limitations or the consultation exercise, the decision did in fact purport to amend Art. 20 or, in any event, the decision did not reflect existing standard banking practice, but merely sought to establish it for the future.

10–044   [62] I am unable to accept the Defendant's submission:

a) U.C.P. is a code produced and published by the I.C.C.

b) It is entirely legitimate for the I.C.C. to seek to resolve any ambiguities in, or difficulties of interpretation of, the code.

c) The decision in 1999 involved discussion with local banking commissions throughout the world (to which all banks, including CIC and CMB were able to contribute).

d) When applied to the facts of the present case, the outcome of the consultation is not inconsistent with the decision on *Glencore* or *Kredietbank*, at least if my earlier analysis is correct.

e) The decision expressly states that it reflects international standard banking practice: at the least, no bank in following the decision could be said to be acting without reasonable care.

f) The consultation exercise began in earnest some 9 months prior to the presentation of the documents in the present case and the decision was promulgated some 2 months prior.

[63] This conclusion is consistent with the commercially beneficial aim of reinforcing standard banking practice in regard to the "appearance" of documents and consequent reduction in the risk of inconsistent decisions, all in a field crying out for international consistency. Further, the conclusion I have reached receives some degree of support from the decision of United States District Court for 5 Circuit in *Voest-Alpine Trading USA Corps v Bank of China* 167 F. Supp. 2nd 940 (FD text 2000) where the I.C.C. policy statement was accepted as determinative:

> "Third, the Bank of China claimed that the failure to stamp the packing list documents as an 'original' was a discrepancy. Again, these documents are clearly originals on their face as they have three slightly differing signatures in blue ink there was no requirement in the letter of credit or the UCP 500 that original documents be marked as such. The I.C.C.'s policy statement on the issue provides that, "banks treat as original any document that appears to be hand signed by the issuer of the document. . . . the failure to mark obvious originals is not a discrepancy."

[64] Whether or not there was any argument on the issue, it follows that the judge must have treated the decision as reflecting international standard banking practice.

Note

The decision avoids the central problems, such as how to treat laser printed **10–045** originals, described above. It may be that for new types of documents, that are difficult to distinguish (*e.g.* typed originals, laser-printed originals and high-quality photocopies), the only workable solution is a requirement clearly to mark original documents as such.

PART D

CARRIAGE

Chapter 11

SUBSTANCE OF CARRIAGE CONTRACTS

THIS is primarily a book on international sale contracts. No more than being a   **11–001**
specialist book on documentary credits is it a specialist book on the law of
carriage of goods by sea. Nevertheless, just as it is not possible fully to understand
international sale contracts without some knowledge of their finance, it is also
necessary to grasp the general principles of carriage contracts. Chapters 12 to 14,
below, examine who are the contracting parties, and how the terms relate to the
terms of, and statements in the bill of lading.

However, carriage of goods by sea is one area of human activity which is
controlled by international convention, adopted as part of UK law by legislation.
For the most part the legislation operates against the interests of carriers. However, the control is not all one way, and represents a compromise between
carrying and cargo-owning interests. The nature of the compromise is the subject
of this chapter. If the legislation is to work, it should be difficult for carriers to
avoid it. It should also be difficult for cargo-owners to take the benefits of the
compromise, while avoiding the burdens.

(1) General Principles of the Common Law

The detailed law of carriage by sea is beyond the scope of this book. Never-   **11–002**
theless, it is important to appreciate that:

1. The bargaining strength of a shipowner is generally greater than that of a
   cargo-owner.[1] Certainly this was true historically, and shipowners could
   use their bargaining power effectively to determine the terms of carriage
   contracts.

2. The common law principle of freedom of contract allowed shipowners to
   reduce the value of bills of lading as negotiable documents.

3. The intervention of the UK legislature, bringing into effect an international
   convention (originally *Hague Rules*, later *Hague-Visby Rules*), was a reaction
   to this problem.

4. Though the international conventions operate primarily for the benefit of
   cargo-owners, they are in the nature of a compromise, and also protect
   shipowners. In particular, they replace a strict liability regime with one
   dependent on lack of due diligence, and provide for time bars, limits to
   liability and excepted perils.

5. The legislation works by incorporation into carriage contracts. It has no
   independent force.

---

[1] Not necessarily however, for example, where the shipowner is an independent tanker
owner and the cargo-owner a large oil company.

Because of point 5, above, the whereabouts of contractual relationships between the parties is a matter of considerable importance; see further chapters 12 and 13, below. In particular, cargo-owners sometimes argue the absence of a contractual relationship, specifically to avoid a provision that protects shipowners, as for example in *Pyrene v Scindia Navigation* in paras 3–004, above and 11–065, below).

At common law, the carrier's liability is, in principle, strict, but freedom of contract allows reduction or even negation of liability, subject to principles of *contra preferentem*. Both these principles have been eroded by legislation. A strict liability regime can operate harshly with modern, more complex ships, where damage to cargoes could often be caused by third parties, including for example, fitters, repairers, shipbuilders, etc. However, the legislation provides a floor of rights for cargo-owners, and minimum obligations, out of which the carrier cannot contract.

(a) From Bailment to Contract

11–003 It is probable that sea carriers were originally regarded as common carriers for reward,[2] to whom a particularly stringent regime applied.[3] They were certainly regarded as bailees for reward, whose duties arose independently of contract.[4] Even today, where the original bailment duties are extensively modified by contract, they can still govern in the absence of privity of contract between the owner of the goods and the bailee,[5] or where the contract has been repudiated, as for example (arguably) where a shipowner wrongfully deviates on the voyage.[6]

The basis of any bailment is a voluntary taking of possession of goods owned by another, from which the law also assumes a voluntary undertaking of duties towards the owner. In the case of gratuitous bailment, these duties are not particularly onerous, the bailee being required only to keep the property as his own. Bailees for reward are subject to the more stringent duty, to take reasonable care to keep them safe[7]:

"If the goods are lost or damaged, whilst they are in [the bailee's] possession, he is liable unless he can show—and the burden is on him to show—that the loss or damage occurred without any neglect or default or misconduct of himself or of any of the servants to whom he delegated his duty."

This is strict liability, unless the bailee can prove lack of neglect, default or misconduct. In the case of a common carrier, this meant strict liability unless the

---

[2] Although the authorities are not unequivocal: see, *e.g.* the material collected by Dockray, *Cases and Materials on the Carriage of Goods by Sea* (2nd ed., Cavendish, 1998), at pp. 22 *et seq.*

[3] Probably for reasons of public policy.

[4] *Morris v Martin*, [1966] 1 Q.B. 716, *per* Diplock L.J. at 732, and also part of the *ratio*. Indeed, the concept of bailment, being derived from Roman law, is much older than modern contractual concepts.

[5] *e.g.* in *Compania Portorafti Commerciale SA v Ultramar Panama Inc (The Captain Gregos)* [1990] 1 Lloyd's Rep. 310 (see below), where a shipowner who misdelivered cargo was held in principle liable to the owner in conversion, even if there was no contractual nexus between plaintiff and defendant.

[6] *e.g. Joseph Thorley Ltd v Orchis S.S. Co Ltd* [1907] 1 K.B. 660, *per* Fletcher Moulton L.J. at 667, who thought that the shipowner might in these circumstances be entitled to freight as a common carrier. It is not clear how far these observations survive the views expressed in the House of Lords, however, in *Hain S.S. Co Ltd v Tate & Lyle Ltd* [1936] 2 All E.R. 597. For a full review, see, *e.g.* Brian Coote's essay, "Deviation and the Ordinary Law", in *Lex Mercatoria*, (Francis Rose ed., L.L.P., 2000), Ch. 2.

[7] *Morris v C.W. Martin & Sons, per* Lord Denning M.R. at 726.

loss were caused by an excepted peril, such as an Act of God, or of the King's (or Queen's) enemies, or an inherent vice of the goods themselves.

Since at the latest the nineteenth century, this strict bailment-based regime has been routinely modified by the parties, by contract, shipowners using their extensive bargaining strength to reduce their liability, and increase the range of excepted perils (to cover, *e.g.* perils of the sea, and negligence in navigation or management). The common law freedom of contract principles allowed them to do this, but bailment remained (and remains) the starting point. Therefore, in interpreting the contractual provisions, the courts took account of the earlier regime. In so doing, the courts developed the idea of fundamental obligations, out of which the carrier could contract only by the clearest words, and breach of which might prevent the application of contractual excepted perils. In *Paterson Steamships Ltd v Canadian Co-Operative Wheat Producers Ltd*,[8] for example, Lord Wright observed[9]:

11–004

> "At common law, [the sea carrier] was called an insurer, that is he was absolutely responsible for delivering in like order and condition at the destination the goods bailed to him for carriage. He could avoid liability for loss or damage only by showing that the loss was due to the act of God or the King's enemies. But it became the practice for the carrier to stipulate that for loss due to various specified contingencies or perils he should not be liable: the list of these specific excepted perils grew as time went on. That practice, however, brought into view two separate aspects of the sea carrier's duty which it had not been material to consider when his obligation to deliver was treated as absolute. It was recognized that his overriding obligations might be analysed into a special duty to exercise due care and skill in relation to the carriage of the goods and a special duty to furnish a ship that was fit for the adventure at its inception. These have been described as fundamental undertakings, or implied obligations. If then goods were lost (say) by perils of the seas, there could still remain the inquiry whether or not the loss was also due to negligence or unseaworthiness. If it was, the bare exception did not avail the carrier."

This was elaborated on in *Smith, Hogg v Black Sea and Baltic General Insurance*[10]:

> "In carriage of goods by sea, the shipowner will in the absence of valid and sufficient exceptions be liable for a loss occasioned by negligence. Apart from express exceptions, the carrier's contract is to deliver the goods safely. But when the practice of having express exceptions limiting that obligation became common, it was laid down that there were fundamental obligations, which were not affected by the specific exceptions, unless that was made clear by express words. Thus an exception of perils of the sea does not qualify the duty to furnish a seaworthy ship or to carry the goods without negligence . . . [11] From the nature of the contract, the relevant cause of the loss is held to be the unseaworthiness or the negligence as the case may be, not the peril of the sea, where both the breach of the fundamental obligation and the objective peril are co-operating causes. The contractual exception of perils of the seas does not affect the fundamental obligation, unless the contract qualifies the latter in express terms."

In sea carriage, therefore, contractual interpretation is still heavily influenced by the bailment duties that existed prior to the development of modern forms of

---

[8] [1934] A.C. 538, PC.
[9] At 544–545.
[10] [1940] A.C. 997 at 1004.
[11] Reference is made to the *Paterson Steamships*.

contract. In particular, the courts require the clearest words to exclude liability for failure to provide a vessel which is seaworthy at the start of the voyage, or for negligence. Moreover, where the loss is caused, wholly or partly, by unseaworthiness or negligence, it is assumed not to be caused by an excepted peril.

(b) Other Implied Terms

11–005   There are other duties, implied by the common law, which probably have bailment origins. The carrier is *prima facie* liable if the goods are not delivered to their destination in the same condition in which they had been shipped (see further chapter 14, below). There is an implied obligation that he will make reasonable dispatch, and that he will not deviate. The detailed law of deviation is beyond the scope of this book, and in any case its effect and juristic basis are still a matter of doubt. What is certain is that:

1. Deviation is permitted, at common law, only to save life at sea (*e.g.* by avoiding dangerous weather). Deviation to save property is not permitted.

2. Deviation is regarded as (at least) a fundamental breach of contract. Deviation by the carrier (however minor in nature) allows the cargo-owner to repudiate the contract, and if he does so the shipowner can thereafter rely on no exemption clauses at all. This will be so even if the cause of any subsequent loss is not in any way related to the deviation.

3. There is some authority that deviation also prevents a carrier from relying on exemption clauses prior to the deviation; if this proposition is correct, it is difficult to reconcile with *Photo Production v Securicor* in chapter 7, above, and unless deviation cases are to be treated as *sui generis*, the better view must surely be that the proposition is wrong.

4. It is possible for a holder of a bill of lading to waive a deviation, but this does not affect subsequent holders of the bill; see *Hain SS Co v Tate and Lyle Ltd* (1936) 41 Com. Cas. 350, HL.

5. Allowable deviations were extended by Article IV(4) of the Hague Rules (see the discussion of *Stag Line v Foscolo Mango* below at para. 11–027), to allow reasonable deviation, or any deviation in saving or attempting to save life *or property*. Article IV(4) was unaltered by the Visby amendments. The Rules do not affect the consequences of an unwarranted deviation, however. Further, if a deviation is warranted neither by Article IV(4) nor by a clause in the bill of lading contract, then on the above principles the carrier may lose the benefit not only of any exemption clauses in the bill of lading, but also of the excepted perils in the Hague or Hague-Visby Rules themselves.

(c) Contracting Out

11–006   At common law the carrier can, in principle, contract out of any of his contractual duties, including those considered above, and the delivery obligations described in chapter 5, above. So for example, frequently there are clauses in carriage contracts which give carriers wide liberties to deviate. In principle such clauses can be effective to define the agreed route, in other words to prevent what would otherwise be a deviation being a breach of contract at all, let alone a breach going to the root of the contract. However, the normal principles of *contra preferentem* interpretation apply to such clauses, and a deviation outside the main object and intent of the contract (*e.g.* in the opposite direction) will not be protected by except by a very clear clause.

The following case has already been considered in another context in paras 6–030 and 6–034, *et seq.*, above.

GLYNN v MARGETSON & CO

House of Lords. [1893] A.C. 351

The bill of lading, for a cargo of oranges, purported to give the carrier the **11–007** "liberty to proceed to and stay at any port or ports in any rotation in the Mediterranean, Levant, Black Sea or Adriatic, or on the coasts of Africa, Spain, Portugal, France, Great Britain and Ireland, for the purpose of delivering coals, cargo or passengers, or for any other purpose whatsoever." On its face, this allowed deviation to a wide variety of ports, including any in Spain, "for . . . any . . . purpose whatsoever."

The ship left Malaga in Spain on a voyage to Liverpool, but called first at Burriana, a port in East Spain and in the opposite direction from Liverpool (*i.e.* further from Liverpool than Malaga). Because of the delay the shipper's cargo of oranges were delivered in a damaged condition, and the shipper sued the shipowner for breach of contract.

Held:
The shipowner could not rely on the deviation clause. The clause must not be construed in such a way as to defeat the main object and intent of the contract, which was to carry the oranges from Malaga to Liverpool, and the liberty to deviate must therefore be restricted to ports which were in the course of the voyage.

Lord Halsbury: . . . It seems to me that in construing this document, **11–008** which is a contract of carriage between the parties, one must in the first instance look at the whole of the instrument and not at one part of it only. Looking at the whole of the instrument, and seeing what one must regard, for a reason which I will give in a moment, as its main purpose, one must reject words, indeed whole provisions, if they are inconsistent with what one assumes to be the main purpose of the contract. The main purpose of the contract was to take on board at one port and to deliver at another port a perishable cargo. . . .

Now if one applies the principle . . . to the present case, in which the parties have in writing expressed the intention that there should be a delivery of goods (and the particular class of goods is not to be omitted from consideration—they were perishable goods taken from one port to another) it seems to me that to apply these general printed words (which might in a particular case receive complete fulfilment) as regards each of these stipulations, to the particular contract as between carrier and customer would manifestly defeat the very object which both the parties had in view.

My Lords, I also concur with my noble and learned friend on the woolsack that the particular words which give the liberty are to be construed to refer to a liberty to deliver in the course of a voyage which has been agreed upon between the parties.

Note

11–009　　This case should be considered along with the case to which the *Hague* or *Hague-Visby Rules* apply, considered below.

Ultimately this decision is based on the construction of the contract, and is unaffected by later developments in the law, such as those in *Suisse Atlantique Societe d'Armement Maritime SA v NV Rotterdamsche Kolen Centrale* [1967] 1 A.C. 361, or *Photo Productions v Securicor* (in para. 7–015, above). It follows that it should be possible to draft a contract which gives the carrier the liberty claimed here. Note also that the perishable nature of the cargo (oranges) was a relevant factor to the decision.

(d) Duties of the Cargo-owner

11–010　　The cargo-owner also has duties under the carriage contract. The most obvious duty is to pay freight, but other charges, such as demurrage, might also be incurred, if for example there is delay at loading or discharge.[12] The shipper is under an obligation (which will be implied if not expressed) not to ship dangerous goods without informing the carrier of their nature. Full discussion is beyond the scope of this book, but see generally on implied obligations into carriage contracts Wilson, *Carriage of Goods by Sea* (4th ed., Pearson Higher Education, 2001), Part 1. The law relating to dangerous goods was fully reviewed by the House of Lords in *Effort Shipping Ltd v Linden Management SA (The Giannis NK)* [1998] A.C. 605, noted by Francis Rose [1998] L.M.C.L.Q. 480.

Generally, the legislation does not affect cargo-owners' duties, but under the *Hague-Visby Rules*, Article IV(6), a carrier is entitled to land, destroy or render harmless dangerous goods which have been shipped without his knowledge, and the shipper is liable for any expenses thereby incurred. The carrier can always enforce the obligations against the shipper, but whether he can enforce them against (for example) the receiver of cargo depends on whether there is a contract with him, on the principles discussed in chapter 13, below. There might also be a common law lien on the freight, which can be asserted against the receiver prior to his taking delivery of the cargo.[13]

(e) The First Legislation

11–011　　The main features of the common law, then, are, first, that the liability of the carrier (in principle) is strict, and not dependent on negligence. Secondly, however, a contract of carriage can contain wide-ranging exemption clauses, to which the common law gives effect.

Neither of these features is commonly regarded as appropriate to modern carriage, and the legislation moves away from both principles. The American Harter Act 1893 was the first legislation, which replaced the strict liability regime with one based on lack of due diligence, properly to equip, man, provision, and outfit said vessel, and to make said vessel seaworthy, and in the proper loading,

---

[12] See paras 2–030 *et seq.*, and 3–016, above for further discussion of demurrage.

[13] Probably only on common law freight, which is payable on delivery, and only on quantity of cargo delivered. Most carriage contracts today provide for advance freight, or freight payable on intaken quantity, to which the common law lien may well not apply, but its existence continues to influence development of the law; *e.g.* paras 12–011 *et seq.*, and 13–056 *et seq.*, below.

stowage, custody, care, and delivery of the cargo. The carriers were not entitled to contract out of these obligations, but were entitled to the benefit of a list of excepted perils as long as they exercised due diligence to make the said vessel in all respects seaworthy and properly manned, equipped, and supplied.

HARTER ACT 1893 (USA)

... it is enacted: **11–012**

1. That it shall not be lawful for the manager, agent, master, or owner of any vessel transporting merchandise or property from or between ports of the United States and foreign ports to insert in any bill of lading or shipping document any clause, covenant, or agreement, whereby it, he, or they shall be relieved from liability for loss or damage arising from negligence, fault, or failure in proper loading, stowage, custody, care, or proper delivery of any and all lawful merchandise or property committed to its or their charge. Any and all words or clauses of such import inserted in bills of lading or shipping receipts shall be null and void and of no effect.

2. That it shall not be lawful for any vessel transporting merchandise or property from or between ports of the United States of America, and foreign ports, her owner, master, agent, or manager, to insert in any bill of lading or shipping document any covenant or agreement whereby the obligations of the owner or owners of the said vessel to exercise due diligence, properly equip, man, provision, and outfit said vessel, and to make said vessel seaworthy, and capable of performing her intended voyage, or whereby the obligations of the master, officers, agents, or servants to carefully handle and stow her cargo, and to care for and properly deliver same, shall in anywise be lessened, weakened, or avoided.

3. That if the owner of any vessel transporting merchandise or property to or from any port in the United States of America shall exercise due diligence to make the said vessel in all respects seaworthy and properly manned, equipped, and supplied, neither the vessel, her owner or owners, agent, or charterers, shall become or be held responsible for damage or loss resulting from faults or errors in navigation or in the management of said vessel nor shall the vessel, her owner or owners, charterers, agent, or master be held liable for losses arising from dangers of the sea or other navigable waters, acts of God, or public enemies, or the inherent defect, quality, or vice of the thing carried, or from insufficiency of package, or seizure under legal process, or for loss resulting from any act or omission of the shipper or owner of the goods, his agent or representative, or from saving or attempting to save life or property at sea, or from any deviation in rendering such service.

4. That it shall be the duty of the owner or owners, masters, or agent of any vessel transporting merchandise or property from or

between ports of the United States and foreign ports to issue to shippers of any lawful merchandise a bill of lading, or shipping document, stating, among other things, the marks necessary for identification, number of packages, or quantity, stating whether it be carrier's or shipper's weight, and apparent order or condition of such merchandise or property delivered to and received by the owner, master, or agent of the vessel for transportation, and such document shall be prima facie evidence of the receipt of the merchandise therein described.

5. That for a violation of any of the provisions of this Act the agent, owner, or master of the vessel guilty of such violation, and who refuses to issue on demand the bill of lading herein provided for, shall be liable to a fine not exceeding two thousand dollars. The amount of the fine and costs for such violation shall be a lien upon the vessel, whose agent, owner, or master is guilty of such violation, and such vessel may be libeled therefor in any district court of the United States, within whose jurisdiction the vessel may be found. One half of such penalty shall go to the party injured by such violation, and the remainder to the Government of the United States.

Notes

11–013   1. This enactment is now of historical interest only, except that it is incorporated into the 1946 revision of the New York Produce Exchange standard form dry-cargo time charterparty, which remains in widespread use throughout the world.

2. The Harter Act applied only to inward and outward voyages to and from the US. However, other jurisdictions also began to adopt similar legislation, *e.g.* the Australian Sea Carriage of Goods Act 1904 and the Canadian Water Carriage of Goods Act 1910, and by 1921 there was pressure to adopt internationally agreed standards.

3. Though the Harter Act was the model for newer regimes, it proved to be incomplete in a number of respects. For example, the extent of shipowners' freedom to limit liability per package was never clear (*e.g. Hordern v Commonwealth and Dominion Line* [1917] 2 K.B. 420, and the cases discussed therein.)

4. Like the Harter Act, the *Hague* (and later *Hague-Visby*) *Rules*, on which see further below, replaced strict liability with a due diligence requirement, and provided a minimum floor of liability, contracting out of which was not allowed. They also produced a more comprehensive regime, which was internationally agreed.

(2) Legislative Intervention and the *Hague-Visby Rules*

11–014   The *Hague-Visby Rules* (in the UK at least, and the other states that have adopted them) are the successors to the *Hague Rules*, which were adopted in the UK in 1924. The Visby amendments were not particularly revolutionary, and did not alter the principles of the Hague Rules. Moreover, the amendments have not been adopted throughout the world, the majority of jurisdictions remaining with the original regime.

It is, therefore, appropriate to begin with the *Hague Rules*, the justifications for them, and their main principles. As harmonisation attempts go, they were probably one of the more successful. Nevertheless, over time, various defects (actual or apparent, depending on your viewpoint) came to light, and it was the response to these which led eventually to the Visby amendments. The argued defects, and the Visby amendments, are also therefore considered here.

There are some who argue that the *Hague-Visby Rules* are themselves inadequate, and a number of states have now adopted the *Hamburg Rules*, drafted by UNCITRAL in 1978. These are considered (in outline) below. They do not form part of U.K. law. Whatever the merits of the *Hamburg Rules*, proponents of harmonisation may observe that whereas there was one regime, adopted pretty well throughout the world, on the carriage of goods by sea, now there are three.

(a) Reasons for the *Hague Rules*

We have seen that, in principle, the carrier's common law liability was strict, **11–015** and that this was seen as inappropriate in an age of complex vessels, which would often be maintained by third parties, of whose activities the carrier had little or no knowledge, and over whom he had no real control. The regime of the Hague Rules is based on due diligence.

As is also apparent from the last section, the freedom of contract prevalent in the 19th century allowed contracts of carriage to contain wide-ranging exemption clauses, to which the common law gave effect. Carriers could use their bargaining strength to insert widely drawn exemption clauses, excluding much liability for loss of, or damage to goods.

This was seen as undesirable, and the US legislature reacted first with the Harter Act 1893, which is the precursor to the *Hague Rules* (the latter of which are still in force in many countries, including the US), and the *Hague-Visby Rules*, which are in force in a small number of countries, including the UK.

For the legislature compulsorily to rewrite contracts between commercial parties requires justification. Inequality of bargaining power may not, in itself, provide sufficient justification, and the legislature would probably not have intervened to protect the original contracting party, the shipper. It was not the shipper who generally suffered from the terms exacted by carriers, however, but the indorsee, who had no say in those terms. Bills of lading were fast becoming worthless documents, and banks also suffered where they took such documents as security on a commercial credit. Thus, the negotiability of the shipping documents was being seriously eroded.

A different justification is advanced by Lord Goff, in an article which argues generally against the rewriting of commercial contracts, but is prepared to accept a limited degree of intervention here. Shipowners might effectively be exercising a monopoly power, which needs to be controlled. This argument might also justify singling out one industry (shipping) and applying a special regime to it, a practice which is surely undesirable in general, if free-market economics are to be encouraged.

GOFF, COMMERCIAL CONTRACTS AND THE COMMERCIAL COURT

[1984] L.M.C.L.Q. 382, at p. 392

Of course, there can be occasions when monopoly or unilateral action can **11–016** lead to too extreme a use of exceptions—as it did in the case of bill of lading exceptions by shipowners in the first part of [the twentieth] century. This led to the Convention we all know as the Hague Rules: though it is of interest that, under the Convention, there are still substantial exceptions from liability on which shipowners can and do rely when sued by bill of lading holders.

DIAMOND, *THE HAGUE-VISBY RULES*

[1978] L.M.C.L.Q. 225

[Footnotes are as in the original, but renumbered for inclusion in this book.]

11–017 . . . the main conceptual idea underlying The Hague Rules was not of English origin. The fundamental conceptual idea of the Rules had previously been embodied in and was taken over from the United States Harter Act of 1893, a statute which has claims to be regarded as one of the most remarkable statutes ever enacted in the field of shipping law. But the draftsmen of the 1924 Convention, who had mostly been brought up on English shipping law, had employed phraseology well known to English maritime law, even to the extent of borrowing many of the detailed exceptions commonly found in English liner bills of lading and inserting a catalogue of those exceptions into the Rules.[14]

It is also true that England cannot be regarded as having been one of the first countries to initiate statutory control of bill of lading clauses. Until 1921 England, then possessed of the largest merchant fleet in the world and having a correspondingly powerful shipowning lobby, had remained faithful to its strong 19th century tradition that Parliamentary interference with the freedom of commercial men to contract as they pleased was to be avoided at almost all cost. But in 1921 there was a change of policy.[15] It had become recognised that the freedom of contract did not exist in the case of bills of lading whose terms were usually dictated by the shipowners. The only freedom of the shipper was to take the bill of lading or leave it. And in view of the Conference system even the latter freedom was often illusory.

It had also become recognised that, due to the invention of the c.i.f. and c. & f. contracts, it was often not the shipper but the indorsee of the bill of lading who had no control over the terms of the bill, who would be affected by them. Finally, by 1921 there was an undesirable diversity among the countries of the British Empire as to the law in force relating to bills of lading. The self-governing dominions, who did not have a

---

[14] Sir Leslie Scott, who led the British delegation at the Brussels Convention in 1922, defended the list of exceptions on the grounds that: "This enumeration contains nothing but the exception clauses which figure in nearly all bills of lading in the world;" see S. Brackhus, *"The Hague Rules Catalogue"* in *Six Lectures on The Hague Rules* (Grunfors ed., Gottenburg, 1967).

[15] The turning point was the report of the Imperial Shipping Committee in February 1921 recommending the introduction of uniform legislation throughout the British Empire on the lines of the Canadian Act. The British Government undertook to take steps to that end: see Colinvaux [*The Carriage of Goods by Sea Act, 1924* (London, 1954)], p. 7.

shipowning lobby, had been quick to follow the lead given by the United States. Australia in 1904, Canada in 1910 and New Zealand in a series of statutes between 1903 and 1922 passed legislation based on the Harter Act. They also distinguished those countries from the remainder of the Empire where no such legislation was in force.

From about 1921, therefore, it became the objective of the United Kingdom Government to do two things; first, to introduce uniform legislation on the subject of bills of lading throughout the Empire; secondly, to do this in such a way that British shipowners would not be at a disadvantage as compared with those in the rest of the world. . . .

Note
The Conference system, which in essence maintained an oligopoly, is described in *Mogul Steamship Co Ltd v Mcgregor, Gow Co* [1892] A.C. 25. It would have seriously restricted the terms upon which shippers could contract. Here, then, we see the two justifications for limited intervention, the distortion of market freedom by the shipowners, and the reduction in negotiability of the shipping documents.

THE BUNGA SEROJA

High Court of Australia. [1999] 1 Lloyd's Rep. 512

The main point arising from this decision was that heavy weather could be a peril of the sea, even if predictable (and indeed predicted). It was not necessary that the hazard also be unpredictable and unforeseen. For present purposes, we are interested in the analysis of the history of the Hague Rules.   **11–018**

GAUDRON, GUMMOW AND HAYNE JJ.:
[Footnotes as in original, but renumbered for inclusion here.]

History of the Hague Rules
   10. By the early 19th century, shipowners had come to be regarded as common carriers by both English and American law.[16] Accordingly, the carrier was strictly liable for damage to or loss of cargo that was damage or loss occurring in the course of carriage unless the carrier could prove not only that its negligence had not contributed to the damage or loss, but also that one of four excepted causes (act of God, act of public enemies, shipper's fault or inherent vice of the goods) was responsible for the loss.[17]
   11. To avoid this liability (sometimes spoken of as tantamount to that of an insurer)[18] carriers began to include more and wider exculpatory

[16] At least where the ship was a "general ship", that is, a ship put up to carry goods for anyone wishing to ship them on the particular voyage on which the ship is bound; see, *e.g.* *Laveroni v Drury* (1852) 8 Ex. 166 at 170 [155 E.R. 1304 at 1306]; *Liver Alkali Co v Johnson* (1874) L.R. 9 Ex. 338 at 340–341.
[17] Benedict on *Admiralty*, 7th ed. (rev.), vol. 2A @ 11 at 2–1. See also *Laveroni v Drury* (1852) 8 Ex. 166 at 170 [155 E.R. 1304 at 1306]; *Nugent v Smith* (1876) 45 L.J. (C.L.) 697 at 701; *Propeller Niagara v Cordes* 62 U.S. 7 at 22–23 (1859).
[18] *Forward v Pittard* (1785) 1 T.R. 27 at 33 [99 E.R. 953 at 956] per Lord Mansfield.

clauses in their bills of lading. In England, it was held that carriers and shippers could agree to terms by which the carrier assumed virtually no liability, even for its own negligence.[19] In *Australasian United Steam Navigation Co Ltd v Hiskens*, Mr Justice Isaacs said[20]:

> "Common law relations based on reasonableness and fairness were in practice destroyed at the will of the shipowners, and as fast as Courts pointed out loopholes in their conditions, so fast did they fill them up, until at last the position of owners of goods became intolerable."

In the United States, however, the Federal Courts held that contractual clauses which purported to exonerate carriers from the consequences of their own negligence were void as against public policy,[21] and strictly interpreted clauses which attempted to exonerate carriers for the failure to provide a seaworthy ship. This did not help United States cargo interests when much of their trade was carried on British ships pursuant to bills of lading containing choice of forum clauses nominating England as the place in which suit must be brought.

12. These problems led, in the United States, to the Harter Act of 1893 ("the Harter Act").[22] This Act was a compromise between the conflicting interests of carriers and shippers. A carrier could not contract out of its obligation to exercise due diligence to furnish a seaworthy vessel[23] or to relieve it from "liability for loss or damage arising from negligence, fault, or failure in proper loading, stowage, custody, care or proper delivery of any and all lawful merchandise or property committed to its or their charge".[24]

13. New Zealand, Australia and Canada each passed legislation modelled on the Harter Act: the Shipping and Seamen Act (NZ), the Sea-Carriage of Goods Act, 1904 (Cth)[25] and the Water Carriage of Goods Act, 1910 (Can). All of these Acts, although modelled on the Harter Act, made some changes to the model. Thus the 1904 Australian Act was, in some respects, more generous to cargo interests than the Harter Act, 1924.[26]

---

[19] *In re Missouri Steamship Company* (1889) 42 Ch.D. 321.

[20] (1914) 18 C.L.R. 646 at 671.

[21] See, *e.g. Railroad Co v Lockwood* 84 U.S. 357 at 384 (1873); *Phoenix Insurance Co v Erie and Western Transportation Co* 117 U.S. 312 at 322 (1886); *Liverpool and Great Western Steam Co v Phoenix Insurance Co.* 129 U.S. 397 at 441–442 (1889); *Compania de Navigacion la Flecha v Brauer* 168 U.S. 104 at 117 (1897).

[22] 46 U.S.C. App. @@ 190–196.

[23] Harter Act @ 2, 46 U.S.C. App. @ 191.

[24] Harter Act @ 1, 46 U.S.C. App. @ 190.

[25] *Australasian United Steam Navigation Co Ltd v Hiskens* (1914) 18 C.L.R. 646 at 672 per Isaacs J.

[26] For example, under the Harter Act, statutory exemptions from liability were available if the owner exercised due diligence to make the ship seaworthy and properly manned, equipped and supplied (@ 3, 46 U.S.C. App. @ 192). By contrast, under the Sea-Carriage of Goods Act 1904 (Cth), the statutory exemptions were available only if the ship was at the beginning of the voyage seaworthy and properly manned, equipped and supplied (s.8(2)).

14. Pressure grew for uniform rules. In February, 1921, the British **11–019** Imperial Shipping Committee recommended uniform legislation throughout the British Empire based on the Canadian Act.[27] Draft rules were prepared, considered and amended. By 1922 the Comite Maritime International had adopted a draft. The Diplomatic Conference on Maritime Law then took up the matter and in August, 1924 the International Convention for the Unification of Certain Rules of Law Relating to Bills of Lading was concluded and opened for signature.[28] Australia enacted the Sea-Carriage of Goods Act (Cth) as soon as the final diplomatic steps had been taken.[29]

15. The new rules quickly gained international acceptance, although United States legislation was not passed until 1936.[30] By the start of World War II "the overwhelming majority of the world's shipping was committed to the Hague Rules".[31]

16. The Hague Rules represent a compromise about the allocation of risk of damage to cargo (a compromise which was different from what had been represented in domestic statutes). Thus, to take only one example, shipping interests gained the advantage in Australia and the United States of elimination of the rule established in *McGregor v Huddart Parker Ltd*[32] and *The Isis*.[33] In those cases, the High Court of Australia and the Supreme Court of the United States held that a carrier could claim exemption from liability on the bases set out in the 1904 Australian Act and the Harter Act if (and only if) the carrier had complied with its obligation relating to the seaworthiness of the vessel, regardless of whether the cargo's loss or damage was caused by lack of seaworthiness. Under the Hague Rules, however, some causal connection must be shown between the loss and the matter in respect of which due diligence was not demonstrated.[34]

17. The complexity of the history which we have touched on is such that, as Mr Justice Dixon said in *William Holyman & Sons Pty Ltd v Foy & Gibson Pty Ltd*,[35] "(the) case law, English, Australian and American, dealing with other legislation thought to be *in pari materia* cannot be applied to the Hague Rules, except with great care and discrimination".

18. Similarly, it may be that similar care and discrimination must be **11–020** shown in applying decisions about marine insurance to the Hague Rules. Many of the issues which arose under the exempting provisions of bills of lading issued before the Hague Rules find parallels with issues arising

---

[27] Sturley (ed.), *The Legislative History of the Carriage of Goods by Sea Act and the Travaux Preparatoires of the Hague Rules* (1990), vol. 2 at 138.
[28] Benedict on *Admiralty*, 7th ed. (rev.), vol. 2A @ 15 at 2–14.
[29] The Act received the Royal Assent on 17 September 1924; the Convention was concluded and opened for signature on 25 August 1924.
[30] Sturley, *The History of COGSA and the Hague Rules* (1991) 22 J.M.L.C. 1 at 36–55.
[31] Benedict on *Admiralty*, 7th ed. (rev.), vol. 2A @ 15 at 2–17. See also Sturley, *The History of COGSA and the Hague Rules*, (1991) 22 J.M.L.C. 1 at 56.
[32] (1919) 26 C.L.R. 336.
[33] *May v Hamburg-Amerikanische Packetfahrt Aktiengesellschaft* 290 U.S. 333 (1933).
[34] Art. IV(1).
[35] (1945) 73 C.L.R. 622 at 633.

under policies of marine insurance. Whether, however, principles developed in connection with one area should be applied in the other was open to argument for many years and may still be so. In *Arbib & Houlberg v Second Russian Insurance Co*,[36] the Court of Appeals for the Second Circuit identified as follows the distinction drawn in the United States between the two areas:

> "The phrase 'perils of the seas' occurs in bills of lading, where it is used as a ground of the carrier's exemption from liability, and it is also employed in policies of insurance in stating the ground of the insurance company's liability. In the interpretation of the phrase when used in bills of lading, the courts have adopted great strictness, as the carrier is seeking exemption of liability; but in the interpretation of the phrase when used in insurance policies, the courts in many cases have given to it great elasticity of meaning."[37]

Further, given the importance of obligations of utmost good faith in insurance law but the absence of any such obligation in a contract for carriage of goods, the possible difficulty resulting from any unthinking application of the decisions made in one area to problems arising in the other is obvious. In addition, the term "perils of the seas" is given a defined meaning in the "Rules for Construction of Policy" contained in the Second Schedule to the Marine Insurance Act, 1909 (Cth).[38] These are not, however, issues which fall for decision in this case.

(b) General Principles and Effect

11–021   The general principles of the legislative intervention were as follows. In general, liability should be for lack of due diligence only (Article III). The carrier should not be liable for excepted perils (Article IV). There are statutory limitations on damage per unit or package, and time for bringing actions (Article IV). Beyond that, however, the carrier is not permitted to reduce the extent of his liability further (Article III(8)).

Thus cargo-owners benefit because they can bring actions where they could not before. On the other hand, various exemptions and limitations on carrier liability are also written into the Rules. If cargo-owners can get round the Rules, *e.g.* by suing in tort where the defendant cannot show that he is protected by the carriage contract, then that aspect of their operation is subverted. This was one of the justifications for the decision in *The Aliakmon*, discussed in para. 13–073, below; see further also below, where defects in the UK law (in this regard) are uncovered.

The Rules affect only bill of lading contracts, and do not apply to charterparties (Article V). However, the shipowner's obligations to any cargo-owner apart from the charterer himself will be governed by the bill of lading, not the charterparty (see paras 12–004 *et seq.*, below).

---

[36] 294 F. 811 at 816 (2nd Cir. 1923).
[37] See also Couch, *Cyclopedia of Insurance Law*, 2nd ed. (1982), vol. 11 @ 43:93.
[38] R7 states: "The term 'perils of the seas' refers only to fortuitous accidents or casualties of the seas. It does not include the ordinary action of the winds and waves."

(i) *Stages of Claim and Burden of Proof*

It is not uncommon for cargo to arrive damaged, with no clear indication as to **11–022**
how the damage occurred. For example, the ship might be very old, but have
encountered unusually stormy weather on the voyage. If there has been a leak,
and seawater damage incurred, it may not be clear whether the cause is the
vessel's unseaworthiness (for which the carrier would normally be liable), or a
peril of the sea (for which normally he would not). Burden of proof issues can,
therefore, be decisive.

Because of the bailment origins of sea carriage, once the cargo-owner proves
loss it is for the carrier to bring himself within a common law or contractual
excepted peril. He will generally be unable to rely on excepted perils if the loss
has been caused, wholly or in part, by the unseaworthiness of the vessel at the
start of the voyage, or by his negligence. If the cause is unseaworthiness, and the
Hague or *Hague-Visby Rules* apply, the carrier has a defence (under Article III(1))
if he can prove that he has exercised due diligence.

THE HELLENIC DOLPHIN

Queen's Bench Division (Admiralty Court). [1978] 2 Lloyd's Rep. 336

Cargo was damaged by incursion of seawater through the vessel's plating. The **11–023**
carriers claimed peril of the sea, and the cargo-owners that the vessel was
unseaworthy at the start of the voyage. The main importance of the case, for
present purposes, lies in Lloyd J.'s description of the stages in such a claim (note
that the action was on bills of lading, to which the *Hague Rules* applied).

LLOYD J.: The cargo-owner can raise a *prima facie* case against the
shipowner by showing that cargo which had been shipped in good order
and condition was damaged on arrival. The shipowner can meet that
prima facie case by relying on an exception, for example, perils at sea. The
position in that respect is exactly the same whether the Hague Rules are
incorporated or not. The cargo-owner can then seek to displace the
exception by proving that the vessel was unseaworthy at commencement
of the voyage and that the unseaworthiness was the cause of the loss. The
burden in relation to seaworthiness does not shift.

Naturally, the Court can draw inferences: ... But if at the end of the
day, having heard all the evidence and drawn all the proper inferences,
the Court is left on the razor's edge, the cargo-owner fails on unseaworthiness and the shipowners are left with their defence of perils of the sea.
If, on the other hand, the Court comes down in favour of the cargo-
owners on unseaworthiness, the shipowners can still escape by proving
that the relevant unseaworthiness was not due to any want of due
diligence on their part or on the part of their servants or agents.

Notes
The stages then are as follows: **11–024**

1. Cargo-owner proves loss (that is sufficient for a cause of action since the
   contract sets up a bailment—it is then for the shipowner to set up a
   defence).

2. Shipowner proves excepted peril.[39]

3. Cargo-owner proves unseaworthiness.

4. (Only if Hague or Hague-Visby apply) shipowner proves due diligence.

In *The Hellenic Dolphin*, there was no doubt that the vessel was unseaworthy by the time of the loss, and the issue was, at what point did she become unseaworthy. The court being "left on the razor's edge", the cargo-owners failed. Even if that conclusion were incorrect, the shipowners had discharged their burden on the due diligence issue. Note that the due diligence stage is only relevant if the Hague or Hague-Visby Rules apply, since at common law, liability in respect of unseaworthiness is strict.

The burdens at stages 1 and 2 are clear. At stage 1 the plaintiff must prove his loss, and at stage 2 it is the carrier who is trying to invoke an exemption, so clearly the burden of proof should be on him. Stage 4 is simply an interpretation of the Rules, but it is arguable, on basic principles of the law of bailment, that the burden of proof remains on the carrier at stage 3.[40] Obviously, *The Hellenic Dolphin* is inconsistent with this view, but consistent with that taken in *The Glendarroch*.[41] There, the shipowner had established a peril of the sea, the issue being whether there was negligence. Lord Esher M.R. reasoned, in effect, that negligence was an exception within an exception, for which it was appropriate for the burden to shift back to the plaintiff:

"When you come to the exceptions, among others, there is that one, perils of the sea. There are no words which say 'perils of the sea not caused by the negligence of the captain or crew.' You have got to read those words in by a necessary inference. How can you read them in? They can only be read in, in my opinion, as an exception upon the exceptions. You must read in, 'Except the loss is by perils of the sea, unless or except that loss is the result of the negligence of the servants of the owner.'

That being so, I think that according to the ordinary course of practice each party would have to prove the part of the matter which lies upon him. The plaintiffs would have to prove the contract and the non-delivery. If they leave that in doubt, of course they fail. The defendants' answer is, 'Yes; but the case was brought within the exception—within its ordinary meaning.' That lies upon them. Then the plaintiffs have a right to say there are exceptional circumstances, viz., that the damage was brought about by the negligence of the defendants' servants, and it seems to me that it is for the plaintiffs to make out that second exception."

In *The Kriti Rex* also, the burden of proof was assumed to be on the cargo-owner.[42] Probably the weight of authority supports *The Glendarroch* and *The Hellenic Dolphin*. Arguably this is undesirable, as Ezeoke observes,[43] because the shipowner is usually in a better position than the cargo-owner, to ascertain the facts.

There are suggestions in *The Bunga Seroja*, below, that common law bailment principles may not have any application where the issue is on interpretation of the

---

[39] In *The Torenia* [1983] 2 Lloyd's Rep. 210, also in an action on a bill of lading contract, the carrier failed to prove that the loss was caused by a peril of the sea (note that it is not enough for him to show that a peril of the sea was partly responsible, if the loss was also partly caused by unseaworthiness).

[40] The authorities are extensively reviewed by Ezeoke: "Allocating onus of proof in sea cargo claims: the contest of conflicting principles" [2001] L.M.C.L.Q. p. 261.

[41] [1894] P. 226. See Lord Esher M.R. at 231.

[42] [1996] 2 Lloyd's Rep. 171. It was an unusual case, though, in which there had been no bailment, the problem arising on the approach voyage.

[43] At pp. 264 *et seq.*

Rules. It is not clear, however, that bailment principles affect the burden of proof anyway at stage 3. The burden of proof reasoning in *The Glendarroch* did not depend on bailment principles, the exception within an exception being an interpretation of a contractual clause,[44] and *The Hellenic Dolphin* was a case to which the Hague Rules applied. Obviously, at stage 4, we are concerned only to interpret the Rules.

MAXINE FOOTWEAR CO LTD v CANADIAN GOVERNMENT MERCHANT MARINE LTD

Privy Council. [1959] A.C. 589

The ship became unseaworthy because of a fire during loading, and had to be **11–025** scuttled. The fire was caused by the negligence of employees of the carrier in their use of an acetylene torch to thaw out frozen scupper pipes.

Held
The carrier was in breach of Article III(1) (duty to make the ship seaworthy), which covered the loading process, and could not rely on the fire immunity contained in Article IV(2)(b).

Lord Somervell of Harrow: (at 602–603) Article III(1) is an overriding obligation. If it is not fulfilled and the non-fulfilment causes the damage the immunities of Art. IV cannot be relied on. This is the natural construction apart from the opening words of Art. III(2). The fact that that rule is made subject to the provisions of Art. IV and that r. 1 is not so conditioned makes the point clear beyond argument.

Notes
The same conclusion was reached in respect of Art. IV(6) (dangerous cargo) in *Northern Shipping Co v Deutsche Seereederei GmbH (The Kapitan Sakharov)*.[45]

Thus, it follows that if the shipowner, going through the four stages in *The Hellenic Dolphin*, does not satisfy the requirements of Art. III(1) (provision of seaworthy vessel), he cannot rely on the excepted perils in Art. IV(2). If he has exercised due diligence to make the ship seaworthy at the start of the voyage, he is not in breach of Art. III(1), but can still be in breach of Art. III(2), if he fails properly and carefully to carry and care for, etc., the cargo. However, unlike Art. III(1), Art. III(2) is expressly made subject to the excepted perils in Art. IV.

In *The Happy Ranger*,[46] the Court of Appeal held that Art. IV(5) (package limitation) applied even if the shipowner was in breach of Art. III(1).

(ii) *Interpretation of the Rules*

The *Hague* and *Hague-Visby Rules* are part of the domestic law of the states **11–026** which have adopted them, but are based upon international convention. The

---

[44] The *existence* of the exception within the exception does depend on bailment principles, but the burden of proof reasoning does not.
[45] [2000] 2 Lloyd's Rep. 255 at 269–270.
[46] [2002] E.W.C.A. Civ. 694.

issue, then, is to what extent pre-1924 domestic law remains relevant in interpreting the Rules.

STAG LINE LTD v FOSCOLO MANGO & CO

House of Lords. [1932] A.C. 328

11–027   The *Ixia* was bound for Constantinople in Turkey from Swansea in South Wales,
and by a clause in the bill of lading the shipowners had "liberty . . . to call at any
ports in any order, for bunkering or other purposes, . . . all as part of the contract
voyage". When the ship set sail she had on board engineers who were testing a
superheater. It was intended to land them at Lundy Island (which was on the
normal route) but the tests were not completed by then, so they were landed
instead at St. Ives (which was off the normal route). After leaving St. Ives, on the
way back to the usual route the ship and cargo were lost.

The cargo-owners sued the shipowner for damages.

Held

1. The deviation was not permitted by the clause in the bill of lading: "other
   purposes" should be construed only to allow a liberty to call at a port which
   had some purpose relating to the contract voyage. This interpretation is in
   line with *Glynn v Margetson*, see para. 11–007, above.

2. The deviation was not reasonable within Article IV(4) of the Hague Rules
   (which was unchanged by the 1971 Act).

3. It therefore followed that the carrier could not take the benefit of the perils
   of the sea exemption under the Hague Rules Article IV(2)(c)—also
   unchanged by the 1971 Act. Therefore, the cargo-owners were entitled to
   succeed.

11–028   LORD ATKIN: My Lords, this case assumes importance because it
involves a question of construction of the Carriage of Goods by Sea Act,
1924, and has evoked a construction of that Act from at least one judge of
great authority on such matters which I venture to think is based on a
wrong method of approach to that Act. The *Ixia*, a ship of 1828 tons net
register, sailed from Swansea to Constantinople with a full and complete
cargo of coal under a charterparty in the terms of the Chamber of
Shipping Welsh Coal Charter, 1896, as amended on various dates, the last
of which was December 21, 1924. A bill of lading was taken by the
charterers making the cargo deliverable to named consignees, Messrs.
Foscolo, Mango & Co, Ltd, "with liberty to call at any ports in any order
for bunkering or other purposes . . . . all as part of the contract voyage; all
the terms conditions and exceptions contained in the charterparty are
herewith incorporated." The liberties given in the bill of lading are the
same liberties as those given in the charterparty, and it appears to me
with respect that whether the plaintiff be the charterer or the consignee
the document to be construed is the charterparty. [See further paras
12–004 *et seq.*, below, on the incorporation of charterparty terms into bills
of lading.]

I do not propose to set out the facts, but to discuss the points of law
raised. The position in law seems to be that the plaintiffs are prima facie

entitled to say that the goods were not carried safely: the defendants are then prima facie entitled to rely on the exception of loss by perils of the sea: and the plaintiffs are prima facie entitled in reply to rely upon a deviation. For unless authorized by the charterparty or the Act the departure to St. Ives from the direct course to Constantinople was admittedly a deviation. I pause here to say that I find no substance in the contention faintly made by the defendants that an unauthorized deviation would not displace the statutory exceptions contained in the Carriage of Goods by Sea Act. I am satisfied that the general principles of English law are still applicable to the carriage of goods by sea except as modified by the Act: and I can find nothing in the Act which makes its statutory exceptions apply to a voyage which is not the voyage the subject of "the contract of carriage of goods by sea" to which the Act applies. It remains therefore for the shipowners to show that the suggested deviation was authorized by the contract including the terms incorporated by the Act. They first rely upon the express liberty given by the charterparty "to call at any ports in any order for bunkering or other purposes . . . . all as part of the contract voyage." What exactly the Chamber of Shipping and the Documentary Council of the Baltic and White Sea Conference (who we are told in the document adopted this form of charterparty) meant by these words I wish they could be asked. We have to struggle to find a meaning. They cannot be unlimited in scope, or they would authorize the shipowner to direct the ship to any part of the globe for any purpose he thought fit. Even if limited to port or ports on the geographical course of the voyage, as I think they clearly must be the purpose of the call must receive some limitation. The liberty could not reasonably be intended to give the right to call or take on board friends of the shipowner for the purposes of a pleasure trip. On the other hand I find it very difficult to adopt the view difficult to adopt the view which has found favour with one of your Lordships that they involve some limitation which is kindred to or associated with bunkering. Even if the purpose be extended beyond taking in motor fuel or supplies necessary for the navigation of the ship to supplies for the maintenance or comfort of passengers I find it difficult to put such a restricted meaning on the words in view of the collocation "any ports in any order" which seems to point to some purposes other than the restricted ones suggested. Logically I find a difficulty in excluding a suggested purpose from a class until I have found some more or less definite conception of the nature of the class. I think myself that the purposes intended are business purposes which would be contemplated by the parties as arising out of the contemplated voyage of the ship. This might include in a contract other than a contract to carry a full and complete cargo a right to call at port or ports on the geographical course to load and discharge cargo for other shippers. It would probably include a right to call for orders. But I cannot think that it would include a right such as was sought to be exercised in the present case to land servants of the shipowners or others who were on board at the start to adjust machinery, and were landed for their own and their owners' convenience because they could not be transferred to any ingoing vessel. I think, therefore, the shipowner is not excused by this clause.

11–029   There remains the provision of Art. IV., r. 4, of the Schedule to the Carriage of Goods by Sea Act, which with the other Rules in the Schedule is incorporated expressly in the bill of lading pursuant to s.3 of the Act. "Any deviation in saving or attempting to save life or property at sea, or any reasonable deviation shall not be deemed to be an infringement or breach of these Rules or of the contract of carriage, and the carrier shall not be liable for any loss or damage resulting therefrom." In approaching the construction of these rules it appears to me important to bear in mind that one has to give the words as used their plain meaning, and not to colour one's interpretation by considering whether a meaning otherwise plain should be avoided if it alters the previous law. If the Act merely purported to codify the law, this caution would be well founded. I will repeat the well known words of Lord Herschell in the *Bank of England v Vagliano Brothers* [1891] A. C. 107, 144. Dealing with the Bills of Exchange Act as a code he says: "I think the proper course is in the first instance to examine the language of the statute and to ask what is its natural meaning, uninfluenced by any considerations derived from the previous state of the law, and not to start with inquiring how the law previously stood, and then, assuming that it was probably intended to leave it unaltered, to see if the words of the enactment will bear an interpretation in conformity with this view. . . . . The purpose of such a statute surely was that on any point specifically dealt with by it, the law should be ascertained by interpreting the language used instead of, as before, by roaming over a vast number of authorities in order to discover what the law was." He then proceeds to say that of course it would be legitimate to refer to the previous law where the provision of the code was of doubtful import, or where words had previously acquired a technical meaning or been used in a sense other than their ordinary one. But if this is the canon of construction in regard to a codifying Act, still more does it apply to an Act like the present which is not intended to codify the English law, but is the result (as expressed in the Act) of an international conference intended to unify certain rules relating to bills of lading. It will be remembered that the Act only applies to contracts of carriage of goods outwards from ports of the United Kingdom: and the rules will often have to be interpreted in the courts of the foreign consignees. For the purpose of uniformity it is, therefore, important that the Courts should apply themselves to the consideration only of the words used without any predilection for the former law, always preserving the right to say that words used in the English language which have already in the particular context received judicial interpretation may be presumed to be used in the sense already judicially imputed to them.

Having regard to the method of construction suggested above, I cannot think that it is correct to conclude, as Scrutton L.J. does, that r. 4 was not intended to extend the permissible limits of deviation as stated in *The Teutonia* L.R. 4 P.C. 171, 179. This would have the effect of confining reasonable deviation to deviation to avoid some imminent peril. Nor do I see any justification for confining reasonable deviation to a deviation in the joint interest of cargo owner and ship, as MacKinnon J. appears to hold, or even to such a deviation as would be contemplated reasonably by both cargo owner and shipowner, as has been suggested by Wright J. in *Foreman and Ellams, Ltd v Federal Steam Navigation Co* [1928] 2 K.B. 424, 431, approved by Slesser L.J. in the present case. A deviation may, and often will, be caused by fortuitous circumstances never contemplated by the original parties to the contract; and may be reasonable, though it is made solely in the interests of the ship or solely in the interests of the cargo, or indeed in the direct interest of neither: as for instance where the presence of a passenger or of a member of the ship or crew was urgently required after the voyage had begun on a matter of national importance; or where some person on board was a fugitive from justice, and there were urgent reasons for his immediate appearance. The true test seems to be what departure from the contract voyage might a prudent person controlling the voyage at the time make and maintain, having in mind all the relevant circumstances existing at the time, including the terms of the contract and the interests of all parties concerned, but without obligation to consider the interests of any one as conclusive. I think this view conforms to that of Greer L.J., the only criticism of whose test I would make is that it appears unnecessary to introduce the reasonable cargo owner into the discussion. The decision has to be that of the master or occasionally of the shipowner; and I conceive that a cargo owner might well be deemed not to be unreasonable if he attached much more weight to his own interests than a prudent master having regard to all the circumstances might think it wise to do.

Applying then this test, was this deviation reasonable? I do not discuss the facts except to say that I see no ground for suggesting that the deviation was due to some default of the shipowner in respect of the firemen. In the absence of evidence directed to that issue it does not seem right to impute blame to the owners in that respect. I desire to refrain from expressing an opinion whether the question of whether a deviation is reasonable is a question of law or fact. In the present case we are judges both of law and of fact; and if the question is of fact the concurrence of the learned judges below seems to me to lose some of its value when regard is had to the meaning they attributed to the issue they were determining. I think that Greer L.J. is plainly right in applying the test of reasonableness to the deviation as a whole. It could not, however, be laid down that as soon as the place was reached to which deviation was justified, there was an obligation to join the original course as directly as possible. A justified deviation to a port of refuge might involve thereafter a shorter and more direct route to the port of destination compared with a route which took the shortest cut to the original course. On the other hand, though the port of refuge was justifiably reached, the subsequent voyage might be so conducted as to amount to an unreasonable deviation. Taking all the facts into account I am pressed with the evidence which the learned judge accepted, that after St. Ives the coasting course directed by the master was not the correct course which would ordinarily be set in those circumstances. It is obvious that the small extra risk to ship and cargo caused by deviation to St. Ives, was vastly increased by the subsequent course. It seems to me not a mere error of navigation but a failure to pursue the true course from St. Ives to Constantinople which in itself made the deviation cease to be reasonable. For these reasons I agree that this appeal should be dismissed.

Note

11–030   Though this speech pays lip service to harmonisation of the law, the reasoning was not necessary for the decision, which was the same as it would have been at common law. Lord Buckmaster "expressed no opinion" "upon the view that the rules in the Schedule did no more than incorporate in a codified form the permissible limits of deviation which had previously been stated" at common law.

In *The Bunga Seroja*,[47] the High Court of Australia observed that:

"9. In understanding the operation of the Hague Rules, there are three important considerations. The rules must be read as a whole, they must be read in the light of the history behind them, and they must be read as a set of rules devised by international agreement for use in contracts that could be governed by any of several different, sometimes radically different, legal systems. . . .

19. It is necessary to recall that the rules were reached as a matter of international agreement. Several things follow from their origin.

20. First, the rules necessarily take a form different from domestic statutes like the Harter Act (and equivalent Australian, Canadian and New Zealand Acts) because, while those domestic acts 'were written to be read in the context of domestic law, the new rules were designed to create a self-contained code (at least in the areas it covered) that would not require reference to domestic law'.[48]

21. Secondly, because the rules were created by international agreement, it is not desirable to begin from an assumption that they are to he construed like a contract governed by Australian law or some other common law system.

22. Thirdly, while any action brought in a national Court on a contract of carriage governed by that nation's law will be framed in a way that reflects that law, it cannot be assumed that the rules take the form which they do in order to reflect some particular cause of action or body of learning that is derived from, say, the common law. Thus questions of burden of proof and the like are questions that may well arise in any action brought in a common law Court but it cannot be assumed that the Hague Rules reflect, say, the rules about burden of proof as between a bailor and bailee for reward at common law. For this reason, we very much doubt that principles established in cases like *The Glendarroch* [above] can be used as an aid to construing the Hague Rules.[49] They are principles which apply in common law actions between bailor and bailee but that is very different from using them as some guide to understanding what the Hague Rules mean."

It may perhaps be concluded that the courts have gone some way towards interpreting the Rules so as to harmonise the law across nations. However,

---

[47] [1999] 1 Lloyd's Rep. 512.
[48] Benedict on *Admiralty* (7th ed. (rev.)) vol. 2A, pp. 2–12 at p. 15.
[49] *cf. The Torenia* [1983] 2 Lloyd's Rep. 210 at 216.

fundamental common law principles remain a bar to harmonisation (see further paras 15–004 *et seq.*, below). Privity of contract principle in particular can thwart the operation of the *Hague Rules*, as in *Midland Silicones* (see para. 11–037, below) and the *Hague-Visby Rules* (see *The Captain Gregos*, see para. 11–061, below). Overall, however, the *Hague Rules* were quite successful at harmonising the law throughout the world.

(c) REASONS FOR *VISBY* AMENDMENTS

The *Hague-Visby Rules* were adopted by the UK legislature through the enact- **11–031** ment of the Carriage of Goods by Sea Act 1971 (brought into force when 20 states had adopted the revisions, in 1977), replacing the Hague Rules, which had been adopted by the 1924 Act of the same name.

The revision process was intended to reverse three decisions of the House of Lords on the *Hague Rules*, the *Vita Food Products Inc v Unus Shipping Co Ltd*; *Scruttons v Midland Silicones* and *The Muncaster Castle* (all discussed below), but the Visby amendments were wholly inadequate to deal with the *Midland Silicones* problem, which has only recently been resolved by independent UK legislation. The main motivation for the revision process was a reaction against the (arguably wholly predictable) view taken by the House of Lords in *Riverstone Meat Co Pty Ltd v Lancashire Shipping Co Ltd (The Muncaster Castle)* [1961] A.C. 807, below, on the definition of unseaworthiness. Ironically, however, the point proved controversial, and the proposal which started the ball rolling was removed from the new Rules, as eventually modified. Only *Vita Food* appears to have been affected by the amendments, the loophole that was opened by that case having probably been closed.

The Visby amendments effected other changes, to the limit of liability (originally £100 per package, which was thought, perhaps wrongly, to have been eroded by inflation: see further below), the *Grant v Norway* rule (see para. 14–033, below, and Article III(4)), and the development of container transport (see para. 15–018, below, and Article IV(5)(c)).

The main principles of the *Hague Rules* were not changed, the Visby amendments being an evolutionary response to subsequent developments. Whatever their merits, it is worth observing that though harmonisation might be fine in a static society, it seems to be more difficult to maintain over time. Before 1977 there was basically one regime which operated throughout the world; after 1977 there were two.

(i) *The Vita Food Problem*

The draftsmen of the original Hague Rules (contained in the Carriage of Goods **11–032** by Sea Act 1924) intended that the Rules should apply to any outward voyage from the United Kingdom, and other contracting states adopted the same principle.

The method used was the so-called "clause paramount" technique. Thus, s.3 of the 1924 Act provided:

> "Every bill of lading or similar document of title issued in Great Britain or Northern Ireland which contains or is evidence of any contract to which the Rules apply shall contain an express statement that it is to have effect subject to the provisions of the said Rules as applied by this Act."

Other contracting states adopted similar sections, with the relevant state inserted instead of "Great Britain or Northern Ireland". Thus, in theory at least, bills of lading issued for all outward voyages from any contracting state ought to have contained a clause expressly applying the Rules (the "clause paramount"), in which case the Rules would be written into all such contracts.

VITA FOOD PRODUCTS INC v UNUS SHIPPING CO LTD

Privy Council. [1939] A.C. 277

11–033   A cargo of herrings was shipped in Newfoundland, bound for New York. The defendant carrier was a Nova Scotian company, and the plaintiff consignee was a New York corporation. The ship ran aground and the cargo was damaged off the coast of Nova Scotia. Newfoundland had adopted the Hague Rules for outward voyages, by virtue of its own Carriage of Goods by Sea Act 1932, and there was a "clause paramount" provision (section 3) similar to that above. In normal circumstances, the parties would have complied with the requirements, and the Hague Rules would have been expressly incorporated.

By mistake, however, old bills of lading were used, the "clause paramount" provision was not complied with, and English law was accidentally chosen to govern the contract. English law at that time also adopted the Hague Rules, but only to outward voyages from the United Kingdom (which this, of course, was not).

The carrier claimed the protection of both the bill of lading contract, and the Hague Rules, since the exemption clauses from either would protect him. The cargo-owner claimed that the exemptions of neither bill of lading nor *Hague Rules* applied, and sued the carrier, not on the contract of carriage, but as a common carrier.

He claimed the bill of lading contract did not apply because, owing to non-compliance with the clause paramount provision, it was void as an illegal contract.

The other issue was whether the Hague Rules applied to the contract of carriage, though the carrier would win if *either* the bill of lading point *or* the *Hague Rules* point was decided in his favour.

Held: (for the carrier)

1. Failure to include a clause paramount did not render the contract of carriage unenforceable, as an illegal contract under Newfoundland law. Therefore, the carrier *could* claim the exemptions in the bill of lading contract.

2. That disposed of the case in favour of the carrier, but *obiter*, the contract of carriage was governed by English law, and as English law applied the Hague Rules only to outward voyages from the United Kingdom, the Rules did not apply in this case, because it was not such a voyage.

11–034   LORD WRIGHT: It will be convenient at this point to determine what is the proper law of the contract. In their Lordships' opinion the express words of the bill of lading must receive effect, with the result that the contract is governed by English law. It is now well settled that by English law (and the law of Nova Scotia is the same) the proper law of the contract "is the law which the parties intended to apply." That intention is objectively ascertained, and, if not expressed, will be presumed from the terms of the contract and the relevant surrounding circumstances. But as Lord Atkin, dealing with cases where the intention of the parties is expressed, said in *Rex v International Trustee for, etc., Bondholders A.-G.* [1937] A.C. 500, 529 (a case which contains the latest enunciation of this principle), "Their intention will be ascertained by the intention expressed in the contract if any, which will be conclusive." It is objected that this is too broadly stated and that some qualifications are necessary. It is true that in questions relating to the conflict of laws rules cannot generally be stated in absolute terms but rather as *prima facie* presumptions. But where the English rule that intention is the test applies, and where there is an express statement by the parties of their intention to select the law of the contract, it is difficult to see what qualifications are possible, provided the intention expressed is *bona fide* and legal, and provided there is no reason for avoiding the choice on the ground of public policy. In the present case, however, it might be said that the choice of English law is not valid for two reasons. It might be said that the transaction, which is one relating to the carriage on a Nova Scotian ship of goods from Newfoundland to New York between residents in these countries, contains nothing to connect it in any way with English law, and therefore that choice could not be seriously taken. Their Lordships reject this argument both on grounds of principle and on the facts. Connection with English law is not as a matter of principle essential. The provision in a contract (*e.g.* of sale) for English arbitration imports English law as the law governing the transaction, and those familiar with international business are aware how frequent such a provision is even where the parties are not English and the transactions are carried on completely outside England. . . . In any case parties may reasonably desire that the familiar principles of English commercial law should apply. The other ground urged is that the choice of English law is inconsistent with the provisions of the bill of lading, that in respect of certain goods the Harter Act or the Canadian Water Carriage of Goods Act of 1910 (now repealed, but in force at the date of the bill of lading) was to apply. It has been explained that the incorporation of these Acts may have only contractual effect, but in any case, though the proper law of the contract is English, English law may incorporate the provisions of the law of another country or other countries as part of the terms of the contract . . . English law will in these and sometimes in other respects import a foreign law, but the contract is still governed by its proper law. The reference to the United States and the Canadian Acts does not on any view supersede English law which is to govern the contract, nor does Newfoundland law, though Newfoundland was the place where the contract was made, apply to oust English law from being the law of the contract, and as such from being the law which defines its nature, obligation and interpretation, though Newfoundland law might apply to the incidents of performance to be done in Newfoundland. There is, in their Lordships' opinion, no ground for refusing to give effect to the express selection of English law as the proper law in the bills of lading. . . .

Notes

11–035   1. Though the country of loading, country of discharge, and the law chosen to govern the contract (England) all applied the *Hague Rules*, Lord Wright held that this contract was not governed by the Rules.

2. The parties' choice of English law to govern the contract was valid, even though the contract had not even a remote connection with England (except that possibly the insurance company was English). The principle stated by Lord Wright was that parties to a contract can choose the law of any state to govern it, as long only as that choice is *bona fide* and legal, and not contrary to public policy. It is not necessary for there to be even a remote connection with the state chosen. In *Vita Food* itself, *both* parties pleaded that the contract was governed by the law of Newfoundland.

3. The advantage of Lord Wright's approach is that where there are a number of re-sales, involving sellers and buyers of many different nationalities, the parties can if they wish ensure (by express choice of law clause) that the law of the same country continues to govern the carriage contract, even where the eventual parties may well have no connection with the law of that country, for example where a bill of lading contract containing an express choice of law clause has been transferred many times under the provisions of the Carriage of Goods by Sea Act 1992 (on which see chapter 13, below).

4. On the other hand, though the *Vita Food* case was brought about by accident, the decision that the parties could choose as proper law the law of any country opened up the possibility of deliberate evasion of the Rules. The parties could choose the law of a state which did not adopt the Rules, or, *e.g.* English law for any voyage apart from an outgoing one from the U.K. Yet a major purpose of the Rules was to prevent carriers, who are usually in a stronger bargaining position than shippers, from limiting their liability to such an extent as to render bills of lading worthless. In *The Hollandia*, see below, Lord Diplock doubted Lord Wright's position.

5. This case showed up the flaw of the "clause paramount" technique. It was because of this decision that the *Hague-Visby Rules* adopt a different drafting technique (Article X: see further below).

RAOUL P. COLINVAUX, "REVISION OF THE HAGUE RULES RELATING TO BILLS OF LADING"

[1963] J.B.L. 341

[Footnotes are as in the original, but renumbered for inclusion in this book.]

Application of Hague Rules to Inward and Outward Shipping

11–036   The last recommendation [of the Stockholm Conference of the International Maritime Committee in June 1963] of particular importance to British shipowners is that the Hague Rules should apply both to inward and outward shipments to or from any state which subscribes to the

Rules. In fact it is already the practice to incorporate the Hague Rules in most bills of lading issued by British shipowners, but this will, to a considerable extent, close the loophole provided by *Vita Food Products Inc v Unus Shipping Co.*[50] The fact is that a carrier, provided he makes his bill of lading subject to English law, may contract on what terms he pleases, in the case of shipments to the United Kingdom. This loophole has been of assistance to shipowners importing fruit and other perishable cargoes, particularly from the Mediterranean, and it might be a matter for consideration whether carriers of such cargoes should not be entitled to contract on special terms.

Note
Though *Vita Food* was addressed by the Visby amendments, the proposal that "the Hague Rules should apply both to inward and outward shipments to or from any state which subscribes to the Rules" was not the solution adopted: see further below.

(ii) *The Midland Silicones Problem*

SCRUTTONS LTD v MIDLAND SILICONES LTD

House of Lords. [1962] A.C. 446

The plaintiffs were consignees of a drum of chemicals. The defendants were a stevedoring company engaged by the carrier to unload his vessels in London. They negligently dropped the drum, thereby causing damage to the value of £593.   **11–037**

The contract of carriage, to which only shippers and carriers were party, incorporated the Hague Rules (by virtue of the United States Carriage of Goods by Sea Act 1936, on an outward voyage from the United States to London). These limited the liability of the carrier for damage to $500 (though the clause did not expressly extend to independent contractors).

The consignee sued the stevedores in negligence, claiming £593 damages. The stevedores claimed the benefit of the limitation of liability clause in the Hague Rules, but the plaintiffs claimed that they were not bound by it: neither they nor the defendants were party to the carriage contract.

Held: (Lord Denning dissenting) The plaintiffs were not bound by the clause in the Hague Rules, and could recover the whole of the £593 from the stevedores.

LORD REID: Although I may regret it, I find it impossible to deny the existence of the general rule that a stranger to a contract cannot in a   **11–038**

[50] [1939] A.C. 277.

question with either of the contracting parties take advantage of provisions in the contract, even where it is clear from the contract that some provision in it was intended to benefit him. That rule appears to have been crystalised a century ago in *Tweddle v Atkinson* (1861) 30 L.J.Q.B. 265, and finally established in this House in *Dunlop Pneumatic Tyre Co Ltd v Selfridge & Co Ltd* [1915] A.C. 847. There are, it is true, certain well-established exceptions to that rule—though I am not sure that they are really exceptions and do not arise from other principles. But none of these in any way touches the present case.

The actual words used by Lord Haldane in the *Dunlop* case were made the basis of an argument that, although a stranger to a contract may not be able to sue for any benefit under it, he can rely on the contract as a defence if one of the parties to it sues him in breach of his contractual obligation—that he can use the contract as a shield though not as a sword. I can find no justification for that. If the other contracting party can prevent the breach of contract well and good, but if he cannot I do not see how the stranger can. As was said in *Tweddle v Atkinson*, the stranger cannot "take advantage" from the contract.

Notes

1. The House of Lords decision in *Midland Silicones* is a reaffirmation of the privity of contract doctrine. The stevedores could not rely on an exemption clause in a contract to which neither they nor the plaintiffs were party. Though the cases revolve around stevedores the principle could be used by cargo-owners in a tort action against any employee or independent contractor of the carrier, or indeed anybody who was not party to the carriage contract (see further the discussion of through bills of lading and multimodal transport documents in chapter 15, below).

2. Lord Denning, in his dissenting speech, noted that before the development of a general tort of negligence in *Donoghue v Stevenson* [1932] A.C. 562, the *Midland Silicones* difficulty could not arise. The shipper or consignee's contractual relationship was with the carrier alone. The privity of contract doctrine, because it allowed only parties to contracts to sue on them, prevented cargo-owners suing servants and independent contractors employed by the carrier *at all*. The only available contract action was against the carrier himself, who could of course claim the benefit of any exemption clauses in the carriage contract. Since 1932, if, *e.g.* stevedores damage goods through their negligence, the cargo-owner has not needed to show a contractual relationship to be able to sue. He can sue directly in tort. Thus the privity of contract doctrine, which originally had protected the stevedores, now had exactly the opposite effect. Because there was no contract with the cargo-owner the stevedores were prevented from relying on exemption clauses in the carriage contract.

3. In the present context, the effect of *Midland Silicones*, that was considered undesirable, was to allow cargo-owners to circumvent the $500 limit imposed by the US Hague Rules, by suing stevedores directly in tort.

4. In fact the exemption clause in *Midland Silicones* did not expressly protect servants and independent contractors engaged by the carrier. This led to carriers re-drafting their exemption clause expressly to cover them (*e.g.* the *Himalaya* clause, named after a ship against which an action was successfully brought).[51]

---

[51] *Adler v Dickson* [1955] 1 Q.B. 158.

The *Himalaya* clause proved a partial solution to the *Midland Silicones* problem.[52]

5. Though the Visby amendments were intended to resolve the *Midland Silicones* problem, they almost certainly failed to do so (see below at paras 11–061, *et seq.*). The development of the *Himalaya* clause was a partial response (but see, *e.g. Raymond Burke Motors Ltd v The Mersey Docks and Harbour Co*,[53] demonstrating the limitations of the *Himalaya* device. The problem was eventually solved by the Contract (Rights of Third Parties) Act 1999, which can also resolve the problems of through bills of lading.

6. Other aspects of privity of contract remain problematic under the present regime, however, for example if the plaintiff/claimant cargo-owner is not party to a carriage contract (see further below at paras 11–061, *et seq.*, below). This is unaffected by the 1999 Act, though the situation should become less common, following the enactment of the Carriage of Goods by Sea Act 1992 (see chapter 13, below).

(iii) *The Muncaster Castle Problem*

As already observed, the Rules substituted for strict liability a due diligence requirement. Given the complexity of modern ships, this was thought desirable, to protect shipowners from suit where they were in no sense responsible for a defect.

RIVERSTONE MEAT CO PTY LTD v LANCASHIRE SHIPPING CO LTD (THE MUNCASTER CASTLE)

House of Lords. [1961] A.C. 807

Facts:

A fitter in a ship repair yard had failed to harden up nuts on some **11–039** inspection covers, with the result that seawater got into the hold, and the cargo (ox tongue) was damaged. The fitters were employed by ship repairers with a good reputation. The cargo-owners sued the shipowners for damages.

Held:

The carrier was liable because the negligence of the fitters constituted a lack of due diligence on the part of the carrier. Therefore the carrier could not rely on the exemption contained in Article IV(1) of the Hague Rules, since that clause requires him to show that he has exercised due diligence to make the ship seaworthy. It follows that the carrier can be liable if the ship becomes unseaworthy because of any negligent work done on the ship prior to the voyage, including that of contractors.

VISCOUNT SIMONDS: The Hague Rules, as is well known, were the result of the Conferences on Maritime Law held at Brussels in 1922 and 1923. Their aim was broadly to standardise within certain limits the rights of every holder of a bill of lading against the shipowner, prescribing an

---

[52] Especially *The Eurymedon* [1975] A.C. 154.
[53] [1986] 1 Lloyd's Rep. 155.

irreducible minimum for the responsibilities and liabilities to be under-taken by the latter. To guide them, the framers of the rules had, amongst other precedents, the American Harter Act of 1893, the Australian Sea Carriage of Goods Act, 1904, the Canadian Water Carriage of Goods Act, 1910, and, though they had no British Act as a model, they had decisions of the English courts in which the language of the Harter Act had fallen to be construed by virtue of its provisions being embodied in bills of lading. In all these Acts the relevant words "exercise due diligence to make the ship seaworthy" are to be found. It was in these circumstances that these words were adopted in the Hague Rules.

My Lords, the question how far their meaning should be governed by previous decisions in the courts of America or this country has been more than once discussed in this House. Notwithstanding some apparent qual-ification of the proposition which is to be found in the speeches of Lord Atkin and Lord Macmillan in *Stag Line Ltd v Foscolo Mango & Co Ltd* [above], I think I am at liberty to adopt emphatically what was said by Viscount Sumner and Lord Hailsham in *Gosse Millerd Ltd v Canadian Government Merchant Marine Ltd (The Canadian Highlander)* [1929] A.C. 223. The former of them said [1929] A.C. at p. 237:

"By forbearing to define 'management of the ship' . . . the legislature has, in my opinion, shown a clear intention to continue and enforce the old clause as it was previously understood and regularly construed by the courts of law":

the latter said [1929] A.C. at p. 230:

"I am unable to find any reason for supposing that the words as used by the legislature in the Act of 1924 have any different meaning from that which has been judicially assigned to them when used in contracts for the carriage of goods by sea before that date, and I think that the decisions which have already been given are sufficient to determine the meaning to be put upon them in the statute now under discussion."

Mutatis mutandis these statements apply to the words we have to construe . . .

First I would refer to *Dobell & Co v S.S. Rossmore Co* [1895] 2 Q.B. 408, a case often referred to in the courts of this country and of the United States and never so far as I am aware dissented from. In that case, the ship was unseaworthy owing to the negligence of the ship's carpenter. Into the bill of lading the words of the Harter Act were introduced, "which" said Lord Esher M.R. ([1895] 2 Q.B. at p. 413): "I decline to construe as an Act, but which we must construe simply as words occurring in this bill of lading". Then he proceeds:

"In the 3rd section of the Act so incorporated the exception which is to relieve the shipowner is made to depend on the condition that the owner of the ship . . . shall exercise due diligence to make the vessel in all respects seaworthy. If he does not do that the exceptions in his favour do not take effect. It is contended that the meaning of the clause is that if the owner personally did all that he could do to make the ship seaworthy when she left America, then, although she was not seaworthy, by the fault of some agent or servant, the owner is not liable."

And the learned Master of the Rolls, after rejecting this contention, went on:

"It is obvious to my mind . . . that the words of the 3rd section which limit the owner's liability if he shall exercise due diligence to make the ship in all respects seaworthy, must mean that this is to be done by the owner by himself or the agents whom he employs to see to the seaworthiness of the ship before she starts out of that port."

So, also, Kay L.J. [1895] 2 Q.B. at p. 416:

"It seems to me to be plain on the face of this contract that what was intended was that the owner should, if not with his own eyes, at any rate by the eyes of proper competent agents, ensure that the ship was in a seaworthy condition before she left port, and that it is not enough to say that he appointed a proper and competent agent."

I have cited from these judgments at some length because they determine decisively the meaning attached by the courts of this country to the relevant words. It is true that the negligence was that of a servant of the shipowner, but the reasoning and the language of the judgments embrace any agent employed by him. These are wide words.

[Viscount Simonds continued with a review of a number of other authorities, both in the UK and US courts.]

Notes

1. The shipowner was not personally at fault, and it was this decision which **11–040** prompted the revision process culminating in the *Hague-Visby Rules*. Because no agreement could be reached, however, *The Muncaster Castle* was left alone by the amendments, and still stands.

2. There was no reason for this decision to have surprised anybody. The *Hague Rules* adopted the drafting of the Harter Act, which the Court of Appeal as long ago as in *Dobell & Co v S.S. Rossmore Co* [1895] 2 Q.B. 408, had interpreted similarly to the House of Lords' interpretation of the *Hague Rules* in *The Muncaster Castle*. Had the Rules required "personal want of due diligence", as in the Gencon voyage charterparty, then the decision in *The Muncaster Castle* would have been different: *cf. The Gundulic* [1981] 2 Lloyd's Rep. 418 (interpreting Gencon).

RAOUL P. COLINVAUX, "REVISION OF THE HAGUE RULES RELATING TO BILLS OF LADING"

[1963] J.B.L. 341

[Footnotes are as in the original, but renumbered for inclusion in this book.]

11–041   There can be no more remarkable event in the history of maritime law than the Stockholm Conference of the International Maritime Committee in June 1963. With British merchant fleets dwindling, with confidence in the decisions of the House of Lords reduced by the unbusinesslike flavour of some of their lordships' speeches, it is heartening to find world accord with the sound and basic way of thinking of London maritime lawyers.

What was particularly significant about this Conference was that British shipping interests, supported by British cargo interests, denied justice by our own highest tribunal, should find the hope of justice at an international Bar. The main decisions of the Conference were in effect to recommend the overruling of the *Muncaster Castle*[54] and the decision in *Midland Silicones v Scruttons*,[55] in so far as it implied that servants of a shipowner should not be able to avail themselves of the benefits of the exceptions in the Hague Rules.

Unseaworthiness Caused by Competent Independent Contractor

The *Muncaster Castle* decided that a carrier was liable for lack of due diligence to make a ship seaworthy, even if he chose with the greatest care a surveyor to see that it was seaworthy. If, for instance a fitter employed by a repairer did his work carelessly the carrier would remain liable. It is only fair to state that this decision seems to have been right in law; it is the view which has been taken in *Carver* for generations. Equally clearly it flouted the intentions of those who framed the Hague Rules relating to bills of lading with the object of protecting the diligent shipowner at the expense of cargo underwriters. To remedy the matter the conference proposed the addition of a proviso to Article 3, rule 1, of the Rules in the following terms[56]:

"Provided that if in the circumstances in which it is proper to employ an independent contractor (including a classification society), the carrier has taken care to appoint one of repute as regards competence, the carrier shall not be deemed to have failed to exercise due diligence

---

[54] *Riverstone Meat Co Pty Ltd v Lancashire Shipping Co Ltd* [1961] A.C. 807; [1961] J.B.L. 199.
[55] [1962] A.C. 446; [1962] J.B.L. 6, 85, 202; see further Jan Sandström, "The Limitation of the Stevedore's Liability" [1962] J.B.L. 340.
[56] *cf.* the suggestions of the Sub-Committee on Bills of Lading Clauses of the International Maritime Committee, quoted by Sandström, *op. cit.*, in [1962] J.B.L. 340, 349.

solely by reason of an act or omission on the part of such an independent contractor, his servants or agents (including any independent subcontractor and his servants or agents) in respect of the construction, repair or maintenance of the ship or any part thereof or of her equipment. Nothing contained in this proviso shall absolve the carrier from taking such precautions by way of supervision or inspection as may be reasonable in relation to any work carried out by such an independent contractor as aforesaid."

One side effect of this proposal would be greatly to enhance the value of Lloyd's Survey Reports, which are accorded international respect, but which, as the law stands, give the shipowner a minimum of protection. . . .

Increase in Minimum Limits of Liability

As for the limitation of liability clause (art. 4, rule 5, of the Hague Rules) the limit of liability, it is proposed, should be increased to 10,000 gold francs (about £235). This would bring the law internationally approximately into line with the limit of £200 in the British Maritime Association's "gold clause agreement" to which most cargo insurers and British shipping interests have subscribed.

Note

As already observed, the proposal of the Conference in response to *The Muncaster Castle* was not adopted, and Article III(1) is unchanged in the Hague-Visby Rules. The proposal to increase liability limits was adopted, but I.M.F. units of account were later substituted for gold francs; unlike gold francs, units of account are not inflation-proofed, and it might in the event have been better to leave the limits alone: see further below.

The remainder of the article comments on other suggestions for reform, dealt with elsewhere in this chapter, and in para. 14–049, below.

The gold clause agreement referred to in the last paragraph set out above is further referred to in *Pyrene v Scindia Navigation Ltd*, below.

11–042

(d) The *Hague-Visby* Rules

In the UK, the *Hague-Visby Rules* were given effect by the Carriage of Goods by Sea Act 1971, which was brought into force internationally in 1977. The Act is set out in full in Appendix D, below.

Article IV *bis* was new in the 1971 Act; its effect, or rather lack of it, is considered below (it was clearly intended to reverse *Midland Silicones*). The second paragraph of Article III(4) was also new, and is considered in para. 14–049, below.

11–043

(i) *Vita Food Resolved?*

Because of the *Vita Food* case, the revised Visby Rules did not continue the "clause paramount" technique, but replaced it with a provision which directly applies the Rules. Thus, Article X provides:

11–044

"The provisions of these Rules shall apply to every bill of lading relating to the carriage of goods between ports in two different States if:

(a) the bill of lading is issued in a contracting State, or
(b) the carriage is from a port in a contracting State, or
(c) the contract contained in or evidenced by the bill of lading provides that these Rules or legislation of any States giving effect to them are to govern the contract,

whatever may be the nationality of the ship, the carrier, the shipper, the consignee, or any other interested person."

Had this provision been in the original Rules, they would have been applicable in *Vita Food*, every sub-section being triggered. The actual decision would have been the same, the carrier still being protected by the bill of lading exceptions.

THE HOLLANDIA

House of Lords. [1983] 1 A.C. 565

11–045 In an outward voyage from Scotland, the bill of lading gave the Court of Amsterdam exclusive jurisdiction (choice of forum clause). The carrier's liability was to be limited to an amount less than that provided for by the Hague-Visby Rules.

Dutch law applies the Hague, but not the Hague-Visby Rules, and the Court of Amsterdam would have upheld the carriers' limitation of liability. However, were the Visby amendments to apply, the limitation would be "null and void and of no effect" by virtue of Article III(8). The question for decision was whether the cargo-owners could sue the carriers in the U.K. courts, and thereby avoid the more stringent limitation of liability.

Held:
Article X applied the Hague-Visby Rules directly to any outward voyage from the UK, and the carrier could not avoid their application by giving Dutch courts exclusive jurisdiction. Further, the choice of forum clause was itself void by virtue of Article III(8), as an attempt to limit the carrier's liability below that permitted by the Rules.

11–046 LORD DIPLOCK: As foreshadowed at an earlier point in this speech I must return in a brief postscript to an argument based on certain passages in an article by a distinguished commentator, Dr. F.A. Mann "*Statutes and the Conflict of Laws*" (1974) 46 B.Y.I.L. 117, and which, it is suggested, supports the view that even a choice of substantive law, which excludes the application of the Hague-Visby Rules, is not prohibited by the 1971 Act notwithstanding that the bill of lading is issued in and is for carriage from a port in the United Kingdom. The passages to which our attention was directed by counsel for the carriers I find myself (apparently in respectable academic company) unable to accept. They draw no distinction between the 1924 Act and the 1971 Act despite the contrast between the legislative techniques adopted in the two Acts, and the express inclusion in the Hague-Visby Rules of Art. X (absent from the Hague Rules), expressly applying the Hague-Visby Rules to every bill of lading falling within the description contained in the article, which article is given the force of law in the United Kingdom by s.1(2) of the 1971 Act. The 1971 Act deliberately abandoned what may conveniently be termed the "clause paramount" technique employed in s.3 of the 1924 Act, the Newfoundland counterpart of which provided the occasion for wide-ranging *dicta* in the opinion of the Privy Council delivered by Lord Wright in *Vita Food Products Inc v Unus Shipping Co Ltd* [above]. Although the actual decision in that case would have been the same if the relevant Newfoundland statute had been in the terms of the 1971 Act, those *dicta* have no application to the construction of the latter Act and this has rendered it no longer necessary to embark on what I have always found to be an unrewarding task of ascertaining precisely what those *dicta* meant.

Notes

1. The issue did not arise directly as to what would have been the effect of choosing Dutch law as the proper law. The bill of lading purported to do this, but Lord Diplock thought that the choice of law clause was ambiguous. The *ratio* of the case is thus confined to the choice of forum clause.   **11–047**

2. However, there are clear *dicta* that even had the choice of law clause been unambiguous it would not have been effective to avoid the Rules. Lord Diplock took the view that Lord Wright's reasoning in *Vita Food* does not survive the change in legislative technique.

General observations on the choice of law clauses

Though Lord Wright's reasoning in *Vita Food* applies directly only to the earlier Act, by taking it to its logical conclusion it would be possible to argue that the re-drafting makes no difference (in effect the argument of Mann to which Lord Diplock alludes in his speech). It could be argued, for example, that Article X itself does not apply if the parties can effectively choose Dutch law to govern the contract, since in that case no UK statutes, including Article X, apply. Had that argument been successful in *The Hollandia*, the 1971 re-drafting would have made no difference.

Lord Diplock's rejection of Mann's view does not necessarily lead to the conclusion that Lord Wright's views on express choice of law clauses *in general* are wrong. A better explanation is probably that this particular English statute, creating as it does a "mandatory rule", overrides an express choice of law clause, on grounds of public policy.

On either argument Article X is not apparently affected by the same difficulties as the "clause paramount".

Postscript: Contracts (Applicable Laws) Act 1990

TODD, BILLS OF LADING AND BANKERS' DOCUMENTARY CREDITS

(3rd ed., LLP, 1998), Ch 8

[Footnotes are as in the original, but renumbered for inclusion in this book.]

11–048   Carriage contracts are now covered by the Contracts (Applicable Laws) Act 1990, Article 3 of which provides:

> "Freedom of choice
>
> 1. A contract shall be governed by the law chosen by the parties. The choice must be expressed or demonstrated with reasonable certainty by the terms of the contract or the circumstances of the case. By their choice the parties can select the law applicable to the whole or a part only of the contract.
> 2. The parties may at any time agree to subject the contract to a law other than that which previously governed it, whether as a result of an earlier choice under this Article or of other provisions of this Convention. Any variation by the parties of the law to be applied made after the conclusion of the contract shall not prejudice its formal validity under Article 9[57] or adversely affect the rights of third parties.
> 3. The fact that the parties have chosen a foreign law, whether or not accompanied by the choice of a foreign tribunal, shall not, where all the other elements relevant to the situation at the time of the choice are connected with one country only, prejudice the application of rules of the law of that country which cannot be derogated from by contract, hereinafter called 'mandatory rules'.
> 4. The existence and validity of the consent of the parties as to the choice of the applicable law shall be determined in accordance with the provisions of Articles 8, 9 and 11."[58]

This differs little substantively from the *Vita Food* common law position. Article 3(1) preserves the right of the parties to choose the applicable law, except to the extent that Article 3(3) preserves the "mandatory rules" of a country where all the elements of the contract, apart from the choice of law clause, point exclusively to that country. Mandatory rules are those from which the parties are not permitted to contract out. Presumably this is intended to mirror the public policy proviso under the common law. Particularly where rules are intended to protect a weaker party, their purpose could be entirely negated were the parties able to choose the law of a country that did not operate them, and it is probable, for example, that Article 3(3) would prevent the parties to an exclusively English contract from contracting out of the provisions of the Unfair Contract Terms Act 1977.

Article 3(3) preserves mandatory rules only where *all* the elements relevant to the situation at the time of the choice are connected with one country only. A question that may well arise with carriage contracts is whether a choice of law clause in the bill of lading can avoid the provisions of the Hague-Visby Rules, which almost certainly fall into the

---

[57] Dealing with formal validity.
[58] Respectively dealing with material validity, formal validity and incapacity.

category of mandatory rules, protecting as they do cargo interests from the stronger bargaining power of carriers.[59] It would be quite rare for all the elements relevant to the situation to point to one country alone. Suppose, for example, a foreign carrier loading British-owned cargo at a United Kingdom port insists on the insertion of a proper law clause choosing a non-contracting state (to the Hague-Visby Rules). The port of loading and shipper's place of business point to the application of the Hague-Visby Rules, but if the carrier is foreign it cannot be said that *all* the relevant elements point to the United Kingdom. However, it does not necessarily follow that the selection of a non-contracting state would be valid. If an action is brought in a United Kingdom court, Article 7(2) provides:

> "Nothing in this Convention shall restrict the application of the rules of the law of the forum in a situation where they are mandatory irrespective of the law otherwise applicable to the contract."

Attention might also be drawn to Article 21:

> "This Convention shall not prejudice the application of international conventions to which a Contracting State is, or becomes, a party."

It appears, then, that potential Hague-Visby difficulties are adequately catered for, albeit not by reference to Article 3 alone.

There are under Article 3 significant departures from the common law position. Article 3(1) allows the parties to select the law applicable to part only of the contract, and Article 3(2) allows the parties to alter their choice of law after the contract has been made, subject to the provisos that a contract validly made cannot be rendered invalid by a variation of the applicable law, not can such variation prejudice the rights of third parties.[60]

Note
Other problems on the application of the Rules are considered below.

(ii) *Package Limitation*

The liability of the carrier was originally limited by the *Hague Rules* to £100 "per package or unit", but this gave rise to two problems. The first was the definition of a package. The second was the figure of £100, which if taken as cash value had quickly become eroded by inflation. **11–049**

---

[59] See, *e.g. The Hollandia* [1983] 1 A.C. 565.
[60] The Article refers only to formal validity, which under art. 9 is determined at the conclusion of the contract. Problems could therefore arise if under the law applicable after the variation, but not under the original proper law, the contract is regarded as having been validly repudiated or frustrated before the date of the variation. Presumably the validity of the variation itself is determined by the earlier choice of law.

The amount

From the paragraph from Colinvaux quoted above, it is clear that the limit (originally of £100) was intended to be increased by the Visby amendments.

It seems to have been the intention of the Brussels International Convention to tie the figure into sterling gold value in 1924, in which case of course, the figure would have been uniform across the world, and would have risen automatically with inflation. Unfortunately, in the UK the drafting of the 1924 Act was ambiguous, so that the figure could have been read as £100 cash. Furthermore, some States expressly adopted a cash value in their domestic legislation (for example, in the United States the figure was set at $500). Thus, the figure was no longer uniform across the world, and at any rate in the United States (if not the United Kingdom also) was not inflation-proofed.

The Visby amendments resolved the issue by substituting for £100 sterling first an amount calculated by reference to the value of a notional gold unit, the gold franc. Since 1981 (by virtue of the Merchant Shipping Act), the amount has instead been calculated by reference to the International Monetary Fund special drawing rights, or "unit of account". It is now set at 666.67 units of account per package. The value of the unit of account can change daily, but is of the order of £500 per package. Unlike the gold franc, however, the value of the unit of account decreases in real terms with inflation, although being based on a basket of currencies it is not significantly affected by depreciation of any one.

However, since in the case of a large container this would lead to a very low package limitation, there is an alternative weight limitation of 2 units of account per kilo of the gross weight of the goods lost or damaged, and the weight limitation applies whenever it is higher than the package limitation. Containers above about a third of a ton therefore come under the weight limitation, rather than the package limitation. The weight limitation works out at around £1.50 per kilo.

While the Hague-Visby limits are being eroded by inflation, it seems that some implementations of the Hague Rules have been inflation-proofed all along.

THE ROSA S

Queen's Bench Division (Admiralty Court). [1989] 1 Q.B. 419

Facts:

11–050   A consignment of 222 cases containing an aluminium casting and rolling plant was shipped in Turin aboard the defendants' vessel, and a bill of lading issued for it, which by clause paramount, incorporated the provisions of the Hague Rules. When the cargo was discharged, it was discovered that one of the cases was badly damaged, and the consignees sued on the bill of lading contract. The defendants admitted liability, and the only dispute was as to the limit of liability per package.

Held:

The limit of liability of £100 per package or unit in the Hague Rules referred not to £100 in today's money, but to £100 sterling gold value in 1924. This was on the relevant date (June 1st 1984) £6,630.50 sterling. Note that this limit is therefore much higher than the limit under the Hague-Visby Rules, based on the I.M.F. unit of account.

HOBHOUSE J.: It is agreed by the parties that the carriage of the goods on **11–051** board *Rosa S* was subject to the provisions of the International Convention relating to Bills of Lading dated Brussels Aug 25, 1924. The defendants further admit that the damage was caused by their breach of their contractual duties as carriers under the bill of lading. The dispute between the parties is what is the limit of the defendants' liability to the plaintiffs in respect of such breach and damage. No value of the goods was declared by the shippers or inserted in the bill of lading.

Clause 2 of the bill of lading provided that:

"Any dispute arising out of this Bill of Lading shall be governed by English law and . . . the High Court of Justice in London shall have exclusive jurisdiction . . . "

Clause 1 of the bill of lading was a paramount clause which read:

"It is mutually agreed that this Bill of Lading shall have effect subject to the provisions of the International Convention relating to Bills of Lading dated Brussels 25th August 1924 (hereafter called the Hague Rules) except where legislation giving effect to the Hague Rules as amended by the protocol signed at Brussels on 23rd February 1968 (hereafter called the Hague Visby Rules) is compulsorily applicable, in which case this Bill of Lading shall have effect subject to such legislation. Neither the Hague Rules nor the Hague Visby Rules shall apply where the goods carried hereunder are live animals.

  Nothing in this bill of lading shall be deemed to be a surrender by the carrier of any of his rights or immunities or an increase of any of his responsibilities under the said rules or enactments and/or their protocols.

  If anything herein contained is inconsistent with the said legislation or Hague Rules or Hague Visby Rules it shall, to the extent and on the occasion of such inconsistency and no further, be null and void."

At the material time Italy had not become a contracting party to the Hague-Visby Rules, hence the parties agreement that this bill of lading was subject to the provisions of the 1934 Convention, the Hague Rules.

Clause 28 of the bill of lading provided, *inter alia*:

" . . . Neither the carrier nor the ship shall in any event be or become liable for any loss or damage to or in connection with goods in an amount exceeding pound sterling 100 per package or unit . . . "

The defendants before me somewhat faintly sought to rely upon this **11–052** clause as showing a contractual intention that whatever might be the true effect of the Hague Rules and the 1924 Convention, they were entitled to a limit of £100 sterling and no more. This contention of course could not survive the concluding words of the clause paramount:

" . . . if anything herein contained is inconsistent with the . . . Hague Rules . . . it shall . . . be null and void . . . "

and Art. III, r. 8 of the Hague Rules which provides that any clause in a contract of carriage purporting to relieve the carrier from liability or lessening his liability otherwise than as provided in the Convention is to be null and void and of no effect. Accordingly the question of what is the limit of the defendants' liability under this bill of lading must be ascertained by reference to the provisions of the 1924 Convention and that alone.

The only authoritative text of the 1924 Convention is the French text. The bureau of the conference did however authorise an English translation. During the argument before me the parties have been content to proceed on the basis of the English translation subject to two points to which I will refer. In this translation Art. IV, r. 5 reads:

"Neither the carrier nor the ship shall in any event be or become liable for any loss or damage to or in connection with goods in an amount exceeding £100 per package or unit, or the equivalent of that sum in other currency unless the nature and value of such goods have been declared by the shipper before shipment and inserted in the bill of lading . . . "

Article IX provides:

"The monetary units mentioned in this Convention are to be taken to be gold value."

Those contracting states in which the pound sterling is not a monetary unit reserve to themselves the right of translating the sums indicated in this Convention in terms of pound sterling into terms of their own monetary system in round figures. . . .

The plaintiffs submit that Art. IV, r. 5 must be read with the first sentence of Art. IX so that instead of saying £100 sterling it says £100 sterling gold value. They say that the gold content of £100 sterling was in 1924 defined as a matter of English law by the Coinage Act, 1870, and was at the date of this bill of lading, and is at today's date, defined by the Coinage Act 1971, as being 798.805 grammes of gold of a millesimal fineness 916.66, which is the same as 732,238 grammes of fine gold. They say that the gold value is therefore the value of that quantity of gold. Taking the relevant date for the assessment of the defendants' liability as being the date of the delivery of the goods, which the parties have agreed can be treated as June 1, 1984, this gives a value of the gold expressed in sterling as being £6630.50p. They therefore say that that is the value which expresses the relevant limit applicable to their claim. Their claim is for a sum in Kenyan pounds. That sum of sterling converted into Kenyan pounds at the same date gives a limit of liability expressed in Kenyan pounds of £6491.25. That is what the plaintiffs say is the correct limit of the defendants' liability in respect of the plaintiffs' claim in the present action.

The defendants on the other hand say that the correct limit is £100 sterling in today's money or its nominal equivalent expressed in Kenyan currency. They say that all considerations of gold value should be excluded. They say that Art. IV should be construed on its own without recourse to Art. IX; that Art. IX is in any event too unclear and unspecific to qualify the words of Art. IV. As a matter of English law a gold clause to be effective must have a greater clarity and degree of definition than Art. IX contains. They sought to rely upon historical arguments to support the conclusion that the Convention treated sterling currency as a nominal money of account and not any gold value of sterling. They finally argued that if any gold value was to be taken into account it was simply the quantity of gold that a £100 sterling would at the date of the accrual of the cause of action have bought and that its purpose was simply to provide stability in terms of sterling between the date of the accrual of the cause of action and any date when judgment might thereafter be given.

Some preliminary observations need to be made. The Court in the present case is concerned to construe a contract, the contract contained in this bill of lading. The parties to this bill of lading have chosen to refer to the provisions of an international Convention. International Conventions are agreements between states not between private individuals, nor as a matter of English law do they of themselves have any legal effect in English law unless made law by some statute. **11–053**

Under the Carriage of Goods by Sea Act, 1924, the substance of what were subsequently to become the Hague Rules were not made part of English law as such, but were compulsorily incorporated into bills of lading issued in this country. That Act was based upon the draft Convention; Art. IX of the final Convention was not part of the draft Convention yet the United Kingdom legislature chose to include in the rules as scheduled to the 1924 Act a sentence which corresponded to the first sentence of Art. IX of the Convention as it was finally agreed to. The 1924 Act has been repealed by the Carriage of Goods by Sea Act 1971 and was not in force at the date of this bill of lading.

. . .

Turning now to the Convention itself, it seems to me clear beyond argument that the first sentence of Art. IX is intended to qualify the reference to £100 sterling in Art. IV(5). No other purpose for the inclusion in the Convention of the relevant sentence of Art. IX has been suggested. There is no reason to suppose that those words were not intended to have any effect. They were clearly intended to have the effect of expressing the sterling figure as a gold value figure. This, in respect of the 1924 Act, was regarded as too obvious for argument by Devlin J. in *Pyrene Co Ltd v Scindia Navigation Co Ltd* [1954] 2 Q.B. 402 at p. 413 where he said:

"The limit stated in that rule is £100, but this is subject to Article IX which prescribes the figures to be taken to be the gold value."

Whether one looks at the matter as at the date of the 1924 Convention or as at the date of this bill of lading contract the provision that the limit in Art. IV, r. 5 is to be treated as a gold value presents no problem. . . .

. . .

In the present case I consider that the intention of the parties is clear and sufficiently precise. I am concerned with the construction of a commercial contract between a goods owner and carrier and there is no reason why the ordinary rules of construction should not be applied to such a document; indeed in so far as there is any rule of certainty applicable to such documents it is that the carrier, if he wishes to exclude or limit his liability, must do so by clear terms. The argument of the defendants in the present case stands that principle on its head.

. . .

. . . The defendants' arguments therefore fail. The gold value provision in Art. IX of the Convention is of sufficient clarity; it is effective. The defendants' submission how the provision should be applied likewise fails.

Notes

11–054   The case is an interpretation of the Hague Rules themselves, or at any rate the English translation of the authoritative French text. The reasoning applies to any bill of lading incorporating the Rules directly, without reference to particular legislation. Some bills of lading, however, expressly incorporate the Rules as set out in the Schedule to the United Kingdom Carriage of Goods by Sea Act 1924. The Schedule to the Carriage of Goods by Sea Act 1924 differed from the authoritative text, being based on an earlier draft. Hobhouse J. thought that his reasoning also applied to the Rules as set out in the 1924 Act, however.

The Rosa S was applied in Australia in *The Nadezhda Krupskaya* [1989] 1 Lloyd's Rep. 518, and also by Hobhouse J. in *Convoy Intercontinental Container Transport v Open Bulk Carriers Ltd.*

CONVOY INTERCONTINENTAL CONTAINER TRANSPORT v OPEN BULK CARRIERS LTD

Queen's Bench Division, 26 July 1990

Issues

11–055   The case involved the construction of a (Gencon) voyage charterparty, which contained the following clause:

> "13. *Amount of limitation.* The responsibility of the carrier shall in no case, whether governed by The Hague Rules or not, exceed the amount of £100 per package or other unit."

In the event, the Hague Rules were held not to have been incorporated into the charterparty, but the £100 in clause 13 was held to refer to the gold value in 1924.

11–056   HOBHOUSE J.: The final point concerned the meaning of £100 in clause 13. If it were not for the inclusion of the phrase "whether governed by The Hague Rules or not", the sum referred to would clearly be a simple monetary sum in the value of the currency at the time of settlement of the claim. £100 in an English law contract is £100 legal tender. But, in my judgment, the inclusion of the phrase "whether governed by The Hague Rules or not" either demonstrates that gold value is being referred to or creates an ambiguity which must be resolved against the carrier. Given that there is an intention to have a limit consistent with The Hague Rules, one has to take into account the provisions of Article 9 as well as Article 4(5) of the Convention. Article 9 provides that:

"The monetary units mentioned in this Convention are to be taken to be gold value."

The effect of this provision for a contract governed by English law was considered in *The Rosa S* [1989] Q.B. 419, a case where The Hague Rules were incorporated by contract. It was held that the limit was a gold value limit. In my judgment the effect of Clause 13 on the present contract is the same. No problem of calculation arises as it is accepted that, on this basis, the claims do not exceed the limit and can therefore be recovered in full.

Notes

American bills of lading may be expressed to "have effect subject to the **11–057** provisions of the Carriage of Goods by Sea Act of the United States, approved April 16, 1936 . . . " The United States Carriage of Goods by Sea Act 1936 fixes its own limit of $U.S. 500, and this figure is not defined in terms of gold value. The reasoning in *The Rosa S* clearly does not therefore apply to a bill of lading which expressly incorporates the United States legislation. In that event the package limitation is simply $500 cash value.

Definition of package:
The main problem on the package definition, which probably could not have been foreseen in 1924, was the development of container transport. Suppose 100 boxes are put into a container. Is the container the package, or is each box a separate package?

The *Hague-Visby Rules* clarify the position, and state that the container is the package, unless its contents are separately enumerated in the bill of lading. This interpretation reduces the value of the regime to cargo-owners, in the absence of separate enumeration, but from the viewpoint of the shipowner, allows easier calculation of potential liabilities, against which he is able to insure.

The Court of Appeal has recently interpreted the original Hague Rules the other way, more favourable to the cargo-owner.

THE RIVER GURARA

Court of Appeal (Civil Division). [1998] Q.B. 610, [1998] 1 Lloyd's Rep. 225

Decision:
It was held that for the purposes of Art. IV(5) of the *Hague Rules*, where parcels of **11–058** cargo were loaded in containers, it was the parcels and not the containers which constituted the relevant "packages".

Another aspect of this case (on which Hirst L.J. dissented in part) is discussed in para. 14–052, below.

PHILLIPS L.J.: The Hague Rules were the product of international con- **11–059** vention. They were incorporated into the domestic legislation of a large number of seagoing nations and became widely used as the terms which governed the international carriage of goods by sea. Two considerations follow from this. First, it is legitimate when construing the rules to have regard to their objects, as disclosed by the *travaux preparatoires* of the convention. Second, particular respect should be paid to decisions of other jurisdictions in respect of the meaning of the rules, for the stated object of the convention was the unification of the domestic laws of the contracting states relating to bills of lading (see *Stag Line Ltd v Foscolo Mango & Co Ltd* [1932] A.C. 328 at 342, 350, *per* Lord Atkin and Lord Macmillan and *The Hollandia* [1983] 1 A.C. 565 at 572 *per* Lord Diplock.)

The objects of the limitation provisions of the Hague Rules are considered in a number of the United States authorities to which we have been referred and in a number of learned articles. For present purposes it is helpful to note that—

"one of the main purposes of limitation was to benefit cargo owners . . . The intention of The Hague Rules was to give cargo a liberal limit of liability so as to preclude shipowners from inserting clauses in their bills of lading purporting to limit liability to ridiculously low figures." (See Anthony Diamond Q.C. "The Hague-Visby Rules" [1978] 2 L.M.C.L.Q. 225 at 229.)

Mr Kay [for the shipowners] did not seek to gainsay this purpose of limitation, but he submitted that there was another purpose, to which he sought to give paramount effect. He contended that one of the objects underlying the rules was to ensure that the shipowner was able to verify the extent of his liability. Where the nature and value of the goods inside a package were not specifically declared, the limit of liability would attach to the package itself. The number of packages would be apparent to the shipowner so that he could verify the limit of his liability. It followed that if a number of smaller packages were encased in a larger package, the appropriate package for limitation purposes was the larger one, for that was the only one that the shipowner could verify. Applying this principle, where packages were put inside a container, the container was the appropriate package for limitation purposes.

Colman J. was not attracted by this argument, nor am I. The verification principle is not apparent from consideration of the *travaux preparatoires* of the convention. Furthermore, as Colman J. observed, rr. 3 to 5 of Art. III [on which see further chapter 14, below] . . . , envisage circumstances in which the shipowner will not be able to verify the number of packages shipped.

Mr Russell [for the cargo-owners] submitted that, when the convention was concluded in 1924, a figure of £100 represented a fair figure for the average value of a package shipped. To apply the same figure to a huge container stuffed with many packages would defeat the object of preventing shipowners from limiting their liability to sums that were absurdly low by reference to the average values of cargoes shipped. I consider that there is force in this submission. If Mr Kay is correct, the change in the method of stowing and carrying cargo that occurred when containerisation was introduced effected a radical change in the limitation regime. I would not readily reach such a conclusion.

Mr Russell further submitted that to describe a container as a package was to strain the natural meaning of that word. With this also I agree. In *Bekol BV v Terracina Shipping Corp* (13 July 1988, unreported), which seems to be the only recorded case in which the English court has considered the meaning of "package" in the Hague Rules, Leggatt J. referred to the definition of that word in the Oxford English Dictionary: "A bundle of things packed up, whether in a box or other receptacle, or merely compactly tied up . . . " A huge metal container stuffed with goods which will normally themselves be made up in individual packages is not naturally described as a package.

These two considerations alone would lead me, in the absence of authority, to conclude that where the Hague Rules limit falls to be computed in relation to parcels of cargo which are loaded in containers, it is the parcels, and not the containers, which constitute the relevant packages.

When I turn to consider decisions on the point in other jurisdictions, they reinforce my conclusion. . . .

. . . The weight of this international authority, coupled with my provisional conclusion formed independently of it, leaves me in no doubt that in the present case the shipowners' limit of liability should be calculated on the basis of the number of packages carried in the containers rather than the number of containers,

Note

Both *The Rosa S* and *The River Gurara* were applied in the Hong Kong High Court in *Center Optical (Hong Kong) Ltd v Jardine Transport Services (China) Ltd* [2001] 2 Lloyd's Rep. 678, a case involving misdelivery of containerised cargo.   **11–060**

Another difficulty about containers is that they are often deck cargo, and the Rules, even as amended, did not apply to deck cargo or live animals. The 1971 Act allows them to apply, however, if the bill of lading or other relevant document is expressly made subject to the Rules.

Conclusion

In this section, therefore, we have seen two respects in which the *Hague Rules* provide the cargo-owner with better protection than *Hague-Visby Rules*, with the proviso that the currency cases depend on the version of the Rules incorporated.

(e) HAGUE-VISBY RULES: RESIDUAL PROBLEMS

(i) *Privity Problems*

The *Hague* and *Hague-Visby Rules* are a compromise between carrying and cargo-owning interests. If a cargo-owner, by suing in tort, can get around the Rules, carriers suffer the burdens of the compromise, without gaining the benefits. Art. IV *bis*, which was added by the Visby amendments, was intended to address   **11–061** this problem, being quite clearly directed at *Midland Silicones* (see above at para. 11–037):

> "1. The defences and limits of liability provided for in these Rules shall apply in any action against the carrier in respect of loss or damage to goods covered by a contract of carriage whether the action be founded in contract or in tort.
>
> 2. If such an action is brought against a servant or agent of the carrier (such servant or agent not being an independent contractor), such servant or agent shall be entitled to avail himself of the defences and limits of liability which the carrier is entitled to invoke under these Rules.
>
> 3. The aggregate of the amounts recoverable from the carrier, and such servants and agents, shall in no case exceed the limit provided for in these Rules.
>
> 4. Nevertheless, a servant or agent of the carrier shall not be entitled to avail himself of the provisions of this article, if it is proved that the damage resulted from an act or omission of the servant or agent done with intent to cause damage or recklessly and with knowledge that damage would probably result."

Unfortunately, the Rules work by being incorporated into bill of lading contracts (Art. II). Therefore, if the parties to the action are not party to a bill of lading contract the Rules do not apply, and Art. IV *bis* is not triggered. Therefore Art. IV *bis* has no effect on *Midland Silicones*, or any attempt by a cargo-owner, by suing in tort and relying on the privity of contract doctrine, to avoid those parts of the Rules which protect the carrier.

This was the view adopted by the Court of Appeal in *The Captain Gregos*,[61] where it became obvious (even if it had not been before) that privity could thwart the operation of the *Hague-Visby Rules*, just as with the earlier *Hague Rules*, in spite of the revisions. If no contract is expressed, or can be implied, between the parties to the action, then the substance of the Rules does not apply. The effect of the case is that, in the absence of a contract between cargo-owner and shipowner, the cargo-owner, by suing in tort, can avoid those parts of the Hague Rules which protect the shipowner. In *The Captain Gregos* itself, the cargo-owner attempted to do this in an attempt to avoid the one-year time bar. In principle, he could do so, but the case later went back to the Court of Appeal on the issue whether there *was* privity of contract between cargo-owner and shipowner. *The Captain Gregos (No. 2)* is considered in detail in para. 13–061, below.

Note that this aspect of privity of contract, whereby someone who is not party to the carriage contract cannot be burdened by its terms, is unaffected by recent legislation amending other aspects of the privity doctrine. The Carriage of Goods by Sea Act 1992 will make it rarer for there to be no contractual relationship between the parties, however.

PAUL TODD, CASENOTE ON THE CAPTAIN GREGOS

[1990] 10 Journal of International Banking Law N232–N234; [1989/90] 4 Oil and Gas Law and Taxation Review D47–D50

[This note covers The Captain Gregos and The Captain Gregos (No. 2). Only those parts relevant to the former are set out here, the remainder are discussed in chapter 13, below.]

---

[61] [1990] 1 Lloyd's Rep. 310.

Hague-Visby Rules: application of time bar where no carriage contract   **11–062**
between parties: misdelivery of cargo: whether contract between carrier
and receiver: Bills of Lading Act 1855, s.1: *Brandt v Liverpool* doctrine
*Compania Portorafti Commerciale SA v Ultramar Panama Inc, The Captain
Gregos* . . . [1990] 1 Lloyd's Rep. 310.
. . .
Bingham, Stocker and Slade L.JJ.

Facts:
The case involved a chain sale of a cargo of some 800,000 barrels, or
110,000 tonnes of Gulf of Suez crude, shipped in Egypt for delivery in
Rotterdam. The last two purchasers in the chain (P.E.A.G. and B.P.)
claimed that some of the cargo had been stolen by the shipowner, and
brought an action against him in conversion.

For various reasons, the action was not brought until more than a year
after the cargo had been discharged, and the carrier claimed the benefit of
the one year time bar in Article III(6) of the Hague-Visby Rules, which
were incorporated into the two bills of lading issued in respect of the
cargo:

" . . . the carrier and the ship shall in any event be discharged from all
liability whatsoever in respect of the goods, unless suit is brought
within one year of their delivery or of the date when they should have
been delivered. This period may, however, be extended if the parties so
agree after the cause of action has arisen."

*[The shippers were Ultramar, who resold the cargo to P.E.A.G., on f.o.b. terms
but such that P.E.A.G. were not party to the carriage contract. P.E.A.G. sold c.i.f.
to B.P. Thus, neither P.E.A.G. nor B.P. were party to an express contract with the
shipowner.]*

The case arose by way of originating summons, the carrier as plaintiff
seeking a determination that he could rely on the one year limitation
period, as against P.E.A.G. and B.P. (Ultramar having apparently dropped
out of the action).

Held . . . :

1. . . . Article III(6) was applicable to theft or misdelivery of the
   cargo.

2. But if the cargo-owners were not party to the carriage contract,
   none of the provisions of the Hague-Visby Rules would apply.
   Insufficient argument was heard on the issue *whether* the cargo-
   owners were party. This therefore was the issue before the court at
   the second hearing.

Comment . . . :

11–063   . . . Since Article III (6) applied on its construction, the question for decision was therefore whether, if the cargo-owners were not party to the carriage contract (the issue decided at the later hearing), the carrier could claim the benefit of the time bar, or by inference any other provision of the Hague-Visby Rules protecting him.

It has been clear since *Leigh & Sillivan Ltd v Aliakmon Shipping Co Ltd, The Aliakmon* [1986] A.C. 785 that a cargo-owner can avoid the *Hague* Rules by suing in tort, but the Hague-Visby Rules differ from the Hague Rules in a number of material respects. For example, Article IV *bis*, para. 1 provides:

> "The defences and limits of liability provided for in these Rules shall apply in any action against the carrier in respect of loss or damage to goods covered by a contract of carriage whether the action be founded in contract or in tort."

Further, the Hague-Visby Rules are given statutory force by the Carriage of Goods by Sea Act 1971, s.1(2) of which provides:

> "The provisions of the Rules, as set out in the Schedule to this Act, shall have the force of law."

Until *The Captain Gregos*, it was therefore possible to argue that the Hague-Visby Rules could have an independent force, rather than working only by incorporation into a carriage contract. Anthony Diamond Q.C., for example, argued that Article IV *bis* allowed the carrier to rely on the Rules "even if the carrier is being sued by someone who is not a party to the bill": [1978] L.M.C.L.Q. 225, 249.

After *The Captain Gregos*, this argument is no longer possible. Like the Hague Rules, the Hague-Visby Rules also operate only by incorporation into the carriage contract. This is in line with other articles, and in particular Article II, which clearly assumes that the responsibilities, liabilities, rights and immunities in the Rules are incorporated into the carriage contract, and have no independent force:

> "Subject to the provisions of Article VI, under every contract of carriage of goods by sea the carrier, in relation to the loading, handling, stowage, carriage, custody, care and discharge of such goods, shall be subject to the responsibilities and liabilities, and entitled to the rights and immunities hereinafter set forth."

Bingham L.J. also thought that the principle that only a party to a contract may sue on it, or be bound by its terms, was so fundamental that had Parliament intended to alter it, it would have used much clearer language than that used in the Carriage of Goods by Sea Act 1971:

"Whatever the law in other jurisdictions, the general principle that only a party to a contract may sue on it is well-established here. If the draftsmen of the 1924 or 1971 Acts had intended the respective rules to infringe that principle or appreciated that that was their effect, I think they would have sought to make that clear in the Acts. It would be strange if so fundamental a principle were to be so inconspicuously abrogated. The effect of Article IV *bis*, therefore, is merely that a cargo-owner who is party to the contract of carriage cannot improve his position suing in tort, rather than on the carriage contract: see, *e.g.* the argument advanced by Professor G.H. Treitel [1986] L.M.C.L.Q. 294, 304."

Another privity problem

The sellers' argument in *Pyrene v Scindia Navigation Co Ltd* was also an attempt by a cargo-owner to avoid the Hague Rules, on the grounds that there was no contract between himself and the shipowners. The argument was rejected, but only because a contract was found between the parties. This involved implying a contract between f.o.b. seller and shipowner, the express carriage contract having been entered into by the f.o.b. buyer (see paras 3–004 *et seq.*, above). **11–064**

PYRENE CO LTD v SCINDIA NAVIGATION CO LTD

Queen's Bench Division. [1954] 2 Q.B. 402

Facts and issues:
The facts were set out in paras 3–004 *et seq.*, above, and are more fully stated at the start of the passage set out from Devlin J.'s judgment at para. 11–073. Essentially, the cargo was dropped and damaged by the negligence of the shipowner during loading, while still the property of the f.o.b. seller. The seller sued the shipowner in tort, and the shipowner claimed the benefit of the Hague Rules liability limit of £200.[62] The issue was whether there was a contractual relationship between the f.o.b. seller and the shipowner. **11–065**

Held:

1. The shipowner was entitled to the benefit of the clause limiting liability to £200.

2. The buyer was shipper.[63] There was therefore no express contractual relationship between seller and shipowner.

3. The Hague Rules, incorporating the clause, applied to the loading process. See further below on this issue.

4. Although the buyer was shipper, the seller was party to an implied contract with the carrier, even though he did not expressly make the contract of carriage. The reasoning adopted was that buyer, seller and carrier were all parties in a joint venture. Therefore the seller was bound by the clause limiting liability to £200, despite not being expressly party to the contract of carriage.

[62] The £200 limit was derived from the British Maritime Law Association's Agreement of Aug. 1, 1950, which is no longer in force, having been superseded in the UK by Art. IV(5) of the Hague-Visby Rules.
[63] See further Ch. 3, above.

DEVLIN J.: *(on the implied contract, starting at 425) [Devlin J. had described the varieties of f.o.b. contract—see chapter 3—and concluded that the buyer was shipper, and continued:]*

11–066   The question at once arises: if, as the plaintiffs contend, there is no contractual relationship between them and the defendants, how do they get these goods on board? If the ship sails off without loading the goods the plaintiffs are in breach of their contract of sale. Have they no redress against the ship? Mr Megaw [for the sellers] argues that they would have none, and that vis-à-vis the sellers the ship in loading acts as a volunteer. This seems to me to be a position which none of the three parties would have accepted for a moment.

Let me look at the situation first from the standpoint of the shipper, I.S.D. In the ordinary case, such as I have been considering above, where the shipper takes out a bill of lading or an insurance policy, he has at the time of the contract himself got the property in the goods; the question whether he contracts for the benefit of subsequent owners depends on proof of his intention at the time of contracting. But where, as in this case, he has not got the property at the time of the contract, and does not intend to acquire it before the contract begins to operate, he must act as agent. He cannot intend otherwise; the intention is inherent in the act; he must either profess agency or confess himself a wrongdoer. For if the shipowner lifts the seller's goods from the dock without the seller's authority he is guilty of conversion to which the shipper, by requiring him to do it, makes himself a party.

Let me look at it now from the standpoint of the ship. If the shipowners were sued for conversion they would surely have redress against the shipper. A person who requests a carrier to handle goods must have the right to deal with them or it would not be safe to contract with him. A shipowner cannot be supposed to inquire whether the goods he handles do or do not belong to the shipper who entrusts them to his care; if the goods are not the shipper's there must be implied a warranty of authority by him that he has the right to contract with regard to them.

Then from the standpoint of the seller, if his goods are left behind, and it is said to him: "You made no contract with the ship; what else did you expect?" he would answer, I think, that he naturally supposed that all the necessary arrangements had been made by the shippers.

In brief, I think the inference irresistible that it was the intention of all three parties that the seller should participate in the contract of affreightment so far as it affected him. If it were intended that he should be a party to the whole of the contract his position would be that of an undisclosed principal and the ordinary law of agency would apply. But that is obviously not intended; he could not, for example, be sued for the freight. This is the sort of situation that is covered by the wider principle; the third party takes those benefits of the contract which appertain to his interest therein, but takes them, of course, subject to whatever qualifications with regard to them the contract imposes. It is argued that it is not reasonable to suppose that the seller would submit to the terms of a contract whose detail he does not know and which might not give him the sort of protection of which he would approve. I do not think that as a matter of business this is so. Most people board a bus or train without considering what protection they will get in the event of an accident. I see nothing unreasonably imprudent in a seller assuming that the buyer, whose stake in the contract is greater than his, would have obtained whatever terms are usual in the trade; if he were legally minded enough to inquire what they were, the answer would be that by statutory require-ment the contract was governed by the Hague Rules.

If this conclusion is wrong, there is an alternative way by which, on the facts of this case, the same result would be achieved. By delivering the goods alongside the seller impliedly invited the shipowner to load them, and the shipowner by lifting the goods impliedly accepted that invitation. The implied contract so created must incorporate the shipowner's usual terms; none other could have been contemplated; the shipowner would not contract for the loading of the goods on terms different from those which he offered for the voyage as a whole. . . . I do not think that the solution fits so well the circumstances of this case. First, it means that if the goods were not lifted there would be no contract; and while that does not arise in this case, a solution that leaves it in the air is not so acceptable as one that covers it. Secondly, I find it difficult to infer that the shipowner by lifting the goods intended to make any new contract; he would not know where the property in the goods lay; I think he must have supposed that he was acting under a contract already made through Bahr Behrend [their agents], and on the assumption that Bahr Behrend had authority to make it. Thirdly, I doubt whether the seller intended to make any sepa-rate contract when he sent down the goods; I think that he, too, would have supposed that they would be dealt with under the contract of affreightment.

Notes

1. The contract between seller and carrier was implied because of the conse-   **11–067**
quences which (according to Devlin J.) would flow if the seller were not party to the venture. For example, if the ship sailed without loading, the seller would thereby be put in breach of the contract of sale, but without any redress against the ship. Conversely, if the shipowner handled the goods in order to load them, he (and the shipper) could be sued by the seller for conversion.

2. This reasoning is not particularly convincing. If the ship sailed without loading the buyer would probably be regarded as having failed to nominate an effective ship, and conversely if the shipowner was sued merely for handling the goods he would have a defence to a conversion action based on the consent of the seller (*volenti non fit iniuria*), whether or not the seller was also party to a con-tract.

3. The decision was no doubt to be welcomed in preventing the f.o.b. seller, in a contract where the buyer was shipper, from by suing not on the contract of carriage, but in negligence, to avoid the exemption clauses in the carriage con-tract. It was assumed throughout, however, that to achieve this result, it was necessary for the plaintiffs and defendants to be party to a contract. Even if *Pyrene v Scindia* is correct, it will not always be possible to imply a contract between

them, so the case lays down no general principle. In *Midland Silicones Ltd v Scruttons Ltd*, above Viscount Simonds said of *Pyrene* that the decision "can be supported only on the facts of the case which may well have justified the implication of a contract between the parties." Whether it was even correct on its facts must surely be doubted in the light of more recent implied contract cases in paras 13–066, *et seq.*, below.

4. Neither the Visby amendments, nor any subsequent legislation sucessfully addresses this privity problem.

(ii) *Construction of Contract Arguments*

11–068   There have been a number of attempts to argue that the provisions of the *Hague-Visby Rules* protecting the shipowner do not, as a matter of construction, apply to certain types of breach of contract. The first such case concerned the time bar.

The time bar in the Hague-Visby Rules is contained in Article III(6), and is in the following terms:

"Subject to paragraph 6 *bis* the carrier and the ship shall in any event be discharged from all liability whatsoever in respect of the goods, unless suit is brought within one year of their delivery or of the date when they should have been delivered. This period may, however, be extended if the parties so agree after the cause of action has arisen."

Article III(6) of the original Hague Rules had been similar, also providing for a one year time bar, but without the word "whatsoever".

Anthony Diamond Q.C. observed ([1978] L.M.C.L.Q 225, at p. 256) that:

"There is the clearest possible evidence that the sole or main purpose of this amendment was to make the time limit apply where the goods had been delivered without production of bills of lading and so to make it unnecessary to require an indemnity given by a receiver to be kept open indefinitely."

Presumably "indefinitely" in this quote means the 6 year common law limitation period.

Diamond's view was based on the recommendations of the C.M.I.'s 26th Conference at Stockholm in 1963, which led to the Brussels Protocol in 1968 and hence the Visby amendments, but it has to be said that this is not entirely clear, because a separate two year time limit had originally been proposed for wrongful delivery, but had later been rejected.

In *The Captain Gregos*, the purchasers of a cargo of crude oil claimed that a quantity of their cargo has been stolen by the carrier, and wished to sue the carrier in tort. The carrier claimed the benefit of the one year time bar in Article III(6) of the Hague-Visby Rules, which were incorporated into the two bills of lading issued in respect of the cargo. The case arose by way of originating summons, the carrier as plaintiff seeking a determination that he could rely on the one year limitation period.

11–069   Hirst J. took the view that on its construction,[64] Article III(6) did not apply to misdelivery of the cargo (*i.e.* delivery to the wrong person). His reasoning was not limited to theft, but applied whether or not there was an allegation of dishonesty. His reasoning was that Article III(6) had to read in the light of Article II:

"Subject to the provisions of Article VI, under every contract of carriage of goods by sea the carrier, in relation to the loading, handling, stowage, carriage,

[64] [1989] 2 All E.R. 54 (first instance).

custody, care and discharge of such goods, shall be subject to the responsibilities and liabilities, and entitled to the rights and immunities hereinafter set forth."

In Hirst J.'s view, Article II limited the scope of the Hague-Visby Rules (including the exemptions and limitations contained therein) to the carrier's duty of care in relation to transportation from loading to discharge. The Rules embodied a compromise between carriers and cargo-owners, and this "package" ended at discharge. Thus, it did not extend to delivery of the cargo. It followed that Article III(6) did not apply to delivery of the cargo to the wrong person. His view was strengthened by Article I(e):

"'Carriage of goods'" covers the period from the time when the goods are loaded to the time they are discharged from the ship."

Hirst J. was not impressed by the view that the word "whatsoever" in Article III(6), which as explained above was added by the Visby amendments, was intended to protect the carrier in the event of delivery without production of a bill of lading. He was not prepared to invoke the discussions of the Stockholm Conference, which in Diamond's view would have led to the contrary conclusion (see above), although these discussions were referred to in the case. His reasoning was not entirely clear, but it seems that he thought the wording of Article II so clear that no argument as to legislative intention was necessary. Although he said he was adopting a purposive approach to construction, his conclusions were in fact the result of an absolutely literal interpretation of Article II.

Had Hirst J.'s reasoning stood it would have had far-reaching consequences for carriers, but the Court of Appeal (see also above) took the opposite view. Bingham L.J. said:

"It seems to me that the acts of which the cargo-owners complain are the most obvious imaginable breaches of Article III(2). A bailee does not properly and carefully carry, keep and care for goods if he consumes them in his ship's boilers or delivers them to an unauthorised recipient during the voyage. A bailee does not properly and carefully discharge goods if, whether negligently or intentionally, he fails to discharge them and so converts them to his own use. If the cargo-owners were to establish the facts they allege, and had brought suit within the year, I cannot see how a claim based on breach of the rules could fail. Both the cargo-owners and the judge tended to treat their claim as one of misdelivery, but that does not strike me as an apt of helpful way of characterising it.

Article III(6) provides that the carrier and the ship shall 'in any event be discharged from *all liability whatsoever in respect of the goods*' (my emphasis) unless suit is brought within one year. I do not see how any draftsman could use more emphatic language . . . I would hold that 'all liability whatsoever in respect of the goods' means exactly what it says. The inference that the one year time bar was intended to apply to all claims arising out of the carriage (or miscarriage) of goods by sea under bills subject to the Hague-Visby Rules is in my judgment strengthened by the consideration that Article III(6) is, like any time bar, intended to achieve finality and, in this case, enable the shipowner to clear his books . . . "

Another line of cases involves cargo which has been wrongly shipped above **11–070** deck. In *Wibau Maschinenefabric Hartman SA v Mackinnon Mackenzie & Co (The Chanda)* [1989] 2 Lloyd's Rep. 494 (applied in New Zealand in *The Pembroke* [1995]

2 Lloyd's Rep. 290), cargo[65] which the carriage contract required to have been shipped below deck was shipped above deck, and was damaged, in heavy weather, by seawater. Hirst J. held that the carrier could not rely on the package limitation clause in Article IV(5) of the unamended Hague Rules (which in the case would have limited the damages to 1,250 Deutschmarks per package). He thought that as a matter of construction, the package limitation clause could not have been intended to protect a shipowner who, by carrying the cargo above deck in breach of contract, so palpably increased the risk of damage to it. Such an interpretation would be repugnant to the main object of the contract, which was to stow the cargo below deck.

The reasoning is similar to that in *Glynn v Margetson* (see above), where a deviation clause was not to be construed in such a way as to defeat the main object and intent of the contract. Another case where similar reasoning is adopted is *Sze Hai Tong v Rambler Cycle Co Ltd* [1959] A.C. 576 (and the *Sze Hai Tong* line of cases—see para. 6–016, above).

At first sight, the reasoning looks similar to the fundamental breach of contract doctrine which was disapproved by the House of Lords in *Suisse Atlantique Societe D'Armement Maritime SA v NV Rotterdamsche Kolen Centrale* [1967] 1 A.C. 361 and *Photo Production Ltd v Securicor Transport Ltd* [1980] A.C. 827, [1980] 1 Lloyd's Rep. 545. Like *Glynn v Margetson*, however (see above), *The Chanda* (which is surely correct in principle) proceeds entirely on the construction of the clause, and Hirst J. clearly did not think his decision in any way inconsistent with anything said by their Lordships in *Suisse Atlantique*.

In *The Antares* [1987] 1 Lloyd's Rep. 424, the shipowner had also broken the carriage contract by carrying cargo above deck. Yet he was able to rely on the one year time bar in the *Hague-Visby Rules*, whereas the shipowner in *The Chanda* could not rely on the package limitation in the *Hague Rules*. In Hirst J.'s view (in *The Chanda*) the cases were quite different. The one year time bar was not of a nature which undermined the purpose of the shipowner's obligation to stow below deck, whereas the same could not be said of the package limitation. Since the principles that apply are of construction, there is no reason why the time bar cannot apply to such a breach, even if the package limitation does not. Attempting to reconcile the various cases, Hirst J. claimed to be adopting a principle of construction:

" . . . that clauses which are clearly intended to protect the shipowner provided he honours his contractual obligation to stow goods under deck do not apply if he is in breach of that obligation. This same principle seems to me to be reflected in . . . Lord Wilberforce's speech in the *Suisse Atlantique* case . . . As Lord Wilberforce said, this rule is quite clearly based on contractual intention.

I am satisfied that the package limitation clause falls fairly and squarely within this category, since it can hardly have been intended to protect the shipowner who, as a result of the breach, exposed the cargo in question to such palpable risk of damage. Otherwise the main purpose of the shipowners' obligation to stow below deck would be seriously undermined . . .

In my judgment there is nothing in the *Antares* case which conflicts with this view. The exception at issue there (the one year limitation clause) not only had statutory force by virtue of the terms of the 1971 Act (unlike the present clause), but was also not of a nature which in any way undermined the purpose of the shipowners' obligation to stow below deck."

---

[65] The control cabin of an asphalt drying and mixing plant, which was described as delicate equipment "which should never be stowed where it may be exposed to violent sea and weather conditions."

(iii) *Application of the Rules*

Article II applies the Rules only to contracts of carriage of goods by sea, and **11–071** Article 1(e) provides that " 'Carriage of goods' covers the period from the time when the goods are loaded to the time they are discharged from the ship." Both these provisions are unchanged from the Hague Rules.

Article 1(b) provides that " 'Contract of carriage' applies only to contracts of carriage covered by a bill of lading or any similar document of title, in so far as such document relates to the carriage of goods by sea, including any bill of lading or any similar document as aforesaid issued under or pursuant to a charter-party from the moment at which such bill of lading or similar document of title regulates the relations between a carrier and a holder of the same." Section 3 of the 1924 Act (set out above) applied to bills of lading. Section 1(2) of the 1971 Act provides that "The provisions of the Rules, as set out in the Schedule to this Act, shall have the force of law", but s.1(4) provides:

"Subject to subsection (6) below, nothing in this section shall be taken as applying anything in the Rules to any contract for the carriage of goods by sea, unless the contract expressly or by implication provides for the issue of a bill of lading or any similar document of title."

Section 1(6) provides:

"(6) Without prejudice to Article X (c) of the Rules, the Rules shall have the force of law in relation to—

(a) any bill of lading if the contract contained in or evidenced by it expressly provides that the Rules shall govern the contract, and

(b) any receipt which is a non-negotiable document marked as such if the contract contained in or evidenced by it is a contract for the carriage of goods by sea which expressly provides that the Rules are to govern the contract as if the receipt were a bill of lading,

but subject, where paragraph (b) applies, to any necessary modifications and in particular with the omission in Article III of the Rules of the second sentence of paragraph 4 and of paragraph 7."

In *Pyrene v Scindia*, the loss occurred before the goods had been shipped, and no bill of lading was therefore issued.

PYRENE CO LTD v SCINDIA NAVIGATION CO LTD

Queen's Bench Division. [1954] 2 Q.B. 402

The facts have already been set out briefly in chapter 3, but are also described **11–072** more fully in Devlin J.'s judgment here. The cargo was damaged during the loading process, before passing the ship's rail, and before a bill of lading had been issued; indeed, no bill of lading was ever issued, but Devlin J. held that the Hague Rules package limitation (at that time £200 in the UK) applied.

DEVLIN J.: This case raises questions of interest and importance upon **11–073** the interpretation of the Hague Rules and their applicability to a f.o.b. seller. The plaintiffs sold a piece of machinery, a fire tender, to the Government of India (which acted in this matter through a department known for short as; I.S.D.) for delivery f.o.b. London. I.S.D. nominated the *Jalazad*, one of the defendants' vessels, as the ship to be loaded under the contract of sale, and through their agents, Bahr Behrend & Co, made all the arrangements for the carriage of the goods. While the tender was being lifted on to the vessel by the ship's tackle, and before it was across the rail it was, through the fault of the ship, dropped and damaged. Under the contract of sale the property had not then passed to I.S.D. The damage to the tender cost £966 to repair and the plaintiffs sue for that sum. The defendants admit liability but claim that the amount is limited under article 4, rule 5, of the Hague Rules. The limit stated in that rule is £100, but this is subject to article 9 which prescribes that the figure is to be taken to be gold value. There are doubts about the interpretation and effect of this latter article, and they have been very sensibly resolved for the parties to this case by the acceptance of the British Maritime Law Association's Agreement of August 1, 1950, which fixes the limit at £200.

It is therefore for the defendants to establish that they are entitled to limit their liability. To do this they must show privity of contract between themselves and the plaintiffs, that the contract incorporated the rules, and that the rules are effective to limit their liability. The plaintiffs dispute all these points: they claim in tort for the damage done to their goods.

The fire tender was not the only piece of machinery supplied by the plaintiffs for shipment on board this ship, though it was the only piece which was damaged before shipment. A bill of lading had been prepared to cover the whole shipment; and it was issued to I.S.D. in due course but with the fire tender deleted from it. The bill of lading incorporated the Hague Rules and was subject to their provisions, as by the Carriage of Goods by Sea Act, 1924, s.3, it was bound to be. It is not disputed that in this case, as in the vast majority of cases, the contract of carriage was actually created before the issue of the bill of lading which evidences its terms.

I think it is convenient to begin by considering the effect of the rules, for Mr Megaw [for the sellers] contends that even if a bill of lading covering the fire tender had been issued incorporating the rules the holder of the bill would not be subject to immunity in respect of an accident occurring at this stage of the loading. If this is so, it disposes of the defendants' plea. If it is not so, I shall have to consider whether the rules affect the contract of affreightment when no bill of lading is issued, and whether the plaintiffs were a party to that or any similar contract.

Mr Megaw's argument turns upon the meaning to be given to article 1(e), which defines "carriage of goods" as covering "the period from the time when the goods are loaded on to the time when they are discharged from the ship." Mr Megaw says that these goods never were loaded on to the ship. In a literal sense obviously they were not. But Mr Megaw does not rely on the literal sense; there are rules which could hardly be made intelligible if they began to operate only after the goods had been landed on deck. He treats the word "on" as having the same meaning as in "free on board"; goods are loaded on the ship as soon as they are put across the ship's rail, which the tender never was. He submits that the rule (which, of course, has effect in English law only by virtue of its place in the Schedule to the Carriage of Goods by Sea Act, 1924) must be construed in accordance with English principles. He relies upon *Harris v Best, Ryley & Co* (1892) 68 L.T. 76 and *Argonaut Navigation Co Ltd v Ministry of Food* [1949] 1 K.B. 572, which lay down the rule that loading is a joint operation, the shipper's duty being to lift the cargo to the rail of the ship (I shall refer to that as the first stage of the loading), and the shipowner's to take it on board and stow it (I shall refer to that as the second stage).

Mr Megaw contends, therefore, that the accident occurred outside the period specified in article 1(e). So, he says, article 4, rule 5 (which limits liability), and, indeed, all the other rules which regulate the rights and responsibilities of the shipowner, do not apply. They are made applicable by article 2, which provides that "under every contract of carriage of goods by sea the carrier, in relation to the loading, handling, stowage, carriage, custody, care and discharge of such goods, shall be subject to the responsibilities and liabilities, and entitled to the rights and immunities hereinafter set forth." "Contract of carriage" is defined in article 1(b); the term "applies only to contracts of carriage covered by a bill of lading or any similar document of title, in so far as such document relates to the carriage of goods by sea." Then it is paragraph (e) of this article 1 which contains the definition of "carriage of goods" on which Mr Megaw relies. It is in this way, he argues, that if the casualty does not fall within the period covered by this last definition the rules do not apply to it.

In my judgment this argument is fallacious, the cause of the fallacy   **11–074** perhaps lying in the supposition inherent in it that the rights and liabilities under the rules attach to a period of time. I think that they attach to a contract or part of a contract. I say "part of a contract" because a single contract may cover both inland and sea transport; and in that case the only part of it that falls within the rules is that which, to use the words in the definition of "contract of carriage" in article 1(b), "relates to the carriage of goods by sea." Even if "carriage of goods by sea" were given by definition the most restricted meaning possible, for example, the period of the voyage, the loading of the goods (by which I mean the whole operation of loading in both its stages and whichever side of the ship's rail) would still relate to the carriage on the voyage and so be within the "contract of carriage."

Article 2 is the crucial article which for this purpose has to be construed. It is this article that gives the carrier all his rights and immunities, including the right to limit his liability. He is entitled to do that "in relation to the loading" and "under every contract of carriage." Now I shall have to consider later the meaning of "loading" in article 2 and whether it is such as to exclude what I have called the first stage, that is, the operations on the shore side of the ship's rail. For the moment I am concerned only to see whether its meaning is cut down by the definition in article 1(e) on which Mr Megaw relies. The only phrase in article 2 that can out it down is the one I have quoted: "under every contract of carriage"; it is only in so far as article 1(e) operates through the definition of "contract of carriage" that it can have any effect on article 2. I have already sought to demonstrate that, however limited the period in article 1(e) may be, the loading in both its stages must still relate to it and so be within the definition of contract of carriage.

A precise construction of article 1(e), while not irrelevant, is in no way conclusive of the point I have to decide, which turns, I think, upon the meaning of "loading" in article 2.

But before I try to elucidate that, let me state my view of article 1(e). For, as I have said, though not dominant, it is not irrelevant; in construing "loading" in article 2 you must have regard to similar expressions throughout the rules, article 1(e) included. In my judgment, no special significance need be given to the phrase "loaded on." It is not intended to specify a precise moment of time. Of course, if the operation of the rules began and ended with a period of time a precise specification would be necessary. But they do not. It is legitimate in England to look at section 1 of the Act, which applies the rules not to a period of time but "in relation to and in connexion with the carriage of goods by sea." The rules themselves show the same thing. The obligations in article 3, rule 1, for example, to use due diligence to make the ship seaworthy and man and equip her properly are independent of time. The operation of the rules is determined by the limits of the contract of carriage by sea and not by any limits of time. The function of article 1(e) is, I think, only to assist in the definition of contract of carriage. As I have already pointed out, there is excluded from that definition any part of a larger contract which relates, for example, to inland transport. It is natural to divide such a contract into periods, a period of inland transport, followed perhaps by a period of sea transport and then again by a period of inland transport. Discharging from rail at the port of loading may fall into the first period; loading on to the ship into the second. The reference to "when the goods are loaded on" in article 1(e) is not, I think, intended to do more than identify the first operation in the series which constitutes the carriage of goods by sea; as "when they are discharged" denotes the last. The use of the rather loose word "cover," I think, supports this view.

11–075 There is another reason for thinking that it would be wrong to stress the phrase "loaded on" in article 1(e). It is no doubt necessary for an English court to apply the rules as part of English law, but that is a different thing from assuming them to be drafted in the light of English law. If one is inquiring whether "loaded on" in article 1(e) has a different meaning from "loaded" or "loading" in other parts of the rules, it would be mistaken to look for the significant distinction in the light of a conception which may be peculiar to English law. The idea of the operation being divided at the ship's rail is certainly not a universal one. It does not, for example, apply in Scotland: *Glengarnock Iron and Steel Co Ld v Cooper & Co* (1895) 22 R. 672, *per* Lord Trayner (at 676). It is more reasonable to read the rules as contemplating loading and discharging as single operations. It is no doubt possible to read article 1(e) literally as defining the period as being from the completion of loading till the completion of discharging. But the literal interpretation would be absurd. Why exclude loading from the period and include discharging? How give effect to the frequent references to loading in other rules? How reconcile it with article 7 which allows freedom of contract "prior to the loading on and subsequent to the discharge from"? Manifestly both operations must be included. That brings me back to the view that article 1(e) is naming the first and last of a series of operations which include in between loading and discharging, "handling, stowage, carriage, custody and care." This is, in fact, the list of operations to which article 2 is by its own terms applied. In short, nothing is to be gained by looking to the terms of article 1(e) for an interpretation of article 2.

I think, therefore, that article 1(e), which was the spearhead of Mr Megaw's argument, turns out to be an ineffective weapon. But that still leaves it necessary to consider the meaning of "loading" in article 2. Just how far does the operation of loading, to which article 2 grants immunity, extend? Now I have already given reasons against presuming that the framers of the rules thought in terms of a divided operation, and in the absence of such a presumption the natural meaning of "loading" covers the whole operation. How far can that be pressed? Article 3, rule 2, for example, provides: "the carrier shall properly and carefully load," etc. If "load" includes both stages, does that oblige the shipowner, whether he wants to or not, to undertake the whole of the loading? If so, it is a new idea to English lawyers, though perhaps more revolutionary in theory than in practice. But if not, and "load" includes only the second stage, then should it not be given a similar meaning in article 2 with the result that immunity extends only to the second stage?

There is, however, a third interpretation to article 3, rule 2. The phrase "shall properly and carefully load" may mean that the carrier shall load and that he shall do it properly and carefully: or that he shall do whatever loading he does properly and carefully. The former interpretation perhaps fits the language more closely, but the latter may be more consistent with the object of the rules. Their object as it is put, I think, correctly in Carver's *Carriage of Goods by Sea*, 9th ed. (1952), p. 186, is to define not the scope of the contract service but the terms on which that service is to be performed. The extent to which the carrier has to undertake the loading of the vessel may depend not only upon different systems of law but upon the custom and practice of the port and the nature of the cargo. It is difficult to believe that the rules were intended to impose a universal rigidity in this respect, or to deny freedom of contract to the carrier. The carrier is practically bound to play some part in the loading and discharging, so that both operations are naturally included in those covered by the contract of carriage. But I see no reason why the rules should not leave the parties free to determine by their own contract the part which each has to play. On this view the whole contract of carriage is subject to the rules, but the extent to which loading and discharging are brought within the carrier's obligations is left to the parties themselves to decide.

11–076   I reject the interpretation of loading in article 2 as covering only the second stage of the operation. Such authority as there is is against it. If loading under the rules does not begin before the ship's rail, by parity of reasoning discharging should end at the ship's rail; but so to hold would be contrary to the decision of Roche J. in *Goodwin, Ferreira & Co Ld v Lamport Holt Ld* (1929) 141 L.T. 494.

Since the shipowner in this case in fact undertook the whole operation of loading it is unnecessary to decide which of the other two interpretations is correct. I prefer the more elastic one, that which I have called the third. There appears to be no binding authority on the point. I have noted the view expressed in Carver; on the other hand, Temperley's *Carriage of Goods by Sea Act, 1924*, 4th ed. (1932), p. 26, and Scrutton on *Charterparties and Bills of Lading*, 15th ed. (1948), p. 160, consider that the carrier is responsible for the whole of the loading. However, it is sufficient for me to say that on the facts of this case the rights and immunities under the rules extend to the whole of the loading carried out by the defendants and, therefore, Mr Megaw's first point fails.

I think, if I may so put it, that it is a good thing that it should fail. There must be many cases of carriage to which the rules apply where the ship undertakes the whole of the loading and discharging; and it would be unsatisfactory if the rules governed all but the extremities of the contract. It so happens that in this case (rather unusually) the exemption of the extremities would benefit the shipper. For the form of bill of lading which would have applied is made subject to the rules *simpliciter*, and does not set out the traditional mass of clauses which the rules have rendered generally ineffective. If they were there the shipper would probably fare worse under them than under the rules. It would certainly be a triumph for the innate conservatism of those who have not scrapped their small print if, though only on the outer fringes, it was to come into its own. But the division of loading into two parts is suited to more antiquated methods of loading than are now generally adopted and the ship's rail has lost much of its nineteenth-century significance. Only the most enthusiastic lawyer could watch with satisfaction the spectacle of liabilities shifting uneasily as the cargo sways at the end of a derrick across a notional perpendicular projecting from the ship's rail.

The next contention on behalf of the plaintiffs is that the rules are incorporated in the contract of carriage only if a bill of lading is issued. The basis for this is in the definition of article 1(b) of "contract of carriage"; I have already quoted it, and it "applies only to contracts of carriage covered by a bill of lading." The use of the word "covered" recognises the fact that the contract of carriage is always concluded before the bill of lading, which evidences its terms, is actually issued. When parties enter into a contract of carriage in the expectation that a bill of lading will be issued to cover it, they enter into it upon those terms which they know or expect the bill of lading to contain. Those terms must be in force from the inception of the contract; if it were otherwise the bill of lading would not evidence the contract but would be a variation of it.

Moreover, it would be absurd to suppose that the parties intend the terms of the contract to be changed when the bill of lading is issued: for the issue of the bill of lading does not necessarily mark any stage in the development of the contract; often it is not issued till after the ship has sailed, and if there is pressure of office work on the ship's agent it may be delayed several days. In my judgment, whenever a contract of carriage is concluded, and it is contemplated that a bill of lading will, in due course, be issued in respect of it, that contract is from its creation "covered" by a bill of lading, and is therefore from its inception a contract of carriage within the meaning of the rules and to which the rules apply. There is no English decision on this point; but I accept and follow without hesitation the reasoning of Lord President Clyde in *Harland & Wolff Ltd v Burns & Laird Lines Ltd* [1931] S.C. 722.

Mr Megaw contends that the parties in this case contemplated a shipped bill of lading and, therefore, that they intended the application of the rules to the contract to be conditional upon the issue of a shipped bill. No doubt the parties contemplated a shipped bill of lading. But then they also contemplated a shipment. When no shipment took place there was nothing in this contract, I think, to prevent the shipper from demanding under article 3, rule 3, a "received for shipment" bill if it were of any use to him. Mr Megaw's point, I think, is that if a bill of lading as contemplated is issued, the terms of it (including the rules) operate retrospectively; if the bill is not issued, the terms do not come into operation at all. But I can see no reason for treating the bill of lading differently from any other formal contractual document. If the agreement was made "subject to" bill of lading there would be room for Mr Megaw's argument; but there would also be no legal contract at all until the bill of lading was issued, and it is not suggested that this is the case here.

[Devlin J. then went on to consider the privity aspects of the case—see further paras 11–065 et seq., above.]

Notes

1. Mr Megaw, for the sellers, advanced a number of arguments here, all of **11–077** which were rejected by Devlin J. The arguments were as follows:

    (a) Article II applies the rights and immunities in the Rules only to "contract[s] of carriage of goods by sea". Contract of carriage in Article 1(b) is envisaged as "relat[ing] to the carriage of goods". Carriage of goods takes place, according to Article 1(e), in "the period from the time when the goods are loaded to the time they are discharged from the ship". This period does not start until the goods were loaded in the f.o.b. sense, that is to say, when they had crossed the ship's rail. Therefore there was no carriage of goods, to which the rights and immunities in the Rules applied. Devlin J.'s view was that even if this definition of carriage of goods were to be accepted, the entire loading process "relates to" it, as required by Article 1(b), and therefore that the time-based argument should fail. Devlin J. also took the view that "loading" in Article II covered the whole loading process, and was not limited to stowage, after the goods had crossed the ship's rail.

(b) Under Article 1(b), the contract of carriage "applies only to contracts of carriage covered by a bill of lading," and here no bill of lading was ever issued (because the goods were never loaded). Devlin J.'s view was that a contract is "covered by" a bill of lading as long as it is "contemplated that a bill of lading will, in due course, be issued".

2. On the application of the Rules, Devlin J. held that, held that, at least where (as in the case itself) the shipowner had undertaken responsibility for the entirety of the loading and discharging process, the Rules should also apply to the entirety of the process. However, the object of the Rules is "to define not the scope of the contract service but the terms on which that service is to be performed." There is therefore nothing in the Rules to prevent the shipowner taking responsibility for part only, or indeed none of the loading and discharge process.[66] On this distinction, see also discussion of *The Coral* in para. 12–017, below.

3. The effect of Article 1(e) was, however, to exclude, for example, inland stages of a multimodal transport operation.

4. The case is an interpretation of the original *Hague Rules*, as enacted in the U.K. in the Carriage of Goods by Sea Act 1924. Though the *Hague Rules* have been replaced, no material changes have occurred in any of the Articles discussed, and all the arguments would apply equally to the *Hague-Visby Rules*. It follows that the case is still an authority on the interpretation of the Rules.

No bill of lading

In *Pyrene v Scindia* it was envisaged that the goods would be carried under a bill of lading, albeit that one was never in fact issued. The combined effect of s.1(6) of the 1971 Act and Article X is that the *Hague-Visby Rules* may not apply where the goods are carried other than under a bill of lading. In *The European Enterprise*,[67] Steyn J. observed that:

"It is the invariable practice of all English cross channel operators not to issue bills of lading for the cross channel Ro-Ro ferry trade. Instead, they issue commercial non-negotiable receipts."

The effect was that the minimum package limitation did not apply, and the carrier was able to substitute a lower limit. This clearly provides a possible loophole for shipowners who wish to avoid the application of the Rules.

THE HAPPY RANGER

Court of Appeal. [2002] E.W.C.A. Civ. 694

11–078 Goods were damaged on loading, *en route* from Italy, which is a contracting state to the *Hague-Visby Rules*. The contract was on the basis of a specimen bill of lading, but no bill of lading was ever issued. Moreover, even if it had been, the terms of the carriage contract had already been settled, so it would have operated merely as a receipt, and not contained the contract of carriage (see further chapter 12, below). The carrier attempted to limit liability to the contractual limit of £100 per package, but the Court of Appeal held (Rix L.J. dissenting) that the *Hague-Visby Rules* applied.

---

[66] Here the shipper would have benefited from the non-application of the Rules, but more usually it is the carrier who benefits from their exclusion.

[67] [1989] 2 Lloyd's Rep. 182.

Tuckey L.J.: [21] ... Based on what Devlin J. said in *Pyrene Co Ltd v* **11–079** *Scindia Steam Navigation Co Ltd* [see above] the judge accepted that the fact that no bill of lading had been issued in respect of the goods in question was not conclusive. Use of the word "covered" reflected the fact that bills of lading were often not issued until after the ship had sailed. A bill of lading evidenced an earlier contract. Provided it was contemplated that a bill of lading would be issued which would contain the terms of the contract it was covered by a bill. But the judge continued ([2002] 1 All E.R. (Comm.) 176 at [25]):

"However, the present is not in my judgment a case in which Parsons [shippers] were entitled to demand, at or after shipment, a bill of lading setting forth the terms of the contract ... The contract of carriage as between Parsons and the Owners was always to be found in the contract of 7 October 1997. Those parties did not intend or expect that as between themselves any bill of lading issued would be of any contractual effect independent of the contract made on 7 October 1997 and in particular they did not intend that any bill of lading issued would evidence the terms of their contract. The terms of their contract were already adequately and completely evidenced by the contract and the specimen form of bill of lading attached thereto. The parties envisaged that any bill of lading issued might in fact contain terms at variance with those which they had already agreed, which latter were to prevail."

[22] Mr Milligan [for the cargo-owners] submits that the judge's approach was wrong. The question was not whether the bill of lading to be issued would contain the terms of the contract of carriage but simply whether one was to be issued. The language of s.1(4) of the 1971 Act makes it clear that Art. I(b) simply requires that the contract should provide for the issue of a bill of lading. Here the contract did so provide so the Hague-Visby Rules apply. The issue of a bill of lading rarely creates a contract. Normally it evidences a contract which pre-exists its issue. Whether it pre-exists it in oral or written form is irrelevant.

[23] Mr Teare Q.C., for the respondents [carriers], supported the judge's reasoning. He accepted that the contract did contemplate the issue of a bill of lading but argued that as this would not contain the terms of the contract it would not be a bill to which the Hague-Visby Rules would apply. He relied by analogy, as did the judge, on *President of India v Metcalfe Shipping Co Ltd* [1970] 1 Q.B. 289 [see chapter 12]. In that case the dispute was between voyage charterers and owners as to whether a claim for short delivery was subject to the jurisdiction clause in the charterparty or in the bills of lading. This court held that as the charterparty authorised the master to sign the bill of lading "without prejudice to the charter party", it operated as a mere receipt for the goods or as a document of title and, whilst forming part of the narrative, had no impact on the charterparty. Mr Teare's alternative submission is that the contract in this

case was a voyage charterparty and he relies on Art. V of the Hague-Visby Rules.

[24] On this issue I accept Mr Milligan's submissions. It does not seem to me that the Hague-Visby Rules are concerned with whether the bill of lading contains terms which have been previously agreed or not. It is the fact that it is issued or that its issue is contemplated which matters. As it was put in one of the cases "the bill of lading is the bedrock on which the mandatory code is founded". If a bill of lading is or is to be issued the contract is "covered" by it or "provides for its issue" within the definitions of Art. I(b) and s.1(4) of the 1971 Act. The Hague-Visby Rules make special provision for charterparties and bills issued under them. I do not think the *President of India* case helps. That case was only concerned with a conflict between the terms of the charterparty and the terms of the bill of lading. It was not concerned with the application of the Hague-Visby Rules. As to Mr Teare's alternative submission, I do not think it is possible to characterise the contract in this case as a voyage charterparty. It was obviously a carefully drawn document and although it does contain terms which are to be found in voyage charterparties, it emphatically calls itself a contract of carriage and that is what I think it is. The fact that the goods to be carried were a part cargo supports this conclusion, although I accept that this factor is not conclusive.

[25] It follows that I think the Hague-Visby Rules applied compulsorily to the contract of carriage and that the judge's conclusion on this issue was wrong. . . .

Second Issue

In *The Rafaela S*,[68] even though it had to be produced for delivery of the cargo to be made, Langley J. held that a straight bill of lading was not a bill of lading for the purposes of s.1(4) of the Carriage of Goods by Sea Act 1971, as indeed it is not for the purposes of the Carriage of Goods by Sea Act 1992 (see chapter 13, below). His view (at para. 21) was that a " 'document of title' . . . is . . . the antithesis of a document which can evidence the title of only one person. It is general not specific to one person." This issue was left open in *The Happy Ranger*, where the Court of Appeal held the bill not to be a straight bill.

11–080   TUCKEY L.J.: [27] A "straight" bill has no English law definition, but the term derives, it appears, from earlier United States legislation referring to a "straight" bill as one in which the goods are consigned to a specific person as opposed to an "order" bill where the goods are consigned to the order of anyone named in the bill or bearer. Bills to "order" or "bearer" are transferable by endorsement and delivery and entitle the holder to possession of the goods upon production of the bill. They will not necessarily transfer title to the goods and are not negotiable in the strict sense of that word either, although colloquially such bills are described as documents of title which are negotiable.

---

[68] [2002] E.W.H.C. 593 (Comm.).

[After concluding that the bill of lading in the case was not a straight bill, he continued:]

[30] Mr Milligan submits that even if the parties contemplated the issue of a "straight" bill, such a bill would be a bill of lading or similar document of title within the meaning of the Hague-Visby Rules. In making this submission he defies the unanimous views of textbook writers. There is no case which decides this point; some of the textbooks are written by the same authors and others rely on one another. *C.P. Henderson & Co v Comptoir d'Escompte de Paris* (1873) L.R. 5 P.C. 253 is only authority for the proposition that a bill naming a consignee which does not contain the words "or order or assigns" is not negotiable (transferable). Mr Milligan says that nevertheless a consignee is within the class which the Hague-Visby Rules are designed to protect and because (as in this case) the bill is his only key to possession of the goods, it must be regarded at least as a document of title in the sense contemplated by the Hague-Visby Rules if it is not a bill of lading within the meaning of those rules. The arguments about this need also to take into account the provisions of the Carriage of Goods by Sea Act 1992 which now define "straight" bills not as bills of lading at all but as sea waybills.

[31] Because I have decided that the bills actually issued in this case were not "straight" bills, it is not and will not be necessary to decide this point in this case. And nor do I think that we should do so. It should be decided in a case where it arises and initially at first instance rather than on appeal. I hope I have said enough to indicate that it is not an easy point. All I need add is that I think it would be unwise to assume that the statements in the textbooks are correct.

(3) HAMBURG RULES

The Hague-Visby regime clearly revolves around the traditional bill of lading, **11–081** a document which is no longer in universal use (see further chapter 15, below). The *Hamburg Rules*, which were devised by a Working Party of the United Nations Commission on International Trade Law (UNCITRAL), favour carriers less than the existing regimes, and apply to contracts of carriage by sea, whether or not a bill of lading is issued (see Articles 2 and 18). The Hamburg Rules have not been adopted in the UK, and appear unlikely to gain widespread international acceptance.

The *Hamburg Rules* are set out in full in Appendix I, below. See also generally *A Guide to the Hamburg Rules, An Industry Report*, prepared by Luddeke and Johnson (LLP, 1991).

Appendix I (below) also sets out a background to the *Hamburg Rules*, which is an explanatory note by the UNCITRAL Secretariat. The following main features can be observed (from the explanatory note):

1. The *Hague Rules* system, which in this context includes the Visby amendments, was seen as heavily favouring carriers at the expense of shippers (para. 3). They were also seen to be out of date technologically.

2. The *Hamburg Rules* apply whether or not a bill of lading is issued, but like the *Hague* and *Hague-Visby Rules*, do not apply to charterparties (paras 11–13).

3. The period of responsibility is defined more widely, but is probably the same as that under the *Hague Rules*, in the light of *Pyrene v Scindia*—see above. (Note that the *Hamburg Rules* cover only sea carriage, and would therefore not resolve the issues of multimodal transport, considered in chapter 15, below.)

4. The extensive exempted perils provided by the Hague Rules system were thought to too favourable to the carrier, and to be out of date (paras 16–18).

5. Deck cargo, and liability for delay, are now specifically covered (paras 19–21).

6. Financial limits are raised (paras 22–27).

7. There is another attempt to deal with the *Midland Silicones* problem (para. 28). However, since Article II applies the Rules to "contracts of carriage by sea", it would probably be subject to precisely the same *Captain Gregos* reasoning as the Hague-Visby regime.

8. There are provisions to deal with through (but not multimodal) transport (paras 30–31).

THE MERCHANTS GUIDE, P & O CONTAINERS

(International ed., 1995), p. 43

11–082   *[Footnotes are mine. Minor grammatical errors are uncorrected.]*

In March 1978 an international conference in Hamburg adopted a new set of rules (the Hamburg Rules) which radically alter the liability which shipowners have to bear for loss or damage to goods in the courts of those nations where the Rules apply. The main differences between the new Rules and the old Hague-Visby Rules are as follows:

(a) The Carrier will be liable for loss, damage or delay to the goods occurring whilst in his charge unless he proves that *"he, his servants or agents took all measures that could reasonably be required to avoid the occurrence and its consequences."* The detailed list of exceptions set out in the Hague and Hague-Visby Rules is no longer available to the Carrier. In particular the Carrier is no longer exonerated from liability arising from errors in navigation, management of the ship or fire. All the case law that has built up over seventy years since the Hague Rules were introduced, and which has largely clarified and made certain the effect of those Rules, to the great benefit of both Merchant and Carrier alike, will be inapplicable where these Rules are applied. They are therefore bound to lead to far more disputes. No less a person than Lord Diplock observed about the requirement that the shipowner is liable unless he proves that he *"Took all measures that could reasonably be required to avoid the occurrence and its consequences"* that *"speaking from many years of experience as a judge I think, given that very broad definition, I could decide almost everything as I personally like and I think other judges may feel exactly the same.*" Hardly a recipe for certainty!

(b) The Carrier is liable for delay in delivery if "*the goods have not been delivered at the port of discharge provided for in the contract of carriage within the time expressly agreed upon or, in the absence of such agreement, within the time which it would be reasonable to require of a diligent carrier having regard to the circumstances of the case.*"[69]

(c) The dual system for calculating the limit of liability, either by reference to package or weight as set out in the Hague-Visby Rules, has been readopted, but the amounts have been increased by about 25% to SDR 835 per package and SDR 2.5 per kilo. The liability for delay is limited to an equivalent of two and a half times the freight payable for the goods delayed, but not exceeding the total freight payable for the whole contract under which the goods were shipped. In no case shall the aggregate liability for both loss/ damage and delay exceed the limit for loss/damage.

(d) The Hamburg Rules cover all contracts for the carriage by sea other than charter parties whereas the Hague/Hague-Visby Rules only apply where a bill of lading is issued. The Hamburg Rules are therefore applicable to Waybills, Consignment Notes, etc. (One of the few advantageous provisions in the Hamburg Rules).

(e) They cover shipment of live animals and deck cargo, whereas Hague/Hague-Visby Rules may not.

(f) They apply to both imports and exports to/from a signatory nation (*i.e.* all that nations trade) whereas Hague/Hague-Visby (if applied as intended by the drafters) apply to exports only. This will create and undesirable forum shopping for litigation.

[The commentator lists the relatively small number of signatories and continues:]

It is unfortunate that we should be burdened with these new rules, which will add to the confusion of practitioners over the recourse to which they are entitled by destroying the uniformity currently in existence, as the Hague and Hague-Visby Rules are complementary. Hamburg, as a third force, introduces conflict and threatens to be a " '*lawyers' charter to print money*"!

Fortunately, unless one trades with Africa, the chances of encountering Hamburg Rules are relatively remote at present, as none of the major trading nations is, or seems likely to become a Hamburg signatory in the near future. . . .

---

[69] Article 5.2.

Note

11–083   It is perhaps unsurprising that P & O are not favourably disposed towards rules under which they would incur greater liability. Cargo-owners, by contrast, would favour the *Hamburg Rules* over the *Hague-Visby Rules*.

UNCITRAL observe (at para. 48) that:

> "The Hamburg Rules offer the potential of achieving greater uniformity in the law relating to the carriage of goods by sea than do the Hague Rules."

Maybe so, but the potential has not been achieved. The *Hague Rules* were remarkably successful, from a harmonisation viewpoint, being adopted almost everywhere in the world. Now, by contrast, there are three regimes in operation. Perhaps this does no more than illustrate the difficulties of harmonisation, in a dynamic situation, where change is required. In fairness, UNCITRAL go on to recommend (at para. 49) that:

> "[i]n order to achieve their potential for uniformity of law in this area, [the Hamburg Rules] must be adhered to by States worldwide."

I do not know the source of the quote near the end of the passage.

CHAPTER 12

THE BILL OF LADING AND THE CONTRACT OF CARRIAGE

(1) RELATIONSHIP BETWEEN BILL OF LADING AND CARRIAGE CONTRACT

(a) BILL OF LADING NOT THE CARRIAGE CONTRACT

THE process of carriage is described in greater detail in chapter 14, below, but a **12–001** shipped bill of lading should be issued only after the goods have been loaded on board the ship. By that stage, however, the carriage contract must already have been concluded. Any terms in the bill of lading are therefore necessarily post-contractual. They may be a statement by the carrier of his view of the terms of the carriage contract. They may be strong evidence of the terms of that contract, especially if the shipper had regularly contracted with the same carrier on the same bill of lading terms. but the carrier cannot unilaterally impose new terms after loading. It follows that the terms in the bill of lading cannot be conclusive evidence of the terms of the carriage contract. Indeed, in *Heskell v Continental Express*, in para. 14–056, below, the bill of lading did not evidence even the existence of a carriage contract.

Probably the commonest situation where the bill of lading terms will differ from the carriage contract is where the shipper is also charterer of the vessel. There the charterparty will be the carriage contract and the bill of lading merely a receipt (see *The El Amria and The El Minia* at para. 3–008, above). Charterparty and bill of lading terms will certainly differ if the charterparty is on a period basis (time or demise), and whereas the *Hague-Visby Rules* apply compulsorily to bill of lading contracts in the UK, they do not apply to charterparties (see also *The Albazero* in para. 13–038, below).

The following case is perhaps rarer, where the shipowner had made promises prior to shipment, which were not incorporated into the bill of lading. The pre-shipment promises were nevertheless incorporated into the carriage contract.

ARDENNES (CARGO OWNERS) v ARDENNES (OWNERS) (THE ARDENNES)

King's Bench Division. [1951] 1 K.B. 55

The goods in question were mandarin oranges to be shipped from Spain to **12–002** England. Before the contract of carriage was concluded the shipowners promised the shippers orally that they would arrive in London by November 30, 1947, but they did not actually arrive until December 5. The arrival date was important to the shipper because import duty was imposed from December 1.

A clause in the bill of lading allowed the shipowners to deviate on the voyage, and the shipowners pleaded that in defence.

Held:

The shippers could not rely on the deviation clause in the bill of lading. It was the oral promise, rather than the bill of lading terms, which were incorporated into the carriage contract.

12–003   LORD GODDARD C.J.: It is, I think, well settled that a bill of lading is not in itself the contract between the shipowner and the shipper of goods, though it has been said to be excellent evidence of its terms ... [1] The contract has come into existence before the bill of lading is signed; the latter is signed by one party only, and handed by him to the shipper usually after the goods have been put on board. No doubt if the shipper finds that the bill contains terms with which he is not content, or does not contain some of the terms for which he has stipulated, he might, if there were time, demand his goods back; but he is not, in my opinion, for that reason, prevented from giving evidence that there was in fact a contract entered into before the bill of lading was signed different from that which is found in the bill of lading or containing some additional term. He is not party to the preparation of the bill of lading, nor does he sign it. It is unnecessary to cite authority further than the two cases already mentioned for the proposition that the bill of lading is not itself the contract; therefore in my opinion evidence as to the true contract is admissible.

Notes

1. Unlike a bill of lading a charterparty is a contract, so if the shipper is also charterer the charterparty terms prevail over bill of lading terms, if there is a conflict, and over any oral pre-shipment promises.

2. It could be very inconvenient if *The Ardennes* position also obtained as between carrier and *indorsee*, especially if the shipper had orally agreed terms more favourable to the carrier. The indorsee would not necessarily know of these terms. In principle his relationship with the carrier should be determined by the bill of lading alone. The next case applies this principle, but its precise juristic basis is unclear.

(b) POSITION WHERE BILL OF LADING NEGOTIATED

LEDUC & CO v WARD

Court of Appeal. (1888) 20 Q.B.D. 475

12–004   In a voyage from Fiume to Dunkirk, the ship deviated to Glasgow, and sank with her cargo. The carrier attempted to rely on a clause exempting him from liability for perils of the sea, but would have been unable to do so had he deviated from the route as defined by the carriage contract.[2] He claimed that the shipper knew,

---

[1] Lord Goddard refers to *Sewell v Burdick* (1884) 10 App. Cas. 74, *per* Lord Bramwell at p. 105 and *Crooks v Allan* (1879) 5 Q.B.D. 38.

[2] The precise juristic basis of deviation remains unclear, and detailed discussion is beyond the scope of this book. Probably it is best analysed as a breach of condition, bringing the contract to an end, but the difficulties of reconciling this with *Photo Production v Securicor* (see Ch. 7, above) are discussed in *The Sara D* [1989] 2 Lloyd's Rep. 277.

before the carriage contract was concluded, that it was intended to sail to Glasgow, and in effect that the deviation was permitted by the contract.

Held:
The pre-contract agreement could not bind the indorsee, who took on bill of lading terms. These did not permit that deviation,[3] and by deviating the carrier lost the benefit of the excepted perils clause.

LORD ESHER M.R. (at 479–480): It has been suggested that the bill of   **12–005**
lading is merely in the nature of a receipt for the goods, and that it contains no contract for anything but the delivery of the goods at the place named therein. It is true that, where there is a charterparty, as between the shipowner and the charterer the bill of lading may be merely in the nature of a receipt for the goods, because all the other terms of the contract of carriage between them are contained in the charterparty; and the bill of lading is merely given as between them to enable the charterer to deal with the goods while in the course of transit; but, where the bill of lading is indorsed over, as between the shipowner and the indorsee the bill of lading must be considered to contain the contract, because the former has given it for the purpose of enabling the charterer to pass it on as the contract of carriage in respect of the goods. Where there is no charterparty, as between the grantee of the bill of lading and the shipowner, the bill of lading is no doubt a receipt for the goods, and as such, like any other receipt, it is not conclusive, for it may be controverted by evidence shewing that the goods were not received; the question whether it will be more than a receipt as between the shipper and the shipowner depends on whether the captain has received the goods, for he has no authority to make a contract of carriage to bind the shipowner, except in respect of goods received by him. If the goods have not been received, the bill of lading cannot contain the terms of a contract of carriage with respect to them as against the shipowner. But, if the goods have been received by the captain, it is the evidence in writing of what the contract of carriage between the parties is; it may be true that the contract of carriage is made before it is given, because it would generally be made before the goods are sent down to the ship: but when the goods are put on board the captain has authority to reduce that contract into writing: and then the general doctrine of law is applicable, by which, where the contract has been reduced into a writing which is intended to constitute the contract, parol evidence to alter or qualify the effect of such writing is not admissible, and the writing is the only evidence of the contract, except where there is some usage so well established and generally known that it must be taken to be incorporated with the contract. In the case of *Fraser v Telegraph Construction Co* (1872) L.R. 7 Q.B. 566 at 571 Blackburn J held that a bill of lading must be taken to be the contract under which the goods were shipped. In *Chartered Mercantile Bank of India v Netherlands India Steam Navigation Co* (1883) 10 Q.B.D. 521 I expressed

---

[3] There was in fact a wide deviation clause in the bill of lading, but it did not protect the shipowner on reasoning that was the precursor to *Glynn v Margetson*, in para. 11–007, above.

the same view that I am now expressing as to the nature of a bill of lading. In *Glyn, Mills & Co v East and West India Dock Co* [in chapter 6, above] Lord Selborne said, "Every one claiming as assignee under a bill of lading must be bound by its terms, and by the contract between the shipper of the goods and the shipowner therein expressed. The primary office and purpose of a bill of lading, although by mercantile law and usage it is a symbol of the right of property in the goods, is to express the terms of the contract between the shipper and the shipowner." The terms of the Bills of Lading Act [see chapter 13, below] shew that the legislature looked upon a bill of lading as containing the terms of the contract of carriage.

Notes

12–006   The contract between carrier and indorsee in *Leduc v Ward* was imputed by the Bills of Lading Act 1855, s.1 (see chapter 13, below), but a *Brandt v Liverpool* contract, where applicable (see paras 13–056, *et seq.*, below) also must be on the terms of the bill of lading (or ship's delivery order) alone. This is because it is a fresh contract, implied from the presentation of the documents, and is not dependent in any way on the original carriage contract.

In *The Ardennes*, Lord Goddard accepted that the bill of lading terms alone would have governed, had the action been brought by a subsequent holder, rather than the shipper[4]:

> "*Leduc v Ward* . . . was a case between shipowner and endorsee of the bill of lading, between whom its terms are conclusively by virtue of the Bills of Lading Act, 1855, so that evidence was admissible in that case to contradict or vary its terms. Between those parties the statute makes it the contract . . . "

One problem is that the last sentence of the above passage suggests that *Leduc v Ward* is merely an interpretation of the 1855 Act, which referred to "the contract contained in the bill of lading". The Carriage of Goods by Sea Act 1992 is in different terms (see chapter 13, below), so it is arguable that the decision no longer applies. A possible justification for the decision, analogous with the estoppel principle discussed in chapter 14, below, is that by issuing a bill of lading in terms less favourable to himself than the oral contract terms, the shipowner was estopped from relying on the more favourable terms against an indorsee who had (by taking up the documents) relied upon the terms in the bill of lading. This justification would be unaffected by the 1992 changes, but would apply only where the bill of lading terms were less favourable to the carrier than the orally agreed terms. It is also subject to the problem, discussed in the next case, that the indorsee is normally bound to take up the bill of lading in any event, as long only as the carriage contract is reasonable, and that therefore no inference should be drawn from his doing so.[5]

(c) Consignee or Indorsee also Charterer

12–007   Because the bill of lading is not the contract in the hands of the shipper, where the shipper is also charterer the charterparty terms prevail, if different from the bill of lading terms. The position should be the same for an indorsee who is also

---

[4] [1951] 1 K.B. 55, at p. 60.
[5] In *Leduc v Ward* itself, the orally agreed contract was probably not reasonable, so the decision itself should survive the 1992 changes.

charterer; the charterparty is the carriage contract, unless a variation can be inferred from his taking up of the bill of lading.

PRESIDENT OF INDIA v METCALFE SHIPPING CO LTD (THE DUNELMIA)

Court of Appeal. [1970] 1 Q.B. 289

The charterers of a vessel were also indorsees of bills of lading issued by the ship's **12–008** master. The charterparty contained an arbitration clause, and provided that the ship's master should "sign bills of lading . . . without prejudice" to the terms of the charterparty. The bills of lading contained the terms "Freight payable by the charterers as per charterparty" and "All conditions and exceptions as per charterparty", but as will become clear at paras 12–020 *et seq.*, below, such wording would not incorporate the arbitration clause.

In a dispute between charterers and shipowners over alleged short delivery on discharge, the charterers sought arbitration, but this was refused by the shipowners. The question was itself referred to arbitration by agreement, and was appealed eventually to the Court of Appeal.

Held:
The arbitration clause in the charterparty was effective, the charterparty being *prima facie* the contract which governed relations between shipowners and charterers, and not being superseded by the bill of lading in the hands of the indorsee.

LORD DENNING M.R.: I will first consider the matter on principle. It **12–009** seems to me that whenever an issue arises between the charterer and the shipowner, *prima facie* their relations are governed by the charterparty. The charterparty is not merely a contract for the hire of the use of a ship. It is a contract by which the shipowners agree to carry the goods and to deliver them. If the shipowners fail to carry the goods safely, that is a breach of the contract contained in the charterparty; and the charterers can claim for the breach accordingly, unless that contract has been modified or varied by some subsequent agreement between the parties. The signature by the master of a bill of lading is not a modification or variation of it. The master has no authority to modify or vary it. His authority is only to sign bills of lading "without prejudice to the terms of the charterparty." There is a long list of cases on this "without prejudice" clause. In *Hansen v Harrold Brothers* [1894] 1 Q.B. 612, Lord Esher M.R. said, at p. 619:

> "The meaning . . . is that it is a term of the contract between the charterers and the shipowners that, notwithstanding any engagements made by the bills of lading, that contract shall remain unaltered."

It is sometimes said that the "without prejudice" clause is put in for the benefit of the shipowners only. But that is not correct. It is for the benefit of both shipowners and charterers. In *Turner v Haji Goolam Mahomed Azam* [1904] A.C. 826, Lord Lindley, giving the judgment of the Privy Council said, at p. 837:

"The words, 'without prejudice to this charter' mean that the rights of the shipowners against the time charterers, and *vice versa*, are to be preserved."

In this case, therefore, the bill of lading did not modify or vary the charter. And there is nothing else. So the charter governs . . .

After full consideration, I am prepared to hold that in a case such as this the relations between shipowner and charterer are governed by the charterparty. Even though the charterer is not the shipper and takes as indorsee of a bill of lading, nevertheless their relations are governed by the charter, at any rate when the master is only authorised to sign bills of lading without prejudice to the charter.

Notes

12–010   Prior to this case the opposite view prevailed, and was expressed by the leading textbook writers,[6] primarily on the basis of *Calcutta Steamship Co Ltd v Andrew Weir & Co*.[7] This view is no longer sustainable after *The Dunelmia*, although it is sometimes argued that *The Dunelmia* is limited to cases where the charterparty requires bills of lading only to be issued without prejudice to its terms. Yet the judgments of at any rate Lord Denning M.R. and Edmund Davies L.J. are stated in the widest terms. They took the view that the leading textbooks were wrong, and that earlier authorities did not support the view of the writers.

This also seems right in principle. Invariably, the charterparty will have been made before the bill of lading is indorsed to the charterer, so that if bill of lading terms were to prevail it would be necessary to infer from the act of taking up the bill an intention to vary already agreed terms. Since the charterer has to take up the bill to collect the goods from the vessel, and indeed is usually bound to do so under the terms of the sale contract,[8] it is difficult to draw any particular inference from this act alone, to provide the basis for a variation or an estoppel.[9] *Calcutta Steamship Co* is distinguishable, because there the charterers took the bill of lading entirely voluntarily, as security for an advance, and the case therefore has no application to the usual position under a sale contract, where the holder has no choice but to take up the bill. In *Leduc v Ward* also, an estoppel or variation could be inferred from the shipowner's issuing of the bill of lading without incorporating the orally agreed terms, since the indorsee would certainly not have been bound to take it up, had he been aware of those terms.

The Dunelmia was distinguished in *The El Amria and The El Minia*, at para. 3–008, above, where the Court of Appeal held that a contract of affreightment had been made by the f.o.b. sellers as principals, and that therefore the only contract the buyers had was on bill of lading terms. Had the sellers been contracting as agents for the buyers, *The Dunelmia* would have applied, the buyers' relationship with the carriers would have been on the terms of the contract of affreightment, and the bill of lading would have acted merely as a receipt.

[6] At that time *Scrutton on Charterparties* (17th ed., 1964) p. 46 and Carver, *Carriage by Sea* (11th ed., 1963) p. 340.
[7] [1910] 1 K.B. 759.
[8] Assuming only that the documentary requirements in Ch. 6, above are satisfied. On the terms of the carriage contract, a c.i.f. seller is required only to enter into a contract of carriage which is reasonable: see, *e.g. Gatoil International Inc v Tradax Petroleum Ltd (The Rio Sun)* [1985] 1 Lloyd's Rep. 350. In *The Dunelmia* the contract was f.o.b., but *Concordia v Richco* (see Ch. 6, above) suggests that similar principles would apply.
[9] [1970] 1 Q.B. 289, *per* Lord Denning M.R., at 306–307.

An observation on arbitration clauses

Disputes over arbitration clauses do not usually arise because one party prefers arbitration to litigation, whereas the other party prefers litigation. Usually one route is barred by limitation, but not the other. In *The Dunelmia* the charterers were out of time to bring a court action, so if they failed on the arbitration issue they lost case entirely. Limitation is also often the disguised reason for the cases at paras 12–020, *et seq.*, below.

(2) Incorporation of Charterparty Terms into Bills of Lading

(a) General principles

Suppose S has a large quantity of a bulk dry cargo commodity to ship. It would   **12–011** be natural for him to charter a vessel in which to do so, for a voyage. But no single buyer has the capacity to take the entire cargo, so S obtains three bills of lading, intending to sell part of the cargo to X, part to Y and part to Z. The sale is on f.o.b. terms, and under the carriage contract, freight is payable on delivery. It is therefore reasonable for X, Y and Z to take on the obligation to pay freight at discharge. The charterparty may also contain a cesser clause, relieving S of this liability and requiring the shipowner to claim instead from the receivers of the cargo.[10] The shipowner will be protected by his common law lien on the cargo for freight.

It is therefore sensible for the bills of lading to impose liability to pay freight on X, Y and Z. The rates should, of course, be the same as under the charterparty, and since freight is normally payable on a tonnage basis, what could be more natural than simply to provide in the bills of lading, "Freight as per charterparty"?

Such was probably the origin of incorporation of charterparty terms into bills of lading. But the original principle has been extended. X, Y and Z also have control of the discharge process, although S controls loading. It is therefore also reasonable for X, Y and Z to take on the obligation to pay demurrage at discharge. The shipowner might also want the bill of lading to incorporate the charterparty excepted perils. So from "freight as per charterparty" developed "freight and other conditions as per charterparty", and eventually wider general words of incorporation, such as "all terms and conditions as per charterparty". Bills of lading incorporating charterparty terms remain common today, expecially for bulk cargoes.

As to which clauses are incorporated by general words, the test from *T.W. Thomas & Co Ltd v Portsea S.S. Co Ltd (The Portsmouth)*,[11] is accepted as being that general words incorporate into a bill of lading only terms which are germane to the bill of lading (*i.e.* to the receipt, carriage or delivery of the cargo or the payment of the freight). There are two main areas of contention. First, what is the effect of the charterparty placing cargo-handling duties on the charterer? Can the shipowner evade liability if damage is caused to the cargo during these processes, bearing in mind that the charterparty does not have to be tendered with the bill of lading, so that the indorsee may be unaware of its terms? Secondly, what about clauses, such as arbitration clauses, which arguably do not relate directly to the cargo?

There are also side issues. If the charterparty terms are written directly into the bill of lading, they may not fit exactly, talking about rights and duties of charterers, for example, rather than cargo-owners. To what extent is it permissible for the courts to "manipulate" the incorporated clauses to fit into the bill of lading?

---

[10] An example of a cesser clause can be found in at paras 13–002, below.
[11] [1912] A.C. 1.

Another problem is that the charterparty is not always identified, and if there is more than one, the courts may be required to determine which.

(b) Ancillary Obligations

12–012   Applying the *Thomas v Portsea* test, in *Garbis Maritime Corporation v Philippine National Oil Co* [1982] 2 Lloyd's Rep. 283 Goff J. said (at 289):

"Provided that such a clause relates to loading, carriage and discharge of the goods, it must surely be sufficient for the purposes of incorporating such clauses that words of incorporation, such as those in the present case, are used. If a receiver of goods accepts a bill of lading in this form without ascertaining the terms of the charter-party, he must accept that his contract with the shipowner for the carriage of goods, contained in or evidenced by the bill of lading, is subject to the charter-party terms relevant to the loading, carriage and discharge of goods, even though they may be unusual terms and may limit the shipowner's liability."

The bill of lading incorporated "all terms whatsoever" of the charterparty (except rate and payment of freight), and Goff J. thought this phrase sufficiently wide to encompass terms relating not only to the carriage itself, but also to loading and discharge. The particular clause held to be incorporated concerned the loading of a clean Napatha parcel into epoxy painted holds.

It appears, then, for example, that terms relating to loading, stowage and discharge) could be incorporated by general words of incorporation in the bill of lading:

"It is established that general words of incorporation in a bill of lading may be effective to incorporate terms of an identifiable charterparty which are relevant to the shipment, carriage and discharge, of the cargo and the payment of freight, provided of course that the terms of the charterparty are consistent with the terms of the bill of lading."

Suppose, then, the charterparty places responsibility for loading and discharge on the charterers,[12] but it is a shipowner's bill (on the principles at paras 12–037, *et seq.*, below). If the charterparty division of responsibilities is incorporated into the bill of lading, and binds the cargo-owner, he will be unable to sue the shipowner for damage during this period, nor will he be able to sue the charterer, at any rate in contract, since the charterer is not party to the bill of lading contract.

(c) Article III(8)

12–013   Surely, if such a clause were so incorporated, it ought to fall foul of Art. III(8) of the Hague or Hague-Visby Rules, if applicable to the bill of lading contract? It seems not, however; the *Hague* and *Hague-Visby Rules* do not determine the scope of the contract, or which duties are undertaken by the shipowner. These are determined solely by the bill of lading contract itself.

A similar argument was attempted in *GH Renton & Co Ltd v Palmyra Trading Corporation of Panama*.

---

[12] As in an f.i.o., or free in and out charterparty.

GH RENTON & CO LTD v PALMYRA TRADING CORPORATION OF PANAMA

House of Lords. [1957] A.C. 957

The bills of lading provided, by clause 14(c) of the printed conditions, that: **12–014**

> "should it appear that . . . strikes . . . would prevent the vessel from . . . entering the port of discharge or there discharging in the usual manner and leaving again . . . safely and without delay, the master may discharge the cargo at port of loading or any other safe and convenient port . . . "

By clause 14(f): "The discharge of and cargo under the provisions of this clause shall be deemed due fulfilment of the contract . . . "

The shipowners argued that this clause allowed them, in the event of strikes at the port of discharge (London), to discharge the goods at Hamburg. The cargo-owners argued that the clause was rendered void by Article III (8) of the Rules, on the grounds that it relieved the carrier of some of his obligations under Article III (2). of the Rules, "properly and carefully to . . . carry . . . and discharge the goods carried."

Held:

1. (Distinguishing *Glynn v Margetson & Co* [1893] A.C. 351, in para. 11–007, above), a clause is not repugnant to the main objects of the contract where it modifies the carrier's obligations in the event of defined events which are outside the control of either party.

2. The Article III(8) argument should be rejected because Article III(2) was held to be directed to the manner of carrying the goods and not to the goods being carried to a particular destination. It applied only to the manner of carrying out the duties agreed by the carrier, but did not alter the agreement itself, by redefining the scope of the agreed duties.

LORD MORETON OF HENRYTON: . . . I construe the words "shall properly   **12–015**
and carefully carry and discharge the goods carried" [in Article III(2)] as meaning that the carrier must perform the duties of carriage and discharge imposed upon him by the contract in a proper and careful manner. In *Pyrene Co Ltd v Scindia Navigation Co Ltd* [1954] 2 Q.B. 402, 417–418, Devlin J. said:

> "There is, however, a third interpretation to article III, rule 2. The phrase 'shall properly and carefully load' may mean that the carrier shall load and that he shall do it properly and carefully: or that he shall do whatever loading he does properly and carefully. The former interpretation perhaps fits the language more closely, but the latter may be more consistent with the object of the rules. Their object as it is put, I think, correctly in Carver's *Carriage of Goods by Sea*, 9th edition (1952), page 186, is to define not the scope of the contract service but the terms on which that service is to be performed. The extent to which the carrier has to undertake the loading of the vessel may depend not only upon different systems of law but upon the custom and practice of the port and the nature of the cargo. It is difficult to believe that the rules

were intended to impose a universal rigidity in this respect, or to deny freedom of contract to the carrier. The carrier is practically bound to play some part in the loading and discharging, so that both operations are naturally included in those covered by the contract of carriage. But I see no reason why the rules should not leave the parties free to determine by their own contract the part which each has to play. On this view the whole contract of carriage is subject to the rules, but the extent to which loading and discharging are brought within the carrier's obligations is left to the parties themselves to decide."

My Lords, I agree with this passage, save that, to my mind, not only is the construction approved by Devlin J. more consistent with the object of the rules, but it is also the more natural construction of the language used.

Now, sub-clauses (*c*) and (*f*) of clause 14 do not seek to relieve the carrier from any liability arising from failure in the duties and obligations imposed by article III, rule 2, as so construed . . .

. . . My Lords, . . . article III, rule 2, as I construe it, does not place any obligation on the carrier to transport the goods at all, unless the contract says he is to transport them; so that if the contract says he need not carry them in a certain event, there is no conflict with article III, rule 2. This is a sufficient answer to counsel's argument . . .

12–016   LORD SOMERVELL OF HARROW: The general ambit of the Hague Rules is to be found in article III, rule 2, which has already been cited. It is, in my opinion, directed and only directed to the manner in which the obligations undertaken are to be carried out. Subject to the later provisions, it prohibits the shipowner from contracting out of liability for doing what he undertakes properly and with care. This question was considered by Devlin J. in *Pyrene Co Ltd v Scindia Navigation Co Ltd* in relation to the words "shall properly and carefully load." I agree with his statement, which has already been cited.

Prima facie, therefore, the rules leave the parties free to contract in the terms in question here. They do not prohibit Hamburg as a destination in the events which happened, but they apply on that voyage as they would have done on the voyage to and discharge at London if there had been no strike.

Interpretation of Hague Rules

Thus, Article III(8) only prevents a carrier from restricting his liability for *the manner of* carrying out an operation which under the contract he has agreed to perform. However, nothing in Article III(8) would prevent a carrier from re-defining his duties so as to exclude responsibility to perform the operation in the first place. Article III(2) does not define the scope of the contract, but only the liability, once its scope has been defined by the parties.

For example, suppose the shipowner *has* agreed to take responsibility for loading and discharge. If he performs the cargo-handling process negligently, Article III(8) prevents him from restricting his liability below the requirements of Article III(2). However, nothing in III(8) prevents him from refusing to undertake responsibility for cargo-handling in the first place, for example by placing it upon the charterer or shipper.

It follows that Article III(8) should not operate in the cases where terms from a free in and out (or f.i.o.) charterparty (under which the charterer is responsible for cargo-handling) are incorporated into a bill of lading. The position is simply that the f.i.o. clause re-defines the shipowner's duties so as to relieve him altogether of the obligation to load and discharge. On the basis of *Renton v Palmyra*, where after all carrier was in effect allowed to modify his obligations relating to discharge, it seems that this is unaffected by Article III(8).

This Hague-Visby Rules construction was endorsed by the Court of Appeal in *The Coral*.

BALLI TRADING LTD v AFALONA SHIPPING CO LTD (THE CORAL)

Court of Appeal. [1993] 1 Lloyd's Rep. 1

The charterparty in question, incorporated into the bill of lading by general words   **12–017**
of incorporation, was on the popular Nype 46 form,[13] clause 8 of which provided:

" . . . charterers are to load, stow and trim and discharge the cargo at their expense under the supervision of the Captain . . . "

Clause 2 provided that:

"Charterers are to provide necessary dunnage and shifting boards, also any extra fitting requisite for a special trade or unusual cargo, but owners to allow them the use of any dunnage and shifting boards already aboard the vessel. Charterers to have the privilege of using shifting boards for dunnage, they making good any damage thereto."

Damage occurred during loading, and the cargo-owners claimed summary judgment.

Held:
The Court of Appeal refused summary judgment on the grounds that the ship-owners had no arguable defence to a breach of contract claim. It was well settled that article III, rule 2 did not impose on the carrier an obligation to load handle stow carry keep care for and discharge the goods carried; the agreement between the defendant owners and the charterers that the latter should undertake responsibility for loading and stowing and discharging could not affect the obligations which the defendant owners had undertaken by the bill of lading.

BELDAM L.J.: . . . It is now settled that art. III, r. 2 does not impose upon   **12–018**
the carrier an obligation to load, handle, stow, carry, keep, etc, the goods
carried. In *Pyrene Co Ltd v Scindia Steam Navigation Co Ltd* [1954] 2 Q.B. 402
at p. 418 Devlin J. accepted that the object of the rules was not to define
the scope of the contract of carriage but the terms upon which the service
was to be performed. And he said:

---

[13] New York Produce Exchange 1946, probably still the most commonly used time charter form in the world, in spite of the extensively-revised and updated 1993 revision.

" . . . The carrier is practically bound to play some part in the loading and discharging so both operations are naturally included in those covered by the contract of carriage. But I see no reason why the rules should not leave the parties free to determine by their own contract the part which each has to play. On this view the whole contract of carriage is subject to the rules but the extent to which loading stowing and discharging are brought within the carrier's obligations is left to the parties themselves to decide."

This exposition of the effect of art. III, r. 2 was approved by the House of Lords in *GH Renton & Co v Palmyra Trading Corporation of Panama* [1957] A.C. 149.

It goes without saying that the agreement between the owner and charterer that the latter should undertake responsibility for loading, stowing and discharging, etc., could not affect the obligations which the defendant owner had undertaken by the bills of lading. The question for decision is the effect of incorporating cll. 2 and 8 of the charter-party on the scope of the obligations the defendant had undertaken in the bill of lading. It is accepted that, subject to questions of compatibility and construction, the language of cl. 1 of the bill of lading is wide enough to incorporate cl. 2 and cl. 8 of the charter-party into the bill of lading. The clauses were—

" . . . directly germane to the shipment, carriage and delivery of goods . . . and such clauses may be treated as incorporated even though the precise words may need some modification."

See *Miramar Maritime Corporation v Holborn Oil Trading Ltd* [1984] A.C. 676 at p. 683 *per* Lord Diplock . . .

[He concluded that cl. 8 was validly incorporated, and continued:]

. . . [T]he defendant contended that the clause must be given the same meaning when read in the bill of lading as it would be construed to have in the charter-party and consequently relieved the owner not only of the obligation to the charterer to load and stow but also of an obligation to the owner of the cargo to be responsible for those services.

I would not accept this argument, as I do not think it follows that in the altered context the clause must have the same meaning. Where between the owner and the charterer it is agreed that loading and stowing shall be carried out by the charterer, it is a necessary implication that the charterer warrants that he will use reasonable care and skill in performing his obligations, and consequently that responsibility for bad stowage will fall upon him. It does not inevitably follow that where the clause is incorporated into a bill of lading and the owner agrees with the shipper that the charterer will load, stow and trim the cargo at the latter's expense, that the shipper's only right of recourse in the event of bad stowage will be against the charterer.

Notes

The only issue was whether the shipowners had an arguable defence, and it **12–019** was never decided whether the incorporated clause did *in fact* protect the shipowner from liability (see the last two paragraphs here). There was thus no decision in *The Coral* that Nype clause 8 necessarily implied that "the shipper's only right of recourse in the event of bad stowage would be against the charterers" (with whom, however, they had no contract). Conversely, nor does the case decide the opposite. Besides, a differently worded clause might clearly relieve the shipowners of responsibility as well. Then the cargo-owners might be left without recourse.

In fact, clause 8 of Nype is frequently amended to the opposite effect, by adding "and responsibility" after "supervision".[14] The shipowner would then clearly be liable to the cargo-owner, and the problems alluded to here would not arise. The clause would merely operate to allocate duties as between shipowner and charterer.

(d) ARBITRATION CLAUSES

It has already been observed, in connection with *The Dunelmia*, that disputes **12–020** about the application of arbitration clauses are often disguised limitation disputes. Whether or not this is the case, there is an argument that a consignee or indorsee should not lightly be bound arbitration clauses of which, on the basis of *Finska* in para. 6–072, above, he might be unaware.

PAUL TODD, "INCORPORATION OF ARBITRATION CLAUSES INTO BILLS OF LADING"

[1997] J.B.L. 331

[Footnotes as in the original, but renumbered and cross-referenced for inclusion here.]

... The following propositions would probably be accepted as an orthodox statement of the law[15]:

(a) An arbitration clause covering disputes under the charterparty is not incorporated by general words of incorporation in the bill of lading, such as "all terms and conditions as per charterparty", on the grounds that it is not directly germane to the subject matter of the bill of lading (that is, to the shipment, carriage and delivery of goods).[16] The position is unaffected even by the addition of a clause in the charterparty requiring all bills of lading issued pursuant to

---

[14] As in, *e.g. The Arctic Trader* [1996] 2 Lloyd's Rep. 449, discussed in a different context in para. 14–014, below.

[15] They are consistent with, *e.g.* Mocatta, Mustill and Boyd, *Scrutton on Charterparties and Bills of Lading*, (19th ed., Sweet & Maxwell, 1984), art. 37(b), p. 68, although art. 37(a) should now be modified in the light of *The Nerano* [below] ... See also R. Merkin, *Arbitration Law*, (LLP, 1991) p. 4–14/1.

[16] The *ratio* of the leading case, *TW Thomas & Co Ltd v Portsea SS Co Ltd (The Portsmouth)* [1912] A.C. 1. There may be an exception for very wide general words of incorporation, on the interpretation of *The Merak* [1965] P. 223, adopted by Oliver L.J. in *The Varenna* [below], at 622 B–E.

the charterparty to incorporate by reference all terms and conditions of the charter including the arbitration clause.[17] However, if an arbitration clause covering disputes under the charterparty is expressly incorporated, the words will be "manipulated" so as to cover disputes under the bill of lading.[18]

(b) An arbitration clause covering disputes under the bill of lading, or under both the charterparty and the bill of lading, is incorporated by general words of incorporation in the bill of lading, since it is germane to the subject matter of the bill,[19] and no manipulation is necessary for such a clause.

(c) An arbitration clause covering disputes under the contract is not incorporated by general words of incorporation in the bill of lading.[20] This outcome is unaffected even by the addition of a clause in the charterparty stating that the contract shall be completed and superseded by the signing of bills of lading, which shall contain the arbitration clause.[21] It is not clear whether, if such a clause is expressly incorporated, once incorporated the word "contract" will be interpreted to refer to the bill of lading contract rather than the charterparty, in which case there would be no need to manipulate it.[22]

Notes

I also suggested that if this was indeed a correct statement of the law, it was far from ideal. Only clauses in paragraph (b), above are incorporated by general words of incorporation in the bill of lading,[23] but unless the indorsee has sight of the charterparty, he will not know whether the arbitration clause is of the type in paragraph (b) or not. I suggested that a better solution would be to concentrate entirely on the words of incorporation in the bill of lading, and generally to take the view that arbitration clauses were special (unlike any other clause in the

---

[17] The *ratio* of *The Varenna*.

[18] *Daval Aciers D'Usinor et de Sacilor v Armare SRL (The Nerano)* [1996] 1 Lloyd's Rep. 1, CA, affirming Clarke J.: [1994] 2 Lloyd's Rep. 50. This is probably quite common in practice, since many standard form charterparty arbitration clauses are expressed to apply only to disputes under the charterparty. See further *Contracts for the Carriage of Goods*, (D. Yates ed., LLP, 1993) pp. 1–123—1–127.

The quotation marks here reflect the uneasiness of the courts to admit that they engage in "manipulation", a phrase described as colourful in *The Varenna, per* Lord Donaldson M.R. at 618B.

[19] The most probable interpretation of *The Merak* [1965] P. 223. *Dicta* in *The Annefield* [1971] P. 168 are also consistent with this interpretation.

[20] The *ratio* of *The Njegos* [1936] P. 90, upheld by the Court of Appeal in *The Annefield*. Both cases concerned the popular Centrocon arbitration clause.

[21] *Federal Bulk Carriers Inc. v C Itoh Ltd (The Federal Bulker)* [1989] 1 Lloyd's Rep. 103.

[22] Bingham L.J. *ibid.* at 108 (col. 2), thought that this "would plainly be understood". However, Dillon L.J. at 110 (col. 2), citing Lord Denning M.R. and Cairns L.J. in *The Annefield* [1968] P. 168, at 185 A–B and 186–187, was doubtful. Bingham L.J.'s view suggests that the clause is not germane to the subject matter of the bill of lading unless it is incorporated, when it becomes germane.

[23] *e.g.* "all conditions and exceptions as per charterparty . . . ".

charterparty), and should never be incorporated by general words of incorporation. I said that[24]:

" . . . Sir John Megaw in *Aughton Ltd v M.F. Kent Services Ltd*,[25] where he observed that there were three inter-related factors peculiar to arbitration agreements. First, an arbitration agreement may preclude the parties to it from bringing a dispute before a court of law. Secondly, an arbitration agreement has to be 'a written agreement'.[26] Thirdly, the arbitration clause differs from other types of clause because it constitutes a 'self-contained contract collateral or ancillary to' the substantive contract.[27] On the second point, Sir John emphasised that the object of the writing requirement was to ensure that nobody is to be deprived of his right to have a dispute decided by a court of law, unless he has consciously and deliberately agreed that it should be so."

The inference from the last sentence is that such deprival should also not result from general words of incorporation. As far as I could see, the recent authorities concentrated on the incorporation clause in the bill of lading, rather than the wording of the clause in the charterparty, and the only authority clearly inconsistent with this approach was *The Merak*.

The starting point is *TW Thomas & Co Ltd v Portsea SS Co Ltd (The Portsmouth)*,[28] where Lord Atkinson gave as his reason for refusing to incorporate the arbitration clause that general words incorporate into a bill of lading only terms which are germane to the bill of lading (*i.e.* to the receipt, carriage or delivery of the cargo or the payment of the freight), and that the arbitration clause was not germane.[29] It is possible that similar reasoning applies to other charterparty clauses, apart from arbitration clauses,[30] but a proper law clause was incorporated by general words of incorporation in *The San Nicholas* (see para. 12–029, below), and an exclusive jurisdiction clause in *The Pioneer Container*.[31] In reality, it seems that only arbitration clauses are caught by the *Thomas v Portsea* test.

One of the problems with the germaneness test is that what is germane can depend on the precise wording of the clause, in this case the arbitration clause, which is what led the Court of Appeal in *The Merak* effectively to decide the proposition in paragraph (b), above. However, recent cases have concentrated on the wording in the bill of lading, rather than the charterparty, and *The Merak* has been treated as anomalous.

---

[24] At 337. Footnotes again as in original, but "manipulated" to fit here.

[25] (1991) 57 Build. L.R. 1; (1991) 31 Con. L.R. 60. The issue concerned incorporation of an arbitration clause into a general commercial contract, and Sir John Megaw thought that the bill of lading authorities were equally applicable to this issue. See also *The Heidberg*, below.

[26] Sir John Megaw cited the Arbitration Act 1950, s.32, as re-enacted in the Arbitration Act 1979, s.7(1)(e). He also observed that a similar provision from Arbitration Act 1889 had been in force at the time of *Thomas v Portsea*. Presumably, however, nothing in these provisions would prevent an unwritten arbitration agreement from being valid at common law, although it would not benefit from the provisions of the Arbitration Acts 1950–1979. See now Arbitration Act 1996, s.5.

[27] The words were taken from Lord Diplock's speech in *Bremer Vulkan v South India Shipping* [1981] A.C. 909.

[28] [1912] A.C. 1.

[29] At 6. Similar views were expressed by Lord Loreburn L.C. at 6, by Lord Gorell at 8, and by Lord Robson at 11.

[30] In *OK Petroleum AB v Vitol Energy SA* [1995] 2 Lloyd's Rep. 160, Colman J. applied similar principles to a time bar, and thought that they might also apply to a jurisdiction clause: at p. 168 (col. 2).

[31] *K.H. Enterprise (cargo owners) v Pioneer Container (owners) (The Pioneer Container)* [1994] 2 A.C. 324.

SKIPS A/S NORDHEIM v SYRIAN PETROLEUM CO LTD (THE VARENNA)

Court of Appeal. [1984] Q.B. 599

12-021 The bill of lading incorporated "all conditions and exceptions" of the charterparty. The charterparty contained a London arbitration clause, and also provided that all bills of lading issued pursuant to the charter were to include all terms and conditions of the charter, including the arbitration clause.[32] In an action by the shipowners against the consignees for demurrage due under the charterparty (the charterers having defaulted), the consignees applied for the action to be stayed, contending that the arbitration clause had been incorporated into the bill of lading contract.

Held:
  1. The question of which terms were incorporated into the bill of lading depended on the construction of the bill of lading, rather than the charterparty.

  2. Arbitration clauses are not incorporated by a bill of lading incorporating conditions and exceptions of a charterparty.

12-022   OLIVER L.J.: The question raised by this appeal is one which, to the tyro, appears deceptively simple. It is whether an arbitration clause contained in a charterparty and which was clearly intended by the parties to that contract to be incorporated referentially in any bill of lading issued thereunder was in fact effectively incorporated by the terms of such a bill of lading. On the face of it that is a comparatively simple question of the true construction of the bill of lading in question and it is discouraging to one whose unfamiliarity with this field is unrivalled to find what appears to be a simple construction point overlaid by a great weight of authority which, it is claimed, compulsively restricts the inquiry to predestinate grooves. In the recent case of *Astro Valiente Compania Naviera SA v Pakistan Ministry of Food and Agriculture (No. 2), (The Emmanuel Colocotronis (No. 2))* [1982] 1 W.L.R. 1096 Staughton J., in construing a bill of lading containing somewhat similar wording to that with which the instant appeal is concerned, considered himself freed from the inhibitions which might be thought to have been imposed by the earlier cases. In the instant case, however, Hobhouse J. felt himself unable to follow Staughton J. in so adventurous an excursion from what clearly has become, to commercial lawyers, a familiar route.

The question squarely raised by this appeal is: which of them was right?

Coming as I do entirely fresh to the field, it seems to me that the primary consideration which must govern any approach to the problem

---

[32] It was this last factor that was new; otherwise the case is essentially the same as *Thomas v Portsea*.

is that the document which falls to be construed is the bill of lading, and not the charterparty. It may well be that, once having arrived at a conclusion that, as a matter of construction of the bill of lading, there fall to be incorporated referentially clauses of a particular type or description in the charterparty, it will then become necessary to construe the charterparty in order to see whether particular terms do or do not fall within that type or description. But the initial task must be to look at the bill of lading and that document alone to see what its terms are and then, so far as it purports to include the terms of some other document by reference, to ascertain what are the terms so included.

One point can be disposed of at the outset of the inquiry. It clearly cannot be sufficient to assert that the bill of lading refers generally to the charterparty and that that reference therefore, as it were, incorporates all the provisions of the charterparty because the holder of the bill of lading has notice (either actual or constructive) of the charterparty. No doubt every holder of a bill of lading knows that there is a charterparty in the background whether referred to or not but such knowledge cannot of itself furnish any reason why, in the construction of his contract, he should be in any way concerned with the terms which have been negotiated altogether separately between the charterer and the shipowner. So elementary a proposition may seem self-evident, but I mention it only because there seemed to be lurking in the [consignees'] argument a suggestion that because the bill of lading in the instant case compels reference to the charterparty to ascertain the contents of some of its clauses, it follows that the whole charterparty must be referred to to ascertain the meaning which the parties to that contract attached to those clauses. That seems to me to be an impermissible approach. The purpose of referential incorporation is not, or at least is not generally, to incorporate the intentions of the parties to the contract whose clauses are incorporated but to incorporate the clauses themselves in order to avoid the necessity of writing them out verbatim. The meaning and effect of the incorporated clause has to be determined as a matter of construction of the contract into which it is incorporated having regard to all the terms of that contract.

There are in fact, as Staughton J. pointed out in the *Astro Valiente* case, likely to be two stages in the inquiry, for it inevitably happens that an incorporation in very wide general terms is appropriate to incorporate into the bill of lading terms not strictly appropriate for such a contract. One then has to see whether the terms are so clearly inconsistent with the contract constituted by the bill of lading that they have to be rejected or whether the intention to incorporate a particular clause is so clearly expressed as to require, by necessary implication, some modification of the language of the incorporated clause so as to adapt it to the new contract into which it is incorporated. The question of consistency is, however, a quite separate question.

The primary contest between the parties to the instant appeal is on the ambit of the provision in the bill of lading that "all conditions and exceptions of which Charter party including the negligence clause, are deemed to be incorporated in Bill of Lading". The plaintiffs say that, as a result of a long line of authorities over the past century and beyond, the words "all conditions and exceptions" in the context of a bill of lading have a well-established and well-recognised commercial meaning. They mean such conditions and exceptions as are appropriate to the carriage and delivery of goods and do not, as a matter of ordinary construction, extend to a collateral term such as an arbitration clause even if that clause is expressed (which they submit this one is not) in terms which are capable, without modification, of referring to the bill of lading contract.

The general proposition contended for by the plaintiffs is clearly established by a line of cases which were extensively reviewed by Hobhouse J. in the instant case, the most striking of which are, perhaps, *Serraino & Sons v Campbell* [1891] 1 Q.B. 283, *TW Thomas & Co Ltd v Portsea Steamship Co Ltd* [1912] A.C. 1 and *Hogarth Shipping Co Ltd v Blyth Greene Jourdain & Co Ltd* [1917] 2 K.B. 534.

The argument has been restricted in fact to the meaning of the word "conditions", for it is unnecessary in the context of the instant case to consider the more extensive formula sometimes found of "terms and conditions". Bailhache J. in *Fort Shipping Co Ltd v Pederson & Co* (1924) 19 Ll.L. Rep. 26 held that the word "terms" was wider than "conditions" and that accordingly in a case in which the incorporation was of "all terms and conditions" the restricted interpretation established by the cases above referred to did not prevent him from treating as incorporated a clause not strictly germane to the carriage and delivery of the goods; but in fact it seems to have been the view of both Lord Atkinson and Lord Gorell in *TW Thomas & Co Ltd v Portsea Steamship Co Ltd* that the addition of "terms", at any rate when conjoined with the word "other", made no difference to the construction, a view apparently shared by Merriman P. in *The Njegos* [1936] P. 90 and, I rather think, by Cairns L.J. in *The Annefield* [1971] P. 168. Whether or not this is so, it is unnecessary to decide for present purposes although speaking for myself I find it difficult to see any logical distinction between "all terms and conditions" and "all conditions". What is, I think, tolerably clear is that, certainly standing alone, an incorporation of the "conditions" of the charterparty does not suffice, as a matter of authority, to incorporate an arbitration clause in the charterparty.

The defendants, however, support the view favoured by Staughton J. in the *Astro Valiente* case [1982] 1 W.L.R. 1096, by reference to the judgment of Kay L.J. in *Serraino & Sons v Campbell* [1891] 1 Q.B. 283 and in particular a passage of the report of that case where Kay L.J. appears to reject any rigid or accepted construction applicable to all cases and to favour a flexible approach dependent on the surrounding circumstances in each case (at 301).

12–023   They also point to the observations of Lord Reid in *Wickman Machine Tools Sales Ltd v L Schuler A.G.* [1974] A.C. 235 at 250–251 that the word "condition" has many meanings and that its use cannot be more than an indication, albeit perhaps a strong indication, of intention. Speaking for myself, I do not find that these references help very much in the context of the instant case. The authorities clearly show that the use of general incorporating words, whether "terms" or "conditions", in a bill of lading are and have for years been normally construed in the restrictive way for which the plaintiffs contend, but no one has argued that there may not be a context or surrounding circumstances from which some wider connotation may be culled, and that, as it seems to me, was all that Kay L.J. was saying, for in fact he concurred in the result in the *Serriano* case.

What does seem to me important is that documents so commonly in use and containing familiar expressions which have a well-established meaning among commercial lawyers should be consistently construed and that a well-established meaning, particularly as regards something like an arbitration clause where clarity and certainty are important to both parties, should not be departed from in the absence of compulsive surrounding circumstances or a context which is strongly suggestive of some other meaning.

It has been submitted that the decision of the Divisional Court in *The Northumbria* [1906] P. 292 in some way justifies the attribution to the word "conditions" of some wider meaning, that word being conjoined in that case (as it is in the present case) with the words "including negligence clause". Again, I do not see how that case helps in the present context. The question there was not what was meant by the word "conditions" but what was brought in by the words "including negligence clause", the fact being that the clause referred to as the "negligence clause" not only excluded liability for accidents occasioned by negligence but also an exception of the warranty of seaworthiness. Thus the question was not what was the ambit of the general words but what was the ambit of an express reference to a particular clause.

I would have considerable sympathy with Staughton J.'s approach in the *Astro Valiente* case were the matter *res integra*, although even then I am impressed by the argument of counsel for the plaintiffs with regard to the importance of clarity in seeking to incorporate an arbitration clause. But the matter is not *res integra* and in the light of the authorities to which we have been referred I am, for my part, compelled to the conclusion that Hobhouse J was right in his approach to the construction of the general words of incorporation in this case.

It is argued, however, that there is another route by which, even though the words of incorporation are, standing by themselves, insufficient to bring in the arbitration clause, that clause can be incorporated. It is said that if you have general words of incorporation in the bill of lading and you find that those general words are coupled with express words in a clause in the charterparty which show that that clause was intended to be or was suitable for incorporation in the bill of lading without adaptation then, even though the clause is not one which is germane to the contract constituted by the bill of lading on an application of the ordinary rule of construction referred to above, the clause will nevertheless be treated as incorporated. That proposition is supported by reference to two more recent cases: *The Annefield* [1971] P. 168, and *The Merak, T.B. & S. Batchelor & Co Ltd v S.S. Merak (owners)* [1965] P. 223. In the former case Brandon J. formulated the result of the authorities in a series of propositions, the fourth of which was that—

"where the arbitration clause by its terms applies both to disputes under the charterparty and to disputes under the bill of lading, general words of incorporation will bring the clause into the bill of lading so as to make it applicable to disputes under that document."

That was echoed in this court by Lord Denning M.R. when he said ([1971] P. 168 at 184):

"But if the clause is one which is not thus directly gername, it should not be incorporated into the bill of lading contract unless it is done explicitly in clear words either in the bill of lading or in the *charterparty.*" (My emphasis.)

On analysis, however, it appears that that view of the matter derives entirely from *The Merak*, where the words of the arbitration clause were such as to make it clear that it was intended to apply, in terms, both to disputes under the charterparty and to disputes under any bill of lading issued under it.

With the greatest deference I am bound to say that I doubt whether that proposition does in fact clearly emerge from *The Merak*. The incorporating words in that case were, it is true, general words but they were as wide as they could possibly be. They purported to incorporate into the bill of lading "All the terms, conditions, clauses and exceptions . . . contained in the charterparty", and the court held that they were of such strength and width that they could not, in the absence of some strong indication to the contrary, be cut down or restricted. Thus there was, as I read the decision, strictly no need to consider whether the incorporation was limited only to those clauses germane to the contract of carriage. All the clauses of the charterparty were to be applied, subject only to the test of carriage. All the clauses of the charterparty were to be applied, subject only to the test of consistency, a test clearly passed by the arbitration clause in that case. Davies L.J., dealing with a submission that *TW Thomas & Co Ltd v Portsea Steamship Co Ltd* established the general proposition that general words could only incorporate those terms gername to the shipment, carriage and delivery of the goods, observed ([1965] P. 230 at 254):

"It is difficult, however, to see that the *Thomas* case, when considered on its facts, does establish such a proposition or that parties to a bill of lading, if *they use wide enough words of incorporation*, cannot, if they are so minded, agree to incorporate into the bill an arbitration clause which expressly applies to disputes arising out of the bill, that is to say,

disputes arising out of the shipment, carriage or delivery of the goods."
(My emphasis.)

An alternative way of putting it is, I suppose, to say that, where the
arbitration clause is so expressed as to make it clear that it is not merely
apt to apply but is intended to apply to disputes arising under bills of
lading, it is to be treated in the same way as clauses which are germane
to the shipment, carriage or delivery of goods. It is not, however, clear
from the case how far this can result in incorporation in the absence of
sufficiently wide words of incorporation in the bill of lading, although it
appears to have been the view of Russell LJ that even the words in *TW
Thomas & Co v Portsea Steamship Co Ltd* would have been sufficient in the
case of an arbitration clause in the charterparty expressed in the terms of
the clause in *The Merak* (see [1965] P. 223 at 260).

It is this proposition which lies at the core of the [consignees'] argument
in the instant case, but they have to face the fact that the clause on which
they have to rely is not, in fact, a *Merak* type of clause. It refers expressly
only to disputes "under this charter" so that it can only be incorporated
on its face, not as a clause which, by its terms, has to be treated as
germane to the shipment, carriage and delivery of goods, but as a clause
which requires verbal manipulation to adapt it to the bill of lading.

The [consignees] seek to escape from this dilemma by reference to cl. 44
of the charterparty, which provides that bills of lading issued under the
charterparty shall incorporate by reference, inter alia, the arbitration
clause. Now it can scarcely be argued that this clause itself is one which
can be incorporated in the bill of lading but what is said is that if you take
the charterparty and construe it as a whole you will then deduce an
intention that the words "this charter" in the arbitration clause have to be
read as including a reference, by adaption or manipulation, to a bill of
lading. Thus, it is argued, the clause so construed becomes a clause of the
same purport if not in the same terms as the clause in *The Merak*.

For the reasons mentioned above, this seems to me not to be a permissible approach. It is, in fact, the same argument as was adduced in *The
Merak* for reading the erroneous reference in that case to cl. 30 as a
reference to cl. 32 (the aritration clause) and it was decisively rejected by
Russell L.J. Although Hobhouse J. appears to have entertained some
reservations about this, I, for my part, find Russell L.J.'s reasoning persuasive. I do not see how it can be permissible to ascertain what the parties
to a particular contract intended to be incorporated by reference to an
entirely different document.

I respectfully concur in the conclusion at which Hobhouse J. arrived
and I agree that the appeal should be dismissed.

Notes

The emphasis here is clearly on interpretation of the bill of lading, rather than   **12–024**
the charterparty, and even *The Merak* is explained on this basis. The consignee
may have no knowledge of the charterparty. Effectively, by refusing to construe

"conditions and exceptions" more widely than in the strict legal sense, the Court of Appeal has pretty well ensured that the only way arbitration clauses can be incorporated is by express words of incorporation in the bill of lading. If correct, the decision reduces the uncertainty inherent in taking up charterparty bills when the charterparty itself is not tendered.

Oliver L.J. thought (but did not need to decide) that "all terms and conditions" would not suffice either, because "terms" is no wider than "conditions". He insisted on a strict legal construction of the words in the bill of lading itself, and refuses to consider a more flexible approach based either on wider commercial usage or any but the most compulsive surrounding circumstances.

A similar approach, emphasising the need for certainty, and concentrating on the words in the bill of lading, was taken in *The Federal Bulker*.

FEDERAL BULK CARRIERS INC v C ITOH & CO LTD (THE FEDERAL BULKER)

Court of Appeal. [1989] 1 Lloyd's Rep. 103

12–025   The charterparty, which was on the Baltimore Grain Form C, contained an amended "Centrocon" Arbitration Clause, which covered "All disputes from time to time arising out of this contract". The bill of lading incorporated:

"All terms, conditions and exceptions as per charterparty dated January 20, 1986, and any addenda thereto to be considered as fully incorporated herein as if fully written."

Like *The Varenna*, the charterparty required the bill of lading to incorporate various clauses, and enumerating the arbitration clause explicitly. It was this factor which distinguished the case from *The Annefield*, for example.

The receivers claimed that the cargo had been damaged, and commenced arbitration proceedings, but the shipowners challenged the jurisdiction of the arbitrators.

The Court of Appeal held that the principle in *The Varenna* extended to this incorporation clause. Neither the inclusion of "terms" nor the phrase "as if fully written" strengthened the case for incorporation. Nor was the wording of the charterparty relevant.

12–026   Bingham L.J.: Generally speaking, the English law of contract has taken a benevolent view of the use of general words to incorporate by reference standard terms to be found elsewhere. But in the present field a different, and stricter, rule has developed, especially where the incorporation of arbitration clauses is concerned. The reason no doubt is that a bill of lading is a negotiable commercial instrument and may come into the hands of a foreign party with no knowledge and no ready means of knowledge of the terms of the charter-party. The cases show that a strict test of incorporation having, for better or worse, been laid down, the Courts have in general defended this rule with some tenacity in the interests of commercial certainty. If commercial parties do not like the English rule, they can meet the difficulty by spelling out the arbitration provision in the bill of lading and not relying on general words to achieve incorporation.

DILLON L.J.: I also agree. The question whether clauses in a charter-party are incorporated in a bill of lading is a question of construction essentially of the bill of lading.

The formula of incorporation used in this bill of lading,

" . . . all terms, conditions and exceptions as per charter-party dated January 20 1986 and any addenda thereto to be considered as fully incorporated . . . "

is quintessentially a formula which is not effective to incorporate into the bill of lading any arbitration clause contained in a charter-party.

This has been well established for over one hundred years. See the decision of this Court in *Hamilton & Co v Mackie & Sons* (1889) 5 T.L.R. 677 and the decision of the House of Lords in *TW Thomas & Co Ltd v Portsea Steamship Co Ltd* [1912] A.C. 1. In both of those cases precisely that formula was used. Also reference may be made to the case of *The Njegos* [1936] P. 90 where again the formula used was "all the terms, conditions and exceptions of the charter-party" including a negligence clause. Extremely experienced Counsel, Sir Robert Aske and Mr Henry Willinck agreed in the course of the argument that the practice in Chambers in the Commercial Court was to refuse applications to stay proceedings under bills of lading because of an arbitration clause in the charter-party where, at any rate, the incorporation clause was so worded. That is recorded at p. 94 of the report and picked up by the President, Sir Boyd Merriman, in his judgment at p. 100.

The correctness of these decisions is in no way challenged by the appellants, but they are said to be distinguishable in this case because of terms in the charter-party not, be it noted, in the bill of lading. It is said on one point that the arbitration clause in this charter-party must refer, or at least is well capable of referring, to disputes under the bill of lading rather than under the charter-party since it refers to disputes "arising out of this contract" in a context in which the clause is set out as a clause to be included in a bill of lading which is later incorporated in the charter-party.

In *The Annefield* [1971] P. 168 to which my Lord has referred, an identically worded arbitration clause was included in the charter-party and it was regarded as, at the highest, ambiguous whether that clause, if transferred to a bill of lading, could be construed as referring to disputes under the bill of lading rather than disputes under the charter-party contract. See the judgment of Lord Denning, M.R. at p. 185 A to B and the judgment of Lord Justice Cairns L.J. at pp. 186 to 187. But whether ambiguous or not, the arbitration clause in the charter-party is still not a term, condition or exception contained in the charter-party as those terms have been construed in the authorities I have mentioned.

Mr Hirst [for the defendant receivers] relies even more on the words in the charter-party (which my Lord has read) whereby it was mutually agreed that

> "this contract shall be completed and superseded by the signing of Bills of Lading in the form customary for such voyages for grain cargoes, which Bills of Lading shall contain the following clauses."

There follow 21 clauses including this clause, 11, the arbitration clause, and added to the charter-party there are further additional clauses, 22 to 44.

It is said that the words of incorporation should be read to pick up all the clauses which the charter-party envisaged as to be included in a bill of lading. Mr Hirst relies in addition on the words in the bill of lading, "fully incorporated as if fully written". I do not, for my part, see that those latter words add anything. If a term is incorporated, it is incorporated as fully written.

I do not see that the words in the charter-party which I have cited impose any obligation to include the particular cll. 1 to 21, let alone the additional cll. 22 to 44, in any bill of lading. The words in the charter-party are only concerned to achieve supersession of liability under the charter-party if there are appropriately-worded bills of lading. The consequence, if relevant, may be that there is no supersession of liability (if there is any under the charter-party) if the terms of the bill of lading do not match up to the provisions envisaged by the charter-party. But there is no obligation and thus there is no basis in the charter-party for construing the bill of lading as importing the clauses, including the arbitration clause, as clauses required by the charter-party to be included in the bill of lading.

Moreover cll. 1 to 44 of the charter-party, save as deleted, include many matters which have no relevance to the bill of lading or which are duplicated by express clauses in the bill of lading. There are many matters also covered by cll. 1 to 44 which are not "terms, conditions and exceptions" as that phrase has been construed in the authorities binding on this Court and, in particular, in *Thomas v Portsea*.

It is well established that there is need for certainty in commercial matters and the only solution, in my judgment, is to adhere to the well established meaning of the words of incorporation which have been used in this bill of lading. They incorporate only "terms, conditions and exceptions as per the charter-party" as those words are generally understood and they do not import the arbitration clause . . .

. . . One has to look at the bill of lading to see what was intended to be incorporated in the bill of lading. Seeing that the bill of lading used terms to which the Courts have given a well-established meaning for over 100 years, I would adhere to that meaning. The arbitration clause is not incorporated and I too would dismiss this appeal.

Conclusion

It looks as though general words of incorporation are unlikely ever to incorporate arbitration clauses, although *The Merak* suggests that "all clauses" might suffice to do so.

The courts also seem to moving towards the principle that which terms are incorporated should be determined by construction of the bill of lading, not the charterparty, because the cargo-owner is not party to the charterparty.

(e) MANIPULATION

In *The Annefield* Lord Denning said[33]:   **12–027**

"I would say that a clause which is directly germane to the subject matter of the bill of lading (that is, to the shipment, carriage and delivery of goods) can and should be incorporated into the bill of lading contract, even though it may involve a degree of manipulation of the words in order to fit exactly the bill of lading."

This suggested that manipulation was acceptable, once the clause had been incorporated into the bill of lading contract. It was, however, *obiter dicta*, since the arbitration clause in the case was not incorporated. It now seems that these views on manipulation are wrong.

In *Miramar Maritime Corporation v Holborn Oil Trading Ltd (The Miramar)* [1984] A.C. 676, Lord Diplock had refused to allow manipulation of a demurrage clause, from an Exxonvoy 1969 form, which had been incorporated into a bill of lading. Under the clause, liability to pay demurrage attached only to the charterers, and Lord Diplock refused to extend liability to the holder of the bill of lading.

At one time it was thought that the reasoning in *The Miramar* did not apply to arbitration clauses from charterparties incorporated into bills of lading, partly because of *The Annefield*. *The Annefield* concerned general words of incorporation, however. In *The Rena K*,[34] Brandon J., took the view that where a bill of lading expressly incorporated an arbitration clause from a charterparty, it was permissible to manipulate the clause in the charterparty in order to make it applicable to disputes under the bill of lading. In *The Nai Matteini*, however, considered further below, the bill of lading purported expressly to incorporate the arbitration clause (although it did not say from which charterparty: see below), but neither arbitration clause, read literally, clearly applied to a dispute between plaintiffs and defendants. Hence, whichever arbitration clause was incorporated, it would have been necessary to manipulate its wording in order to fit the bill of lading. The clause in the head charterparty applied only to disputes between the owners and head-charterers. The clause in the sub-charterparty also was clearly only apposite to disputes between owners and charterers (presumably this time, however, the parties to the sub-charterparty), there being no mention of other cargo-owners. The defendants were cargo-owners, but neither head nor sub-charterers, and hence not clearly within the ambit of either arbitration clause.

Gatehouse J. took the view that the observations referred to above from *The Annefield* and *The Rena K* could not stand in the light of the House of Lords decision in *The Miramar*. Although *The Miramar* was not concerned directly with

---

[33] [1971] P. 168, at 184.
[34] [1978] 1 Lloyd's Rep. 545.

the incorporation of an arbitration clause, Gatehouse J. thought that Lord Dip-lock's reasoning applied at any rate to every clause in the Exxonvoy 1969 form. He also saw no reason to treat the incorporation of arbitration clauses differently from incorporation of any other clauses in the charterparty. It followed that the defendants failed, since they were unable to show the incorporation of any clause which literally applied to disputes between themselves and the plaintiffs.

Express words of incorporation in bill of lading

12–028   *The Nai Matteini* differed from both *The Annefield* and *The Miramar* in that there were express words of incorporation in the bill of lading. Webster J. regarded this as a proper basis for distinction in *The Oinoussin Pride*,[35] where he refused to follow *The Nai Matteini*:

"In the absence of authority I would conclude that, if practical, effect should be given to the expressed intention of the parties to the bills, namely, to incorpo-rate the arbitration clause in them, and that it is not only practical but necessary to do so by adding those words to [the arbitration clause] in order to give effect to that expressed intention. Authority however, is not absent. In *The Rena K* [1978] 1 Lloyd's Rep. 545, in a case virtually on all fours with the present one in that the incorporation clause of the bills of lading specifically incorporated the arbitration clause of the charter-party, and which is to be distinguished only of the ground that the charter-party there was a voyage charter-party, whereas here there is a time charter-party, Brandon J. at p. 551, col. 1 said:

'The addition of these words ("including the arbitration clause") must, as it seems to me, mean that the parties to the bills of lading intended the provisions of the arbitration clause in the charter-party to apply in principle to disputes arising under the bills of lading, and if it is necessary, as it obviously is, to manipulate or adapt part of the wording of that clause in order to give effect to that intention, then I am clearly of the opinion that this should be done.'

I would follow that decision without hesitation, were it not for the recent decision of Gatehouse J. in *The Nai Matteini* [1988] 1 Lloyd's Rep. 452. That case is different from the present one in that there were two charter-parties to choose from, a head charter-party and a sub charter-party, and in that both of those charter-parties were voyage charter-parties. I have been tempted to treat that difference as a factor which entitles me to distinguish Gatehouse J.'s decision in that case so that I need not follow it for that reason, but on reflection I have concluded that I cannot treat that difference as constituting a distinction so as to avoid the difficulty in that way; for the reasoning in reliance upon which Gatehouse J. arrived at his decision in that case included a conclusion that he should not follow Brandon J.'s decision in *The Rena K* because that decision was inconsistent with the decision of the House of Lords in *Miramar Maritime Corporation v Holborn Oil Trading Ltd* [1984] 1 A.C. 676. With great respect to Gatehouse J. however, I have, with diffidence, to disagree with that conclusion for the following reasons; the words of incorporation in *Miramar* were general words, not including any specific incorporation of the arbitration clause in the charter-party into the bills of lading. The issue in that case has nothing to do with the question whether the receivers were bound by the arbitration clause contained in that charter-party, but only with the question whether they were liable for demurrage under it. Mr Steyn, as he then was, in argument, submitted that the case before their Lordships House was entirely different from cases which concerned the question whether arbitration clause had been incorpo-rated, and I can find no indication in the speech of Lord Diplock, with which all

[35] [1991] 1 Lloyd's Rep. 126.

the other members of their Lordships House agreed, that the principle he was enunciating, or any of his reasoning, applied to cases of specific incorporation of an arbitration clause such as exists in this case and such as existed in *The Rena K*. Lord Diplock only referred to arbitration clauses at p. 683 where he said:

'In strictness, what is said by Russell L.J. and Lord Denning M.R. in *The Merak* [1965] P. 223 and *The Annefield* [1971] P. 168 was *obiter* as respects the correct approach to the extent to which incorporation clauses in bills of lading issued in standard forms annexed to charter-parties, are effective to impose upon the bill of lading holder personal liability for non performance of obligations undertaken by the charterer that are contained in clauses of the charter-party, other than an arbitration clause. Nevertheless, those *dicta* are a clear distinction as respects incorporation in the bill of lading between an arbitration clause in the charter-party and a clause therein "Which is directly germane to the shipment, carriage and delivery of goods". A clause which falls within this latter category, it was said, is to be treated as incorporated in the bill of lading even though it may involve a degree of "Manipulation" of the words in order to fit exactly the bill of lading.'

Even if that passage is to be read as extending the principles enunciated by the House of Lords in *Miramar* so as to apply to cases of general words of incorporation, and the application of those general words to arbitration clauses in charter-parties, I do not read them as constituting a *dictum*, still less a decision, that those principles should be extended to cases where the words of incorporation expressly and specifically include the arbitration clause. In both *The Merak* and *The Annefield*, the words of incorporation were general, not specific. Finally, the House of Lords in *Miramar* did not overrule *The Rena K*, though I can attach little weight to this point because that case was not referred to in the speech of Lord Diplock and, according to the report, was not even cited in argument.

For these reasons I follow the decision of Brandon J. rather than the reasoning of Mr Justice Gatehouse in *The Nai Matteini* . . . "

Similar sentiments were expressed by Clarke J. in *Daval Aciers D'Usinor et de Sacilor v Armare SRL (The Nerano)*,[36] and it appears, therefore, that clauses of this type can be manipulated as appropriate for a bill of lading contract.

No manipulation required?
As noted at paras 12–025, *et seq.*, in *The Federal Bulker* the arbitration clause was not incorporated by general words of incorporation, and that was sufficient to decide the case in the owners' favour. Had it been incorporated, arguably no manipulation would have been necessary, since the phrase in the charterparty applying to disputes "arising out of this contract" was equally apposite both to disputes under the charterparty and (by incorporation) under the bill of lading. This was not decided, and of course, with an arbitration clause it cannot matter, because it can only be incorporated by express words, and if so it will be manipulated. It might become an issue if similar wording were used in other clauses, incorporated by general words.

(f) From Which Charterparty?

Suppose there is more than one charterparty (*e.g.* if the ship is sub-chartered), **12–029** and the bill of lading does not state whether terms are to be incorporated from the head or sub-charterparty. Usually this is because gaps in the bill of lading, identifying the charterparty, are not filled in, so that the incorporation clause

---

[36] [1994] 2 Lloyd's Rep. 50, affirmed by the Court of Appeal [1996] 1 Lloyd's Rep. 1.

refers only to "the charterparty", without specifying which. The question now is which charterparty terms are incorporated (the courts having rejected the view that the clause is too uncertain to be given any effect).

The general position was stated by the Court of Appeal in *The San Nicholas*, who agreed with a statement made in what was then the current edition of *Scrutton on Charterparties*[37]:

> "It is submitted that a general reference will normally be construed as relating to the head charter, since this is the contract to which the shipowner, who issues the bill of lading, is a party."

In *The San Nicholas* only the head charterparty, and not the sub-charterparty, was subject to English law (the sub-charterparties being subject to the law of the flag of the vessel), and it was necessary for the plaintiff cargo-owners to show that English law applied to the bill of lading contract in order to obtain leave to serve a writ on the defendant shipowners out of the jurisdiction. The vessel and cargo had sunk and been totally lost. Because spaces in the incorporation clause in the bill of lading, which should have been filled in, had been left blank, it was not clear which charterparty terms were incorporated. The Court of Appeal held the head charter, so the cargo-owners obtained leave to serve the writ.

The San Nicholas was followed in *The Sevonia Team*,—see below. A general reference will therefore normally be construed as relating to the head charter.[38] The explicit justification is that the shipowners are party to the head, but not the sub-charterparty. The courts seem also concerned to protect the shipowner's lien for freight (see the discussion of general principles at para. 12–011). For these purposes, head charter freight is obviously more appropriate.

In both *The San Nicholas* and *The Sevonia Team* both head and sub-charterparty were voyage charters, however, and the position is different where the head charter is a time charterparty. It is clear that many of the terms of a time charterparty are quite inappropriate for incorporation into a bill of lading, for example reference to the period, delivery, re-delivery, and hire. So if the head charterparty is in time form, and the sub-charter in voyage form, the general rule will not apply, and the sub-charter will be incorporated.

BANGLADESH CHEMICAL INDUSTRIES CORPORATION v HENRY STEPHENS SHIPPING CO LTD (THE SLS EVEREST)

Court of Appeal. [1981] 2 Lloyd's Rep. 389

12–030   A cargo of 20,000 tonnes of phosphate of lime aboard the *SLS Everest* was lost when water entered the engineroom and the ship eventually sank. The shipowners had claimed on their hull insurance policy. The cargo-owners (plaintiffs) sued them for damages, and for a *Mareva* injunction to prevent them removing the insurance moneys from the jurisdiction. It was accepted that in order to obtain the injunction, the plaintiffs had to show that the carriage contract was governed by English law.

The bill of lading contained the statement:

> "Freight and other conditions as per —— including the exoneration clause . . ."

---

[37] *Scrutton on Charterparties* (18th ed., 1974) at p. 63.
[38] Scrutton's justification is that the shipowner is party to the head charter, the courts historically being anxious to protect the shipowner's lien for freight.

The blank was never filled in.

The vessel was chartered and sub-chartered. The head charterparty was a time charterparty, and was governed by French law, whereas the sub-charterparty, which was governed by English law, was a voyage charterparty.

Held:
The carriage contract was governed by English law. The terms of the sub-charterparty prevailed over those of the head charterparty, and were incorporated. The of the head charterparty, because it was a time charterparty, were inapposite.

LORD DENNING M.R.:

The Blank in the Bill of Lading
The question is: What is to be done about the blank in the sentence,

"Freight and other conditions as per —— including the exoneration clause."

In the case of *The San Nicholas* [1976] 1 Lloyd's Rep. 8, blanks were left in the bill of lading. That bill of lading said:

"This shipment is carried under and pursuant to the terms of the Charter dated —— at —— between —— and —— as Charterer."

This court held that, on its true construction, the blanks could be filled in according to the terms of the charter in that case: following a passage from *Scrutton on Charterparties* at p. 63:

"It not infrequently happens that where a printed form of bill provides for the incorporation of 'the charterparty dated . . . ', the parties omit to fill in the blank. It is submitted that the effect is the same as if the reference were simply to 'the charterparty', and that omission does not demonstrate an intent to negative the incorporation."

It seems to me that that reasoning is applicable here. Even though our clause does not say "the charter" or "the charterparty", I should have thought it is quite obvious to anyone that the sentence should read "Freight and other conditions as per charterparty including the exoneration clause". Unless the charter-party was incorporated, all sorts of terms and arrangements would have to be implied—or discovered in some other way—in order to make the whole thing workable. But it works simply and completely by incorporating the terms of the charter—that is, the terms of the voyage charter.

If it were a head charter, it might be another matter. *Scrutton on Charterparties* says:

"It is submitted that the general reference would normally be construed as relating to the head charter."

Then there is a note which says:

> "At any rate if it is a voyage charter. The position is less clear where it is a time charter, the terms of which are in many respects inapposite to the carriage of goods on a voyage. The court might well hesitate to hold the consignee liable for, say, unpaid time charter hire."

The charter here is the voyage charter. Therefore, I would write into the clause: "Freight and other conditions as per the charterparty"—that is, the charter-party . . . between Drumplace Ltd (the voyage charterers) and the Bangladeshi corporation [plaintiffs].

DUNN L.J.: That brings me to the second question: What charter-party is incorporated in the bill of lading and what is its proper law? Mr Hobhouse did not seriously suggest that the head charter-party . . . was incorporated, and he was right not to do so. The terms of that charter, which was a time charter, would have been quite inapplicable.

Note

12–031   In *The Sevonia Team*, Lloyd J. regarded *The SLS Everest* as an exception to the general rule, taking the view that a general reference will normally be construed as incorporating the head charterparty, as in *The San Nicholas* (because that is the only charterparty to which the shipowner is party). The reason for the opposite result in *The SLS Everest* was simply that the head charterparty was a time charter, and its terms therefore inapposite; while voyage charter terms, such as freight, laytime and demurrage, can make perfect sense in a bill of lading contract, time charter terms, such as hire, off-hire, delivery and redelivery, do not. Other common time charter clauses, such as speed warranties and trading limits, also make little sense in a bill of lading.

K/S A/S SEATEAM & CO v IRAQ NATIONAL OIL CO (THE SEVONIA TEAM)

Commercial Court. [1983] 2 Lloyd's Rep. 640

12–032   The facts have already been set out in chapter 3, above. The Bills of Lading Act aspects of this case have ceased to have any relevance following the enactment of the Carriage of Goods by Sea Act 1992 (see further chapter 13, above). It was also necessary, however, for the shipowners to show that the bill of lading incorporated the head charterparty, in order to claim freight from the receivers (who were also holders of the bill of lading). They succeeded in so doing, Lloyd J. following *The San Nicholas*, and distinguishing *The SLS Everest*.

LLOYD J.: *(after discussing the application of the 1855 Act)* I turn now to the second main point in the case: which, if either, of the two charter-parties is incorporated in the bill of lading? Mr Gilman [for the third defendant cargo-owners] submitted that the incorporation clause is so vague and uncertain, that neither of the charters is effectively incorporated. For that submission he relied on *Smidt v Tiden* (1874) L.R. 9 Q.B. 446. But, as the editors of Scrutton point out in a footnote, a court would nowadays hesitate long before reaching that conclusion. In two recent decisions, the Court of Appeal has held that the bill of lading was effective to incorporate the terms of a charter, even though in each case there were two charters to chose from: see *The San Nicholas* and *The SLS Everest* [above].

Mr Gilman sought to distinguish those decisions on the grounds that in both cases there was a space left blank in the printed form of bill of lading for the date of the charter to be inserted, and the date had been left blank; whereas in the present case there is no space for the date to be filled in. I am unable to follow that distinction. The fact that there is no space left blank would, if anything, make the incorporation clause less, not more, uncertain.

As to the choice between the two charters, the general rule is stated in Scrutton (at p. 63) as follows:

"It is submitted that a general reference will normally be construed as relating to the head charter, since this is the contract to which the shipowner, who issues the bill of lading, is a party."

That passage was expressly approved by Lord Denning, M.R., in *The San Nicholas*, at p. 11:

" . . . It seems to me plain that the shipment was carried under and pursuant to the terms of the head charter . . . the head charter was the only charter to which the shipowners were parties; and they must, in the bill of lading, be taken to be referring to that head charter. I find myself in agreement with the statement in *Scrutton on Charterparties* . . . "

Of course there are exceptions. In *The SLS Everest*, the head charter was a time charter. I held, following a suggestion in another footnote in Scrutton, that the reference was to the sub-charter in that case, since the terms of the time charter were largely inapposite. That decision was upheld in the Court of Appeal. Here it is the other way round. The head charter is a voyage charter, and the terms are wholly apposite. It is the sub-charter, or transportation agreement, whose terms may be regarded as inapposite . . .

[*Lloyd J. concluded that there were no sufficient grounds "to displace the normal rule that the reference in the bill of lading is a reference to the head charter."*]

Notes

The problem with incorporating terms from a time charterparty is not that it is a long-term charterparty, but that it contains terms which are wholly different in type from a voyage charterparty or bill of lading. A consecutive voyage charter can also be very long-term, but its terms are of a type that can easily be incorporated into a bill of lading. In principle, therefore, a consecutive voyage charterparty should be treated like a voyage charterparty, and in *The Nai Matteini*, *The San Nicholas*, rather than *The SLS Everest*, was followed.

NAVIGAZIONNE ALTA ITALIA SpA v SVENSKA PETROLEUM A/B (THE NAI MATTEINI)

Queen's Bench Division (Commercial Court). [1988] 1 Lloyd's Rep. 452

Facts:

12–033 The facts boil down to the following. The plaintiffs, who were owners of *The Nai Matteini*, were an Italian corporation. They chartered the vessel to Montedison S.p.A., also an Italian corporation, on a long-term consecutive voyage charterparty, of over 13 years' duration. This head charterparty, which was expressly governed by Italian law, contained an arbitration clause, which (read literally) applied only to disputes between the owner and head-charterer.

Montedison sub-chartered the vessel to Saudi Arabian Maritime Co for a voyage (on an Asbatankvoy—formerly Exxonvoy 1969—form). The sub-charterparty provided for arbitration in London, and was to be governed by English law.

The defendants were purchasers of a cargo of crude oil, shipped aboard The *Nai Matteini*. The bill of lading purported to incorporate all the terms, conditions and exceptions contained in the Charter Party, including (among other clauses) the arbitration clause. In other words, the arbitration clause (or at least the arbitration clause from one of the charterparties) was *expressly* incorporated.[39] The defendants alleged short delivery of the oil at discharge, and just under a year later telexed commenced arbitration proceedings in London, on the basis of the arbitration clause in the Asbatankvoy sub-charter. No further proceedings were taken, however.

Exactly 5 years and a day after the alleged short delivery had taken place, the plaintiffs (*i.e.* the shipowners) sought a declaration that there was no agreement between plaintiffs and defendants to submit disputes between them, relating to the carriage of that cargo, to arbitration.[40]

Held:

In the Commercial Court, Gatehouse J. found in favour of the shipowners, on the grounds that there was no arbitration agreement in force between the parties. The arbitration clause from the head charterparty, not the sub-charterparty was incorporated. This clause applied only to disputes between the owner and head-

---

[39] Thus, the problems considered in cases such as *The Varenna* did not apply; there was, however, a manipulation issue (see above).

[40] It is not made clear in the report why exactly five years had been allowed to pass before this declaration was sought, but it would be no surprise if this is connected with the limitation period under Italian law.

The plaintiffs also claimed that arbitration proceedings had been abandoned, but had decided to defer the issue of abandonment pending an appeal to the House of Lords (presumably now reported as *Food Corporation of India v Antclizo Shipping Corporation (The Antclizo)* [1988] 1 W.L.R 603). A major difference between arbitration and litigation is that arbitrators have no power to strike out claims because of delay in pursuing them, even after years have elapsed. This can be extremely inconvenient for a respondent, where the claimant has started arbitration proceedings, but has taken no further action, but where the claim has not been formally abandoned.

charterer, and therefore could not (without manipulation) apply to disputes between the plaintiffs and defendants. Gatehouse J. was not prepared to manipulate the clause, on the principles considered in the previous section.

Comment:
The clause in the bill of lading referred only to the "Charter Party", without specifying which. The head-charterparty here was in consecutive voyage form, but Gatehouse J. was not persuaded by arguments for the defendants (based on *The SLS Everest*—see above at para. 12–030), that the provisions of the head-charterparty were inapposite for incorporation into the bill of lading, and that the general rule should not apply. He concluded, therefore, that the arbitration clause in the head-charterparty was incorporated into the bill of lading, but that it did not apply to disputes between the plaintiffs and defendants.

    The San Nicholas states only the normal position, however, and was distinguished by His Honour Judge Diamond Q.C. in *The Heidberg*.

PAUL TODD, CASENOTE ON THE HEIDBERG[41]

[1994] 6 Oil and Gas Law and Taxation Review D67

Charterparty
    Incorporation of arbitration clause in charterparty into bill of lading   **12–034**
—clause from which charterparty incorporated?
    Partenreederei M/S "Heidberg" v Grosvenor Grain and Feed Co Ltd, The "Heidberg"
    Queen's Bench Division (Commercial Court)
    His Honour Judge Diamond Q.C. (sitting as a judge of the High Court).
    Commercial Court, 21 March 1994.

Facts:
The full facts are very complicated but stripped of inessential details amount to the following.

    In July 1990 a contract of affreightment was concluded between UNCAC (shippers) and Peter Dohle, neither of whom were parties to the action. The contract was on the SYNACOMEX form, for a minimum of 6 and a maximum of 12 voyages over a period, and provided for arbitration in Paris.

    In February 1991 UNCAC gave notice, in accordance with the contract of affreightment, for a vessel to load at Bordeaux, the cancelling date being 8th March 1991. Peter Dohle had no vessel available which could meet the cancelling date, and so arranged to charter *The Heidberg* for a voyage from the plaintiff shipowners. The charter was arranged at short notice by telephone, later followed up by a recap telex. It was intended to use the SYNACOMEX 90 form, but amended so as to replace the Paris arbitration clause with a Centrocon arbitration clause providing for arbitration in London. At the time of shipment and issue of bills of lading the voyage charterparty had not been reduced to writing (indeed, it was not until about 2 years later).

[41] Now reported at [1994] 2 Lloyd's Rep. 287.

UNCAC accordingly shipped cargo aboard *The Heidberg* and obtained a bill of lading, incorporating the terms and conditions of the charter-party, including the arbitration clause, but not identifying which charter-party. The bill of lading was later indorsed in favour of the defendants (as c.i.f. buyers), and it was common ground that under the terms of the Bills of Lading Act 1855, s.1, which was the operative provision at the time, only the defendants could sue or be sued on the bill of lading.

Soon after leaving Bordeaux *The Heidberg* collided with another vessel and the plaintiffs' cargo was damaged. The plaintiff owners issued a writ in London claiming (*inter alia*) general average from the defendants, and a declaration that they were not liable for breach of contract and/or duty in respect of the collision. Six days later the defendants' insurers to whom the defendant's claims were subrogated claimed against the owners in the Tribunal de Commerce in Paris, and the owners claimed that the Tribunal had no jurisdiction. They claimed that the dispute should be resolved by arbitration in London, in accordance with the Centrocon arbitration clause in the March 1991 voyage charterparty. The Tribunal de Commerce handed down judgment in September 1993, holding (*inter alia*) that the Centrocon arbitration clause was not incorporated in the bill of lading (it was common ground that this conclusion was correct according to French law).

Held (for the defendants):

1. The Court was bound by the Brussels Convention to recognise the decision of the Tribunal de Commerce that the Centrocon arbitration clause was not incorporated in the bill of lading.

2. If the court was wrong on the first issue then the question whether the Centrocon arbitration clause was incorporated should be determined by English law, not French law.

3. Under English law also, however, the Centrocon clause was not incorporated into the bill of lading.

Comment:

12–035   The most interesting issues arise on point 3. The bill of lading clearly incorporated an arbitration clause from a charterparty, but did not specify which, referring only to a "charterparty dated . . . .", but with the blank not filled in. The courts have long held that the absence of the date does not render the incorporation clause void for uncertainty, and the general position was stated by the Court of Appeal in *The San Nicholas* [1976] 1 Lloyd's Rep. 8, who agreed with a statement made in what was then the current edition of *Scrutton on Charterparties*:

> "It is submitted that a general reference will normally be construed as relating to the head charter, since this is the contract to which the shipowner, who issues the bill of lading, is a party."

The San Nicholas was followed in *The Sevonia Team* [1983] 2 Lloyd's Rep. 640 and *The Nai Matteini* [1988] 1 Lloyd's Rep. 452 (see [1987/88] 12 OGLTR D136–D138). Until the present decision, therefore, it was assumed that a general reference would therefore normally be construed as relating to the head charter. In *The Heidberg*, the head charterparty was the March 1991 voyage charter, so an application of these principles would have led to the Centrocon clause being incorporated. In rejecting this conclusion His Honour Judge Diamond Q.C. cast doubt on the generality of "normal rule" from *The San Nicholas*.

Undoubtedly there are exceptions to the "normal rule". In *The San Nicholas* and *The Sevonia Team* both the above cases head and sub-charterparty were voyage charters, and in *The Nai Matteini* the head charter was for 13 years' consecutive voyages, but where the head charter is a time (or presumably demise) charterparty it has long been recognised that different principles apply, since many terms of a time charterparty would be inapposite for incorporation into a bill of lading (for example period, delivery, re-delivery, and hire clauses). Hence, in *The SLS Everest* [1981] 2 Lloyd's Rep. 289, where the head-charterparty was a time charterparty, the Court of Appeal did not apply the general rule: the terms of the sub-charter were incorporated.

In *The Heidberg*, however, the head charterparty was a voyage charterparty, and His Honour Judge Diamond Q.C. had therefore to find other reasons for displacing the "normal rule" in *The San Nicholas*. He would have been prepared to decide the issue on the narrow ground that a bill of lading is not capable of incorporating a charterparty whose terms had not, at the time of its issue, been reduced into writing, on the grounds first that the wording in the bill of lading, "in accordance with the Charter Party dated" referred more aptly to a written than to an oral contract, secondly that a bill of lading is a transferable document whose terms in the hands of an indorsee do not, in the interests of certainty, include oral terms, on analogy with *Leduc v Ward* (1888) 20 Q.B.D. 475, and thirdly that an arbitration agreement has to be in writing to come within the Arbitration Act 1950 and the New York Convention, and it would be strange if the bill of lading were capable of incorporating an agreement which fell outside these provisions.

His Honour Judge Diamond Q.C. would have gone further, however, and doubted the generality of "the normal rule" from *The San Nicholas*. Scrutton's observation that the head charter is the one to which the shipowner is party ignored the position of the shipper, who is the other (original) party to the bill of lading contract. While there may be reasons for adopting *The San Nicholas* approach where there is a cesser clause in the head charterparty and the incorporation clause was intended to give the shipowner a lien on the cargo for freight or demurrage, there was no reason for doing so here, where there was no cesser clause in the head charterparty applying to demurrage and no possibility of a lien for freight, since it did not become payable until after delivery. It followed that, taking into account all commercial reasons for incorporating either document in the bill of lading, there was no reason to prefer the voyage charterparty to the contract of affreightment (which His Honour Judge Diamond Q.C. thought could properly be referred to as a charterparty, although this was not the usual usage of that term).

Comments

12–036   There were therefore a number of reasons why the head charter terms were not incorporated, including doubts as to whether *The San Nicholas* should be of general application; its rationale was to protect the shipowner's lien, and that rationale could not possibly apply here.

His Honour Judge Diamond Q.C. also emphasised that the head charterparty was oral (although I do not think this was essential to the decision in *The Heidberg*). There was, however, a recap telex, and this aspect of the decision was doubted in *The Epsilon Rosa*.[42] In that case, the defendant shipowners claimed that an arbitration clause from a charterparty had been incorporated (by express words of incorporation) into the bill of lading. The claimant cargo-owners claimed that there was no arbitration clause in force, partly on the basis that the charterparty had not been reduced to writing. David Steel J.:

"[24] It was the claimant's submission that the recap telex and the associated documentation did not constitute a charterparty for the purposes of the clause . . .

. . .

[25] The claimants derived some support for their approach from the decision of Judge Diamond Q.C. in *Partenreederei M/S Heidberg v Grosvenor Grain and Feed Co, The Heidberg* [1994] 2 Lloyd's Rep. 287. The judge was there concerned with a fixture agreed over the telephone. It was followed up by a recap telex. The recap telex was in fact erroneous in referring to the wrong standard form of charterparty (which contained a Paris arbitration clause) in comparison with that which had been agreed (which contained a London arbitration clause). Although in due course the charterers sent a form of charterparty to the owners for signature, that was not acted on as the casualty had already occurred.

[26] Amongst the many issues upon which the judge was asked to rule was whether 'an incorporation clause in a bill of lading can have the effect of incorporating oral terms which have not been reduced into writing'. Having set out his reasons for concluding that it would be commercially unsound to hold that a bill of lading (in like terms to the present) was capable of incorporating the terms of an oral agreement, the judge concluded (at 311):

'I therefore consider that, as a matter of the construction of the bill of lading, it does not incorporate the terms of the charter-party which, at the date of the bill of lading is issued, had not been reduced to writing. For the reasons given earlier an oral contract, evidenced only by a recap telex, does not seem to me to qualify for this purpose.'

[27] I am unable to accept the claimant's submission . . .

. . .

[28] I fully accept and adopt the decision in *The Heidberg* to the extent that the transferee of a bill of lading should not be affected by oral terms. But I cannot accede to the further proposition that where the contract is contained in or evidenced by a recap telex, this does not qualify for the purposes of having been reduced to writing. This conclusion of Judge Diamond Q.C. was expressed to be 'for the reasons given earlier'. The only earlier reference to this matter is in his comment ([1994] 2 Lloyd's Rep. 287 at 310):

'[Counsel for the plaintiff owner's] submissions can only suggest, at most, that where an oral contract is evidenced by a written document such as a 'recap telex', the terms set out in that document may perhaps be treated as capable of being incorporated into a bill of lading. The argument cannot reasonably be pressed so far as to suggest that an oral term, which is not contained in or evidenced by any document at all, is capable of being incorporated.'

[42] [2002] E.W.H.C. 762 (Comm.).

[29] In my judgment, commercial realities are wholly inconsistent with the claimant's submission. Indeed, the claimant was aware of and had approved the fixture.[43] I find the 'Charter Party' referred to in the bill of lading was the agreement contained in the recap telex (and the standard form to which it refers). This conclusion seems to me to accord with the duty on the court to give an intelligent meaning to documents surrounding this commercial transaction."

Whereas a bill of lading must be in writing in order to constitute a valid document of title, and for the purposes of Art. III(3) of the *Hague-Visby Rules*, there are no formality requirements for either charterparties or sale contracts, although arbitration clauses must be in writing. It is common for charterparty fixtures to be made by telephone, or on the Internet, with details following on a fax or recap telex, and perhaps eventually a formal signed document. The extent to which terms must be agreed for a contract to become binding, and the meaning of writing in the Internet age, are considered further in chapter 16, below.

(3) IDENTITY OF CARRIER

Bills of lading are not issued personally by shipowners and charterers, but by **12–037** the master, or perhaps charterers' agents or loading brokers (see further chapter 14, below for a description of these roles). Usually the person signing signs for the shipowner, but in some cases he will sign as agent for the charterer.

Shippers (and subsequent holders) need to know whether the bills of lading are issued on behalf of the shipowner or charterer. The *Hague Rules* and *Hague-Visby Rules* impose a time bar, and delays pursuing the wrong party are clearly to be avoided. Other reasons why the issue is important are:

1. The charterer may have gone into liquidation, as in *The Nea Tyhi* (see para. 14–037, below), or stolen the cargo and disappeared (as in *Manchester Trust*, below), in which case if there is no action against the shipowner there is no action against anyone.
2. If, *e.g.* a shipowner is sued in tort, he can only rely on exemption clauses in the bill of lading (subject to the bailment on terms principle set out at para. 12–046, and in appropriate circumstances to the Contract (Rights of Third Parties) Act 1999) if he is party to the carriage contract.

As between shipowner and charterer, the issue is simply this: on whose authority does the master (or other person signing) issue bills of lading? The terms of the charterparty are likely to be relevant. Even where cargo-owners are concerned, ultimately the issue is one of agency, but apparent as well as actual authority can now be relevant. Moreover, the cargo-owner may have no knowledge of the charterparty, and the courts have been reluctant to import equitable notice doctrines to impose charterparty terms upon him. Ideally, then, at least from the cargo-owner's viewpoint, it should not be necessary to examine the charterparty in detail to determine for whom the master (or other person signing) acts. The law should adopt presumptions, or concentrate on the bill of lading, rather than the terms of the charterparty.

There are indeed rebuttable presumptions. In general, where a charterparty is by demise the master signs on behalf of the charterer. In the case of time and voyage charterparties there is a rebuttable presumption that the *master* signs on behalf of the shipowner. Issues tend to arise today where the bill of lading is signed by someone other than the master.

Sometimes the charterparty itself will contain a demise (or identity of carrier) clause, which states whether the master signs on behalf of owner or charterer. Though this is enforceable as between owners and charterers, it will not usually bind a cargo-owner, who is not party to the charterparty.

---

[43] He had also paid freight on the basis of the recap telex [author's footnote].

(a) Demise Charterparty

BAUMWOLL MANUFACTUR VON CARL SCHEIBER v FURNESS

House of Lords. [1893] A.C. 8

12–038   A vessel was chartered for a term of four months, the charter providing that the captain and crew should be servants of the charterer, and paid and appointed by him (except the chief engineer, who was appointed by the shipowner, but paid for by the charterer).[44]

Goods were shipped under bills of lading signed by the captain and some of the charterer's agents, without any actual authority from the owner. The bills of lading contained no reference to the charterparty and the shippers had no notice of its terms. Due, it was alleged, to the unseaworthiness of the ship the goods were lost at sea. The shippers sued the owner.

The issue was whether the owners or charterers were liable on the bills of lading, or alternatively in tort.

Held:
The owner was not liable, the bills of lading not having been signed on his behalf.

Lord Herschell L.C.: My Lords, this case in my opinion turns on the construction of the charterparty, and the question is what was the relation created by it between the parties? Was is a "demise" of the ship, or of not strictly speaking a demise was it an agreement which put the vessel altogether out of the power and control of the then owner, and vested that power and control in the charterers, so that during the time that this hiring lasted she must be regarded as the vessel of the charterers, and not as the vessel of the owner?

In order to create what has been called a demise, it is obvious that the use of the word "demise" is not necessary. When this charterparty was entered into the vessel was let by the one party, and hired by the other for a term at a lump sum, to be paid month by month during that term. The use which was to be made of the vessel during that term rested entirely with the charterers. The then owner had no voice whatever in it. The charterers might send her on such voyages as they pleased; and the only right which the owner had to object was that he had limited and restricted to a slight extent the use of the vessel by the terms of the charterparty. The master of the vessel and the crew were appointed as well as paid by the charterers. The owner had no voice in this at all. All that he had a voice in was the nomination of the chief engineer, but even that officer was to be paid by the charterers. Now how would it be possible so far (I will come to the other clauses which are relied on presently) more completely to let and hire this ship—demise it, if you will—put it out of the power and control of the owner, and put it in the

---

[44] This was a hire purchase arrangement, where the vessel was let for a period of months, after which the charterers were obliged to purchase her. Demise charterparties are still used for hire purchase.

power and control of the charterers than by such provisions as these? It is said that the charterers could not use the vessel for all voyages, and that there was a certain restriction placed on their right so to use her. That certainly is not conclusive against a demise, otherwise there would be no demise of half the houses in this metropolis which are subject to restrictions as to the uses to which they can be put.

Then it is said that there are other provisions which shew that the owner was not entirely parting with his possession or control of the vessel, inasmuch as he was to insure her. The remark which I have just made applies equally to that provision. But in addition to that, he was to keep the hull and machinery in thoroughly efficient repair for the sevice. Would it be the less a demise of a house or of a chattel because the owner who demised it undertook to keep it in repair during the term for which it was demised?

What are the other stipulations which are relied upon? There is a provision that "the charterers hereby agree to indemnify the owners from all consequences or liabilities that may arise from the captain signing bills of lading, or in otherwise complying with the same." It is said that the insertion of that clause shews that the parties contemplated that the signing of the bills of lading by the captain might impose a liability upon Furness. I think a just observation was made with regard to some of these provisions by the learned Master of the Rolls; namely, that this is a document which is not prepared specially for this purpose; a good deal of it is in print, altered in writing to suit the particular arrangement; but some of the provisions that have been left standing were undoubtably not specifically inserted with a view to this agreement, but have been left standing it may be more or less through an oversight. I do not, of course, for a moment dispute that in reading this document you must construe together the written and the printed parts. But it is not a question what liability is imposed by the clause I have just read. It imposes no liability at all. It says that the charterers shall indemnify the owners from all liability. So they undertake to do, no doubt, and effect must be given to it, if such a liability is imposed. But to infer from the presence of such a provision in the charterparty that the parties must have had it in contemplation that a liability would be imposed, inasmuch as otherwise they would not have provided for an indemnity against it, appears to me to be straining the effect of a printed provision in a document of this sort much beyond the extent to which it is legitimate to do so.

The only other provision I think on which reliance is placed is this, "that the owners shall have a lien upon all cargoes, and all sub-freights, for freight or chater-money due under this charter." It does not appear to me that there is anything in that provision, which is a provision as between charterer and shipowner, which stands in the way of the view I have suggested to your Lordships that this is acase in which by the charterparty the charterer has become, *pro hac vice* and during the term of the charter, the owner of the vessel, when one is considering the rights and liabilities which arise from the acts of the master, and the crew of the vessel, who during that time are the servants of the charterer, appointed and paid by him.

It cannot be disputed as a general proposition of law, that a person who does not himself enter into a contract, can only be made liable upon the contract if it was entered into by one who was his agent or servant acting within the scope of his authority; and it is equally indisputable that a liability by reason of a wrong or tort can only be established by proving, either that the person charged himself committed the wrong, or that it was committed by his servants or agents acting within the scope of their authority.

In the present case the right of the plaintiffs to complain of the loss of their goods by reason of the facts alleges, may be regarded as arising as a matter of contract out of the bills of lading that were signed. Is it established that the persons who signed those bills of lading, with whom in the first instance the contract was made, the master, or Messrs. Ross and Keen the agents at the port, in making that contract were acting for the defendant Furness? It seems to me impossible to contend that these were contracts made either with the master or the agents on behalf of the defendant Furness.

Notes

12–039   1. This case should be contrasted with *Manchester Trust v Furness, Withy,* below, where there is a clear presumption that the captain acts as agent for the owners. The reason for there being no such presumption here was that the House of Lords regarded this as a demise charterparty, although it did not share many of the features commonly found in demise charters. There was no use of the word "demise", there was some restriction on the use to which the ship could be put, and the owner undertook to keep the hull and machinery in repair. The main reasoning lay in the provisions in the charter as to the employment of captain and crew, putting the ship out of the power and control of the owner, and into the power and control of the charterer.

2. Whether the action was regarded as one in contract or tort, it was held that the ordinary principles of agency applied, there being nothing special about the relationship between shipper and shipowner:

"A contract of affreightment is only like any other contract".

It mattered not that the shippers had no notice of the terms of the charter.

3. One reason for the opposite conclusion being reached in *Manchester Trust,* below (which was not, however, a charterparty by demise), was that it would have been unfair on the holder of the bill of lading had the owner been able to evade liability.

(b) Time and Voyage Charters

MANCHESTER TRUST LTD v FURNESS, WITHY & CO LTD

Queen's Bench Division. [1895] 2 Q.B. 539

12–040   A vessel (the Boston City) was chartered under a time charterparty, which contained the following provision (demise clause):

"The captain and crew, although paid by the owners, shall be agents and servants of the charterers for all purposes, whether of navigation or otherwise, under the charter. In signing bills of lading it is especially agreed that the captain shall only do so as agent for the charterers; and the charterers hereby agree to indemnify the owners from all consequences or liabilities (if any) that may arise from the captain signing bills of lading, or in otherwise complying with the same."

The charterers shipped coal aboard the vessel, and the master issued bills of lading to them as shippers: "and other conditions as per charterparty", but not containing the above clause from the charterparty. The bill of lading stated Rio de Janeiro as port of destination, but the charterers tricked the master instead to unload at Buenos Ayres, without production of the bills. The charterers indorsed the bills to the plaintiff's bank to secure an advance, but fraudulently sold the coal to a third party.

The plaintiffs sued the defendant shipowners for damages for non-delivery at Rio. The shipowners denied liability on the basis of the clause in the charterparty.

Held:
For the plaintiffs, that the clause in the charterparty was ineffective to rebut the presumption that the master acted as servant of the shipowners, being effective only as an undertaking between shipowners and charterers.

LINDLEY L.J.:   **12–041**
... The plaintiffs, who are holders of the bills of lading, rely upon the general rule of law that primâ facie at all events a bill of lading signed by the master is signed by the master as the servant or agent of the shipowner. Of course, in the ordinary course of business that is so; but it may turn out that the master is not the servant or agent of the shipowner, and in the case to which we were referred of *Baumwoll Manufactur v Furness* [above], the charter was such that the master was not the servant of the shipowner, but was the servant of the charterer. The peculiarity of that case was this, that although the charterparty there contained a great many clauses similar to those which we find in the charterparty in this case, the hiring of the master was by the charterer and not by the shipowner. The charterer employed him, paid him, dismissed him, and upon the strength of that clause the House of Lords held, affirming the decision of this Court, that the master was in fact the servant of the charterer, and was not in fact the servant of the shipowner. Now it is said that, notwithstanding that case, the peculiar clause [demise clause] to which I have alluded shews that in truth the master here had ceased to be or was not the servant of the owner, but had become the servant of the charterer, and the real question we have to consider is what is the effect of that clause as between the holder of the bill of lading and the shipowner. Let us look first of all at the true construction of the clause as between the shipowner and the charterer. They are the persons who make that bargain, and as between them the captain and crew, although paid by the owners, are to be the agents and servants of the charterers. Then the clause contains an indemnity, which to my mind is extremely significant. It seems as if these parties felt that, notwithstanding this clause, the owners might be held

liable for the acts of the master; and they stipulated in that event, notwith-standing the previous bargain that the captain is to be the agent and servant of the charterer—the charterer shall indemnify the shipowner. The view taken by Mathew J. is that that is a stipulation which is valid as between the charterers and the owners, but which does not affect the true position of the captain and the crew, and has no effect at all upon the holder of the bill of lading, although the bill of lading refers in terms to this charterparty. Upon reflection, I am of opinion that that is the true and correct view. I cannot regard all these clauses taken together without coming to the conclusion that the master was, and continued to be in fact, the servant of the owner, subject to a stipulation that as between the owner and the charterers the charterers should treat him as his servant, and indemnify the owners from the consequences of what the captain might do as regards signing bills of lading and so on.

Now, if that is the true view it settles the question. But then we are pressed with the fact that in this case the bill of lading referred to the charterparty, and it is said that the holder of the bill of lading took it with notice of the charterparty, and with notice therefore of this contract, and with notice that the master was the servant of the charterers. That argu-ment appears to me to be pushing the doctrine of constructive notice a great deal too far . . . What is wanted in this case is to say that by reason of the reference to the charterparty the holder of the bill of lading and the person who takes it in the ordinary course of business are to be treated as having notice of all the contents of the charterparty. There is no doctrine that goes to anything like that extent; and as regards the extension of the equitable doctrines of constructive notice to commercial transactions, the Courts have always set their faces resolutely against it. The equitable doctrines of constructive notice are common enough in dealing with land and estates, with which the Court is familiar; but there have been repeated protests against the introduction into commercial transactions of anything like an extension of those doctrines, and the protest is founded on perfect good sense. In dealing with estates in land title is everything, and it can be leisurely investigated; in commercial transactions posses-sion is everything, and there is no time to investigate title; and if we were to extend the doctrine of constructive notice to commercial transactions we should be doing infinite mischief and paralyzing the trade of the country . . .

Notes

12–042   Lindley L.J.'s reluctance to import equitable notice doctrines into the field of commerce has often been cited with approval. The logic must be that the charter-party is not scrutinised too closely. Here, a presumption was applied that the master signed for the shipowner. The clause in the charterparty was not a good ground for rebutting the presumption, and *Baumwoll* reasoning, applying as it did only to charters by demise, was inapposite.

The decision is also consistent with the general principle of agency that as against a third party, a principal (here the shipowner) cannot limit the usual authority of his agent (master) without informing third parties who deal with him of the agent's limited authority.

Similar reasoning would not apply to a demise clause in a bill of lading.

The *Manchester Trust* presumption only applies, on its terms, to bills of lading signed by the master. Time and voyage charters are sometimes used by liner operators to charter in additional tonnage. Often in such cases, the ship will be painted in the charterers' colours, and bills of lading issued by the charterers, or their agents, possibly on their own standard forms with their own logo. Clearly it would be inappropriate, in such cases, to conclude that the carriage contract is made with the shipowner.

THE OKEHAMPTON

Court of Appeal. [1913] P. 173

The plaintiffs were sub-charterers (both head and sub-charters being by way of **12–043** voyage charterparty) of a vessel which was sunk by collision with the defendants' vessel (*The Okehampton*). The defendants admitted that the collision was caused by the negligent navigation of their vessel. The plaintiffs sued for the bill of lading freight which they would have earned but for the collision, either on the basis that they would have been contractually entitled to it, or on the grounds of their right to possession as bailees of the goods.

The issue was whether the bill of lading had been signed by the plaintiffs (themselves, not by the ship's master) on their own behalf as principals, in which case they would have sufficient possessory interest in ship and cargo to bring the action, or whether they were signing as agents for the shipowners, in which case they had not sufficient interest.

Held:

Reversing the decision of Bargreave Deane J., the plaintiffs signed the bill of lading on their own behalf, as principals. *As a matter of fact* the Court of Appeal held that the contract of carriage was made with the plaintiff sub-charterers.

Note

The *Manchester Trust* presumption was not applied, though both head and sub-charters were by way of voyage, not demise charterparty. Two factors considered relevant by Hamilton L.J. were first, that the plaintiffs seemed merely to be making a casual addition to their own line of steamers, and secondly that the bill of lading was signed by the sub-charterers themselves, and not by the ship's master.

(c) Demise Clauses in Bills of Lading

THE BERKSHIRE

Queen's Bench Division (Admiralty). [1974] 1 Lloyd's Rep. 185

Goods were shipped on board *The Lancashire*, a ship owned by the same owners **12–044** (Bibby Line Ltd) as *The Berkshire*, in apparent good order and condition. *The Lancashire* was operating under a time charterparty at all material times. The bill of lading was issued by Ayers Steamship Co on behalf of the charterers' agents, Ocean Wide. By order of the charterers the ship deviated during the voyage, and the goods were transhipped on to a vessel not owned by the same owners. At some later time, but before delivery at the port of discharge, the goods were damaged by sea water.

The shippers and indorsees brought an action *in rem* against the owners of *The Lancashire.*

Two main issues arose: first, whether the owners were party to the contract of carriage, and whether therefore the indorsees could sue by virtue of the Bills of Lading Act 1855, s.1 (see chapter 13, below), and secondly, whether, if the owners were party to such a contract, they were liable for damage that occurred after transhipment.

Held

1. The owners were party to the contract of carriage. On the question of whether the charterer signed the bill of lading as agent for the shipowner, a demise clause in the bill of lading was read literally:

   "If the ship is not owned or chartered by demise to the company or line by whom the Bill of Lading is issued (as may be the case notwithstanding anything that appears to the contrary) the Bill of Lading shall take effect as a contract with the Owner or demise charterer as the case may be as principal made through the agency of the said company or line who act as agents only and shall be under no personal liability whatsoever in respect thereof."

2. The owners were liable for damage that occurred after transhipment.

BRANDON J.: *(on the demise clause)* Despite arguments to the contrary put forward for the shipowners, I see no reason not to give effect to the demise clause in accordance with its terms. The company or line by whom the bill of lading was issued, within the meaning of the clause, is clearly in this case Ocean Wide. It is not in dispute that the ship was not owned or chartered by demise to that company, but was on the contrary owned by the shipowners. It follows that the bill of lading is, by its express terms, intended to take effect as a contract between the shippers and shipowners made on behalf of the shipowners by Ocean Wide as agents only. The circumstance that Ayers signed the bill of lading for Ocean Wide does not affect the position, which is the same as if Ocean Wide had signed it themselves.

On the first point, therefore, I hold that the contract contained in or evidenced by the bill of lading purports to be a contract between the shippers and shipowners, and not between the shippers and charterers.

Notes

This bill of lading was not signed by the master, so the *Manchester Trust v Furness* presumption did not apply. It may well be that, in the absence of the demise clause, the charterers' agents, on whose behalf the bill was signed, would have been taken to be signing for the time charterers. The explicit demise clause in the bill of lading gave notice to the holders that the bill of lading was signed only with the owners' authority, and the holders were entitled to rely on that representation.

In *The Mica* [1973] 2 Lloyd's Rep. 478, a demise clause was held by Heald J. in the Canada Federal Court, Trial Division, to be ineffective to relieve charterers from liability, being contrary to Article III(8) of the *Hague Rules*. As with *The Berkshire*, it must be presumed that the charterers would have been regarded as the contracting party, apart from the clause. If *The Mica* is correct, then it suggests that the charterers would not have been able to escape liability, had they (rather than the shipowners) been sued in *The Berkshire*.

(d) Other Factors

Bill of lading signed by master:
The *Manchester Trust* reasoning starts with a presumption, which was not rebutted **12–045** by any of the factors present in the case. In principle it could presumably be rebutted. *Elder Dempster & Co v Paterson, Zochonis & Co* was similar to *The Okehampton*, in that the time charterers were liner operators, adding temporary additional tonnage to their fleet. The bills of lading were however signed by the master, albeit on the directions of the charterers. Rowlatt J. held that these were charterers' bills, an assumption that both Court of Appeal and House of Lords were content to accept.[45] However, even where the charterers were liner operators, adding temporary additional tonnage, the Court of Appeal in *The Rewia* refused to depart from the general principle that a bill of lading signed by the master is an owner's bill.[46] Leggatt L.J. said that:

"a bill of lading signed for the master cannot be a charterer's bill unless the contract was made with the charterers alone, and the person signing has authority to sign, and does sign, on behalf of the charterers and not the owners."

Of *Elder Dempster*, he said:

"*Paterson Zochonis v Elder Dempster* concerned a claim for cargo damage which occurred on a vessel chartered for use in the Elder Dempster Line. The bills of lading were issued in the name of the first three defendants, of whom African Shipping Co were the time charterers. The question of liability on the bills was dealt with only in passing, Rowlatt J. observing:

'. . . it seems to me that there is a contract with the African Shipping Co on this bill of lading. This is a case where a well-known line of ships found it necessary to supplement its fleet by getting in another upon a time charter; and people in the commercial world who use the line know nothing at all about that. They think they are shipping by this line; and unless it is clear to the contrary the contract should be regarded as being made with the line. In this case the mate's receipt as the bill of lading itself which goes just as far it is the more material document proclaims to the people who took the bill of lading that those who are going to carry the goods are the African Steamship Co; and there is the signature at the bottom which may be the signature of the master without qualification. Therefore, I think, in these circumstances it is a bill of lading with the African Steamship Co.'

[The plaintiffs] relied on this case as an example of a vessel chartered on a line. The report of the case in the Court of Appeal ([1923] 1 K.B. 420 at page 422) shows that, as the judge held, the contract on the bill of lading was with the charterers. But no impetus is to be derived from that case for present purposes, because although the bills were liner bills all the tonnage used by the first defendants appears to have been chartered in."

Elder Dempster is, therefore, regarded as exceptional, but still presumably applicable where the bill of lading represents clearly enough that the contracting

---

[45] (1922) 12 Ll. L.R. 69, affirmed [1923] 1 K.B. 420; reversed on other grounds [1924] A.C. 522
[46] [1991] 2 Lloyds Rep. 325.

carriers are charterers, and where they are a well-known line chartering in additional tonnage (but apparently not where they charter in all their tonnage).

Bill of lading signed other than by master:
Where the bill of lading is signed by, for example charterers' agents, no rules can be stated with any confidence. Usually these will be liner bills, and the factual situation will often be similar to *Elder Dempster* or *The Okehampton*, above. There appears to be no presumption that such bills are signed on behalf of charterers, however.

In a line of cases culminating in *Homburg Houtimport v Agrosin Private Ltd (The Starsin)*,[47] the courts have taken into account a number of factors, including the wording of any demise clause in the charter or identity of carrier clause in the bill of lading, and the wording in the signature box. In *The Starsin* these tended to contradict, the former lending weight to the shipowner, and the latter the charterer as contracting carrier. In other words, from the signature box, the bills of lading appeared clearly to have been signed on behalf of the charterers, not the shipowners. Yet the majority of the Court of Appeal, having satisfied itself that the charterers had ostensible authority to bind the owners, reversing Colman J. but following Moore-Bick J.'s decision in *Fetim BV v Oceanspeed Shipping Ltd (The Flecha)*,[48] concluded that this was an owners' bill. The weighting of the various factors is still not certain, however, since in both *The Starsin* and *The Flecha*, not only was there a clear identity of carrier clause, but also a clause providing that the bill of lading would take effect only as a contract of carriage with the owner, even if the vessel were not owned by the line by whom it was issued (*i.e.* expressly providing for the situation which had occurred, where the bill was issued by the charterers). The reasoning in *The Starsin* expressly depended on the last of these factors, so neither case therefore stands for much that is of general application.

(e) BAILMENT ON TERMS

12–046   If a plaintiff (or claimant) can sue in tort, and there is no contract between himself and the defendant, he can avoid any contractual exemption clauses. In *The Starsin* at first instance,[49] Colman J. held that the cargo-owners had title to sue the shipowners in tort, but that the bills of lading were issued on behalf of the charterers. Except to the extent that they were protected by a *Himalaya* clause, therefore, the shipowners were unable to rely on exemption clauses in the carriage contract. The problem went away in the Court of Appeal, which reversed Colman J. By a 2–1 majority, the bills of lading were issued on behalf of the shipowners, and in any case the cargo-owners had no title to sue in tort.[50]

Cargo-owners also sometimes try to take advantage of tort actions to sue actual (rather than contracting) carriers where through bills of lading, or multimodal transport documents are issued (see further paras 15–024, *et seq.*, below). With the enactment of the Contract (Rights of Third Parties) Act 1999, *Himalaya* clauses can nearly always be made to protect actual carriers, but the tort action remains problematic in the present context, unless the principles in *Elder Dempster* provide protection.

---

[47] [2001] 1 Lloyd's Rep. 437.
[48] Respectively [2000] 1 Lloyd's Rep. 85; [1999] 1 Lloyd's Rep. 612.
[49] [2000] 1 Lloyd's Rep. 85.
[50] On the last point, see para. 13–083, below.

ELDER DEMPSTER & CO v PATERSON, ZOCHONIS & CO

House of Lords. [1924] A.C. 522

A shipping company which ran a line of ships chartered an additional **12–047** ship on time charter to supplement their fleet. The additional ship was not, like the rest of the fleet, fitted with 'tween decks. As a result the shipper's goods (casks of palm oil) were damaged. The bills of lading under which the goods were shipped protected the charterers from damage due to bad stowage. An action was brought by the shippers against both shipowners and charterers.

The questions arising were whether the damage fell within the exemption clause in the bill of lading, and whether the charterers and shipowners were protected by the clause.

Held:

1. (Reversing the Court of Appeal on this issue) the damage was not due to unseaworthiness (Viscount Finlay dissenting), but to bad stowage, and so the exemption clause in the bill of lading applied to it.

2. The contract of carriage was between shippers and charterers, but both shipowners and charterers were protected by the clause. It is the basis of the shipowners' protection that is problematic.

SCRUTTON L.J.: (in the Court of Appeal)

[Note that Scrutton L.J. dissented, taking the view that this was not unseaworthiness, and therefore in principle, the bill of lading clauses afforded protection:]

The above considerations lead to the conclusion that the charterers, with **12–048** whom in my opinion the bill of lading contract was made, and who include the first three defendants, were protected by the exceptions in their bill of lading. But it was argued that the fourth defendant, the owner, was liable in tort because he was not a party to the bill of lading and therefore could not claim the benefit of the exceptions contained in it, but was a bailee liable for negligence—*i.e.* bad stowage. To this counsel for the owner made reply that the owner in the case of a time charter like the present one was not in possession of the goods. This in my opinion is contrary to all the authorities ... The real answer to the claim is in my view that the shipowner is not in possession as a bailee, but as the agent of a person, the charterer, with whom the owner of the goods has made a contract defining his liability, and that the owner as servant or agent of the charterer can claim the same protection as the charterer. Were it otherwise there would be an easy way round the bill of lading in the case of every chartered ship; the owner of the goods would simply sue the owner of the ship and ignore the bill of lading exceptions, though he had contracted with the charterer for carriage on those terms and the owner had only received the goods as agent for the charterer.

LORD SUMNER: (in the House of Lords) There was, finally, an argument that the shipowners might be liable in tort, or at any rate, as bailees quasi ex contractu, though the charterers and their agents were not. This fails, to my mind ... It may be, that in the circumstances of this case the obligations to be inferred from the reception of the cargo for carriage to the United Kingdom amount to a bailment upon terms, which include the exceptions and limitations of liability stipulated in the known and contemplated form of bill of lading. It may be, that the vessel being placed in the Elder, Dempster & Co's line, the captain signs the bills of lading and takes possession of the cargo only as agent for the charterers, though the time charter recognizes the ship's possessory lien for hire. The former I regard as the preferable view, but, be this as it may, I cannot find here any such bald bailment with unrestricted liability, or such tortious handling entirely independent of contract, as would be necessary to support the contention.

Notes

12–049   It is not obvious here what principle is operating. *Elder Dempster* was heavily criticised in *Midland Silicones* (see para. 11–037, above). Lord Reid (at 479) treated the decision as[51]:

> "an anomalous and unexplained exception to the general principle that a stranger cannot rely for his protection on provisions in a contract to which he is not a party."

In other words, he thought the decision wrong, but at this time, the House of Lords still regarded itself as bound by its previous decisions. However, *Elder Dempster* certainly cannot be taken to lay down a general principle that shipowners can take advantage of exemptions in charterers' bills.

Lord Sumner talks of bailment on terms. In *Morris v C.W. Martin & Son*, Lord Denning M.R. thought that if there were a bailment on terms, and the bailee subbailed the goods with the owner's consent[52]:

> "the owner is bound by the conditions if he has expressly or impliedly consented to the bailee making a sub-bailment containing those conditions, but not otherwise."

This principle would allow the sub-bailee to take advantage of exemption clauses between bailor and head bailee, and was applied by the Privy Council in *The Pioneer Container*.[53]

The problem is that whereas there is usually a bailment, followed by a subbailment, where through bills of lading or combined transport documents are used,[54] cargo on a chartered ship is usually simply handed over to the contracting

---

[51] [1962] A.C. 446, at 479.
[52] [1966] 1 Q.B. 716 at 729.
[53] [1994] 2 A.C. 324. The goods owner had authorised the carrier so to sub-contract "on any terms", so the sub-bailee (shipowner in the case itself) was entitled to enforce an exclusive jurisdiction clause contained in the bill of lading against the owners of the goods, against the goods owner as head bailor.
[54] *e.g.* bailment to the inland forwarding agent, as contracting carrier, who then sub-bails to the actual carriers for each leg.

carrier. There is no sub-bailment.[55] Bailment on terms does not explain *Elder Dempster* itself, where again there was just one bailment, so another explanation must be sought. In *Midland Silicones*, Viscount Simonds said (at 470):

> "In my opinion, what the *Elder Dempster* case decided, and all that it decided, is that in such a case, the master having signed the bill of lading, the proper inference is that the shipowner, when he receives the goods into his possession, receives them on the terms of the bill of lading. The same inference might perhaps be drawn in some cases even if the charterer himself signed the bill of lading, but it is unnecessary to consider any such question."

In other words, the decision applies only where the bill of lading is signed by the master, and yet the contracting carriers are the charterers. In the light of *The Rewia*, we must consider that to be quite a rare situation.

---

[55] In *The Mahkutai* [1996] 3 W.L.R. 1, the Privy Council thought that the reasoning in The Pioneer Container had no application in the absence of a sub-bailment.

CHAPTER 13

TRANSFER OF CARRIAGE CONTRACTS

(1) GENERAL PRINCIPLES

13–001 IN a c.i.f. or classic f.o.b. contract, the purchaser or receiver of goods will not be party to an express contract with the carrier. Nor will a bank which finances the transaction on the security of the bill of lading, under a commercial credit. The contract of carriage is usually made by the seller as shipper of the goods. F.o.b. purchasers may sometimes be party to the carriage contract (in which case none of the difficulties discussed in this article apply), but banks never are.

The privity of contract doctrine states that only a party to a contract may sue, or be sued on it. Third parties can neither sue nor be sued, however closely connected with it they may be. Nor can they benefit directly from any exemption clauses or defences in the contract.

Thus at common law the shipper, and only the shipper, can sue the carrier in contract, and only he can also be sued by the carrier on the contract of carriage. Generally, however, once the goods are sold, the shipper will have no interest in suing the carrier, because goods which are lost or damaged at sea are at the buyer's risk. Assuming they were in apparent good order and condition when loaded, the buyer will therefore have to take up the documents and pay for the goods, and will have no recourse against the seller, whether or not they have been damaged or destroyed at sea. The seller on the other hand, will either have already been paid for the goods, or he will be entitled to payment from the buyer, so will not be interested in taking any action. If the goods are re-sold, then risk passes to the sub-purchaser in the same way, and in general it can be said that the risk is transferred, as from shipment, to the eventual purchaser of the goods. Therefore the buyer (or eventual purchaser in a chain sale) may well wish to sue the carrier, but he is not party to any express contract with him.

As an alternative to suing the carrier, the party at risk can claim on the marine insurance policy if the goods are lost or damaged at sea, and indeed is probably more likely to do this. Actions on the carriage contract are still important if the insurance policy does not cover the loss, either through some oversight or accident, or where for example war risk is not covered. But even if (as is usually the case) the policy covers the loss, the insurance company, having paid the buyer, may itself attempt to recover from the carrier under the subrogation doctrine.[1] The issues remain the same in that event.

Note also that the marine insurance policy will not compensate for, *e.g.* a drop in value due to late delivery, whereas a contract action against the carrier may (see *The Heron II* [1969] 1 A.C. 350).

(a) VALUE OF BILL OF LADING REDUCED

13–002 Much of the value of a bill of lading lies in the contractual actions it gives the holder for the time being against the carrier. It is essential that he can sue the

---

[1] In *The Aliakmon* at first instance, Staughton J. thought that the issue was in reality between two insurance companies: [1983] 1 Lloyd's Rep. 203 at 205 (col. 1).

carrier, if bills of lading are to be used as freely negotiable documents, since it is vital for a purchaser who takes up a bill to acquire contractual rights against the carrier should the cargo be lost or damaged at sea. Similarly, if a bank takes a bill of lading as security under a documentary credit, its security is seriously impaired if it does not also acquire contractual rights against the carrier.

Conversely, carriers would not willingly carry cargo if they thought that the exemption clauses in the bill of lading contract would not protect them. Since the Hague or Hague-Visby Rules operate only by incorporation into contracts of carriage, the time limits, limits to liability and excepted perils also only protect the carrier if there is a contractual relationship between himself and the cargo-owner. It follows that if the buyer can sue in tort, he will avoid the bill of lading exemptions unless there is contract between buyer and carrier (see, *e.g. The Captain Gregos*, in paras 11–061 *et seq.*, above, and the discussion of *The Aliakmon*, para. 13–073, below).

The carrier may also wish to sue the buyer, or eventual receiver of the cargo, for example for outstanding freight or demurrage. Indeed, he may have no option but to proceed against the receiver of the cargo. Suppose the vessel is chartered under a voyage charterparty. The charterer ships his own cargo, which is sold to the receiver on the voyage. Because of delay by the receiver in discharging the cargo, demurrage is incurred at the discharge port.

Voyage charterparties commonly contain cesser clauses, the usual effect of which is to relieve the charterer of liability once the cargo is shipped. For claims arising after shipment the shipowner must look to the receiver of the cargo, and not to the charterer. A typical cesser clause can be found in Norgrain (North American Grain Charterparty), clause 34:

> "Charterers' liability under this Charterparty is to cease on cargo being shipped except for payment of freight, deadfreight, and demurrage at loading, and except for all other matters provided for in this Charterparty where the Charterers' responsibility is specified."

The effect of this clause is that the shipowner must look to the receiver, and not to the charterer, for the demurrage that has been incurred at discharge. Sometimes, where freight is payable on delivery of the cargo, the cesser clause will apply to the freight payment as well. But if there is no contract between shipowner and receiver of the cargo, the shipowner will be unable to claim freight or any other payment from him. See, for example, *The Sevonia Team* (para. 12–032, above) and *Sewell v Burdick*.

(b) Common Law did not Transfer Contract with Bill of Lading

THOMPSON v DOMINY

Exchequer. (1845) 14 M. & W. 403

The plaintiff indorsees for value of a bill of lading sued the carrier for alleged short delivery.   **13–003**

Held

The transfer of a bill of lading does not enable the transferee to bring an action in his own name on the carriage contract.

PARKE B: I have never heard it argued that a contract was transferable, except by the law merchant, and there is nothing to shew that a bill of lading is transferable under any custom of merchants. It transfers no more than the property in the goods; it does not transfer the contract.

ALDERSON B: Because, in *Lickbarrow v Mason* [see chapter 6, above], a bill of lading was held to be negotiable, it has been contended that that instrument possesses all the properties of a bill of exchange; but it would lead to absurdity to carry the doctrine to that length. The word "negotiable" was not used in the sense in which it is used as applicable to a bill of exchange, but as passing the property in the goods only.

Note:

13–004   *Thompson v Dominy* decided that merely because it had been established that transfer of the bill of lading could transfer property in the goods, it did not follow that it also transferred the carriage contract: there is no common law doctrine whereby rights and liabilities under the carriage contract are *automatically* transferred, as a matter of law, on transfer of the bill of lading.

It was a very awkward decision, which almost certainly delayed development of c.i.f., and more sophisticated varieties of f.o.b. contract. The legislature quickly reacted to reverse it, with the Bills of Lading Act 1855, s.1. By 1990 at the latest (with the decision in *The Delfini*), it had become clear that the 1855 Act was not well-suited suited to modern trade conditions, and it was replaced by the much more comprehensive Carriage of Goods by Sea Act 1992.

Other devices, such as the implied contract, and tort actions, were also used to avoid the consequences of *Thompson v Dominy*, where the 1855 Act did not apply. These devices retain a reduced importance since 1992, but there are still gaps in the legislation, and it is still necessary to cover them.

Even if the contract is transferred, it does not follow that all the statements in the bill of lading are contracutual undertakings, nor even necessarily that the master has the authority to make them, so as to bind the shipowner (or charterer, if it is a charterer's bill).[2] These issues are considered further in chapter 14, below.

(2) BILLS OF LADING ACT 1855, s.1

(a) THE 1855 ACT

13–005   The 1855 Act was intended to deal with the difficulties alluded to above. The Bills of Lading Act 1855, s.1, and the relevant part of the Preamble, enacted:

BILLS OF LADING ACT 1855, s.1

Whereas by the custom of merchants a bill of lading of goods being transferable by indorsement the property in the goods may thereby pass to the indorsee, nevertheless all rights in respect of the contract contained in that bill of lading continue in the original shipper or owner and it is expedient that such rights should pass with property... 1. Every consignee of goods named in a bill of lading, and every indorsee of a bill of

---

[2] On which see paras 12–037, *et seq.*, below.

lading to whom property in the goods therein mentioned shall pass, upon or by reason of such consignment or indorsement shall have transferred to and vested in him all rights of suit and be subject to the same liabilities in respect of such goods as if the contract in the bill of lading had been made with himself.

BILLS OF LADING ACT 1855, s.2

Nothing herein contained shall prejudice or affect any right of stoppage **13–006** *in transitu*, or any right to claim freight against the original shipper or owner, or any liability of the consignee or indorsee by reason or in consequence of his being such consignee or indorsee, or of his receipt of the goods by reason or in consequence of such consignment or indorsement.

Note
These sections were a legislative reaction to *Thompson v Dominy*, the reasoning of which decision was that merely because transfer of the bill of lading could transfer property in the goods, it did not follow that it transferred contractual rights and liabilities also. In the words of Parke B.:

"[The bill of lading] transfers no more than the property in the goods; it does not transfer the contract."

Section 1 did little more than reverse this reasoning, enacting in effect: insofar that transfer of the bill of lading passes property in goods, it is expedient that it should also pass contractual rights and liabilities, and it *shall* heretofore do so. The important point to note is the tie-in with property. Only if transfer of the bill of lading passed property did it also pass contractual rights.

Section 2 preserved the right to claim freight from the shipper. The liability of shippers and intermediate holders remains a live issue under the Carriage of Goods by Sea Act 1992 (see further below).

Section 3, which (ineffectually) addressed different issues, is discussed in para. 14–048, below.

(b) A Summary of the Problems

The problems of s.1 of the 1855 Act may be summarised as follows: **13–007**

1. Documentation. Only the shipped bill of lading was covered.

2. The property link. The Act was dependent on the passing of property, and on the manner of its passing.

3. Rights and liabilities linked.

4. Because of 2, bulk cargoes were not generally catered for.

5. Because of 2, banks (under documentary credits) were not generally covered.

6. Late arrival of bill of lading. Stale bills of lading were probably outside the 1855 Act, and even if they were not, there were often property difficulties (*e.g. The Delfini* [1990] 1 Lloyd's Rep. 252).[3]

---

[3] See also para. 5–066, above.

7. Exemption clauses. This is *The Captain Gregos* problem considered in paras 11–061, *et seq.*, above.

These problems have been solved by the 1992 Act, but others may have been created. It should also be remembered that parts of the common law world (*e.g.* Malaysia) continue to operate the 1885 regime, although others (*e.g.* Singapore) have enacted their own versions of the 1992 Act.

(c) Documentation

13–008   Section 1 applied only where a shipped bill of lading was used. Presumably no other documentation was commonly used in 1855. Even a received for shipment bill of lading would not suffice,[4] still less a delivery order, combined transport document, waybill or electronic document.

(d) Property Link

13–009   If property did not pass on the voyage, as with undivided bulk cargoes, then the section would not operate.[5] There were also restrictions on the timing of the passing of property, the manner of its passing, and whether the bill of lading named a consignee or was made out to order.[6]

(e) Rights and Liabilities Linked

13–010   Rights and liabilities were dealt with together under the 1855 Act. It was not possible to obtain benefits without being subject to liabilities. Banks under documentary credits would obviously have wanted statutory assignment of rights of action, but would not have been willing to incur liability for freight and demurrage merely by virtue of holding a bill of lading.

(f) Bulk Cargoes

13–011   This point has already been covered. But see also *The Aramis*, considered further at para. 13–067, below.

(g) Banks

13–012   The House of Lords held in *Sewell v Burdick* (1884) 10 App. Cas. 74 that s.1 did not affect a bank who held a bill of lading merely as pledgee. This case, which was

---

[4] See the discussion of *Diamond Alkali* in para. 6–060, above.

[5] *Aramis (cargo owners) v Aramis (owners)*, (*The Aramis*) [1989] 1 Lloyd's Rep. 213. S.1 could never operate where the sale is of an unascertained part of an undivided bulk cargo, except for the very unusual circumstances that occurred in *Karlshamns Oljefabriker v Eastport Navigation (The Elafi)* (see para. 5–015, above). After discharge of parts of the bulk to various buyers *en route*, all that remained was destined for the same buyer, and property passed (on the voyage) by process of exhaustion.

Some of the bulk cargo problems might have been avoided, had the 1995 amendments to the Sale of Goods Act been in force, but by the time they were, the 1855 Act had already been repealed.

[6] See, *e.g. Hispanica de Petroleos SA v Vencedora Oceania Navegacion SA (The Kapetan Markos) (No.2)* [1987] 2 Lloyd's Rep. 321; *Enichem Anic SpA v Ampelos Shipping Co Ltd (The Delfini)* [1990] 1 Lloyd's Rep. 252.

the earliest House of Lords decision on the 1855 Act, was of great importance to the banking community, and even after 1992, is still of importance in addressing the nature of the bank's property under a documentary credit. The case has already been discussed, at para. 8–039, above. Because as pledgee a bank obtains only a special property in the goods, and not the general property, s.1 was not triggered.

Obviously, the bank welcomed the decision in *Sewell v Burdick*, since it was not, merely by virtue of holding the bill of lading, liable to the shipowner for freight, but it also followed, since rights and liabilities were transferred together under s.1, that a bank could never rely on the section. Nor could it be sued for freight or demurrage even if it took delivery of the goods.

(h) Late Bills

Stale bills of lading were probably outside the 1855 Act. For s.1 to operate it was **13–013** probably necessary for the bill of lading still to be valid as a document of title when it is indorsed, and property thereby passes. In the oil trade especially, bills of lading may well be negotiated after the cargo has been discharged. This is what happened in *The Delfini*, and at first instance Phillips J. held that the bill of lading had ceased to be effective as a transferable document of title when the cargo was discharged (see the discussion at para. 6–040, above). Hence the ultimate receiver (who claimed short delivery) could not rely on s.1, primarily on the grounds that indorsement and transfer of the bill of lading could not be instrumental in conferring upon the indorsee either proprietary or possessory title ([1988] 2 Lloyd's Rep. 599, 607 (col. 2)). The decision of the Court of Appeal was on different grounds, but exactly the same result was reached by Phillips J. in *The Sirina* [1988] 2 Lloyd's Rep. 613, for the same reasons that he had adopted in *The Delfini*.

(i) Exemption Clauses

If the carrier was sued in tort, he was unable to limit his liability, even by **13–014** invoking the provisions of the *Hague-Visby Rules*, unless he had a contract with the cargo-owner. Not only did this mean that the amount of liability was unlimited, but also that the common law limitation period applied, of six years, rather than the more favourable one year under the Rules. See further the discussion of *The Captain Gregos* at paras 11–061, *et seq.*, above.[7]

(j) Law Commission

The Law Commission appears to have been persuaded of the inadequacies of **13–015** the 1855 Act, probably by the Court of Appeal decisions in *The Aramis* and *The Delfini*. At any rate, its recommendations in "Rights of Suit in Respect of Carriage of Goods by Sea",[8] led to the enactment of the Carriage of Goods by Sea Act 1992.

---

[7] In the event, the case went back to the Court of Appeal, where there was a partial application of the *Brandt v Liverpool* doctrine (see below). Were similar facts to arise today, the decision would be the same, since the cargo-owners never became lawful holders of a bill of lading, to trigger the Carriage of Goods by Sea Act 1992.

[8] Law Commission Report No. 196 (1991).

(3) Carriage of Goods by Sea Act 1992

(a) The 1992 Act in General

13–016   The Act is set out in full in Appendix E, below. It was intended to give effect to the recommendations of the report of the Law Commission and the Scottish Law Commission, "Rights of Suit in Respect of Carriage of Goods by Sea", Law Commission Report No. 196 (1991), and the authorities suggest that the Law Commission report can be called in aid not only to the mischief that the Act was intended to cure but also to the meaning of the Act itself, in the event of ambiguity.[9]

Sections 1–3 (and the definition in s.5) are relevant to this chapter; s.4 deals with another problem, considered in para. 14–050, below.

(b) Section 1 (Documentation)

13–017   Section 1 of the 1992 Act enumerates and extends the documents to which the Act applies.

There are three categories set out in s.1(1), the bill of lading, the sea waybill and the ship's delivery order. Section 1(2)(a) appears to exclude a bill of lading naming a consignee, but this is not in fact the case, since although it does not come within the definition of a bill of lading, it does fall within the definition of the sea waybill. By virtue of s.1(2)(b), the received for shipment bill is expressly included. The sea waybill is defined in s.1(3) and the ship's delivery order in s.1(4), the definition of the ship's delivery order being similar to the common law definition.

Note that only the ship's delivery order is covered, merchants' delivery orders continuing to be excluded, as before. As we saw in paras 6–096, *et seq.*, above, it will not always be possible in practice to obtain a ship's delivery order, in which case this is a significant omission. As we will see below, however, the documentary gaps in the 1992 Act are precisely the areas where the *Brand v Liverpool* doctrine is most likely to remain applicable.

Provision for electronic documentation is made in s.1(5), should the Secretary of State choose to make the appropriate regulations, the definition of information technology and telecommunication system being set out in s.5(1). This provision does not appear to have been very well thought through. The first point to note is that no guidelines are laid down in s.1(5), for example as to the type of electronic documentation that ought in principle to be covered. It would be sensible to allow only electronic documentation which performs a similar function to the other documentation covered by the Act, for example, to amount to an undertaking and receipt by the carrier, and to be transferred to lawful holders, assuming that they could be defined, without the carrier necessarily being further involved. Secondly, the definition of information technology in s.5(1) assumes that information recorded on a computer system is not itself documentary in form. There are good arguments that this is legally incorrect. Thirdly, the provision in s.1(5)(a) and (b) seems to assume the transmission of a single computer-generated document from trader to trader, which is quite unlike either the C.M.I.

---

[9] As in *Factortame Ltd v Secretary of State for Transport* [1990] 2 A.C. 85. See also *Pepper v Hart* [1993] 1 All E.R. 42, and in particular the comments of Lord Browne-Wilkinson at 61.

or B.I.M.C.O. models (although analogous to Bolero). The whole issue of electronic documentation is considered further in chapter 16, below.

(c) Documentation not Covered by the Act

As already observed, only ship's delivery orders are covered, but to obtain a **13–018** ship's delivery order you need to contact the carrier. This cannot always be done. For merchants' delivery orders, the position is the same as before. Mate's receipts are also outside the Act.[10]

Stale bills of lading are covered, but the ultimate receiver has to obtain the document eventually to sue; if arrives too late there could be Hague-Visby time bar problems. It will not be possible to advance the argument in *The Captain Gregos*, in para. 11–063, above, since there will now be a statutory contact between receiver and shipowner.

A general problem with documentation is that only contractual issues are resolved by the new Act (this is not intended as a criticism). There is no change, for example, to the definition of a document of title, so that new forms of documentation may give no better security than before. No doubt it is possible effectively to transfer constructive possession, by conferring contractual rights on the holder of a document, but property is needed to protect a party against the bankruptcy of another merchant, and (of course) this is not addressed in the 1992 Act.

(d) Specific Enumeration of Documents Covered

Section 1 operates by enumeration, rather than setting out more general **13–019** requirements for documents to satisfy the Act. The problem with enumeration is that it does not easily allow for development, since new documentation could arise which has not yet been conceived. The Law Commission considered this point and felt that certainty was more important than a long shelf-life.

(e) Section 2 (Rights Under Shipping Documents)

Section 2(1)(a) transfers rights of suit under the contract of carriage to the **13–020** lawful holder of a bill of lading. The property requirement of the old Act has entirely disappeared. Section 2(1)(b) transfers contractual rights to the named consignee under a sea waybill, and s.2(1)(c) makes appropriate provision for ship's delivery orders.

Section 2(2)(a) deals with the problem of the stale bill of lading. Bills of lading negotiated after delivery are included, so long as the underlying transaction preceded delivery. The Law Commission did not wish to encourage sales of bills of lading which gave nothing more than contractual rights of action (para. 2.43). Section 2(2)(b) covers the situation where the buyer rejects the goods on their arrival, after they have been delivered to him. His immediate seller will become lawful holder after the bill of lading has become stale, but will obtain contractual rights under the Act.[11]

Section 2(3) addresses an obvious problem with delivery orders, where the consignment is part of a larger undivided bulk. The rights transferred relate only to the part of the goods to which the order relates, although the delivery order

---

[10] Unless perhaps they can be construed as received for shipment bills of lading, but a mate's receipt is usually intended as a preliminary document only, unlike a received for shipment bill of lading.

[11] It is necessary to re-transfer rights to him, as they would have been divested by s.2(5).

will often make reference to the entire bulk. Section 2(4) addresses the problem where somebody other than the person with rights under the 1992 Act suffers loss, to deal with the possible argument that only nominal damages should be awarded.[12]

(f) Residual Rights of Shipper and Intermediate Holders

13–021   Section 2(5) extinguishes rights on re-transfer, including the shipper's rights (but note that the section does not affect the rights of charterers, because of the definition of contract of carriage in s.5(1)). It also excludes original holders of waybills and ship's delivery orders. Tort actions are not divested, however, giving rise to potential double liability problems (see para. 13–041, below).

Section 2(5) clearly assumes that the holders, rather than the shippers, are the correct persons to sue, and effectively that risk has passed to them on shipment. This is of course true generally for c.i.f. and f.o.b. contracts. It would not be true of an ex-ship contract, nor necessarily of c.i.f. out-turn, at least if such a contract leaves risks of transportation losses on the seller (see paras 2–024, *et seq.*, above). In such cases, the seller will need to take an assignment of the buyer's rights, or ensure that the buyer will sue on his behalf,[13] if loss occurs through the carrier's breach of contract. If the buyer rejects the bill of lading then the problem is dealt with by s.2(2)(b), but the buyer would not necessarily reject for minor loss or damage.

EAST WEST CORPORATION v DKBS 1912

Queen's Bench Division (Commercial Court). [2002] E.W.H.C. 83 (Comm.), [2002] 2 Lloyd's Rep. 182

13–022   The claimants[14] were Hong Kong merchants who had sold goods, cash on delivery, to a company in Chile (Gold Crown). They arranged for shipping documents to be forwarded to banks in Chile, to be released against payment. The Chilean banks were simply to act as the correspondents of the claimant's bankers, to obtain payment from Gold Crown, in exchange for the bills of lading. All but one of the bills of lading were made out to the order of the relevant Chilean bank, the exception mistakenly simply naming the bank as consignee. The buyers did not pay for all the goods, but the defendant carriers (Maersk and P. & O.) delivered the goods to them, without production of bills of lading. The banks returned the bills of lading to the claimants, but without indorsing them back. One of the issues was whether the claimants had title to sue.

---

[12] For example, in *The Sanix Ace* [1987] 1 Lloyd's Rep. 465 (see below). The plaintiff would still be the proper person to sue, but is suing on behalf of the parties at risk. In *The Sanix Ace* itself the nominal damages argument failed because the plaintiff had property in the goods, but suppose he had the bill of lading but no property, for example because he had himself purchased only part of the undivided bulk. Then this subsection would be necessary to prevent the nominal damages argument from succeeding. *The Albazero* (see below) is unaffected by this section, as the plaintiff would not be the proper person to sue under the Act: as charterer, his rights would not be divested by s.2(5), so the position would be exactly as before.

[13] Note that the buyer can obtain substantial damages, and hold them for the shipper, under s.2(4)(b).

[14] Newspeak for plaintiffs, in the UK, if not elsewhere in the common law world.

Held:

1. Except in the case of the bill of lading naming the bank as consignee (which counted as a waybill within s.2(5)), the claimant shippers' contractual rights were divested by s.2(5).

2. Because the banks had not indorsed the bills of lading back to the claimants, the claimants could not rely on s.2(2)(b). It would have been different if the bills of lading had been stale by the time they were returned, but they were not, delivery not having been made to the person entitled.

3. Any bailment claim the claimants might otherwise have had, had been modified by the bill of lading contracts, and likewise transferred and divested. There was no longer an independent bailment claim.

4. However, as owners of the goods, the claimants retained an independent negligence action, and could succeed on that basis.

THOMAS J.:

The Facts

[3] The claimants are related companies and carry on in Hong Kong a   **13–023** business of exporting goods manufactured in China to other countries in the world. For some time they had been selling goods to Gold Crown, a company based in Santiago, Chile. In 1998 they agreed to sell further consignments to them on terms of cash against delivery. The claimants shipped goods at Hong Kong in containers on liner services for delivery in Chile. Those that were carried by the defendants in the first action (Maersk) were shipped between 22 September 1998 and 19 October 1998 and those carried by the defendants in the second action (P. & O.) were shipped on 5 February 1999.

[4] The claimants had made arrangements with their bankers for the shipping documents to be remitted to banks in Chile so that the documents would only be released on payment. Liner bills of lading were duly issued for each of the nine shipments and delivered to the claimants. The claimants were named as the shippers in each bill of lading and the notify party was Gold Crown. The goods were consigned to the order of named Chilean banks in all the bills of lading, save one of the Maersk bills where the goods were simply consigned to a named Chilean bank and not to its order; these banks were to act as the correspondents of the claimant's bankers to obtain payment from Gold Crown in return for the bills of lading.

[5] The bills of lading were indorsed by the claimants and sent by the claimants' bankers to their correspondent bankers in Chile for them to obtain payment. There were some transfers between the banks in Chile to which it will be necessary to refer.

[6] The containers carried by Maersk arrived at San Antonio, Chile between the end of October and November 1998; those carried by P. & O. (on a chartered vessel) arrived at San Antonio and were discharged from the vessel on 10 March 1999. The bills of lading issued by P. & O. provided for them to be shipped to Valparaiso, but no point arose on this for various reasons which it is not necessary to set out. In accordance with the customs laws of Chile, as duty had not been paid in advance, the containers had to be placed on arrival in a licensed customs warehouse. The goods carried by Maersk were placed by their agents A.J. Broom in a customs warehouse operated by Seaport S.A. at San Antonio. Those carried by P. & O. were placed by the ship's agents, Agencias Universales S.A., first in a container yard and then moved to a licensed customs warehouse operated by Empressa Porturia de Chile de San Antonio at San Antonio. It will be necessary to examine in more detail the detailed provisions of these laws and the arrangements for the operation of licensed warehouses and customs clearance.

[7] Customs duty was paid on the goods and the goods in the containers were released to the customs agent of Gold Crown without presentation of the original bills of lading and handed over to Gold Crown. Four of the seven containers carried by Maersk were released in November 1998, two after 19 January 1999 and one at an unknown date. Those carried by P. & O. were released on 15 March 1999.

[8] Although Gold Crown made some payments to the claimants, they did not pay for the goods in two of the containers carried by P. & O. and seven of the containers carried by Maersk. The banks were requested to return the bills of lading to the claimants which they did without indorsing them back.

[9] Each of the bills of lading contained a clause subjecting the contract to English law and jurisdiction. The claimants commenced proceedings in this court against P. & O. and Maersk on the basis that they had delivered the cargo without presentation of the bills of lading. They claimed $US 134,807.40 against Maersk and $US 95,147.20 against P. & O.

[10] In the ordinary case, a carrier would have no defence to such a claim properly made by a person entitled to bring a claim under the bill of lading. However, Maersk and P. & O. have raised a number of defences. (1) The claimants had no title to sue. (2) Under the law of Chile carriers were required to deliver the goods to the licensed customs warehouse. Once they had delivered the goods to the licensed customs warehouse which they had to do without presentation of the bills of lading, they had discharged their obligations and the contract of carriage came to an end. Furthermore the Hamburg Rules were in force in Chile; under art. 4 of the Hamburg Rules, Maersk and P. & O. were discharged from responsibility in such circumstances. As they had acted in accordance with the law of Chile, they were not liable for delivery without presentation of the bills of lading. (3) If they were not correct in their contentions as to the law of Chile, the express terms of the bills of lading exempted

them from liability. (4) They were not negligent in delivering the goods without production of the bills of lading.

[11] At an earlier stage, Maersk and P. & O. both contended that the claimants had not properly mitigated their loss, but at the conclusion of the evidence that allegation was quite properly abandoned.

[12] It is convenient to consider the issues that arise under four main headings—(1) title to sue, (2) the delivery obligation, (3) the exceptions in the bill of lading and (4) the claim in negligence. I was greatly assisted by the very thorough and detailed research and submissions made by counsel for the parties.

Issue (1): Do the Claimants Have Title to Sue?

[13] The claimants contended that they had title to sue on a number of different bases. (i) They had retained their rights of suit as shippers and these had not transferred to the Chilean banks even though the banks were named as consignees and the banks had obtained physical possession of the bills of lading. (ii) If the rights of suit had been transferred to the Chilean banks, the claimants had title to sue as undisclosed principals of the Chilean banks named as consignees. (iii) If they had lost their rights of suit and did not have them as undisclosed principals of the Chilean banks, the rights of suits had been transferred back to them. (iv) They had, in any event, title to sue in bailment. (v) They had the right to sue in negligence for the loss of their proprietary interest. Before considering each of these contentions, it is necessary to set out my further findings of fact.   **13–024**

Further findings of fact
[14] It was quite clear on the evidence that the capacity in which the claimants' own bankers in Hong Kong acted was to put in place arrangements for payment to be made by Gold Crown to the correspondent bank before the bills of lading were transferred to Gold Crown. The correspondent banks in Chile which were named as the consignees were appointed only for the purpose of collecting the price from the buyers as the agents (or sub-agents) of the claimants. The goods remained in the ownership of the claimants and neither their bankers in Hong Kong nor the correspondent bankers in Chile obtained any security or other interest in them. As between the banks in Chile and the claimants, the banks had no right to take delivery from the carrier.   **13–025**

[15] That was all clear both from the documents and from the evidence of Mr Deepak Balani, a director and principal in the claimants, which I accept; he was an honest and clear witness. His evidence was that the claimants had named the banks as consignees as that was their practice. Their own bankers wanted this done so that the payments were routed through their correspondent banks in Chile.

[16] I am also satisfied on his evidence and from the documents that the claimants retained full control over the documents, as the banks at all times held them to the order and direction of the claimants. The clearest proof of this was the transfers of the documents between banks in Chile to which I briefly referred at paragraph. For example, one of the Maersk bills for goods which the claimants intended to sell to Gold Crown was issued with the Banco Credito e Inversiones as consignee; the claimants decided to sell the goods to another buyer and recalled the bills from that bank. The claimants then asked Maersk to issue new bills naming Banco de Chile as consignee and the new buyer as the notify party. Maersk issued a new bill. All of this was done on the instructions of the claimants; it was a clear illustration of the fact that they exercised control over the bills, even though the banks were the named consignees and the bills were in the possession of the banks. At the time the goods were delivered to Gold Crown, five of the seven Maersk bills were in the hands of a bank other than the bank named in the bill of lading as the consignee.

(i) Did the claimants lose their rights of suit?

13–026 [17] The position was agreed to be the same for all the bills of lading, save for the Maersk bill of lading no 4 where the goods were consigned simply to a bank in Chile and not to its order. It is therefore convenient to consider first all the bills of lading except no 4.

[18] It is clear that the Chilean banks were named as the consignees in the bills of lading, the bills of lading were indorsed by the claimants to them and they obtained physical possession of the bills of lading. Maersk and P. & O. contended that on these facts and by reason of the provisions of the 1992 Act, the Chilean banks became the persons entitled to sue and the claimants lost their rights of suit.

[19] Under s.2(1) of the 1992 Act, the lawful holder of a bill of lading, by virtue of becoming the lawful holder of the bill of lading, has transferred to him and vested in him all rights of suit under the contract of carriage. A holder of a bill of lading includes, under s.5(2)(a) of the 1992 Act "a person with possession of the bill, who by virtue of being identified in the bill, is the consignee of the goods to which the bill relates". Section 2(5) provides for the extinguishment of the shippers' rights:

"Where rights are transferred by virtue of the operation of subsection (1) above in relation to any document, the transfer for which the subsection provides shall extinguish any entitlement to those rights which derives—(a) where that document is a bill of lading, from a person's having been an original party to the contract of carriage . . ."

[20] The submission of Maersk and P. & O. was that on an ordinary reading of the 1992 Act, the Chilean banks to which the bills of lading were originally indorsed and transferred became the lawful holder of

those bills of lading as they obtained possession of the bills in which they were the named consignees. These banks therefore obtained the rights of suit and those of the claimants as the shippers were extinguished.

[21] The claimants' submission was more complex. Section 2(1) and s.5(2)(a) of the 1992 Act (as defined in [19], above) should not be read in the way suggested by Maersk and P. & O. These provisions were only intended to apply where the person who became the lawful holder was not only in physical possession of the bill and the named consignee, but was also in fact in control of the goods and the bills and entitled to take delivery of the goods. Where the person was not entitled to take delivery of the goods, such a person was not in truth the consignee. It was not enough that he was named on the face of the bill as consignee; the true position had to be ascertained. If the person named as consignee did not have authority to take delivery, then he should not be treated as a "consignee" of the bill for the purposes of s.5(2)(a) and hence was not a holder. Section 2(1) and s.5(2)(a) did not apply where the shipper still retained constructive possession of the bills and the physical possession was held by a person acting in a ministerial capacity. In this case, control remained in the claimants and the banks never treated their physical possession of the bills as giving them a right to possess the goods. The claimants as shippers had retained constructive possession of the bills, as they had complete control over them.

[22] Although the claimants' submission was complex, there is, in my view, a short answer, as the issue depends upon the construction of the 1992 Act. It is clear, in my judgment, that the Chilean banks to whom the bills of lading were sent initially were the consignees identified in the bills of lading within the ordinary meaning of those words in the 1992 Act. I cannot see that it is possible to give the word "consignee" any other construction. When they received the bills, they held possession of them. They therefore fulfilled the definition set out in s.5(2)(a) and became the lawful holders. In my view it is not appropriate to go behind the facts as they would appear from the face of the bill of lading. As the Law Commission pointed out in their joint Report with the Scottish Law Commission which led to the passing of the 1992 Act, *Rights of Suit in Respect of Carriage of Goods by Sea* (Law Com. No. 196, Scot. Law Com. No. 130), under the law as it then stood a carrier was bound to make delivery against presentation of the bill of lading without enquiry as to the way in which he had acquired the property in the goods; the object of the change was to simplify the law. The construction advanced by the claimants would return a substantial degree of complexity. For example, if the claimants were correct, there would need to be an enquiry into the question as to whether the consignee named on the face of the bill of lading had, as between the shipper and the person named as consignee, an entitlement to delivery. It would in another guise re-open the enquiry into the contractual arrangements that the reform brought about by the 1992 Act sought to remove. It will be necessary to consider whether the

Chilean banks held them as agents and other issues raised by the claimants, but as regards this first question, the answer is in my view clear.

Maersk Bill of Lading No. 4

13–027   [23] Maersk bill of lading no. 4 was, it seems, originally issued as a bill of lading where the goods were consigned to the order of the Banco de Credito e Inversiones. The claimants wanted it amended to the order of the Banco de Chile; a new bill of lading was issued with the consignee named as the Banco de Chile, but the words "or order" omitted, in error. Maersk decided to make no claim to rectify this bill of lading.

[24] The claimants contended that in these circumstances the bill of lading was therefore a "straight" or "non-negotiable" bill—whatever is the appropriate terminology in English law: see Carver on *Bills of Lading* (13th edn, 2001) at para. 1–007; that therefore the claimants' rights had not been extinguished by the provisions of the 1992 Act. The position under such a bill of lading is summarised in Carver on *Bills of Lading* at para. 6–007. The bill is not a document of title at common law, the transfer does not operate as a transfer of constructive possession; the carrier is bound to deliver to the consignee without presentation of the bill.

[25] The effect of s.2(5) of the 1992 Act in such circumstances is not to extinguish the rights of the claimants as the original party to this bill of lading, as Maersk accepted would follow if they did not seek to rectify this bill of lading. The claimants are therefore entitled to maintain their claim in respect of this bill as the shippers. . . .

(iii) Were the rights of suit transferred back to the claimants?

13–028   [32] Although the bills of lading were delivered back to the claimants, they were never indorsed by the banks to them. Was indorsement necessary? The issue turned substantially upon the meaning of the definitions of "holder" in s.5(2)(b) and (c) of the 1992 Act.

[33] The simple contention advanced by Maersk and P. & O. was that by reason of s.5(2)(b) of the 1992 Act, the rights of suit could only be transferred back by indorsement. This sets out the second definition of a holder as—

> "a person with possession of the bill as a result of the completion, by delivery of the bill, of any indorsement of the bill, or in the case of a bearer bill, of any other transfer of the bill".

There had been no indorsement back; therefore, as the claimants accepted, they could not establish title to sue on this basis. Maersk and P. & O. stressed that the simple step of indorsement back could have been taken and there was no need to attempt to complicate the simple scheme of the 1992 Act.

[34] The claimants contended that indorsement was unnecessary because by the time of the return of the bills of lading to the claimants, the goods had been delivered and the bills of lading therefore no longer gave

a right to possess as against the carrier. If the goods had not been delivered, then the bills would have been indorsed back to the claimants to enable them to take delivery of them. The claimants were therefore holders of the bills under s.5(2)(c) of the 1992 Act and rights of suit vested in them; s.5(2)(c) sets out the third definition of a holder as—

"a person with possession of the bill as a result of any transaction by virtue of which he would have become a holder falling within paragraph (a) or (b) above had not the transaction been effected at a time when possession of the bill no longer gave a right (as against the carrier) to possession of the goods to which the bill relates . . . "

They contended that once the cargo had been discharged, the bill of lading no longer gave a right to possession, only to a claim for damages; they relied on a series of decisions to which I refer at [35] below and following. As holders they were entitled to bring a claim under s.2(2):

"Where, when a person becomes the lawful holder of a bill of lading, possession of the bill no longer gives a right (as against the carrier) to possession of the goods to which the bill relates, that person shall not have any rights transferred to him by virtue of subsection (1) above unless he becomes the holder of the bill—(a) by virtue of a transaction effected in pursuance of any contractual or other arrangements made before the time when the right to possession ceased to attach to possession of the bill . . . "

[35] The first question which arises is whether there was a right to possess as against the carrier after the goods had been wrongly delivered to Gold Crown. There are a number of cases prior to the 1992 Act where the courts considered the circumstances in which a bill of lading is discharged or spent. In *Barclays Bank Ltd v Customs and Excise Comrs.* [1963] 1 Lloyd's Rep. 81 at 89, Diplock L.J. summarised the general rule: **13–029**

"The contract for the carriage of goods by sea is a combined contract of bailment and transportation . . . Such a contract is not discharged by performance until the shipowner has actually surrendered possession (that is divested himself of all powers to control any physical dealing in the goods) to the person entitled under the terms of the contract to obtain possession of them."

[36] The specific issue, however, is whether the contract of carriage is discharged if the goods are delivered to a person other than the person entitled under the bill of lading. In *Meyerstein v Barber* (1866) L.R. 2 C.P. 38 at 53, Willes J. said in the Court of Common pleas:

"I think the bill of lading remains in force at least so long as complete delivery of possession of the goods has not been made to some person having a right to claim under it. I believe that will be found not only to be the law, but also to be in accordance with the convenience and practice of carriers and merchants."

In the House of Lords, Lord Hatherley L.C. agreeing with this went on to state ((1870) L.R. 4 H.L. 317 at 330):

"When they have arrived at the dock, until they are delivered to some person who has the right to hold them the bill of lading remains the only symbol that can be dealt with by way of assignment, or mortgage, or otherwise ... Until that time bills of lading are effective representations of the ownership of the goods, and their force does not become extinguished until possession, or what is equivalent in law to possession, has been taken on the part of the person having the right to demand it."

In *London Joint Stock Bank Ltd v British Amsterdam Maritime Agency Ltd* (1910) 16 Com. Cas. 102, Channell J. observed that the question as to whether the bill of lading was discharged depended upon whether the person who took delivery was entitled to delivery.

[37] Although Diplock L.J. left the question open in the *Barclays Bank* case, in *Enichem Anic SpA v Ampelos Shipping Co Ltd (The Delfini)* [1988] 2 Lloyd's Rep. 599, the correctness of the observations of Channell J. was accepted by the parties. In that case, it was contended that a bill of lading for 24,540 mt. of oil remained in force because 275 mt. had been short-delivered; the bill of lading would only be discharged upon delivery of the full cargo. Phillips J. rejected that argument; after analysing the cases to which I have referred, he added (at 608):

"So long as the contract is not discharged, the bill of lading in my view, remains a document of title by endorsement and delivery of which the rights of property in the goods can be transferred ... The discharge of the contract referred to by Diplock J. occurs, in my view, when the primary obligations of the contract of carriage come to an end, notwithstanding that the carrier may have incurred secondary obligations as a consequence of the breach of those primary obligations. In this case, once the *Delfini* had arrived at [the discharge port], discharged the vast majority of the cargo loaded ... and sailed away, the contract of carriage was discharged by performance. Thereafter any remedy against the defendants lay in a claim for damages for breach."

In the Court of Appeal ([1990] 1 Lloyd's Rep. 252) the court did not find it necessary to deal with the issue as to whether the bills of lading were discharged.

13–030   [38] In *The Future Express* [1992] 2 Lloyd's Rep. 79, the cargo was delivered against an indemnity to a person who did not have a right to delivery under the bill of lading; one of the many issues that arose was whether the bill of lading was spent. Judge Diamond Q.C. held, following the passage from the judgment of Willes J., that the bill of lading had not become spent, as the goods had not been delivered to a person who had a right to demand delivery or was entitled to them. He went on to observe that it was a difficult question as to whether the bill of lading was spent as a document of title if the cargo was delivered against an indemnity to a person authorised to receive delivery; he said:

"To hold that a bill of lading becomes spent when goods are delivered against an indemnity would greatly detract from the value of bills of lading as documents of title to goods, would diminish their value to bankers and other persons who have to rely upon them for security and would facilitate fraud."

He held that it was not necessary to decide the question, in view of the fact that the bill was not in any event spent as delivery had not been made to the person entitled. In the Court of Appeal the decision was affirmed ([1993] 2 Lloyd's Rep. 542) on grounds which made it unnecessary for the Court of Appeal to decide the issue on whether the bill of lading was spent.

[39] As Gold Crown had no right to take delivery, it is my view that the bills of lading were not spent when the goods were delivered to them. It is clear on the basis of the long-accepted dictum of Willes J. that a bill of lading remains in force even if the goods are misdelivered to a person not entitled to them. The reason is clear. At or after the time of misdelivery to a person not entitled, the bill of lading may be being negotiated between banks on the basis that it is still a valid document of title. In short-haul bulk trades, it is not uncommon that the cargo arrives at the port of destination whilst the documents are still being negotiated (see for example the practice in the European oil trade described by Staughton J. in *A/S Hansen-Tangens Rederi III v Total Transport Corp, (The Sagona)* [1984] 1 Lloyd's Rep. 194 at 200). Until the goods are delivered to the person actually entitled, the bill of lading must remain the document of title to the goods. Although there may be a debate as to whether a bill is or is not spent when the goods are delivered against an indemnity to a person entitled to them (*cf.* Carver on *Bills of Lading* para. 6–009), there can be no doubt that they are not spent when the goods are delivered to a person not entitled.

[40] But even if the bill of lading is not in these circumstances spent and thus remains the document of title to the goods, can it be said that there is still a right to possess as against the carrier within the meaning of the 1992 Act, when the carrier no longer has the goods? The claimants contended that there was no right to possess, as there could not be a right to posses that which the carrier did not have; there only existed a secondary right to damages. I do not agree. It seems to me clear from the 1992 Act that the reference to the right to possess is a reference to one of the primary rights emanating from the bill of lading's function as a document **13–031**

of title. Even if it were not clear from the wording of the 1992 Act, the explanatory notes to s.2(2) and s.5(2) make it clear that the references are to circumstances where the bill of lading has ceased to be a transferable document of title; the note also refers to paras. 2.43–2.44 of the Law Commissions' Report which also makes this clear.

[41] I therefore conclude that s.2(2) was not applicable, as the bills of lading still gave a right to possession of the goods as against the carrier. If, contrary to that view, I had concluded that s.2(2) was applicable, then I would have been satisfied that there were arrangements in force from the outset of the transaction under which the Chilean banks would return the documents to the claimants in the event that they were not taken up by Gold Crown. This seems to me to have been implicit in the way in which the Chilean banks were retained in this case to collect payment from Gold Crown.

(iv) Did the claimants have rights of suit in bailment?

13–032 [42] The claimants contended that rights of suit in bailment subsisted, even if they had no rights of suit under the bill of lading contract because of the provisions of the 1992 Act. As bailors they were entitled to sue Maersk and P. & O. in conversion.

[43] The principal question to which the submission gave rise was whether the claimants retained an immediate right as against Maersk and P. & O. as carriers to possess the goods. It was common ground that the claimants could only claim in bailment if they were at all times entitled to immediate possession of the goods.

[44] Maersk and P. & O. contended that as the Chilean banks became the lawful holders of the bills under the provisions of the 1992 Act, they became the parties entitled to immediate possession. The claimants could not therefore be entitled to immediate possession.

[45] The claimants' answer to this short contention was as follows.

— A bailment arose on shipment between the claimants as shippers and the carriers (Maersk and P. & O.).

— At common law the transfer of a bill of lading to another did not transfer constructive possession unless that was the intention of the parties; they relied on the judgment of Lloyd L.J. in *The Future Express* in the Court of Appeal [1993] 2 Lloyd's Rep. 542 at 547.

— There had been no such intention, as the claimants intended to retain control over the goods. There was also no attornment as there was no intention to transfer title to the goods; the claimants relied on the judgment of Judge Diamond Q.C. in *The Future Express* [1992] 2 Lloyd's Rep. 79 at 95 and a passage in the speech of Lord Brandon of Oakbrook in *Leigh & Sillavan Ltd v Aliakmon Shipping Co Ltd, The Aliakmon* [1986] A.C. 785 at 818.

— The 1992 Act did not affect that position; the Act only transferred rights in contract and not in bailment. Furthermore the only rights of suit transferred in contract were "rights of suit" and not primary rights such as the right to possess.

— As between the Chilean banks and the claimants, it was the claimants as the owners of the goods and the persons entitled to them who were entitled to immediate possession of the goods; Maersk and P. & O. would have been bound to deliver to the claimants as the true owners, if the claimants had sought delivery.

— The Chilean banks had at most a contractual right to possession under the bills of lading. A mere contractual right to possession was not sufficient to found a right to sue in conversion: *Jarvis v Williams* [1955] 1 W.L.R. 71; *International Factors Ltd v Rodriguez* [1979] Q.B. 351 at 357.

— If, contrary to their submissions, the Chilean banks had a right to immediate possession, they had a right to do so only as agents of the claimants. It is necessary to examine each stage of this argument, beginning with the position at common law.

[46] At common law, the right to possession under the bailment created on the issue of the bill of lading was, by mercantile custom, capable of transfer by indorsement of the bill of lading; the indorsement and delivery of the bill of lading were capable of transferring the indorser's right to possession of the goods to the indorsee. What effect that had on rights of property depended on the intention of the parties. A special or general property in goods was only passed if that was the intention; as Lord Bramwell said in *Sewell v Burdick* (1884) 10 App. Cas. 74 at 105, "the property does not pass by the indorsement, but by the contract in pursuance of which the indorsement is made". For example, if the bill was indorsed to an agent to enable him to sell the goods, no property would pass to the agent: see Scrutton on *Charterparties and Bills of Lading* (20th edn., 1996): art. 104(3) and the old cases of *Waring v Cox* (1808) 1 Camp. 369, 170 E.R. 989 and *Patten v Thompson* (1816) 5 M. & S.350, 105 E.R. 1079 (which explains this partly on the grounds that no consideration or value was given for the transfer). The position was summarised by Lloyd L.J. in *The Future Express* in accepting the correctness of counsel's submission that—

"just as the transfer of the bill of lading only operates to transfer the general property in the goods if that is the intention of the parties, so it only operates to transfer the special property when the transferor so intends."

[47] Contractual rights were not transferred by mercantile custom and **13–033** so the transferee of the bill of lading could not sue under the contract of carriage contained in the bill of lading; the purpose of the Bills of Lading Act 1855 was to remedy this in situations where the common law had been unable to provide a remedy—see the analysis of Lord Hobhouse of

Woodborough in *Borealis AB (formerly Borealis Petrokemi AB) v Stargas Ltd
(Bergesen DY A/S, third party), The Berge Sisar* [2001] U.K.H.L. 17 at [18] to
[21], [2001] 2 W.L.R. 1118 [below]. Under the law prior to the 1855 Act, the
rights and obligations in contract could become separated from the right
of the indorsee to the possession, and to demand delivery, of the goods
(see [2001] 1 All E.R. (Comm.) 673 at [19], [2001] 2 W.L.R. 1118). The 1855
Act, however, only transferred the rights under the contract contained in
the bill of lading when the property in the goods passed upon or by
reason of the consignment or indorsement; this gave rise to difficulties
where the property did not pass in such circumstances.

[48] The intention and effect of the 1992 Act was to sever the link
between the transfer of rights under the contract of carriage and the
passing of property which the Law Commission considered had caused
the difficulties. The effect of the 1992 Act was, however, only on the
contract of carriage. This was made clear by Lord Hobhouse in *The Berge
Sisar*. After referring to the Report of the Law Commissions, he stated
([2001] 1 All E.R. (Comm.) 673 at [31], [2001] 2 W.L.R. 1118)[15]:

"But it must be observed that all these statements in the report, like the
terminology used in the 1992 Act, are expressed in terms which refer
explicitly to 'the contract of carriage' and not to the right of the holder
of the endorsed bill of lading to the possession of the goods as the
bailor as against the bailee. It is thus categorising the delivery up of the
goods in this context as the performance of a contractual obligation not
a bailment obligation. This is not objectionable since where there is a
contract of carriage the contract certainly includes a contractual obligation to deliver the goods . . . the bailment is a contractual bailment. The
relationship of the original parties to the contract of carriage is a
contractually mutual relationship, each having contractual rights
against the other. The important point which is demonstrated by this
part of the report, and carried through into the 1992 Act is that it is the
contractual rights, not the proprietary rights (be they general or special), that are to be relevant. The relevant consideration is the mutuality
of the contractual relationship transferred to the endorsee and the
reciprocal contractual rights and obligations which arise from that
relationship."

[49] Thus rights are acquired under the 1992 Act irrespective of the
contractual provisions as to the passing of property between the shipper
and the person who becomes the holder.

[50] The rights transferred to the lawful holder under the 1992 Act are
the "rights of suit"; this phrase was taken from the 1855 Act. Although
"rights of suit" have been described as rights of "suing upon the contract" (as in *The Freedom* (1871) L.R. 3 P.C. 594 at 599), the phrase was not
used to distinguish "rights of suit" from "rights under the contract". It is

---

[15] This paragraph is also set out at para. 13–048, below.

clear, in my view, that the phrase refers not merely to the right to sue, but the rights under the contract. These include the contractual right as against the carrier to demand delivery against presentation of the bill of lading and hence the right to possess. Not only is the language of the 1992 Act clear, but it is also clear from the Law Commissions' Report and in particular paras. 2.34 and 3.13–3.21 that it was intended that "rights of suit" include the right to demand delivery. It would make no sense to the scheme of the 1992 Act if the contractual right to demand delivery from the carrier was excluded from the rights transferred.

[51] The 1992 Act does not in terms affect rights in bailment: see the Report of the Law Commissions and the speech of Lord Hobhouse to which I have referred. But the question arises as to whether there are rights in bailment to immediate possession independent of the contract contained in the bill of lading. Rights in bailment subsist in many cases independent of a contract, as the obligations between bailor and bailee arise out of the bailment and are not dependent on there being a contract. I accept that the analysis of Professor Palmer in *Palmer on Bailment* (2nd edn., 1991) can apply in such cases and the duties of the bailor can be seen as arising out of the voluntary assumption of possession of another's goods.

[52] However, the rights as between bailor and bailee are often gov- **13–034** erned by a contract; where there is a contract, the contract may modify or define the obligations in bailment. In the present case, the right to possess the goods entrusted to the carrier was governed by the contract contained in the bill of lading; it was not independent of it. As between the carriers (P. & O. and Maersk) and the claimants as shippers, there was no agreement as to the terms of the bailment other than the terms set out in the bill of lading. Under the terms of the contract contained in the bill of lading, the goods were to be delivered against presentation of the bill of lading (as I subsequently discuss at [120] to [129], below, where I accept the submissions of the claimants on that issue). There was no separate agreement with the claimants as shippers that the rights of the consignees or holders of the bill of lading should be other than those set out in the bill of lading. When these contractual rights were transferred by s.2(1) of the 1992 Act to the Chilean banks, the claimants lost their contractual right to immediate possession under s.2(5) of the Act for the reasons set out. As between themselves and the carriers (Maersk and P. & O.) their rights in bailment and their rights under the contract were the same; there were no separate rights. It was only as between the claimants and the Chilean banks that the rights were different, but the position under the arrangements between the Chilean banks and the claimants did not affect the contractual rights under the bills of lading between the carriers and the Chilean banks.

[53] The lawful holder of a bill of lading clearly cannot acquire under the 1992 Act rights which the transferor did not have (see the discussion of *Finlay v Liverpool and Great Western Steamship Co Ltd* (1870) 23 L.T. 251 at para. 5–027 of Carver on *Bills of Lading* and at p. 578 of *The Bill of Lading*

as a Document of Title at ch. 22 of Palmer and McKendrick *Interests in Goods* (1st edn., 1993)). Therefore as between the carrier and the lawful holder of the bill of lading, the right of the lawful holder to immediate possession of the goods can be defeated where the transferor to him did not have the right to transfer the bill. However, if the shipper was the true owner of the goods and had the right to immediate possession under the bill of lading, then by operation of the 1992 Act that contractual right to immediate possession is transferred, even if the shipper remained as between the shipper and the transferee the party entitled to delivery. The rights under the bill of lading operate independently of the arrangements under the banking relationships.

[54] The right so transferred is not a "mere contractual" right to possession of the goods of the kind discussed in *Jarvis v Williams* and the *International Factors Ltd* case. The contractual rights that are transferred by transfer of the bill of lading include the obligation to delivery under the bailment. Though the rights under the contract and possessory rights can be separated, they are not separated in these circumstances for the reasons I have given.

[55] Thus I have reached the view that there were no separate rights in bailment that were retained by the claimants. But the question remains as to whether the Chilean banks acquired the rights as agents for the claimants? It seems clear that if an agent has a right to possession for an undisclosed principal that right can in many circumstances be exercised by the principal: see the judgment of Hope J.A. in *Maynegrain Pty. Ltd v Compafina Bank* [1982] 2 N.S.W.L.R. 141. However, in this case the rights so obtained were obtained by the Chilean banks as consignees under the 1992 Act and for the reasons given in [31], above, they could not have been acquired by them in their capacity as agents.

(v) A claim in negligence

13–035 [56] As a final alternative, the claimants contended that they could maintain a claim for negligence against Maersk and P. & O. based on their possessory and proprietary interest in the goods.

[57] For the reasons given, I have concluded that the claimants did not have any possessory rights. However, the claimants relied on the fact that a claim for negligence could be brought by a person who only had a proprietary right without the immediate right to possess.

[58] Maersk and P. & O. accepted that there could be a claim if the goods had been damaged or destroyed (by, for example being thrown overboard); in such a case there would have been damage to that bare proprietary right and, if negligent, there would have been a claim. They also accepted that there could be a claim for negligent damage to a proprietary interest, provided there was damage to that interest by physical damage to the property or through the extinguishment of the claimant's proprietary interest through transfer of title to a third party. They contended that as the goods carried by them were only in the hands of a person not entitled to them, then there was no damage to the claimants'

proprietary rights. The claimants still owned the goods as Gold Crown had no proper title to them; they were not physically damaged and the claimants' title was not extinguished. The actual claim of the claimants was damage to their possessory rights and not to their proprietary rights as those had not been interfered with.

[59] The circumstances in which a claim lies in negligence for damage to a proprietary interest are set out in Clerk and Lindsell on *Torts* (18th edn., 2000) at para. 14–142 and the cases there referred to, in particular *Mears v London and South Western Rly Co* (1862) 11 C.B.N.S. 850. The claimants must prove that the negligence of Maersk and P. & O. deprived them of their interest in circumstances in which the goods could not be recovered. At one stage in the proceedings it was suggested that the claimants should have sued to recover the goods from Gold Crown, but quite rightly that was not pursued. I am quite satisfied that it was wholly impracticable for the claimants to have sought to recover the goods from Gold Crown in Chile; thus they were permanently deprived of their proprietary interest and thus they can maintain this claim against Maersk and P. & O.

[60] This claim based on their proprietary rights is outside the scope of and independent of the 1992 Act.

Conclusion on Title to Sue

[61] I have therefore come to the view that the claimants can maintain a claim on one of the grounds they have advanced on all the bills of lading and also a claim under Maersk bill no. 4 on a further ground.

[Thomas J. concluded that the law of Chile did not require the defendants to deliver without production of original bills of lading, and that they were accordingly liable in negligence.]

Notes

The arguments in paras. 35—38 are essentially a reiteration, albeit in a different **13–036** context, of those already rehearsed at paras 6–046, *et seq.*, above. Thomas J.'s judgment does not really advance the position; since the goods were delivered to someone not entitled, there was no need to reach a conclusion on the other issues.

The Berge Sisar (in paras. 47 and 48) is considered further below.

Ultimately, the claimants failed in contract (except for the straight bill—Maersk bill of lading no. 4) and bailment, but succeeded in an independent negligence action. The 1992 Act had no effect on negligence actions, and the consequences of this are also considered further below.

There were a number of other defences raised, as outlined in para. 10, above. The defendants claimed to be protected by exemption clauses in the carriage contracts, this being rejected on arguments similar to those in *Motis Exports* in para. 6–034, see above. They also claimed that Chilean law required them to deliver without production, a claim that failed on its facts. Thomas J. did not decide whether the defendants would have had a defence, had he come to the opposite conclusion on Chilean law.

Many of the arguments on the defences reiterate those already considered in para. 6–034, above.

(g) Shipper or Intermediate Holder also Charterer

13–037   By virtue of s.5(5) of the Act, the contractual rights of shippers and intermediate holders are extinguished, except where they derive from a charterparty. Independent rights of charterers, who are not the lawful holders of a bill of lading, have not been considered directly under the 1992 Act, but there are two authorities under the old Act, whose reasoning appears to differ, however.

THE ALBAZERO

House of Lords. [1977] A.C. 774

13–038   The facts have already been set out in chapter 5, above. The Court of Appeal had held that property had passed to the c.i.f. purchaser by the time the goods were lost, and there was no appeal on the property issue. The purchasers were out of time to sue on the bill of lading contract, and the issue was whether the sellers, who were time charterers, could sue on their behalf, there being no similar time bar in the charterparty.

The shippers claimed (on the basis of an old Scots case, *Dunlop v Lambert* (1839) 6 Cl. & F. 600) substantial damages to be held in trust for the indorsee. The shipowners argued that property in the goods having passed to the indorsees by the time of their loss, the shippers were entitled to nominal damages only. This argument was based on the general contractual principle that damages are compensatory only, and that the shippers had suffered no loss.

Held:
The shippers could recover only nominal damages on the charterparty.

13–039   Lord Diplock: The question of law of general importance . . . to which your Lordships' answer is sought on this appeal can be stated thus: Where goods which have been shipped on a chartered vessel under a bill of lading issued by the shipowner are lost or damaged as a result of conduct which constitutes a breach of the charterparty by the shipowner, can the charterer recover in an action against the shipowner as damages for breach of the charterparty the full value of the goods lost or the full amount of the diminution in value of the goods damaged, notwithstanding that the charterer had no proprietary interest in the goods at the time when they were damaged and had himself sustained no loss or damage as a consequence of the breach?'

The only way in which I find it possible to rationalise the rule in *Dunlop v Lambert* so that it may fit into the pattern of English law is to treat it as an application of the principle, accepted also in relation to policies of insurance upon goods, that in a commercial contract concerning goods where it is in the contemplation of the parties that the proprietary interests in the goods may be transferred from one owner to another after the contract has been entered into and before the breach which causes loss or damage to the goods, an original party to the contract, if such be the intention of them both, is to be treated in law as having entered into the contract for the benefit of all persons who have or may acquire an interest in the goods before they are lost or damaged, and is entitled to recover by way of damages for breach of contract the actual loss sustained by those for whose benefit the contract is entered into.

With the passing of the Bills of Lading Act 1855 the rationale of *Dunlop v Lambert* could no longer apply in cases where the only contract of carriage into which the shipowner had entered was that contained in a bill of lading, and the property in the goods passed to the consignee or indorsee named in the bill of lading by reason of the consignment or indorsement. Upon that happening the right of suit against the shipowner in respect of obligations arising under the contract of carriage passes to him from the consignor. Furthermore, a holder of the bill for valuable consideration in exercising his own right of suit has the benefit of an estoppel not available to the consignor that the bill of lading is conclusive evidence against the shipowner of the shipment of the goods described in it.

The rationale of the rule is in my view also incapable of justifying its extension to contracts for carriage of goods which contemplate that the carrier will also enter into separate contracts of carriage with whoever may become the owner of goods carried pursuant to the original contract.

A charterparty which provides for the issue of bills of lading covering the carriage of particular goods shipped on the chartered vessel is such a contract, whether it be a voyage or time charter. While it is generally the case with a voyage charter that the terms of the charterparty are incorporated in the bills of lading required or authorised to be issued under it by the shipowner, even if the contractual rights of the parties under the charter were identical with those of the parties under the bill of lading, there would be no sensible business reason for inferring that the shipowner in entering into the charterparty intended to accept concurrent liabilities to be sued for the same loss or damage by the charterer and by the consignee or indorsee of the bill of lading.

A fortiori there can be no sensible business reason for extending the rule to cases where the contractual rights of the charterer under the charterparty are not identical with those of the bill of lading holder whose goods are lost or damaged; and this must always be the case as respects holders for valuable consideration because of the statutory estoppel to which I have referred. But there may be, and in time charters there often are, considerable other differences between the contractual rights of the charterer under the charterparty and those of the bill of lading holder under the bill of lading. In the absence of a clause paramount in the charterparty, the limit upon the amount recoverable per package under the Hague Rules would not be applicable to claims under the charterparty, nor would the one year prescription period, the exceptions from liability under the charterparty might be different and either more or less extensive than those under the bill of lading, the standard of care required of the shipowner and his vicarious liability for its observance would generally be governed by different norms, and the arbitration clause might be different in the two contracts or present in one and absent in the other.

The complications, anomalies and injustices that might arise from the co-existence in different parties of rights of suit to recover, under separate contracts of carriage which impose different obligations upon the parties to them, a loss which a party to one of those contracts alone has sustained, supply compelling reasons why the rule in *Dunlop v Lambert* should not be extended to cases where there are two contracts with the carrier covering the same carriage and under one of them there is privity of contract between the person who actually sustains the loss and the carrier by whose breach of that contract it was caused.

Notes

13–040 In *Dunlop v Lambert* (1839) 6 Cl. & F. 600, the consignor of goods had recovered substantial damages from the carrier, although risk, and possibly property, had passed to the purchaser of the cargo.[16] It appears to be an exception to the general principle that a contracting party can recover only for his own loss. Lord Diplock certainly treated the case as anomalous, based on early practices of international trade. He held that in the light of the Bills of Lading Act 1855, it was now reasonable to assume that all the rights and obligations under the contract of carriage pass to the indorsee. Where there were two contracts, the shipper should be able to recover nominal damages only, on the original contract of carriage.

This principle ought to be of direct application to the 1992 Act. However, in *The Sanix Ace*,[17] Hobhouse J. distinguished *The Albazero*, on the grounds that the property in the goods remained in the original shipper (who was also charterer of the vessel). He rejected the carrier's argument that the plaintiffs had suffered no recoverable loss and hence were limited to nominal damages alone[18]:

"The argument is patently unsustainable and I did not feel it necessary to call upon the claimants' Counsel. It has long been settled law that the owner of goods is entitled to sue and recover damages in respect of loss or damage to those goods. The only qualification is that, if he is suing in tort, his claim may be defeated if his title was a bare proprietary one and did not include any right to possession of the goods. In English law it is the claimants' property in the goods which gives the right to recover substantial damages. In tort the title to sue and recovery of substantial damages are concurrent. There is no such thing in the relevant context as a right to sue in tort for merely nominal damages. In contract, although nominal damages can be awarded, the right to recover substantial damages can be proved by proving possession or ownership of the relevant goods. The carriers' argument before me that the claimants had suffered no damage because they had subsequently been paid by the end users is misconceived. As soon as the goods are damaged the owner of the goods suffers loss. Formerly he was the owner of the goods of full value and subsequently he is the owner of the goods with only a reduced value. He has suffered a loss. Whether or not he may be able to recoup his loss from others is a separate question."

What was crucial in Hobhouse J.'s view was whether the plaintiffs had property in the goods at the time they were damaged.

---

[16] In fact, the *ratio* of this case has never been very clear; it may have been an *ex ship* contract, in which case the consignor was simply suing for damage to his own property.

[17] *Obestain Inc v National Mineral Development Corporation Ltd (The Sanix Ace)* [1987] 1 Lloyd's Rep. 465.

[18] [1987] 1 Lloyd's Rep. 465, 468 (col. 1).

Of course, under the 1855 Act, if property remained in the seller then no right of suit would be transferred to any other party, so there would be no possibility of the two contracts mentioned by Lord Diplock. No doubt, *The Albazero* itself would have been decided the other way, had property not passed, and indeed, the property issue was litigated as far as the Court of Appeal. But under the 1992 Act, it is possible for property to remain in the seller, even where the buyer obtains an action under s.2. This can possibly give rise to injustice; see the example in the following section, but with the seller as charterer, suing on the charterparty, rather than in tort.

(h) An Independent Tort Action?

Tort actions are unaffected by the 1992 Act, and we saw the value of an independent negligence action in *East West Corporation v DKBS 1912*, above. In that case the Chilean banks must also have had a contractual claim against the carrier, as lawful holders under the 1992 Act. In the event, they had no interest in bringing a claim, but suppose the following situation, based on facts which are a variation of *The Aliakmon*, below. Under the sale contract, property passes on payment, because of a reservation of title clause, but the bill of lading is released to the buyer, who therefore becomes lawful holder. The goods are damaged through the shipowner's negligence, which is also a breach of the bill of lading contract. Buyer sues under the 1992 Act, recovers substantial damages, and goes bankrupt before paying the price. Seller sues in tort. There is no obvious principle which prevents the shipowner being liable twice over.[19] Yet neither seller nor buyer has been over-compensated, and it is difficult to see upon what principle either has been unjustly enriched.

13–041

As will become apparent below, a negligence action can generally only be brought by someone with property in the goods, at the time of the breach of duty that causes the damage. Under the regime of the 1855 Act the dual role of contract and tort actions would have been unlikely to give rise to difficulty, since only the owner had an action in tort, and the property link ensured that nobody apart from the owner was likely to have a contractual action. The 1992 Act does away with the property link; hence the problem.

(i) Section 3 (Liabilities Under Shipping Documents)

The 1855 Act transferred rights and liabilities together, so that anyone who obtained contractual rights was also subject to contractual liability. The effect of the decision in *Sewell v Burdick* was to prevent banks as pledgees from becoming automatically liable for bill of lading freight, but also as a necessary consequence deprived them of any right to sue under the Act. An important feature of the new legislation is that liabilities are now dealt with separately from rights.

13–042

The view taken by the Law Commission (part III(e)) was that a bank as pledgee should not thereby become automatically under the carriage contract, but should be able to sue on it as lawful holder. However, if the bank did sue, or demanded delivery of the goods, it would also become subject to liabilities. This is essentially what is provided for by ss.3(1)(a)–(c).

Section 3(2) addresses an obvious problem where the goods are part of a larger bulk. A buyer of part of a bulk should not become liable for freight or demurrage (for example) on the entire cargo. Under s.3(3), the original contracting party also remains liable. This was also the case under the 1855 Act, at any rate as far as

---

[19] Unless the seller's title is regarded as a bare proprietary one which does not include any right to possession of the goods, the bill of lading having been transferred. In that case, change the document to a waybill and the seller certainly retains title to sue.

freight was concerned, by virtue of s.2 of that Act, and it may be justified in that a carrier who has contracted with a shipper of substance should not be forced instead to sue the lawful holder who may be less reputable.

A holder only becomes liable on the documents under s.3(1) where he:

"(a) takes or demands delivery from the carrier of any of the goods to which the document relates;

(b) makes a claim under the contract of carriage against the carrier in respect of any of those goods; or

(c) is a person who, at a time before those rights were vested in him, took or demanded delivery from the carrier of any of those goods."

Were the facts of *Sewell v Burdick* to arise again today, therefore, the bank would still not be liable for freight, even under the 1992 Act. Note that whereas the liabilities of the original shipper are not divested by the Act, the Act is silent on whether, once a holder becomes liable under s.3, that liability is divested on re-transfer of the bill of lading (or other document).

The courts have considered the circumstances under which a holder of a bill of lading can become liable under s.3, and (less conclusively) whether liability is divested on reindorsement. In *The Aegean Sea* [1998] 2 Lloyd's Rep. 39, ROIL, who had purchased a cargo of oil f.o.b., were voyage charterers of the vessel (an oil tanker). They ordered the vessel to an unsafe port, where she grounded, exploded and was destroyed; moreover, the shipowners incurred liability for the pollution caused. They sued not only the charterers, but also Repsol who (they claimed) became the holders of the bills of lading under the 1992 Act. (Repsol owned ROIL, and purchased the cargo from them, on *ex ship* terms.) Mistakenly, the bills of lading were sent to Repsol, not ROIL, and Repsol also telexed a letter of indemnity to the owners (because the shipowners demanded an indemnity from Repsol, not ROIL), but the ship and cargo were lost before it could be delivered. The shipowners did not succeed in their action against Repsol on the bill of lading contract (based on the safe port clause and an implied indemnity); because the bills of lading had been indorsed and sent to them in error, and Thomas J. therefore took the view that they never became lawful holders at all, nor had they requested delivery, so as to fall within s.3. (The shipowners were, however, able to sue ROIL under the charterparty.) Thomas J. also thought, however, *obiter* because it was not necessary for his decision, that once liability had been imposed under s.3, it was not divested by later re-indorsement of the bills of lading.

In *The Berge Sisar* [1998] 2 Lloyd's Rep. 475, the Court of Appeal differed from Thomas J. and held, as part of the *ratio*, that the liability of an intermediate holder is divested on re-transfer. In *Smurthwaite v Wilkins* (1862) 11 C.B. (N.S.) 842, Erle C.J. had held that an intermediate holder of a bill of lading did not remain liable for freight after divestment of the bill, under the Bills of Lading Act 1855. In *The Berge Sisar*, Millett L.J., who gave the only majority speech, approved of this decision, taking the view that that the same position obtained under the 1992 Act as would have obtained under the Bills of Lading Act. What was unclear was whether divestment was automatic on re-transfer, or not until the new holder satisfied the s.3 conditions; if the former, the shipowner could find himself with nobody to sue. (See further Reynolds [1999] L.M.C.L.Q. 161.)

The House of Lords did not need to decide this point, because they held that the intermediate holder had not become liable at all, under s.3. Lord Hobhouse, however, also thought that *Smurthwaite v Wilkins* should still be regarded as good law under the 1992 Act. His talk in terms of mutuality (see the passage set out below) suggests that divestment should be automatic on re-transfer, there being no additional requirement for liability to be imposed on the new holder.

BOREALIS v STARGAS, THE BERGE SISAR

House of Lords. [2001] U.K.H.L. 17, [2001] 2 W.L.R. 1118

(noted by Treitel [2001] L.M.C.L.Q. 344)

Borealis were intermediate purchasers of corrosive cargo which caused damage to **13–043** the ship, and were sued as intermediate holders of the bills of lading, the bills of lading having subsequently been further indorsed to their buyers. Borealis had, before becoming lawful holders of the bills of lading, requested delivery of the cargo but having taken samples for testing, thereafter rejected it.

Held in the Court of Appeal:
By a 2–1 majority, the Court of Appeal held Stargas not liable on the bills of lading; although they had become liable, by their request for delivery, under subsection (c) above, that liability had been divested on re-indorsement of the bills, since they had not irrevocably taken delivery.

Held in the House of Lords:
Merely requesting samples for testing was not taking or demanding delivery within s.3.

Lord Hobhouse:

The 1992 Act: Its Genesis
[18] The predecessor of the 1992 Act was the Bills of Lading Act 1855. **13–044** It was a short Act consisting of only three sections, of which only the first two are of present relevance. The preamble explained why it had been passed:

> "Whereas by the custom of merchants a bill of lading of goods being transferable by endorsement, the property in the goods may thereby pass to the endorsee, but nevertheless all rights in respect of the contract contained in the bill of lading continue in the original shipper or owner; and it is expedient that such rights should pass with the property"

Endorsed bills of lading were recognised by the law merchant to be symbols of the goods by the delivery of which the goods covered by the bill of lading could likewise be delivered. This was an application of the principles of bailment and attornment (*Sanders Bros v Maclean & Co* (1883) 11 Q.B.D. 327; *Dublin City Distillery Ltd v Doherty* [1914] A.C. 823). In the *Sanders Bros* case Bowen L.J. said (at 341):

> "The law as to the indorsement of bills of lading is as clear as in my opinion the practice of all European merchants is thoroughly understood. A cargo at sea while in the hands of the carrier is necessarily incapable of physical delivery. During this period of transit and voyage, the bill of lading by the law merchant is universally recognised

as its symbol, and the indorsement and delivery of the bill of lading operates as a symbolical delivery of the cargo. Property in the goods passes by such indorsement and delivery of the bill of lading, whenever it is the intention of the parties that the property should pass, just as under similar circumstances the property would pass by an actual delivery of the goods. And for the purpose of passing such property in the goods and completing the title of the indorsee to full possession thereof, the bill of lading, until complete delivery of the cargo has been made on shore to some one rightfully claiming under it, remains in force as a symbol, and carries with it the full ownership of the goods. It is a key which in the hands of a rightful owner is intended to unlock the door of the warehouse, floating or fixed, in which the goods may chance to be."

The bill of lading acknowledges the receipt of the goods from the shipper for carriage to a destination and delivery there to the consignee. It therefore evidences a bailment with the carrier who has issued the bill of lading as the bailee and the consignee as bailor. This analysis was already well recognised before 1855 as is demonstrated by *Bryans v Nix* (1839) 4 M. & W. 775, 150 E.R. 1634 and *Evans v Nichol* (1841) 3 M. & G. 614, 133 E.R. 1286. But the consignee need not be named and the bill of lading may simply say "deliver to the bearer" or to "order" or "to order or assigns" or similar words. The contribution of the law merchant had been to recognise the attornment as transferrable and therefore the indorsement and delivery of the bill of lading as capable of transferring the endorser's right to the possession of the goods to the endorsee (*Lickbarrow v Mason* (1787) 2 Term. Rep. 63, [1775–1802] All E.R. Rep. 1; *Kum v Wah Tat Bank* [1971] 1 Lloyd's Rep. 439 at 446–449 per Lord Devlin). What effect this would have on the title to the goods depended on the circumstances and the intention of the transferor and transferee (*Sewell v Burdick* (1884) 10 App. Cas. 74; *Glyn Mills, Currie & Co v East and West India Dock Co* (1880) 6 Q.B.D. 475).

13–045   [19] However, as the preamble stated, the law merchant had not recognised any similar transfer of the contractual rights (*Thompson v Dominy* (1845) 14 M. & W. 403, 153 E.R. 532) [above]. The bill of lading evidences a contract of carriage. The parties to that contract are the issuing carrier, usually the shipowner although it may be a charterer, and the shipper or his principal. Where there is a named consignee it may be inferred that the contracting party is the consignee not the shipper: *Dawes v Peck* (1799) 8 Term. Rep. 330, 101 E.R. 1417 and the other cases cited by Brandon J. in *The Albazero* [1977] A.C. 774 at 786. But, where the principal was the shipper, the contract was with him and remained with him. The rights and obligations in contract became separated from the right of the endorsee to the possession, and to demand the delivery up, of the goods.

[20] There was a qualification of this. The bill of lading evidenced a bailment upon terms, typically conditions which qualified the obligation

to deliver up the goods to the bailor, including the discharge of liens or the performance of any requirements for unloading the goods from the ship. These conditions would be stated in the bill of lading or incorporated from a charterparty. For liens which are common law liens, *e.g.*, the lien for freight or for general average, unless the bill of lading contained words waiving or negativing the lien (as by stamping the bill of lading "freight prepaid"), the bill of lading holder had no right to the possession of the goods without first discharging the liens. At the time of the passing of the 1855 Act, the recognition of the carrier's liens as a qualification of the rights of the endorsee against the shipowner was well established: *Cock v Taylor* (1811) 13 East. 399, 104 E.R. 424; *Sanders v Vanzeller* (1843) 4 Q.B. 260, 114 E.R. 897; *Stindt v Roberts* (1848) 17 L.J.Q.B. 166; and *Young v Moeller* (1855) 5 E. & B. 755, 119 E.R. 662. It took a bit longer fully to work out all the contractual implications. In 1883, Cave J., following the earlier decisions, said in *Allen v Coltart* (1883) 11 Q.B.D. 782 at 785:

"where goods are deliverable to the holder of a bill of lading on certain conditions being complied with, the act of demanding delivery is evidence of an offer on his part to comply with those conditions, and the delivery accordingly by the master is evidence of his acceptance of that offer."

In 1923 the Court of Appeal authoritatively expanded the inferred contract as fully encompassing the rights and obligations of the carrier on the terms of the bill of lading: *Brandt & Co v Liverpool Brazil and River Plate Steam Navigation Co Ltd* [1924] 1 K.B. 575, Bankes, Scrutton and Atkin L.JJ., affirming a decision of Greer J. (a combination of unparalleled distinction in this field). The plaintiff was a person who was claiming damages from the shipowner for negligence in the carriage of a consignment of goods. He was not able to bring himself within the terms of the 1855 Act but he succeeded on the contract to be inferred from the presentation of the bill of lading and the delivery of the goods against it. Atkin L.J. ([1924] 1 K.B. 575 at 598–599) outlined the route by which the law had developed. He referred to the inferred undertaking by the bill of lading holder to pay the sums due in respect of the carriage of the goods and asked whether there was any corresponding obligation on the part of the shipowner in that inferred contract. He continued:

"It appears to me that just as plainly the assignee is bound by an implied contract, so is the shipowner, and the shipowner's obligation in the case where freight has in fact been paid by the holder of the bill of lading, is that he will deliver the goods. Is it a contract to deliver the goods on the terms of the bill of lading? Shipowners would be surprised to hear it suggested that having undertaken to carry goods upon terms in their bill of lading qualifying and limiting their liability they are nevertheless under an absolute obligation to deliver the goods and not an obligation qualified by the exceptions in the bill of lading; no other contract could be properly inferred." (See [1924] 1 K.B. 575 at 599–600.)

The inferred contract is not a fiction. It is a contract which the court concludes has come into existence because that is the proper finding of fact to make on the evidence in the case. Thus there has to be the requisite element of offer and acceptance and mutuality. This has been stressed in the modern authorities such as *The Aramis* [1989] 1 Lloyd's Rep. 213 and *Mitsui & Co Ltd v Novorossiysk Shipping Co (The Gudermes)* [1993] 1 Lloyd's Rep. 311 [below]; if the facts do not justify it, the court will decline to find that there was a contract.

[21] The common law was thus able, without the assistance of statute, to accommodate the contractual position of the consignee who was the person for whom the shipper was entrusting the goods to the carrier and the position of the holder of the bill of lading who was taking delivery from the carrier at destination against presentation of the bill of lading. The 1855 Act was primarily concerned with the position of endorsees who did not come into either category but the drafting was sufficiently wide to be all embracing. Sections 1 and 2 provided:

[LORD HOBHOUSE set out the two sections and continued:]

The drafting of the 1855 Act gave rise to criticisms and difficulties. Two of them are presently relevant and of importance to the understanding of the 1992 Act.

The Passing of "Property" "Upon or by Reason of" the Endorsement

13–046   [22] This problem was the subject of the decision of your Lordships' House in *Sewell v Burdick* (1884) 10 App. Cas. 74. It has two aspects. The first is what does the word "property" encompass. Is it limited to the general property in the goods, that is, the legal title to the goods as is transferred by a sale? Or does it include the special property which signifies the right to possession? In *Sewell's* case it was decided that it should be limited to the passing of the general property. The primary reason for reaching that conclusion was that bills of lading are as often as not used as security documents facilitating the financing by banks of merchants' sale transactions (*e.g.*, under documentary letters of credit). A bank's interest is to use the possessory right to the document and the goods it represents as security; its interest is not to enter into contractual relations with the carrier, still less, to undertake contractual obligations towards the carrier. The decision in *Sewell's* case was that a transaction of pledge accompanied by the endorsement of the bill of lading over to the pledgee did not come within the scope of s.1 and did not transfer to the pledgee any contractual rights nor subject the pledgee to any contractual liabilities under the bill of lading.

[23] The other aspect was that the passing of the property had to be "upon or by reason of [the] consignment or endorsement". But property

under a contract of sale passes when the parties to that contract intend it to pass; it passes by reason of the contract of sale, not by reason of the endorsement of the bill of lading (s. 18 of the Sale of Goods Acts 1893 and 1979). Under an f.o.b. contract, the property in the goods prima facie passes upon shipment not upon the endorsement of or other dealing with the bills of lading. A contract for the international sale of goods commonly includes an express term covering the transfer of title. Similarly, ss. 18(2) and 19(2) of the Sale of Goods Acts made relevant the question whether the seller has by taking a bill of lading making the goods deliverable to his own order reserved the right of disposal. The difficulties of using the criterion in the 1855 Act were increased by simple logistics. The goods would arrive and be discharged and delivered before the documents had completed their progress down the chain of the intermediate buyers and sellers and their banks. The endorsement of those documents ceases to have any role in relation to the possession or legal ownership of the goods (*Enichem Anic SpA v Ampelos Shipping Co Ltd (The Delfini)* [1990] 1 Lloyd's Rep. 252) [see chapter 5, above]. In the present case, by January 1994, the cargo of propane had probably long since been processed at Terneuzen and had ceased to exist.

[24] There were cases therefore where the 1855 Act could not be used and where the tool of inferring a *Brandt* contract became less and less useful (*e.g. The Aramis*). There were related problems arising from changed patterns of trade. Cargoes were shipped in bulk. Bills of lading were issued for quantities out of undivided consignments and those quantities were then sold to different buyers and the various bills of lading endorsed over to them. Such endorsements were ineffective to pass the legal title in part of an undivided whole to a purchaser (*Re Wait* [1927] 1 Ch. 606). Further, the practice of issuing delivery orders for parcels out of a bulk cargo were similarly ineffective and the intended buyers were left without remedy against the carrier (*Margarine Union GmbH v Cambay Prince Steamship Co Ltd, The Wear Breeze* [1969] 1 Q.B. 219; *Leigh & Sillavan Ltd v Aliakmon Shipping Co Ltd, The Aliakmon* [1986] A.C. 785) [below].

"Subject to the Same Liabilities"

[25] The use of this phrase in the 1855 Act gave rise to immediate   **13–047**
difficulty. What was the position of an endorser after he had endorsed over the bill of lading to another? How did endorsement affect the liabilities of the shipper? The answer was given in *Fox v Nott* (1861) 6 H. & N. 630, 158 E.R. 260 and *Smurthwaite v Wilkins* (1862) 11 C.B.N.S. 842, 142 E.R. 1026. The endorser is not liable after he has endorsed over the bill of lading to another who is; the shipper remains liable as an original party to the contract. Two considerations seem to have weighed with the courts in these and the later cases (see *Effort Shipping Co Ltd v Linden Management SA, The Giannis NK* [1998] A.C. 605 at 615–618 per Lord Lloyd of Berwick). The words "subject to the same liabilities" were to be contrasted with the words "have transferred to him". The liability of the endorsee was

to be additional to that of the original contracting party. The other was to follow the reasoning which underlay the *Allen v Coltart* line of authority. It is the use of the bill of lading to demand and take delivery of the goods which is the basis of liability. Thus Erle C.J. said in *Smurthwaite's* case:

"Looking at the whole statute, it seems to me that the obvious meaning is that the assignee *who receives the cargo* shall have all the rights and bear all the liabilities of a contracting party; but that, if he passes on the bill of lading by indorsement to another, he passes on all the rights and liabilities which the bill of lading carries with it." (See (1862) 11 C.B.N.S. 842 at 848, 142 E.R. 1026 at 1028–1029; Erle C.J.'s emphasis.)

He rejected the argument that the endorser having passed on all his rights to the endorsee should retain all his liabilities in respect of the goods, saying:

"Such a construction might be very convenient for the ship-owner but it would be clearly repugnant to one's notions of justice." (See 11 C.B.N.S. 842 at 849, 142 E.R. 1026 at 1029.)

The judgment of Erle C.J. was approved by the Earl of Selborne L.C. in *Sewell v Burdick* (1884) 10 App. Cas. 74 at 86–88 (see also 83) and he echoed his language when he referred to a person who had had the bill of lading endorsed to him while the goods were at sea and who then chooses to take advantage of his possession of the bill of lading to "take the position of full proprietor upon himself with its corresponding burdens if he thinks fit"; "and that he actually does so as between himself and the ship-owner if and when he claims and takes delivery of the goods by virtue of that title".

The Drafting of the 1992 Act

[26] By 1980 the difficulties in the 1855 Act had assumed serious proportions and the 1855 Act was failing to meet the needs of the mercantile community and the changed pattern of international trade and carriage by sea. There were other points of concern as well. In certain trades the use of paper bills of lading was becoming increasingly obsolete. Electronic documents were coming into use [see chapter 16, below]. Documents other than bills of lading were being used for the purposes previously served by bills of lading [see chapter 15, below]. Another related question which had to be considered particularly in the drafting of any new legislation was the concept when a bill of lading became "accomplished", *i.e.*, ceased to be capable of transferring rights to an endorsee (save by estoppel). This was always a potential problem under the 1855 Act but did not cause significant problems in practice. It was however a problem which would have to be faced by the draftsman of a replacement for the 1855 Act.

[27] The existing state of the law having been recognised to be unsatisfactory, the question was referred to the Law Commission and the Scottish Law Commission. Their joint report, *Rights of suit in respect of carriage of goods by sea* (Law Com. No. 196, Scot. Law Com. No. 130), was published in March 1991 and appended a draft bill. They concentrated upon the carriage of goods by sea and the adequacy of the 1855 Act and did not in that report make recommendations for the amendment of the Sale of Goods Act 1979. They reviewed in detail the various aspects to which I have referred. They made recommendations for reform. They rejected as inadequate amendments to s.1 of the 1855 Act which would simply have removed the requirement that the holder should have become the owner of the goods "upon or by reason of" the endorsement or which would have removed all reference to property in s.1, so that it sufficed for the purposes of both rights and liabilities that the person was the holder of the bill of lading. They preferred instead an approach which severed the link between property and right of action and transferred the rights of suit to the holder without more, but not the liabilities. They recommended that there should not be an automatic linking of contractual rights and liabilities; pledgees would not be liable "unless they sought to enforce their security" (para. 2.31). In support of their recommendation they said (para. 2.34 (iv)):

"The statutory assignment model of the 1855 Act is familiar to international traders. Our reform is an evolutionary one which recognises that those parts of the 1855 Act which have worked well should be retained."

As regards the point at which the bill of lading ceases to be a transferable document of title, they adopted the existing test of delivery of the goods to the person entitled to receive them (para. 2.42). As regards the liability of the holder under the bill of lading, their recommendation was in essence that a holder who seeks to take the benefit of the contract of carriage should not be permitted to do so without the corresponding burdens (paras 3.15–3.22). I will come back later to what they said.

[28] The recommendations are summarised in Pt VII of the report and the appended draft bill was designed to reflect those recommendations. The bill was enacted without substantive amendment. Your Lordships are entitled to look at the report in order to identify the mischief to which the Act is directed and, in the case of ambiguity, to help in resolving any such ambiguity.

The 1992 Act

[29] Not the whole of the 1992 Act is relevant to the present appeal. It **13–048** is not necessary to quote those provisions which extend the descriptions of documents which are to be recognised as having a similar function to bills of lading nor the sections which revise s.3 of the 1855 Act. I will

confine my quotation to what is directly relevant to bills of lading and the present appeal.

[Lord Hobhouse set out the relevant parts of the statute, and continued:]

[30] This Act, in accordance with the view expressed in the report, retains much of the basic structure of the 1855 Act. Much of its increased length and complexity derives from the fact that it covers other documents—waybills and delivery orders—besides bills of lading. It makes separate provision for the rights and the liabilities of a bill of lading holder. Section 2(1) makes being the lawful holder of the bill of lading the sole criterion for the right to enforce the contract which it evidences and this transfer of the right extinguishes the right of preceding holders to do so (s.2(5)). There are two qualifications: in simplified terms, the holder can sue and recover damages on behalf of another with an interest in the goods (s.2(4)), and the transfer of a bill of lading after it has ceased to give a right to the possession of the goods does not confer any right of suit against the carrier unless the transfer was pursuant to an earlier contract or to the revesting of that right after a rejection by a buyer (s.2(2) and s.5(2)). In the present case the provisions of s.2 do not give rise to any problem. ...

[31] Section 2 of the 1992 Act has adopted a different and more generous approach to the transfer of contractual rights than that adopted by s.1 of the 1855 Act in that it wholly omits the "property" criterion. A party who takes a bill of lading as security, as a pledgee, has the contractual rights transferred to him under s.2. He can enforce them against the carrier or not as he chooses and may, if he chooses to do so, recover from the carrier also on behalf of the person with the full legal title (s. 2(4)). This leaves the question whether the pledgee or similar person should come under any liability to the carrier. Under the 1855 Act he did not because he did not come within s.1 of that Act and acquired neither rights nor liabilities. The draftsman of the 1992 Act respected the commercial reasoning upon which *Sewell's* case was based and did not require bankers and others taking the documents as security to have to accept any liabilities merely by reason of being the holders of the bills of lading. Section 3(1) imposes additional requirements before a holder of a bill of lading comes under any contractual liability to the carrier. The solution adopted by the draftsman was to use the principle that he who wishes to enforce the contract against the carrier must also accept the corresponding liabilities to the carrier under that contract. This was the view expressed by the Earl of Selborne L.C. It is the rationale of the cases leading up to the *Brandt* case. It is a principle of mutuality. It was spelled out in the commissions' report.

"3.15. However, where the holder of the bill of lading enforces any rights conferred on him under the contract of carriage he should do so on condition that he assumes any liabilities imposed on him under that contract . . .

3.18. We see in general no unfairness in making the person who either claims delivery or who takes delivery of the goods, from being subject to the terms of the contract of carriage, since in both cases the person is enforcing or at least attempting to enforce rights under the contract of carriage . . .

3.22. Furthermore, it is unfair that the carrier should be denied redress against the indorsee of the bill of lading who seeks to take the benefit of the contract of carriage without the corresponding burdens."

But it must be observed that all these statements in the report, like the terminology used in the 1992 Act, are expressed in terms which refer explicitly to "the contract of carriage" and not to the right of the holder of the endorsed bill of lading to the possession of the goods as the bailor as against the bailee. It is thus categorising the delivery up of the goods in this context as the performance of a contractual obligation not a bailment obligation. This is not objectionable since where there is a contract of carriage the contract certainly includes a contractual obligation to deliver the goods. A bill of lading invariably includes words evidencing the carrier's agreement to deliver the goods at destination to "or order or assigns" or words to that effect; the bailment is a contractual bailment. The relationship of the original parties to the contract of carriage is a contractually mutual relationship, each having contractual rights against the other. The important point which is demonstrated by this part of the report, and carried through into the 1992 Act is that it is the contractual rights, not the proprietary rights (be they general or special), that are to be relevant. The relevant consideration is the mutuality of the contractual relationship transferred to the endorsee and the reciprocal contractual rights and obligations which arise from that relationship.

[32] In giving effect to this intention, s.3 of the 1992 Act postulates first **13–049** that the holder in question must be a person in whom the contractual rights of suit have been vested by s.2(1). The language of s.2(1) adopts and is identical to the corresponding words in the 1855 Act, "shall have transferred [to] and vested in him all rights of suit". Section 3(1)(a) and (b) relate to a person who, being a person who has those rights, chooses to exercise them either (a) by taking or demanding delivery of the goods or (b) by making a claim under the contract of carriage contained in or evidenced by the bill of lading. Both involve an enforcement by the endorsee of the contractual rights against the carrier transferred to him by s.2(1). Under (a) it is by enjoying or demanding the performance of the carrier's contractual delivery obligation. Under (b) it is by claiming a remedy for some breach by the carrier of the contract of carriage. Each of (a) and (b) involves a choice by the endorsee to take a positive step in relation to the contract of carriage and the rights against the carrier

transferred to him by s.2(1). It has the character of an election to avail himself of those contractual rights against the carrier. There are however difficulties which neither the drafting nor the report faces up to. Whilst taking delivery is a clear enough concept—it involves a voluntary transfer of possession from one person to another—making a "demand" or "claim" does not have such a specific character and, what is more, may be tentative or capable of being resiled from, a point commented upon by Millett L.J. in the Court of Appeal ([1999] Q.B. 863 at 884). Delivery brings an end to the actual bailment of the goods and is (save in special circumstances) the final act of contractual performance on the part of the carrier. Claims or demands may on the other hand be made at any stage (although usually only made after the end of the voyage) and there may at the time still be performance obligations of the carrier yet to be performed.

[33] To "make a claim" may be anything from expressing a view in the course of a meeting or letter as to the liability of the carrier to issuing a writ or arresting the vessel. A "demand" might be an invitation or request, or, perhaps, even implied from making arrangements; or it might be a more formal express communication, such as would have sufficed to support an action in detinue. From the context in the 1992 Act and the purpose underlying s.3(1), it is clear that s.3 must be understood in a way which reflects the potentially important consequences of the choice or election which the bill of lading holder is making. The liabilities, particularly when alleged dangerous goods are involved, may be disproportionate to the value of the goods; the liabilities may not be covered by insurance; the endorsee may not be fully aware of what the liabilities are. I would therefore read the phrase "demands delivery" as referring to a formal demand made to the carrier or his agent asserting the contractual right as the endorsee of the bill of lading to have the carrier deliver the goods to him. And I would read the phrase "makes a claim under the contract of carriage" as referring to a formal claim against the carrier asserting a legal liability of the carrier under the contract of carriage to the holder of the bill of lading.

13–050   [34] But this is not the end of this problem. The use of the word "demand" is problematic as is the phrase "or at least attempting to enforce rights" in para. 3.18 of the report. (It seems that those who wrote para. 3.18 had in mind such exceptional situations as where the cargo is destroyed while the vessel is waiting to discharge at the discharge port and after a demurrage liability recoverable under the bill of lading has arisen — an intriguing and, if I may be forgiven for saying so, a relatively unilluminating example.) If the carrier accedes to the demand and gives delivery as demanded, the demand is subsumed in the taking of delivery. If the carrier rejects the demand, a new scenario arises: is the endorsee going to make a claim against the carrier for refusing to comply with the demand? If the endorsee chooses to let the matter drop and not to make a claim, what significance of the demand remains? What principle of mutuality requires that the endorsee shall nevertheless be made subject to the liabilities of a contracting party? What if the endorsee chooses to endorse over the bill of lading to another to whom the carrier is willing to and does deliver the goods? The task of the judge, arbitrator or legal adviser attempting to construe s.3(1) is not an easy one and it is necessary to try and extract from it some self-consistent structure.

[35] So far I have been concentrating on paras. (a) and (b). Paragraph (c) presents further problems. It raises the relatively common situation where the vessel and its cargo arrive at the destination before the bills of lading have completed their journey down the chain of banks and buyers. The intended receiver has not yet acquired any rights under s.2(1). He is not entitled to demand delivery of the goods from the carrier. He may or may not be the owner of the goods but he quite probably will not at that time have the right to the possession of the goods; an earlier holder of the bill of lading may be a pledgee of the goods. This situation is dealt with commercially by delivering the goods against a letter of indemnity provided by the receiver (or his bank) which will include an undertaking by the receiver to surrender the bill of lading to the carrier as soon as it is acquired and will include any other stipulations and terms which the situation calls for. It may well at that time, either expressly or by implication, give rise to a *Brandt* type of contract on the terms of the bill of lading. But again the question arises: what is the character and the role of the demand referred to in para. (c)? Ex hypothesi, the intended receiver had no right to make the demand and the carrier had no obligation to accede to it unless there was some other contract between the receiver and the carrier, *e.g.*, a charterparty, which gave rise to that right and obligation in which case ss.2 and 3 have no application to that transaction.

Paragraph (c) clearly involves an anticipation that the s.2(1) rights will be transferred to the receiver. The parenthesis which follows emphasises this "by virtue of having the rights vested in him". This shows that it is a necessary condition of the receiver's becoming liable under s.3(1) that the rights are vested in him by the operation of s.2(1). The inclusion of the word "demanded" remains problematical. A rightly rejected demand for delivery by one who is not entitled to delivery is an act devoid of legal significance. What is significant is if the carrier decides (voluntarily) to accede to the demand and deliver the goods to the receiver notwithstanding the non-arrival of the bill of lading. Paragraph (c) does not include the making of a claim. The draftsman has accepted the irrelevance of a claim made by one who has no contractual standing to make it. Unless facts occur which give a relevance to the inclusion of the word "demanded" in para. (c), in my view the scheme of ss.2 and 3 requires that any such demand be treated as irrelevant for the purposes of s.3(1) and that the 1992 Act be construed accordingly. A "demand" made without any basis for making it or insisting upon compliance is not in reality a demand at all. It is not a request made "as of right", which is the primary dictionary meaning of "demand". It is not accompanied by any threat of legal sanction. It is a request which can voluntarily be acceded to or refused as the person to whom it is made may choose. Accordingly it will be unlikely in the extreme that para. (c) will ever apply save where there has been an actual delivery of the cargo.

13–051   [36] Taking delivery in paras. (a) and (c) means, as I have said, the voluntary transfer of possession from one person to another. This is more than just co-operating in the discharge of the cargo from the vessel. Discharge and delivery are distinct aspects of the international carriage of goods (see generally Scrutton on *Charterparties* (20th edn., 1996) section XIII). Although the normal time for delivering cargo to the receiver may be at the time of its discharge from the vessel, that is not necessarily so. There may be a through contract of carriage. The goods may need to be unpacked from a container. The vessel may need to discharge its cargo without delay into a terminal. The discharge of the vessel is a necessary operation in the interests of the ship as well as of the cargo and requires the cooperation of others besides the shipowner. Providing that coopera-tion should not be confused with demanding delivery. The unloading of one cargo is for the shipowner the necessary preliminary to the loading of the next. Damaged or contaminated cargoes may need especial discharge because they may cause damage or pollution. Any unnecessary delays will cost the shipowner money and a loss to the charterer through incurring demurrage or forfeiting dispatch. Where the vessel is operating under a charterparty it is more likely than not that the obligation to discharge will be that of the charterer. The charterer will be responsible for providing or arranging a berth at which the vessel can discharge. Where the cargo is a bulk cargo which has been sold by the charterer to the intended receiver, the contract of sale may require the buyer to perform the seller's charterparty obligations in relation to the discharge of the vessel. The delivery to which s.3 is referring is that which involves a full transfer of the possession of the relevant goods by the carrier to the holder of the bill of lading. The surrender of the relevant endorsed bill of lading to the carrier or his agent before or at the time of delivery will ordinarily be an incident of such delivery. Where that is not done, the carrier will ordinarily require a letter of indemnity. The letter of indem-nity will probably be the best evidence of what arrangement has been made and will probably contain appropriate express terms.

The Facts: The "Demand"

[Lord Hobhouse reviewed the facts and continued:]

13–052   [38] It will be apparent that in my judgment what occurred fell far short of amounting to the making of any demand for delivery on the part of Borealis. ... The only thing done by Borealis appears to have been to direct the master to their import jetty and then, having allowed her to berth there, to take the routine samples from the cargo tanks before clearing the vessel for discharge into their terminal. These are exactly the type of co-operative acts, assisting the shipowners and charterers, to which I have referred earlier and which cannot on any view be treated as a demand by Borealis to deliver. Further, the trade in which these parties were involved necessitates the routine sampling of the cargo before it can be decided whether the vessel can be allowed to discharge its cargo into the terminal. It is elementary that in the ordinary course the nature and quality of the cargo must be established first. As the facts of the present case illustrate, it is always possible that the cargo may unexpectedly turn out to be contaminated or have some other characteristic which makes it unfit or unsafe for discharge into the terminal. What occurred did not get even as far as the stage of Borealis expressing their willingness to receive this cargo into their terminal. It fell a long way short of amounting to any demand or request that it should be. Once Borealis knew what the true characteristics of the cargo were, they refused to accept it from the ship.

[39] It follows that, as a matter of fact, Bergesen have failed on the agreed primary facts to make out even an arguable case that Borealis demanded the delivery of this cargo. If the facts had disclosed something more positive on the part of Borealis, it is difficult to visualise that it could have had an appropriately unequivocal character or could have amounted to a demand for the purposes of para. (c) of s.3(1). The considerations discussed in [35] and [36] above would apply both as a matter of the proper use of language and as a matter of the interpretation of s.3(1) in its schematic context including the guidance given by a consideration of the report.

The Secondary Question: Endorsement On and s.3(1)

[40] The answer which I have given to the question whether there was **13–053** a demand is decisive of the appeals. If there was no demand by Borealis, there cannot be any liability of Borealis under s.3(1) whatever answer is given to the secondary question which was decisive in the Court of Appeal. The secondary question is easily formulated: when an endorsee of a bill of lading who has both had transferred to and vested in him all the rights of suit under the contract of carriage pursuant to s.2(1) and become subject to the liabilities under that contract pursuant to s.3(1), does he cease to be so liable when he endorses over the bill of lading to another so as to transfer his rights of suit to that other?

[41] The remarkable thing is that the report does not refer to this question at all and the 1992 Act contains no express provision covering it even though there are express provisions dealing with similar matters such as s.2(5) (extinction of rights) and s.3(3) (preservation of liabilities). It clearly was not foreseen as being a live issue. One of the reasons, I believe, must have been that they did not visualise there being anything tentative about any of the triggering steps referred to in the three paragraphs of s.3(1). They were contemplating actions of the bill of lading holder or receiver which would take place after the completion of the voyage. They did not have in mind conduct which could be resiled from or circumstances which would leave open the possibility of doing so. They did not visualise that casualties and disputes might arise during the

course of a voyage which could give rise to the possible operation of s.3(1) and yet, in the event, not put an end to the carriage or the subsequent onward transfer of the bills of lading. Three things follow from this. The first is that no special significance can be attached to the fact that there is no express provision which provides the answer one way or the other in the 1992 Act. The problem was not seen to be a problem and the question was not seen to require an answer. Secondly, it underlines that a relatively stringent approach should be adopted to the interpretation of s.3(1). The character of the conduct which attracts the liability imposed by s.3(1) is expected to have an element of relative finality; it is not conduct which is tentative or equivocal nor conduct which is equally consistent with the person leaving it to a later endorsee to exercise the rights transferred by s.2(1). Thirdly, the answer to the question must be found by seeking out from the drafting of the 1992 Act and the report, pursuant to which the 1992 Act was drafted, what is the scheme of the statutory provisions and what principles they reflect.

[42] Valuable discussions of the various countervailing arguments for one view or the other are to be found in the judgments of the Court of Appeal, particularly the dissenting judgment of Sir Brian Neill ([1999] Q.B. 863 at 878–881) who was able to draw upon his particular experience in this field of law. Similarly your Lordships have had the assistance of citation from the judgment of Thomas J. in *Aegean Sea Traders Corp v Repsol Petroleo SA, The Aegean Sea* [1998] 2 Lloyd's Rep. 39 which dealt with a number of other points besides this one. Your Lordships were also referred to a short article by Francis Reynolds Q.C. in [1999] L.M.C.L.Q. 161 which draws attention to the importance of the factual context in which any such question arises and notes the importance of the concession which was made in the present case in the Court of Appeal and the artificiality of the situation which resulted with liability being said to arise from a momentary passage of the bills of lading two months later through the hands of Borealis.

[43] I agree with the sentiment of Professor Reynolds that it is likely that the particular facts will be of importance in any subsequent case concerning the interrelation of ss.2 and 3 of the 1992 Act. It is possible that the conduct of one or other party may give rise to estoppels as where one party has been led to exercise forbearance in reliance upon some conduct of the other. In most cases there will be other documents or agreements to take into account besides the bill of lading such as charterparties, letters of indemnity, non-separation agreements, or ad hoc agreements. With these caveats, I will shortly state my conclusion on the secondary question itself as a matter of the construction of the 1992 Act unqualified by any special factors.

13–054   [44] I consider that there are two principles which are stated in the report and reflected in the drafting of the 1992 Act which show an intention on the part of the draftsman to preserve the decision in *Smurthwaite's* case. The first is the intention to preserve the well tried and familiar structure of the 1855 Act having removed its dependence upon concepts of the passing of property. In the report, this approach surfaces in most of the relevant discussion and recommendations: see [27] above and paras. 2.22, 2.34, 2.40–2.41 and 3.9–3.24 of the report. In the 1992 Act s.2(1) and s.(1) adopt the crucial wording of the 1855 Act which formed the basis of *Smurthwaite's* case and similar cases "shall have transferred to and vested in him all rights of suit under the contract of carriage as if" — "shall become subject to the same liabilities under that contract as if". Those words having been previously construed as having a certain effect, their repetition in the 1992 Act implies that the draftsman expected them to continue to be construed in the same way. *Smurthwaite's* case is referred to in the report and is adopted rather than criticised. There is no provision in the 1992 Act which contradicts the intention that that decision should still have force.

[45] The second principle is that of mutuality (or, if preferred, reciprocity or fairness). I have already quoted passages from the report demonstrating that this was the guiding principle in arriving at the recommendations which have led to s.3(1). Section 3(1) is drafted following this principle because it makes it fundamental that, for a person to be caught by s.3(1), he must be the person in whom the rights of suit under the contract of carriage are vested pursuant to s.2(1). The liability is dependant upon the possession of the rights. It follows that, as there is no provision to the contrary, the 1992 Act should be construed as providing that, if the person should cease to have the rights vested in him, he should no longer be subject to the liabilities. The mutuality which is the rationale for imposing the liability has gone. There is no longer the link between benefits and burdens. I have already commented upon the fact that the report refers to *Smurthwaite's* case and adopts it without criticism. It was in that case that Erle C.J. said:

> " ... The contention is that the consignee or assignee shall always remain liable, like the consignor, although he has parted with all interest and property in the goods by assigning the bill of lading to a third party before the arrival of the goods. The consequences which this would lead to are so monstrous, so manifestly unjust, that I should pause before I consented to adopt this construction of the Act of Parliament." (See (1862) 11 C.B.N.S. 842 at 848, 142 E.R. 1026 at 1028.)

I recognise, and emphasise yet again, that it is likely that individual cases will be more complicated than that here visualised by Erle C.J. and other factors are likely to come into play which, maybe decisively, will affect the respective rights and liabilities of the relevant parties. But as a matter of the construction of the 1992 Act per se, what he says remains apt and reflects the same principle as that adopted by the report and is supported, not contradicted, by the 1992 Act.

Notes

13–055   Paras. 18–21 describe how the bill of lading developed to transfer constructive possession, and (later) contractual rights and liabilities. The cases on implied contracts at common law, which were fully reviewed by the Court of Appeal in *Brandt v Liverpool*,[20] and the later cases, such as *The Aramis* and *The Gudermes*, both referred to in para. 20, are considered fully at paras 13–067, *et seq.*, below.

Paras. 22 and 24 summarise the problems of tying in transfer of contractual rights and liabilities with the passing of property, culminating with the Court of Appeal decisions in *The Delfini*, in para. 23, and *The Aramis*, in para. 24. It was probably these decisions that finally persuaded the Law Commission that legislative change was needed.

The restrictive interpretation of s.3 is to be welcomed. The shipowners in *The Aegean Sea* succeeded against the charterers, and there was no doubt in *The Berge Sisar* that the charterers would have been liable. Because the liability of the shipper is not divested, s.3 only adds potential defendants, where action is brought by the carrier. No great injustice is therefore done by refusing to impose liability on persons whose relationship to the cargo is tenuous.

It also follows that no injustice is done by divesting liability on re-transfer, even where the subsequent holder incurs no liability under s.3. The shipowner can still sue the shipper, and the mutuality arguments in Lord Hobhouse's speech are surely convincing.

Note however that the mutuality argument does not apply to the original shipper, who remains liable,[21] in spite of having rights under the carriage contract divested. From the shipowner's viewpoint this is reasonable, since otherwise he would have substituted for a shipper with whom (in principle) he could choose whether or not to do business, a receiver of cargo of whom he may know nothing. The shipper could, however, remain liable (for example) for demurrage due at discharge, even though the fault may lie firmly with the receiver. Cesser clauses deal with this in charterparties, but they are rare in bills of lading.

(4) *Brandt v Liverpool* Contracts

(a) Application of the *Brandt v Liverpool* Doctrine to Bills of Lading

13–056   Even where (before 1992) the Bills of Lading Act 1855 did not apply, it was sometimes possible to imply a contract between the carrier and the receiver of the cargo at common law. Prior to the Court of Appeal decision in *Brandt v Liverpool*,[22] the implied contract had always been used to enable the carrier to sue the receiver of cargo for freight; by delivering the cargo, the carrier released his lien for freight, and it was reasonable to infer that he would only do this on the basis that he would be paid freight by the receiver of the cargo.[23]

In *Brandt v Liverpool*, a contract was successfully implied for the first time in favour of a receiver of cargo, a bank which had realised the security of its pledge, but was unable to rely on the 1855 Act.[24] The receiver having paid the freight was able to sue the carrier for damages for delay, and for the return of a reconditioning

---

[20] [1924] 1 K.B. 575.
[21] By virtue of s.3(3).
[22] *Brandt v Liverpool, Brazil & River Plate SN Co* [1924] 1 K.B. 575.
[23] *Cock v Taylor* (1811) 13 East 399; *Sanders v Vanzeller* (1843) 4 Q.B. 260; *Stindt v Roberts* (1848) 17 L.J.Q.B. 166; *Young v Moeller* (1855) 5 El. & Bl. 755; *Allen v Coltart* (1883) 11 Q.B.D. 782; *W.N. White & Co, Ltd v Furness, Withy & Co, Ltd* [1895] A.C. 40.
[24] Because of *Sewell v Burdick*.

cost of the cargo (which they had paid to the carrier under protest), where a clean bill of lading had been issued for defective cargo.[25] The Court of Appeal was prepared to imply a new contract between receiver and carrier: on delivery of the cargo against tender of a bill of lading, a contract was implied that delivery would be on the terms of the bill of lading.[26]

BRANDT v LIVERPOOL, BRAZIL & RIVER PLATE SN CO

Court of Appeal. [1924] 1 K.B. 575

Goods (zinc ashes) were shipped damaged, but the shipowner nevertheless **13–057** issued a bill of lading stating that they were shipped in apparent good order and condition.

Subsequently, the goods had to be unloaded and reconditioned, at a cost of £748, and re-shipped on another vessel, being forwarded late to their destination.

The bill of lading was indorsed in favour of the plaintiff pledgees (a bank), who advanced money on it in good faith. When the goods arrived at their destination, the indorsees presented the bill of lading, paid the freight and (under protest) the sum of £748, which the shipowner demanded, and took delivery of the goods.

The indorsee bank then sued the shipowners for damages due to delay (the general value of the goods having fallen), and for repayment of the £748 (as pledgees they had no action based on the Bills of Lading Act 1855).

Held:

1. The indorsee could sue on the basis of a common law implied contract. By the acts of presenting the bill of lading, payment of the freight and delivery of the goods, a contract was implied between the indorsees and shipowners on the terms of the bill of lading (for the terms of the contract, see the quote from Atkin L.J.'s judgment, quoted in para. 20 of Lord Hobhouse's speech in *The Berge Sisar*, above).

2. Some (but not all) of the damage occurred before shipment, and the shipowners tried to avoid liability for this damage, for which they were obviously not directly responsible. The Court of Appeal held that they were estopped from so pleading by virtue of the statement in the bill of lading that the goods were shipped in apparent good order and condition.

Notes

1. In *Brandt v Liverpool* the plaintiff paid the freight, and the bill of lading was presented in exchange for the discharge of the goods from the ship.

---

[25] The shipowner was liable although (because the damage had occurred before shipment) he had not damaged the cargo, because he had issued a clean bill of lading. However, statements in bills of lading describing the condition of the goods on loading are not contractual promises (see *Compania Naviera Vasconzada v Churchill & Sim* [1905] 1 K.B. 237), and the shipowner's liability depended on him being estopped from denying the truth of the statements that had been relied on by the receiver. This is not a satisfactory basis for liability, since the buyer must show reliance, and it is possible to envisage circumstances where the buyer might have taken up the bill in any event, as argued (unsuccessfully) in *Cremer v General Carriers SA (The Dona Mari)* [1974] 1 W.L.R. 341. See also the extensive discussion in paras 14–021, *et seq.*, below.

[26] In *Brandt v Liverpool* itself, the shipowner delivered the goods against presentation of the bill of lading, and the receiver (a bank as pledgee) paid the freight. The Court of Appeal was prepared to imply a fresh contract between receiver and carrier, on the terms of the bill of lading.

2. The payment of freight (or other charges) constitutes the consideration for the implied contract. Since freight and other charges are often pre-paid by the seller, the action would be seriously limited were it necessary for an indorsee to pay them to rely on the action.

3. The consideration moving from the carrier is to deliver the goods on the terms of the bill of lading. He also releases his lien on the cargo for freight (and possibly other charges).

4. There is no need for the document tendered to be a bill of lading.

CREMER v GENERAL CARRIERS SA (THE DONA MARI)

Queen's Bench Division. [1974] 1 W.L.R. 341

13–058   Two consignments of 486 tons of tapioca were shipped aboard the *Dona Mari*, for each of which a bill of lading was issued by the shipowner. On loading the goods were clearly defective; they smelt bitter and were not dry, and the chief officer therefore indorsed the mate's receipts "Not quite dry" and "Not quite dried" respectively. But these indorsements were not transferred to the bills of lading, which were therefore issued clean. Though the goods were loaded in separate bags of 486 tons each, they were stored on the ship as a single bulk, and not split again until unloading.

There were two buyers. The first buyer (c.i.f.) paid cash against the bills of lading for both consignments, and indorsed one of the bills in favour of the second buyer, who had purchased the first consignment afloat.

The other bill of lading (for the second consignment) was exchanged with the shipowners' agents in Bremen for two ship's delivery orders, on exactly the same terms as the bill of lading, one for 120 tons, one for 366 tons. One of these (120 tons) was presented to the second buyer to effect a resale to him of part of that consignment. The first buyer retained 366 tons himself. The second buyer paid the first buyer cash against documents.

Freight was paid to the shipowners when the goods were unloaded, each buyer paying as appropriate for the amount in which he had an interest. Actions were commenced against the carrier when the condition of the goods was discovered.

The main difficulty related to the second buyers. No property had passed to them until unloading, and in respect of part of the bulk (the second consignment) a bill of lading was not tendered by the second buyers, but a ship's delivery order.

Held:
The plaintiffs were entitled to succeed. Kerr J. saw no reason for distinguishing *Brandt v Liverpool* on either of the above grounds.

13–059   KERR J.: The case . . . raises a number of points of law and a large number of authorities were cited. I will deal first with the position of the second plaintiffs, but I will do so shortly because the defendants accept that the first plaintiff could in any event sue for damage to the entire cargo, holding any recovery as trustee for the second plaintiffs to the extent of their interest, and because I do not consider that the second plaintiffs are in a better position in relation to the defendants than the first plaintiff.

The defendants contend that the first plaintiff became the owner of the entire undivided bulk on or by reason of the endorsement and delivery to him of the two bills of lading by the shippers. I agree with this. They also contend, and I again agree, that the second plaintiffs did not become owners of any part of this bulk until after it had been delivered by the defendants in bulk and subsequently separated from the first plaintiff's portion, so that the second plaintiffs were never owners of any part of the cargo at the relevant time so far as the defendants were concerned. The defendants therefore submit that the second plaintiffs have no cause of action either in contract or tort. This has not been challenged so far as tort is concerned in the light of *Margarine Union GmbH v Cambay Prince Steamship Co Ltd (The Wear Breeze)* [1969] 1 Q.B. 219.[27] But it was there stressed that on the facts of that case there was no possibility of any contractual nexus between the parties (see in particular [1969] 1 Q.B. at 228, 232). The facts of the present case are quite different and *prima facie* analogous to the position in *Brandt v Liverpool* [above]. The plaintiffs in that case were bankers to whom a bill of lading had been endorsed and delivered by way of pledge. They were accordingly at no time the owners of the cargo, and neither they nor the defendant carriers were able to rely on s.1 of the Bills of Lading Act 1855 to create a transfer to the plaintiffs of the rights and liabilities under the contract of carriage. But the plaintiffs had paid to the defendants or to their agents the freight due on the cargo covered by the bill of lading, and the defendants thereupon delivered the goods to the plaintiffs against surrender of the bill of lading. The Court of Appeal affirmed the decision of Greer J. that a contract incorporating the terms of the bill of lading was to be implied between the plaintiffs and the defendants by reason of the payment of the freight by the plaintiffs and the delivery of the goods by the defendants against the bill of lading. The court similarly held that in those circumstances the plaintiffs were entitled to rely as against the defendants by way of estoppel on the representation in the bill of lading that the goods had been shipped in apparent good order and condition.

In the present case it was submitted on behalf of the defendants that the decision in *Brandt v Liverpool* should be distinguished on two grounds. First, reference was made to observations in the judgment of Scrutton L.J. that the plaintiffs in that case had a special property in the goods as pledgees and that this was sufficient to found an action in tort. I cannot however see that this has any bearing on the position of the parties in contract. The inference which the court in that case drew from the circumstances, in particular the payment of freight to the defendants and the delivery of the goods to the plaintiffs against surrender of the bill of lading, was to the effect that the defendants agreed to deliver the goods to the plaintiffs in the condition in which, under the terms of the contract of carriage, they should have been delivered. This conclusion appears to me to be unaffected by any consideration whether or not the plaintiffs might have had some alternative claim in tort. But secondly and more

---

[27] See now *The Aliakmon*, below; neither plaintiff would have had property in any of the cargo, so a tort claim would have been impossible.

substantially, counsel for the defendants relied on the fact that part of the bulk delivered to the second plaintiffs was not delivered in exchange for a bill of lading but in exchange for one of the delivery orders ex bill of lading B3 [relating to the second consignment]. He sought on this ground to distinguish *Brandt v Liverpool* and to this extent to deny the second plaintiffs' right to sue.

13–060   There have been a number of cases in which the courts have considered the nature and effect of delivery orders. There are different types of documents which are so described. In many cases they may be issued by a seller to his buyer, in which case they will not confer any rights against the carrier without an attornment by the carrier: see *e.g. J. & J. Cunningham v Guthrie* (1886) 26 Sc. L.R. 208. In other cases, they may be what are sometimes referred to as "ship's delivery orders", *i.e.,* documents which are usually issued by shipowners' agents addressed to the master or chief officer or other persons authorising delivery to the holder or to the order of a named person. In the latter class of case the nexus between the carrier and the holder of the delivery order may, as here, be still closer by reason of the fact that the holder is required to pay the freight to the carrier before the cargo is released to him against the surrender of the delivery order. In such cases, but depending on the circumstances, the holder of a delivery order may in practice be in much the same position in relation to the carrier as if he had taken delivery under a bill of lading: see *Comptoir d'Achat et de Vente du Boerenbond Belge SA v Luis de Ridder Ltda, The Julia* [1949] A.C. 293 [see para. 2–015, above], per Lord Porter at 311 and Lord Normand at 322, and *Colin & Shields v W. Weddel & Co Ltd* [see para. 6–097, above], per Singleton L.J. Denning L.J. Similarly, if a bailee concludes a contract with A on the terms of a warrant or similar document issued to A, and A then transfers the subject-matter of the bailment and the document to B, and the bailee recognises the transfer to B, then the terms of the original contract will come into force between the bailee and B: see *HMF Humphrey Ltd v Baxter, Hoare & Co Ltd* [1933] All E.R. 457 and *Britain & Overseas Trading (Bristles) Ltd v Brooks Wharf & Bull Wharf Ltd* [1967] 2 Lloyd's Rep. 51.

Following those authorities, I not only consider that there is nothing in them which prevents me from reaching the same conclusion on the facts of this case as was reached in *Brandt v Liverpool*, but that the only sensible inference is that a contract in the terms of the two original bills of lading came into effect between the defendants and the second plaintiffs so far as concerns that portion of the bulk which was delivered to the second plaintiffs. It does not of course follow that the same conclusion would be reached on the facts of other cases involving delivery orders which are not ship's delivery orders and where there are no facts from which a direct contract between the holder and the carrier can be implied. But the facts of the present case appear to me to be as strong as they can be in favour of inferring such a contract. I also consider that the second plaintiffs' right to claim damages for breach of that contract is unaffected by the fact that prior to delivery they were not owners of any part of the undivided bulk. First, the whole of the bulk was affected uniformly by damage due to one cause, so that no difficulty arises in that connection. Secondly, the plaintiffs in *Brandt v Liverpool* had also not been the owners of any part of the cargo at any time but nevertheless succeeded in contract.

I therefore hold that the second plaintiffs have a good cause of action against the defendants for breach of the contract of carriage. Further, since it is agreed that any clausing of bills of lading B3 would also have appeared on the second plaintiffs' delivery order issued under this bill of lading, I hold that, as in *Brandt v Liverpool* the second plaintiffs can rely against the defendants on the estoppel created by the representation that the goods were shipped in apparent good order and condition if they are able to establish the necessary facts for this purpose.

Notes

1. The plaintiffs were correct not to challenge the defendants' contention that **13–061** there was no possibility of a tort action: *The Wear Breeze* referred to in the above extract, has been expressly upheld by the House of Lords in *The Aliakmon* (below).

2. The main importance of the case is in holding that the *Brandt v Liverpool* action works, even where a ship's delivery order is presented, rather than a bill of lading.

3. It is important to note that the delivery order was issued by the carrier. Delivery orders addressed only to the seller's agent will not suffice. Sometimes (*e.g.* where the carrier has no land based agent) it will be impossible to obtain ship's delivery orders, but buyers should note that only those issued by the ship offer any protection. In *The Wear Breeze* by contrast, none of the documents, which included delivery orders, was issued by the shipowner, and Kerr J. mentions in the above extract that "there was no possibility of any contractual nexus between" buyer and carrier.

4. There was also an estoppel point, the bill of lading having falsely stated that the goods had been shipped in apparent good order and condition. On this aspect of the case, see further para. 14–022, below.

5. In *The Elli 2*, delivery was not made against bills of lading at all, merely a guarantee that the receiver would produce them later. In *The Captain Gregos (No. 2)*,[28] below, the receiver (B.P.) never became lawful holder of the bills of lading at all, delivery having been made against a letter of indemnity. In the last of these cases, the 1992 Act would not have applied, had the same facts arisen today, since it transfers rights only to lawful holders of documents. The *Brandt v Liverpool* doctrine would, however.

THE ELLI II

Court of Appeal. [1985] 1 Lloyd's Rep. 107

A quantity of cement was sold c.i.f. Jeddah to the defendant receiver (Mr Bamao- **13–062** dah). Bills of lading incorporating charterparty terms were issued and signed and sent to the receiver, but it was not clear whether he presented those against discharge or merely guaranteed that he would produce them later. In an *ex parte*

---

[28] *Compania Portorafti Commerciale SA v Ultramar Panama Inc (The Captain Gregos (No. 2))* [1990] 2 Lloyd's Rep. 395.

application to serve the defendant out of the jurisdiction, the shipowners claimed demurrage due under the charterparty.

Held

1. There was at least a good arguable case that shipowners were entitled to demurrage on the basis of a *Brandt v Liverpool* contract.

2. It was assumed (though for the purposes of the application it was only necessary for the owners to show a good arguable case) that the contract could be implied notwithstanding that the evidence did not make clear whether the buyer tendered the bills of lading in exchange for the goods, or whether on occasions he gave a guarantee or undertaking that they would be forthcoming as soon as they came into his possession.

3. There was a good arguable case that English law governed the implied contract, so the owners were entitled to succeed under RSC, Order 11, rule 1(1)(f) (which required a good arguable case that there was a contract between the parties governed by English law). The bill of lading incorporated a charterparty containing a London arbitration clause.

13–063   ACKNER L.J.: It is common ground that the implication of [a *Brandt v Liverpool* contract is a matter of fact to be decided on the circumstances of each case. Indeed, that is made clear by *Brandt's* case. Mr Gross [for the defendant] accepts that although one usually finds that freight has been paid, this is not essential, nor was it to be expected in Mr Bamaodah's case since he had no obligation for freight. Had the owners been able to prove, which they were not, that Mr Bamaodah had on presenting the bill taken delivery of the cargo, I cannot see how any possible criticism could have been made of the learned Judge's implication, particularly since, as he said, there had been a course of dealing in the past, including cases in which demurrage had been earned and paid. The essential point, as I see it, raised by Mr Gross, is that it makes all the difference that Mr Bamaodah may not have presented a bill of lading, but instead may have given an undertaking to do so when he received the bill of lading. Like the learned Judge, I cannot see that this makes any difference.

Presenting the bill of lading and supplying a guarantee that it will be presented on arrival can both equally lead to the inference that the delivery and acceptance of the goods was on the terms of the bill of lading produced, or to be produced, so far as they were applicable to discharge at the port of discharge . . .

13–064   MAY L.J.: I . . . move to the implied contract point. This raises the question whether it is to be inferred that an implied contract in the terms of the bill of lading came into existence between the parties when the appellant presented the bills of lading in exchange for the delivery of the goods, or alternatively gave a guarantee that they would be handed over as soon as they became available. It is accepted on both sides that this is a question of fact. In the first place I also respectfully agree with the learned Judge that it can make no difference at all whether the appellant actually tendered the bills of lading, or some of them, in exchange for the delivery of the goods, or whether on occasions he gave a guarantee or undertaking that they would be forthcoming as soon as they came into his possession.

That such a contract can and indeed must be implied as a matter of fact in appropriate circumstances is based, insofar as recent authority is concerned, on the well-known case of *Brandt & Co v Liverpool Steam Navigation Co Ltd* [1924] 1 K.B. 575. Mr Gross submitted that although the boundaries of this doctrine are not clear, nevertheless certain minimal conditions have to be satisfied. The first and fourth of these can be combined and considered together. In effect they amount to the contention that before any such contract can be inferred the receiver of the goods should be the holder of the bill of lading at the time and that the goods should be taken in actual exchange for it. As I have already indicated, I do not think that this is necessarily a condition precedent to the implication of the relevant contract.

Mr Gross secondly submitted that it is another prerequisite that some right of property should pass to the ultimate receiver of the goods by virtue of the endorsement of the bill of lading. In the instant case property probably passed at the latest when the cement was shipped. Consequently, as between the appellant and respondents, no property was passed in the cement by virtue of the endorsement on the bills of lading. This may be so, but I do not think it necessarily precludes the implication of any contract. A bill of lading is frequently, and maybe usually a document of title. However, in appropriate circumstances its endorsement and transfer will transfer a right to possession, even though property in the relevant goods may already have passed between the respective parties. This is clearly what happened in the instant case.

Finally, Mr Gross submitted that the other minimal condition which has to be satisfied is that usually the freight still remains payable under the contract of carriage. That which may "usually" be the situation, but which *ex hypothesi* may not always be so, cannot in my view properly be described as a condition precedent to the creation of the suggested contract. That the freight is still payable and is paid by the ultimate receiver of the goods may well in a number of cases be the consideration passing from him supporting the relevant contract. Nevertheless, the earlier authority, to which I shall refer in a moment, makes it quite clear that other considerations, such as demurrage, will be sufficient.

Nevertheless, I agree that the boundaries of the doctrine are not clear. I would not expect them to be so. As the question whether or not any such contract is to be implied is one of fact, its answer must depend on the circumstances of each particular case—and the different sets of facts which arise for consideration in these cases are legion. However, I also agree that no such contract should be implied on the facts of any given case unless it is necessary to do so: necessary, that is to say, in order to give business reality to a transaction and to create enforceable obligations between parties who are dealing with one another in circumstances in which one would expect that business reality and those enforceable obligations to exist . . .

Applying those principles to the instant case, and having regard particularly to the earlier course of dealing between the parties to which my Lord has referred, I have no doubt that on the evidence before us there is a good arguable case that an implied contract did arise between the appellant and the respondents when the bill of lading, or the guarantee, were given in exchange for the delivery of the goods, and that that contract was in the terms to be found in the bills of lading themselves . . .

[*May L.J. then went on to conclude that the implied contract was governed by English law.*]

Notes

13–065   The main importance of the case is that a *Brandt v Liverpool* was implied, even though no document was tendered to obtain delivery of the cargo.

Note also that the *Brandt v Liverpool* doctrine was invoked despite freight not being paid. There was, however, other financial consideration (demurrage). It is also made clear, however, that the implication of the implied contract is not automatic, but depends on the facts. There must be offer, acceptance and consideration. If there is nothing for the receiver to pay, it will not be easy to find consideration. There must also be implied an offer and acceptance. There is no reason to imply a contract simply from the act of presenting a bill of lading and taking delivery of the cargo.

(b) No Contract Implied on Facts

13–066   In order to be able to imply a contract, it is necessary to be able to infer offer, acceptance and consideration. In *Brandt v Liverpool* itself the payment of freight (and other charges)[29] constituted the consideration, moving from the receiver of the cargo. The consideration moving from the carrier was delivery of the cargo, on the terms of the bill of lading, but it is not always possible to find acceptance by the shipowner of an obligation to deliver on bill of lading terms, and consideration moving from the receiver. If, for example, freight and other charges are paid by the shipper,[30] it will be difficult to find any consideration moving from the receiver, and if delivery is not made, for example if the goods do not arrive, it is difficult to infer acceptance of any contract by the carrier.

The Court of Appeal has made clear twice in recent years that a real (rather than fictitious) contract must be implied, and that the courts will not artificially extend the doctrine in order to reach a commercially just solution.

ARAMIS (CARGO OWNERS) v ARAMIS (OWNERS) (THE ARAMIS)

Court of Appeal. [1989] 1 Lloyd's Rep. 213

13–067   The two plaintiffs, Unigrain and Van der Valk, had each purchased consignments of a little over 200 tonnes of Argentine linseed expellers, and were holders of bills of lading in respect of these consignments. Their cargo was part of an undivided

---

[29] Including the £748 reconditioning cost, which they had paid under protest.
[30] Freight is commonly prepaid for dry-cargo shipments, but not for tankers.

bulk, being mixed also with other consignments of Argentine linseed expellers, destined for other receivers.

The trial was conducted without oral evidence or full discovery, so that the facts found were rather sparse, but it seems that the vessel called at various ports en route, where some of the bulk was discharged in favour of other buyers. It seems that there was over-discharge, because when the vessel arrived (at Rotterdam) there was insufficient cargo left aboard to satisfy the plaintiffs' bills of lading. Only 11,550 kilos was discharged in favour of Van der Valk, and none at all in favour of Unigrain.

Both plaintiffs sued the carrier, and lost. Various grounds were advanced, Van der Valk bringing a claim based on s.1 of the 1855 Act. Their problem was that property in their part of the undivided bulk cargo could not pass to them until division of the bulk at discharge (this is no longer a problem in the light of the Carriage of Goods by Sea Act 1992). Until then it was not ascertained, and property could not therefore pass by virtue of the Sale of Goods Act 1979, s.16. Van der Valk therefore failed.

Unigrain did not even attempt to advance an argument based on s.1 in *The Aramis*, facing as they did the additional difficulty that none of their cargo at all was discharged. Hence, they never obtained any property in any of the cargo (again, this would not be a problem under the Carriage of Goods by Sea Act 1992, as long as they were lawful holders of a bill of lading).

Note that this case is not like *The Elafi*, in para. 5–015, above, where all the cargo that remained aboard was destined for the *same* buyer, so that it could be said to have been ascertained by process of exhaustion. Here, even after the over-discharge had occurred en route, there were two rival claims, and the remaining cargo could not be said to belong to Van der Valk, rather than Unigrain, until discharge had taken place at Rotterdam.

Both plaintiffs also failed on the basis of *Brandt v Liverpool*, not having paid freight or (in one case) taken delivery of any cargo. A narrow view was taken of when *Brandt v Liverpool* would be implied. Bingham L.J. took the view that it would[31]:

" . . . be contrary to principle to countenance the implication of a contract from conduct if the conduct relied upon is no more consistent with an intention to contract than with an intention not to contract. It must, surely, be necessary to identify conduct referable to the contract contended for or, at the very least, conduct inconsistent with there being no contract made between the parties to the effect contended for. Put another way, I think it must be fatal to the implication of a contract if the parties would or might have acted exactly as they did in the absence of a contract."

He continued[32]: "One cannot cast principle aside, and simply opt for a commercially convenient solution." Stuart-Smith L.J. took a similar position on when a contract would be implied:

"If their conduct is equally referable to and explicable by their existing rights and obligations, albeit such rights and obligations are not enforceable against each other, there is no material from which the Court can draw the inference. It is only if their conduct is unequivocally referable to or explicable by one or more of the rights or obligations contained in the bill of lading that there is factual material from which the Court can draw the inference that a contract has been entered into between them."

---

[31] *Aramis (cargo owners) v Aramis (owners) (The Aramis)* [1989] 1 Lloyd's Rep. 213, at 244. See also Treitel, "Bills of Lading and Implied Contracts" [1989] L.M.C.L.Q. 162, at pp. 168 *et seq.*
[32] At 225 (col. 2).

Note

13–068   This case made clear that *Brandt v Liverpool* was not merely a remedial device, that would be used to plug the gaps in the 1855 Act. There really must be a contract. It is not enough for the receiver simply to present a bill of lading and collect the cargo, because that no more points to the existence of a contract than not. An even stronger statement can be found in *The Gudermes* three years later. Staughton L.J. (following *The Aramis*) said that[33]:

> " . . . it is not enough to show that the parties have done something more than, or something different from, what they were already bound to do under obligations owed to others. What they do must be consistent only with there being a new contract implied, and inconsistent with there being no such contract."

In effect, the parties must change their position, in a way which is only consistent with the implication of a contract.[34] In *The Gudermes*, Staughton L.J. thought that this was not particularly problematic where, as in *Brandt v Liverpool* itself, or *The Dona Mari*, the receiver paid the freight, or the in earlier cases, the carrier had, by delivering, released his lien for freight. It is another matter where no freight or other charges are paid. One wonders whether, on this basis, a contract would have been implied in *Pyrene v Scindia*, in para. 11–065, above. Was the seller's conduct really "consistent only with there being a new contract implied, and inconsistent with there being no such contract"?

However, the parties may change their position, by doing something they do not have to do, leading to the implication of a contract, even in the absence of financial consideration. In *The Elli* 2, the shipowners were under no obligation to deliver without production of the bills of lading, and also by so doing released their lien for demurrage (which was payable by the receiver of the cargo), so it was reasonable to infer a contract. There was financial consideration there, of course, but in *The Captain Gregos (No. 2)*, the shipowners were under no obligation to deliver to B.P. without production of the bills of lading, although it was to their advantage to do so, and B.P. were under no obligation either to provide an indemnity, or to cooperate with the carrier by allowing the cargo to be discharged into their tanks. Again, therefore, the parties had altered their position, consistently with the implication of a new contract.

COMPANIA PORTORAFTI COMMERCIALE SA v ULTRAMAR PANAMA INC (THE CAPTAIN GREGOS (No. 2))

Court of Appeal. [1990] 2 Lloyd's Rep. 395

13–069   The facts of *The Captain Gregos* have already been set out in para. 11–061, above. The case went back to the Court of Appeal, to decide whether there was a

---

[33] *Mitsui & Co Ltd v Novorossiysk Shipping Co (The Gudermes)* [1993] 1 Lloyd's Rep. 311.

[34] The statements in *The Aramis* and *The Gudermes* are not easy to reconcile with *New Zealand Shipping Co Ltd v AM Satterthwaite & Co Ltd (The Eurymedon)* [1975] A.C. 154, where a *Brandt v Liverpool* contract was implied where freight had been prepaid by the shipper, and the carrier was under an obligation, under the carriage contract with the shipper, to deliver the cargo anyway. Indeed, the Privy Council affirmed, as part of the *ratio* of the case, that consideration for a new contract can include the performance of obligations already owed under an existing contract. However, it is not easy to see how either carrier or consignee did anything that they would not have done in the absence of the *Brandt v Liverpool* contract. If the cases cannot be reconciled, the Court of Appeal cases are binding and the Privy Council case is not.

contractual nexus between cargo-owners and shipowners. It was abundantly clear that neither P.E.A.G. nor B.P. were party to the bills of lading under s.1 of the Bills of Lading Act 1855, nor would B.P. be covered by the 1992 Act, since the bills of lading were only transferred to them after discharge, and never indorsed to them at all. Hence, they never became lawful holders, and the bills of lading took no part in the delivery process. Nevertheless, the Court of Appeal held that B.P. were party to a *Brandt v Liverpool* contract. It follows that *Brandt v Liverpool* may apply, even where the 1992 Act does not.

Brandt v Liverpool might have been thought to be a hopeless argument after *The Aramis*; B.P. did not pay the freight, nor even undertake to do so although it was outstanding at the time of delivery. Nor, of course, did they present bills of lading, nor undertake to do so.

Nevertheless, B.P. were held to be bound by an implied contract, since in their agreement with P.E.A.G. they had agreed that P.E.A.G. should arrange shipment on terms normally in use for tankships. Such terms, at any rate for an Egyptian shipment, would incorporate the Hague-Visby Rules, so that "there was . . . an identity of understanding on the part of the shipowners and B.P., the shipowners knowing and B.P. having every reason to believe that the cargo was carried on Hague-Visby terms".

This approach, depending as it does on the terms of the *sale* contract, seems difficult to reconcile with *The Aramis*, and indeed the test adopted, whether it was necessary to imply a contract (between B.P. and shipowner) in order to give business reality to the transaction, comes from May L.J.'s judgment in the earlier case of *The Elli 2* [1985] 1 Lloyd's Rep. 107.

Bingham L.J. noted that *The Aramis* had been adversely criticised by distinguished commentators, and its correctness was even doubted. It was distinguished on the grounds that B.P. were already owners of the cargo when discharge began, and also that:

> "B.P. had [under its agreement with P.E.A.G.] very clearly and explicitly consented to the carriage of the goods on terms incorporating any of the charterparty conditions normally in use for tankships, which would include the Hague-Visby Rules."

The first of these does not seem to be a good ground for distinguishing the earlier case. If the implication of a contract depends on the facts, the second might be.

In any case, neither distinction applied to P.E.A.G. They did not have property at the time of discharge, it having already passed to B.P., and Ultramar undertook no shipment obligations in their (f.o.b.) contract with P.E.A.G. Therefore no contract could be implied between them and the shipowners.

Note

In this case, unlike *The Aramis*, consideration moved from both parties. No **13–070** financial consideration moved from B.P., but their co-operation was needed in the discharge, and the shipowners clearly benefited from being able to discharge into B.P.'s tanks. Also, B.P. gave the shipowners the benefit of the indemnity, and the protection of the time bar and other protective clauses of the Hague-Visby Rules.

As for the shipowners, they did not give up lien against freight or demurrage, as in all previous successful cases, but obviously they were not obliged to deliver without production of bills of lading, and took a risk by so doing. They provided consideration for a new contract, but also changed their position, whereas neither feature was present in *The Aramis*.

Of *The Aramis* it was said "no doubt its correctness may fall to be reviewed hereafter", but the principles in the earlier case were later applied in *The Gudermes*, above. *The Gudermes* is really a stronger case than *The Aramis*, because there was co-operation between the parties, and both parties changed their position. This did not necessarily lead to the inference of a contract, however. It could equally well be explained as a means of getting round a problem that had developed. Co-operation, and change of position, may lead to the implication of a contract, but it need not. Ultimately, it is a factual question.

(c) Conclusions on *Brandt v Liverpool* Today

13–071 *The Aramis* limited the application of the implied contract doctrine, by requiring a real, not just a fictitious contract. Though its correctness was doubted in *The Captain Gregos (No. 2)*, it was followed in *The Gudermes*, and is probably good law. In any case, it seems right in principle; contracts should not be implied merely to remedy supposed defects in the law.

The 1992 Act is of course wider in application than its predecessor, so one must question whether *Brandt v Liverpool* retains any relevance at all today.

If *The Captain Gregos (No. 2)* is correct, cases involving delivery without production of a bill of lading may well continue to come under *Brandt v Liverpool*, rather than the 1992 Act, especially if the receiver never becomes lawful holder. Another possibility is where delivery is made other than against a document of title. In all such cases the carrier is under no obligation to deliver the cargo, and changes his position by so doing. The positive choice of the parties to act in a particular manner was absent in *The Aramis*, but will be present in these cases. There are documents which come outside the scope of the 1992 Act. Against any such document the shipowner is not required to deliver the cargo. If he does, he changes his position. In such cases, it might still be possible to imply a contract, and distinguish *The Aramis* and *The Gudermes*. It would be dangerous to generalise, however, since we are told that the implication of a contract is a matter of fact.

Of course, if *Brandt v Liverpool* retains any relevance, it depends on delivery of the cargo, so cannot apply where the goods have been totally lost at sea.

(5) Tort Actions Against Carriers

13–072 If the carrier damages cargo negligently, he can be sued in tort. While the 1855 Act was in force, the tort action was seen to be a possible way around its deficiencies, although as will become apparent below, its usefulness was significantly limited by the House of Lords decision in *The Aliakmon*.

Since 1992 tort actions have probably become even less important, since the party at risk will nearly always be able to sue in contract. However, the shipper's independent negligence action was crucial in *East West Corporation v DKBS 1912*, above, and might (as we saw at para. 13–022, above) give rise to double liability problems against carriers.

Tort actions have also been used to avoid the *Hague Rules* or *Hague-Visby Rules*, where there is no contractual nexus between the parties, as (successfully) in *Midland Silicones* and *The Captain Gregos* in para. 11–061, above, and unsuccessfully in *Pyrene v Scindia* (also in para. 11–065, above) and *The Starsin* in para. 13–083, below. The usefulness of this action has been limited by the 1992 Act, which makes a contractual nexus more likely, and by the Contract (Rights of Third Parties) Act 1999, which makes it easier to extend the protection of contractual exemption clauses to non-contracting parties (see further below).

In spite of its reduced role, negligence actions should be considered for completeness. The most important limitation is that negligence protects property, so that only those who have property at the time of the breach of duty can sue. It was for this reason that it was ineffective at avoiding the limitations of the 1855 Act, since often the reason for its non-application was precisely that the plaintiff did not have property at the time of the damage.

In general, given the reliance by carriers, their servants, agents and independent contractors, on excepted perils, time bars, limitations to damages, etc., policy arguments could be advanced for limiting the scope of tort actions in this area of activity.

LEIGH & SILLAVAN LTD v ALIAKMON SHIPPING CO LTD (THE ALIAKMON)

Court of Appeal. [1985] Q.B. 350, affirmed in House of Lords [1986] A.C. 785

The buyers agreed to buy a quantity of steel coils to be shipped from Korea, c. & f. **13–073** Immingham. A clean bill of lading was issued by the shipowners, although the steel was badly stowed aboard *The Aliakmon*, and because of this it was further damaged during the voyage to the United Kingdom.

When the sellers tendered the bill of lading the buyers were unable to pay, so after re-negotiation the contract was varied, so that, although the bill of lading would be delivered to the buyers to enable them to take delivery of the steel, payment would not become due until 180 days after sight. The buyers discovered the damage to the goods on unloading and brought actions against the shipowners in contract and tort.

Had the contract been performed as originally agreed the buyers would have obtained property in the steel on indorsement, and could have relied on s.1 of the 1855 Act. The effect of the variation was first, that the sellers reserved a right of disposal against payment, so that property did not pass to the buyers, then or at any later time, and secondly that the buyers presented the bill of lading and took delivery of the steel not as principals on their own account, but as agents of the sellers.

Held

1. No right of action accrued to the buyers under the Bills of Lading Act 1855, s.1, because property did not pass to them on indorsement and delivery of the bill of lading.

2. On the facts of the case no contract could be implied on the basis of *Brandt v Liverpool* (see above), because the buyers took delivery of the goods only as agents for the sellers.

3. The buyers could not bring an action in negligence against the carriers, because (by virtue of the variation) they had no property in the goods at the time they were damaged.

The contract issues were dealt with more fully in the Court of Appeal, the issue in the House of Lords (which upheld the decision of the court below), being confined to the question of tort liability.

SIR JOHN DONALDSON M.R.: *(On the contract issues in the Court of Appeal)*

[The Master of the Rolls held that s.1 did not apply because the sellers had reserved title until payment, under s.19(1) of the Sale of Goods Act 1979, and continued:]

It then becomes necessary to consider whether the buyers can rely **13–074** upon an implied contract between them and the shipowners on the terms of the bill of lading as was done in *Brandt v Liverpool* [see above]. In that case the bill of lading was endorsed to pledgees and no general property in the goods therefore passed to them by virtue of the endorsement. Accordingly, when they wished to sue the shipowners for damage to the goods, they too were unable to take advantage of the provisions of s.1 of the Bills of Lading Act. However the pledgees had tendered the bill of lading to the shipowners, paid the freight and taken delivery of the goods. Bankes L.J., after referring to older authorities, said, at p. 589:

"By those authorities it has been clearly established that where the holder of a bill of lading presents it and offers to accept delivery, if that offer is accepted by the shipowner, the holder of the bill of lading comes under an obligation to pay the freight and to pay the demurrage, if any, and there are general expressions in all those three cases, I think, in which the learned judges have said that the contract so made by that offer and acceptance covers, so as to include, the terms of the bill of lading."

But for one crucial difference, that decision would entitle the buyers to sue the shipowners in the present case. They presented the bill of lading to the shipowners on 12 November 1976, they took delivery of the steel, they paid the discharging costs and they undertook to pay the import duty. The crucial difference between *Brandt's* case and this case is that in the covering letter with which the bill of lading was sent to the ship's agents, the buyers said that the material was to be placed into covered warehouse to the sole order of the sellers, who would be responsible for all discharging costs, adding that they, the buyers, accepted liability for the duty acting as the sellers' agents. In that situation the only contract which, in my judgment, could be implied was a contract between the sellers and the shipowners. This is of no assistance to the buyers. The judge so held and I agree with him.

This conclusion disposes of all contractual claims by the buyers against the shipowners. But it still leaves a claim in tort. Here again their right to sue is very much in issue.

LORD BRANDON: *(In the House of Lords)*

13–075 My lords, under the usual kind of c.i.f. or c & f. contract of sale, the risk in the goods passes from the seller to the buyer on shipment, as is exemplified by the obligation of the buyer to take up and pay for the shipping documents even though the goods may already have suffered damage or loss during their carriage by sea. The property in the goods, however, does not pass until the buyer takes up and pays for the shipping documents. These include a bill of lading relating to the goods which has been endorsed by the seller in favour of the buyer. By acquiring the bill of lading so endorsed the buyer becomes a person to whom the property in the goods has passed upon or by reason of such endorsement, and so by virtue of section 1 of the Bills of Lading Act 1855, has vested in him all the rights of suit, and is subject to the same liabilities in respect of the goods, as if the contract contained in the bill of lading had been made with him.

In terms of the present case this means that, if the buyers had completed the c. & f. contract in the manner intended, they would have been entitled to sue the shipowners for the damage to the goods in contract under the bill of lading, and no question of any separate duty of care in tort would have arisen. In the events which occurred, however, what had originally been a usual kind of c. & f. contract of sale had been varied so as to become, in effect, a contract of sale ex-warehouse at Immingham. The contract as so varied was, however, unusual in an important respect. Under an ordinary contract of sale ex-warehouse both the risk and the property in the goods would pass from the seller to the buyer at the same time, that time being determined by the intention of the parties. Under this varied contract, however, the risk had already passed to the buyers on shipment because of the original c. & f. terms, and there was nothing in the new terms which caused it to revert to the sellers. The buyers, however, did not acquire any rights of suit under the bill of lading by virtue of s.1 of the Bills of Lading Act 1855. This was because, owing to the sellers' reservation of the right of disposal of the goods, the property in the goods did not pass to the buyers upon or by reason of the endorsement of the bill of lading, but only upon payment of the purchase price by the buyers to the sellers after the goods had been discharged and warehoused at Immingham. Hence the attempt of the buyers to establish a separate claim against the shipowners founded in the tort of negligence.

My lords, there is a long line of authority for a principle of law that, in order to enable a person to claim in negligence for loss caused to him by reason of loss of or damage to property, he must have had either the legal ownership of or a possessory title to the property concerned at the time when the loss or damage occurred. It is not enough for him to have only had contractual rights in relation to such property which have been adversely affected by the loss of or damage to it. The line of authority to which I have referred includes the following cases: *Cattle v Stockton Waterworks Co* (1875) L.R. 10 Q.B. 453 (contractor doing work on another's land unable to recover from a waterworks company loss suffered by him by reason of that company's want of care in causing or permitting water to leak from a water pipe laid and owned by it on the land concerned); *Simpson & Co v Thomson* (1877) 3 App. Cas. 279 (insurers of two ships A and B, both owned by C, unable to recover from C loss caused to them by want of care in the navigation of ship A in consequence of which she collided with and damaged ship B); *Société Anonyme de Remorquage à Helice v Bennetts* [1911] 1 K.B. 243 (tug owners engaged to tow ship A unable to recover from owners of ship B loss of towage remuneration caused to them by want of care in the navigation of ship B in consequence of which she collided with and sank ship A); *Chargeurs Réunis Compagnie Francaise de Navigation à Vapeur v English & American Steamship Co*

(1921) 9 Ll. L.R. 464 (time charterer of ship A unable to recover from owners of ship B loss caused to them by want of care in the navigation of ship B in consequence of which she collided with and damaged ship A); *The World Harmony* [1967] P. 341 (same as preceding case). The principle of law referred to is further supported by the observations of Scrutton L.J. in *Elliott Steam Tug Co Ltd v The Shipping Controller* [1922] 1 K.B. 127, 139–140.

13–076   None of these cases concerns a claim by c.i.f. or c. & f. buyers of goods to recover from the owners of the ship in which the goods are carried loss suffered by reason of want of care in the carriage of the goods resulting in their being lost or damaged at a time when the risk in the goods, but not yet the legal property in them, has passed to such buyers. The question whether such a claim would lie, however, came up for decision in *Margarine Union GmbH v Cambay Prince Steamship Co Ltd (The Wear Breeze)* [1969] 1 Q.B. 219. In that case c.i.f. buyers had accepted four delivery orders in respect of as yet undivided portions of a cargo of copra in bulk being shipped under two bills of lading. It was common ground that, by doing so, they did not acquire either the legal property in, nor a possessory title to, the portions of copra concerned: they only acquired the legal property later when four portions each of 500 tons were separated from the bulk on or shortly after discharge in Hamburg. The copra having been damaged by want of care by the shipowners' servants or agents in not properly fumigating the holds of the carrying ship before loading, the question arose whether the buyers were entitled to recover from the shipowners in tort for negligence the loss which they had suffered by reason of the copra having been so damaged. Roskill J held that they were not, founding his decision largely on the principle of law established by the line of authority to which I have referred. He derived further support for his decision by reference to *Brandt v Liverpool, Brazil and River Plate Steam Navigation Co Ltd* [see above at para. 13–057]. In that case it was held by the Court of Appeal that, although the plaintiffs could not bring themselves within s.1 of the Bills of Lading Act 1855 because they were neither consignees named in nor endorsees of bills of ladings relating to goods carried in the defendant shipowners' ship, nevertheless a contract between the plaintiffs and the defendants on the terms of the bills of lading could by implied from the fact that the plaintiffs had themselves presented the bills of lading to, and obtained delivery of the goods to which they related from, the ship at the port of discharge; and secondly, that the plaintiffs were entitled to sue the defendants under such implied contract for loss suffered by them by reason of the want of care of the defendants in the carriage of the goods. Roskill J. asked himself the rhetorical question why, if the plaintiffs had a right to sue the defendants in tort for negligence, should there have been any reason or need for implying a contract between them.

My Lords, counsel for the buyers, Mr Anthony Clarke, Q.C., did not question any of the cases in the long line of authority to which I have referred except *The Wear Breeze*. He felt obliged to accept the continuing correctness of the rest of the cases ("the other non-recovery cases") because of the recent decision of the Privy Council in *Candlewood Navigation Corporation v Mitsui OSK Lines Ltd (The Mineral Transporter)* [1986] A.C. 1, in which those cases were again approved and applied, and to which it will be necessary for me to refer more fully later. He contended, however, that *The Wear Breeze* [1969] 1 Q.B. 269 was either wrongly decided at the time, or at any rate should be regarded as wrongly decided today, and should accordingly be overruled.

In support of this contention Mr Clarke relied on five main grounds. The first ground was that the characteristics of a c.i.f. or c. & f. contract for sale differed materially from the characteristics of the contracts concerned in the other non-recovery cases. The second ground was that under a c.i.f. or c. & f. contract the buyer acquired immediately on shipment of the goods the equitable ownership of them. The third ground was that the law of negligence had developed significantly since 1969 when *The Wear Breeze* was decided, in particular as a result of the decisions of your Lordships' House in *Anns v Merton London Borough Council* [1975] A.C. 728 and *Junior Books Ltd v Veitchi Co Ltd* [1983] 1 A.C. 520. In this connection reliance was placed on two decisions at first instance in which *The Wear Breeze* [1969] 1 Q.B. 269 had either not been followed or treated as no longer being good law. The fourth ground was that any rational system of law would provide a remedy for persons who suffered the kind of loss which the buyers suffered in the present case. The fifth ground was the judgment of Goff L.J. in the present case, so far as it related to the buyer's right to sue the shipowners in tort for negligence. I shall examine each of these grounds in turn.

Ground (1): Difference in Characteristics of a c.i.f. or c. & f. Contract

My Lords, under this head Mr Clarke said that in the other non-recovery cases the plaintiffs who failed were not persons who had contracted to buy the property to which the defendants' want of care had caused loss or damage; they were rather persons whose contractual rights entitled them either to have the use or services of the property concerned and thereby made profits (*e.g.* the time charter cases), or to render services to the property concerned and thereby earn remuneration (e.g., the towage cases). By contrast buyers under a c.i.f. or c. & f. contract of sale were persons to whom it was intended that the legal ownership of the goods should later pass, and who were therefore prospectively, though not presently, the legal owners of them.

13–077

I recognise that this difference in the characteristics of a c.i.f. or c. & f. contract of sale exists, but I cannot see why it should of itself make any difference to the principle of law to be applied. In all these cases what the plaintiffs are complaining of is that, by reason of their contracts with others, loss of or damage to the property, to which, when it occurred, they had neither a proprietary nor a possessory title, has caused them to suffer loss; and the circumstance that, in the case of c.i.f. or c.and f. buyers, they are, if the contract of sale is duly completed, destined later to acquire legal ownership of the goods after the loss or damage has occurred, does not seem to me to constitute a material distinction in law.

Ground (2): Equitable Ownership
[This part of Lord Brandon's speech has already been set out, at para. 5–028, above]

Ground (3): Development of the Law of Negligence Since 1969
[Lord Brandon was not persuaded that the law had developed since 1969, and that if it had, there should be a retrenchment.]

13–078   ... Counsel for the buyers said, rightly in my view, that the policy reason for excluding a duty of care in cases like *The Mineral Transporter* [1986] A.C. 1 and what I earlier called the other non-recovery cases was to avoid the opening of the floodgates so as to expose a person guilty of want of care to unlimited liability to an indefinite number of other persons whose contractual rights have been adversely affected by such want of care. Counsel for the buyers went on to argue that recognition by the law of a duty of care owed by shipowners to a c.i.f. or c. & f. buyer, to whom the risk but not yet the property in the goods carried in such shipowners' ship has passed, would not of itself open any floodgates of the kind described. It would, he said, only create a strictly limited exception to the general rule, based on the circumstance that the considerations of policy on which that general rule was founded did not apply to that particular case. I do not accept that argument. If an exception to the general rule were to be made in the field of carriage by sea, it would no doubt have to be extended to the field of carriage by land, and I do not think that it is possible to say that no undue increase in the scope of a person's liability for want of care would follow. In any event, where a general rule, which is simple to understand and easy to apply, has been established by a long line of authority over many years, I do not think that the law should allow special pleading in a particular case within the general rule to detract from its application. If such detraction were to be permitted in one particular case, it would lead to attempts to have it permitted in a variety of other particular cases, and the result would be that the certainty, which the application of the general rule presently provides, would be seriously undermined. Yet certainty of the law is of the utmost importance, especially, but by no means only, in commercial matters. I therefore think that the general rule, re-affirmed as it has been so recently by the Privy Council in *The Mineral Transporter*, ought to apply to a case like the present one, and that there is nothing in what Lord Wilberforce said in the *Anns* case which would compel a different conclusion.

Counsel for the buyers sought to rely also on *Junior Books Ltd v Veitchi Co Ltd* [1983] 1 A.C. 520. ... The decision is of no direct help to the buyers in the present case . . . But counsel for the buyers relied on certain observations in the speech of Lord Roskill as supporting the proposition that a duty of care in tort might, as he submitted it should be in the present case, be qualified by reference to the terms of a contract to which the defendant was not a party. In this connection Lord Roskill said, at p. 546:

"During the argument it was asked what the position would be in a case where there was a relevant exclusion clause in the main contract. My Lords, that question does not arise for decision in the instant appeal, but in principle I would venture the view that such a claim according to the manner in which it was worded might in some circumstances limit the duty of care just as in the *Hedley Byrne* case the plaintiffs were ultimately defeated by the defendants' disclaimer of responsibility."

As is apparent this observation was no more than an obiter dictum. Moreover, with great respect to Lord Roskill there is no analogy between the disclaimer in the *Hedley Byrne & Co Ltd v Heller & Partners Ltd* [1964] A.C. 465, which operated directly between the plaintiffs and the defendants, and an exclusion of liability clause in a contract to which the plaintiff is a party but the defendant is not. I do not therefore find in the observation of Lord Roskill relied on any convincing legal basis for qualifying a duty of care owed by A to B by reference to a contract to which A is, but B is not, a party.

As I said earlier, counsel for the buyers submitted that your Lordships **13–079** should hold that a duty of care did exist in the present case, but that it was subject to the terms of the bill of lading. With regard to this suggestion Sir John Donaldson M.R. said in the present case ([1985] Q.B. 350 at 368:

"I have, of course, considered whether any duty of care in tort to the buyer could in some way be equated to the contractual duty of care owed to the shipper, but I do not see how this could be done. The commonest form of carriage by sea is one on the terms of the Hague Rules. But this is an intricate blend of responsibilities and liabilities (Article III), right and immunities (Article IV), limitations to the amount of damages recoverable (Article IV, r. 5), time bars (Article III, r. 6), evidential provisions (Article III, rr. 4 and 6), indemnities (Article III, r. 5 and Article IV, r. 6) and liberties (Article IV, rr. 4 and 6). I am quite unable to see how these can be synthesized into a standard of care."

I find myself suffering from the same inability to understand how the necessary synthesis could be made as the Master of the Rolls.

As I also said earlier, counsel for the buyers sought to rely on the concept of a bailment on terms as a legal basis for qualifying the duty of care for which he contended by reference to the terms of the bill of lading. He argued that the buyers, by entering into a c. & f. contract with the sellers, had impliedly consented to the sellers bailing the goods to the shipowners on the terms of a usual bill of lading which would include a paramount clause incorporating the Hague Rules. I do not consider that this theory is sound. The only bailment of the goods was one by the sellers to the shipowners. That bailment was certainly on the terms of a usual bill of lading incorporating the Hague Rules. But, so long as the sellers remained the bailors, those terms only had effect as between the sellers and the shipowners. If the shipowners as bailors had ever attorned to the buyers, so that they became the bailors in place of the sellers, the terms of the bailment would then have taken effect as between the shipowners and the buyers. Because of what happened, however, the bill of lading never was negotiated by the sellers to the buyers and no attornment by the shipowners ever took place. I would add that, if the argument for the buyers on terms of bailment were correct, there would never have been any need for the Bills of Lading Act 1855 or for the decision of the Court of Appeal in *Brandt v Liverpool, Brazil and River Plate Steam Navigation Co Ltd* [above] to which I referred earlier.

Ground (4): The Requirements of a Rational System of Law

13–080 My Lords, under this head counsel for the buyers submitted that any rational system of law ought to provide a remedy for persons who suffered the kind of loss which the buyers suffered in the present case, with the clear implication that, if your Lordships' House were to hold that the remedy for which he contended was not available, it would be lending its authority to an irrational feature of English law. I do not agree with this submission for, as I shall endeavour to show, English law does, in all normal cases, provide a fair and adequate remedy for loss of or damage to goods the subject matter of a c.i.f. or c. & f. contract, and the buyers in this case could easily, if properly advised at the time when they agreed to the variation of the original c. & f. contract, have secured to themselves the benefit of such a remedy.

As I indicated earlier, under the usual c.i.f. or c. & f. contract the bill of lading issued in respect of the goods is indorsed and delivered by the seller to the buyer against payment by the buyer of the price. When that happens, the property in the goods passes from the sellers to the buyers upon or by reason of such indorsement, and the buyer is entitled, by virtue of s.1 of the Bills of Lading Act 1855, to sue the shipowners for loss of or damage to the goods on the contract contained in the bill of lading. The remedy so available to the buyer is adequate and fair to both parties, and there is no need for any parallel or alternative remedy in tort for negligence. In the present case, as I also indicated earlier, the variation of the original c. & f. contract agreed between the sellers and the buyers produced a hybrid contract of an extremely unusual character. It was extremely unusual in that what had originally been an ordinary c. & f.

contract became, in effect, a sale ex-warehouse at Immingham, but the risk in the goods during their carriage by sea remained with the buyers as if the sale had still been on a c. & f. basis. In this situation the persons who had a right to sue the shipowners for loss of or damage to the goods on the contract contained in the bill of lading were the sellers, and the buyers, if properly advised, should have made it a further term of the variation that the sellers should either exercise this right for their account (see *The Albazero* [above]) or assign such right to them to exercise for themselves. If either of these two precautions had been taken, the law would have provided the buyers with a fair and adequate remedy for their loss.

These considerations show, in my opinion, not that there is some lacuna in English law relating to these matters, but only that the buyers, when they agreed to the variation of the original contract of sale, did not take the steps to protect themselves which, if properly advised, they should have done. To put the matter quite simply the buyers, by the variation to which they agreed, were depriving themselves of the right of suit under s.1 of the Bills of Lading Act 1855 which they would otherwise have had, and commercial good sense required that they should obtain the benefit of an equivalent right in one or other of the two different ways which I have suggested.

Ground (5): The Judgment of Robert Goff L.J.
My Lords, after a full examination of numerous authorities relating to **13–081** the law of negligence Goff L.J. (now Lord Goff of Chieveley) said ([1985] 2 W.L.R. 289 at 330):

"In my judgment, there is no good reason in principle or in policy, why the c. & f. buyer should not have . . . a direct cause of action. The factors which I have already listed point strongly towards liability. I am particularly influenced by the fact that the loss in question is of a character which will ordinarily fall on the goods owner who will have a good claim against the shipowner, but in a case such as the present the loss may, in practical terms, fall on the buyer. It seems to me that the policy reasons pointing towards a direct right of action by the buyer against the shipowner in a case of this kind outweigh the policy reasons which generally preclude recovery for purely economic loss. There is here no question of any wide or indeterminate liability being imposed on wrongdoers; on the contrary, the shipowner is simply held liable to the buyer in damages for loss for which he would ordinarily be liable to the goods owner. There is a recognised principle underlying the imposition of liability, which can be called the principle of transferred loss. Furthermore, that principle can be formulated. For the purposes of the present case, I would formulate it in the following deliberately narrow terms, while recognising that it may require modification in the light of experience. Where A owes a duty of care in tort not to cause physical damage to B's property, and commits a breach of that duty in circumstances in which the loss of or physical damage to the property will ordinarily fall on B but (as is reasonably foreseeable by A) such loss or damage, by reason of a contractual relationship between B and C, falls upon C, then C will be entitled, subject to the terms of any contract restricting A's liability to B, to bring an action in tort against A in respect of such loss or damage to the extent that it falls on him, C. To that proposition there must be exceptions. In particular, there must, for the reasons I have given, be an exception in the case of contracts of insurance. I have also attempted so to draw the principle as to exclude the case of the time charterer who remains liable for hire for the chartered ship while under repair following collision damage, though this could if necessary be treated as another exception having regard to the present state of the authorities."

With the greatest possible respect to Robert Goff L.J., the principle of transferred loss which he there enunciated, however useful in dealing with special factual situations it may be in theory, is not only not supported by authority, but is on the contrary inconsistent with it. Even if it were necessary to introduce such a principle in order to fill a genuine lacuna in the law, I should myself, perhaps because I am more faint hearted than Robert Goff L.J., be reluctant to do so. As I have tried to show earlier, however, there is in truth no such *lacuna* in the law which requires to be filled. Neither Sir John Donaldson M.R. nor Oliver L.J. (now Lord Oliver of Aylmerton) was prepared to accept the introduction of such a principle and I find myself entirely in agreement with their unwillingness to do so.

My Lords, I have now examined and rejected all the five grounds on which counsel for the buyers relied in support of his contention that *The Wear Breeze* [1969] 1 Q.B. 219 was either wrongly decided at the time, or at any rate should be regarded as wrongly decided today, and should accordingly be overruled. The conclusion which I have reached is that *The Wear Breeze* was good law at the time when it was decided and remains good law today. It follows that I consider that the decision of Lloyd J. in *The Irene's Success* [1982] Q.B. 481, which even counsel for the buyers did not seek to support in its entirety, was wrong and should be overruled, and the observations of Sheen J. with regard to it in *The Nea Tyhi* [1982] 1 Lloyd's Rep. 606 should be disapproved [contractual aspects of this case, which are not subject to this criticism, are considered in para. 14–037, below].

My Lords, if I had reached a different conclusion on the main question of the existence of a duty of care, and held that such a duty of care, qualified by the terms of the bill of lading, did exist, it would have been necessary to consider the further question whether, on the rather special facts of this case, the shipowners committed any breach of such duty. As it is, however, the answer to that further question is not required.

For the reasons which I have given, I would affirm the decision of the Court of Appeal and dismiss the appeal with costs.

Notes

On the contractual issues, the reason why property had not passed to the buyer **13–082** was because when the contract was varied the sellers were taken to have reserved a right of disposal in the goods until payment, the price being payable by 180–day bill of exchange. This inference was made, notwithstanding the delivery of the bill of lading, in the light of the Sale of Goods Act 1979, s.19(1).

On the *Brandt v Liverpool* issue, the reason given by the Court of Appeal was that the buyers were acting as agents for the sellers in presenting the bill of lading. A possible additional difficulty (alluded to by Staughton J. at first instance) was that they did not pay the freight, and so it might have been difficult to find consideration for an implied contract (see further above).

The real interest in the case lies in the discussion of the negligence action, since the buyers did not have property in the goods when the damage occurred. From one perspective, this is simply a very conservative decision, but had the tort action succeeded, because no contract could be implied or inferred between buyer and carrier, the carrier would be unable to rely on exemption clauses in the contract of carriage (often written in by the Hague or Hague-Visby Rules—see Chapter 11). This argument was particularly heavily with Lord Donaldson M.R. in the Court of Appeal, who noted that the carrier might never have agreed to carry the goods at all but for the protection of the exemption clauses in the bill of lading contract.

Lord Roskill's views in *Junior Books* (in which Lord Brandon dissented), in the passage quoted in the above extract, would have avoided the difficulty alluded to in the previous paragraph, because he postulated that the exemption clauses in the carriage contract might have the effect of limiting the duty of care owed by the carrier to the buyer. Because Lord Brandon rejected this approach, the court was necessarily faced with the stark choice of either allowing a negligent carrier to escape with impunity, or allowing the buyer to sue at large leaving the carrier unprotected by exemption clauses. Lord Brandon chose the former course.

The same conservative approach has also been taken to conversion, by the Court of Appeal in *MCC Proceeds Inc v Lehman Brothers International (Europe)* [1998] 4 All E.R. 675, [1998] 2 B.C.L.C. 659.

Continuing damage

In *The Wear Breeze* and *The Aliakmon*, both damage and breach of duty occurred **13–083** before property passed to the plaintiffs, but it is possible for damage to occur on an ongoing basis, as a result of a single prior breach, in which case the breach, but not the damage, may occur prior to the passing of property. For example, a breach by the shipowner, in failing to provide a seaworthy vessel at the start of the voyage, may allow seawater to leak in gradually, causing incremental damage to the cargo. If the plaintiff can claim only in respect of damage occurring after he becomes owner of the cargo, this can give rise to evidential problems as to apportionment, when property passes from seller to buyer at some time during the voyage, but the damage, caused by exposure to seawater, for example, occurs continuously, some before and some after the passing of property.[35] If on the other hand, in order to claim the claimant must have legal title at the time of the breach of duty, the evidential problems will be reduced, but so will the prospects of successful recovery.

---

[35] As in *The Nea Tyhi* [1982] 1 Lloyd's Rep. 606. The tort aspects of that decision must now be regarded as wrong, however, in the light of *The Aliakmon*.

This issue had not been dealt with in either *The Wear Breeze* or *The Aliakmon*, but in *The Starsin*,[36] the Court of Appeal decided that in a case involving incremental damage, the cause of action arose when (more than negligible) damage was first caused. The allegation was that bad stowage had caused damage to the cargo by condensation, but whereas stowage had occurred at the start of the voyage, most of the damage had occurred during the course of it. Property passed to the plaintiff buyers during the voyage, after the breach, and after some, but not all the damage had occurred. In the event a contract action succeeded,[37] on the bills of lading (see para. 12–045, above), but the Court of Appeal also considered the position in tort, the shipowners having argued (unsuccessfully) that the bills of lading were issued on behalf of the charterers, rather than themselves. Had the contract action not succeeded, the tort action would have failed also. The plaintiffs must have property at the time of the breach, not just at the time of the damage.

The authorities were fully reviewed, in particular by Rix L.J., who had dissented on the contract issue. In *Weller*, the claim failed because no duty of care was owed. Since the reasoning was in terms of duty of care, the relevant time was arguably the breach of duty, rather than the occurrence of the damage. On the other hand, in many personal injury cases, including *Donoghue v Stevenson* itself,[38] the breach preceded the injury, and yet the claim succeeded. The decision in *The Starsin* is effectively to adopt one rule for both personal injury and property damage cases, in line with the decisions in *Cartledge v Jopling & Sons Ltd*[39] and *Pirelli General Cable Works Ltd v Oscar Faber & Partners*.[40]

Special pleading for sea carriage

13–084 A view that comes across clearly from *The Aliakmon* that it is for the parties to adapt themselves to the law, rather than for the law to adapt itself to the needs of the parties. This was, of course, the old (pre-1992) law, but even then, the buyer could easily have protected himself by taking an assignment, for example. In other cases it could have been difficult, in reality, to do this. If there were 50 sales in a chain, one would have to have 50 assignments, and if one were missing none thereafter would mend the gap. Moreover, contractual burdens cannot be assigned. Anyway, whatever view one takes of this argument (which is essentially against special pleading), the legislature has now been prepared to intervene twice, to provide a special contractual regime for sea transport.

(6) Other Privity Issues

13–085 The *Himalaya* clause problem, alluded to at para. 11–038, above, has been resolved, not by the Hague-Visby amendments discussed at para. 11–061 (which did not work), but by the Contract (Rights of Third Parties) Act 1999. Section 1 provides:

"(1) Subject to the provisions of this Act, a person who is not a party to a contract (a third party) may in his own right enforce a term of the contract if—

---

[36] *Homburg Houtimport BV v Agrosin Private Ltd (The Starsin)* [2001] 1 Lloyd's Rep. 437.
[37] Rix L.J. dissenting on this issue.
[38] [1932] A.C. 562.
[39] [1963] A.C. 758.
[40] [1983] 2 A.C. 1.

(a) the contract expressly provides that he may, or

(b) ... the term purports to confer a benefit on him.

...

(3) The third party must be expressly identified in the contract by name, as a member of a class or as answering a particular description but need not be in existence when the contract is entered into."

The stevedores, or other independent contractors engaged by the carrier clearly fall within the class description in subs. (3), and a *Himalaya* clause confers the benefit of exemption clauses in the carriage contract. The same reasoning also allows actual carriers to be similarly protected under through bills of lading or multimodal transport documents (see chapter 15, below). Prior to the 1999 Act, *Himalaya* clauses could not be guaranteed to work, although they usually did.[41]

The privity problem in *Pyrene v Scindia* (again see para. 11–065, above) remains outstanding, where in a type 3 f.o.b. contract the seller sues in tort, to avoid carriage contract clauses protecting the shipowner. In *Pyrene v Scindia* Devlin J. was able to construe an implied contract, but as we saw there, this aspect of the decision must be regarded as highly doubtful.

[41] See nn. 51–53 in Ch. 11, above.

Chapter 14

REPRESENTATIONS IN BILLS OF LADING

(1) Introduction

(a) Importance of Representations in Bills of Lading

14–001   A bill of lading, as a document of title, represents the goods. A purchaser, or a bank advancing money on a documentary credit, cannot inspect the goods while they are at sea, and has to rely instead on representations in the shipping documents, and in particular in the bill of lading. These representations provide him with evidence that the seller has performed the sale contract, by shipping conforming goods. He can therefore confidently pay on the strength of the representations therein. Should any problems arise after negotiation of the bill of lading, he knows that goods of the stated description have been loaded on board. They are his security, very important if an overseas seller, about whose solvency he knows nothing, goes bankrupt.

Modern international trade depends on the accuracy of these representations. As Colman J. recently observed in *The Starsin*[1]:

> " . . . if an innocent shipper, indorsee or consignee could not rely on statements on the face of a bill of lading as to such matters as the date of shipment and the absence of clausing and was obliged to verify the accuracy of the date and the apparent good order and condition of the goods each time he took a bill of lading, that would represent a most serious impediment to international trade which depends so heavily on the accuracy of bills of lading as negotiable instruments."

The same reasoning applies to descriptions of the goods, and of the fact of their shipment. If any of these representations are false, the person taking up the bill can suffer loss, for which ideally there should be redress. It has been said that "[the] accuracy of the bill of lading statements is a matter which is generally within the control of the shipowner"[2] and he is therefore the appropriate person to take responsibility for them. But the law has never systematically provided a cause of action against the shipowner, and recent decisions do not improve the position of the holder of the bill.

Note
     I shall assume, for the purposes of this discussion, that the master signs bills of lading for the shipowner (*i.e.* we are avoiding the problems discussed at paras 12—037, *et seq*, above).

---

[1] [2000] 1 Lloyd's Rep. 85, reversed on other grounds: [2001] 1 Lloyd's Rep. 437, CA.
[2] Carver (1890) 6 L.Q.R. 289, 303–304. The passage continues "although no doubt the shipper has often very much to do with it." The notion that the shipper is the originator of statements in bills of lading has placed an undesirable brake on the development of the law: see further below at paras 14–019, *et seq.*, below.

(b) Initial Observations

Two general observations need to be made, both of which can detrimentally **14–002** affect the representee's prospects of recovering.

Misrepresentation could be innocently made

The first observation is that misrepresentations in bills of lading do not normally occur without fraud or negligence. If the master has been fraudulent, then there should be no difficulty in suing him for deceit, and if the representation is within the scope of his authority, the shipowner also. If he is negligent, *Hedley Byrne* liability may attach (this is discussed further below at para. 14–024).

However, whereas there will probably be fraud or negligence somewhere,[3] the person who actually made the representation (master or loading broker) may well be innocent.[4] In most cases where the shipping date is altered, fraud is often involved somewhere, as in *Kwei Tek Chao v British Traders and Shippers*,[5] where the shipment date on the bill of lading had been forged. However, the fraud was not that of the master who issued the bill, or of the immediate c.i.f. seller, but of forwarding agents acting without the seller's authority, on behalf of earlier sellers on a domestic supply contract, to enable them to claim payment under a documentary credit. The person defrauded was not the bank, but a c.i.f. purchaser two further down the chain.[6]

In *V/O Rasnoimport v Guthrie & Co Ltd*,[7] a theft occurred of most of the cargo prior to shipment, followed by a misstatement in the bill of lading that all the cargo had been shipped. A bill of lading had been signed and issued by the defendants, who were agents of the shipowners, stating that 225 bales of rubber had been shipped on board the vessel. In reality, unbeknown to the agents, only 90 bales had been shipped. Yet Mocatta J. found, not only that the defendants had not been fraudulent, but that they had not even been negligent in issuing the bill. The remaining bails had been stolen before loading by employees of Malayan Railways, which was supposed to have carried them to lighters, and thence to the vessel. They were not however placed aboard the lighters, but left on the wagons and thereafter misappropriated. In consequence of a go-slow movement by the railway union, no railway tally clerks were available to take a tally from the railway wagons into the lighter, and the defendants were unaware that the bales were missing. The defendants were held to have acted "without negligence and in accordance with the usual practice of ship's agents in the Far East and elsewhere".[8] The incorrect bill of lading was issued to the shippers of the cargo, who

---

[3] In *Gill & Duffus SA v Berger & Co Inc* [1984] A.C. 382 (see para. 7–022, above), for example, Lord Diplock observed at 390, in parenthesis, that " . . . in the case of a c.i.f. contract it is difficult to see how, without fraud upon his part, the seller could ship beans but nevertheless be in a position to tender shipping documents conforming to those called for by a c.i.f. contract to sell peas . . . ", admittedly a rather extreme misrepresentation, but the same could no doubt also be said of less serious representations.

[4] Not always of course. In *The American Accord* [1983] 1 A.C. 168 (see Ch. 10, above) it was the loading broker who was fraudulent.

[5] [1954] 2 Q.B. 459. See also para. 7–033, above.

[6] Another example might be thought to be *Discount Records Ltd v Barclays Bank Ltd* [1975] 1 W.L.R. 315 (see also para. 10–012, above). There, the master had the true facts hidden from him by the shipper, who was alleged to be fraudulent. This is a poor example, however, because there was also no misstatement in the bill of lading. The goods really were in apparent good order and condition.

[7] [1966] 1 Lloyd's Rep. 1. See further below, para. 14–059.

[8] At 3, col. 2.

had contracted to sell the bales of rubber to the plaintiff purchasers.[9] Accordingly, they indorsed the bill of lading and delivered it to the plaintiffs, against which delivery, believing 225 bales to have been shipped, the plaintiffs paid. It was found as a fact that[10]:

> "In taking up and paying for the said Bill of Lading the Plaintiffs acted on the faith of the statement contained therein to the effect that bales had been shipped thereunder, believing the said statement to be true."

Here then, there was a criminal act, and the representee relied to his detriment on a related misstatement in a bill of lading. That statement had however been made entirely innocently, so that no tortious liability could attach to the defendants, nor, had the statement been within the scope of their authority, the shipowners.[11]

Misstatement may not be relied upon

14–003
The second observation is that there are there are at least two distinct ways in which the holder of a bill of lading might suffer from the inaccuracy of statements contained therein. The most obvious is that he may not have taken up, and paid against, the bill of lading at all, had the truth been known. What has actually been shipped (if anything)[12] may be worthless to him; had he known the truth he would have re-entered the market and purchased elsewhere, perhaps also suing his seller for breach of the sale contract. Alternatively, on a falling market, he might have decided to reject anyway, even if there was little or nothing wrong with the goods. In both these cases, the falsity of the representation has led him to take up the bill of lading, where otherwise he would have rejected it. The appropriate remedy would be, as far as possible, to unravel the transaction; damages should be what the holder has paid, less the value of the actual goods received. Merely to give him the difference in value between the goods as described and the actual goods will not fully compensate the holder, on a falling market, since it will exclude the market loss.[13] For the same reason, to hold the representor to what he has represented is insufficient; the holder should be put into the position he would have occupied had the misrepresentation not been made. This is effectively a tortious, not contractual basis of compensation, therefore.

On the other hand, on a rising market, the holder might, in order to protect his market gain, have decided to accept the bill of lading anyway, even had he known the truth, relying on a damages action against the seller. This is easier to explain with some real figures. Suppose there are two grades of widget, A and B, for which at the time of contracting the market prices are respectively £50 and £40 per ton. I contract to purchase grade A widgets; the bill of lading falsely states that grade A widgets have been loaded, although in fact the widgets are grade B. In

---

[9] The sale was f.o.b., and the seller's obligations would have been to load the goods on board the vessel. The bill of lading wrongly implied that they had fully performed this obligation.

[10] At 4, col. 1.

[11] The defendants were, however, liable for breach of contract, for which of course liability is strict.

[12] Nothing had been shipped in *Heskell v Continental Express* [1950] 1 All E.R. 1033 (see para. 14–056, below) or *Hindley & Co Ltd v East Indian Produce Co Ltd* [1973] 2 Lloyd's Rep. 515. In *Etablissment Esefka International Anstalt v Central Bank of Nigeria* [1979] 1 Lloyd's Rep. 445 (see para. 10–020, above), it was alleged that neither ship nor cargo existed. If so, of course, there would be no shipowner to sue.

[13] The value of the goods, as described, on a falling market being less than the holder has paid. One of the problems with the *Churchill & Sim* estoppel, described below, is that it requires reliance, which is easier to prove on a falling market, precisely the circumstance in which it fails fully to compensate.

the meantime the market price of both has doubled, respectively to £100 and £80 per ton. Even if I knew the truth, that the widgets were grade B, I could rationally have accepted the bill, paying the contract price of £50 for widgets that are now worth £80. I would then resell at £80, purchase the widgets I wanted for £100, and would be left to claim from the seller just £20 per ton damages. Rejecting the bill would have saved me the contract price of £50, but required me to go back into the market for widgets at £100. This would have left me to recover £50 per ton from the seller, a position less satisfactory than if I had accepted the lower grade widgets.

In this case the holder does not rely, at any rate directly, on the truth of the representation. There might also be other reasons why he would have accepted the bill of lading anyway, whatever the state of the market.[14] It might be objected that, since he has not relied directly on the misrepresentation in the bill, he is not truly a victim, and should have no action. It is true that the document he has, representing goods other than as stated, is of less value than he expected. It is also true that the bill of lading is the "key to the warehouse", and security for the goods. If the seller becomes bankrupt the holder expects to receive the goods as described, whereas in fact he has lesser security. This, however, is not a convincing argument, if he would have been prepared to accept a truthful bill in any event, relying for compensation on an action against the seller. He would in any event have been prepared to take the risk of the seller's bankruptcy, and has therefore lost nothing. **14–004**

Reliance is not the only reason for compensating the holder, however. Before 1992, he might, merely by becoming holder, have incurred contractual liability to the shipowner,[15] for example to pay any outstanding freight or demurrage due, and he would have inherited any liability incurred by the shipper for shipping dangerous goods. Since 1992, this liability is not imposed on all holders, but it certainly would be on the ultimate receiver of the cargo, whether or not he has relied on any statements in the bill of lading.[16] If he takes the burdens of the carriage contract, he should also be able to take the benefits of any contractual promises the shipowner has made. This argument might seem less convincing if freight has been prepaid, no demurrage is incurred and there is no liability for shipment of dangerous cargo, but even then, the holder's position has been changed by taking up the bill. No longer can he sue in tort, for example, for post-shipment damage, without being bound by bill of lading exemption clauses.

In the rising market example, since he would have taken up the bill of lading in any event, the loss the holder suffers is the difference in value between the goods as described and as received. To hold the representor to the truth of the representation is sufficient to compensate, but it should not be necessary for the holder to have to rely on the representation. Nor should it be necessary to prove fraud or negligence by the master, since the contractual liabilities incurred are independent of his state of mind.

---

[14] For example, the sale contract might provide for the price to depend on the shipment date, as in *Rudolf A Oetker v IFA Internationale Frachagentur AG (The Almak)* [1985] 1 Lloyd's Rep. 557 (see below), *Procter & Gamble v Becher GmbH* [1988] 2 Lloyd's Rep. 21 (see para. 7–050, above), or *The Eurus* [1998] 1 Lloyd's Rep. 351. A false shipment date in the bill of lading would not therefore lead the buyer to take up a bill of lading which (had he known the truth) he would otherwise have rejected, but merely to pay more for the cargo.

For other reasons why there may be no direct reliance, see the discussion of *The Dona Mari*, at para. 14–022, below.

[15] Under the Bills of Lading Act 1855, s.1.

[16] Carriage of Goods by Sea Act 1992, s.3.

(c) Conflicting Viewpoints of Holder and Shipowner

Viewpoint of holder

14–005   All the above scenarios have in common that the holder (who will typically be a purchaser or bank) has a document which appears to be a document of title to goods, but does not in fact represent the goods it purports to represent. The goods are not as stated therein, and in this sense at least, he has suffered a loss as the result of the misrepresentation. Moreover, the holder has had little prospect of protecting himself, for example by investigating the matter and so rejecting the documents. Banks under documentary credits have little time to make investigations, and unless they can prove fraud by the beneficiary, must take up apparently conforming documents.[17] The position is essentially similar for buyers under c.i.f. contracts.[18]

The representee must be assumed to be innocent, then, and ideally should be able to recover compensation. The proper defendant is the shipowner,[19] who has deep pockets, whose vessel can be arrested, and who is (in some sense at least) responsible for the representation. A purchaser might also, it is true, be able to sue his immediate seller, as in *Kwei Tek Chao*,[20] or *Hindley & Co Ltd v East Indian Produce Co Ltd*,[21] but one of the functions of the bill of lading is to provide buyers with security against the seller's bankruptcy. An action against a foreign seller will in any case not always be satisfactory. If the seller is not only foreign but also party to the fraud, as was alleged in *Discount Records v Barclays Bank*,[22] then any action against him will almost certainly be worthless. In holding the shipowner liable in *The Saudi Crown*,[23] for a fraudulent representation in a bill of lading, Sheen J. observed that:

> " . . . great injustice may be done to the innocent third party if he is left to pursue whatever remedy he may have against a person of unknown financial means in some distant land."

Moreover, the defendant should ideally have deep pockets; a bill of lading offers little security if it provides an action only against the master, even though the statement has emanated from him.[24]

Viewpoint of shipowner

14–006   The law cannot revolve solely around the position of the holder. Liability can only be imposed on someone to whom the statement can be attributed, and even then, regard should be had to the capacity in which he made it. The shipowner should be entitled to claim, in his defence, "I did not make the representation", or "I made the representation only as a statement of fact, not as a contractual

---

[17] *United City Merchants (Investments) Ltd v Royal Bank of Canada (The American Accord)*. It is not enough to show that someone else has been fraudulent (as in the case itself), or merely to suspect fraud: *Discount Records Ltd v Barclays Bank Ltd*. The test was elaborated in *Bolivinter Oil SA v Chase Manhattan Bank* [1984] 1 Lloyd's Rep. 251. All these cases are discussed in Ch. 10, above.

[18] *Gill & Duffus SA v Berger & Co Inc*, in para. 7–022, above.

[19] Assuming (as we are for the present purposes) that the shipowner is the contracting carrier.

[20] In para. 7–033, above.

[21] In para. 2–012, above.

[22] In para. 10–012, above; the seller was French.

[23] [1986] 1 Lloyd's Rep. 261.

[24] The loading broker may have deep pockets, and was successfully sued in *Rasnoimport*, below, where the shipowner would have been able to rely on *Grant v Norway*, also discussed below.

promise." It is, of course, unlikely that the shipowner will have made any statement directly, bills of lading being issued and signed by masters, or loading brokers or charterers' agents. Even leaving aside the possibility that it might be a charterer's bill,[25] it would be unreasonable to impose liability on the shipowner for statements for which the person making them had neither his actual nor ostensible authority to make. Moreover, the nature of the statements has to be considered; if (for example) they were not made as contractual promises, then it would be unreasonable to treat them as such. Conversely, of course, if the statement, objectively viewed, was a contractual warranty, then the shipowner should be strictly liable for its breach.

The law must therefore strike a balance, protecting the position of the representee, but only by imposing liability on the party responsible for the representation. Ultimately, though, authority questions should surely be issues of fact, whereas the courts adopt inflexible rules. Worse, the rules are often derived from 19th, or early 20th century case law, when the parties' expectations differed from what they are today.[26] In recent years it is true that the law has developed, and the worst anomalies have been dealt with by legislation, but the lack of an underlying rationale is still apparent, and there are still gaps.

Organisation of the chapter

The later part of the chapter considers a specific (and arguably anomalous) aspect of the law of agency, which limits the authority of the ship's master to make statements on the shipowners' behalf, and hence make the shipowner liable if they are untrue. To a large extent this problem (which now seems exclusively to be concerned with quantity statements) has been resolved by legislation, at any rate in the UK, but there is an associated problem with such statements, that they are so qualified as not really to be statements at all. There are several recent cases, where the value of the bill of lading as a negotiable document has been significantly reduced.

For the first part of the chapter, however, we assume the statement in the bill of lading to be one which, in principle, the master has actual or apparent authority to make,[27] such as a description of the apparent condition of the goods, or the date of shipment. The well-known case of *Lloyd v Grace Smith & Co*[28] tells us that merely because an act is performed fraudulently does not take it outside the scope of the agent's authority, and therefore the statement will be attributed to the shipowner, whatever the master's state of mind in making it. It might be thought that such statements should pose no problem, but even if the statement is attributed to the shipowner, the question still needs to be asked, in what context was the statement made? Is it a contractual promise, for example?

Arguably, the position ought to be straightforward, but the law has been influenced by two factors:

(a) The bill of lading contract is made between carrier and shipper. The common law did not, as we saw in chapter 13, above, recognise that the bill of lading transferred the contract, and although such transfer was later provided by statute, what is transferred is the contract made between carrier and shipper; the terms of the transferred contract are the same as those of the original contract.

(b) Many of the statements made in the bill of lading either originate with information supplied by the shipper, or the information is known to him. It

---

[25] We are assuming not, for the present discussion.

[26] The inability of the common law to adapt to changing trade practices might become problematic again, given the present need for it to adapt to e-commerce.

[27] *i.e.* no *Grant v Norway* problem (see further paras 14–033, *et seq.*, below).

[28] [1912] A.C. 716.

would therefore be surprising if the carrier were to warrant their accuracy.

(2) WHO PROVIDES THE INFORMATION?

14-007   In *Heskell v Continental Express*,[29] Devlin J. described the shipment process (at least where shipping with a line), and the functions of loading broker and forwarding agent, as follows[30]:

"A contract of carriage is rarely made with any formality. Sometimes it is done by means of the engagement of shipping space, but in many cases the shipper, having learned from an advertisement or otherwise of a date and place of sailing, sends forward his goods and no contract is concluded until the goods are loaded or accepted for loading. The bill of lading is a receipt for the goods and a document of title to them. It is not the contract, for that has already been made, but it usually—I suppose almost always when there is no charterparty —contains its terms. When a shipment is made, as in this case, by a regular line, there are usually agents on each side intervening between the shipper and the shipowner. The shipper frequently employs a forwarding agent and the shipowner a loading broker. The forwarding agent's normal duties are to ascertain the date and place of sailing, obtain a space allocation if that is required, and prepare the bill of lading. The different shipping lines have their own forms of bill of lading which can be obtained from stationers in the city, and it is the duty of the forwarding agent to put in the necessary particulars and to send the draft stamped to the loading broker. His duties include also arranging for the goods to be brought alongside, making the customs entry and paying any dues on the cargo. After shipment he collects the completed bill of lading and sends it to the shipper. All the regular shipping lines operating from the United Kingdom appear to entrust the business of arranging for cargo to a loading broker. He advertises the date of sailings in shipping papers or elsewhere, and generally prepares and circulates to his customers a sailing card. It is his business to supervise the arrangements for loading, though the actual stowage is decided on by the cargo superintendent, who is in the direct service of the shipowner. It is the broker's business also to sign the bill of lading, and issue it to the shipper or his agent in exchange for the freight. His remuneration is by way of commission on freight, and that is doubtless an inducement to him to carry out his primary function, at any rate when shipping is plentiful, of securing enough cargo to fill the ship. Under ordinary conditions shippers may send cargo to the quay without notifying the broker, though the broker much prefers to know of it, but during the war and in the post-war period this was impossible. The docks would have become cluttered up with cargo for which no room could be found. Therefore, there was introduced a registration system, which was still in force in 1946. The cargo could not be sent down to the docks unless the loading broker had been notified and his permission obtained in the appropriate form. The form is in two parts which are detachable. They have been called respectively the black form and the red form. The shipper or his agent sends both parts to the loading broker. After space has been allocated, the red form is sent back to the shipper with instructions about sending the cargo forward. The shipper then returns the red form to the loading broker accompanied by the draft bill of lading. The loading broker and the forwarding agent thus appear to discharge well-defined and separate functions, but in practice the same firm

---

[29] (1950) 83 Ll.L. Rep. 438; [1950] 1 All E.R. 1033.
[30] At 1037 of the All E.R. Reports.

is often both the loading broker and the forwarding agent, though the two sets of dealings may be kept in separate compartments of the business. The firm generally acts as loading broker only for one line and does all that line's business, so that it is free in respect of other business to act as it will, but even in the case of the same transaction, it appears to be customary for the firm to act both as loading broker and as forwarding agent. Strick did both, and that the practice is general is shown by the form of freight account that Strick use and which is similar to those of other firms. Items for preparing bills of lading, canal tolls, agency, customs clearance charges, etc., which all fall within the scope of forwarding agency, are added to the freight and collected as one sum."

Note that in 1946, when the shipment in the case occurred, there was a considerable shortage of shipping space, so that more formal methods of shipment could not be used.

Devlin J. observes that the bill of lading cannot be the contract, because it is **14–008** issued after the contract has been made; the contract is made, at the latest, when the goods are loaded or accepted for loading. The relationship between the bill of lading and the carriage contract was considered at paras 12–001, *et seq.*, above. More important to note for this chapter is that it is the forwarding agent, acting for the shipper, who prepares the bill of lading. Statements in the bill emanate from the shipper, not the shipowner. Devlin J. then continues, on the particular cargo[31]:

"The way in which the bill of lading came to be issued was this. No. 9 shed is the property of the Manchester port authority, the Manchester Ship Canal Co. This company, whom I will call the dock-owners, are employed by the loading brokers to receive the cargo and check it, and their stevedores do the loading into the ship. In so employing them, Strick are acting for the ship, and the charge that is made by the dock-owners for loading, storing and receiving is a disbursement that is debited to the shipowner. The loading brokers have ready prepared in their office a cargo book, in which are entered all the consignments for which space on the ship has been allocated. As the cargo arrives at No. 9 shed the dock-owners' checker records the receipt of the goods on a receiving pad. The sheets are torn off and sent to the loading brokers and a circle is made round the number of each consignment in the cargo book that is noted as received. Bills of lading are then prepared in respect of these consignments, and as each bill of lading is passed a stroke in addition to the circle is made through the number. The bill of lading is then passed out for the freight to be calculated and for it to be signed by the responsible official as opportunity arises. It is then retained in the office until the ship has completed its loading. When the loading is finished there is prepared from the cargo left on the quay a list of goods shut out or shipment of which has been stopped. The bills of lading relating to the consignments on this list are taken out of the pile of signed bills, and the remainder are issued. There is also prepared by comparison between the receiving sheets and the cargo book a list of goods advised and not received: this is doubtless intended as a further check."

While this description is useful for an understanding of the older cases, the advent of containerisation, and also use of computers, has changed the practice. Dockray summarises (*Cases and Materials on the Carriage of Goods by Sea* (2nd ed.) at p. 14) the *Heskell* description as follows:

"Having learned from an advertisement or otherwise of a date and place of sailing, a shipper would forward his goods to the dock or berth. At the docks, a dock receipt or a mate's receipt would be given in exchange for the goods. The

---

[31] At 1039.

shipper or his agent would then prepare a draft bill of lading in the form used by the particular line and deliver it to the shipowner or his agent.... After loading, the draft bill of lading would be compared against the earlier receipt, signed by the master or more often an agent employed by the shipping line and issued to the shipper or his agent in exchange for the freight."

He then goes on to describe the development of modern container traffic, and observes (at p. 16):

"A number of... important changes have... occurred since *Heskell* was decided. In UK outbound liner shipping, the mate's receipt is now a comparative rarity. Export cargo to be carried by a line is forwarded for shipment accompanied by a Standard Shipping Note or a Dangerous Goods Note... prepared in several copies by or on behalf of the shipper. A copy of the Shipping Note is signed and returned to the shipper to acknowledge receipt. And it is now common for the bill of lading to be prepared by the carrier by computer from details supplied when the shipper reserved space on a vessel."

Dockray also observes that a sea waybill is often used in liner shipments, in place of a bill of lading. The use of alternative documentation is considered further in chapter 15, below. Traditional documentation continues to be used outside the liner trade.

Whatever their practical significance, the ramifications of these changes are not great, from a lawyers' viewpoint. Details in the bill of lading are still provided initially by the shipper, not the carrier. Where the mate's receipt is still used, it continues to be a preliminary document, given up in return for the bill of lading (see further para. 6–047, above). For the purposes of para. 12–001, it remains true, as Devlin J. observed, that "The bill of lading ... is not the contract, for that has already been made ... "—indeed, the contract will often be made earlier today than it was in *Heskell*.

The reason for setting out the extract here from *Heskell v Continental Express* is because the representations that eventually appeared in the bill of lading were originally made by the forwarding agent, acting for the seller (or shipper). This is also true whether a mate's receipt is used, or a Standard Shipping Note or a Dangerous Goods Note, as described by Dockray. Thus, information in the bill of lading about the goods originates with the shipper, not the master. However, the master (or loading broker) should not simply sign and issue the bill of lading without checking the truth of the statements made by the shipper. He adds his own confirmation, rather than simply transferring the information.

NAVIERA MOGOR SA v SOCIETE METALLURGIQUE DE NORMANDIE (THE NOGAR MARIN)

Court of Appeal. [1988] 1 Lloyd's Rep. 412

Facts:

14–009   The (voyage) charterers of *The Nogar Marin* shipped coils of wire rods, which they had themselves manufactured. Some of the coils were rusty when shipped, because they had been stored in the open, unprotected against the weather, and had suffered from the effects of rain during storage and loading. The charterparty required the master to sign bills of lading as presented by the charterers.

The ship's agents mistakenly signed two bills of lading, as presented by the charterers, which were not claused, and stated that the goods were in apparent good order and condition when loaded. It seems that the reason for the mistake was that the mate's receipt, which was signed by the master, bore the typewritten notation "clean on board", and the ship's agents were presented with this, along with two bills of lading presented for signature by the charterers. In the subsequent arbitration proceedings from which the case came to the courts on appeal, the master was found to have been guilty of an error of judgment, but not reckless.

When the goods arrived at their destination, the receivers, who had taken up the bills of lading in good faith, discovered the true condition of the goods, and arrested the vessel. The shipowners, who had no answer to the receivers' claim except on *quantum*,[32] came to a reasonable settlement. They attempted to claim the costs of the settlement from the charterers on the basis that the charterers were in breach of contract in presenting inaccurate documents for signature, or alternatively on the basis of an implied indemnity.

Held:
Mustill L.J., delivering the judgment of the Court of Appeal, held the charterers not liable.

In the arbitration proceedings, the main reason for the decision had **14–010** been causation. The ship's agents were not obliged simply to sign the bills of lading as presented, without further enquiry; the master should have claused the mate's receipts, and claused bills should have been issued. The shipowners' loss was caused not by the presentation by the charterers of inaccurate documents for signature, therefore, but the chain of causation was broken by the error of judgment of the master.

Mustill L.J. agreed with the arbitrators on the causation issue, but also thought that no liability arose in any event, because the charterers were not in breach of contract in tendering a clean mate's receipt, and no liability to indemnify therefore arose. The mate's receipt is simply an acknowledgement to the shippers that the ship has taken delivery of the goods. It does not need to be signed as presented, or indeed at all, and the master can choose for himself how to act. Mustill L.J. also thought that the charterers were under no duty to present accurate bills of lading, where the inaccuracy related only to statements of fact which the shipowners' servants could check. The charterers must not present bills under which the legal obligations of the shipowners towards the cargo-owners are greater than under the charterparty itself, but the duty is limited to that, and does not extend to factual representations in the bills.

Mustill L.J.: (*after reviewing authorities on implied terms and implied indemnities*)

[32] The nature of the receivers' claim is not discussed in the case, but must have been on the basis of the estoppel considered below.

14–011   We now return to the issues in the present case, the first of which concerns the mate's receipt. Counsel for the owners disclaimed any contention that an implied contract to indemnify arose from the fact of presenting the mate's receipt for signature: rightly so in our opinion. The mate's receipt said nothing about the condition of the goods. All that the charterers were inviting the master to do, when they tendered it, was to acknowledge that the goods had been received into the custody of the ship. This cannot be said to have involved any request to the owners that they should do the act which led to the incurring of liability, namely the signing of clean bills of lading. Nor does the award state any facts from which it would be possible to infer a promise by the charterers to the remarkable effect that if the master did not clause the receipt, they would indemnify the owners if they subsequently became liable for their subsequent failure to see that the bills were claused.

The owners do however contend that the charterers committed a breach of the charter-party by tendering a clean mate's receipt. We do not agree. As we shall later suggest, the authorities do not establish that there is invariably an implied term of the charter that the bill as presented shall correctly state the apparent condition of the cargo. But even if we are wrong in this, a mate's receipt is in a quite different category from a bill of lading. No doubt the parties foresee that some such document will be signed. But the mate's receipt is what its name indicates: an acknowledgment to the shippers that the ship has taken delivery of the goods. It is not part of the mechanism established by the charter-party, which does not stipulate that it is to be signed "as presented", or indeed at all. Nor does it share the prime characteristic of a bill of lading, of being a document which can be negotiated to third parties, thereby putting the shipowners into a new contractual relationship over which they have no control. It is a simple receipt. True it is, that if the mate or master signs it without qualification, it may put his owners into difficulties with the shipper who bails the goods into the custody of the ship, because it is *prima facie* evidence of receipt in good order and condition. But this creates no new liability, and no new party is involved. The master must choose for himself how to act, and the notion that if the charterer happens also to be the shipper he is in breach of duty under the charter-party by offering the master a document which, if carelessly signed by the master without proper enquiry, will constitute evidence in favour of the person who tenders it, is not a concept which we can grasp. Furthermore, on the facts of the present case (and we would suspect on the facts of most cases) the argument must founder on causation. The charterers tender the document. The master has a free choice whether or not to clause it. He chooses not to do so. Later, those acting for the owners have the opportunity to clause the bill of lading, so as to protect the owners. Again they let the opportunity pass. The resulting estoppel and liability must surely have only a distant connection with the original tender of the mate's receipt.

The problems arising from the signature of the bill of lading as tendered are altogether more difficult to analyse. . . .

. . . But this is in our judgment some way removed from the case where the complaint about the bill concerns . . . a representation of fact on its face backed by the signature of those acting for the owners; where the shipowner's servants have the opportunity to check the accuracy of the representation to which they are committing the shipowner; and where the making of which is a tortious act towards those who become transferees for value in reliance on the fact that the document is a clean bill of lading.

Again, although it is evident . . . that a term requiring representations **14–012** on the face of the bill to correspond with the true facts may be implied as against a charterer, when those facts are uniquely within the knowledge of the charterer and are not within the scope of a reasonable investigation on the part of the shipowner's servants, it seems to us that a case such as the present stands on a different footing. Granted, the arguments before this Court have assumed that the charterers were well aware of the defective state of the goods. Nevertheless, the arbitrators' findings show that the master should at least have recognized enough of the true facts to require the bill to be qualified. The making of a proper inspection is not just a matter between the master and his owners; it affects the transferees as well. We see no reason to imply a term which takes the ultimate financial responsibility for this task, away from the master's employers and places it on the shoulders of the charterer.

Moreover, from a strictly practical point of view, we cannot see the point of the suggested term. Two situations may be envisaged. First, the defects in the goods are not such as to be apparent on a reasonable examination at the point of shipment. It is a common place that in such a situation the signature of the bill of lading without qualification does not preclude the owners from establishing the true condition of the goods. There is thus no enhanced exposure, beyond that which existed under the charter, and no need for an implied term to protect the owners against it. In the second case, the defective condition of the cargo is to be apparent on reasonable examination. If this is so, the master should not issue clean bills. Why imply a term to protect the owners against the consequences of the master failing to do his job, when this failure will present the charterers in almost every case with an unanswerable argument on causation? We can see no reason.

The present situation is rather more complicated, because the master's mistake took place at an earlier stage of the transaction, and the history of events at Caen is not fully known. In the end, however, we do not regard this as decisive. The fact that the master signed the earlier document and Sogena [the agents] the later was adventitious. Both signed on behalf of the owners and the division of function should not place the owners in a more favourable position than if (in the more traditional mode) the chief officer had signed the receipt, and the master the bill of lading.

Finally, on this part of the case, we believe that, although the arbitrators may perhaps have been compressed, the position as regards causation, the analysis, is essentially correct. True, the master did not sign the bill. But it was his mistake concerning the receipt which permitted Sogena to sign the bills without qualification, and if his act was not strictly "intervening", it can justly be regarded as predominant, on the arbitrators' findings, over whatever breach the charterers may have committed by presenting for signature bills of lading which conformed with the receipt which the master had previously signed.

[*Mustill L.J. then went on to consider implied indemnity arguments, continuing:*]

14–013   ... It seems to us plain and the authorities leave us in no doubt that the implication of an obligation to indemnify is not automatic. It must always depend on the facts of the individual case, and on the terms of any underlying contractual relationship. The first step is always to indemnify the express or implied request by the person called upon to indemnify. Here, if the request is to be understood as meaning: "Kindly sign this bill, just as it stands, with its acknowledgment of receipt in apparent good order and condition", the claim for an indemnity must be sound, for the agents did precisely what they were asked; and the defence based on an intervening act must fail, since no act intervened, or ever could intervene, in such a situation. In the present case, we do not regard this as the correct reading of what happened. Everyone in the shipping trade knows that the master need not sign a clean bill just because one is tendered; everyone knows that it is the master's task to verify the condition of the goods before he signs. This being so, we cannot understand the request implicit in the tender as being more than this:

"The charter requires you to bind your owners to the contract of carriage contained in the bill of lading, and please do so. The bill of lading also constitutes a receipt, and please sign it as such, with whatever appropriate qualification you may think fit".

If this is a right account of the transaction, as we believe it to be, the claim for an indemnity must fail.

Notes
    1. There is also in the case much discussion of the nature of the liability in cases such as these, under an implied term or implied indemnity.
    2. From the above quote, it can be seen:

(a) that the mate's receipt is issued much earlier than the shipped bill,

(b) that it is merely a receipt for the goods,

(c) that it is not negotiated, but is given up in return for a bill of lading (see further the discussion in para. 6–047, above),

(d) that the statements contained in it, and indeed in the bill of lading, are made by the shipper; all the master does, when issuing the bill of lading, is to certify that the shipper's statements are correct, state that the goods have been shipped, and make associated statements as to shipment date, name of vessel, etc.,

(e) that the master should clause the bill of lading if it does not accurately describe the condition of the goods. Indeed, the master is obliged to check the accuracy of any statements made in the bill of lading.[33]

3. From (d) and (e), it can be seen that statements originating in the mate's receipt are originally made by the shipper, not the carrier. The carrier certifies quantity loaded, and apparent order and condition, but these should also be known by the shipper. There is no basis, therefore, at least *vis-a-vis* the shipper, for implying that the carrier warrants their accuracy.

4. There are, however, statements in the bill of lading, such as whether the goods are loaded on or under deck, which originate with the carrier, and are not necessarily within the shipper's knowledge. There is a greater case, therefore, for holding that the carrier warrants the accuracy of these statements.

Nature of obligation towards shipper

In *The Nogar Marin* the shipowner, having been sued by the receivers, **14–014** attempted unsuccessfully to recoup from the charterers, who were also the shippers. It was for the master himself to check the accuracy of statements in the bill of lading, and it was his failure to do so, rather than the presentation of the bill by the charterers for signature, which caused the shipowners' loss.

It does not follow that the master owes any positive obligation towards the shippers of goods to clause the bill of lading, or indeed to ensure the accuracy of any statements therein, of which the shippers should have been aware (see also *The Almak*, below). In *The Arctic Trader*,[34] similar principles were applied as between shipper and time charterer, even where the time charterer did not ship the cargo on his own account. Though the cargo of salt was clearly contaminated, the master did not clause either the mate's receipt or the bill of lading. The vessel was delayed at the discharge port, partly because of claims by the receivers, and since the vessel was not off-hire for the entirety of this period, the time charterers suffered loss. They failed in their claim that a term should be implied into the charterparty requiring the shipowners accurately to state the apparent order and condition of the goods. Delivering the judgment of the court, Evans L.J. said[35]:

"(5) If the time charterer is himself the shipper, then an implied term of the kind suggested by charterers would impose a duty on the master to tell the charterer/shipper what he already knows, namely, the apparent order and condition of the goods which he has shipped.

(6) We would accept Mr Goldstone's submission [for the charterers] that a time charterer is much less likely than a voyage charterer to ship goods for his own account. When there is a long-term charter to another shipowner or the operator of a line, the likelihood is that this will rarely, if ever, occur. So, Mr

[33] In *Stumore, Weston & Co v Breen* (1886) 12 App. Cas. 698, Lord Fitzgerald agrees (at 708) with Bowen L.J.'s view in the Court of Appeal, that the master's duty is "to sign the bill of lading for the cargo received, and to use reasonable care and skill in seeing that the bill of lading is properly drawn up which he does sign." In that case the master was held liable to his employer (who had been sued by the receiver of the cargo) for issuing a bill of lading containing a false shipment date.
[34] *Trade Star Line Corporation v Mitsui & Co Ltd (The Arctic Trader)* [1996] 2 Lloyd's Rep. 449, CA.
[35] At 458–459.

Goldstone submits, the existence or otherwise of an implied term should depend, not upon that unlikely possibility, but upon what will be, perhaps invariably, the situation in practice. . . .

(7) The next question is whether there is the same objection to implying a term that the mate's receipt will be accurate in those cases where the charterer does not, and is unlikely to, know for himself what the apparent order and condition of the goods on shipment was. It cannot then be said that the document would merely tell the charterer what he already knows—unless as a matter of law the third-party shipper's knowledge is attributed to him. In other words, does the shipper act as the charterer's agent for the purposes of his contract with the shipowners?

(8) It is clear, in our judgment, that when the time charterer instructs the master . . . to receive certain cargo on board, and the cargo is loaded at the charterer's expense, although under the supervision and maybe at the risk of the shipowner, then the cargo is loaded by or on behalf of the charterer for the purposes of the charter-party, and a third party shipper should be regarded as the charterer's agent accordingly.

(9) It follows from this that whether or not the charterer is also the shipper there is the same objection to implying a term that the master or chief officer will tell the charterer what he already knows, or is deemed to know."

(3) Legal Effect of Representations

(a) Evidence of Truth

14-015   In *Henry Smith & Co v Bedouin Steam Navigation Co Ltd*,[36] a shipowner was held bound to deliver the full amount of goods signed for by the master in a bill of lading, unless he could prove that the whole or some part of it was in fact not shipped. The case is authority simply that quantity statements in bills of lading are evidence, and in the absence of other evidence will conclude the issue as to the quantity of goods shipped. Presumably the same reasoning would apply to any other statement of fact in a bill of lading.

(b) Warranty of Truth?

14-016   The problem discussed in this section is the effect, if any, of a representation that is shown to be untrue. Does the shipowner warrant to the holder the truth of bill of lading statements?

There are advantages for a holder to sue in contract. Liability is strict, so it is unnecessary to examine the master's state of mind. There is no need to show detrimental reliance, and damages are such, in principle, as to put the representee into the position he would have been in, had the statement been true. This will fully compensate on a static or rising, but not (as we have seen) on a falling market.[37] However, the shipowner will not normally be liable in contract, for false representations in bills of lading.

---

[36] [1896] A.C. 70, HL.
[37] The market loss results from the misstatement being made. Had the statement been true, the representee would still have suffered the market loss.

COMPANIA NAVIERA VASCONZADA v CHURCHILL & SIM

King's Bench Division. [1906] 1 K.B. 237

Facts:

The master signed a bill of lading containing the clauses "shipped in **14–017** good order and condition, and to be delivered in the like good order and condition", and "quality and measure unknown". In fact the goods had been clearly damaged prior to shipment. The purchasers paid the contract price to the shippers against tender of the bill of lading, and sued the shipowners, the shippers being a foreign company (although not in liquidation).

Decision:

1. Statements as to the apparent condition, but not the actual quality of the goods shipped,[38] were within the master's authority. They could therefore be attributed to the shipowner.

2. However, the clause in the bill of lading: "shipped in good order and condition, and to be delivered in the like good order and condition" did not amount to a contractual warranty, by the shipowner, that the goods would be delivered in good order and condition.

3. It was, however, a statement of fact, which was reasonably relied upon by the purchasers to their detriment. Accordingly, the shipowners were estopped from denying the truth of the statement. Since they were therefore unable to explain how the damage occurred, they were liable for it.

4. The qualification "quality and measure unknown" did not protect the shipowners, since "quality and measure" were not the same as "order and condition".

CHANNELL J.: (*at 246—247*) The [purchasers] put their case alternatively **14–018** either as a claim on the contract contained in the bill of lading, or by way of estoppel. First, as to the suggested breach of contract—no doubt by the Bills of Lading Act the indorsee to whom the property has passed becomes a party to the contract made originally between the shipper and shipowner and evidenced by the bill of lading. But, as has been pointed out in more than one case, the contract must be construed in the same way between the original parties and the substituted parties, and it is necessary to see exactly what the original contract is. It seems to me that

---

[38] Distinguishing *Grant v Norway* (1851) 10 C.B. 665, discussed below, where a bill of lading was issued although no goods were shipped, and *Cox v Bruce* (1886) 18 Q.B.D. 147 (see at 152), where the master misstated the actual quality of the goods. In neither case was the shipowner bound by these statements, which were not made within the master's actual or apparent authority.

the contract is to deliver the goods in the same condition as that in which they are shipped, coupled with an acknowledgment that the condition at the time of shipment was good. The words "shipped in good order and condition" are not words of contract in the sense of a promise or under-taking. The words are an affirmation of fact, or perhaps rather in the nature of an assent by the captain to an affirmation of fact which the shipper may be supposed to make as to his own goods. So far, therefore, as the words of the bill of lading . . . are concerned, I see no contract that the condition of the goods is correctly described. . . . I think, therefore, . . . that the cause of action must be based on estoppel, and not on breach of contract. It seems to me, however, that the case does come within the recognized rules as to estoppel. The statement, as I have pointed out, is one of fact. If not exactly intended to be acted on, it must be known that it would probably be acted on. Bills of lading are transferable, and the object of the shipper in asking for the insertion of the statement that the goods are in good condition at the time of shipment is clearly rather to have evidence to offer to his transferee than for his own direct benefit. The advantage of what is known as a clean bill of lading is obvious, and I think it would be idle for a master of a ship to say that he did not contemplate a purchaser of the goods acting on the statement that the goods were shipped in good condition.

Comment:

14–019   The contractual reasoning is essentially that the carriage contract is originally made with the shipper, from whom the representations originated, and that it would be absurd to warrant the accuracy of what the shipper already knew. Moreover, although the action was brought on the contract transferred to the purchaser, this contract was made originally between shipper and shipowner, and "the contract must be construed in the same way between the original parties and the substituted parties". No new contract with the indorsee springs up, on different terms.

The estoppel gave the purchasers the result they wanted, but it is dependent on reliance, which will not always be present (see further below).

To which statements does Churchill & Sim apply?

It may be observed that there are two grounds for the conclusion in *Churchill & Sim*, that a statement as to the apparent order and condition of the goods is not a contractual warranty. The first is its form; it is in the form of an affirmation of fact, and is not expressly a promise. Yet statements of fact can, at least in principle, imply a promise as to their truth. For example, in *V/O Rasnoimport v Guthrie*,[39] from the factual statement that 225 bales were loaded on board was implied not only a statement, but a warranty by the loading broker that he had the ship-owner's authority to make the statement. This constituted an offer, at large, accepted by the purchaser (plaintiff) taking up the bill of lading. Moreover, if the form of the statement is crucial, then the same reasoning would also apply to other statements of fact in the bill, but in *The Nea Tyhi*,[40] a statement that goods were "shipped under deck" was treated as a contractual undertaking. This sug-gests that the form of the statement is not critical.

---

[39] See para. 14–059, below.
[40] [1982] 1 Lloyd's Rep. 606.

The other strand of reasoning in *Churchill & Sim* is that the description of the goods originated with the shipper.[41] If so, then the reasoning only applies to statements which emanate originally from the shipper, such as description and apparent quality. The shipper also states the quantity delivered into the carrier's care, but not the quantity loaded,[42] so in principle, *Churchill & Sim* might be argued not apply to quantity statements. Mocatta J. thought in *Rasnoimport* that the reasoning should be extended to quantity statements, on the grounds that "words in a bill of lading as to the quantity of goods shipped, like those as to their apparent order and condition, are not, whether made with or without the authority of the owners, words of contract in the sense of a promise or undertaking. They are at most an affirmation of fact or a representation." This, however, looks solely at the form of the statements; quantity statements are surely distinguishable on the grounds that the shipper need not be aware of their accuracy, and that it is the master who states the quantity actually loaded.[43]

It may also be usual for the carrier to state the shipment date, but not necessarily. In *The Almak*,[44] the issue (in effect) was whether shippers of cargo, who were also charterers of the vessel, could sue the shipowners on the carriage contract where the bill of lading had been backdated, the effect of the misstatement being to increase the price they paid under what was probably an f.o.b. sale contract. In refusing to imply such a term, Mustill J. was attracted by the following argument:

"One may begin with the most straightforward case, where a charterer, who is shipping goods for his own account, presents the bill of lading to the master for signature and retains it throughout the transaction. Here, since the inclusion of a wrong date in the bill tendered for signature must have involved a want of care on the part of the charterer, the test for an implied term will not be satisfied unless it can be shown that the charter-party will not work properly as a commercial contract without a term requiring the owner to take reasonable care to protect the charterer against the consequences of his own mistake. In my judgment, the matter has only to be stated in this way to show clearly that no such term need be implied. The straightforward commercial view of the situation is that if the charterer suffers damage through the misdating, he has only himself to blame."

No contractual duty arises, in other words, to check the accuracy of statements **14–020** which emanate from the other party. In this case, the shipment date must already have been on the bill of lading presented by the charterer for the master's signature. However, the shipment date will not always originate with the shippers, and if the statement emanates from the carrier, *Churchill & Sim* reasoning ought not to apply.[45] The reasoning may then be limited to statements of apparent quality and, perhaps, quantity.[46]

The principle that one party to a contract should not be presumed to warrant the accuracy of a statement made by the other party seems eminently reasonable,

---

[41] Presumably in the mate's receipt.

[42] The quantities differed in *Heskell* and *Rasnoimport*, the shipper being unaware in both cases that goods had been left behind.

[43] Note that s.4 of the Carriage of Goods by Sea Act 1992 merely makes them conclusive evidence against the carrier. It does not address the cause of action that follows from that. This would matter if the misstatement was innocently made, and not relied upon, since then only a contractual action would assist.

[44] *Rudolf A. Oetker v IFA Internationale Frachagentur AG (The Almak)* [1985] 1 Lloyd's Rep. 557. The facts are more complex than stated here, but the issues in essence boil down to these.

[45] This matters, because an estoppel is likely to be useless.

[46] *e.g.* Carver on *Bills of Lading* at 3–011 (applies reasoning to quantity), but *cf.* 2–007.

if it is assumed that those are the only two parties to the communication.[47] *The Almak* concerned only the relationship between shipper/charterer and shipowner, and in that context, the reasoning is beyond reproach. In *Churchill & Sim*, by contrast, the action was brought by a subsequent holder, yet the case assumes that the master is communicating with the shipper alone, and that the contract between shipper and shipowner is transferred with the bill of lading. But this is a terribly old-fashioned view of international trade. Since 1855 it has been known that the shipowner is potentially contracting with all holders of the bill of lading, and since *Leduc & Co v Ward*,[48] it has been known that the transferred contract is not necessarily the same as the original. If, as seems likely, *Churchill & Sim* has established a rigid rule, then the common law has got stuck in the early part of the nineteenth century, and is allowing trade practices of that time to influence the law of today.[49]

As an aside, the *Churchill & Sim* reasoning is also not easy to justify where a contract is separately implied, as in *Brandt v Liverpool*,[50] rather than being statutorily transferred, yet in that case the Court of Appeal followed *Churchill & Sim*.

In the event the purchaser won in *Churchill & Sim*, on the estoppel reasoning considered below, and it seems likely that had the master been negligent, there would also now be tortious liability (see also below). The lack of a contract action caused no injustice, therefore. However, both estoppel and tort depend on reliance, whereas (as we saw above) there will not necessarily be reliance by the holder. We also saw above that negligence by the master cannot be assumed. In any case, if the shipowner has made a statement to the holder, which can be interpreted as a contractual warranty, then he should be strictly liable in contract, just as the loading broker was in *Rasnomiport*. In the 21st century, it is surely reasonable to assume (as Mocatta J. did in *Rasnoimport*) that statements in a bill of lading will be communicated other than to the original shipper, and that although the shipper should be expected to be aware of the facts, the subsequent holder will not. Moreover, though the statements are originally made by the shipper, they are confirmed by the master, and not merely as a ministerial act.[51] The master is not simply repeating what has been said to him.

Surely there is a case for arguing that this aspect of *Churchill & Sim* is regrettable, a potential source of injustice, and based on an outdated view of international trade.

(c) Estoppels

14–021　　In *Churchill & Sim*, the shipowner was, however, estopped from denying the truth of the statements as to apparent order and condition. He was therefore unable to resist a claim that the goods delivered were not the same as those loaded, so "not being able to deny that the goods were in good condition at the time of shipment, must pay the damage which was on delivery found to be done to the goods".[52] The estoppel does not depend on the statement being fraudulent, and no fraud was proved in *Churchill & Sim*. Nor, indeed, is it dependent on

---

[47] See also statements by Evans L.J. in *Trade Star Line Corporation v Mitsui & Co Ltd (The Arctic Trader)* [1996] 2 Lloyd's Rep. 449, at 458–459.

[48] (1888) 20 Q.B.D. 475.

[49] Bools regards the position as a historical quirk: *The Bill of Lading: A Document of Title to Goods* (LLP, 1997) pp. 118–119.

[50] *Brandt v Liverpool, Brazil and River Plate SN Co, Ltd* [1924] 1 K.B. 575.

[51] *Naviera Mogor SA v Societe Metallurgique de Normandie (The Nogar Marin)* [1988] 1 Lloyd's Rep. 412.

[52] At 251.

negligence. It does, however, depend on the purchaser relying on the representation. In *Silver v Ocean SS Co Ltd*,[53] where *Churchill & Sim* was adopted in the Court of Appeal, the court applied a presumption that someone taking up a clean bill relies on the statements in it, but it is clear that this presumption is rebuttable, for example, in the face of clear evidence that he would have accepted the bill of lading in any event, whatever statements it contained as to the apparent condition of the goods. In *The Skarp*,[54] the sale contract required the buyer to take up the bill in any event, submitting the dispute to arbitration, and Langton J. observed that the courts would not be astute to assume traders would break their contracts. We have also seen how it might be rational, on a rising market, for a purchaser to take up a bill of lading, even in the knowledge that the goods are non-conforming.

CREMER v GENERAL CARRIERS SA (THE DONA MARI)

Queen's Bench Division. [1974] 1 W.L.R. 341

The facts and issues were set out at para. 13–058, above. The plaintiffs successfully **14–022** argued title to sue on a *Brandt v Liverpool* implied contract. The damage had however occurred pre-shipment, and clean documents issued for the goods. The shipowner argued that the *Churchill & Sim* estoppel did not work, because there was no reliance on the statement in the bill of lading, as to the apparent order and condition of the goods; under the sale contract the purchasers would have been obliged to take up the documents anyway, even had they been claused.

Kerr J.: I therefore turn to the question whether the first and second plaintiffs can succeed against the defendants because the cargo was damaged on delivery in Bremen. Since this damage was due to the pre-shipment condition of the cargo, they can only do so on the basis that the defendants are estopped from relying on this defence by reason of the statement in the bills of lading that the goods were shipped in apparent good order and condition. The nature of this estoppel is well established . . . the only ingredient of this estoppel which is in issue is whether or not the [first] plaintiffs relied on the representation in the clean bills of lading in the sense of having acted on it to their detriment . . . The defendants . . . contended that . . . reliance was displaced by the fact that the [first] plaintiffs were in any event bound to take up the documents by reason of the terms of the contracts of sale . . .

Looking at the matter broadly, it seems to me contrary to all principle that an issue should be tried, as in the present case, between a carrier and a cargo owner in which the carrier seeks to say that by operation of law he can avoid liability under the contract of carriage because, on the true construction of a contract of sale to which he was not a party and of which he knew nothing, the holder of a clean bill of lading (which should have been claused by the carrier) would have been in breach and liable to

---

[53] [1930] 1 K.B. 416.
[54] [1935] P. 134. The decision was criticised, and not followed, in *The Dona Mari* [1974] 1 W.L.R. 341, Kerr J. observing that the terms of the sale contract should in principle be irrelevant to the relationship between cargo-owner and shipowner. No doubt they should, but they cannot be, as long as reliance is a requirement of estoppel.

pay damages to his supplier if he had rejected the claused bill, notwith-standing the fact that the court may be wholly satisfied that this would indeed have happened, as in this case. I therefore reject the defendants' submissions that the plaintiffs are not entitled to rely on the estoppel created by the clean bills of lading and delivery orders.

Notes

14–023   1. A point taken by the shipowners in *The Dona Mari* in respect of both buyers, was that the damage had occurred pre-shipment. As in *Brandt v Liverpool* itself, the buyers argued that the owners were estopped from so pleading, by virtue of their issue of clean bills of lading.

2. The owners claimed that no estoppel arose because the first buyer would have had to accept the bill of lading even if it had been claused, on the grounds that under the sale contract a quality and analysis certificate was to be regarded as final. Kerr J. did not accept this view of the sale contract, finding as a fact that had the bills of lading been claused as had the mate's receipts, the first buyer would probably have compromised with the shippers and paid only a lower price, and would not have presented the documents at all to the second buyer.

3. Even on the defendants' view of the sale contract Kerr J. indicated that he would have regarded the point as bad: it was enough that there was therefore a detriment in *fact* whatever the sale contract said. In principle, he thought that the position as between carrier and cargo owner should not depend on the inter-pretation of the sale contract, to which the carrier was not a party and of which he knew nothing.

4. No estoppel arose either in *The Skarp* (above), where the court took account of the clear terms of the sale contract, which barred the right of the buyers to reject the bills of lading. Kerr J. did not think *The Skarp* laid down any rule of law in that regard, but simply decided that no detriment had been suffered in fact in that case. In principle, there is a lot to be said for the view that the sale contract terms should be irrelevant, but one of the problems with estoppel reasoning is the detriment requirement. Necessarily, the sale contract could in some cases it could be relevant to the question whether there was a detriment suffered in fact.

Further observations on estoppel

Apart from the reliance problems, a more serious limitation, given that estoppel is not a cause of action, is that it assists only for representations the truth of which assist a pre-existing contract or tort claim. Effectively this limits its use to state-ments about the apparent condition of the goods on loading, and (subject to the discussion below) the fact of their having been loaded.[55] Suppose, however, the bill of lading is backdated. The purchaser may well be induced to take up and pay for goods which otherwise he would have rejected, for example if the market is falling, or because he needs the goods by a certain date to fulfil another commit-ment. The shipowner may be estopped from denying the truth of the shipment date stated in the bill of lading, but it is difficult to see that this could be of any possible use, except (perhaps) in an action for failure to proceed with reasonable despatch, where it is alleged that the goods have deteriorated on the voyage. Usually for backdated bills of lading, however, it will be necessary to show an alternative cause of action. As we saw above, sometimes there might (but will not

---

[55] In *The River Gurara* [1998] Q.B. 610, Phillips L.J. said (at 625): "Nor, prior to the Carriage of Goods by Sea Act 1992, did a statement in a bill of lading give rise to an estoppel against the shipowner: *Grant v Norway* (1851) 10 C.B. 665." This would surely have been because the master had no authority to make the statement, not because he was not estopped in principle.

always) be a contract action, since that aspect of *Churchill & Sim* does not always apply to the shipment date.

Another problem is that the estoppel method will not always fully compensate.[56] Suppose the market has fallen since the contract date and the purchaser would have rejected a claused bill. He would not have paid the contract price for the goods, let us say £X. The goods in the condition described in the bill are worth £Y, and the goods actually received £Z. *Churchill & Sim* reasoning calculates the loss as Y–Z. But the actual loss caused by the misstatement is X–Z. On a falling market Y is less than X; therefore the victim is not fully compensated. A tort action is necessary fully to compensate in these circumstances.

(d) Fraudulent and Negligent Misstatement

Suppose that, as in *Kwei Tek Chao*,[57] the shipment date is misstated, for example   **14–024**
August 31, 2002, whereas the goods were actually loaded on September 1st. If the contract was for goods shipped in August and the market is falling I would have rejected the bill of lading, had it truthfully stated the shipment date. My loss is the contract price less the (lower) market price. An estoppel will not help me. Whether I have a contract action depends on whether the contract reasoning in *Churchill & Sim* extends to shipment dates (see above), but in any case, it is not clear that it would compensate me for the market fall; goods shipped on September 1 are probably worth exactly the same as those shipped on August 31.

In *Kwei Tek Chao* the (c.i.f.) purchaser successfully sued the seller, but the seller's solvency might be doubtful, and in any case nobody wants to be left with an action against another trader abroad.[58] It is the shipowner's misrepresentation that has led to my loss; I should be able to recover from him.

If the representation results from the fraud of the master himself, then a deceit action will lie, as in *The Saudi Crown*.[59] Moreover, the shipowner can be vicariously liable, even though the master has acted fraudulently. It is well-established that where an agent is performing acts within his actual or apparent authority, for him to act fraudulently does not take him outside that authority.[60] In *The Saudi Crown*, the shipowner was held directly liable for the fraudulent misrepresentation of a shipment date, made by the master. Of course, the reasoning would apply to any fraudulent misrepresentation causing loss, not just to representations about shipment dates.

It is not clear whether liability would lie in the event of a negligent misrepresentation by the master, the fraud being that of another party, but in principle *Hedley Byrne* liability might arise.[61] In *Heskell v Continental Express*,[62] a bill of lading had been issued for goods which were not on board the ship at all,[63] due to the negligence of the loading broker. Devlin J. thought that the loading broker would not be liable in tort, but only because of *"Le Lievre v Gould*,[64] and other similar decisions which make it plain that negligent mis-statement can never give

---

[56] This would probably also have been true of contractual reasoning, on a falling market.
[57] In para. 7–033, above.
[58] In *Churchill & Sim*, being left to sue a foreign seller was regarded as a detriment for the purposes of establishing an estoppel.
[59] See para. 14–039, below.
[60] Sheen J. cited *Lloyd v Grace Smith & Co* [1912] A.C. 716. See also the discussion of *Grant v Norway*, below, which it was necessary for Sheen J. to distinguish.
[61] *Hedley Byrne & Co Ltd v Heller & Partners Ltd* [1964] A.C. 465.
[62] See para. 14–056, below.
[63] This was an application of *Grant v Norway*—see below.
[64] [1893] 1 Q.B. 491.

rise to a cause of action."[65] In *Hedley Byrne* itself, now as Lord Devlin he thought that[66]:

> "*Le Lievre v Gould* and all decisions based on its reasoning (in which I specifically include, lest otherwise it might be thought that *generalia specialibus non derogant*, the decision of Devlin J. in *Heskell v Continental Express Ltd*) can no longer be regarded as authoritative; and, when similar facts arise in the future, the case will have to be judged afresh in the light of the principles which the House has now laid down."

This suggests that a *Hedley Byrne* action should at least be regarded as a possibility. A master who negligently makes a false statement in a bill of lading can surely anticipate that it might be relied upon by a holder in due course, causing him economic loss, but *Caparo Industries Plc v Dickman*[67] tells us that it is not enough merely for economic loss to be reasonably foreseeable. There, the House of Lords was also reluctant to impose liability:

> "where a statement is put into more or less general circulation and may foreseeably be relied on by strangers to the maker of the statement for any one of a variety of different purposes which the maker of the statement has no specific reason to anticipate."

Here by contrast, however, the statement is circulated not generally, but only to those who will become holders of the bill, who will rely on the statement in a fairly obvious way.[68] *Caparo* is distinguishable, therefore. Ultimately, the question is whether there is an assumption of responsibility by the master to the holder of the bill of lading.[69] In the circumstances of today's trade, such a conclusion would surely be justified?

The passage from *The David Agmashenbeli*, below, also suggests the possibility of *Hedley Byrne* liability, although the duty of care would there have been owed to the shipper, and one of the reasons for the courts' reluctance to extend tort liability, the fear expressed in *Ultramares Corporation v Touche*,[70] of:

> " . . . a liability in an indeterminate amount for an indeterminate time to an indeterminate class"

would clearly not apply.

The tort action is not a panacea, though. It depends on reliance, and in the case of an innocent representation, as in *Rasnoimport*, there could of course be no liability in tort. For quantity statements, there is an additional problem, which might prevent the shipowner being vicariously liable, even where personal liability for a misstatement could be established against the master (see below).

(e) Nature of Master's Obligation to State Truth

14–025   The bill of lading in *Churchill & Sim* incorporated the American Harter Act (see para. 11–012, above), which imposed on the shipowners the duty to issue a bill of

[65] [1950] 1 All E.R. 1033, at 1042.

[66] [1964] A.C. 465, at 532, cited by Reynolds: (1967) 83 L.Q.R. 189, n. 16.

[67] [1990] 2 A.C. 605.

[68] Although it was not a *Hedley Byrne* case, the arguments against extension of negligence liability in *The Aliakmon*, at para. 13–073, above, might nonetheless be considered analogous, at least if floodgates is the perceived problem, the class of potential claimants being the same.

[69] *Henderson v Merrett Syndicates* [1995] 2 A.C. 145, *per* Lord Goff at 181; see also *White v Jones* [1995] 2 A.C. 207.

[70] (1931) 174 N.E. 441, at 444.

lading stating, among other things, "the apparent order and condition" of the goods. Of this Channell J. ("not without some doubt") made the following observation (at 437):

> "The 4th section of the Harter Act makes it the duty of the captain to insert in the bill of lading a statement as to the condition of the goods, and I agree that this means that he is to make a true statement; but I have a difficulty in seeing that the clause that the bill of lading is to be "subject to all the terms and provisions and to the exemptions from liability contained in" the Harter Act imports a contract that the statement as to the condition of the goods is true."

The Harter Act is of historical interest only, but Article III(3)(c) of the *Hague Rules* and *Hague-Visby Rules*, one of which is in force in most jurisdictions in the world, also requires the shipowner to issue a bill of lading (if demanded) showing "the apparent order and condition of the goods". Channell J. thought that he was obliged to make a true statement, but nevertheless was not required to warrant that the statement is true. This apparent paradox is only resolvable on the basis that the shipper can demand that the bill of lading be issued clean, if the goods are in apparent good order and condition. He has no interest in requiring the bill of lading to be claused, and suffers no loss if it is issued clean when it should have been claused. It also follows, however, that the shipowner is entitled to refuse to issue a clean bill, if the goods are not in apparent good order and condition.

Of Article III(3)(c), Evans L.J. said the following in *The Arctic Trader*:

> "This requires an accurate statement of fact. (We would reject [the shipowner's] somewhat extreme submission that the duty can be discharged by making any such statements, whether accurate or not.) It is moreover, in our judgment, an unqualified or 'absolute' contractual undertaking, not merely one which the shipowner, or the master, must take reasonable care to perform. However, since making an accurate statement as to the apparent order and condition of goods may involve some degree of skill and expertise, though it does not necessarily do so, then in such cases the distinction between a duty to exercise reasonable skills and care in making an accurate statement, on the one hand, and a contractual duty to base the statement on the exercise of reasonable skill and care, is of no practical relevance. But one should not, in our judgment, lose sight of the fact that the duty is to make an accurate statement in the circumstances of the case."

The issue arose directly in *The David Agmashenbeli* (see below) where the shipper claimed that a bill of lading had been wrongly claused, when it should have been issued clean.

THE DAVID AGMASHENBELI

Commercial Court. [2002] E.W.H.C. 104 (Admiralty)

The master insisted on clausing a bill of lading for a cargo of urea, to show that it was discoloured. The cargo-owners claimed that they were entitled to clean bills of lading, and sued the shipowner for loss incurred.   **14-026**

Held:
The master was required to exercise his own judgment on the appearance of the cargo being loaded. On the facts, though the master was in breach of his duty, the

cargo-owners failed to establish that the bill of lading should have been issued clean, and that the breach by the master had caused them any loss.

Colman J.:

Introduction

This action arises out of a dispute between cargo and shipowners relating to the nature of the duty of a master into whose vessel goods are loaded for carriage under a bill of lading contract as to the issue and clausing of bills of lading. In particular, it raises the question in what circumstances is a master entitled to decline to sign clean bills of lading.

The answer to that question is of considerable importance to the shipping industry. Clean bills of lading are essential documents for the purpose of triggering the right to receive payment under documentary credits issued in respect of contracts for the international sale of goods. If claused bills of lading are presented under such documentary credits they will ordinarily be rejected by the buyers' banks and sellers will be unable to obtain payment in the absence of special agreements with the buyers to permit the banks to make payment. Indeed, the inability of sellers to present clean bills of lading may operate as a repudiatory breach of the sale contract.

Conversely, if clean bills of lading are issued in respect of goods received by the vessel otherwise than in apparent good order and condition, the shipowners will be estopped as against an indorsee for value or against a person taking delivery against the bills from asserting that, at the time of loading, the goods were not in apparent good order and condition. In cases where the Hague-Visby Rules apply, and nowadays there are very few cases where they do not, a clean bill of lading is, by operation of Article III rule 4, prima facie evidence of the receipt of the cargo by the carrier in apparent good order and condition and when the bill has been transferred to a third party acting in good faith it is conclusive evidence of the apparent order and condition. Consequently, issue of a clean bill when the goods are not in truth in apparent good order and condition will in many cases expose the shipowners to a high risk of liability for defects in the order or condition of the goods which existed at the time when they were received by the vessel.

It may therefore fairly be said that the statement in bills of lading as to the apparent order and condition of the goods will in many cases be of fundamental importance to the operation of international contracts for the sale of goods carried by sea and to the operation of contracts for the carriage of goods by sea. Whereas it is common enough to encounter an allegation that a master has issued clean bills of lading notwithstanding the apparent condition of the goods when they were received on board, it is relatively uncommon to encounter an allegation, like that in the present case, that the master has claused bills of lading when he had no basis for doing so. . . .

The Clausing Issue: the Duty of the Shipowners

The claimants' submissions may be summarised as follows: **14–027**

(i) Article III rule 3 of the Hague-Visby Rules, which both sides accept were incorporated into the bill of lading contract, provides as follows: SU11'After receiving the goods into his charge, the carrier, or the master or agent of the carrier shall, on demand of the shipper, issue to the shipper a bill of lading showing, among other things—

"(c) The apparent order and condition of the goods . . . "

In particular, it is not sufficient for the bills of lading to show the apparent order and condition which the master or other agent of the carrier honestly believed them to be in if the description does not accurately describe the actual apparent order and condition.

(ii) The claimants argue that, as a matter of principle, the commercial function of a bill of lading demands that it should objectively accurately describe the apparent order and condition of the goods. To limit the duty to one of honesty would greatly decrease the utility of a bill of lading as a key document in particular as a negotiable instrument under the sale contract and as evidence of the condition.

(iii) The claimants rely in particular on the judgment of the Court of Appeal in *The Arctic Trader* [1996] 2 Lloyd's Rep. 449 at pp. 456 to 459 and in particular the passage at p. 458R in which Evans L.J. described as an "unqualified or absolute contractual undertaking" the duty of the owners to the shipper under Article III(3) to issue on demand a bill of lading which stated the apparent order and condition of the goods.

(iv) The claimants further rely on a passage from the judgment of Channell J. in *Compania Naviera Vasconzada v Churchill & Sim* [1906] 1 K.B. 237 at p. 245 which refers to the "duty" imposed on the master under the Harter Act, s.4, to insert in the bill of lading a "true statement" as to the condition of the goods.

(v) Alternatively, apart from the Hague Visby Rules, there was an implied term of the contract of carriage under which the owners were under a duty to the shippers that the master would only sign bills of lading which accurately stated the apparent order and condition of the goods, the specific duty of the master being to exercise the judgment of a responsible and reasonable ship's officer when assessing the apparent order and condition of the goods and when deciding whether or not to clause the bills of lading. In this connection the claimants rely on *The Arctic Trader, supra*, at p. 456L, *The Hawk* [1999] 1 Lloyd's Rep. 176 at p. 185R and the earlier decision of the Court of Appeal in *The Nogar Marin* [1988] 1 Lloyd's Rep. 412 at p. 422.

(vi) If the master is unsure whether to clause the bills of lading, the claimants submit that he should take advice, if necessary, from a source independent of the shippers.

(vii) Apart from the terms of the contract of carriage, the owners, through their master were under a duty of care in tort owed to the shipper to exercise reasonable care not to misrepresent in the bills of lading the apparent order and condition of the goods. The claimants rely on the developing law with regard to liability for negligent misstatements following *Hedley Byrne v Heller & Partners* [1964] A.C. 465 and *Caparo v Dickman* [1990] 2 A.C. 605, culminating in *Spring v Guardian Assurance* [1995] 2 A.C. 296. It is submitted that the three tests in *Caparo* are satisfied. In particular (a) loss to the shipper/holder caused by inaccurate clausing is reasonably foreseeable; (b) a relationship of proximity exists between the shipper/holder and the carrier arising out of their direct relationship as parties to the bill of lading contract and (c) it is fair, just and reasonable to impose a duty of care for otherwise the shipper/holder cannot use the bill of lading for one of its most important purposes, namely as a negotiable instrument and cannot recover damages from the shipowner whose negligence has caused the loss.

(viii) The claimants further support their submission on duty of care by reference to the considerations identified by Neill L.J. in *James McNaughton Paper Group v Hicks Anderson* [1991] 2 Q.B. 113 at p. 125. In particular they submit that:

(a) the master's statement as to the apparent order and condition of the goods is made for the purpose of the indorsement of the bill as a key document in the transfer of title to the goods conformably with a sale contract;

(b) that statement is communicated for the purpose of sending it to the shipper who is an immediate party to the bill of lading contract and not a remote party;

(c) the relationship between the shipowner, shipper and any subsequent holder is a direct contractual relationship and the imposition of a duty of care would not conflict with any pre-existing or relevant contractual matrix, there being hypothetically, no alternative remedy for the shipper;

(d) the fact that the Hague-Visby Rules do not, on the relevant hypothesis, provide a remedy for the failure of a master to exercise reasonable care in respect of the issue of clean or claused bills of lading does not lead to the conclusion that there is no room for the co-existence of a duty in tort, for the function of the Rules is to identify an irreducible minimum obligation regime which cannot be diminished by contract. For example, there is the parallel duty of the carrier as bailee at Common Law;

(e) the class of those to whom any such duty of care would be owed is very small, namely the shipper and holders of the bill;

(f) the master as representor must know that the shipper and holders will rely on the accuracy of his statement for the purposes of transference of the bill as evidence of the apparent condition of the goods and as a document of title;

(g) it was reasonable for the shipper, as representee, to rely on the exercise of reasonable skill and care by the master in describing the apparent order and condition of the goods because the shipper is entirely in the master's hands in relation to clausing.

(ix) Finally, the claimants submit that there was a duty of care arising from the relationship of bailment between the shipper as bailor and the master as bailee.

The defendants' submissions are as follows: **14–028**

(i) For the purposes of the representation as to the apparent order and condition of the goods to be stated in the bill of lading by reason of Article III(3) what matters is not the actual apparent order and condition but what the representor as an ordinary and reasonably skilled master reasonably and honestly believes to be the apparent order and condition. For this purpose the master is not required to be a cargo surveyor or expert or to conduct tests or even a detailed examination or to engage cargo experts to advise him.

(ii) In any event, the representation in a bill of lading as to the apparent order and condition of the cargo does not give rise to a contractual undertaking either as to its accuracy or as to the skill and care employed by the master in reaching the conclusion expressed in the representation.

(iii) In support of proposition (i) the defendants rely on *C.N. Vasconzada v Churchill & Sim, supra*, at p. 245, and the observation of Channell J. in relation to the Harter Act, s.4, as an unskilled person the master is expected "to notice the apparent condition of the goods but not their quality" and to qualify the standard words of the bill, "shipped in good order and condition" . . . "according to the truth", which, the defendants say, means conforming with the sincere and honest belief of the master. They also rely on the judgment of Scrutton L.J. in *Silver v Ocean Steamship Co Ltd* [1930] 1 K.B. 416 at pp. 425–426 approving the judgment of Sir Robert Phillimore in *The Peter de Grosse* (1875) 1 P.D. 414 at p. 420 that "shipped in apparent good order and condition" means that "apparently and so far as met the eye, and externally they were placed in good order on board", and further on the observations of Greer L.J. at p. 434—"such reasonable examination as can be expected when goods of this kind are delivered for shipment under the conditions necessarily prevailing, that is to say, delivery by night" and of Slesser L.J. at p. 439—"what was apparent to anyone". They also rely on the judgment of Branson J. in *National Petroleum Co v Athelviscount* (1934) 48 Ll.L. Rep. 164 at p. 170.

14–029   (iv) In support of proposition (i) the defendants also relied on a number of Continental and American authorities. The decision of the High court at Brussels in *The S.S. Rosario* (3 Nov 1967) is summarised as concluding:

> "In order to satisfy his legal obligation to describe the apparent order and condition of the goods in the bill of lading, the Master is not held to be a surveyor or to proceed to research and exhaustive examination.
>
> When there is nothing to stop the conclusion that a superficial thawing of frozen meat would not but escape a normal examination by a competent and conscientious Master, the latter cannot be held liable for having omitted to insert exceptions in the bill of lading."

(v) Mr Hofmeyr Q.C. on behalf of the defendants also unearthed the decision of the US District Court for the Southern District of New York in Sidney J. *Groban and Union Tractor Ltd v S.S. Pegu and Elder Dempster Lines Ltd* (1971) 331 F. Supp. 883 in which the issue was whether the master had claused the bills so as to indicate adequately the apparent order and condition of a cargo of tractor parts by the words "cargo loaded in secondhand condition". I shall have to return to this decision in this judgment. However, it was observed that the carrier was under no obligation to detail the specific reasons for that description. The ship's officers "could scarcely be expected to be expert in describing the condition of a shipment of tractor parts such as this. The bill . . . was claused to indicate the condition of the goods as it reasonably appeared to them".

(vi) It is submitted these cases support the proposition that all that a master is required to do is honestly to state the external condition of the cargo as it meets the eye of a master who is not an expert in the cargo in question.

(vii) As to proposition (ii) that the statement as to the apparent order and condition of the goods are not words of contract, the Defendants rely on the judgment of Channell J. in *C.N. Vasconzada v Churchill and Sim*, *supra*, in relation to s.4 of the Harter Act and in particular the following passage at pp. 246–247:

"It seems to me that the contract is to deliver the goods in the same condition as that in which they are shipped, coupled with an acknowledgment that the condition at the time of shipment, was good. The words 'shipped in good order and condition' are not words of contract in the sense of a promise or undertaking. The words are an affirmation of fact, or perhaps rather in the nature of an assent by the captain to an affirmation of fact which the shipper may be supposed to make as to his own goods. So far, therefore, as the words of the bill of lading, apart from the incorporation of the Harter Act, are concerned, I see no contract that the condition of the goods is correctly described. The 4th section of the Harter Act makes it the duty of the captain to insert in the bill of lading a statement as to the condition of the goods, and I agree that this means that he is to make a true statement; but I have difficulty in seeing that the clause that the bill of lading is to be 'subject to all the terms and provisions and to the exemptions from liability contained' in the Harter Act imports a contract that the statement as to the condition of the goods is true. I think, therefore, though not without some doubt so far as the effect of the incorporation of the Harter Act is concerned, that the cause of action must be based on estoppel, and not on breach of contract".

(viii) The Defendants also rely on observations of Devlin J. in *Heskell v Continental Express* (1950) 83 Ll.L. Rep. 438 at p. 455 and of Mocatta J. in *V/O Rasnoimport v Guthrie & Co Ltd* [1966] 1 Lloyd's Rep. 1 at p. 7R to the effect that "words in a bill of lading as to the quantity of goods shipped, like those as to their apparent order and condition are not ... words of contract in the sense of a promise or undertaking. They are at most an affirmation of fact or a representation."

(ix) In *The River Gurara* [1998] Q.B. 610 at 625 Phillips L.J. held that as a matter of construction of Article III of the Hague Rules "an unqualified description of the goods in the bill of lading does not constitute a binding agreement between the shipper and the carrier that the goods have been shipped as stated, but merely *prima facie* evidence of that fact." The defendants rely strongly on Article III(3) which they submit contains no requirement of accuracy in such statements and rule 4 which explicitly defines the function of the statement in the bill of lading as "prima facie evidence of the receipt by the carrier of the goods as therein described ... "

(x) The Defendants criticise the judgment of Evans L.J. in the Court of Appeal in *The Arctic Trader* [1996] 2 Lloyd's Rep. 449 at p. 458 in as much as it referred to an absolute contractual duty under Article III(3) to issue a bill of lading which stated the apparent order and condition of the goods. Such a duty was inconsistent with the wording of Rule 3(3) and (4). The latter expressly confined the consequences of the bill of lading stating the order and condition to be *prima facie* evidence of the facts stated and did not extend to any promissory effect. Further Rule 3(5) made it clear that, at least as regards marks, number, quantity and weight, the shipper having been deemed to guarantee the accuracy of what he informed the carrier, there could be no countervailing obligation of accuracy on the part of the carrier.

(xi) In *The Boukadoura* [1989] 1 Lloyd's Rep. 393 at p. 399L, Evans L.J. had held that there was an implied term of a charterparty that the bills presented by the charterer for signature should not contain a description of the goods which was known to be incorrect. By parity of reasoning the shipper must be under a similar duty to the owner in respect of the apparent order and condition of the goods as described in the bill.

The Clausing Issue: Discussion

14–030   It is necessary to keep in mind two areas of distinction which underlie the analysis of this issue.

First, a bill of lading has two distinct functions:

"(i) as evidence of the contract of carriage and (ii) as a receipt and document of title to the goods laden on board."

Secondly, whether the carrier's duty in respect of the statement in the bill of lading as to the apparent order and condition is of a contractual nature is a distinct issue from the question what scope that duty has and in particular whether it is duty of care or analogous to a duty of care or whether it is merely a duty honestly to state the apparent order and condition of the goods.

The starting point in this analysis is to identify the function of the statement of the order and condition of the goods in a bill of lading. For this purpose it is necessary to go back to the issue of the bill. It is the shipper or the shipper's agent who in the ordinary way tenders the bill to the carrier or the carrier's agent, usually the master, for signature. In so doing, the shipper invites the carrier to acknowledge the truth of the statement in the tendered bill as to the order and condition of the goods which the shipper has delivered into the possession of the carrier pursuant to the contract of affreightment. In determining whether the carrier by the master's or other agent's signature accepts contractual responsibility for the accuracy of the statement as to the condition of the goods it is relevant to take account of the fact that it is the shipper or his agent who is delivering the goods and that accordingly any such statement would be as to facts of which he must already have actual or imputed knowledge. Further, because the shipper already has that knowledge he cannot be said to rely on the accuracy of the statement. His requirement goes no further than the need to obtain from the carrier a receipt for the goods in appropriate form. The tender for signature of a bill which states the order and condition of the goods is thus an invitation to the carrier to express his acknowledgment of the truth of the statements in the bill. As such it is an invitation to make a representation of fact as distinct from a binding promise as to the accuracy of the represented facts. The purpose of making that representation is to record the carrier's evidence as to his receipt of the goods and as to their apparent condition when he did receive them for carriage. Given that bills of lading are negotiable instruments, the specific function of recording that evidence is to inform subsequent holders of the facts represented, for those facts are likely to be relevant to their exercise of contractual rights against sellers of the goods or, indeed, the carriers themselves.

Against this background, it is not difficult to see why it has been said in many of the authorities on the Harter Act, the Hague Rules and the Hague-Visby Rules that those codes stop short of imposing on the carrier any contractual obligation as to the accuracy of that which is stated in the bill as to the order and condition of the goods.

Moreover, the wording of Article 3(3), (4) and (5) of the Hague Rules and their successor, the Hague-Visby Rules, is clearly consistent with this analysis. It imposes a contractual duty to issue a bill of lading containing the information specified but by Rule 4 provides only that such statements are to be *prima facie* evidence of the facts stated. That is to say, it is always open to the carrier to adduce evidence displacing what would otherwise be concluded from the statements in the bill of lading. Where, however, the bill has been transferred to a third party acting in good faith there is an estoppel as to the accuracy of the statements: the carrier is precluded from proving the contrary. Whereas at common law the rules of estoppel may in certain circumstances preclude the carrier as against the lawful holder of the bill from the opportunity to displace such conclusion: *cf. C.N. Vasconzada v Churchill* [1906] 1 K.B. 237, and see generally Scrutton on *Charterparties*, 20th ed., pp. 111–112, there is no decision in any authority before *The Arctic Trader* which suggests that the carrier contractually warrants either the accuracy or the exercise of reasonable care in relation to the accuracy of such statements in the bill of lading.

The Arctic Trader, supra, raised the question whether there was to be implied into a time charter a term which imposed on the shipowners through their master a duty of care to clause mate's receipts if the cargo was not in apparent good order and condition. The arbitrator concluded that there was such a term and that the shipowners through their master were in breach of it. The Court of Appeal dismissed an appeal from Tuckey J. who allowed an appeal against the arbitrator's conclusion. He did so on the ground that there was no such contractual duty owed to the charterer or person who presented the bill of lading. The Court of Appeal concluded that the existence of such a duty was not relevant on the facts because the shipowners could not have been in breach of it. The shippers and charterers' agent had persuaded the master to issue mate's receipts which inaccurately stated that the goods were in apparent good order and condition. In any event, since the charterers knew that the condition of the goods was such that bills of lading ought to have been claused, they could not have suffered any loss by reason of the issue of clean mate's receipts. At pp. 458–459 Evans L.J. referred to the objections to implying such a term into a time charter in respect of statements in a bill of lading by reference to the observations of Mustill L.J. in *The Nogar Marin* [1998] 1 Lloyd's Rep. 412 at p. 421 in respect of what was described as the "unanswerable argument on causation". Against this background Evans L.J. left open the question whether there was any such implied term in the time charter (p. 459L).

The claimants rely heavily on a passage in the Court of Appeal judgment at p. 458L.

"The duty owed to shippers under art. III(3) of the Hague Rules is to issue, on demand, a bill of lading which states '(c) the apparent order and condition of the goods'. This requires an accurate statement of fact. (We would reject Mr Hamblen's somewhat extreme submission that the duty can be discharged by making any such statements, whether accurate or not.) It is moreover, in our judgment, an unqualified or 'absolute' contractual undertaking, not merely one which the shipowner, or the master, must take reasonable care to perform. However, since making an accurate statement as to the apparent order and condition of goods may involve some degree of skill and expertise, though it does not necessarily do so, then in such cases the distinction between a duty to exercise reasonable skills and care in making an accurate statement, on the one hand, and a contractual duty to base the statement on the exercise of reasonable skill and care, is of no practical relevance. But one should not, in our judgment, lose sight of the fact that the duty is to make an accurate statement in the circumstances of the case."

It is common ground that this observation was *obiter*. That the effect of Art. III(3) is to impose some contractual duty on the carrier is beyond argument. The master or carrier's agent must at least issue to the shipper on demand a bill of lading showing the specified information. Refusal to issue any bill of lading accurate or not in respect of the goods received on board would thus be a breach of the contract of carriage in respect of which the shipowner would be liable to the shipper. But that duty is more specifically defined in as much as Rule 3(a), (b) and (c) specify those matters which the bill of lading is required to show, including "the apparent order and condition of the goods".

A refusal to issue a bill which made any statement as to the apparent order and condition of the goods would thus be a failure to comply with the contractual obligation imposed by the rule.

14–031   If there is a contractual obligation to the shipper that the bill of lading should state the apparent order and condition of the goods, how is that duty to be performed? In my judgment, the general effect of the authorities is that the duty requires that the master should make up his mind whether in all the circumstances the cargo, in so far as he can see it in the course and circumstances of loading, appears to satisfy the description of its apparent order and condition in the bills of lading tendered for signature. If in doubt, a master may well consider it appropriate to ask his owners to provide him with expert advice, but that is a matter for his judgment. In the normal case, however, he will be entitled to form his own opinion from his own observations and the failure to ask for expert advice is unlikely to be a matter of criticism. For this purpose the law does not cast upon the master the role of an expert surveyor. He need not possess any greater knowledge or experience of the cargo in question than any other reasonably careful master. What he is required to do is to exercise his own judgment on the appearance of the cargo being loaded. If he honestly takes the view that it is not or not all in apparent good order and condition and that is a view that could properly be held by a reasonably observant master, then, even if not all or even most such masters would necessarily agree with him, he is entitled to qualify to that effect the statement in the bill of lading. This imposes on the master a duty of a relatively low order but capable of objective evaluation. However, the defendant's submission that he need do no more than honestly state his view is, in my judgment, to put it too low, although no doubt in most cases the result will be the same. Nevertheless, the master who honestly takes an eccentric view of the apparent condition of the cargo which would not be shared by any other reasonably observant master would not be justified in issuing bills of lading which were qualified to reflect his view. In so far as the observations of the Court of Appeal in *The Arctic Trader, supra,* which were strictly *obiter,* suggest any higher duty on the master, I am not persuaded that they accurately express the effect of Article III(3).

Likewise, the extent to which and the terms in which the master considers it appropriate to qualify the bills of lading statement as to the order and condition of the cargo is again a matter for his judgment. Reasonably careful masters might use different words to describe the reason why and the extent to which the cargo was not in their view in apparent good order and condition. In many cases they may only have a limited command of English and little knowledge of the nature of the cargo. The approach which, in my judgment, properly reflects the master's duty is that the words used should have a range of meaning which reflects reasonably closely the actual apparent order and condition of the cargo and the extent of any defective condition which he, as a reasonably observant master, considers it to have.

Against this background, the shipowners' duty is to issue a bill of lading which records the apparent order and condition of the goods according to the reasonable assessment of the master. That is not, as I have indicated, any contractual guarantee of absolute accuracy as to the order and condition of the cargo or its apparent order and condition.

There is no basis, in my judgment, for the implication of any such term either on the proper construction of Article III(3) or at common law. The shipper is taken to know the actual apparent order and condition of his own cargo. What the Hague-Visby Rules require is no more than that the bill of lading in its capacity of a receipt expresses that which is apparent to the master or other agent of the carrier, according to his own reasonable assessment.

In the present case the mate's receipt was necessarily the basis of the statement as to the order and condition of the goods in the bill of lading and there is therefore no practical reason to distinguish between the duty owed by the shipowners in respect of what the master wrote on the mate's receipt and that which in consequence was stated in the bills of lading.

No doubt where a master proposes to qualify the statement as to the good order and condition of the cargo in a mate's receipt or bill of lading it would be sensible for him to warn the shipper's representative that he proposes to do so. That is a matter of common sense so as to give the opportunity to avoid disputes which may involve delays to the vessel, but in the last resort it is the master's own judgment which is to be recorded and it is open to him to record it by words which reasonably reflect that judgment.

14–032   As to the Claimant's submission that there is a duty of care upon the carrier through the master or other agent accurately to state the apparent order and condition of the cargo, I am not persuaded that the application of now well-established considerations relevant to the existence of such a duty lead to that conclusion. The starting point is that the relationship between the shipper and the carrier is such that the knowledge of the actual apparent condition of the cargo is possessed by both parties. The purpose of the requirement that the carrier should record in the bill of lading the order and condition as it appears to the master is to enable the shipper to transmit that information by means of the bill to subsequent holders of the bill to enable them to facilitate its functions as a document of title to the goods and as a mode of assignment of the contract of affreightment. That function is reflected in the requirements of the Code set out in Article III(3). That is an international code which has created an internationally known duty regime to the effect that all holders of bills of lading subject to the Hague Rules or Hague-Visby Rules can be expected to know that, when bills of lading are presented to them, the statements as to the apparent order and condition of the cargo can be relied upon to reflect the reasonable judgment of a reasonably competent and observant master in all the circumstances. There is no reason why, if the master consciously exercises his judgment in the manner which I have described, there should be superadded to that obligation a duty of care which would impose upon him any stricter obligation than that. If the master fails to comply with the contractual duty of properly exercising his judgment, the shipper will have his remedy against the carrier for breach of contract. If a stricter duty were to be imposed, there would be a real danger that the master would inevitably be driven to conduct detailed investigations of the cargo as it was loaded and to consult expert advice as to whether and how he should clause the bills of lading and that carriers would often be subjected to a time-consuming exercise which would in any case add little or nothing to what could be expected from the master using his own judgment. This prospect would involve objectionable interference with the speedy movement of cargo and vessels and would at best be likely to offer only marginal advantages in the accurate observation and recording of the order and condition of the cargo.

For these reasons, I consider that, at least where the Hague Rules or Hague Visby Rules govern the bills of lading, the third "test" in *Caparo v Dickman, supra*,—that it is fair, just and reasonable to impose a duty of care in all the circumstances is not satisfied.

Nor do I consider that where the Hague Rules or Hague-Visby Rules apply there is any room for a term to be implied in the contract of carriage imposing on the carrier any higher duty than that required under Art. 3(3). The implication is not necessary for the proper working of the contract of carriage or for the use of the bill of lading as a document of title or as a means of assigning the contract. Similarly, the relationship of bailment being on the terms contained in Art. 3, there is no conceptual justification for introducing any higher duty. The issue of a bill of lading recording the apparent order and condition of the goods is purely ancillary to the bailment: it has no bearing on the care of the goods and I see no reason why it should attract the duty of care which rests upon a bailee in consequence of the bailment relationship.

[*Colman J. then applied these tests to the facts.*]

Note

There was a secondary issue, on the Carriage of Goods by Sea Act 1992, s.2.

(4) Statements as to Quantity

(a) Grant v Norway

Since the shipper ought normally to know the quantity of goods shipped,[71] and to originate the statement of quantity in the bill of lading, *Churchill & Sim* would suggest that statements by the shipowner as to the quantity of goods shipped should not normally be contractual statements. Yet quantity statements are statements of fact, and if relied upon by the holder of the bill, ought to trigger the estoppel reasoning from that case, but only if the statement in the bill of lading can be attributed to the shipowner. However, the well-known case of *Grant v Norway* established that the master has neither actual nor apparent authority to issue bills of lading for goods which are not loaded on board the ship. Thus, at common law at least, a shipowner will not be bound by a statement in a bill of **14–033**

[71] Not necessarily, since what he left with the carrier may not have been loaded, as in *Heskell*. (There was no carriage contract in *Heskell*, however.)

lading (whether fraudulent, negligent or innocent) issued where no goods have been shipped, nor one which overstates the quantity of goods shipped.

GRANT v NORWAY

Court of Common Pleas. (1851) 138 E.R. 263

14–034 The master signed bills acknowledging the shipment of 12 bales of silk which were never shipped. The plaintiffs had taken the bills of lading as security against a pledge. They sued the shipowners in tort.

Held
The shipowner was not liable. The master had no authority, by signing and issuing bills of lading, to bind the shipowner for goods which were not aboard the ship.

JERVIS C.J.: The master is a *general agent* to perform all things relating to the usual employment of the ship: and the authority of such agent to perform all things *usual in the line of business in which he is employed*, cannot be limited by any order or direction not known to the party dealing with him . . .

Is it then, usual in the management of a ship carrying goods or freight, for the master to give a bill of lading for goods not put on board? For, all parties concerned have a right to assume that agent has authority to do all which is usual. The very nature of a bill of lading shows that it ought not to be signed until goods are on board; for, it begins by describing them as *shipped*. It was not contended that such a course was usual. In *Lickbarrow v Mason* [see para. 6–044, above] Buller J. says:

> "A bill of lading is an acknowledgement by the captain, of having received the goods on board his ship: therefore, it would be a fraud in the captain to sign such bills of lading, if he had not received the goods on board; and the consignee would be entitled to his action against the captain for his fraud."

It is not contended that the captain had any real authority to sign bills of lading, unless the goods had been shipped: nor can we discover any ground upon which a party taking a bill of lading by indorsement, would be justified in assuming that he had authority to sign such bills, whether the goods were on board or not.

. . . a party taking a bill of lading, either originally, or by indorsement, for goods which have not been put on board, is bound to shew some particular authority given to the master to sign it.

Notes
14–035   The case decides that a ship's master has neither the actual nor ostensible authority of the shipowner to sign bills of lading for goods which are not loaded on board the ship. By analogy bills neither can bills issued by loading brokers or

charterers' agents bind shipowners or charterers for goods not loaded on board the ship.

It is, of course, perfectly reasonable for a shipowner to defend an action, whether in contract or tort, or founded on an estoppel, by saying that he did not make the statement; the master did. Under normal circumstances, the master will not have actual authority to make any false statements, but "[a]ctual authority and apparent authority are quite independent of one another",[72] and the general principle is that a principal will be bound by statements which are within the usual authority of his agent to make, even if they are made wrongfully, or indeed fraudulently. In the case of a ship's master, then, the issue is what is his usual authority? It might reasonably be thought to encompass (for example) making statements in bills of lading as to the description of the goods, and their apparent (but not actual) order and condition, shipment date, and whether they have been loaded on or under deck. The same might also be said of the statement that the goods have been loaded on board, but for that last, *Grant v Norway* tells us otherwise.

I suggested earlier that one of the problems in this area of law is that the principles have become ossified. Twenty-first century law is being dictated to by nineteenth century trading practice. Issues which should really be of fact, or at least capable of changing with general trends in trade practice, were established in the nineteenth and early twentieth centuries, and have not been allowed to adapt. *Grant v Norway* proceeded on a narrow view of agency, the master's authority being defined by the usage of trade and the general practice of ship-masters, almost certainly a narrower test than a definition in terms of the scope of a general authority, as adopted by the House of Lords in *Lloyd v Grace Smith & Co*.[73] This case concerned the vicarious liability of a master for the tortious acts of his servant.[74] A firm of solicitors was liable for the conduct of its clerk, who was employed to conduct conveyancing transactions, but who in doing so defrauded one of the clients. Though clearly the clerk was not employed to defraud clients, and had no actual authority to do so, the basis of the master's liability was that he had a general authority to conduct conveyancing transactions, even though he had not the specific authority to act wrongfully.

Like *Grant v Norway*, *Lloyd v Grace Smith & Co* was an action in tort, rather than contract, but it is difficult to see why the test of ostensible authority should differ from that of course of employment for vicarious liability purposes. In *The Ocean Frost*, below, the Court of Appeal at any rate treated ostensible authority as co-extensive with course of employment for vicarious liability purposes (though statements in the House of Lords in the same case are in less general terms).

Grant v Norway almost limits the liability of the shipowner to the actual authority given to the master. Agency tests have widened since *Grant v Norway*; ostensible has diverged from actual authority, and indeed it seems likely the usage of trade and the general practice of shipmasters has changed since 1851. Ultimately, surely, tests as to apparent authority are a matter of fact, which can change over time and place. The decision also reduces the value of a bill of lading in the hands of an indorsee for value.

Yet at common law at least, the decision remains to this day set in stone, an anomalous nineteenth century rule operating in the twenty-first century world. Lord Esher purported to follow *Grant v Norway* in *Cox v Bruce* (1886) 18 Q.B.D. 147, and extended the reasoning to hold that the master or captain has no authority to bind the shipowner by statements as to "the particular mercantile quality of the goods before they are put on board". But there is no reason to

---

[72] *Freeman & Lockyer v Buckhurst Park Properties (Mangal) Ltd* [1964] 2 Q.B. 480, *per* Diplock L.J. at 502.
[73] [1912] A.C. 716.
[74] On this principle, masters can be sued for torts committed by their servants acting in the course of their employment.

assume a ship's master *would* have any knowledge of the mercantile quality of goods, whereas he ought to know whether they have been loaded on board. In other words, *Cox v Bruce* is probably consistent with ordinary principles of agency, and does not depend on the correctness or otherwise of *Grant v Norway.*[75]

The House of Lords approved *Grant v Norway*, in a different context, in *George Whitechurch Ltd v Cavanagh* [1902] A.C. 117, also discussed in *The Saudi Crown*, and it must be regarded as a correct, if anomalous and inconvenient authority.

(b) GRANT V NORWAY NOT EXTENDED

14–036   In recent years, the courts have refused to extend *Grant v Norway*, taking the view that it is out of line with out of line with the general law, and anomalous. In *The Nea Tyhi*,[76] for example, Sheen J. refused to extend the reasoning to a misstatement that goods had been shipped under deck, and in *The Saudi Crown*,[77] he held that the master had ostensible authority to issue backdated bills. It is now clear that *The Saudi Crown* holds, even where the bills were signed before the goods were loaded.[78] Nonetheless, in all these cases, *Grant v Norway* was accepted as entrenched authority, at least for the narrow proposition that a master has no authority to sign bills of lading for goods which are not loaded on board the ship. In *Rasnoimport v Guthrie*,[79] the purchasers were forced to sue the person in the position of the master, for breach of warranty of authority.[80] This will normally be pointless, but in *Rasnoimport* the defendants were loading brokers, and thus a substantial concern.

THE NEA TYHI

Admiralty Court. [1982] 1 Lloyd's Rep. 606

14–037 Bills of lading were issued by a charterer's agent, claused "shipped under deck", for goods which were actually shipped above deck. The goods were damaged by rainwater, and the indorsee sued the shipowners.[81]

Held:

1. The shipowner was bound by the statement in the bills, *Grant v Norway* being limited to the situation where the goods are not loaded on board at all. The plaintiffs could therefore succeed against the shipowner in contract.

2. An alternative action in tort also succeeded, but this aspect of the case can no longer stand in the light of the decision of the House of Lords in *The Aliakmon* (see para. 13–073, above).

[75] All relevant passages from *Cox v Bruce* can be found in the judgment in *The Saudi Crown*, below.
[76] See below.
[77] See below.
[78] *The Starsin* [2000] 1 Lloyd's Rep. 85. This aspect of the decision was not subject to appeal: [2001] 1 Lloyd's Rep. 437.
[79] See below. The usefulness of the breach of warranty of authority action is significantly reduced by s.4 of the Carriage of Goods by Sea Act 1992, especially if the damages reasoning in *Heskell* is correct, in one of the situations where the 1992 Act does not work.
[80] An action that worked precisely because of the rule in *Grant v Norway.*
[81] The charterers had gone into liquidation, but these were assumed to be shipowners' bills.

SHEEN J.: Mr Colman on behalf of the defendants commenced his **14–038** submissions on this question by saying that he relied upon the well-known case of *Grant v Norway*, which is authority for the proposition that a master or ship's agent has no ostensible authority to sign a bill of lading for goods not on board, and the shipowner cannot be held liable to a third party who relies upon such a statement. To those who are not familiar with the law relating to the carriage of goods by sea, but who are familiar with general principles of agency and, in particular, with the decision of the House of Lords in *Lloyd v Grace, Smith and Co* [see above] the decision in *Grant v Norway* may come as a surprise. But that decision has survived for 130 years and has been quoted with approval in the Court of Appeal and House of Lords; see *Kleinwort, Sond & Co v Associated Automatic Machine Corporation Ltd* (1934) 151 L.T. 1. Accordingly I am bound by it. The decision in *Grant v Norway* and the cases which followed it were fully considered in the judgment of Mocatta J. in *V/O Rasnoimport v Guthrie and Co Ltd* [see below]. It is unnecessary for me to repeat in this judgment all that Mocatta J. stated in that case. It is however noticeable that, in order to achieve a result which did justice in that case without declining to follow the decision in *Grant v Norway*, Mocatta J. was driven to complex and tortuous reasoning. I confess that I find it impossible to reconcile the decision in *Lloyd v Grace, Smith and Co* with the decision in *Grant v Norway*, and yet the earlier case cannot have been overlooked by the House of Lords when giving judgment in the later one. *Lloyd v Grace Smith* was decided at first instance by Scrutton J., with a special jury at Liverpool Assizes and he gave judgment for the plaintiff. Only two years earlier he had been Counsel in *Russo-Chinese Bank v Li Yan San* [1910] A.C. 174, in which case he had successfully relied upon *Grant v Norway*. The Court of Appeal by a majority, namely Farwell and Kennedy L.JJ., allowed the appeal. In the judgment of Farwell L.J. the decision in *Grant v Norway* and *Russo-Chinese Bank v Li Yan San* played a prominent part. In the House of Lords no mention is made of the decision in *Grant v Norway* in any of the speeches. The main speech was made by Lord Macnaghten, who was a member of the Privy Council in the *Russo-Chinese Bank* case, and who also wrote the principal speech in *George Whitechurch Ltd v Cavanagh*, [1902] A.C. 117 in which *Grant v Norway* was approved. I can only conclude that the decision in *Grant v Norway* is to be regarded as an exception and not as laying down a general principle. Indeed in *Uxbridge Permanent Benefit Building Society v Pickard* [1939] 2 K.B. 248 MacKinnon L.J. sought to rationalize the distinction between the liability of the principal in *Lloyd v Grace Smith* and the non-liability of the principal in *Grant v Norway* with the words:

" . . . anyone dealing with the captain of a ship must be taken to know that he has, and can only have, authority to sign a bill of lading for goods which have been in fact shipped, and therefore he can have no ostensible authority to sign a bill of lading for goods which have not been shipped."

I do not understand how the conclusion follows from the premise.

The decision in *Grant v Norway* is the first stepping stone in the submissions of Mr Colman. In this Court it gives him a firm foothold. But his next step is to say that the misdescription of the shipment, the erroneous statement that the plywood was under deck, is an act of such gravity of quality between shipowner and shipper that it is similar to a statement that goods have been shipped when in fact they have not been shipped. Mr Colman says that accordingly it should be treated in a similar manner and that no liability should fall on the shipowner. In order to tempt me to extend the protection to shipowners which is afforded by the decision in *Grant v Norway*, Mr Colman submitted that I have to decide which of two innocent parties should suffer and where the line should be drawn.

In the light of the comments which I have already made about the decision in *Grant v Norway* it must already be clear that I can see no justification for extending that protection. Furthermore there is a distinction between the case of a master issuing a bill of lading in respect of goods which have not in fact been shipped and the case of a master issuing a bill of lading which states that the goods are under deck when in truth they are on deck. In the former case the shipper ought to know that his goods have not been shipped, whereas in the latter case there is not necessarily any reason for the shipper to know that there is an erroneous statement on the bill of lading. If the shipper does know of the error in the bill of lading he has no right to endorse it to a purchaser for value. As to Mr Colman's submission that one of two "innocent" parties must suffer, if I had to choose whether the shipowners or the endorsee of a bill of lading should be the loser I would have no hesitation in saying that there is more reason that he who contracts with the charterer and puts trust and confidence in him to the extent of authorizing the charterer's agent to issue and sign bills of lading should be a loser, than a stranger. This principle was stated by Holt C.J. in *Hern v Nichols* in 1701.

In my judgment the charterer's agents had ostensible authority to sign bills of lading on behalf of the master. Accordingly that signature binds the shipowners as principals to the contract contained in or evidenced by the bills of lading. It follows that the defendants are liable in damages to the plaintiffs for breach of that contract. . . .

THE SAUDI CROWN

Queen's Bench Division (Admiralty Court). [1986] 1 Lloyd's Rep. 261

14–039   The plaintiffs were purchasers of just over 4,000 tonnes of ricebran extractions, which were loaded on board "The Saudi Crown", a vessel owned by the defendant shipowners. The sale contract called for bills of lading dated not later than 15th July 1982. Loading was not actually completed until July 26th, but the five bills of lading, issued by Rathaji Agencies on behalf of the owners, were dated 15th. Therefore at least some of the bills were falsely dated.

There was a conflict of evidence as to whether the bills were signed on 15th, before the goods were loaded, or were not signed until after all the goods were put on board, and backdated. Sheen J. found that they were not signed and issued until after all the cargo was loaded.

When the plaintiffs accepted the bills they were unaware of the true shipment date, and would have rejected them had they known. It later became clear that they could not use that cargo to meet other commitments, so they had to purchase a further 1,200 tonnes from other suppliers.

They claimed damages for misrepresentation from the shipowners.

Held:
The owners were liable in damages. *Grant v Norway* was again restricted.

SHEEN J.: It seems to me that if Rajathi Agencies were authorised to sign **14–040** bills of lading on behalf of the shipowners, as is admitted, they must have had authority to insert the name of the place at which and the date on which each bill of lading was issued. It is clearly within the authority of an agent to put the date of issue on a bill of lading. If that agent puts the wrong date on a bill of lading he must do so by mistake or deliberately. It can be assumed that the agent has no actual authority to insert the wrong date on a bill of lading, but the question is: can that affect any liability of the principal which may arise from the fact that his agent was within the scope of his apparent authority when inserting the wrong date?

In this context it is relevant to quote the words of Lord Robertson in *George Whitechurch Ltd v Cavanagh* [1902] A.C. 117, at p. 137:

"It seems to me extremely doubtful whether *Grant v Norway* can be held, or has ever been held, to represent the general law, or to do more than determine the law about ship-masters and bills of lading; and whether, assuming it to have the wider bearing, it is reconcilable with the doctrine of Lord Selbourne in *Houldsworth v City of Glasgow Bank*. I find it extremely difficult on principle to hold that the scope of an agent's employment can be limited to the right performance of his duties, or to say that an agent within whose province it is truly to record a fact is outside the scope of his duties when he falsely records it, when the question of liability to be decided is whether a loss is to be borne by the principal who placed him there, or by an innocent third party who had no voice in selecting him."

That passage is precisely in point in this action. It was within the province of Rajathi Agencies to record the date of issue on each bill of lading. One of the questions which arises is whether the loss resulting from a false statement as to that date is to be borne by the defendants, who employed Rajathi Agencies to act for them, or by the plaintiff, who had no voice in selecting that agent.

The general principle is well known. An innocent principal is civilly responsible for the fraud of his authorised agent, acting within his authority, to the same extent as if it was his own fraud. (See Lord Macnaughten in *Lloyd v Grace Smith and Co* [1912] A.C. 716 at p. 736.)

Mr Clarke contends that there is an exception to this general principle which affords protection to the defendants. He relies upon the decision in *Grant v Norway* which was approved by the House of Lords in *George Whitechurch Ltd v Cavanagh* [1902] A.C. 117.

In *Cox v Bruce* (1886) 18 Q.B.D. 147 at p. 151 Lord Esher said:

"That raises a question as to the true meaning of the doctrine of *Grant v Norway*. It is clearly impossible, consistently with that decision, to assert that the mere fact of a statement being made in a bill of lading estops the ship-owner and gives a right of action against him if untrue, because it was there held that a bill of lading signed in respect of goods not on board the vessel did not bind the ship-owner. The ground of that decision, according to my view, was not merely that the captain had no authority to sign a bill of lading in respect of goods not on board, but that the nature and limitation of the captain's authority are well known among mercantile persons, and that he is only authorised to perform all things usual in the line of business in which he is employed. Therefore the doctrine of that case is not confined to the case where the goods are not put on board the ship. That the captain has authority to bind his owners with regard to the weight, condition and value of the goods under certain circumstances may be true; but it appears to me absurd to contend that he has authority, though his owners really gave him no such authority, to estimate and determine and state on the bill of lading so as to bind his owners the particular mercantile quality of the goods before they are put on board, as, for instance, that they are goods containing such a percentage of good or bad material, or such and such a season's growth. To ascertain such matters is obviously quite outside the scope of the functions and capacities of a ship's captain and of the contract of carriage with which he has to do . . . Furthermore, I doubt very much whether the endorsee, being placed by the Bills of Lading Act [see chapter 13, above] in the same position as if the contract between the shippers and ship-owners had been made with him, can stand for this purpose in any different position from that of the shipper."

Putting the correct date on a bill of lading is a routine clerical task which does not require any skill. An erroneous date may be inserted negligently or fraudulently. There is nothing on the document to put its recipient on enquiry. The date may or may not be of any materiality. But when it is material, as in this case, it seems to me that great injustice may be done to the innocent third party if he is left to pursue whatever remedy he may have against a person of unknown financial means in some distant land. If I am driven to reach that conclusion I will do so, but not otherwise. I can see no ground for extending *Grant v Norway* to protect shipowners from liability for the errors of their duly appointed agents. It cannot be said that the nature and limitations of the agents' authority are known to exclude authority to insert the date on the grounds that the ascertainment of the correct date is "obviously quite outside the scope and functions or capacities" of those agents. It was immaterial that the misdated document was a bill of lading. The plaintiffs suffered loss as a result of a false statement made by the defendants' agents as to the date on which cargo was loaded.

If the bills of lading had been correctly dated the plaintiffs would have rejected them. In their claim for damages for misrepresentation the plaintiffs are not relying upon the rights of suit which they have by reason of being endorsees of the bills of lading [see chapter 13]. The complaint made by the plaintiffs is that they were induced to become endorsees by reason of a misrepresentation as to the date when the cargo was loaded. That misrepresentation was made by the agents of the shipowners in the course of their normal duties. It was a fraud committed by the defendants' representatives in the course of their employment.

Notes

Two specific points might be worth noting, because they relate to the discussion earlier in the chapter. First, the statement that the goods were shipped under deck in *The Nea Tyhi* was taken to amount to a contractual warranty. Secondly, once the misstatement had been attributed to the shipowner, there was no cause of action problem in *The Saudi Crown*, because it was made fraudulently. **14–041**

More generally, the effect of these decisions is (if anything) further to entrench *Grant v Norway*,[82] while refusing to extend it to statements other than quantity of good loaded. *Grant v Norway* continues to stand (apart from legislation), but only as an anomalous exception to general principles of agency.

It was not necessary in either or these cases to decide whether *Grant v Norway* would have applied where, at the time the bills of lading were signed, loading had not been completed. In each case, it was found as a fact that loading had been completed first. However, the issue of the pre-dated bill of lading did arise in *The Starsin*, where at first instance,[83] Colman J. refused to extend *Grant v Norway* to this situation:

"The defendant owners submit that the authority given by them to time charterers was to issue bills of lading in accordance with the mate's receipts and not otherwise. They rely on [clause] 8 . . . of the time charter which provided as follows: **14–042**

'8. The Captain (although appointed by the Owners), shall be under the orders and directions of the Charterers as regards employment and agency; and Charterers are to load, stow, trim, tally/lash/unlash/secure/unsecure/demurrage/undemurrage and discharge the cargo at their expense under the supervision of the Captain, who is to sign bills of lading for cargo as presented, in conformity with Mate's or Tally Clerk's receipts . . . '

. . .

The defendant owners submit that in as much as these bills of lading were antedated and were not claused to reflect the apparent condition of the goods as recorded on the mate's receipts, they were issued without their actual authority.

---

[82] Note that the speech of Lord Robertson in *George Whitechurch Ltd v Cavanagh*, quoted by Sheen J. in the above extract, was a dissenting speech, and that the House of Lords case followed *Grant v Norway* and extended it.
[83] [2000] 1 Lloyd's Rep. 85 (reversed on other grounds); [2001] 1 Lloyd's Rep. 437.

Further, there was no ostensible authority. The . . . authority point was to be approached on the basis that these bills were (a) owners' bills of lading (b) negligently completed by the local agents. The owners' case must therefore be that, so far as these claimants were concerned, the agents were not held out by the owners as having authority to sign bills which were incorrect as regards date or apparent pre-shipment condition. There was, it was argued, no evidence that these claimants had knowledge of the functions of the local agents as general agents for the owners. All they had to rely on was the bill of lading in each case and there was nothing in the bill to suggest that the agents had authority to issue bills which did not comply with the mate's receipt. Indeed, an indorsee could be taken to assume that a local port agent would not in the ordinary way have actual authority to issue such disconforming bills.

[Evidence was given] that it was common knowledge in the shipping industry that where a ship is time chartered the authority given to the charterer to issue bills of lading on behalf of the master is confined to bills of lading which adhere to any remarks on the mate's receipts and tally records and that specific letters of authority do not ordinarily authorise bills of lading to be issued by or on behalf of shipowners which permit disconformity with the statements in the mate's receipts. It was argued that such assumption would be inconsistent with ostensible authority in the absence of holding out to the contrary by the shipowner.

There can be no doubt that ostensible or apparent authority is founded upon the principal's representation to the party relying on the contract that the agent has authority to enter into it on the agreed terms. That representation may be made either specifically in relation to a particular contract or generally by reason of the principal's placing the agent in a ministerial position in which an agent would ordinarily have actual authority to enter into transactions of the kind in question: see generally *Armagas v Mundogas (The Ocean Frost)* [1986] A.C. 717 (see Lord Keith at p. 777 A–C).

In testing the presence of ostensible authority it is, however, necessary not to lose sight of the need to identify the scope of the representation. This is particularly so in the case of an agent who has been placed in a ministerial position in which one would normally be expected to have actual authority to enter into a particular kind of transaction. Thus, if a director of a company were authorised by the Board or other internal approval committee to enter into a contract with a supplier of goods on certain specific terms and due to a negligent oversight the director signed the contract on terms which omitted certain of the details included in the draft approved by the Board, or other approval body, it would normally not be open to the company to assert that it was not bound by the contract signed by a director who could normally be expected by a third party to have actual authority to bind the company to contracts of that kind. That consequence would follow from the scope of the representation arising from the company having placed the director in that position *vis-à-vis* the third party. The representation in such a case is not that the director is acting with the approval of the company in respect of each detail of the contract but that the transaction is one of a kind to which the director has authority to bind the company and that his conduct in relation to the entering into of transactions of that kind may be relied upon as conduct authorised by the company and as giving rise to obligations by which the company will treat itself as bound. Notwithstanding that the director may not have had actual authority to agree to the details of the transaction and that the third party may have appreciated that the director would ordinarily need such authority, the company will still be bound under the ostensible authority principle unless the third party knew that the director did not have the requisite authority.

14–043   This concept of ostensible or apparent authority based on the usual authority of a representative of the principal has for long been firmly implanted in

English commercial law outside the sphere of maritime contracts: see, for example, *Freeman & Lockyer v Buckhurst Park Properties (Mangal) Ltd* [1964] 2 Q.B. 480, *per* Diplock L.J. at p. 503.... I would hold that ... it would be unconscionable for a principal to deny that he was bound by a transaction which had been entered into apparently on his behalf by someone whom he had permitted to represent to third parties that he had the principal's authority to bind the principal to transactions of the kind in question. To permit the principal to rely on lack of actual authority in such circumstances to the prejudice of the third party would be to permit a similarly prejudicial inconsistency of conduct to that against which the law of estoppel is directed. Finally, the fact that the agent represents that he has that actual authority to enter into a contract of a kind which a person holding his representative position or appointment on behalf of the principal would have does not offend against the principle that ostensible authority cannot be based on a representation of actual authority given by the agent alone: see *The Ocean Frost per* Robert Goff L.J. at pp. 730–735 (CA) and Lord Keith at p. 777 (HL). This is because the representation in such a case is that attributable to the principal's conduct in placing his representative in a position to deal with the third party in respect of that kind of transaction.

It is against that background that the position of the time charterer and the loading port agent respectively authorised to issue bills of lading by the terms of the time charter and the master's letters of authority falls to be analysed. Once such a time charter has been entered into or letter issued, the shipowners have placed the time charterer or local agent in the position of their representative in respect of the issue of bill of lading contracts relating to the cargo to be loaded and have thereby indirectly represented to the shippers and to indorsees of the bills that they, the shipowners, have authorised the time charterers or agents to bind them to contracts of that kind. Consequently, the shippers and indorsees are entitled to assume that the owners are content to be bound by the terms of the bill even if, unknown to them, there was no actual authority to issue the bill in precisely the terms in which the bill was issued.

Furthermore, although it may be common knowledge that time charterers and local agents are not authorised to sign bills of lading which do not conform with the contents of mate's receipts, this does not assist the defendant owners for it has no impact whatever on the scope of their representation, namely of a general authority to sign bills of lading in respect of cargo loaded so as to bind the owners. The common knowledge that there would be no actual authority to sign clean bills against claused master's receipts does not disturb the basis for the time charterers' or agents' ostensible authority any more than the lack of board or other approval in respect of a supply contract in the example which I have given would disturb the ostensible authority of the director to bind his company to the kind of contracts which directors normally sign.

These being the underlying principles, are there any authorities which disturb this conclusion? **14–044**

The defendants rely on *Grant v Norway* (1851) 10 C.B. (N.S.) 665. That case decided that the master had no authority, actual or ostensible to bind the shipowner in respect of goods that were never shipped. The law has subsequently been changed by the Carriage of Goods by Sea Act 1992, s.4 [below], to enable a third party indorsee to rely on the bill of lading as binding in respect of goods even if not shipped. The defendants argue that by parity of reasoning, just as there is no authority to issue bills of lading for goods never shipped, nor is there authority to issue bills of lading dated before the actual date of shipment or which are clean when the mate's receipts were checked.

The decision of Rix J. in *The Hector* [1998] 2 Lloyd's Rep. 287 is also relied on. In two passages, at pp. 297L and 298R it was held *obiter* that where an owner puts his vessel under his time charterer' orders and directions regarding employment, he gives his time charterer ostensible authority to bind the owner by signing bills of lading on behalf of the master. He added, pertinently to the facts in that case:

'For these purposes, I would regard an owner as giving his time charterer ostensible authority to bind him (in signing bills of lading on the master's behalf) by reason of putting his vessel under his time charterer's orders and directions regarding employment. That is not simply a matter of private contract: it is reflected in the reality of what happens when a time chartered vessel enters port in order to load cargo. An owner in such circumstances holds out his time charterer as a disponent owner with powers over the employment of his vessel, and thus as having power to bind him by signing a bill of lading. However, my views to this effect are ultimately irrelevant, for in my judgment it cannot in any event be said that a time charterer has his owner's usual or ostensible authority to sign a bill of lading not in conformity with mate's receipts or to sign a predated bill of lading.'

Rix J. gave no explanation for this conclusion, no doubt because this part of his judgment was *obiter*. However, having regard to the principles to which I have already referred, I am unable to agree with this view. In this connection also, the weight of such authority as exists is to the contrary.

In *The Nea Tyhi* [1982] 1 Lloyd's Rep. 606 the issue was whether the ship-owner was bound by bills of lading issued by time charterer's agents which stated that the cargo was shipped under deck whereas in truth it was shipped on deck. On the facts there was no actual authority and the major issue was whether there was ostensible authority having regard to the reasoning in *Grant v Norway, supra* Sheen J. declined to extend the scope of that decision to bills of lading which were inaccurate in the manner before him. While recognising that *Grant v Norway, supra*, had been approved by the Court of Appeal and the House of Lords in *George Whitechurch Ltd v Cavanagh* [1902] A.C. 117 and *Kleinwort Sons & Co v Associated Automatic Machine Corporation Ltd* (1934) 151 L.T. 1, Sheen J. held that it could not be reconciled with the decision of the House of Lords in *Lloyd v Grace Smith & Co* [1912] A.C. 716. No doubt Sheen J. had in mind that the policy considerations which underlie the imposition of contractual liability on the grounds of the usual authority of an agent as held out by the principal, which I have already discussed, are substantially the same as those which underlie the imposition of the vicarious liability of the employer in tort in respect of the fraud or negligence of his employee in the course of his employment. Whereas dislocation between the considerations giving rise to a contractual nexus and those giving rise to vicarious liability is certainly theoretically possible, it is acutely objectionable in principle given the similarity between the underlying policy considerations.

At p. 611L of his judgment Sheen J. drew attention to that passage in the judgment of MacKinnon L.J. in *Uxbridge Permanent Benefit Building Society v Pickard* [1939] 2 K.B. 248, in which he had attempted to rationalise the distinction between *Grant v Norway* and *Lloyd v Grace Smith*. Sheen J. commented that he did not understand how the conclusion (that there was no ostensible authority) followed from the premise (that anyone dealing with the Captain of a ship must be taken to know that he could only have authority to sign a bill of lading for goods which have been in fact shipped). In my judgment, this explanation is not consistent with the true conceptual basis of ostensible authority to which I have referred. The application of that basis would not lead to any distinction between the contractual rights acquired by the innocent shipper or consignee under a bill of lading issued by a time charterer or other agent clothed by the shipowner with authority to issue bills of lading generally, where the bill was issued negligently or fraudulently in respect of goods not shipped, (and therefore without actual authority) and the contractual rights of a third party in respect of a contract signed by an agent who had been placed by his principle in a position to conclude contracts of the kind in question. In this connection the words of Lord Robertson in *George Whitechurch Ltd v Cavanagh* [1902] A.C. 117 at page 137 are directly in point:

'It seems to me extremely doubtful whether *Grant v Norway* can be held, or has ever been held, to represent the general law, or to do more than determine the law about ship-masters and bills of lading; and whether, assuming it to have the wider bearing, it is reconcilable with the doctrine of Lord Selbourne in *Houldsworth v City of Glasgow Bank*. I found it extremely difficult on principle to hold that the scope of an agent's employment can be limited to the right performance of his duties, or to say that an agent within whose province it is truly to record a fact is outside the scope of his duties when he falsely records it, when the question of liability to be decided is whether a loss is to be borne by the principal who placed him there, or by an innocent third party who had no voice in selecting him.'

Accordingly, as the law has now developed, *Grant v Norway* should be treated **14–045** as conceptually aberrant and should not be used as a basis for the extension of the protection of shipowners against being bound by bills of lading issued by time charterers, or other agents on behalf of the owners, which by reason of some inaccuracy on their face, have been issued without actual authority. Not only does this conclusion give effect to the conceptual basis of ostensible authority but it also reflects a further important policy consideration. That is that if an innocent shipper, indorsee or consignee could not rely on statements on the face of a bill of lading as to such matters as the date of shipment and the absence of clausing and was obliged to verify the accuracy of the date and the apparent good order and condition of the goods each time he took a bill of lading, that would represent a most serious impediment to international trade which depends so heavily on the accuracy of bills of lading as negotiable instruments.

The conclusion at which I have arrived on this point is supported not only by the decision of Sheen J. in *The Nea Tyhi, supra*, but also by a decision of the same judge in *The Saudi Crown* [1986] 1 Lloyd's Rep. 261, in which he observed (at p. 265R of the former report):

[*Coleman J. quoted the passage from* The Saudi Crown, *above, beginning "Putting the correct date on a bill of lading is a routine clerical task which does not require any skill", and continued:*]

I have also been referred to the decision of H.H. Judge Diamond Q.C. in *The Hawk* [1999] 1 Lloyd's Rep. 176 and in particular to his observations at p. 185R as to the effect of the master issuing clean bills of lading in spite of the goods not being in apparent good order and condition—not, as he commented, a ground for concluding that the bills were unauthorised.

As to reliance on the shipowners' representation that the bill of lading contracts were in terms entered into with their authority, the evidence establishes that the claimants relied on the fact that the bills were clean, . . . and it is to be inferred that they were taken up in reliance on that statement being authorised by the carriers, that is to say the shipowners on this hypothesis. It is true that there is no mention in the statements of the claimants having relied on the accuracy of the dates of shipment. However, it is, in my judgment, a proper inference that the dates were relied on as accurate and represented as such with the carrier's authority: cf. *Silver v Ocean Steamship Co* [1930] 1 K.B. 417, *per* Scrutton L.J. at page 428 and Greer L.J. at page 434 with reference to clean bills. It is inconceivable that the claimants in the present case would have taken up the bills if they had known that the dates were inaccurate without first requiring fresh bills to be issued.

Accordingly, I hold that, if these were owners' bills, the fact that they were ante-dated and failed to conform with the notations on the mate's receipts does not prevent them from being binding on the defendant owners, the local agents having ostensible authority to issue bills of lading to the shippers of goods loaded on to the vessel."

14–046 Yet however restrictively the case has been interpreted, to the situation where goods mentioned in the bill of lading are never shipped *Grant v Norway* still applies, except to the extent that it has been curtailed by legislation.

(c) LEGISLATION

14–047 There have been three legislative attempts, in the UK, to overturn *Grant v Norway*. The first was s.3 of the Bills of Lading Act 1855, which (in the UK at least) is now of historical interest only (although it remains in force in parts of the common law world). It became clear, however, that s.3, providing as it did for neither cause of action, nor conclusive evidence of shipment, as against the shipowner, made no difference to the common law.[84]

BILLS OF LADING ACT 1855, S.3

14–048   . . . And whereas it frequently happens that the goods in respect of which bills of lading purport to be signed have not been laden on board, and it is proper that such bills of lading in the hand of a bona fide holder for value should not be questioned by the master or other person signing the same on the ground of the goods not having been laden as aforesaid:

3. Every bill of lading in the hands of a consignee or indorsee for valuable consideration, representing goods to have been shipped, shall be conclusive evidence of such shipment as against the master or other person signing the same, notwithstanding that such goods or some part thereof may not have been so shipped, unless such holder of the bill of lading shall have had actual notice at the time of receiving the same that the goods had not in fact been laden on board: Provided that the master or other person so signing may exonerate himself in respect of such misrepresentation by showing that it was caused without any default on his part, and wholly by the fraud of the shipper, or of the holder, or some person under whom the holder claims.

Notes

14–049   This section (which remains in force in parts of the common law world) was presumably intended to reverse *Grant v Norway* when the bill of lading had been transferred to a consignee or indorsee, but was ineffective to do so. It provided conclusive evidence only against the master, not the shipowner, and it provided

---

[84] There is extensive discussion of s.3 in *V/O Rasnoimport v Guthrie*. The reaction of the courts, to the admittedly poorly-drafted s.3, is definitely not an example of the mischief principle at work, and those who think judges bend the law to arrive at a fair result would be well-advised to look at the s.3 cases.

no cause of action, only conclusive evidence, even against him. But usually there would be no contract with the master personally, and no bailment in respect of the goods left behind. See further *V/O Rasnoimport v Guthrie*, below, where Mocatta J. was unable to find a cause of action against a loading broker in respect of which the conclusive evidence provision in s.3 could operate. The indorsee in *Rasnoimport* succeeded on another issue, but independently of s.3.

The *Hague-Visby Rules* (where they apply—see chapter 11, above) address the *Grant v Norway* problem more effectively, where a third party (subsequent holder) is involved. The important part is Article III(4), 2nd sentence:

" . . . a bill of lading shall be prima facie evidence of the receipt by the carrier of the goods as therein described . . . However, proof to the contrary shall not be admissible when the bill of lading has been transferred to a third party in good faith."

This appears to be effective in principle, although two difficulties could arise. First, the Article applies only to proof of *receipt* of the goods, not to their shipment, and secondly, if Devlin J. is right in *Heskell*, below, it may be possible to argue that where no goods at all are shipped, the bill of lading is a nullity, and there is no contract of carriage, so that the section may not be triggered at all.

More recently, the position has been addressed more comprehensively by s.4 of the Carriage of Goods by Sea Act 1992:

CARRIAGE OF GOODS BY SEA ACT 1992, S.4

A bill of lading which—   14–050

(a) represents goods to have been shipped on board a vessel or to have been received for shipment on board a vessel; and

(b) has been signed by the master of the vessel or by a person who was not the master but had the express, implied or apparent authority of the carrier to sign bills of lading,

shall, in favour of a person who had become the lawful holder of the bill, be conclusive evidence against the carrier of the shipment of the goods or, as the case may be, of their receipt for shipment.

Comment

Though this provision appears to deal with the problem, by attributing statements in para. (a) to the shipowner (or carrier), there are a number of ways in which this provision is deficient. The most obvious is that a bill of lading is defined, for the purposes of the Act, as a negotiable bill, and therefore statements in "straight" bills of lading, or waybills, are excluded.[85]

There are, however, less obvious problems. First, there is authority that a bill of lading, issued where no goods at all are shipped, is a complete nullity.[86] It represents no goods, and is not really a bill of lading at all. Therefore even the comprehensive 1992 Act will not apply to it. Moreover, where no goods are

---

[85] See s.1(2) in App. E, below.
[86] *e.g. Heskell v Continental Express Ltd.* See also *Hindley*, para. 14–005, above, at 518, *per* Kerr J. A forged bill of lading might also be a nullity: *e.g.* Stuart-Smith L.J. in *Motis Exports Ltd v Dampskibsselskab AF 1912 (Aktieselskab)* [2000] 1 Lloyd's Rep. 211. See also *The American Accord*, at 187–188 (*per* Lord Diplock).

shipped there may also be no contract of carriage,[87] and hence nothing for the Carriage of Goods by Sea Act 1992 to transfer. Neither of these arguments apply where some goods are shipped, but the bill of lading overstates the quantity. Here, the Act will apply, as long as a quantity is stated. However, its efficacy is severely curtailed by recent statements that qualifications in bills of lading, such as "weight or quantity unknown" negate statements of quantity altogether,[88] and the same might also be true of "said to contain".[89] A bill of lading fraudulently misstating the quantity of goods shipped as 10,000 tons will not represent the shipment of 10,000 tons when so qualified, and thus will not bind the shipowner where only 9,000 tons have been shipped.

AGROSIN PTE LTD v HIGHWAY SHIPPING CO LTD (THE MATA K)

Queen's Bench Division (Commercial Court). [1998] 2 Lloyd's Rep. 614

14–051 The bill of lading showed 11,000 tons of cargo loaded, "weight, measure, quality, quantity, condition, contents and value unknown." In an action for short delivery, Clarke J. held that the shipowners were not bound by any bill of lading quantity statement, even under s.4 of the 1992 Act. They had not, in fact, stated any quantity of goods loaded.

CLARKE J.: The plaintiffs' case depends upon satisfying s.4 of the Carriage of Goods by Sea Act, 1992 . . .

[*Clarke J. set out the section, and continued:*]

14–052   The plaintiffs' case is that the bill of lading described above meets those requirements. If it does, it follows that it is conclusive evidence in favour of Mitsui and against the defendants of the shipment of 11,000 tonnes of muriate of potash. It further follows . . . that it is conclusive evidence of that fact in favour of the plaintiffs as assignees of [notify party] Mitsui's rights, notwithstanding the fact that it would not be conclusive evidence in favour of the plaintiffs as shippers. I say nothing about the position as between the plaintiffs as charterers and the defendants as owners under the charter-party.

The essential question under this head is whether s.4(a) is satisfied, namely whether the bill of lading represents 11,000 tonnes of goods to have been shipped because, for present purposes, I assume that s.4(b) has been satisfied and that the plaintiffs had the express, implied or apparent authority of the defendants to sign the bill of lading on their behalf . . .

Does the bill of lading represent that 11,000 tonnes of muriate of potash were shipped?

If this question is to be answered on the construction of the bill of lading as it stands, the answer, in my judgment, is No. The reason is that given

---

[87] There was none in *Heskell*.
[88] *The Atlas* [1997] 1 Lloyd's Rep. 225, *The Mata K* [1998] 2 Lloyd's Rep. 614.
[89] *The River Gurara* [1998] Q.B. 610, though this issue was left open.

in a number of decided cases, namely that a bill of lading which states that 11,000 tonnes of cargo were shipped "quantity unknown" is not a representation that 11,000 tonnes were shipped. Any other conclusion would give no meaning to the expression "quantity... unknown".

The same point was put thus by Viscount Reading C.J. in *New Chinese Antimony Co Ltd v Ocean Steamship Co Ltd* [1917] 2 K.B. 664 at p. 669:

"Where in a bill of lading, which is prepared by the shippers for acceptance by the defendants' agent, the agent accepts in the margin a quantity 'said to be 937 tons,' and in the body of the bill of lading there is a clause 'weight, &c., unknown,' there is no *prima facie* evidence that 937 tons have been shipped. Sankey J. in my judgment omitted to give proper effect to the words 'weight, &c, unknown.' He based his judgment on the decision in *Smith & Co v Bedouin Steam Navigation Co* [1896] A.C. 70, but he omitted to notice that in that case a definite quantity was given in the bill of lading and that there were no qualifying words such as 'said to be' or 'weight unknown.' I think that the true effect of this bill of lading is that the words 'weight unknown' have the effect of a statement by the shipowners' agent that he has received a quantity of ore which the shippers' representative says weight of 937 tons but which he does not accept as being of that weight, the weight being unknown to him and that he does not accept the weight of 937 tons except for the purpose of calculating freight and for that purpose only."

In *Noble Resources Ltd v Cavalier Shipping Corporation (The Atlas)* [1996] 1 Lloyd's Rep. 642 Longmore J. rejected an argument that the same approach should not be adopted where the bill of lading contained no equivalent of "said to be" but only "weight unknown". He said at p. 646:

" . . . it is impossible to imagine that the *New Chinese Antimony* case would have been decided differently if the bill in that case had said merely 'weight unknown'; one has to construe the bill of lading to determine whether it is an unqualified assertion or representation of the shipment of a particular quantity of goods. If the bill of lading provides that the weight is unknown it cannot be an assertion or representation of the weight in fact shipped. Mr Jacobs said that the typed figures should prevail over printed 'weight unknown' but, if Russian bills are construed as a whole, they must be held to mean that the shipowners are not committing themselves, one way or the other, as to the weight of the cargo shipped."

Mr Davey invites me to refuse to follow part of the reasoning of Longmore J. in that case but not, as I understand it, that part. In any event I entirely agree with Longmore J. for the reasons which he gave. See also to the same effect *River Gurara (Cargo Owners) v Nigerian National Shipping Line Ltd* [1997] 3 W.L.R. 1128, at 1141 *per* Phillips L.J.

Notes

14–053   Clarke J. went on to consider the effect of the *Hague Rules*, Article III(3) and (4)[90]:

> "3. After receiving the goods into his charge, the carrier, or the master or agent of the carrier, shall, on demand of the shipper, issue to the shipper a bill of lading showing among other things— . . . (b) either the number of packages or pieces, or the quantity, or weight, as the case may be, as furnished in writing by the shipper; provided that no carrier, master or agent of the carrier, shall be bound to state or show in the bill of lading any marks, number, quantity, or weight which he has reasonable grounds for suspecting not accurately to represent the goods actually received, or which he has had no reasonable means of checking.
>
> 4. Such a bill of lading shall be *prima facie* evidence of the receipt by the carrier of the goods as therein described in accordance with paragraphs (a), (b) and (c)."

Article III(3) is triggered, however, only if the shipper demands such a bill, and:

> "There is no suggestion or evidence that the plaintiffs asked the defendants to issue a bill of lading showing the shipment of 11,000 tonnes without the qualification 'weight . . . unknown'. The only evidence relied upon is the bill of lading itself. I do not however think that it is a fair inference from the form of the bill of lading that the plaintiffs made such a request. On the contrary the natural inference is that the shippers were content with a bill of lading in standard Congenbill form, which includes the provision 'weight . . . unknown' as part of its printed form. The plaintiffs signed the bill of lading on behalf of the defendants. They were surely happy with it. If they had wanted a bill of lading in a different form they would surely have drafted one."

Note that the reasoning in *The Mata K* is not in any sense an application of *Grant v Norway*; in *The Mata K*, there was simply no quantity statement in the bill.

(d) Quantity Statements and Tort Actions

14–054   Where s.4 applies, quantity statements are attributed to the shipowner, who will be liable in contract or tort, or on the basis of an estoppel, on the principles described above.[91]

Where s.4 does not help, it might be thought possible to avoid the problem by suing the shipowner in tort, vicariously for the master's deceit (or negligent misstatement if the fraud is that of another party). There are, however, two problems with this. First, where the bill of lading is qualified as above, there is no misstatement, even by the master. Secondly, whether or not there is such a

---

[90] Art. III(3) was unchanged by the Visby amendments, but on Art. III(4), see above.
[91] In *Rasnoimport*, as we saw above, Mocatta J. thought that quantity statements were not contractual, but he also saw no reason why they should not give rise to a *Churchill & Sim*, or *Silver v Ocean* estoppel, all the elements of estoppel being present. Of course, the shipowner was not estopped in fact, because of *Grant v Norway*. See also the comment on *The River Gurara*, para. 14–029, above.

qualification, there is nothing in s.4 explicitly to extend the master's actual or apparent authority, and at least in cases of fraud, his course of employment for vicarious liability purposes is coextensive with his ostensible authority for agency purposes.[92] Though there is no UK authority, in *Blue Nile Co Ltd v Emery Customs Brokers (S) Pte Ltd*,[93] Chan Sek Keong J. observed that if "the defendants [shipowners] are not liable for the fraud of their servant [master] they cannot, rationally, be liable for his negligence." If this is correct, course of employment would also be coextensive with ostensible authority in negligence actions. Therefore, since misstatements as to quantity are outside the master's apparent authority, they are also outside his course of employment, and will therefore not impose vicarious liability on the shipowner.

(e) Breach of Warranty of Authority

Since the curtailment of *Grant v Norway* by the 1992 Act this action has reduced practical importance,[94] but the cases continue to raise issues of general application.   **14–055**

Even if the shipowner himself cannot be sued it may still be possible to sue the master or agent signing the bill for breach of warranty of authority. The argument is that since the master has only actual and apparent authority to sign bills of lading for goods which are actually loaded on board the ship, it follows that by signing bills of lading for goods which are not loaded, he is purporting to exercise authority which he does not have. Where the indorsee is suing (as in *Rasnoimport*) the cause of action is based on an implied contract between himself and the master, the master's warranty of authority (by issuing the bill of lading) being regarded as an offer to all the world, accepted by the act of the indorsee in taking up the bill of lading.

HESKELL v CONTINENTAL EXPRESS LTD

King's Bench Division. [1950] 1 All E.R. 1033

Heskell, who had agreed to sell 3 bales of poplin to a Persian buyer, Mishan, arranged through his forwarding agents for their shipment from Manchester to Teheran, aboard S.S. *Mount Orford Park*. He did not at this time enter into a contract of carriage with the shipowner.   **14–056**

Strick Ltd, the shipowner's loading brokers, instructed Heskell, through his forwarding agents, to send the goods down to the dock, and Heskell instructed Continental Express, Ltd, who were warehousing the goods, to despatch them to the ship. Continental Express failed to do so, and did not inform Heskell of their failure. Heskell, in ignorance therefore of the true position, applied through his forwarding agents for a bill of lading and Strick Ltd issued one, despite the fact that none of the goods were never received by them.

Heskell forwarded the bill of lading to Mishan (the buyer) and received payment. Later, the true position was discovered and eventually Heskell settled a damages claim from Mishan, for non-delivery. He in turn claimed damages from Continental Express and Strick. He did not sue the shipowners because of the rule in *Grant v Norway*, above.

---

[92] This is clear from the House of Lords decision in *The Ocean Frost* [1986] A.C. 717, at any rate in fraud cases. The case also decided that an agent without ostensible authority cannot give himself authority by representing that he has it.
[93] [1990] 2 M.L.J. 385 (Singapore).
[94] There will still be a breach of warranty of authority, but because of s.4, no loss, the shipowner being liable in any event.

Held

1. Heskell was able to succeed in contract against Continental Express, Ltd This claim is of no relevance to this chapter.

2. His claim against Strick failed in contract, because no contract had ever been made with Strick.

3. He sued Strick also for breach of warranty of authority, and failed on that ground because the breach of warranty had caused no loss. The damages were what the plaintiff had lost by being unable to sue the shipowner, and since there was no contract of carriage there would have been no useful action against the shipowner even if Strick had the authority he warranted. In the absence of a contract of carriage the bill of lading was a nullity, and the fact that it was issued without the authority of the shipowners robbed it of no virtue.

D<small>EVLIN</small> J.:

[*Devlin J. discussed the contractual claim with Strick and moved on to the breach of warranty of authority action. Heskell's difficulty was as to damages*].

14–057   The right way of testing the matter is, I think, to treat the bill of lading as if it had been signed personally by the owner and issued personally by him.

On that supposition how does the matter stand? In considering this, it seems to me of the first importance to remember that the bill of lading is not itself a contract of carriage and that it is not contended that any contract of carriage was ever made. The carelessness of Strick played no part in this. Whether they had acted with or without authority, there would still have been no contract of carriage. The reason why it was not made was because of a fault or breakdown on the plaintiff's side. He did not assume himself nor did he entrust to his forwarding agents the general duty of superintendence and of seeing that no hitch in tendering the goods occurred and as between himself and Strick the failure was his. On this basis, therefore, that there was no contract of affreightment, what would be the nature of the plaintiff's claim against the shipowner if the owner had himself personally signed and issued the bill of lading? In order to save the constant repetition of this hypothesis, in the next paragraph of the judgment I deal with this case as if it were a claim against the shipowner on a bill signed by him.

. . . The whole truth of this matter is that, in the absence of a contract of carriage, the bill of lading is a nullity, and it would have been none the less so even if it had been issued at a board meeting of Strick Line, Ltd, or passed by a resolution of the company in general meeting. The fact that it was issued without authority robbed it of no virtue. It would never have been more than a bit of paper purporting to record a bargain that had never been made. The plaintiff's liability to Mishan arose because he failed to make a contract of carriage. He cannot allege that that failure was a consequence of any breach of duty which the shipowner committed. Accordingly, he would have no claim against the shipowner, and so can recover no damages against the broker.

Notes

1. The essential difficulty facing Heskell was that no contract of carriage was **14–058** ever made. The bill of lading could not itself be the contract, and Strick could not bind the owners for goods which were never loaded. Nor could an estoppel against the carrier work, because estoppel cannot be used as a cause of action, in the absence of a carriage contract.

2. Because there was no contract of carriage, the action, for breach of warranty of authority, against the loading broker also failed, because only nominal damages could be awarded. Whether they had acted with or without authority, there would still have been no action against the shipowner. This approach seems unsound, however, because if Strick had had the authority he warranted, the goods would have been shipped, and there would have been a carriage contract. Doubt was cast on Devlin J.'s approach in *V/O Rasnoimport v Guthrie*, Mocatta J. taking the view that the correct approach was not to examine the position of the plaintiffs on the hypothesis that the owners themselves signed the bill of lading, but on the basis that the defendants had the authority which they warranted they had.

3. Devlin J.'s conclusion that there was no carriage contract, and that the bill of lading was a nullity, suggest that the 1992 Act would not apply, were the same facts to arise today.

Where some goods are left behind, but some shipped, the damages problem alluded to in *Heskell* disappears.

V/O RASNOIMPORT v GUTHRIE & CO LTD

Commercial Court. [1966] 1 Lloyd's Rep. 1

The defendant loading brokers issued shipped bills of lading for 225 bales of **14–059** rubber, whereas only 90 bales had been loaded on board. The plaintff indorsees for value sued the loading brokers for breach of warranty of authority, and under s.3 of the Bills of Lading Act 1855 (see above).

Held:

1. Since s.3 provided only conclusive evidence and not a cause of action, even if the defendants were "other persons" within the section, the plaintiffs could not rely on the section.

2. But the plaintiffs were entitled to succeed on the breach of warranty of authority claim, and could claim substantial damages.

MOCATTA J.: A preliminary point on this question was what was meant by Devlin J. in *Heskell's* case . . . , when he said:

" . . . The right way of testing the matter is, I think, to treat the bill of lading as if it had been signed personally by the shipowner and issued personally by him."

One view of this passage is that the learned Judge was not laying down any principle of law, but was for brevity and convenience putting the case for the plaintiff there as high as it could be put. Another is that the learned Judge was in error. It would not greatly matter which view were right had it not been that . . . the learned Judge, treating the shipowners as having signed the bill of lading for goods not on board and assuming that the indorsee, who had relied upon that statement in the bill of lading to his detriment, sued the shipowner for non-delivery, said that the shipowner would be prevented from alleging non-shipment by s.3 of the Bills of Lading Act. With great reapect, I do not think it correct, when a breach of warranty of authority has been established by an agent purporting to make a contract for his principal, to consider the rights of the third party on the assumption that the principal had himself signed the unauthorized contract, though in most cases the assumption would not affect the result.

In my judgment, the correct approach is not to examine the position of the plaintiffs on the hypothesis that the owners themselves signed the bill of lading, but on the basis that the defendants had the authority which I have held them to have warranted they had. If on that basis the plaintiffs could have recovered the appropriate damages from the owners for the non-delivery of the 135 bales, then they have plainly suffered detriment and damage by reason of the breach of warranty since, the breach having occurred, they are without remedy against the owners.

Note

14–060   On this basis *Heskell* is wrong on the damages issue, but in any case it is distinguishable, because here there *was* a contract of carriage, some goods having been shipped.

Except perhaps for straight bills of lading, which are outside s.4, *Rasnoimport* would appear to have no direct application today. It remains of interest, however, because of a finding of fact that the misrepresentation in the bill of lading was innocently made, and because (unlike *Churchill & Sim*) a factual statement in a bill of lading was held to amount to a contractual warranty to the indorsee. Of course, unlike *Churchill & Sim*, the indorsee took the benefit of a new contract, whereas in the earlier case his contract was assumed to be simply transferred from the shipper.

Part E

THE FUTURE

Chapter 15

PROBLEMS AND PROPOSED SOLUTIONS

INTERNATIONAL trade practices have changed considerably over the last thirty **15–001** years or so. Consequently, the legal framework no longer protects the parties as well as once it did. There are (logically) three basic solutions to the crisis, change the law, change commercial practice, or do neither, accepting the deficiencies of the present system. It is impossible to predict which of these solutions will prevail.

This chapter covers a diversity of issues, and possible solutions (although some of the problems may be insoluble). The next chapter looks in particular at technological solutions which the parties could adopt, should the present inadequacies overcome what appears to be a strong conservative streak among commercial people.

(1) STANDARDISATION AND UNIFICATION OF INTERNATIONAL SALES

(a) STANDARD FORMS AND DEFINITIONS OF TRADE TERMS

In the interests of certainty, it is clearly desirable for trade terms, such as c.i.f., **15–002** f.o.b., to be defined with a reasonable degree of precision.[1] Against that, one of the attractions of the f.o.b. term, in particular, is its flexibility. Flexibility and precision in a definition are obviously at odds with one another. To the extent that the common law promotes flexibility, therefore, it must be for the parties themselves to fill out the flexible terms with as much detail as they require. Many trades have developed standard forms which achieve greater or lesser degrees of certainty.

The common law process is ill-suited, on its own, to standardising definitions of trade terms. In Treitel's casenote on *The Naxos* (see chapter 3, above), he had previously observed that the "common law can only solve problems . . . by applying standards which, because they operate *ex post facto*, or because of their inherent flexibility, lack the commercially desirable qualities of predictability and precision." This is particularly true, for example, of the f.o.b. contract described in para. 3–031, above, a term which is sufficiently flexible to accommodate a wide range of varieties of contract.

Part of the problem is that the definitions, *e.g.* f.o.b. and c.i.f., evolved through cases where the courts were concerned not to define the terms as such, but simply to determine the intentions of the two parties to the action. Since evidence of their intentions is often not readily available, the courts have generally had regard to

---

[1] This is especially true of chain sales (see paras 15–009, *et seq.*, below), where it is important that each contract in the chain is interpreted similarly.

the practice of merchants. Thus, for example, in *Tregelles v Sewell* (see para. 2–005, above), where the Court of Exchequer had to construe what is possibly the first reported c.i.f. contract, Martin B. observed that "a document of this kind ought to be construed according to the known practice of merchants in respect of such transactions."[2] It follows that, because the nature of the exercise is to interpret the contract according to the intention of the parties to the transaction, other factors, apart from the written terms, can be taken into account.[3] This means that the same trade term can have different meanings in different contexts, and in particular, can be affected by what is customary in a particular trade. Moreover, unless the written terms are sufficiently detailed to allow the contract to be interpreted largely independently of other factors, it is by no means certain that the same written contract will be interpreted in the same way between different parties in the chain. In reality, whereas the common law definition of c.i.f. does not permit of radical variations, this is not true at all of f.o.b.

15–003   It is also worth observing that insofar that they were defined at all, the trade terms were defined by the courts very early in their development, the contracts later being adapted for different purposes by the commercial parties. When *Tregelles v Sewell* was decided, nobody could have foreseen the modern development of the c.i.f. contract. In another early c.i.f. case, Lord Blackburn in *Ireland v Livingston* observed that already, by 1871, "The terms [c.i.f.] are very usual, and are perfectly well understood in practice."[4] Not only, therefore, may the common law definitions be relatively imprecise, but they may also not accord well with twenty-first, as opposed to nineteenth-century usage.

It is true that where a term, such as f.o.b, is flexible, the courts will sometimes presume a meaning in the absence of contrary intention,[5] but even that approach was not taken in *Pound v Hardy*, in para. 3–047, above. In any case, it cannot be entirely satisfactory for the duties of the parties to be determined by trying to glean some meaning from exchanges of letters, as for example in *N.V. Handel My. J. Smits Import-Export v English Exporters (London) Ltd* or *Federspiel v Twigg* in paras 3–013 and 3–015, above. It must be better for the parties themselves to address the issue by the use of standard forms. Extensive reference has already been made, for example, to GAFTA 64 and GAFTA 100. An advantage of leaving detailed definitions to the parties themselves is that they can write contracts to suit their particular trade.

Partly, perhaps, because of the need for back-to-back chain sales to be on identical terms, there have been various initiatives to standardise definitions of trade terms.[6] These have, however, met with limited success, partly perhaps because the main motivation seems to have been to achieve standardisation internationally, rather than merely to ensure consistency within the law of the U.K. International harmonisation has met with only mixed success, and there is really no alternative to parties drafting their contracts in considerable detail. Most

---

[2] (1862) 7 H. & N. 574, 158 E.R. 600 at 602. While this may be the first case where the courts have had expressly to construe the term "c.i.f." (or more accurately, the older formulation "c.f. and i."), it is probable that the contract in the earlier House of Lords decision in *Couturier v Hastie* (1856) 5 H.L.C. 673, although described as "f.o.b.", was what we would now describe as a c.i.f. contract.

[3] See, *e.g. Pyrene v Scindia* in para. 3–004, above; there was nothing in the written contract to determine that the buyer, rather than the seller, was responsible for making the carriage contract.

[4] (1872) L.R. 5 H.L. 395, 406.

[5] *e.g.* in *Ian Stach Ltd v Baker Bosley Ltd* [1958] 2 Q.B. 130, considered in this context at paras 3–016, *et seq.*, above.

[6] See below.

international sale contracts are therefore made on fairly detailed standard forms.[7]

(b) Harmonisation and Globalisation

It is arguable that, since international trade is by definition international, it is **15–004** advantageous to have definitions which are similar throughout the world. This is the thinking behind publications such as Incoterms (see below). The position in the UK, however, is that Incoterms does not have the force of law, but must be adopted by the parties, if they so wish. Its position is effectively the same as that of the commercial standard form contracts. The UK position allows the parties to adopt definitions of their choice, but does not impose any definitions on them.

Another argument is that legal principles, for example of liability, or of contract formation, interpretation, repudiation, etc., should be unified across differing legal systems throughout the world. International trade is an area which particularly lends itself to this argument.[8] There are also some good examples of successful unification, such as U.C.P. 500 and the original Hague Rules.

National legal systems have their own traditions, however, held on to tenaciously, and so far, harmonisation in general has not enjoyed a particularly successful history. For example, e-commerce (of which there is some discussion in chapter 16, below), is another area which lends itself well to harmonisation arguments, for example for digital signatures, ID certificates and certification authorities. There is the obvious practical point that ID certificates will be used across national boundaries.[9] There are also single market justifications within the EU.[10]

Since requirements for conventional hand-written signatures tend to impede e-commerce (and not least in international trade—see further chapter 16, below), a number of states have enacted legislation whose effect is to give varying degrees of validity to their electronic equivalents, but very little consensus can be discerned. Agreement has not been reached even on the most fundamental matters. Some the legislation is technology-specific, covering only "digital signatures", which are defined strictly in terms of asymmetric cryptography.[11] Later legislation has tended, following the trend of the UNCITRAL Model Laws, to adopt a

---

[7] For example, The Grain and Feed Trade Association (GAFTA) which (in August 2000) described itself (at *www.gafta.com*) as "a world wide organisation promoting international trade in grains, animal feeding stuffs, pulses and rice," went on to say:

"GAFTA has a range of more than 75 standard forms of contracts available for the Trade, covering CIF, FOB, and delivered terms. The contracts provide the terms of trade for different commodities which include those covered by the generic terms 'grain' and 'feed'. They cover the principal cereals such as wheat, barley, maize (corn), as well as oilseed cakes and meals, fishmeal, pulses and rice, from different origins worldwide, and for different methods of transportation or for different terms of trade.

Internationally more than 80% of the world's trade in cereals, and a significant proportion of trade in animal feeds, moves on the terms of GAFTA contracts."

[8] For a thorough review, see Fletcher, Mistelis and Cremona, *Foundations and Perspectives of International Trade Law* (Sweet & Maxwell, 2001). Two comments: first, the various harmonisation initiatives discussed do not always harmonise with each other; secondly, there is virtually a total absence of UK law input into the discussion. Presumably these ideas (or whichever one of them prevails) would be forced upon us, were we to go down the harmonisation route.

[9] *e.g.* Reed, *Internet Law: Text and Materials*, p. 146. Also *A European Initiative in Electronic Commerce*, COM(97) 157 (available at *www.cordis.lu/esprit/src/ecomcom.htm*), para. 16 (on p. 5).

[10] *e.g.* the discussion in Lodder and Kaspersen, *eDirectives: Guide to European Union Law on E-Commerce* (Kluwer, 2002), p. 37. See also the explanatory text to the EU Directive, para. 10.

[11] *e.g.* Utah Digital Signature Act 1996, full text of which is available at *www.jmls.edu/cyber/statutes/udsa.html*.

functionally-equivalent definition of "electronic signature".[12] Such definitions look to what the signature does, and do not assume asymmetric cryptography. It may be that the trend is in that direction,[13] since better methods appear to be emerging, of certifying identity, than asymmetric cryptography.[14] Nonetheless, technology-specific legislation remains, and there are still good arguments in its favour.[15] There is also two-tier legislation, according differing weights to differing types of signature.[16] Even on such fundamental issues, therefore, no international consensus can be discerned; there are at least three fundamentally different types of legislation, and indeed, many states have still not adopted any legislation at all. Liability provisions also vary widely. In some cases no provision is made, but legislation can also be found providing for negligence liability, perhaps reversing the usual burden of proof, and yet another possibility is to require particular procedures, with liability if the procedures are not followed.[17]

15–005 This is not an e-commerce book, and the above examples are included here to demonstrate that merely because harmonisation is a good idea, it by no means follows that it will happen. Given the tendency of states jealously to guard the principles they hold dear, it will only happen if either they are persuaded to abandon those principles (a possibility with digital signatures, where the debate is still young), or they are forced to do so. Probably the Hague Rules succeeded partly because the arguments on negotiability were convincing, and partly because the UK's position became untenable internationally, and the Hague Rules represented the best compromise a shipowning nation could get.

When it comes to harmonisation of international sales contracts, considered below, persuasion ought not to succeed because the Vienna Convention is worse, for some purposes, than existing UK law. International pressure might conceivably persuade the UK to adopt the Vienna Convention, but if that happens, it seems likely that the major trading parties will simply contract out of it. The Vienna Convention is discussed in more detail below.

There are also quite major differences between some legal systems, for example between the US and the UK on many contractual issues. More significant are the truly fundamental differences between common and civil law traditions. Even the *Hague Rules* and *Hague-Visby Rules* have been (and continue to be) to some extent frustrated by the UK privity of contract principles (see paras 11–061, *et seq.*, above), and present UK contract law does not sit well with the Vienna Convention. Whatever the merits of harmonisation across these two traditions, it will probably be an uphill struggle to achieve it.

---

[12] Conventional usage appears to define "digital signature" in terms of specific technology, and "electronic signature" more widely, in terms of function. See also, B.P. Aalberts & S. van der Hof, *Digital Signature Blindness, Analysis of Legislative Approaches Toward Electronic Authentication* (November 1999) section 1.2, available at *http://rechten.kub.nl/simone/ds-fr.htm*, where this usage is insisted upon.

[13] Notably, perhaps, after initially enacting a technology-specific provision, Germany has replaced its "Signaturgesetz" with functionally-equivalent legislation: Law Governing Framework Conditions for Electronic Signatures and Amending Other Regulations, (2001) section 2. For an English language version, see *www.regtp.de/imperia/md/content/tech_reg_t/digisign/119.pdf*. The earlier, technology-specific German law is described in Lodder and Kaspersen, p. 36.

[14] *e.g.* use of biometric data, such as a thumbprint, or handwritten signature data—see *www.penop.com/home.asp*.

[15] *e.g.* Elizabeth Beary, *The Digital Signature Debate: Technology Neutral or Specific?* (1998) at *http://raven.cc.ukans.edu/~cybermom/CLJ/beary.html*. Essentially, technology-specific legislation promotes certainty, functional equivalence flexibility.

[16] For a thorough survey of legislation throughout the world, see *www.ilpf.org/groups/survey.htm* (*Survey of International Electronic and Digital Signature Initiatives* (Internet Law and Policy Forum, February 1999)).

[17] See, *e.g.* Reed (2000a), pp. 145–146. Note again the lack of any international consensus.

Harmonisation has also enjoyed little success dynamically. Even the *Hague Rules* have not survived the revision process, and as we saw in chapter 11, above, whereas once there was one set of Conventions in force pretty well throughout the world, now there are three. A similar fate appears to have befallen the partially-successful attempts to harmonise control of oil pollution at sea, where it now seems likely that the EU, like the US, will go its own way. The U.C.P. continues to be a success story, but its adaptations have tended to facilitate changing practices, rather than control one of the parties.

There is finally the point that much harmonisation is industry-specific. The Hague Rules and the oil pollution conventions affect only sea carriers, for example. There is an argument that in a competitive society disparate activities should compete on a level playing field; that necessarily argues against industry-specific legislation.

(c) INCOTERMS 2000

Incoterms is a set of international rules, published by the International Chamber of Commerce, for the interpretation of the terms most commonly used in international sale contracts. It was first published in 1936, and was previously updated in 1953, 1967, 1976, 1980 and 1990, in order to bring the rules into line with current international trade practices. The latest version is Incoterms 2000. In the 1990 revision, which was the most substantial, at least in recent years,[18] the layout of Incoterms was also changed, contracts being grouped for the first time, depending on the delivery point, and extent of the seller's duties. This grouping continues to be adopted in the 2000 revision, and the respective obligations of the parties have also been grouped under the ten headings apparent from the extract in Appendix B—see below (the same headings being used across the different contracts). **15–006**

There is only one contract in the first group, Group E, the *ex works* (or EXW) contract, where delivery is made from the seller's place of business. Next comes Group F contracts (FCA (free carrier), FAS and FOB), where the seller is required to deliver the goods to the carrier, but where the buyer arranges and pays for the sea carriage. Delivery under Group C contracts (CFR (c. & f.), CIF, CPT (carriage paid to destination) and CIP (carriage and insurance paid to name place of destination)) is also to the carrier, but here it is the seller who arranges and pays for the sea carriage. Finally, Group D contracts (delivered at frontier or DAF, delivered ex ship or DES, delivered ex quay or DEQ, delivered duty unpaid or DDU, and delivered duty paid or DDP) require the seller actually to deliver the goods to an arrival destination, rather than merely to the carrier, and differ from Group C contracts primarily in that risk of loss or damage remains with the seller until the goods arrive. Group C differs from Group F in the identity of the shipper, seller in Group C and buyer in Group F.

The main substantive motivation, particularly for the 1990 revisions, as with the latest revision to the U.C.P. (on which see chapter 8, above and Appendix C, below), was to bring the terms into line with the increase use of new forms of transport documentation, and in particular electronic data interchange. A good example of the changes can be found in the documentation requirements for CIF contracts. Incoterms 1980 was unequivocal, requiring the seller to furnish a clean, shipped bill of lading, which was also negotiable, "clean bill of lading" being defined in a note at the end of the appropriate clause. If the bill of lading contained reference to a charterparty, a copy of the charterparty had also to be

---

[18] Incoterms 2000, by contrast, seems mostly to be a tidying up operation. Though there are no substantial changes, however, at least for f.o.b. and c.i.f. contracts, there are improvements, particularly for example in the explanation of the c.i.f. contract.

provided. No provision was made for the tender of alternative shipping documents, such as non-negotiable waybills, or combined transport documents.

As can be seen from Appendix B, below, Incoterms 2000 gives far greater documentary leeway, the changes dating from the 1990 revision. For example, no longer is a shipped bill of lading necessarily required, reference instead being made to "the usual transport document for the agreed port of destination".[19]

To have effect, the current version of Incoterms must be incorporated expressly into the sale contract. Incoterms publications, including Incoterms 2000 (and 1990) are available through their website (link tested August 2002) at *www. iccwbo.org*.

The full text of Incoterms 2000, for f.o.b. and c.i.f. contracts, is set out in Appendix B, below.

INCE & CO, *INTERNATIONAL TRADE LAW UPDATE*

(Tradewatch, Spring 2000) Issue 4. Available (link tested August 2002) at www.ince.co.uk/index.cfm

Incoterms 2000

15–007   At the end of the last Millennium, ICC unveiled a new edition of Incoterms—Incoterms 2000. Whilst the process of revision took about two years, there are fcw significant changes from the 1990 edition.

The main changes are in relation to:

(a) customs clearance and payment of duty obligations under FAS (free alongside ship (. . . named port of shipment)) where the obligations are now placed upon the seller and DEQ (delivered ex quay named port of destination)), where the obligations are now placed upon the buyer and

(b) the loading obligations under FCA (free carrier (. . . named place)) which now depend on whether delivery is given at the sellers' premises or elsewhere.

It may well be that a substantial amount of time was spent during the revision process considering whether to adopt the suggestion that the maritime based Incoterms (*e.g.* FOB and CIF etc.) be abolished as anachronistic. It was apparently argued by some that such terms were surplus to requirements and a duplication of the more flexible terms which could easily be used in substitution. For example, it is understood that it was suggested that FCA could be used instead of FOB and CIP (carriage and insurance paid to (. . . named place of destination)) could be used instead of CIF. On this basis, FOB Barcelona would become FCA Barcelona port and CIF Rotterdam presumably CIP Rotterdam port. Ultimately, the drafting committee rejected the suggestions as too revolutionary, fearing that an abandonment of the traditional maritime based terms would

---

[19] See c.i.f. A8, in Appendix B, below. There is a list of documentation, including electronic varieties.

result in substantial confusion. As a result, the "status quo" was fortunately (in our view) maintained.

Some Observations on Incoterms

Incoterms covers only sale contracts, and so excludes carriage contracts, and   **15–008**
contracts made with or between banks under a documentary credit, even though
the obligation to enter into such ancillary contracts will nearly always befall one
or other party to the sale contract. Contracts involving banks under a documentary credit are usually covered by the Uniform Customs and Practice on
Documentary Credits, another International Chamber of Commerce publication
(see Appendix C, below).

Given that the common law has developed fairly precise definitions of the f.o.b.
and c.i.f. contract, it may be that Incoterms is more useful for the other international sale contracts, some of which are variations on the traditional contracts.
The observation in the Tradewatch extract, that the drafting committee seriously
considered the possibility that the c.i.f. and f.o.b. terms were anachronistic,
suggests the converse, that they should be seen as specific examples of the more
general contracts in Incoterms, such as FCA and CIP. The emphasis in Incoterms
is on the new, rather than the traditional international trade contracts.

Contracting f.o.b. Incoterms fills out a flexible common law definition, and
determines that the contract is *Pyrene v Scindia* type 3. C.i.f. Incoterms largely
describes the common law definition, except that there is greater documentary
leeway in A8 (although the delivery order in *The Julia* appears to be excluded,
since it does not "enable the buyer to claim the goods from the carrier at
destination").[20] Buyers contracting c.i.f. Incoterms should be aware that the documentation may give less security than the traditional documentation, and might
also affect the timing of the passing of property.

Incoterms may provide insufficiemt detail for many traders. For example, while
it covers the division of responsibilities between the parties, and in appropriate
circumstances the passing of risk, it is silent on the passing of property. Standard
forms such GAFTA 64 and 100 are far more detailed, and for example there is no
equivalent in Incoterms of the detailed nomination provisions considered in paras
3–017, *et seq.*, above. Moreover, while the f.o.b. contract is clearly tied down to the
third *Pyrene v Scindia* variety,[21] litigation is unlikely to be entirely avoided, as long
as phrases of such generality as "necessary information for procuring insurance"
(in f.o.b. A10) continue to be used. On the other hand, Incoterms can be used to
fill out a contract, which is otherwise silent in some areas.[22]

Incoterms is not well-suited to bulk commodity contracts, where (as was
explained in paras 1–015, *et seq.*, above) long chains are almost inevitable. For
example, under Incoterms 2000, a c.i.f. seller must:

" . . . contract on the usual terms at his own expense for the carriage of the
goods to the named port of destination by the usual route in a seagoing vessel
(or inland waterway vessel as the case may be) of the type normally used for
the transport of goods of the contract description."

---

[20] Indeed, c.i.f. Incoterms may not be regarded by the courts as a true c.i.f. contract, but this
may not matter overly, since there are in any event express provisions as to the transfer of
risk.
[21] See paras 3–004, *et seq.*, above.
[22] *e.g.* in *The Albazero*, the shipper's general terms and conditions provided that "Whenever
the provisions of the contract are not contrary to Incoterms 1953, the latter shall be
applicable to the contract." See [1975] 3 W.L.R. 491 at 498; Schmitthoff's *Export Trade* (10th
ed.), p. 673, n. 19.

This implies that the seller must actually make the carriage contract, suitable for a single sale, but appropriate only for the original seller in a long chain. Intermediate purchasers would merely process documents. There is no equivalent of this obligation in GAFTA 100, by contrast, although documentary obligations are set out. Perhaps one should conclude from this that Incoterms is not intended for the bulk commodity trade, which has in any case its own developed standard forms. Surprisingly, Incoterms was used for the c.i.f. contract in *The Delfini*, a case involving bulk oil carriage, but the transactions there were relatively simple, being an f.o.b. contract, followed by a c.i.f.[23]

(d) CHAINS AND CIRCLES

15–009   It will be apparent from the discussion in chapter 1, above that both c.i.f. and f.o.b. contracts proved well-suited to chain sales. Whereas in the nineteenth century cases the parties are often relatively small-time merchants, today it is far more likely for them to be commodity traders, either acting as middlemen to organise the trade, or as speculators hoping to re-sell the goods at a profit.

We have also seen in earlier chapters that documentation is used to effect each transfer (see, *e.g. Concordia v Richco* in para. 6–087, above, where there was a circle followed by a chain, and the documents were never sent around the circle).

Circles, as in *The Filipinas I*, are less common than chain sales. A number of features can be identified as desirable in chain sales, especially where finance is by documentary credit. For example[24]:

1. Where back-to-back contracts are used for the chain, where the only difference between each contract is the price, each contract should also be interpreted in the same way, whoever are the parties.

2. If a buyer is required to accept the documents and the goods, it is essential that he should be able to use the same documents and goods for the resale.

3. Where payment is by documentary credit, the documentary requirements under the credit should mirror those under the sale contract.

Documentary requirements are covered in chapter 6, above, for the sale contract, and chapter 10, above, for the documentary credit. Generally, the common law promotes quite well the second desirable feature identified above.

(e) NEGOTIABILITY OF DOCUMENTS

15–010   The courts have developed their interpretation of international sale contracts to a considerable extent to give effect to feature 2 above. The existence of chain sales, and the need for a party in the middle of the chain to be able to enforce a contract on c.i.f. terms, were explicitly recognised by Atkin J. as a justification for his decision in *C. Groom Ltd v Barber*, at paras 4–011, *et seq.*, above. The reasoning in *Gill & Duffus v Berger* in para. 7–022, above, takes express account of the realities of the bulk commodities trade. Many of the principles in chapter 10, above, such as the doctrine of strict compliance, where payment is by documentary credit, are easier to justify for chain than for single sales.[25] It is because of the common law's suitability for this type of transaction that I think it unlikely that U.L.I.S., or the

---

[23] See also *Universal Petroleum Co Ltd v Handels und Transport GmbH* [1987] 1 W.L.R. 1178.
[24] But see further the discussion of commodity contracts at paras 1–015, *et seq.*
[25] See also *Ian Stach Ltd v Baker Bosley Ltd* [1958] 2 Q.B. 130, in para. 9–017, above.

Vienna Convention considered below, are unlikely to have any significant role to play in this area of law, at any rate for the foreseeable future.

Certainty is an important consideration. Lord Roskill in *The Salem* (see below) observed that[26]:

" . . . this House has on many recent occasions stressed the need for certainty in the law and especially in the field of commercial law".

It is particularly important to be able to determine with certainty whether a breach of contract by the seller allows the buyer to repudiate the contract. This argues for a classification of terms into conditions and warranties, rather than innominate terms.[27] Again the common law has obliged, showing a willingness to embrace the realities of the situation.[28]

(f) Reluctance to Embrace *Hongkong Fir*

If any of the sale contracts in a chain or circle can be repudiated, it is desirable **15–011** that they all can be. This requires a greater degree of certainty than in domestic sales of goods. It may be partly in the interests of certainty that the courts look to the form rather than the substance. For example, whether a buyer can reject depends on whether the seller has broken a condition of the contract, and not at all on the buyer's motives for rejecting (which are often, as we have seen in chapter 7, above, simply that the market has dropped). In a passage already set out from *Diamond Alkali* in para. 6–061, above, McCardie J. observed:

"Nor is it material that a buyer objects to the document for ulterior motives: see, for example, Lord Cairns' judgment in *Bowes v Shand* (1877) 2 App. Cas. 455, 465, 476 and Lord Hatherley's judgment in the same case. A buyer, as these noble Lords pointed out, is entitled to insist on the letter of his rights. As Lord Hatherley said: 'If you seek to fasten upon him the engagement, you must first bring him'—the buyer—'within the four corners of the contract.' A buyer, moreover, may have obvious business reasons for so insisting, as he may have to implement his own bargain with rigorous sub-vendees."

On similar reasoning, it is preferable to categorise terms as conditions rather than innominate terms; the effect of the latter depends on the effect of the breach, which could obviously differ as between the various parties in the chain.

The Sale of Goods Act 1979 still largely adopts the condition/warranty distinction, although there is some erosion in s.15A, added by the Sale and Supply of Goods Act 1994, and set out in para. 4–039, above. The courts are also reluctant to extend *Hongkong Fir* to all types of term, and recognise the importance of certainty in chain sales.[29]

PAUL TODD, "REJECTION OF SHIPPING DOCUMENTS"

Documentary Credits Insight (1999) (section on strict compliance)

[Footnotes as in the original, but renumbered for inclusion here.]

---

[26] [1983] 2 A.C. 375, at 389.
[27] See generally Treitel, *The Law of Contract* (10th ed., 1999), pp. 738–743.
[28] In addition to the cases here, note that the delivery term in *The Jambur*, in para. 2–021, above, was held to be a condition, entitling the buyers to reject the documents tendered.
[29] See, *e.g.* the discussion of *Bunge v Tradax* in paras 3–024, *et seq.*, above.

15–012   It might be thought that the discrepancy problem is exacerbated by the doctrine of strict compliance, and that a fairer system might result from relaxing the doctrine. No doubt, the rigour of the present doctrine allows buyers to use technicalities to avoid sale contracts on falling markets,[30] especially if the documentary requirements are very strict, and the sellers have difficulty in complying. Moreover, in respect of many other breaches of contract, the UK courts at any rate have tended to move away from treating terms as conditions, any breach of which, however trivial, allows the other party to repudiate, in favour of the innominate, or intermediate term, where the lawfulness of repudiation depends on the effect of the breach.[31]

Though developments along those lines may well enhance the security of the credit from the seller's viewpoint, I would argue that if there are other possibilities, relaxation of the strict compliance doctrine is not a desirable method of achieving this goal. If the rule were changed to require rejection of documents only where discrepancies were material, the bank would have to judge materiality, but they do not have the relevant expertise. Both the general law and the U.C.P. reflect the actuality, that whereas banks can check documents they probably have no knowledge of the goods underlying the transaction, nor of relations or disputes between buyer and seller. Thus, for example, Article 4 of the U.C.P. provides: "In credit operations all parties concerned deal in documents, and not in goods, services and/or other performances to which the documents may relate."

There is a more fundamental reason for caution when considering relaxation of strict compliance. The international sales that are the underlying basis of many documentary credits are merely parts of a wider transaction, since multiple resales while the goods are at sea are commonplace. Since it is impossible to inspect the goods while they are at sea, even a buyer (who unlike a bank may well be presumed to have expertise in the goods themselves) can only form a judgment on the basis of inspection of documents. Moreover, it is vital that if the nth buyer is required to accept the documents, he can use those same documents in his resale to buyer (n + 1). Yet the effect of a discrepancy on buyer n may be totally different from its effect on buyer (n + 1). Obviously therefore, the effect of such a discrepancy must be disregarded where there are likely to be multiple resales. The prospect of multiple resales was a factor in requiring certainty, and hence a preference in international sale contracts for conditions over innominate terms, in the well-known House of Lords decision in *Bunge Corporation v Tradax SA*.[32] In *Seng Co Ltd v Glencore Grain Ltd*,[33] Mance J. adopted a test similar to common law strict

---

[30] The reason for the rejection in *Glencore*.
[31] *Hongkong Fir Shipping Co Ltd v Kawasaki Kisen Kaisha Ltd* [1962] 2 Q.B. 26.
[32] [1981] 1 W.L.R. 711.
[33] [1996] 1 Lloyd's Rep. 398, applied in *Soules CAF v PT Transap of Indonesia* [1999] 1 Lloyd's Rep. 917. See also *SIAT di dal Ferro v Tradax Overseas SA* [1980] 1 Lloyd's Rep. 53, where Megaw L.J. also adopted a strict test as to documentation, subject only to a *de minimis* exception.

compliance for documentation under a c. & f. sale contract, and in refusing leave to appeal,[34] Hobhouse L.J. was clearly unimpressed by the seller's contention that "there is a distinction to be drawn between a case which requires documents to be tendered to the Buyer, and where they are to be tendered to a bank under a letter of credit."

There are other arguments, perhaps of lesser substance, but which lend   **15–013**
further support to retention of a strict doctrine. It may be a technicality, but the contract between confirming bank and beneficiary must be unilateral, since the beneficiary makes no undertaking to the bank. Acceptance is tender of documents, and innominate terms reasoning simply has no place in unilateral contracts. The other contracts to which the bank are party are bilateral, but clearly the same documentary requirements must apply to all these contracts, if the credit is to be workable. A more convincing argument, perhaps, is that the courts do sometimes intervene to import requirements of fairness or good faith whatever the contracting parties have stipulated, but usually only where there is an inequality of bargaining power between the parties; there is no reason to assume that this is normally the case in international trade transactions.

(g) U.L.I.S. AND THE VIENNA CONVENTION

Chapter 14 of Schmitthoff's *Export Trade* (9th ed.) entitled "The Unification of   **15–014**
International Sales Law", began[35]:

" . . . it would be of great value to the international business community if the law relating to international sales were unified and no longer determined by different national legal systems which provide different answers to questions such as when an offer or acceptance becomes effective, when possession, property or risk in the goods sold passes, what the rights of the buyer are when goods not conforming to the contract are tendered, and similar questions. A unification of the law of international sales would reduce the danger of a conflict of laws in a particularly sensitive area of international business relations. Aware of the value of a unified sales law for the international business community, the International Institute for the Unification of Private Law in Rome, on the suggestion of the great German comparativist Ernst Rabel, drafted two Uniform Laws on International Sales and after 30 years' preparation these Laws were adopted by a conference at the Hague on April 25, 1964.

The two Uniform Laws are *Uniform Law on the International Sale of Goods* (Uniform Law on Sales) and the *Uniform Law on the Formation of Contracts for the International Sale of Goods* (Uniform Law on Formation) . . . "

So U.L.I.S. (and the later Vienna Convention)[36] deal with unification of the laws of different countries. They are set out in full in the appendices because[37]:

---

[34] Unreported, CA, July 4, 1996.
[35] See also Ch. 32 of 10th ed., where however this passage is not repeated.
[36] Also known as CISG, standing for "Convention on Contracts for the International Sale of Goods".
[37] Observations from Bernstein and Lookofsky *Understanding the CISG in Europe* (Kluwer Law International, 1997).

"More than 40 countries, accounting for two-thirds of all world trade, have ratified the Convention on Contracts for the International Sale of Goods. In Europe and elsewhere, the age of internationalization and the global market is upon us, and the CISG sets the ground rules for international contracts of sale."

. . .

"[The] CISG is fast becoming the sales law of the world."[38]

U.L.I.S. is part of UK law (but applies only if the parties choose it). CISG is not part of UK law, but in principle it could apply anyway, whether or not the parties have a place of business in a Contracting State, through the express adoption by the parties of a proper law clause, choosing as the applicable law a jurisdiction which is a CISG Contracting State.

Nonetheless, it seems (to the author, at any rate) unlikely that either will have a significant impact the UK law of international sales, at any rate during the lifetime of this book. The reasons for this pessimism are that:

(a) although U.L.I.S. has been part of UK law for over 30 years, it is hardly ever adopted by the parties;

(b) private UK law does not always incorporate well international conventions—see further above;

(c) neither U.L.I.S. nor the Vienna Convention appear to provide well for re-sales, in particular in their failure to construe terms as conditions.

The Uniform Law on the International Sale of Goods (U.L.I.S.) and the Uniform Law on the Formation of Contracts for the International Sale of Goods (U.L.F.I.S.), which were sponsored by the International Institute for the Unification of Private Law (UNIDROIT), were signed at a Diplomatic Conference in the Hague in April 1964. They were introduced into the law of the UK by the Uniform Laws on International Sales Act 1967, which was brought into force in August 1973, by the Uniform Law on International Sales Order 1972. UNCITRAL's later revisions, culminating in the United Nations Convention on Contracts for the International Sale of Goods (Vienna Convention) 1980, have not been adopted in the UK.

15–015   The following points of interest may be noted:

1. Sections 1(3) and 1(4) (the latter as amended by the Sale of Goods Act 1979) of the Uniform Laws on International Sales Act 1967 provide:

"(3) While an Order of Her Majesty in Council is in force declaring that a declaration by the United Kingdom under Article V of the First Convention (application only by choice of parties) has been made and not withdrawn the Uniform Law on Sales shall apply to a contract of sale only if it has been chosen by the parties to the contract as the law of the contract.

(4) In determining the extent of the application of the Uniform Law on Sales by virtue of Article 4 thereof (choice of parties)—

(a) in relation to a contract made before 18th May 1973, no provision of the law of any part of the United Kingdom shall be regarded as a mandatory provision within the meaning of that Article;

(b) in relation to a contract made on or after 18th May 1973 and before 1st February 1978, no provision of that law shall be so regarded except sections 12 to 15, 55 and 56 of the Sale of Goods Act 1979;

---

[38] Though not in large parts of the common law world, *e.g.* India, Malaysia [author's footnote].

(c) in relation to a contract made on or after 1st February 1978, no provision of that law shall be so regarded except sections 12 to 15 of the Sale of Goods Act 1979."

The contracting in requirement of s.1(3) will be replaced by contracting out should the Vienna Convention be adopted in the UK.

2. The condition / warranty distinction adopted by the Sale of Goods Act 1979 is replaced by a notion of fundamental breach in Article 10, which (unlike the condition / warranty distinction) has regard to the effects of the breach, and is therefore similar in principle to the innominate term developed from the Court of Appeal decision in *Hongkong Fir Shipping Co Ltd v Kawasaki Kisen Kaisha Ltd* [1962] 2 Q.B. 26. The Vienna Convention (Article 25) adopts a similar distinction, but with a more objective definition of fundamental breach. This is strikingly at odds with the UK development, especially that described in chapter 3, above.

3. The property provisions in Articles 52–53 of U.L.I.S. deal only with encumbrances, and not with the timing of passing of property as between the seller and buyer. A similar provision can be found in the Vienna Convention (Article 42).

4. Article 9 of U.L.I.S. (and indeed of the Vienna Convention) would appear to allow the parties to continue to adopt terms such as c.i.f. and f.o.b., in which case presumably those terms would take precedence over any other parts of either convention with which they conflicted. This could obviously give rise to interpretation problems where, for example, the UK law would regard a term of a c.i.f. or f.o.b. contract as a condition.

The full text of U.L.I.S. and the Vienna Convention (which are in any case set out in the appendices) can be found respectively (links tested in August 2002) at: *www.jus.uio.no/lm/unidroit.ulis.convention.1964/doc.html* and *www.jus.uio.no/lm/un. contracts.international.sale.of.goods.convention.1980/index.html*.

Reference might also usefully be made to UNCITRAL's and UNIDROIT's home pages, respectively (links tested in August 2002) at: *www.uncitral.org/en-index.htm* and *www.jus.uio.no/lm/unidroit.doc.html*.

See also, on The Vienna Convention, Bernstein and Lookofsky, *Understanding the CISG in Europe* (Kluwer Law International, 1997); the Vienna Convention is also known as the "Convention on Contracts for the International Sale of Goods", or "CISG".

U.L.I.S., as enacted in Schedule 1 of the Uniform Laws on International Sales Act 1967, is set out in Appendix G, below. The Vienna Convention is set out in Appendix H, below.

J.D. FELTHAM, "THE APPROPRIATION TO A C.I.F. CONTRACT OF GOODS LOST OR DAMAGED AT SEA"

[1975] J.B.L. 273

[Footnotes are as in the original, but renumbered for inclusion in this book.]

If a contract governed by the Uniform Law on the International Sale of **15–016** Goods[39] provides that the goods are to be sold on c.i.f. terms, a difficult

---

[39] If the proper law of the contract is English law, the Uniform Law on Sales will apply to the contract only if it has been chosen by the parties to the contract as the law of the contract: Uniform Laws on International Sales Act 1967, s.1(3).

question arises as to how the reference to c.i.f. terms shows an intention to incorporate the normal incidents of a c.i.f. contract at common law, even when inconsistent with the provisions of the Uniform Law.[40] But so far as the provisions of the Uniform Law are relevant, a basic rule is that the risk shall pass to the buyer when delivery is effected in accordance with the provisions of the contract and the Uniform Law.[41] Under Article 19.2 where the contract of sale involves the carriage of goods and no other place for delivery has been agreed upon, delivery shall be effected by handing over the goods to the carrier for transmission to the buyer. The words "for transmission to the buyer" appear to necessitate an appropriation for risk to pass at this stage under this provision. It is provided in Article 19.3 that where goods handed over to a carrier are not clearly appropriated to performance of the contract, the seller shall, in addition to handing over the goods, send to the buyer notice of the consignment and, if necessary, some document specifying the goods. Article 100 provides that, in a case to which Article 19.3 applies, the seller, at the time of sending the notice or other document referred to in that paragraph, knew or ought to have known that the goods had been lost or had deteriorated after they were handed over to the carrier, the risk shall remain with the seller until the time of sending such notice or document. There appears to be an implication that, in a case where the seller neither knew nor ought to have known of the loss or deterioration, he may by his notice pass the risk to the buyer as from some earlier time, presumably shipment. But on the other hand a seller c.i.f. appears to be precluded from effectively appropriating to his contract goods known to have been lost or to have deteriorated[42] at sea so as to pass the risk of such earlier loss or deterioration to the buyer.

Article 99.1 states the general rule that where the sale is of goods in transit by sea, the risk shall be borne by the buyer as from the time at which the goods were handed over to the carrier. But Article 99.2 provides that where the seller, at the time of the conclusion of the contract, knew or ought to have known that the goods had been lost or had deteriorated, the risk shall remain with him until the time of conclusion of the contract. In view of Article 100, the main bite of Article 99.2 is probably as to the sale afloat of specific goods. But it implies that, in a case where the seller neither knows nor ought to know of the loss or deterioration of goods, that he may appropriate to a contract goods which have been lost or deteriorated at sea before the conclusion of the contract so as to pass the risk of such loss or deterioration to the buyer.

Notes
1. As to whether the U.L.I.S. position mirrors that of the common law, see further the discussion in chapter 4, above. If it does not (and surely that must be

---

[40] See Uniform Law on the International Sale of Goods, Art. 9.
[41] *ibid.* Art. 97.1.
[42] Presumably "deterioration" includes impairment in quality or value otherwise than by natural decay.

the right conclusion?), then there is, of course, the problem of which regime prevails.

2. The risk provisions in Article 67(2) of the Vienna Convention (see Appendix H, below), depending as they do on appropriation, probably do not mirror the common law rules discussed in chapter 4, above: *cf.*, for example, *C. Groom v Barber*, where the loss almost certainly preceded any appropriation to the contract.

3. This is but one example, but it is perhaps sufficient to give an inkling as to the types of problems that may be encountered, under UK law, when the parties adopt U.L.I.S., but contract on c.i.f. (or indeed f.o.b.) terms. These problems seem no less severe under the Vienna Convention, were that convention to become part of UK law.

GAFTA 100, CLAUSE 33 (INTERNATIONAL CONVENTIONS)

The following shall not apply to this contract: **15–017**

(a) The Uniform Law on Sales and the Uniform Law on Formation to which effect is given by the Uniform Laws on International Sales Act 1967;

(b) the United Nations Convention on Contracts for the International Sale of Goods of 1980; and

(c) the United Nations Convention on Prescription (Limitation) in the International Sale of Goods of 1974 and the amending Protocol of 1980.

Comment

Para. (b) is, of course, the Vienna Convention. Whether or not the Vienna Convention is adopted in the U.K., then, it will not be adopted by GAFTA members, or (presumably) other large commodity traders.

(2) Containerisation and Multimodal Transport

As was explained in chapter 1, above, one of the revolutions in maritime   **15–017A**
transport in the second half of the 20th century was the introduction of containerisation. Containerisation has a number of features, all of which have potential consequences for the law of international trade:

1. Container ships are fast, and also allow fast cargo-handling. There has not been a similar increase, however, in speed of processing documentation.

2. Containers carry high value cargo which is not generally re-sold on the voyage. Hence, the need for negotiable documentation is reduced.

3. Containers lend themselves to multimodal transport operations, where they are stuffed and loaded, not at the port of shipment, and discharged, not at the port of discharge, but in each case at an inland container depot.

There will typically be, therefore, a land leg, followed by a sea and a second land leg. Over that time the container will not be inspected.

(a) Fast Ships and Use of Non-negotiable Documentation

15–018   The emphasis with container operations is speed, and perhaps because of the relatively high value of the goods being moved, the market demands fast container ships, such as, for example, those operating in the North Atlantic. Unfortunately documentation still has to be processed and posted, and so the speed of the documents has not kept pace; North Atlantic voyages are relatively short, in fast vessels. Also with liner shipments, processing by the loading brokers often takes place after the ship has departed, and can take time.

If the ship arrives before the documents the shipowner faces the unappetising choice of waiting around (and not earning freight) until the documents catch up, or risk delivering without production of a bill of lading. The latter course of action is exceedingly risky: see, *e.g. Sze Hai Tong Bank Ltd v Rambler Cycle Co Ltd*, and other cases discussed in para. 6–016, above.

A possible solution is to use, instead of a bill of lading, a document which the consignee does not need to present to obtain delivery of the goods. The sea waybill or liner waybill is such a document, which for this reason can be carried on the ship itself. It is not, unlike the bill of lading, a negotiable document, and delivery is made to a named consignee.

KURT GRUNFORS (PROFESSOR OF MARITIME LAW AND TRANSPORT LAW, UNIVERSITY OF GOTHENBURG) "CONTAINER BILLS OF LADING AND MULTIMODAL TRANSPORT DOCUMENTS"

Paper presented to the UNCTAD Seminar on Ocean Transport Documentation and its Simplification, 1980

Bills of Lading and Waybills—Two Types of Documents Having Different Origins

15–019   There exist two main types of transport documents—the ocean bill of lading and the land or air waybill (consignment note). Their legal effects differ very much from each other. The reason why is to be found in their origin.

Historically the bill of lading constitutes a document developed in order to meet the need of ocean transportation, where carriage takes a long time and there is a need for a document representing the goods for transactional purposes in the meantime. The first bill of lading in the modern sense of this word dates from about 1500, and the first time the document is mentioned in a statutory text is in a provision of the Swedish Maritime Code of 1667.

In practice, the waybill was developed within the framework of land transportation in the 17th and 18th centuries. Originally it was regulated in detail in the first version of the Convention on rail transport (CIM 1890), and these rules were copied later, as for their main lines, in the Warsaw Convention on air carriage and in the Convention on road transport (CMR, 1956 [incorporated into UK law by the Schedule to the Carriage of Goods by Road Act 1965]). In these branches of the transport industry, the time of transit was not as long as in ocean transportation, and thus there was no need of buying and selling the goods when in transit. As a consequence the waybill was not representing the goods.

The main difference as to the legal effects cannot be explained by the difference of the scope of application only. The character of the documents in question is best understood if we keep in mind the following two historical starting points:

(1) the bill of lading is a promise from the carrier to his customer;

(2) the waybill is a notice from the sender to the receiver, without the carrier even being involved . . .

This basic difference explains why the waybill does not represent the goods, and why the possession of the waybill is no prerequisite for the delivery of the goods at the place of final destination. The receiver is the party named as receiver in the waybill. If (1) he can identify himself, and if (2) he requests the delivery of the goods by the carrier or his agent at the place of final destination, he has the right to have the goods delivered as soon as they have arrived.

These very clear border-lines relating to the contract of carriage, however, were somewhat confused later on. The particulars on the goods, given in a waybill, were naturally binding upon the carrier, as he kept outside the notice. But gradually carriers were more and more interested in controlling what particulars were given by the senders, writing letters to receivers. The first step of involving the carrier seems to have been that the sender showed the letter to the carrier and had him confirm the correctness of the details given in the waybill by writing a short sentence of confirmation and his name. The next step was that the carrier himself issued the waybill, which thereby was based on the contract of carriage and thus also included a promise from the carrier to his customer, just like the bill of lading. In spite of this, commercial life still kept to the special character of the waybill as not representing the goods, possible to explain only by having its history in mind. The details of this historical development have not yet been fully investigated by legal historians, but the main lines of the evolution are ostensible from the materials available.

Today both types of document can be said to fulfil three main functions: the receipt of the goods that have been taken in charge by the carrier, the evidence of the contract of carriage and the basis for security in the goods as to the money in settlement.

UNITED NATIONS CONFERENCE ON TRADE AND DEVELOPMENT (UNCTAD). TRADE AND DEVELOPMENT BOARD AD HOC INTERGOVERNMENTAL GROUP TO CONSIDER MEANS OF COMBATING ALL ASPECTS OF MARITIME FRAUD, INCLUDING PIRACY

Second session, October 1985

Chapter III

Reduction in the Number of Bills of Lading or their Replacement by Another Document

15–020   53. The bill of lading has always been an extremely important document in international trade. Nevertheless, many problems are connected with its use. Owing to its being a negotiable document it has unfortunately also been used as a tool in fraudulent transactions, particularly because of the practice of issuing bills in several originals [see chapter 1]. Owing to reduced transit times in maritime carriage and slow mail service, the bills of lading system is close to collapse where goods arrive at destination before the bill of lading.

A. Contribution by the International Maritime Committee (CMI)

54. In response to the request of the Ad hoc Intergovernmental Group, the International Maritime Committee (CMI) replied that at the end of the CMI Venice Colloquium [1983] eight recommendations were adopted and then unanimously approved by the CMI Assembly. The first, third and fourth recommendations are worded as follows:

> "1. The practice of issuing bills of lading in sets of two or more originals should cease.
>
>   . . .
>
> 3. The practice of issuing a bill of lading when a negotiable document is not required should be discouraged.
> 4. Uniform rules for incorporation in sea waybills should be prepared and their adoption encouraged."

55. With respect to the first and third recommendations, the Colloquium could not find any real practical need for maintaining the practice—or rather malpractice—of issuing bills of lading in more than one original. In particular, keeping one original on board and tendering that original to someone at destination would at best upset the very function of a negotiable transport document, which is to enable the transfer of property while the goods are being carried by sea and, at worst, engage

the shipowner in a heavy liability where the bill of lading by mistake was tendered to the wrong party. But, even more important, in the great majority of cases a bill of lading is not necessary at all. As has been said, its main function is to enable the goods to be sold in transit by the transfer of the very document from one party to another. This is only required with respect to bulk commodities and very seldom, if ever, with respect to general cargo. In the debate it was suggested that shipping lines should charge a considerable amount for a bill of lading, particularly if requested in several originals, in order to discourage merchants from requesting bills of lading where this is not absolutely necessary. Such charges may well be required only because of the additional costs and risks which the bills of lading system carries with it . . .

B. Contribution by the International Chamber of Shipping (ICS)

Sea waybills

59. With regard to the replacement of the bill of lading by another **15–021** document, such as a non-negotiable document, ICS has recently participated in a meeting of the CMI in which the CMI agreed to establish a working group to examine the legal issues involved in substitution of non-negotiable documentation for the currently widely used negotiable bill of lading. Some of the members of the ICS have taken this issue up nationally. The brochure issued by their United Kingdom member, the General Council of British Shipping is worded as follows:

"Twenty years ago, when most cargo was carried on conventional vessels, documentary delays were not a serious problem, as there was usually time for negotiable bills of lading to catch up with the cargo. Containerization, faster vessels, fewer ports of call and improved terminal facilities have greatly reduced transit time but often the processing of bills of lading fails to match this. The result is that many consignments arrive at their destinations before the necessary documentation. This is inefficient and costly for all concerned. To bridge this gap between the movement times of goods and essential documents, a new form—the waybill—was developed. A waybill is a non-negotiable document, which does not have to be presented at destination. The named consignee or his authorized agent takes delivery of the goods subject to proof of identity and authority, although in certain countries national law still demands presentation of a bill of lading. Waybills have been in limited but successful use for several years, notably on the Scandinavian and North American services, where the problems of delayed documents and faster transit times were particularly acute. In January 1977, the General Council of British Shipping (GCBS) and SITPRO [Simplification of International Trade Procedures Board] took these developments further with the introduction of the GCBS Common Short Form Sea Waybill. The sea waybill is recommended by GCBS and SITPRO, and is already acceptable to carriers in many trades."

60. A separate publication by SITPRO provides details of the Common Short Form Bill of Lading which can be used where a bill of lading is still required. At this stage, however, it may be of some value to note briefly the nature of the GCBS Common Short Form Sea Waybill. The sea waybill is non-negotiable and acts as both a receipt and evidence of the contract of carriage. It not only reduces direct documentation costs, but also by helping to solve the problems caused by late documentation, it eliminates many indirect costs. Unlike existing sea waybills, the form does not bear individual shipping line logos and the exporter or freight forwarder merely has to insert the name of the carrier being used. Instead of containing conditions and clauses in small print on the form, the sea waybill contains an incorporation clause referring to the detailed conditions of carriage which are available separately. The sea waybill is a "received for carriage" document which can be converted into a "shipped" or "loaded on board" document by means of appropriate notations by the carrier as provided for by the Carriage of Goods by Sea Act 1971 [see chapter 11]. Since the sea waybill is not a document of title the consignee does not usually need to take possession of the goods and the release is given on the basis of conditions laid down by the carrier or other persons controlling the cargo at its destination. In this way the importer can be provided with a complete set of other documents and arrange clearance much sooner than if negotiable bills of lading were awaited.

61. The sea waybill is not intended to replace the bill of lading where it is necessary for the exporter to retain clear title to the goods until security for payment is assured, although there are numerous instances where the sea waybill could be acceptable, for example, trade between multinational and associated companies or open-account sales. It could also be used for shipments which involve no payment, for example, shipments of samples or household effects.

62. Use of the sea waybill is not restricted to members of the GCBS but is available to all carriers for outward liner shipments from the United Kingdom. It is acceptable for United Kingdom value added tax purposes as evidence of exportation provided it is fully completed.It can be used in the system of documentary credits provided that it is authorised for such use by the instructions of the buyer and seller. It is also fully acceptable as proof of shipment when converted into a "shipped" or "loaded on board" document for the purposes of the Export Credit Guarantee Department. Further, as a "shipped on board" document, it is acceptable to the Intervention Board for Agricultural Produce as evidence of shipment and intended destination for the purpose of payment of refunds or collection of levies under the terms of the Common Agricultural Policy.

takes charge of the goods. When shipping goods in containers, whether as full container load (FCL) or less than full container load (LCL), the exporter should give preference to one of the container terms rather than uses a term appropriate to non-container shipment. The UCPDC provide that transport documents used in container transport are acceptable to banks under letters of credit unless the credit calls for a marine bill of lading, a post receipt or a certificate of posting.[44]

(ii) *Multimodal Transport Documents*

Though the arrangements for the entire carriage will usually be undertaken by one person (typically a freight forwarder) there are likely to be three different actual carriers, one for each leg. Diana Faber distinguishes between two types of operation[45]: **15–027**

"A combined transport contract is one under which the person contracting with the cargo interests undertakes legal responsibility for the entire transportation of the goods using different means of transport between the points named in the contract. Under this type of contract the cargo interests can claim against that person for damage to their goods which was caused at any point in the journey. Through transport contracts are those under which that person undertakes responsibility for the care of the goods only when he has control of them. He acts as agent for the cargo interests in entering into contracts with the carriers and others involved in the transportation."

The essence of the combined (or multimodal) transport document proper is that one carrier, usually the forwarding agent, makes himself responsible for the entire operation. He may sub-contract each stage, or more commonly each stage after the initial land leg, but he contracts with the shipper as principal, undertaking primary liability himself. He is therefore liable in contract if the goods are damaged on any of the three stages, although if he is sued for damage caused while the goods are in the custody of another carrier, he should be able to recoup his costs from that other carrier.[46] The only contract of carriage, however, is with the single contracting carrier, often referred to as a Combined Transport Operator (C.T.O.).

The multimodal transport document, used for the combined transport contract is therefore similar, in principle, to the through bill of lading described in chapter 6, except that the through bill of lading covers successive stages of sea transit, where there is transhipment. As with a through bill, one carrier takes on responsibility for the entire enterprise, but may sub-contract each leg. However, whereas the through bill of lading will be issued by a shipowner or charterer (see paras 12–037 *et seq.*, above), a combined transport document may be issued by a non-vessel operating carrier (N.V.O.C.) such as a freight forwarder, but contracting as principal, as observed in the previous paragraph.

By contrast, under the through transport contract, the forwarding agent acts as shipper's agent in arranging each stage of carriage, the other contracting party being the actual carrier for each stage. Thus there will be three separate carriage contracts with three separate carriers, though made through the agency of the freight forwarder. Alternatively, the forwarding agent may contract as principal

---

[44] U.C.P. 500, Art. 26.
[45] Faber, "The problems arising from multimodal transport" [1996] L.M.C.L.Q. 503, at p. 503.
[46] An issue considered by Faber at pp. 515 *et seq.*

for the first stage and agent for the shipper in arranging carriage for the on stages. In this case he will issue a through transport document (T.T.D.).

KURT GRUNFORS (PROFESSOR OF MARITIME LAW AND TRANSPORT LAW, UNIVERSITY OF GOTHENBURG) "CONTAINER BILLS OF LADING AND MULTIMODAL TRANSPORT DOCUMENTS"

Paper presented to the UNCTAD Seminar on Ocean Transport Documentation and its Simplification, 1980

Bills of Lading Covering Land Transportation and Waybills Covering Ocean Transportation

15–028   The idea of a bill of lading exclusively applicable to maritime transport and the waybill (consignment note) exclusively to land and air transportation is in conformity with the origin of the respective documents. However, the evolution has expanded the scope of both types of documents both ways. In traditional bills of lading the pre-carriage and on-carriage were often by rail or road, though mostly of a very limited length (perhaps of an auxiliary or accessory nature). The modern container bills of lading, introduced in the 60s, expanded the carriage to include the land part, also of a considerable length. Today bills of lading have "gone ashore", if I may put it that way, and cover both land and sea legs of a multi-modal transport, and they are still recognized as bills of lading. At the same time, forwarding agents have "gone to sea" and issued their bills of lading, covering a land-sea-land transport. As bills of lading require much work of issuing and handling, there is today a trend of issuing simpler waybills in cases, where a multimodal transport, including a sea leg, or a single-mode ocean transport do not require the negotiability of the bill of lading; there does not exist any need or any intention to sell the goods to a third person when in transit. Such documents are, since the beginning of the 70s, more and more used and accepted by banks. Thus the traditions of land documentation have been successfully introduced into the maritime milieu . . . It is obviously possible to transfer the pattern of land waybills to cover sea transport also.

ERIK CHRISPEELS (LEGAL OFFICER IN THE UNCTAD SECRETARIAT) "THE CONVENTION AND THE MULTIMODAL TRANSPORT DOCUMENT"

Paper presented to the UNCTAD Seminar on Ocean Transport Documentation and its Simplification, 1980

The Status, Functions and Legal Effects of the Multimodal Transport Document

15–029   The multimodal transport operator contracts and assumes liability for the goods as a principal, not as an agent, in relation to he consignor and his sub-contracting carriers, and he assumes liability for the goods during the entire multimodal transport transit. The contractual undertaking of the multimodal transport operator and the liability assumed by him confer a unique status on the multimodal transport document as compared with traditional transport documents.

By issuing the multimodal transport document, the multimodal transport operator acknowledges that he has received and taken in charge the goods as they are described in that document—quantity, weight, description, marks. The multimodal transport document thus serves as evidence of the receipt by the multimodal transport operator of the identified goods.

By issuing the multimodal transport document, the multimodal transport operator also acknowledges that he will organise the transport of the goods from an agreed place to another against payment of freight, and subject to the liabilities assumed by him and his standard conditions of transport. The multimodal transport document also serves as evidence and as a memorandum of the multimodal transport contract.

The multimodal transport document can be made a document of title to the goods, in which case it symbolically represents the goods. Title in the goods can be transferred to another person by transferring the document.

The multimodal transport document controls delivery of the goods at destination. If it names a consignee, delivery can be made only to that person, without the need to surrender a document. If it is made out to bearer, delivery of the goods at destination can be made to the person surrendering the document, and in such circumstances the multimodal transport document serves as a quasi-negotiable document.

In summary the [United Nations Convention on International Multimodal Transport of Goods, 1980] confers on the multimodal transport document the legal and commercial functions both of a traditional negotiable ocean bill of lading, and of its modern corollary, the non-negotiable sea waybill.

(iii) *Unification of International Conventions*

With combined transport operations, different liability conventions may govern **15–030** each part of the operation, so that the liability regime varies, depending on where damage to the cargo occurs. Road transport, for example, is governed by the C.M.R. Convention, adopted in the UK by the Carriage of Goods by Road Act 1965. The basis of, and limits to, liability are different from those under the Hague and Hague-Visby Rules, so that the basis of liability, limitations and time limits may vary depending on whether damage occurs during the sea carriage, or over land. But if the goods are in a container, it may be difficult to ascertain precisely when the loss occurs; damage which only becomes apparent at stage 3 may have been caused by an event that occurs at stage 1. Arguably, then, it would be better if there were a uniform basis of liability for the entire voyage.

The Hamburg Rules (discussed in paras 11–081, *et seq.*, above and Appendix I, below) look (in principle) well-suited to adaptation to multimodal transport, providing as they do for a single "carrier", who remains liable during the entire operation, whether or not he is also the "actual carrier", who is the person actually entrusted with the goods at the time the damage occurs. Usually the "carrier" is a forwarding agent, but the sea carrier could also undertake this responsibility. Article 1.6, however, provides that " 'Contract of carriage by sea' means any contract whereby the carrier undertakes against payment of freight to carry goods by sea from one port to another; however, a contract which involves carriage by sea and also carriage by some other means is deemed to be a contract of carriage by sea for the purposes of this Convention only in so far as it relates to the carriage by sea." Since the liability limits are lower than those under both the Geneva Convention on Carriage of Goods by Road 1956 and the Berne Convention Concerning International Carriage by Rail 1980, Hamburg does not really address the problems of multimodal transport.

(iv) *Residual Difficulties*

15–031   Even if the problems discussed so far are solved, there are still documentation difficulties. Combined transport documents can be either negotiable or non-negotiable, but as a combined transport document is necessarily issued before shipment, it is conceptually closer to the received for shipment than to the shipped bill of lading.

Received for shipment bills may not be documents of title (see chapter 6, above), and although the Carriage of Goods by Sea Act 1992 applies to received for shipment bills (see chapter 13, above) the definition of a received for shipment bill may not extend to a document issued by an agent of the shipper, possibly hundreds of miles from the loading port. It follows that a bank (or purchaser) which advances money against even a negotiable combined transport document may well obtain security which is inferior to that provided by a shipped bill of lading.

(3) OIL CARGOES AND STANDBY LETTERS OF CREDIT

15–032   We saw at paras 1–047 *et seq.*, that bulk commodities, and in particular bulk oil, are often sold many times on the voyage. Each sale requires an inspection of the documents, perhaps by two banks, as well as transmission between the parties. Obviously, this is a time-consuming process, and so the documents frequently do not arrive until months, or even years after the cargo. Nor is it reasonable to assume that even a seller who is a late participant in the chain will ever have a document of title to tender.

This had led to two major changes in trade practice. First, though the seller may be required to present documents, payment is no longer necessarily triggered by tender of an original bill of lading. In *The Delfini*, for example, payment was by guarantee (standby letter of credit) in the following terms[47]:

"This guarantee is payable at first beneficiary's written request to us in the case of our principals Enichemica S.p.A. fail to pay any amount up to the sum of U.S.$ 6,015,000 within the terms above indicated and against presentation of the following documents:

    (a) a copy or photocopy of the commercial invoice,
    (b) a copy or photocopy of the bill of lading,

---

[47] *Enichem Anic SpA v Ampelos Shipping Co Ltd (The Delfini)* [1990] 1 Lloyd's Rep. 252. See further para. 5–066, above. The terms of the guarantee are set out at 256 (col. 1).

(c) seller's certificate stating that payment has not been made by Enichemica S.p.A. within the due date."

In *The Filiatra Legacy*,[48] the sellers were required to certify that the buyer had failed to fulfil its payment obligation within 30 days from the bill of lading date under the contract, and were entitled to tender a letter of indemnity authorising the shipowners to discharge the cargo to the buyers without production of the bills of lading *in lieu* of original bills of lading.

Secondly, delivery is not made against production of an original bill of lading, but usually on the instructions of the time charterer (who before the oil crisis of 1973 would often have owned the cargo throughout, and even now, will know the identity of the final purchaser in the chain), subject to an indemnity, should the person to whom delivery is made not be entitled. The charterer will also indemnify the shipowner, either expressly or impliedly.[49] In *The Sagona*, Staughton J. commented as follows on the practice in the oil industry at the time (delivery of the cargo was in July 1978):

STAUGHTON J.: . . . What remains is an allegation as to the ordinary **15–033** practice of the oil cargo trade for at least 30 years, and the course of dealing between the owners and the charterers throughout the chartered service. The principal relevance of the practice and course of dealing is, to my mind, as an aid to the interpretation of the orders which the charterers gave, either by their radio-telegram or through the words and conduct of their agent, Mr. Friederichs. But they are also relevant if a question of causation arises, as to whether the misfortune that befell the vessel was a consequence of the charterers' orders, or of the master's failure to ask for a bill of lading. The practice, but not the course of dealing, is further relevant to the interpretation of the charter-party.

Every one of the nine witnesses who gave evidence had something to say on this issue . . . Considerable differences of view emerged from this evidence. In addition it has to be considered whether the practice and course of dealing were different when a vessel was carrying an in-house cargo, from that which prevailed when the vessel was sub-chartered or otherwise carrying a cargo which had no connection with the Total group.

Furthermore it is plain that the practice changed after July, 1978, partly as a direct consequence of the events that occurred in this case and partly as a result of changes in the nature and structure of the oil industry which had been occurring since 1973. So I am concerned with the practice and course of dealing which existed up to and including July, 1978. I shall consider the topic under two sub-headings: (i) was it the practice and course of dealing for the master to check that the receivers had a properly endorsed bill of lading? (ii) Was it the practice and course of dealing for the agent to check that the receivers had a properly endorsed bill of lading?

---

[48] *Anonima Petroli Italiana SpA v Marlucidez Armadora SA (The Filiatra Legacy)* [1991] 1 Lloyd's Rep. 337, also at paras 5–070, *et seq.*, above.
[49] Expressly, for example, in *The Houda*—see paras 6–007, *et seq.*, above, impliedly in *The Sagona* [1984] 1 Lloyd's Rep. 194.

(i) *The master*

15–034 It was not disputed that the owners by their master have, in law, the right to withhold delivery until a properly endorsed bill of lading is produced. (No doubt that proposition assumes that a bill of lading has been issued.) Equally it was not disputed that, in law, if the cargo is delivered without production of a bill of lading to someone who is not entitled to it, the owners are liable in damages for breach of contract, and the owners and their master are liable in damages for conversion, to the holder of the bill of lading. Candidates for a British master's certificate are taught their legal responsibilities in this respect when studying for the examinations set by the Department of Trade. So too the protection and indemnity associations from time to time issue circulars to their members, emphasizing the duty of masters to obtain appropriate security if cargo is to be delivered without production of a bill of lading, and the limitation or exclusion which would affect the association's cover if that were not done.

Those considerations are only directly relevant to the duties and obligations owed by owners and masters to the holders of bills of lading. They do not bear directly on the question of what duty is owed by an owner, through his master, to a time charterer. But one might have thought from that material, or indeed from the limited perspective of the practice in carriage of goods by sea which is enjoyed by lawyers, that a bill of lading or letter of indemnity always would be obtained by a ship's master before delivering cargo, with perhaps rare exceptions such as would stimulate the P. and I. associations to issue their circulars. Whether that happens in the carriage of dry cargo, either in bulk or in many different parcels separately shipped, is not a question upon which I need make any finding in this case. In the oil cargo trade, I am convinced by the evidence that it by no means always happens. One circumstance peculiar to the oil cargo trade is that a very quick turnround of the vessel in port is expected (in this case the vessel spent a total of some 42 hours at the berth in Nordenham). Others may be that a bill of lading is less likely to reach the receivers in time to be presented at the port of discharge; or that it is less easy to store a bulk oil cargo to the order of the shipowners, thus suspending delivery but allowing the ship to leave; or that there is a much higher proportion of in-house shipments in the carriage of oil; or that participants in the oil industry, at any rate until 1973, were all substantial companies who would not disappear or become insolvent.[50] Only the last two of those reasons would explain the failure to ask for a letter of indemnity, if there were no bill of lading. But the circumstances peculiar to the oil industry were not much explored in evidence, and I make no finding upon them. I merely indicate that, if there was a difference between the practice for dry cargo and that for bulk oil, there may have been facts which justified it.

---

[50] See further para. 1–047, above, on developments in oil trading following the Yom Kippur war of 1973 [footnote author's own].

Captain Elvehoy, the master of the *Sagona*, had been at sea in command of tankers since 1970. Asked how often an original bill of lading had been presented to him prior to discharge, he answered: "I have never seen it". On a number of occasions he had been given one original of the bill of lading, at the port of loading, in a sealed envelope which was addressed to the receivers, *eo nomine*, or to the agent, or to the receivers through the agent. That had not happened on the voyage to Nordenham in this case. The master's practice was to hand the envelope, when there was one, to the agent at the port of discharge.

That evidence was supported by Captain Bardset, who served as alternate master to Captain Elvehoy during the period when the vessel was on charter to the charterers; and by Captain Rodahl, Captain Rutherford and Captain English, expert witnesses called on behalf of the owners. In particular, Captain Rodahl said that at college he had been taught that, in practice, a master seldom saw an original bill of lading at the port of discharge. He for his part had never carried an original bill of lading, even in a sealed envelope; but he had heard of the practice. Captain Rutherford said that what he learnt at college differed greatly from his experience in practice. He could not recall having been presented with a bill of lading, except in rare circumstances. All five witnesses justified their failure to enquire whether the receiver had a bill of lading, by saying that it was up to the agent to see to the receiver's title.

The expert witnesses called by the owners were all men of great experience and were impressive witnesses. I cannot and do not reject their evidence. It is confirmed to some extent by an incident that happened to Captain Bardset at Immingham on a later voyage. The log extract for Nov. 12 and 13, 1978, reads as follows:

"12.11.78 1900 hrs. Discharge hoses connected Representatives for the Cargo Receivers arrived on board and enquired about loading papers. I then asked for original B/L which he did not have, but would enquire about them ashore (the office). Chief Supervisor C. Samuel came on board immediately after and asked if it was true that I would not discharge before having the original B/L. I confirmed this, and said either the original B/L, Bank Guarantees or 'Letter of Indemnity'. He got quite annoyed and told us to leave berth and go to anchor and wait there until Tuesday, which was the earliest he could get an original B/L.

13.11.78 0905 hrs. A representative from Cargo Receivers came on board and asked if it was true that I would not discharge without an original B/L. He thought this strange because he had never before been asked to produce an original B/L. As he said, a copy, but no-one had ever asked for the original B/L. He said it was unusual that an original B/L had to be produced.

2230 hrs. Mr. Heinz Schmidt from Vlissingen came on board with the original B/L. I had to sign a photocopy of the original B/L to confirm that I had received original B/L. C. Supervisor P. Karton advised us that they had about 4 VLCC and 25 coast boats and 4 others at the yard a month, but none had ever asked for an original B/L."

It was agreed that all the documents in the bundle could be read as evidence of the facts stated therein. Further confirmation came from two documents disclosed by the charterers on discovery. These related to the discharge of vessels in different ownership at Wilhelmshaven. In each case Lehnkering A.G. were the agents and Total the charterers. In neither case was an original bill of lading produced. It was common ground that at Wilhelmshaven, in contrast with other ports, the master of a vessel would deal directly with receivers. Evidently the masters did not insist on an original bill of lading on those two occasions.

15–035   The evidence to the contrary was that of Captain Michaels, who was also a man of great experience and an impressive witness. He said that on only one occasion had he been asked by receivers to discharge a cargo without presentation of an original bill of lading, and had eventually agreed to do so against a letter of indemnity. On a very few other occasions he had been authorized to discharge without a bill of lading —but not at the request of the receivers. In the great majority of cases he had always insisted that an original bill of lading be presented.

There are two reasons why I do not think that Captain Michaels' experience was representative of the general practice. First, he seemed to me to be an exceptionally careful and meticulous man—and as it turned out he was right, as he told me. Secondly, his experience was very much confined to in-house cargoes, or tonnage exchange contracts where the same considerations applied. Those comprised between 80 and 90 per cent. of his voyages. He had an original bill of lading on board, in an envelope, for 85 per cent. of all cargoes. Sometimes the envelope containing the bill of lading was unsealed; in that event he would take the bill of lading out on arrival in order to save time. When the envelope was sealed, he would produce it to the receiver and ask if he could see the bill of lading; the receiver would allow him to do so. In either case he would mark the bill of lading to show that he had seen it, and the time when he had done so. He had never commanded a time chartered ship. He did not regard it as the agent's function to deal with documentation for the cargo.

There is also the Civil Evidence Act statement of Mr. Jegede. He states, and I accept, that of the 26 voyages performed by the *Sagona* under the time charter before the Nordenham voyage, 13 involved discharge at Lagos (of those 13, eight were very short voyages on a shuttle from Port Harcourt refinery); and an original bill of lading was carried on board the vessel for the consignee. He also states that a representative of his operations department attended on board the vessel and—

" . . . received the original bill of lading plus a copy bill of lading from the master personally."

On the completion of discharge, the master's copy of the bill of lading was signed as accomplished. What Mr. Jegede does not state is whether the original bill of lading was extracted from its envelope and examined by the master, or whether the master merely handed over the envelope. Mr. Jegede could not be asked as he did not give oral evidence. On that state of the evidence I do not consider that I should reject the version put forward by Captain Elvehoy and Captain Bardset, that bills of lading were not presented to them during this time charter at the ports of discharge.

Documentary evidence also shows that of the 26 voyages only two involved a sub-charter. It is not wholly clear that the remaining 24 were all concerned with in-house cargoes; but I am prepared to assume, in favour of the charterers, that they were.

On the evidence as a whole I conclude (1) that it was a common but not universal practice in the carriage of oil cargoes up to July, 1978, for the master not to insist upon presentation of an original bill of lading or a letter of indemnity at the port of discharge; and (2) that the common practice formed part of the course of dealing under this charter, whether the vessel was carrying in-house cargo or (as on two occasions) cargo procured by sub-charterers.

[Staughton J. then went on to discuss the practices of the agent at the discharge port.]

Comment

Staughton J.'s findings of fact were important because, had the time charterers' order to discharge, without production of an original bill, been manifestly unlawful, the master should have disregarded it. The charterers would then not have caused any loss occasioned to the shipowners, and would not have been liable on the implied indemnity. However, because delivery without production was normal, there was no reason for the master, or the charterers, to suppose that the receivers were not entitled to the cargo.[51] The instruction to discharge was normal, and apparently legitimate. There was no reason for the master to disregard it. It was the order, and not the master's obedience of it, that caused loss to the shipowners, and the charterers were accordingly liable to indemnify.

Let us suppose, anyway, that the practices described in *The Delfini*; *The Filiatra Legacy*; *The Houda* and *The Sagona* are commonplace. The bill of lading would provide a bank (for example), on a documentary credit, no security at all. Realistically, the cargo would be delivered without its production, and property would necessarily pass to the receivers, on mixing the cargo with his own oil, already in the refinery. The bill of lading holder would be left with personal actions against the receiver (for conversion) and the shipowner, and the shipowner would have personal actions on indemnities (as in *The Sagona*).

A form of security is still built into the system, but it depends entirely on personal actions, fine as long as nobody goes bankrupt. Clearly the bill of lading is no longer performing any of its traditional security functions. Perhaps it is no wonder that the banks are content to advance money on standby letters of credit, since their security would not be significantly improved, in practice, by their demanding a document of title.

15–036

---

[51] One of the banks earlier in the chain had not been reimbursed.

The system could also be potentially fraud-prone, in that a criminal, purporting to be the time charterer, could instruct the master, perhaps by telex, to deliver to an accomplice. There is no bill of lading to provide an independent check. Frauds similar to this are described by Barbara Conway, in her book entitled *Maritime Fraud* (in para. 10–018, above).

Note also that none of the solutions discussed earlier in this chapter are appropriate here, for clearly a non-negotiable document is not the answer. Computerised documentation may be, at least in principle: see further chapter 16, below.

(4) Fraud and Maritime Crime

15–037   All businesses are exposed to a risk of fraud and other crimes, and although there is a lot of concern about maritime crime, the figures suggest that its extent can probably be measured in tenths of one per cent of the total maritime industry.[52] If the costs could be spread evenly across the industry, in other words, they would be regarded as fairly insignificant. Readers might object to this conclusion, but surely it must be true, if (as the evidence suggests) traders are prepared to tolerate, decade upon decade, a system which is extraordinarily vulnerable to fraud.

In reality, of course, the costs are not spread evenly; there is little redress for individual fraud and maritime crime victims, and it is proper to consider their position as serious. Maritime crime can certainly have serious consequences for individuals, not necessarily financial; in extreme cases, for example where ships and cargoes are taken by pirates, it is not unknown for entire crews to be killed and thrown overboard. The ships may then reappear as "phantom ships", ostensibly trading legitimately, but in reality with a view to stealing the cargoes of those who are induced into using them.

It is also reasonable to argue that preventive steps need to be taken, to keep the costs of maritime crime to reasonable proportions.

There are features of maritime fraud which are peculiar to the maritime enterprise:

1. The system has been developed to promote speed and convenience, with low transaction costs. This is the whole point of container transport, and in bulk commodity trading it manifests itself in negotiability of documentation. These aims are, however, the antithesis of fraud prevention, and almost any attempts to reduce fraud will tend increase both costs and delay.[53] It is hardly an exaggeration, therefore, to say that the system positively encourages fraud.

   The courts also seem to have developed the law on the assumption that this is what the parties want. "The object of mercantile usages is to prevent the risk of insolvency, not of fraud" is a well-known quote,[54] and the sentiment has been oft-repeated. The law has developed, apparently in

---

[52] Definitive figures are naturally hard to find. Most estimates suggest $US billions, but probably not tens of billions, against legitimate trade of about $US 4,000 billion a year.

[53] An example of this is the deferred payment credit, which allows the bank greater time to investigate whether false or forged documents have been tendered. But sellers are not prepared to wait for their money, and payment by time draft, which can be negotiated for cash, has rendered the deferred payment credit almost obsolete. A bank would be ill-advised to negotiate a deferred payment credit, since it would then bear the risk of fraud being discovered before payment: *Banco Santander SA v Bayfern Ltd* [2000] Lloyd's Rep. Bank. 165.

[54] *Sanders v Maclean* (1883) 11 Q.B.D. 327, 343, *per* Bowen L.J.

accordance with commercial practice,[55] to promote negotiability, but with that comes an inevitable increase in fraud risk.[56] The system described in this book protects the commercial parties against the non-performance of other traders, and against their bankruptcy if they have no assets, but is vulnerable to fraudulent attack.

2. Relatively little maritime crime is committed by insiders. Fraudsters will rarely be fiduciaries, and equitable tracing of proceeds, and associated actions, will not normally be available.

3. The necessarily international nature of the crime gives rise to jurisdictional problems.

(a) Types of Maritime Crime

(i) *Piracy, Phantom Ships and Non-existent Cargoes*

Piracy

At the serious end of the spectrum is piracy. This is necessarily a violent crime,[57] **15–038** and has become more serious over the last decade or so. No longer is it confined largely to thefts of equipment and other valuables from ships. Thefts of entire ships and cargoes are now common, the vessels being forcibly taken, often with loss of life, in the most serious cases of the entire crew. The ISF and ICF observe that perennial danger areas include the

> "Malacca and Singapore Straits and the whole area in the vicinity of Singapore (though usually not in Singapore territorial waters). Attacks usually occur whilst ships are transiting the Straits, sometimes up to 15 miles offshore, when embarking or disembarking pilots and even during lightening operations. The majority of cases in this area have involved pirates operating from Indonesian islands."[58]

In *Petro Pirates*,[59] Captain Ken Blyth describes how the *Cheung Son*, which was hijacked in March 1998, was seized off Hong Kong by a gang posing as Chinese customs officials, the entire crew of 23 being murdered. From the viewpoint of the people directly involved, these are brutal crimes, which could hardly be more serious. Moreover, it is estimated that they cost insurers some $ US 200 to 400 million annually.[60] It is essential that these crimes be effectively countered, for example by tracking of vessels, training of crews,[61] and collection of information by the International Maritime Bureau.

---

[55] The justification for the decision in *Gill & Duffus SA v Berger & Co Inc* [1984] A.C. 382, which surely promotes negotiability at the expense of security, is that the contrary view, "if correct, would destroy the very roots of the system by which international trade, particularly in commodities, is enabled to be financed", *per* Lord Diplock at 392.

[56] A fairly extreme case, where the law could not be invoked to prevent what appears to have been a very clear fraud, is *Discount Records Ltd v Barclays Bank Ltd* [1975] 1 W.L.R. 315, [1975] 1 Lloyd's Rep. 444.

[57] As defined by Staughton J. (at any rate for marine insurance purposes) in *Athens Maritime v Hellenic Mutual War Risks (The Andreas Lemos)* [1983] Q.B. 647.

[58] *Pirates & armed robbers—A master's guide* (3rd ed., 1999), at p. 7.

[59] Blyth *Petro Pirates* (Allen Unwin) p. 149.

[60] *ibid.* at p. 146.

[61] Ken Blyth records an attack on an Australian tanker which was thwarted by a well-trained crew and officers *ibid.* at pp. 139 and 157.

The cargo-owner will usually suffer a total loss of cargo, and there will be no redress against the carrier. Bill of lading contracts will usually be governed by the *Hague Rules* or *Hague-Visby Rules*, Article III(2) of which requires the shipowner "properly and carefully [to] load, handle, stow, carry, keep, care for, and discharge the goods carried". As long as he has done this, he will incur no liability for failure to deliver the cargo. Piracy is in any case normally regarded as peril of the sea,[62] which is an excepted peril under Article IV(2)(c). The shipowner will also usually lose his ship, without redress from the cargo-owner. As between shipowner and cargo-owner, therefore, the losses will usually lie where they fall, but marine insurance policies will often cover the loss.

15–039   One of the best documented recent pirate attacks is that of *The Petro Ranger* in April 1998,[63] where an oil tanker was seized, a few hours out from Singapore, on a two-day voyage to Vietnam. She later reappeared as the *Wilby*, the pirates having also placed false registration papers on board and created false bills of lading for the cargo. Most of the cargo was stolen by the pirates, and smuggled into China. Had events gone to plan, from the pirates' viewpoint, the remaining cargo would also have been stolen and sold, the vessel sold (as *Wilby*) and the crew killed (this would probably already have occurred, had their co-operation not been required in transferring the cargo to other vessels). The vessel was however detained by the Chinese authorities, after which the crew were able to escape,[64] and the pirates discovered.

The vessel was eventually recovered by the owners, slightly but not particularly badly damaged. When the vessel was recovered by the Chinese authorities, some cargo remained on board, and another small quantity had been transhipped by the pirates aboard a lighter, *Jin Chao*, which was also captured. All of it was eventually transferred into shore tanks controlled by the Chinese authorities, but (it was alleged) on the basis that the owners and Chinese authorities (into whose tanks the cargo was eventually discharged) had reached an "unspoken understanding". In respect of this recovered cargo alone could the shipowners thereby incur liability. This was successfully argued in respect of the cargo still on board the tanker, although in respect of the *Jin Chao* cargo, the case was remitted to the arbitrators, and eventual liability not determined.

In *The Petro Ranger*, the cargo-owners sued on the charterparty to which they were party, property presumably not having passed by the time of the piracy event. The charterparty constituted piracy as a specific exception[65]:

"19. General exceptions clause . . . And neither the Vessel nor Master or Owner nor the Charterer, shall, unless otherwise in this Charter expressly provided, be responsible for any loss or damage or delay or failure in performing hereunder, arising or resulting from . . . perils of the sea; act of public enemies, pirates or assailing thieves; arrest or restraint of princes, rulers or people, or seizure under legal process provided bond is promptly furnished to release the Vessel or cargo."

The shipowners unsuccessfully argued this clause in *The Petro Ranger*, failing on causation, the court refusing to interfere with the findings of the arbitrators, at

---

[62] *The Bunga Seroja* [1999] 1 Lloyd's Rep. 512.

[63] [2001] 2 Lloyd's Rep. 348. The case arose as a challenge to an arbitration award, so although the facts are interesting, and are discussed at length here, the case does not create any binding legal principles that are relevant to the present discussion.

[64] One of the reasons why this case is unusually well documented; Captain Blyth later publishing *Petro Pirates*, referred to above at n. 59.

[65] By no means all charterparties do this, but piracy might also amount to a riot, which is also often expressly excepted. Riot was defined by Phillimore J. in *Field v Receiver of Metropolitan Police* [1907] 2 K.B. 853 at 860.

least for the cargo that had not already been discharged on to the lighter.[66] An argument was also advanced, but ultimately not pursued, on arrest or restraint of princes (the acts of the Chinese authorities).

Had the cargo-owners been purchasers of the cargo, and holders of bills of lading, rather than the charterers, then their relationship with the shipowner would have been on bill of lading, rather than charterparty terms.[67] Even if the bill of lading incorporated charterparty terms, Singapore is a contracting state to the Hague-Visby Rules, so clause 19 would not in any event have helped the shipowner if he would otherwise have been liable under the Rules, because of Article III(8).

The shipowners in *The Petro Ranger* also argued that the piracy event had frustrated the carriage contract. If the vessel and cargo had been lost forever then a frustration argument might well have succeeded (although then, of course, it would not have been needed, since no cargo would have been recovered to attract liability), but of course in *The Petro Ranger*, the vessel and some of the cargo were recovered. Whether the contract is frustrated will depend on the length of time the vessel is lost, but it will not lightly be inferred. In *The Petro Ranger*, Lord Simon's test was adopted from *National Carriers Ltd v Panalpina (Northern) Ltd*[68]:

"Frustration of a contract takes place when there supervenes an event (without default of either party and for which the contract makes no sufficient provision) which so significantly changes the nature (not merely the expense or onerousness) of the outstanding contractual rights and/or obligations from what the parties could reasonably have contemplated at the time of its execution that it would be unjust to hold them to the literal sense of its stipulations in the new circumstances; in such case the law declares both parties to be discharged from further performance."

In *The Petro Ranger*, the vessel was discovered by the Chinese authorities after only 10 days, and although she was detained for a further three weeks or so, the court refused to interfere with the arbitrators' findings that the charterparty had not been frustrated.

To turn to cargo-owner liabilities, cargo that is lost will obviously not be delivered. Whether any bill of lading freight is payable depends on whether it is earned in advance or on delivery; if earned in advance it is of no consequence that the goods are later lost, that the carriage contract is frustrated, or even that the shipowner is in repudiatory breach of it.[69] Most tanker carriage contracts provide for freight to be payable on delivery, in which case it will not be payable on stolen cargo.

Ghost ships

Piracy is not usually an end in itself. The ISF and ICF observe that[70]: **15–040**

"In recent years, evidence collected by the IMB, among others, suggests that a growing number of attacks, particularly in the Far East, involve 'mafia-style'

---

[66] It would have been difficult to prove that Chinese government officials were implicated in the piracy, although suspicions were voiced: "The fact that the pirates were not prosecuted and ultimately returned to Indonesia or Malaysia gave serious grounds for such suspicions."

[67] See paras 12–004, *et seq.*, above.

[68] [1981] A.C. 675, 700.

[69] *The Dominique* [1989] 2 W.L.R. 440.

[70] See n.58, at p.10.

organised crime. Rather than simple robbery, the motive for such attacks is often the seizure of the ship itself with a view to stealing the entire cargo. Hijacked vessels have also been falsely registered as 'ghost ships' that have become involved in organised criminal activity such as stealing subsequent cargoes or trafficking drugs and illegal immigrants.

The criminal gangs involved in such attacks are likely to be especially violent and ruthless. Occasional, but horrific, instances have been reported of an entire ship's crew being cold-bloodedly murdered during such criminal operations."

The piracy, then, might be merely a prelude to a "ghost ship" crime. The purpose of a ghost ship is to reappear with a changed identity, posing as a legitimate trader, loading cargoes for which shipping documents are issued. Ship and cargo then disappear again, the cargo being stolen, leaving a purchaser or bank with worthless documents,[71] for which he has paid. The process may then be repeated, the vessel being given another new identity, and loading more cargo.

A variation on the ghost ship crime is *The Salem*, below, where the fraudsters really did own the ship. These cases may involve no violence, they are not much better from the cargo-owner's viewpoint than the piracy scenario already considered. When the shipowner, master and crew are all party to the fraud, and the shipper has been duped, the ultimate purchaser of cargo who suffers loss will have difficulty finding a defendant worth suing. Shippers will typically be innocent, and c.i.f. or f.o.b. sellers (whether the original shipper or further down the chain) not even in breach of contract. In exceptional cases, it might be possible to recover the stolen property.[72] The victim might also have an outside chance of tracing the proceeds, or going after accomplices involved in laundering them, either for common law conspiracy, or knowing receipt and knowing assistance.[73]

An all risks insurance policy might protect the victim, but unlike piracy, it might otherwise be difficult to find a risk insured against.

SHELL INTERNATIONAL PETROLEUM CO v GIBBS (THE SALEM)

House of Lords. [1983] 2 A.C. 775

15–041 *The Salem* became infamous because of the enormous value of the cargo which was stolen, and the lengths to which the conspirators went, purchasing a tanker specifically for the crime, and deliberately scuttling her afterwards. The crime was committed by shipowners (albeit only for the one voyage), through the innocent agency of the charterers, the victim being the cargo-owner.

The conspirators began by contracting with the South African Government, or more specifically, the South African Strategic Fuel Fund Association (S.F.F.), for

---

[71] Worthless at least in the sense that they provide the holder with no useful action against the carrier.

[72] The victim will have to show that property had passed to him prior to the theft, to have title to sue in conversion.

[73] The difficulties of tracing the proceeds of fraud are well illustrated by *Bank Tejarat v Hong Kong and Shanghai Banking Corporation Ltd* [1995] 1 Lloyd's Rep. 239, where a London branch of an issuing bank was defrauded into paying, under a documentary credit, against forged (but apparently genuine) shipping documents, for a non-existent cargo. It had paid by issuing a telegraphic transfer order to a German bank with which it had an account. It was unable to trace the money at all, because at common law, the money that had been transferred from Germany could not be identified as its money. Knowing assistance claims also failed, due to lack of requisite knowledge on the part of the defendants.

the sale of 200,000 tons of Saudi Arabian Crude Oil c.i.f. Durban, at a time when ordinarily, the South African Government would have been unable to obtain Saudi Arabian Crude, owing to an oil embargo placed on her by Arab countries in the Middle East.

The conspirators were then able to use that contract to obtain finance from Mercabank Ltd, a South African bank, for the purchase of a tanker. They used the advance to purchase a ship, *The South Sun*, for $12.3 million, which they re-registered as *The Salem*, and appointed parties to the conspiracy as master and principal officers of the vessel. At this stage, however, they were legitimate shipowners with a legitimate contract for the sale of oil, funded by a legitimate documentary credit.

They chartered the ship to innocent voyage charterers, Pontoil S.A. Pontoil purchased (from innocent Kuwaiti shippers) 200,000 tons of crude oil, and about 195,000 tons was actually aboard the ship, supposedly destined for Italy. By another innocent transaction, Pontoil sold the cargo afloat (c.i.f.) to Shell. Thus Shell became the owners of the cargo.

Meanwhile the parties to the fraud re-negotiated with the S.F.F., who agreed to accept the Kuwaiti oil in place of the originally agreed quantity of Saudi oil, albeit at a reduced price. The shipowners used the oil aboard the *Salem* in order to fulfil this contract. This was, of course, theft. They changed the name of the ship to the *Lema*, and *en route* deviated to a sea buoy one and a half miles offshore at Durban, where they discharged as much of the oil as they could (just over 180,000 tons). This they sold to the S.F.F., who paid the fraudsters approximately $45 million under the documentary credit.

Shortly after the ship had sailed from Durban the owners deliberately scuttled her, along with the remaining 15,000 tons of cargo, in an attempt to conceal what had occurred.

The cargo was insured on the terms of a standard Lloyd's marine insurance policy, which did not provide for an all risks cover, but which covered "takings at sea" and "barratry of the master and mariners". Shell, as assignees of the rights under the insurance policy, claimed the insured sum (just over US $ 56 million).

Held

The House of Lords held that though the policy covered the 15,000 tons scuttled (as a peril of the sea), it did not cover the 180,000 tons discharged in Durban. "Takings at sea" did not cover wrongful misappropriation by the shipowner, and "barratry" could only be committed against a shipowner.

The extract from Mustill J.'s judgment at first instance ([1982] Q.B. 946) presents a fuller view of the facts.

MUSTILL J.: *(stating the facts, at first instance)* The history of this affair, **15–042** apart from a few inevitable but important omissions, is set out in a long and comprehensive statement of facts agreed between the parties for the purposes of this action. I will return to certain aspects of the facts in more detail at a later stage, but the following summary, contained in paragraph 2 of the agreed statement, is sufficient to enable the issues of law to be stated:

"The conspirators were planning and preparing the fraud from at least as early as October 1979. In the result the conspirators achieved their object as follows. (i) They obtained a purchase contract from the South African Strategic Fuel Fund Association ('S.F.F.') providing for the delivery of a cargo of Saudi Arabian crude-oil to Durban. (ii) They used that contract to obtain an advance payment from a South African bank (Mercabank Ltd) sufficient to finance the purchase of a suitable tanker to carry such a cargo from the Arabian Gulf. (iii) They purchased such a tanker (the Salem). (iv) They manned that tanker with a master and principal officers ... who were parties to the conspiracy and with a crew which was likely to be amenable to the conspirators' instructions. (v) They chartered out the tanker to an innocent charterer (Pontoil S.A.) for a laden voyage (in the event) from Kuwait to Europe. (vi) They deceived the charterer (Pontoil S.A.) and the shipper (Kuwait Oil Co) of this cargo and the Kuwaiti authorities none of whom would have permitted the loading of the cargo nor the departure of the vessel had they known the conspirators' actual instructions. (vii) Either before or after loading they procured the agreement of S.F.F. to accept a cargo of Kuwaiti oil in place of Saudi Arabian oil and at a slightly reduced price. (viii) They carried the cargo to and discharged as much as possible of it at Durban. (ix) They collected the price from S.F.F. (x) They scuttled the tanker in the Atlantic so as to attempt to conceal what had occurred. The final event in this sequence—the scuttling of the vessel—was completed on January 17, 1980."

. . .

Adding a little detail to this summary, it can be said that Pontoil had brought the cargo on f.o.b. terms from Kuwait Oil Co. They then declared the goods under an open cover written by the defendant and his fellow underwriters. After the cargo had been loaded at Mina al Ahmadi ("Mina"), but before the vessel reached Durban, they resold the cargo on c.i.f. terms to Shell. After the loss of the vessel had become known to both parties, Pontoil tendered to Shell the documents of title, including a certificate of insurance relating to the voyage cover. After some discussion, it was agreed that Shell would pay the full price of the goods and pursue the claim against underwriters. There is no dispute as to the right of Shell to bring the present proceedings, and to recover to the same extent and on the same basis, as if Pontoil had retained the documents and brought the claim themselves.

15–043   As I have said, the goods were declared under an open cover. This related primarily to the carriage of crude oil in bulk from the Persian Gulf, Kuwait, and ports in the Gulf of Suez, to Italy, together with voyages from Italy to various destinations. The cover also provided: "other voyages held covered." It was an express term of the contract that Pontoil were obliged to declare all shipments and that the underwriters were obliged to accept such declarations. The risks comprised in the open cover were those of the Lloyd's S.G. policy, together with the Institute Cargo Clauses (F.P.A.) and the Institute Strikes, Riots and Civil Commotions Clauses. The relevant part of the Lloyd's S.G. policy reads:

"Touching the adventures and perils which we the assurers are contented to bear and do take upon us in this voyage: they are of the seas, men of war, fire, enemies, pirates, rovers, thieves, jettisons, letters of mart and countermart, surprisals, takings at sea, arrests, restraints, and detainments of all kings, princes, and people, of what nation, condition, or quality soever, barratry of the master and mariners, and of all other perils, losses, and misfortunes, that have or shall come to the hurt, detriment or damage of the said goods and merchandises, and ship &c., or any part thereof."

The Institute Cargo Clauses (F.P.A.) contain the following material provisions:

"1. This insurance attaches from the time the goods leave the warehouse or place of storage at the place named in the policy for the commencement of the transit, continues during the ordinary course of transit and terminates either on delivery (a) to the consignees' or other final warehouse or place of storage at the destination named in the policy... 4. Held covered at a premium to be arranged in case of change of voyage or of any omission or error in the description of the interest vessel or voyage. 5. Warranted free from particular average unless the vessel or craft be stranded, sunk, or burnt . . . 8. The seaworthiness of the vessel as between the assured and underwriters is hereby admitted. In the event of loss the assured's right of recovery hereunder shall not be prejudiced by the fact that the loss may have been attributable to the wrongful act or misconduct of the shipowners or their servants, committed without the privity of the assured . . . It is necessary for the assured when they become aware of an event which is 'held covered' under this insurance to give prompt notice to underwriters and the right to such cover is dependent upon compliance with this obligation."

. . .

I now return to the facts in more detail. Crude oil and its derivatives are attractive goods to steal. They are valuable, readily handled, and almost impossible to trace. The most obvious place to steal them is the port of destination. One way to carry out such a theft is to persuade an innocent carrier to deliver the goods against letters of indemnity which subsequently prove to be worthless. The present scheme was more ambitious, for it involved delivery at the wrong place, as well as to the wrong person. The fact that South Africa was the place where the goods were to be landed was a great advantage to the conspirators, for it meant that the persons to whom they would make delivery would realise that some devious means had been adopted to evade the embargo, and would therefore recognise that some aspect of the transaction and perhaps also of the documentation might not bear too close a scrutiny. On the other hand, the discharge of the goods at South Africa could scarcely be accomplished with the consent of an honest shipowner. Few shipowners would be prepared to take the risk of sailing from the Gulf under papers for

Europe whilst actually bound for South Africa. Moral considerations apart, the deception would in all likelihood be discovered, and that would be the end of any further trade with states applying the embargo. So the carrier would have to be persuaded to divert the cargo en route. No honest person would consent to do this unless he was given, first, a convincing explanation why the cargo was being landed thousands of miles short of its destination, and, second, either the full set of bills of lading or a totally ironclad indemnity against liabilities to any potential claimant. Moreover, if the conspirators were to be sure of getting safely away with the proceeds, they would need as long as possible to elapse between the landing of the cargo and the moment when the true owner began to ask questions about its whereabouts. For this purpose, it would be necessary for the ship to resume the intended voyage after the diversion and then unobtrusively disappear.

All this pointed to the employment of a dishonest shipowner. Whether the conspirators could not find one or whether they thought it too risky to try, I do not know. Instead, they decided to become shipowners themselves. This required a great deal of money, which no doubt they did not have. But they would be paid a much greater amount of money when the goods were ultimately delivered to the buyers. This provided the opportunity for the most striking feature of the scheme, namely, that if the buyers could be persuaded to advance the price of the ship against the future price of the oil, the scheme would become self-financing.

The plot thus conceived had five essential elements: (i) a firm purchase commitment on terms which did not involve the tender of negotiable documents; (ii) an assurance that the price would be payable against delivery of the goods; (iii) an agreement by the importer that part of the price could be used to finance the purchase of the ship; (iv) the acquisition of a ship and the provision of a dishonest crew; (v) a cargo of oil ready for export from the Gulf which would be shipped without the conspirators having to pay for it, and a means of convincing the authorities of the exporting country that the goods would not go to South Africa.

The way in which these various elements came to be fulfilled may be summarised as follows. I must emphasise that this summary is based entirely on the statement of facts, which was a document agreed between Shell and the underwriters alone. The allegations contained in the statement have not been investigated in any way by the court, and neither they nor any inferences drawn from them have any status, except in relation to the dispute between these two parties.

(i) The Sale Contracts

15–044   The first contract with the South African importers was made during October 1979 when intermediaries introduced one of the conspirators to a South African governmental agency known as Sasol, acting on behalf of S.F.F. Discussions took place which resulted in a written contract for the sale to S.F.F. by American Polamax International Inc., a company controlled by the conspirators, of four shipments of light crude oil, delivery to be at 30 day intervals commencing during February 1980. Soon afterwards, Sasol, through the same intermediaries, inquired of American Polamax whether an additional cargo could be acquired at an earlier date. This inquiry led in due course to the conclusion of a contract, probably oral, on or about November 23, 1979, whereby S.F.F. agreed to purchase and American Polamax agreed to sell about 1.5 million barrels of Saudi Arabian light crude oil or equivalent crude to be delivered to Durban in December 1979.

(ii) Payment of the Price

The price of the cargo was to be about U.S. $50 million, depending on actual out-turn quantity. The sellers were to furnish, after the vessel sailed, a certified invoice from American Polamax to S.F.F., a copy of a certified original bill of lading and a certified copy of the certificate of origin. Prior to coupling, discharge and payment, the sellers were to produce to the buyers the original bills of lading and a certified certificate of origin. A surveyor appointed by the buyers was then to inspect the cargo. Upon receipt of this certificate of quantity and quality 90 per cent. of the price was to be paid, the remainder being payable on completion of discharge. Payment was to take place by means of a letter of credit. Subsequently, important amendments were made to this sale contract. I will return to these later.

(iii) The Finance for the Ship

When the contract for the sale of the December delivery was first proposed, American Polamax made it a condition of the sale that finance should be arranged for the purchase of a suitably situated tanker. Sasol agreed, and it was arranged that a bank would make available a letter of credit for $12.3 million against an undertaking by Sasol's bank that this sum would be deducted from the purchase price and used to repay the loan. It was the understanding that the credit would be available for 21 days. This arrangement was complete and the letter of credit opened by November 26, 1979.

(iv) The Ship and the Crew

The precise manner in which the ship was acquired is not important. It is sufficient to say that the conspirators negotiated the purchase of the *South Sun* at a price of $12.3 million, payable by means of the letter of credit established by the South African bank. Meanwhile, the conspirators had been arranging for the purchase of an "off-the-shelf" Liberian company, named Oxford Shipping Co Inc. The price of the shares was $300,000, payable on or about December 27, 1979, upon arrival of the

South Sun off Durban, or any other discharge port. The agreement was declared to be subject to the contingency that the *South Sun* would lift a cargo of crude oil, arrive at Durban and commence discharge. If the contingency was not fulfilled, the price was to be only $25,000. The sale of the ship went through as planned, the memorandum of agreement being signed on November 27, 1979. The ship was re-registered as the *Salem* in the name of Oxford Shipping on December 3, 1979. There was a hitch as regards the sale of the shares in Oxford Shipping to the conspirators and the transaction was not completed until the middle of January 1980. Nothing turns on this. Whilst these negotiations were in progress, the conspirators had been assembling a suitably malleable crew, the principal members of which were parties to the conspiracy. The crew was ready and waiting in South Africa by the beginning of November 1979.

(v) Finding and Shipping the Cargo

15–045
As soon as the conspirators had concluded a firm agreement to purchase the ship, they offered her on the market (in the name of Oxford Shipping) for a voyage to carry crude oil from the Persian Gulf to the usual European and Caribbean discharge options. A fixture was rapidly arranged with Pontoil who in turn nominated the *Salem* under a contract with Kuwait Oil Co to lift about 200,000 tons of crude oil. The terms of this contract were such that the property and risk in the oil passed from the Kuwaiti sellers to Pontoil upon shipment.

The *Salem* arrived at Kuwait on December 5, 1979, and three days later commenced loading at a berth which (it may be assumed) was within the harbour. Subsequently a series of documents came into existence, all of which ostensibly related to an orthodox voyage outside the terms of the embargo. The bill of lading, certificate of origin, certificate of quantity and quality, master's receipt of documents and master's receipt of samples, all spoke of a voyage to Italy. As a result of these documents and other representations made by the master, the Kuwaiti authorities were willing to allow the goods out of the country. If they had known the true facts, they would not have permitted the vessel to be loaded with oil or to sail from Mina, nor would Pontoil have nominated the vessel to load the oil which they had agreed to purchase.

The remaining events may now be summarised in chronological order. A few days before the loading of the vessel, the conspirators informed the South African intermediaries, giving a pretext, that the cargo would have to be Kuwaiti crude and not Saudi Arabian light. After the vessel sailed she proceeded on a course out of the Arabian Gulf and southwards along the east coast of Africa. Such a course was usual for vessels bound for Europe but was likewise the route to follow if sailing to Durban. The vessel was steaming more slowly than would be normal for a tanker of her type.

On December 19, nine days after the *Salem* sailed from Kuwait, a meeting took place in Johannesburg between a group of the conspirators and representatives of Sasol, in the course of which there was handed to Sasol a document which had, or purported to have, the following effect. (i) A concern named Beets Trading A.G. ("Beets") controlled by one of the conspirators, which had previously been mentioned to Sasol as the suppliers of the goods, declared itself to be the sole owner of the cargo, and agreed to transfer title irrevocably to S.F.F. upon receipt of payment; (ii) the cargo was described as Kuwaiti crude oil; (iii) the price was fixed at US $34.50 per barrel, a discount of 20 cents per barrel on the price previously agreed; (iv) payment of 90 per cent. of the price was to be made (a) as to $11,361,500 to the financing bank; (b) as to the balance, to a bank in Switzerland for account of Beets. The remaining 10 per cent. was to be paid 48 hours after completion of discharge on actual out-turn volume.

In the course of the meeting on December 19, the conspirators produced a bill of lading in which the name of the consignees had been deleted, and stated that the bill was not intended to constitute a document of title but was only evidence that cargo had been shipped. In the document to which I have just referred there was an express agreement by Beets and American Polamax to indemnify S.F.F. against all claims which might be made as a result of the bills of lading not being presented.

On December 27 the vessel, now bearing the name *Lema*, arrived off Durban and on the following day she made fast to the single buoy mooring ("S.B.M.") about one and a half miles offshore. The S.B.M. is owned by a consortium of South African companies whose members respectively own refineries and tank farms in Durban and elsewhere in South Africa and is operated by another such company on behalf of the consortium. On December 28, on the coupling of the vessel to the S.B.M., payments were made by S.F.F. of (i) U.S. $12,469,875 to the financing bank; (ii) US $31,108,500 to the Swiss Bank for the account of Beets. The balance of US $1,064,333 was paid to the Swiss Bank for the account of Beets on January 15, 1980. The sums remitted to Switzerland were immediately on their receipt distributed among the conspirators via other Swiss bank accounts.

The vessel sailed from Durban on January 2, 1980, with about 15,840 tons of crude oil still on board. The presence of this quantity was due, at least in part, to problems experienced by the vessel with her pumps during discharge. Shortly after sailing the cargo tanks were filled with seawater in order to give her a laden appearance. Thereafter the vessel followed the usual route for ships bound for Europe. Meanwhile the conspirators caused a series of telex messages to be sent, all designed to give the impression that the voyage was proceeding normally, apart from a reduction in speed due to boiler damage.

As I have said, the final instalment of the price was paid by Sasol on January 15, 1980. On the following day when the vessel was off the coast

of Senegal, she was deliberately flooded and abandoned by the master
and crew, acting upon the instructions of the conspirators. On January 17
she sank, taking with her the remainder of the cargo. It had at all material
times been the intention of the conspirators that the vessel should be
scuttled with a view to concealing the evidence of the fraud.

Finally, reference must be made to the cargo which was discharged at
Durban. This was resold by S.F.F. to a number of oil companies carrying
on business in South Africa. As a result, the oil was sub-divided and
transferred to storage tanks in a number of locations in South Africa. The
persons who had thus acquired possession of the oil then began to refine
some of it. When the cargo interests came to realise what had happened,
they began proceedings in South Africa with a view to recovering possession of any of the remaining oil. Interim preservation orders were
obtained, but since by this date the greater part of the oil had already
been refined or mixed with other oil, cargo interests were advised that
they would not obtain court orders for the return of any of the cargo,
having regard to the discretion of the court and the balance of convenience. This advice was accepted. Shell did, however, maintain proceedings for compensation against those in South Africa who had had
possession of any of the oil after its discharge from Durban. Ultimately
these proceedings were reasonably settled by Shell in the sum of $
30,500,000.

LORD ROSKILL: *(in the House of Lords)*
*[Lord Roskill considered the definition of "taking at sea", the discussion of which
turned almost entirely on whether the decision of the Court of Appeal in* Nishina
Trading Co Ltd v Chiyoda Fire and Marine Insurance Co Ltd (The
Mandarin Star) *[1969] 2 Q.B. 449 should be overruled (it was). Of "deemed
barratry", which was claimed to be covered by clause 8, he said:]*

15–046   The present argument proceeded on the basis that the clause achieved its
objective by treating the loss by scuttling as a loss by perils of the sea by
excluding from consideration that element of privity of the shipowner to
the scuttling which alone prevented the loss from being treated as a loss
by that insured peril. Mr. Pollock called this a "deemed loss" by perils of
the sea. He then sought to apply that reasoning to a loss by barratry.

"Barratry," as rule 11 of the rules of construction and indeed the
common law made plain, involves a wrongful act being committed by the
master or crew to the prejudice of the shipowners. In the present case
there was a wrongful act, indeed there were several wrongful acts, wilfully committed by the master and crew. But what prevented that act or
those acts giving rise to a loss by barratry was that so far from being
wilfully committed to the prejudice of the shipowners the master and
crew were acting in conspiracy with the shipowners. But, it was argued,
clause 8 [the Lloyd's S.G. clause, set out in Mustill J.'s judgment], in the
interest of the innocent assured, enjoined that the assured's right of
recovery should not be prejudiced by the fact that the loss might be and

in this case was attributable to the wrongful act of the shipowners without which there would be a loss by barratry. Therefore it was argued there is a loss by "deemed barratry".

My Lords, one cannot fail to admire the ingenuity which devised this submission to which I hope my summary does not do injustice. But Kerr L.J. disposed of the submission in a single sentence of his judgment [1982] Q.B. 946, 997 with a succinctness upon which I cannot hope to improve and which I gratefully adopt. "The one peril to which this sentence [i.e. the second sentence of clause 8] clearly cannot apply is barratry, since this is by definition one which can only be committed *against* the shipowners . . . " The emphasis is that of the learned Lord Justice. This submission therefore fails for that reason . . .

Note

Though the saga of *The Salem* is often described as a fraud, including in the **15–047** House of Lords itself, by Mustill J., and in Barbara Conway's books on *The Piracy Business* and *Maritime Fraud*,[74] it was rather (at any rate as far as Shell were concerned) a theft of the cargo, and differs in marked respects from the frauds considered later in this section. This is also true of the growing phantom ships phenomenon.

There were, of course, a number of deceptions on loading in *The Salem* (set out in Mustill J.'s judgment), which were worked primarily on the shippers of the cargo, but the direct cause of loss was theft. It seems that the property was still in Pontoil, since the documents were transferred only after the theft, but it was at Shell's risk, and Shell bore the loss. In these cases, therefore, the shipper (who is the person actually deceived) loses nothing. The purchaser loses the cargo, in which he may or may not have property at the time of the theft. By contrast, in *Etablissment Esefka International Anstalt v Central Bank of Nigeria*, below, the deception was worked directly on the victim, whose loss is purely economic, there being nothing physical to lose.[75]

There also appears to have been a deception carried out on S.F.F. and those who took delivery of the cargo, that the conspirators owned it. This was a genuine fraud, which resulted in the victims having to make reparation to Shell, in the subsequent proceedings.

The profit to the conspirators, even after taking into account the loss of the tanker, was about US $ 32 million, at the time the largest in known maritime history.

The crime was undoubtedly abetted by S.F.F.'s anxiety to get hold of oil on almost any terms, and by those who accepted delivery of the cargo, to do so without a proper document of title. These people were victims to the extent that they were forced to settle with Shell, and in theory could have protected themselves, simply by insisting on proper documents proving title. It is not easy to see how Shell could have protected themselves, within the normal parameters of a c.i.f. contract. The sellers (Pontoil) had fully performed, and even if status checks had been run on the shipowners, the sellers had also presumably entered into a reasonable carriage contract. Presumably the insurance was also as customary in the trade. In theory, Shell could no doubt have contracted on terms which required all risks cover, as Mustill J. observed:

---

[74] The saga of *The Salem* is described by Barbara Conway: *The Piracy Business* (Hamlyn, 1981), Ch. 6, and *Maritime Fraud* (Lloyds of London Press, 1990), Ch. 2.
[75] Not much turns on this, but had property passed to Shell in *The Salem*, they could probably have sued S.F.F. in conversion.

"Finally, it is necessary to mention a submission advanced on behalf of Shell to the effect that the defendant was taking a formalistic and unpraiseworthy stand on the precise words of the policy, and that the court ought to lean in favour of an interpretation permitting a recovery which, according to Shell, has all the commercial merits. This submission is to my mind entirely misconceived. It has been recognised for centuries that the Lloyd's S.G. form confers a haphazard kind of cover, full of duplication and gaps. The addition of the Institute cargo clauses removes some of the anomalies, but not all. If the assured wishes to have a seamless cover, insuring against all forms of fortuitous losses in transit, he can obtain it by insuring on the terms of the Institute cargo clauses (all risks); and in a case such as the present this would give him substantial grounds for arguing that a wrongful conversion by a bailee is covered, without the need to bring the loss within the ancient words of the standard policy: see, for example, *London and Provincial Leather Processes Ltd v Hudson* [1939] 2 K.B. 724. But this comprehensive form of insurance is more expensive. Shell could, if they had wished, have made it a term of their c.i.f. purchase that the sellers would provide all risk cover. They chose not to do so. This being the case, there is no warrant for criticising the underwriters for insisting that Shell found their claim on the cover for which they have paid, receiving neither less nor more than they were entitled to on the true interpretation of the contract of insurance."

It may be that this course of action was more theoretical than practical, however. The cargo was already afloat when the sale contact was concluded. In any case, the shipment would have been at the time of the 1979 oil shortages caused by the Iran-Iraq war, and Shell may have been anxious to secure the purchase quickly, on whatever terms.

The reality surely is that when commodity prices fluctuate wildly (as with oil at the end of 1979), trades occur very quickly, increasing significantly the difficulties of protecting oneself against becoming the victim of crime. Of course, large amounts of money can also be made by trading quickly on fluctuating markets, which may make the risks worthwhile.

The balance of the cargo in The Salem

15–048 Shell were able to recover in respect of the scuttled cargo, lost through a peril of the sea. An interesting side issue was that the underwriters argued that it was lost through fraud or fraudulent conspiracy, which was not covered by the policy, and indeed would not generally be covered by a marine insurance policy. Ultimately this was a causation issue; Lord Roskill did not think the fraud or fraudulent conspiracy caused the loss (at 393):

"I am very far from satisfied that when the Salem sailed from Mina the fraud or fraudulent conspiracy was bound to succeed, or, to use the phrase used in argument, the cargo was 'doomed.' In connection with another part of his argument Mr. Pollock drew your Lordships' attention to the details of a remarkable document evidencing an agreement concluded between the conspirators and the South African authorities as late as December 19, 1979, by which date the Salem was proceeding slowly down the east coast of Africa awaiting final instructions. He also referred your Lordships to paragraph 27 of the agreed statement of facts. In short, the conspirators at that date had still to persuade the South African authorities to accept Kuwaiti oil and no Saudi Arabian oil and documentation which bore no relationship to that which ought to have been tendered to them. It is perhaps eloquent of the determination of the South African authorities to get this oil to Durban under any circumstances that they were willing at that late date to accept what was proffered against an indemnity in circumstances which even the most credulous buyer in the open market would not have considered for one moment, thus enabling the conspirators to succeed in their objective."

Note that the fraud was taken to have occurred at Mina, the misrepresentations having been made at loading.

Thefts by charterers
In *Manchester Trust v Furness* (see para. 12–040, above) the charterers fraudulently induced the master to discharge the cargo en route. The master need not be party to the fraud, and clearly the practice with oil cargoes (discussed above), whereby original bills of lading are not tendered, and cargo delivered on charterers' instructions, can encourage frauds of this type.

The cargo-owner's position is protected if the bill of lading contract is with the shipowner, as in *Manchester Trust* itself, but this merely shifts the loss to another innocent party.

No ship or cargo
Unlike the cases considered so far, this is a true fraud, as was alleged in *Etablissment Esefka International Anstalt v Central Bank of Nigeria*,[76] one of the many frauds (or alleged frauds) arising from the Nigerian cement fiasco in the mid-1970s.[77] In *Etablissment Esefka* (also in para. 10–020, above), it was alleged that ship and cargo were simply invented, and documents forged for a non-existent cargo on board a non-existent ship. In this type of situation the shipper, who is necessarily party to the fraud, negotiates the worthless documents to his purchaser against payment. Here, the deception is worked directly on the victim, whose loss is purely economic, there being nothing physical to lose.

From the victim's viewpoint the position is even worse than with piracy and ghost ships, since the "shipper" is also inevitably party to the fraud, and even if the maritime insurance policy has not itself been forged, it will not cover the loss. Nor is there any property to recover. Prevention is the only safe option, for example by insisting on status checks of shippers and shipowners, or using Lloyd's to discover whether the ship exists, and could have loaded the cargo at the indicated port of loading at the time. Since the bill of lading will be a nullity, cases such as *Gill & Duffus v Berger* in para. 7–022, above, or *The American Accord* in para. 10–003, above, will not apply. As with all prevention options, there is a cost, of course, and transactions might be delayed.

(ii) *Lesser Sellers' Frauds*

The use of documents to represent goods, and their ready acceptance by banks and buyers, gives enormous possibilities to fraudulent sellers. The most extreme is what was alleged in *Etablissment Esefka*, but another possibility was the allegation in *Discount Records v Barclays Bank*, in para. 10–012, above. We also saw in chapter 10, above, how the decision in *The American Accord* can assist fradusters who obtain bills of lading which mis-describe the goods. If the facts alleged were true, the master was himself deceived in *Discount Records*. Alternatively, the quality of the goods may be very poor, but beyond the competence of the master to certify, so that again, clean shipping documents will be tendered.[78] **15–049**

[76] [1979] 1 Lloyd's Rep. 445. This was not a final trial, but the CA observed that there were many doubts in the plaintiff sellers' claim.
[77] Described in Conway, *The Piracy Business* (Hamlyn, 1981), Ch. 4. The situation also gave rise to many fraudulent demurrage claims, made easier by the huge delays encountered at Lagos, and the fact that the Nigerian government, as buyers, had agreed to pay demurrage (against which claims there were no proper safeguards). There is also a good description of the situation in *Trendtex Trading Corporation v Central Bank of Nigeria* [1977] Q.B. 529 at 548–549.
[78] As apparently occurred in *Midland Bank Ltd v Seymour* [1955] 2 Lloyd's Rep. 147.

It is difficult for buyers to guard against this type of fraud, because they will not have time to make extensive investigations, and because of *The American Accord.* The protection against becoming a victim in the *Etablissment Esefka* type of case will not assist here, because the ship was at the loading port and really did load the cargo. The master is innocent, so there is no action against either him or the carrier. Really, the only protection is to take care who one deals with.

If the master colludes with the fraud, as in *Brown Jenkinson v Percy Dalton* (at paras 7–066 *et seq.,* above), the position is very different, because the carrier is liable, and the law is generous to plaintiffs/claimants if the fraudster can be brought to court.[79] This is not as outlandish as it may seem. Especially where a trader has merely crossed the line, perhaps inadvertently, between acceptable business practice and what the law regards as dishonesty (as indeed in *Brown Jenkinson* itself), it will often be possible to sue the fraudster himself, or his accomplices.[80]

(iii) *Buyers' Frauds*

15–050   We have already seen a number of frauds by buyers, or people in the position of buyers, against other traders. Nearly all result from wrongful dealings with the bill of lading, and are in principle preventable. The *Glyn Mills* type of fraud, for example, where originals of a set of three are separately negotiated, would be preventable were bills of lading not issued in sets, or if purchasers and banks demanded all the originals in a set. Merchants would have to stipulate expressly, however; in an ordinary c.i.f. contract the seller needs tender only one original (see para. 6–080, above).

There is nothing a merchant can do to protect himself against the *Motis Exports* fraud (see paras 6–026 *et seq.,* above). In *Motis Exports* he was able to shift the loss on to the carrier, however (see futher below on loss-shifting), and carriers can protect themselves, by making bills of lading more difficult to forge.

(iv) *Other Frauds*

Third party thefts and frauds

15–051   Purchasers of cargo are also vulnerable to third party thefts and frauds, such as those which occurred in *Rasnoimport v Guthrie* (see para. 14–002, above), *Kwei Tek Chao v British Traders & Shippers* (see paras 7–033 and 14–002, above). In both these cases, a bill of lading was issued which did not accurately describe the goods; in the first the mis-description was as to quantity loaded, and in the second as to shipment date. Neither the master nor the seller was aware of the mis-description; in the first case a theft of cargo, prior to loading, had gone undetected, and in the second the date on the bill of lading had been fraudulently altered by a third party.

In both cases the purchaser, who was the initial victim of the fraud, was able to shift the loss, in the first case on to the loading brokers, and in the second case on to the sellers. Were the facts of *Rasnoimport* to recur today the shipowner would be liable. These cases basically shift the loss from one innocent party on to another. Perhaps there is justice in these cases. As between the loading broker who misstated the quantity loaded in *Rasnoimport,* and the purchaser who relied

---

[79] *e.g.* in an action for fraudulent misrepresentation, or deceit, damages will fully compensate the plaintiff's loss, without regard to normal remoteness of damage rules: *Doyle v Olby (Ironmongers) Ltd* [1969] 2 Q.B. 158. Nor are damages for deceit subject to reduction on the grounds of contributory negligence: *Edgington v Fitzmaurice* (1884) 29 Ch. D. 459.
[80] *e.g. Niru Battery Manufacturing Co v Milestone Trading Ltd* [2002] E.W.H.C. 1425 (Comm.), where various deceit actions were successfully brought.

on the misstatement, arguably the loading broker should bear the loss, even though no negligence was shown. The seller in *Kwei Tek* had broken the sale contract by shipping late, although he was unaware of this, and as between himself and purchaser arguably should bear the loss (in this case, a market loss). Shifting of losses is covered further below.

Insurance frauds

For completeness, there are other types of maritime fraud, which do not impinge directly on bills of lading and international sale contracts. One of the most common is the insurance fraud, where (for example) a ship is scuttled for her insurance value.[81] These (apparently quite widespread) frauds are beyond the scope of this book.

Frauds by charterers on shipowners

A typical fraud by a time charterer against a shipowner may be as follows: the charterer arranges to hire the ship, loads cargo freight prepaid, and disappears with the freight once the ship has sailed, without paying the shipowner the hire under a time charter.[82] Although this type of fraud is theoretically possible with a voyage charter,[83] in reality the risk to the shipowner is greater with a time charterer, especially if long-term. In return (typically) for one month's hire in advance, the shipowner not only loses the remainder of the hire, but remains under a contractual obligation to the cargo-owners to deliver the cargo, now however at his own expense.[84]

Barbara Conway observes that a shipowner in this position has three choices[85]:

15–052

> "The first is that he soldiers on to deliver the goods, bearing all the additional costs from having to pay wages, port dues, bunker fees, canal tolls etc out of his own pocket.
>
> "The second is an attempt to come to an agreement with the shipper of the goods in question. After all, the shipowner may not have the funds to carry out course one and he may, not entirely unreasonably, feel that it was the shipper's fault that he was in this jam in the first place—if proper care had been taken over the transport of the goods the situation might never have arisen."

There are two additional points to note about this second choice. The first is that if the shipper has sold c.i.f., he will have no interest in coming to an agreement; the goods are at the buyer's risk after shipment, and the shipowner will incur liability to the buyer, rather than the shipper, under the Carriage of Goods by Sea Act 1992. Unlike the shipper, the buyer will not feel that he was in any way at fault. Secondly, if the shipowner attempts to come to an agreement with the cargo-owner, he does so from a position of weakness, since in the absence of the agreement he is liable for all the costs identified in course one. Barbara Conway then describes course three, where "the shipowner will himself divert the vessel

---

[81] Note however that there was no attempt at an insurance fraud in *The Salem.*

[82] Except, perhaps, for the first month, which would typically be payable in advance.

[83] It is theoretically possible to work a freight fraud with a voyage charter, if charter freight is payable in arrears but sub-charter freight payable in advance, but in reality voyage charter freight is nearly always payable in advance, except in tanker charters where the charterer is a major oil company, such as Exxon or Shell. The fraudulent re-sale considered below is also theoretically possible, but a master is far more likely to obey the instructions of a time charterer to deliver the cargo without production of a bill of lading.

[84] At any rate if the bill of lading is signed on behalf of the shipowner—see paras 12–037, *et seq.*, above.

[85] *Maritime Fraud*, at p. 12.

to the nearest suitable port and will sell the cargo to defray the costs he has already incurred and avoid new ones. No matter how great the provocation and the threatening financial problems caused by the original fraudster, this action means that the shipowner (often himself the master of the vessel) is now also a fraudster."[86]

None of these choices is attractive, but the reality is that the shipowner's legal position is weak. The payment of a month's hire in advance affords shipowners some protection against this type of fraud, but since the essence of the fraud is that the freights are worth far more than the month's hire, it is necessarily limited. It might be thought that a lien on sub-freights can also provide some protection, but it does not in fact because it kicks in too late; by the time the charterer defaults on the second month's hire, the freights will already have been paid to the charterer.[87] The only effective protection is to make status checks on charterers, at any rate before entering into long-term time charterparties. If there is any doubt about the honesty of a voyage charterer, an alternative form of protection is to require freight (or at least a bank guarantee) in advance.

Frauds by shipowners against charterers

Apart from theft of the charterer's cargo, there is little scope for frauds by shipowners against charterers. In time charterparties shipowners or masters may be in a position to overcharge on deliveries of bunker fuel, as the charterers suspected in *The Leon*.[88] In tanker voyage charterparties shipowners have been known to steal charterers' cargo for use as bunker fuel, as the charterers suspected in *The Ypatianna*, although in the particular case no deliberate wrongdoing was proved.[89]

(b) PREVENTION AND CURE

(i) *Shifting the Loss*

15–053   If the fraudster is in court redress will not necessarily be problematic. This is likely to be the case only with trivial, or technical frauds, but where the fraudster can be sued the law most certainly does not treat him favourably. In an action for fraudulent misrepresentation, or deceit, for example, damages will fully compensate the plaintiff's loss, without regard to normal remoteness of damage

---

[86] Elsewhere, she illustrates the unwisdom of relative innocents becoming involved in the same criminal enterprise as professional fraudsters: *The Piracy Business* (Hamlyn, 1981), chapter 9, the case of the *Delta Sigma Pi*.

[87] As in *The Spiros C* [2000] 2 Lloyd's Rep. 319, a case involving the bankruptcy rather than the fraud of the charterer. The Court of Appeal held, in effect, that the shipowner had delegated the method of collecting freight to the charterer, and that once it had been paid to the charterer, it could no longer be intercepted by the shipowner's lien. Rix L.J. observed (at para. 38) that under an ordinary time charterparty, "the owner has been prepared to leave all matters relating to the freight to his time charterer, at any rate as long as the time charter hire payments are kept up, and where the risk of non-payment of that hire rests on the owner and no one else." It follows that, as long as the bill of lading freights are paid before the charterer defaults on hire, the shipowner cannot claim them again from the cargo-owner.

[88] *Leon Corporation v Atlantic Lines and Navigation Co Ltd (The Leon)* [1985] 2 Lloyd's Rep. 470.

[89] *Indian Oil Corporation Ltd v Greenstone Shipping SA (The Ypatianna)* [1988] 1 Q.B. 345. There was inter-connection, however, between the vessel's cargo, ballast and fuel oil systems, in breach of the International Maritime Organisation and classification society rules, so that inter-tank transfers could have occurred.

rules.[90] Nor are damages for deceit subject to reduction on the grounds of contributory negligence.[91]

In more serious cases it is unlikely that the fraudster is worth suing, or that the proceeds will be traceable, although it might be possible to sue conspirators, knowing receivers and assisters.[92] One problem with maritime frauds is that they are often committed by strangers, making it difficult to establish the necessary fiduciary relationship to follow the proceeds in equity. In most cases the victim's only realistic redress is to shift the loss on to another party, who will usually be innocent.

For example, in *Discount Records Ltd v Barclays Bank Ltd*,[93] as we saw in para. 10–012, above, the plaintiff purchasers were left with cartons which contained largely rubbish. The report suggests that they might have had a contractual action against the issuing bank, arising from an independent breach, and might therefore have been able to shift the loss on to the bank. Other cases that we have already considered, where the immediate victim has been able to shift the loss, include *V/O Rasnoimport v Guthrie & Co Ltd*,[94] where the indorsee, who (as we saw in para. 14–059, above) was the immediate victim of the crime, having been induced to pay the entirety of the price for a part cargo, successfully sued the loading broker for breach of warranty of authority, but could also presumably instead have sued the seller. Either way the loss would have been shifted.

Shifting loss from buyer to seller:
Where fraud is committed against a cargo owner, the identity of both the initial victim, and the person who eventually bears the cost, will depend on the terms of the contract of sale.

If the sale is on ex-ship terms, the seller will not be entitled to claim payment unless the goods are delivered to their destination, and will therefore have to bear the cost, even if the goods are loaded on board the vessel, if they are then diverted by the carrier on the voyage. If the sale is c.i.f., c. & f., f.o.b. or f.a.s., the loss is likely to fall, at least initially, on the ultimate receiver, who will have paid, or be obliged to pay, for the cargo which has not arrived, or never been shipped. This follows from the principles as to risk discussed in chapter 4, above. If the goods are lost after shipment, for example by being diverted elsewhere than the destination port by the shipowner or charterer, the loss is, at least as between buyer and seller, at the buyer's risk.[95] It is another matter if some or all of the goods were never loaded. Then there is no doubt that at any rate a c.i.f. of c. & f. seller is in breach of contract, whether or not he was responsible for, or aware of the situation.[96]

In the cases just described, we are assuming that it is the effect of the fraud itself to put the seller in breach of contract,[97] but the loss can be shifted whether or not the breach bears any relation to the fraud. Suppose, for example, under a c.i.f. contract goods are shipped, packed in bags of the wrong size, and the goods are

---

[90] *Doyle v Olby (Ironmongers) Ltd* [1969] 2 Q.B. 158.

[91] *Edgington v Fitzmaurice* (1884) 29 Ch. D. 459, cited in *Standard Chartered Bank*, per Evans L.J. at 226 (paras 40–41).

[92] e.g. *Bank Tejarat v Hong Kong and Shanghai Banking Corporation (Ci) Ltd and Hong Kong and Shanghai Bank Trustee (Jersey) Ltd*, above, where attempts were (unsuccessfully) made to do this, in relation to money obtained fraudulently under a documentary credit.

[93] [1975] 1 W.L.R. 315.

[94] [1966] 1 Lloyd's Rep. 1.

[95] Except in *The Playa Larga*, in para. 2–040, above, where the seller had an involvement in the diversion, and where the carrier might have been required to divert, under the carriage contract.

[96] *Hindley & Co Ltd v East Indian Produce Co Ltd* [1973] 2 Lloyd's Rep. 515, in para. 2–012, above, where the fault was that of a seller earlier in the chain.

[97] Another example is *Kwei Tek Chao v British Traders and Shippers*, in Ch. 7, above.

later diverted at sea by a fraudulent shipowner or charterer. Normally the risk of loss after shipment falls on the buyer, but if the size of the bags is stated in the bill of lading, the buyer can reject it and not pay for the goods.[98] This shifts the loss back to the seller just as surely as the previous example, but the breach of contract has nothing to do with the fraud.

Shifting loss from cargo-owner to carrier

One of the frauds discussed above was the type where the charterer, possibly in collusion with the master, directs the goods elsewhere than to the destination port, with a view to stealing them. The immediate victim is the receiver of the goods, but if his contract of carriage is with the shipowner he can shift the loss on to him. In *Manchester Trust v Furness, Withy & Co Ltd*,[99] the master had been induced to unload the goods, by a fraudulent charterer, without production of the bill of lading. The effect was to put the shipowner in breach of contract, and the cargo-owner was thereby able to recover the entirety of his loss (see paras 12–040 *et seq.*, above). There is perhaps justice in this, because the master, who acted for the shipowner, must have been party to the crime.

Another example where loss was shifted from cargo-owner to carrier was *Motis Exports*, in paras 6–026, *et seq.*, above, where the master was innocent, but had been induced to deliver against a forged bill of lading. Generally, however, the courts have tended to take the view that if the carrier acts properly, he should not be expected to bear the risk of fraud committed against one of the merchants, a good example of this principle being *Glyn Mills Currie & Co v East and West India Dock Co*,[1] in para. 6–010, above.

(ii) *Prevention*

15–054		Shifting loss is entirely satisfactory from a victim's viewpoint, but obviously it creates problems for the other party, and it would undoubtedly be preferable to prevent, or at least reduce fraud.

One of the reasons why maritime fraud is relatively easy to commit is that the commercial parties are ignorant of the true facts. For example, phantom ship frauds are possible because there is no centrally-kept register of shipping, or means of tracking where ships are. Nigerian cement type frauds could be prevented, or at least reduced, by relatively simple enquires as to whether the vessel identified in the bill of lading could have been at the stated port of loading at the stated time.

It follows that in order to prevent fraud, it is a good idea to equip oneself with as much information as possible. Much of the information is relatively easily available.[2] To do this, however, inevitably increases the cost of transactions. It is also much more difficult for a buyer in a chain sale, who may have no control over the identity of the original shipper, or indeed the vessel, but who may be required to pay, without delay, against any bill of lading tendered.

Buyers can make enquiries to ensure that they deal only with reputable sellers. They can demand certificates from independent survey firms that goods of the correct quality have been loaded. In order to ensure their independence it is important that the buyer employs and pays these survey firms, but this is of

---

[98] *e.g. Manbre Saccharine Company Ltd v Corn Products Co Ltd* [1919] 1 K.B. 198, in para. 4–014, above. The loss in *Manbre Saccharine* was caused by a German submarine in wartime, but the position would have been exactly the same had it been caused by fraud.
[99] [1895] 2 Q.B. 282.
[1] (1882) 7 App. Cas. 591.
[2] There are various organisations which can provide information on ships, owners, charterers, etc., such as Lloyd's, the International Chamber of Commerce, the Baltic Exchange and the International Maritime Bureau, as well as reputable ship brokers.

course only possible on the first sale. On the second sale the intermediate seller will have paid, so the survey ceases to be independent as between him and sub-buyer.

It is much more difficult for sub-buyers in chain sales, especially of generic goods, to protect themselves. They may be sure of the honesty of their particular seller, but will have no control over the seller from whom he buys, or earlier sellers in the chain (the problem, for example, in *Hindley*, above). In any event, they will have to show that their immediate seller has been fraudulent, if they are to avoid having to pay against documents. Normally this will not be the case, the fraud having been committed by the original seller and/or carrier.

Ultimately, it may be that the whole system of documentary sales, allowing long chains to develop, and finance by documentary credit, is fraud-prone, and that serious attempts to curtail fraud would essentially destroy the system.

HON. TAN BOON TEIK (ATTORNEY-GENERAL FOR THE RUPUBLIC OF SINGAPORE) "TRANSNATIONAL FRAUD"

[1985] L.M.C.L.Q. 418. (It is a shortened version of a lecture delivered at Queen Mary College, London, on June 4, 1985 under the auspices of the I.C.C. International Maritime Bureau)

[References included as footnotes in the original article appear here in the text.]

Transnational fraud has paralleled the growth of world trade, the development of a global system of financial services and the emergence of a sophisticated communications network that is shrinking one's sense of time and space. Singapore is a major link in this network of world trade, finance and communications. **15–055**

Fraud requires a clever manipulation of this global network. Given our regard for intelligence and our opprobrium for violence, and the blurring of one's notion of honesty by avarice stimulated by commerce, there is much less outrage against frauds than less social crimes such as rape, murder and robbery. Besides, victims of frauds are often institutions rather than people and it is perhaps an ironic confirmation of humanity that people have less sympathy for the defrauded corporation. Another feature of fraud is that while social crimes are more or less exclusively national in context economic crimes like fraud overlap boundaries and continents. And criminal jurisdiction is, almost without exception, based on the notion of territoriality.

What I want to put forward for your consideration is the sort of strategy which should be advanced and the change of mental perspective or "mind-set" that is involved. Reality is largely a matter of habit and we need to alter our habitual approaches in the light of changed circumstances.

Part I: Spreading the Costs

Increasingly we must see and regard ourselves as part of an emerging world community. A comprehensive internationalization of trade has set **15–056** the stage. Where world economies in the past were the result of empires, the present world economy grew out of relatively free exchange. Today's trading community comprises shippers, charterers, shipowners, bankers, insurers, importers and exporters and the system designed for the transfer of goods is simple and efficient.

But the sea remains the lifeblood of trade. Delivery of goods still takes time. As a matter of custom, the seller gets paid before the buyer receives the goods. The system of letters of credit evolved with banks as the intermediaries in the transaction. Documents rather than goods are the focal point of these transactions. Article 8 of the *Uniform Customs and Practice for Documentary Credits* issued by the International Chamber of Commerce [see now Article 4 of U.C.P. 500, in Appendix C] states:

> "In documentary credit operations, all parties concerned deal in documents and not in goods."

The simplicity of the system makes it potentially efficient. That the system is efficient derives from the convention of trust. As long as parties to the transaction realize that trust makes the simplicity of the system practicable, all the parties derive a benefit. People can buy and sell, taking advantage of the global communications and financial networks, and transaction costs are kept minimal.

Without trust, all parties would have to adopt measures to inspect and verify at every stage of the transaction. Duties of inquiry would raise costs. Inquiry would increase bank charges and delay payments. Negotiations would take longer. Given the volume of transactions involved, the system would become no better if not worse than the customs and excise system of a repressive regime. Transaction costs would simply become prohibitive.

The threat of fraud is that it undermines the system by putting trust at risk. The simplicity of the system makes it attractive and vulnerable to forgers, scuttlers and cheats. What is one to do? Protection and care can be devised, inquiry implimented and some inspection required: in other words some sort of policing. But the danger of this approach is that it requires too much policing to make it effective. Policing raises transaction costs. Clever criminals will always devise a slightly more elaborate scheme—in a sense they always have the advantage of being one step ahead. The stakes are also high enough to make it economically viable for the criminal to bribe away obstacles. That is commonly the way in which important insiders are brought within a criminal enterprise and it has been a feature in many of the prosecutions in Singapore (*e.g. Isaac Paul Ratnam v Public Prosecutor* [1984] 1 MLJ cxliii).

The expense of policing is, however, not a convincing reason for ignoring the victims of frauds, whose losses are often massive. Can the system remain in its present simple and cost-efficient form without having victims becoming disenchanted with it and withdrawing from international trade? What I wish to propose may seem contoversial and at first sight may seem impracticable. I only wish to say that if the practical problems could be resolved, it would have the merit of preserving a trading infrastructure that is efficient.

An analogy can be drawn between fraud in trade and accidents on the road. They are the unavoidable cost of community. Just as there are costs in social life within national communities, there will be costs within an international trading community. But we persist with the notion of community because there are gains. The principle I have in mind is that participants in any form of community must share the gains and spread the losses. This is the shift in the "mind-set" which I alluded to earlier. Instead of assigning social costs to specific individuals, a better approach may be to spread the costs.

Since all the members of the trading community on the whole benefit from an increase in the volume of international trade, it seems quite inequitable that a particular member should have to cope with an inevitable loss from fraud that arises from the simple system based on trust. There is a simple procedure in the system of documentary credits. The same contract applies to countless transactions. This is a considerable saving in costs. Parties and their lawyers do not need to sit down and negotiate for days specifying special duties of inquiry and inspection which in their discharge would increase the cost of each transaction. Trading would become more expensive and the volume would be likely to fall.

This seems to be an area where empirical work and economic analysis of tort and contract rules pioneered by Professors Coase, Posner and Calabresi at the law schools of Chicago and Yale can be extremely fruitful. Professor Atiyah of Oxford University has also discussed this approach in the area of torts, and it also featured in the report and recommendations of the Pearson Commission.

The system of documentary credits keeps transaction costs minimal. I would be interested to know what are the losses arising from maritime fraud and what this would be as a fraction of the volume of world trade. To abstract further, supposing we divide the aggregate losses by the number of transactions and based on this impose a surcharge to be paid for by the parties to each individual transaction. I doubt if the cost of each transaction would increase substantially. Certainly we can compare this to the costs of policing.

The problem is a practical one of how such a surcharge could be **15–057** devised and administered. Perhaps an international organization like the I.C.C. International Maritime Bureau, or a conglomerate of insurance companies could administer it. Insurance actuaries with their experience could certainly devise a calculus which would set premiums at a rate to encourage all members of the trading community to take the necessary degree of care. This would also make costs more determinate, allowing parties to have a better idea of their expected profits.

Once we see losses from fraud as essentially a distributive problem as far as the economics of trade are concerned, it would be easier to devise uniform policies or conventions and allow the system to continue on the basis of trust. The approach I have suggested is an alternative method of distributing the inevitable losses of the trading community. Instead of either having specific individuals bearing losses or having individuals involving themselves in interminable and expensive negotiations as to who should bear the losses, who should exercise greater vigilance, who could be called upon to inspect, losses can be spread. This is another way of re-conceiving the problem that fraud poses for an existing system which is otherwise efficient.

There may be objections to loss spreading. In the contemporary system of civil liability, the knowledge that there exists a rule which makes one liable for losses encourages the potential defendant to take care by adopting suitable measures. Therefore, the counter argument may allege that the spreading of losses would not create enough incentives for the parties to take care. This is really a variation of the police proposal. Since trust is the premise of the system, it is difficult and inequitable for individual parties to take a practically "optimal" level of care. Insurance rates can be so arranged to create the necessary incentives. To combat maritime fraud requires a joint effort.

This shift to a perspective of "community" is also important when we try to improve means of catching the criminals. Since criminal sanctions have traditionally been regarded as an exercise of sovereignty, our concepts are perhaps a little parochial and ineffective in dealing with transnational fraud. Of course, the time involved in co-ordinating complex investigations across boundaries is a great boon to criminals. Unfortunately, international police investigations do not mirror the efficiency of international trade and no positive convention has been established in this regard. What is also regrettable is that since most of these frauds involve conspiracy, prosecution often requires the grant of immunity to accomplices or to the "supergrasses" who act as witnesses and informers. In this regard investigators should always be given guidelines by the prosecuting authority.

One problem is that though we are a comity of nations, the vision is still obscured by the concept of sovereignty. For many States, sovereignty is, in fact, still a vision. In matters of sovereignty much depends on political will. Therefore, I propose to leave this vexing problem of international co-ooperation to be discussed in other fora. I should, however, say that many international organizations such as the International Maritime Bureau, and Commonwealth groups like the Commonwealth Secretariat have made significant contributions.

Part II: Making Criminals Pay

15–058   So far I might have seemed a little sanguine in my approach to the problem of transnational fraud, and these words might perhaps be read with encouragement by the cosmopolitan criminal. I have dealt with one approach to the losses from transnational fraud. I would now like to concentrate on the strategy one should take towards this new species of criminal.

Unlike social crimes which are often irrationally motivated, a person who commits economic crime is capable of rational reasoning and works out his "trade-offs". He is guided by the likelihood of his arrest and the efficiency with which the crime can be committed, and he may probably even think a term of imprisonment would justify the crime if the returns are sufficiently high. The strategy must be to make the price of crime prohibitive . . .

[There follow arguments for restitution of proceeds. The article continues:]

The lesson to draw is that economic crimes must be met with economic measures. If there is a real likelihood that the criminal could lose all the proceeds this may deter him by reducing the attractiveness of such crimes . . .

CHAPTER 16

COMPUTERISATION

16–001   COMPUTERS have already affected international trade to a considerable extent. The use of the Internet for contracting, both for sale and carriage contracts, is now commonplace.

Developments have also begun on dematerialisation of shipping documents. It is relatively easy to dematerialise non-negotiable documents, such as waybills, and non-negotiable multimodal transport documents. Negotiable documentation presents greater difficulties, with the need to prove title, and to transfer of contractual rights and liabilities. These are, however, quite easily resolvable in principle. It is more debatable whether practical difficulties in implementing the computerised bill of lading, and making it useful, will be overcome in the near future.

(1) Contracting Over the Internet

(a) How Much Do You Need to Agree?

16–002   The problem addressed here is not Internet-specific, but no doubt e-mail (and possibly web-based contracting) will tend to exacerbate, if anything, these issues.

Unlike bills of lading (on which see further below), most contracts do not need to be in writing, and this includes both international sale contracts, and charter-parties. Quite apart from the Internet, many fixtures are made by telephone, with only the broadest of details being given, and then confirmed by fax or recap telex, before being reduced to a more formal written form. A typical firm offer for a voyage charter, for example, from a shipowner, might include[1]:

Period for which the offer is valid

Freight rate

Name of vessel

Lay days

Vessel's carrying capacity of the cargo in question

Loading and discharging ports

Loading/discharge costs

Demurrage/dispatch

Commission

---

[1] UNCTAD report on *Charterparties* (1974) para. 129. See also generally, paras. 125–135 (on fixing a voyage charter), and paras. 136–140 (on fixing a time charter). See also Dockray, *Cases and Materials on the Carriage of Goods by Sea* (2nd ed., Cavendish, 1998), pp. 22–25.

Charterparty form to be used

If the charterer suggests modifications these will take effect as a counter offer, but if he agrees an enforceable agreement will be taken to have been concluded, even though it is only later that the other (lees important) details will be agreed, and the written form drawn up and signed. The fact that the parties intend later to record their agreement in a written form does not prevent the agreement being enforceable earlier.[2]

On fluctuating markets, there is always the temptation for one of the parties, whether to sale or carriage contract, to try to get out of it. The simplest argument is that no valid contract has been made in the first place. It is therefore necessary to decide when there is a binding contract in principle, and if so, the effect of a qualification such as "subject details".

At least for charterparties, there is a comprehensive analysis in Debattista: "Charter-party Fixtures "Subject Details"—Further Reflections" [1985] L.M.C.L.Q. 241. (Though the article is now quite old, later authorities largely support his conclusions.) At p. 245 he suggests the following presumptions:

"(a) where the parties leave something unmentioned, it is easier to find that there is a contract;

(b) where the parties mention an issue which they leave unresolved, it is easier to find that there is no contract."

A good summary of the general law can be found in Maugham L.J.'s judgment in *Foley v Classique Coaches Ltd*[3]:

"It is indisputable that unless all the material terms of the contract are agreed there is no binding obligation. An agreement to agree in the future is not a contract; nor is there a contract if a material term is neither settled nor implied by law and the document contains no machinery for ascertaining it."

It needs also to be added, however, that otherwise the courts are quite happy to conclude that an enforceable agreement has been reached. They are not out to frustrate commercial expectations. *Foley* itself concerned an agreement for the supply of petrol "at a price to be agreed by the parties in writing and from time to time", and despite lack of precise agreement as to price the Court of Appeal held that there was an enforceable contract. Scrutton L.J. said[4]:

16–003

"In the present case the parties obviously believed they had a contract and they acted for three years as if they had; they had an arbitration clause which relates to the subject-matter of the agreement as to the supply of petrol, and it seems to me that this arbitration clause applies to any failure to agree as to the price. By analogy to the case of a tied house there is to be implied in this contract a term that the petrol shall be supplied at a reasonable price and shall be of reasonable quality. For these reasons I think the Lord Chief Justice was right in holding that there was an effective and enforceable contract, although as to the future no definite price had been agreed with regard to the petrol."

The courts are prepared to fill in details, where the parties apparently intend to be bound, as long as there is sufficient certainty to determine the fundamentals of

---

[2] *WJ Rossiter v Miller* (1878) 3 App. Cas. 1124; *The Blankenstein* [1985] 1 All E.R. 475 (valid contract sale of ship, although memorandum of agreement not signed and deposit not paid). See also Debattista, *op. cit.*, p. 243.

[3] [1934] 2 K.B. 1, at 13.

[4] *Foley v Classique Coaches Ltd* [1934] 2 K.B. 1 at 10.

an agreement. *Foley* also implies that even where material terms are not agreed, there might still be an enforceable contract if the agreement contains machinery for ascertaining them, such as the arbitration clause in the case itself.

As was observed in *Foley*, however, the courts do not recognise the notion of an agreement to agree.[5] Moreover, if the parties expressly make the contract "subject to" something which is not yet agreed, the courts will generally infer a lack of agreement at this stage. In *The Solholt*,[6] for example, Staughton J. said (of a contract for the sale of a ship that):

> "She is described as having on that day been 'fixed subject to details'. That means that the main terms were agreed, but until the subsidiary terms and the details had also been agreed no contract existed."

16–004 This was *obiter*, but other authorities point in the same direction. In *The Samah*,[7] Parker J. refused to hold a charterparty agreement concluded at the recap telex stage, where agreement still had to be reached on modifications to the vessel:

> "At this time very little was known at all about the proposed modifications.[8] The telex specifically provides that the details are to be agreed and that the modification of plans, other than the water ballast tanks, is to be discussed with the owners. The owners had not then seen the charterers' proforma. It is undoubtedly possible to contract when much is left outstanding and for a party to commit himself to the acceptance of certain conditions which he has not seen. The present case is, however, not one of certain matters merely being left unmentioned. The parties have specifically stated that the details of the main modifications are to be agreed and the possible modification of other tanks is to be discussed. Furthermore, when Hellenic Seaways Overseas Corporation, the agents in Piraeus for the plaintiffs [would-be charterers], sent forward to Mr. Maris the proforma charter-party, they stated:
>
> > ' . . . you can add or alter clauses considering the special trading in which above mentioned vessels will be employed.'
>
> This recognizes that the fixture was an unusual one for which special clauses would be required, as indeed they ultimately were. Mr. Rokison [for the charterers] submits that the introduction of the special clauses later was merely a variation of an already binding fixture of the terms of the charterers' NYPE proforma. But I cannot accept this. The reality of the situation is that both parties recognized that special provisions would have to be made. The charterers indeed set about drafting them. In my judgment neither party intended the final telexes to constitute a binding contract and neither party considered at the time that they had done so. Furthermore, even if they had so intended or considered, they would not have succeeded. The parties having expressly stated that certain further matters were to be agreed or discussed, the Court cannot fill the gap. I therefore reject the plaintiffs' claim that a binding charter was made on Jan. 3 [date of telex exchange]."

---

[5] *May & Butcher v R.* [1934] 2 K.B. 17.
[6] [1981] 2 Lloyd's Rep. 574.
[7] [1981] 1 Lloyd's Rep. 40.
[8] It seems that a Ro-Ro vessel was to be adapted for the import of bagged cement into Nigeria (author's footnote).

Later cases are to the same effect.[9] Debattista suggests that even where matters remain explicitly to be agreed, the inclusion of an arbitration clause as a mechanism to resolve any outstanding uncertainties might still save the contract.[10] However, if the parties expressly use terminology such as "subject to details", which clearly indicates an intention not yet to be bound, the courts will give effect to that intention.

(b) When is Contract Made?

For paper-based contracts, it is well-known that acceptance takes place on posting,[11] so that there can be a valid contract, even though the acceptance never reaches the offeror.[12] There is also authority that the rule does not apply to "instantaneous" methods of communication, such as telex.[13] The question is, does the paper-based postal rule apply to Internet communications, such as e-mail and the W.W.W.?   **16–005**

This depends on the rationale for the postal rule, upon which opinions differ. In *Harris' Case*, Mellish L.J. justified it on the grounds of commercial convenience[14]:

"Now throughout the argument I have been forcibly struck with the extraordinary and very mischievous consequences which would follow if it were held that an offer might be revoked at any time until the letter accepting it had been actually received. No mercantile man who has received a letter making him an offer, and has accepted the offer, could safely act on that acceptance after he has put it into the post until he knew that it had been received. Every day, I presume, there must be a large number of mercantile letters received which require to be acted upon immediately. A person, for instance, sends an order to a merchant in London offering to pay a certain price for so many goods. The merchant writes an answer accepting the offer, and goes that instant into the market and purchases the goods in order to enable him to fulfil the contract. But according to the argument presented to us, if the person who has sent the offer finds that the market is falling, and that it will be a bad bargain for him, he may at any time, before he has received the answer, revoke his offer. The consequences might be very serious to the merchant, and might be much more serious when the parties are in distant countries. Suppose that a dealer in Liverpool writes to a dealer in New York and offers to buy so many quarters of corn or so many bales of cotton at a certain price, and the dealer in New York, finding that he can make a favourable bargain, writes an answer accepting the offer. Then, according to the argument that has been presented to us to-day, during the whole time that the letter accepting the offer is on the Atlantic, the dealer who is to receive it in Liverpool, if he finds that the market has fallen, may send a message by telegraph and revoke his offer."

The commercial convenience argument, then, depends on the offeree being unaware whether his acceptance has been received, and prevents the offeror from

---

[9] *e.g. The Nissos Samos* [1985] 1 Lloyd's Rep. 378, *Granit SA v Benship International Inc* [1994] 1 Lloyd's Rep. 526 (where in the absence of the words "subject to details" a contract was held to have been concluded), *Ignazio Messina & Co v Polskie Linie Oceaniczne* [1995] 2 Lloyd's Rep. 566.
[10] He cites Lord Denning M.R. in *F & G Sykes (Wessex) v Fine Fare Ltd* [1967] 1 Lloyd's Rep. 53, at 57–58.
[11] *Adams v Lindsell* (1818) 1 B. Ald. 681.
[12] *Household Fire and Carriage Accident Insurance Co Ltd v Grant* (1879) 4 Ex. D. 216, CA.
[13] *Entores Ltd v Miles Far East Corporation* [1955] 2 Q.B. 327. See para. 16–006, below.
[14] *Imperial Land Co of Marseilles, Re (Harris' Case)* (1872) L.R. 7 Ch. App. 587, at 594.

taking advantages of delays and uncertainties a communication method which he has himself chosen.

A different justification for the postal rule can be found in *Household Fire and Carriage Accident Insurance Co Ltd v Grant*,[15] where Thesiger L.J. treated delivery to the post office as delivery to the parties' common agent. He also said[16]:

> "The acceptor, in posting the letter, has, to use the language of Lord Blackburn, in *Brogden v Directors of Metropolitan Ry. Co* 2 App. Cas. 666, 691, 'put it out of his control and done an extraneous act which clenches the matter, and shews beyond all doubt that each side is bound.' "

16–006   The emphasis here, then, is on the relinquishing of control to a third party. But this is also true of a telephone conversation, or communication by fax or telex, to which, it seems, the postal rule does not apply. One possibility is that, unlike communications by ordinary post, the sender of such a communication will know, either immediately or very quickly, whether the communication has been received. This distinction harks back to that in *Harris' Case*, and suggests that though entrusting the communication to a third party might be a necessary precondition for the application of the postal rule, it is not sufficient.

In *Entores Ltd v Miles Far East Corporation*, the Court of Appeal held that the rule did not apply to instantaneous communications, the decision and reasoning later being upheld by the House of Lords in *Brinkibon v Stahag Stahl Und Stahlwarenhandels-Gesellschaft mbH*.[17] This is an alternative ground for distinguishing between postal and, *e.g.* telephone and fax communications,[18] but it may effectively be a restatement of the same distinction, since unlike a postal communication, with "instantaneous" communication, the offeree should know immediately if his communication has failed to reach the offeror. Telex and fax both work on circuit-switched telephone lines, and fax machines certainly normally show up an error if there is a transmission failure.

An important factor, then, seems to be whether the offeree can discover quickly whether his acceptance has reached the offeror. However, in *Brinkibon* Lord Wilberforce also said that[19]:

> "No universal rule can cover all such cases: they must be resolved by reference to the intentions of the parties, by sound business practice and in some cases by a judgment where the risks should lie."

With several different justifications for the postal rule, and the view in *Brinkibon* that there is no universal rule, it would be difficult to predict with any degree of certainty whether the postal rule will apply to Internet communications. However, e-mail, like postal mail (often referred to as snailmail by computer users), is transmitted by third parties. Though usually fast, it is questionable whether it can normally be regarded as instantaneous (at least if it travels over the Internet), since there is a time delay (from fractions of a second to hours, depending on traffic) between leaving the sender's mailbox and reaching the recipient's.[20] It will not be known whether the recipient has actually read it, but that is also true of telex, fax and indeed postal communications. There is additionally, however, a risk of non-delivery, even to the recipient's mailbox, and the sender may not know whether there has been receipt (confirm receipt options being no more

---

[15] (1879) 4 Ex. D. 216, especially at 221.
[16] *ibid*. at 223.
[17] [1983] 2 A.C. 34.
[18] The communication in *Entores* was in fact by telex, effectively a printed form of telephone communication.
[19] *Brinkibon v Stahag Stahl Und Stahlwarenhandels-Gesellschaft mbH* [1983] 2 A.C. 34 at 42.
[20] Because the Internet is a packet-switched network.

reliable than the mail itself). In all these respects, e-mail bears closer similarities to snailmail than it does to telephone, fax or telex communication, so there is a case for applying the postal rule.

By contrast, e-mail can move instantaneously (and be confirmed) between two users of the same system, *e.g.* a communication between one *Hotmail* user and another,[21] or presumably between two *Bolero* users. For such communications, it would be difficult to justify application of the postal rule. It is true that a third party is involved in the communication, but that is equally true of the telex. Not only is communication instantaneous, but the message does not need to move anywhere; all that needs to happen is for the recipient to be able to access it from his mailbox.

Web-based contracts must surely be in the same position as e-mail over the Internet. They are no more instantaneous than e-mail, and although the sender might immediately be aware of non-delivery (because his browser will show an error message), he will not be if the message reaches the recipient but the returned webpage is lost. Communication is by a third party, and there is surely a good case for applying the postal rule to web-based contracting.

(c) Writing and Signatures

For most contracts, including charterparties and international sale contracts, **16–007** there are no formal requirements, but a bill of exchange, as often used for payments under documentary credits is "an unconditional order in writing".[22] A bill of lading, to be valid as a document of title, must be in writing and signed, and orally agreed terms are not transferred into any contract between carrier and consignee or indorsee.[23] Also, an arbitration clause must be in writing. For this reason, in *The Heidberg* (discussed at paras. 12–034, *et seq.*, above) His Honour Judge Diamond Q.C. refused to incorporate into a bill of lading an arbitration clause from the head charterparty, one reason being that the head charterparty was "oral", although there was a recap telex. We also saw in para. 12–036, above, that a charterparty evidenced by recap telex was regarded as being in writing in *The Epsilon Rosa*. Writing is defined in s.1. of the Interpretation Act 1978 as follows:

> " 'Writing' includes typing, printing, lithography, photography and other modes of representing or reproducing words in a visible form, and expressions referring to writing are construed accordingly."

There is therefore surely a good argument that a recap telex, or even an e-mail message, can constitute writing.

There is no statutory definition of a signature.

CHRIS REED, "WHAT IS A SIGNATURE?"

2000 (3) J.I.L.T. http://elj.warwick.ac.uk/jilt/00–3/reed.html/

[Footnotes as in original, but renumbered for present purposes. Some cross-references to elsewhere in the article have also been removed.]

---

[21] The mail does not need to go anywhere, simply being stored on the system, for access by another user.

[22] Bills of Exchange Act 1882, s.3(1). See Ch. 8, above, for their use in documentary credit payments.

[23] See *Leduc v Ward*, in para. 12–004, above.

16–008   English law has rarely found it necessary to define what is meant by a signature, dealing with new signature methods by analogy with the ways in manuscript signatures have previously been treated by the law. Now, the increasingly widespread use of electronic communications demands a reassessment of what constitutes a valid signature. . . .

1.1 A shortage of definitions

16–009   Signing a document is a fundamental legal act, so much so that almost every commercial document of any importance is signed. In spite of this, the signature as a legal artefact has received very little analytical attention.[24] This is perhaps unsurprising; the paradigm case of signature is the signatory's name, written in his or her[25] own hand, on a paper document[26] (a "manuscript signature"), and this is so universally understood by lawyers and non-lawyers alike that it requires no special treatment. Variations on this theme have been considered by the English courts from time to time, ranging from simple modifications such as crosses[27] or initials,[28] through pseudonyms[29] and identifying phrases,[30] to printed names[31] and rubber stamps.[32] In all these cases the courts have been able to resolve the question whether a valid signature was made by drawing an analogy with a manuscript signature.

For this reason, perhaps, it has never been felt necessary to define the term "signature" in the Interpretation Act, nor in general have definitions

---

[24] Authors have examined specific issues, such as the signing of wills and deeds by the use of a mark (Meston & Cusine, *"Execution of Deeds by a Mark"* (1993) J.L.S.S. 270), the effectiveness of signatures on faxed indictments (Queries (1993) 157 J.P. 736), electronic signatures of international trade documents (Economic Commission for Europe, Committee on the Development of Trade Working Party of Facilitation of International Trade Procedures, "Review of definitions of 'Writing', 'Signatures' and 'Document' employed in multilateral conventions and agreements relating to international trade" [1998] 5 E.D.I. L.R. 3) and signatures of telexes (Smith, "Electronic Signatures" [1996] 2 C.T.L.R. T–17). However, no detailed analysis of English law's basic requirements for a valid signature appears to have been undertaken, although some short articles on digital signatures do make reference to these matters—see, *e.g.* Davies, "Legal aspects of digital signatures" (1995) 11 C.L.&P. 165.

[25] For ease of reading "he" and "his" are used hereafter to stand for "he/she" and "his/her", following the convention used for statutory drafting.

[26] This distinction of "paper document" is important, as will be seen below. The legal concept of document is extremely wide, extending to such things as photographs of tombstones and houses (*Lyell v Kennedy (No. 3)* (1884) 27 Ch.D. 1), account books (*Hill v R.* [1945] K.B. 329) and drawings and plans (*Hayes v Brown* [1920] 1 K.B. 250; *JH Tucker & Co, Ltd v Board Of Trade* [1955] 2 All E.R. 522). For evidential purposes in civil actions, a document is "anything in which information of any description is recorded" (Civil Evidence Act 1995 s.13).

[27] *Baker v Dening* (1838) 8 A. & E. 94.

[28] *Hill v Hill* [1947] Ch. 231.

[29] *Redding, Re* (1850) 14 Jur. 1052, 2 Rob. Ecc. 339.

[30] *Cook, In the Estate of (Deceased). Murison v Cook* [1960] 1 All E.R. 689 (holograph will signed "your loving mother").

[31] *Brydges v Dix* (1891) 7 T.L.R. 215; *France v Dutton* [1891] 2 Q.B. 208. Typewriting has also been considered in *Newborne v Sensolid (Great Britain), Ltd* [1954] 1 Q.B. 45.

[32] *Lazarus Estates, Ltd v Beasley* [1956] 1 Q.B. 702; *London County Council v Vitamins Ltd; London County Council v Agricultural Food Products Ltd* [1955] 2 Q.B. 218.

been included in those statutes which specifically impose requirements for signatures . . .

. . .

1.3 Form versus function

There are two ways in which the law might set out to test the validity and **16–010** effectiveness of a signature. The first is to determine whether the signature has the required *form*. This approach would result in a list of acceptable forms of signature, foremost among which would be the manuscript signature. The list could be extended ad hoc to cover new forms of signature which are sufficiently similar to those already on the list.

The alternative approach is to determine the functions which a signature must perform, and then to provide that all signature methods which effect those functions will be treated for legal purposes as valid signatures.

As will be apparent from what follows, English law initially assessed the validity of signatures by reference to their form, but has since moved towards assessing validity in terms of the functions performed by the signature method. . . .

2. Form

There is very little legislation which attempts to define what constitutes a signature. . . .

So far as case law is concerned, there is a long history of judicial recognition of new forms of signature. In a series of cases during the nineteenth and early twentieth centuries, the courts recognised as valid signature methods the use of initials,[33] marks,[34] seals (for some but not all types of document),[35] the adoption of a printed name[36] and the use of rubber stamps.[37] The approach adopted by the courts in these cases was to determine whether the particular form of signature adopted had already been recognised as valid in previous decisions, and if not, to decide whether it was acceptable in the particular circumstances. Often no reasons were given to explain why the signature method in question was legally acceptable; it appears that the judges in each case simply satisfied themselves that the method adopted achieved the same authentication effects as a manuscript signature.

These judgments only decided whether the particular form of signature at issue was valid, and did not attempt to lay down any general principles for determining valid forms of signature.

---

[33] *Re Hinds* 16 Jur. 1161, *Re Savory* 15 Jur. 1042 (signature of wills); *Hill v Hill* [1947] Ch. 231 (signature of contract).
[34] *Re Clarke* 27 L.J.P.M. & A. 18 (illiterate testator made his mark on will but wrong name written against the mark—extrinsic evidence admitted to show true identity of maker of mark); *Re Field* 3 Curt. 752; *Baker v Dening* 8 A. & E. 94 (signature valid even though signatory could write his name).
[35] *Re Doe d. Phillips v Evans* 2 L.J. Ex. 193 (signature by seal valid for purposes of Insolvency Act); *Re Byrd* 3 Curt. 117 (signature by seal invalid for purposes of Wills Act).
[36] *Schneider v Norris* 2 M. & S. 286.
[37] *Schneider v Norris* 2 M. & S. 286 (*obiter per* Le Blanc J. at 289).

[Professor Reid then considers cases where the legislation, or other context, requires a personal signature, requiring the signatory to write his name (or some equivalent) in his own handwriting. He continues:]

The leading case . . . is *Goodman v J. Eban Ltd,*[38] where the Court of Appeal reviewed the relevant authorities when holding (by a 2:1 majority, Denning L.J. dissenting) that a solicitor's bill did not require a personal signature, and thus a signature by rubber stamp was valid . . .

2.4 Marks

16–011   A possible further requirement of form, for which there is ambiguous authority that it is an essential element of *all* signatures, is that the signature should take the form of some mark made on a document. In *Morton v Copeland*[39] Maule J. stated that signing:

> "does not necessarily mean writing a person's Christian and surname, but any mark which identifies it as the act of the party."[40]

It might be thought that until recently it would have been impossible to conceive of a signature method which did not mark the document, and thus that the description by the courts of a signature as a "mark" should not be taken as stating any more than the obvious. Surprisingly, this precise issue did arise in the case of *in re Cunningham.*[41] In that case a validly attested will was revised by making alterations on its face, and the testator and witnesses then traced their original signatures with a dry pen. Although it was clear from the other evidence in the case that they all intended to make their signatures, the court held that the revised version of the will was not validly attested. The reason for the decision appears to be that no physical mark was made on the will, but unfortunately this point was not fully addressed in the judgment, the court simply asserting that these acts did not produce a valid signature.

The requirement for signatures to take the form of a mark seems to have been assumed in more recent cases,[42] and is also found in s.1(4) of the Law of Property (Miscellaneous Provisions) Act 1989:

---

[38] [1954] 1 Q.B. 550.

[39] (1855) 16 C.B. 517, 535.

[40] See also *Baker v Dening* (1838) 8 A. & E. 94; *Re Field* 3 Curt. 752; *Re Clarke* 27 L.J.P.M. & A. 18.

[41] 29 L.J.P.M. & A. 71.

[42] For example, in *Goodman v J Eban Ltd* [1954] 1 Q.B. 550, 557 Sir Raymond Evershed M.R. adopted the definition in the *Shorter Oxford English Dictionary* (2nd ed.) vol. 2, p. 1892: "(ii) to place some distinguishing mark upon (a thing or person) . . . (iv) to attest or confirm by adding one's signature; to affix one's name to (a document, etc.)." See also *R v Moore ex parte Myers* (1884) 10 V.L.R. 322.

"In subsections (2) and (3) above 'sign', in relation to an instrument,[43] includes making one's mark on the instrument and 'signature' is to be construed accordingly."

If the requirement for a mark still subsists, and is not a mere historical curiosity, then it will be impossible to sign most electronic documents. This is because the term "mark" would appear to require some signature process whose result:

- is visible to the eye; and

- produces a physical alteration to the thing marked.

As will be explained . . . below, neither of these can be achieved in respect of an electronic document.

3. From form to function

The more modern judicial approach to the validity of signatures concentrates not on form as a test for validity, but rather on function. This line of authority can be traced back over 150 years, and now represents the standard judicial test for validity. Under this line of cases a signature will be valid, irrespective of the form it takes, if it performs the functions which the law requires of a signature (but possibly subject to the formal requirement that it be a mark—see . . . above). The case law suggests that these functions are primarily (if not exclusively) evidential. However, additional functional requirements can be detected in some of the legislation, and these also need to be investigated to ensure that electronic signatures can achieve those functions.

16–012

3.1 The primary function—authentication

The history of the requirements of form for documentary transactions (primarily writing and signature) suggests that the reason why the law required them was for authentication purposes. Many of the requirements for writing and signature have their origin in the Statute of Frauds 1677, and Fifoot makes a convincing argument that the Statute of Frauds was enacted to deal with perceived evidential problems. He suggests that the intention behind the legislation was to remove the possibility that oral evidence could be adduced to deny the apparent accuracy of a document or explain its true meaning[44]:

---

[43] Note, though, that the term 'instrument' is normally used only to mean a hard copy document, and that in respect of dealings in land ss.2(1) and 2(3) of the Act require a signed writing, which again must be a hard copy document—see further Reed, *Digital Information Law: electronic documents and requirements of form* (Centre for Commercial Law Studies, London, 1996) Chs. 1 and 4. It is not conclusive, then, that signatures of non-hard copy documents also require a mark.

[44] Fifoot, *History and Sources of the Common Law* (Stevens & Sons Ltd, London, 1949) p. 360, discussing *Pinchon's Case* (1612) 9 Co Rep. 866 in which an oral agreement was enforced against the deceased's personal representatives.

... In order to achieve this aim, formal requirements for writings and signatures were imposed to ensure the evidential reliability of documents before the courts.[45]

...

3.1.1 Cases

16–013   The modern approach to the validity of signature methods is set out in *Goodman v J Eban Ltd*[46] In that case a solicitor's bill had been "signed" with a facsimile of the firm's name imposed by means of a rubber stamp. The defendant client of the firm argued that the bill was unenforceable because it had not validly been signed[47] but the majority of the Court of Appeal disagreed. They held that it was sufficient if the rubber stamp were placed on the bill by the solicitor with the intention of authenticating the document as his own. Sir Raymond Evershed M.R. said:

> "It follows, then, I think, that the essential requirement of signing is the affixing, either by writing with a pen or pencil or by otherwise impressing on the document, one's name or 'signature' so as personally to authenticate the document."[48]

and Romer L.J. agreed:

> "The first reaction of many people, I think, would be that the impression of a name produced by a rubber stamp does not constitute a signature, and, indeed, in some sense, is the antithesis of a signature. When, however, the matter is further considered in the light of authority and also of the function which a signature is intended to perform one arrives, I think, at a different result ... The letter was type-written and concludes with the words (also typed) 'Yours faithfully, Goodman, Monroe & Company'. This was immediately followed by a repetition of the firm name, in the form Goodman, Monroe & Co, which looks at first sight as though it had been written by hand, but which in reality was impressed by the plaintiff through the medium of a rubber stamp. This repetition would be plainly otiose were it merely intended to repeat the typed name of the firm, and the obvious intention of the plaintiff was that it should be regarded as a signature for the purpose of authenticating the letter."[49]

---

[45] Salmond, "The Superiority of Written Evidence" (1890) 6 L.Q.R. 75.

[46] [1954] 1 Q.B. 550.

[47] As required by s.65(2)(i) Solicitors Act, 1932, the legislation then governing solicitors' bills, which provided:

> "(1) Subject to the provisions of this Act, no action shall be brought to recover any costs due to a solicitor until one month after a bill thereof has been delivered in accordance with the requirements of this section ...
>
> (2) The said requirements are as follows: (i) The bill must be signed by the solicitor, or, if the costs are due to a firm, one of the partners of that firm, either in his own name or in the name of the firm, or be enclosed in, or accompanied by, a letter which is so signed and refers to the bill ... ".

[48] [1954] 1 Q.B. 550, 557.

[49] [1954] 1 Q.B. 550, 563.

This judgment clearly demonstrates that the validity of a particular signature method is to be tested by reference to the functions it performs. The purported signature will be valid if it provides evidence of authentication of the document by the purported signatory.

Goodman v J Eban also determined that there was no requirement for a signature to be in the form of the name of a natural person, and thus that when signing on behalf of an organisation it is sufficient to sign in the name of the organisation.[50] Furthermore, the signature does not need to take the form of handwriting, so that it is permissible to affix the signature to the document mechanically by such means as a rubber stamp,[51] printing[52] or typewriting.[53]

Other cases which have considered the validity of signature methods have held that:

- it is sufficient to constitute a valid signature if the name of the signatory is placed on the document by a third party, acting under authority from the signatory[54];

- there is no need for the signature to take the form of a legal or natural person's name, and that the signature may be some mark or symbol, provided there is extrinsic evidence which can identify the placer of the mark and his intention that the mark should be his signature[55];

---

[50] See also *Bartletts de Reya (A Firm) v Byrne* (1983) *The Times* January, 14 1983; 127 S.J. 69, CA (Civil Division).

[51] *Beauvais v Green* 22 T.L.R. 816; *Bennett v Brumfitt* (1867) L.R. 3 C.P. 30; *British Estate Investment Society Ltd v Jackson (HM Inspector of Taxes)* [1956] T.R. 397, 37 Tax. Cas. 79, 35 A.T.C. 413, 50 R. & I.T. 33, High Court of Justice (Chancery Division); *Lazarus Estates Ltd v Beasley* [1956] 1 Q.B. 702; *London County Council v Vitamins Ltd London County Council v Agricultural Food Products, Ltd* [1955] 2 Q.B. 218.

[52] *Brydges v Dix* (1891) 7 T.L.R. 215; *France v Dutton* [1891] 2 Q.B. 208.

[53] *Newborne v Sensolid (Great Britain) Ltd* [1954] 1 Q.B. 45.

[54] In *Jenkins v Gaisford & Thring, In the Goods of Jenkins* (1863) 3 Sw. & Tr. 93 a testator made his signature on a codicil to a will using an engraved stamp of his signature which had been made because an illness had left him too weak to write. The stamp was applied by a servant in the testator's presence and under his direction. The court held that the codicil was validly signed under the Statute of Wills s.9 (1 Vict. c. 26). Sir C. Cresswell said, "It has been decided that a testator sufficiently signs by making his mark, and I think it was rightly contended that the word 'signed' in [s.9] must have the same meaning whether the signature is made by the testator himself, or by some other person in his presence or by his direction . . . *The mark made by the instrument or stamp was intended to stand for and represent the signature of the testator.*" ((1863) 3 Sw. & Tr. 93 at p. 96, emphasis added). In later cases, signature by an agent has been held to be valid even though not made in the presence of the signatory (*R v Kent JJ.* (1873) L.R. 8 Q.B. 305; *London County Council v Vitamins Ltd London County Council v Agricultural Food Products Ltd* [1955] 2 Q.B. 218; *Tennant v London County Council* (1957) 55 L.G.R. 421) or if not specifically authorised but made under a general authority to sign on behalf of the principal (*France v Dutton* [1891] 2 Q.B. 208).

[55] *Baker v Dening* (1838) 8 A. & E. 94; *Field, Re* 3 Curt. 752. In *Clarke, Re* 27 L.J.P.M. & A. 18, an illiterate testator made his mark on the will, but the wrong name was written against the mark. Extrinsic evidence was permitted to show the true identity of the maker of the mark. See also *Morton v Copeland* (1855) 16 C.B. 517, 535 *per* Maule J., who said that signing "does not necessarily mean writing a person's Christian and surname, but any mark which identifies it as the act of the party."

- words other than the name of the signatory can be used to effect a signature if there is extrinsic evidence that they were intended by the writer to identify him or herself and to adopt the document.[56]

This examination of the case law demonstrates that the English courts are prepared, at least in the case of hard copy documents, to accept signatures made in any manner which provides evidence of:

- the identity of the signatory;

- that the signatory intended the 'signature' to be his signature; and

- that the signatory approves of and adopts the contents of the document.

. . .

Notes

16–014   On this basis, and assuming that a personal signature is not required, the common law takes a liberal view of the signature requirement. Rubber stamps, printing and typewriting all seem to be regarded as valid. Further, as the Law Commission observed in December 2001[57]:

"Indeed many functions are not fulfilled, or are only partly fulfilled, by the use of paper. Thus English law has long accepted a 'signature' in the form of an 'X' though this does not identify the 'signatory' in any real sense."

However, though the definition of writing (above) might conceivably be wide enough to encompass e-mail,[58] it seems unlikely, even if a functional (rather than formal) approach is taken, that any definition of signature is wide enough to encompass electronic documents.[59] At the very least, a physical mark on a document seems to be required.

Chris Reed's article is primarily about electronic signatures, which will be essential if full dematerialisation of shipping documents is to take place. Electronic signatures are examined further below. Essentially, it is necessary to replicate, through electronic means, the functional requirements of a written signature

---

[56] *Redding, Re* (1850) 14 Jur. 1052, 2 Rob. Ecc. 339, where the testator executed a will in the assumed name of the man with whom she was cohabiting and two years later erased that signature and re-signed in her real name. The court held that probate could be granted in the first name because the second signature, while not itself valid as execution, was not intended to revoke the will but merely to clarify her identity. See also *Hill v Hill* [1947] Ch. 231 (initials); *Cook, In the Estate of (Deceased) Murison v Cook* [1960] 1 All E.R. 689 (holograph will validly signed "your loving mother"); *Rhodes v Peterson* (1972) S.L.T. 98 ("Mum" a valid signature under Scots law).
[57] Law Commission, *"Electronic Commerce: Formal Requirements in Commercial Transactions" (Advice from the Law Commission)* (2001) para. 2.7, available at *www.lawcom.gov.uk*
[58] Also the view of the Law Commission (2001) at para. 3.10.
[59] Clearly not if a physical mark is required.

identified by Reed (identity of signatory, intention to sign, and intention to adopt document).

(2) FACILITATION OF PAPERLESS DOCUMENTATION

One of the changes made in the 1990 revision of Incoterms was to allow **16–015** electronic in place of paper documents. This is continued in the 2000 revision, for example in clause A8 (see Appendix B, below).

The eUCP (set out in Appendix M, below) is more sophisticated, dealing with issues that might arise as to the acceptability of electronic documentation, such as the place of presentation in Articles e3(a) and e5(a), and date of issuance in Article e9, which may not be as obvious as with their paper counterparts. No doubt the banking community is gearing itself up for a possible change in transport community practice, as it did twenty years or so ago, with the increased use of non-negotiable documentation, in place of the traditional bill of lading.[60]

Facilitation such as this is essential if the use of electronic documentation is to develop, but it is only the starting point. There has long been provision, in both the U.C.P. and Incoterms, for tender of waybills in place of traditional bills of lading, but that does not provide the parties who use them with equivalent security. So with electronic documentation, merely making provision for it does not ensure that such documentation is functional and safe. We need to consider in depth how such documentation might work.

(3) PAPERLESS BILLS OF LADING IN REALITY

A bill of lading provides proof that the shipper has loaded conforming goods, **16–016** and also of entitlement of the holder to the goods. Unlike a waybill it does not merely record information. In a paper bill, these functions are provided respectively by the master's signature and statement that the goods were loaded in apparent good order and condition, and physical delivery and (in the case of an order bill) successive indorsements to the person entitled. The bill of lading also transfers contractual rights and liabilities, and possibly property in the goods.

All these functions would need to be replicated in an electronic equivalent. They fall into two general categories. First, there needs to be electronic authentication, not only of the master's signature but also of subsequent indorsements (or their equivalent). Nobody should be able to impersonate the master, and only the current holder of the document should be able to trasnfer it. Secondly, the other attributes of a document of title are essentially bundles of rights and obligations, which can (in principle at least) be replicated by contract actions.

More specifically, the following considerations need to be addressed. First, an electronic equivalent needs to be found for the master's written signature, and indorsement by the current holder. Secondly, some means needs to be found to transmit the document electronically. Thirdly, rights and obligations under the carriage contract need to be transferred. Fourthly, property needs to be transferred.

---

[60] This was one of the major differences between the 1983 and 1974 revisions of the U.C.P., the later making provision for alternative documentation.

There is also, ideally at least, a fifth requirement. Transmission speed is not the only reason why bills of lading often lag behind the cargo. Checking is also a slow process. This also needs to be addressed if computerised bills of lading are to become not only possible, but also useful.

(a) Open and Closed Systems

16–017   Bills of lading can be used by traders and carriers anywhere in the world, and this should ideally also be true of their electronic equivalents. Of the two schemes discussed below, C.M.I. is in principle open, whereas Bolero is closed, depending on membership of an organisation. In practice, even C.M.I. could operate securely only with a certification infrastructure, and it is probable that a fully open system is impossible, if it is also to be secure.

A closed system can be far more secure than the present system. It is also easier to make appropriate contractual provision between the parties. Moreover, the Law Commission observed in 2001 that[61]:

"Because electronic contracts for carriage are not bills of lading, and do not satisfy the narrow common law definition of a 'document of title',[62] they are not within the ambit of the Carriage of Goods by Sea Act 1971 (which applies the Hague-Visby Rules to the contract for carriage) or the Carriage of Goods by Sea Act 1992 (which gives the holder of the bill of lading rights of suit under the contract for carriage). However the provisions of these Acts can be replicated by contract, if parties using electronic contracts for carriage choose to do so."

Article III(3) of the *Hague-Visby Rules* allows the shipper to demand a paper bill of lading, but in a closed system it would be possible to contract out of this. On the basis of *The Happy Ranger* (discussed in para. 11–078, above) the *Hague-Visby Rules* would not apply as long as it was not contemplated that a bill of lading would be issued, and a closed system could ensure this.

However, apart from the obvious limitation of a closed system, it can also be undesirable to give too much power to a single organisation, part of the reason for the downfall of the abortive Seadocs project in 1983.

The Seadocs experience

16–018   An attempt partially to computerise documentation in the bulk oil trade was actually made in the Seadocs project (Seaborne Trade Documentation System), instigated in 1983 by Intertanko (the International Association of Independent Tanker Owners) and the Chase Manhattan Bank, which failed to get beyond an initial testing stage. Seadocs was envisaged as a compromise between traditional paper documentation and a fully electronic system. The essential idea of Seadocs was to avoid delay by lodging the bill of lading with a central registry, from which it did not move, and notifying change of ownership electronically. Delays would in theory be significantly reduced, the documents would be available for inspection, and the shipowner could always be certain that he was delivering to the correct party.

---

[61] At para. 4.9.
[62] The note states: "Mercantile custom and usage has recognised only a (paper) bill of lading as satisfying the narrow common law definition of a 'document of title'."

Leaving aside the numerous detailed problems with the scheme, among the reasons for the failure of the project was the monopoly position of the registry, which was perceived to be acting in its own interests rather than those of the trading parties. This may well be a problem with any closed system, although it would be less so if there were a number of registries competing for business. Another problem was the lack of enthusiasm from the P. & I. Clubs, and hence ultimately the shipowners. It is clear, however, that major problems were also caused by the retention of the paper bill of lading, albeit that it was centrally lodged. Kathy Love wrote[63]:

"A more serious problem, from the point of view of the banks, was that without physical presentation of the bill a bank would not be able to scrutinise the bill (and the documents associated with it, which could also be lodged in the Registry) for conformity with a letter of credit. In order to meet this objection the Registry, somewhat grudgingly, undertook to examine a bill, if requested to do so, to see whether it complied with particular requirements stated by the requesting party. It was hoped that this facility would also go some way towards satisfying the concerns of cargo buyers who, particularly in view of the frequency of fraudulent bills, often had careful in-house programmes for scrutinising documents.

However, this offer by the Registry was perceived to be seriously flawed . . ."

Apart from a pilot project using shadow documents, Seadocs was never operated and therefore was not examined by the courts. Had it been, it might well have been perceived to be flawed in other respects as well, since no provision was made for the transfer of contractual rights and liabilities to holders of the bill, apart from the original shipper. The Bills of Lading Act 1855, s.1, which was then the operative legislation, would certainly not have applied in the absence of physical indorsement and transfer, and it is by no means certain that the common law would have recognised the static bill as a document of title. It is by no means clear, for example, who if anyone could have sued the shipowner had he delivered to the wrong person, or what protection a bank as holder under a documentary credit might have had in the event of the bankruptcy of the buyer. In any system of electronic documentation the parties themselves must make provision for these eventualities, and cannot rely on legal mechanisms already being in place once they move away from traditional documentation.

Lessons from Seadocs

1. It is a mistake to grant monopoly power to a registry or (on the same reasoning) any institution setting up a closed group.

2. In retrospect, Seadocs can be seen to have been insufficiently ambitious (perhaps justifiable given the state of computer and communications technology of the day). You have to take *all* of the functions of the paper bill, and replicate them in an electronic system. This requires (at least) the use of cryptography or some other electronic method of replicating a signature, and the setting up of contractual rights and liabilities, as similar as possible to those created by the paper bill it replaces.

---

[63] Kathy Love, "*Seadocs: The Lessons Learned*", [1992] 2 Oil and Gas Law and Taxation Review 53, at p. 55.

(b) Electronic Signatures

16–019   In a closed system the parties can agree on whatever formalities are necessary, and (as in Bolero) agree that formality requirements will be satisfied by a "Signed Message", as defined by Bolero.[64] However, you have to be very certain that all parties to litigation are also members of Bolero. Reed observes (*"What is a Signature?"*—see above at para. 16–008):

> "One solution available to those who wish to use electronic signatures is to make provision in a contract for the acceptability of the signature method.[65] Even if the use of the technology does not create what the courts would recognise as a valid signature, at worst the contractual term would raise an estoppel in favour of the party seeking to rely on the electronic signature.[66] However, the estoppel will not bind a third party, who will be able to plead the lack of signature as a defence and, as a corollary, will not be able to found his own action on the estoppel; and it will be ineffective if the result would be to declare valid a transaction which is in fact *void* according to the law for lack of formalities.[67] . . .
>
> For these reasons electronic signatures cannot remain creatures of contract. An assessment of the validity and effectiveness of these new types of signature therefore requires a fundamental review of the nature of signatures in English law."

It is also possible, in a closed system, for the functions of a signature to be reproduced electronically, within the system itself. For example, if users need a password to access the system, the password itself can authenticate the identity of a sender of the message.

---

[64] *Bolero Rulebook*, rule 2.2.2 (set out in App. L, below).

[65] See, *e.g.* American Bar Association, *Model Electronic Data Interchange Trading Partner Agreement* (American Bar Association, 1990) para. 1.5:
  "Each party shall adopt as its signature an electronic identification consisting of symbol(s) or code(s) which are to be affixed to or contained in each Document transmitted by such party ('Signatures'). Each party agrees that any Signature of such party affixed to or contained in any transmitted Document shall be sufficient to verify such party originated such Document."
See further Baum & Pettit, *Electronic Contracting, Publishing and EDI Law* (John Wiley & Sons, New York, 1991) para 2.16. See also *Trading Partner Agreement to Authorize EDI for Defense Transportation* (Logistics Management Institute, Bethesda, Maryland, 1990) para. XIV:
  "Vendor will use a code as specified in each transaction set addendum as its discrete authenticating code in lieu of signature and as the equivalent of a signature."

[66] This estoppel will arise even if the parties know that their agreed electronic signature technology is ineffective as a matter of law:
  "The full facts may be known to both parties; but if, even knowing those facts to the full, they are clearly enough shown to have assumed a different state of facts *as between themselves* for the purposes of a particular transaction, then their assumption will be treated, as between them, as true, in proceedings arising out of the transaction. The claim of the party raising the estoppel is, not that he believed the assumed version of the facts was true, but that he believed (and agreed) that it should be *treated as true*."
Spencer Bower & Turner, *The Law Relating to Estoppel by Representation* (3rd ed., Butterworths, London, 1977) p. 160, citing *Newis v General Accident Fire & Life Assurance Corporation* (1910) 11 C.L.R. 620 at 636 *per* Isaacs J. (High Court of Australia). See also *TCB Ltd v Gray* [1986] Ch. 621 (estoppel relating to the absence of a seal on a deed).

[67] See, *e.g. Swallow & Pearson v Middlesex County Council* [1953] 1 All E.R. 580 (in respect of the formality of writing). An estoppel can arise, however, if the requirement for a signature is imposed by the law solely to protect the parties to the transaction, as opposed to the public interest—see Spencer Bower & Turner, *The Law Relating to Estoppel by Representation* (3rd ed., Butterworths, London, 1977) pp. 142–4.

In an open system, on the other hand, there is no inbuilt authentication, and a digital signature, or other secure means of identification, needs to be used instead. A digital signature relies on asymmetric encryption, and certification authorities to certify identity.

STEFFAN HINDELANG "NO REMEDY FOR DISAPPOINTED TRUST—THE LIABILITY REGIME FOR CERTIFICATION AUTHORITIES TOWARDS THIRD PARTIES OUTWITH THE EC DIRECTIVE IN ENGLAND AND GERMANY COMPARED"

[2002] 1 J.I.L.T., available at http://elj.warwick.ac.uk/jilt/02–1/hindelang.html

[Footnotes as in original, but renumbered for inclusion here—figures are omitted.]

2.1 Technology

No attempt will be made here to explain the rather complex underlying **16–020** technology in any detail. Readers who are unfamiliar with cryptographic terminology and techniques should consult, in addition to what is stated here, the many excellent sources available which can provide the relevant technical background (see for example, Reed, 2000, ABA, 1996). The importance of understanding the technology cannot be overstated. In order to facilitate the reconstruction of the technological operations the reader might be advised to make use of the appendices and glossary at the end of this dissertation.

2.1.1 What is "Public Key Cryptography"?

Public key encryption uses two different but mathematically related keys,[68] each of which will decrypt documents encrypted by the other key. One key, chosen arbitrarily, is used to transform data into a seemingly unintelligible form and is kept secret,[69] while the other is made public.[70] All effective electronic signatures require the use of a "one-way function" (irreversibility). This means that if a document, signed electronically by Alice with her private key, is sent to Bob, Bob must be able to decrypt the document's signature element with the help of Alice's public key, but must not be able to re-encrypt it with this key (Reed, 2000a). In other words it must be "computationally infeasible" to derive the private key from the knowledge of the public key. Otherwise the discovered private key could be used to forge digital signatures of the holder (ABA, 1996).

---

[68] The pair of keys is usually provided by a CA as part of its services.
[69] The private key is usually stored on a smart card and can be accessed only through entering a personal identification number.
[70] The system derives its name from this idea.

2.1.2 How Does the "Public Key Cryptography" Process Work?
Alice wants to send a word document to Bob . . .

1. Alice passes the document through an algorithm, called a *"digest"* or *"hash" function*. This function carries out a mathematical operation on the original document. It creates a unique and concise version of the original text—the *"message digest"*.[71]

2. Alice then encrypts the message digest with her *private key*. Encryption is carried out by performing a series of mathematical functions (an encryption algorithm) which has two inputs: the "message digest" which is nothing more than a string of 1s and 0s and the private key which is itself also a number. The result of this operation is a series of different numbers, which (in a technical sense) form the actual *electronic signature* (Reed, 2000a).

3. Alice sends the plain word document and her electronic signature to Bob.

4. When Bob receives the message, his computer and software perform mathematical operations in order to determine whether the document was altered in transit (**Integrity** of the document) and whether Alice's public and private key correspond (See Figure 2: Validating an Electronically Signed Document).

5. Bob's system takes Alice's digital signature, and uses her *public key*[72] to decrypt the digital signature. This operation will (re-)produce the "message digest" of the document Alice **sent**. If a private key other than the one corresponding to the public key of Alice was used to encrypt the sent message digest, the electronic signature will not be verified.[73] At the same time the plain document Bob received is run through the same hash function (!) that Alice used. This will provide Bob with the message digest of the document he **received**.

7. Bob will then compare the two message digests. Any change in the word document while in transit, no matter how slight, would lead to a significant change of the message digest generated out of the received word document when the same hash function is used. Each document has its unique message digest. However, if the

---

[71] Also called *"hash value"* or *"hash result"*. The result of the operation of the hash function is a very short file in comparison to the word document but nevertheless substantially unique to it. In the case of a secure hash function it is "computationally infeasible" to derive the original message from knowledge of its "hash value".

[72] Bob may get Alice's public key either from her (as part of a certificate, if certified), or from Alice's (or the CA's) web page, etc. In some cases, the choice might affect the legal regime that applies to the CA.

[73] If the "message digest" had been encoded with the private key of a person other than Alice, the usage of Alice's public key on this electronic signature will result in the awareness that the message has been sent by someone else than Alice, since in theory only the person behind the synonym "Alice" is in possession of the private key.

message digest produced from the electronic signature and the message digest produced from the plain document received are the same, Bob will know that the document he received, had not been altered in transit. Alice's signature has been validated.

2.2.3 Certification Infrastructure . . .
Certification Authorities

However, the utility of an electronic signature as an **authenticating tool** **16–021** is limited by the ability of the recipient to ensure the authenticity of the key used to verify the message digest. In other words, it proves only that private key and public key belong together. If the evil Dr. No is forging a message from Alice he will send his own public key as well, claiming that it actually belongs to Alice. In order to rely on the authenticity of that public key, however, Bob needs to get it from some source other than Alice. If Bob has access to Alice's public key from some outside source, and uses it to verify the message signed with Dr. No's private key, purporting to be Alice, the verification will fail, revealing the forgery.

In a nutshell, if Alice and Bob had no previous dealings, are strangers, then no electronic signature will reliably identify them to each other without assistance of some outside source to provide a link between their identities and their public keys. Any outside source that reasonably inspires trust will suffice. Here certification authorities (CA) come in.

A *certification authority* is a body, either public or private, that seeks to fill the need for trusted third party services in electronic commerce by issuing electronic certificates, signed electronically, that attest to some fact about the subject of the certificate (Froomkin, 1996). In order to be willing to accept certificates issued by a CA 1 the recipient of this certificate, in our case Bob, must have confidence that the CA 1's public key is really the CA 1's and not another manifestation of the wily Dr. No. One way to achieve this confidence is to have an identifying certificate from another CA (CA 2), certifying CA 1's key. The public key of CA 2 might be certified by a CA 3 and so on. Ultimately, this will lead to a *certificate chain*, with a root certificate at the bottom of the tree.[74] However, this just shifts the problem to the validity of the last CA's public key. One solution to this problem is to establish a governmental root CA, which usually inspires trust. Another solution is to establish a business self-regulatory body monitored by governmental authorities.

Certificates

A *certificate* is a digitally signed statement by a CA that provides **16–022** independent confirmation of an attribute claimed by a person proffering

---

[74] Hierarchical CA structures are not the only solution. Confidence may also be achieved by cross-certification. This means that two CA's certify each other's public key. It is also possible that CAs certify themselves by simply signing their own public keys and posting the certificate on their own web sites. Self-certification is possible because the CAs rely on trust gained from other activities, such as postal services or banking activities (Angel, 1999).

a digital signature. In technical words, a certificate is a computer based record which:

(1) identifies the CA issuing it,

(2) names, identifies, or describes an attribute of the subscriber (*e.g.*; a subject's name,[75] where a subject resides, the subject's age, a subject's membership in an organisation[76])

(3) contains the subscriber's public key, and

(4) is digitally signed by the issuing CA
(Froomkin, 1996).

Usually it also contains information about the level of inquiry used to confirm the fact. Since personal circumstances change and the reality represented by the certificate is out of date, certificates have limited periods of validity or are subject to periodic re-confirmation by the CA. Certificates which are outdated or have been compromised, *e.g.* by disclosing the private key, are listed in so-called *certificate revocation list* (CRL), which is maintained by the issuing CA.

Recalling our example given above, if Alice wants Bob to enter into dealings with her, she will not only send the plain word document and her electronic signature but will also ensure that Bob has access to her certificate, which links her electronic signature, or more precisely her public key, to her identity. Alice's certificate might be sent by Alice (most common situation), or posted on a web page of her CA or it could also be e-mailed by Alice's CA to Bob. In some cases, the choice might affect the legal regime that applies to the CA.

Bibliography

American Bar Association (*ABA*) (1996), *Digital Signature Guidelines* —Legal Infrastructures for Certification Authorities and Secure Electronic Commerce, American Bar Association, Chicago.

Froomkin, M A (1996), The Essential Role of Trusted *Third Parties* in Electronic Commerce, Oregon Law Review, 1996 (75) 49.

Reed, C (2000a), *Internet Law: Text and Materials*, Butterworths, London, Edinburgh, Dublin.

Reed, Christopher (2000b), *What is a Signature?*, Journal of Information, Law & Technology (JILT) 2000 (3) <http://elj.warwick.ac.uk/jilt/00–3/reed.html>.

---

[75] So-called *identifying certificates*; The CA connects (binds) a name to a public key. The act of the CA in checking that the name corresponds to something in the non-digital world binds the name to an identity (Froomkin, 1996).
[76] So-called *authorising certificates*.

Roßnagel, A (1998), Das Gesetz und die Verordnung zur digitalen Signatur—Entstehung und Regelungsgehalt, Recht der Datenverarbeitung (RDV), 1998 (5).

Notes

Briefly[77]:

1. A message signed using Alice's private key can only be accurately decrypted **16–023** using her public key. It also follows that if the message content is known, and the encrypted message, decrypted using her public key, reveals the known content, then the message must have been signed with her private key.

2. It is computationally infeasible (*i.e.* takes an infeasible amount of computer time, such as many years) to deduce Alice's private key from her public key.

3. The role of the certification authority (or C.A.) is to certify that the public key really does belong to Alice, and not, for example, to someone impersonating Alice, such as Eve.

Communications between an innocent Alice (or somebody purporting to be her) and an equally innocent Bob, with attempts at interception by the evil Eve, seem to be conventional in discussions involving cryptography, having originated with the original discussions of the RSA asymmetric encryption system in 1977.[78] Certification authorities are usually identified, in such discussions, as Carol.

Legislation and digital signatures

At the time of writing (September 2002), Article 5(1) of EC Directive 1999/93/EC on a Community framework for electronic signatures requires member states to ensure that "advanced electronic signatures which are based on a qualified certificate and which are created by a secure-signature-creation device" are admissible in evidence and for validity purposes, in essence accorded the same weight as a conventional hand-written signature.[79] Article 5(2) requires member states to ensure that any "electronic signature is not denied legal effectiveness and admissibility as evidence in legal proceedings solely on the grounds that it is" in electronic form, even if it does not satisfy the stringent requirements of Article 5(1). Obviously, the weight given to an electronic signature under Article 5(2) is inferior to that given under Article 5(1), and the requirements are accordingly less stringent. The definition of an "electronic signature", for the purposes of Article 5(2) is sufficiently wide to include an e-mail signature, or scanned handwritten signature incorporated into an electronic document, but the definitions of "advanced electronic signature", "qualified certificate" (which must be issued by a "certification-service-provider"), and "secure-signature-creation device", required to satisfy Article 5(1) are significantly more stringent. Nonetheless, the digital signature described here, certified by an approved C.A., would satisfy the requirements of Article 5(1).

The UK has, however, not implemented the EC Directive fully. Section 7 of the Electronic Communications Act 2000, when it comes into force, is broadly in line with Article 5(2) of the Directive, albeit with an added requirement for the

---

[77] There is also a brief description in bolero.net's document, "Digital Signatures in the Bolero System", available at *www.bolero.net/downloads/digisigs.pdf*

[78] Steven Levy, *Crypto* (Allen Lane, 2000), at p. 102.

[79] The full text of the Directive can be downloaded (in pdf format) from *http://appia .rechten.vu.nl/~CLI//directives/1999_93.pdf*

signature to be certified,[80] but there is no equivalent of Article 5(1).[81] However, none of the suggested electronic bills of lading described here require any legislation to operate in a secure and functional manner.

(c) Transmission of Document

16–024   Section 1(5) of the Carriage of Goods by Sea Act 1992 (in Appendix E) allows the Secretary of State, by regulations, to provide for the application of the Act to electronic documentation. No such regulations have been promulgated. However, the section appears to assume that an electronic document, like its paper equivalent, will be issued by the carrier to the shipper, and then transferred down the chain to successive holders by indorsement.[82] No doubt, this would be in principle possible, with each holder adding his digital signature to the indorsement, so as to create a chain of digital signatures. The eventual holder could thereby prove the route by which the document had reached him, and also its content (from the message digest). He could therefore prove title, and also the contents of the bill of lading when it was issued.

However, neither of the two main proposed systems for electronic bills of lading adopts this model. Some means has also to be found to transfer contractual rights and liabilities to the electronic holder (assuming no regulations are likely to be forthcoming under the 1992 Act), to transfer the right to take delivery, and also perhaps property in the goods. While transferring contractual rights from holder to holder would not be particularly problematic, assigning rights, along with the electronic document, with each transfer, transfer of liabilities would be more difficult; other models may be better suited to this.

The most important requirement is that the carrier needs to be informed of the identity of the ultimate receiver of the cargo, to whom (and to whom alone) he would be under an obligation to deliver. He does not need to know this prior to delivery, as indeed he does not with conventional documentation. Bolero adopts the method of maintaining a title database, allowing the holder to transfer possession of the bill to somebody else, to whom control would then pass. The document does not move in any meaningful sense, but remains on the closed computer system, appropriate persons (who are all members of the system) having access to it, and control over it being passed from holder to holder (by e-mail). The carrier, as a member of the system, will be able to discover, when the ship arrives, to whom to deliver. Under this system, all members have a contract with all other members, so in principle at least, all appropriate rights and liabilities can be created contractually.

The C.M.I. model involves the carrier at every stage, the carrier being notified of every transfer of the bill of lading, and transferring control of the document to the new holder. Although C.M.I. does not expressly provide for this, there would be no difficulty in making a new contract with each holder, thereby involving effectively transfer of contractual rights and liabilities. It is fair to point out, though, that the C.M.I. model is quite old, and while in outline sound, would need filling out to work properly (see below).

---

[80] The requirements of s.7 are not particularly stringent, and are defined in terms of functional equivalence, rather than being technology-specific.
[81] The full text of the Act is available at *www.hmso.gov.uk/acts/acts2000/20000007.htm*
[82] This was also the only form of transfer which was considered by the Law Commission in 2001 to be the true electronic equivalent of a bill of lading, since no third party needed to be involved in the transfer process: at para. 4.7.

(d) Contracts Between Holder and Carrier

Essentially, then, there are two ways of dealing with contractual rights and **16–025** liabilities. One is to involve the carrier with each transfer, assuming communication with the carrier to be possible at all times on the voyage (not really a problem today, although it was when paper bills of lading were devised). The other is to operate a closed system, where all trading parties are members, and each therefore in an existing contractual relationship with each other. The contracts of membership are essential for the operation of such a scheme (see further below).

(e) Transfer of Property

Where a paper bill of lading is issued to the order of the seller, we saw in **16–026** chapter 5 that s.19(2) of the Sale of Goods Act 1979 creates a presumption that the property will pass only when the seller is paid, usually against tender and indorsement of the bill of lading. Where payment is by documentary credit, the pledge is created, transferring special property to the bank, on tender of documents by the seller. It seems unlikely that s.19(2), or indeed the common law presumption upon which it was based, would apply to a paperless bill. There is, however, no necessary connection between indorsement and delivery of the bill of lading and the passing of property. Ultimately, the passing of property depends on the intention of the parties,[83] and therefore can be determined by specific provision in the contract of sale. It will however be necessary for the parties to make express provision in the sale contract, should they wish the paperless bill of lading to perform this function.

(f) Two Models

Two main models have been proposed, C.M.I. (see Appendix K, below) and **16–027** Bolero (see Appendix L, below). C.M.I. is an open system, which in principle can be used by any trader, contractual issues being soluble because the carrier is involved in each transfer. Bolero is a closed system, which can be used only by traders who have signed up to it (for a fee). Contractual issues can be dealt with (ultimately) by the rule book, by which all parties agree to be bound.

PAUL TODD, "DEMATERIALISATION OF SHIPPING DOCUMENTS"

Published as Ch. 3 in Cross-Border Electronic Banking (Reed, Walden and Edgar ed.), (2nd ed., Lloyd's of London Press, 2000)

[Footnotes as in original, but renumbered, and in some cases updated and revised slightly for present purposes.]

---

[83] Sale of Goods Act 1979, s.17.

II. Electronic bills of lading

16–028   In order to establish minimum requirements for any electronic replacement for a bill of lading, we must identify the functions of the paper bill
of lading it has to replace. Some of these are straightforward enough. On
the back of the bill of lading is a statement of the terms of the carriage
contract. On the front there will typically be a description of the goods,
and a statement, signed by the master, such as that they were loaded in
apparent good order and condition on board a named ship on a stated
date. There is no particular difficulty about any of these, except to observe
that the signature of carrier will require electronic authentication procedures. Moreover, in order to speed up the documentation process, there
is no reason why the carriage contract terms could not be public, and the
other matters made known to all parties likely to be interested (for
example all purchasers in the chain) as soon as the master has signed the
bill. This was the reason for the retention of the paper bill in Seadocs, to
allow advance inspection by the parties, but today there is no need to
retain a paper bill to do this.

Malcolm Clarke has recently observed that the electronic bill of lading
must "be recognised not only by merchants but also by courts as having
the same legal effect as its paper predecessor".[84] Clearly this is likely to be
problematic where courts require written evidence, but this problem has
been addressed by Bolero.[85] It would be more difficult to deal with this
difficulty in an open system, however, since Bolero works by getting the
consent of all parties not to take such evidential points.

Any electronic bill of lading must at least do all of this, and replicate the
bill's functions as a document of title (this aspect is given separate
treatment below). It also needs to provide some security against fraud.
This is not an absolute requirement, since the present system is by no
means proof against fraud, which suggests that commerce is prepared to
accept a certain level of fraud in order to effect speedier and less costly
transactions. The system needs only to be at least as good as the present
system in this respect, but in reality, a far greater degree of security is
possible, and Bolero ought to be very secure.

If electronic documentation is to be truly equivalent to the present-day
bill of lading, then it should also be open to anyone to use. As will appear
from the discussion below, complete openness is not compatible with
complete security, and it may be necessary to compromise on one or other
of these requirements, or on both.

Finally, if it is intended to speed up the documentary process, which as
we have seen is the real problem with bulk oil carriage, it ought to be
possible not only to transfer but also to check the documentation electronically. Using present-day levels of technology, this would require a considerable degree of standardisation of documentation, which may not be

---

[84] Malcolm Clarke, "*A black letter lawyer looks at Bolero*" [1999] I.T.L.Q. 69, at p. 69.
[85] See the discussion below of paragraph 2.2.2 of the *Rule Book*, "Validity and Enforceability".

acceptable to the commercial parties.[86] An alternative would be to allow publication to interested parties of all evidential functions of the bill of lading in advance, before the bill of lading is actually transferred. An electronic system could separate the evidential from the transfer functions of the bill, and could therefore allow this, as long as the identity of the interested parties were known in advance.[87]

III. Replacing the document of title: property and privity problems
More difficult to dematerialise are the bill of lading's functions as a document of title. One of these is its ability to transfer property in the goods. Where the bill of lading is issued to the order of the seller, s.19(2) of the Sale of Goods Act 1979 creates a presumption that the property will pass only when the seller is paid, usually against tender and indorsement of the bill of lading. Where payment is by documentary credit, the pledge is created, transferring special property to the bank, on tender of documents by the seller. But there is no necessary connection between the bill of lading and the passing of property, the latter of which depends on the intention of the parties.[88] Depending as it does on intention, it can be determined by specific provision in the contract of sale. Since s.19(2) will probably not apply to a paperless bill of lading, the parties will have to

16–029

---

[86] The 967 pages of documentation in *Bankers Trust Co v State Bank of India* [1991] 2 Lloyd's Rep. 443 could probably not be processed any faster electronically than they were by hand.

UCP 500 & 400 Compared (I.C.C. Publication No. 511, 1993), notes at p. 40 that "a considerable degree of standardisation of formatting and message content practice has been attained by SWIFT, and more will be obtained once a uniform EDIFACT document 'syntax' becomes operative". The comments in I.C.C. Publication No. 511 (1993) are directed towards the development of internationally standardised banking practice, and something like this would obviously be necessary for the speed potential of EDI fully to be recognised.

Even without electronic checking, in chain sales where the identity of successive holders is known by the time of shipment, there is no reason why electronic copies could not be circulated for inspection purposes, well in advance of the actual transfers. As long as the transfer itself is rigorously controlled, and as long as *each* electronic copy is properly authenticated by the carrier, perhaps using public and private key systems similar to that described below, there is no obvious reason why as many copies as one wished could not be circulating simultaneously. This would effect a significant speed advantage. Obviously, the copy could not be used as proof of title, although it could (subject to the proper authentication) be used as evidence that the shipper had shipped goods of the contract description. With a closed system, it would be necessary only to place a single authenticate copy on the system, and allow access to interested parties.

[87] Even with long chains, all or most of the parties will often be known from the time of shipment; see, *e.g. The Sevonia Team* [1983] 2 Lloyd's Rep. 640, where there were three successive f.o.b. purchasers, all of whom were known at the time of shipment. The position will be different if the contract of sale is not made until after the cargo is shipped, as in *The Epaphus* [1987] 2 Lloyd's Rep. 215, but as Croom-Johnson observed in that case, "a sale afloat in a named ship is rare." Indeed, it had only arisen because the original sale had fallen through. It might also be different in a case like *C Groom Ltd v Barber* [1915] 1 K.B. 316, where the seller could appropriate goods satisfying the contract description from any vessel. In *Groom*, the identity of the purchasers was unknown to shipper and carrier, until just before the bill of lading was tendered to them. Often, however, it will be possible to make known the information in the bill of lading, to people whose identity is known well in advance of actual tender.

[88] Sale of Goods Act 1979, s.17.

make alternative express provision. Bolero is also confident that a pledge can, in principle, be created by an electronic bill of lading.[89]

Possibly the most difficult function is the transfer of constructive possession. Only the lawful holder of the bill of lading should be able to require the carrier to deliver to him, and the carrier should not be required, or allowed, to deliver to anyone else. It is therefore absolutely fundamental that the carrier knows the identity of this person at the port of discharge. The person claiming the cargo must be able to prove, in the absence of a paper document, that he has become the lawful holder of the virtual bill of lading. ...

[The author discusses the functions of a document of title, on which see chapter 6, above, and continues:]

Any dematerialisation would have to fix the carrier with equivalent liabilities and defences. For the most part, this can be done by contract, as long as the carrier, holder of the electronic bill of lading and (if a different person) the true owner of the goods, are parties to the contract. With a conventional paper transaction, however, only the shipper is expressly party to a contract with the carrier, contractual rights and liabilities being transferred to subsequent holders by the Carriage of Goods by Sea Act 1992. Since it cannot be assumed that the 1992 Act will apply to a paperless bill,[90] whatever system is adopted will have to address the privity issue. As will appear from the discussion below, the C.M.I. model is capable of doing this, because the carrier is directly involved in every transaction, and can therefore contract expressly with every holder. This is not true of Bolero, which addresses the problem differently, by requiring all members to contract with each other on the basis of the *Bolero Rule Book*.[91] The Rule Book is therefore absolutely essential to the operation of Bolero.[92] Paragraph 3.5 of the Rule Book provides for novation of the carriage contract with each appropriate transfer of the electronic bill.[93]

In principle, therefore, both C.M.I. and Bolero can deal with the problems of transferring contractual rights and liabilities. Malcolm Clarke has questioned whether there would be consideration for the new contract, arising by novation in Bolero, and by express communication between

---

[89] Mallon and Tomlinson, "*Bolero: electronic 'bills of lading' and electronic contracts of sale*" [1998] I.T.L.Q. 257, at p. 264.

[90] Although provision has also been made (in s.1(5)) for the inclusion by regulation of electronic documentation, it would probably be a mistake to assume that appropriate regulations will necessarily be forthcoming.

[91] Para. 2.1.1 of the Rule Book provides that "The Rule Book constitutes an agreement between Users, and between each User and the Bolero Association acting on its own behalf, and on behalf of all other Users from time to time, and, where necessary, on behalf of Bolero International." All carriers and merchants are members, and the Rule Book establishes a contractual nexus between each member and every other member.

[92] See also further below...

[93] This will not apply to every transfer, because a pledgee ought not necessarily become liable for, *e.g.* freight or demurrage due under the carriage contract: *cf. Sewell v Burdick* (1884) 10 App. Cas. 74, for the position with a conventional bill of lading.

carrier and holder in C.M.I.[94] Consideration is clearly provided by the carrier, in delivering (or presumably promising to deliver) the goods. The problem, he argues, is as to consideration moving from the consignee, a problem similar to *Brandt v Liverpool* contracts [see paras 13–056, *et seq.*, above], where freight and other charges have been prepaid by the shipper.[95] He suggests that consideration might be found in the co-operation required in the delivery process by the receiver of the cargo, as in *The Captain Gregos (No. 2)*.[96] In principle, consideration might also be provided in relieving the carrier from claims from other parties for misdelivery, or indeed, for Bolero (but not C.M.I.) the consideration may be found in the original contract of membership. The problems in cases such as *The Aramis* and *The Gudermes* do not arise,[97] since there it was necessary, in order to imply a contract, to find conduct which was inconsistent with there being no such contract. The problems, in other words, were not limited to consideration. Since we are envisaging express contracts, those problems would not arise here.

By providing a contractual nexus between all interested parties, it is possible to provide each holder with contractual rights against the carrier, thereby rendering the carrier liable for misdelivery or, if appropriate, damage to the goods. If the carrier delivers to a holder of an electronic document, even if the holder is not the true owner of the cargo,[98] the true owner will be unable to sue as long as there is privity between himself and the carrier. Past holders will fall into this category under C.M.I., and any owner who is a member will be covered under Bolero. The problems in a case such as *Glyn Mills* [in chapter 6, above] would not arise since electronic bills of lading would not be issued in sets.[99] A problem might arise for goods stolen prior to shipment, since no contractual scheme can prevent someone from outside the scheme from suing in conversion, even if the carrier delivers against an electronic bill of lading. By contrast, the justification for *Glyn Mills* is either that the plaintiff bank, knowing of the existence of the other originals, was *volenti*,[1] or that delivering against a paper document of title is not wrongful, and therefore not a conversion.[2] Neither of these justifications would apply to this situation if a paperless bill were used, whereas the second (but not the first) would in the case of a paper bill. This may therefore be one situation where the protection

---

[94] [[1999] I.T.L.Q. 69,] at pp. 72 *et seq.* Clarke considers only Bolero, but if he is right, the same problems would also affect C.M.I.

[95] From *Brandt v Liverpool, Brazil and River Plate Navigation Co Ltd* [1924] 1 K.B. 575. There is no problem where, as in *Brandt* itself, freight and/or other charges are paid by the receiver.

[96] [1990] 2 Lloyd's Rep. 395.

[97] Respectively [1989] 1 Lloyd's Rep. 213; [1993] 1 Lloyd's Rep. 311.

[98] Obviously this ought not to happen, if Bolero procedures are properly used. The most likely scenario would be a fraud, if the fraudster were able to discover the true owner's private key.

[99] [See ch. 6, above].

[1] The views of Lords Blackburn and Watson are consistent with this: *Glyn Mills* at 606 and 614.

[2] Probably Lord Selborne's view, *Glyn Mills* at 596. See also Bools, *The Bill of Lading: A Document of Title to Goods* (L.L.P., 1997), at p. 166.

given to the paper document cannot be replicated by an electronic system, but it is hardly likely to be commonplace.

IV. The C.M.I. model

16–030   In 1990 the C.M.I. published its *Rules for Electronic Bills of Lading* [see Appendix K, below], which represent an ingenious method of overcoming the problems of proving title to goods by electronic means.[3] The essence of the system is as follows. Article 4 provides for an electronic document containing information similar to that on a paper bill of lading to be sent by the carrier to an electronic address specified by the shipper. In addition a private key is sent to the shipper to be used in subsequent transactions. The private key is known only by the shipper and the carrier. The shipper (and any subsequent holder) can transfer what the C.M.I. calls the "Right of Control and Transfer" to a subsequent holder (Clause 7):

> "(i) by notification of the current Holder to the carrier of its intention to transfer its Right of Control and Transfer to a proposed new Holder, and (ii) confirmation by the carrier of such notification message, whereupon (iii) the carrier shall transmit the information as referred to in article 4 (except for the Private Key) to the proposed new Holder, whereafter (iv) the proposed new Holder shall advise the carrier of its acceptance of the Right of Control and Transfer, whereupon (v) the carrier shall cancel the current Private Key and issue a new Private Key to the new Holder."

Article 4(c) allows the proposed new holder to advise the carrier that he refuses to accept the transfer, and requires the carrier to assume this unless the new holder accepts within a reasonable time. In this event the carrier advises the current holder, and the current private key retains its validity. Under Article 7(a), only the holder can claim delivery of the goods from the carrier, nominate a consignee or substitute for a consignee already nominated, or transfer the right of control and transfer to anybody else.

The C.M.I. system satisfies one of the most important requirements explained . . . above, that the carrier needs to be informed of (and have proof of) the identity of the ultimate receiver of the cargo, to whom (and to whom alone) he would be under an obligation to deliver. Because of the requirements of Article 4, the electronic message performs evidential functions similar to the traditional bill of lading, stating the name of the shipper, the description of the goods, representations and reservations as with a paper bill of lading, the date and place of receipt and/or shipment of the goods, and a reference to the terms of the carriage contract.[4] No

---

[3] This was essentially the solution suggested by Jan Ramberg in his contribution to Thomsen and Wheble, *Trading with EDI—The Legal Issues* (I.B.C. Financial Books, 1989), pp. 193 *et seq.*

[4] It does not seem to be envisaged that the terms are themselves transmitted electronically, but that they are readily available.

doubt the parties could vary these requirements if additional evidential functions were required. Furthermore, the proposed new holder gets the opportunity to inspect the electronic documentation before accepting it, and if he does not accept he does not obtain any right of control and transfer over the goods. Those rights remain in the seller just as is the case if a paper bill of lading is rejected.

The system is also theoretically open to anyone to use. There is no need for the parties to be members of a group, and any carrier with the necessary technology can operate the system. In fact, the system requires no more than that all parties are in telephone or radio communication with the carrier, and have [computer access to a telecommunication network].

In its original unmodified form, there are weakness to C.M.I., but in principle, these can be overcome. For example, C.M.I. appears to make no provision for contractual rights and liabilities to be transferred along with the documentation. If the carrier refused to deliver to the eventual holder, he would certainly be in breach of contract, but only the original shipper could sue him. It would not be difficult to make appropriate provision, however, since (unlike the conventional position, with paper bills of lading) each holder is inevitably in direct communication with the carrier. It would not be difficult for the carrier to offer a new contract to each holder, and for each holder to accept when the right to control and transfer is accepted.[5] There is no need for legislation to enable this to operate smoothly.

The second problem is that it is not clear what happens if a holder who **16–031** has accepted the right of control and transfer does not pay for the goods. The previous holder must not be allowed to retain any right, as against the carrier, in the goods after a transfer, since otherwise a subsequent holder who does pay would be obtaining no security of any value. This is not a problem that is unique to electronic documentation, since s.19(3) of the Sale of Goods Act 1979 was enacted specifically to deal with a similar problem with a conventional bill of lading. There can be no equivalent of s.19(3) operating in the present situation, but there is no reason why a seller should not make equivalent provision by an express term in the contract of sale, requiring the buyer to re-transfer the right of control and transfer to him in the event of non-payment, and reserving a right of disposal in the goods until paid. Just as with s.19(3), this would protect the seller in the event of the buyer's bankruptcy, but would not necessarily protect against a fraud, where for example, the defaulting buyer re-sold the goods to a third party who bought in good faith. The best method of protection for the seller in this case would be to require

---

[5] Subject to addressing [the consideration problems discussed above]. It is not clear what would happen if either party refused the contract offered. In the absence of a Bolero-style Rule Book, the sale contract would have to require the seller to provide a carriage contract on reasonable (or other specified) terms, and upon whether the carrier offered this would depend the buyer's obligation to accept the transfer. The seller would then have to make appropriate provision in his own carriage contract to require the carrier to offer terms to the transferee.

payment by an electronic equivalent of a documentary credit, and only to transfer the right of control and transfer to a reputable bank against payment.[6]

A third point, which is related to the second, is that the C.M.I. rules make no provision for the passing of property in the goods. But transfer of even a conventional paper document of title will not necessarily pass property in the goods.[7] It would be necessary for the parties to make appropriate provision in the sale contract, and in the other contracts making up the credit. This would obviously require new contracts to be drafted, but this is unavoidable in any case, since special forms of agreement will be required whenever electronic forms of transmission are used. It is of course to be hoped that industry-standard contracts can be developed, in order to avoid the necessity to engage lawyers to draft each individual transaction. One of the advantages of, for example, the c.i.f. contract, is that its meaning is well-known anywhere in the world, and a c.i.f. purchaser can re-sell c.i.f. without the need for complex negotiations and re-drafting.

I would suggest, however, that the greatest difficulty with the C.M.I. proposals is that they seem to be relatively insecure against fraud.[8] It is undoubtedly possible to modify the system so as to make it as secure as is wished, and far more secure than any paper system, but it is difficult to see how this can be achieved without imposing additional levels of bureaucracy, possibly to the extent of militating against a truly open system. It may well be impossible to provide a system which is both completely open and completely secure, although either one or the other ought to be possible. No doubt different compromises will be reached between these conflicting objectives in differing trades.

16–032   The essential problem with the C.M.I. model is that it assumes transmission of secret codes between ship and shore. The C.M.I. calls the secret

[6] The mechanism of payment would probably have to be constrained, since it is likely that the law would not recognise the concept of an electronic bill of exchange. It is not easy to see how an unconfirmed negotiation credit, such as that in *Maran Road Saw Mill v Austin Taylor Ltd* [1975] 1 Lloyd's Rep. 156, for example [see Ch. 8, above], could operate entirely electronically. [Since the chapter was published, the Law Commission, in 2001, recommended no change to the law on bills of exchange, observing at para. 9.7 that: "We are not however aware of any demand to create an electronic equivalent of a bill of exchange, with negotiable status. If such a demand did arise, reform should be approached internationally."]

[7] See [*Sewell v Burdick*, in Ch. 8, above, at paras. 8–038, *et seq.*]. It is clear that new forms of contract will need to be drafted for electronic documentation, and when they are property issues should also be considered.

[8] At any rate by comparison with what is theoretically possible. It may well be that even as it stands, it is more secure than present-day paper systems. After all, signatures, and even entire bills of lading for non-existent goods, are not difficult to forge under the present system. The carrier who issued the document was deceived in *Motis Exports* [see para. 6–026, above]. There are those who argue that so long as we can produce a system which is as secure as the present we should be content. That attitude seems to me to be the very negation of progress. The present paper system is insecure because it is difficult to make a paper system secure. Electronic systems can be made much more secure, and that should therefore be the aim. The fact that the railway locomotive could replace the horse was not a good reason for limiting it to that role.

code the private key, but I prefer to use "secret code" for reasons which will become apparent in a moment. It is difficult to see how this transmission can be other than by radio communication, into which anybody can in principle listen. Furthermore, any fraudster who by listening obtains the secret code thereby obtains directly the key to the goods. He can now pretend to be the genuine holder and re-sell or pledge the goods to an innocent third party. No doubt the fraud would be discovered when the ship discharged, but by then the fraudster would presumably have banked the money and departed the scene. If the C.M.I. model is to be secure, it is essential that the secret code is encrypted.

There are no problems about transmission of the secret code to the original shipper, or of receiving the secret code from the ultimate receiver.[9] There is also no problem about the first stage of the first transaction, since only the shipper knows the secret code, and even if it is intercepted during transmission to the carrier, this will be of no use to a fraudster, since the code is used only once. The problems arise with transmissions from the carrier to subsequent holders. If the fraudster intercepts a ship-to-shore transmission of the code, he can in principle use this information to impersonate the holder and steal the goods.

The problem with encrypting the code before transmission is that the trader or carrier (but not the fraudster) needs to be able to decrypt it. There needs therefore to be a key, but how do you transmit the key? If all the trading parties were known in advance this would not be a problem, since the encryption algorithm and keys could be agreed between them privately, and nobody else would be able to encrypt or decrypt the secret code. However, the C.M.I. model assumes that the goods can be sold by anybody to anybody. The problem is that the key has to be notified to each recipient, and since this must itself be done over an insecure channel, this lets the fraudster in, since with the key he can obtain the secret code, and hence deal with the goods.

The problem of encrypting without insecure distribution of keys was only solved relatively recently, using public-key/private-key encryption. Details are beyond the scope of this chapter,[10] but in its essentials the C.M.I. model using public key/private key encryption could work as follows. We need to make four assumptions:

1. Each party has a unique public key which is known to everyone.

2. Each party has a unique private key which is kept secret, and never disclosed or transmitted.

---

[9] At least as far as the carrier is concerned. A weakness is that there is no authentication of the carrier's signature (although this could be provided using a public/private key system described below). The transferee needs assurance that the message he is receiving is in fact from the carrier.

[10] For a good recent description, including of the bureaucracy needed to operate it, see Adams and Bond, *"Secure E-commerce as a competitive weapon"* [1999] I.T.L.Q. 241.

3. The encryption method (or algorithm) is publicly available, and universally adopted in the trade. The system can only work if everybody uses the same encryption algorithm.

4. Any message sent from A to B encrypted with A's private key and B's public key can only be decrypted using A's public key and B's private key. This is not reversible.[11] Thus, only B should be able to decrypt the message, and B can also tell that the message must have come from A.

16–033   The system is modified on the basis of these assumptions to work as follows:

1. Each trader knows everybody else's public key, because it is public.

2. The carrier gives the shipper the secret code as before. There is no need for this communication to be encrypted, since there is no need to use an insecure channel of communication.

3. The shipper performs a transaction by returning the secret code (and the identity of the transferee) to the carrier, the secret code being encrypted using his private key and the carrier's public key. The carrier, and only the carrier, can decrypt this using his private key and the shipper's public key.

4. The carrier sends the electronic bill of lading and a new secret code to the transferee, the secret code being encrypted using his private key and the transferee's public key.[12] The transferee, and only the transferee, can decrypt this using his private key and the carrier's public key, and he also knows that the transmission must have come from the carrier.

5. Further transactions are performed in the same way.

6. The ultimate receiver uses the secret code as before to obtain the goods.[13] No encryption is necessary at this stage.

It is essential to this system that the private keys remain secret and never need to be transmitted, so that the fraudster never gets the opportunity to discover any private key, and therefore cannot encrypt or decrypt any secret codes.

---

[11] [It is easy to derive the public key from the private, but not vice-versa.]

[12] Only the secret code needs to be encrypted. The contents of the bill of lading should be sent in the clear, as should most certainly (if they are sent at all) the terms of the carriage contract. This is because if the fraudster can discover the plaintext by other means (and carriage contracts are usually easy to obtain) and the encrypted text it will be easier for him (knowing, like everyone else, the public keys) to discover the private keys, and hence to discover the secret code.

[13] Since the other holders in the chain are identified by decoding using their public key, it is only at this stage that it matters that the "secret code" is secret. Since any holder could, in principle, be an ultimate receiver, however, it is best to keep it secret throughout.

The system needs actually to be slightly more complex than we have so far described, because we have not authenticated the carrier's identity. All holders apart from the original shipper need to be able to verify that the secret code has been sent by the carrier, not only to prevent impersonation, but also to ensure that the carrier has really made the representations in the bill of lading. The problem is that the secret code is not known to the recipient until it is decoded, so decoding it cannot verify the carrier's identity. Some piece of information, already known to the recipient, must also be decoded using the carrier's private key, so that by decoding using his public key, he can be certain that the message really was sent by the carrier.[14]

Obviously, for encryption and decryption to work between the legitimate parties, there must be a relationship between the public and private keys. However, whereas it should be easy to encrypt and decrypt messages using the public key, discovering the private key from a knowledge of the public key should be infeasible (*i.e.* a computer could do it, but it would take many years).[15] The C.M.I. system can therefore be made secure, since neither the secret code nor any encryption key needs to be sent over insecure channels in plaintext. Nor do private keys ever need to be disclosed or transmitted. Only if a fraudster is able to obtain a private key does it break down.

However, the very idea of a public key suggests a central authority at a minimum to keep a directory of keys. For maximum security, each trader's public and private keys need to be changed regularly, since if the same keys are used over and over again a fraudster has an increased chance of discovering a private key. If new keys are frequently to be generated and (in the case of public keys) circulated, then the central authority has a far greater role to play. Authenticating the carrier's signature needs further regulation. The more secure the system, the greater the role of the central authority, until we no longer have a truly open system.[16]

---

[14] Alternatively, the newly emerging Certification Authorities might be used for this purpose. They take physical evidence of identity, and then issue an electronic certificate which links the holder's identity with that person's digital signature key. The certificate is signed with the Certification Authority's own private key, and if the recipient recognises that signature he has received reliable independent evidence of the certificate holder's identity.

[15] It is not possible to devise one-way algorithms which are truly irreversible, but it is quite easy to devise algorithms which are quick to operate one way but not the other. A commonly-used public key/private key technique is to derive the private key from two or more very large prime numbers, and the public key from the product of those numbers. Generating these keys is easy (they are just functions of the numbers), but if the numbers are sufficiently large (*e.g.* numbers of 200 digits) and are kept secret, the reverse process (finding prime factors of very large numbers) can be computationally infeasible. Exhaustive search (division of the public key by all known prime numbers up to its square root) is the only known method for very large numbers, and as long as the numbers are sufficiently large this can take even a fast computer many years, by which time one would hope the cargo has been legitimately discharged.

[16] See Adams and Bond, above, . . . at pp. 248–249.

No doubt, if a certain level of fraud can be tolerated by the trade (and it is by no means entirely absent in the present system), then the role of the central authority can be reduced. Signature authentication may still be needed for legal purposes, however, when things go wrong, so a truly open system may never be possible.

V. Further comments on the C.M.I. model

16–034   Any type of electronic communication poses problems that are not posed by ordinary paper transactions, and Article 3 of the C.M.I. rules provide rules of procedure to deal with this. It is particularly important to adopt rigorous procedures in case of dispute, since it may be intended to use the electronic record as evidence. One problem, for example, is the fleeting nature of an electronic record[17]:

> "Because of its physical characteristics, the traditional paper document is accepted as evidence. It is durable, and changes or additions will normally be clearly visible. The electronic document is quite different. It takes the form of a magnetic medium whose data content can be changed at any time. Changes or additions will not appear as such."

Even for these records to be acceptable as evidence between the parties to the transaction, therefore, some method must be found to ensure that all changes appear as such, and can be authenticated. Standards need to be agreed between the parties to ensure that the information sent is accurate, that it reaches the recipient, and that any changes are recorded as changes.

Article 3(a) of the C.M.I. rules provides for U.N.C.I.D.[18] to govern the communications between the parties. U.N.C.I.D. is intended to provide the procedures necessary for the accurate transmission of electronic data. For example, Article 10 makes provision for the keeping of a "Trade Data Log", which is intended to ensure that all changes are properly recorded. It is also necessary to agree on lower-level communication protocols, just to ensure that the computers understand the strings of data transmitted.[19]

VI. An alternative model: Bolero

16–035   The C.M.I. model assumes reliable communication between ship and shore, over channels that are essentially open and insecure. In principle, the C.M.I. model is an open system, but less so if it is to be operated

---

[17] *U.N.C.I.D. Uniform Rules of Conduct for Interchange of Trade Data by Teletransmission* (I.C.C. Publication No. 452, 1988), p. 8. Today, not all storage is magnetic, but the principle remains applicable.

[18] The *Uniform Rules of Conduct for Interchange of Trade Data by Teletransmission*, as adopted by the I.C.C. Executive Board at its 51st Session (Paris, September 22, 1987).

[19] Article 3(a) of the C.M.I. rules accordingly provide for communications to conform with the relevant UN/EDIFACT standards (United Nations Rules for Electronic Data Interchange for Administration, Commerce and Transport), unless the parties choose some other protocol acceptable to all the users. UN/EDIFACT is an example of what is referred to in U.N.C.I.D. as a trade data interchange application protocol (TDI-AP).

securely. It does not operate by transferring electronic documents, as much as issuing new documents to each trader.

Bolero operates quite differently. It is necessarily a closed system, to which all trading parties have to register. It does not rely on insecure communication between ship and shore, but on Internet communication, and in any case authenticates messages using public and private keys, the issuance of which it administers itself. It also maintains a register of titles, allowing the owner of goods on board a ship to transfer them to other members, and updating the title accordingly. The carrier can therefore be reliably informed, at the port of discharge, of the identity of the ultimate receiver to whom he is to discharge the goods.

A major difference between C.M.I. and Bolero is that in the former the carrier is party to every transfer, and can therefore, in principle, make contracts with every transferee.[20] With Bolero there is no need for the carrier to be party to every transfer, as long as he is aware of the identity of the eventual receiver of the cargo. A contractual nexus must exist between the carrier and the person entitled to the cargo at discharge. Bolero provides this by the Rule Book, which binds all members contractually to each other, and by novation of the carriage contract as appropriate on each transfer. The Rule Book is absolutely central to the operation of the scheme, the following paragraphs being taken from Bolero's website (as of December 1999)[21]:

"The Rule Book is a multi-lateral contract which binds each User to every other user in relation to their use of the bolero.net service. The purpose of this contract, which is at the core of the bolero.net structure, is to ensure that every User agrees to be governed by a common set of rules enshrining the key elements of the bolero.net service. For example, that Users agree, as between each other, that electronic communications will be treated as valid, that no User will deny that it sent a message bearing its digital signature and that messages so signed will bind the User (the company).

In addition, the Rule Book provides the legal rules which underpin the system for the ability to transact electronic bills of lading (Bolero Bills of Lading) through an application that mirrors the rights and obligations of those Users in relation to the international carriage of goods (importers and exporters, banks, carriers, forwarders and other intermediaries)."

As the second paragraph states, the Rule Book also systematically provides for every function previously performed by the paper bill of lading, including transfers, pledges, etc. The whole system, which is

---

[20] [Subject to the consideration problems discussed above.]

[21] *The Rule Book* provides for membership of Bolero Association Limited. The service is operated by Bolero International Ltd, which is a joint venture between S.W.I.F.T. (Society for Worldwide Interbank Financial Telecommunications) and Through Transport Mutual Insurance Association Ltd (T.T. Club).

made subject to UK law, is obviously extremely thorough,[22] and a full description is entirely beyond the scope of this chapter... Full documentation is in any case available from the website.[23] Obviously, however, matters such as communication protocols, and required format for documents, are provided by the Rule Book and detailed Operating Procedures.

As can be seen from the end of the first paragraph set out above, provision is also made in the Rule Book to deal with legal evidential requirements. Essentially, the members agree under the contract of membership not to stand upon formality requirements. Hence, paragraph 2.2.2 of the Rule Book states:

> "2.2.2. *Validity and Enforceability*
>
> (1) *Writing Requirements*. Any applicable requirement of law, contract, custom or practice that any transaction, document or communication shall be made or evidenced in writing, signed or sealed shall be satisfied by a Signed Message.
>
> (2) *Signature Requirements*. The contents of a Message Signed by a User, or a portion drawn from a Signed Message, are binding upon that User to the same extent, and shall have the same effect at law, as if the Message or portion thereof had existed in a manually signed form.
>
> (3) *Undertaking not to Challenge Validity*. No User shall contest the validity of any transaction, statement or communication made by means of a Signed Message, or a portion drawn from a Signed Message, on the grounds that it was made in electronic form instead of by paper and/or signed or sealed."

16–036   C.M.I. was a good idea, in principle, conceived at a time when the ease of internet communication enjoyed today was probably unthinkable. It never developed beyond the in principle stage. Bolero, by contrast, is a fully thought through scheme, ready for operation. Because it is a closed system, apart from the advantages of being easily able to make provision for everything contractually, it has advantages in terms of security over the C.M.I. model, and it is easier to provide inspection facilities for documentation. The only real problem is precisely that the system is not open, but depends on membership.

The issue is how much this really matters, bearing in mind that to operate C.M.I. securely would in any case have required considerable organisational overheads. Obviously, there can be problems in cases like *The Epaphus*,[24] where the sale falls through, if the re-sale is to someone

---

[22] A feasibility study into the legal issues to which the Bolero concept gives rise was undertaken by Allen & Overy and Richards Butler, both large London law firms.

[23] [The original footnote is no longer apposite. Downloads are available via *www.bolero.net/content/search/library/*

[24] [[1987] 2 Lloyd's Rep. 215, where the contract of sale was not made until after the cargo is shipped.]

outside the scheme.[25] It might also be problematic to operate in cases like *Groom v Barber*,[26] where the carrier is not identified until just before the documents are tendered.

It seems unlikely, however, that Bolero will suffer the same fate as Seadocs. There, the central registry operated effectively as a monopoly, and seems to have been distrusted. Bolero, by contrast, appears to have wider support from merchants and the banks. On their website they say:

"Given its cross-industry pedigree, and that its core messaging services will be operated under contract by S.W.I.F.T., an organisation with an outstanding record as a trusted third party for the banking industry, Bolero International Ltd. believes that it is in an unprecedented position to gain the trust of all participants in global trade."

Also, as has already been observed, setting up a secure internet-based database is relatively easy, and the thinking behind Bolero has all been made public. If a carrier, or group of carriers, or traders, or indeed any individual, wanted to operate his or their own scheme, it would be reasonably straightforward to do so. Obviously, banks advancing money on the security of electronic bills of lading would need to define required standards (perhaps a role for a future U.C.P.), but the monopoly associated with Seadocs really does not exist here.

Notes

Since writing this chapter I have realised that I overestimated the requirements **16–037** necessary to make C.M.I. work securely. It is not generally necessary to encrypt the information in the bill of lading, since it is unlikely to contain sensitive information. It is not necessary, therefore, at any stage to use the recipient's public key. No more is therefore necessary than that each party communicating, whether carrier or trader, digitally signs the communication, using his private key. If the communication itself is sent in the clear, a digitally signed digest will enable the recipient to verify the identity of the sender, and the authenticity of the substantive communication (since any tampering will be shown up when the message digest is decrypted).

The central authority referred to in the chapter should more conventionally be referred to as a certification authority.

(g) Security of Electronic Bills of Lading

Compared with the ease with which paper bills of lading can be fraudulently **16–038** altered, as in *Kwei Tek Chao* (discussed in para. 7–033, above) or even entirely forged, as in *Motis Exports* (discussed in para. 6–026, above) the use of digital encryption techniques should enable electronic bills of lading to be far more secure.

[25] *The Bolero Rule Book* allows for a switch to a paper bill of lading, however: paragraph 3.7.
[26] [[1915] 1 K.B. 316, where the seller could appropriate goods satisfying the contract description from any vessel. In *Groom*, the identity of the purchasers was unknown to shipper and carrier, until just before the bill of lading was tendered to them.]

Closed systems, in particular, can be very secure. Bolero's documentation on enrolment into the system (available from their website) states that:

"all users[27] are identified and listed in a shared registry, so the risk of dealing with an unidentified party or impostor is minimal. To confirm identification of the new user, proof of incorporation, authorisation, and authenticity must accompany the application."

They then set out eligibility criteria:

"The following criteria which must be satisfied by all applicants to become a User

  (a) has satisfied the Registrar that it has an active business;
  (b) has satisfied the Registrar that it has a reasonably favourable business reputation;
  (c) has signed and agreed to be bound by the Rule Book;
  (d) has paid all fees and deposits due;
  (e) is properly incorporated according to the law of the jurisdiction in which it is registered and is a Member or Participant of BAL as prescribed by it, and has entered into this agreement with BAL for the services provided by BAL;"

No doubt, this reduces the risk of an impostor trader, as in *Motis Exports*, or a phantom carrier (as described in paras 15–038, *et seq.*, above).

Both closed systems, such as Bolero, and open systems depend on encryption, the security of which depends fundamentally on the private key not being compromised. Probably the easiest way to break into either system described in detail here is to obtain a private key, and responsibility must be placed on traders to keep them secret. Accordingly, the *Bolero Rulebook* provides:

"*2.2.4. Responsibility for Messages*

  (1) *Private Key Security.* Each User is responsible for all Messages Signed by means of its Private Key, regardless of any failure to maintain the security of its own Private Key.
  (2) *Site Security.* Each User is responsible for implementing all necessary security procedures and measures at its site to ensure that data transmissions to and from the Bolero System are protected against unauthorised access, alteration, delay, loss or destruction.

2.2.5. *Notice*

Each User undertakes to give immediate notice to Bolero International and to comply with the relevant Operational Rules, in the event that its Private Key has been lost or compromised or it has reasonable grounds for believing that such Private Key has been or may be misused, or used by an unauthorised person."

It seems likely that smart cards would be used to store private keys, in which case compromise would most likely arise from straightforward theft. But an impostor might impersonate a trader at the stage of applying for a public key; guarding against this ought really be the responsibility of the system, rather than the user.

---

[27] Legally, a user in the bolero.net system is a company, so the enrolment process focuses on ensuring that the company and the officer acting for it exist and are sufficiently identified.

Apart from impersonation by an impostor obtaining a private key, it is also   **16–039**
necessary to guard against the encryption system being broken by a fraudster.
There is probably little that can be done to guard against this, apart from using
reputable and trusted systems, but even reputable systems in the past have had
unintended back doors, allowing intruders in. For example, Netscape was said to
be vulnerable in 1995, because the output of the Random Number Generator,
essential to the cryptosystem, was apparently found to be predictable,[28] and there
have been other similar well-publicised examples. A properly designed cryptosystem ought to be unbreakable within a feasible time, but the possibility of poor
design, or a mistake, needs to be provided for, by appropriate provisions for
primary liability and insurance. Consideration also needs to be given to the
method by which the cryptosystem is provided; if on a CD, for example, it would
be necessary to guard against the fraudster substituting his own, appearing
genuine but with an unseen but intended back door. A similar guard would need
to be maintained, of course, however the system were supplied.

Open systems also require certification authorities to match persons to public
keys, and it is obviously important for this to be done accurately. Presently in the
UK, there is no legislation on the liability of CAs, the government initially taking
the view that liability should best be governed by the existing law, although it
now recognises that it will need to bring UK law into line with the EC Directive.[29]
For the time being, however, the liability of a C.A. for issuing an inaccurate
certificate is governed by principles of contract and tort. The problem is that the
only express contract is likely to be with the person to whom the certificate is
issued, although it might be possible to imply a contract with anyone relying on
the certificate.[30] Nor is it clear that there would be *Hedley Byrne* liability, given the
number of people who might rely on a certificate, and the multifarious uses to
which it might be put.[31]

(h) Conclusions

This chapter has considered two methods of replacing the paper bill of lading   **16–040**
with an electronic equivalent, both of which could work in a secure and practical
manner, in principle. Each requires an infrastructure, however. It would not be
possible for any one trader, or number of traders unilaterally to move to electronic
bills of lading. There would probably have to be a critical mass, for any system to
work in reality.

The infrastructure requirements increase if standardisation of documents is also
required, to allow for automatic checking, for example, and indeed, there is
arguably little point in having an electronic system at all, unless this is done. It
seems from their website that most of Bolero's work is in the direction of standardisation, rather than developing electronic bills of lading, and also that is where
they are enjoying commercial success.

---

[28] *Crypto*, pp. 281–282.
[29] "The Government has decided that the liability of Trust Service Providers (TSPs), both to
their customers and to parties relying on their certificates, is best left to existing law and to
providers' and customers' contractual arrangements." (*"Promoting Electronic Commerce"*,
(Cm 4417, 1999) para. 4(e), available at *www.dti.gov.uk/cii/docs/ecbill0799.pdf*).

However, the new government accepts that legislation will be needed to bring UK law
into line with Article 6 of the EU Directive: "DTI *Consultation on EC Directive 1999/93/EC of
the European Parliament and Council on a Community Framework for Electronic Signatures*"
(2001), paras. 39–42, available from *www.dti.gov.uk/cii/ecommerce/europeanpolicy/esign
condoc.pdf*

[30] The principles would have to be similar to the breach of warranty of authority reasoning
in *V/O Rasnoimport v Guthrie* see para. 14–059, above.
[31] See the authorities at paras. 14–024, above, but noting that the context here is different.

So will electronic bills of lading catch on? They could allow all the original functions of a bill of lading to be replicated, and offer far greater security in addition. On the other hand, commercial parties have been putting up with a system based on indemnities and personal liabilities for decades now, which though providing inferior security to the original, clearly still works. Given the infrastructure requirements, and critical mass needed for any change, I suspect the paper bill of lading will not be replaced for years yet, or even decades.

Another possibility is a more radical change in commercial practices. The bill of lading developed at a time when a ship at sea was out of contact, but this is no longer true. Its use, and the sale contracts which developed around it, also assumed that inspection of the goods at sea was impossible, but even if that is still the case today, technology will certainly allow remote inspection in the near future. Why transfer risk on shipment, if the goods can be inspected at any time? Why set any store by the statements in bills of lading considered in chapter 14, above? Technological change could therefore have far more radical effects than those considered in this chapter. It would still be necessary to have a method of transferring title, however, and contractual rights and liabilities between cargo-owner and shipowner, so some form of documentation, whether paper or electronic, would continue to be required.

APPENDIX A

SALE OF GOODS ACT 1979

(1979 c. 54)

Author's Comment

The Sale of Goods Act 1979, as subsequently amended, is set out here **A–001**
almost in full, because nearly every section has relevance to the law of
international sales, and in particular the discussion in chapters 2 to 5,
above and the discussion of rights of rejection in chapter 7, above.

Many of the cases discussed there were decided before 1979, but the
Sale of Goods Act 1979 replaced the 1893 Act of the same name. The 1979
Act, whose Preamble states that it is "An Act to consolidate the law
relating to the sale of goods" incorporates the amendments to the 1893
Act which had been made by the Misrepresentation Act 1967, the Supply
of Goods (Implied Terms) Act 1973 and the Unfair Contract Terms Act
1977), but these amendments were, for the most part, aimed at the
protection of consumers, and did not significantly affect the law of international trade. For the purposes of this book, therefore, the 1979 provisions can generally be regarded as identical to those of 1893.[1] Moreover,
the 1893 Act, whose Preamble is in identical terms to that of 1979, was
itself intended to consolidate rather than alter the previous law, so that
even decisions prior to 1893 can still be regarded as authoritative.

The Sale of Goods Act 1979 was itself amended by the Sale and Supply
of Goods Act 1994, which came into force on January 3, 1995, and which
carried into effect the recommendations of the Law Commission.[2] Its
principal amendments are to ss.12–15, with major changes especially to
s.14.[3] Also, although the implied terms continue to be conditions, ss.13–15
are now made subject to the new s.15A, which places restrictions on the
buyer's right to reject: see further the discussion in chapter 4, above.

---

[1] The Supply of Goods (Implied Terms) Act 1973 did not have retrospective effect, and
earlier sections are retained in those parts of Sched. 1 which are here set out. The cases on
merchantable quality, such as *Mash & Murrell, Ltd v Joseph I Emanuel, Ltd* [1962] 1 W.L.R. 16;
[1962] 1 All E.R. 77; [1961] 2 Lloyd's Rep. 326; reversing [1961] 1 All E.R. 485; [1961] 1 W.L.R.
862; [1961] 1 Lloyd's Rep. 46; which are discussed in paras 4–031 *et seq.*, above, were decided
on the basis of the original s.14(2): see further Sched. 1, s.6, and notes thereto.
[2] Law Commission Report No. 160, Scot. Law Commission Report No. 104 (1987), "Sale and
Supply of Goods."
[3] See generally, Patrick Milne, "Goodbye to Merchantable Quality" (1995) 145 N.L.J. 683.

A–002   The other main change affected by the Sale and Supply of Goods Act 1994 was to introduce a partial right of rejection in the new s.35A, to which s.11 is made subject. This has some bearing on the discussion of rejection of documents and goods in chapter 7, above.

The other recent amendment was the Sale of Goods (Amendment) Act 1995, which came into force on September 19, 1995. This altered the previously-absolute rule in s.16, making it subject to the new s.20A, with other consequential additions (*e.g.* s.20B) and amendments (*e.g.* in s.61): see further the discussion of the passing of property in chapter 5, above.

All the cases discussed in this book are based on the law prior to the recent amendments, and it is likely, given the delay in the judicial system, that cases on the unamended 1979 Act will continue to be litigated for the foreseeable future.

SALE OF GOODS ACT 1979 (c. 54)

A–003   An Act to consolidate the law relating to the sale of goods.

Part I

Contracts to Which Act Applies

1. Contracts to which Act applies
A–004   (1) This Act applies to contracts of sale of goods made on or after (but not to those made before) 1 January 1894.

(2) In relation to contracts made on certain dates, this Act applies subject to the modification of certain of its sections as mentioned in Schedule 1 below.[4]

(3) Any such modification is indicated in the section concerned by a reference to Schedule 1 below.

(4) Accordingly, where a section does not contain such a reference, this Act applies in relation to the contract concerned without such modification of the section.

Part II

Formation of the Contract

Contract of sale

2. Contract of sale
A–005   (1) A contract of sale of goods is a contract by which the seller transfers or agrees to transfer the property in goods to the buyer for a money consideration, called the price.

---

[4] This section as a whole is derived from the Sale of Goods Act 1893, but sub-section (2) is consequent upon the Misrepresentation Act 1967, s.5, the Criminal Law Act 1967, s.12(1), the Supply of Goods (Implied Terms) Act 1973, s.18(5), the Consumer Credit Act 1974, s.192(4), and the Unfair Contract Terms Act 1977, s.31(2), which had altered the law of sale between 1893 and 1979. Because the changes made between 1893 and 1979 were not retrospective, it was necessary to retain the old provisions in Sched. 1.

(2) There may be a contract of sale between one part owner and another.

(3) A contract of sale may be absolute or conditional.

(4) Where under a contract of sale the property in the goods is transferred from the seller to the buyer the contract is called a sale.

(5) Where under a contract of sale the transfer of the property in the goods is to take place at a future time or subject to some condition later to be fulfilled the contract is called an agreement to sell.

(6) An agreement to sell becomes a sale when the time elapses or the conditions are fulfilled subject to which the property in the goods is to be transferred.

3. Capacity to buy and sell

(1) Capacity to buy and sell is regulated by the general law concerning capacity to contract and to transfer and acquire property.   **A–006**

(2) Where necessaries are sold and delivered to a minor or to a person who by reason of mental incapacity or drunkenness is incompetent to contract, he must pay a reasonable price for them.

(3) In subsection (2) above "necessaries" means goods suitable to the condition in life of the minor or other person concerned and to his actual requirements at the time of the sale and delivery.

Formalities of contract

4. How contract of sale is made

(1) Subject to this and any other Act, a contract of sale may be made in writing   **A–007**
(either with or without seal), or by word of mouth, or partly in writing and partly by word of mouth, or may be implied from the conduct of the parties.

(2) Nothing in this section affects the law relating to corporations.

Subject matter of contract

5. Existing or future goods

(1) The goods which form the subject of a contract of sale may be either existing   **A–008**
goods, owned or possessed by the seller, or goods to be manufactured or acquired by him after the making of the contract of sale, in this Act called future goods.

(2) There may be a contract for the sale of goods the acquisition of which by the seller depends on a contingency which may or may not happen.

(3) Where by a contract of sale the seller purports to effect a present sale of future goods, the contract operates as an agreement to sell the goods.

6. Goods which have perished

Where there is a contract for the sale of specific goods, and the goods without   **A–009**
the knowledge of the seller have perished at the time when the contract is made, the contract is void.

7. Goods perishing before sale but after agreement to sell

Where there is an agreement to sell specific goods and subsequently the goods,   **A–010**
without any fault on the part of the seller or buyer, perish before the risk passes to the buyer, the agreement is avoided.

The price

8. Ascertainment of price

A–011   (1) The price in a contract of sale may be fixed by the contract, or may be left to be fixed in a manner agreed by the contract, or may be determined by the course of dealing between the parties.

(2) Where the price is not determined as mentioned in subsection (1) above the buyer must pay a reasonable price.

(3) What is a reasonable price is a question of fact dependent on the circumstances of each particular case.

9. Agreement to sell at valuation

A–012   (1) Where there is an agreement to sell goods on the terms that the price is to be fixed by the valuation of a third party, and he cannot or does not make the valuation, the agreement is avoided; but if the goods or any part of them have been delivered to and appropriated by the buyer he must pay a reasonable price for them.

(2) Where the third party is prevented from making the valuation by the fault of the seller or buyer, the party not at fault may maintain an action for damages against the party at fault.

Implied terms etc.[5]

10. Stipulations about time

A–013   (1) Unless a different intention appears from the terms of the contract, stipulations as to time of payment are not of the essence of a contract of sale.

(2) Whether any other stipulation as to time is or is not of the essence of the contract depends on the terms of the contract.

(3) In a contract of sale "month" *prima facie* means calendar month.

11. When condition to be treated as warranty

A–014   (1) This section does not apply to Scotland.

(2) Where a contract of sale is subject to a condition to be fulfilled by the seller, the buyer may waive the condition, or may elect to treat the breach of the condition as a breach of warranty and not as a ground for treating the contract as repudiated.

(3) Whether a stipulation in a contract of sale is a condition, the breach of which may give rise to a right to treat the contract as repudiated, or a warranty, the breach of which may give rise to a claim for damages but not to a right to reject the goods and treat the contract as repudiated, depends in each case on the construction of the contract; and a stipulation may be a condition, though called a warranty in the contract.

(4) Subject to section 35A below[6] where a contract of sale is not severable and the buyer has accepted the goods or part of them, the breach of a condition to be fulfilled by the seller can only be treated as a breach of warranty, and not as a

---

[5] Prior to the coming into force of the Sale and Supply of Goods Act 1994, this sub-heading was Conditions and warranties."One of the effects of the 1994 Act has been to move away from the rigid distinction drawn in the 1893 Act between conditions and warranties, but by comparison with the Uniform Law on the International Sale of Goods (see App. G, below), the move has not been especially radical: see, however, s.15A, below.

[6] This qualification, and indeed s.35A itself, was added by the Sale and Supply of Goods Act 1994.

ground for rejecting the goods and treating the contract as repudiated, unless there is an express or implied term of the contract to that effect.

(5) [repealed by the Sale and Supply of Goods Act 1994].

(6) Nothing in this section affects a condition or warranty whose fulfilment is excused by law by reason of impossibility or otherwise.

(7) Paragraph 2 of Schedule 1 below applies in relation to a contract made before 22 April 1967 or (in the application of this Act to Northern Ireland) 28 July 1967.

12. Implied terms about title, etc.

(1) In a contract of sale, other than one to which subsection (3) below applies, there is an implied term on the part of the seller that in the case of a sale he has a right to sell the goods, and in the case of an agreement to sell he will have such a right at the time when the property is to pass. **A–015**

(2) In a contract of sale, other than one to which subsection (3) below applies, there is also an implied term that—

(a) the goods are free, and will remain free until the time when the property is to pass, from any charge or encumbrance not disclosed or known to the buyer before the contract is made, and

(b) the buyer will enjoy quiet possession of the goods except so far as it may be disturbed by the owner or other person entitled to the benefit of any charge or encumbrance so disclosed or known.

(3) This subsection applies to a contract of sale in the case of which there appears from the contract or is to be inferred from its circumstances an intention that the seller should transfer only such title as he or a third person may have.

(4) In a contract to which subsection (3) above applies there is an implied term that all charges or encumbrances known to the seller and not known to the buyer have been disclosed to the buyer before the contract is made.

(5) In a contract to which subsection (3) above applies there is also an implied term that none of the following will disturb the buyer's quiet possession of the goods, namely—

(a) the seller;

(b) in a case where the parties to the contract intend that the seller should transfer only such title as a third person may have, that person;

(c) anyone claiming through or under the seller or that third person otherwise than under a charge or encumbrance disclosed or known to the buyer before the contract is made.

(5A) As regards England and Wales and Northern Ireland, the term implied by subsection (1) above is a condition and the terms implied by subsections (2), (4) and (5) above are warranties.[7]

(6) Paragraph 3 of Schedule 1 below applies in relation to a contract made before 18 May 1973.

13. Sale by description

(1) Where there is a contract for the sale of goods by description, there is an implied term that the goods will correspond with the description. **A–016**

---

[7] This subsection was added by the Sale and Supply of Goods Act 1994, prior to which the words "implied condition" and "implied warranty" were used in the substantive sections, instead of "implied term". The same applies also (for the same reasons) to ss.13(1A), 14(6) and 15(3).

(1A) As regards England and Wales and Northern Ireland, the term implied by subsection (l) above is a condition.

(2) If the sale is by sample as well as by description it is not sufficient that the bulk of the goods corresponds with the sample if the goods do not also correspond with the description.

(3) A sale of goods is not prevented from being a sale by description by reason only that, being exposed for sale or hire, they are selected by the buyer.

(4) Paragraph 4 of Schedule 1 below applies in relation to a contract made before 18th May 1973.

14. Implied terms about quality or fitness

A–017   (1) Except as provided by this section and section 15 below and subject to any other enactment, there is no implied term about the quality or fitness for any particular purpose of goods supplied under a contract of sale.

(2) Where the seller sells goods in the course of a business, there is an implied term that the goods supplied under the contract are of satisfactory quality.

(2A) For the purposes of this Act, goods are of satisfactory quality if they meet the standard that a reasonable person would regard as satisfactory, taking account of any description of the goods, the price (if relevant) and all the other relevant circumstances.

(2B) For the purposes of this Act, the quality of goods includes their state and condition and the following (among others) are in appropriate cases aspects of the quality of goods—

(a) fitness for all the purposes for which goods of the kind in question are commonly supplied,

(b) appearance and finish,

(c) freedom from minor defects,

(d) safety, and

(e) durability.

(2C) The term implied by subsection (2) above does not extend to any matter making the quality of goods unsatisfactory—

(a) which is specifically drawn to the buyer's attention before the contract is made,

(b) where the buyer examines the goods before the contract is made, which that examination ought to reveal, or

(c) in the case of a contract for sale by sample, which would have been apparent on a reasonable examination of the sample.[8]

(3) Where the seller sells goods in the course of a business and the buyer, expressly or by implication, makes known—

(a) to the seller, or

(b) where the purchase price or part of it is payable by instalments and the goods were previously sold by a credit-broker to the seller, to that credit-broker,

---

[8] Subsections (2)–(2C) have been significantly altered by the Sale and Supply of Goods Act 1994; for the original section, see Sched. 1, s.6, and the note thereto.

any particular purpose for which the goods are being bought, there is an implied term that the goods supplied under the contract are reasonably fit for that purpose, whether or not that is a purpose for which such goods are commonly supplied, except where the circumstances show that the buyer does not rely, or that it is unreasonable for him to rely, on the skill or judgment of the seller or credit-broker.

(4) An implied term about quality or fitness for a particular purpose may be annexed to a contract of sale by usage.

(5) The preceding provisions of this section apply to a sale by a person who in the course of a business is acting as agent for another as they apply to a sale by a principal in the course of a business, except where that other is not selling in the course of a business and either the buyer knows that fact or reasonable steps are taken to bring it to the notice of the buyer before the contract is made.

(6) As regards England and Wales and Northern Ireland, the terms implied by subsections (2) and (3) above are conditions.

(7) Paragraph 5 of Schedule 1 below applies in relation to a contract made on or after 18 May 1973 and before the appointed day, and paragraph 6 in relation to one made before 18th May 1973.

(8) In subsection (7) above and paragraph 5 of Schedule 1 below references to the appointed day are to the day appointed for the purposes of those provisions by an order of the Secretary of State made by statutory instrument.

15. Sale by sample

(1) A contract of sale is a contract for sale by sample where there is an express   **A–018** or implied term to that effect in the contract.

(2) In the case of a contract for sale by sample there is an implied term—

(a) that the bulk will correspond with the sample in quality;

(b) [repealed by the Sale and Supply of Goods Act 1994].

(c) that the goods will be free from any defect, making their quality unsatisfactory, which would not be apparent on reasonable examination of the sample.

(3) As regards England and Wales and Northern Ireland, the term implied by subsection (2) above is a condition.

(4) Paragraph 7 of Schedule 1 below applies in relation to a contract made before 18 May 1973.

Miscellaneous[9]

15A. Modification of remedies for breach of condition in non-consumer cases

(1) Where in the case of a contract of sale—   **A–019**

(a) the buyer would, apart from this subsection, have the right to reject goods by reason of a breach on the part of the seller of a term implied by section 13, 14 or 15 above, but

(b) the breach is so slight that it would be unreasonable for him to reject them, then, if the buyer does not deal as consumer, the breach is not to be treated as a breach of condition but may be treated as a breach of warranty.

[9] The sub-heading and sub-section were added by the Sale and Supply of Goods Act 1994.

(2) This section applies unless a contrary intention appears in, or is to be implied from, the contract.

(3) It is for the seller to show that a breach fell within subsection (1)(b) above.

(4) This section does not apply to Scotland.

PART III

EFFECTS OF THE CONTRACT

Transfer of property as between seller and buyer

16. Goods must be ascertained

A–020   Subject to section 20A below[10] where there is a contract for the sale of unascertained goods no property in the goods is transferred to the buyer unless and until the goods are ascertained.

17. Property passes when intended to pass

A–021   (1) Where there is a contract for the sale of specific or ascertained goods the property in them is transferred to the buyer at such time as the parties to the contract intend it to be transferred.

(2) For the purpose of ascertaining the intention of the parties regard shall be had to the terms of the contract, the conduct of the parties and the circumstances of the case.

18. Rules for ascertaining intention

A–022   Unless a different intention appears, the following are rules for ascertaining the intention of the parties as to the time at which the property in the goods is to pass to the buyer.

Rule 1—

Where there is an unconditional contract for the sale of specific goods in a deliverable state the property in the goods passes to the buyer when the contract is made, and it is immaterial whether the time of payment or the time of delivery, or both, be postponed.

Rule 2—

Where there is a contract for the sale of specific goods and the seller is bound to do something to the goods for the purpose of putting them into a deliverable state, the property does not pass until the thing is done and the buyer has notice that it has been done.

Rule 3—

Where there is a contract for the sale of specific goods in a deliverable state but the seller is bound to weigh, measure, test, or do some other act or thing with reference to the goods for the purpose of ascertaining the price, the property does not pass until the act or thing is done and the buyer has notice that it has been done.

Rule 4—

When goods are delivered to the buyer on approval or on sale or return or other similar terms the property in the goods passes to the buyer—

---

[10] This qualification was added by the Sale of Goods (Amendment) Act 1995, prior to which s.16 operated as an absolute bar on the passing of property in unascertained goods.

(a) when he signifies his approval or acceptance to the seller or does any other act adopting the transaction;

(b) if he does not signify his approval or acceptance to the seller but retains the goods without giving notice of rejection, then, if a time has been fixed for the return of the goods, on the expiration of that time, and, if no time has been fixed, on the expiration of a reasonable time.

Rule 5—

(1) Where there is a contract for the sale of unascertained or future goods by description, and goods of that description and in a deliverable state are unconditionally appropriated to the contract, either by the seller with the assent of the buyer or by the buyer with the assent of the seller, the property in the goods then passes to the buyer; and the assent may be express or implied, and may be given either before or after the appropriation is made.

(2) Where, in pursuance of the contract, the seller delivers the goods to the buyer or to a carrier or other bailee or custodier (whether named by the buyer or not) for the purpose of transmission to the buyer, and does not reserve the right of disposal, he is to be taken to have unconditionally appropriated the goods to the contract.

(3) Where there is a contract for the sale of a specified quantity of unascertained goods in a deliverable state forming part of a bulk which is identified either in the contract or by subsequent agreement between the parties and the bulk is reduced to (or to less than) that quantity, then, if the buyer under that contract is the only buyer to whom goods are then due out of the bulk—

(a) the remaining goods are to be taken as appropriated to that contract at the time when the bulk is so reduced; and

(b) the property in those goods then passes to that buyer.

(4) Paragraph (3) above applies also (with the necessary modifications) where a bulk is reduced to (or to less than) the aggregate of the quantities due to a single buyer under separate contracts relating to that bulk and he is the only buyer to whom goods are then due out of that bulk.[11]

19. Reservation of right of disposal

(1) Where there is a contract for the sale of specific goods or where goods are subsequently appropriated to the contract, the seller may, by the terms of the contract or appropriation, reserve the right of disposal of the goods until certain conditions are fulfilled; and in such a case, notwithstanding the delivery of the goods to the buyer, or to a carrier or other bailee or custodier for the purpose of transmission to the buyer, the property in the goods does not pass to the buyer until the conditions imposed by the seller are fulfilled.

(2) Where goods are shipped, and by the bill of lading the goods are deliverable to the order of the seller or his agent, the seller is *prima facie* to be taken to reserve the right of disposal.

(3) Where the seller of goods draws on the buyer for the price, and transmits the bill of exchange and bill of lading to the buyer together to secure acceptance or payment of the bill of exchange, the buyer is bound to return the bill of lading if he does not honour the bill of exchange, and if he wrongfully retains the bill of lading the property in the goods does not pass to him.

A–023

[11] Sub-paragraphs (3) and (4) were added by the Sale of Goods (Amendment) Act 1995, entrenching *The Elafi* (in para. 5–015).

20. Risk *prima facie* passes with property

A–024 (1) Unless otherwise agreed, the goods remain at the seller's risk until the property in them is transferred to the buyer, but when the property in them is transferred to the buyer the goods are at the buyer's risk whether delivery has been made or not.

(2) But where delivery has been delayed through the fault of either buyer or seller the goods are at the risk of the party at fault as regards any loss which might not have occurred but for such fault.

(3) Nothing in this section affects the duties or liabilities of either seller or buyer as a bailee or custodier of the goods of the other party.

20A. Undivided shares in goods forming part of a bulk

A–025 (1) This section applies to a contract for the sale of a specified quantity of unascertained goods if the following conditions are met—

(a) the goods or some of them form part of a bulk which is identified either in the contract or by subsequent agreement between the parties; and

(b) the buyer has paid the price for some or all of the goods which are the subject of the contract and which form part of the bulk.

(2) Where this section applies, then (unless the parties agree otherwise), as soon as the conditions specified in paragraphs (a) and (b) of subsection (1) above are met or at such later time as the parties may agree—

(a) property in an undivided share in the bulk is transferred to the buyer, and

(b) the buyer becomes an owner in common of the bulk.

(3) Subject to subsection (4) below, for the purposes of this section, the undivided share of a buyer in a bulk at any time shall be such share as the quantity of goods paid for and due to the buyer out of the bulk bears to the quantity of goods in the bulk at that time.

(4) Where the aggregate of the undivided shares of buyers in a bulk determined under subsection (3) above would at any time exceed the whole of the bulk at that time, the undivided share in the bulk of each buyer shall be reduced proportionately so that the aggregate of the undivided shares is equal to the whole bulk.

(5) Where a buyer has paid the price for only some of the goods due to him out of a bulk, any delivery to the buyer out of the bulk shall, for the purposes of this section, be ascribed in the first place to the goods in respect of which payment has been made.

(6) For the purposes of this section payment of part of the price for any goods shall be treated as payment for a corresponding part of the goods.

20B. Deemed consent by co-owner to dealings in bulk goods

A–026 (1) A person who has become an owner in common of a bulk by virtue of section 20A above shall be deemed to have consented to—

(a) any delivery of goods out of the bulk to any other owner in common of the bulk, being goods which are due to him under his contract;

(b) any dealing with or removal, delivery or disposal of goods in the bulk by any other person who is an owner in common of the bulk in so far as the goods fall within that co-owner's undivided share in the bulk at the time of the dealing, removal, delivery or disposal.

(2) No cause of action shall accrue to anyone against a person by reason of that person having acted in accordance with paragraph (a) or (b) of subsection (1) above in reliance on any consent deemed to have been given under that subsection.

(3) Nothing in this section or section 20A above shall—

(a) impose an obligation on a buyer of goods out of a bulk to compensate any other buyer of goods out of that bulk for any shortfall in the goods received by that other buyer;

(b) affect any contractual arrangement between buyers of goods out of a bulk for adjustments between themselves; or

(c) affect the rights of any buyer under his contract.[12]

Transfer of title

21. Sale by person not the owner

(1) Subject to this Act, where goods are sold by a person who is not their owner,   **A–027** and who does not sell them under the authority or with the consent of the owner, the buyer acquires no better title to the goods than the seller had, unless the owner of the goods is by his conduct precluded from denying the seller's authority to sell.

(2) Nothing in this Act affects—

(a) the provisions of the Factors Acts or any enactment enabling the apparent owner of goods to dispose of them as if he were their true owner;

(b) the validity of any contract of sale under any special common law or statutory power of sale or under the order of a court of competent jurisdiction.

22. Market overt

[This section has been substantively repealed by the Sale and Supply of Goods   **A–028** Act 1994].

23. Sale under voidable title

When the seller of goods has a voidable title to them, but his title has not been   **A–029** avoided at the time of the sale, the buyer acquires a good title to the goods, provided he buys them in good faith and without notice of the seller's defect of title.

24. Seller in possession after sale

Where a person having sold goods continues or is in possession of the goods,   **A–030** or of the documents of title to the goods, the delivery or transfer by that person, or by a mercantile agent acting for him, of the goods or documents of title under any sale, pledge, or other disposition thereof, to any person receiving the same in good faith and without notice of the previous sale, has the same effect as if the person making the delivery or transfer were expressly authorised by the owner of the goods to make the same.

---

[12] Sections 20A and 20B were added by the Sale of Goods (Amendment) Act 1995.

25. Buyer in possession after sale

A–031   (1) Where a person having bought or agreed to buy goods obtains, with the consent of the seller, possession of the goods or the documents of title to the goods, the delivery or transfer by that person, or by a mercantile agent acting for him, of the goods or documents of title, under any sale, pledge, or other disposition thereof, to any person receiving the same in good faith and without notice of any lien or other right of the original seller in respect of the goods, has the same effect as if the person making the delivery or transfer were a mercantile agent in possession of the goods or documents of title with the consent of the owner.

(2) For the purposes of subsection (1) above—

(a) the buyer under a conditional sale agreement is to be taken not to be a person who has bought or agreed to buy goods, and

(b) "conditional sale agreement" means an agreement for the sale of goods which is a consumer credit agreement within the meaning of the Consumer Credit Act 1974 under which the purchase price or part of it is payable by instalments, and the property in the goods is to remain in the seller (notwithstanding that the buyer is to be in possession of the goods) until such conditions as to the payment of instalments or otherwise as may be specified in the agreement are fulfilled.

(3) Paragraph 9 of Schedule 1 below applies in relation to a contract under which a person buys or agrees to buy goods and which is made before the appointed day.

(4) In subsection (3) above and paragraph 9 of Schedule 1 below references to the appointed day are to the day appointed for the purposes of those provisions by an order of the Secretary of State made by statutory instrument.

26. Supplementary to sections 24 and 25

A–032   In sections 24 and 25 above "mercantile agent" means a mercantile agent having in the customary course of his business as such agent authority either—

(a) to sell goods, or

(b) to consign goods for the purpose of sale, or

(c) to buy goods, or Sale of Goods Act 1979, s.26

(d) to raise money on the security of goods.

PART IV

PERFORMANCE OF THE CONTRACT

27. Duties of seller and buyer

A–033   It is the duty of the seller to deliver the goods, and of the buyer to accept and pay for them, in accordance with the terms of the contract of sale.

28. Payment and delivery are concurrent conditions

A–034   Unless otherwise agreed, delivery of the goods and payment of the price are concurrent conditions, that is to say, the seller must be ready and willing to give possession of the goods to the buyer in exchange for the price and the buyer must be ready and willing to pay the price in exchange for possession of the goods.

29. Rules about delivery

(1) Whether it is for the buyer to take possession of the goods or for the seller **A–035** to send them to the buyer is a question depending in each case on the contract, express or implied, between the parties.

(2) Apart from any such contract, express or implied, the place of delivery is the seller's place of business if he has one, and if not, his residence; except that, if the contract is for the sale of specific goods, which to the knowledge of the parties when the contract is made are in some other place, then that place is the place of delivery.

(3) Where under the contract of sale the seller is bound to send the goods to the buyer, but no time for sending them is fixed, the seller is bound to send them within a reasonable time.

(4) Where the goods at the time of sale are in the possession of a third person, there is no delivery by seller to buyer unless and until the third person acknowledges to the buyer that he holds the goods on his behalf; but nothing in this section affects the operation of the issue or transfer of any document of title to goods.

(5) Demand or tender of delivery may be treated as ineffectual unless made at a reasonable hour; and what is a reasonable hour is a question of fact.

(6) Unless otherwise agreed, the expenses of and incidental to putting the goods into a deliverable state must be borne by the seller.

30. Delivery of wrong quantity

(1) Where the seller delivers to the buyer a quantity of goods less than he **A–036** contracted to sell, the buyer may reject them, but if the buyer accepts the goods so delivered he must pay for them at the contract rate.

(2) Where the seller delivers to the buyer a quantity of goods larger than he contracted to sell, the buyer may accept the goods included in the contract and reject the rest, or he may reject the whole.

(2A) A buyer who does not deal as consumer may not—

(a) where the seller delivers a quantity of goods less than he contracted to sell, reject the goods under subsection (1) above, or

(b) where the seller delivers a quantity of goods larger than he contracted to sell, reject the whole under subsection (2) above,

if the shortfall or, as the case may be, excess is so slight that it would be unreasonable for him to do so.

(2B) It is for the seller to show that a shortfall or excess fell within subsection (2A) above.

(2C) Subsections (2A) and (2B) above do not apply to Scotland.[13]

(3) Where the seller delivers to the buyer a quantity of goods larger than he contracted to sell and the buyer accepts the whole of the goods so delivered he must pay for them at the contract rate.

(4) [repealed by the Sale and Supply of Goods Act 1994].

(5) This section is subject to any usage of trade, special agreement, or course of dealing between the parties.

31. Instalment deliveries

(1) Unless otherwise agreed, the buyer of goods is not bound to accept delivery **A–037** of them by instalments.

---

[13] Subsections (2)–(2C) were significantly altered by the Sale and Supply of Goods Act 1994, which provided for partial rejection.

(2) Where there is a contract for the sale of goods to be delivered by stated instalments, which are to be separately paid for, and the seller makes defective deliveries in respect of one or more instalments, or the buyer neglects or refuses to take delivery of or pay for one or more instalments, it is a question in each case depending on the terms of the contract and the circumstances of the case whether the breach of contract is a repudiation of the whole contract or whether it is a severable breach giving rise to a claim for compensation but not to a right to treat the whole contract as repudiated.

32. Delivery to carrier

A–038   (1) Where, in pursuance of a contract of sale, the seller is authorised or required to send the goods to the buyer, delivery of the goods to a carrier (whether named by the buyer or not) for the purpose of transmission to the buyer is *prima facie* deemed to be a delivery of the goods to the buyer.

(2) Unless otherwise authorised by the buyer, the seller must make such contract with the carrier on behalf of the buyer as may be reasonable having regard to the nature of the goods and the other circumstances of the case; and if the seller omits to do so, and the goods are lost or damaged in course of transit, the buyer may decline to treat the delivery to the carrier as a delivery to himself or may hold the seller responsible in damages.

(3) Unless otherwise agreed, where goods are sent by the seller to the buyer by a route involving sea transit, under circumstances in which it is usual to insure, the seller must give such notice to the buyer as may enable him to insure them during their sea transit; and if the seller fails to do so, the goods are at his risk during such sea transit.

33. Risk where goods are delivered at distant place

A–039   Where the seller of goods agrees to deliver them at his own risk at a place other than that where they are when sold, the buyer must nevertheless (unless otherwise agreed) take any risk of deterioration in the goods necessarily incident to the course of transit.

34. Buyer's right of examining the goods

A–040   Unless otherwise agreed, when the seller tenders delivery of goods to the buyer, he is bound on request to afford the buyer a reasonable opportunity of examining the goods for the purpose of ascertaining whether they are in conformity with the contract and, in the case of a contract for sale by sample, of comparing the bulk with the sample.[14]

35. Acceptance

A–041   (1) The buyer is deemed to have accepted the goods subject to subsection (2) below—

(a) when he intimates to the seller that he has accepted them, or

(b) when the goods have been delivered to him and he does any act in relation to them which is inconsistent with the ownership of the seller.

(2) Where goods are delivered to the buyer, and he has not previously examined them, he is not deemed to have accepted them under subsection (1) above until he has had a reasonable opportunity of examining them for the purpose—

---

[14] This section, and s.35, were amended into their current form by the Sale and Supply of Goods Act 1994.

(a) of ascertaining whether they are in conformity with the contract, and

(b) in the case of a contract for sale by sample, of comparing the bulk with the sample.

(3) Where the buyer deals as consumer or (in Scotland) the contract of sale is a consumer contract, the buyer cannot lose his right to rely on subsection (2) above by agreement, waiver or otherwise.

(4) The buyer is also deemed to have accepted the goods when after the lapse of a reasonable time he retains the goods without intimating to the seller that he has rejected them.

(5) The questions that are material in determining for the purposes of subsection (4) above whether a reasonable time has elapsed include whether the buyer has had a reasonable opportunity of examining the goods for the purpose mentioned in subsection (2) above.

(6) The buyer is not by virtue of this section deemed to have accepted the goods merely because—

(a) he asks for, or agrees to, their repair by or under an arrangement with the seller, or

(b) the goods are delivered to another under a sub-sale or other disposition.

(7) Where the contract is for the sale of goods making one or more commercial units, a buyer accepting any goods included in a unit is deemed to have accepted all the goods making the unit; and in this subsection "commercial unit" means a unit division of which would materially impair the value of the goods or the character of the unit.

(8) Paragraph 10 of Schedule 1 below applies in relation to a contract made before 22nd April 1967 or (in the application of this Act to Northern Ireland) 28th July 1967.

35A. Right of partial rejection

(1) If the buyer—   A–042

(a) has the right to reject the goods by reason of a breach on the part of the seller that affects some or all of them, but

(b) accepts some of the goods, including, where there are any goods unaffected by the breach, all such goods,

he does not by accepting them lose his right to reject the rest.

(2) In the case of a buyer having the right to reject an instalment of goods, subsection (1) above applies as if references to the goods were references to the goods comprised in the instalment.

(3) For the purposes of subsection (1) above, goods are affected by a breach if by reason of the breach they are not in conformity with the contract.

(4) This section applies unless a contrary intention appears in, or is to be implied from, the contract.[15]

36. Buyer not bound to return rejected goods

Unless otherwise agreed, where goods are delivered to the buyer, and he   A–043
refuses to accept them, having the right to do so, he is not bound to return them

---

[15] Section 35A was added by the Sale and Supply of Goods Act 1994.

to the seller, but it is sufficient if he intimates to the seller that he refuses to accept them.

37. Buyer's liability for not taking delivery of goods

A–044   (1) When the seller is ready and willing to deliver the goods, and requests the buyer to take delivery, and the buyer does not within a reasonable time after such request take delivery of the goods, he is liable to the seller for any loss occasioned by his neglect or refusal to take delivery, and also for a reasonable charge for the care and custody of the goods.

(2) Nothing in this section affects the rights of the seller where the neglect or refusal of the buyer to take delivery amounts to a repudiation of the contract.

Part V

Rights of Unpaid Seller Against the Goods

Preliminary

38. Unpaid seller defined

A–045   (1) The seller of goods is an unpaid seller within the meaning of this Act—

(a) when the whole of the price has not been paid or tendered;

(b) when a bill of exchange or other negotiable instrument has been received as conditional payment, and the condition on which it was received has not been fulfilled by reason of the dishonour of the instrument or otherwise.

(2) In this Part of this Act "seller" includes any person who is in the position of a seller, as, for instance, an agent of the seller to whom the bill of lading has been indorsed, or a consignor or agent who has himself paid (or is directly responsible for) the price.

39. Unpaid seller's rights

A–046   (1) Subject to this and any other Act, notwithstanding that the property in the goods may have passed to the buyer, the unpaid seller of goods, as such, has by implication of law—

(a) a lien on the goods or right to retain them for the price while he is in possession of them;

(b) in case of the insolvency of the buyer, a right of stopping the goods in transit after he has parted with the possession of them;

(c) a right of re-sale as limited by this Act.

(2) Where the property in goods has not passed to the buyer, the unpaid seller has (in addition to his other remedies) a right of withholding delivery similar to and co-extensive with his rights of lien or retention and stoppage in transit where the property has passed to the buyer.
[Repealed by the Debtors (Scotland) Act 1987, s 108(3), Sch 8.]

40. Attachment by seller in Scotland

A–047   In Scotland a seller of goods may attach them while in his own hands or possession by arrestment or poinding, and such arrestment or poinding shall have the same operation and effect in a competition or otherwise as an arrestment or poinding by a third party.

Unpaid seller's lien

41. Seller's lien

(1) Subject to this Act, the unpaid seller of goods who is in possession of them   **A–048** is entitled to retain possession of them until payment or tender of the price in the following cases–

   (a) where the goods have been sold without any stipulation as to credit;

   (b) where the goods have been sold on credit but the term of credit has expired;

   (c) where the buyer becomes insolvent.

(2) The seller may exercise his lien or right of retention notwithstanding that he is in possession of the goods as agent or bailee or custodier for the buyer.

42. Part delivery

Where an unpaid seller has made part delivery of the goods, he may exercise   **A–049** his lien or right of retention on the remainder, unless such part delivery has been made under such circumstances as to show an agreement to waive the lien or right of retention.

43. Termination of lien

(1) The unpaid seller of goods loses his lien or right of retention in respect of   **A–050** them—

   (a) when he delivers the goods to a carrier or other bailee or custodier for the purpose of transmission to the buyer without reserving the right of disposal of the goods;

   (b) when the buyer or his agent lawfully obtains possession of the goods;

   (c) by waiver of the lien or right of retention.

(2) An unpaid seller of goods who has a lien or right of retention in respect of them does not lose his lien or right of retention by reason only that he has obtained judgment or decree for the price of the goods.

Stoppage in transit

44. Right of stoppage in transit

Subject to this Act, when the buyer of goods becomes insolvent the unpaid   **A–051** seller who has parted with the possession of the goods has the right of stopping them in transit, that is to say, he may resume possession of the goods as long as they are in course of transit, and may retain them until payment or tender of the price.

45. Duration of transit

(1) Goods are deemed to be in course of transit from the time when they are   **A–052** delivered to a carrier or other bailee or custodier for the purpose of transmission

to the buyer, until the buyer or his agent in that behalf takes delivery of them from the carrier or other bailee or custodier.

(2) If the buyer or his agent in that behalf obtains delivery of the goods before their arrival at the appointed destination, the transit is at an end.

(3) If, after the arrival of the goods at the appointed destination, the carrier or other bailee or custodier acknowledges to the buyer or his agent that he holds the goods on his behalf and continues in possession of them as bailee or custodier for the buyer or his agent, the transit is at an end, and it is immaterial that a further destination for the goods may have been indicated by the buyer.

(4) If the goods are rejected by the buyer, and the carrier or other bailee or custodier continues in possession of them, the transit is not deemed to be at an end, even if the seller has refused to receive them back.

(5) When goods are delivered to a ship chartered by the buyer it is a question depending on the circumstances of the particular case whether they are in the possession of the master as a carrier or as agent to the buyer.

(6) Where the carrier or other bailee or custodier wrongfully refuses to deliver the goods to the buyer or his agent in that behalf, the transit is deemed to be at an end.

(7) Where part delivery of the goods has been made to the buyer or his agent in that behalf, the remainder of the goods may be stopped in transit, unless such part delivery has been made under such circumstances as to show an agreement to give up possession of the whole of the goods.

46. How stoppage in transit is effected

A–053   (1) The unpaid seller may exercise his right of stoppage in transit either by taking actual possession of the goods or by giving notice of his claim to the carrier or other bailee or custodier in whose possession the goods are.

(2) The notice may be given either to the person in actual possession of the goods or to his principal.

(3) If given to the principal, the notice is ineffective unless given at such time and under such circumstances that the principal, by the exercise of reasonable diligence, may communicate it to his servant or agent in time to prevent a delivery to the buyer.

(4) When notice of stoppage in transit is given by the seller to the carrier or other bailee or custodier in possession of the goods, he must re-deliver the goods to, or according to the directions of, the seller; and the expenses of there-delivery must be borne by the seller.

Re-sale etc. by buyer

47. Effect of sub-sale etc. by buyer

A–054   (1) Subject to this Act, the unpaid seller's right of lien or retention or stoppage in transit is not affected by any sale or other disposition of the goods which the buyer may have made, unless the seller has assented to it.

(2) Where a document of title to goods has been lawfully transferred to any person as buyer or owner of the goods, and that person transfers the document to a person who takes it in good faith and for valuable consideration, then—

(a) if the last-mentioned transfer was by way of sale the unpaid seller's right of lien or retention or stoppage in transit is defeated; and

(b) if the last-mentioned transfer was made by way of pledge or other disposition for value, the unpaid seller's right of lien or retention or stoppage in transit can only be exercised subject to the rights of the transferee.

48. Rescission: and re-sale by seller

(1) Subject to this section, a contract of sale is not rescinded by the mere exercise   **A–055** by an unpaid seller of his right of lien or retention or stoppage in transit.

(2) Where an unpaid seller who has exercised his right of lien or retention or stoppage in transit re-sells the goods, the buyer acquires a good title to them as against the original buyer.

(3) Where the goods are of a perishable nature, or where the unpaid seller gives notice to the buyer of his intention to re-sell, and the buyer does not within a reasonable time pay or tender the price, the unpaid seller may re-sell the goods and recover from the original buyer damages for any loss occasioned by his breach of contract.

(4) Where the seller expressly reserves the right of re-sale in case the buyer should make default, and on the buyer making default re-sells the goods, the original contract of sale is rescinded but without prejudice to any claim the seller may have for damages.

Part VI

Actions for Breach of the Contract

Seller's remedies

49. Action for price

(1) Where, under a contract of sale, the property in the goods has passed to the   **A–056** buyer and he wrongfully neglects or refuses to pay for the goods according to the terms of the contract, the seller may maintain an action against him for the price of the goods.

(2) Where, under a contract of sale, the price is payable on a day certain irrespective of delivery and the buyer wrongfully neglects or refuses to pay such price, the seller may maintain an action for the price, although the property in the goods has not passed and the goods have not been appropriated to the contract.

(3) Nothing in this section prejudices the right of the seller in Scotland to recover interest on the price from the date of tender of the goods, or from the date on which the price was payable, as the case may be.

50. Damages for non-acceptance

(1) Where the buyer wrongfully neglects or refuses to accept and pay for the   **A–057** goods, the seller may maintain an action against him for damages for non-acceptance.

(2) The measure of damages is the estimated loss directly and naturally resulting, in the ordinary course of events, from the buyer's breach of contract.

(3) Where there is an available market for the goods in question the measure of damages is *prima facie* to be ascertained by the difference between the contract price and the market or current price at the time or times when the goods ought to have been accepted or (if no time was fixed for acceptance) at the time of the refusal to accept.

Buyer's remedies

51. Damages for non-delivery

A–058   (1) Where the seller wrongfully neglects or refuses to deliver the goods to the buyer, the buyer may maintain an action against the seller for damages for non-delivery.

(2) The measure of damages is the estimated loss directly and naturally resulting, in the ordinary course of events, from the seller's breach of contract.

(3) Where there is an available market for the goods in question the measure of damages is *prima facie* to be ascertained by the difference between the contract price and the market or current price of the goods at the time or times when they ought to have been delivered or (if no time was fixed) at the time of the refusal to deliver.

52. Specific performance

A–059   (1) In any action for breach of contract to deliver specific or ascertained goods the court may, if it thinks fit, on the plaintiff's application, by its judgment or decree direct that the contract shall be performed specifically, without giving the defendant the option of retaining the goods on payment of damages.

(2) The plaintiff's application may be made at any time before judgment or decree.

(3) The judgment or decree may be unconditional, or on such terms and conditions as to damages, payment of the price and otherwise as seem just to the court.

(4) The provisions of this section shall be deemed to be supplementary to, and not in derogation of, the right of specific implement in Scotland.

53. Remedy for breach of warranty

A–060   (1) Where there is a breach of warranty by the seller, or where the buyer elects (or is compelled) to treat any breach of a condition on the part of the seller as a breach of warranty, the buyer is not by reason only of such breach of warranty entitled to reject the goods; but he may—

(a) set up against the seller the breach of warranty in diminution or extinction of the price, or

(b) maintain an action against the seller for damages for the breach of warranty.

(2) The measure of damages for breach of warranty is the estimated loss directly and naturally resulting, in the ordinary course of events, from the breach of warranty.

(3) In the case of breach of warranty of quality such loss is *prima facie* the difference between the value of the goods at the time of delivery to the buyer and the value they would have had if they had fulfilled the warranty.

(4) The fact that the buyer has set up the breach of warranty in diminution or extinction of the price does not prevent him from maintaining an action for the same breach of warranty if he has suffered further damage.

(5) This section does not apply to Scotland.

Interest, etc.

54. Interest, etc.

A–061   Nothing in this Act affects the right of the buyer or the seller to recover interest or special damages in any case where by law interest or special damages may be recoverable, or to recover money paid where the consideration for the payment of it has failed.

Part VII

Supplementary

55. Exclusion of implied terms

(1) Where a right, duty or liability would arise under a contract of sale of goods by implication of law, it may (subject to the Unfair Contract Terms Act 1977) be negatived or varied by express agreement, or by the course of dealing between the parties, or by such usage as binds both parties to the contract.   **A–062**

(2) An express [term] does not negative a [term] implied by this Act unless inconsistent with it.

(3) Paragraph 11 of Schedule 1 below applies in relation to a contract made on or after 18th May 1973 and before 1st February 1978, and paragraph 12 in relation to one made before 18th May 1973.

56. Conflict of laws

Paragraph 13 of Schedule 1 below applies in relation to a contract made on or after 18th May 1973 and before 1st February 1978, so as to make provision about conflict of laws in relation to such a contract.   **A–063**

57. Auction sales

(1) Where goods are put up for sale by auction in lots, each lot is *prima facie* deemed to be the subject of a separate contract of sale.   **A–064**

(2) A sale by auction is complete when the auctioneer announces its completion by the fall of the hammer, or in other customary manner; and until the announcement is made any bidder may retract his bid.

(3) A sale by auction may be notified to be subject to a reserve or upset price, and a right to bid may also be reserved expressly by or on behalf of the seller.

(4) Where a sale by auction is not notified to be subject to a right to bid by or on behalf of the seller, it is not lawful for the seller to bid himself or to employ any person to bid at the sale, or for the auctioneer knowingly to take any bid from the seller or any such person.

(5) A sale contravening subsection (4) above may be treated as fraudulent by the buyer.

(6) Where, in respect of a sale by auction, a right to bid is expressly reserved (but not otherwise) the seller or any one person on his behalf may bid at the auction.

58. Payment into court in Scotland

In Scotland where a buyer has elected to accept goods which he might have rejected, and to treat a breach of contract as only giving rise to a claim for damages, he may, in an action by the seller for the price, be required, in the discretion of the court before which the action depends, to consign or pay into court the price of the goods, or part of the price, or to give other reasonable security for its due payment.   **A–065**

59. Reasonable time a question of fact

Where a reference is made in this Act to a reasonable time the question what is a reasonable time is a question of fact.   **A–066**

60. Rights etc. enforceable by action

A–067 Where a right, duty or liability is declared by this Act, it may (unless otherwise provided by this Act) be enforced by action.

61. Interpretation

A–068 (1) In this Act, unless the context or subject matter otherwise requires—
"action" includes counterclaim and set-off, and in Scotland condescendence and claim and compensation;
'bulk" means a mass or collection of goods of the same kind which—

(a) is contained in a defined space or area; and

(b) is such that any goods in the bulk are interchangeable with any other goods therein of the same number or quantity;[16]

"business" includes a profession and the activities of any government department (including a Northern Ireland department) or local or public authority;
"buyer" means a person who buys or agrees to buy goods;
"consumer contract" has the same meaning as in section 25(1) of the Unfair Contract Terms Act 1977; and for the purposes of this Act the onus of proving that a contract is not to be regarded as a consumer contract shall lie on the seller
"contract of sale" includes an agreement to sell as well as a sale;
"credit-broker" means a person acting in the course of a business of credit brokerage carried on by him, that is a business of effecting introductions of individuals desiring to obtain credit—

(a) to persons carrying on any business so far as it relates to the provision of credit, or

(b) to other persons engaged in credit brokerage;

"delivery" means voluntary transfer of possession from one person to another except that in relation to sections 20A and 20B above it includes such appropriation of goods to the contract as results in property in the goods being transferred to the buyer;
"document of title to goods" has the same meaning as it has in the Factors Acts;
"Factors Acts" means the Factors Act 1889, the Factors (Scotland) Act 1890, and any enactment amending or substituted for the same;
"fault" means wrongful act or default;
"future goods" means goods to be manufactured or acquired by the seller after the making of the contract of sale;
"goods" includes all personal chattels other than things in action and money, and in Scotland all corporeal moveables except money; and in particular "goods" includes emblements, industrial growing crops, and things attached to or forming part of the land which are agreed to be severed before sale or under the contract of sale and includes an undivided share in goods;
"plaintiff" includes pursuer, complainer, claimant in a multiplepoinding and defendant or defender counter-claiming;

---

[16] This definition was added by the Sale of Goods (Amendment) Act 1995, which also amended the definitions of "delivery", "goods" and "specific goods". The Sale and Supply of Goods Act 1994 also made some minor amendments to s.61, including the addition of sub-section (5A).

"property" means the general property in goods, and not merely a special property;

"sale" includes a bargain and sale as well as a sale and delivery;

"seller" means a person who sells or agrees to sell goods;

"specific goods" means goods identified and agreed on at the time a contract of sale is made and includes an undivided share, specified as a fraction or percentage, of goods identified and agreed on as aforesaid;

"warranty" (as regards England and Wales and Northern Ireland) means an agreement with reference to goods which are the subject of a contract of sale, but collateral to the main purpose of such contract, the breach of which gives rise to a claim for damages, but not to a right to reject the goods and treat the contract as repudiated.

(2) [repealed by the Sale and Supply of Goods Act 1994].

(3) A thing is deemed to be done in good faith within the meaning of this Act when it is in fact done honestly, whether it is done negligently or not.

(4) A person is deemed to be insolvent within the meaning of this Act if he has either ceased to pay his debts in the ordinary course of business or he cannot pay his debts as they become due.

(5) Goods are in a deliverable state within the meaning of this Act when they are in such a state that the buyer would under the contract be bound to take delivery of them.

(5A) References in this Act to dealing as consumer are to be construed in accordance with Part I of the Unfair Contract Terms Act 1977; and, for the purposes of this Act, it is for a seller claiming that the buyer does not deal as consumer to show that he does not.

(6) As regards the definition of "business" in subsection (1) above, paragraph 14 of Schedule 1 below applies in relation to a contract made on or after 18th May 1973 and before 1st February 1978, and paragraph 15 in relation to one made before 18th May 1973.

62. Savings: rules of law etc.

(1) The rules in bankruptcy relating to contracts of sale apply to those contracts, **A–069** notwithstanding anything in this Act.

(2) The rules of the common law, including the law merchant, except in so far as they are inconsistent with the provisions of this Act, and in particular the rules relating to the law of principal and agent and the effect of fraud, misrepresentation, duress or coercion, mistake, or other invalidating cause, apply to contracts for the sale of goods.

(3) Nothing in this Act or the Sale of Goods Act 1893 affects the enactments relating to bills of sale, or any enactment relating to the sale of goods which is not expressly repealed or amended by this Act or that.

(4) The provisions of this Act about contracts of sale do not apply to a transaction in the form of a contract of sale which is intended to operate by way of mortgage, pledge, charge, or other security.

(5) Nothing in this Act prejudices or affects the landlord's right of hypothec or sequestration for rent in Scotland.

63. Consequential amendments, repeals and savings

(1) Without prejudice to section 17 of the Interpretation Act 1978 (repeal and **A–070** re-enactment), the enactments mentioned in Schedule 2 below have effect subject to the amendments there specified (being amendments consequential on this Act).

(2) The enactments mentioned in Schedule 3 below are repealed to the extent specified in column 3, but subject to the savings in Schedule 4 below.

(3) The savings in Schedule 4 below have effect.

64. Short title and commencement

A–071   (1) This Act may be cited as the Sale of Goods Act 1979.

(2) This Act comes into force on 1st January 1980.

Schedule 1

Modification of Act for Certain Contracts (s.1)

Preliminary

A–072   1. (1) This Schedule modifies this Act as it applies to contracts of sale of goods made on certain dates.

(2) In this Schedule references to sections are to those of this Act and references to contracts are to contracts of sale of goods.

(3) Nothing in this Schedule affects a contract made before 1 January 1894.

Section 11: condition treated as warranty

A–073   2. In relation to a contract made before 22 April 1967 or (in the application of this Act to Northern Ireland) 28 July 1967, in section 11(4) after "or part of them," insert "or where the contract is for specific goods, the property in which has passed to the buyer,".

Section 12: implied terms about title, etc.

A–074   3. In relation to a contract made before 18 May 1973 substitute the following for section 12:—

12. Implied terms about title, etc.

A–075   In a contract of sale, unless the circumstances of the contract are such as to show a different intention, there is—

(a) an implied condition on the part of the seller that in the case of a sale he has a right to sell the goods, and in the case of an agreement to sell he will have such a right at the time when the property is to pass;

(b) an implied warranty that the buyer will have and enjoy quiet possession of the goods;

(c) an implied warranty that the goods will be free from any charge or encumbrance in favour of any third party, not declared or known to the buyer before or at the time when the contract is made.

Section 13: sale by description

A–076   4. In relation to a contract made before 18 May 1973, omit section 13(3).

Section 14: *quality or fitness* (i)

5. In relation to a contract made on or after 18 May 1973 and before the **A–077** appointed day,[17] substitute the following for section 14:—

14. Implied terms about quality or fitness

(1) Except as provided by this section and section 15 below and subject to any **A–078** other enactment, there is no implied condition or warranty about the quality or fitness for any particular purpose of goods supplied under a contract of sale.

(2) Where the seller sells goods in the course of a business, there is an implied condition that the goods supplied under the contract are of merchantable quality, except that there is no such condition—

(a) as regards defects, specifically drawn to the buyer's attention before the contract is made; or

(b) if the buyer examines the goods before the contract is made, as regards defects which that examination ought to reveal.

(3) Where the seller sells goods in the course of a business and the buyer, expressly or by implication, makes known to the seller any particular purpose for which the goods are being bought, there is an implied condition that the goods supplied under the contract are reasonably fit for that purpose, whether or not that is a purpose for which such goods are commonly supplied, except where the circumstances show that the buyer does not rely, or that it is unreasonable for him to rely, on the seller's skill or judgment.

(4) An implied condition or warranty about quality or fitness for a particular purpose may be annexed to a contract of sale by usage.

(5) The preceding provisions of this section apply to a sale by a person who in the course of a business is acting as agent for another as they apply to a sale by a principal in the course of a business, except where that other is not selling in the course of a business and either the buyer knows that fact or reasonable steps are taken to bring it to the notice of the buyer before the contract is made.

(6) Goods of any kind are of merchantable quality within the meaning of subsection (2) above if they are as fit for the purpose or purposes for which goods of that kind are commonly bought as it is reasonable to expect having regard to any description applied to them, the price (if relevant) and all the other relevant circumstances.

(7) In the application of subsection (3) above to an agreement for the sale of goods under which the purchase price or part of it is payable by instalments any reference to the seller includes a reference to the person by whom any antecedent negotiations are conducted; and section 58(3) and (5) of the Hire-Purchase Act 1965, section 54(3) and (5) of the Hire-Purchase (Scotland) Act 1965 and section 65(3) and (5) of the Hire-Purchase Act (Northern Ireland) 1966 (meaning of antecedent negotiations and related expressions) apply in relation to this subsection as in relation to each of those Acts, but as if a reference to any such agreement were included in the references in subsection of each of those sections to the agreements there mentioned.

Section 14: *quality or fitness* (ii)

6. In relation to a contract made before 18 May 1973 substitute the following for **A–079** section 14:—

---

[17] Under the Consumer Credit Act 1974.

14. Implied terms about quality or fitness[18]

A–080   (1) Subject to this and any other Act, there is no implied condition or warranty about the quality or fitness for any particular purpose of goods supplied under a contract of sale.

(2) Where the buyer, expressly or by implication, makes known to the seller the particular purpose for which the goods are required, so as to show that the buyer relies on the seller's skill or judgment, and the goods are of a description which it is in the course of the seller's business to supply (whether he is the manufacturer or not), there is an implied condition that the goods will be reasonably fit for such purpose, except that in the case of a contract for the sale of a specified article under its patent or other trade name there is no implied condition as to its fitness for any particular purpose.

(3) Where goods are bought by description from a seller who deals in goods of that description (whether he is the manufacturer or not), there is an implied condition that the goods will be of merchantable quality; but if the buyer has examined the goods, there is no implied condition as regards defects which such examination ought to have revealed.

(4) An implied condition or warranty about quality or fitness for a particular purpose may be annexed by the usage of trade.

(5) An express condition or warranty does not negative a condition or warranty implied by this Act unless inconsistent with it.

Section 15: sale by sample

A–081   7. In relation to a contract made before 18 May 1973, omit section 15(3).

Section 22: market overt

A–082   8. In relation to a contract under which goods were sold before 1 January 1968 or (in the application of this Act to Northern Ireland) 29 August 1967, add the following paragraph at the end of section 22(1)–

"Nothing in this subsection affects the law relating to the sale of horses."

Section 25: buyer in possession

A–083   9. In relation to a contract under which a person buys or agrees to buy goods and which is made before the appointed day, omit section 25(2).

Section 35: acceptance

A–084   10. In relation to a contract made before 22 April 1967 or (in the application of this Act to Northern Ireland) 28 July 1967, in section 35(1) omit" (except where section 34 above otherwise provides)".

---

[18] This is essentially the same as the original 1893 section, except that s.14(1) here is unnumbered in the original, s.14(2) here is s.14(1) in the original, and subsequent subsections are also consequently renumbered, s.14(3) here becoming s.14(2) in the original, etc.

11. In relation to a contract made on or after 18 May 1973 and before 1 February   **A–085**
1978 substitute the following for section 55:—

55. Exclusion of implied terms

(1) Where a right, duty or liability would arise under a contract of sale of goods   **A–086**
by implication of law, it may be negatived or varied by express agreement, or by
the course of dealing between the parties, or by such usage as binds both parties
to the contract, but the preceding provision has effect subject to the following
provisions of this section.

(2) An express condition or warranty does not negative a condition or warranty
implied by this Act unless inconsistent with it.

(3) In the case of a contract of sale of goods, any term of that or any other
contract exempting from all or any of the provisions of section 12 above is
void.

(4) In the case of a contract of sale of goods, any term of that or any other
contract exempting from all or any of the provisions of section 13, 14 or 15 above
is void in the case of a consumer sale and is, in any other case, not enforceable to
the extent that it is shown that it would not be fair or reasonable to allow reliance
on the term.

(5) In determining for the purposes of subsection (4) above whether or not
reliance on any such term would be fair or reasonable regard shall be had to all
the circumstances of the case and in particular to the following matters –

(a) the strength of the bargaining positions of the seller and buyer relative to
each other, taking into account, among other things, the availability of
suitable alternative products and sources of supply;

(b) whether the buyer received an inducement to agree to the term or in
accepting it had an opportunity of buying the goods or suitable alternatives
without it from any source of supply;

(c) whether the buyer knew or ought reasonably to have known of the existence and extent of the term (having regard, among other things, to any
custom of the trade and any previous course of dealing between the parties);

(d) where the term exempts from all or any of the provisions of section 13, 14
or 15 above if some condition is not complied with, whether it was reasonable at the time of the contract to expect that compliance with that condition
would be practicable;

(e) whether the goods were manufactured, processed, or adapted to the special
order of the buyer.

(6) Subsection (5) above does not prevent the court from holding, in accordance
with any rule of law, that a term which purports to exclude or restrict any of the
provisions of section 13, 14 or 15 above is not a term of the contract.

(7) In this section "consumer sale" means a sale of goods (other than a sale by
auction or by competitive tender) by a seller in the course of a business where the
goods—

(a) are of a type ordinarily bought for private use or consumption; and

(b) are sold to a person who does not buy or hold himself out as buying them
in the course of a business.

(8) The onus of proving that a sale falls to be treated for the purposes of this section as not being a consumer sale lies on the party so contending.

(9) Any reference in this section to a term exempting from all or any of the provisions of any section of this Act is a reference to a term which purports to exclude or restrict, or has the effect of excluding or restricting, the operation of all or any of the provisions of that section, or the exercise of a right conferred by any provision of that section, or any liability of the seller for breach of a condition or warranty implied by any provision of that section.

(10) It is hereby declared that any reference in this section to a term of a contract includes a reference to a term which although not contained in a contract is incorporated in the contract by another term of the contract.

(11) Nothing in this section prevents the parties to a contract for the international sale of goods from negativing or varying any right, duty or liability which would otherwise arise by implication of law under sections 12 to 15 above.

(12) In subsection (11) above "contract for the international sale of goods" means a contract of sale of goods made by parties whose places of business (or, if they have none, habitual residences) are in the territories of different States (the Channel Islands and the Isle of Man being treated for this purpose as different States from the United Kingdom) and in the case of which one of the following conditions is satisfied:—

(a) the contract involves the sale of goods which are at the time of the conclusion of the contract in the course of carriage or will be carried from the territory of one State to the territory of another; or

(b) the acts constituting the offer and acceptance have been effected in the territories of different States; or

(c) delivery of the goods is to be made in the territory of a State other than that within whose territory the acts constituting the offer and the acceptance have been effected.

Section 55: exclusion of implied terms (ii)

A–087   12. In relation to a contract made before 18 May 1973 substitute the following for section 55:—

55. Exclusion of implied terms
A–088   Where a right, duty or liability would arise under a contract of sale by implication of law, it may be negatived or varied by express agreement, or by the course of dealing between the parties, or by such usage as binds both parties to the contract.

Section 56: conflict of laws

A–089   13. (1) In relation to a contract on or after 18 May 1973 and before 1 February 1978 substitute for section 56 the section set out in sub-paragraph (3) below.

(2) In relation to a contract made otherwise than as mentioned in sub-paragraph (1) above, ignore section 56 and this paragraph.

(3) The section mentioned in sub-paragraph (1) above is as follows–

56. Conflict of laws
A–090   (1) Where the proper law of a contract for the sale of goods would, apart from a term that it should be the law of some other country or a term to the like effect,

be the law of any part of the United Kingdom, or where any such contract contains a term which purports to substitute, or has the effect of substituting, provisions of the law of some other country for all or any of the provisions of sections 12 to 15 and 55 above, those sections shall, notwithstanding that term but subject to subsection (2) below, apply to the contract.

(2) Nothing in subsection (1) above prevents the parties to a contract for the international sale of goods from negativing or varying any right, duty or liability which would otherwise arise by implication of law under sections 12 to 15 above.

(3) In subsection (2) above "contract for the international sale of goods" means a contract of sale of goods made by parties whose places of business (or, if they have none, habitual residences) are in the territories of different States (the Channel Islands and the Isle of Man being treated for this purpose as different States from the United Kingdom) and in the case of which one of the following conditions is satisfied:—

(a) the contract involves the sale of goods which are at the time of the conclusion of the contract in the course of carriage or will be carried from the territory of one State to the territory of another; or

(b) the acts constituting the offer and acceptance have been effected in the territories of different States; or

(c) delivery of the goods is to be made in the territory of a State other than that within whose territory the acts constituting the offer and the acceptance have been effected.

Section 61(1): *definition of "business"* (i)

14. In relation to a contract made on or after 18 May 1973 and before 1 February **A–091** 1978, in the definition of "business" in section 61(1) for "or local or public authority" substitute "local authority or statutory undertaker".

Section 61(1): *definition of "business"* (ii)

15. In relation to a contract made before 18 May 1973 omit the definition of **A–092** "business" in section 61(1).

[Schedules 2–4 (consequential amendments, repeals and savings) are not set out].

INCOTERMS 2000

B–001 *[Footnotes are the author's—the footnotes in the original all refer back to introductory documentation. Only the f.o.b. and c.i.f. trade terms are set out here.]*

FOB
FREE ON BOARD
(. . . named port of shipment)

B–002 "Free on Board" means that the seller fulfils his obligation to deliver when the goods passed the ship's rail at the port of shipment. This means that the buyer has to bear all costs and risks of loss of or damage to the goods from that point. The FOB term requires the seller to clear the goods for export.[1] This term can only be used for sea and inland waterway transport. If the parties do not intend to deliver the goods across the ship's rail,[2] the FCA term is more appropriate to use.

A   THE SELLER'S OBLIGATIONS

A1   Provision of goods in conformity with the contract

B–003 The seller must provide the goods and the commercial invoice, or its equivalent electronic message, in conformity with the contract of sale and any other evidence of conformity which may be required by the contract.

A2   Licences, authorisations and formalities

B–004 The seller must obtain at his own risk and expense any export licence or other official authorisation and carry out, where applicable, all customs formalities necessary for the exportation of the goods.

A3   Contract of carriage and insurance

B–005 a) Contract of carriage
No obligation.

---

[1] *cf. Pound v. Hardy,* in para. 3–047, above; the common law position is extremely uncertain, making it desirable for the parties to state. The Incoterms position is suitable for an export sale, whereas the reverse would be true of a domestic supply contract, as in *Brandt v. Morris,* also in para. 3–046, above.
[2] As in roll-on, roll-off vessels, container ships, and the like.

b) Contract of insurance
No obligation.

A4 Delivery

The seller must deliver the goods on the date or within the agreed period **B–006** at the named port of shipment and in the manner customary at the port on board the vessel nominated by the buyer.

A5 Transfer of risks

The seller must, subject to the provisions of B5, bear all risks of loss of or **B–007** damage to the goods until such time as they have passed the ship's rail at the named port of shipment.

A6 Division of costs

The seller must, subject to the provisions of B6, pay **B–008**

* all costs relating to the goods until such time as they have passed the ship's rail at the named port of shipment; and

* where applicable, the costs of customs formalities necessary for exportation as well as all duties, taxes and other official charges payable upon export.

A7 Notice to the buyer

The seller must give the buyer sufficient notice that the goods have been **B–009** delivered in accordance with A4.

A8 Proof of delivery, transport document or equivalent electronic message

The seller must provide the buyer at the seller's expense with the usual **B–010** proof of delivery in accordance with A4.

Unless the document referred to in the preceding paragraph is the transport document, the seller must render the buyer, at the latter's request, risk and expense, every assistance in obtaining a transport document for the contract of carriage (for example, a negotiable bill of lading, a non-negotiable sea waybill, an inland waterway document, or a multimodal transport document).

Where the seller and the buyer have agreed to communicate electronically, the document referred to in the preceding paragraphs may be replaced by an equivalent electronic interchange (EDI) message.

A9 Checking—packaging—marking

The seller must pay the costs of those checking operations (such as checking **B–011** quality, measuring, weighing, counting) which are necessary for the purpose of delivering the goods in accordance with A4.

The seller must provide at his own expense packaging (unless it is usual for the particular trade to ship the goods of the contract description unpacked) which is required for the transport of the goods, to the extent that the circumstances relating to the transport (for example, modalities, destination) are made known to the seller before the contract of sale is concluded. Packaging is to be marked appropriately.

A10 Other obligations

B–012

The seller must render the buyer at the latter's request, risk and expense, every assistance in obtaining any documents or equivalent electronic messages (other than those mentioned in A8) issued or transmitted in the country of shipment and/or of origin which the buyer may require for the import of the goods and, where necessary, for their transit through any country.

The seller must provide the buyer, upon request, with the necessary information for procuring insurance.[3]

B THE BUYER'S OBLIGATIONS

B1 Payment of the price

B–013

The buyer must pay the price as provided in the contract of sale.

B2 Licences, authorizations and formalities

B–014

The buyer must obtain at his own risk and expense any import licence or other official authorisation and carry out, where applicable, all customs formalities for the importation of the goods and, where necessary, for their transit through any country.

B3 Contracts of carriage and insurance

B–015

a) Contract of carriage
The buyer must contract at his own expense for the carriage of the goods from the named port of shipment.[4]

b) Contract of insurance
No obligation.[5]

B4 Taking delivery

B–016

The buyer must take delivery of the goods when they have been delivered in accordance with A4.

[3] This provision is similar to s.32(3) of the Sale of Goods Act 1979, considered in para. 4–022, above, but *Wimble v. Rosenberg*, also discussed there, suggests that the buyer will typically have the necessary information.
[4] This is, therefore, a contract of the third *Pyrene v. Scindia* variety, as discussed in para. 3–004, above.
[5] Unlike c. & f., where there is a positive obligation on the buyer. It is assumed with a c. & f. contract that the seller will retain a security interest in the goods after shipment, but in cases such as *Concordia v. Richco* in para. 6–087, above, that can also be true in an f.o.b. contract.

B5 Transfer of risks

The buyer must bear all risks of loss of or damage to the goods   **B–017**

- from the time they have passed the ship's rail at the port of shipment; and

- from the agreed date or the expiry date of the agreed period for delivery which arise because he fails to give notice in accordance with B7, or because the vessel nominated by him fails to arrive on time, or is unable to take the goods, or closes for cargo earlier than the time notified in accordance with B7, provided, however, that the goods have been duly appropriated to the contract, that is to say, clearly set aside or otherwise identified as the contract goods.[6]

B6 Division of costs

The buyer must pay   **B–018**

- all costs relating to the goods from the time they have passed the ship's rail at the named port of shipment; and

- any additional costs incurred, either because the vessel named by him fails to arrive on time, or is unable to take the goods, or closes for cargo earlier than the time notified in accordance with B7, or because the buyer has failed to give appropriate notice in accordance with B7, provided, however, that the goods have been duly appropriated to the contract, that is to say, clearly set aside or otherwise identified as the contract goods; and

- where applicable, all duties, taxes and other charges as well as the costs of carrying out customs formalities payable upon import of the goods and for their transit through any country.

B7 Notice to the seller

The buyer must give the seller sufficient notice of the vessel name, loading   **B–019**
point and required delivery time.

B8 Proof of delivery, transport document or equivalent electronic message

The buyer must accept the proof of delivery in accordance with A8.   **B–020**

B9 Inspection of goods

The buyer must pay the costs of any pre-shipment inspection except when   **B–021**
such inspection is mandated by the authorities of the country of export.

B10 Other obligations

The buyer must pay all costs and charges incurred in obtaining the docu-   **B–022**
ments or equivalent electronic messages mentioned in A10 and reimburse
those incurred by the seller in rendering his assistance in accordance
therewith.

---

[6] This provision bears some similarities with *J & J Cunningham v. Munro*, in para. 4–040, above.

CIF
COST INSURANCE AND FREIGHT
(. . . named port of destination)

B–023   "Cost, Insurance and Freight" means that the seller delivers when the goods pass the ship's rail in the port of shipment.

The seller must pay the costs and freight necessary to bring the goods to the named port of destination BUT the risk of loss of or damage to the goods, as well as any additional costs due to events occurring after the time of delivery, are transferred from the seller to the buyer. However, in CIF the seller also has to procure marine insurance against the buyer's risk of loss of or damage to the goods during the carriage.

Consequently the seller contracts for insurance and pays the insurance premium. The buyer should note that under the CIF term the seller is only required to obtain insurance on minimum cover.[7] Should the buyer wish to have the protection of greater cover, he would either need to agree as much expressly with the seller or to make his own extra insurance arrangements.

The CIF term requires the seller to clear the goods for export.

This term can only be used for sea and inland waterway transport. If the parties do not intend to deliver the goods across the ship's rail,[8] the CIP term should be used instead.

A   THE SELLER'S OBLIGATIONS

A1   Provision of goods in conformity with the contract

B–024   The seller must provide the goods and the commercial invoice, or its equivalent electronic message, in conformity with the contract of sale and any other evidence of conformity which may be required by the contract.

A2   Licences, authorisations and formalities

B–025   The seller must obtain at his own risk and expense any export licence or other official authorisation and carry out, where applicable, all customs formalities necessary for the export of the goods.

A3   Contract of carriage and insurance

B–026   a) Contract of carriage
The seller must contract on the usual terms at his own expense for the carriage of the goods to the named port of destination by the usual route in a seagoing vessel (or inland waterway vessel as the case may be) of the type normally used for the transport of goods of the contract description.

---

[7] Compare the common law position, discussed in para. 6–113, above.
[8] As in the case of roll-on/roll-off or container traffic.

b) Contract of insurance

The seller must obtain at his own expense cargo insurance as agreed in the contract, that the buyer, or any other person having an insurable interest in the goods, shall be entitled to claim directly from the insurer and provide the buyer with the insurance policy or other evidence of insurance cover.[9]

The insurance shall be contracted with underwriters or an insurance company of good repute and, failing express agreement to the contrary, be in accordance with minimum cover of the institute Cargo Clauses (Institute of London Underwriters) or any similar set of clauses. The duration of insurance cover shall be in accordance with B5 and B4. When required by the buyer, the seller shall provide at the buyer's expense war, strikes, riots and civil commotion risk insurances if procurable. The minimum insurance shall cover the price provided in the contract plus ten per cent (*i.e.* 110%) and shall be provided in the currency of the contract.

A4 Delivery

The seller must deliver the goods on board the vessel at the port of shipment on the date or within the agreed period. **B–027**

A5 Transfer of risks

The seller must, subject to the provisions of B5, bear all risks of loss of or damage to the goods until such time as they have passed the ship's rail at the port of shipment. **B–028**

A6 Division of costs

The seller must, subject to the provisions of B6, pay **B–029**

- all costs relating to the goods until they have been delivered in accordance with A4; and

- the freight and all other costs resulting from A3 a), including costs of loading the goods on board; and

- the costs of insurance resulting from A3 b); and

- any charges for unloading at the port of discharge which were for the seller's account under the contract of carriage; and

- where applicable, the costs of customs formalities necessary for export as well as all duties, taxes and other official charges payable upon export, and for their transit through any country if they were for the seller's account under the contract of carriage.

---

[9] Compare the common law position in para. 6–108, above.

A7 Notice to the buyer

B–030 The seller must give the buyer sufficient notice that the goods have been delivered in accordance with A4 as well as any other notice required in order to allow the buyer to take measures which are normally necessary to enable him to take the goods.

A8 Proof of delivery, transport document or equivalent electronic message

B–031 The seller must, at his own expense, provide the buyer without delay with the usual transport document for the agreed port of destination.

This document (for example, a negotiable bill of lading, a non-negotiable sea waybill or an inland waterway document) must cover the contract goods, be dated within the period agreed for shipment, enable the buyer to claim the goods from the carrier at destination and, unless otherwise agreed, enable the buyer to sell the goods in transit by the transfer of document to a subsequent buyer (the negotiable bill of lading) or by notification to the carrier.[10]

When such a transport document is issued in several originals, a full set of originals must be presented to the buyer.[11]

Where the seller and the buyer have agreed to communicate electronically, the document referred to in the preceding paragraphs may be replaced by an equivalent electronic data interchange (EDI) message.

A9 Checking—packaging—marking

B–032 The seller must pay the costs of those checking operations (such as checking quality, measuring, weighing, counting) which are necessary for the purpose of delivering the goods in accordance with A4.

The seller must provide at his own expense packaging (unless it is usual for the particular trade to ship the goods of the contract description unpacked) which is required for the transport of the goods arranged by him. Packaging is to be marked appropriately.

A10 Other obligations

The seller must render the buyer at the latter's request, risk and expense, every assistance in obtaining any documents or equivalent electronic messages (other than those mentioned in A8) issued or transmitted in the country of shipment and/or of origin which the buyer may require for the

---

[10] The method conceived for the C.M.I. electronic bill lading discussed in paras 16–030 *et seq.*, above. It now seems more likely that Bolero will be adopted, in preference to C.M.I., in which case title changes are recorded on a register. The carrier will be able to check the register, so this may also count as notification to the carrier.

[11] The 1990 revision also required that "If the transport document contains reference to a charter party, the seller must also provide a copy of this latter document." The dropping of this requirement mirrors the changes to U.C.P. 500 in 1993 (see para. 6–113, above).

import of the goods and, where necessary, for their transit through any country.

The seller must provide the buyer, upon request, with the necessary information for procuring any additional insurance.[12]

B. THE BUYER'S OBLIGATIONS

B1 Payment of the price

The buyer must pay the price as provided in the contract of sale.   **B–033**

B2 Licences, authorisations and formalities

The buyer must obtain at his own risk and expense any import licence or other official authorisation and carry out, where applicable, all customs formalities for the import of the goods and for their transit through any country.   **B–034**

B3 Contracts of carriage and insurance

a) Contract of carriage
No obligation.
b) Contract of insurance
No obligation.   **B–035**

B4 Taking delivery

The buyer must accept delivery of the goods when they have been delivered in accordance with A4 and receive them from the carrier at the named port of destination.   **B–036**

B5 Transfer of risks

The buyer must bear all risks of loss of or damage to the goods from the time they have passed the ship's rail at the port of shipment.   **B–037**

The buyer must, should he fail to give notice in accordance with B7, bear all risks of loss of or damage to the goods from the agreed date or the expiry date of the period fixed for shipment provided, however, that the goods have been duly appropriated to the contract, that is to say, clearly set aside or otherwise identified as the contract goods.

B6 Division of costs

The buyer must, subject to the provisions of A3, pay   **B–038**

- all costs relating to the goods from the time they have been delivered in accordance with A4; and

---

[12] *e.g.* war risks—see also the discussion in para. 4–027 and para. 6–113, above.

- all costs and charges relating to the goods whilst in transit until their arrival at the port of destination, unless such costs and charges were for the seller's account under the contract of carriage; and

- unloading costs including lighterage and wharfage charges, unless such costs and charges were for the seller's account under the contract of carriage; and

- all additional costs incurred if he fails to give notice in accordance with B7, for the goods from the agreed date or the expiry date of the period fixed for shipment, provided, however, that the goods have been duly appropriated to the contract, that is to say, clearly set aside or otherwise identified as the contract goods.

- where applicable, all duties, taxes and other charges as well as the costs of carrying out customs formalities payable upon import of the goods and, where necessary, for their transit through any country unless included within the contract of carriage.

B7 Notice to the seller

B–039

The buyer must, whenever he is entitled to determine the time for shipping the goods and/or the port of destination, give the seller sufficient notice thereof.

B8 Proof of delivery, transport document or equivalent electronic message

The buyer must, accept the transport document in accordance with A8 if it is in conformity with the contract.

B9 Inspection of goods

B–040

The buyer must pay the costs of pre-shipment inspection except when mandated by the authorities of the country of export.

B10 Other obligations

The buyer must pay all costs and charges incurred in obtaining the documents or equivalent electronic messages mentioned in A10 and reimburse those incurred by the seller in rendering his assistance in accordance therewith.

The buyer must provide the seller, upon request, with the necessary information for procuring insurance.

Appendix C

UNIFORM CUSTOMS AND PRACTICE ON DOCUMENTARY CREDITS (1993 REVISION) OF THE INTERNATIONAL CHAMBER OF COMMERCE

A. GENERAL PROVISIONS AND DEFINITIONS

Article 1

Application of the UCP

The Uniform Customs and Practice for Documentary Credits, 1994 Revision,   **C–001**
Publication No. 500, shall apply to all documentary credits (including to the
extent to which they may be applicable standby letters of credit), where they are
incorporated into the text of the credit. They are binding on all parties thereto
unless otherwise expressly stipulated in the credit.

Article 2

Meaning of Credit

For the purposes of these articles, the expressions "documentary credit(s)" and   **C–002**
"standby letter(s) of credit" (hereinafter referred to as "Credit(s)"), mean any
arrangement, however named or described, whereby a bank (the "Issuing Bank")
acting at the request and on the instructions of a customer (the "Applicant") or on
its own behalf,

    i. is to make a payment to or to the order of a third party (the "Beneficiary"),
       or is to accept and pay bills of exchange ("Draft(s)") drawn by the Benefi-
       ciary,
       or

    ii. authorizes another bank to effect such payment, or accept and pay such
       bills of exchange (Draft(s)),
       or

    iii. authorizes another bank to negotiate,

against stipulated document(s), provided that the terms and conditions of the
Credit are complied with.
For the purposes of these articles, branches of a bank in different countries are
considered another bank.

Article 3

Credits v. Contracts

C–003   a. Credits, by their nature, are separate transactions from the sales or other contract(s) on which they may be based and banks are in no way concerned with or bound by such contract(s), even if any reference whatsoever to such contract(s) is included in the credit. Consequently, the undertaking of a bank to pay, accept and pay Draft(s) or negotiate and/or to fulfil any other obligation under the Credit is not subject to claims or defences by the Applicant resulting from his relationships with the Issuing Bank or the Beneficiary.

   b. A Beneficiary can in no case avail himself of the contractual relationships existing between the banks or between the Applicant and the Issuing Bank.

Article 4

Documents v. Goods/Services/Performance

C–004   In credit operations all parties concerned deal with documents, and not with goods, services and/or other performances to which the documents may relate.

Article 5

Instructions to Issue/Amend credits

C–005   a. Instructions for the issuance of a Credit, the Credits itself, instructions for an amendment thereto and the amendment itself must be complete and precise.

   In order to guard against confusion and misunderstanding, banks should discourage any attempt:

   i. to include excessive detail in the credit or in any amendment thereto;

   ii. to give instructions to issue, advise or confirm a Credit by reference to a Credit previously issued (similar Credit) where such a previous Credit has been subject to accepted amendment(s), and/or unaccepted amendment(s).

   b. All instructions for the issuance of a Credit and the Credit itself and, where applicable, all instructions for an amendment thereto and the amendment itself, must state precisely the document(s) against which payment, acceptance or negotiation is to be made.

A beneficiary can in no case avail himself of the contractual relationship existing between the banks or between the applicant for the credit and the issuing bank.

B.   FORM AND NOTIFICATION OF CREDITS

Article 6

Revocable v. Irrevocable Credits

C–006   a. A Credit may be either

   i. revocable,

or

ii. irrevocable.

b. The Credit, therefore, should clearly indicate whether it is revocable or irrevocable.

c. In the absence of such indication the Credit shall be deemed to be irrevocable.

Article 7

Advising Bank's Liability

a. A Credit may be advised to a beneficiary through another bank (the "Advising Bank") without engagement on the part of the Advising Bank, but that bank, if it elects to advise the Credit, shall take reasonable care to check the apparent authenticity of the Credit which it advises. If the bank elects not to advise the Credit, it must so inform the Issuing Bank without delay.   **C–007**

b. If the Advising Bank cannot establish such apparent authenticity it must inform, without delay, the bank from which the instructions appear to have been received that it has been unable to establish the authenticity of the Credit and if it elects nonetheless to advise the Credit it must inform the beneficiary that it has not been able to establish the authenticity of the Credit.

Article 8

Revocation of a Credit

a. A revocable Credit may be amended or cancelled by the Issuing Bank at any moment and without prior notice to the beneficiary.   **C–008**

b. However, the Issuing Bank must:

i. reimburse another bank with which a revocable Credit has been made available for sight payment, acceptance or negotiation—for any payment, acceptance or negotiation made by such bank—prior to receipt by it of notice of amendment or cancellation, against documents which appear on their face to be in accordance with the terms and conditions of the Credit.

ii. reimburse another bank with which a revocable Credit has been made available for deferred payment, if such bank has, prior to receipt by it of notice of amendment or cancellation, taken up documents which appear on their face to be in accordance with the terms and conditions of the Credit.

Article 9

Liability of Issuing and Confirming Bank

a. An irrevocable Credit constitutes a definite undertaking of the Issuing Bank, provided that the stipulated documents are presented to the Nominated Bank or to the Issuing Bank and that the terms and conditions of the credit are complied with: **C–009**

    i. if the Credit provides for sight payment—to pay at sight;

    ii. if the Credit provides for deferred payment—to pay on the maturity date(s) determinable in accordance with the stipulations of the Credit;

    iii. if the Credit provides for acceptance:

        a. by the Issuing Bank—to accept Draft(s) drawn by the Beneficiary on the Issuing Bank and pay them at maturity,
        or

        b. by another drawee bank—to accept and pay at maturity Draft(s) drawn by the Beneficiary on the Issuing Bank in the event the drawee bank stipulated in the Credit does not accept the Draft(s) drawn on it, or to pay Draft(s) accepted but not paid by such drawee bank at maturity.

    iv. if the Credit provides for negotiation—to pay, without recourse, to drawers and/or bona fide holders, Draft(s) drawn by the Beneficiary and/or document(s) presented under the Credit. A Credit should not be issued available by Draft(s) on the Applicant. If the Credit nevertheless calls for a Draft(s) on the Applicant, banks will consider such Draft(s) as an additional document(s).

b. A confirmation of an irrevocable Credit by another bank (the "Confirming Bank") upon the authorization or request of the Issuing Bank constitutes a definite undertaking of the Confirming Bank, in addition to that of the Issuing Bank, provided that the stipulated documents are presented to the Confirming Bank or to any other Nominated Bank and that the terms and conditions of the credit are complied with:

    i. if the Credit provides for sight payment—to pay at sight;

    ii. if the Credit provides for deferred payment—to pay on the maturity date(s) determinable in accordance with the stipulations of the Credit;

    iii. if the Credit provides for acceptance:

        a. by the Confirming Bank—to accept Draft(s) drawn by the Beneficiary on the Confirming Bank and pay them at maturity,
        or

        b. by another drawee bank—to accept and pay at maturity Draft(s) drawn by the Beneficiary on the Confirming Bank in the event the drawee bank stipulated in the Credit does not accept the Draft(s) drawn on it, or to pay Draft(s) accepted but not paid by such drawee bank at maturity;

    iv. if the Credit provides for negotiation—to negotiate, without recourse, to drawers and/or bona fide holders, Draft(s) drawn by the Beneficiary and/or document(s) presented under the Credit. A Credit should not be issued available by Draft(s) on the Applicant. If the Credit nevertheless calls for a Draft(s) on the applicant, banks will consider such Draft(s) as an additional document(s).

c.   **i.** If another bank is authorized or requested by the Issuing Bank to add its confirmation to a Credit but is not prepared to do so, it must so inform the Issuing Bank without delay.

    ii. Unless the Issuing Bank specifies otherwise in its authorization or request to add confirmation, the Advising Bank may advise the Credit to the Beneficiary without adding its confirmation.

d. i. Except as otherwise provided by Article 48, an irrevocable Credit can neither be amended nor cancelled without the agreement of the Issuing Bank, the Confirming Bank, if any, and the Beneficiary.

ii. The Issuing Bank shall be irrevocably bound by an amendment(s) issued by it from the time of the issuance of such amendment(s). A Confirming Bank may extend its confirmation to an amendment and shall be irrevocably bound as of the time of its advice of the amendment. A Confirming Bank may, however, choose to advise an amendment to the Beneficiary without extending its confirmation and if so it must so inform the Issuing Bank and the Beneficiary without delay.

iii. The terms of the original Credit (or a Credit incorporating previously accepted amendment(s)) will remain in force for the Beneficiary until the Beneficiary communicates his acceptance of the amendment to the bank that advised such amendment. The Beneficiary should give notification of acceptance or rejection of amendment(s). If the Beneficiary fails to give such notification, the tender of documents, to the Nominated Bank or Issuing Bank, that conform to the Credit and not yet accepted amendment(s) will be deemed to be notification of acceptance by the Beneficiary of such amendment(s) and as of that moment the Credit will be amended.

iv. Partial acceptance of amendments contained in one and the same advice of amendment is not allowed and consequently will not be given any effect.

Article 10

Types of Credit

a. All credits must clearly indicate whether they are available by sight payment, by deferred payment, by acceptance or by negotiation.   **C–010**

b. i. Unless the Credit stipulates that it is available only with the Issuing Bank, all credits must nominate the bank (the "Nominated Bank") which is authorized to pay, to incur a deferred payment undertaking, to accept Draft(s) or to negotiate. In a freely negotiable Credit, and bank is a Nominated Bank.

ii. Negotiation means the giving of value for Draft(s) and/or document(s) by the bank authorized to negotiate. Mere examination of the documents without giving value does not constitute a negotiation.

c. Unless the Nominated Bank is the Confirming Bank, nomination by the Issuing Bank does not constitute any undertaking by the Nominated Bank to pay, to incur a deferred payment undertaking, to accept Draft(s) or to negotiate. Except where expressly agreed to by the Nominated Bank and so communicated to the Beneficiary, the Nominated Bank's receipt and/or examination of the documents does not make that bank liable to pay, to incur a deferred payment undertaking, to accept Draft(s) or to negotiate.

d. By nominating another bank, or by allowing for negotiation by any bank, or by authorizing or requesting another bank to add its confirmation, the Issuing Bank authorizes such bank to pay, accept Draft(s) or negotiate as the case may be, against documents which appear on their face to be in compliance with the terms and conditions of the credit and undertakes to reimburse such bank in accordance with the provisions of these articles.

Article 11

Tele-transmitted and Pre-Advised Credits

C–011   a. i. When an Issuing Bank instructs an Advising Bank by an authenticated teletransmission to advise a Credit or an amendment to a Credit, the teletransmission will be deemed to be the operative Credit instrument or the operative amendment, and no mail confirmation should be sent. Should a mail confirmation nevertheless be sent, it will have no effect and the Advising Bank will have no obligation to check such mail confirmation against the operative Credit instrument or the operative amendment received by teletransmission.

ii. If the teletransmission states "full details to follow" (or words of similar effect), or states that the mail confirmation is to be the operative Credit instrument or the operative amendment, then the teletransmission will not be deemed to be the operative Credit instrument or the operative amendment. The issuing bank must forward the operative Credit instrument or the operative amendment to such Advising Bank without delay.

b. If a bank uses the services of an Advising Bank to have the credit advised to the Beneficiary, it must also use the services of the same banks for advising any amendment(s).

c. A preliminary advice of the issuance or amendment of an irrevocable Credit (pre-advice) shall only be given by an Issuing Bank if such bank is prepared to issue the operative Credit instrument or the operative amendment thereto. Unless otherwise stated in such preliminary advice by the Issuing Bank, an Issuing Bank having given such pre-advice shall be irrevocably committed to issue and amend the Credit, in terms not inconsistent with the pre-advice, without delay.

Article 12

Incomplete or Unclear Instructions

C–012   If incomplete or unclear instructions are received to advise, confirm or amend a Credit, the bank requested to act on such instructions may give preliminary notification to the Beneficiary for information only and without responsibility. This preliminary notification should state clearly that the notification is provided for information only and without the responsibility of the Advising Bank. In any event the Advising Bank must inform the Issuing Bank of the action taken and request it to provide the necessary information.

The Issuing Bank must provide the necessary information without delay. The Credit will be advised, confirmed or amended only when complete and clear instructions have been received and if the Advising Bank is then prepared to act on the instructions.

C. LIABILITIES AND RESPONSIBILITIES

Article 13

Standard for Examination of Documents

C–013   a. Banks must examine all documents stipulated in the Credit with reasonable care to ascertain whether or not they appear on their face to be in compliance with the terms and conditions of the Credit. Compliance of the stipulated documents on their face with the terms and conditions of the Credit shall be determined by international standard banking practice as reflected in these Articles. Documents which appear on their face to be inconsistent with one another will be considered as not appearing on their face to be in accordance with the terms and conditions of the Credit.

Documents not stipulated in the Credit will not be examined by banks. If they receive such documents, they shall return them to the presenter or pass them on without responsibility.

b. The Issuing Bank, the Confirming Bank, if any, or a Nominated Bank acting on their behalf, shall each have a reasonable time, not to exceed seven banking days following the receipt of the documents, to examine the documents and determine whether to take up or to refuse the documents and inform the party from which it received the documents accordingly.

c. If a Credit contains conditions without stating the document(s) to be presented in compliance therewith, banks will deem such conditions as not stated and will disregard them.

Article 14

Discrepant Documents and Notice

a. When the Issuing Bank authorizes another bank to pay, incur a deferred payment undertaking, accept Draft(s), or negotiate against documents which appear on their face to be in compliance with the terms and conditions of the Credit, the Issuing Bank and the Confirming Bank, if any, are bound: **C–014**

    i. to reimburse the Nominated Bank which has paid, incurred a deferred payment undertaking, accepted Draft(s), or negotiated

    ii. to take up the documents.

b. Upon receipt of the documents the Issuing Bank and/or Confirming Bank, if any, or a Nominated Bank acting on their behalf, must determine on the basis of the documents alone whether or not they appear on their face not to be in compliance with the terms and conditions of the Credit. If the documents appear on their face not to be in accordance with the terms and conditions of the Credit such banks may refuse to take up the documents.

c. If the Issuing Bank determines that the documents appear, on their face, not to be in compliance with the terms and conditions of the Credit it may in its sole judgment approach the Applicant for a waiver of the discrepancy(ies). This does not, however, extend the period mentioned in Article 13 (b).

d. i. If the Issuing Bank and/or Confirming Bank, if any, or a Nominated Bank acting on their behalf, decides to refuse the documents, it must give notice to that effect by telecommunication or, if that is not possible, by other expeditious means, without delay but no later than the close of the seventh banking day following the day of receipt of the documents. Notice shall be given to the bank from which it received the documents, or to the Beneficiary, if it received the documents directly from him.

    ii. Such notice must state all discrepancies in respect of which the bank refuses the documents and must also state whether it is holding the documents at the disposal of, or is returning them to, the presentor.

    iii. The Issuing Bank and/or Confirming Bank, if any, shall then be entitled to claim from the remitting bank refund, with interest, of any reimbursement which may have been made to that bank.

  e. If the Issuing Bank and/or Confirming Bank, if any, fails to act in accordance with the provisions of this article and/or fails to hold the documents at the disposal of, or return them to the presentor, the Issuing Bank and/or Confirming Bank, if any, shall be precluded from claiming that the documents are not in compliance with the terms and conditions of the Credit.

  f. If the remitting bank draws the attention of the Issuing Bank and/or Confirming Bank, if any, to any discrepancy(ies) in the document(s) or advises such banks that it has paid, incurred a deferred payment undertaking, accepted Draft(s) or negotiated under reserve or against an indemnity in respect of such discrepancy(ies), the Issuing Bank and/or Confirming Bank, if any, shall not be thereby relieved from any of its obligations under any provisions of this article. Such reserve or indemnity concerns only the relations between the remitting bank and the party towards whom the reserve was made or from whom, or on whose behalf, the indemnity was obtained.

Article 15

Disclaimer on Effectiveness of Documents

C–015   Banks assume no liability or responsibility for the form, sufficiency, accuracy, genuineness, falsification or legal effect of any documents, or for the general and/or particular conditions stipulated in the document(s) or superimposed thereon; nor do they assume any liability or responsibility for the description, quantity, weight, quality, condition, packing, delivery, value or existence of the goods represented by any document(s), or for the good faith or acts and/or omissions, solvency, performance or standing of the consignor, the carriers, or the insurers of the goods or of any other person whomsoever.

Article 16

Disclaimer on the Transmission of Messages

C–016   Banks assume no liability or responsibility for the consequences arising out of delay and/or loss in transit of any message(s), letter(s) or document(s), or for delay, mutilation or other error(s) arising in the transmission of any telecommunication. Banks assume no liability or responsibility for errors in translation and/or interpretation of technical terms, and reserve the right to transmit Credit terms without translating them.

Article 17

Force Majeure

C–017   Banks assume no liability or responsibility for the consequences arising out of the interruption of their business by Acts of God, riots, civil commotions, insurrections, wars or any causes beyond their control, or by any strikes or lockouts. Unless specifically authorized, banks will not, upon resumption of their business, pay, incur a deferred payment undertaking, accept Draft(s) or negotiate under Credits which expired during such interruption of their business.

Article 18

a. Banks utilizing the services of another bank or other banks for the purpose   **C–018** of giving effect to the instructions of the Applicant do so for the account and at the risk of such Applicant.

b. Banks assume no liability or responsibility should the instructions they transmit not be carried out, even if they have themselves taken the initiative in the choice of such other bank(s).

c.   i. A party instructing another party to perform services is liable for any charges, including commissions, fees, costs or expenses incurred by the instructed party in connection with the instructions.

  ii. Where a Credit stipulates that such charges are for the account of a party other than the instructing party, and charges cannot be collected, the instructing party remains ultimately liable for the payment thereof.

d. The Applicant shall be bound by and be liable to indemnify the banks against all obligations and responsibilities imposed by foreign laws and usages.

Article 19

a. If an Issuing Bank intends that the reimbursement to which a paying,   **C–019** accepting or negotiating bank is entitled shall be obtained by such bank (the "Claiming Bank") claiming on another party (the "Reimbursing Bank") it shall provide such Reimbursing Bank in good time with proper instructions or authorization to honour such reimbursement claims.

b. Issuing Banks shall not require a Claiming Bank to supply a certificate of compliance with the terms and conditions of the Credit to the Reimbursing Bank.

c. An Issuing Bank shall not be relieved from any of its obligations to provide reimbursement itself if and when reimbursement is not received by the Claiming Bank from the Reimbursing Bank.

d. The Issuing Bank shall be responsible to the Claiming Bank for any loss of interest if reimbursement is not provided by the Reimbursing Bank on first demand, or as otherwise specified in the Credit, or mutually agreed, as the case may be.

e. Reimbursing Bank's charges should be for the account of the Issuing Bank. However in cases where the charges are for the account of another party it is the responsibility of the Issuing Bank to so indicate in the original Credit and in the reimbursement authorization. In cases where the Reimbursing Bank's charges are for the account of another party they shall be collected from the Claiming Bank when the Credit is drawn under. In cases where the Credit is not drawn under, the Reimbursing Bank's charges remain the obligation of the Issuing Bank.

D. DOCUMENTS

Article 20

Ambiguity as to the Issuers of Documents

C–020 **a.** Terms such as "first class", "well known", "qualified", "independent", "official", "competent", "local" and the like shall not be used to describe the issuers of any document(s) to be presented under a Credit. If such terms are incorporated in the Credit, banks will accept the relevant document(s) as presented, provided that it appears on its face to be in accordance with the other terms and conditions of the Credit and not to have been issued by the Beneficiary.

b. Unless otherwise stipulated in the Credit, banks will also accept as originals document(s) produced or appearing to have been produced:

    i. by reprographic, automated or computerized systems;

    ii. as carbon copies;

provided that it is marked as original and, where necessary, appears to be signed.
A document may be signed by handwriting, by facsimile signature, by perforated signature, by stamp, by symbol, or by any other mechanical or electronic method of authentication.

c. **i.** Unless otherwise stipulated in the Credit, banks will accept as a copy-(ies), a document(s) either labelled copy or not marked as an original and a copy(ies) need not be signed.

    ii. Credits that require multiple document(s) such as "duplicate", "two fold", "two copies" and the like, will be satisfied by the presentation of one original and the remaining number in copies except where the document itself indicates otherwise.

d. Unless otherwise stipulated in the Credit, a condition under a Credit calling for a document to be authenticated, validated, legalised, visaed, certified or indicating a similar requirement, will be satisfied by any signature, mark, stamp or label on such document that on its face appears to satisfy the above condition.

Article 21

Unspecified Issuers of Contents of Documents

C–021 When documents other than transport documents, insurance documents and commercial invoices are called for, the Credit should stipulate by whom such documents are to be issued and their wording or data content. If the Credit does not so stipulate, banks will accept such documents as presented, provided that their data content is not inconsistent with any other stipulated document presented.

Article 22

Issuance Date of Documents v. Credit Date

C–022 Unless otherwise stipulated in the Credit, banks will accept a document bearing a date of issuance prior to that of the Credit, subject to such document being presented within the time limits set out in the Credit and in these articles.

Article 23

Marine/Ocean Bill of Lading

a. If a Credit calls for a bill of lading covering port-to-port shipment, banks **C–023** will, unless otherwise stipulated in the Credit, accept a document, however named, which:

i. appears on its face to indicate the name of the carrier and to have been signed or otherwise authenticated by:

- the carrier or a named agent for or on behalf of the carrier, or
- the master or a named agent for or on behalf of the master.

Any signature or authentication of the carrier or master must be identified as carrier or master, as the case may be. An agent signing or authenticating for the carrier or master must also indicate the name and capacity of the party, *i.e.*, carrier or master, on whose behalf that agent is acting,
and

ii. indicates that the goods have been loaded on board, or shipped on a named vessel.
Loading on board or shipment on board a named vessel may be indicated by pre-printed wording on the bill of lading that the goods have been loaded on board a named vessel, in which case the date of issuance of the bill of lading will be deemed to be the date of loading on board, and the date of shipment.
In all other cases loading on board a named vessel must be evidenced by a notation on the bill of lading which gives the date on which the goods have been loaded on board, in which case the date of the on board notation will be deemed to be the date of shipment.

If the bill of lading contains the indication "intended vessel", or similar qualification in relation to the vessel, loading on board a named vessel must be evidenced by an on board notation on the bill of lading which, in addition to the date on which the goods have been loaded on board also includes the name of the vessel on which the goods have been loaded, even if they have been loaded on the vessel named as the "intended vessel".

If the bill of lading indicates a place of receipt or taking in charge different from the port of loading, the on board notation must also include the port of loading stipulated in the Credit and the name of the vessel on which the goods have been loaded, even if they have been loaded on the vessel named in the bill of lading. This provision also applies whenever loading on board the vessel is indicated by pre-printed wording on the bill of lading,
and

iii. indicates the port of loading and the port of discharge stipulated in the Credit, notwithstanding that it:

a. indicates a place of taking in charge different from the port of loading, and/or a place of final destination different from the port of discharge,
and/or

b. contains the indication "intended" or similar qualification, in relation to the port of loading and/or port of discharge, as long as the

document also states the ports of loading and/or discharge stipulated in the Credit.
and

   iv. consists of a sole original bill of lading or, if issued in more than one original, the full set as so issued,
and

   v. appears to contain all of the terms and conditions of carriage, or some of such terms and conditions by reference to a source of document other than the bill of lading (short form/blank back bill of lading) and banks will not examine the contents of such terms and conditions,
and

   vi. contains no indication that it is subject to a charter party and/or no indication that the carrying vessel is propelled by sail only,
and

   vii. in all other respects meets the stipulations of the Credit.

b. For the purpose of this article, transhipment means unloading and reloading from one vessel to another vessel during the course of ocean carriage from the port of loading to the port of discharge as stipulated in the Credit.

c. Unless transhipment is prohibited by the terms of the Credit, banks will accept a bill of lading which indicates that the goods will be transhipped, provided that the entire ocean carriage is covered by one and the same bill of lading.

d. Even if the Credit prohibits transhipment, banks will accept a bill of lading which:

   i. indicates that transhipment will take place as long as the relative cargo is shipped in Container(s), Trailer(s) and "LASH" barge(s) as evidenced by the bill of lading, provided that the entire ocean carriage is covered by one and the same bill of lading.
and/or

   ii. incorporates clauses stating that the carrier reserves the right to tranship.

Article 24

Non-Negotiable Sea Waybill

C–024   **a.** If a Credit calls for a non-negotiable sea waybill covering port-to-port shipment, banks will, unless otherwise stipulated in the Credit, accept a document, however named, which:

   i. appears on its face to indicate the name of the carrier and to have been signed or otherwise authenticated by:

     ● the carrier or a named agent for or on behalf of the carrier, or
     ● the master or a named agent for or on behalf of the master.

Any signature or authentication of the carrier or master must be identified as carrier or master, as the case may be. An agent signing or authenticating for the carrier or master must also indicate the name and capacity of the party, *i.e.,* carrier or master, on whose behalf that agent is acting,
and

ii. indicates that the goods have been loaded on board, or shipped on a named vessel.

Loading on board or shipment on board a named vessel may be indicated by pre-printed wording on the non-negotiable sea waybill that the goods have been loaded on board a named vessel, in which case the date of issuance of the non-negotiable sea waybill will be deemed to be the date of loading on board, and the date of shipment.

In all other cases loading on board a named vessel must be evidenced by a notation on the non-negotiable sea waybill which gives the date on which the goods have been loaded on board, in which case the date of the on board notation will be deemed to be the date of shipment.

If the non-negotiable sea waybill contains the indication "intended vessel", or similar qualification in relation to the vessel, loading on board a named vessel must be evidenced by an on board notation on the non-negotiable sea waybill which, in addition to the date on which the goods have been loaded on board also includes the name of the vessel on which the goods have been loaded, even if they have been loaded on the vessel named as the "intended vessel".

If the non-negotiable sea waybill indicates a place of receipt or taking in charge different from the port of loading, the on board notation must also include the port of loading stipulated in the Credit and the name of the vessel on which the goods have been loaded, even if they have been loaded on the vessel named in the non-negotiable sea waybill. This provision also applies whenever loading on board the vessel is indicated by pre-printed wording on the non-negotiable sea waybill, and

iii. indicates the port of loading and the port of discharge stipulated in the Credit, notwithstanding that it:

a. indicates a place of taking in charge different from the port of loading, and/or a place of final destination different from the port of discharge, and/or

b. contains the indication "intended" or similar qualification, in relation to the port of loading and/or port of discharge, as long as the document also states the ports of loading and/or discharge stipulated in the Credit. and

iv. consists of a sole original non-negotiable sea waybill or, if issued in more than one original, the full set as so issued, and

v. appears to contain all of the terms and conditions of carriage, or some of such terms and conditions by reference to a source of document other than the non-negotiable sea waybill (short form/blank back non-negotiable sea waybill) and banks will not examine the contents of such terms and conditions, and

vi. contains no indication that it is subject to a charter party and/or no indication that the carrying vessel is propelled by sail only, and

vii. in all other respects meets the stipulations of the Credit.

b. For the purpose of this article, transhipment means unloading and reloading from one vessel to another vessel during the course of ocean carriage from the port of loading to the port of discharge as stipulated in the Credit.

c. Unless transhipment is prohibited by the terms of the Credit, banks will accept a non-negotiable sea waybill which indicates that the goods will be transhipped, provided that the entire ocean carriage is covered by one and the same non-negotiable sea waybill.

d. Even if the Credit prohibits transhipment, banks will accept a non-negotiable sea waybill which:

i. indicates that transhipment will take place as long as the relative cargo is shipped in Container(s), Trailer(s) and "LASH" barge(s) as evidenced by the non-negotiable sea waybill, provided that the entire ocean carriage is covered by one and the same non-negotiable sea waybill. and/or

ii. incorporates clauses stating that the carrier reserves the right to tranship.

Article 25

Charter Party Bill of Lading

C–025   **a.** If a Credit calls for or permits a charter party bill of lading banks will, unless otherwise stipulated in the Credit, accept a document, however named, which:

i. contains any indication that it is subject to a charter party and

ii. appears on its face to indicate the name of the carrier and to have been signed or otherwise authenticated by:

- the master or a named agent for or on behalf of the master, or.
- the owner or a named agent for or on behalf of the owner.

Any signature or authentication of the master or owner must be identified as master or owner, as the case may be. An agent signing or authenticating for the carrier or master must also indicate the name and capacity of the party, *i.e.* master or owner, on whose behalf that agent is acting, and

iii. does or does not indicate the name of the carrier, and

iv. indicates that the goods have been loaded on board or shipped on a named vessel.

Loading on board or shipment on board a named vessel may be indicated by pre-printed wording on the bill of lading that the goods have been loaded on board a named vessel or shipped on a named vessel, in which case the date of issuance of the bill of lading will be deemed to be the date of loading on board, and the date of shipment.

In all other cases loading on board a named vessel must be evidenced by a notation on the bill of lading which gives the date on which the goods have been loaded on board, in which case the date of the on board notation will be deemed to be the date of shipment, and

     v. indicates the port of loading and the port of discharge stipulated in the Credit,
and

     vi. consists of a sole original bill of lading or, if issued in more than one original, the full set as so issued,
and

     vii. contains no indication that the carrying vessel is propelled by sail only,
and

     viii. in all other respects meets the stipulations of the Credit.

  b. Even if the Credit requires the presentation of a charter party contract in connection with a charter party bill of lading, banks will not examine such charter party contract, but will pass it on without responsibility on their part.

Article 26

Multimodal Transport Document

  a. If a Credit calls for a transport document covering at least two different   **C–026** modes of transport (multimodal transport), banks will, unless otherwise stipulated in the Credit, accept a document, however named, which:

     i. appears on its face to indicate the name of the carrier or multimodal transport operator and to have been signed or otherwise authenticated by:

- the carrier or multimodal transport operator or a named agent for or on behalf of the carrier or multimodal transport operator, or
- the master or a named agent for or on behalf of the master.

Any signature or authentication of the carrier, multimodal transport operator or master must be identified as carrier multimodal transport operator or master, as the case may be. An agent signing or authenticating for the carrier multimodal transport operator or master must also indicate the name and capacity of the party, *i.e.*, carrier multimodal transport operator or master, on whose behalf that agent is acting,
and

     ii. indicates that the goods have been dispatched, taken in charge or loaded on board.

Dispatch, taking in charge or loading on board may be indicated by wording to that effect on the multimodal transport document and the date of issuance will be deemed to be the date of dispatch, taking in charge or loading on board, and the date of shipment. However, if the document indicates, by stamp or otherwise, a date of dispatch, taking in charge or loading on board such date will be deeded to the date of shipment,
and

     iii. a. indicates the place of taking in charge stipulated in the Credit which may be different from the port, airport or place of loading, and the place of final destination which may be different from the port, airport or place of discharge,
and/or

    b. contains the indication "intended" or similar qualification, in relation to vessel and/or port of loading and/or port of discharge.
and

    iv. consists of a sole original multi-modal transport document or, if issued in more than one original, the full set as so issued,
and

    v. appears to contain all of the terms and conditions of carriage, or some of such terms and conditions by reference to a source of document other than the multi-modal transport document (short form/blank back multi-modal transport document) and banks will not examine the contents of such terms and conditions,
and

    vi. contains no indication that it is subject to a charter party and/or no indication that the carrying vessel is propelled by sail only,
and

    vii. in all other respects meets the stipulations of the Credit.

    b. Even if the Credit prohibits transhipment, banks will accept a multi-modal transport document which indicates that transhipment will or may take place, provided that the entire ocean carriage is covered by one and the same multi-modal transport document.

Article 27

Air Transport Document

C–027   **a.** If a Credit calls for an air transport document banks will, unless otherwise stipulated in the Credit, accept a document, however named, which:

    i. appears on its face to indicate the name of the carrier and to have been signed or otherwise authenticated by:

- the carrier, or
- a named agent for or on behalf of the carrier.

Any signature or authentication of the carrier must be identified as carrier. An agent signing or authenticating for the carrier must also indicate the name and capacity of the party, *i.e.*, carrier, on whose behalf that agent is acting,
and

    ii. indicates that the goods have been accepted for carriage,
and

    iii. where the Credit calls for an actual date of dispatch, indicates a specific notation of such date and the date of dispatch so indicated on the air transport document will be deemed to be the date of shipment.

For the purposes of this article, the information appearing in the box on the air transport document (marked "For Carrier Use Only" or similar expression) relative to the flight number and date will not be considered as a specific notation of such date of dispatch.

    iv. In all other cases, the date of issuance of the air transport document will be deemed to be the date of shipment.
and

v. indicates the airport of departure and the airport of destination stipulated in the Credit,
and

vi. appears to be the original for consignor/shipper even if the Credit stipulates a full set of originals, or similar expression,
and

vii. appears to contain all of the terms and conditions of carriage, or some of such terms and conditions by reference to a source of document other than the air transport document, and banks will not examine the contents of such terms and conditions,
and

viii. in all other respects meets the stipulations of the Credit.

b. For the purpose of this article, transhipment means unloading and reloading from one aircraft to another aircraft during the course of carriage from the airport of departure to the airport of destination as stipulated in the Credit.

c. Even if the Credit prohibits transhipment, banks will accept an air transport document which indicates that transhipment will or may take place, provided that the entire carriage is covered by one and the same air transport document.

Article 28

Road, Rail or Inland Waterway Transport Documents

a. If a Credit calls for a road, rail or inland waterway transport document banks will, unless otherwise stipulated in the Credit, accept a document of the type called for, however named, which: **C–028**

i. appears on its face to indicate the name of the carrier and to have been signed or otherwise authenticated by the carrier, or a named agent for or on behalf of the carrier.

Any signature, authentication, reception stamp or other indication of the carrier, must be identified on its face as that of the carrier. An agent signing or authenticating for the carrier, must also indicate the name and capacity of the party, *i.e.*, carrier, on whose behalf that agent is acting,
and

ii. indicates that the goods have been received for shipment, dispatch or carriage or wording to this effect. The date of issuance will be deemed to be the date of shipment unless the transport document contains a reception stamp in which case the date of the reception stamp will be deemed to be the date of shipment,
and

iii. indicates the place of shipment and the place of destination stipulated in the Credit,
and

iv. in all other respects meets the stipulations of the Credit.

b. In the absence of any indication on the transport document as to the numbers issued, banks will accept the transport document(s) presented as constituting a full set. Banks will accept as original(s) the transport document(s) whether marked as original(s) or not.

c. For the purpose of this article, transhipment means unloading and reloading from one means of conveyance to another means of conveyance, in different modes of transport, during the course of carriage from the place of shipment to the place of destination as stipulated in the Credit.

d. Even if the Credit prohibits transhipment, banks will accept an road, rail or inland waterway transport document which indicates that transhipment will or may take place, provided that the entire carriage is covered by one and the same transport document and within the same mode of transport.

Article 29

Courier and Post Receipts

C–029   a. If the credit calls for a post receipt or certificate of posting, banks will, unless otherwise indicated in the Credit, accept a post receipt or certificate of posting which:

     i. appears on its face to have been stamped or otherwise authenticated and dated in the place from which the Credit stipulates the goods are to be shipped or dispatched and such date will be deemed to be the date of shipment or dispatch,
and

     ii. in all other respects meets the stipulations of the Credit.

   b. If the credit calls for a document issued by a courier or expedited delivery service evidencing receipt of the goods for delivery, banks will, unless otherwise indicated in the Credit, accept a document, however named, which:

     i. appears on its face to indicate the name of the courier/service, and to have been stamped, signed or otherwise authenticated by such named courier/service (unless the Credit specifically calls for a document issued by a named Courier/Service, banks will accept a document issued by any Courier/Service),
and

     ii. indicates a date or pick-up or of receipt or wording to that effect, and such date will be deemed to be the date of shipment or dispatch,
and

     iii. in all other respects meets the stipulations of the Credit.

Article 30

Transport Documents issued by Freight Forwarders

C–030   Unless otherwise authorized in the Credit, banks will only accept a transport document issued by a freight forwarder if it appears on its face to indicate:

     i. the name of the freight forwarder as a carrier or multimodal transport operator and to have been signed or otherwise authenticated by the freight forwarder as carrier or multimodal transport operator
or

     ii. the name of the carrier or multimodal transport operator and to have been signed or otherwise authenticated by the freight forwarder as a named agent for or on behalf of the carrier or multimodal transport operator.

Article 31

"On Deck", "Shipper's Load and Count", Name of Consignor

Unless otherwise stipulated in the Credit, banks will accept a transport document   **C–031**
which:

    i. does not indicate, in the case of carriage by sea or by more that one conveyance including carriage by sea, that the goods are or will be loaded on deck. Nevertheless, banks will accept a transport document which contains a provision that the goods may be carried on deck, provided it does not specifically state that they are or will be loaded on deck,
      and/or

    ii. bears a clause on the face thereof such as "shippers load and count" or "said by shipper to contain" or words of similar effect,
      and/or

    iii. indicates as the consignor of the goods a party other than the Beneficiary of the Credit.

Article 32

Clean Transport Documents

    a. A clean transport document is one which bears no clause or notation which   **C–032** expressly declares a defective condition of the goods and/or the packaging.

    b. Banks will refuse transport documents bearing such clauses or notations unless the Credit expressly stipulates the clauses or notations which may be accepted.

    c. Banks will regard a requirement in a Credit for a transport document to bear the clause "clean on board" as complied with if such transport document meets the requirements of this Article and of Articles 23, 24, 25, 26, 27, 28 or 30.

Article 33

Freight Prepaid/Payable Transport Documents

    a. Unless otherwise stipulated in the Credit, or inconsistent with any of the   **C–033** documents presented under the Credit, banks will accept transport documents stating that freight or transportation charges (hereinafter referred to as "freight") have still to be paid.

    b. If a Credit stipulates that the transport document has to indicate that freight has been paid or prepaid, banks will accept a transport document on which words clearly indicating payment or prepayment of freight appear by stamp or otherwise, or on which payment of freight is indicated by other means. If the Credit requires courier charges to be paid or prepaid banks will accept a transport document issued by a courier or expedited delivery service evidencing that courier charges are for the account of a party other than the consignee.

c. The words "freight prepayable" or "freight to be prepaid" or words of similar effect, if appearing on transport documents, will not be accepted as constituting evidence of the payment of freight.

d. Banks will accept transport documents bearing reference by stamp or otherwise to costs additional to the freight, such as costs of, or disbursements incurred in connection with, loading, unloading or similar operations, unless the conditions of the Credit specifically prohibit such reference.

Article 34

Insurance Documents

C–034   a. Insurance documents must appear on their face to be issued and/or signed by insurance companies or underwriters or their agents.

b. If the insurance document indicates that it has been issued in more than one original, all the originals must be presented unless otherwise authorized by the Credit.

c. Cover notes issued by brokers will not be accepted, unless specifically authorized by the Credit.

d. Unless otherwise stipulated in the Credit, banks will accept an insurance certificate or a declaration under an open cover pre-signed by insurance companies or underwriters or their agents. If a Credit specifically calls for an insurance certificate or a declaration under an open cover, banks will accept, in lieu thereof, an insurance policy.

e. Unless otherwise stipulated in the Credit, or unless it appears from the insurance document(s) that the cover is effective at the latest from the date of loading on board or taking in charge of the goods, banks will refuse documents which bear a date later than the date of loading on board or dispatch or taking in charge of the goods as indicated by the transport document(s).

f.   i. Unless otherwise stipulated in the Credit, the insurance document must be expressed in the same currency as the Credit.

  ii. Unless otherwise stipulated in the Credit, the minimum amount for which the insurance document must indicate the insurance cover to have been effected is the CIF (cost, insurance and freight (. . . "named port of destination")) or CIP (carriage and insurance paid to freight (. . . "named port of destination")) value of the goods, as the case may be, plus 10%, but only when the CIF or CIP value can be determined from the documents on their face. Otherwise banks will accept as such minimum amount 110% of the amount for which payment, acceptance or negotiation is requested under the Credit, or 110% of the amount of the gross amount of the invoice, whichever is the greater.

Article 35

Type of Insurance Coverage

C–035   a. Credits should stipulate the type of insurance required and, if any, the additional risks which are to be covered. Imprecise terms such as "usual risks" or "customary risks" should not be used; if they are used, banks will accept insurance documents as presented, without responsibility for any risks not being covered.

b. Failing specific instructions, banks will accept insurance cover as presented, without responsibility for any risks not being covered.

c. Unless otherwise stipulated in the Credit, banks will accept an insurance document which indicates that the cover is subject to a franchise or an excess (deductible).

Article 36

All Risk Insurance Coverage

Where a Credit stipulates "insurance against all risks", banks will accept an insurance document which contains any "all risks" notation or clause, whether or not bearing the heading "all risks", even if the insurance document indicates that certain risks are excluded, without responsibility for any risk(s) not being covered. **C–036**

Article 37

Commercial Invoice

a. Unless otherwise stipulated in the Credit, commercial invoices: **C–037**

   i. must appear on their face to be issued by the Beneficiary named in the Credit (except as provided in Article 48), and

   ii. must be made out in the name of the Applicant, (except as provided in Article 48(h)), and

   iii. need not be signed.

b. Unless otherwise stipulated in the Credit, banks may not accept commercial invoices issued for amounts in excess of the amount permitted by the Credit. Nevertheless, if a bank authorized to pay, incur a deferred payment undertaking, accept Draft(s), or negotiate under a Credit accepts such invoices, its decision will be binding on all parties, provided such bank has not paid, incurred a deferred undertaking, accepted Draft(s) or negotiated for an amount in excess of that permitted by the Credit.

c. The description of the goods in the commercial invoice must correspond with the description in the Credit. In all other documents, the goods may be described in general terms not inconsistent with the description of the goods in the Credit.

Article 38

Other Documents

If a credit calls for an attestation or certification of weight in the case of transport other than by sea, banks will accept a weight stamp or declaration of weight which appears to have been superimposed on the transport document unless the **C–038**

Credit specifically stipulates that the attestation or certification of weight must be by a separate document.

E. MISCELLANEOUS PROVISIONS

Article 39

Allowances in Credit Amount, Quantity and Unit Prices

C–039   a. The words "about", "approximately", "circa" or similar expressions used in connection with the amount of the Credit or the quantity or the unit price stated in the Credit are to be construed as allowing a difference not to exceed 10% more or 10% less than the amount or the quantity or the unit price to which they refer.

b. Unless a Credit stipulates that the quantity of the goods specified must not be exceeded or reduced, a tolerance of 5% more or 5% less will be permissible, even if partial shipments are not permitted, always provided that the amount of the drawings does not exceed the amount of the Credit. This tolerance does not apply when the Credit stipulates the quantity in terms of a stated number of packing units or individual items.

c. Unless a Credit which prohibits partial shipments stipulates otherwise, or unless b. above is applicable, a tolerance of 5% less in the amount of the drawing will be permissible provided that if the Credit stipulates the quantity of the goods, such quantity is shipped in full and if the Credit stipulates a unit price such price is not reduced. This provision does not apply when expressions referred to in a. above are used in the Credit.

Article 40

Partial Shipments/Drawings

C–040   a. Partial drawings and/or shipments are allowed, unless the Credit stipulates otherwise.

b. Transport documents which appear on their face to indicate that shipment has been made on the same means of conveyance and for the same journey, provided that they indicate the same destination, will not be regarded as covering partial shipments, even if the transport documents indicate different dates of shipment and/or different ports of shipment, taking in charge, or despatch.

c. Shipments made by post will not be regarded as partial shipments if the post receipts or certificates of posting or courier's receipts or dispatch notes appear to have been stamped, signed or otherwise authenticated in the place from which the Credit stipulates the goods are to be dispatched, and on the same date.

Article 41

Instalment Shipment/Drawings

C–041   If drawings and/or shipments by instalments within given periods are stipulated in the Credit and any instalment is not drawn and/or shipped within the period allowed for that instalment, the Credit ceases to be available for that and any subsequent instalments, unless otherwise stipulated in the Credit.

Article 42

Expiry Date and Place for Presentation of Documents

a. All Credits must stipulate an expiry date for presentation of documents for   **C–042**
payment, acceptance or, with the exception of freely negotiable Credits, a
place for presentation of documents for negotiation. An expiry date stipulated for payment, acceptance or negotiation will be construed to express
and expiry date for presentation of documents.

b. Except as provided in Article 44(a), documents must be presented on or
before such expiry date.

c. If an Issuing Bank states that the Credit is to be available "for one month",
"for six months" or the like, but does not specify the date from which the
time is to run, the date of issuance of the Credit by the Issuing Bank will be
deemed to be the first day from which such time is to run. Banks should
discourage indication of the expiry date of the Credit in this manner.

Article 43

Limitation on the Expiry Date

a. In addition to stipulating an expiry date for presentation of documents,   **C–043**
every Credit which calls for a transport document(s) should also stipulate a
specified period of time after the date of shipment during which presentation must be made in compliance with the terms and conditions of the
Credit. If no such period of time is stipulated, banks will refuse documents
presented to them later than 21 days after the date of shipment. In any event,
documents must be presented not later than the expiry date of the credit.

b. In cases in which sub-Article 40(b) applies, the date of shipment will be
considered to be the latest shipment date on which any of the transport
documents presented.

Article 44

Extension of Expiry Date

a. If the expiry date of the Credit and/or the last day of the period of time for   **C–044**
presentation of documents stipulated by the Credit or applicable by virtue of
Article 43 falls on a day on which the bank to which presentation has to be
made is closed for reasons other than those referred to in Article 17, the
stipulated expiry date and/or the last day of the period of time after the date
of shipment for presentation of documents, as the case may be, shall be
extended to the first following business day on which such bank is open.

b. The latest date for shipment shall not be extended by reason of the extension
of the expiry date and/or the period of time after the date of shipment for
presentation of document(s) in accordance with this article. If no such latest
date for shipment is stipulated in the Credit or amendments thereto, banks
will reject transport documents indicating a date of shipment later than the
expiry date stipulated in the Credit or amendments thereto.

c. The bank to which presentation is made on such first following business day
must provide a statement that the documents were presented within the

time limits extended in accordance with Article 44(a) of the Uniform Customs and Practice for Documentary Credits, 1994 Revision. I.C.C. Publication No. 500.

Article 45

Hours of Presentation

C–045   Banks are under no obligation to accept presentation of documents outside their banking hours.

Article 46

General Expressions as to Dates

C–046
   a. Unless otherwise stipulated in the Credit, the expression "shipment" used in stipulating an earliest and/or latest shipment date will be understood to include the expressions "loading on board", "dispatch", "accepted for carriage", "date of post receipt", "date of pick-up", and in the case of a Credit calling for or allowing a multimodal transport document the expression "taking in charge".

   b. Expressions such as "prompt", "immediately", "as soon as possible", and the like should not be used. If they are used banks will disregard them.

   c. If the expression "on or about" and similar expressions are used, banks will interpret them as a stipulation that shipment is to be made during the period from five days before to five days after the specified date, both end days included.

Article 47

Date Terminology for Periods of Shipment

C–047
   a. The words "to", "until", "till", "from" and words of similar import applying to any date or period in the Credit referring to shipment will be understood to include the date mentioned.

   b. The word "after" will be understood to exclude the date mentioned.

   c. The terms "first half", "second half" of a month shall be construed respectively as the 1st to the 15th, and the 16th to the last day of each month, all dates inclusive.

   d. The terms "beginning", "middle", or "end" of a month shall be construed respectively as from the 1st to the 10th, the 11th to the 20th,and the 21st to the last day of each month, all dates inclusive.

F.   TRANSFER

Article 48

Transferable Credit

C–048
   a. A transferable credit is a credit under which the Beneficiary (First Beneficiary) may request the bank authorized to pay, incur a deferred payment undertaking, accept or negotiate (the "Transferring Bank") or in the case of a freely negotiable Credit the bank specifically authorized in the Credit as a

Transferring Bank, to make the Credit available in whole or in part to one or more other Beneficiary(ies) (Second Beneficiary(ies)).

b. A credit can be transferred only if it is expressly designated as "transferable" by the Issuing Bank. Terms such as "divisible", "fractionable", "assignable", and "transmissible" do not render the Credit transferable. If such terms are used they shall be disregarded.

c. The Transferring Bank shall be under no obligation to effect such transfer except to the extent and in the manner expressly consented to by such bank.

d. At the time of making a request or transfer and prior to the transfer of the Credit, the First Beneficiary must irrevocably instruct the Transferring Bank whether or not he retains the right to refuse to allow the Transferring Bank to advise amendments to he Second Beneficiary(ies). If the Transferring Bank consents to the transfer under these conditions, it must, at the time of transfer, advise the Second Beneficiary(ies) of the First Beneficiary's instructions regarding amendments.

e. If a Credit is transferred to more than one Second Beneficiary(ies), refusal of an amendment by one or more Second Beneficiary(ies) does not invalidate the acceptance(s) by the other Second Beneficiary(ies) with respect to whom the Credit will be amended accordingly. With respect to the Second Beneficiary(ies) who rejected the amendment, the Credit will remain unamended.

f. Transferring Bank charges in respect of transfers including, commissions, fees, costs or expenses are payable by the First Beneficiary unless otherwise agreed. If the Transferring Bank agrees to transfer the Credit it shall be under no obligation to effect the transfer until such charges are paid.

g. Unless otherwise stated in the Credit a transferable credit can be transferred once only. Consequently the Credit cannot be transferred at the request of the Second Beneficiary to any subsequent Third Beneficiary. For the purpose of this article, a retransfer to the First Beneficiary does not constitute a prohibited transfer.
Fractions of a transferable Credit (not exceeding in the aggregate the amount of the Credit) can be transferred separately, provided partial shipments/drawings are not prohibited, and the aggregate of such transfers will be considered as constituting only one transfer of the Credit.

h. The credit can be transferred only on the terms and conditions specified in the original credit, with the exception of:

- the amount of the Credit,
- any unit price stated therein,
- the expiry date,
- the last date for presentation of documents in accordance with Article 43,
- the period for shipment,

any or all of which may be reduced or curtailed. The percentage for which insurance cover must be effected may be increased in such a way as to provide the amount of cover stipulated in the original credit, or these articles.

In addition, the name of the First Beneficiary can be substituted for that of the Applicant, but if the name of the Applicant is specifically required by the original Credit to appear in any document(s) other than the invoice, such requirement must be fulfilled.

i. The First Beneficiary has the right to substitute his own invoice(s) (and Draft(s)) for those of the Second Beneficiary(ies), for amounts not in excess of the original amount stipulated in the Credit and for the original unit prices if stipulated in the Credit, and upon such substitution of invoice(s) (and Draft(s)) the First Beneficiary can draw under the Credit for the difference, if any, between his invoice(s) and the Second Beneficiary's(ies') invoice(s).

When a Credit has been transferred and the First Beneficiary is to supply his own invoice(s) (and Draft(s)) in exchange for the Second Beneficiary's(ies') invoice(s) (and Draft(s)) but fails to do so on first demand, the Transferring Bank has the right to deliver to the Issuing Bank the documents received under the Credit, including the Second Beneficiary's(ies') invoice(s) (and Draft(s)) without further responsibility to the First Beneficiary.

j. The First Beneficiary may request that payment or negotiation be effected to the Second Beneficiary(ies) at the place to which the Credit has been transferred, up to and including the expiry date of the Credit, unless the original Credit expressly states that it may not be made available for payment of negotiation at a place other than that stipulated in the Credit. This is without prejudice to the Beneficiary's right to substitute subsequently his own invoice(s) (and Draft(s)) for those of the Second Beneficiary(ies) and to claim any difference due to him.

G.   ASSIGNMENT OF PROCEEDS

Article 49

Assignment of Proceeds

C–049   The fact that a Credit is not stated to be transferable shall not affect the Beneficiary's right to assign any proceeds to which he may be, or may become, entitled under such Credit, in accordance with the provisions of the applicable law. This Article relates only to the assignment of proceeds and not to the assignment of the right to perform under the Credit itself.

CARRIAGE OF GOODS BY SEA ACT 1971

(as amended by the Merchant Shipping Acts 1981 and 1995)

Be it enacted by the Queen's most Excellent Majesty, by and with the advice and **D–001**
consent of the Lords Spiritual and Temporal, and Commons, in this present
Parliament assembled, and by the authority of the same, as follows:

1. Application of The Hague Rules as amended

(1) In this Act, "the Rules" means the International Convention for the unifica- **D–002**
tion of certain rules of law relating to bills of lading signed at Brussels on 25th
August 1924, as amended by the Protocol signed at Brussels on 23rd February
1968 and [inserted by the Merchant Shipping Act 1981, s.2(1) and by the Merchant
Shipping Act 1995, s.314(2)] by the Protocol signed at Brussels on 21st December
1979.

(2) The provisions of the Rules, as set out in the Schedule to this Act, shall have
the force of law.

(3) Without prejudice to subsection (2) above, the said provisions shall have
effect (and have the force of law) in relation to and in connection with the carriage
of goods by sea in ships where the port of shipment is a port in the United
Kingdom, whether or not the carriage is between ports in two different States
within the meaning of Article X of the Rules.

(4) Subject to subsection (6) below, nothing in this section shall be taken as **D–003**
applying anything in the Rules to any contract for the carriage of goods by sea,
unless the contract expressly or by implication provides for the issue of a bill of
lading or any similar document of title.

(5) The Secretary of State may from time to time by order made by statutory
instrument specify the respective amounts which for the purposes of paragraph
5 of Article IV of the Rules and of Article IV *bis* of the Rules are to be taken as
equivalent to the sums expressed in francs which are mentioned in subparagraph
(a) of that paragraph. [Note: this subsection has now been repealed].

(6) Without prejudice to Article X (c) of the Rules, the Rules shall have the force
of law in relation to—

(a) any bill of lading if the contract contained in or evidenced by it expressly
provides that the Rules shall govern the contract, and

(b) any receipt which is a non-negotiable document marked as such if the
contract contained in or evidenced by it is a contract for the carriage of
goods by sea which expressly provides that the Rules are to govern the
contract as if the receipt were a bill of lading,

but subject, where paragraph (b) applies, to any necessary modifications and in
particular with the omission in Article III of the Rules of the second sentence of
paragraph 4 and of paragraph 7.

D–004/7   (7) If and so far as the contract contained in or evidenced by a bill of lading or receipt within paragraph (a) or (b) of subsection (6) above applies to deck cargo or live animals, the Rules as given the force of law by that subsection shall have effect as if Article I(c) did not exclude deck cargo and live animals.

In this subsection "deck cargo" means cargo which by the contract of carriage is stated as being carried on deck and is so carried.

[The next section was added by the Merchant Shipping Act 1995, s.314(2).]

1A. Conversion of special drawing rights into sterling

D–008   (1) For the purposes of Article IV of the Rules the value on a particular day of one special drawing right shall be treated as equal to such a sum in sterling as the International Monetary Fund have fixed as being the equivalent of one special drawing right—

(a) for that day; or

(b) if no sum has been so fixed for that day, for the last day before that day for which a sum has been so fixed.

(2) A certificate given by or on behalf of the Treasury stating—

(a) that a particular sum in sterling has been fixed as aforesaid for a particular day; or

(b) that no sum has been so fixed for a particular day and that a particular sum in sterling has been so fixed for a day which is the last day for which a sum has been so fixed before the particular day,

shall be conclusive evidence of those matters for the purposes of subsection (1) above; and a document purporting to be such a certificate shall in any proceedings be received in evidence and, unless the contrary is proved, be deemed to be such a certificate.

(3) The Treasury may charge a reasonable fee for any certificate given in pursuance of subsection (2) above, and any fee received by the Treasury by virtue of this subsection shall be paid into the Consolidated Fund.

2. Contracting States, etc.

D–009   (1) If Her Majesty by Order in Council certifies to the following effect, that is to say, that for the purposes of the Rules—

(a) a State specified in the Order is a contracting State, or is a contracting State in respect of any place or territory so specified; or

(b) any place or territory specified in the Order forms part of a State so specified (whether a contracting State or not), the Order shall, except so far as it has been superseded by a subsequent Order, be conclusive evidence of the matters so certified.

(2) An Order in Council under this section may be varied or revoked by a subsequent Order in Council.

3. Absolute warranty of seaworthiness not to be implied in contracts to which Rules apply

D–010   There shall not be implied in any contract for the carriage of goods by sea to which the Rules apply by virtue of this Act any absolute undertaking by the carrier of the goods to provide a seaworthy ship.

4. Application of Act to British possessions, etc.

(1) Her Majesty may by Order in Council direct that this Act shall extend, **D–011** subject to such exceptions, adaptations and modifications as may be specified in the Order, to all or any of the following territories, that is—

(a) any colony (not being a colony for whose external relations a country other than the United Kingdom is responsible),

(b) any country outside Her Majesty's dominions in which Her Majesty has jurisdiction in right of Her Majesty's Government of the United Kingdom.

(2) An Order in Council under this section may contain such transitional and other consequential provisions as appear to her Majesty to be expedient, including provisions amending or repealing any legislation about the carriage of goods by sea forming part of the law of any of the territories mentioned in paragraphs (a) and (b) above.

(3) An Order in Council under this section may be varied or revoked by a subsequent Order in Council.

5. Extension of application of Rules to carriage from ports in British possessions, etc.

(1) Her Majesty may by Order in Council provide that section 1 (3) of this Act **D–012** shall have effect as if the reference therein to the United Kingdom included a reference to all or any of the following territories, that is—

(a) the Isle of Man;

(b) any of the Channel Islands specified in the Order;

(c) any colony specified in the Order (not being a colony for whose external relations a country other than the United Kingdom is responsible);

(d) any associated state (as defined by section 1(3) of the West Indies Act 1967) specified in the Order;

(e) any country specified in the Order, being a country outside Her majesty's dominions in which Her Majesty has jurisdiction in right of Her Majesty's Government of the United Kingdom.

(2) An Order in Council under this section may be varied or revoked by a subsequent Order in Council.

6. Supplemental

(1) This Act may be cited as the Carriage of Goods by Sea Act 1971. **D–013**

(2) It is hereby declared that this Act extends to Northern Ireland.

(3) The following enactments shall be repealed, that is—

(a) the Carriage of Goods by Sea Act 1924,

(b) section 12(4)(a) of the Nuclear Installations Act 1965, and without prejudice to section 38(1) of the Interpretation Act 1889, the reference to the said Act of 1924 in section 1 (1) (i) (ii) of the Hovercraft Act 1968 shall include a reference to this Act.

[This subsection was substituted by the Merchant Shipping Act 1995, s.314(2).]

(4) It is hereby declared that for the purposes of Article VIII of the Rules section 186 of the Merchant Shipping Act 1995 (which entirely exempts shipowners and

others in certain circumstances for loss of, or damage to, goods) is a provision relating to limitation of liability.

(5) This Act shall come into force on such day as Her Majesty may by Order in Council appoint, and, for the purposes of the transition from the law in force immediately before the day appointed under this subsection to the provisions of this Act, the Order appointing the day may provide that those provisions shall have effect subject to such transitional provisions as may be contained in the Order.

SCHEDULE

THE HAGUE RULES AS AMENDED BY THE BRUSSELS PROTOCOL 1968

Article I

D–013A In these Rules the following words are employed, with the meanings set out below:

   (a) "Carrier" includes the owner or the charterer who enters into a contract of carriage with the shipper.

   (b) "Contract of carriage" applies only to contracts of carriage covered by a bill of lading or any similar document of title, in so far as such document relates to the carriage of goods by sea, including any bill of lading or any similar document as aforesaid issued under or pursuant to a charter-party from the moment at which such bill of lading or similar document of title regulates the relations between a carrier and a holder of the same.

   (c) "Goods" includes goods, wares, merchandise, and articles of every kind whatsoever except live animals and cargo which by the contract of carriage is stated as being carried on deck and is so carried.

   (d) "Ship" means any vessel used for the carriage of goods by sea.

   (e) "Carriage of goods" covers the period from the time when the goods are loaded to the time they are discharged from the ship.

Article II

D–014 Subject to the provisions of Article VI, under every contract of carriage of goods by sea the carrier, in relation to the loading, handling, stowage, carriage, custody, care and discharge of such goods, shall be subject to the responsibilities and liabilities, and entitled to the rights and immunities hereinafter set forth.

Article III

D–015 1. The carrier shall be bound before and at the beginning of the voyage to exercise due diligence to—

   (a) Make the ship seaworthy.

   (b) Properly man, equip and supply the ship.

   (c) Make the holds, refrigerating and cool chambers, and all other parts of the ship in which the goods are carried, fit and safe for their reception, carriage and preservation.

2. Subject to the provisions of Article IV, the carrier shall properly and carefully load, handle, stow, carry, keep, care for, and discharge the goods carried.

3. After receiving the goods into his charge the carrier or the master or agent of the carrier shall, on demand of the shipper, issue to the shipper a bill of lading showing among other things—

(a) The leading marks necessary for identification of the goods as the same are furnished in writing by the shipper before the loading of such goods starts, provided such marks are stamped or otherwise shown clearly upon the goods if uncovered, or on the cases or coverings in which such goods are contained, in such a manner as should ordinarily remain legible until the end of the voyage.

(b) Either the number of packages or pieces, or the quantity, or weight, as the case may be, as furnished in writing by the shipper.

(c) The apparent order and condition of the goods. Provided that no carrier, master or agent of the carrier shall be bound to state or show in the bill of lading any marks, number, quantity or weight which he has reasonable ground for suspecting not accurately to represent the goods actually received, or which he has had no reasonable means of checking.

4. Such a bill of lading shall be *prima facie* evidence of the receipt by the carrier **D–016** of the goods as therein described in accordance with paragraph 3 (a), (b), and (c). However, proof to the contrary shall not be admissible when the bill of lading has been transferred to a third party in good faith.

5. The shipper shall be deemed to have guaranteed to the carrier the accuracy at the time of shipment of the marks, number, quantity and weight, as furnished by him, and the shipper shall identify the carrier against all loss, damages and expenses arising or resulting from inaccuracies in such particulars. The right of the carrier to such indemnity shall in no way limit his responsibility and liability under the contract of carriage to any person other than the shipper.

6. Unless notice of loss or damage and the general nature of such loss or damage be given in writing to the carrier or his agent at the port of discharge before or at the time of the removal of the goods into the custody of the person entitled to delivery thereof under the contract of carriage, or, if the loss or damage be not apparent, within three days, such removal shall be *prima facie* evidence of the delivery by the carrier of the goods as described in the bill of lading.

The notice in writing need not be given if the state of the goods has, at the time **D–017** of their receipt, been the subject of joint survey or inspection.

Subject to paragraph 6 *bis* the carrier and the ship shall in any event be discharged from all liability whatsoever in respect of the goods, unless suit is brought within one year of their delivery or of the date when they should have been delivered. This period may, however, be extended if the parties so agree after the cause of action has arisen.

In the case of any actual or apprehended loss or damage the carrier and the receiver shall give all reasonable facilities to each other for inspecting and tallying the goods.

6. *bis.* An action for an indemnity against a third person may be brought even **D–018** after the expiration of the year provided for in the preceding paragraph if brought within the time allowed by the law of the Court seized of the case. However, the time allowed shall be not less than three months, commencing from the day when the person bringing such action for indemnity has settled the claim or has been served with process in the action against himself.

7. After the goods are loaded the bill of lading to be issued by the carrier, master, or agent of the carrier, to the shipper shall, if the shipper so demands, be a "shipped" bill of lading, provided that if the shipper shall previously have taken up any document of title to such goods, he shall surrender the same as against the issue of the "shipped" bill of lading, but at the option of the carrier such document of title may be noted at the port of shipment by the carrier, master, or agent with the name or names of the ship or ships upon which the goods have been shipped and the date or dates of shipment, and when so noted, if it shows the particulars mentioned in paragraph 3 of Article III, shall for the purpose of this article be deemed to constitute a "shipped" bill of lading.

8. Any clause, covenant or agreement in a contract of carriage relieving the carrier or the ship from liability for loss or damage to or in connection with goods arising from negligence, fault or failure in the duties and obligations provided in this article or lessening such liability otherwise than as provided in these Rules, shall be null and void and of no effect. A benefit of insurance in favour of the carrier or similar clause shall be deemed to be a clause relieving the carrier from liability.

Article IV

D–019 **1.** Neither the carrier nor the ship shall be liable for loss or damage arising or resulting from unseaworthiness unless caused by want of due diligence on the part of the carrier to make the ship seaworthy, or to secure that the ship is properly manned, equipped and supplied, and to make the holds, refrigerating and cool chambers and all other parts of the ship in which the goods are carried fit and safe for their reception, carriage and preservation in accordance with paragraph 1 of Article III. Whenever loss or damage has resulted from unseaworthiness the burden of proving the exercise of due diligence shall be on the carrier or other person claiming exemption under this article.

2. Neither the carrier nor the ship shall be responsible for loss or damage arising or resulting from—

(a) Act, neglect, or default of the master, mariner, pilot, or the servants of the carrier in the navigation or in the management of the ship.

(b) Fire, unless caused by the actual fault or privity of the carrier.

(c) Perils, dangers and accidents of the sea or other navigable waters.

(d) Act of God.

(e) Act of war.

(f) Act of public enemies.

(g) Arrest or restraint of princes, rulers or people, or seizure under legal process.

(h) Quarantine restrictions.

(i) Act or omission of the shipper or owner of the goods, his agent or representative.

(j) Strikes or lockouts or stoppage or restraint of labour from whatever cause, whether partial or general.

(k) Riots and civil commotions.

(l) Saving or attempting to save life or property at sea.

(m) Wastage in bulk or weight or any other loss or damage arising from inherent defect, quality or vice of the goods.

(n) Insufficiency of packing.

(o) Insufficiency or inadequacy of marks.

(p) Latent defects not discoverable by due diligence.

(q) Any other cause arising without the actual fault or privity of the carrier, or without the fault or neglect of the agents or servants of the carrier, but the burden of proof shall be on the person claiming the benefit of this exception to show that neither the actual fault or privity of the carrier nor the fault or neglect of the agents or servants of the carrier contributed to the loss or damage.

3. The shipper shall not be responsible for loss or damage sustained by the carrier or the ship arising or resulting from any cause without the act, fault or neglect of the shipper, his agents or his servants.

4. Any deviation in saving or attempting to save life or property at sea or any   **D–020** reasonable deviation shall not be deemed to be an infringement or breach of these Rules or of the contract of carriage, and the carrier shall not be liable for any loss or damage resulting therefrom.

5. (a) [as amended by Merchant Shipping Act 1981, s.2(3), and by the Merchant Shipping Act 1995, s.314(2)] Unless the nature and value of such goods have been declared by the shipper before shipment and inserted in the bill of lading, neither the carrier nor the ship shall in any event be or become liable for any loss or damage to or in connection with the goods in an amount exceeding the equivalent of 666.67 units of account per package or unit or 2 units of account per kilogramme of gross weight of the goods lost or damaged, whichever is the higher.

(b) The total amount recoverable shall be calculated by reference to the value of such goods at the place and time at which the goods are discharged from the ship in accordance with the contract or should have been so discharged.

The value of the goods shall be fixed according to the commodity exchange price, or, if there is no such price, according to the current market price, or, if there be no commodity exchange price or current market price, by reference to the normal value of goods of the same kind and quality.

(c) Where a container, pallet or similar article of transport is used to consolidate goods, the number of packages or units enumerated in the bill of lading as packed in such article of transport shall be deemed the number of packages as far as these packages or units are concerned. Except as aforesaid such article of transport shall be considered the package or unit.

(d) [as amended by Merchant Shipping Act 1981, s.2(4), and by the Merchant Shipping Act 1995, s.314(2)] The unit of account mentioned in this Article is the special drawing right as defined by the International Monetary Fund. The amounts mentioned in sub-paragraph (a) of this paragraph shall be converted into national currency on the basis of the value of that currency on a date to be determined by the law of the Court seized of the case [at the date of the judgment in question: Merchant Shipping Act 1981, section 2(5)].

(e) Neither the carrier nor the ship shall be entitled to the benefit of the limitation of liability provided for in this paragraph if it is proved that the damage resulted from an act or omission of the carrier done with intent to cause damage, or recklessly and with knowledge that damage would probably result.

(f) The declaration mentioned in sub-paragraph (a) of this paragraph, if embodied in the bill of lading, shall be *prima facie* evidence, but shall not be binding or conclusive on the carrier.

(g) By agreement between the carrier, master or agent of the carrier and the shipper other maximum amounts than those mentioned in sub-paragraph (a) of this paragraph may be fixed, provided that no maximum amount so fixed shall be less than the appropriate maximum mentioned in that sub-paragraph.

(h) Neither the carrier nor the ship shall be responsible in any event for loss or damage to, or in connection with, goods if the nature or value thereof has been knowingly mis-stated by the shipper in the bill of lading.

6. Goods of an inflammable, explosive or dangerous nature to the shipment whereof the carrier, master or agent of the carrier has not consented with knowledge of their nature and character, may at any time before discharge be landed at any place, or destroyed or rendered innocuous by the carrier without compensation and the shipper of such goods shall be liable for all damages directly or indirectly arising out of or resulting from such shipment. If any goods shipped with such knowledge and consent shall become a danger to the ship or cargo, they may in like manner be landed at any place, or destroyed or rendered innocuous by the carrier without liability on the part of the carrier except to general average, if any.

Article IV Bis

D–021   1. The defences and limits of liability provided for in these Rules shall apply in any action against the carrier in respect of loss or damage to goods covered by a contract of carriage whether the action be founded in contract or in tort.

2. If such an action is brought against a servant or agent of the carrier (such servant or agent not being an independent contractor), such servant or agent shall be entitled to avail himself of the defences and limits of liability which the carrier is entitled to invoke under these Rules.

3. The aggregate of the amounts recoverable from the carrier, and such servants and agents, shall in no case exceed the limit provided for in these Rules.

4. Nevertheless, a servant or agent of the carrier shall not be entitled to avail himself of the provisions of this article, if it is proved that the damage resulted from an act or omission of the servant or agent done with intent to cause damage or recklessly and with knowledge that damage would probably result.

Article V

D–022   A carrier shall be at liberty to surrender in whole or in part all or any of his rights and immunities or to increase any of his responsibilities and liabilities under these Rules, provided such surrender or increase shall be embodied in the bill of lading issued to the shipper. The provisions of these Rules shall not be applicable to charter-parties, but if bills of lading are issued in the case of a ship under a charter-party they shall comply with the terms of these Rules. Nothing in these Rules shall be held to prevent the insertion in a bill of lading of any lawful provision regarding general average.

Article VI

Notwithstanding the provisions of the preceding articles, a carrier, master or agent of the carrier and the shipper shall in regard to any particular goods be at liberty to enter any agreement in any terms as to the responsibility and liability of the carrier in respect of such goods, or his obligation as to seaworthiness, so far as this stipulation is not contrary to public policy, or the care or diligence of his servants or agents in regard to the loading, handling, stowage, carriage, custody, care and discharge of the goods carried by sea, provided that in this case no bill of lading has been or shall be issued and that the terms agreed shall be embodied in a receipt which shall be a non-negotiable document and shall be marked as such.   **D–023**

Any agreement so entered into shall have full legal effect.

Provided that this article shall not apply to ordinary commercial shipments made in the ordinary course of trade, but only to other shipments where the character or condition of the property to be carried or the circumstances, terms and conditions under which the carriage is to be performed are such as reasonably to justify a special agreement.

Article VII

Nothing herein contained shall prevent a carrier or a shipper from entering into any agreement, stipulation, condition, reservation or exemption as to the responsibility and liability of the carrier or the ship for the loss or damage to, or in connection with, the custody and care and handling of the goods prior to the loading on, and subsequent to the discharge from, the ship on which the goods are carried by sea.   **D–024**

Article VIII

The provisions of these Rules shall not affect the rights and obligations of the carrier under any statute for the time being in force relating to the limitation of the liability of owners of sea-going vessels.   **D–025**

Article IX

These Rules shall not affect the provisions of any international Convention or national law governing liability for nuclear damage.   **D–026**

Article X

The provisions of these Rules shall apply to every bill of lading relating to the carriage of goods between ports in two different States if: **D–027**

(a) the bill of lading is issued in a contracting State, or

(b) the carriage is from a port in a contracting State, or

(c) the contract contained in or evidenced by the bill of lading provides that these Rules or legislation of any States giving effect to them are to govern the contract,

whatever may be the nationality of the ship, the carrier, the shipper, the consignee, or any other interested person.

[Articles 11 to 16 deal with the coming into force of the Convention, procedure for ratification, accession and denunciation, and the right to call for a fresh conference to consider amendments to the Rules contained in the Convention.]

CARRIAGE OF GOODS BY SEA ACT 1992

(1992 c.50)

An Act to replace the Bills of Lading Act 1855 with new provision with respect to **E–001** bills of lading and certain other shipping documents. [16th July 1992]

Be it enacted by the Queen's most Excellent Majesty, by and with the advice and consent of the Lords Spiritual and Temporal, and Commons, in this present Parliament assembled, and by the authority of the same, as follows:

1.—(1) This Act applies to the following documents, that is to say— **E–002**

(a) any bill of lading;

(b) any sea waybill; and

(c) any ship's delivery order.

(2) References in this Act to a bill of lading—

(a) do not include references to a document which is incapable of transfer either by indorsement or, as a bearer bill, by delivery without indorsement; but

(b) subject to that, do include references to a received for shipment bill of lading.

(3) References in this Act to a sea waybill are references to any document which is not a bill of lading but—

(a) is such a receipt for goods as contains or evidences a contract for the carriage of goods by sea; and

(b) identifies the person to whom delivery of the goods is to be made by the carrier in accordance with that contract.

(4) References in this Act to a ship's delivery order are references to any document which is neither a bill of lading nor a sea waybill but contains an undertaking which—

(a) is given under or for the purposes of a contract for the carriage of goods to which the document relates, or to goods which include those goods; and

(b) is an undertaking by the carrier to a person identified in the document to deliver the goods to which the document relates to that person.

(5) The Secretary of State may by regulations make provision for the application of this Act to cases where a telecommunication system or any other information technology is used for effecting transactions corresponding to—

(a) the issue of a document to which this Act applies;

(b) the indorsement, delivery or other transfer of such a document; or

(c) the doing of anything else in relation to such a document.

(6) Regulations under subsection (5) above may—

(a) make any such modifications of the following provisions of this Act as the Secretary of State considers appropriate in connection with the application of this Act to any case mentioned in that subsection; and

(b) contain supplemental, incidental, consequential and transitional provision;

and the power to make regulations under that subsection shall be exercisable by statutory instrument subject to annulment in pursuance of a resolution of either House of Parliament.

E–003   **2.**—(1) Subject to the following provisions of this section, a person who becomes—

(a) the lawful holder of a bill of lading;

(b) the person who (without being an original party to the contract of carriage) is the person to whom delivery of the goods to which the sea waybill relates is to be made by the carrier in accordance with the contract; or

(c) the person to whom delivery of the goods to which a ship's delivery order relates is to be made in accordance with the undertaking contained in the order, shall (by virtue of becoming the holder of the bill, or, as the case may be, the person to whom delivery is to be made) have transferred to him and vested in him all rights of suit under the contract of carriage as if he had been a party to that contract.

(2) Where, when a person becomes the lawful holder of a bill of lading, possession of the bill no longer gives a right (as against the carrier) to possession of the goods to which the bill relates, that person shall not have any rights transferred to him by virtue of subsection (1) above unless he becomes the holder of the bill—

(a) by virtue of a transaction effected in pursuance of any contractual or other arrangements made before the time when such a right of possession ceased to attach to possession of the bill; or

(b) as a result of the rejection to that person by another person of goods or documents delivered to the other person in pursuance of any such arrangements.

(3) The rights vested in any person by virtue of the operation of subsection (1) above in relation to a ship's delivery order—

(a) shall be so vested subject to the terms of the order; and

(b) where the goods to which the order relates form a part only of the goods to which the contract of carriage relates, shall be confined to rights in respect of the goods to which the order relates.

(4) Where, in the case of any document to which this Act applies—

(a) a person with any interest or right in or in relation to goods to which the document relates sustains loss or damage in consequence of a breach of the contract of carriage; but

(b) subsection (1) above operates in relation to that document so the rights of suit in respect of that breach are vested in another person,

the other person shall be entitled to exercise those rights for the benefit of the person who sustained the loss or damage to the same extent as they could have been exercised if they had been vested in the person for whose benefit they are exercised.

(5) Where rights are transferred by virtue of the operation of subsection (1) above in relation to any document, the transfer for which that subsection provides shall extinguish any entitlement to those rights which derives—

(a) where that document is a bill of lading, from a person's having been an original party to the contract of carriage; or

(b) in the case of any document to which this Act applies, from the previous operation of that subsection in relation to that document;

but the operation of that subsection shall be without prejudice to any rights which derive from a person's having been an original party to the contract contained in, or evidenced by, a sea waybill and, in relation to a ship's delivery order, shall be without prejudice to any rights deriving otherwise than from the previous operation of that subsection in relation to that order.

3.—(1) Where subsection (1) of section 2 of this Act operates in relation to any document to which this Act applies and the person in whom rights are vested by virtue of that subsection— **E–004**

(a) takes or demands delivery from the carrier of any goods to which the document relates;

(b) makes a claim under the contract of carriage against the carrier in respect of any of those goods; or

(c) is a person who, at a time before those rights were vested in him, took or demanded delivery from the carrier of any of these goods,

that person shall (by virtue of taking or demanding delivery or making the claim or, in a case falling within paragraph (c) above, of having the rights vested in him) become subject to the same liabilities under that contract as if he had been party to that contract.

(2) Where the goods to which a ship's delivery order relates form a part only of the goods to which the contract of carriage relates, the liabilities to which any person is subject by virtue of the operation of this section in relation to that order shall exclude liabilities in respect of any goods to which the order does not relate.

(3) This section, so far as it imposes liabilities under any contract on any person, shall be without prejudice to the liabilities under the contract of any person as an original party to the contract.

4. A bill of lading which— **E–005**

(a) represents goods to have been shipped on board a vessel or to have been received for shipment on board a vessel; and

(b) has been signed by the master of the vessel or by a person who was not the master but had the express, implied or apparent authority of the carrier to sign bills of lading, shall, in favour of a person who had become the lawful holder of the bill, be conclusive evidence against the carrier of the shipment of the goods or, as the case may be, of their receipt for shipment.

E–006   5.—(1) In this Act—
"bill of lading", "sea waybill" and "ship's delivery order" shall be construed in accordance with section 1 above;
"the contract of carriage"—

(a) in relation to a bill of lading or sea waybill, means the contract contained in or evidenced by that bill or waybill; and

(b) in relation to a ship's delivery order, means the contract under or for the purposes of which the undertaking contained in the order is given;

"holder", in relation to a bill of lading, shall be construed in accordance with subsection (2) below;
"information technology" includes any computer or other technology by means of which information or other matter may be recorded or communicated without being reduced to documentary form; and
"telecommunication system" has the same meaning as in the Telecommunications Act 1984.

(2) References in this Act to the holder of a bill of lading are references to any of the following persons, that is to say—

(a) a person with possession of the bill who, by virtue of being the person identified in the bill, is the consignee of the goods to which the bill relates;

(b) a person with possession of the bill as a result of the completion, by delivery of the bill, of any indorsement of the bill or, in the case of a bearer bill, of any other transfer of the bill;

(c) a person with possession of the bill as a result of any transaction by virtue of which he would have become a holder falling within paragraph (a) or (b) above had not the transaction been effected at a time when possession of the bill no longer gave a right (as against the carrier) to possession of the goods to which the bill relates;

and a person shall be regarded for the purposes of this Act as having become the lawful holder of a bill of lading wherever he has become the holder of the bill in good faith.

(3) References in this Act to a person's being identified in a document include references to his being identified by a description which allows for the identity of the person in question to be varied, in accordance with the terms of the document, after its issue; and the reference to section 1(3)(b) of this Act to a document's identifying a person shall be construed accordingly.

(4) Without prejudice to sections 2(2) and 4 above, nothing in this Act shall preclude its operation in relation to a case where the goods to which a document relates—

(a) cease to exist after the issue of the document; or

(b) cannot be identified (whether because they are mixed with other goods or for any other reason);

and references in this Act to the goods to which a document relates shall be construed accordingly.

(5) The preceding provisions of this Act shall have effect without prejudice to the application, in relation to any case, of the rules (the Hague-Visby Rules) which

for the time being have the force of law by virtue of section 1 of the Carriage of Goods by Sea Act 1971.

(1) This Act may be cited as the Carriage of Goods by Sea Act 1991.

(2) The Bills of Lading Act 1855 is hereby repealed.

(3) This Act shall come into force at the end of the period of two months beginning with the day on which it is passed, but nothing in the Act shall have effect in relation to any document issued before the coming into force of this Act.

(4) This Act shall not extend to Northern Ireland.

APPENDIX F

FACTORS ACT 1889

F–001   **1.** For the purposes of this Act—

(1) The expression "mercantile agent" shall mean a mercantile agent having in the customary course of his business as such agent authority either to sell goods, or to consign goods for the purpose of sale, or to buy goods, or to raise money on the security of goods:

(2) A person shall be deemed to be in possession of goods or of the documents of title to goods, where the goods or documents are in his actual custody or are held by any other person subject to his control or for him or on his behalf:

(3) The expression "goods" shall include wares and merchandise:

(4) The expression "document of title" shall include any bill of lading, dock warrant, warehouse-keeper's certificate, and warrant or order for the delivery of goods, and any other document used in the ordinary course of business as proof of the possession or control of goods, or authorising or purporting to authorise, either by endorsement or by delivery, the possessor of the document to transfer or receive goods thereby represented:

(5) The expression "pledge" shall include any contract pledging, or giving a lien or security on, goods, whether in consideration of an original advance or of any further or continuing advance or of any pecuniary liability:

(6) The expression "person" shall include any body of persons corporate or unincorporate.

F–002   **2.** (1) Where a mercantile agent is, with the consent of the owner, in possession of goods or of the documents of title to goods, any sale, pledge, or other disposition of the goods, made by him when acting in the ordinary course of business of a mercantile agent, shall, subject to the provisions of this Act, be as valid as if he were expressly authorised by the owner of the goods to make the same; provided that the person taking under the disposition acts in good faith, and has not at the time of the disposition notice that the person making the disposition has not authority to make the same.

(2) Where a mercantile agent has, with the consent of the owner, been in possession of goods or of the documents of title to goods, any sale, pledge, or other disposition, which would have been valid if the consent had continued, shall be valid notwithstanding the determination of the consent: provided that the person taking under the disposition has not at the time thereof notice that the consent has been determined.

(3) Where a mercantile agent has obtained possession of any documents of title to goods by reason of his being or having been, with the consent of the owner, in possession of the goods represented thereby, or of any other documents of title to the goods, his possession of the first-mentioned documents shall, for the purposes of this Act, be deemed to be with the consent of the owner.

(4) For the purposes of this Act the consent of the owner shall be presumed in the absence of evidence to the contrary.

3. A pledge of the documents of title to goods shall be deemed to be a pledge of the goods.

F–003

4. Where a mercantile agent pledges goods as security for a debt or liability due from the pledgor to the pledgee before the time of the pledge, the pledgee shall acquire no further right to the goods than could have been enforced by the pledgor at the time of the pledge.

F–004

5. The consideration necessary for the validity of a sale, pledge, or other disposition, of goods, in pursuance of this Act, may be either a payment in cash, or the delivery or transfer of other goods, or of a document of title to goods, or of a negotiable security, or any other valuable consideration; but where goods are pledged by a mercantile agent in consideration of the delivery or transfer of other goods, or of a document of title to goods, or of a negotiable security, the pledgee shall acquire no right or interest in the goods so pledged in excess of the value of the goods, documents, or security when so delivered or transferred in exchange.

F–005

6. For the purposes of this Act an agreement made with a mercantile agent through a clerk or other person authorised in the ordinary course of business to make contracts of sale or pledge on his behalf shall be deemed to be an agreement with the agent.

F–006

7. (1) Where the owner of goods has given possession of the goods to another person for the purpose of consignment or sale, or has shipped the goods in the name of another person, and the consignee of the goods has not had notice that such person is not the owner of the goods, the consignee shall, in respect of advances made to or for the use of such person, have the same lien on the goods as if such person were the owner of the goods, and may transfer any such lien to another person.

(2) Nothing in this section shall limit or affect the validity of any sale, pledge, or disposition, by a mercantile agent.

F–007

8. Where a person, having sold goods, continues, or is, in possession of the goods or of the documents of title to the goods, the delivery or transfer by that person, or by a mercantile agent acting for him, of the goods or documents of title under any sale, pledge or other disposition thereof, or under any agreement for sale, pledge or other disposition thereof, to any person receiving the same in good faith and without notice of the previous sale, shall have the same effect as if the person making the delivery or transfer were expressly authorized by the owner of the goods to make the same.

F–008

9. Where a person, having bought or agreed to buy goods, obtains with the consent of the seller possession of the goods or the documents of title to the goods, the delivery or transfer, by that person or by a mercantile agent acting for him, of the goods or the documents of title under any sale, pledge or other disposition thereof, or under any agreement for sale, pledge or other disposition thereof, to any person receiving the same in good faith and without notice of any lien or other right of the original seller in respect of the goods, shall have the same effect as if the person making the delivery or transfer were a mercantile agent in possession of the goods or documents of title with the consent of the owner.

For the purposes of this section—

(i) the buyer under a conditional sale agreement shall be deemed not to be a person who has bought or agreed to buy goods, and

F–009

(ii) "conditional sale agreement" means an agreement for the sale of goods which is a consumer credit agreement within the meaning of the Consumer Credit Act 1974 under which the purchase price or part of it is payable by instalments, and the property in the goods is to remain in the seller (notwithstanding that the buyer is to be in possession of the goods) until such conditions as to the payment of instalments or otherwise as may be specified in the agreement are fulfilled.

F–010   **10.** Where a document of title to goods has been lawfully transferred to a person as a buyer or owner of the goods, and that person transfers the document to a person who takes the document in good faith and for valuable consideration, the last-mentioned transfer shall have the same effect for defeating any vendor's lien or right of stoppage in transitu as the transfer of a bill of lading has for defeating the right of stoppage in transitu.

F–011   **11.** For the purposes of this Act, the transfer of a document may be by endorsement, or, where the document is by custom or by its express terms transferable by delivery, or makes the goods deliverable to the bearer, then by delivery.

F–012   **12.** (1) Nothing in this Act shall authorise an agent to exceed or depart from his authority as between himself and his principal, or exempt him from any liability, civil or criminal, for so doing.

(2) Nothing in this Act shall prevent the owner of goods from recovering the goods from an agent or his trustee in bankruptcy at any time before the sale or pledge thereof, or shall prevent the owner of goods pledged by an agent from having the right to redeem the goods at any time before the sale thereof, on satisfying the claim for which the goods were pledged, and paying to the agent, if by him required, any money in respect of which the agent would by law be entitled to retain the goods or the documents of title thereto, or any of them, by way of lien as against the owner, or from recovering from any person with whom the goods have been pledged any balance of money remaining in his hands as the produce of the sale of the goods after deducting the amount of his lien.

(3) Nothing in this Act shall prevent the owner of goods sold by an agent from recovering from the buyer the price agreed to be paid for the same, or any part of that price, subject to any right of set-off on the part of the buyer against the agent.

F–013   **13.** The provisions of this Act shall be construed in amplification and not in derogation of the powers exercisable by an agent independently of this Act.

. . .

17. This Act may be cited as the Factors Act 1889.

Appendx G

THE UNIFORM LAW ON THE INTERNATIONAL SALE OF GOODS

Set out in this appendix is U.L.I.S., as enacted in Schedule 1 of the Uniform Laws **G–001**
on International Sales Act 1967.

SCHEDULE 1 TO THE UNIFORM LAWS ON INTERNATIONAL SALES ACT 1967

CHAPTER 1

SPHERE OF APPLICATION OF THE LAW

Article 1

1. The present Law shall apply to contracts of sale of goods entered into by **G–002**
parties whose places of business are in the territories of different Contracting
States, in each of the following cases:

(a) where the contract involves the sale of goods which are at the time of the
conclusion of the contract in the course of carriage or will be carried from
the territory of one State to the territory of another;

(b) where the acts constituting the offer and the acceptance have been effected
in the territories of different States;

(c) where delivery of the goods is to be made in the territory of a State other
than that within whose territory the acts constituting the offer and the
acceptance have been effected.

2. Where a party to the contract does not have a place of business, reference
shall be made to his habitual residence.

3. The application of the present Law shall not depend on the nationality of the
parties.

4. In the case of contracts by correspondence, offer and acceptance shall be
considered to have been effected in the territory of the same State only if the
letters, telegrams or other documentary communications which contain them
have been sent and received in the territory of that State.

5. For the purpose of determining whether the parties have their places of
business or habitual residences in "different States", any two or more States shall
not be considered to be "different States" if a valid declaration to that effect made

under Article II of the Convention dated the 1st day of July 1964 relating to a Uniform Law on the International Sale of Goods is in force in respect of them.

Article 2

G–003   Rules of private international law shall be excluded for the purposes of the application of the present Law, subject to any provision to the contrary in the said Law.

Article 3

G–004   The parties to a contract of sale shall be free to exclude the application thereto of the present Law either entirely or partially. Such exclusion may be express or implied.

Article 4

G–005   The present Law shall also apply where it has been chosen as the law of the contract by the parties, whether or not their places of business or their habitual residences are in different States and whether or not such States are Parties to the Convention dated the 1st day of July 1964 relating to the Uniform Law on the International Sale of Goods, to the extent that it does not affect the application of any mandatory provisions of law which would have been applicable if the parties had not chosen the Uniform Law.

Article 5

G–006   1. The present Law shall not apply to sales:

(a) of stocks, shares, investment securities, negotiable instruments or money;

(b) of any ship, vessel or aircraft, which is or will be subject to registration;

(c) of electricity;

(d) by authority of law or on execution or distress.

2. The present Law shall not affect the application of any mandatory provision of national law for the protection of a party to a contract which contemplates the purchase of goods by that party by payment of the price by instalments.

Article 6

G–007   Contracts for the supply of goods to be manufactured or produced shall be considered to be sales within the meaning of the present Law, unless the party who orders the goods undertakes to supply an essential and substantial part of the materials necessary for such manufacture or production.

Article 7

G–008   The present Law shall apply to sales regardless of the commercial or civil character of the parties or of the contracts.

Article 8

The present Law shall govern only the obligations of the seller and the buyer arising from a contract of sale. In particular, the present Law shall not, except as otherwise expressly provided therein, be concerned with the formation of the contract, nor with the effect which the contract may have on the property in the goods sold, nor with the validity of the contract or of any of its provisions or of any usage. **G–009**

CHAPTER II

GENERAL PROVISIONS

Article 9

1. The parties shall be bound by any usage which they have expressly or impliedly made applicable to their contract and by any practices which they have established between themselves. **G–010**

2. They shall also be bound by usages which reasonable persons in the same situation as the parties usually consider to be applicable to their contract. In the event of conflict with the present Law, the usages shall prevail unless otherwise agreed by the parties.

3. Where expressions, provisions or forms of contract commonly used in commercial practice are employed, they shall be interpreted according to the meaning usually given to them in the trade concerned.

Article 10

For the purposes of the present Law, a breach of contract shall be regarded as fundamental wherever the party in breach knew, or ought to have known, at the time of the conclusion of the contract, that a reasonable person in the same situation as the other party would not have entered into the contract if he had foreseen the breach and its effects. **G–011**

Article 11

Where under the present Law an act is required to be performed "promptly", it shall be performed within as short a period as possible, in the circumstances, from the moment when the act could reasonably be performed. **G–012**

Article 12

For the purposes of the present Law, the expression "current price" means a price based upon an official market quotation, or, in the absence of such a quotation, upon those factors which, according to the usage of the market, serve to determine the price. **G–013**

Article 13

For the purposes of the present Law, the expression "a party knew or ought to have known", or any similar expression, refers to what should have been known to a reasonable person in the same situation. **G–014**

Article 14

G–015   Communications provided for by the present Law shall be made by the means usual in the circumstances.

Article 15

G–016   A contract of sale need not be evidenced by writing and shall not be subject to any other requirements as to form. In particular, it may be proved by means of witnesses.

Article 16

G–017   Where under the provisions of the present Law one party to a contract of sale is entitled to require performance of any obligation by the other party, a court shall not be bound to enter or enforce a judgment providing for specific performance except in accordance with the provisions of Article VII of the Convention dated the 1st day of July 1964 relating to a Uniform Law on the International Sale of Goods.

Article 17

G–018   Questions concerning matters governed by the present Law which are not expressly settled therein shall be settled in conformity with the general principles on which the present Law is based.

Chapter III

Obligations of the Seller

Article 18

G–019   The seller shall effect delivery of the goods, hand over any documents relating thereto and transfer the property in the goods, as required by the contract and the present Law.

Section I

Delivery of the Goods

Article 19

G–020   1. Delivery consists in the handing over of goods which conform with the contract.

2. Where the contract of sale involves carriage of the goods and no other place for delivery has been agreed upon, delivery shall be effected by handing over the goods to the carrier for transmission to the buyer.

3. Where the goods handed over to the carrier are not clearly appropriated to performance of the contract by being marked with an address or by some other

means, the seller shall, in addition to handing over the goods, send to the buyer notice of the consignment and, if necessary, some document specifying the goods.

Sub-Section 1. Obligations of the seller as regards the date and place of delivery

A.—Date of Delivery
Article 20

Where the parties have agreed upon a date for delivery or where such date is fixed by usage, the seller shall, without the need for any other formality, be bound to deliver the goods at that date, provided that the date thus fixed is determined or determinable by the calendar or is fixed in relation to a definite event, the date of which can be ascertained by the parties. **G–021**

Article 21

Where by agreement of the parties or by usage delivery shall be effected within a certain period (such as a particular month or season), the seller may fix the precise date of delivery, unless the circumstances indicate that the fixing of the date was reserved to the buyer. **G–022**

Article 22

Where the date of delivery has not been determined in accordance with the provisions of Articles 20 or 21, the seller shall be bound to deliver the goods within a reasonable time after the conclusion of the contract, regard being had to the nature of the goods and to the circumstances. **G–023**

B.—Place of Delivery
Article 23

1. Where the contract of sale does not involve carriage of the goods, the seller shall deliver the goods at the place where he carried on business at the time of the conclusion of the contract, or, in the absence of a place of business, at his habitual residence. **G–024**

2. If the sale relates to specific goods and the parties knew that the goods were at a certain place at the time of the conclusion of the contract, the seller shall deliver the goods at that place. The same rule shall apply if the goods sold are unascertained goods to be taken from a specified stock or if they are to be manufactured or produced at a place known to the parties at the time of the conclusion of the contract.

C.—Remedies for the seller's failure to perform his obligations as regards the date and place of delivery

Article 24

1. Where the seller fails to perform his obligations as regards the date or the place of delivery, the buyer may, as provided in Articles 25 to 32: **G–025**

(a) require performance of the contract by the seller;

(b) declare the contract avoided.

2. The buyer may also claim damages as provided in Article 82 or in Articles 84 to 87.

3. In no case shall the seller be entitled to apply to a court or arbitral tribunal to grant him a period of grace.

Article 25

G–026   The buyer shall not be entitled to require performance of the contract by the seller, if it is in conformity with usage and reasonably possible for the buyer to purchase goods to replace those to which the contract relates. In this case the contract shall be *ipso facto* avoided as from the time when such purchase should be effected.

(a) Remedies as regards the date of delivery

Article 26

G–027   **1.** Where the failure to deliver the goods at the date fixed amounts to a fundamental breach of the contract, the buyer may either require performance by the seller or declare the contract avoided. He shall inform the seller of his decision within a reasonable time; otherwise the contract shall be *ipso facto* avoided.

2. If the seller requests the buyer to make known his decision under paragraph 1 of this Article and the buyer does not comply promptly, the contract shall be *ipso facto* avoided.

3. If the seller has effected delivery before the buyer has made known his decision under paragraph 1 of this Article and the buyer does not exercise promptly his right to declare the contract avoided, the contract cannot be avoided.

4. Where the buyer has chosen performance of the contract and does not obtain it within a reasonable time, he may declare the contract avoided.

Article 27

G–028   **1.** Where failure to deliver the goods at the date fixed does not amount to a fundamental breach of the contract, the seller shall retain the right to effect delivery and the buyer shall retain the right to require performance of the contract by the seller.

2. The buyer may however grant the seller an additional period of time of reasonable length. Failure to deliver within this period shall amount to a fundamental breach of the contract.

Article 28

G–029   Failure to deliver the goods at the date fixed shall amount to a fundamental breach of the contract whenever a price for such goods is quoted on a market where the buyer can obtain them.

Article 29

Where the seller tenders delivery of the goods before the date fixed, the buyer may accept or reject delivery; if he accepts, he may reserve the right to claim damages in accordance with Article 82.

G–030

(b) Remedies as regards the place of delivery

Article 30

1. Where failure to deliver the goods at the place fixed amounts to a fundamental breach of the contract, and failure to deliver the goods at the date fixed would also amount to a fundamental breach, the buyer may either require performance of the contract by the seller or declare the contract avoided. The buyer shall inform the seller of his decision within a reasonable time; otherwise the contract shall be *ipso facto* avoided.

G–031

2. If the seller requests the buyer to make known his decision under paragraph 1 of this Article and the buyer does not comply promptly, the contract shall be *ipso facto* avoided.

3. If the seller has transported the goods to the place fixed before the buyer has made known his decision under paragraph 1 of this Article and the buyer does not exercise promptly his right to declare the contract avoided, the contract cannot be avoided.

Article 31

1. In cases not provided for in Article 30, the seller shall retain the right to effect delivery at the place fixed and the buyer shall retain the right to require performance of the contract by the seller.

G–032

2. The buyer may however grant the seller an additional period of time of reasonable length. Failure to deliver within this period at the place fixed shall amount to a fundamental breach of the contract.

Article 32

1. If delivery is to be effected by handing over the goods to a carrier and the goods have been handed over at a place other than that fixed, the buyer may declare the contract avoided, whenever the failure to deliver the goods at the place fixed amounts to a fundamental breach of the contract. He shall lose this right if he has not promptly declared the contract avoided.

G–033

2. The buyer shall have the same right, in the circumstances and on the conditions provided in paragraph 1 of this Article, if the goods have been despatched to some place other than that fixed.

3. If despatch from a place or to a place other than that fixed does not amount to a fundamental breach of the contract, the buyer may only claim damages in accordance with Article 82.

Sub-section 2. Obligations of the seller as regards the conformity of the goods

A. Lack of conformity

Article 33

G–034   1. The seller shall not have fulfilled his obligation to deliver the goods, where he has handed over:

(a) part only of the goods sold or a larger or a smaller quantity of the goods than he contracted to sell;

(b) goods which are not those to which the contract relates or goods of a different kind;

(c) goods which lack the qualities of a sample or model which the seller has handed over or sent to the buyer, unless the seller has submitted it without any express or implied undertaking that the goods would conform therewith;

(d) goods which do not possess the qualities necessary for their ordinary or commercial use;

(e) goods which do not possess the qualities for some particular purpose expressly or impliedly contemplated by the contract;

(f) in general, goods which do not possess the qualities and characteristics expressly or impliedly contemplated by the contract.

2. No difference in quantity, lack of part of the goods or absence of any quality or characteristic shall be taken into consideration where it is not material.

Article 34

G–035   In the cases to which Article 33 relates, the rights conferred on the buyer by the present Law exclude all other remedies based on lack of conformity of the goods.

Article 35

G–036   1. Whether the goods are in conformity with the contract shall be determined by their conditions at the time when risk passes. However, if risk does not pass because of a declaration of avoidance of the contract or of a demand for other goods in replacement, the conformity of the goods with the contract shall be determined by their condition at the time when risk would have passed had they been in conformity with the contract.

2. The seller shall be liable for the consequences of any lack of conformity occurring after the time fixed in paragraph 1 of this Article if it was due to an act of the seller or of a person for whose conduct he is responsible.

Article 36

G–037   The seller shall not be liable for the consequences of any lack of conformity of the kind referred to in sub-paragraphs (d), (e) or (f) of paragraph 1 of Article 33, if at the time of the conclusion of the contract the buyer knew, or could not have been unaware of, such lack of conformity.

Article 37

If the seller has handed over goods before the date fixed for delivery he may, up to that date, deliver any missing part or quantity of the goods or deliver other goods which are in conformity with the contract or remedy any defects in the goods handed over, provided that the exercise of this right does not cause the buyer either unreasonable inconvenience or unreasonable expense. **G–038**

B. Ascertainment and notification of lack of conformity

Article 38

1. The buyer shall examine the goods, or cause them to be examined, promptly. **G–039**

2. In case of carriage of the goods the buyer shall examine them at the place of destination.

3. If the goods are redespatched by the buyer without transhipment and the seller knew or ought to have known, at the time when the contract was concluded, of the possibility of such redespatch, examination of the goods may be deferred until they arrive at the new destination.

4. The methods of examination shall be governed by the agreement of the parties or, in the absence of such agreement, by the law or usage of the place where the examination is to be effected.

Article 39

1. The buyer shall lose the right to rely on a lack of conformity of the goods if he has not given the seller notice thereof promptly after he has discovered the lack of conformity or ought to have discovered it. If a defect which could not have been revealed by the examination of the goods provided for in Article 38 is found later, the buyer may nonetheless rely on that defect, provided that he gives the seller notice thereof promptly after its discovery. In any event, the buyer shall lose the right to rely on a lack of conformity of the goods if he has not given notice thereof to the seller within a period of two years from the date on which the goods were handed over, unless the lack of conformity constituted a breach of a guarantee covering a longer period. **G–040**

2. In giving notice to the seller of any lack of conformity, the buyer shall specify its nature and invite the seller to examine the goods or to cause them to be examined by his agent.

3. Where any notice referred to in paragraph 1 of this Article has been sent by letter, telegram or other appropriate means, the fact that such notice is delayed or fails to arrive at its destination shall not deprive the buyer of the right to rely thereon.

Article 40

G–041   The seller shall not be entitled to rely on the provisions of Articles 38 and 39 if the lack of conformity relates to facts of which he knew, or of which he could not have been unaware, and which he did not disclose.

C. Remedies for lack of conformity

Article 41

G–042   1. Where the buyer has given due notice to the seller of the failure of the goods to conform with the contract, the buyer may, as provided in Articles 42 to 46:

(a) require performance of the contract by the seller;

(b) declare the contract avoided;

(c) reduce the price.

2. The buyer may also claim damages as provided in Article 82 or in Articles 84 to 87.

Article 42

G–043   1. The buyer may require the seller to perform the contract:

(a) if the sale relates to goods to be produced or manufactured by the seller, by remedying defects in the goods, provided the seller is in a position to remedy the defects;

(b) if the sale relates to specific goods, by delivering the goods to which the contract refers or the missing part thereof;

(c) if the sale relates to unascertained goods, by delivering other goods which are in conformity with the contract or by delivering the missing part or quantity, except where the purchase of goods in replacement is in conformity with usage and reasonably possible.

2. If the buyer does not obtain performance of the contract by the seller within a reasonable time, he shall retain the rights provided in Articles 43 to 46.

Article 43

G–044   The buyer may declare the contract avoided if the failure of the goods to conform to the contract and also the failure to deliver on the date fixed amount to fundamental breaches of the contract. The buyer shall lose his right to declare the contract avoided if he does not exercise it promptly after giving the seller notice of the lack of conformity or, in the case to which paragraph 2 of Article 42 applies, after the expiration of the period referred to in that paragraph.

Article 44

G–045   1. In cases not provided for in Article 43, the seller shall retain, after the date fixed for the delivery of the goods, the right to deliver any missing part or quantity of the goods or to deliver other goods which are in conformity with the contract or to remedy any defect in the goods handed over, provided that the exercise of this right does not cause the buyer either unreasonable inconvenience or unreasonable expense.

2. The buyer may however fix an additional period of time of reasonable length for the further delivery or for the remedying of the defect. If at the expiration of the additional period the seller has not delivered the goods or remedied the defect, the buyer may choose between requiring the performance of the contract or reducing the price in accordance with Article 46 or, provided that he does so promptly, declare the contract avoided.

Article 45

1. Where the seller has handed over part only of the goods or an insufficient quantity or where part only of the goods handed over is in conformity with the contract, the provisions of Articles 43 and 44 shall apply in respect of the part or quantity which is missing or which does not conform with the contract.

G–046

2. The buyer may declare the contract avoided in its entirety only if the failure to effect delivery completely and in conformity with the contract amounts to a fundamental breach of the contract.

Article 46

Where the buyer has neither obtained performance of the contract by the seller nor declared the contract avoided, the buyer may reduce the price in the same proportion as the value of the goods at the time of the conclusion of the contract has been diminished because of their lack of conformity with the contract.

G–047

Article 47

Where the seller has proffered to the buyer a quantity of unascertained goods greater than that provided for in the contract, the buyer may reject or accept the excess quantity. If the buyer rejects the excess quantity, the seller shall be liable only for damages in accordance with Article 82. If the buyer accepts the whole or part of the excess quantity, he shall pay for it at the contract rate.

G–048

Article 48

The buyer may exercise the rights provided in Articles 43 to 46, even before the time fixed for delivery, if it is clear that goods which would be handed over would not be in conformity with the contract.

G–049

Article 49

1. The buyer shall lose his right to rely on lack of conformity with the contract at the expiration of a period of one year after he has given notice as provided in Article 39, unless he has been prevented from exercising his right because of fraud on the part of the seller.

G–050

2. After the expiration of this period, the buyer shall not be entitled to rely on the lack of conformity, even by way of defence to an action. Nevertheless, if the buyer has not paid for the goods and provided that he has given due notice of the lack of conformity promptly, as provided in Article 39, he may advance as a defence to a claim for payment of the price a claim for a reduction in the price or for damages.

Section II

Handing over of Documents

Article 50

G–051   Where the seller is bound to hand over to the buyer any documents relating to the goods, he shall do so at the time and place fixed by the contract or by usage.

Article 51

G–052   If the seller fails to hand over documents as provided in Article 50 at the time and place fixed or if he hands over documents which are not in conformity with those which he was bound to hand over, the buyer shall have the same rights as those provided under Articles 24 to 32 or under Articles 41 to 49, as the case may be.

Section III

Transfer of Property

Article 52

G–053   1. Where the goods are subject to a right or claim of a third person, the buyer, unless he agreed to take the goods subject to such right or claim, shall notify the seller of such right or claim, unless the seller already knows thereof, and request that the goods should be freed therefrom within reasonable time or that other goods free from all rights and claims of third persons be delivered to him by the seller.

2. If the seller complies with a request made under paragraph 1 of this Article and the buyer nevertheless suffers a loss, the buyer may claim damages in accordance with Article 82.

3. If the seller fails to comply with a request made under paragraph 1 of this Article and a fundamental breach of the contract results thereby, the buyer may declare the contract avoided and claim damages in accordance with Articles 84 to 87. If the buyer does not declare the contract avoided or if there is no fundamental breach of the contract, the buyer shall have the right to claim damages in accordance with Article 82.

4. The buyer shall lose his right to declare the contract avoided if he fails to act in accordance with paragraph 1 of this Article within a reasonable time from the moment when he became aware or ought to have become aware of the right or claim of the third person in respect of the goods.

Article 53

G–054   The rights conferred on the buyer by Article 52 exclude all other remedies based on the fact that the seller has failed to perform his obligation to transfer the property in the goods or that the goods are subject to a right or claim of a third person.

Section IV

Other obligations of the Seller

Article 54

1. If the seller is bound to despatch the goods to the buyer, he shall make, in the usual way and on the usual terms, such contracts as are necessary for the carriage of the goods to the place fixed. **G–055**

2. If the seller is not bound by the contract to effect insurance in respect of the carriage of the goods, he shall provide the buyer, at his request, with all information necessary to enable him to effect such insurance.

Article 55

1. If the seller fails to perform any obligation other than those referred to in Articles 20 to 53, the buyer may: **G–056**

(a) where such failure amounts to a fundamental breach of the contract, declare the contract avoided, provided that he does so promptly, and claim damages in accordance with Articles 84 to 87, or

(b) in any other case, claim damages in accordance with Article 82.

2. The buyer may also require performance by the seller of his obligation, unless the contract is avoided.

Chapter IV

Obligations of the Buyer

Article 56

The buyer shall pay the price for the goods and take delivery of them, as required by the contract and the present law. **G–057**

Section I

Payment of the Price

A. Fixing the price

Article 57

Where a contract has been concluded but does not state a price or make provision for the determination of the price, the buyer shall be bound to pay the **G–058** price generally charged by the seller at the time of the conclusion of the contract.

Article 58

G–059   Where the price is fixed according to the weight of the goods, it shall, in case of doubt, be determined by the net weight.

B. Place and date of payment

Article 59

G–060   1. The buyer shall pay the price to the seller at the seller's place of business or, if he does not have a place of business, at his habitual residence, or, where the payment is to be made against the handing over of the goods or of documents, at the place where such handing over takes place.

2. Where, in consequence of a change in the place of business or habitual residence of the seller subsequent to the conclusion of the contract, the expenses incidental to payment are increased, such increase shall be borne by the seller.

Article 60

G–061   Where the parties have agreed upon a date for the payment of the price or where such date is fixed by usage, the buyer shall, without the need for any other formality, pay the price at that date.

C. Remedies for non-payment

Article 61

G–062   1. If the buyer fails to pay the price in accordance with the contract and with the present law, the seller may require the buyer to perform his obligation.

2. The seller shall not be entitled to require payment of the price by the buyer if it is in conformity with usage and reasonably possible for the seller to resell the goods. In that case the contract shall be *ipso facto* avoided as from the time when such resale should be effected.

Article 62

G–063   1. Where the failure to pay the price at the date fixed amounts to a fundamental breach of the contract, the seller may either require the buyer to pay the price or declare the contract avoided. He shall inform the buyer of his decision within a reasonable time; otherwise the contract shall be *ipso facto* avoided.

2. Where the failure to pay the price at the date fixed does not amount to a fundamental breach of the contract, the seller may grant to the buyer an additional period of time of reasonable length. If the buyer has not paid the price at the expiration of the additional period, the seller may either require the payment of the price by the buyer or, provided that he does so promptly, declare the contract avoided.

Article 63

1. Where the contract is avoided because of failure to pay the price, the seller shall have the right to claim damages in accordance with Articles 84 to 87. **G–064**

2. Where the contract is not avoided, the seller shall have the right to claim damages in accordance with Articles 82 and 83.

Article 64

In no case shall the buyer be entitled to apply to a court or arbitral tribunal to grant him a period of grace for the payment of the price. **G–065**

Section II

Taking Delivery

Article 65

Taking delivery consists in the buyer's doing all such acts as are necessary in order to enable the seller to hand over the goods and actually taking them over. **G–066**

Article 66

1. Where the buyer's failure to take delivery of the goods in accordance with the contract amounts to a fundamental breach of the contract or gives the seller good grounds for fearing that the buyer will not pay the price, the seller may declare the contract avoided. **G–067**

2. Where the failure to take delivery of the goods does not amount to a fundamental breach of the contract, the seller may grant to the buyer an additional period of time of reasonable length. If the buyer has not taken delivery of the goods at the expiration of the additional period, the seller may declare the contract avoided, provided that he does so promptly.

Article 67

1. If the contract reserves to the buyer the right subsequently to determine the form, measurement or other features of the goods (sale by specification) and he fails to make such specification either on the date expressly or impliedly agreed upon or within a reasonable time after receipt of a request from the seller, the seller may declare the contract avoided, provided that he does so promptly, or make the specification himself in accordance with the requirements of the buyer in so far as these are known to him. **G–068**

2. If the seller makes the specification himself, he shall inform the buyer of the details thereof and shall fix a reasonable period of time within which the buyer may submit a different specification. If the buyer fails to do so the specification made by the seller shall be binding.

Article 68

G–069   1. Where the contract is avoided because of the failure of the buyer to accept delivery of the goods or to make a specification, the seller shall have the right to claim damages in accordance with Articles 84 to 87.

2. Where the contract is not avoided, the seller shall have the right to claim damages in accordance with Article 82.

Section III

Other Obligations of the Buyer

Article 69

G–070   The buyer shall take the steps provided for in the contract, by usage or by laws and regulations in force, for the purpose of making provision for or guaranteeing payment of the price, such as the acceptance of a bill of exchange, the opening of a documentary credit or the giving of a banker's guarantee.

Article 70

G–071   1. If the buyer fails to perform any obligation other than those referred to in Sections I and II of this Chapter, the seller may:

(a) where such failure amounts to a fundamental breach of the contract, declare the contract avoided, provided that he does so promptly, and claim damages in accordance with Articles 84 to 87; or

(b) in any other case, claim damages in accordance with Article 82.

2. The seller may also require performance by the buyer of his obligation, unless the contract is avoided.

Chapter V

Provisions Common to the Obligations of the Seller and of the Buyer

Section I

Concurrence between Delivery of the Goods and Payment of the Price

Article 71

G–072   Except as otherwise provided in Article 72, delivery of the goods and payment of the price shall be concurrent conditions. Nevertheless, the buyer shall not be obliged to pay the price until he has had an opportunity to examine the goods.

Article 72

G–073   1. Where the contract involves carriage of the goods and where delivery is, by virtue of paragraph 2 of Article 19, effected by handing over the goods to the carrier, the seller may either postpone despatch of the goods until he receives payment or proceed to despatch them on terms that reserve to himself the right of disposal of the goods during transit. In the latter case, he may require that the goods shall not be handed over to the buyer at the place of destination except against payment of the price and the buyer shall not be bound to pay the price until he has had an opportunity to examine the goods.

2. Nevertheless, when the contract requires payment against documents, the buyer shall not be entitled to refuse payment of the price on the ground that he has not had the opportunity to examine the goods.

Article 73

1. Each party may suspend the performance of his obligations whenever, after the conclusion of the contract, the economic situation of the other party appears to have become so difficult that there is good reason to fear that he will not perform a material part of his obligations.   **G–074**

2. If the seller has already despatched the goods before the economic situation of the buyer described in paragraph 1 of this Article becomes evident, he may prevent the handing over of the goods to the buyer even if the latter holds a document which entitles him to obtain them.

3. Nevertheless, the seller shall not be entitled to prevent the handing over of the goods if they are claimed by a third person who is a lawful holder of a document which entitles him to obtain the goods, unless the document contains a reservation concerning the effects of its transfer or unless the seller can prove that the holder of the document, when he acquired it, knowingly acted to the detriment of the seller.

Section II

Exemptions

Article 74

1. Where one of the parties has not performed one of his obligations, he shall not be liable for such non-performance if he can prove that it was due to circumstances which, according to the intention of the parties at the time of the conclusion of the contract, he was not bound to take into account or to avoid or to overcome; in the absence of any expression of the intention of the parties, regard shall be had to what reasonable persons in the same situation would have intended.   **G–075**

2. Where the circumstances which gave rise to the non-performance of the obligation constituted only a temporary impediment to performance, the party in default shall nevertheless be permanently relieved of his obligation if, by reason of the delay, performance would be so radically changed as to amount to the performance of an obligation quite different from that contemplated by the contract.

3. The relief provided by this Article for one of the parties shall not include the avoidance of the contract under some other provision of the present Law or deprive the other party of any right which he has under the present Law to reduce the price, unless the circumstances which entitled the first party to relief were caused by the act of the other party or of some person for whose conduct he was responsible.

Section III

Supplementary Rules Concerning the Avoidance of the Contract

A. Supplementary grounds for avoidance

Article 75

G–076   1. Where, in the case of contracts for delivery of goods by instalments, by reason of any failure by one party to perform any of his obligations under the contract in respect of any instalment, the other party has good reason to fear failure of performance in respect of future instalments, he may declare the contract avoided for the future, provided that he does so promptly.

2. The buyer may also, provided that he does so promptly, declare the contract avoided in respect of future deliveries or in respect of deliveries already made or both, if by reason of their interdependence such deliveries would be worthless to him.

Article 76

G–077   Where prior to the date fixed for performance of the contract it is clear that one of the parties will commit a fundamental breach of the contract, the other party shall have the right to declare the contract avoided.

Article 77

G–078   Where the contract has been avoided under Article 75 or Article 76, the party declaring the contract avoided may claim damages in accordance with Articles 84 to 87.

B. Effects of avoidance
Article 78

G–079   1. Avoidance of the contract releases both parties from their obligations thereunder, subject to any damages which may be due.

2. If one party has performed the contract either wholly or in part, he may claim the return of whatever he has supplied or paid under the contract. If both parties are required to make restitution, they shall do so concurrently.

Article 79

G–080   1. The buyer shall lose his right to declare the contract avoided where it is impossible for him to return the goods in the condition in which he received them.

2. Nevertheless, the buyer may declare the contract avoided:

(a) if the goods or part of the goods have perished or deteriorated as a result of the defect which justifies the avoidance;

(b) if the goods or part of the goods have perished or deteriorated as a result of the examination prescribed in Article 38;

(c) if part of the goods have been consumed or transformed by the buyer in the course of normal use before the lack of conformity with the contract was discovered;

(d) if the impossibility of returning the goods or of returning them in the condition in which they were received is not due to the act of the buyer or of some other person for whose conduct he is responsible;

(e) if the deterioration or transformation of the goods is unimportant.

Article 80

The buyer who has lost the right to declare the contract avoided by virtue of Article 79 shall retain all the other rights conferred on him by the present Law.   **G–081**

Article 81

1. Where the seller is under an obligation to refund the price, he shall also be liable for the interest thereon at the rate fixed by Article 83, as from the date of payment.   **G–082**

2. The buyer shall be liable to account to the seller for all benefits which he has derived from the goods or part of them, as the case may be:

(a) where he is under an obligation to return the goods or part of them,

(b) where it is impossible for him to return the goods or part of them, but the contract is nevertheless avoided.

Section IV

Supplementary Rules Concerning Damages

A. Damages where the contract is not avoided

Article 82

Where the contract is not avoided, damages for a breach of contract by one party shall consist of a sum equal to the loss, including loss of profit, suffered by the other party. Such damages shall not exceed the loss which the party in breach ought to have foreseen at the time of the conclusion of the contract, in the light of the facts and matters which then were known or ought to have been known to him, as a possible consequence of the breach of the contract.   **G–083**

Article 83

Where the breach of contract consists of delay in the payment of the price, the seller shall in any event be entitled to interest on such sum as is in arrear at a rate   **G–084** equal to the official discount rate in the country where he has his place of business or, if he has no place of business, his habitual residence, plus 1 per cent.

B. Damages where the contract is avoided

Article 84

G–085   1. In case of avoidance of the contract, where there is a current price for the goods, damages shall be equal to the difference between the price fixed by the contract and the current price on the date on which the contract is avoided.

2. In calculating the amount of damages under paragraph 1 of this Article, the current price to be taken into account shall be that prevailing in the market in which the transaction took place or, if there is no such current price or if its application is inappropriate, the price in a market which serves as a reasonable substitute, making due allowance for differences in the cost of transporting the goods.

Article 85

G–086   If the buyer has bought goods in replacement or the seller has resold goods in a reasonable manner, he may recover the difference between the contract price and the price paid for the goods bought in replacement or that obtained by the resale.

Article 86

G–087   The damages referred to in Articles 84 and 85 may be increased by the amount of any reasonable expenses incurred as a result of the breach or up to the amount of any loss, including loss of profit, which should have been foreseen by the party in breach, at the time of the conclusion of the contract, in the light of the facts and matters which were known or ought to have been known to him, as a possible consequence of the breach of the contract.

Article 87

G–088   If there is no current price for the goods, damages shall be calculated on the same basis as that provided in Article 82.

C. General provisions concerning damages

Article 88

G–089   The party who relies on a breach of the contract shall adopt all reasonable measures to mitigate the loss resulting from the breach. If he fails to adopt such measures, the party in breach may claim a reduction in the damages.

Article 89

G–090   In case of fraud, damages shall be determined by the rules applicable in respect of contracts of sale not governed by the present law.

Section V

Expenses

Article 90

The expenses of delivery shall be borne by the seller; all expenses after delivery shall be borne by the buyer. **G–091**

Section VI

Preservation of the Goods

Article 91

Where the buyer is in delay in taking delivery of the goods or in paying the price, the seller shall take reasonable steps to preserve the goods; he shall have the right to retain them until he has been reimbursed his reasonable expenses by the buyer. **G–092**

Article 92

1. Where the goods have been received by the buyer, he shall take reasonable steps to preserve them if he intends to reject them; he shall have the right to retain them until he has been reimbursed his reasonable expenses by the seller. **G–093**

2. Where goods despatched to the buyer have been put at his disposal at their place of destination and he exercises the right to reject them, he shall be bound to take possession of them on behalf of the seller, provided that this maybe done without payment of the price and without unreasonable inconvenience or unreasonable expense. This provision shall not apply where the seller or a person authorised to take charge of the goods on his behalf is present at such destination.

Article 93

The party who is under an obligation to take steps to preserve the goods may deposit them in the warehouse of a third person at the expense of the other party provided that the expense incurred is not unreasonable. **G–094**

Article 94

1. The party who, in the cases to which Articles 91 and 92 apply, is under an obligation to take steps to preserve the goods may sell them by any appropriate means, provided that there has been unreasonable delay by the other party in accepting them or taking them back or in paying the costs of preservation and provided that due notice has been given to the other party of the intention to sell. **G–095**

2. The party selling the goods shall have the right to retain out of the proceeds of sale an amount equal to the reasonable costs of preserving the goods and of selling them and shall transmit the balance to the other party.

Article 95

G–096   Where, in the cases to which Articles 91 and 92 apply, the goods are subject to loss or rapid deterioration or their preservation would involve unreasonable expense, the party under the duty to preserve them is bound to sell them in accordance with Article 94.

Chapter VI

Passing of the Risk

Article 96

G–097   Where the risk has passed to the buyer, he shall pay the price notwithstanding the loss or deterioration of the goods, unless this is due to the act of the seller or of some other person for whose conduct the seller is responsible.

Article 97

G–098   1. The risk shall pass to the buyer when delivery of the goods is effected in accordance with the provisions of the contract and the present Law.

2. In the case of the handing over of goods which are not in conformity with the contract, the risk shall pass to the buyer from the moment when the handing over has, apart from the lack of conformity, been effected in accordance with the provisions of the contract and of the present Law, where the buyer has neither declared the contract avoided nor required goods in replacement.

Article 98

G–099   1. Where the handing over of the goods is delayed owing to the breach of an obligation of the buyer, the risk shall pass to the buyer as from the last date when, apart from such breach, the handing over could have been made in accordance with the contract.

2. Where the contract relates to a sale of unascertained goods, delay on the part of the buyer shall cause the risk to pass only when the seller has set aside goods manifestly appropriated to the contract and has notified the buyer that this has been done.

3. Where unascertained goods are of such a kind that the seller cannot set aside a part of them until the buyer takes delivery, it shall be sufficient for the seller to do all acts necessary to enable the buyer to take delivery.

Article 99

G–100   1. Where the sale is of goods in transit by sea, the risk shall be borne by the buyer as from the time at which the goods were handed over to the carrier.

2. Where the seller, at the time of the conclusion of the contract, knew or ought to have known that the goods had been lost or had deteriorated, the risk shall remain with him until the time of the conclusion of the contract.

Article 100

If, in a case to which paragraph 3 of Article 19 applies, the seller, at the time of   **G–101**
sending the notice or other document referred to in that paragraph knew or ought
to have known that the goods had been lost or had deteriorated after they were
handed over to the carrier, the risk shall remain with the seller until the time of
sending such notice or document.

Article 101

The passing of the risk shall not necessarily be determined by the provisions of   **G–102**
the contract concerning expenses.

APPENDIX H

UNITED NATIONS CONVENTION ON CONTRACTS FOR THE INTERNATIONAL SALE OF GOODS, 1980 (CISG)

H–001 [Note that the full text can be found at UNCITRAL's website, at *www. uncitral.org*]

THE STATES PARTIES TO THIS CONVENTION, BEARING IN MIND the broad objectives in the resolutions adopted by the sixth special session of the General Assembly of the United Nations on the establishment of a New International Economic Order, CONSIDERING that the development of international trade on the basis of equality and mutual benefit is an important element in promoting friendly relations among States, BEING OF THE OPINION that the adoption of uniform rules which govern contracts for the international sale of goods and take into account the different social, economic and legal systems would contribute to the removal of legal barriers in international trade and promote the development of international trade, HAVE DECREED as follows:

PART I

SPHERE OF APPLICATION AND GENERAL PROVISIONS

CHAPTER I

SPHERE OF APPLICATION

Article 1

H–002 (1) This Convention applies to contracts of sale of goods between parties whose places of business are in different States:

(a) when the States are Contracting States; or

(b) when the rules of private international law lead to the application of the law of a Contracting State.

(2) The fact that the parties have their places of business in different States is to be disregarded whenever this fact does not appear either from the contract or from any dealings between, or from information disclosed by, the parties at any time before or at the conclusion of the contract.

(3) Neither the nationality of the parties nor the civil or commercial character of the parties or of the contract is to be taken into consideration in determining the application of this Convention.

Article 2

This Convention does not apply to sales: **H–003**

(a) of goods bought for personal, family or household use, unless the seller, at any time before or at the conclusion of the contract, neither knew nor ought to have known that the goods were bought for any such use;

(b) by auction;

(c) on execution or otherwise by authority of law;

(d) of stocks, shares, investment securities, negotiable instruments or money;

(e) of ships, vessels, hovercraft or aircraft;

(f) of electricity.

Article 3

(1) Contracts for the supply of goods to be manufactured or produced are to be   **H–004** considered sales unless the party who orders the goods undertakes to supply a substantial part of the materials necessary for such manufacture or production.

(2) This Convention does not apply to contracts in which the preponderant part of the obligations of the party who furnishes the goods consists in the supply of labour or other services.

Article 4

This Convention governs only the formation of the contract of sale and the   **H–005** rights and obligations of the seller and the buyer arising from such a contract. In particular, except as otherwise expressly provided in this Convention, it is not concerned with:

(a) the validity of the contract or of any of its provisions or of any usage;

(b) the effect which the contract may have on the property in the goods sold.

Article 5

This Convention does not apply to the liability of the seller for death or   **H–006** personal injury caused by the goods to any person.

Article 6

The parties may exclude the application of this Convention or, subject to article   **H–007** 12, derogate from or vary the effect of any of its provisions.

CHAPTER II

GENERAL PROVISIONS

Article 7

(1) In the interpretation of this Convention, regard is to be had to its inter-   **H–008** national character and to the need to promote uniformity in its application and the observance of good faith in international trade.

(2) Questions concerning matters governed by this Convention which are not expressly settled in it are to be settled in conformity with the general principles on which it is based or, in the absence of such principles, in conformity with the law applicable by virtue of the rules of private international law.

Article 8

H–009   (1) For the purposes of this Convention statements made by and other conduct of a party are to be interpreted according to his intent where the other party knew or could not have been unaware what that intent was.

(2) If the preceding paragraph is not applicable, statements made by and other conduct of a party are to be interpreted according to the understanding that a reasonable person of the same kind as the other party would have had in the same circumstances.

(3) In determining the intent of a party or the understanding a reasonable person would have had, due consideration is to be given to all relevant circumstances of the case including the negotiations, any practices which the parties have established between themselves, usages and any subsequent conduct of the parties.

Article 9

H–010   (1) The parties are bound by any usage to which they have agreed and by any practices which they have established between themselves.

(2) The parties are considered, unless otherwise agreed, to have impliedly made applicable to their contract or its formation a usage of which the parties knew or ought to have known and which in international trade is widely known to, and regularly observed by, parties to contracts of the type involved in the particular trade concerned.

Article 10

H–011   For the purposes of this Convention:

   (a) if a party has more than one place of business, the place of business is that which has the closest relationship to the contract and its performance, having regard to the circumstances known to or contemplated by the parties at any time before or at the conclusion of the contract;

   (b) if a party does not have a place of business, reference is to be made to his habitual residence.

Article 11

H–012   A contract of sale need not be concluded in or evidenced by writing and is not subject to any other requirement as to form. It may be proved by any means, including witnesses.

Article 12

H–013   Any provision of article 11, article 29 or Part II of this Convention that allows a contract of sale or its modification or termination by agreement or any offer, acceptance or other indication of intention to be made in any form other than in writing does not apply where any party has his place of business in a Contracting State which has made a declaration under article 96 of this Convention. The parties may not derogate from or vary the effect or this article.

Article 13

For the purposes of this Convention "writing" includes telegram and telex.　**H–014**

Part II

Formation of the Contract

Article 14

(1) A proposal for concluding a contract addressed to one or more specific　**H–015** persons constitutes an offer if it is sufficiently definite and indicates the intention of the offeror to be bound in case of acceptance. A proposal is sufficiently definite if it indicates the goods and expressly or implicitly fixes or makes provision for determining the quantity and the price.

(2) A proposal other than one addressed to one or more specific persons is to be considered merely as an invitation to make offers, unless the contrary is clearly indicated by the person making the proposal.

Article 15

(1) An offer becomes effective when it reaches the offeree.　**H–016**

(2) An offer, even if it is irrevocable, may be withdrawn if the withdrawal reaches the offeree before or at the same time as the offer.

Article 16

(1) Until a contract is concluded an offer may be revoked if the revocation　**H–017** reaches the offeree before he has dispatched an acceptance.

(2) However, an offer cannot be revoked:

(a) if it indicates, whether by stating a fixed time for acceptance or otherwise, that it is irrevocable; or

(b) if it was reasonable for the offeree to rely on the offer as being irrevocable and the offeree has acted in reliance on the offer.

Article 17

An offer, even if it is irrevocable, is terminated when a rejection reaches the　**H–018** offeror.

Article 18

(1) A statement made by or other conduct of the offeree indicating assent　**H–019** to an offer is an acceptance. Silence or inactivity does not in itself amount to acceptance.

(2) An acceptance of an offer becomes effective at the moment the indication of assent reaches the offeror. An acceptance is not effective if the indication of assent does not reach the offeror within the time he has fixed or, if no time is fixed, within a reasonable time, due account being taken of the circumstances of the transaction, including the rapidity of the means of communication employed by the offeror. An oral offer must be accepted immediately unless the circumstances indicate otherwise.

(3) However, if, by virtue of the offer or as a result of practices which the parties have established between themselves or of usage, the offeree may indicate assent by performing an act, such as one relating to the dispatch of the goods or payment of the price, without notice to the offeror, the acceptance is effective at the moment the act is performed, provided that the act is performed within the period of time laid down in the preceding paragraph.

Article 19

H–020
(1) A reply to an offer which purports to be an acceptance but contains additions, limitations or other modifications is a rejection of the offer and constitutes a counter-offer.

(2) However, a reply to an offer which purports to be an acceptance but contains additional or different terms which do not materially alter the terms of the offer constitutes an acceptance, unless the offeror, without undue delay, objects orally to the discrepancy or dispatches a notice to that effect. If he does not so object, the terms of the contract are the terms of the offer with the modifications contained in the acceptance.

(3) Additional or different terms relating, among other things, to the price, payment, quality and quantity of the goods, place and time of delivery, extent of one party's liability to the other or the settlement of disputes are considered to alter the terms of the offer materially.

Article 20

H–021
(1) A period of time for acceptance fixed by the offeror in a telegram or a letter begins to run from the moment the telegram is handed in for dispatch or from the date shown on the letter or, if no such date is shown, from the date shown on the envelope. A period of time for acceptance fixed by the offeror by telephone, telex or other means of instantaneous communication, begins to run from the moment that the offer reaches the offeree.

(2) Official holidays or non-business days occurring during the period for acceptance are included in calculating the period. However, if a notice of acceptance cannot be delivered at the address of the offeror on the last day of the period because that day falls on an official holiday or a non-business day at the place of business of the offeror, the period is extended until the first business day which follows.

Article 21

H–022
(1) A late acceptance is nevertheless effective as an acceptance if without delay the offeror orally so informs the offeree or dispatches a notice to that effect.

(2) If a letter or other writing containing a late acceptance shows that it has been sent in such circumstances that if its transmission had been normal it would have reached the offeror in due time, the late acceptance is effective as an acceptance unless, without delay, the offeror orally informs the offeree that he considers his offer as having lapsed or dispatches a notice to that effect.

Article 22

An acceptance may be withdrawn if the withdrawal reaches the offeror before   **H–023**
or at the same time as the acceptance would have become effective.

Article 23

A contract is concluded at the moment when an acceptance of an offer becomes   **H–024**
effective in accordance with the provisions of this Convention.

Article 24

For the purposes of this Part of the Convention, an offer, declaration of accep-   **H–025**
tance or any other indication of intention "reaches" the addressee when it is made
orally to him or delivered by any other means to him personally, to his place of
business or mailing address or, if he does not have a place of business or mailing
address, to his habitual residence.

Part III

Sale of Goods

Chapter I

General Provisions

Article 25

A breach of contract committed by one of the parties is fundamental if it results   **H–026**
in such detriment to the other party as substantially to deprive him of what he is
entitled to expect under the contract, unless the party in breach did not foresee
and a reasonable person of the same kind in the same circumstances would not
have foreseen such a result.

Article 26

A declaration of avoidance of the contract is effective only if made by notice to   **H–027**
the other party.

Article 27

Unless otherwise expressly provided in this Part of the Convention, if any   **H–028**
notice, request or other communication is given or made by a party in accordance
with this Part and by means appropriate in the circumstances, a delay or error in
the transmission of the communication or its failure to arrive does not deprive
that party of the right to rely on the communication.

Article 28

If, in accordance with the provisions of this Convention, one party is entitled to   **H–029**
require performance of any obligation by the other party, a court is not bound

to enter a judgement for specific performance unless the court would do so under its own law in respect of similar contracts of sale not governed by this Convention.

Article 29

H–030 (1) A contract may be modified or terminated by the mere agreement of the parties.

(2) A contract in writing which contains a provision requiring any modification or termination by agreement to be in writing may not be otherwise modified or terminated by agreement. However, a party may be precluded by his conduct from asserting such a provision to the extent that the other party has relied on that conduct.

CHAPTER II

OBLIGATIONS OF THE SELLER

Article 30

H–031 The seller must deliver the goods, hand over any documents relating to them and transfer the property in the goods, as required by the contract and this Convention.

SECTION I

DELIVERY OF THE GOODS AND HANDING OVER OF DOCUMENTS

Article 31

H–032 If the seller is not bound to deliver the goods at any other particular place, his obligation to deliver consists:

(a) if the contract of sale involves carriage of the goods—in handing the goods over to the first carrier for transmission to the buyer;

(b) if, in cases not within the preceding subparagraph, the contract related to specific goods, or unidentified goods to be drawn from a specific stock or to be manufactured or produced, and at the time of the conclusion of the contract the parties knew that the goods were at, or were to be manufactured or produced at, a particular place—in placing the goods at the buyer's disposal at that place;

(c) in other cases—in placing the goods at the buyer's disposal at the place where the seller had his place of business at the time of the conclusion of the contract.

Article 32

H–033 (1) If the seller, in accordance with the contract or this Convention, hands the goods over to a carrier and if the goods are not clearly identified to the contract by markings on the goods, by shipping documents or otherwise, the seller must give the buyer notice of the consignment specifying the goods.

(2) If the seller is bound to arrange for carriage of the goods, he must make such contracts as are necessary for carriage to the place fixed by means of transportation appropriate in the circumstances and according to the usual terms for such transportation.

(3) If the seller is not bound to effect insurance in respect of the carriage of the goods, he must, at the buyer's request, provide him with all available information necessary to enable him to effect such insurance.

Article 33

The seller must deliver the goods: H–034

(a) if a date is fixed by or determinable from the contract, on that date;

(b) if a period of time is fixed by or determinable from the contract, at any time within that period unless circumstances indicate that the buyer is to choose a date; or

(c) in any other case, within a reasonable time after the conclusion of the contract.

Article 34

If the seller is bound to hand over documents relating to the goods, he must   H–035
hand them over at the time and place and in the form required by the contract. If the seller has handed over documents before that time, he may, up to that time, cure any lack of conformity in the documents, if the exercise of this right does not cause the buyer unreasonable inconvenience or unreasonable expense. However, the buyer retains any right to claim damages as provided for in this Convention.

Section II

Conformity of the Goods and Third Party Claims

Article 35

(1) The seller must deliver goods which are of the quantity, quality and descrip-   H–036
tion required by the contract and which are contained or packaged in the manner required by the contract.

(2) Except where the parties have agreed otherwise, the goods do not conform with the contract unless they:

(a) are fit for the purposes for which goods of the same description would ordinarily be used;

(b) are fit for any particular purpose expressly or impliedly made known to the seller at the time of the conclusion of the contract, except where the circumstances show that the buyer did not rely, or that it was unreasonable for him to rely, on the seller's skill and judgement;

(c) possess the qualities of goods which the seller has held out to the buyer as a sample or model;

(d) are contained or packaged in the manner usual for such goods or, where there is no such manner, in a manner adequate to preserve and protect the goods.

(3) The seller is not liable under subparagraphs (a) to (d) of the preceding paragraph for any lack of conformity of the goods if at the time of the conclusion of the contract the buyer knew or could not have been unaware of such lack of conformity.

Article 36

H–037
(1) The seller is liable in accordance with the contract and this Convention for any lack of conformity which exists at the time when the risk passes to the buyer, even though the lack of conformity becomes apparent only after that time.

(2) The seller is also liable for any lack of conformity which occurs after the time indicated in the preceding paragraph and which is due to a breach of any of his obligations, including a breach of any guarantee that for a period of time the goods will remain fit for their ordinary purpose or for some particular purpose or will retain specified qualities or characteristics.

Article 37

H–038
If the seller has delivered goods before the date for delivery, he may, up to that date, deliver any missing part or make up any deficiency in the quantity of the goods delivered, or deliver goods in replacement of any non-conforming goods delivered or remedy any lack of conformity in the goods delivered, provided that the exercise of this right does not cause the buyer unreasonable inconvenience or unreasonable expense. However, the buyer retains any right to claim damages as provided for in this Convention.

Article 38

H–039
(1) The buyer must examine the goods, or cause them to be examined, within as short a period as is practicable in the circumstances.

(2) If the contract involves carriage of the goods, examination may be deferred until after the goods have arrived at their destination.

(3) If the goods are redirected in transit or redispatched by the buyer without a reasonable opportunity for examination by him and at the time of the conclusion of the contract the seller knew or ought to have known of the possibility of such redirection or redispatch, examination may be deferred until after the goods have arrived at the new destination.

Article 39

H–040
(1) The buyer loses the right to rely on a lack of conformity of the goods if he does not give notice to the seller specifying the nature of the lack of conformity within a reasonable time after he has discovered it or ought to have discovered it.

(2) In any event, the buyer loses the right to rely on a lack of conformity of the goods if he does not give the seller notice thereof at the latest within a period of two years from the date on which the goods were actually handed over to the

buyer, unless this time-limit is inconsistent with a contractual period of guarantee.

Article 40

The seller is not entitled to rely on the provisions of articles 38 and 39 if the lack **H–041** of conformity relates to facts of which he knew or could not have been unaware and which he did not disclose to the buyer.

Article 41

The seller must deliver goods which are free from any right or claim of a third **H–042** party, unless the buyer agreed to take the goods subject to that right or claim. However, if such right or claim is based on industrial property or other intellectual property, the seller's obligation is governed by article 42.

Article 42

(1) The seller must deliver goods which are free from any right or claim of a **H–043** third party based on industrial property or other intellectual property, of which at the time of the conclusion of the contract the seller knew or could not have been unaware, provided that the right or claim is based on industrial property or other intellectual property:

- (a) under the law of the State where the goods will be resold or otherwise used, if it was contemplated by the parties at the time of the conclusion of the contract that the goods would be resold or otherwise used in that State; or

- (b) in any other case, under the law of the State where the buyer has his place of business.

(2) The obligation of the seller under the preceding paragraph does not extend to cases where:

- (a) at the time of the conclusion of the contract the buyer knew or could not have been unaware of the right or claim; or

- (b) the right or claim results from the seller's compliance with technical drawings, designs, formulae or other such specifications furnished by the buyer.

Article 43

(1) The buyer loses the right to rely on the provisions of article 41 or article 42 **H–044** if he does not give notice to the seller specifying the nature of the right or claim of the third party within a reasonable time after he has become aware or ought to have become aware of the right or claim.

(2) The seller is not entitled to rely on the provisions of the preceding paragraph if he knew of the right or claim of the third party and the nature of it.

Article 44

Notwithstanding the provisions of paragraph (1) of article 39 and paragraph (1) **H–045** of article 43, the buyer may reduce the price in accordance with article 50 or claim damages, except for loss of profit, if he has a reasonable excuse for his failure to give the required notice.

Section III

Remedies for Breach of Contract by the Seller

Article 45

H–046   (1) If the seller fails to perform any of his obligations under the contract or this Convention, the buyer may:

(a) exercise the rights provided in articles 46 to 52;

(b) claim damages as provided in articles 74 to 77.

(2) The buyer is not deprived of any right he may have to claim damages by exercising his right to other remedies.
(3) No period of grace may be granted to the seller by a court or arbitral tribunal when the buyer resorts to a remedy for breach of contract.

Article 46

H–047   (1) The buyer may require performance by the seller of his obligations unless the buyer has resorted to a remedy which is inconsistent with this requirement.
(2) If the goods do not conform with the contract, the buyer may require delivery of substitute goods only if the lack of conformity constitutes a fundamental breach of contract and a request for substitute goods is made either in conjunction with notice given under article 39 or within a reasonable time thereafter.
(3) If the goods do not conform with the contract, the buyer may require the seller to remedy the lack of conformity by repair, unless this is unreasonable having regard to all the circumstances. A request for repair must be made either in conjunction with notice given under article 39 or within a reasonable time thereafter.

Article 47

H–048   (1) The buyer may fix an additional period of time of reasonable length for performance by the seller of his obligations.
(2) Unless the buyer has received notice from the seller that he will not perform within the period so fixed, the buyer may not, during that period, resort to any remedy for breach of contract. However, the buyer is not deprived thereby of any right he may have to claim damages for delay in performance.

Article 48

H–049   (1) Subject to article 49, the seller may, even after the date for delivery, remedy at his own expense any failure to perform his obligations, if he can do so without unreasonable delay and without causing the buyer unreasonable inconvenience or uncertainty of reimbursement by the seller of expenses advanced by the buyer. However, the buyer retains any right to claim damages as provided for in this Convention.

(2) If the seller requests the buyer to make known whether he will accept performance and the buyer does not comply with the request within a reasonable time, the seller may perform within the time indicated in his request. The buyer may not, during that period of time, resort to any remedy which is inconsistent with performance by the seller.

(3) A notice by the seller that he will perform within a specified period of time is assumed to include a request, under the preceding paragraph, that the buyer make known his decision.

(4) A request or notice by the seller under paragraph (2) or (3) of this article is not effective unless received by the buyer.

Article 49

(1) The buyer may declare the contract avoided: **H–050**

(a) if the failure by the seller to perform any of his obligations under the contract or this Convention amounts to a fundamental breach of contract; or

(b) in case of non-delivery, if the seller does not deliver the goods within the additional period of time fixed by the buyer in accordance with paragraph (1) of article 47 or declares that he will not deliver within the period so fixed.

(2) However, in cases where the seller has delivered the goods, the buyer loses the right to declare the contract avoided unless he does so:

(a) in respect of late delivery, within a reasonable time after he has become aware that delivery has been made;

(b) in respect of any breach other than late delivery, within a reasonable time:

   (i) after he knew or ought to have known of the breach;

   (ii) after the expiration of any additional period of time fixed by the buyer in accordance with paragraph (1) of article 47, or after the seller has declared that he will not perform his obligations within such an additional period; or

   (iii) after the expiration of any additional period of time indicated by the seller in accordance with paragraph (2) of article 48, or after the buyer has declared that he will not accept performance.

Article 50

If the goods do not conform with the contract and whether or not the price has already been paid, the buyer may reduce the price in the same proportion as the value that the goods actually delivered had at the time of the delivery bears to the value that conforming goods would have had at that time. However, if the seller remedies any failure to perform his obligations in accordance with article 37 or article 48 or if the buyer refuses to accept performance by the seller in accordance with those articles, the buyer may not reduce the price. **H–051**

Article 51

(1) If the seller delivers only a part of the goods or if only a part of the goods delivered is in conformity with the contract, articles 46 to 50 apply in respect of the part which is missing or which does not conform. **H–052**

(2) The buyer may declare the contract avoided in its entirety only if the failure to make delivery completely or in conformity with the contract amounts to a fundamental breach of the contract.

Article 52

H–053   (1) If the seller delivers the goods before the date fixed, the buyer may take delivery or refuse to take delivery.

(2) If the seller delivers a quantity of goods greater than that provided for in the contract, the buyer may take delivery or refuse to take delivery of the excess quantity. If the buyer takes delivery of all or part of the excess quantity, he must pay for it at the contract rate.

CHAPTER III

OBLIGATIONS OF THE BUYER

Article 53

H–054   The buyer must pay the price for the goods and take delivery of them as required by the contract and this Convention.

SECTION I

PAYMENT OF THE PRICE

Article 54

H–055   The buyer's obligation to pay the price includes taking such steps and complying with such formalities as may be required under the contract or any laws and regulations to enable payment to be made.

Article 55

H–056   Where a contract has been validly concluded but does not expressly or implicitly fix or make provision for determining the price, the parties are considered, in the absence of any indication to the contrary, to have impliedly made reference to the price generally charged at the time of the conclusion of the contract for such goods sold under comparable circumstances in the trade concerned.

Article 56

H–057   If the price is fixed according to the weight of the goods, in case of doubt it is to be determined by the net weight.

Article 57

H–058   (1) If the buyer is not bound to pay the price at any other particular place, he must pay it to the seller:

(a) at the seller's place of business; or

(b) if the payment is to be made against the handing over of the goods or of documents, at the place where the handing over takes place.

(2) The seller must bear any increases in the expenses incidental to payment which is caused by a change in his place of business subsequent to the conclusion of the contract.

Article 58

(1) If the buyer is not bound to pay the price at any other specific time, he must **H–059** pay it when the seller places either the goods or documents controlling their disposition at the buyer's disposal in accordance with the contract and this Convention. The seller may make such payment a condition for handing over the goods or documents.

(2) If the contract involves carriage of the goods, the seller may dispatch the goods on terms whereby the goods, or documents controlling their disposition, will not be handed over to the buyer except against payment of the price.

(3) The buyer is not bound to pay the price until he has had an opportunity to examine the goods, unless the procedures for delivery or payment agreed upon by the parties are inconsistent with his having such an opportunity.

Article 59

The buyer must pay the price on the date fixed by or determinable from the **H–060** contract and this Convention without the need for any request or compliance with any formality on the part of the seller.

Section II

Taking Delivery

Article 60

The buyer's obligation to take delivery consists: **H–061**

(a) in doing all the acts which could reasonably be expected of him in order to enable the seller to make delivery; and

(b) in taking over the goods.

Section III

Remedies for Breach of Contract by the Buyer

Article 61

(1) If the buyer fails to perform any of his obligations under the contract or this **H–062** Convention, the seller may:

(a) exercise the rights provided in articles 62 to 65;

(b) claim damages as provided in articles 74 to 77.

(2) The seller is not deprived of any right he may have to claim damages by exercising his right to other remedies.

(3) No period of grace may be granted to the buyer by a court or arbitral tribunal when the seller resorts to a remedy for breach of contract.

Article 62

H–063   The seller may require the buyer to pay the price, take delivery or perform his other obligations, unless the seller has resorted to a remedy which is inconsistent with this requirement.

Article 63

H–064   (1) The seller may fix an additional period of time of reasonable length for performance by the buyer of his obligations.

(2) Unless the seller has received notice from the buyer that he will not perform within the period so fixed, the seller may not, during that period, resort to any remedy for breach of contract. However, the seller is not deprived thereby of any right he may have to claim damages for delay in performance.

Article 64

H–065   (1) The seller may declare the contract avoided:

(a) if the failure by the buyer to perform any of his obligations under the contract or this Convention amounts to a fundamental breach of contract; or

(b) if the buyer does not, within the additional period of time fixed by the seller in accordance with paragraph (1) of article 63, perform his obligation to pay the price or take delivery of the goods, or if he declares that he will not do so within the period so fixed.

(2) However, in cases where the buyer has paid the price, the seller loses the right to declare the contract avoided unless he does so:

(a) in respect of late performance by the buyer, before the seller has become aware that performance has been rendered; or

(b) in respect of any breach other than late performance by the buyer, within a reasonable time:

(i) after the seller knew or ought to have known of the breach; or
(ii) after the expiration of any additional period of time fixed by the seller in accordance with paragraph (1) or article 63, or after the buyer has declared that he will not perform his obligations within such an additional period.

Article 65

H–066   (1) If under the contract the buyer is to specify the form, measurement or other features of the goods and he fails to make such specification either on the date agreed upon or within a reasonable time after receipt of a request from the seller, the seller may, without prejudice to any other rights he may have, make the specification himself in accordance with the requirements of the buyer that may be known to him.

(2) If the seller makes the specification himself, he must inform the buyer of the details thereof and must fix a reasonable time within which the buyer may make a different specification. If, after receipt of such a communication, the buyer fails to do so within the time so fixed, the specification made by the seller is binding.

CHAPTER IV

PASSING OF RISK

Article 66

Loss of or damage to the goods after the risk has passed to the buyer does not **H–067** discharge him from his obligation to pay the price, unless the loss or damage is due to an act or omission of the seller.

Article 67

(1) If the contract of sale involves carriage of the goods and the seller is not **H–068** bound to hand them over at a particular place, the risk passes to the buyer when the goods are handed over to the first carrier for transmission to the buyer in accordance with the contract of sale. If the seller is bound to hand the goods over to a carrier at a particular place, the risk does not pass to the buyer until the goods are handed over to the carrier at that place. The fact that the seller is authorized to retain documents controlling the disposition of the goods does not affect the passage of the risk.

(2) Nevertheless, the risk does not pass to the buyer until the goods are clearly identified to the contract, whether by markings on the goods, by shipping documents, by notice given to the buyer or otherwise.

Article 68

The risk in respect of goods sold in transit passes to the buyer from the time of **H–069** the conclusion of the contract. However, if the circumstances so indicate, the risk is assumed by the buyer from the time the goods were handed over to the carrier who issued the documents embodying the contract of carriage. Nevertheless, if at the time of the conclusion of the contract of sale the seller knew or ought to have known that the goods had been lost or damaged and did not disclose this to the buyer, the loss or damage is at the risk of the seller.

Article 69

(1) In cases not within articles 67 and 68, the risk passes to the buyer when he **H–070** takes over the goods or, if he does not do so in due time, from the time when the goods are placed at his disposal and he commits a breach of contract by failing to take delivery.

(2) However, if the buyer is bound to take over the goods at a place other than a place of business of the seller, the risk passes when delivery is due and the buyer is aware of the fact that the goods are placed at his disposal at that place.

(3) If the contract relates to goods not then identified, the goods are considered not to be placed at the disposal of the buyer until they are clearly identified to the contract.

Article 70

H–071   If the seller has committed a fundamental breach of contract, articles 67, 68 and 69 do not impair the remedies available to the buyer on account of the breach.

Chapter V

Provisions Common to the Obligations of the Seller and of the Buyer

Section I

Anticipatory Breach and Instalment Contracts

Article 71

H–072   (1) A party may suspend the performance of his obligations if, after the conclusion of the contract, it becomes apparent that the other party will not perform a substantial part of his obligations as a result of:

(a) a serious deficiency in his ability to perform or in his creditworthiness; or

(b) his conduct in preparing to perform or in performing the contract.

(2) If the seller has already dispatched the goods before the grounds described in the preceding paragraph become evident, he may prevent the handing over of the goods to the buyer even though the buyer holds a document which entitles him to obtain them. The present paragraph relates only to the rights in the goods as between the buyer and the seller.

(3) A party suspending performance, whether before or after dispatch of the goods, must immediately give notice of the suspension to the other party and must continue with performance if the other party provides adequate assurance of his performance.

Article 72

H–073   (1) If prior to the date for performance of the contract it is clear that one of the parties will commit a fundamental breach of contract, the other party may declare the contract avoided.

(2) If time allows, the party intending to declare the contract avoided must give reasonable notice to the other party in order to permit him to provide adequate assurance of his performance.

(3) The requirements of the preceding paragraph do not apply if the other party has declared that he will not perform his obligations.

Article 73

H–074   (1) In the case of a contract for delivery of goods by instalments, if the failure of one party to perform any of his obligations in respect of any instalment constitutes a fundamental breach of contract with respect to that instalment, the other party may declare the contract avoided with respect to that instalment.

(2) If one party's failure to perform any of his obligations in respect of any instalment gives the other party good grounds to conclude that a fundamental breach of contract will occur with respect to future instalments, he may declare the contract avoided for the future, provided that he does so within a reasonable time.

(3) A buyer who declares the contract avoided in respect of any delivery may, at the same time, declare it avoided in respect of deliveries already made or of future deliveries if, by reason of their interdependence, those deliveries could not be used for the purpose contemplated by the parties at the time of the conclusion of the contract.

SECTION II

DAMAGES

Article 74

Damages for breach of contract by one party consist of a sum equal to the loss, including loss of profit, suffered by the other party as a consequence of the breach. Such damages may not exceed the loss which the party in breach foresaw or ought to have foreseen at the time of the conclusion of the contract, in the light of the facts and matters of which he then knew or ought to have known, as a possible consequence of the breach of contract.   **H–075**

Article 75

If the contract is avoided and if, in a reasonable manner and within a reasonable time after avoidance, the buyer has bought goods in replacement or the seller has resold the goods, the party claiming damages may recover the difference between the contract price and the price in the substitute transaction as well as any further damages recoverable under article 74.   **H–076**

Article 76

(1) If the contract is avoided and there is a current price for the goods, the party claiming damages may, if he has not made a purchase or resale under article 75, recover the difference between the price fixed by the contract and the current price at the time of avoidance as well as any further damages recoverable under article 74. If, however, the party claiming damages has avoided the contract after taking over the goods, the current price at the time of such taking over shall be applied instead of the current price at the time of avoidance.   **H–077**

(2) For the purposes of the preceding paragraph, the current price is the price prevailing at the place where delivery of the goods should have been made or, if there is no current price at that place, the price at such other place as serves as a reasonable substitute, making due allowance for differences in the cost of transporting the goods.

Article 77

A party who relies on a breach of contract must take such measures as are reasonable in the circumstances to mitigate the loss, including loss of profit,   **H–078** resulting from the breach. If he fails to take such measures, the party in breach may claim a reduction in the damages in the amount by which the loss should have been mitigated.

Section III

Interest

Article 78

H–079   If a party fails to pay the price or any other sum that is in arrears, the other party is entitled to interest on it, without prejudice to any claim for damages recoverable under article 74.

Section IV

Exemptions

Article 79

H–080   (1) A party is not liable for a failure to perform any of his obligations if he proves that the failure was due to an impediment beyond his control and that he could not reasonably be expected to have taken the impediment into account at the time of the conclusion of the contract or to have avoided or overcome it or its consequences.

(2) If the party's failure is due to the failure by a third person whom he has engaged to perform the whole or a part of the contract, that party is exempt from liability only if:

(a) he is exempt under the preceding paragraph; and

(b) the person whom he has so engaged would be so exempt if the provisions of that paragraph were applied to him.

(3) The exemption provided by this article has effect for the period during which the impediment exists.

(4) The party who fails to perform must give notice to the other party of the impediment and its effect on his ability to perform. If the notice is not received by the other party within a reasonable time after the party who fails to perform knew or ought to have known of the impediment, he is liable for damages resulting from such non-receipt.

(5) Nothing in this article prevents either party from exercising any right other than to claim damages under this Convention.

Article 80

H–081   A party may not rely on a failure of the other party to perform, to the extent that such failure was caused by the first party's act or omission.

Section V

Effects of Avoidance

Article 81

(1) Avoidance of the contract releases both parties from their obligations under it, subject to any damages which may be due. Avoidance does not affect any provision of the contract for the settlement of disputes or any other provision of the contract governing the rights and obligations of the parties consequent upon the avoidance of the contract. **H–082**

(2) A party who has performed the contract either wholly or in part may claim restitution from the other party of whatever the first party has supplied or paid under the contract. If both parties are bound to make restitution, they must do so concurrently.

Article 82

(1) The buyer loses the right to declare the contract avoided or to require the seller to deliver substitute goods if it is impossible for him to make restitution of the goods substantially in the condition in which he received them. **H–083**

(2) The preceding paragraph does not apply:

(a) if the impossibility of making restitution of the goods or of making restitution of the goods substantially in the condition in which the buyer received them is not due to his act or omission;

(b) if the goods or part of the goods have perished or deteriorated as a result of the examination provided for in article 38; or

(c) if the goods or part of the goods have been sold in the normal course of business or have been consumed or transformed by the buyer in the course normal use before he discovered or ought to have discovered the lack of conformity.

Article 83

A buyer who has lost the right to declare the contract avoided or to require the seller to deliver substitute goods in accordance with article 82 retains all other remedies under the contract and this Convention. **H–084**

Article 84

(1) If the seller is bound to refund the price, he must also pay interest on it, from the date on which the price was paid. **H–085**

(2) The buyer must account to the seller for all benefits which he has derived from the goods or part of them:

(a) if he must make restitution of the goods or part of them; or

(b) if it is impossible for him to make restitution of all or part of the goods or to make restitution of all or part of the goods substantially in the condition in which he received them, but he has nevertheless declared the contract avoided or required the seller to deliver substitute goods.

Section VI

Preservation of the Goods

Article 85

H–086 If the buyer is in delay in taking delivery of the goods or, where payment of the price and delivery of the goods are to be made concurrently, if he fails to pay the price, and the seller is either in possession of the goods or otherwise able to control their disposition, the seller must take such steps as are reasonable in the circumstances to preserve them. He is entitled to retain them until he has been reimbursed his reasonable expenses by the buyer.

Article 86

H–087 (1) If the buyer has received the goods and intends to exercise any right under the contract or this Convention to reject them, he must take such steps to preserve them as are reasonable in the circumstances. He is entitled to retain them until he has been reimbursed his reasonable expenses by the seller.

(2) If goods dispatched to the buyer have been placed at his disposal at their destination and he exercises the right to reject them, he must take possession of them on behalf of the seller, provided that this can be done without payment of the price and without unreasonable inconvenience or unreasonable expense. This provision does not apply if the seller or a person authorized to take charge of the goods on his behalf is present at the destination. If the buyer takes possession of the goods under this paragraph, his rights and obligations are governed by the preceding paragraph.

Article 87

H–088 A party who is bound to take steps to preserve the goods may deposit them in a warehouse of a third person at the expense of the other party provided that the expense incurred is not unreasonable.

Article 88

H–089 (1) A party who is bound to preserve the goods in accordance with article 85 or 86 may sell them by any appropriate means if there has been an unreasonable delay by the other party in taking possession of the goods or in taking them back or in paying the price or the cost of preservation, provided that reasonable notice of the intention to sell has been given to the other party.

(2) If the goods are subject to rapid deterioration or their preservation would involve unreasonable expense, a party who is bound to preserve the goods in accordance with article 85 or 86 must take reasonable measures to sell them. To the extent possible he must give notice to the other party of his intention to sell.

(3) A party selling the goods has the right to retain out of the proceeds of sale an amount equal to the reasonable expenses of preserving the goods and of selling them. He must account to the other party for the balance.

Part IV

Final Provisions

Article 89

The Secretary-General of the United Nations is hereby designated as the   **H–090**
depositary for this Convention.

Article 90

This Convention does not prevail over any international agreement which has   **H–091**
already been or may be entered into and which contains provisions concerning
the matters governed by this Convention, provided that the parties have their
places of business in States parties to such agreement.

Article 91

(1) This Convention is open for signature at the concluding meeting of the   **H–092**
United Nations Conference on Contracts for the International Sale of Goods and
will remain open for signature by all States at the Headquarters of the United
Nations, New York until 30 September 1981.

(2) This Convention is subject to ratification, acceptance or approval by the
signatory States.

(3) This Convention is open for accession by all States which are not signatory
States as from the date it is open for signature.

(4) Instruments of ratification, acceptance, approval and accession are to be
deposited with the Secretary-General of the United Nations.

Article 92

(1) A Contracting State may declare at the time of signature, ratification,   **H–093**
acceptance, approval or accession that it will not be bound by Part II of this
Convention or that it will not be bound by Part III of this Convention.

(2) A Contracting State which makes a declaration in accordance with the
preceding paragraph in respect of Part II or Part III of this Convention is not to be
considered a Contracting State within paragraph (1) of article 1 of this Convention
in respect of matters governed by the Part to which the declaration applies.

Article 93

(1) If a Contracting State has two or more territorial units in which, according   **H–094**
to its constitution, different systems of law are applicable in relation to the matters
dealt with in this Convention, it may, at the time of signature, ratification,
acceptance, approval or accession, declare that this Convention is to extend to all
its territorial units or only to one or more of them, and may amend its declaration
by submitting another declaration at any time.

(2) These declarations are to be notified to the depositary and are to state
expressly the territorial units to which the Convention extends.

(3) If, by virtue of a declaration under this article, this Convention extends to
one or more but not all of the territorial units of a Contracting State, and if the
place of business of a party is located in that State, this place of business, for the

purposes of this Convention, is considered not to be in a Contracting State, unless it is in a territorial unit to which the Convention extends.

(4) If a Contracting State makes no declaration under paragraph (1) of this article, the Convention is to extend to all territorial units of that State.

Article 94

H–095   (1) Two or more Contracting States which have the same or closely related legal rules on matters governed by this Convention may at any time declare that the Convention is not to apply to contracts of sale or to their formation where the parties have their places of business in those States. Such declarations may be made jointly or by reciprocal unilateral declarations.

(2) A Contracting State which has the same or closely related legal rules on matters governed by this Convention as one or more non-Contracting States may at any time declare that the Convention is not to apply to contracts of sale or to their formation where the parties have their places of business in those States.

(3) If a State which is the object of a declaration under the preceding paragraph subsequently becomes a Contracting State, the declaration made will, as from the date on which the Convention enters into force in respect of the new Contracting State, have the effect of a declaration made under paragraph (1), provided that the new Contracting State joins in such declaration or makes a reciprocal unilateral declaration.

Article 95

H–096   Any State may declare at the time of the deposit of its instrument of ratification, acceptance, approval or accession that it will not be bound by subparagraph (1)(b) of article 1 of this Convention.

Article 96

H–097   A Contracting State whose legislation requires contracts of sale to be concluded in or evidenced by writing may at any time make a declaration in accordance with article 12 that any provision of article 11, article 29, or Part II of this Convention, that allows a contract of sale or its modification or termination by agreement or any offer, acceptance, or other indication of intention to be made in any form other than in writing, does not apply where any party has his place of business in that State.

Article 97

H–098   (1) Declarations made under this Convention at the time of signature are subject to confirmation upon ratification, acceptance or approval.

(2) Declarations and confirmations of declarations are to be in writing and be formally notified to the depositary.

(3) A declaration takes effect simultaneously with the entry into force of this Convention in respect of the State concerned. However, a declaration of which the depositary receives formal notification after such entry into force takes effect on the first day of the month following the expiration of six months after the date of its receipt by the depositary. Reciprocal unilateral declarations under article 94 take effect on the first day of the month following the expiration of six months after the receipt of the latest declaration by the depositary.

(4) Any State which makes a declaration under this Convention may withdraw it at any time by a formal notification in writing addressed to the depositary. Such

withdrawal is to take effect on the first day of the month following the expiration of six months after the date of the receipt of the notification by the depositary.

(5) A withdrawal of a declaration made under article 94 renders inoperative, as from the date on which the withdrawal takes effect, any reciprocal declaration made by another State under that article.

Article 98

No reservations are permitted except those expressly authorized in this Convention.   **H–099**

Article 99

(1) This Convention enters into force, subject to the provisions of paragraph (6)   **H–100** of this article, on the first day of the month following the expiration of twelve months after the date of deposit of the tenth instrument of ratification, acceptance, approval or accession, including an instrument which contains a declaration made under article 92.

(2) When a State ratifies, accepts, approves or accedes to this Convention after the deposit of the tenth instrument of ratification, acceptance, approval or accession, this Convention, with the exception of the Part excluded, enters into force in respect of that State, subject to the provisions of paragraph (6) of this article, on the first day of the month following the expiration of twelve months after the date of the deposit of its instrument of ratification, acceptance, approval or accession.

(3) A State which ratifies, accepts, approves or accedes to this Convention and is a party to either or both the Convention relating to a Uniform Law on the Formation of Contracts for the International Sale of Goods done at The Hague on 1 July 1964 (1964 Hague Formation Convention) and the Convention relating to a Uniform Law on the International Sale of Goods done at The Hague on 1 July 1964 (1964 Hague Sales Convention) shall at the same time denounce, as the case may be, either or both the 1964 Hague Sales Convention and the 1964 Hague Formation Convention by notifying the Government of the Netherlands to that effect.

(4) A State party to the 1964 Hague Sales Convention which ratifies, accepts, approves or accedes to the present Convention and declares or has declared under article 52 that it will not be bound by Part II of this Convention shall at the time of ratification, acceptance, approval or accession denounce the 1964 Hague Sales Convention by notifying the Government of the Netherlands to that effect.

(5) A State party to the 1964 Hague Formation Convention which ratifies, accepts, approves or accedes to the present Convention and declares or has declared under article 92 that it will not be bound by Part III of this Convention shall at the time of ratification, acceptance, approval or accession denounce the 1964 Hague Formation Convention by notifying the Government of the Netherlands to that effect.

(6) For the purpose of this article, ratifications, acceptances, approvals and accessions in respect of this Convention by States parties to the 1964 Hague Formation Convention or to the 1964 Hague Sales Convention shall not be effective until such denunciations as may be required on the part of those States in respect of the latter two Conventions have themselves become effective. The depositary of this Convention shall consult with the Government of the Netherlands, as the depositary of the 1964 Conventions, so as to ensure necessary co-ordination in this respect.

Article 100

H–101   (1) This Convention applies to the formation of a contract only when the proposal for concluding the contract is made on or after the date when the Convention enters into force in respect of the Contracting States referred to in subparagraph (1)(a) or the Contracting State referred to in subparagraph (1)(b) of article 1.

(2) This Convention applies only to contracts concluded on or after the date when the Convention enters into force in respect of the Contracting States referred to in subparagraph (1)(a) or the Contracting State referred to in subparagraph (1)(b) of article 1.

Article 101

H–102   (1) A Contracting State may denounce this Convention, or Part II or Part III of the Convention, by a formal notification in writing addressed to the depositary.

(2) The denunciation takes effect on the first day of the month following the expiration of twelve months after the notification is received by the depositary. Where a longer period for the denunciation to take effect is specified in the notification, the denunciation takes effect upon the expiration of such longer period after the notification is received by the depositary.

DONE at Vienna, this day of eleventh day of April, one thousand nine hundred and eighty, in a single original, of which the Arabic, Chinese, English, French, Russian and Spanish texts are equally authentic.

IN WITNESS WHEREOF the undersigned plenipotentiaries, being duly authorized by their respective Governments, have signed this Convention.

APPENDIX I

TEXT AND COMMENTARY ON THE HAMBURG RULES

[This material can be found at UNCITRAL's website: *www.uncitral.org*]   **I–001**

UNITED NATIONS CONVENTION ON THE CARRIAGE OF GOODS BY SEA (1978)

Hamburg Rules

PREAMBLE

THE STATES PARTIES TO THIS CONVENTION,

HAVING RECOGNIZED the desirability of determining by agreement certain rules   **I–002**
relating to the carriage of goods by sea,

HAVING DECIDED to conclude a convention for this purpose and have thereto
agreed as follows:

PART I

GENERAL PROVISIONS

Article 1. *Definitions*

In this Convention: **I–003**

1. "Carrier" means any person by whom or in whose name a contract of
carriage of goods by sea has been concluded with a shipper.

2. "Actual carrier" means any person to whom the performance of the carriage
of the goods, or of part of the carriage, has been entrusted by the carrier, and
includes any other person to whom such performance has been entrusted.

3. "Shipper" means any person by whom or in whose name or on whose
behalf a contract of carriage of goods by sea has been concluded with a carrier, or
any person by whom or in whose name or on whose behalf the goods are actually
delivered to the carrier in relation to the contract of carriage by sea.

4. "Consignee" means the person entitled to take delivery of the goods.

5. "Goods" includes live animals; where the goods are consolidated in a
container, pallet or similar article of transport or where they are packed, goods
includes such article of transport or packaging if supplied by the shipper.

6. "Contract of carriage by sea" means any contract whereby the carrier undertakes against payment of freight to carry goods by sea from one port to another; however, a contract which involves carriage by sea and also carriage by some other means is deemed to be a contract of carriage by sea for the purposes of this Convention only in so far as it relates to the carriage by sea.

7. "Bill of lading" means a document which evidences a contract of carriage by sea and the taking over or loading of the goods by the carrier, and by which the carrier undertakes to deliver the goods against surrender of the document. A provision in the document that the goods are to be delivered to the order of a named person, or to order, or to bearer, constitutes such an undertaking.

8. "Writing" includes, *inter alia*, telegram and telex.

Article 2. Scope of application

I–004   **1.** The provisions of this Convention are applicable to all contracts of carriage by sea between two different States, if:

(a) the port of loading as provided for in the contract of carriage by sea is located in a Contracting State, or

(b) the port of discharge as provided for in the contract of carriage by sea is located in a Contracting State, or

(c) one of the optional ports of discharge provided for in the contract of carriage by sea is the actual port of discharge and such port is located in a Contracting State, or

(d) the bill of lading or other document evidencing the contract of carriage by sea is issued in a Contracting State, or

(e) the bill of lading or other document evidencing the contract of carriage by sea provides that the provisions of this Convention or the legislation of any State giving effect to them are to govern the contract.

2. The provisions of this Convention are applicable without regard to the nationality of the ship, the carrier, the actual carrier, the shipper, the consignee or any other interested person.

3. The provisions of this Convention are not applicable to charter-parties. However, where a bill of lading is issued pursuant to a charter-party, the provisions of the Convention apply to such a bill of lading if it governs the relation between the carrier and the holder of the bill of lading, not being the charterer.

4. If a contract provides for future carriage of goods in a series of shipments during an agreed period, the provisions of this Convention apply to each shipment. However, where a shipment is made under a charter-party, the provisions of paragraph 3 of this article apply.

Article 3. Interpretation of the Convention

I–005   In the interpretation and application of the provisions of this Convention regard shall be had to its international character and to the need to promote uniformity.

PART II

LIABILITY OF THE CARRIER

Article 4. Period of responsibility

1. The responsibility of the carrier for the goods under this Convention covers **I–006** the period during which the carrier is in charge of the goods at the port of loading, during the carriage and at the port of discharge.

2. For the purpose of paragraph 1 of this article, the carrier is deemed to be in charge of the goods

(a) from the time he has taken over the goods from:

  (i) the shipper, or a person acting on his behalf; or
  (ii) an authority or other third party to whom, pursuant to law or regulations applicable at the port of loading, the goods must be handed over for shipment;

(b) until the time he has delivered the goods:

  (i) by handing over the goods to the consignee; or
  (ii) in cases where the consignee does not receive the goods from the carrier, by placing them at the disposal of the consignee in accordance with the contract or with the law or with the usage of the particular trade, applicable at the port of discharge; or
  (iii) by handing over the goods to an authority or other third party to whom, pursuant to law or regulations applicable at the port of discharge, the goods must be handed over.

3. In paragraphs 1 and 2 of this article, reference to the carrier or to the consignee means, in addition to the carrier or the consignee, the servants or agents, respectively of the carrier or the consignee.

Article 5. Basis of liability

1. The carrier is liable for loss resulting from loss of or damage to the goods, as **I–007** well as from delay in delivery, if the occurrence which caused the loss, damage or delay took place while the goods were in his charge as defined in article 4, unless the carrier proves that he, his servants or agents took all measures that could reasonably be required to avoid the occurrence and its consequences.

2. Delay in delivery occurs when the goods have not been delivered at the port of discharge provided for in the contract of carriage by sea within the time expressly agreed upon or, in the absence of such agreement, within the time which it would be reasonable to require of a diligent carrier, having regard to the circumstances of the case.

3. The person entitled to make a claim for the loss of goods may treat the goods as lost if they have not been delivered as required by article 4 within 60 consecutive days following the expiry of the time for delivery according to paragraph 2 of this article.

4. (a) The carrier is liable

  (i) for loss of or damage to the goods or delay in delivery caused by fire, if the claimant proves that the fire arose from fault or neglect on the part of the carrier, his servants or agents;

     (ii) for such loss, damage or delay in delivery which is proved by the claimant to have resulted from the fault or neglect of the carrier, his servants or agents in taking all measures that could reasonably be required to put out the fire and avoid or mitigate its consequences.

  (b) In case of fire on board the ship affecting the goods, if the claimant or the carrier so desires, a survey in accordance with shipping practices must be held into the cause and circumstances of the fire, and a copy of the surveyors report shall be made available on demand to the carrier and the claimant.

5. With respect to live animals, the carrier is not liable for loss, damage or delay in delivery resulting from any special risks inherent in that kind of carriage. If the carrier proves that he has complied with any special instructions given to him by the shipper respecting the animals and that, in the circumstances of the case, the loss, damage or delay in delivery could be attributed to such risks, it is presumed that the loss, damage or delay in delivery was so caused, unless there is proof that all or a part of the loss, damage or delay in delivery resulted from fault or neglect on the part of the carrier, his servants or agents.

6. The carrier is not liable, except in general average, where loss, damage or delay in delivery resulted from measures to save life or from reasonable measures to save property at sea.

7. Where fault or neglect on the part of the carrier, his servants or agents combines with another cause to produce loss, damage or delay in delivery, the carrier is liable only to the extent that the loss, damage or delay in delivery is attributable to such fault or neglect, provided that the carrier proves the amount of the loss, damage or delay in delivery not attributable thereto.

Article 6. Limits of liability

I–008   1. (a) The liability of the carrier for loss resulting from loss of or damage to goods according to the provisions of article 5 is limited to an amount equivalent to 835 units of account per package or other shipping unit or 2.5 units of account per kilogram of gross weight of the goods lost or damaged, whichever is the higher.

  (b) The liability of the carrier for delay in delivery according to the provisions of article 5 is limited to an amount equivalent to two and a half times the freight payable for the goods delayed, but not exceeding the total freight payable under the contract of carriage of goods by sea.

  (c) In no case shall the aggregate liability of the carrier, under both subparagraphs (a) and (b) of this paragraph, exceed the limitation which would be established under subparagraph (a) of this paragraph for total loss of the goods with respect to which such liability was incurred.

2. For the purpose of calculating which amount is the higher in accordance with paragraph 1 (a) of this article, the following rules apply:

(a) Where a container, pallet or similar article of transport is used to consolidate goods, the package or other shipping units enumerated in the bill of lading, if issued, or otherwise in any other document evidencing the contract of carriage by sea, as packed in such article of transport are deemed packages or shipping units. Except as aforesaid the goods in such article of transport are deemed one shipping unit.

(b) In cases where the article of transport itself has been lost or damaged, that article of transport, if not owned or otherwise supplied by the carrier, is considered one separate shipping unit.

3. Unit of account means the unit of account mentioned in article 26.

4. By agreement between the carrier and the shipper, limits of liability exceeding those provided for in paragraph 1 may be fixed.

Article 7. Application to non-contractual claims

1. The defences and limits of liability provided for in this Convention apply in any action against the carrier in respect of loss of or damage to the goods covered by the contract of carriage by sea, as well as of delay in delivery whether the action is founded in contract, in tort or otherwise.   **I–009**

2. If such an action is brought against a servant or agent of the carrier, such servant or agent, if he proves that he acted within the scope of his employment, is entitled to avail himself of the defences and limits of liability which the carrier is entitled to invoke under this Convention.

3. Except as provided in article 8, the aggregate of the amounts recoverable from the carrier and from any persons referred to in paragraph 2 of this article shall not exceed the limits of liability provided for in this Convention.

Article 8. Loss of right to limit responsibility

1. The carrier is not entitled to the benefit of the limitation of liability provided for in article 6 if it is proved that the loss, damage or delay in delivery resulted from an act or omission of the carrier done with the intent to cause such loss, damage or delay, or recklessly and with knowledge that such loss, damage or delay would probably result.   **I–010**

2. Notwithstanding the provisions of paragraph 2 of article 7, a servant or agent of the carrier is not entitled to the benefit of the limitation of liability provided for in article 6 if it is proved that the loss, damage or delay in delivery resulted from an act or omission of such servant or agent, done with the intent to cause such loss, damage or delay, or recklessly and with knowledge that such loss, damage or delay would probably result.

Article 9. Deck cargo

1. The carrier is entitled to carry the goods on deck only if such carriage is in accordance with an agreement with the shipper or with the usage of the particular trade or is required by statutory rules or regulations.   **I–011**

2. If the carrier and the shipper have agreed that the goods shall or may be carried on deck, the carrier must insert in the bill of lading or other document evidencing the contract of carriage by sea a statement to that effect. In the absence of such a statement the carrier has the burden of proving that an agreement for carriage on deck has been entered into; however, the carrier is not entitled to invoke such an agreement against a third party, including a consignee, who has acquired the bill of lading in good faith.

3. Where the goods have been carried on deck contrary to the provisions of paragraph 1 of this article or where the carrier may not under paragraph 2 of this article invoke an agreement for carriage on deck, the carrier, notwithstanding the provisions of paragraph 1 of article 5, is liable for loss of or damage to the goods, as well as for delay in delivery, resulting solely from the carriage on deck, and the extent of his liability is to be determined in accordance with the provisions of article 6 or article 8 of this Convention, as the case may be.

4. Carriage of goods on deck contrary to express agreement for carriage under deck is deemed to be an act or omission of the carrier within the meaning of article 8.

Article 10. *Liability of the carrier and actual carrier*

I–012   **1.** Where the performance of the carriage or part thereof has been entrusted to an actual carrier, whether or not in pursuance of a liberty under the contract of carriage by sea to do so, the carrier nevertheless remains responsible for the entire carriage according to the provisions of this Convention. The carrier is responsible, in relation to the carriage performed by the actual carrier, for the acts and omissions of the actual carrier and of his servants and agents acting within the scope of their employment.

2. All the provisions of this Convention governing the responsibility of the carrier also apply to the responsibility of the actual carrier for the carriage performed by him. The provisions of paragraphs 2 and 3 of article 7 and of paragraph 2 of article 8 apply if an action is brought against a servant or agent of the actual carrier.

3. Any special agreement under which the carrier assumes obligations not imposed by this Convention or waives rights conferred by this Convention affects the actual carrier only if agreed to by him expressly and in writing. Whether or not the actual carrier has so agreed, the carrier nevertheless remains bound by the obligations or waivers resulting from such special agreement.

4. Where and to the extent that both the carrier and the actual carrier are liable, their liability is joint and several.

5. The aggregate of the amounts recoverable from the carrier, the actual carrier and their servants and agents shall not exceed the limits of liability provided for in this Convention.

6. Nothing in this article shall prejudice any right of recourse as between the carrier and the actual carrier.

Article 11. *Through carriage*

I–013   **1.** Notwithstanding the provisions of paragraph 1 of article 10, where a contract of carriage by sea provides explicitly that a specified part of the carriage covered by the said contract is to be performed by a named person other than the carrier, the contract may also provide that the carrier is not liable for loss, damage or delay in delivery caused by an occurrence which takes place while the goods are in the charge of the actual carrier during such part of the carriage. Nevertheless, any stipulation limiting or excluding such liability is without effect if no judicial proceedings can be instituted against the actual carrier in a court competent under paragraph 1 or 2 of article 21. The burden of proving that any loss, damage or delay in delivery has been caused by such an occurrence rests upon the carrier.

2. The actual carrier is responsible in accordance with the provisions of paragraph 2 of article 10 for loss, damage or delay in delivery caused by an occurrence which takes place while the goods are in his charge.

PART III

LIABILITY OF THE SHIPPERS

Article 12. General rule

The shipper is not liable for loss sustained by the carrier or the actual carrier, or for damage sustained by the ship, unless such loss or damage was caused by the fault or neglect of the shipper, his servants or agents. Nor is any servant or agent of the shipper liable for such loss or damage unless the loss or damage was caused by fault or neglect on his part. **I–014**

Article 13. Special rules on dangerous goods

1. The shipper must mark or label in a suitable manner dangerous goods as dangerous. **I–015**

2. Where the shipper hands over dangerous goods to the carrier or an actual carrier, as the case may be, the shipper must inform him of the dangerous character of the goods and, if necessary, of the precautions to be taken. If the shipper fails to do so and such carrier or actual carrier does not otherwise have knowledge of their dangerous character:

(a) the shipper is liable to the carrier and any actual carrier for the loss resulting from the shipment of such goods, and

(b) the goods may at any time be unloaded, destroyed or rendered innocuous, as the circumstances may require, without payment of compensation.

3. The provisions of paragraph 2 of this article may not be invoked by any person if during the carriage he has taken the goods in his charge with knowledge of their dangerous character.

4. If, in cases where the provisions of paragraph 2, subparagraph (b), of this article do not apply or may not be invoked, dangerous goods become an actual danger to life or property, they may be unloaded, destroyed or rendered innocuous, as the circumstances may require, without payment of compensation except where there is an obligation to contribute in general average or where the carrier is liable in accordance with the provisions of article 5.

PART IV

TRANSPORT DOCUMENTS

Article 14. Issue of bill of lading

1. When the carrier or the actual carrier takes the goods in his charge, the carrier must, on demand of the shipper, issue to the shipper a bill of lading. **I–016**

2. The bill of lading may be signed by a person having authority from the carrier. A bill of lading signed by the master of the ship carrying the goods is deemed to have been signed on behalf of the carrier.

3. The signature on the bill of lading may be in handwriting, printed in facsimile, perforated, stamped, in symbols, or made by any other mechanical or electronic means, if not inconsistent with the law of the country where the bill of lading is issued.

Article 15. Contents of bill of lading

I–017   **1.** The bill of lading must include, *inter alia*, the following particulars:

(a) the general nature of the goods, the leading marks necessary for identification of the goods, an express statement, if applicable, as to the dangerous character of the goods, the number of packages or pieces, and the weight of the goods or their quantity otherwise expressed, all such particulars as furnished by the shipper;

(b) the apparent condition of the goods;

(c) the name and principal place of business of the carrier;

(d) the name of the shipper;

(e) the consignee if named by the shipper;

(f) the port of loading under the contract of carriage by sea and the date on which the goods were taken over by the carrier at the port of loading;

(g) the port of discharge under the contract of carriage by sea;

(h) the number of originals of the bill of lading, if more than one;

(i) the place of issuance of the bill of lading;

(j) the signature of the carrier or a person acting on his behalf;

(k) the freight to the extent payable by the consignee or other indication that freight is payable by him;

(l) the statement referred to in paragraph 3 of article 23;

(m) the statement, if applicable, that the goods shall or may be carried on deck;

(n) the date or the period of delivery of the goods at the port of discharge if expressly agreed upon between the parties; and

(o) any increased limit or limits of liability where agreed in accordance with paragraph 4 of article 6.

2. After the goods have been loaded on board, if the shipper so demands, the carrier must issue to the shipper a "shipped" bill of lading which, in addition to the particulars required under paragraph 1 of this article, must state that the goods are on board a named ship or ships, and the date or dates of loading. If the carrier has previously issued to the shipper a bill of lading or other document of title with respect to any of such goods, on request of the carrier the shipper must surrender such document in exchange for a "shipped" bill of lading. The carrier may amend any previously issued document in order to meet the shippers demand for a "shipped" bill of lading if, as amended, such document includes all the information required to be contained in a "shipped" bill of lading.

3. The absence in the bill of lading of one or more particulars referred to in this article does not affect the legal character of the document as a bill of lading provided that it nevertheless meets the requirements set out in paragraph 7 of article 1.

Article 16. Bills of lading: reservations and evidentiary effect

1. If the bill of lading contains particulars concerning the general nature, **I–018** leading marks, number of packages of pieces, weight or quantity of the goods which the carrier or other person issuing the bill of lading on his behalf knows or has reasonable grounds to suspect do not accurately represent the goods actually taken over or, where a "shipped" bill of lading is issued, loaded, or if he had no reasonable means of checking such particulars, the carrier or such other person must insert in the bill of lading a reservation specifying these inaccuracies, grounds of suspicion or the absence of reasonable means of checking.

2. If the carrier or other person issuing the bill of lading on his behalf fails to note on the bill of lading the apparent condition of the goods, he is deemed to have noted on the bill of lading that the goods were in apparent good condition.

3. Except for particulars in respect of which and to the extent to which a reservation permitted under paragraph 1 of this article has been entered:

(a) the bill of lading is *prima facie* evidence of the taking over or, where a "shipped" bill of lading is issued, loading, by the carrier of the goods as described in the bill of lading; and

(b) proof to the contrary by the carrier is not admissible if the bill of lading has been transferred to a third party, including a consignee, who in good faith has acted in reliance on the description of the goods therein.

4. A bill of lading which does not, as provided in paragraph 1, subparagraph (k), of article 15, set forth the freight or otherwise indicate that freight is payable by the consignee or does not set forth demurrage incurred at the port of loading payable by the consignee, is *prima facie* evidence that no freight or such demurrage is payable by him. However, proof to the contrary by the carrier is not admissible when the bill of lading has been transferred to a third party, including a consignee, who in good faith has acted in reliance on the absence in the bill of lading of any such indication.

Article 17. Guarantees by the shipper

1. The shipper is deemed to have guaranteed to the carrier the accuracy of **I–019** particulars relating to the general nature of the goods, their marks, number, weight and quantity as furnished by him for insertion in the bill of lading. The shipper must indemnify the carrier against the loss resulting from inaccuracies in such particulars. The shipper remains liable even if the bill of lading has been transferred by him. The right of the carrier to such indemnity in no way limits his liability under the contract of carriage by sea to any person other than the shipper.

2. Any letter of guarantee or agreement by which the shipper undertakes to indemnify the carrier against loss resulting from the issuance of the bill of lading by the carrier, or by a person acting on his behalf, without entering a reservation relating to particulars furnished by the shipper for insertion in the bill of lading, or to the apparent condition of the goods, is void and of no effect as against any third party, including a consignee, to whom the bill of lading has been transferred.

3. Such a letter of guarantee or agreement is valid as against the shipper unless the carrier or the person acting on his behalf, by omitting the reservation referred to in paragraph 2 of this article, intends to defraud a third party, including a consignee, who acts in reliance on the description of the goods in the bill of lading. In the latter case, if the reservation omitted relates to particulars furnished by the shipper for insertion in the bill of lading, the carrier has no right of indemnity from the shipper pursuant to paragraph 1 of this article.

4. In the case of intended fraud referred to in paragraph 3 of this article, the carrier is liable, without the benefit of the limitation of liability provided for in this Convention, for the loss incurred by a third party, including a consignee, because he has acted in reliance on the description of the goods in the bill of lading.

Article 18. *Documents other than bills of lading*

I–020 Where a carrier issues a document other than a bill of lading to evidence the receipt of the goods to be carried, such a document is *prima facie* evidence of the conclusion of the contract of carriage by sea and the taking over by the carrier of the goods as therein described.

Part V

Claims and Actions

Article 19. *Notice of loss, damage or delay*

I–021   **1.** Unless notice of loss or damage, specifying the general nature of such loss or damage, is given in writing by the consignee to the carrier not later than the working day after the day when the goods were handed over to the consignee, such handing over is *prima facie* evidence of the delivery by the carrier of the goods as described in the document of transport or, if no such document has been issued, in good condition.

2. Where the loss or damage is not apparent, the provisions of paragraph 1 of this article apply correspondingly if notice in writing is not given within 15 consecutive days after the day when the goods were handed over to the consignee.

3. If the state of the goods at the time they were handed over to the consignee has been the subject of a joint survey or inspection by the parties, notice in writing need not be given of loss or damage ascertained during such survey or inspection.

4. In the case of any actual or apprehended loss or damage, the carrier and the consignee must give all reasonable facilities to each other for inspecting and tallying the goods.

5. No compensation shall be payable for loss resulting from delay in delivery unless a notice has been given in writing to the carrier within 60 consecutive days after the day when the goods were handed over to the consignee.

6. If the goods have been delivered by an actual carrier, any notice given under this article to him shall have the same effect as if it had been given to the carrier; and any notice given to the carrier shall have effect as if given to such actual carrier.

7. Unless notice of loss or damage, specifying the general nature of the loss or damage, is given in writing by the carrier or actual carrier to the shipper not later than 90 consecutive days after the occurrence of such loss or damage or after the delivery of the goods in accordance with paragraph 2 of article 4, whichever is later, the failure to give such notice is *prima facie* evidence that the carrier or the actual carrier has sustained no loss or damage due to the fault or neglect of the shipper, his servants or agents.

8. For the purpose of this article, notice given to a person acting on the carriers or the actual carriers behalf, including the master or the officer in charge of the ship, or to a person acting on the shippers behalf is deemed to have been given to the carrier, to the actual carrier or to the shipper, respectively.

Article 20. Limitation of actions

1. Any action relating to carriage of goods under this Convention is time- I–022 barred if judicial or arbitral proceedings have not been instituted within a period of two years.

2. The limitation period commences on the day on which the carrier has delivered the goods or part thereof or, in cases where no goods have been delivered, on the last day on which the goods should have been delivered.

3. The day on which the limitation period commences is not included in the period.

4. The person against whom a claim is made may at any time during the running of the limitation period extend that period by a declaration in writing to the claimant. This period may be further extended by another declaration or declarations.

5. An action for indemnity by a person held liable may be instituted even after the expiration of the limitation period provided for in the preceding paragraphs if instituted within the time allowed by the law of the State where proceedings are instituted. However, the time allowed shall not be less than 90 days commencing from the day when the person instituting such action for indemnity has settled the claim or has been served with process in the action against himself.

Article 21. Jurisdiction

1. In judicial proceedings relating to carriage of goods under this Convention I–023 the plaintiff, at his option, may institute an action in a court which according to the law of the State where the court is situated, is competent and within the jurisdiction of which is situated one of the following places:

(a) the principal place of business or, in the absence thereof, the habitual residence of the defendant; or

(b) the place where the contract was made, provided that the defendant has there a place of business, branch or agency through which the contract was made; or

(c) the port of loading or the port of discharge; or

(d) any additional place designated for that purpose in the contract of carriage by sea.

2. (a) Notwithstanding the preceding provisions of this article, an action may be instituted in the courts of any port or place in a Contracting State at which the carrying vessel or any other vessel of the same ownership may have been arrested in accordance with applicable rules of the law of that State and of international law. However, in such a case, at the petition of the defendant, the claimant must remove the action, at his choice, to one of the jurisdictions referred to in paragraph 1 of this article for the determination of the claim, but before such removal the defendant must furnish security sufficient to ensure payment of any judgement that may subsequently be awarded to the claimant in the action.

(b) All questions relating to the sufficiency or otherwise of the security shall be determined by the court of the port or place of the arrest.

3. No judicial proceedings relating to carriage of goods under this Convention may be instituted in a place not specified in paragraph 1 or 2 of this article. The provisions of this paragraph do not constitute an obstacle to the jurisdiction of the Contracting States for provisional or protective measures.

4. (a) Where an action has been instituted in a court competent under paragraphs 1 or 2 of this article or where judgement has been delivered by such a court, no new action may be started between the same parties on the same grounds unless the judgement of the court before which the first action was instituted is not enforceable in the country in which the new proceedings are instituted;

(b) For the purpose of this article, the institution of measures with a view to obtaining enforcement of a judgement is not to be considered as the starting of a new action;

(c) For the purpose of this article, the removal of an action to a different court within the same country, or to a court in another country, in accordance with paragraph 2 *(a)* of this article, is not to be considered as the starting of a new action.

5. Notwithstanding the provisions of the preceding paragraphs, an agreement made by the parties, after a claim under the contract of carriage by sea has arisen, which designates the place where the claimant may institute an actions, is effective.

Article 22. Arbitration

I–024   1. Subject to the provisions of this article, parties may provide by agreement evidenced in writing that any dispute that may arise relating to carriage of goods under this Convention shall be referred to arbitration.

2. Where a charter-party contains a provision that disputes arising thereunder shall be referred to arbitration and a bill of lading issued pursuant to the charter-party does not contain special annotation providing that such provision shall be binding upon the holder of the bill of lading, the carrier may not invoke such provision as against a holder having acquired the bill of lading in good faith.

3. The arbitration proceedings shall, at the option of the claimant, be instituted at one of the following places:

(a) a place in a State within whose territory is situated:

    (i) the principal place of business of the defendant or, in the absence thereof, the habitual residence of the defendant; or

    (ii) the place where the contract was made, provided that the defendant has there a place of business, branch or agency through which the contract was made; or

    (iii) the port of loading or the port of discharge; or

(b) any place designated for that purpose in the arbitration clause or agreement.

4. The arbitrator or arbitration tribunal shall apply the rules of this Convention.

5. The provisions of paragraphs 2 and 4 of this article are deemed to be part of every arbitration clause or agreement, and any term of such clause or agreement which is inconsistent therewith is null and void.

6. Nothing in this article affects the validity of an agreement relating to arbitration made by the parties after the claim under the contract of carriage by sea has arisen.

Part VI

Supplementary Provisions

Article 23. *Contractual stipulations*

1. Any stipulation in a contract of carriage by sea, in a bill of lading, or in any other document evidencing the contract of carriage by sea is null and void to the extent that it derogates, directly or indirectly, from the provisions of this Convention. The nullity of such a stipulation does not affect the validity of the other provisions of the contract or document of which it forms a part. A clause assigning benefit of insurance of goods in favour of the carrier, or any similar clause, is null and void.

    I–025

2. Notwithstanding the provisions of paragraph 1 of this article, a carrier may increase his responsibilities and obligations under this Convention.

3. Where a bill of lading or any other document evidencing the contract of carriage by sea is issued, it must contain a statement that the carriage is subject to the provisions of this Convention which nullify any stipulation derogating therefrom to the detriment of the shipper or the consignee.

4. Where the claimant in respect of the goods has incurred loss as a result of a stipulation which is null and void by virtue of the present article, or as a result of the omission of the statement referred to in paragraph 3 of this article, the carrier must pay compensation to the extent required in order to give the claimant compensation in accordance with the provisions of this Convention for any loss of or damage to the goods as well as for delay in delivery. The carrier must, in addition, pay compensation for costs incurred by the claimant for the purpose of exercising his right, provided that costs incurred in the action where the foregoing provision is invoked are to be determined in accordance with the law of the State where proceedings are instituted.

Article 24. *General average*

I–026   **1.** Nothing in this Convention shall prevent the application of provisions in the contract of carriage by sea or national law regarding the adjustment of general average.

2. With the exception of article 20, the provisions of this Convention relating to the liability of the carrier for loss of or damage to the goods also determine whether the consignee may refuse contribution in general average and the liability of the carrier to indemnify the consignee in respect of any such contribution made or any salvage paid.

Article 25. *Other conventions*

I–027   **1.** This Convention does not modify the rights or duties of the carrier, the actual carrier and their servants and agents provided for in international conventions or national law relating to the limitation of liability of owners of seagoing ships.

2. The provisions of articles 21 and 22 of this Convention do not prevent the application of the mandatory provisions of any other multilateral convention already in force at the date of this Convention relating to matters dealt with in the said articles, provided that the dispute arises exclusively between parties having their principal place of business in States members of such other convention. However, this paragraph does not affect the application of paragraph 4 of article 22 of this Convention.

3. No liability shall arise under the provisions of this Convention for damage caused by a nuclear incident if the operator of a nuclear installation is liable for such damage:

(a) under either the Paris Convention of 29 July 1960 on Third Party Liability in the Field of Nuclear Energy as amended by the Additional Protocol of 28 January 1964, or the Vienna Convention of 21 May 1963 on Civil Liability for Nuclear Damage, or

(b) by virtue of national law governing the liability for such damage, provided that such law is in all respects as favourable to persons who may suffer damage as is either the Paris Convention or the Vienna Convention.

4. No liability shall arise under the provisions of this Convention for any loss of or damage to or delay in delivery of luggage for which the carrier is responsible under any international convention or national law relating to the carriage of passengers and their luggage by sea.

5. Nothing contained in this Convention prevents a Contracting State from applying any other international convention which is already in force at the date of this Convention and which applies mandatorily to contracts of carriage of goods primarily by a mode of transport other than transport by sea. This provision also applies to any subsequent revision or amendment of such international convention.

Article 26. *Unit of account*

I–028   **1.** The unit of account referred to in article 6 of this Convention is the special drawing right as defined by the International Monetary Fund. The amounts mentioned in article 6 are to be converted into the national currency of a State according to the value of such currency at the date of judgement or the date agreed upon by the parties. The value of a national currency, in terms of the special drawing right, of a Contracting State which is a member of the International Monetary Fund is to be calculated in accordance with the method of valuation applied by the International Monetary Fund in effect at the date in question for its operations and transactions. The value of a national currency, in terms of the special drawing right, of a Contracting State which is not a member of the International Monetary Fund is to be calculated in a manner determined by that State.

2. Nevertheless, those States which are not members of the International Monetary Fund and whose law does not permit the application of the provisions of paragraph 1 of this article may, at the time of signature, or at the time of ratification, acceptance, approval or accession or at any time thereafter, declare that the limits of liability provided for in this Convention to be applied in their territories shall be fixed as 12,500 monetary units per package or other shipping unit or 37.5 monetary units per kilogram of gross weight of the goods.

3. The monetary unit referred to in paragraph 2 of this article corresponds to sixty-five and a half milligrams of gold of millesimal fineness nine hundred. The conversion of the amounts referred to in paragraph 2 into the national currency is to be made according to the law of the State concerned.

4. The calculation mentioned in the last sentence of paragraph 1 and the conversion mentioned in paragraph 3 of this article is to be made in such a manner as to express in the national currency of the Contracting State as far as possible the same real value for the amounts in article 6 as is expressed there in units of account. Contracting States must communicate to the depositary the manner of calculation pursuant to paragraph 1 of this article, or the result of the conversion mentioned in paragraph 3 of this article, as the case may be, at the time of signature or when depositing their instruments of ratification, acceptance, approval or accession, or when availing themselves of the option provided for in paragraph 2 of this article and whenever there is a change in the manner of such calculation or in the result of such conversion.

PART VII

FINAL CLAUSES

Article 27. Depositary

The Secretary-General of the United Nations is hereby designated as the depositary of this Convention.   **I–029**

Article 28. Signature, Ratification, Acceptance, Approval, Accession

1. This Convention is open for signature by all States until 30 April 1979 at the Headquarters of the United Nations, New York.   **I–030**

2. This Convention is subject to ratification, acceptance or approval by the signatory States.

3. After 30 April 1979, this Convention will be open for accession by all States which are not signatory States.

4. Instruments of ratification, acceptance, approval and accession are to be deposited with the Secretary-General of the United Nations.

Article 29. Reservations

I–031   No reservations may be made to this Convention.

Article 30. Entry into force

I–032   **1.** This Convention enters into force on the first day of the month following the expiration of one year from the date of deposit of the twentieth instrument of ratification, acceptance, approval or accession.

2. For each State which becomes a Contracting State to this Convention after the date of the deposit of the twentieth instrument of ratification, acceptance, approval or accession, this Convention enters into force on the first day of the month following the expiration of one year after the deposit of the appropriate instrument on behalf of that State.

3. Each Contracting State shall apply the provisions of this Convention to contracts of carriage by sea concluded on or after the date of the entry into force of this Convention in respect of that State.

Article 31. Denunciation of other conventions

I–033   **1.** Upon becoming a Contracting State to this Convention, any State Party to the International Convention for the Unification of certain Rules relating to Bills of Lading signed at Brussels on 25 August 1924 (1924 Convention) must notify the Government of Belgium as the depositary of the 1924 Convention of its denunciation of the said Convention with a declaration that the denunciation is to take effect as from the date when this Convention enters into force in respect of that State.

2. Upon the entry into force of this Convention under paragraph 1 of article 30, the depositary of this Convention must notify the Government of Belgium as the depositary of the 1924 Convention of the date of such entry into force, and of the names of the Contracting States in respect of which the Convention has entered into force.

3. The provisions of paragraphs 1 and 2 of this article apply correspondingly in respect of States Parties to the Protocol signed on 23 February 1968 to amend the International Convention for the Unification of certain Rules relating to Bills of Lading signed at Brussels on 25 August 1924.

4. Notwithstanding article 2 of this Convention, for the purposes of paragraph 1 of this article, a Contracting State may, if it deems it desirable, defer the denunciation of the 1924 Convention and of the 1924 Convention as modified by the 1968 Protocol for a maximum period of five years from the entry into force of this Convention. It will then notify the Government of Belgium of its intention.

During this transitory period, it must apply to the Contracting States this Convention to the exclusion of any other one.

Article 32. *Revision and amendment*

1. At the request of not less than one third of the Contracting States to this **I–034** Convention, the depositary shall convene a conference of the Contracting States for revising or amending it.

2. Any instrument of ratification, acceptance, approval or accession deposited after the entry into force of an amendment to this Convention is deemed to apply to the Convention as amended.

Article 33. *Revision of the limitation amounts and unit of account or monetary unit*

1. Notwithstanding the provisions of article 32, a conference only for the **I–035** purpose of altering the amount specified in article 6 and paragraph 2 of article 26, or of substituting either or both of the units defined in paragraphs 1 and 3 of article 26 by other units is to be convened by the depositary in accordance with paragraph 2 of this article. An alteration of the amounts shall be made only because of a significant change in their real value.

2. A revision conference is to be convened by the depositary when not less than one fourth of the Contracting States so request.

3. Any decision by the conference must be taken by a two-thirds majority of the participating States. The amendment is communicated by the depositary to all the Contracting States for acceptance and to all the States signatories of the Convention for information.

4. Any amendment adopted enters into force on the first day of the month following one year after its acceptance by two thirds of the Contracting States. Acceptance is to be effected by the deposit of a formal instrument to that effect with the depositary.

5. After entry into force of an amendment a Contracting State which has accepted the amendment is entitled to apply the Convention as amended in its relations with Contracting States which have not within six months after the adoption of the amendment notified the depositary that they are not bound by the amendment.

6. Any instrument of ratification, acceptance, approval or accession deposited after the entry into force of an amendment to this Convention is deemed to apply to the Convention as amended.

Article 34. *Denunciation*

1. A Contracting State may denounce this Convention at any time by means of **I–036** a notification in writing addressed to the depositary.

2. The denunciation takes effect on the first day of the month following the expiration of one year after the notification is received by the depositary. Where a longer period is specified in the notification, the denunciation takes effect upon the expiration of such longer period after the notification is received by the depositary.

Done at Hamburg, this thirty-first day of March, one thousand nine hundred and seventy-eight, in a single original, of which the Arabic, Chinese, English, French, Russian and Spanish texts are equally authentic.

In witness whereof the undersigned plenipotentiaries, being duly authorized by their respective Governments, have signed the present Convention.

COMMON UNDERSTANDING ADOPTED BY THE UNITED NATIONS CONFERENCE ON THE CARRIAGE OF GOODS BY SEA

I–037   It is the common understanding that the liability of the carrier under this Convention is based on the principle of presumed fault or neglect. This means that, as a rule, the burden of proof rests on the carrier but, with respect to certain cases, the provisions of the Convention modify this rule.

EXPLANATORY NOTE BY THE UNCITRAL SECRETARIAT ON THE UNITED NATIONS CONVENTION ON THE CARRIAGE OF GOODS BY SEA, 1978 (HAMBURG)*

INTRODUCTION

I–038   1. The United Nations Convention on the Carriage of Goods by Sea, 1978 (Hamburg) (hereinafter referred to as the "Hamburg Rules") was adopted on 31 March 1978 by a diplomatic conference convened by the General Assembly of the United Nations at Hamburg, Federal Republic of Germany. The Convention is based upon a draft prepared by the United Nations Commission on International Trade Law (UNCITRAL).

2. The Hamburg Rules establish a uniform legal regime governing the rights and obligations of shippers, carriers and consignees under a contract of carriage of goods by sea. Their central focus is the liability of a carrier for loss of and damage to the goods and for delay in delivery. They also deal with the liability of the shipper for loss sustained by the carrier and for damage to the ship, as well as certain responsibilities and liabilities of the shipper in respect of dangerous goods. Other provisions of the Hamburg Rules deal with transport documents issued by the carrier, including bills of lading and non-negotiable transport documents, and with limitation of actions, jurisdiction and arbitral proceedings under the Convention.

3. The Convention entered into force on 1 November 1992 for the following twenty States: Barbados, Botswana, Burkina Faso, Chile, Egypt, Guinea, Hungary, Kenya, Lebanon, Lesotho, Malawi, Morocco, Nigeria, Romania, Senegal, Sierra Leone, Tunisia, Uganda, United Republic of Tanzania, and Zambia. As of 1 August 1994, an additional two States, Austria and Cameroon, had become party to the Convention.

---

* This note has been prepared by the secretariat of the United Nations Commission on International Trade Law (UNCITRAL) for informational purposes only; it is not an official commentary on the Convention.

A. Background to the Hamburg Rules

1. The Hague Rules

4. The Hamburg Rules are the result of a movement to establish a modern and **I–039** uniform international legal regime to govern the carriage of goods by sea. For many years, a large proportion of the carriage of goods by sea has been governed by a legal regime centred around the International Convention relating to the Unification of Certain Rules relating to Bills of Lading, adopted on 25 August 1924 at Brussels, otherwise known as the "Hague Rules".

5. The Hague Rules establish a mandatory legal regime governing the liability of a carrier for loss of or damage to goods carried under a bill of lading. They cover the period from the time the goods are loaded onto the ship until the time they are discharged. According to their provisions, the carrier is liable for loss or damage resulting from his failure to exercise due diligence to make the ship seaworthy, to properly man, equip and supply the ship or to make its storage areas fit and safe for the carriage of goods. However, the Hague Rules contain a long list of circumstances that exempt the carrier from this liability. Perhaps the most significant of these exemptions frees the carrier from liability if the loss or damage arises from the faulty navigation or management of the ship.

6. The Hague Rules have been amended twice since their adoption, first in 1968 (by means of a protocol hereinafter referred to as the "Visby Protocol") and again in 1979 (by means of a protocol hereinafter referred to as the "1979 Additional Protocol"). These amendments deal mainly with the financial limits of liability under the Hague Rules. They do not alter the basic liability regime of the Hague Rules or the allocation of risks effected by it.

2. Dissatisfaction with the Hague Rules system

7. There emerged over the course of time increasing dissatisfaction with the **I–040** Hague Rules system. This dissatisfaction was based in part upon the perception that the overall allocation of responsibilities and risks achieved by the Hague Rules, which heavily favoured carriers at the expense of shippers, was inequitable. Several provisions of the Hague Rules were regarded as ambiguous and uncertain, which was said to result in higher transportation costs and to add further to the risks borne by shippers. The dissatisfaction with the Hague Rules was also based upon the perception that developments in conditions, technologies and practices relating to shipping had rendered inappropriate many features of the Hague Rules that may have been appropriate in 1924.

3. Steps towards revising the law governing the carriage of goods by sea

8. The question of revising the law governing the carriage of goods by sea was **I–041** first raised by the delegation of Chile at the first session of UNCITRAL in 1968. Shortly afterwards, the General Assembly recommended that UNCITRAL should consider including the question among the priority topics in its programme of work. UNCITRAL did so at its second session in 1969.

9. At about the same time, the law relating to bills of lading and the carriage of goods by sea had come under study within a working group of the United Nations Conference on Trade and Development (UNCTAD). The Working Group concluded that the rules and practices concerning bills of lading, including those contained in the Hague Rules and the Hague Rules as amended by the Visby Protocol, should be examined and, where appropriate, revised and amplified and that a new international convention should be prepared. The objective of that work would be to remove the existing uncertainties and ambiguities in the existing law and to establish a balanced allocation of responsibilities and risks between cargo interests and the carriers. The Working Group recommended that the work be undertaken by UNCITRAL. In 1971, UNCITRAL decided to proceed accordingly.

10. By 1976, UNCITRAL had finalized and approved the text of a draft Convention on the Carriage of Goods by Sea. Thereafter, the General Assembly convened the diplomatic conference at Hamburg, which adopted the Hamburg Rules in 1978.

B. Salient Features of the Hamburg Rules

1. Scope of application

I–042 11. In order to achieve international uniformity in the law relating to the carriage of goods by sea, the Hamburg Rules have been given a relatively wide scope of application—substantially wider than that of the Hague Rules. The Hamburg Rules are applicable to all contracts for the carriage of goods by sea between two different States if, according to the contract, either the port of loading or the port of discharge is located in a Contracting State, if the goods are discharged at an optional port of discharge stipulated in the contract and that port is located in a Contracting State, or if the bill of lading or other document evidencing the contract is issued in a Contracting State. In addition to those cases, the Hamburg Rules apply if the bill of lading or other document evidencing the contract of carriage provides that the rules are to apply. The application of the Rules does not depend upon the nationality of the ship, the carrier, the shipper, the consignee or any other interested person.

12. The Hamburg Rules do not apply to charter-parties. However, they apply to bills of lading issued pursuant to charter-parties if the bill of lading governs the relation between the carrier and a holder of the bill of lading who is not the charterer.

13. Unlike the Hague Rules, which apply only when a bill of lading is issued by the carrier, the Hamburg Rules govern the rights and obligations of the parties to a contract of carriage regardless of whether or not a bill of lading has been issued. This is becoming increasingly important as more and more goods are carried under non-negotiable transport documents, rather than under bills of lading.

2. Period of responsibility

I–043 14. The Hague Rules cover only the period from the time the goods are loaded onto the ship until the time they are discharged from it. They do not cover loss or damage occurring while the goods are in the custody of the carrier prior to loading or after discharge.

15. In modern shipping practice carriers often take and retain custody of goods in port before and after the actual sea carriage. It has been estimated that most loss and damage to goods occurs while the goods are in port. In order to ensure

that such loss or damage is the responsibility of the party who is in control of the goods and thereby best able to guard against that loss or damage, the Hamburg Rules apply to the entire period the carrier is in charge of the goods at the port of loading, during the carriage and at the port of discharge.

3. Basis of carrier's liability

16. The basis of the carrier's liability under the Hague Rules system was one of **I–044** the principal concerns of the movement for reform that eventually resulted in the Hamburg Rules. While the Hague Rules provide that the carrier is liable for loss or damage resulting from his failure to exercise due diligence to make the ship seaworthy, to properly man, equip and supply the ship or to make its storage areas fit and safe for the carriage of goods, a long list of circumstances exempts the carrier from this liability. These provisions are based upon exemption clauses that commonly appeared in bills of lading when the Hague Rules were adopted in the early 1920's. Perhaps the most significant of these exemptions frees the carrier from liability if the loss or damage arises from the faulty navigation or management of the ship, the so-called "nautical fault" exception. As a result of these exemptions, the shipper bears a heavy portion of the risk of loss of or damage to his goods.

17. The original justifications for this liability scheme, and in particular the nautical fault exception, were the inability of the shipowner to communicate with and exercise effective control over his vessel and crew during long voyages at sea, and the traditional concept of an ocean voyage as a joint adventure of the carrier and the owner of the goods. However, subsequent developments in communications and the reduction of voyage times have rendered those justifications obsolete. The liability scheme has no parallel in the law governing other modes of transport. Moreover, it is viewed as contrary both to the general legal concept that one should be liable to pay compensation for loss or damage caused by his fault or that of his servants or agents, and to the economic concept that loss should fall upon the party who is in a position to take steps to avoid it.

18. The Hamburg Rules effect a more balanced and equitable allocation of risks and responsibilities between carriers and shippers. Liability is based on the principle of presumed fault or neglect. That is, the carrier is liable if the occurrence that caused the loss, damage or delay took place while the goods were in his charge, and he may escape liability only if he proves that he, his servants or agents took all measures that could reasonably be required to avoid the occurrence and its consequences. This principle replaces the itemization of the carrier's obligations and the long list of his exemptions from liability under the Hague Rules, and eliminates the exemption from liability for loss or damage caused by the faulty navigation or management of the ship. The liability of the carrier under the Hamburg Rules corresponds with the liability imposed upon carriers under international conventions governing carriage of goods by other modes of transport, such as road and rail.

4. Deck cargo

19. Sea cargo carried on deck was traditionally subject to high risk of loss or **I–045** damage from the elements or other causes. For this reason the Hague Rules do not cover goods carried on deck by agreement of the parties, permitting the carrier to disclaim all liability for such cargo. However, developments in transport and packaging techniques, and in particular containerization, have made it possible for cargo to be carried on deck with relative safety. It is common for containers to be stored on deck in modern container ships.

20. The Hamburg Rules take these developments into account. Firstly, they expressly permit the carrier to carry goods on deck not only if the shipper so agrees, but also when such carriage is in accordance with the usage of the particular trade or if it is required by law. Secondly, they hold the carrier liable on the basis of presumed fault or neglect for loss, damage or delay in respect of goods that he is permitted to carry on deck. If he carries goods on deck without being permitted to do so, he is made liable for loss, damage or delay resulting solely from the carriage on deck, without being able to exclude that liability by proving that reasonable measures were taken to avoid the loss, damage or delay.

5. Liability for delay

I–046　**21.** Historically, sea voyages were subject to innumerable uncontrollable hazards, which frequently resulted in delays and deviations. Because of this unpredictability, the Hague Rules do not cover the liability of the carrier for delay in delivery. However, as a result of modern shipping technology, the proper charting of the oceans and sophisticated and efficient methods of navigation, voyages have become less subject to delays and more predictable. Shippers have come to rely upon and expect compliance with undertakings by carriers to deliver the goods within a specified period of time. Thus, the Hamburg Rules govern the liability of the carrier for delay in delivery in the same manner as liability for loss of or damage to the goods, *i.e.*, in accordance with the principle of presumed fault or neglect.

6. Financial limits of liability

I–047　**22.** The Hamburg Rules limit the liability of the carrier for loss of or damage to the goods to an amount equal to 835 units of account per package or other shipping unit, or 2.5 units of account per kilogram of gross weight of the goods lost or damaged, whichever is the higher. The carrier and the shipper can agree to limits higher than those, but not to lower limits.

23. The unit of account is the Special Drawing Right (SDR) as defined by the International Monetary Fund (IMF). The Rules set forth detailed provisions as to the manner in which the limits expressed in units of account are to be converted into national currencies with special provisions for certain States that are not members of the IMF. The limits of liability under the Hamburg Rules are 25 per cent higher than those established under the 1979 Additional Protocol, which also uses the SDR as the unit of account. In the Hague Rules and the Visby Protocol the limits of liability are expressed in units of account based upon a certain quantity of gold. Because national currencies no longer have fixed values in relation to gold, the values of those limits in national currencies vary.

24. The Hamburg Rules maintain the dual per package/per kilogram system established in the Visby Protocol. The purpose of this system is to take account of the fact that the value/weight ratios of goods carried by sea differ markedly. Sea cargo ranges from cargo such as bulk commodities, which have a low value relative to their weight, to cargo such as complex heavy machinery, which has a much higher value/weight ratio.

25. Under the dual system, the relatively low limit of 2.5 units of account per kilogram would apply to unpackaged commodities carried in bulk, while the higher per-package limit would apply to items carried in packages or other shipping units. The break-even point is 334 kilograms: if a package or shipping unit is under that weight, the per-package limit would apply; above that weight, the per-kilogram limit would apply. For the purpose of calculating the limits of liability, the packages or shipping units contained in a container are deemed to be those enumerated in the bill of lading or other transport document evidencing the contract of carriage.

26. The liability of the carrier for delay in delivering the goods is limited to $2\frac{1}{2}$ times the freight payable for the goods delayed, but not exceeding the total freight payable under the contract of carriage.

27. The Hamburg Rules contain an expedited procedure for revising the limits of liability in the event of a significant change in the real value of the limits resulting, for example, from inflation.

7. Rights of carrier's servants and agents

28. If a servant or agent of the carrier proves that he acted within the scope of his employment, he is entitled to avail himself of the defences and limits of liability that the carrier is entitled to invoke under the Hamburg Rules. I–048

8. Loss of benefit of limits of liability

29. A carrier loses the benefit of the limits of liability if it is proved that the loss, damage or delay resulted from an act or omission of the carrier done with intent to cause the loss, damage or delay, or recklessly and with knowledge that the loss, damage or delay would probably result. A servant or agent of the carrier loses the benefit of the limits of liability in the event of such conduct on his part. I–049

9. Liability of the carrier and actual carrier; through carriage

30. A carrier may enter into a contract of carriage by sea with a shipper but entrust the carriage, or a part of it, to another carrier. The contracting carrier in such cases often includes in the bill of lading a clause that exempts him from liability for loss or damage attributable to the actual carrier. Shippers face difficulties in legal systems that uphold those exemption clauses because they have to seek compensation from the actual carrier; that carrier might be unknown to the shipper, might have effectively restricted or excluded his liability or might not be subject to suit by the shipper in an appropriate jurisdiction. The Hague Rules do not deal with the liability of the actual carrier. I–050

31. The Hamburg Rules balance the interests of shippers and carriers in such cases. They enable the contracting carrier to exempt himself from liability for loss, damage or delay attributable to an actual carrier only if the contract of carriage specifies the part of carriage entrusted to the actual carrier and names the actual carrier. Moreover, the exemption is effective only if the shipper can institute judicial or arbitral proceedings against the actual carrier in one of the jurisdictions set forth in the Hamburg Rules. Otherwise, the contracting carrier is liable for loss, damage or delay in respect of the goods throughout the voyage, including loss, damage or delay attributable to the actual carrier. Where the contracting carrier and the actual carrier are both liable, their liability is joint and several.

10. Liability of the shipper

32. Under the Hamburg Rules a shipper is liable for loss sustained by the carrier or the actual carrier, or for damage sustained by the ship, only if the loss or damage was caused by the fault or neglect of the shipper, his servants or agents. I–051

33. Particular obligations are imposed upon the shipper with respect to dangerous goods. He is obligated to mark or label the goods in a suitable manner and, where he hands over dangerous goods to a carrier, he must inform the carrier of their dangerous character and, if necessary, of the precautions to be taken. Failure to meet these obligations could, in particular cases, entitle the carrier to be compensated for loss suffered from the shipment of the goods. The carrier may be entitled to dispose of dangerous goods or render them innocuous without compensating the shipper if the shipper fails to meet his obligations with respect to the goods, or if the goods become an actual danger to life or property.

11. Transport documents

(a) *Bills of lading*

I–052   **34.** Under both the Hague Rules and the Hamburg Rules, the carrier must issue a bill of lading if the shipper requests one. However, the Hamburg Rules take into account modern techniques of documentation by providing that a signature on a bill of lading not only may be handwritten but also may be made by any mechanical or electronic means, if not inconsistent with the law of the country where the bill of lading is issued.

35. The Hamburg Rules itemize the types of information required to be set forth in the bill of lading. Among other things, these include the general nature of the goods, the number of packages or pieces, their weight or quantity, and their apparent condition. The itemization is more extensive than that under the Hague Rules, since the additional information is needed in order to implement the liability regime of the Hamburg Rules, which is more comprehensive than that of the Hague Rules.

36. Under the Hamburg Rules the absence of one of the required particulars does not affect the legal character of the document as a bill of lading. This resolves a question which is not dealt with in the Hague Rules and which has been resolved in disparate ways in national legal systems.

I–053   **37.** Under the Hamburg Rules as well as the Hague Rules, the information set forth in the bill of lading is *prima facie* evidence of the taking over or loading by the carrier of the goods as so described. The Hamburg Rules and the Visby Protocol further provide that the description of the goods is conclusive in favor of a third-party transferee of the bill of lading who in good faith has acted in reliance on the description. The Hamburg Rules provide that if the carrier did not note the apparent condition of the goods on the bill of lading, they are deemed to have been in apparent good condition. This, too, resolves a question that is uncertain under the Hague Rules.

38. If the carrier knows or reasonably suspects that information in the bill of lading concerning the general nature of the goods, the number of packages or pieces, or their weight or quantity, is not accurate, or if he had no reasonable means of checking that information, he may, under the Hamburg Rules, insert in the bill of lading a reservation specifying the inaccuracies, grounds of suspicion or the absence of reasonable means of checking. The *prima facie* or conclusive evidentiary effect of the bill of lading is not applicable in respect of such information. These provisions are more explicit than comparable provisions of the Hague Rules.

39. Sometimes, a shipper asks the carrier to issue a "clean" bill of lading (*i.e.,* without inserting a reservation) even though the carrier may have grounds to question the accuracy of information supplied by the shipper for insertion in the bill of lading or may have no reasonable means of checking the information, or may have discovered defects in the condition of the goods. In return, the shipper agrees to indemnify the carrier against loss suffered by him as a result of issuing the bill of lading without a reservation. The Hamburg Rules provide that such an agreement is valid as against the shipper, unless the carrier intends to defraud a third party who relies on the description of the goods in the bill of lading. However, the agreement has no effect as against a third-party transferee of the bill of lading, including a consignee.

(b) *Other transport documents*

40. There is a growing practice in maritime transport for carriers to issue non-negotiable transport documents, such as sea waybills, rather than bills of lading. Although non-negotiable documents have been used in certain trades for some time, the use of such documents is spreading to other trades. Non-negotiable documents avoid certain problems that have arisen in connection with the use of bills of lading, such as the arrival of the goods at their destination before the bill of lading reaches the consignee.   **I–054**

41. The Hamburg Rules accommodate these developments firstly, by applying to contracts for carriage of goods by sea regardless of whether or not a bill of lading is issued, and secondly, by providing that a transport document issued by the carrier, which is not a bill of lading, is nevertheless *prima facie* evidence of the conclusion of the contract of carriage by sea and of the taking over of the goods by the carrier as described in the document.

42. Since the Hague Rules apply only when a bill of lading has been issued, they do not deal with other types of transport documents.

12. Claims and actions

43. The Hamburg Rules contain provisions governing judicial as well as arbitral proceedings brought under the Rules. They expressly permit the parties to agree to submit their disputes under the Convention to arbitration. This is important because some legal systems preclude the settlement by arbitration of disputes relating to the carriage of goods by sea. Arbitration has become recognized as an effective means of resolving such disputes; thus the Hamburg Rules contain provisions to settle questions such as limitation of actions and jurisdiction in connection with arbitration. The Hague Rules do not provide for arbitration.   **I–055**

(a) *Limitation of actions*

44. A claim under the Hamburg Rules must be brought in judicial or arbitral proceedings within a two-year limitation period. The period may be extended by the party against whom the claim is made. Under the Hague Rules suit must be brought within one year. The Hamburg Rules further provide that a party held liable under the Hamburg Rules has an additional period of time after the expiration of the two-year period to institute an action for indemnity against   **I–056**

another party who may be liable to him. Comparable provisions are not contained in the Hague Rules, but were added by the Visby Protocol.

(b) *Jurisdiction*

I–057   **45.** The Hamburg Rules require judicial or arbitral proceedings to be brought in one of the places specified in the Rules. The specified places are broad enough to meet the practical needs of the claimant. These include the following: the principal place of business or habitual residence of the defendant; the place where the contract of carriage was made, if made through the defendant's place of business, branch or agency there; the port of loading; the port of discharge; any other place designated in the contract of carriage or arbitration agreement. Judicial proceedings may also be instituted in a place where a vessel of the owner of the carrying vessel has been validly arrested, subject to the right of the defendant to have the action removed to one of the places mentioned in the preceding sentence. Notwithstanding those options, if, after a claim has arisen, the parties by agreement designate a place where the claimant may institute judicial proceedings, the proceedings must be instituted in that place; the same is true with respect to an agreement as to the place of arbitral proceedings, if the agreement is otherwise valid. The Hague Rules do not contain provisions with respect to jurisdiction.

13. Selected provisions

I–058   **46.** The Hamburg Rules are mandatory in the sense that the parties to a contract of carriage by sea may not by agreement reduce the carrier's responsibilities and obligations under the Rules. However, those responsibilities and obligations may be increased.

47. Other provisions of the Hamburg Rules pertain to the relationship between the Rules and the law of general average and other international conventions. Upon becoming a party to the Hamburg Rules, a State that is a party to the Hague Rules or the Hague Rules as amended by the Visby Protocol must denounce them. Under certain conditions the denunciation may be deferred for a period of up to five years.

C. Uniformity of Law

I–059   **48.** The Hamburg Rules offer the potential of achieving greater uniformity in the law relating to the carriage of goods by sea than do the Hague Rules. Firstly, since the Hague Rules apply only when a bill of lading is issued, the significant and growing portion of maritime transport in which bills of lading are not issued is not covered by them. Secondly, even when the Hague Rules do apply, many aspects of the rights and obligations of the parties to a contract of carriage are not dealt with. A question or issue that is not covered by the Hague Rules will be resolved by rules of national law, which often produce disparate solutions, or by clauses in bills of lading, which may unfairly favor one of the parties and which may be given effect to differing degrees in national legal systems.

49. The Hamburg Rules, by comparison, deal much more comprehensively with the rights and obligations of the parties to a contract of carriage. In order to achieve their potential for uniformity of law in this area, they must be adhered to by States worldwide.

Further information about the Convention may be obtained from:

UNCITRAL Secretariat
Vienna International Centre
P.O. Box 500
A–1400 Vienna
Austria

Telephone: (43–1) 26060–4060 or 4061

Telefax: (43)(1) 26060–5813

e-mail: *uncitral@uncitral.org*

APPENDIX J

CMI UNIFORM RULES FOR SEA WAYBILLS

J–001 [The full text of these rules can be found at CMI's website: *www.comitemaritime.org/rules/rulessaway*]

1. Scope of Application

J–002 (i) These Rules shall be called the "CMI Uniforms Rules for Sea Waybills".

(ii) They shall apply when adopted by a contract of carriage which is not covered by a bill of lading or similar document of title, whether the contract be in writing or not.

2. Definitions

J–003 In these Rules:

"Contract of carriage" shall mean any contract of carriage subject to these Rules which is to be performed wholly or partly by sea.

"Goods" shall mean any goods carried or received for carriage under a contract of carriage.

"Carrier" and "Shipper" shall mean the parties named in or identifiable as such from the contract of carriage.

"Consignee" shall mean the party named in or identifiable as such from the contract of carriage, or any person substituted as consignee in accordance with rule 6(i).

"Right of Control" shall mean the rights and obligations referred to in rule 6.

3. Agency

J–004 (i) The shipper on entering into the contract of carriage does so not only on his own behalf but also as agent for and on behalf of the consignee, and warrants to the carrier that he has authority so to do.

(ii) This rule shall apply if, and only if, it be necessary by the law applicable to the contract of carriage so as to enable the consignee to sue and be sued thereon. The consignee shall be under no greater liability than he would have been had the contract of carriage been covered by a bill of lading or similar document of title.

4. Rights and Responsibilities

J–005 (i) The contract of carriage shall be subject to any International Convention or National Law which is, or if the contract of carriage had been covered by a bill of lading or similar document of title would have been, compulsorily applicable thereto. Such convention or law shall apply notwithstanding anything inconsistent therewith in the contract of carriage.

(ii) Subject always to subrule (i), the contract of carriage is governed by:

(a) these Rules;

(b) unless otherwise agreed by the parties, the carrier's standard terms and conditions for the trade, if any, including any terms and conditions relating to the non-sea part of the carriage;

(c) any other terms and conditions agreed by the parties.

(iii) In the event of any inconsistency between the terms and conditions mentioned under subrule (ii)(b) or (c) and these Rules, these Rules shall prevail.

5. Description of the Goods

(i) The shipper warrants the accuracy of the particulars furnished by him relating   **J–006** to the goods, and shall indemnify the carrier against any loss, damage or expense resulting from any inaccuracy.

(ii) In the absence of reservation by the carrier, any statement in a sea waybill or similar document as to the quantity or condition of the goods shall

(a) as between the carrier and the shipper be prima facie evidence of receipt of the goods as so stated;

(b) as between the carrier and the consignee be conclusive evidence of receipt of the goods as so stated, and proof to the contrary shall not be permitted, provided always that the consignee has acted in good faith.

6. Right of Control

(i) Unless the shipper has exercised his option under subrule (ii) below, he shall   **J–007** be the only party entitled to give the carrier instructions in relation to the contract of carriage. Unless prohibited by the applicable law, he shall be entitled to change the name of the consignee at any time up to the consignee claiming delivery of the goods after their arrival at destination, provided he gives the carrier reasonable notice in writing, or by some other means acceptable to the carrier, thereby undertaking to indemnify the carrier against any additional expense caused thereby.

(ii) The shipper shall have the option, to be exercised not later than the receipt of the goods by the carrier, to transfer the right of control to the consignee. The exercise of this option must be noted on the sea waybill or similar document, if any. Where the option has been exercised the consignee shall have such rights as are referred to in subrule (i) above and the shipper shall cease to have such rights.

7. Delivery

(i) The carrier shall deliver the goods to the consignee upon production of proper   **J–008** identification.

(ii) The carrier shall be under no liability for wrong delivery if he can prove that he has exercised reasonable care to ascertain that the party claiming to be the consignee is in fact that party.

8. Validity

J–009   In the event of anything contained in these Rules or any such provisions as are incorporated into the contract of carriage by virtue of rule 4, being inconsistent with the provisions of any International Convention or National Law compulsorily applicable to the contract of carriage, such Rules and provisions shall to that extent but no further be null and void.

APPENDIX **K**

CMI RULES ON ELECTRONIC BILLS OF LADING

[The full text of these rules can be found at CMI's website: *www.* **K–001**
comitemaritime.org/rules/rulesebla]

1. Scope of Application

These Rules shall apply whenever the parties so agree. **K–002**

2. Definitions

a. "Contract of Carriage" means any agreement to carry goods wholly or **K–003**
partly by sea.

b. "EDI" means Electronic Data Interchange, *i.e.* the interchange of trade
data effected by teletransmission.

c. "UN/EDIFACT" means the United Nations Rules for Electronic Data
Interchange for Administration, Commerce and Transport.

d. "Transmission" means one or more messages electronically sent
together as one unit of dispatch which includes heading and terminating
data.

e. "Confirmation" means a Transmission which advises that the content
of a Transmission appears to be complete and correct, without prejudice
to any subsequent consideration or action that the content may
warrant.

f. "Private Key" means any technically appropriate form, such as a
combination of numbers and/or letters, which the parties may agree for
securing the authenticity and integrity of a Transmission.

g. "Holder" means the party who is entitled to the rights described in
Article 7(a) by virtue of its possession of a valid Private Key.

h. "Electronic Monitoring System" means the device by which a computer system can be examined for the transactions that it recorded, such
as a Trade Data Log or an Audit Trail.

i. "Electronic Storage" means any temporary, intermediate or permanent
storage of electronic data including the primary and the back-up storage
of such data.

3. Rules of procedure

K–004 a. When not in conflict with these Rules, the Uniform Rules of Conduct for Interchange of Trade Data by Teletransmission, 1987 (UNCID) shall govern the conduct between the parties.

b. The EDI under these Rules should conform with the relevant UN/EDIFACT standards. However, the parties may use any other method of trade data interchange acceptable to all of the users.

c. Unless otherwise agreed, the document format for the Contract of Carriage shall conform to the UN Layout Key or compatible national standard for bills of lading.

d. Unless otherwise agreed, a recipient of a Transmission is not authorised to act on a Transmission unless he has sent a Confirmation.

e. In the event of a dispute arising between the parties as to the data actually transmitted, an Electronic Monitoring System may be used to verify the data received. Data concerning other transactions not related to the data in dispute are to be considered as trade secrets and thus not available for examination. If such data are unavoidably revealed as part of the examination of the Electronic Monitoring System, they must be treated as confidential and not released to any outside party or used for any other purpose.

f. Any transfer of rights to the goods shall be considered to be private information, and shall not be released to any outside party not connected to the transport or clearance of the goods.

4. Form and content of the receipt message

K–005 a. The carrier, upon receiving the goods from the shipper, shall give notice of the receipt of the goods to the shipper by a message at the electronic address specified by the shipper.

b. This receipt message shall include:

(i) the name of the shipper;

The shipper must confirm this receipt message to the carrier, upon which Confirmation the shipper shall be the Holder.

c. Upon demand of the Holder, the receipt message shall be updated with the date and place of shipment as soon as the goods have been loaded on board.

d. The information contained in (ii), (iii) and (iv) of paragraph (b) above including the date and place of shipment if updated in accordance with paragraph (c) of this Rule, shall have the same force and effect as if the receipt message were contained in a paper bill of lading.

5. Terms and conditions of the Contract of Carriage

a. It is agreed and understood that whenever the carrier makes a reference   **K–006**
to its terms and conditions of carriage, these terms and conditions shall
form part of the Contract of Carriage.

b. Such terms and conditions must be readily available to the parties to
the Contract of Carriage.

c. In the event of any conflict or inconsistency between such terms and
conditions and these Rules, these Rules shall prevail.

6. Applicable law

The Contract of Carriage shall be subject to any international convention   **K–007**
or national law which would have been compulsorily applicable if a
paper bill of lading had been issued.

7. Right of Control and Transfer

a. The Holder is the only party who may, as against the carrier: **K–008**

(i) claim delivery of the goods;

b. A transfer of the Right of Control and Transfer shall be effected: (i) by
notification of the current Holder to the carrier of its intention to transfer
its Right of Control and Transfer to a proposed new Holder, and
(ii) confirmation by the carrier of such notification message, whereupon
(iii) the carrier shall transmit the information as referred to in article 4
(except for the Private Key) to the proposed new Holder, whereafter
(iv) the proposed new Holder shall advise the carrier of its acceptance of
the Right of Control and Transfer, whereupon (v) the carrier shall cancel
the current Private Key and issue a new Private Key to the new
Holder.

c. If the proposed new Holder advises the carrier that it does not accept
the Right of Control and Transfer or fails to advise the carrier of such
acceptance within a reasonable time, the proposed transfer of the Right of
Control and Transfer shall not take place. The carrier shall notify the
current Holder accordingly and the current Private Key shall retain its
validity.

d. The transfer of the Right of Control and Transfer in the manner
described above shall have the same effects as the transfer of such rights
under a paper bill of lading.

8. The Private Key

a. The Private Key is unique to each successive Holder. It is not transfer-   **K–009**
able by the Holder. The carrier and the Holder shall each maintain the
security of the Private Key.

b. The carrier shall only be obliged to send a Confirmation of an electronic message to the last Holder to whom it issued a Private Key, when such Holder secures the Transmission containing such electronic message by the use of the Private Key.

c. The Private Key must be separate and distinct from any means used to identify the Contract of Carriage, and any security password or identification used to access the computer network.

9. Delivery

K–010 a. The carrier shall notify the Holder of the place and date of intended delivery of the goods. Upon such notification the Holder has a duty to nominate a consignee and to give adequate delivery instructions to the carrier with verification by the Private Key. In the absence of such nomination, the Holder will be deemed to be the consignee.

b. The carrier shall deliver the goods to the consignee upon production of proper identification in accordance with the delivery instructions specified in paragraph (a) above; such delivery shall automatically cancel the Private Key.

c. The carrier shall be under no liability for misdelivery if it can prove that it exercised reasonable care to ascertain that the party who claimed to be the consignee was in fact that party.

10. Option to receive a paper document

K–011 a. The Holder has the option at any time prior to delivery of the goods to demand from the carrier a paper bill of lading. Such document shall be made available at a location to be determined by the Holder, provided that no carrier shall be obliged to make such document available at a place where it has no facilities and in such instance the carrier shall only be obliged to make the document available at the facility nearest to the location determined by the Holder. The carrier shall not be responsible for delays in delivering the goods resulting from the Holder exercising the above option.

b. The carrier has the option at any time prior to delivery of the goods to issue to the Holder a paper bill of lading unless the exercise of such option could result in undue delay or disrupts the delivery of the goods.

c. A bill of lading issued under Rules 10(a) or (b) shall include: the information set out in the receipt message referred to in Rule 4 (except for the Private Key); and (ii) a statement to the effect that the bill of lading has been issued upon termination of the procedures for EDI under the CMI Rules for Electronic Bills of Lading. The aforementioned bill of lading shall be issued at the option of the Holder either to the order of the

Holder whose name for this purpose shall then be inserted in the bill of lading or "to bearer".

d. The issuance of a paper bill of lading under Rule 10(a) or (b) shall cancel the Private Key and terminate the procedures for EDI under these Rules. Termination of these procedures by the Holder or the carrier will not relieve any of the parties to the Contract of Carriage of their rights, obligations or liabilities while performing under the present Rules nor of their rights, obligations or liabilities under the Contract of Carriage.

e. The Holder may demand at any time the issuance of a print-out of the receipt message referred to in Rule 4 (except for the Private Key) marked as "non-negotiable copy". The issuance of such a print-out shall not cancel the Private Key nor terminate the procedures for EDI.

11. Electronic data is equivalent to writing

The carrier and the shipper and all subsequent parties utilizing these **K–012** procedures agree that any national or local law, custom or practice requiring the Contract of Carriage to be evidenced in writing and signed, is satisfied by the transmitted and confirmed electronic data residing on computer data storage media displayable in human language on a video screen or as printed out by a computer. In agreeing to adopt these Rules, the parties shall be taken to have agreed not to raise the defence that this contract is not in writing.

Appendix L

BOLERO RULEBOOK

L–001 [This is the first, and as yet only, edition of the Rule book (September 1999). It is available from Bolero's website: *www.boleroassociation.org/downloads/rulebook1*

More detailed operating procedures can also be found at: *www.boleroassociation.org/downloads/op_procs*]

PART 1

DEFINITIONS AND INTERPRETATION

1.1. DEFINITIONS

L–002 **(1) Applicant User**: A User who instructs a bank to issue a Documentary Credit.

(2) Authority: Any central, national, state, provincial or local government; any agency of such government; or any body or person empowered to make regulations or issue directions or requirements legally enforceable against the User in relation to the:

    (a) administration of any seaport, canal, waterway, airport, road or railway;

    (b) import, export or transport of goods;

    (c) transfer of any cash or securities;

    (d) imposition of any tax or duty; or

    (e) enforcement of law.

L–003 **(3) Accept, Acceptance**: In relation to a Certificate, to manifest approval of a Certificate, whether expressly or by implication such as by creating a Digital Signature Verifiable by reference to that Certificate.

(4) Annual Charge: The lump sum fee payable annually by a User as set out in the Charges Schedule to the Operational Service Contract.

(5) BAL Service Contract: The contract between Bolero Association Limited and each User, as amended from time to time.

(6) BBL Text: A Document which:

    (a) is sent into the Core Messaging Platform and recorded in the Title Registry as the documentary component of the Bolero Bill of Lading; and

    (b) acknowledges the receipt of goods by a Carrier for carriage by sea.

(7) Bearer Holder: A User who is or becomes Designated a Holder of a Blank Endorsed Bolero Bill of Lading.   **L–004**

(8) Beneficiary User: A User who is designated under a Documentary Credit as the party to whom, or to whose order, payment is to be made or whose bills of exchange are to be accepted and paid.

(9) Blank Endorse: To render, by the process described in the Operating Procedures, a Bolero Bill of Lading capable of transfer simply by Designation of a new Bearer Holder.

(10) Bolero Association: The Bolero Association Limited, a corporate body created to represent the Users of the Bolero System and to perform administrative and disciplinary functions assigned to it by the BAL Service Contract.   **L–005**

(11) Bolero Bill of Lading: A BBL Text together with its related Title Registry Record.

(12) Bolero Certificate: A Certificate for use in the Bolero System and listing a Public Key used to Verify the Digital Signature on a Message Digitally Signed by a User.

(13) Bolero Header: The part of a Message indicating its type and function within the Bolero System and conveying data into the Bolero System's logs, User Database, Title Registry, and other records, and, in some cases, prompts one or more actions by the Bolero System.   **L–006**

(14) Bolero International: The owners or operators of the Bolero System for the time being, or their successors in title.

(15) Bolero Services: The services supplied by the Bolero System as set out in the Operational Service Contract.

(16) Bolero System: The business processes and methods, together with the digital information system, which are provided by Bolero International for communicating Messages and Documents and facilitating business transactions, as well as the Bolero Rulebook and Operating Rules governing their use. The Bolero System does not include any   **L–007**

system, software, or equipment whose use is expressly limited to testing and/or non-binding transactions by agreement with Bolero International.

(17) Carrier: A User which contracts with another User to carry goods by any means of transport, regardless of whether the Carrier is the owner or operator of the means of transport used. Synonym: Originator.

(18) Certificate: A unit of information which, at a minimum:

    (a) lists its Issuer by name;

    (b) lists a Public Key;

    (c) lists by name, or otherwise indicates, a User holding the Private Key corresponding to the listed Public Key;

    (d) is Digitally Signed by its Issuer; and

    (e) has the meaning consistent with this definition ascribed to it in its Documentary Form.

L–008 **(19) Certifier**: A person that Issues one or more Certificates to Users. The Certifier which issued a particular Certificate is also termed its "Issuer".

(20) Chartered Bill of Lading: An acknowledgement by a Carrier of the receipt of goods for carriage on board its ship in respect of which there is a charterparty, other than a bareboat or demise charter, concurrently in force in respect of the use of the ship either for the same voyage (voyage charter) or for a period of time (time charter) within which the said carriage is to take place.

(21) Consignee: A User Designated as such, being thereby identified as the party to whom delivery of the goods must be made by the Carrier and also indicating the intention to make the Bolero Bill of Lading non-transferable

L–009 **(22) Consignee Holder**: A User simultaneously Designated as Consignee and Holder of a Bolero Bill of Lading.

(23) Core Messaging Platform: The messaging system of the Bolero System as described in the Operating Procedures.

(24) Designate: To name or appoint a User to a role in the Title Registry. "Designation" means the act of Designating or the state of having been Designated.

L–010 **(25) Digital Signature**: A mathematical result calculated from a unit of digital information and a Private Key, such that one having the unit of information and the corresponding Public Key can, through Verification, accurately determine (1) whether that mathematical result was created using that Private Key, and (2) whether the unit of information has been altered since that mathematical result was calculated.

(26) Document: A contract, bill, or other unit of substantive, often textual, information sent as a subdivided part of a Message. Synonyms: Attachment, attached Document.

(27) Documentary Credit: Any documentary credit, including standby letters of credit, as defined by The Uniform Customs and Practice for Documentary Credits or the International Standby Practices 1998, both of the International Chamber of Commerce, in effect at the time of the issue of the documentary credit.

(28) Documentary Form of a Certificate: A textual interpretation of a Certificate authorised by its Issuer. 　　　　　　　　　　　　　　　L–011

(29) Enrol: To become a User of the Bolero System through the BAL Service Contract and Operational Service Contract. "Enrolled" means to have become and to remain a User in accordance with those contracts.

(30) Head Charter: A charterparty contract, other than a charter by demise or bareboat charter, between a Carrier, as owner or disponent owner of a ship and another User as charterer, for the use of the Carrier's ship for the purpose of carrying cargo either for a specific voyage or series of voyages or for a period of time.

(31) Head Charterer: A User who has entered into a Head Charter with a Carrier. 　　　　　　　　　　　　　　　　　　　　　L–012

(32) Holder-to-order: A User who is or becomes simultaneously Designated both Holder and To Order Party of a Bolero Bill of Lading.

(33) Holder: A User who is or becomes Designated to the role of Holder. "Holdership" is the status of being a Holder. A User may be the Holder of a Bolero Bill of Lading without occupying another Role, or Holdership may be joined to another role as in the case of a Holder-to-order, Bearer Holder, Pledgee Holder, or Consignee Holder.

(34) Issue a Certificate: To list oneself as Issuer in a Certificate and Digitally Sign that Certificate. 　　　　　　　　　　　　　　L–013

(35) Issuer: With reference to a Certificate, the Certifier which Issued the Certificate.

(36) Key Pair: In a scheme of asymmetric or Public K cryptography, a Private Key and its mathematically related Public Key, which together have the property that the Public Key can Verify a Digital Signature that the Private Key creates.

L–014 **(37) Message**: Any communication, notice or other information sent through the Bolero System as described in the Operating Procedures.

(38) Operating Procedures: The document by that title appended to the Rulebook.

(39) Operational Rules: Those parts of the Operating Procedures which contain mandatory provisions and designated as Operational Rules in the Operating Procedures.

L–015 **(40) Operational Service Contract**: The standard form contract between each User and Bolero International, as amended from time to time.

(41) Originator: See "Carrier", paragraph (17) above.

(42) Pledgee Holder: A User who is or becomes Designated as both Pledgee and Holder simultaneously.

L–016 **(43) Private Key**: The key of a Key Pair used to create a Digital Signature.

(44) Public Key: The key of a Key Pair used to Verify a Digital Signature.

(45) Revoke: In relation to a Certificate, to include the Certificate in a class of Certificates, for which the Issuer of the Certificates gives notice that they (each or together) are Revoked.

L–017 **(46) Rulebook**: The Bolero Rulebook, as amended from time to time, governing the relationship between Users and their rights and obligations arising from the Bolero System.

(47) Sea Waybill: A Document, other than a BBL Text or a Ship's Delivery Order, which is such a receipt for goods as contains or evidences a contract for the carriage of goods by sea and identifies a User to whom delivery of the goods is to be made by the Carrier in accordance with that contract.

L–018 **(48) Shipper**: A User which is the original contracting party with whom a Carrier enters into the contract for the carriage of goods.

(49) Ship's Delivery Order: A Document, other than a BBL Text or a Sea Waybill, which contains an undertaking to the User identified in the Document to deliver identified goods to that User, given under or for the purposes of a contract of carriage of those goods or of goods which include those goods.

(50) Signed: Properly Digitally Signed, which is to say, bearing a Digital Signature which can be Verified using the Public Key listed in a Certificate Issued by Bolero International and which was a Valid Certificate when the Digital Signature was created.

(51) Surrender: The presentation of a Bolero Bill of Lading to the Carrier L–019 or another User appointed by the Carrier, in accordance with the Operational Rules, in order to obtain delivery of the goods at the end of the carriage.

(52) Surrender Party: A User who is or becomes Designated as such and thereby identified as the person to whom the Bolero Bill of Lading must be presented to obtain delivery of the goods at the end of the carriage.

(53) Title Registry: An application operated by Bolero International and providing:

(a) the means to execute the functions relating to Holdership and transfer of Bolero Bill of Lading;

(b) a record of the status of current Bolero Bills of Lading; and

(c) an audit trail of dealings with such Bolero Bills of Lading.

(54) Title Registry Instruction, Instruction: The portion of a Bolero L–020 Header which directs the Title Registry to enter or change certain specified information in the Title Registry Record for a specified Bolero Bill of Lading.

(55) Title Registry Record: The structured information kept in the Title Registry, linked to the BBL Text, and derived from Title Registry Instructions involving the related Bolero Bill of Lading.

(56) Transport Document: Any Document originated by a Carrier which is either a Sea Waybill or a Ship's Delivery Order.

(57) To Order Party: A User Designated as such who is not also desig- L–021 nated as the Holder of the Bolero Bill of Lading.

(58) User: A person who is Enrolled as a User of the Bolero System.

(59) User Database: The records concerning Users kept in the Bolero System.

L–022 **(60) Root Identifier**: A name uniquely identifying a User within the Bolero System.

(61) User Support Resources: The support services as well as the online information and functions provided by the Bolero System via a secured WorldWide Web interface.

(62) User System: The means by which a User connects with and utilises the Bolero System. It includes the digital networking connection to the Bolero System to be established by the User pursuant to the Operational Service Contract, software and hardware for composing, sending, and receiving Messages, reading or processing Documents, as well as computer security facilities and other components.

L–023 **(63) Valid Certificate**: A Certificate which is valid according to the terms specified in its Documentary Form. If no such terms are specified or available to a User relying on that Certificate, the Certificate is valid if has been signed by its Issuer and has not expired on its face or been Revoked as set out in the Operating Procedures.

(64) Verify, Verification: In relation to a given Digitally Signed Message and Public Key, to determine accurately that:

    (a) the Digital Signature on the Message was created by the Private Key corresponding to that Public Key; and

    (b) that the Message has not been altered since its Digital Signature was created.

1.2. Interpretation

L–024 **(1) "May" and "Shall"**. "May" shall be construed as permissive. "Shall" shall be construed as imperative.

(2) Singular Includes Plural. Words importing only the singular number shall include the plural number and vice versa.

(3) Gender. Words importing only the neuter gender shall include the masculine and feminine genders. Words importing persons shall include companies or associations or bodies of persons whether incorporated or unincorporated.

(4) English. This document is drafted in the English language, and its original English version is controlling in all questions of interpretation.

PART 2

GENERAL PROVISIONS

2.1. SCOPE AND APPLICATION

2.1.1. *Parties*

(1) Effect as Agreement between Users. The Rulebook constitutes an agreement between Users, and between each User and the Bolero Association acting on its own behalf, and on behalf of all other Users from time to time, and, where necessary, on behalf of Bolero International. **L–025**

(2) Obligations between Users. The Bolero Association and Bolero International do not undertake or accept any responsibility for the performance of any obligation or duty owed by one User to any other User under this Rulebook or otherwise.

(3) Effect of Service Contracts. No liability on the part of the Bolero Association or Bolero International to any User shall arise except under and in accordance with the terms of, in the case of the Bolero Association, the BAL Service Contract, and in the case of Bolero International, the Operational Service Contract.

2.1.2. *Applicability*

(1) Rulebook. Each User agrees, when Enrolling into the Bolero System, to be bound by this Rulebook. **L–026**

(2) Incorporation of Operating Procedures. The Operating Procedures describe the Bolero System and provide factual background. They are hereby incorporated into it as if fully set forth herein.

(3) Operational Rules. Portions of the Operating Procedures are labelled "Operational Rules" (abbreviated "Op. Rule"). The Operational Rules are binding obligations according to their terms, the same as any other obligation of this Rulebook. The remaining descriptive portions of the Operating Procedures are in the nature of non-mandatory recitals.

(4) Inapplicable to Bolero Test Bed and Other Systems. This Rulebook and the Operating Rules shall not apply to any Message, Document, or Title Registry Instruction that is not sent via the Bolero System, or to a Bolero Bill of Lading whose BBL Text was not a Document sent via the Bolero System.

2.1.3. *Enrolment*

L–027 **(1) Bolero Association's Requirements**. Each User affirms that it has fully complied with the requirements of the Bolero Association regarding Enrolment.

(2) Information Provided During Enrolment. Each User warrants that the information that it provides to the Bolero Association and/or Bolero International in connection with Enrolment is accurate and complete. Further, the User shall promptly notify the Bolero Association and Bolero International if any information previously provided becomes inaccurate or misleading.

2.2. MESSAGES

2.2.1. *Operations*

L–028 **(1) Authentication**. Each User agrees that all Messages sent by it or on its behalf via the Bolero System shall:

    (a) be Signed by it;

    (b) identify the sender; and

    (c) identify the recipient.

(2) Presumption of Sending. A User shall be presumed to have sent a Message as soon as the User has Signed and sent the Message in accordance with the Operational Rules.

(3) Presumption of Receipt. A User shall be presumed to have received a Message as soon as Bolero International has correctly forwarded the Message to such User in accordance with the Operational Rules.

(4) Equipment and Applications. Each User shall operate a User System that the User shall take all reasonable care to maintain in good order.

(5) Misdelivery. If a Message which is clearly addressed to one User is delivered to another, the User in receipt of the misdelivered Message shall:

    (a) return the Message to its sender via the Bolero System as soon as the error is discovered;

    (b) take reasonable measures to refrain from storing or retaining any copy of the Message; and

    (c) treat the information contained in the Message as confidential and not use or disclose it for any purpose.

2.2.2. *Validity and Enforceability*

(1) Writing Requirements. Any applicable requirement of law, contract, custom or practice that any transaction, document or communication shall be made or evidenced in writing, signed or sealed shall be satisfied by a Signed Message. **L–029**

(2) Signature Requirements. The contents of a Message Signed by a User, or a portion drawn from a Signed Message, are binding upon that User to the same extent, and shall have the same effect at law, as if the Message or portion thereof had existed in a manually signed form.

(3) Undertaking not to Challenge Validity. No User shall contest the validity of any transaction, statement or communication made by means of a Signed Message, or a portion drawn from a Signed Message, on the grounds that it was made in electronic form instead of by paper and/or signed or sealed.

2.2.3. *Messages as Evidence*

(1) Admissibility. Each User agrees that a Signed Message or a portion drawn from a Signed Message will be admissible before any court or tribunal as evidence of the Message or portion thereof. **L–030**

(2) Primary Evidence. In the event that a written record of any Message is required, a copy produced by a User, which Bolero International has authenticated, shall be accepted by that User and any other User as primary evidence of the Message.

(3) Authenticated Copies to Prevail. Each User agrees that if there is a discrepancy between the record of any User and the copy authenticated by Bolero International, such authenticated copy shall prevail.

2.2.4. *Responsibility for Messages*

(1) Private Key Security. Each User is responsible for all Messages Signed by means of its Private Key, regardless of any failure to maintain the security of its own Private Key. **L–031**

(2) Site Security. Each User is responsible for implementing all necessary security procedures and measures at its site to ensure that data transmissions to and from the Bolero System are protected against unauthorised access, alteration, delay, loss or destruction.

2.2.5. *Notice*

Each User undertakes to give immediate notice to Bolero International and to comply with the relevant Operational Rules, in the event that its **L–032**

Private Key has been lost or compromised or it has reasonable grounds
for believing that such Private Key has been or may be misused, or used
by an unauthorised person.

2.3. ILLEGALITY

L–033   **(1) Compulsory Requirements**. Each User undertakes to comply with
any compulsorily applicable legal requirements as to the permitted form
in which data may be transmitted electronically and as to the content of
such data.

(2) Illegal Trading and Transfers. Users shall not use the Bolero System
for the transmission of Messages in the course of or to facilitate any:

(a) illegal trading,

(b) trading of goods which are contraband, or

(c) illegal transfers of money.

(3) Compliance with Regulations. Each User is responsible for ensuring
that it complies with any law or regulation applicable to any transaction
in which it participates via the Bolero System and for the observance of
regulations relating to data protection or encryption.

2.4. CONSEQUENCES OF RESIGNATION OR TERMINATION

L–034   **(1) Messages**. When a User ceases to be Enrolled, that User shall ensure
that:

(a) all its existing Messages sent from the Bolero System before the
     effective date of termination are collected and read;

(b) all other Users from whom it expects to receive Messages are
     advised of its departure from the Bolero System; and

(c) it takes all reasonable steps to give other Users the necessary
     information to enable future communications to be received by it.

(2) Switch to Paper by Terminated User. If, at the time of the termination
of a User's right of access in accordance with the provisions of the
Operational Service Contract or the BAL Service Contract, that User is a
Holder, Holder-to-order, Bearer Holder, or a Pledgee Holder of a Bolero
Bill of Lading, it shall follow such instructions as Bolero International or
Bolero Association may give, including, but not limited to, an instruction
to initiate the Switch to Paper procedure under Rule

3.7 (Switch to Paper). Neither Bolero International nor the Bolero Association shall, however, be under any obligation to issue such instructions.

2.5. Miscellaneous

(1) Partial Invalidity. If any provision in this Rulebook is held to be L–035
invalid, illegal or unenforceable by any competent court, tribunal or regulatory body, such invalidity, illegality or unenforceability shall attach only to that provision, and:

  (a) the validity legality or enforceability of the remaining provisions shall not be affected and this Rulebook shall apply as if such invalid, illegal or unenforceable provisions had not been included;

  (b) the validity, legality or enforceability in any other jurisdiction of the offending or

any other provision shall not be affected.

(2) Applicable Law. This Rulebook is governed by and shall be interpreted in accordance with English Law.

(3) English Jurisdiction. Where the sole matter at issue between the parties is a claim for non-compliance with or breach of this Rulebook, all proceedings in respect of such claim shall be subject to the exclusive jurisdiction of the English courts.

(4) Non-exclusive Jurisdiction. Any other dispute arising out of this Rulebook shall be subject to the non-exclusive jurisdiction of the English courts. Nothing in this Rule 2.5 limits the right of a User to bring proceedings in connection with this Rulebook, other than those which fall within paragraph (3) of Rule 2.5, in any other court or tribunal of competent jurisdiction.

Part 3

Bolero Title Registry

3.1. Creation of a Bolero Bill of Lading

(1) Contents of BBL Text and Identification. Each Carrier agrees that any L–036
Message sent by him as a Bolero Bill of Lading other than a Message intended to operate as a Chartered Bill of Lading shall, within the BBL Text:

(a) include an acknowledgement by the Carrier of the receipt of goods shipped on board a vessel or received for shipment by that Carrier; and

(b) contain or evidence the terms of the contract of carriage.

The Message shall be transmitted to the Title Registry.

(2) Chartered Bills of Lading. Where a Carrier creates a Bolero Bill of Lading intended to operate as a Chartered Bill of Lading and Designates the Head Charterer as Shipper and Holder, the BBL Text need not contain or evidence the terms of the contract of carriage between the Carrier and Head Charterer. The BBL Text shall, however, include an acknowledgement by the Carrier of the receipt of goods shipped on board a vessel or received for shipment by that Carrier.

(3) Statements Relating to Goods Received. Without prejudice to the generality of section 2.2.2, any statement a Carrier makes as to the leading marks, number, quantity, weight, or apparent order and condition of the goods in the BBL Text will be binding on the Carrier to the same extent and in the same circumstances as if the statement had been contained in a paper bill of lading.

(4) Original Parties. When a Carrier creates a Bolero Bill of Lading the Carrier must:

(a) Designate a Shipper; and

(b) Designate a Holder of the Bill of Lading, and

(c) Either:

> (1) Designate a To Order Party (who shall not be the same as the Designated Holder),
> (2) Designate a Consignee (who shall not be the same as the Designated Holder), or
> (3) Blank Endorse the Bolero Bill of Lading, thereby Designating the Holder as a Bearer Holder, in accordance with the Shipper's instructions. In the absence of any instructions as to (b) or (c), the Carrier shall Designate the Shipper as the Bearer Holder.

3.2. Incorporation by Reference

L–037 **(1) Standard Terms and Conditions**. In order to incorporate its standard terms and conditions, otherwise than by setting the said terms and conditions out in full in the BBL Text, a Carrier shall:

(a) Express in the BBL Text that external terms and conditions be incorporated into the BBL Text; and

(b) Indicate where such terms and conditions can be found and read, electronically or otherwise.

(2) Effect of Incorporation. Each User agrees that such incorporation shall be effective to make such terms and conditions binding upon the parties to the contract of carriage.

(3) Incorporation of Charterparty Terms. Without prejudice to the generality of section 2.2.2, each User agrees that words contained in the BBL Text incorporating the provisions of any charterparty shall have the same effect as if such wording had appeared as part of the written terms of a paper bill of lading issued by the Carrier.

(4) International Conventions. A contract of carriage in respect of which the Carrier has created a Bolero Bill of Lading shall be subject to any international convention, or national law giving effect to such international convention, which would have been compulsorily applicable if a paper bill of lading in the same terms had been issued in respect of that contract. Such international convention or national law shall be deemed incorporated into the Bolero Bill of Lading. In the event of a conflict between the provisions of any international convention or national law giving effect to such international convention and the other provisions of the contract of carriage as contained in the BBL Text, the provisions of that national law or that international convention shall prevail.

(5) Special Clauses. The clause set out in the Annex shall form part of this Rulebook, in the circumstances in which it is applicable.

3.3. Rights over a Bolero Bill of Lading

(1) Transferability. A Bolero Bill of Lading may be transferable or non-transferable.   L–038

(2) Making Transferable. Where the Carrier intends to create a transferable Bolero Bill of Lading it shall Designate a To Order Party or Blank Endorse the Bill.

(3) Effect of Designating To Order Party. If the Carrier Designates a To Order Party, the Carrier is thereby deemed to have agreed that:

(a) such To Order Party who becomes the Holder-to-order of the Bolero Bill of Lading can Designate a new To Order Party, a Pledgee Holder, a Bearer Holder or a Consignee; and

(b) any subsequent Holder-to-order, Pledgee Holder or Bearer Holder can do likewise.

L–039   **(4) Effect of Blank Endorsement.** If the Carrier gives a Title Registry Instruction that the Bolero Bill of Lading shall be Blank Endorsed, it is thereby deemed to have agreed that:

> (a) the Holder is a Bearer Holder and can Designate a new Bearer Holder, a To Order Party, a Holder-to-order, a Pledgee Holder or a Consignee; and

> (b) any subsequent Holder-to-order, Pledgee Holder or Bearer Holder can do likewise.

(5) Holder To Order or Bearer Holder Not Shipper. By creating a Bolero Bill of Lading in which it Designates a Bearer Holder who is not the Shipper, the Carrier thereby acknowledges that it holds the goods described in the Bolero Bill of Lading to the order of that Bearer Holder.

(6) Making Non-transferable. If a Carrier Designates a Consignee, the Bolero Bill of Lading shall be non– transferable.

(7) Carrier's Responsibility for Compliance with Contract of Carriage. The Carrier shall ensure that the Designations it makes in the Title Registry Instruction accurately reflect:

> (a) the express or implied instructions of the Shipper and;

> (b) the terms and effect of the contract of carriage as contained in or evidenced by the BBL Text; or

> (c) in the case of a Chartered Bill of Lading in which the Head Charterer is Designated Shipper, the terms set out in the BBL Text as if the same were the terms of the contract of carriage.

3.4. Transfer of Possession

3.4.1. *Procedure for Transfer of Possession*

L–040   **(1) By Designation.** The transfer of constructive possession of the goods, after the creation of a transferable Bolero Bill of Lading, shall be effected by the Designation of:

> (a) a new Holder-to-order,

> (b) a new Pledgee Holder,

> (c) a new Bearer Holder, or

> (d) a Consignee Holder.

(2) Effect of Designations. The Carrier shall, upon Designation of such Holder-to-order, Pledgee Holder, Bearer Holder or Consignee Holder, acknowledge that from that time on it holds the goods described in the Bolero Bill of Lading to the order of the new Holder-to-order, Pledgee Holder, Bearer Holder or Consignee Holder, as the case may be.

(3) To Order Party Becomes Holder. Where a new To Order Party is Designated, no transfer of constructive possession of goods shall take place until such time as the To Order Party also becomes Designated as Holder and so becomes a Holder-to-order.

(4) Consignee Becomes Holder. Where a new Consignee is Designated, no transfer of constructive possession shall take place until such time as the Consignee also becomes Designated Holder.

(5) Refusal by Transferee. If any Designated Holder-to-order or Con- L–041
signee Holder refuses to accept the novation of the contract of carriage in accordance with Rule 3.5.2, the Carrier shall cease to hold the goods to the order of such Designated Holder-to-order or Consignee Holder and constructive possession of the goods shall remain with the immediately preceding Holder-to-order, Bearer Holder, Pledgee Holder or, if none, to the Shipper.

(6) Rejection by Pledgee. Where a Designated Pledgee Holder rejects the Bolero Bill of Lading by returning Holdership to the immediately preceding Holder, the Carrier shall cease to hold the goods to the order of such Designated Pledgee Holder and the constructive possession of the goods will automatically revert to the immediately preceding Holder-to-order, Bearer Holder, Pledgee Holder or, if none, to the Shipper.

3.4.2. *Bolero International as Carrier's Agent*

Each Carrier hereby irrevocably appoints Bolero International as its agent L–042
for the following purposes:

(a) To acknowledge that the Carrier holds the goods to the order of any Designated Holder-to-order, Pledgee Holder, Bearer Holder or Consignee Holder or Shipper under Rule 3.4.1 paragraphs 3.4.1(2), 3.4.1(5), or 3.4.1(6) (Procedure for Transfer of Possession.), and.

(b) To receive notice of any refusal of any such transfer of possession by such Designated Holder-to-order, Pledgee Holder, Bearer Holder, or Consignee Holder.

3.5. NOVATION OF THE CONTRACT OF CARRIAGE

3.5.1. *Occurrence and Effect*

The Designation of a new Holder-to-order or a new Consignee Holder L–043
after the creation of the Bolero Bill of Lading, other than one who is also

the Head Charterer, shall mean that the Carrier, the Shipper, the immediately preceding Holder-to-order, if any, and the new Holder-to-order or
Consignee Holder agree to all of the following terms in this section
3.5.1:

(1) New Parties to Contract of Carriage. Upon the acceptance by the new
Holder-to-order or Consignee Holder of its Designation as such, or, at the
expiry of the 24 hour period allowed for the refusal of the transfer under
Rule 3.5.2 (New Holder's Right to Refuse Designation), whichever is the
earlier, a contract of carriage shall arise between the Carrier and the new
Holder-to-order or Consignee Holder either:

  (a) on the terms of the contract of carriage as contained in or evidenced
      by the BBL Text; or

  (b) when the Shipper is a Head Charterer, on the terms set out or
      incorporated in the BBL Text, as if this had contained or evidenced
      the original contract of carriage.

(2) Accession to Rights and Liabilities. The new Holder-to-order or
Consignee Holder shall be entitled to all the rights and accepts all the
liabilities of the contract of carriage as contained in or evidenced by, or
deemed to be so contained in or evidenced by, the Bolero Bill of Lading.

(3) Prior Designee's Rights and Liabilities Extinguished. The immediately preceding Holder-to-order's rights and liabilities under its contract of carriage with the Carrier shall immediately cease and be
extinguished, unless:

  (a) such immediately preceding Holder-to-order is also the Shipper, in
      which case its rights but not its liabilities under its contract of
      carriage with the Carrier shall cease and be extinguished; or

  (b) such immediately preceding Holder-to-order is the Head Charterer,
      in which case neither its rights nor its liabilities under its contract
      of carriage with the Carrier shall cease or be extinguished.

3.5.2. *New Holder's Right to Refuse Designation*

L–044   **(1) Refusal**. The new Holder-to-order or Consignee Holder may, within
24 hours of having received notification thereof, reject his Designation as
new Holder-to-order or Consignee Holder in accordance with Operational Rule 30, in which case all rights and obligations under the contract
of carriage between the previous Holder-to-order and the Carrier remain
vested in the previous Holder-to-order, or if none, the Shipper, as if no
attempt to novate the contract had been made.

(2) Acceptance. If within the 24 hour period and before rejection of his Designation, the Designated Holder-to-order or Consignee Holder represents that it accepts the novation or attempts to exercise any rights to the goods, by taking delivery or commencing proceedings against the Carrier for loss of or damage to the goods or otherwise, it shall be deemed to have accepted its Designation at the time it was made for the purposes of Rule 3.5 (Novation of the Contract of Carriage). Any subsequent refusal given pursuant to paragraph (1) of this Rule 3.5.2 shall be void.

3.5.3. *Pledgee Holders*

(1) No Novation. There shall be no novation of the contract of carriage   **L–045** between the Carrier and a Pledgee Holder as such.

(2) Pledgee Holder who is also To Order Party. A Pledgee Holder that is also the current To Order Party enforcing its pledge over a Bolero Bill of Lading shall automatically become the Holder-to-order, with the consequence that the contract of carriage is novated in accordance with the provisions of Rule 3.5. (Novation of the Contract of Carriage).

(3) Enforcement by Pledgee Holder who is Not To Order Party. When a Pledgee Holder, who is not the current To Order Party, enforces its pledge over a Bolero Bill of Lading, the current To Order Party, if any, shall be automatically deleted from the Title Registry Record, and the Pledgee Holder shall automatically become the Bearer Holder.

3.5.4. *Bearer Holders*

(1) No Novation. There shall be no novation of the contract of carriage   **L–046** between the Carrier and a Bearer Holder as such.

(2) Exercise of Rights. A Bearer Holder who wishes either to claim delivery of the goods or commence proceedings against the Carrier for failure to deliver the goods shall first Designate itself as Holder-to-order, whereupon it shall become a party to the contract of carriage in accordance with the provisions of Rule 3.5. (Novation of the Contract of Carriage).

3.5.5. *Bolero Bill of Lading Terms and Conditions to Apply*

For the avoidance of doubt, any User who is or was the Holder, Pledgee   **L–047** Holder, Bearer Holder, Holder-to-order or Consignee Holder of a Bolero Bill of Lading, irrespective of whether such Designation has been rejected, agrees that any claim against the Carrier for loss of or damage to the goods shall be subject to the terms of the contract of carriage as contained in or evidenced by the BBL Text.

3.6. Delivery of the Goods

L–048   **(1) Persons Entitled to Delivery.** Under a contract of carriage in respect of which a Bolero Bill of Lading has been created, delivery of the goods shall only be made by the Carrier to, or to the order of, a Holder-to-order or Consignee Holder which duly Surrenders the Bolero Bill of Lading.

Note
Pledgee Holders and Bearer Holders are also entitled to delivery of the goods, but have to make themselves into Holders-to-order first. This is a matter entirely within their power and discretion, and is therefore no fetter on their immediate right to possession of the goods.

(2) Surrender of the Bolero Bill of Lading. The Bolero Bill of Lading shall be Surrendered either to the User identified as the Surrender Party or, if none, to the Carrier in accordance with the Operational Rules.

(3) Termination of Bolero Bill of Lading. Once the Title Registry Record has recorded that the Bolero Bill of Lading has been Surrendered, the Bolero Bill of Lading shall cease to be effective as a Bolero Bill of Lading and no further dealings with it through the Title Registry shall be possible.

3.7. Switch to Paper

L–049   **(1) Persons Entitled to Switch to Paper.** At any time before the goods to which the Bolero Bill of Lading relates have been delivered by the Carrier, a current Holder, Holder-to-order, Pledgee Holder or Bearer Holder shall be entitled to demand that the Carrier issue a paper bill of lading in accordance with the Operational Rules.

(2) Form of Paper Bill of Lading. The Carrier shall, immediately upon receipt of such a demand, issue a paper bill of lading which sets out:

   (a) all the data contained in and all of the terms and conditions contained in or evidenced by the original BBL Text;

   (b) a statement to the effect that it originated as a Bolero Bill of Lading,

   (c) the date upon which it was issued in paper form; and

   (d) a record issued by Bolero International of the chain of Users which have been parties to contracts of carriage with the Carrier, from the date of the creation of the Bolero Bill of Lading until the date on which its switch to paper demand was sent by Bolero International.

(3) Discrepancies. In the event of any discrepancy between the paper bill of lading so issued and the electronic record of the Bolero Bill of Lading, the electronic record shall prevail.

(4) Delivery of Paper Bill of Lading. The Carrier shall deliver that paper bill of lading in accordance with the instructions of the person currently entitled to hold it, being:

    (a) the current Pledgee Holder; or if none

    (b) the current Holder-to-order or Bearer Holder; or if none

    (c) the current Holder.

(5) End of Bolero Bill of Lading. A User that has knowledge or notice that the switch to paper has been demanded shall give no further Title Registry Instructions in relation to the Bolero Bill of Lading. The Bolero Bill of Lading shall cease to be effective as from the moment of the issue of the paper bill of lading by the Carrier.

3.8. Powers of Parties to a Bolero Bill of Lading

(1) Table of Powers. The parties to a Bolero Bill of Lading, as defined   **L–046** below, shall be entitled to execute functions in relation to that Bolero Bill of Lading in accordance with the following table:

[There follows a table of functions.]

(2) Timing of Carrier's Rights. The Carrier may perform the functions indicated in the table, other than grant or deny amendments, only at the time of the creation of the Bolero Bill of Lading and only in accordance with the provisions of paragraph 3.1(4) of Rule 3.1 (Creation of a Bolero Bill of Lading).

(3) Shipper Holder Designating To Order. A Shipper which is also a Bearer Holder of a Bolero Bill of Lading can Designate a To Order Party.

(4) Shipper, Consignee, or To Order Party Not Holder. Unless a Shipper, Consignee, or To Order Party is also simultaneously the Holder, it is not empowered to give any Title Registry Instructions.

(5) One Holder Only. There shall not be more than one Holder (whether Bearer Holder, Holder-to-order, Pledgee Holder, Consignee Holder or Holder) of a Bolero Bill of Lading at any one time.

(6) Pledgee Automatically Holder. The Designation of a Pledgee shall   **L–047** cause the removal of the previous Holder and the automatic Designation of the Pledgee as Holder. Any To Order Party also then Designated remains so Designated until the pledge is either relinquished or enforced.

(7) Pledgee Not Bearer Holder. Where a Bolero Bill of Lading is Blank Endorsed, the Designation of a Pledgee shall make the User so Designated a Pledgee Holder, not a Bearer Holder.

(8) Underlying Contractual Obligations. Nothing in this Rulebook shall be construed as permitting any User to Designate any person in breach of the User's obligations or duties arising under or in relation to any underlying contract governing the transaction.

(9) Non-limitation. Nothing in this Rule shall limit the right of a Shipper, who is the Holder of a Bolero Bill of Lading, to insist upon an amendment of the Bolero Bill of Lading.

Note
The purpose of this Rule is to preserve the Shipper's right in appropriate cases, prior to delivery of the goods or of the bill of lading, to redirect the goods away from the original consignee or To Order Party.

(10) Instructions to Carrier under Bolero Bill of Lading. Where a Bolero Bill of Lading is currently in force or the relevant shipping documents exist in electronic form, the Carrier may require that all instructions to the Carrier shall only be given by Messages.

3.9. Transport Documents

L–048 **(1) Creation of Transport Documents.** Where, instead of creating a Bolero Bill of Lading, a Carrier by a Message creates a Transport Document, such Message will take effect, for the purposes of the operation of any international convention or national law, as if it were a Transport Document which had been issued by the Carrier in paper form.

(2) Rights and Liabilities of User Identified. Any User identified in a Transport Document will obtain the same rights and liabilities under the contract of carriage, by reason of having been so identified, as it would have done under a paper version of such a Transport Document.

(3) Rights and Liabilities of Named User. Where a User is named by a party entitled to do so under a contract of carriage made with a Carrier as the person to whom delivery of the goods is to be made, that User shall acquire the same rights and liabilities as it would have done if the relevant Transport Document had been issued in paper form.

(4) Duration. In no circumstances shall any rights or liabilities created by the operation of this Rule be any greater or continue for any longer period of time, than would have been the case if the relevant Transport Document had been issued in paper form.

(5) Paper copies of Transport Documents. Once a Carrier has created a Transport Document any subsequent paper copy of such document shall clearly state that it is a copy only. In the event of any discrepancy between the paper copy and the electronic record, the electronic record shall prevail.

(6) Termination of Rights and Liabilities. In the event that the right to the delivery of the goods under a contract of carriage to which this Rule applies, is transferred to a party who is not a User, all rights and liabilities created by the operation of this Rule shall immediately be terminated.

3.10. Ownership and Contracts of Sale

(1) Transfer of Ownership. If as a result of either the intention of the parties to the transaction or the effect of any applicable law, the transfer of constructive possession of the goods and/or the novation of the contract of carriage as provided for in this Rulebook have the effect of transferring the ownership or any other proprietary interest in the goods (in addition to constructive possession thereof), then nothing in this Rulebook shall prevent such transfer of ownership or other proprietary interest from taking place.   L–049

(2) Rulebook Does not Effect Transfer. Nothing in this Rulebook shall be construed as effecting the transfer by the owner of property in the goods which are subject to a contract of carriage contained in or evidenced by a Bolero Bill of Lading or other Transport Document.

(3) Validity of Electronic Tender of Documents. Each User agrees that, where a contract of sale between Users requires that shipping documents are to be tendered to the buyer of those goods or to another party nominated by the buyer, a tender of documents by means of the Bolero System shall not be rejected on the grounds that the documents tendered are in the form of electronic messages or images provided that they contain all of the information required by the contract of sale.

(4) Sale Concluded by Electronic Interchange. Where a contract of sale between Users is concluded (in whole or in part) by means of a Message or by a series of Messages, each User agrees that such Message or Messages shall constitute or evidence the contract concluded between them.   L–050

(5) Switch to Paper for Contracts of Sale. Upon a request from any User entitled to demand the original contract of sale, a contracting User will print and sign in writing the Message or Messages in accordance with any and all formalities required by any applicable law to give effect to the contract.

(6) Date of Contract of Sale. A sale contract switched to paper by the procedure set out in paragraph (5) shall take effect as if the sale contract had been made and signed in writing on the date of the relevant Message or Messages.

3.11. DOCUMENTARY CREDITS

L–051 **(1) Validity of Electronic Presentation of Documents**. This Rulebook will apply and the presentation of any Documents by electronic transmission through the Bolero System will be accepted as if they were the equivalent paper documents, where a User issues, advises or confirms a Documentary Credit on the instructions of an Applicant User under which a Beneficiary User is required to present stipulated documents in order to operate the Documentary Credit, provided that:

(a) the Documentary Credit expressly indicates that presentation under the Bolero System is acceptable; and

(b) the data contained in such transmissions is presented in Documents whose description matches that of the documents required to be presented by the terms of the credit; and

(c) where the Documentary Credit requires that a particular document is issued, authenticated or signed by a particular person, the data transmission is Signed by that person or by a User who is authorised to act and take responsibility on his behalf.

(2) Electronic Documents to be "Originals". Any requirement under the terms of a Documentary Credit, to which this Rulebook apply, that an "original" document be presented shall be satisfied by the presentation of a Document from a Message bearing the Signature of the person said to have issued or created the document or that of a User who is authorised to act and to take responsibility on his behalf.

(3) Copies. Where the terms of a Documentary Credit, to which this Rulebook apply, require that a number of copies of a document be presented by a Beneficiary User to another User ("the recipient User"):

(a) such a requirement shall be satisfied by a single transmission of the equivalent Document to such recipient User; and

(b) The recipient User shall be entitled or empowered to make the number of onward transmissions, or, as the case may be, to create the number of copies, of that document as would have been necessary to complete the transaction in a paper environment, provided always that no Bolero Bill of Lading shall have more than one Holder (whether Holder-to-order, Bearer Holder, Pledgee Holder, Consigneee Holder or Holder) at any one time.

(4) Banks as Holders of Bolero Bills of Lading. Where a User acting as an issuing or confirming bank is designated as a Pledgee Holder or Bearer Holder of a Bolero Bill of Lading for the purposes of the performance of a Documentary Credit, the User shall only acquire such property in and responsibility for the goods as the parties to the Documentary Credit transaction intend.

ANNEX

US LAW CLAUSES

These Clauses are to form part of this Rulebook and where applicable   **L–052** shall do so as part of the provisions of Rule 3.2 (Incorporation by Reference).

(1) Ad valorem Declarations. If the carriage covered by a Bolero Bill of Lading includes carriage to or from a port or place in the United States of America, the Carrier shall provide the Shipper of the Bolero Bill of Lading the opportunity to declare a value of the goods to be carried by him and will include any such declaration in the Bolero Bill of Lading. Any declaration or absence thereof will be binding on the first Holder and any successive Holder to the same extent as if the opportunity to declare a value had been contained in a paper bill of lading.

(2) International Conventions. Where the carriage covered by the Bolero Bill of Lading evidences Carriage to or from a port or place in the United States, the United States Carriage of Goods by Sea Act 1936 shall be deemed to be incorporated and form part of the contract of carriage contained in or evidenced by the Bolero Bill of Lading.

eUCP

(SUPPLEMENT TO UCP 500 FOR ELECTRONIC PRESENTATION—VERSION 1.0)

Article e1

Scope of the eUCP

M–001   a   The Supplement to the Uniform Customs and Practice for Documentary Credits for Electronic Presentation ("eUCP") supplements the Uniform Customs and Practice for Documentary Credits (1993 Revision ICC Publication No. 500,) ("UCP") in order to accommodate presentation of electronic records alone or in combination with paper documents.

      b   The eUCP shall apply as a supplement to the UCP where the credit indicates that it is subject to eUCP.

      c   This version is Version 1.0. A Credit must indicate the applicable version of the eUCP. If it does not do so, it is subject to the version in effect on the date the Credit is issued or, if made subject to eUCP by an amendment accepted by the Beneficiary, on the date of that amendment.

Article e2

Relationship of the eUCP to the UCP

M–002   a   A Credit subject to the eUCP ("eUCP Credit") is also subject to the UCP without express incorporation of the UCP.

      b   Where the eUCP applies, its provisions shall prevail to the extent that they would produce a result different from the application of the UCP.

      c   If an eUCP Credit allows the Beneficiary to choose between presentation of paper documents or electronic records and it chooses to present only paper documents, the UCP shall apply to that presentation. If only paper documents are permitted under an eUCP Credit, the UCP alone shall apply.

Article e3

Definitions

a Where the following terms are used in the UCP, for the purposes of applying the UCP to an electronic record presented under an eUCP Credit, the term: **M–003**

    i. **"appears on its face"** and the like shall apply to examination of the data content of an electronic record.

    ii. **"document"** shall include an electronic record.

    iii. **"place for presentation"** of electronic records means an electronic address.

    iv. **"sign"** and the like shall include an electronic signature.

    v. **"superimposed", "notation" or "stamped"** means data content whose supplementary character is apparent in an electronic record.

b The following terms used in the eUCP shall have the following meanings:

    i. **"electronic record"** means

- data created, generated, sent, communicated, received, or stored by electronic means
- that is capable of being authenticated as to the apparent identity of the sender and the apparent source of the data contained in it, and as to whether it has remained complete and unaltered, and
- is capable of being examined for compliance with the terms of the eUCP Credit.

    ii. **"electronic signature"** means a data process attached to or logically associated with an electronic record and executed or adopted by a person in order to identify that person and to indicate that person's authentication of the electronic record.

    iii. **"format"** means the data organisation in which the electronic record is expressed or to which it refers.

    iv. **"paper document"** means a document in traditional paper form.

    v. **"received"** means the time when an electronic record enters the information system of the applicable recipient in a form capable of being accepted by that system. Any acknowledgement of receipt does not imply acceptance or refusal of the electronic record under an eUCP Credit.

Article e4

Format

M–004 An eUCP Credit must specify the formats in which electronic records are to be presented. If the format of the electronic record is not so specified, it may be presented in any format.

Article e5

Presentation

M–005 **a** An eUCP Credit allowing presentation of:

> **i.** electronic records must state a place for presentation of the electronic records.
>
> **ii.** both electronic records and paper documents must also state a place for presentation of the paper documents.

b Electronic records may be presented separately and need not be presented at the same time.

c If an eUCP Credit allows for presentation of one or more electronic records, the Beneficiary is responsible for providing a notice to the Bank to which presentation is made signifying when the presentation is complete. The notice of completeness may be given as an electronic record or paper document and must identify the eUCP Credit to which it relates. Presentation is deemed not to have been made if the Beneficiary's notice is not received.

d **i.** Each presentation of an electronic record and the presentation of paper documents under an eUCP Credit must specify the eUCP Credit under which it is presented.

> **ii.** A presentation not so identified may be treated as not received.

e If the Bank to which presentation is made is open but its system is unable to receive a transmitted electronic record on the stipulated expiry date and/or the last day of the period of time after the date of shipment for presentation, as the case may be, the Bank will be deemed to be closed and the date of presentation and/or the expiry date shall be extended to the first following banking day on which such Bank is able to receive an electronic record. If the only electronic record remaining to be presented is the notice of completeness, it may be given by telecommunications or by paper document and will be deemed timely, provided that it is sent before the bank is able to receive an electronic record.

f An electronic record that cannot be authenticated is deemed not to have been presented.

Article 6

Examination

a If an electronic record contains a hyperlink to an external system or **M–006** a presentation indicates that the electronic record may be examined by reference to an external system, the electronic record at the hyperlink or the referenced system shall be deemed to be the electronic record to be examined. The failure of the indicated system to provide access to the required electronic record at the time of examination shall constitute a discrepancy.

b The forwarding of electronic records by a Nominated Bank pursuant to its nomination signifies that it has checked the apparent authenticity of the electronic records.

c The inability of the Issuing Bank, or Confirming Bank, if any, to examine an electronic record in a format required by the eUCP Credit or, if no format is required, to examine it in the format presented is not a basis for refusal.

Article e7

Notice of Refusal

a   **i.** The time period for the examination of documents commences **M–007** on the banking day following the banking day on which the Beneficiary's notice of completeness is received.

   ii. If the time for presentation of documents or the notice of completeness is extended, the time for examination of documents commences on the first following banking day on which the bank to which presentation is to be made is able to receive the notice of completeness.

b If an Issuing Bank, the Confirming Bank, if any, or a Nominated Bank acting on their behalf, provides a notice of refusal of a presentation which includes electronic records and does not receive instructions from the party to which notice of refusal is given within 30 calendar days from the date the notice of refusal is given for the disposition of the electronic records, the Bank shall return any paper documents not previously returned to the presenter but may dispose of the electronic records in any manner deemed appropriate without any responsibility.

Article e8

Originals and Copies

M–008 Any requirement of the UCP or an eUCP Credit for the presentation of one or more originals or copies of an electronic record is satisfied by the presentation of one electronic record.

Article e9

Date of Issuance

M–009 Unless an electronic record contains a specific date of issuance, the date on which it appears to have been sent by the issuer is deemed to be the date of issuance. The date of receipt will be deemed to be the date it was sent if no other date is apparent.

Article e10

Transport

M–010 If an electronic record evidencing transport does not indicate a date of shipment or dispatch, the date of issuance of the electronic record will be deemed to be the date of shipment or dispatch. However, if the electronic record bears a notation that evidences the date of shipment or dispatch, the date of the notation will be deemed to be the date of shipment or dispatch. A notation showing additional data content need not be separately signed or otherwise authenticated.

Article e11

Corruption of an Electronic Record after Presentation

M–011 a If an electronic record that has been recieved by the Issuing Bank, Confirming Bank, or another Nominated Bank appears to have been corrupted, the Bank may inform the presenter and may request that the electronic record be re-presented.

    b If the Bank requests that the electronic record be re-presented:

       i. the time for examination is suspended and resumes when the presenter re-presents the electronic record; and

       ii. if the Nominated Bank is not the Confirming Bank, it must provide the Issuing Bank and any Confirming Bank with notice of the request for re-presentation and inform it of the suspension; but

       iii. if the same electronic record is not re-presented within thirty (30) calendar days, the Bank may treat the electronic record as not presented, and

       iv. any deadlines are not extended.

Article e12

Additional Disclaimer of Liability for Presentation of Electronic Records under eUCP

By checking the apparent authenticity of the electronic record, Banks assume no liability for the identity of the sender, source of the information, or its complete and unaltered character other than that which is apparent in the electronic record received by the use of commercially acceptable data process for the receipt, authentication, and identification of electronic records. **M–012**

INDEX

*[Paragraph references in **bold** indicate that the text is reproduced in full]*

ACCOMPLISHED BILLS OF LADING,
13–047

ACTIONS FOR PRICE
general position, 5–081—5–084
waiver of right of disposal,
5–085—5–086

AGENTS
CMI Uniform Rules, **J–004**
identifying the carrier,
12–037—12–039, 12–045
representations in bills of lading
restrictions on implied or
apparent authority,
14–007—14–008,
14–035—14–053
warranties of authority,
14–055—14–060

ANTICIPATORY BREACHES
grounds for repudiation,
7–007—7–014

APPROPRIATION OF GOODS
mistake means qualified acceptance
of goods, 7–045—7–049
passing of property
ascertained goods, 5–012—5–025
c.i.f. contracts, 5–056—5–059
"contractual" and "proprietary"
distinguished, 5–013
depends upon intention of
parties, 5–049
equitable rights, 5–028
rebuttable presumption, 5–022
unascertained goods,
5–008—5–011
rejection of documents for non-
conforming goods, 7–030,
7–031
tender of documents, 4–018—4–019

ARBITRATION
internet trading, 16–004
relationship between carriage
contract and bill of lading,
12–020—12–028
sub-charterers, 12–034—12–036

ASCERTAINED GOODS
passing of property, 5–012—5–025

ASCERTAINED GOODS—*cont.*
intention of parties, 5–030–032

BACKDATED DOCUMENTS
acceptance of goods by inference,
7–039—7–049
measure of damages, 7–050—7–064
rejection of documents and rejection
of goods distinguished,
7–032—7–039

BACK-TO-BACK DOCUMENTARY CREDITS,
8–029

BAILMENT
early common law, 13–044—13–045
influence on carriage contracts,
11–003—11–004
relationship between carriage
contract and bill of lading,
12–046—12–049
transfer of carriage contracts
modern legislative changes,
13–032—13–034

BANKS
see also DOCUMENTARY CREDITS;
requirements for credit *under*
SALE CONTRACTS
early legislative problems with
transfer of carriage contracts,
13–007, 13–012

BARRATRY
insurance cover against fraud and
piracy, 15–041, 15–046

BEARER BILLS, 8–003

BILLS OF EXCHANGE
defined, 8–002
documentary bills, 8–006
negotiation, 8–004
parties, 8–003
sight and time bills, 8–005

BILLS OF LADING
see also COMITÉ MARITIME
INTERNATIONAL;
REPRESENTATIONS IN BILLS OF
LADING
accomplished, 13–047

BILLS OF LADING—*cont.*
advantages and disadvantages of traditional documentation, 1–080
appropriation of goods at moment of tender, 4–018—4–019
backdated
acceptance of goods by inference, 7–039—7–049
measure of damages, 7–050—7–064
rejection of documents and rejection of goods distinguished, 7–032—7–039
Bolero Title Registry, **L–036, L–050—L–052**
"clause paramount" technique, 11–032—11–036, 11–044—11–047
containerisation, 15–024
documentary bills, 8–006
electronic transmission, 16–024, 16–028
fraud, 16–038—16–039
security, 16–038—16–039
evidence of carriage contract, 3–008—3–009
f.o.b. and c.i.f. contract requirements
clean, 6–066—6–070
issued to agent of buyer, 3–005
shipped, 6–057, 6–060—6–065
through bills, 6–076—6–080
time for tendering, 6–084—6–094
fraud by sellers, 15–049
functions, 14–030
Hague-Visby Rules, 11–041—11–048, 11–071—11–080
origins, 11–015—11–020
Hamburg Rules, 11–081, **I–016—I–020,** I–052—I–053
interrelationship of sale and carriage contracts, 2–028—2–038
master's authority, 15–034—15–036
multimodal transport, 15–027—15–028
origins and evolution, 1–012
passing of property, 2–027
c.i.f. contracts, 5–069—5–070
effect of delivery on, 5–012, 5–013, 5–023, 5–040—5–048
effect on reservation of title, 5–060—5–064
reduction recommended by UNCTAD, 15–020

BILLS OF LADING—*cont.*
security of documentary credits, 8–035—8–037
simplified forms from SITPRO, 15–021
title documents, 6–043—6–046
delivery of goods without, 6–022—6–024
received for shipment, 6–050—6–051
spent bills of lading, 6–040—6–042
transfer of carriage contracts
common law, 13–003—13–004
early legislative intervention, 13–005—13–014
early legislative problems, 13–007, 13–013
essential to value, 13–002
implied contracts, 13–056—13–065, 13–071
modern legislative changes, 13–018, 13–020
no contracts implied, 13–066—13–070
transfer of contractual rights, 1–013
UCP provisions, **C–023**
waybills distinguished, 15–019
BOLERO
electronic trading
closed system, 16–027
C.M.I. system distinguished, 16–035—16–036
Rule Book, 16–035
transfer of title, 16–029
Rule Book
applicability, **L–026**
definitions, **L–002—L–023**
enrolment, **L–017**
governing law, **L–056**
illegality, **L–033**
messages, **L–028—L–032**
resignation or termination, **L–034**
scope, **L–025**
Title Registry
bills of lading, **L–036, L–050—L–052**
delivery, **L–048**
documentary credits, **L–055**
incorporation, **L–037**
novation, **L–043—L–047**
passing of property, **L–040—L–042, L–053—L–054**
rights conferred, **L–038—L–039**
sale contracts, **L–053—L–054**
switching to paper, **L–049**

BOLERO—*cont.*
  Title Registry—*cont.*
    transport documents, **L–052**
BREACH OF CONTRACT
  backdated bills of lading,
    acceptance of goods by inference,
      7–039—7–049
    measure of damages,
      7–050—7–064
    rejection of documents and
      rejection of goods
      distinguished, 7–032—7–039
  carrier indemnities, 7–065—7–070
  conditions
    breach giving right to repudiate,
      7–006, 7–012—7–013
    c.i.f. contracts, 7–055, 7–058,
      7–062
    f.o.b. contracts, 3–023—3–039
    meaning, 12–022—12–023
    requirements for credit,
      9–010—9–013
    shipping dates, 7–018—7–020
    terms relating to goods, 7–018
    warranty distinction abolished by
      U.L.I.S., 15–014
  damages
    backdated bills of lading,
      7–050—7–064
    breach of condition, 7–006
    breach of warranty, 7–006
    market fluctuations, 7–001—7–002
    repudiation, 7–003—7–005
    rejection of documents, 7–026
    U.L.I.S. provisions,
      G–083—G–090
  market fluctuations
    measure of damages,
      7–001—7–002
  rejection of documents,
    7–021—7–031, 7–034
  rejection of goods, 7–021, 7–030
  repudiation
    anticipatory breaches,
      7–007—7–014
    breach of condition, 7–006
    reach of innominate term, 7–006
    carriage contracts, 11–003
    hain sales and circles, 15–011
    effect, 7–015—7–017
    measure of damages,
      7–003—7–005
    transfer of risk, 4–046—4–047

BREACH OF CONTRACT—*cont.*
  rejection of documents,
    7–021—7–031
    rejection of goods distinguished,
      7–032—7–039
  warranties
    breaches of authority,
      14–055—14–060
    reach giving right to damages,
      7–006
    condition distinction abolished by
      U.L.I.S., 15–014
    representations in bills of lading,
      14–016—14–020
BROKERS
  representations in bills of lading,
    14–007—14–008
BULK CARGOES
  see also GRAIN TRADES; OIL
  INCOTERMS 2000, 15–008
  passing of property affecting
    equitable rights, 5–026—5–029
  property and risk divorced,
    4–003—4–006
  retreat from traditional
    documentation, 1–049
  spent bills of lading, 6–040—6–042
  transfer of carriage contracts
    early legislative problems,
      13–007, 13–011
    modern legislative changes,
      13–020
  unsuitability of f.o.b. and c.i.f.
    contracts, 1–002
BULK COMMODITY CONTRACTS
  advantages of traditional bills of
    lading, 1–050
  distinguishing features, 1–048
  futures delivery contacts, 1–041
  passing of property, 5–008—5–011,
    5–018, 5–021, 5–024—5–025,
    5–080
BURDEN OF PROOF
  Hague Rules, 11–022—11–025
BUYERS' CALL CONTRACTS
  term of f.o.b., 3–021—3–023

C. & F. CONTRACTS, 3–059
CF CONTRACTS, 3–059
C.I.F. CONTRACTS
  backdated bills of laden
    rejection of documents and
      rejection of goods
      distinguished, 7–032—7–039
  bills of lading necessary for modern
    development, 1–012

C.I.F. CONTRACTS—*cont.*
chain sales and circles,
1–018—1–031, 1–048
commodity futures markets,
1–032—1–040
delivered contracts, 2–019—2–023
documents
additional requirements, 6–095
charterparty bills, 6–070—6–075
clean bills of lading,
6–066—6–070
delivery orders, 6–096—6–100
extent of insurance cover,
6–113—6–114
invoices, 6–101
role, 6–002
sets of three, 6–080—6–083
shipped bills of lading, 6–057
tender of insurance policy,
6–108—6–112
through bills of lading,
6–076—6–080
time for tendering bills of lading,
6–084—6–088
early insurance arrangements,
1–012
evolution from f.o.b. contracts,
1–009
fats and oils, 1–023—1–031
features shared with f.o.b. contracts,
1–001
f.o.b. contract compared, 2–004
advantages, 3–006
goods must be shipped, 2–011,
2–012—2–013
grain trades, 1–016—1–022
INCOTERMS 2000, 15–008
buyers' obligations,
B–033—B–040
sellers' obligations, **B–024—B–032**
meaning
common law definitions,
2–002—2–005
freight and insurance included,
2–006—2–008, 2–011
terms net cash, 2–009, 2–011
modern problems, 1–015
obligation to present correctly
dated bill of lading, 7–055,
7–058, 7–062
origins and evolution, 1–005
out-turn contracts, 2–025—2–026
passing of property, 5–017, 5–022,
5–033, 5–039
appropriation, 5–056—5–059

C.I.F. CONTRACTS—*cont.*
passing of property—*cont.*
effect of transferring bills of
lading, 5–069—5–070
rejection of documents,
7–021—7–031
relationship with carriage contracts,
2–028—2–038
requirements for credit,
9–015—9–016
retreat from traditional
documentation, 1–049
risk
notice by seller to buyer of route,
4–026—4–028
passes on shipment, 4–011
sale of documents not goods, 4–015,
4–017
sellers' duties, limited to loading
goods, 2–014—2–018
standardisation of terms, 15–002
tender of documents for lost goods,
4–012—4–014, 4–017
transfer of contractual rights, 1–013
U.L.I.S., 15–014—15–016
unsuitability,
container shipping,
15–025—15–026
modern trading, 1–002
CARRIAGE CONTRACTS
see also HAGUE RULES; HAGUE-VISBY
RULES; TRANSFER OF CARRIAGE
CONTRACTS
application of Hague-Visby Rules,
11–071—11–080
cargo-owner's duties, 11–010
central role of sale contracts, 2–001
CMI
requirements, **K–006**
Uniform Rules, **J–007**
common law principles, 11–002
conflict of laws
"clause paramount" technique,
11–032—11–036,
11–044—11–047
statutory freedom of choice,
11–048
contracting out, 11–006—11–009
demise clauses, 12–044—12–045
deviation, 11–005—11–006
distinguishing feature of f.o.b.
contracts, 3–004, 3–005,
3–015—3–016
delivery of goods on production of
documents, 6–008

CARRIAGE CONTRACTS—*cont.*
electronic transmission of
documents, 16–025
evidenced by bills of lading,
3–008—3–009
governing law
"clause paramount" technique,
11–032—11–036,
11–044—11–047
statutory freedom of choice,
11–048
Hamburg Rules, 11–081—11–083
liability under, **I–006—I–013**,
I–044
identifying the carrier,
12–037—12–039
agents, 12–037—12–039, 12–045
time and voyage charters,
12–040—012–043
implied terms, 11–005
INCOTERMS 2000
buyers' obligations, **B–015**
excluded from, 15–008
sellers' obligations, **B–005**
indemnities for defective
documents or goods,
7–065—7–070
influence of bailment duties,
11–003—11–004
legislative intervention, replacement
of strict liability,
11–011—11–013
multimodal transport, 15–027
package value limits,
11–049—11–060
relationship with bill of lading
arbitration clauses,
12–020—12–028
bailment on terms,
12–046—12–049
consignee or indorsee of
charterer, 12–007—12–010
incorporation of charterparty
terms in bill of lading,
12–011—12–019
incorporation of arbitration
clauses, 12–020—12–028
loading follows contract, 12–001
pre-contract agreements,
12–004—12–006
pre-shipment promises,
12–002—12–003
sub-charterers, 12–029—12–036
relationship with sale contracts,
2–028—2–038, 3–059
U.L.I.S. provisions, **G–073**

CARRIAGE CONTRACTS—*cont.*
waybills and bills of lading
distinguished, 15–019
CERTIFICATION AUTHORITIES
authentication of electronic
signatures, 16–021—16–023
CHAIN SALES
see also TRANSFER OF CARRIAGE
CONTRACTS
back-to-back credits, 8–029
disadvantages of traditional bills of
lading, 1–050
fats and oils, 1–023—1–031
fraud prevention, 15–054
governing law, 11–035
grain trades, 1–016—1–018
INCOTERMS 2000, 15–008
negotiability of documents,
15–009—15–010
oil trades, 1–048, 15–032
repudiation, 15–011
requirement that documents
conform, 6–001
strict compliance, 15–012—15–013
tender of documents for lost goods,
4–012
CHARTERPARTIES
delivery of goods without title
documents, 6–007, 6–019, 6–027
demise clauses, 12–044—12–045
documentary credits
documentary requirements,
10–001
requirement for original
documents, 10–034
effect of bills of lading on
reservation of title,
5–063—5–064
f.o.b. contracts, 3–008
fraud
by shipowners, 15–052
on shipowners, 15–051—15–052
Hamburg Rules, I–042
identifying the carrier,
12–037—12–039
agents, 12–037—12–039
time and voyage charters,
12–040—012–043
interrelationship of sale and
carriage contracts, 2–033, 2–035,
2–037
liability for piracy, 15–039
ostensible authority of owners,
14–044

CHARTERPARTIES—*cont.*
  relationship between carriage
      contract and bill of lading
    arbitration clauses,
        12–020—12–028,
        12–034—12–036
    bailment on terms,
        12–046—12–049
    consignee or indorsee of
        charterer, 12–007—12–010
    incorporation of charterparty
        terms in bill of lading,
        12–011—12–019
    pre-contract agreements,
        12–004—12–006
    pre-shipment promises,
        12–002—12–003
    sub-charterers, 12–029—12–036
  repudiation for anticipatory
      breaches, 7–007—7–014
  requirement for charterparty bills,
      6–070—6–075
  theft of cargoes, 15–048
  time charters
    identifying the carrier,
        12–040—012–043
    ostensible authority of owners,
        14–044
    transfer of carriage contracts,
        13–039
  transfer of carriage contracts
    modern legislative changes,
        13–021, 13–037—13–040
  UCP provisions, **C–025**
  voyage charters
    identifying the carrier,
        12–040—012–043
  withdrawal clauses, 7–005
CIRCLES
  chain sales, 1–018
  fats and oils, 1–023—1–031
  GAFTA 100 clause, 1019
  negotiability of documents,
      15–009—15–010
  oil trades, 1–047
  sham trades, 1–020—1–022
  strict compliance, 15–012—15–013
  repudiation, 15–011
CLAIMS
  meaning, 13–049, 13–052
"CLAUSE PARAMOUNT"
  Hague-Visby Rules, 11–032—11–036,
      11–044—11–047

COMITÉ MARITIME INTERNATIONAL
    (CMI)
  electronic trading
    Bolero system distinguished,
        16–035—16–036
    encryption, 16–032
    evidential problems, 16–034
    non-payment and passing of
        property, 16–031
    open system, 16–027
    transfer of title, 16–029—16–030
    working assumptions, 16–033
  rules
    application, **K–002**
    authentication, **K–012**
    carriage contracts, **K–006**
    definitions, **K–003**
    delivery, **K–008, K–010**
    governing law, **K–007**
    messages, **K–005**
    paper documents, **K–011**
    passing of property, **K–008**
    private keys, **K–009**
    procedure, **K–004**
  Uniform Rules (sea waybills)
    agency, **J–004**
    control of goods, **J–007**
    definitions, **J–003**
    delivery, J–008
    description of goods, **J–006**
    rights and responsibilities, **J–005**
    scope, **J–002**
    validity, **J–009**
COMMODITY BROKERS
  speculation on fluctuating markets,
      1–018
COMMODITY FUTURES MARKETS
  see FUTURES MARKETS
COMPUTERISATION
  see also INTERNET TRADING
  Data Freight Receipt system, 15–022
  dematerialisation, 16–001
CONDITIONS
  see also WARRANTIES
  breach giving right to repudiate,
      7–006, 7–012—7–013
  c.i.f. contracts
    obligation to present correctly
        dated bill of lading, 7–055,
        7–058, 7–062
  f.o.b. contracts
    additional terms, 3–023—3–039
    meaning, 12–022—12–023
    requirements for credit,
        9–010—9–013
    shipping dates, 7–018—7–020

CONDITIONS—*cont.*
terms relating to goods, 7–018
warranty distinction abolished by
U.L.I.S., 15–014
CONDUCT
see ESTOPPEL
CONFIRMED DOCUMENTARY CREDITS,
8–022—8–025, 8–028
workings, 1–014
CONFLICT OF LAWS
"clause paramount" technique,
11–032—11–036,
11–044—11–047
statutory freedom of choice, 11–048
CONTAINERISATION
see also BULK CARGOES
consequences on international trade
law, 15–017
Hamburg Rules, I–045
need for fast documentation, 15–018
unsuitability
of c.i.f. and f.o.b. contracts, 1–002,
15–025—15–026
of bills of lading, 15–024
CONVENTION FOR THE INTERNATIONAL
SALE OF GOODS (CISG)
application, H–002—H–007
buyers
obligations, H–054—H–066
remedies, H–046—H–053
conformity, H–036—H–045
delivery
sellers' obligations,
H–032—H–035
buyers' obligations, H–061
final provisions, H–090—H–102
formation of contract,
H–015—H–025
general provisions, H–008—H–014
provisions common to buyers and
sellers, H–072—H–089
risk, H–067—H–070
sale of goods, H–026—H–030
sellers' obligations, H–031—H–053
CONVERSION
security of documentary credits,
8–034—8–035
COPIES
documentary credits,
10–034—10–045
COST INSURANCE FREIGHT CONTRACTS
see C.I.F. CONTRACTS
CREDIT
see also DOCUMETARY CREDITS;
FINANCE; requirements for
credit *under* SALE CONTRACTS

CREDIT—*cont.*
advantages of traditional bills of
lading, 1–050
origins and evolution of c.i.f.
contracts, 1–005
CRIME
see FRAUD; PIRACY; THEFT
CUSTOM
delivery of goods without title
documents, 6–022—6–024
role in establishing intention, 6–001
title documents
bills of lading, 6–043—6–046
effect of proving custom,
6–052—6–056
received for shipment bills of
lading, 6–050—6–051

DAMAGES
backdated bills of lading,
7–050—7–064
breach of warranty, 7–006
market fluctuations, 7–001—7–002
repudiation, 7–003—7–005
rejection of documents, 7–026
U.L.I.S. provisions, G–083—G–090
DATA FREIGHT RECEIPT SYSTEM
computerised bills of lading, 15–022
DECEIT
carrier indemnities, 7–070
quantities in bills of lading, 14–054
DECK CARGOES *see* CONTAINERISATION
"DELIVERED" CONTRACTS
named destination, 3–059
DELIVERY
see also PASSING OF PROPERTY
additional terms in f.o.b. contracts,
3–052—3–055
Bolero Title Registry, L–048
c.i.f. contracts
c.i.f. delivered contracts,
2–019—2–023
completed by transfer of
documents, 2–010, 2–011
CISG
buyers' obligations, H–061
sellers' obligations,
H–032—H–035
CMI
Rules, K–008, K–010
Uniform Rules, J–008
continuing duties of seller,
2–039—2–046
early difficulties, 1–011
early f.o.b. contracts, 1–008, 1–009

DELIVERY—*cont.*
electronic documents
difficulties with electronic
trading, 16–029
effect on traditional rules of
delivery, 6–033
INCOTERMS 2000
buyers' obligations, **B–006, B–016**
sellers' obligations, **B–006, B–009,
B–010**
master's authority, 15–034—15–036
multimodal transport documents,
15–029
passing of property
appropriation of unascertained
goods, 5–010, 5–033
bills of lading ceasing to be
effective, 5–066—5–068
effect on actions for price, 5–081
physical and constructive, 5–003
production of title documents
delivery of goods against forged
title documents, ,
6–026—6–035
delivery without production,
6–015—6–028
functions, 6–003
locus standi required to sue,
6–036—6–039
obligation to deliver goods,
6–008—6–014
refusal by carrier, 6–004—6–007
spent bills of lading,
6–040—6–042
security of documentary credits,
8–034
transfer of carriage contracts,
13–048—13–049, 13–051
U.L.I.S.
sellers' obligations,
**G–020—G–033,
G–066—G–069, G–072**
DELIVERY ORDERS
implied contracts, 13–060—13–061
requirements of c.i.f contracts,
6–096—6–100
transfer of carriage contracts,
13–018
modern legislative changes,
13–020, 13–021
DEMANDS
meaning, 13–049, 13–052—13–053
DEMISE CLAUSES
carriage contracts, 12–044—12–045

DEMURRAGE
damages for anticipatory breach,
7–008
cargo-owner's duties, 11–010
fraudulent claims, 15–048
transfer of carriage contracts
implied contracts,
13–056—13–065
DEVIATION
contracting out, 11–006—11–009
Hague Rules, 11–027—11–030
implied terms in carriage contracts,
11–005
relationship between carriage
contract and bill of lading,
12–004
DOCUMENTARY CREDITS, 8–007—8–008
see also eUCP; requirements for
credit *under* SALE CONTRACTS
back-to-back, 8–029
bank's right to reject documents
conforming documents,
10–002—10–024
doctrine of strict compliance,
10–025—10–029
fraud, 10–003—10–024
fundamental principles,
10–002—10–011
non-conforming documents,
10–025—10–029
Bolero Title Registry, **L–055**
confirmed, 8–022—8–025, 8–028
workings, 1–014
documentary requirements
originals, 10–034—10–045
U.C.P., 10–001
effects
absolute payment, 9–033,
9–035—9–037
conditional payment, 9–033,
9–034, 9–035—9–037
no payment, 9–033, 9–035—9–037
excluded from INCOTERMS 2000,
15–008
functions, 1–014
fundamental principles
autonomy of contract documents,
8–007, 8–010
banks deal with documents not
goods, 8–012
four essential contracts,
8–008—8–009
matching contractual obligations,
8–011
insolvent banks, 9–031—9–032

Documentary Credits—*cont.*
  irrevocable, 8–016, 8–020—8–021
    problems between confirming
      bank and seller,
      8–047—8–050
    requirements of sale contract,
      9–002—9–004
  origins and evolution, 1–014
  rejection of documents, 7–023,
    7–025
  revocable , 8–016, 8–017—8–019
  revolving, 8–029
  security
    constructive possession,
      8–031—8–040
    equitable title, 8–041—8–042
    fraud, 8–043—8–046
    legal title, 8–038—8–040
    problems between confirming
      bank and seller,
      8–047—8–050
  short-circuiting, 9–028—9–030
  sight and time bills, 8–005
  standby letters of credit, 8–030
  title documents issued in triplicate,
    6–013
  transferrable, 8–029
  trivial defects
    bank's duties, 10–031—10–033
    consultation and negotiation,
      10–033
    reasons, 10–030
  UCP
    application, 8–014
    banks deal with documents not
      goods, 8–012
    harmonisation of law, 8–013
    unconfirmed, 8–026—8–028
Documents
  see also Bills of Lading;
    Documentary Credits;
    Internet Trading
  backdated bills of lading
    acceptance of goods by inference,
      7–039—7–049
    measure of damages,
      7–050—7–064
    rejection of documents and
      rejection of goods
      distinguished, 7–032—7–039
  bills of lading
    received for shipment,
      6–050—6–051
    spent, 6–040—6–042
    time for tendering, 6–084—6–094
    title documents, 6–043—6–046

Documents—*cont.*
  c.i.f. contracts
    additional rerquirements, 6–095
    charterparty bills, 6–071—6–075
    delivery orders, 6–096—6–100
    effect on seller's duties,
      2–014—2–018
    invoices, 6–101
    role, 6–002
    sets of three, 6–080—6–083
    transfer to complete delivery,
      2–010, 2–011
  clean bills of lading
    f.o.b. and c.i.f contract
      requirements, 6–066—6–070
  custom, 6–052—6–056
  endorsement
    bills of exchange, 8–004
    bills of lading, 6–044
    Bolero Title Registry,
      L–038—L–039
    documents of title, 6–005
    early legislative problems, 13–046
    symbolic delivery of cargo,
      13–044
  f.o.b. contracts, 6–002
  forgeries, 6–026—6–035
  Hamburg Rules, **I–016—I–020,**
    I–052—I–054
  importance in passing of risk
    role in evidencing valid contract,
      4–007—4–009
    role in passing of property, 4–010
  UCP, **C–004**
  insurance requirements
    extent of cover, 6–113—6–114
    tender, 6–108—6–112
    valid policy, 6–107
  loss of control prior to development
    of bankers' documentary
    credits, 1–014
  lost, 6–022, 6–023, 6–025
  mates' receipts, 6–047—6–049
  origins and variations, 6–001
  quality certificates, 6–102—6–106
  rejection for non-conforming goods,
    7–021—7–031
  shipped bills of lading
    c.i.f. contract requirements, 6–057,
      6–060—6–065
    f.o.b. contract requirements,
      6–057—6–059
  theft, 6–023, 6–025
  through bills of lading
    f.o.b. and c.i.f contract
      requirements, 6–076—6–080

Documents—*cont.*
title to goods
indorsement, 6–005
delivery of goods against forged
title documents,
6–026—6–035
delivery, 6–003
delivery without production,
6–015—6–028
issued in triplicate, 6–010—6–013,
6–031
locus standi required to sue,
6–036—6–039
obligation to deliver goods,
6–008—6–014
refusal by carrier, 6–004—6–007
transfer of carriage contracts
delivery orders, 13–018
early legislative problems, 13–007
mates' receipts, 13–018
modern legislative changes,
13–017
specific enumeration, 13–019
transfer of carriage contracts, stale
bills of lading, 13–018
UCP provisions, **C–020—C–038**
Due Diligence
Hague Rules, 11–011—11–013,
11–039—11–040
Durability
merchantable quality, 4–036
satisfactory condition, 4–038—4–039

Electronic Documents
see Internet Trading
Encryption
C.M.I. model, 16–032—16–033,
16–037
internet trading, 16–020
Endorsement
see also Transfer of Carriage
Contracts
bills of exchange, 8–004
bills of lading
passing of property, 6–044
Bolero Title Registry, **L–038—L–039**
documents of title, 6–005
early legislative problems, 13–046
symbolic delivery of cargo, 13–044
Estoppel
backdated bills of lading
acceptance of goods by inference,
7–039—7–049
carrier indemnities, 7–068
condition of goods,. 13–057, 13–061

Estoppel—*cont.*
credit requirements in sale contract,
9–020—9–027
electronic signatures, 16–019
passing of property, effect on
actions for price, 5–084
representations in bills of lading
quantities, 14–054
warranties of condition,
14–017—14–019,
14–021—14–023
substitution of nominated vessel
recovery of additional expense,
4–043—4–045
transfer of carriage contracts,
13–039
transfer of risk, 4–040—4–042
εUCP
copies, **M–008**
corruption of records, **M–011**
date of issue, **M–009**
definitions, **M–003**
disclaimers, **M–012**
examination, M–006
format, **M–004**
presentation, **M–005**
refusal, **M–007**
relationship to UCP, **M–002**
transport, **M–010**
Evidence
anticipatory breach, 7–010
"Ex Quay" Contracts, 3–059, 3–060
"Ex Ship" Contracts, 3–059, 3–060
"Ex Works/Warehouse" Contracts,
3–059, 3–060
Exclusion Clauses
theft and piracy, 15–038
carriage contracts, 11–006—11–009
scope, 11–038
delivery of goods
against forged title documents,
6–034
without title documents,
6–016—6–018—6–025
origins of Hague Rules, 11–016,
11–018
transfer of carriage contracts
early legislative problems,
13–007, 13–014
Exports
acceptable documents to Credit
Guarantee Department, 15–021
additional terms relating to licences
in f.o.b. contracts, 3–046—3–050

F.A.S. CONTRACTS
  named ports, 3–059, 3–060
  origins, 1–006
F.O.B. CONTRACTS
  additional terms
    as conditions, 3–023—3–039
    buyer's calls', 3–021
    delivery, 3–052—3–055
    export licences, 3–046—3–050
    market fluctuations, 3–056—3–057
    notice stipulations, 3–023—3–028
    shipment dates, 3–023
    substitution of vessel,
      3–040—3–045
  advantages over c.i.f. contracts,
    3–006
  application of Hague-Visby Rules,
    11–071—11–080
  bills of lading necessary for modern
    development, 1–012
  classic example, 3–005
  commodity futures markets,
    1–032—1–040
  common law definitions,
    2–002—2–003
  defined, 3–002
  desire to move away from, 1–010
  documents
    clean bills of lading,
      6–066—6–070
    role, 6–002
    shipped bills of lading,
      6–057—6–059
    through bills of lading,
      6–076—6–080
    time for tendering bills of lading,
      6–089—6–094
  evolution, 1–009
  features shared with c.i.f. contracts,
    1–001
  flexibility, 3–001—3–002, 3–005
  INCOTERMS 2000, 15–008
    buyers obligations, **B–013—B–020**
    definition, **B–002**
    sellers' obligations, **B–003—B–012**
  named ports, 3–059
  nomination of vessels
    distinguishing feature, 3–004,
      3–005, 3–013
    obligation on either party, 3–017
    shipment period, 3–018—3–020
  obligation to make carriage
    contract, 3–004, 3–005,
    3–015—3–016
  origins and evolution, 1–004

F.O.B. CONTRACTS—*cont.*
  passing of property, 1–007—1–008,
    5–010, 5–033, 5–039
    affect on actions for price, 5–083
  privity problems under Hague-
    Visby Rules, 11–064—11–067
  requirements for credit,
    9–017—9–019
  retreat from traditional
    documentation, 1–049
  risk
    notice by seller to buyer of route,
      4–021—4–026
    principles, 4–040—4–042
  scope, 3–003
  seller contracting as principal,
    3–007—3–012
    implied obligations,
    presumption that buyer ships
      goods,
    specific goods, 4–005—4–006
  standardisation of terms,
    15–002—15–003
  transfer of contractual rights, 1–013
  U.L.I.S., 15–014
  unsuitability
    for container shipping,
      15–025—15–026
    for modern trading, 1–002
  use in chains and circles, 1–048
  variants, 3–004, 3–005, 3–014
FALSITY
  see BACKDATED BILLS OF LADING;
    FORGERY; FRAUD
FINANCE
  see also BILLS OF EXCHANGE; CREDIT;
    DOCUMENTARY CREDITS; eUCP;
    requirements for credit *under*
    SALE CONTRACTS
  bills of exchange, 8–001—8–005
  documentary bills, 8–006
FLUCTUATING MARKETS
  absence of early protection, 1–014
  additional terms in f.o.b. contracts,
    3–056—3–057
  backdated bills of lading
    measure of damages,
      7–050—7–064
    rejection of documents and
      rejection of goods
      distinguished, 7–032—7–039
  damages
    general measure for breach of
      contract, 7–001—7–002
    repudiation, 7–003—7–005

FLUCTUATING MARKETS—*cont.*
GAFTA clause dealing with circles,
1–019
grain trades, 1–017—1–018
oil, 1–047
reliance on misrepresentations in
bills of lading, 14–003—14–004
scope of internet trading, 16–002
U.L.I.S. provisions, **G–074**

FOODSTUFFS
see also GRAIN TRADES
chain sales and circles,
1–023—1–031

FOREIGN EXCHANGE
restricted to f.o.b. values, 1–005

FORGERY
delivery of goods without proper
title documents, 6–026—6–035
incidence of risk, 6–031—6–035

FORWARD DELIVERY CONTRACTS
characteristics, 1–034
drawbacks, 1–033
futures markets distinguished,
1–036

FORWARDING AGENTS
representations in bills of lading,
14–007—14–008

FRAUD
see also FORGERY; PIRACY; THEFT
absence of protection, 1–051
backdated bills of lading,
7–032—7–033
bills of lading, electronic
transmission, 16–038—16–039
buyers, 15–050
carrier indemnities, 7–065—7–070
documentary credits, bank's right
to reject documents,
10–003—10–024
electronic trading, 16–033
features peculiar to maritime
enterprises, 15–037
incidence of risk, 6–013, 6–032
making criminals pay, 15–058
no ship or cargo, 15–048
prevention, 15–054
rejection of documents, 7–025,
7–027, 7–030—7–031
representations in bills of lading,
14–024
responsibility of innocent
principal, 14–040—14–041
security of documentary credits,
8–043—8–046
sellers, 15–049
shifting the loss, 15–053

FRAUD—*cont.*
spreading the cost, 15–056—15–058
theft of cargoes, 15–040—15–048
third parties, 15–051
transnational, 15–055—15–058

FREE ALONGSIDE SHIP CONTRACTS *see*
F.A.S. CONTRACTS

FREE ON BOARD CONTRACTS *see* F.O.B.
CONTRACTS

FREIGHT
see also CARRIAGE CONTRACTS
included in c.i.f. contracts,
2–006—2–008, 2–011

FRUSTRATION
effect on transfer of risk,
4–051—4–053
ground for repudiation, 7–009
piracy, 15–039

FUTURES
delivery contracts,
1–039—1–040—1–047
relationship with futures markets,
1–042—1–046
markets
characteristics, 1–035
c.i.f annd f.o.b. contracts,
1–032—1–040
forward delivery contracts
distinguished, 1–036
relationship with futures delivery
contracts, 1–042—1–046
requirements, 1–041
traders dealing short,
1–037—1–038
relationship between sale and
carriage contracts,
2–034—2–035

GENERAL COUNCIL OF BRITISH SHIPPING
(GCBS)
introduction of waybills, 15–021

GHOST SHIPS
re-appearance following piracy,
15–040
theft of cargoes, 15–040—15–048

GLOBALISATION, 15–004—15–005

GOODS
see also BULK CARGOES; GRAIN; OIL;
SUGAR
afloat
conclusion of sale contracts,
15–047
importance of representations in
bills of lading, 14–001
liens arising from insolvency,
5–005

GOODS—*cont.*
  afloat—*cont.*
    transfer of risk, 4–048—4–049
  cargo-owner's duties, 11–010
  durability
    implied term affecting risk,
        4–030—4–036
    meaning durable, 4–036, 4–039
    merchantable quality, 4–036
    satisfactory condition,
        4–038—4–039
  implied terms, 11–005
  quality
    f.o.b. and c.i.f contract
        requirements, 6–102—6–106
    fraud prevention, 15–054
    INCOTERMS 2000, **B–011, B–040**
    rejection of goods, 7–022—7–025,
        7–028, 7–029
    terms of credit, 9–005—9–008
  quantities
    representations in bills of lading,
        14–033—14–034,
        14–051—14–054
  risk
    existence of goods fundamental
        to contract, 4–046—4–047
  satisfactory condition
    implied term affecting risk,
        4–038—4–039
GOVERNING LAW
  Bolero Title Registry, **L–056**
  clause paramount technique,
      11–032—11–036,
      11–044—11–047
  CMI Rules, **K–007**
  Hamburg Rules, I–040
  statutory freedom of choice, 11–048
GRAIN
  c.i.f. contracts
    market fluctuations, 1–017
    sham trades, 1–020—1–022
    suitability, 1–016
GRAIN AND FEED TRADE ASSOCIATION
    (GAFTA)
  circles, 1–019
  failure to deal with passing of
      property, 2–003, , 5–001, 15–008
  unification of international sales
      law, 15–017

HAGUE RULES
  application, 11–071—11–080
  bills of lading, 11–041—11–048
  clause paramount technique,
      11–032—11–036

HAGUE RULES—*cont.* ·
  construction of contract arguments,
      11–06811–070
  due diligence, 11–039—11–040
  general principles, 11–021
  interpretation, 11–026—11–030
  origins, 11–015—11–020
  package limitation, 11–049—11–060
  predecessors to Hague-Visby Rules,
      11–014
  problems with privity of contract,
      11–037—11–038, 11–061
  stages of claim and burden of
      proof, 11–022—11–025
  UNCITRAL explanatory notes on
      Hamburg Rules, I–039—I–040
  unseaworthiness, 11–022,
      11–039—11–040
HAGUE-VISBY RULES
  application, 11–071—11–080
  bills of lading, 11–041—11–048
  clause paramount' technique,
      11–032—11–036,
      11–044—11–047
  interpretation, 11–026—11–030
  limits on liability, 11–042, 11–061
  origins, 11–031
  package limitation, 11–049—11–060
  problems with privity of contract,
      11–061
    application by incorporation,
        11–062—11–063
    carriers remain with burden,
        11–061
    f.o.b. contracts, 11–064—11–067
  resolution of difficulties, 11–048
  statutory effect, 11–043
  unseaworthiness, 11–041
HAMBURG RULES
  adaption for multimodal transport,
      15–030
  carriage contracts, 11–081—11–083
  carriers' liability, **I–006—I–013**,
      I–044
  claims and actions, **I–021—I–024**,
      I–055—I–058
  common understanding, **I–037**
  containerisation, I–045
  definitions, **I–003—I–006**
  delay, I–046
  final clauses, **I–029—I–036**
  governing law, I–041
  liability limits, I–047—I–050
  mandatory responsibilities, I–058
  period of responsibility, I–043
  scope, I–042

HAMBURG RULES—*cont.*
shippers' liability, **I–014—I–015,**
I–051
supplementary provisions,
I–025—I–028
transport documents, **I–016—I–020,**
I–052—I–054
UNCITRAL explanatory notes,
I–038—I–059
uniformity, I–059
vicarious liability, I–048
HARMONISATION, 15–004—15–005
HEDGING
meaning, 1–041

IMPLIED TERMS
restrictions on implied or apparent
authority in bills of lading,
14–035—14–053
risk
durability, 4–038—4–039
merchantable condition,
4–030—4–036
satisfactory condition,
4–038—4–039
transfer of carriage contracts,
13–056—13–065
IMPORTS
restricted to f.o.b. values, 1–005
IMPOSSIBLITY *see* FRUSTRATION
INCORPORATION CLAUSES
Bolero Title Registry, **L–037**
sale contracts, 2–036, 2–037
waybills, 15–021
INCOTERMS 2000
buyers's obligations
c.i.f.contracts, **B–033—B–040**
f.o.b. contracts, **B–013—B–020**
costs, **B–008**
f.o.b. contracts
choice of shipment dates, 3–023
failure to deal with basic
definitions, 2–003
interpretation of sale contracts,
15–006
limitations, 15–008
meaning of f.o.b., **B–002**
nomination of vessel, 3–005
paperless documentation, 16–015
passing of property, 5–001
quality and packaging, **B–011**
revision, 15–007
seller's obligations
c.i.f. contracts, **B–024—B–032**
f.o.b. contracts, **B–003—B–012**

INDEMNITIES
defective documents or goods,
7–065—7–070
delivery of goods
against forged title documents,
6–029
without title documents, 6–019,
6–021, 6–026
INJUNCTIONS
documentary credits, bank's right
to reject forged documents,
10–015—10–024
INNOMINATE TERMS
breach giving right to repudiate,
7–006
repudiation for anticipatory
breaches, 7–007—7–014
INSOLVENCY
early difficulties, 1–011
effect of passing of property, 5–004,
5–005
role of bills of lading, 1–012
safeguard of bankers' documentary
credits, 1–014
INSPECTION
early difficulties, 1–011
relevance of passing of risk, 4–002
INSURANCE
central role of sale contracts, 2–001
c.i.f. contracts, 1–012
clauses covering fraud and piracy,
15–040—15–048
documentary requirements
extent of cover, 6–113—6–114
tender, 6–108—6–112
valid policy, 6–107
fraud, 15–048
included in c.i.f. contracts,
2–006—2–008, 2–011
INCOTERMS 2000, sellers'
obligations, **B–005**
third party fraud, 15–051
U.L.I.S. provisions, **G–055**
UCP provisions, **C–034—C–036**
INTENTION OF PARTIES
electronic signatures,
16–013—16–014
passing of property
appropriation, 5–049
ascertained or specific goods,
5–030–032, 5–033
importance, 5–050—5–053
role of custom, 6–001
standardisation of terms, 15–002